PEARSON ALWAYS LEARNING

Anita E. Woolfolk • Philip H. Winne • Nancy E. Perry

Educational Psychology

Third Custom Edition for the Ontario Institute for Studies in Education of the University of Toronto

Taken from:
Educational Psychology, Fifth Canadian Edition
by Anita E. Woolfolk, Philip H. Winne, and Nancy E. Perry

Cover Art: Courtesy of PhotoDisc/Getty Images

Taken from:

Educational Psychology, Fifth Canadian Edition
by Anita E. Woolfolk, Philip H. Winne, and Nancy E. Perry

Published by Prentice Hall
Upper Saddle River, New Jersey 07458

This special edition published in cooperation with Pearson Learning Solutions.

Pearson Learning Solutions, 501 Boylston Street, Suite 900, Boston, MA 02116
A Pearson Education Company
www.pearsoned.com

Printed in Canada

3 4 5 6 7 8 9 10 XXXX 16 15 14 13 12

000200010270772675

SD

ISBN 10: 1-256-34610-1
ISBN 13: 978-1-256-34610-4

BRIEF CONTENTS

CONTENTS

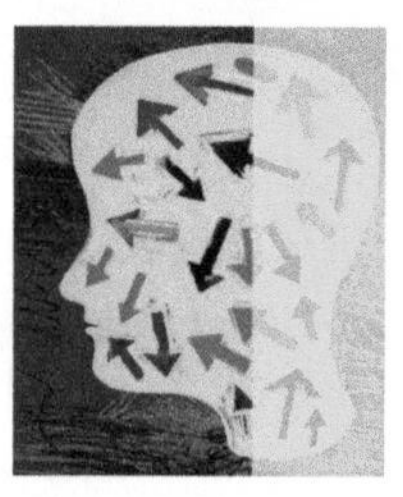

PART 2 LEARNING AND MOTIVATION

6 Behavioural Views of Learning 196

PREFACE

Many of you reading this book will be enrolled in an educational psychology course as part of your professional preparation for teaching, counselling, speech therapy, or psychology. The material we present will interest anyone who is concerned about education and learning, from the nursery school volunteer to the instructor in a community program for adults with learning disabilities. If you are not planning to work in the educational system, you're probably reading this text because you are interested in what educational psychology can reveal about teaching and learning in various settings. We have written the book for everyone so that no background in psychology or education is necessary to understand this material. It is as free of jargon and technical language as possible, while preserving accurate descriptions of the discipline and research. Many people have worked to make this edition clear, relevant, and interesting.

Since the first Canadian edition of *Educational Psychology* appeared, there have been many exciting developments in the field. This fifth Canadian edition incorporates many new insights and current trends in Canada while retaining the best features of the previous book. The new edition continues to emphasize the educational implications and applications of research on child development, cognitive science, learning, teaching, and assessment. Theory and practice are not separated but are considered together. We show how information and ideas drawn from research in educational psychology can be applied to address everyday issues of teaching. To help you explore connections between knowledge and practice, we have included many **examples, lesson segments**, **case studies**, **guidelines**, and **practical tips** from experienced teachers. Throughout the text, you will be challenged to think about the values and uses of ideas in each chapter, and you will see principles of educational psychology in action. Both professors and students find these features very helpful.

As you read *Educational Psychology*, you will notice that the authors are referred to by name when they share their personal experiences. Anita Woolfolk, Phil Winne, and Nancy Perry have been studying, researching, and practising the strategies, methods, and theories discussed in this text for many years. We hope you enjoy our stories and use them to gain insights into your own experiences.

NEW CONTENT AND ORGANIZATION IN THIS EDITION

In this fifth edition, we include the most currently available statistics about Canada and the implications for education in a rapidly changing Canadian mosaic. We continue to highlight the latest research on uniquely Canadian issues concerning programming for students with exceptional learning needs, multicultural education, and second-language learning. Issues and approaches to meeting the diverse needs of learners are presented in a more integrated way throughout the text. Also, we end each chapter with a new section titled "Diversity and Convergences" that highlights similarities and differences among children.

New Topics

Hundreds of new citations have been added to this edition to bring prospective teachers the most current information. Across the book there is increased coverage of a number of important topics. Some of these include:

- Increased coverage of the **brain, neuroscience**, and **teaching** integrated into several chapters.
- Increased attention to the role of social and contextual factors in developing and learning, including **Bronfenbrenner's** ecological theory and **Vygotsky's** sociocultural theory.
- Increased emphasis on **diversity in today's classrooms** (see especially Chapters 4 and 5).
- An emphasis on **integrating across theories** to understand teaching and learning. Examples include:

Chapter 2: Three questions across the theories

Chapter 5: Creating culturally compatible classrooms

Chapter 10: Looking across theories of learning

Chapter 11: Key concepts in motivation

Key content changes in each chapter include:

- Chapter 1: a **preview of the important theories** in the text, a discussion of the concerns of beginning teachers today, and new content on the demographics of Canadian students.
- Chapter 2: new sections on **language and cultural differences** in development, how and when **language develops, emergent literacy**, and enhanced discussion of the "magic middle."
- Chapter 3: new sections on **physical activity** and recess, and **gender development**, as well as enhanced coverage of **families** and **parenting,** and **peer relationships** and **friendships**.
- Chapter 4: new sections on **intellectual styles, neuroscience** and **learning challenges**, and response to intervention (**RTI**).
- Chapter 5: increased attention to **fostering resilience**.
- Chapter 6: expanded coverage of **positive behaviour supports** and cautions about using **punishment**, and new coverage of **functional behaviour assessments** and the **challenges to behavioural views.**
- Chapter 7: expanded coverage of the **brain** and learning, **cognitive load** and working memory, and **concept formation.**
- Chapter 8: new sections on **metacognition** and **critical thinking** in specific school subjects.
- Chapter 9 (**NEW CHAPTER)** ***The Learning Sciences and Constructivism:*** new material on neuroscience and teaching, collaboration and cooperative learning, service learning, and learning in a digital world.
- Chapter 10 (**NEW CHAPTER)** ***Social Cognitive Views of Learning and Motivation***: significantly expanded coverage of self-regulated learning.
- Chapter 11: new sections on **epistemological beliefs, Maslow's hierarchy of needs,** and **curiosity** and **emotions in motivation.**
- Chapter 12: new section on **developing caring relationships** and **classroom connections, bullying and cyberbullying,** and **violence in schools.**
- Chapter 13: new section on **differentiated instruction** and **universal design**.
- Chapter 14: combined assessment and testing chapter that is streamlined, current, and complete, and includes a new section on the merits and demerits of using **tests from textbooks**.

The Plan of the Book

The introductory chapter begins with you and the questions you may be asking yourself about teaching. What is good teaching, and what does it take to become an excellent teacher? How can educational psychology help you to understand what good teaching is and, if you choose a career in teaching, become such a teacher?

Part 1, "Students," focuses on learners, including how students develop mentally, physically, emotionally, and socially, and how all these aspects fit together. We then look at various types of diversity in the classroom. How do students differ in their abilities and preferences for learning, and how can teachers accommodate these differences? What does it mean to create a culturally compatible classroom, one that makes learning accessible to all students?

Part 2, "Learning and Motivation," looks at learning and motivation from four major perspectives—behavioural, cognitive, constructivist, and social cognitive. Learning theories have important but different implications for instruction at every level. Cognitive research is particularly vital right now and promises to be a wellspring of ideas for teaching in the immediate future.

Part 3, "Teaching and Assessing," discusses the ever-present, linked issues of motivating, managing, teaching, and assessing today's students. The material in these chapters is based on the most recent research in real classrooms and includes information on both teacher-centred and student-centred approaches to teaching. The chapter on classroom assessment looks at many ways to assess and evaluate students' learning.

Aids to Understanding

At the beginning of each chapter you will find an **Outline** of the key topics with page numbers for quick reference. Then you are confronted with a question, "What Would You Do?" about a real-life classroom situation related to the information in the chapter. By the time you reach the Teachers' Casebook at the end of the chapter, you should have even more ideas about how to solve the problem raised, so be alert as you read. Each chapter begins with a preview and questions to focus your thinking about the upcoming pages.

Within the chapter, headings point out themes, questions, and problems as they arise, so you can look up information easily. These can also serve as a quick review of important points. When a new term or concept is introduced, it appears in boldface type along with a brief marginal definition. These **Key Terms** are also defined in the **Glossary** at the end of the book. Throughout the book, graphs, tables, photos, and cartoons have been chosen to clarify and extend the text material—and to add to your enjoyment.

Each chapter ends with a **Summary** of the main ideas, as well as an alphabetical list of the key terms from the chapter, along with the page number where each term is discussed.

Text Features

The text emphasizes educational psychology's practical relevance for teachers and students in classrooms through the following features:

Guidelines. An important reason for studying educational psychology is to gain skills in solving classroom problems. Often texts give pages of theory and research findings, but little assistance in translating theory into practice. This text is different. Included in each chapter are several sets of guidelines, teaching tips, and practical suggestions based on the theory and research discussed in the chapter. Each suggestion is clarified by two or three specific examples. Although the guidelines cannot cover every possible situation, they do provide a needed bridge between knowledge and practice and should help you apply the text's information to new situations. In addition, every chapter after the first has one set of guidelines that provides ideas for working with families and the community—an area of growing importance today.

MyEducationLab margin notes. Look for the MyEducationLab logo and directives in the margins and at the end of each chapter. Follow the simple navigation instructions to access the multimedia content, including the **Study Plan (Pre- and Post-Tests)**, **Review, Practice, and Enrichment Activities**, **Activities and Applications**, **Building Teaching Skills and Dispositions**, **Podcasts**, and many more tools and activities to help you better understand the concepts in the text and get a better grade. A margin note near the beginning of each chapter directs you to the **Connect and Extend** section of MyEducationLab, where you will find further content that links to teaching, students' thinking, research, and the news.

Teachers' Casebook. At the end of each chapter, teachers from across Canada offer their own solutions to the problem presented at the beginning of each chapter. Teachers' Casebook: What Would They Do? gives you insight into the thinking of expert teachers; compare their solutions to the ones you devised. Their ideas truly show educational psychology at work in a range of everyday situations. The Teachers' Casebook brings to life the topics and principles discussed in each chapter.

Point/Counterpoint. There is a section in each chapter called Point/Counterpoint, a debate that examines two contrasting perspectives on an important question or controversy related to research or practice in educational psychology. Many of the topics considered in these Point/Counterpoint features have been in the news recently and are central to the discussions of educational reformers.

What Would You Say? Two or three times in every chapter, you are asked how you would answer possible job interview questions based on the text material. These questions were suggested by practising principals and superintendents.

Reaching Every Student. This feature provides ideas for assessing, teaching, and motivating all students in today's classroom. Some describe teaching strategies to reach students with learning problems. Some explain ways of using technology to reach every student. Others present creative ways to teach complex concepts.

Diversity and Convergences. Throughout the book you will find an increased emphasis on diversity. "Diversity and Convergences" sections at the end of every chapter examine the role of diversity in the chapter topics, as well as pull together content that shows similarities and differences among students.

Student Supplements

PEARSON myeducationlab

MyEducationLab (www.myeducationlab.com). This online tool will help you improve your understanding of the concepts taught in this textbook and in your course. Resources include videos of real classroom experiences, sample lesson plans, simulations, case studies, and links to important educational and teaching websites that will help you make the transition from student to teacher. As you study in your course and with this textbook, please follow along in MyEducationLab. Use it! Explore it! And improve your knowledge and your grade!

Features Include the Following

Study Plan: Self-grading quizzes assist you in identifying which areas of each chapter you need to review and provides review exercises to help you deepen your knowledge of the chapter concepts.

Activities and Applications: These exercises present thought-provoking questions that probe your understanding of chapter material through videos, simulations, and teacher and student artifacts.

Building Teaching Skills and Dispositions: Based on classroom video footage and simulations, these assignments help you practise and strengthen skills that are essential to quality teaching.

Podcasts: Listen to Dr. Woolfolk talk about how chapters in the text relates to the profession of teaching.

CourseSmart for Students

CourseSmart goes beyond traditional expectations—providing instant, online access to the textbooks and course materials you need at an average savings of 60%. With instant access from any computer and the ability to search your text, you'll find the content you need quickly, no matter where you are. And with online tools like highlighting and note-taking, you can save time and study efficiently. See all the benefits at **www.coursesmart.com/students**.

Instructor Supplements

Instructor's Resource CD-ROM (978-0-13-266837-8). This resource CD includes the following instructor supplements:

Instructor's Manual. This manual includes a variety of resources for instructors, including teaching outlines; cooperative, research, and field experience activities, supported by handouts; discussion questions; and suggested videos and websites.

PowerPoint Presentations. This instructor resource contains key points, lecture notes, and figures to accompany each chapter in the text.

Test Item File. This test bank contains approximately 2000 test questions, including multiple-choice, fill-in-the-blank, true/false, short answer, and case studies.

These instructor supplements are also available for download from a password-protected section of Pearson Canada's online catalogue (**vig.pearsoned.ca**). Navigate to your book's catalogue page to view a list of the supplements that are available. See your local sales representative for details and access.

MyTest. The test bank is also available as a MyTest, a powerful assessment generation program that helps instructors easily create and print quizzes, tests, exams, as well as homework or practice handouts. Questions and tests can all be authored online, allowing instructors ultimate flexibility and the ability to efficiently manage assessments at anytime, from anywhere. The MyTest can be accessed by visiting **www.pearsonmytest.com**.

Technology Specialists. Pearson's Technology Specialists work with faculty and campus course designers to ensure that Pearson technology products, assessment tools, and online course materials are tailored to meet your specific needs. This highly qualified team is dedicated to helping schools take full advantage of a wide range of educational resources by assisting in the integration of a variety of instructional materials and media formats. Your local Pearson Canada sales representative can provide you with more details on this service program.

CourseSmart for Instructors. CourseSmart goes beyond traditional expectations—providing instant, online access to the textbooks and course materials you need at a lower cost for students. And even as students save money, you can save time and hassle with a digital eTextbook that allows you to search for the most relevant content at the very moment you need it. Whether it's evaluating textbooks or creating lecture notes to help students with difficult concepts, CourseSmart can make life a little easier. See how when you visit **www.coursesmart.com/instructors**.

Feedback

You are invited to respond to any aspect of this text. We welcome your feedback. You may wish to criticize the solutions in the Teachers' Casebook, for example, or suggest topics or materials you think should be added to future editions. We would also like to know what you think of the text features and student supplements. Please send letters to

Acquisitions Editor, Education
Pearson Canada
26 Prince Andrew Place
Don Mills, ON M3C 2T8

ACKNOWLEDGMENTS

Our work on this project benefited immensely from consultations with friends and colleagues. Especially, we thank Anita Woolfolk for continuing to support this Canadian adaptation of her excellent textbook. Also, we thank teachers across this country who responded to the cases and who allowed us to describe their exemplary classroom practices. They are an inspiration to us.

The following Canadian reviewers contributed thoughtful comments:

Jill Singleton-Jackson, University of Windsor
Carlin J. Miller, University of Windsor
Anne MacGregor, Douglas College
John C. Nesbit, Simon Fraser University
Kenneth A. Pudlas, Trinity Western University
Jeff St. Pierre, University of Western Ontario
Noella Piquette-Tomei, University of Lethbridge
Irina Tzoneva, University of Fraser Valley

Thanks also to the MyEducationLab authors:

Latika Nirula, Ph.D.
Curriculum/Faculty Development Specialist, Centre for Learning and Innovation
Michener Institute for Applied Health Sciences

Barbara van Ingen
Registered Psychologist
Concordia University College of Alberta

Kim MacKinnon, Ph.D.
Department of Curriculum, Teaching and Learning
University of Toronto

Thanks to the entire team at Pearson Canada.

1 Learning, Teaching, and Educational Psychology

SuperStock/Photodisc

TEACHERS' CASEBOOK

WHAT WOULD YOU DO?

It is your second year as a teacher at John A. Macdonald Public School (kindergarten–grade 8). One of your colleagues has been nominated for a Prime Minister's Award for Teaching Excellence. This person has been a role model to you in your first two years as a teacher, providing advice and encouragement. You would like to support her by writing a letter of recommendation to the Prime Minister's Office highlighting her exemplary teaching practices, commitment, and leadership. The deadline for submissions is a week away. How will you prepare to write the letter?

CRITICAL THINKING

- What do you need to know about teaching to complete this task?
- What are some indicators of excellent teaching?
- Do different philosophies of teaching provide different answers to this question?
- What points will you make in your letter, and how will you back them up?

If you are like many students, you begin this course with a mixture of anticipation and wariness. Perhaps you are required to take educational psychology as part of a program in teacher education, speech therapy, nursing, or counselling. Or you may have chosen this class as an elective because you are interested in education or psychology. Whatever your reason for enrolling, you probably have questions about teaching, schools, students—or even about yourself—that you hope this course may answer. The fifth Canadian edition of *Educational Psychology* has been written with questions such as these in mind.

In this first chapter, we begin not with the concept of educational psychology but rather with education—more specifically, with the state of teaching today. Teachers have been both criticized as ineffective and lauded as the best hope for young people. Do teachers make a difference in students' learning? What characterizes good teaching? Only when you are aware of the challenges teachers face can you appreciate the contributions of educational psychology. After a brief introduction to the world of the teacher, we turn to a discussion of educational psychology itself. How can principles identified by educational psychologists benefit teachers, therapists, parents, and others who are interested in teaching and learning? What exactly is the content associated with the field of educational psychology, and where does this information come from?

By the time you have completed this chapter, you should be able to answer these questions:

- Does teaching matter?
- What is good teaching?
- What do expert teachers know?
- Why should I study educational psychology?
- What roles do theory and research play in this field?
- What are the greatest concerns of beginning teachers?

Connect and **Extend**
Go to the "Connect and Extend" section in Chapter 1 of MyEducationLab to find further content that links to teaching, students' thinking, research, and the news.

LEARNING AND TEACHING TODAY

Welcome to one of our favourite topics—educational psychology—the study of development, learning, and motivation that takes place in and out of schools. We believe this is the most important course you will take to prepare for your future as an educator, whether your "students" are children or adults learning in classrooms or in environments that are outside schools. In fact, there is evidence that new teachers who have completed coursework in development and learning are twice as likely to stay in teaching (National Commission on Teaching and America's Future, 2003). This may be a required course for you, so let us make the case for educational psychology, first by introducing you to classrooms today.

Dramatic Diversity: Students Today

Who are the students in Canadian classrooms today? Where do they come from? Here are a few facts (taken from Campaign 2000, 2009; Canadian Teachers Federation, 2009; Free the Children, 2005; Statistics Canada, 2010d):

- By 2031, projections indicated that Canada's foreign-born population will increase from 20 percent to 25–28 percent, and 55 percent of these immigrants will come from Asian countries.
- Between 29 and 32 percent of the population will be members of visible minority groups, nearly twice this population's size in the 2006 census.
- Diversity is most concentrated in our largest cities. For example, visible minorities will comprise more than half the population in Toronto and Vancouver, but no more than 5 percent of the population in St. John's and Trois-Rivières or Saguenay.
- Currently, there are classrooms in Vancouver where more than 80 percent of children are English language learners.
- Similarly, children come from a wide range of religious communities. Participation in religions other than Christianity has doubled since 2006 (from 6 to 14 percent), and approximately 50 percent of people with a religious affiliation other than Christian identify themselves as Muslim.
- Currently, approximately one in nine children in Canada lives in poverty. In 2007, 280 000 children were regular users of food banks, which represents an increase of 86 percent since 1989.
- Children in classrooms have diverse abilities and disabilities. Our inclusive policies mean that children with disabilities spend the majority of their school day in general education classrooms.
- Children are surviving diseases as serious as cancer and returning to school, but sometimes with after-effects related to the treatment they underwent that have implications for learning (Daly, Kral, & Brown, 2008).
- Finally, children's families are diverse. Some children live with a mom and dad, but many live with a mom or dad, and some live with two moms or two dads, or with grandparents, or aunts and uncles.

Dealing with such diversity in the classroom can be daunting. It presents unique challenges to schools and communities, but it presents opportunities too. These statistics are dramatic, but a bit impersonal. As a teacher, counsellor, recreational worker, speech therapist, or family member, you will encounter real children. You will meet many individual children in this book too. Even though students in classrooms are increasingly diverse in race, ethnicity, language, and economic level, the teaching force remains very homogeneous. Clearly, it is important for all teachers to understand and work effectively with all their students. Several chapters in this book are devoted to understanding students. In addition, many times within each chapter we will explore the concepts of student diversity and inclusion through research, cases, and practical applications.

DIVERSITY MATTERS Students in today's classrooms are increasingly diverse in race, ethnicity, language, and economic level. Clearly, it is important for all teachers to understand and work effectively with all of their students.

Do Teachers Make a Difference?

For a while, some researchers reported findings suggesting that wealth and social status, not teaching, were the major factors determining who learned in schools (e.g., Coleman, 1966). In fact, much of the early research on teaching was conducted by educational psychologists who refused to accept these claims that teachers were powerless in the face of poverty among students and other societal problems (Wittrock, 1986).

How could you decide if teaching makes a difference in the lives of students? You could look to your own experience. Did you have teachers who had an impact on your life? Perhaps one of your teachers even influenced your decision to become an educator. That said, one of the purposes of educational psychology in general is to go beyond individual experiences and testimonies, powerful as they are, to systematically examine the impact of teaching on the lives of students by using carefully designed research studies. Several of these studies are described below.

RELATIONSHIPS MATTER Research has shown that the quality of the teacher–student relationship in kindergarten predicts a number of academic and behavioural outcomes, particularly for students with behaviour problems, who are less likely to have problems later in school if their teachers are sensitive to their needs and provide frequent, consistent feedback.

Teacher–Student Relationships. Bridget Hamre and Robert Pianta (2001) followed 179 children in a small school district from the time that they entered kindergarten right through to the end of grade 8. The researchers concluded that the quality of the teacher–student relationship in kindergarten (defined in terms of level of conflict with the child, the child's dependency on the teacher, and the teacher's affection for the child) predicted a number of academic and behavioural outcomes through grade 8, particularly for students with high levels of behavioural problems. Even when the gender, ethnicity, cognitive ability, and behaviour ratings of the student were accounted for, the relationship with the teacher still predicted aspects of school success. According to these researchers, "The association between the quality of early teacher–child relationships and later school performance can be both strong and persistent" (p. 636). In a more recent study that followed children from four and a half years of age through grade 5, Pianta and his colleagues found that the degree of emotional warmth of the teacher–child interactions and the teacher's degree of skill in recognizing and responding to children's needs consistently predicted the child's growth in reading and mathematics (Pianta, Belsky, Vandergrift, Houts, & Morrison, 2008).

Based on these results, it appears that students who have significant behaviour problems in the early years are less likely to have problems later in school if their teachers are sensitive to their needs and provide frequent, consistent feedback. Paula Stanovich and Anne Jordan (1998), two researchers at the Ontario Institute for Studies in Education of the University of Toronto (OISE/UT), found that teachers who believed that it was their responsibility to include and instruct all the students in their classrooms (including students with disabilities and English language learners) engaged in more academic interactions with their students and were more persistent in helping students to succeed in school.

Effective teachers who establish positive relationships with their students appear to be a powerful force in those students' lives. Students who have problems seem to benefit the most from good teaching. What makes a teacher effective? What is good teaching? We consider those points next.

Teacher Preparation and Quality. Linda Darling-Hammond (2000), a researcher at Stanford University, examined the ways in which teacher qualifications are related to student achievement using data from several U.S.-based sources, including a survey of policies in the 50 states, case study analyses, the 1993–1994 Schools and Staffing Surveys, and the National Assessment of Educational Progress (NAEP). Her findings indicated that the quality of teachers—as measured by whether the teachers were fully certified and earned a major in their teaching field—was related to student performance. In fact, measures of teacher preparation and certification were by far the strongest predictors of student achievement in reading and mathematics, both before and after controlling for student poverty and English language proficiency. For example, look at Table 1.1. In the first row, all the correlations are positive and significant. This means that the higher the percentage of teachers who earned full certification and a major in their teaching field, the higher their students' achievement in math and in reading. All but one of the correlations in the second row are negative and significant. This indicates that the higher the percentage of teachers who are teaching outside their field, the lower their students' achievement tends to be. So there is evidence that more qualified teachers make a difference in student learning. (Later in the chapter, we will look closely at how to interpret these statistics.)

Setting standards for teacher qualification is controversial, however. The *Point/Counterpoint* box examines issues in the debate about whether or not to set teaching standards.

POINT/COUNTERPOINT

Standards for Teachers

RESEARCH HAS REVEALED many teaching practices that are highly effective. Some educators argue that all teachers should demonstrate a "standard" of performance relating to these practices to earn their teaching certificates. Other educators believe that excellent teachers don't just implement a set of standard practices; excellent teachers are reflective—thoughtful and inventive—about teaching. Teaching standards are being developed and used as measures of teaching quality in several provinces across Canada (e.g., in British Columbia, Alberta, Ontario, and Quebec), in the United States, and around the world (e.g., in New Zealand and the United Kingdom). Is this how we should evaluate teaching quality? Should teachers demonstrate performance to a set of standards in order to be certified?

POINT

School renewal depends on what teachers know and can do to enhance their students' learning.

Advocates of the teaching standards movement claim that teaching standards honour and advance the profession by highlighting the complex and varied nature of educators' work (BC College of Teachers, 2008). Furthermore, proponents of teaching standards argue that the role of standards is to articulate the knowledge, skills, and attitudes that professional educators should possess and to outline the responsibilities that accrue to them as professionals who hold the public trust. The proponents believe that professional standards will contribute to a safe and high-quality learning environment for students.

Many educators are welcoming teaching standards as a basis for educational reform, believing that such standards will lead to higher status and to greater autonomy for the teaching profession (Beck, Hart, & Kosnik, 2002). Teachers' talents and effectiveness often are underestimated by the public and in the media. Standards can lift the morale of teachers by informing others about their skills and accomplishments. Standards can also clarify how teachers contribute to the lives of students through caring, reflective, and innovative practices.

In the past, standards movements have tended to focus on knowledge and skills that students need to acquire, assuming that once educators know *what* students need to learn, getting them to learn it will be relatively easy. There is widespread agreement among teaching experts, however, that teaching and learning are complex processes and that some pedagogical approaches are more effective than others for supporting learning. Shouldn't all teachers be required to learn and effectively implement these approaches?

COUNTERPOINT

The teaching standards movement has more to do with punishing teachers than with enhancing their professionalism.

Those who oppose the teaching standards movement are concerned about how standards will be used in practice. Will they become the basis for disciplining teachers? Will they drive the curricula in teacher education programs, just as high-stakes assessments of students have led to a narrowing of curricula in kindergarten through grade 12? Who will set the standards? How specific will they be?

One of the *Standards for Education, Competence and Professional Conduct of Educators in BC* indicates that teachers should have "a broad knowledge base and understand the subject areas they teach" (BC College of Teachers, 2008). Most teachers agree that this is ideal. However, many teachers are assigned to teach classes or topics for which they have no expertise, often as a result of conditions that exist within a school or district and that are beyond the teachers' control (e.g., budget cutbacks, shortage of teachers with particular qualifications). The BC Teachers' Federation argues that it is unfair to create standards as a set of responsibilities for teachers without also acknowledging the responsibility of employers (school and district administrators, governments) to ensure that conditions are met that enable teachers to meet the standards (BCTF, 2003).

In the United Kingdom, the government's standards for teaching imposed a very narrow definition of both professionalism and failure to meet these standards, which resulted in funding sanctions. A similar model is reflected in the *No Child Left Behind* legislation in the United States. These outcomes reinforce the skepticism of opponents of the teaching standards movement.

It appears that many educators welcome standards that elevate the teaching profession and articulate what effective teachers know and do with respect to instruction. Concern arises from the potential for governments to use standards that create a high-stakes and punitive environment for teachers that could end up having a negative impact on students' ability to learn.

Sources: BC College of Teachers. (2008). *Standards for the competence, professional conduct and ethical behaviour of educators in British Columbia,* 3rd ed. Retrieved from www.bcct.ca/documents/AboutUs/Standards/edu_stds.pdf; BCTF. (2003). *Summary analysis of the BC College of Teachers' standards for the education competence and professional conduct of educators in BC.* Retrieved from www.bctf.ca/.

WHAT IS GOOD TEACHING?

Educators, psychologists, philosophers, novelists, journalists, filmmakers, mathematicians, scientists, historians, policymakers, and parents, to name only a few groups, have examined the question "what is good teaching?" There are hundreds of answers. And good teaching is not confined to classrooms—it occurs in homes and hospitals, in museums and sales meetings, and in therapists' offices and summer camps. In this book we are primarily concerned with teaching in classrooms, but much of what you will learn applies to teaching in other settings as well.

Inside Three Classrooms

To begin our examination of good teaching, let's step inside the classrooms of several outstanding teachers. All the situations that follow reflect the conditions in real classrooms today.

A Multilingual Grade 1 Class. Anne Lee-Hawman teaches grade 1 in Mississauga, Ontario. Of the 22 children in her classroom, half speak English as a second language (ESL). As is true for most linguistically diverse students in Canada, they spend 100 percent of their school day using English as opposed to their native language. This immersion, or submersion, approach to second-language learning contrasts with the bilingual approaches to language learning used in many American states.

An ESL teacher helps Anne to integrate these students by working in Anne's classroom each day. Together Anne and the ESL teacher support students in small groups and make modifications to the curriculum that enable students who speak English as a second language to participate in all the activities of the classroom. One strategy the two teachers have found useful is to make information available through visual materials (e.g., pictures, diagrams, and word or concept maps). Anne also makes use of peer tutors and, whenever possible, offers one-on-one instruction to students who need it.

In addition to supporting students' acquisition of English, Anne encourages students and their parents to continue talking, reading, and writing in their first language at home. As well, she fosters an appreciation for diverse languages and cultures in her classroom by celebrating multicultural holidays and by having students compare and contrast their home or community experiences and practices during classroom discussions and sharing times.

Anne makes a point of learning as much as she can about her students' linguistic and cultural heritages. She recognizes how important it is for teachers to understand how issues of language and culture influence children's learning, so that they don't misinterpret children's motivation and behaviour. This year, five languages are represented in Anne's classroom: English, Hindi, Punjabi, Chinese, and Malaysian. She has a lot of learning to do.

A Suburban Grade 6 Class. Ken teaches grade 6 in a suburban elementary school in Richmond, BC. Students in the class have varying racial, ethnic, family income, and language backgrounds. Ken emphasizes "process writing." His students complete first drafts, discuss them with others in the class, revise, edit, and "publish" their work. The students also keep daily journals and often use these to share personal concerns with Ken. They tell him of problems at home, fights, and fears; he always takes the time to respond in writing. The study of science is also placed in the context of the real world. The students use a National Geographic Society computer network to link with other schools in order to identify acid rain patterns around the world. For social studies, the class plays simulation games; for example, in two games that focused on the first half of the 1800s, the students "lived" as trappers collecting animal skins and as pioneers heading west.

Throughout the year, Ken is very interested in the social and emotional development of his students—he wants them to learn about responsibility and fairness as well as science and social studies. This concern is evident in the way he develops his class rules at the beginning of the year. Rather than specifying dos and don'ts, Ken and his students generate a list of rights and responsibilities for their class. This list covers most of the situations that might need a "rule."

TABLE 1.1 **Correlations Between Teacher Quality Variables and Student Achievement, United States**

	Grade 4 Math, 1992	Grade 4 Math, 1996	Grade 8 Math, 1996	Grade 4 Reading, 1992	Grade 4 Reading, 1994
Percentage of teachers well-qualified (with full certification and a major in their field)	.71**	.61**	.67**	.80**	.75**
Percentage of teachers out of field (with less than a minor in the field they teach)	−.48*	−.44*	−.42*	−.56*	−.33

*p < .05; **p < .01

Source: Darling-Hammond, L. (2000). Teacher quality and student achievement: A review of state policy evidence. *Educational Policy Analysis Archives*, 8, pp. 1–48. Retrieved January 27, 2005, from http://epaa.asu.edu/epaa/v8n1. Copyright © Educational Policy Analysis Archives. Adapted with permission of the EPAA.

An Advanced Math Class. Hilda Borko and Carol Livingston (1989) describe how Randy, an expert secondary school mathematics teacher, worked with his students' confusion to construct a review lesson about strategies for doing integrals. When one student said that a particular section in the book seemed "haphazard," Randy led the class through a process of organizing the material. He asked the class for general statements about useful strategies for doing integrals. He clarified their suggestions, elaborated on some, and helped students improve others. He asked the students to relate their ideas to passages in the text. Even though he accepted all reasonable suggestions, he listed only the key strategies on the board. By the end of the period, the students had transformed the disorganized material from the book into an ordered and useful outline to guide their learning. They also had a better idea about how to read and understand difficult material.

One thing that's noticeable in all three of these classrooms is the teachers' commitment to their students. These teachers must deal with a wide range of student abilities and challenges: different languages, different home situations, and different abilities and disabilities. They must adapt instruction and assessment to students' needs. They must make the most abstract concepts, such as integrals, real and understandable for their particular students. Then there is the challenge of how to use new technologies and techniques. The teachers must use them appropriately to accomplish important goals, not just to entertain the students. And the whole time these experts are navigating through the academic material, they are also taking care of the emotional needs of their students, propping up sagging self-esteem and encouraging responsibility. If we followed these individuals from the first day of class, we would see that they carefully plan and teach the basic procedures for living and learning in their classes. These teachers can efficiently collect and correct homework, regroup students, give directions, distribute materials, collect lunch money, and deal with disruptions—and they can do all this while also making a mental note to find out why one of their students is so tired. Finally, these teachers are also reflective—they constantly think back over situations to analyze what they did and why and to consider how they might improve learning for their students.

So, What Is Good Teaching? Is good teaching science or art, the application of research-based theories or the creative invention of specific practices? Is a good teacher an expert explainer—"a sage on the stage"— or a great coach—"a guide by the side"? These debates have raged for years. In your other education classes, you probably will encounter criticisms of the scientific, teacher-centred sages. You will be encouraged to be inventive, student-centred guides. *But beware of either/or choices.* Teachers must be both knowledgeable and inventive. They must be able to use a range of strategies, and they must also be able to invent new strategies. They must have some basic research-based routines for managing classes, but they must also be willing and able to break from

Reflective Thoughtful and inventive. Reflective teachers think back over situations to analyze what they did and why, and to consider how they might improve learning for their students.

MENTORS MATTER Teaching is one of the few professions in which a new teacher must assume all the responsibilities of an experienced "pro" during the first week on the job. Veteran teachers can be an excellent source of information and support during these early weeks.

the routine when the situation calls for change. They must know the research on student development, "patterns common to particular ages, culture, social class, geography, and gender" (Ball, 1997, p. 773), and they also need to know their own particular students who are unique combinations of culture, gender, and geography. Personally, we hope you all become teachers who are both "sages" and "guides," wherever you stand.

Anne, Ken, and Randy are examples of expert teachers, but they have been teaching for a long time. What about you? Let's look at what it's like to be a new teacher.

What Are the Concerns of Beginning Teachers?

STOP & THINK Imagine walking into class on your first day of teaching. List the concerns, fears, and worries you have. What assets do you bring to the job?

Beginning teachers everywhere share many concerns, including how to maintain classroom discipline, motivate students, accommodate differences among students, evaluate students' work, deal with parents, and get along with other teachers (Conway & Clark, 2003; Melnick & Meister, 2008; Veenman, 1984). Many teachers also experience what has been called "reality shock" when they take their first job because they really cannot ease into their responsibilities. On the first day of their first job, beginning teachers face the same tasks as teachers with years of experience. Student teaching, while a critical element of becoming a good teacher, does not really prepare prospective teachers for starting off a school year with a new class. Here is some advice from Dave Brown, a fantastic teacher who has taught junior high school students in Toronto and middle school students in Lethbridge, Alberta:

> I think one of the most difficult things new teachers face is the almost immediate realization that the environment they find themselves in after being hired is quite different from the one they experienced in their practicum, when they essentially had backup from the sponsor teacher should any negative situation arise. In contrast, many teaching positions are filled mere days before school starts. A new teacher may find that he or she is starting tomorrow, handed a schedule, and offered a "welcome aboard" along with an evening to prepare his or her program. Moreover, you may find that it is a tricky balancing act satisfying the needs of the school's administration, the curriculum, and most importantly, yourself.
>
> The assumption that a new teacher can be expected to come in on short notice and perform in a manner that makes the transition seamless for students, staff, and administration is unrealistic. In fact, most good administrators and staff members know this and are very approachable and helpful. In addition, when I was thrust into my first position—covering a maternity leave—I quickly learned that it's important to know and rely on your strengths in delivering the material, and to be aware of what doesn't work for you. I think this is especially important as a beginning teacher since you are essentially test-driving your lessons for the first time.

With experience, hard work, and good support, seasoned teachers can focus on students' needs and judge their teaching success by the accomplishments of their students (Fuller, 1969; Pigge & Marso, 1997). Here's how one experienced teacher described the shift from concerns about yourself to concerns about your students: "The difference between a beginning teacher and an experienced one is that the beginning teacher asks, 'How am I doing?' and the experienced teacher asks, 'How are the children doing?'" (Codell, 2001, p. 191).

Our goal in writing this book is to give you the foundation to become an expert as you gain experience. One thing experts do is listen to their students. Table 1.2 shows some advice students in a grade 1 class gave to their student teacher: It looks like the students know about good teaching, too.

TABLE 1.2 **Advice for Student Teachers From Their Students**

The students in Ms. Amato's elementary school class gave this advice as a gift to their student teacher on her last day.

1. Teach us as much as you can.
2. Give us homework.
3. Help us when we have problems with our work.
4. Help us to do the right thing.
5. Help us make a family in school.
6. Read books to us.
7. Teach us to read.
8. Help us write about faraway places.
9. Give us lots of compliments, like "Oh, that's so beautiful."
10. Smile at us.
11. Take us for walks and on trips.
12. Respect us.
13. Help us get our education.

Source: From Nieto, Sonia. *Affirming Diversity: The Sociopolitical Context of Multicultural Education,* 4e. Published by Allyn and Bacon, Boston, MA. Copyright © 2004 by Pearson Education. Reprinted by permission of the publisher.

We began this chapter claiming that educational psychology is the most important course you will take. Okay, maybe we are a bit biased—we have been teaching the subject for decades! So let us now turn to our favourite topic.

THE ROLE OF EDUCATIONAL PSYCHOLOGY

For as long as the field of educational psychology has existed—about 100 years—there have been debates about what it really is. Some people believe educational psychology is simply knowledge gained from psychology and applied to the activities of the classroom. Others believe it involves applying the methods of psychology to study classroom and school life (Brophy, 2003; Wittrock, 1992). A look at history shows the close connections between educational psychology and teaching.

In the Beginning: Linking Educational Psychology and Teaching

In one sense, educational psychology is very old. Topics that Plato and Aristotle discussed—the role of the teacher, the relationship between teacher and student, methods of teaching, the nature and order of learning, the role of affect in learning—are still studied by educational psychologists today. From its beginning, psychology in North America was linked to teaching. In 1890, William James officially founded the field of psychology and developed a lecture series for teachers entitled *Talks to Teachers on Psychology*. These lectures were given in summer schools for teachers and then published in 1899. James's student, G. Stanley Hall, founded the American Psychological Association. His dissertation was about children's understandings of the world; teachers helped him collect data. Hall encouraged teachers to make detailed observations to study their students' development—as his mother had done when she was a teacher. Hall's student, John Dewey, founded the Laboratory School at the University of Chicago and is considered the father of the progressive education movement (Berliner, 2006; Hilgard, 1996; Pajares, 2003).

Another of William James's students, E. L. Thorndike, wrote the first educational psychology text in 1903 and founded the *Journal of Educational Psychology* in 1910. Thorndike began a shift from the classroom to the laboratory to study learning but his view proved to be too narrow. It still took 50 years to return to the psychological study of learning in classrooms (Hilgard, 1996).

In the 1940s and 1950s, the study of educational psychology concentrated on individual differences, assessment, and learning behaviours. In the 1960s and 1970s, the focus of research shifted to

Educational psychology The discipline concerned with teaching and learning processes; it applies the methods and theories of psychology and has its own as well.

the study of cognitive development and learning, with attention to how students learn concepts and remember. Recently, educational psychologists have investigated how culture and social factors affect learning and development (Pressley & Roehrig, 2003).

Educational Psychology Today

What is educational psychology today? The view generally accepted is that educational psychology is a distinct discipline with its own theories, research methods, problems, and techniques. Both in the past and today, educational psychologists study learning and teaching and, at the same time, strive to improve educational practice (Pintrich, 2000). In order to understand as much as possible about learning and teaching, educational psychologists examine what happens when *someone* (a teacher or parent) or *something* (a computer) teaches *something* (math or weaving or dancing) to *someone else* (a student or co-worker or team) in some *setting* (a classroom or theatre or gym) (Berliner, 2006; Schwab, 1973). So educational psychologists study child and adolescent development; learning and motivation, including how people learn different academic subjects such as reading or mathematics; social and cultural influences on learning; teaching and teachers; and assessment including testing (Alexander & Winne, 2006).

But even with this long history of interest in teaching and learning, are the findings of educational psychologists really that helpful for teachers? After all, most teaching is just common sense, isn't it? Let's take a few minutes to examine these questions.

Is It Just Common Sense?

In many cases, the principles set forth by educational psychologists—after spending much thought, research, and money—sound pathetically obvious. People are tempted to say, and usually do say, "Everyone knows that!" Consider these examples:

Taking Turns. What method should a teacher use in selecting students to participate in a primary-grade reading class?

Common-Sense Answer. Teachers should call on students randomly so that everyone will have to follow the lesson carefully. If a teacher were to use the same order every time, the students would know when their turn was coming up.

Answer Based on Research. Research by Ogden, Brophy, and Evertson (1977) indicates that the answer to this question is not so simple. In grade 1 reading classes, for example, going around the circle in order and giving each child a chance to read led to better overall achievement than calling on students randomly. The critical factor in going around the circle may be that each child has a chance to participate. Without a system for calling on everyone, many students can be overlooked or skipped. Research suggests there are better alternatives for teaching reading than going around the circle, but if teachers choose one of these alternatives, they should make sure that everyone has the chance for practice and feedback (Tierney, Readence, & Dishner, 1990).

Classroom Management. Students are engaged in an appropriate and educationally meaningful task, but still, some students are repeatedly out of their seats without permission, wandering around the room. What should the teacher do?

Common-Sense Answer. Each time the wanderers get up, the teacher should remind students to remain in their seats. If the teacher does not remind them and lets them get away with breaking the rules, both the out-of-seat students and the rest of the class may decide the teacher is not really serious about the rule.

Answer Based on Research. In a now-classic study, Madsen, Becker, Thomas, Koser, and Plager (1968) found that the more often a teacher told students to sit down when they were out of their seats, the more often the students got out of their seats without permission. When the teacher ignored students who were out of their seats and praised students who were sitting down, the rate of out-of-seat behaviour dropped greatly. When the teacher returned to the previous system of telling students to sit down, the rate of out-of-seat behaviour increased once again. It seems that—at least under some conditions—the more a teacher says, "Sit down!" the more the students stand up!

Skipping Grades. Should a school encourage exceptionally bright students to skip grades or to enter university or college early?

Common-Sense Answer. No! Very intelligent students who are a year or two younger than their classmates are likely to be social misfits. They are neither physically nor emotionally ready for dealing with older students and would be miserable in the social situations that are so important in school, especially in the later grades.

Answer Based on Research. Maybe. According to Samuel Kirk and his colleagues (1993), "from early admissions to school to early admissions to college, research studies invariably report that children who have been accelerated have adjusted as well as or better than have children of similar ability who have not been accelerated" (p. 105). Whether acceleration is the best solution for a student depends on many specific individual characteristics, including the intelligence and maturity of the student, and on the other available options. For some students, moving quickly through the material and working in advanced courses with older students is a very good idea.

Obvious Answers? Lily Wong (1987) demonstrated that just seeing research results in writing can make them seem obvious. She selected 12 findings from research on teaching; one of them was the "taking turns" result noted above. She presented six of the findings in their correct form and six in *exactly the opposite form* to college students and to experienced teachers. Both the college students and teachers rated about half of the *wrong* findings as "obviously" correct. In a follow-up study, other participants were shown the 12 findings and their opposites and were asked to pick which ones were correct. For 8 of the 12 findings, the participants chose the wrong result more often than the right one.

You may have thought that educational psychologists spend their time discovering the obvious. The examples above point out the danger of this kind of thinking. When a principle is stated in simple terms, it can sound simplistic. A similar phenomenon takes place when we see a gifted dancer or athlete perform; the well-trained performer makes it look easy. But we see only the results of the training, not all the work that went into mastering the individual movements. And bear in mind that any research finding—or its opposite—may sound like common sense. The issue is not what *sounds* sensible, but what is demonstrated when the principle is put to the test (Gage, 1991).

Using Research to Understand and Improve Learning

STOP & THINK Quickly, list all the different research methods you can name.

Conducting research to test possible answers is one of two major tasks of educational psychologists. The other task is combining the results of various studies into theories that attempt to present a unified view of such things as teaching, learning, and development.

Descriptive Studies. Educational psychologists design and conduct many different kinds of research studies in their attempts to understand teaching and learning. Some of these studies are "descriptive"—that is, their purpose is to describe events in a particular class or several classes. Reports of **descriptive studies** often include survey results, interview responses, samples of actual classroom dialogue, or observations of class activities.

One descriptive approach, classroom **ethnography**, is borrowed from anthropology. Ethnographic methods involve studying naturally occurring events in the life of a group and trying to understand the meaning of these events to the people involved. For example, the description of an expert high school mathematics teacher that appears earlier in this chapter was taken from an ethnographic study by Hilda Borko and Carol Livingston (1989). The researchers made detailed in-class observations and analyzed these observations, along with audio recordings and information from interviews with the teachers, in order to describe differences between novice and expert teachers.

Descriptive studies Studies that collect detailed information about specific situations, often using observation, surveys, interviews, recordings, or a combination of these methods.

Ethnography A descriptive approach to research that focuses on life within a group and tries to understand the meaning of events to the people involved.

In some descriptive research, researchers carefully analyze videotapes of classes to identify recurring patterns of teacher and student behaviour. In other studies, the researcher uses participant observation and works within the class or school to understand the actions from the perspectives of the teacher and the students. Researchers also may employ case studies. A case study investigates in depth how a teacher plans courses, for example, or how a student tries to learn specific material.

Correlational Studies. Often the results of descriptive studies include reports of correlations. We will take a minute to examine this concept, because you will encounter many correlations in the coming chapters. A correlation is a number that indicates both the strength and the direction of a relationship between two events or measurements. Correlations range from 1.00 to –1.00. The closer the correlation is to either 1.00 or –1.00, the stronger the relationship. For example, the correlation between height and weight is about .70 (a strong relationship); the correlation between height and number of languages spoken is about .00 (no relationship at all).

The sign of the correlation tells the direction of the relationship. A positive correlation indicates that the two factors increase or decrease together. As one gets larger, so does the other. Height and weight are positively correlated because greater height tends to be associated with greater weight. A negative correlation means that increases in one factor are related to decreases in the other. For example, the correlation between outside temperature and the weight of clothing worn is negative, since people tend to wear clothing of increasing weight as the temperature decreases.

It is important to note that correlations do not prove cause and effect (see Figure 1.1). Height and weight are correlated—taller people tend to weigh more than shorter people. But gaining weight obviously does not cause you to grow taller. Knowing a person's height simply allows you to make a general prediction about that person's weight. Educational psychologists identify correlations so that they can make predictions about important events in the classroom.

Experimental Studies. A second type of research—experimentation—allows educational psychologists to go beyond predictions and actually study cause and effect. Instead of just observing and describing an existing situation, the investigators introduce changes and note the results. First, a number of comparable groups of subjects are created. In psychological research, the term subjects generally refers to the people being studied—teachers or grade 8 students, for example—not to subjects such as math or science. One common way to make sure that groups of subjects are essentially the same is to assign each subject to a group using a random procedure. Random means that each subject has an equal chance to be in any group.

In one or more of these groups, the experimenters change some aspect of the situation to see if this change or "treatment" has an expected effect. The results in each group are then compared. Usually statistical tests are conducted to see if the differences between the groups are significant. When differences are described as statistically significant, it means that they probably did not happen simply by chance. A number of the studies we will examine attempt to identify cause-and-effect

Participant observation A method for conducting descriptive research in which the researcher becomes a participant in the situation in order to better understand life in that group.

Case study Intensive study of one person or one situation.

Correlation Statistical description of how closely two variables are related.

Positive correlation A relationship between two variables in which the two increase or decrease together. Example: calorie intake and weight gain.

Negative correlation A relationship between two variables in which a high value on one is associated with a low value on the other. Example: height and distance from top of head to the ceiling.

Experimentation Research method in which variables are manipulated and the effects recorded.

Subjects People or animals participating in a study.

Random Without any definite pattern; following no rule.

Statistically significant Not likely to be a chance occurrence.

FIGURE 1.1 **Correlations Do Not Show Causation**

When research shows that broken homes and crime are correlated, it does not show causation. Poverty, a third variable, may be the cause of both crime and broken homes.

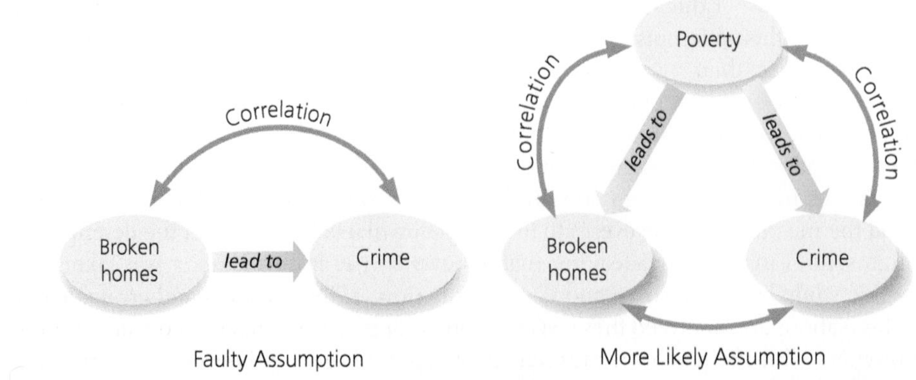

relationships by asking questions such as this: If teachers ignore students who are out of their seats without permission and praise students who are working hard at their desks (cause), will students spend more time working at their desks (effect)?

In many cases, both descriptive and experimental research occur together. The study by Ogden, Brophy, and Evertson (1977) described earlier in this section is a good example. To answer questions about the relationship between how students are selected to read in a primary-grade class and their achievement in reading, these investigators first observed students and teachers in a number of classrooms and then measured the reading achievement of the students. The researchers found that having students read in a predictable order was associated, or correlated, with gains in reading scores. With a simple correlation such as this, however, the researchers could not be sure that the strategy was actually causing the effect. In the second part of the study, Ogden and her colleagues asked several teachers to call on each student in turn. They then compared reading achievement in these groups with achievement in groups where teachers used other strategies. This second part of the research was thus an experimental study.

Single-Subject Experimental Studies. The goal of single-subject experimental studies is to determine the effects of a therapy, teaching method, or other intervention. One common approach is to observe an individual for a baseline period (A) and assess the behaviour of interest; then try an intervention (B) and note the results; then remove the intervention and go back to baseline conditions (A); and finally reinstate the intervention (B). This form of single-subject design is called an ABAB experiment. For example, a teacher might record how often a student is out of her seat without permission during a week-long baseline (A), and then, for the following week, ignore her when she is up but praise her when she is seated (B), recording how many times she is wandering out of her seat. Next, the teacher returns to the baseline conditions (A) and records results. Finally, the teacher reinstates the intervention (B) and observes whether it works again. Years ago, when this very intervention was tested, the praise-and-ignore strategy proved effective in increasing the time students spent in their seats (Madsen, Becker, Thomas, Koser, & Plager, 1968).

Microgenetic Studies. The goal of microgenetic studies is to intensively study cognitive processes in the midst of change—as the change is actually happening. For example, researchers might analyze how children learn a particular strategy for adding two-digit numbers over the course of several weeks. The microgenetic approach has three basic characteristics: (a) researchers observe the entire period of the change—from when it starts to the time it is relatively stable; (b) many observations are made, often using videotape recordings, interviews, and transcriptions of the exact words of the individuals being studied; (c) the behaviour that is observed is "put under a microscope," that is, examined moment by moment or trial by trial. The goal is to explain the underlying mechanisms of change—for example, what new knowledge or skills are developing to allow change to take place (Siegler & Crowley, 1991). This kind of research is expensive and time-consuming, so often only one or a few children are studied.

The Role of Time in Research. Another distinction is useful in understanding research—a distinction based on time. Many things that psychologists want to study, such as cognitive development, happen over several months or years. Ideally, researchers would study the development by observing their subjects over many years as changes occur. These are called longitudinal studies. They are informative, but time-consuming, expensive, and not always practical—keeping up with subjects over years as they grow up and move can be impossible. So instead, much research involves cross-sectional studies, which focus on groups of children at different ages. For example, to study how children's conceptions of "alive" change from ages 3 to 16, researchers can interview children of several different ages rather than following the same children for 14 years.

Teachers as Researchers. Research can also be a way to improve teaching in one classroom or one school. The same kind of careful observation, intervention, data gathering, and analysis that occurs in large research projects can be applied in any classroom to answer questions such as: Which writing prompts seem to encourage the best descriptive writing in my class? When does Kenyon seem to have the greatest difficulty concentrating on academic tasks? Would assigning task roles in science groups lead to more equitable participation of girls and boys in the work? This kind of problem-solving investigation is called action research. By focusing on a specific problem and

Single-subject experimental studies Systematic interventions to study effects with one person, often by applying and then withdrawing a treatment.

Microgenetic studies Detailed observation and analysis of changes in a cognitive process as the process unfolds over several days or weeks.

Longitudinal studies Studies that document changes that occur in subjects over time, often many years.

Cross-sectional studies Studies that focus on groups of subjects at different ages rather than following the same group for many years.

Action research Systematic observations or tests of methods conducted by teachers or schools to improve teaching and learning for their students.

making careful observations, teachers can learn a great deal about both their teaching and their students.

There has been great debate about the importance of experimental research in applied settings, such as in education. Many feel that utilizing systematic, controlled *experimental research* designs and rigorous data analyses enhances the usefulness of educational research (Slavin, 2002; Whitehurst, 2003). David Olson (2004), a professor emeritus at the Ontario Institute for Studies in Education of the University of Toronto, disagrees strongly with Slavin's position. Olson claims that we cannot use medicine as an analogy to education. "Treatments" in education are much more complex and unpredictable than administering one drug or another in medicine. And every educational program is changed by classroom conditions and the way it is implemented. David Berliner (2002) makes a similar point, arguing that "doing science and implementing scientific findings are so difficult in education because humans in schools are embedded in complex and changing networks of social interaction" and that "compared to designing bridges and circuits or splitting either atoms or genes, the science to help change schools and classrooms is harder to do because context cannot be controlled" (p. 20). Berliner concludes that a complex problem like education needs a whole range of methods for study: "Ethnographic research is crucial, as are case studies, survey research, time series, design experiments, action research, and other means to collect reliable evidence for engaging in unfettered argument about education issues. A single method is not what the government should be promoting for educational researchers" (Berliner, 2002, p. 20).

Theories for Teaching

A major goal of research in educational psychology is to understand teaching and learning; however, reaching this goal is a slow process. For instance, very few landmark studies exist that answer a question once and for all. Also, there are so many different kinds of students, teachers, tasks, and settings—and besides, human beings are pretty complicated. To deal with this complexity, research in educational psychology examines limited aspects of a situation—perhaps a few variables at a time, or life in one or two classrooms. If enough studies are completed in a certain area and findings repeatedly point to the same conclusions, we eventually arrive at a **principle**. This is the term for an established relationship between two or more factors—between a certain teaching strategy, for example, and student achievement.

Another tool for building a better understanding of the teaching and learning processes is **theory**. The common-sense notion of theory (as in "Oh well, it was only a theory") is that it is a guess or a hunch. But the scientific meaning of theory is quite different. According to Keith Stanovich at the Ontario Institute for Studies in Education of the University of Toronto, "A theory in science is an interrelated set of concepts that is used to explain a body of data and to make predictions about the results of future experiments" (1992, p. 21). Given a number of established principles, educational psychologists have developed explanations for the relationships among many variables and even whole systems of relationships. There are theories to explain how language develops, how differences in intelligence occur, and, as noted earlier, how people learn.

Few theories explain and predict perfectly. In this book, you will see many examples of educational psychologists taking different theoretical positions and disagreeing on the overall explanations of such issues as learning and motivation. Since no one theory offers all the answers, it makes sense to consider what each has to offer.

So why, you may ask, is it necessary to deal with theories? Why not just stick to principles? The answer is that both are useful. Principles of classroom management, for example, will give you help with specific problems. A good theory of classroom management, on the other hand, will give you a new way of thinking about discipline problems; it will give you tools for creating solutions to many different problems and for predicting what might work in new situations. A major goal of this book is to provide you with the best and the most useful theories for teaching—those that have solid evidence behind them. Although you may prefer some theories over others, consider them all as ways to understand the challenges teachers face.

The theories you encounter in this text should be used as cognitive tools to help you examine, inspect, and interpret the claims you will hear and read throughout your career (Leinhardt, 2001). To give you a frame for thinking about theories, consider the following families of theories, which we will be discussing in the next 10 chapters.

Principle Established relationship between factors.

Theory Integrated statement of principles that attempts to explain a phenomenon and make predictions.

PREVIEW: THEORIES FOR EDUCATIONAL PSYCHOLOGY

There are literally hundreds of theories to explain human development, learning, motivation, and teaching—we couldn't possibly consider them all. To see a small sampling of theories of learning, go to http://tip.psychology.org/theories.html. And that is just theories of learning!

As you will see many times in this book, one way to learn and remember complex information is to organize it, so we have organized eight major theories of development, learning, and motivation into three groupings or families: stage theories, learning theories, and contextual theories.

Stage Theories: Piaget, Freud, and Erikson

Over the years, some psychologists have explained changes from infancy to adulthood as a passage through a series of stages.

Jean Piaget. Piaget (1896–1980) created one of the best known stage theories describing four qualitatively different stages of cognitive development (Piaget, 1970a, 1971). From one stage to the next, the thinking of the child changes in ways that involve more than the addition of knowledge and skills. According to Piaget's stage theory, all the explanation and practice in the world will not help a child functioning at one stage to understand the ways of thinking at a higher stage. We consider Piaget's theory in depth in Chapter 2 on cognitive development and explore his four stages of thinking: sensorimotor, preoperational, concrete operational, and formal operational.

Sigmund Freud. Even if you have not heard of Jean Piaget, we'll bet you have heard of Sigmund Freud (1856–1939). By analyzing the dreams and childhood memories of his patients, mostly upper-middle-class women, Freud established five stages of psychosexual development—and he applied the same five stages in the same order for all people. If the conflicts of one stage are not resolved, Freud suggested that the individual could become fixated at that stage. When you hear a comedian refer to someone as an "anal personality," obsessed with order and control, for example, you are hearing the popular culture version of Freud's idea of fixation at the anal stage—the time when children are experiencing toilet training.

Freud was criticized for overemphasizing sex and aggression; for basing his theories on the memories of wealthy, female, European women with very specific mental problems; for creating stages of development in childhood without ever studying children; and for collecting no experimental data that might support or refute his theories. But his concepts of unconscious motivation and the importance of early experiences, especially parent–child relationships, were powerful influences in the field and also in literature, art, psychology, anthropology, religion, sociology, therapy, and history, to name only a few areas (Miller, 2002).

Erik Erikson. Freud also was an important influence on the life and work of Erik Erikson (1902–1994), who offered a basic framework for understanding the needs of young people in relation to society. In his psychosocial theory, Erikson, like Piaget and Freud, saw development as a passage through a series of stages, each with its particular goals, concerns, accomplishments, and dangers. The stages are interdependent: Accomplishments at later stages depend on how conflicts are resolved in the earlier years, similar to Freud's theory. At each stage, Erikson suggests that the individual faces a developmental crisis—a conflict between a positive alternative and a potentially unhealthy alternative. The way in which the individual resolves each crisis will have a lasting effect on that person's self-image and view of society. For example, the conflict during adolescence is *identity versus role confusion*. Achieving *identity* means making deliberate choices, particularly about work, values, and commitments to people and ideas (Marcia, 1999; Penuel & Wertsch, 1995). If adolescents fail to integrate all these choices, or if they feel unable to choose at all, *role confusion* threatens. We will talk more about all of Erikson's stages in Chapter 3.

Cognitive development Gradual, orderly changes by which mental processes become more complex and sophisticated.

Psychosocial theory Describes the relation of the individual's emotional needs to the social environment.

Developmental crisis A specific conflict whose resolution prepares the way for the next stage.

Learning and Motivation Theories: Behaviourism, Information Processing, and Social Cognitive Theory

A fundamental idea behind many of the theories in the learning family is that most of the changes in cognitive and emotional/social development, knowledge, motivation, and skills are consequences of learning. Children learn language, problem solving, taking the perspectives of others, mathematics, karate, and ways of coping with fears, for example. Learning theorists criticized Freud's ideas about unconscious motivations and fixations because these processes could not be proved wrong; they were interesting stories—but the stories couldn't be tested. Learning theories developed to be more systematic and scientific.

Behaviourism. One strand of learning theories focuses on something that can be observed—*behaviours*—so these theories are often classified under the general category of behaviourism. Conceptually, we may think of a behaviour as sandwiched between two sets of environmental influences: those that precede it (its antecedents) and those that follow it (its consequences) (Skinner, 1950). This relationship can be shown very simply as antecedent–behaviour–consequence, or A–B–C. Behavioural theories carefully analyze the A–B–C relationships with special attention to the C (consequences). The consequences of a behaviour can increase or decrease the chances that the behaviour will occur again. As you will see in Chapter 6, key concepts in behavioural theories are conditioning, reinforcement, punishment, and cueing.

Information Processing. Even though research on behavioural views of learning continues today, the computer revolution, breakthroughs in understanding language development, and Piaget's work all stimulated cognitive research. How people process and remember information became an important focus for research, and information processing theories of learning, development, and motivation appeared. So we now have a strand of cognitive learning theory that focuses on attention, types of memory, how knowledge is represented and stored, how it is forgotten, and the cognitive systems that make all this possible. Important concepts in cognitive information processing theories of learning are attention, perception, working memory, long-term memory, and types of knowledge. We examine these ideas in Chapter 7.

Social Cognitive Theory. Over 30 years ago, Albert Bandura (1925–) noted that the traditional behavioural views of learning were accurate but incomplete because they gave only a partial explanation of learning and overlooked important elements, particularly beliefs and social influences. Bandura's social cognitive theory of learning and motivation combines behavioural concerns with consequences and cognitive interests in thinking. Key concepts in social cognitive theory are the interactions between behaviour, environment, and personal characteristics; beliefs about personal capabilities; learning through observation and models; and guiding your own learning through self-regulation. We explore social cognitive theories in Chapter 10.

Contextual Theories: Vygotsky and Bronfenbrenner

One criticism of many of the theories described above, such as Piaget's theory or information processing theory, is that they overlook the important effects of culture and social context. Psychologists today recognize that culture shapes individuals by determining what and how they learn about the world. For example, in Brazil, without going to school, children who sell candy on the streets learn sophisticated mathematics in order to buy from wholesalers, sell, barter, and make a profit (Bakerman, Adamson, Koner, & Barr, 1990; Ceci & Roazzi, 1994). The stages observed by Piaget are not necessarily "natural" for all children because to some extent they reflect the expectations and activities of Western cultures (Kozulin, 2003; Rogoff, 2003). Two theories that take into account the critical role of cultural and social contexts are Vygotsky's sociocultural theory of learning and Bronfenbrenner's bioecological model of development.

Vygotsky. Lev Vygotsky (1896–1934) believed that human activities take place in cultural settings and cannot be understood apart from these settings. One of his key ideas was that our specific mental structures and processes can be traced to our interactions with others. These social interactions are

Behaviourism Explanations of learning that focus on external events as the cause of changes in observable behaviours.

Information processing The human mind's activity of taking in, storing, and using information.

Social cognitive theory Theory that adds concern with cognitive factors such as beliefs, self-perceptions, and expectations to social learning theory.

Context The total setting or situation that surrounds and interacts with a person or event.

more than simple influences on cognitive development—they actually create our cognitive structures and thinking processes (Palincsar, 1998). You may have noticed that Piaget and Vygotsky were born in the same year, but Piaget lived almost 50 years longer. They were aware of each other's work, but disagreed on some key questions about learning and development. In Chapter 2 we will examine three themes in Vygotsky's writings that explain how social processes form learning and thinking: the social sources of individual thinking; the role of cultural tools in learning and development, especially the tool of language; and the **zone of proximal development** (Wertsch & Tulviste, 1992).

Bronfenbrenner. Urie Bronfenbrenner (1917–2005) developed a frame to map the many interacting social contexts that affect development. He called his theory a **bioecological model** of development (Bronfenbrenner & Morris, 2006). The *bio* aspect of the model recognizes that people bring their biological selves to the developmental process. The *ecological* part recognizes that the social contexts in which we develop are ecosystems because they are in constant interaction and influence each other. Bronfenbrenner suggested that every person lives, learns, and develops within a set of nested systems from the immediate family to neighbourhoods and schools, the community, and society. The influences in all social systems are reciprocal. For example, a defiant teenager may lead parents to impose punishments and punished teenagers can become more defiant. There are many dynamic forces that interact to create the context for individual development. Moreover, the contexts in which we live and develop are incredibly diverse. Bronfenbrenner's theory is one of the most widely used today. We will examine it more closely in Chapter 3 because understanding contexts—cultural and social diversity—is an important part of educational psychology today.

Table 1.3 organizes and summarizes the theory families we have been discussing. You will encounter every one of these theories again in the next 10 chapters.

Zone of proximal development Phase at which a child can master a task if given appropriate help and support.

Bioecological model Bronfenbrenner's theory describing the nested social and cultural contexts that shape development.

TABLE 1.3 A Preview of Theories of Development, Learning, and Motivation

	Theory Family							
	Stage Theories			Learning Theories			Contextual Theories	
	Piaget	Freud	Erikson	Behaviourism	Information Processing	Social Cognitive	Vygotsky	Bronfenbrenner
Focus on...	Cognitive development; qualitative changes in thinking through four stages	Psychosexual development; changes through five stages of personality development	Psychosexual development; successful resolution of conflicts through eight stages of development	Systematic analysis of antecedents and consequences of behaviour	How attention, perception, representation, and knowledge affect memory and problem solving	The interactive effects of behaviour, environment, and personal characteristics on learning and motivation	The role more knowledgeable others, culture, and history play in learning and development	The bioecological system; the individual influenced by nested and interacting social and cultural systems Example concepts
Concrete operations,	formal operations	Unconscious, dream analysis	Developmental crisis, identity crisis	Reinforcement, punishment, conditioning	Perception, working memory, long-term memory	Triadic reciprocal interactions, self-efficacy	Cultural tools, zone of proximal development	Nested, interacting social systems
Discussed in...	Chapter 2	Chapter 1	Chapter 3	Chapter 6	Chapter 7	Chapter 10	Chapter 2	Chapter 3

PREVIEW: THE CONTENTS OF THIS BOOK

Part 1 of this text focuses on students. First we examine how students develop—how they change as they age. Because children may differ from adolescents and adults in their thinking, language, and images of themselves, they may require different kinds of teaching. Teachers must take into account the cognitive, physical, emotional, and social abilities and limitations of their students. Children differ from one another in their abilities and in their previous learning, cultural, and community experiences. Classrooms today are becoming more and more diverse. Teachers are expected to work with students with learning disabilities and visual or hearing impairments, for example, and with students who have developmental disabilities or who are developmentally advanced. As well, in Canada, most classrooms today are multicultural, with students who speak different languages and come from a variety of cultural backgrounds. Teachers must be able to recognize, respect, and adapt to these individual and group differences to create classroom communities that allow students to belong and to thrive.

Having introduced the students, in Part 2 we move to two of the most important topics in both educational psychology and the classroom: learning and motivation. Part 2 explores several theories of learning and motivation, and we will see how these theories can be applied in a number of practical ways. Understanding how students learn and what motivates learning is the basis for teachers' professional knowledge.

Having covered the dual foundations of teaching—the students and the processes of learning and motivation—we concentrate in Part 3 on actual practice. Here we examine how to organize and manage a classroom full of active learners. And because teachers deal with individuals as well as groups, we will spend some time discussing communication and interpersonal relationships. In this part of the book, we will look at approaches to instruction that are teacher-directed and student-centred. Teachers owe it to their students to design powerful environments for learning, so teachers must understand how different approaches can influence students' learning.

Finally, we consider how to evaluate what has been taught. Because to learn is to become more knowledgeable and competent, teachers must know how to assess knowledge and competence. Good assessment tools give teachers information they need to both guide students and give them useful information so that they can guide themselves.

The goal of this book is to help you become an excellent beginning teacher, one who can both apply and improve many techniques. Even more important, we hope that this book will cause you to think about students and teaching in new ways, so that you will have the foundation for becoming an expert teacher as you gain experience.

DIVERSITY AND CONVERGENCES IN EDUCATIONAL PSYCHOLOGY

The last section of every chapter in this book is called "Diversity and Convergences." This section will examine the topic of the chapter in relation to student differences in race, ethnicity, family income, abilities/disabilities, or gender. Then, we will consider the convergences—the principles or practices that hold well for all students. This first chapter has been about teaching and educational psychology.

Diversity

Ministries of Education across Canada have adopted policies of inclusion that reflect their commitment to provide *all* students with meaningful learning experiences that address their unique needs and differences. This is somewhat different from the United States where legislation, such as the *Individuals with Disabilities Education Act* (IDEA) and the *No Child Left Behind Act* (NCLB), specifies that Adequate Yearly Progress goals have to be set and tested specifically for racial and ethnic minority students, students with disabilities, students whose first language is not English, and students from low-income homes. Policies are somewhat less binding than legislation and, some would argue, offer more flexibility in developing locally responsive programs for children.

MyEducationLab
Go to the Activities and Applications section in Chapter 1 of MyEducationLab and complete Activity 3. As you watch the video and answer the accompanying questions, think about how your personal experiences inform your vision of yourself as a teacher.

In this chapter, we examined the diversity of research methods available in educational psychology—from descriptive studies to experimental studies to teachers' action research. You can find reports of the findings from all types of studies in books and journals that are referenced in this book. Table 1.4 provides a list of some of the major journals that publish work in educational and developmental psychology. We have published articles in many of these journals and served on many of their editorial boards, reviewing manuscripts to decide what will be published. For instance, Anita is the editor of the journal *Theory Into Practice*, and Nancy serves on its editorial board. Our goal for that journal is just what the title says—to bring the most useful theories into educational practice and also to bring the wisdom of practice back to researchers who study education.

TABLE 1.4 **Examples of Journals in Educational Psychology and Child Development**

Journal	Organization/Publisher	Website
Canadian Journal of Behavioural Science	Canadian Psychological Association	www.apa.org/pubs/journals/cbs/
Canadian Journal of Experimental Psychology	Canadian Psychological Association	www.apa.org/pubs/journals/cep/
Canadian Psychology	Canadian Psychological Association	www.apa.org/pubs/journals/cap/
Child Development	Society for Research in Child Development	www.srcd.org
Cognitive Development	Jean Piaget Society	www.piaget.org
Contemporary Educational Psychology	Elsevier	www.elsevier.com
Developmental Psychology	American Psychological Association	www.apa.org/journals/dev/
Developmental Review	Thompson Scientific	—
Early Childhood Research Quarterly	National Association for the Education of Young Children (NAEYC)	www.naeyc.org
Educational Psychologist	The Division of Educational Psychology (15) of the American Psychological Association	www.tandf.co.uk/journals/
Educational Psychology Review	Springer	www.springer.com
Journal of Applied Developmental Psychology	Elsevier	www.elsevier.com
Journal of Educational Psychology	American Psychological Association	www.apa.org/journals/edu/
Learning and Instruction	European Association for Research on Learning and Instruction (EARLI)	www.elsevier.com
Merrill Palmer Quarterly	Wayne State University	www.asu.edu/clas/ssfd/mpq/
Psychology in the Schools	Wiley	www.wiley.com/WileyCDA/
School Psychology Quarterly	American Psychological Association	www.apa.org/journals/spq/
Teaching and Teacher Education	Elsevier	www.elsevier.com
The British Journal of Educational Psychology	British Psychological Society	www.bpsjournals.co.uk
The Elementary School Journal	University of Chicago Press	www.journals.uchicago.edu
Theory Into Practice	Taylor Francis and The Ohio State University	http://ehe.osu.edu/tip/

Convergences

We can see two convergences in this chapter. No matter what educators believe about the challenges inherent in teaching diverse groups of learners, they share the goal of wanting all students to succeed in school, and in their classrooms. We think educational psychology has much to offer teachers who want to see all students achieve. Regardless of which research methods are used, education and psychology have had a long relationship. Educational psychology stands with a foot in two worlds: scholarship and practice. Merle Wittrock (1992, p. 138) sums it up well, saying that educational psychology focuses on "the psychological study of the everyday problems of education, from which one derives principles, models, theories, teaching procedures, and practical methods of instruction and evaluation, as well as research methods, statistical analyses, and measurement and assessment procedures appropriate for studying the thinking and affective processes of learners and the socially and culturally complex processes of schools." That about covers it.

SUMMARY TABLE

Learning and Teaching Today (pp. 6–8)

Projections indicate that 25–28 percent of Canada's population will be foreign-born by the year 2031, and 29–32 percent will be members of visible minorities. Diversity continues to be concentrated in our largest cities (Toronto, Montreal, and Vancouver) and schools in these areas can have a majority of children who are English language learners. Too many children (one in nine) live in poverty, and these figures are higher for Aboriginal and immigrant populations. Classrooms include children with a wide range of abilities and disabilities. These statistics represent a challenge and an opportunity for Canada's teaching force, which is very homogeneous.

What evidence is there that teachers make a difference? Three studies speak to the power of teachers in the lives of students. The first found that the quality of the teacher–student relationship in kindergarten predicted several aspects of school success through grade 8. The second study examined mathematics achievement for students in two large school districts as they moved through grades 3, 4, and 5. Again, the quality of the teacher made a difference—students who had three high-quality teachers in a row were way ahead of students who spent one or more years with less competent teachers. Finally, a Canadian study showed how teachers' beliefs about their role in helping *all* children in their classrooms learn affects the qualities of their practices and, hence, outcomes for children.

What Is Good Teaching? (pp. 6–9)

What is good teaching? Good teachers are committed to their students. They must deal with a wide range of student abilities and challenges: different languages, different home situations, and different abilities and disabilities. They must adapt instruction and assessment to students' needs. The whole time that these experts are navigating through the academic material, they also are taking care of the emotional needs of their students, propping up sagging self-esteem, and encouraging responsibility. From the first day of class, they carefully plan and teach the basic procedures for living and learning in their classes.

What are the concerns of beginning teachers? Learning to teach is a gradual process. The concerns and problems of teachers change as they progress through their careers. During the beginning years, attention tends to be focused on maintaining discipline, motivating students, evaluating students' work, and dealing with parents. Even with these concerns, many beginning teachers bring creativity and energy to their teaching and improve every year. The more experienced teacher can move on to concerns about professional growth and effectiveness with a wide range of students.

Reflective Thoughtful and inventive. Reflective teachers think back over situations to analyze what they did and why, and to consider how they might improve learning for their students.

The Role of Educational Psychology (pp. 9–14)

What is educational psychology? Educational psychology has been linked to teaching since the field of psychology was established in the United States over a century ago. The goals of educational psychology are to understand and to improve the teaching and learning processes. Educational psychologists develop knowledge and methods; they also use the knowledge and methods of psychology and other related disciplines to study learning and teaching in everyday situations. Educational psychologists examine what happens when *someone* (a teacher or parent) teaches *something* (math or weaving or dancing) to *someone else* (a student or co-worker or team) in some *setting* (a classroom or theatre or gym).

What are descriptive studies? Reports of descriptive studies often include survey results, interview responses, samples of actual classroom dialogue, or records of the class activities. Ethnographic methods involve studying the naturally occurring events in the life of a group and trying to understand the meaning of these events to the people involved. A case study investigates in depth how a teacher plans courses, for example, or how a student tries to learn specific material.

What are correlations and experimental studies? Correlations allow you to predict events that are likely to occur in the classroom. A correlation is a number that indicates both the strength and the direction of a relationship between two events or measurements. The closer the correlation is to either 1.00 or –1.00, the stronger the relationship. Experimental studies can indicate cause-and-effect relationships and should help teachers implement useful changes. Instead of just observing and describing an existing situation, the investigators introduce changes and note the results.

What are single-subject and microgenetic studies? In single-subject experimental studies, researchers examine the effects of treatments on one person, often by using a baseline/intervention/baseline/intervention, or ABAB, approach. Microgenetic studies take many detailed observations of subjects to track the progression of change from the very beginning until a process becomes stable.

What is action research? When teachers or schools make systematic observations or test out methods to improve teaching and learning for their students, they are conducting action research.

What is the difference between principles and theories? A principle is an established relationship between two or more factors—between a certain teaching strategy, for example, and student achievement. A theory is an interrelated set of concepts that is used to explain a body of data and to make predictions about the results of future experiments. The principles from research offer a number of possible answers to specific problems, and the theories offer perspectives for analyzing almost any situation that may arise.

Educational psychology The discipline concerned with teaching and learning processes; it applies the methods and theories of psychology and has its own as well.

Descriptive studies Studies that collect detailed information about specific situations, often using observation, surveys, interviews, recordings, or a combination of these methods.

Ethnography A descriptive approach to research that focuses on life within a group and tries to understand the meaning of events to the people involved.

Participant observation A method for conducting descriptive research in which the researcher becomes a participant in the situation in order to better understand life in that group.

Case study Intensive study of one person or one situation.

Correlation Statistical description of how closely two variables are related.

Positive correlation A relationship between two variables in which the two increase or decrease together. Example: calorie intake and weight gain.

Negative correlation A relationship between two variables in which a high value on one is associated with a low value on the other. Example: height and distance from top of head to the ceiling.

Experimentation Research method in which variables are manipulated and the effects recorded.

Subjects People or animals participating in a study.

Random Without any definite pattern; following no rule.

Statistically significant Not likely to be a chance occurrence.

Single-subject experimental studies Systematic interventions to study effects with one person, often by applying and then withdrawing a treatment.

Microgenetic studies Detailed observation and analysis of changes in a cognitive process as the process unfolds over several days or weeks.

Longitudinal studies Studies that document changes that occur in subjects over time, often many years.

Cross-sectional studies Studies that focus on groups of subjects at different ages rather than following the same group for many years.

Action research Systematic observations or tests of methods conducted by teachers or schools to improve teaching and learning for their students.

Principle Established relationship between factors.

Theory Integrated statement of principles that attempts to explain a phenomenon and make predictions.

Preview: Theories for Educational Psychology (pp. 15–17)

There are literally hundreds of theories to explain human development, learning, motivation, and teaching, and many different ways to organize these theories. Some theories explore development as a series of stages that everyone passes through. Freud, Piaget, and Erikson are examples of stage theorists. Other theories focus on learning and use concepts of learning to explain motivation and development. Examples are behaviourism, information processing, and social cognitive theory. Finally, many theories today, including the theories of Vygotsky and Bronfenbrenner, emphasize the role of social and historical contexts.

Cognitive development Gradual, orderly changes by which mental processes become more complex and sophisticated.

Psychosocial theory Describes the relation of the individual's emotional needs to the social environment.

Developmental crisis A specific conflict whose resolution prepares the way for the next stage.

Behaviourism Explanations of learning that focus on external events as the cause of changes in observable behaviours.

Information processing The human mind's activity of taking in, storing, and using information.

Social cognitive theory Theory that adds concern with cognitive factors such as beliefs, self-perceptions, and expectations to social learning theory.

Context The total setting or situation that surrounds and interacts with a person or event.

Zone of proximal development Phase at which a child can master a task if given appropriate help and support.

Bioecological model Bronfenbrenner's theory describing the nested social and cultural contexts that shape development.

Preview: The Contents of This Book (p. 18)

How can this book help you? Becoming a good teacher means being a good learner. Much of the information in this text will help you become a more expert learner if you take the ideas personally and apply them to your own life. Take advantage of the book's features—the tables of contents, chapter outlines, the Stop & Think questions, organizational headings, Guidelines boxes, Point/Counterpoint debates, key terms, and the Teachers' Casebooks—to become an expert learner.

PEARSON myeducationlab

MyEducationLab is an interactive, virtual learning tool that will help improve your understanding of the concepts taught in this textbook and in your course. Through this engaging resource, you will have access to simulations of real classroom experiences, exercises that will help you improve your knowledge of key concepts, and additional resources that will help you in your teaching career. Use this online tool with your textbook to help you succeed in your studies and beyond!

TEACHERS' CASEBOOK

It is your second year as a teacher at John A. Macdonald Public School (kindergarten–grade 8). One of your colleagues has been nominated for a Prime Minister's Award for Teaching Excellence. This person has been a role model to you in your first two years as a teacher, providing advice and encouragement. You would like to support her by writing a letter of recommendation to the Prime Minister's Office highlighting her exemplary teaching practices, commitment, and leadership. The deadline for submissions is a week away. How will you prepare to write the letter?

What Would *They* Do?

Here is how two practising teachers responded to the teaching situation described above.

Sally Bender

George Fitton School, Brandon, MB

While, individually, we have our ideas about what an exemplary teacher is and should be, it is important to look at what the profession is saying about the same issue. Taking time to read the professional journals and other literature would help in determining what a letter describing a colleague's performance should include. The granting of such a prestigious award could well depend on your words.

To prepare for writing the letter, I would list qualities describing my colleague's commitment to the profession and to the children whose lives are touched by excellent teaching practice. The list would include the following:

- builds close relationships with students and the school community through respect and example;
- creates a classroom that encourages and honours diversity in thinking and response;
- provides ongoing opportunities for children to take responsibility and ownership for what happens in the classroom and beyond;
- knows about child growth and development and uses that knowledge to drive the teaching and learning that occur in the classroom;
- manages the classroom with respect for the rights of the children and encourages them to take responsibility for their own actions at all times;
- is flexible enough to respond to "teachable moments" by giving up the "teaching" agenda for the "learning" one;
- models patience, tolerance, and respect for all;
- shares learning and teaching practice with colleagues;
- works as a team member and shares responsibility;
- is enthusiastic, challenging, and responsive to all students and colleagues;
- has consistent expectations and evaluates regularly the learning that is taking place for all students;
- provides a positive and encouraging atmosphere where children are free to take risks while learning and to learn from and through their mistakes;
- sees learning as a process that results in better performance;
- is knowledgeable about learning styles and uses that knowledge when planning lessons and learning experiences for all children;
- provides opportunities for learning that begin with the child's experiences and develop from the child's perspective;

- plans activities where cooperation is a necessity, for it is a life skill;
- ensures a classroom environment that is rich in print and language-stimulating possibilities;
- provides a balance between teacher-directed and child-initiated experiences;
- encourages parent support through regular communication.

By determining the qualities that you value in your colleague, you will be better prepared to write the letter of recommendation to accompany the nomination for such a prestigious award.

Barb Popoff

Lord Baden-Powell Elementary, Coquitlam, BC

Following are the qualities that I consider important in being an effective teacher.

An effective teacher:

- demonstrates his or her love of teaching and working with children by providing a warm and caring environment for learning. In a positive learning environment, children take risks without feeling threatened or insecure. They feel safe making decisions about their learning. A happy environment balances hard work and fun.
- considers the self-esteem of children and provides opportunities for children to feel successful and to take pride in their accomplishments. Balancing encouragement, motivation, and constructive criticism allows self-esteem to grow within the structure of the curriculum.
- knows the children—their strengths and their needs. An effective teacher is flexible and can modify the curriculum or teaching lesson to fit the needs and/or strengths of the children. Such a learning environment accommodates children with learning problems, as well as those who need to be challenged.
- works cooperatively and collaboratively with colleagues. The teaching profession can be quite overwhelming, especially to a teacher just starting out. Advising, encouraging, and showing direction and support lessens the anxiety and confusion felt by beginning teachers.
- continues to develop professionally and seeks self-improvement by attending regular professional seminars and conferences. Growth and learning are lifelong, and new ideas and skills are an asset and an exciting part of teaching in any classroom.

2 Cognitive Development and Language

Arrowhead © Diana Ong/SuperStock

TEACHERS' CASEBOOK

WHAT WOULD YOU DO?

The provincial curriculum guide calls for a unit on poetry, including lessons on *symbolism* in poems. You are concerned that many of your grade 5 students may not be ready to understand this abstract concept. To test the waters, you ask a few students to describe a symbol.

"It's sorta like a big metal thing that you bang together." Tracy waves her hands like a drum major.

"Yeah," Sean adds, "my sister plays one in the high school band."

You realize they are on the wrong track here, so you try again. "I was thinking of a different kind of symbol, like a ring as a symbol of marriage or a heart as a symbol of love, or . . ."

You are met with blank stares.

Trevor ventures, "You mean like the Olympic torch?"

"And what does that symbolize, Trevor?" you ask.

"Like I said, a torch." Trevor wonders how you could be so dense.

CRITICAL THINKING

- What do these students' reactions tell you about children's thinking?
- How would you approach this unit?
- What more would you do to "listen" to your students' thinking so that you could match your teaching to their level of thinking?
- How would you give your students concrete experience with the concept of symbolism?
- How will you decide if the students are not developmentally ready for this material?

What is going on with Trevor? In this chapter, you will find out. We begin with a definition of development and three questions that have intrigued psychologists who study it: nature versus nurture, continuity versus discontinuity, and critical versus sensitive periods. Next we examine the general principles of human development and take a brief look at the human brain. Then we will examine the ideas of two of the most influential cognitive developmental theorists, Jean Piaget and Lev Vygotsky. Piaget's ideas have implications for teachers about what their students can learn and when the students are ready to learn it. We will consider important criticisms of his ideas as well. The work of Lev Vygotsky, a Russian psychologist, has become very influential. His theory highlights the important role that teachers and parents play in the cognitive development of children. Finally, we will explore language development, including what is involved in learning two languages, and discuss the role of schools in developing and enriching language skills.

By the time you have completed this chapter, you should be able to answer these questions:

- What are three questions that cut across theories of development and three general principles of agreement?
- How does children's thinking differ at each of Piaget's four stages of development?
- How do cultural tools and social influences shape thinking according to Vygotsky's theory of cognitive development?
- What is the zone of proximal development?
- What are the similarities and differences between Piaget's and Vygotsky's ideas about cognitive development?

- What are the implications of Piaget's and Vygotsky's theories for teaching students of different ages?
- How does language develop during the school years, and what happens if children are learning two languages at once?

Connect and **Extend**
Go to the "Connect and Extend" section in Chapter 2 of MyEducationLab to find further content that links to teaching, students' thinking, research, and the news.

A DEFINITION OF DEVELOPMENT

For the next few chapters, we will explore how students develop and we will encounter some surprising situations. In this chapter, you will learn why the following children behave in peculiar ways:

- Leah, a 5-year-old, is certain that rolling out a ball of clay into a snake makes more clay.
- A 9-year-old child in Geneva, Switzerland, firmly believes that it is impossible to be Swiss and Genevan at the same time, insisting, *"I'm already Swiss, I can't also be Genevan."*
- Jamal, a very bright elementary school student, cannot answer the question, "How would life be different if people did not have to sleep?" because he insists, *"People HAVE TO SLEEP!"*
- A young girl who once said her *feet* hurt suddenly begins to refer to her *foots* hurting, then describes her *footses*, before she finally returns to talking about her *feet*.
- A 2-year-old brings his own mother to comfort a friend who is crying, even though the friend's mother is available too.

What explains these interesting events? You will soon find out, because you are entering the world of child and adolescent development.

The term **development** in its most general psychological sense refers to certain changes that occur in human beings (or animals) between conception and death. The term is not applied to all changes, but rather to those that appear in orderly ways and remain for a reasonably long period of time. A temporary change caused by a brief illness, for example, is not considered a part of development. Psychologists also make a value judgment in determining which changes qualify as development. The changes, at least those that occur early in life, are generally assumed to be for the better and to result in behaviour that is more adaptive, more organized, more effective, and more complex (Mussen, Conger, & Kagan, 1984).

Human development can be divided into a number of different aspects. **Physical development**, as you might guess, deals with physiological changes in the body. **Social and emotional development** refers to changes in the way an individual relates to others, as well as to an individual's personality and emotional understanding. **Cognitive development** implies changes in thinking.

Many changes that occur during development are simply matters of growth and maturation. **Maturation** refers to changes that occur naturally and spontaneously and that are, to a large extent, genetically programmed. Such changes emerge over time and are relatively unaffected by environment, except in cases of malnutrition or severe illness. Much of a person's physical development falls into this category. Other changes are brought about through learning, as individuals interact with their environment. Such changes make up a large part of a person's social development. What about the development of thinking and personality? Most psychologists agree that in these areas, both maturation and interaction with the environment (or nature and nurture, as they are sometimes called) are important, although they may disagree about the amount of emphasis to place on each. Nature versus nurture is one of three continuing discussions in theories of development.

Development Orderly, adaptive changes that humans (or animals) go through from conception to death.

Physical development Changes in body structure that take place as one grows.

Social and emotional development Changes over time in the ways in which one relates to others and the self.

Cognitive development Gradual, orderly changes by which mental processes become more complex and sophisticated.

Maturation Genetically programmed, naturally occurring changes over time.

Three Questions Across the Theories

Because there are many different approaches to research and theory, as you saw in Chapter 1, there are some continuing debates about key questions surrounding development.

What Is the Source of Development? Nature Versus Nurture. Which is more important in development, the "nature" of an individual (heredity, genes, biological processes, maturation, etc.) or the "nurture" of environmental contexts (education, parenting, culture, social policies, etc.)? This debate has raged for at least 2000 years and has had many labels along the way—"heredity versus environment," "biology versus culture," "maturation versus learning," and "innate versus acquired abilities." In earlier centuries, philosophers, poets, religious leaders, and politicians argued the question. Today scientists bring new tools to the discussion as they can map genes or trace the effects of drugs on brain activity, for example (Gottlieb, Wahlsten, & Lickliter, 2006). Even in scientific explanations, the pendulum has swung back and forth between nature and nurture (Cairns & Cairns, 2006; Lerner, Theokas, & Bobek, 2005; Overton, 2006).

Today the environment is seen as critical, but so are biological factors and individual differences. In fact, some psychologists assert that behaviours are determined 100 percent by biology *and* 100 percent by environment—they can't be separated (Miller, 2002). Current views emphasize complex coactions (joint actions) of nature and nurture. For example, a child born with a very easygoing, calm disposition will likely elicit different reactions from parents, playmates, and teachers compared to a child who is often upset and difficult to soothe, so individuals are active in constructing their own environments. But environments shape individuals as well—if not, what good would education be? So today, the either/or debates about nature and nurture are of less interest to educational and developmental psychologists. As a pioneering developmental psychologist said over 100 years ago, the more exciting questions involve understanding how "both causes work together" (Baldwin, 1895, p. 77).

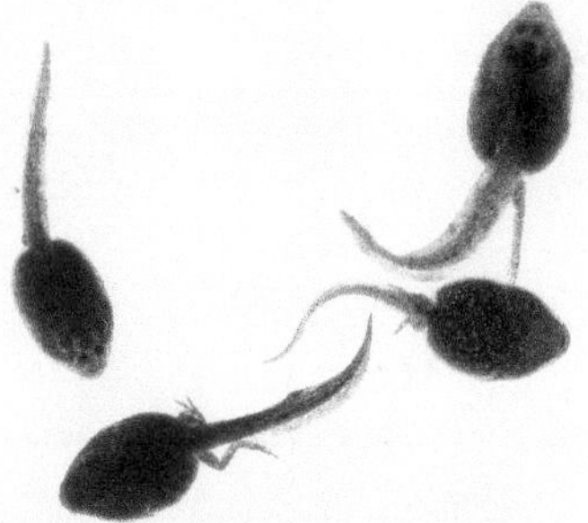

QUALITATIVE AND QUANTITATIVE CHANGES Some changes are qualitative—like a tadpole whose qualities change dramatically as it becomes a frog. Other changes are quantitative—like Jared, whose size changed as he dieted.

What Is the Shape of Development? Continuity Versus Discontinuity. Is human development a continuous process of adding to and increasing abilities or are there leaps or moves to new stages when abilities actually change? A continuous process would be like gradual improvement in your running endurance through systematic exercise. A discontinuous change would be like many of the changes that occur in humans during puberty, such as the ability to reproduce—an entirely different ability. Qualitative changes are contrasted with purely *quantitative* change, such as an adolescent growing taller.

You can think of continuous or quantitative change like walking up a ramp to go higher and higher. Progress is steady. A discontinuous or qualitative change is more like walking up stairs—there are level periods, then you move up to the next step all at once. Piaget's theory of cognitive development, described in the next section, is an example of qualitative, discontinuous change in children's thinking abilities. But other explanations of cognitive development based on learning theories emphasize gradual, continuous change.

Timing: Is It Too Late? Critical Periods and Earlier Versus Later Experiences. Are there critical periods when certain abilities, such as language, need to develop? If those opportunities are missed, can the child still "catch up"? These are questions about timing and development. You will see later in this chapter that there seems to be a critical period for learning accurate language pronunciation. The earlier people learn a second language, the more likely it is that their pronunciation will be near-native. After adolescence it is difficult to learn a new language without speaking with an accent (Anderson & Graham, 1994).

Many earlier psychologists, particularly those influenced by Freud, believed that early childhood experiences were critical, especially for emotional/social and cognitive development. But does early toilet training really set all of us on a particular life path? Probably not. More recent research shows that later experiences are powerful too and can change the direction of development (Kagan & Herschkowitz, 2005). Today most psychologists talk about sensitive periods—not critical periods. There are times when a person is especially ready for or responsive to certain experiences. So the best time to learn a second language on your own without direct instruction is childhood, but adults can and do learn second languages all the time.

Beware of Either/Or. As you might imagine, the debates above proved too complicated to be settled by splitting alternatives into either/or possibilities (Griffins & Gray, 2005). Today, most psychologists see human development, learning, and motivation as a set of interacting and coacting contexts, from the inner biological structures and processes that influence development, such as genes, cells, nutrition, and disease, to the external factors of families, neighbourhoods, social relationships, educational and health institutions, public policies, time periods, historical events, and so on. So the effects of a childhood disease on the cognitive development of a child born in the 16th century to a poor family and treated by bloodletting or leeches will be quite different from the effect of the same disease on a child born in 2010 to a wealthy family and given the best treatment available for that time period. Throughout the rest of this book, we will try to make sense of development, learning, motivation, and teaching without falling into the *either/or trap*.

Coactions Joint actions of individual biology and environment—each shapes and influences the other.

Sensitive periods Times when a person is especially ready for or responsive to certain experiences.

General Principles of Development

Although there is disagreement about what is involved in development and about the way it takes place, there are a few general principles that almost all theorists would support.

1. *People develop at different rates.* In your own classroom, you will have a whole range of examples of different developmental rates. Some students will be larger, better coordinated, or more mature in their thinking and social relationships. Others will be much slower to mature in these areas. Except in rare cases of very rapid or very slow development, such differences are normal and are to be expected in any large group of students.
2. *Development is relatively orderly.* People develop certain abilities before others. In infancy, they sit before they walk, babble before they talk, and see the world through their own eyes before they can begin to imagine how others see it. In school, they master addition before algebra, Bambi before Shakespeare, and so on. Theorists may disagree on exactly what comes before what, but they all seem to find a relatively logical progression.
3. *Development takes place gradually.* Very rarely do changes appear overnight. A student who cannot manipulate a pencil or answer a hypothetical question may well develop this ability, but the change is likely to take time.

The Brain and Cognitive Development

If you have taken an introductory psychology class, you have read about the brain and nervous system. You probably remember that there are several different areas of the brain and that certain areas are involved in particular functions. For example, the feathery looking cerebellum coordinates and orchestrates balance and smooth, skilled movements—from the graceful gestures of the dancer to the everyday action of eating without stabbing yourself in the nose with a fork. The cerebellum may also play a role in higher cognitive functions such as learning. The hippocampus is critical to recalling new information and recent experiences, while the amygdala directs emotions. The thalamus is involved in our ability to learn new information, particularly if it is verbal. The reticular formation plays a role in attention and arousal, blocking some messages and sending others on to higher brain centres for processing, and the corpus callosum moves information from one side of the brain to the other.

Some researchers have described the brain as a jungle of layers and loops, an interconnected and complex organic system (Edelman, 1992). The outer 0.3-centimetre-thick covering of the cerebrum is the wrinkled-looking cerebral cortex—the largest area of the brain. The cerebral cortex allows the greatest human accomplishments, such as complex problem solving and language. In humans, this area of the brain is much larger than it is in lower animals. The cortex is the last part of the brain to develop, so it is believed to be more susceptible to environmental influences than other areas of the brain (Gluck, Mercado, & Myers, 2008; Meece & Daniels, 2008; Schater, Gilbert, & Wenger, 2009). The cerebral cortex accounts for about 85 percent of the brain's weight in adulthood and contains the greatest number of **neurons**—the tiny structures that store and transmit information. Let's see how neurons develop.

The Developing Brain: Neurons. Neuron cells send out long arm- and branch-like fibres called *axons* and *dendrites* to connect with other neuron cells. They share information by releasing chemicals that jump across the tiny spaces, called **synapses**, between the fibre ends. Axons transmit information out to muscles, glands, or other neurons; dendrites receive information and transmit it to the neuron cells themselves. Figure 2.1 shows these components of the neuron system.

By the time we are born, we have all the neurons we will ever have, about 100 to 200 billion, and each neuron has about 2500 synapses. However, the fibres that reach out from the neurons and the synapses between the fibre ends increase during the first years of life, perhaps into adolescence or longer.

By age 2 to 3, each neuron has around 15 000 synapses; children this age have many more synapses than they will have as adults. In fact, they are *oversupplied* with the neurons and synapses that they will need to adapt to their environments. However, only those neurons that are used will survive, and unused neurons will be "pruned" (Bransford, Brown, & Cocking, 2000). This pruning is necessary and supports cognitive development. In fact, some forms of mental retardation are associated with a gene defect that interferes with pruning (Cook & Cook, 2005).

Neurons Nerve cells that store and transfer information.

Synapses The tiny space between neurons; chemical messages are sent across these gaps.

FIGURE 2.1

A Single Neuron

Each neuron (nerve cell) includes dendrites that bring in messages and an axon that sends out messages. This is a single neuron, but each neuron is in a network with many others.

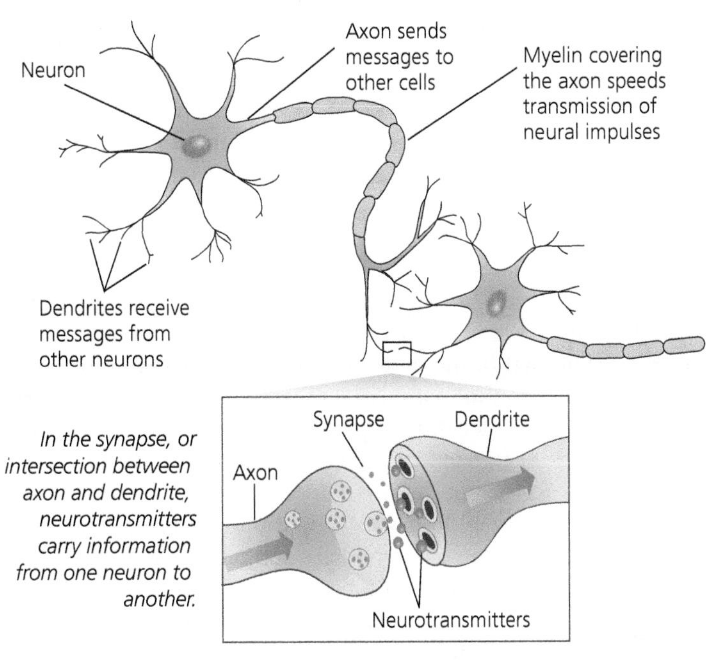

Source: Adapted from Berger, K. S. (2006). *The developing person: Through childhood and adolescence* (7th ed.). New York: Worth, p. 140. With permission of Worth Publishers.

Two kinds of overproduction and pruning processes take place. One is called *experience-expectant* because synapses are overproduced in certain parts of the brain during certain developmental periods, awaiting (expecting) stimulation. For example, during the first months of life, the brain expects visual and auditory stimulation. If a normal range of sights and sounds occurs, then the visual and auditory areas of the brain develop. But children who are born completely deaf receive no auditory stimulation and, as a result, the auditory processing area of their brains becomes devoted to processing visual information. Similarly, the visual processing area of the brain for children blind from birth becomes devoted to auditory processing (Nelson, 2001; Neville, 2007). Experience-expectant overproduction and pruning processes are responsible for general development in large areas of the brain. This may explain why adults have difficulty with pronunciations that are not part of their native language. The neurons and synapses that are not involved in recognizing native language sounds may have been "pruned." Therefore, learning these sounds as an adult requires intense instruction and practice (Bransford et al., 2000).

The second kind of synaptic overproduction and pruning is called *experience-dependent.* Here, synaptic connections are formed based on the individual's experiences. New synapses are formed in response to neural activity in very localized areas of the brain when the individual is not successful in processing information. Again, more synapses are produced than will be kept after "pruning." Experience-dependent processes are involved in individual learning, such as learning unfamiliar sound pronunciations in a second language you are studying.

Stimulating environments may help in the pruning process in early life (experience-expectant period) and support increased synapse development in adulthood (experience-dependent period) (Cook & Cook, 2005). In fact, animal studies have shown that rats raised in stimulating environments (with toys, tasks for learning, other rats, and human handling) develop and retain 25 percent more synapses than rats who are raised with little stimulation. Even though the research with rats may not apply directly to humans, it is clear that extreme deprivation can have negative effects on brain development. But extra stimulation will not necessarily improve development for young children who are getting adequate or typical amounts (Byrnes & Fox, 1998; Kolb & Whishaw, 1998). So spending money on expensive toys or baby education programs probably provides more stimulation than is necessary. Pots and pans, blocks and books, and sand and water all provide excellent stimulation—especially if accompanied by caring conversations with parents or teachers.

Another factor that influences thinking and learning is **myelination**, or the coating of axon neuron fibres with an insulating fatty covering shown in Figure 2.1—look back at that picture and find the myelin. This process is something like coating bare electrical wires with rubber or plastic. This myelin coating makes message transmission faster and more efficient. Myelination happens quickly in the early years, but continues gradually into adolescence and is the reason the child's brain grows rapidly in size during the first few years of life. In fact, by age 5 most children's brains weigh about 90 percent of what they will weigh in adulthood.

The Developing Brain: Cerebral Cortex. Let's move from the neuron level to the brain itself. The cerebral cortex develops more slowly than other parts of the brain, and parts of the cortex mature at different rates. The part of the cortex that controls physical motor movement matures first, followed by the areas that control complex senses such as vision and hearing, and then the frontal lobe that controls higher-order thinking processes. The temporal lobes of the cortex that play major roles in emotion and language creation do not develop fully until the high school years and maybe later.

Different areas of the cortex seem to have different functions, as shown in Figure 2.2. Even though different functions are found in different areas of the brain, these specialized functions are quite specific and elementary. To accomplish more complex functions such as speaking or reading, the various areas of the cortex must communicate and work together (Byrnes & Fox, 1998).

Another aspect of brain functioning that has implications for cognitive development is **lateralization**, or the specialization of the two hemispheres of the brain. We know that each half of the brain controls the opposite side of the body. Damage to the right side of the brain will affect movement of the left side of the body and vice versa. In addition, certain areas of the brain affect particular behaviours. For most of us, the left hemisphere of the brain is a major factor in language processing, and the right hemisphere handles much of the spatial-visual information and emotions (non-verbal information). For some left-handed people, the relationship may be reversed, but for most left-handers, and for females on average, there is less hemispheric specialization altogether (Berk, 2005; O'Boyle & Gill, 1998). The brains of young children show more **plasticity** (adaptability)

FIGURE 2.2 **A View of the Cerebral Cortex**

This is a simple representation of the left side of the human brain, showing the cerebral cortex. The cortex is divided into different areas, or lobes, each having a variety of regions with different functions. A few of the major functions are indicated here.

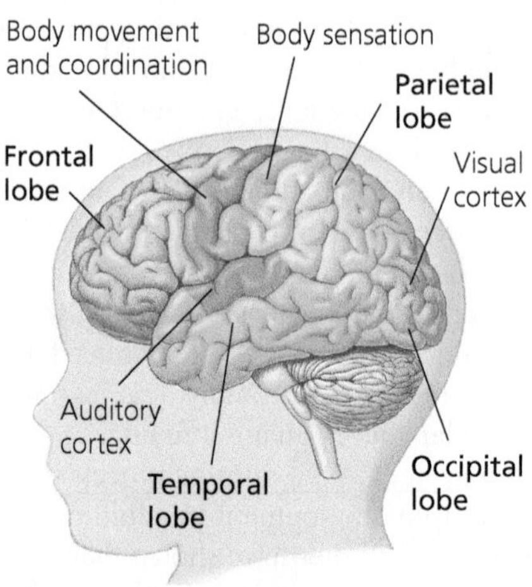

Myelination The process by which neural fibres are coated with a fatty sheath called *myelin* that makes message transfer more efficient.

Lateralization The specialization of the two hemispheres (sides) of the brain cortex.

Plasticity The brain's tendency to remain somewhat adaptable or flexible.

because they are not as specialized or lateralized as the brains of older children and adults. Damage to the left side of the brain in young children can be somewhat overcome to allow language development to proceed. Different areas of the brain take over. But this compensation is less likely to occur after damage to the left brain hemispheres of older children and adults.

These differences in performance by the brain's hemispheres, however, are more relative than absolute; one hemisphere is just more efficient than the other in performing certain functions. Nearly any task, particularly the complex skills and abilities that concern teachers, requires participation of many different areas of the brain in constant communication with each other. For example, the right side of the brain is better at figuring out the meaning of a story, but the left side is where grammar and syntax are understood, so both sides of the brain have to work together during reading tasks. "The primary implication of these findings is that the practice of teaching to 'different sides of the brain' is not supported by the neuroscientific research" (Byrnes & Fox, 1998, p. 310). Remember, no mental activity is exclusively the work of a single part of the brain—so there is no such thing as a "right-brained student" unless that individual has had the left hemisphere removed, a rare and radical treatment for some forms of epilepsy.

Many publications for parents and teachers have useful ideas about the brain and education, but beware of suggestions that oversimplify. As you will see in Chapter 9, the jury still is out on many of these "brain-based" programs.

We turn next to examine a theory of cognitive development offered by a biologist turned psychologist, Jean Piaget.

PIAGET'S THEORY OF COGNITIVE DEVELOPMENT

STOP & THINK Can you be in Montreal, Quebec, and Canada at the same time? Is this a difficult question for you? How long did it take you to answer?

Swiss psychologist Jean Piaget devised a model describing how humans go about making sense of their world by gathering and organizing information (Piaget, 1954, 1963, 1970a, 1970b). We will examine Piaget's ideas closely because they provide an explanation of the development of thinking from infancy to adulthood.

According to Piaget (1954), certain ways of thinking that are quite simple for an adult, such as the Montreal question above, are not so simple for a child. For example, do you remember the 9-year-old child at the beginning of the chapter who was asked if he could be Genevan? He answered, *"No, that's not possible. I'm already Swiss, I can't also be Genevan"* (Piaget, 1965/1995, p. 252). Imagine teaching this student geography. The student has trouble with classifying one concept (Geneva) as a subset of another (Switzerland). There are other differences between adult and child thinking. Children's concepts of time may be different from your own. They may think, for example, that they will someday catch up to a sibling in age, or they may confuse the past and the future. Let's examine why.

Influences on Development

Cognitive development is much more than the addition of new facts and ideas to an existing store of information. According to Piaget, our thinking processes change radically, though slowly, from birth to maturity because we constantly strive to make sense of the world. How do we do this? Piaget identified four factors—biological maturation, activity, social experiences, and equilibration—that interact to influence changes in thinking (Piaget, 1970a). Let's briefly examine the first three factors. We'll return to a discussion of equilibration in the next section.

One of the most important influences on the way we make sense of the world is *maturation*, the unfolding of the biological changes that are genetically programmed in each human being at conception. Parents and

STUDYING CHILDREN'S THINKING Jean Piaget was a Swiss psychologist whose insightful descriptions of children's thinking changed the way we understand cognitive development.

teachers have little impact on this aspect of cognitive development, except to ensure that children get the nourishment and care they need to be healthy.

Activity is another influence on cognitive development. With physical maturation comes the increasing ability to act on the environment and learn from it. When a young child's coordination is reasonably developed, for example, the child may discover principles about balance by experimenting with a see-saw. Thus, as we act on the environment—as we explore, test, observe, and eventually organize information—we are likely to alter our thinking processes at the same time.

As we develop, we also interact with the people around us. According to Piaget, our cognitive development is influenced by *social transmission*, or learning from others. Without social transmission, we would need to reinvent all the knowledge already offered by our culture. Of course, the amount people can learn from social transmission varies according to their stage of cognitive development.

Maturation, activity, and social transmission all work together to influence cognitive development. How do we respond to these influences?

Basic Tendencies in Thinking

Piaget's original work was in biology. As such, he felt that all species inherit two basic instincts, or "invariant functions." The first of these tendencies is toward **organization**—the combining, arranging, recombining, and rearranging of behaviour and thoughts into coherent systems. The second tendency is toward **adaptation**, or adjusting to the environment.

Organization. People are born with a tendency to organize their thinking and knowledge into psychological structures or schemes. These psychological structures are our systems for understanding and interacting with the world. Simple structures are continually combined and coordinated to become more sophisticated and thus more effective. Very young infants, for example, can either look at an object or grasp it when it comes in contact with their hands. They cannot coordinate looking and grasping at the same time. As they develop, however, infants organize these two separate behavioural structures into a coordinated higher-level structure of looking at, reaching for, and grasping the object. They can, of course, still use each structure separately (Ginsburg & Opper, 1988; Miller, 2002).

Piaget gave a special name to these structures: **schemes**. In his theory, schemes are the basic building blocks of thinking. They are organized systems of actions or thought that allow us to mentally represent or "think about" the objects and events in our world. Schemes may be very small and specific—for example, the sucking-through-a-straw scheme or the recognizing-a-rose scheme. Or they may be more general—the drinking scheme or the categorizing-plants scheme. As a person's thinking processes become more organized and new schemes develop, behaviour also becomes more sophisticated and better suited to the environment.

Adaptation. In addition to the tendency to organize their psychological structures, people are born with the tendency to adapt to their environment. Two basic processes are involved in adaptation: assimilation and accommodation.

Assimilation takes place when people use their existing schemes to make sense of events in their world. Assimilation involves trying to understand something new by fitting it into what we already know. At times, we may have to distort the new information to make it fit. For example, the first time many children see a skunk, they call it a "kitty." They try to match the new experience with an existing scheme for identifying animals.

Accommodation occurs when a person must change existing schemes to respond to a new situation. If data cannot be made to fit any existing schemes, more appropriate structures must be developed. We adjust our thinking to fit the new information, instead of adjusting the information to fit our thinking. Children demonstrate accommodation when they add the scheme for recognizing skunks to their other systems for identifying animals.

People adapt to their increasingly complex environments by using existing schemes whenever these schemes work (assimilation) and by modifying and adding to their schemes when something new is needed (accommodation). In fact, both processes are required most of the time. Even using an established pattern such as sucking through a straw may require some accommodation, if you are used to a straw of a different size or length. If you have tried drinking juice from box packages, you know that you have to add a new skill to your sucking scheme—don't squeeze the box or you

Organization Ongoing process of arranging information and experience into mental systems or categories.

Adaptation Adjustment to the environment.

Schemes Mental systems or categories of perception and experience.

Assimilation Fitting new information into existing schemes.

Accommodation Altering existing schemes or creating new ones in response to new information.

will shoot juice through the straw, straight up into the air and into your lap. Whenever new experiences are assimilated into an existing scheme, the scheme is enlarged and changed somewhat, so assimilation involves some accommodation (Mascolo & Fischer, 2005).

There are also times when neither assimilation nor accommodation is used. If people encounter something that is too unfamiliar, they may ignore it. Experience is filtered to fit the kind of thinking a person is doing at a given time. For example, if you overhear a conversation in a foreign language, you probably will not try to make sense of the exchange unless you have some knowledge of the language.

Equilibration. According to Piaget, organizing, assimilating, and accommodating can be seen as a kind of complex balancing act. In his theory, the actual changes in thinking take place through the process of **equilibration**—the act of searching for a balance. Piaget assumed that people continually test the adequacy of their thinking processes in order to achieve that balance.

Briefly, the process of equilibration works as follows. If we apply a particular scheme to an event or situation and the scheme works, equilibrium exists. If the scheme does not produce a satisfying result, **disequilibrium** exists, and we become uncomfortable. This motivates us to keep searching for a solution through assimilation and accommodation, and thus our thinking changes and moves ahead. Of course, the level of disequilibrium must be just right or optimal—too little and we aren't interested in changing, too much and we may be discouraged or anxious and not change.

Four Stages of Cognitive Development

Now we turn to the actual differences that Piaget hypothesized for children as they grow. As you saw in Chapter 1, Piaget believed that all people pass through the same four stages in exactly the same order. These stages are generally associated with specific ages, as shown in Table 2.1, but these are only general guidelines, not labels for all children of a certain age. Piaget noted that individuals may go through long periods of transition between stages and that a person may show characteristics of one stage in one situation, but characteristics of a higher or lower stage in other situations. Therefore, knowing a student's age is never a guarantee of knowing his or her level of cognitive development (Orlando & Machado, 1996).

Infancy: The Sensorimotor Stage. The earliest period is called the **sensorimotor** stage, because the child's thinking involves the major senses of seeing, hearing, moving, touching, and tasting. During this period, the infant develops **object permanence**, the understanding that objects in the environment exist whether the baby perceives them or not. As most parents discover, before infants develop object permanence, it is relatively easy to take something away from them.

Equilibration Search for mental balance between cognitive schemes and information from the environment.

Disequilibrium In Piaget's theory, the "out-of-balance" state that occurs when a person realizes that his or her current ways of thinking are not working to solve a problem or understand a situation.

Sensorimotor Involving the senses and motor activity.

Object permanence The understanding that objects have a separate, permanent existence.

TABLE 2.1 Piaget's Stages of Cognitive Development

Stage	Approximate Age	Characteristics
Sensorimotor	0–2 years	Begins to make use of imitation, memory, and thought. Begins to recognize that objects do not cease to exist when they are hidden. Moves from reflex actions to goal-directed activity.
Preoperational	2–7 years	Gradually develops use of language and ability to think in symbolic form. Is able to think operations through logically in one direction. Has difficulties seeing another person's point of view.
Concrete operational	7–11 years	Is able to solve concrete (hands-on) problems in logical fashion. Understands laws of conservation and is able to classify and seriate. Understands reversibility.
Formal operational	11–adult	Is able to solve abstract problems in logical fashion. Becomes more scientific in thinking. Develops concerns about social issues, identity.

Source: From Wadsworth, B. J. (1996). *Piaget's theory of cognitive and affective development* (5th ed.). Boston: Allyn & Bacon. Copyright © 1996 by Pearson Education. Adapted by permission of the publisher.

"I can't tell you 'cause I'm wearin' my mittens."

Family Circus © Bil Keane, Inc. King Features Syndicate

The older infant who searches for the ball that has rolled out of sight is indicating an understanding that objects still exist even when they are not in view (Moore & Meltzoff, 2004). Recent research, however, suggests that infants as young as three to four months may know that the object still exists, but they do not have the memory skills to "hold on" to the location of the object or the motor skills to coordinate a search for it (Baillargeon, 1999; Flavell, Miller, & Miller, 2002).

A second major accomplishment in the sensorimotor period is the beginning of logical, goal-directed actions. Think of the familiar container toy for babies. It is usually plastic, has a lid, and contains several colourful items that can be dumped out and replaced. A six-month-old baby is likely to become frustrated trying to get to the toys inside. An older child who has mastered the basics of the sensorimotor stage will probably be able to deal with the toys in an orderly fashion. Through trial and error, the child will slowly build a "container toy" scheme: (1) get the lid off; (2) turn the container upside down; (3) shake if the items jam; (4) watch the items fall. Separate lower-level schemes have been organized into a higher-level scheme to achieve a goal.

The child is soon able to reverse this action by refilling the container. Learning to reverse actions is a basic accomplishment of the sensorimotor stage. As we will soon see, however, learning to reverse thinking—that is, learning to imagine the reverse of a sequence of actions—takes much longer.

Early Childhood to the Early Elementary Years: The Preoperational Stage. By the end of the sensorimotor stage, the child can use many action schemes. As long as these schemes remain tied to physical actions, however, they are of no use in recalling the past, keeping track of information, or planning. For this, children need what Piaget called operations, or actions that are carried out and reversed mentally rather than physically. At the preoperational stage the child has not yet mastered these mental operations but is moving toward mastery (so thinking is *pre*operational).

ACTIVE LEARNING The ability to manipulate concrete objects helps children understand abstract relationships such as the connection between symbols and quantity.

According to Piaget, the first type of thinking that is separate from action involves making action schemes symbolic. The ability to form and use symbols—words, gestures, signs, images, and so on—is thus a major accomplishment of the preoperational period and moves children closer to mastering the mental operations of the next stage. This ability to work with symbols, such as using the word *horse* or a picture of a horse or even pretending to ride a horse to represent a real horse that is not actually present, is called the semiotic function. In fact, the child's earliest use of symbols occurs during pretending. Children who are not yet able to talk will often use action symbols—pretending to drink from an empty cup or touching a comb to their hair, showing that they know what each object is for. This behaviour also shows that their schemes are becoming more general and less tied to specific actions. The eating scheme, for example, can be used in playing house. During the preoperational stage, there is also rapid development of that very important symbol system, language. Between the ages of 2 and 4, most children enlarge their vocabulary from about 200 to 2000 words.

As the child moves through the preoperational stage, the developing ability to think about objects in symbolic form remains somewhat limited to thinking in one direction only, or using *one-way logic*. It is very difficult for the child to "think backwards," or imagine how to reverse the steps in a task. Reversible thinking is involved in many tasks that are difficult for the preoperational child, such as the conservation of matter.

Conservation is the principle that the amount or number of something remains the same even if the arrangement or appearance is changed, as long as nothing is added and nothing is taken away. You know that if you tear a piece of paper into several pieces, you will still have the same amount of paper. To prove this, you know that you can reverse the process by taping the pieces back together. Here is a classic example of difficulty with the principle of conservation. Leah, a 5-year-old, is shown two identical glasses, both short and wide in shape. Both have exactly the same amount of coloured water in them. She agrees that the amounts are "the same." The experimenter then pours the water from one of the glasses into a taller, narrower glass and asks, "Now, does one glass have more water, or are they the same?" Leah responds that the tall glass has more because "It goes up more here" (she points to the higher level on the taller glass).

Piaget's explanation for Leah's answer is that she is focusing, or centring, attention on the dimension of height. She has difficulty considering more than one aspect of the situation at a time, or decentring. The preoperational child cannot understand that increased diameter compensates for decreased height, since this would require taking into account two dimensions at once. Thus, children

Goal-directed actions Deliberate actions toward a goal.

Operations Actions that a person carries out by thinking them through instead of literally performing them.

Preoperational The stage of development before a child masters logical mental operations.

Semiotic function The ability to use symbols—language, pictures, signs, or gestures—to represent actions or objects mentally.

Reversible thinking Thinking backward, from the end to the beginning.

Conservation Principle that some characteristics of an object remain the same despite changes in appearance.

at the preoperational stage have trouble freeing themselves from their own perceptions of how the world appears.

This brings us to another important characteristic of the preoperational stage. Preoperational children, according to Piaget, are very egocentric; they tend to see the world and the experiences of others from their own viewpoints. Egocentric, as Piaget intended it, does not mean selfish; it simply means that children often assume that everyone else shares their feelings, reactions, and perspectives. For example, if a little girl at this stage is afraid of dogs, she may assume that all children share this fear. The 2-year-old at the beginning of this chapter who brought his own mother to comfort a friend who was crying, even though the friend's mother was available, was simply seeing the situation through his own eyes. Very young children centre on their own perceptions and on the way the situation appears to them. This is one reason it is difficult for these children to understand that your right hand is not on the same side as theirs when you are facing them.

Research has shown that young children are not totally egocentric in every situation, however. Children as young as 4 change the way they talk to 2-year-olds by speaking in simpler sentences, and even before the age of 2 a child shows a toy to an adult by turning the front of the toy to face the other person. So young children do seem quite able to take the needs and different perspectives of others into account, at least in certain situations (Flavell et al., 2002). And in fairness to young children, even adults can make assumptions that others feel or think as they do. For example, have you ever received a gift that the giver loved but was clearly inappropriate for you? The *Guidelines* box offers a few ideas for how to work with preoperational thinkers in the classroom.

Decentring Focusing on more than one aspect at a time.

Egocentric Assuming that others experience the world the way you do.

GUIDELINES: Teaching the Preoperational Child

Use concrete props and visual aids whenever possible.

EXAMPLES

1. When you discuss concepts such as "part," "whole," or "one-half," use shapes on a felt board or cardboard "pizzas" to demonstrate.
2. Let children add and subtract with sticks, rocks, or coloured chips.

Make instructions relatively short—not too many steps at once. Use actions as well as words.

EXAMPLES

1. When giving instructions about how to enter the room after recess and prepare for social studies, ask a child to demonstrate the procedure for the rest of the class by walking in quietly, going straight to his or her seat, and placing the text, paper, and a pencil on his or her desk.
2. Explain a game by acting out one of the parts.
3. Show children what their finished papers should look like. Use an overhead projector or display examples where children can see them easily.

Help students develop their ability to see the world from someone else's point of view.

EXAMPLES

1. Relate social studies lessons about different people or places back to the children's experiences, pointing out similarities and differences.
2. Be clear about rules for sharing or use of material. Help children understand the value of the rules and develop empathy in children by asking them to think about how they would like to be treated. Avoid giving long lectures on "sharing" or being "nice."

Be sensitive to the possibility that children may have different meanings for the same word or different words for the same meaning. Children may also expect everyone to understand words they have invented.

EXAMPLES

1. If a child protests, "I won't take a nap. I'll just rest!" be aware that a nap may mean something like "changing into pyjamas and being in my bed at home."
2. Ask children to explain the meanings of their invented words.

Give children a great deal of hands-on practice with the skills that serve as building blocks for more complex skills such as reading comprehension.

EXAMPLES

1. Provide cut-out letters to build words.
2. Supplement paper-and-pencil tasks in arithmetic with activities that require measuring and simple calculations—cooking, building a display area for class work, dividing a batch of popcorn equally.

Provide a wide range of experiences in order to build a foundation for concept learning and language.

EXAMPLES

1. Take field trips to zoos, gardens, theatres, and concerts; invite storytellers to the class.
2. Give children words to describe what they are doing, hearing, seeing, touching, tasting, and smelling.

Later Elementary to the Middle School Years: The Concrete Operational Stage. Piaget coined the term **concrete operations** to describe this stage of "hands-on" thinking. The basic characteristics of the stage are the recognition of the logical stability of the physical world, the realization that elements can be changed or transformed and still conserve many of their original characteristics, and the understanding that these changes can be reversed.

Look at Figure 2.3, which shows examples of the different tasks given to children to assess conservation and the approximate age ranges when most children can solve these problems. According to Piaget, a student's ability to solve conservation problems depends on an understanding of three basic aspects of reasoning: identity, compensation, and reversibility. With a complete mastery of **identity**, the student knows that if nothing is added or taken away, the material remains the same. With an understanding of **compensation**, the student knows that an apparent change in one direction can be compensated for by a change in another direction. That is, if the liquid rises higher in the glass, the glass must be narrower. And with an understanding of **reversibility**, the student can mentally cancel out the change that has been made. Leah apparently knew it was the same water (identity), but lacked compensation and reversibility, so she was still moving toward conservation.

Another important operation mastered at this stage is **classification**. Classification depends on a student's abilities to focus on a single characteristic of objects in a set (for example, colour) and group the objects according to that characteristic. More advanced classification at this stage involves recognizing that one class fits into another. A city can be in a particular province and also in Canada. As children apply this advanced classification to locations, they often become fascinated with "complete" addresses, such as this one: Lee Jary, 5116 Forest Hill Drive, Richmond Hill, Ontario, Canada, North America, Northern Hemisphere, Earth, Solar System, Milky Way, Universe.

Classification is also related to reversibility. The ability to reverse a process mentally now allows the concrete operational student to see that there is more than one way to classify a group of objects. The student understands, for example, that buttons can be classified by colour and then reclassified by size or by the number of holes they have.

FIGURE 2.3 **Some Piagetian Conservation Tasks**

In addition to the tasks shown here, other tasks involve the conservation of number, length, weight, and volume. These tasks are all achieved over the concrete operational period.

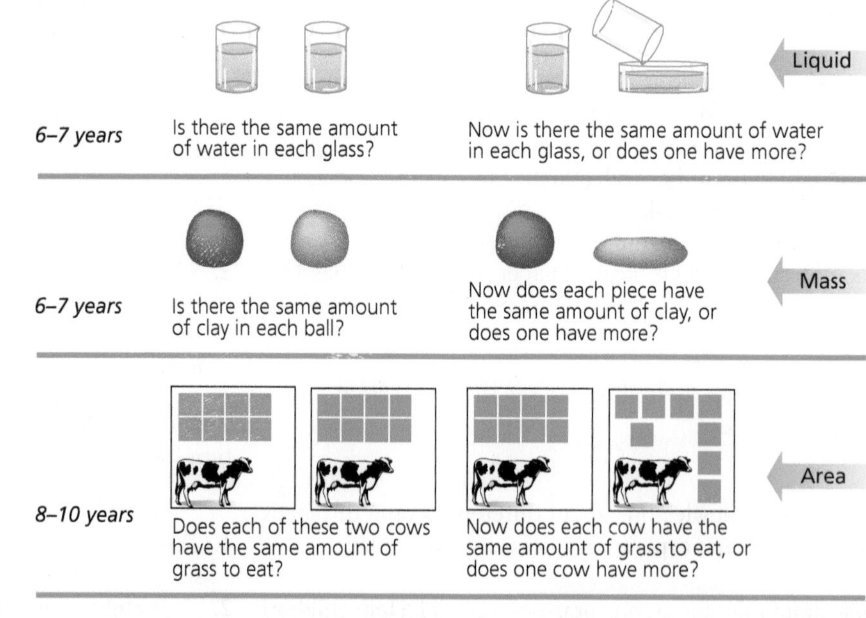

Source: Berk, L., *Child Development*, p. 231, Figure 6.7, © 1997 by Pearson Education, Inc. Reproduced by permission of Pearson Education, Inc. All rights reserved.

Concrete operations Mental tasks tied to concrete objects and situations.

Identity The principle that a person or object remains the same over time.

Compensation The principle that changes in one dimension can be offset by changes in another dimension.

Reversibility A characteristic of Piagetian logical operations—the ability to think through a series of steps, then mentally reverse the steps and return to the starting point; also called reversible thinking.

Classification Grouping objects into categories.

Seriation is the process of making an orderly arrangement from large to small or vice versa. This understanding of sequential relationships permits a student to construct a logical series in which A < B < C (A is less than B is less than C) and so on. Unlike the preoperational child, the concrete operational child can grasp the notion that B can be *larger* than A but *smaller* than C.

With the abilities to handle operations such as conservation, classification, and seriation, the student at the concrete operational stage has finally developed a complete and very logical system of thinking. This system of thinking, however, is still tied to physical reality. The logic is based on concrete situations that can be organized, classified, or manipulated. For example, children at this stage can imagine several different arrangements for the furniture in their rooms before they move it. They do not have to solve the problem strictly through trial and error by actually making the arrangements. However, the concrete operational child is not yet able to reason about hypothetical, abstract problems that involve the coordination of many factors at once. This kind of coordination is part of Piaget's next and final stage of cognitive development.

In any grade you teach, knowledge of concrete operational thinking will be helpful. In the early grades, the students are moving toward this logical system of thought. In the middle grades, it is in full flower, ready to be applied and extended by your teaching. Students in high school and even adults still commonly use concrete operational thinking, especially in areas that are new or unfamiliar. The *Guidelines* box should give you ideas for how to teach children who can apply concrete operations.

Seriation Arrangement of objects in sequential order according to one aspect, such as size, weight, or volume.

GUIDELINES: Teaching the Concrete Operational Child

Continue to use concrete props and visual aids, especially when dealing with sophisticated material.

EXAMPLES

1. Use timelines in history lessons and three-dimensional models in science lessons.
2. Use diagrams to illustrate hierarchical relationships, such as branches of government and the agencies under each branch.

Continue to give students a chance to manipulate and test objects.

EXAMPLES

1. Set up simple scientific experiments like the following involving the relationship between fire and oxygen. What happens to a flame when you blow on it from a distance? (If you don't blow it out, the flame gets larger briefly, because it has more oxygen to burn.) What happens when you cover the flame with a jar?
2. Ask students to make candles by dipping wicks in wax, to weave cloth on a simple loom, to bake bread, to set type by hand, or to do other craftwork that illustrates the daily occupations of people during the pioneer period.

Make sure that presentations and readings are brief and well organized.

EXAMPLES

1. Assign stories or books with short, logical chapters, moving to longer reading assignments only when students are ready.
2. Break up a presentation with a chance to practise the first steps before introducing the next.

Use familiar examples to explain more complex ideas.

EXAMPLES

1. Compare students' lives with those of characters in a story. For example, after reading *Island of the Blue Dolphins* (the true story of a girl who grew up alone on a deserted island), ask, "Have you ever had to stay alone for a long time? How did you feel?"
2. Teach the concept of area by having students measure two rooms in the school that are different sizes.

Give opportunities to classify and group objects and ideas on increasingly complex levels.

EXAMPLES

1. Give students slips of paper that each have one sentence written on them and ask the students to group the sentences into paragraphs.
2. Compare the systems of the human body to other kinds of systems: the brain to a computer, the heart to a pump. Break down stories into components, from the broad to the specific: author; story; characters, plot, theme; place, time; dialogue, description, actions.

Present problems that require logical, analytical thinking.

EXAMPLES

1. Use mind twisters, brainteasers, Mastermind games, and riddles.
2. Discuss open-ended questions that stimulate thinking, such as "Are the brain and the mind the same thing?" "How should the city deal with stray animals?" "What is the largest number?"

High School and University: The Formal Operational Stage. Some students remain at the concrete operational stage throughout their school years, even throughout life. However, new experiences, usually those that take place in school, eventually present most students with problems that they cannot solve using concrete operations. What happens when a number of variables interact, as in a laboratory experiment? In such a situation, a mental system for controlling sets of variables and working through a set of possibilities is needed. These are the abilities that Piaget called formal operations.

> **STOP & THINK** You are packing for a long trip, but you want to pack light. How many different three-piece outfits (slacks, shirt, jacket) will you have if you include three shirts, three slacks, and three jackets (assuming of course that they all go together in fashion perfection)? Time yourself to see how long it takes to arrive at the answer.

At the level of formal operations, the focus of thinking can shift from what *is* to what *might be*. Situations do not have to be experienced to be imagined. You met Jamal at the beginning of this chapter. Even though he is a bright elementary school student, he could not answer the question, "How would life be different if people did not have to sleep?" because he insisted, "People HAVE TO SLEEP!" In contrast, the adolescent who has mastered formal operations can consider contrary-to-fact questions. In answering, the adolescent demonstrates the hallmark of formal operations—hypothetico-deductive reasoning. The formal thinker can consider a hypothetical situation (people do not have to sleep) and reason deductively (from the general assumption to specific implications, such as longer workdays, more money spent on lighting, or new entertainment industries). Formal operations also include inductive reasoning, or using specific observations to identify general principles. For example, the economist observes many specific changes in the stock market and attempts to identify general principles about economic cycles.

PLAYING FOR AN IMAGINARY AUDIENCE Adolescents may seem "alone in a crowd." They can become very focused on their own ideas and feel everyone is noticing their every mistake.

Abstract formal operational thinking is necessary for success in many advanced high school and college courses (Meece & Daniels, 2008). For example, most math is concerned with hypothetical situations, assumptions, and givens: "Let $x = 10$," or "Assume $x^2 + y^2 = z^2$," or "Given two sides and an adjacent angle . . ." Work in social studies and literature requires abstract thinking, too: "What did Woodrow Wilson mean when he called the First World War the 'war to end all wars'?" "What are some metaphors for hope and despair in Shakespeare's sonnets?" "What symbols of old age does T. S. Eliot use in *The Waste Land*?" "How do animals symbolize human character traits in Aesop's fables?"

The organized, scientific thinking of formal operations requires that students systematically generate different possibilities for a given situation. For example, if a child capable of formal operations is asked, "How many different meat/vegetable/salad meals can you make using three meats, three vegetables, and three salads?" the child can systematically identify the 27 possible combinations. A concrete thinker might name just a few meals, focusing on favourite foods or using each food only once. The underlying system of combinations is not yet available to the concrete thinker.

Another characteristic of this stage is adolescent egocentrism. Unlike egocentric young children, adolescents do not deny that other people may have different perceptions and beliefs; the adolescents simply become very focused on their own ideas. They analyze their own beliefs and attitudes. This can lead to what Elkind (1981) calls the sense of an imaginary audience—the feeling that everyone is watching. Thus, adolescents believe that others are analyzing them (e.g., "Everyone noticed that I wore this shirt twice this week." "The whole class thought my answer was dumb!" "Everybody is going to love this CD."). You can see that social blunders or imperfections in appearance can be devastating to an adolescent if he or she believes that "everybody is watching." In fact, Schonert-Reichl (1994) at the University of British Columbia has linked adolescent egocentrism with adolescent depression. In particular, she found that girls from high-socioeconomic-status (SES) families

Formal operations Mental tasks involving abstract thinking and coordination of a number of variables.

Hypothetico-deductive reasoning A formal-operations problem-solving strategy in which an individual begins by identifying all the factors that might affect a problem and then deduces and systematically evaluates specific solutions.

Adolescent egocentrism Assumption that everyone else is interested in one's thoughts, feelings, and concerns.

tended to be overly self-conscious and more at risk for depression. In contrast, boys from high-SES families reported a heightened sense of omnipotence, uniqueness, and invulnerability. Luckily, this feeling of being "on stage" seems to peak in early adolescence, by age 14 or 15.

The ability to think hypothetically, consider alternatives, identify all possible combinations, and analyze one's own thinking has some interesting consequences for adolescents. Since they can think about worlds that do not exist, they often become interested in science fiction. Because they can reason from general principles to specific actions, they are often critical of people whose actions seem to contradict their principles. Adolescents can deduce the set of "best" possibilities and imagine ideal worlds (or ideal parents and teachers, for that matter). This explains why many students at this age develop interests in utopias, political causes, and social issues. They want to design better worlds, and their thinking allows them to do so. Adolescents can also imagine many possible futures for themselves and may try to decide which is best. Feelings about any of these ideals may be strong.

Do We All Reach the Fourth Stage? Most psychologists agree that there is a level of thinking more sophisticated than concrete operations. But the question of how universal formal operational thinking actually is, even among adults, is a matter of debate. The first three stages of Piaget's theory are forced on most people by physical realities. Objects really are permanent. The amount of water doesn't change when it is poured into another glass. Formal operations, however, are not so closely tied to the physical environment. They may be the product of practice in solving hypothetical problems and using formal scientific reasoning—abilities that are valued and taught in literate cultures, particularly in college and university. Even so, only about 30 to 40 percent of high school students can perform Piaget's formal operational tasks (Meece & Daniels, 2008).

Piaget himself (1974) suggested that most adults may be able to use formal operational thought in only a few areas where they have the greatest experience or interest. Taking a college or university class fosters formal operational abilities in that subject, but not necessarily in others (Lehman & Nisbett, 1990). So expect many students in your junior high or high school class to have trouble thinking hypothetically, especially when they are learning something new. Sometimes, students find shortcuts for dealing with problems that are beyond their grasp; they may memorize formulas or lists of steps. These systems may be helpful for passing tests, but real understanding will take place only if students are able to go beyond this superficial use of memorization. The accompanying *Guidelines* box may help you to support the development of formal operations in your students.

GUIDELINES: Helping Students Use Formal Operations

Continue to use concrete operational teaching strategies and materials.

EXAMPLES

1. Use visual aids, such as charts and illustrations, as well as somewhat more sophisticated graphs and diagrams.
2. Compare the experiences of characters in stories to students' experiences.

Give students the opportunity to explore many hypothetical questions.

EXAMPLES

1. Ask students to write position papers, to exchange their papers with students who embraced the opposing side of the issue, and then to participate in debates about topical social issues—the environment, the economy, national unity.
2. Ask students to write about their personal vision of a utopia, a description of a universe that has no gender differences, a description of Earth after humans are extinct, and so forth.

Give students opportunities to solve problems and to reason scientifically.

EXAMPLES

1. Set up group discussions in which students design experiments to answer questions.
2. Ask students to justify two different positions on animal rights, with logical arguments for each position.

Whenever possible, teach broad concepts, not just facts, using materials and ideas relevant to the students' lives.

EXAMPLES

1. When discussing Native land claims, consider other issues that have divided Canadians (e.g., Quebec separation).
2. Use lyrics from popular songs to teach poetic devices, to reflect on social problems, and to stimulate discussion on the place of popular music in our culture.

Information Processing and Neo-Piagetian Views of Cognitive Development

As you will see in Chapter 7, there are explanations for why children have trouble with conservation and other Piagetian tasks. These explanations focus on the child's developing information processing skills, such as attention, memory capacity, and learning strategies. As children mature and their brains develop, they are better able to focus their attention, process information more quickly, hold more information in memory, and use thinking strategies more easily and flexibly. Siegler (2000) proposed that as children grow older, they develop progressively better rules and strategies for solving problems and thinking logically. Teachers can help students to develop their capacities for formal thinking by putting the students in situations that challenge their thinking and reveal the shortcomings of their logic. Siegler's approach is called *rule assessment* because it focuses on understanding, challenging, and changing the rules that students use for thinking.

Some developmental psychologists have formulated **neo-Piagetian theories** that retain Piaget's insights about children's construction of knowledge and the general trends in children's thinking, but add findings from information processing about the role of attention, memory, and strategies. For example, Robbie Case (1992, 1998), who was a professor at both Stanford University and the Ontario Institute for Studies in Education of the University of Toronto before his untimely death in 2000, devised an explanation of cognitive development suggesting that children develop in stages within specific domains such as numerical concepts, spatial concepts, social tasks, storytelling, reasoning about physical objects, and motor development. As children practise using the schemes in a particular domain (for example, using counting schemes in the number concept area), accomplishing the schemes takes less attention. The schemes become more automatic because the child does not have to "think so hard" about it. This frees up mental resources and memory to do more. The child now can combine simple schemes into more complex ones and invent new schemes when needed (assimilation and accommodation in action).

Within each domain such as numerical concepts or social skills, children move from grasping simple schemes during the early preschool years, to merging two schemes into a unit (between about ages 4 and 6), to coordinating these scheme units into larger combinations, and finally, by about ages 9 to 11, to forming complex relationships that can be applied to many problems (Berk, 2005; Case, 1992, 1998). Children do progress through these qualitatively different stages within each domain, but Case argued that progress in one domain, such as number concepts, does not automatically affect movement in another, such as storytelling or social skills. The child must have experience and involvement with the content and the ways of thinking within each domain in order to construct increasingly complex and useful schemes and coordinated conceptual understandings about the domain.

Limitations of Piaget's Theory

Although most psychologists agree with Piaget's insightful descriptions of *how* children think, many disagree with his explanations of *why* thinking develops as it does.

The Trouble With Stages. Some psychologists have questioned the existence of four separate stages of thinking, even though they agree that children do go through the changes that Piaget described (Mascolo & Fischer, 2005; Miller, 2002). One problem with the stage model is the lack of consistency in children's thinking. For example, children can conserve number (the number of blocks does not change when they are rearranged) a year or two before they can conserve weight (the weight of a ball of clay does not change when you flatten it). Why can't they use conservation consistently in every situation? In fairness, we should note that in his later work, even Piaget put less emphasis on *stages* of cognitive development and gave more attention to how thinking *changes* through equilibration (Miller, 2002).

Another problem with the idea of separate stages is that the processes may be more continuous than they seem. Changes may seem like discontinuous, qualitative leaps when we look across longer time periods. The 3-year-old persistently searching for a lost toy seems qualitatively different from the infant who doesn't seem to miss a toy or to search when the toy rolls under a sofa. But if we watched a developing child very closely and observed moment-to-moment or hour-to-hour changes, we might see that indeed there are gradual, continuous changes. Rather than appearing

Neo-Piagetian theories More recent theories that integrate findings about attention, memory, and strategy use with Piaget's insights about children's thinking and the construction of knowledge.

all at once, the knowledge that a hidden toy still exists may be a product of the older child's more fully developed memory: He knows that the toy is under the sofa because he remembers seeing it roll there, whereas for the infant the toy is "out of sight, out of mind." The longer you require children to wait before searching—the longer you make them remember the object—the older they have to be to succeed (Siegler & Alibali, 2005).

Change can be both continuous and discontinuous, as described by a branch of mathematics called *catastrophe theory*. Changes that appear suddenly, like the collapse of a bridge, are preceded by many slowly developing changes such as gradual, continuous corrosion of the metal structures. Similarly, gradually developing changes in children can lead to large changes in abilities that seem abrupt (Dawson-Tunik, Fischer, & Stein, 2004; Siegler & Alibali, 2005).

Underestimating Children's Abilities. It now appears that Piaget underestimated the cognitive abilities of children, particularly younger ones. The problems he gave young children may have been too difficult and the directions too confusing. His subjects may have understood more than they could show on these problems. For example, work by Gelman and her colleagues (Gelman, 2000; Gelman & Cordes, 2001) shows that preschool children know much more about the concept of number than Piaget thought, even if they sometimes make mistakes or get confused. As long as preschoolers work with only three or four objects at a time, they can tell that the number remains the same, even if the objects are spread far apart or clumped close together. In other words, we may be born with a greater store of cognitive tools than Piaget suggested. Some basic understandings, such as the sense of number or understanding what other people know, may be part of our evolutionary equipment, ready for use in our cognitive development (Geary & Bjorklund, 2000).

Piaget's theory also does not explain how even young children can perform at an advanced level in certain areas where they have highly developed knowledge and expertise. For example, Marion Porath (1996, 1997), a former student of Robbie Case who is now at the University of British Columbia, found the drawings of artistically gifted children and the story plots of verbally gifted children to be far more elaborate than those of children in a same-age control group. Similarly, an expert 9-year-old chess player can think abstractly about chess moves, whereas a novice 20-year-old player may have to resort to more concrete strategies to plan and remember moves (Siegler, 1998).

Finally, Piaget argued that the development of cognitive operations such as conservation or abstract thinking cannot be accelerated. He believed that children had to be developmentally ready to learn. Quite a bit of research, however, has shown that children can learn to perform cognitive operations such as conservation with effective instruction. They do not have to naturally discover these ways of thinking on their own. Knowledge and experience in a situation affect the kind of thinking that students can do (Brainerd, 2003).

Cognitive Development and Culture. One final criticism of Piaget's theory is that it overlooks the important effects of the child's cultural and social group. Research across different cultures has generally confirmed that Piaget was accurate about the sequence of the stages in children's thinking he described, but age ranges for the stages vary. Western children typically move to the next stage about two to three years earlier than children in non-Western societies. But careful research has shown that these differences across cultures depend on the subject or domain tested and whether the culture values and teaches knowledge in that domain. For example, children in Brazil who sell candy in the streets instead of attending school appear to fail a certain kind of Piagetian task—class inclusion (e.g., "Are there more daisies, more tulips, or more flowers in the picture?"). But when the tasks are phrased in concepts they understand—selling candy—then these children perform better than Brazilian children the same age who attend school (Saxe, 1999).

Even concrete operations such as classification may not be so basic to people of other cultures. For example, when individuals from the Kpelle people of Africa were asked to sort 20 objects, they created groups that made sense to them—a hoe with a potato, a knife with an orange. The experimenter could not get the Kpelle to change their categories; they said this is how a wise man would do it. Finally, the experimenter asked in desperation, "Well, how would a fool do it?" Then the subjects promptly created the four neat classification piles the experimenter had expected—food, tools, and so on (Rogoff & Morelli, 1989).

There is another increasingly influential view of cognitive development. Proposed years ago by Lev Vygotsky and recently rediscovered, this theory ties cognitive development to culture.

VYGOTSKY'S SOCIOCULTURAL PERSPECTIVE

Psychologists today recognize that the child's culture shapes cognitive development by determining what and how the child will learn about the world. For example, young Zinacanteco Indian girls of southern Mexico learn complicated ways of weaving cloth through informal instruction by adults in their communities. Cultures that prize cooperation and sharing teach these skills early, whereas cultures that encourage competition nurture competitive abilities in their children (Bakerman et al., 1990; Ceci & Roazzi, 1994). The stages observed by Piaget are not necessarily "natural" for all children because to some extent they reflect the expectations and activities of the children's culture (Kozulin, 2003; Rogoff, 2003).

A major spokesperson for this sociocultural theory (also called *sociohistoric theory*) was a Russian psychologist who died more than 70 years ago. Lev Semenovich Vygotsky was only 38 when he died of tuberculosis, but during his life he produced more than 100 books and articles. Some of his translations are now available (Vygotsky, 1978, 1986, 1987a, 1987b, 1993, 1997). Vygotsky's work began when he was studying learning and development to improve his own teaching (Wink & Putney, 2002). He wrote about language and thought, the psychology of art, learning and development, and educating students with special needs. His work was banned in Russia for many years because he referenced Western psychologists. But in the past 30 years, with the rediscovery of his work, Vygotsky's ideas about language, culture, and cognitive development have become major influences in psychology and education and have provided alternatives to many of Piaget's theories (Kozulin, 2003; Van Der Veer, 2007; Wink & Putney, 2002).

SOCIOCULTURAL THEORY Lev Vygotsky elaborated the sociocultural theory of development. His ideas about language, culture, and cognitive development have become major influences in the fields of psychology and education.

Vygotsky believed that human activities take place in cultural settings and cannot be understood apart from the settings. One of his key ideas was that our specific mental structures and processes can be traced to our interactions with others. These social interactions are more than simple influences on cognitive development—they actually create our cognitive structures and thinking processes (Palincsar, 1998). In fact, "Vygotsky conceptualized development as the transformation of socially shared activities into internalized processes" (John-Steiner & Mahn, 1996, p. 192). We will examine two themes in Vygotsky's writings that explain how social processes form learning and thinking: the social sources of individual thinking and the role of tools in learning and development, especially the tool of language (Driscoll, 2005; Wertsch & Tulviste, 1992).

The Social Sources of Individual Thinking

Vygotsky assumed that:

> Every function in a child's cultural development appears twice: first on the social level and later on the individual level; first between people (interpsychological) and then inside the child (intrapsychological). This applies equally to voluntary attention, to logical memory, and to the formation of concepts. All the higher functions originate as actual relations between human individuals. (1978, p. 57)

In other words, higher mental processes, such as directing your own attention and thinking through problems, first are co-constructed during shared activities between the child and another person. Then the processes are internalized by the child and become part of that child's cognitive development (Gredler, 2007). For example, children first use language in activities with others, to regulate the behaviour of the others ("No nap!" or "I wanna cookie"). Later, however, children can regulate their own behaviour using private speech ("Don't spill"), as you will see in a later section. So, for Vygotsky, social interaction was more than influence—it was the origin of higher mental processes such as problem solving. Consider this example:

Sociocultural theory Theory that emphasizes the role in development of cooperative dialogues between children and more knowledgeable members of society; children learn the culture of their community (ways of thinking and behaving) through these interactions.

Co-constructed Constructed through a social process in which people interact and negotiate (usually verbally) to create an understanding or to solve a problem; the final product is shaped by all participants.

> A six-year-old has lost a toy and asks her father for help. The father asks her where she last saw the toy; the child says, "I can't remember." He asks a series of questions—did you have it in your room? Outside? Next door? To each question, the child answers, "no." When he says "in the car?" she says "I think so" and goes to retrieve the toy. (Tharp & Gallimore, 1988, p. 14)

Who remembered? The answer is really neither the father nor the daughter, but the two together. The remembering and problem solving was co-constructed—between people—in the interaction.

But the child may have internalized strategies to use next time something is lost. At some point, the child will be able to function independently to solve this kind of problem. So, as the strategy for finding the toy indicates, higher functions appear first between a child and a "teacher" before they exist within the individual child (Kozulin, 1990, 2003).

Here is another example of the social sources of individual thinking. Richard Anderson and his colleagues (2001) studied how grade 4 students in small-group classroom discussions *appropriate* (take for themselves and use) argument stratagems that occur in the discussions. An argument stratagem is a particular form such as "I think [POSITION] because [REASON]," where the student fills in the position and the reason. For example, a student might say, "I think that the wolves should be left alone because they are not hurting anyone." Another strategy form is "If [ACTION], then [BAD CONSEQUENCE]," as in "If they don't trap the wolves, then the wolves will eat the cows." Other forms manage participation, for example, "What do you think, [NAME]?" or "Let [NAME] talk."

Anderson's research identified 13 forms of talk and argument that helped to manage the discussions, to get everyone to participate and present and defend positions, and to handle confusion. The researchers found that the use of these different forms of talking and thinking *snowballed*—once a useful argument was employed by one student, it spread to other students, and the argument stratagem form appeared more and more in the discussions. Open discussions—students asking and answering each other's questions—were better than teacher-dominated discussion for the development of these argument forms. Over time, these ways of presenting, attacking, and defending positions could be internalized as mental reasoning and decision making for the individual students.

Both Piaget and Vygotsky emphasized the importance of social interactions in cognitive development, but Piaget saw a different role for interaction. He believed that interaction encouraged development by creating disequilibrium—cognitive conflict—that motivated change. Thus, Piaget believed that the most helpful interactions were between peers because peers are on an equal basis and can challenge each other's thinking. Vygotsky (1978, 1986, 1987a, 1987b, 1993), on the other hand, suggested that children's cognitive development is fostered by interactions with people who are more capable or advanced in their thinking—people such as parents and teachers (Moshman, 1997; Palincsar, 1998). Of course, as we have seen above, students can learn from both adults and peers.

Cultural Tools and Cognitive Development

Vygotsky believed that **cultural tools**, including real tools (such as printing presses, rulers, the abacus—today, we would add PDAs, computers, the internet) and psychological tools (sign and symbol systems such as numbers and mathematical systems, maps, works of art, signs, codes, Braille, language, and sign language), play very important roles in cognitive development. For example, as long as the culture provides only Roman numerals for representing quantity, certain ways of thinking mathematically—from long division to calculus—are difficult or impossible. But with a number system that has a zero, fractions, positive and negative values, and an infinite quantity of numbers, much more is possible. The number system is a cultural tool that supports thinking, learning, and cognitive development. This symbol system is passed from adult to child and from child to child through formal and informal interactions and teachings.

Vygotsky believed that all higher-order mental processes, such as reasoning and problem solving, are *mediated* by (accomplished through and with the help of) psychological tools, such as language, signs, and symbols. Adults teach these tools to children during day-to-day activities and the children internalize them. Then the psychological tools can help students advance their own development (Karpov & Haywood, 1998). The process goes something like this: As children engage in activities with adults or more capable peers, they exchange ideas and ways of thinking about or representing concepts—drawing maps, for example, as a way to represent spaces and places. Children internalize these co-created ideas. Thus, children's knowledge, ideas, attitudes, and values develop through appropriating or "taking for themselves" the ways of acting and thinking provided by their culture and by the more capable members of their group (Wertsch, 2007).

In this exchange of signs and symbols and explanations, children begin to develop a "cultural tool kit" to make sense of and learn about their world (Wertsch, 1991). The kit is filled with physical tools such as pencils or paint brushes directed toward the external world and with psychological tools such as problem solving or memory strategies for acting mentally. Children do not just receive the tools transmitted to them by others, however. Children transform the tools as they construct their

Cultural tools The real tools (computers, scales, etc.) and symbol systems (numbers, language, graphs, etc.) that allow people in a society to communicate, think, solve problems, and create knowledge.

CULTURAL TOOLS Vygotsky emphasized the tools that particular cultures provide to support thinking, and the idea that children use the tools they're given to construct their own understanding of the physical and social worlds.

own representations, symbols, patterns, and understandings. As we learned from Piaget, children's constructions of meaning are not the same as those of adults. In the exchange of signs and symbols such as number systems, children create their own understandings (a skunk is a "kitty"). These understandings are gradually changed (a skunk is a skunk) as the children continue to engage in social activities and try to make sense of their world (John-Steiner & Mahn, 1996; Wertsch, 1991).

In Vygotsky's theory, language is the most important symbol system in the tool kit, and it is the one that helps fill the kit with other tools.

The Role of Language and Private Speech

Language is critical for cognitive development. It provides a means for expressing ideas and asking questions, the categories and concepts for thinking, and the links between the past and the future (Das, 1995; Driscoll, 2005). When we consider a problem, we generally think in words and partial sentences. Vygotsky thought that:

> The specifically human capacity for language enables children to provide for auxiliary tools in the solution of difficult tasks, to overcome impulsive action, to plan a solution to a problem prior to its execution, and to master their own behavior. (Vygotsky, 1978, p. 28)

Vygotsky placed more emphasis than Piaget on the role of learning and language in cognitive development. He believed that "thinking deepens on speech, on the means of thinking, and on the child's socio-cultural experience" (Vygotsky, 1987a, p. 120). In fact, Vygotsky believed that language in the form of *private speech* (talking to yourself) guides cognitive development.

Private Speech: Vygotsky's and Piaget's Views Compared. If you have spent much time around young children, you know that they often talk to themselves as they play. This can happen when the child is alone or, even more often, in a group of children—each child talks enthusiastically, without any real interaction or conversation. Piaget called this the collective monologue and he called all of the children's self-directed talk "egocentric speech." He assumed that this egocentric speech is another indication that young children can't see the world through the eyes of others. They talk about what matters to them, without taking into account the needs or interests of their listeners. As they mature, and especially as they have disagreements with peers, Piaget believed, children develop socialized speech. They learn to listen and exchange (or argue) ideas.

Vygotsky had very different ideas about young children's private speech. He suggested that, rather than being a sign of cognitive immaturity, these mutterings play an important role in cognitive development by moving children toward self-regulation—the ability to plan, monitor, and guide one's own thinking and problem solving (see Chapter 10 for a detailed description of this highly effective form of learning).

Vygotsky believed that self-regulation develops in a series of stages. First, the child's behaviour is regulated by others, usually parents, using language and other signs such as gestures. For example, the parent says "No!" when the child reaches toward a candle flame. Next, the child learns to regulate the behaviour of others using the same language tools. The child says "No!" to another child who is trying to take away a toy, often even imitating the parent's voice tone. The child also begins to use private speech to regulate her own behaviour, saying "no" quietly to herself as she is tempted to touch the flame. Finally, the child learns to regulate her own behaviour by using silent inner speech (Karpov & Haywood, 1998). For example, in any preschool room, you might hear 4- or 5-year-olds saying, "No, it won't fit. Try it here. Turn. Turn. Maybe this one!" while they do puzzles. As these children mature, their self-directed speech goes underground, changing from spoken to whispered speech and then to silent lip movements. Finally, the children just "think" the guiding words. The use of private speech peaks at around age 9, although one study found that some students from ages 11 to 17 still spontaneously muttered to themselves during problem solving (McCafferty, 2004; Winsler, Carlton, & Barry, 2000; Winsler & Naglieri, 2003).

Collective monologue Form of speech in which children in a group talk but do not really interact or communicate.

Private speech Children's self-talk, which guides their thinking and action; eventually, these verbalizations are internalized as silent inner speech.

This series of steps is another example of how higher mental functions appear first between people as they communicate and regulate each other's behaviour—what McCaslin and Good (1996) refer to as co-regulating learning—and then appear again within the individual as a cognitive process. Through this process, the child is using language to accomplish important cognitive activities such as directing attention, solving problems, planning, forming concepts, and gaining self-control. Research supports Vygotsky's ideas (Berk & Spuhl, 1995; Emerson & Miyake, 2003). Children and adults tend to use more private speech when they are confused, having difficulties, or making mistakes (Duncan & Cheyne, 1999). Have you ever thought to yourself something like, "Let's see, the first step is . . ." or "Where did I use my glasses last?" or "If I work to the end of this page, then I can . . ."? You were using inner speech to remind, cue, encourage, or guide yourself. In a really tough situation, you might even find that you return to muttering out loud. Because private speech helps students to regulate their thinking, it makes sense to allow, and even encourage, students to use private speech in school. Teachers' insisting on total silence when young students are working on difficult problems may make the work even harder for them. Note when muttering increases in your class—this could be a sign that students need help.

Table 2.2 contrasts Piaget's and Vygotsky's theories of private speech. We should note that Piaget accepted many of Vygotsky's arguments and came to agree that language could be used in both egocentric and problem-solving ways (Piaget, 1962).

The Zone of Proximal Development

According to Vygotsky, at any given point in development, there are certain problems that a child is on the verge of being able to solve. The child just needs some structure, clues, reminders, help with remembering details or steps, encouragement to keep trying, and so on. Some problems, of course, are beyond the child's capabilities, even if every step is explained clearly. The zone of proximal development (ZPD) is the area between the child's current developmental level "as determined by independent problem solving" and the level of development that the child could achieve "through adult guidance or in collaboration with more peers" (Vygotsky, 1978, p. 86). It is a dynamic and changing space as student and teacher interact and understandings are exchanged. This is the area where instruction can succeed. Kathleen Berger (2006) called this area the "magic middle"—somewhere between what the student already knows and what the student isn't ready to learn (see Figure 2.4).

Zone of proximal development (ZPD) Phase at which a child can master a task if given appropriate help and support.

Private Speech and the Zone. We can see how Vygotsky's beliefs about the role of private speech in cognitive development fit with the notion of the zone of proximal development. Often, an adult helps a child to solve a problem or accomplish a task using verbal prompts and structuring. We

TABLE 2.2 Differences Between Piaget's and Vygotsky's Theories of Egocentric or Private Speech

	Piaget	Vygotsky
Developmental significance	Represents an inability to take the perspective of another and engage in reciprocal communication	Represents externalized thought; its function is to communicate with the self for the purpose of self-guidance and self-direction
Course of development	Declines with age	Increases at younger ages and then gradually loses its audible quality to become internal verbal thought
Relationship to social speech	Negative; least socially and cognitively mature children use more egocentric speech	Positive; private speech develops out of social interaction with others
Relationship to environmental contexts	—	Increases with task difficulty; private speech serves a helpful self-guiding function in situations where more cognitive effort is needed to reach a solution

Source: From Berk, L. E., & Garvin, R. A. (1984). Development of private speech among low-income Appalachian children. *Developmental Psychology, 20*, 272.

FIGURE 2.4 **Teaching in the Magic Middle**
The zone of proximal development is the teaching space between the boring and the impossible. In that space, scaffolding from the teacher or a peer can support learning.

Source: Adapted from K. S. Berger (2006). *The developing person through childhood and adolescence* (7th ed.). New York: Worth, p. 51. With permission of Worth Publishers.

will see later that this type of support has been called *scaffolding*. This support can be gradually reduced as the child takes over the guidance, perhaps first by giving the prompts as private speech and finally as inner speech. Let's move forward to a future day in the life of the girl in the earlier example who had lost her toy and *listen to* her thoughts when she realizes that a school book is missing. They might sound something like this:

> "Where's my math book? Used it in class. Thought I put it in my book bag after class. Dropped my bag on the bus. That dope Larry kicked my stuff, so maybe . . ."

The girl can now systematically search for ideas about the lost book without help from anyone else.

The Role of Learning and Development. Piaget defined *development* as the active construction of knowledge and *learning* as the passive formation of associations (Siegler, 2000). He was interested in knowledge construction and believed that cognitive development has to come before learning—the child has to be cognitively "ready" to learn. He said that "learning is subordinated to development and not vice-versa" (Piaget, 1964, p. 17). Students can memorize, for example, that Geneva is in Switzerland but still insist that they cannot be Genevan and Swiss at the same time. True understanding will happen only when the child has developed the operation of *class inclusion*—the idea that one category can be included in another. But as we saw earlier, research has not supported Piaget's position on the need for cognitive development to precede learning (Brainerd, 2003).

In contrast, Vygotsky believed that learning is an active process that does not have to wait for readiness. In fact, "properly organized learning results in mental development and sets in motion a variety of developmental processes that would be impossible apart from learning" (Vygotsky, 1978, p. 90). He saw learning as a tool in development—learning pulls development up to higher levels, and social interaction is a key in learning (Glassman, 2001; Wink & Putney, 2002). Vygotsky's belief that learning pulls development to higher levels means that other people, including teachers, play a significant role in cognitive development.

Limitations of Vygotsky's Theory

Vygotsky's theory added important considerations by highlighting the role of culture and social processes in cognitive development, but he may have gone too far. As we have seen in this chapter, we may be born with a greater store of cognitive tools than either Piaget or Vygotsky suggested. Some basic understandings, such as the idea that adding increases quantity, may be part of our biological predispositions, ready for use to guide our cognitive development. Young children appear to figure out much about the world before they have the chance to learn from either their culture or teachers (Schunk, 2008). Also, Vygotsky did not detail the cognitive processes underlying developmental changes—which cognitive processes allow students to engage in more advanced and independent participation in social activities? The major limitation of Vygotsky's theory, however, is that it consists mostly of general ideas; Vygotsky died before he could expand and elaborate on his ideas and pursue his research. His students continued to investigate his ideas, but much of that work was suppressed until the 1950s and 1960s by Stalin's regime (Gredler, 2005; Kozulin, 1990, 2003). A final limitation might be that Vygotsky did not have time to detail the applications of his theories for teaching, even though he was very interested in instruction. So most of the applications described today have been created by others—and we don't even know if Vygotsky would agree with them.

IMPLICATIONS OF PIAGET'S AND VYGOTSKY'S THEORIES FOR TEACHERS

Piaget did not make specific educational recommendations and Vygotsky did not have time to make a complete set of applications. But we can still glean some guidance from both of them.

Piaget: What Can We Learn?

Piaget was more interested in understanding children's thinking than in guiding teachers. He did express some general ideas about educational philosophy, however. He believed that the main goal of education should be to help children learn how to learn, and that education should "form not furnish" the minds of students (Piaget, 1969, p. 70). Piaget has taught us that we can learn a great deal about how children think by listening carefully, by paying close attention to their ways of solving problems. If we understand children's thinking, we will be better able to match teaching methods to children's abilities.

Even though Piaget did not design programs of education based on his ideas, his influence on 20th-century education is huge (Hindi & Perry, 2007). For example, the National Association for the Education of Young Children has guidelines for developmentally appropriate practice (DAP) that incorporate Piaget's findings (Bredekamp & Copple, 1997).

Understanding and Building on Students' Thinking. The students in any class will vary greatly both in their level of cognitive development and in their academic knowledge. As a teacher, how can you determine whether students are having trouble because they lack the necessary thinking abilities or because they simply have not learned the basic facts? To do this, Robbie Case (1985b) suggested that you observe your students carefully as they try to solve the problems you have presented. What kind of logic do they use? Do they focus on only one aspect of the situation? Are they fooled by appearances? Do they suggest solutions systematically or by guessing and forgetting what they have already tried? Ask your students how they tried to solve the problem. Listen to their strategies. What kind of thinking is behind repeated mistakes or problems? Students are the best sources of information about their own thinking abilities (Confrey, 1990a).

An important implication of Piaget's theory for teaching is what J. M. Hunt (1961) years ago called the "problem of the match." Students must be neither bored by work that is too simple nor left behind by teaching they cannot understand. According to Hunt, disequilibrium must be kept "just right" to encourage growth. Setting up situations that lead to errors can help create an appropriate level of disequilibrium. When students experience some conflict between what they think should happen (a piece of wood should sink because it is big) and what actually happens (it floats!), they may rethink their understanding, and new knowledge may develop.

Many materials and lessons can be understood at several levels and can be "just right" for a range of cognitive abilities. Classics such as *Alice in Wonderland,* myths, and fairy tales can be enjoyed at both concrete and symbolic levels. It is also possible for students to be introduced to a topic together and then work individually on follow-up activities matched to their level. Tom Good and Jere Brophy (2003) describe activity cards for three or four ability levels. These cards provide different readings and assignments, but all are directed toward the overall class objectives. One of the cards should be a good "match" for each student. Often it makes sense to let students choose their own follow-up activities—with encouragement from the teacher to tackle challenges. Using multi-level lessons is called *differentiated instruction* (Tomlinson, 2005b). We look at this approach more closely in Chapter 13.

Activity and Constructing Knowledge. Piaget's fundamental insight was that individuals *construct* their own understanding; learning is a constructive process. At every level of cognitive development, you will also want to see that students are actively engaged in the learning process. In his words:

> Knowledge is not a copy of reality. To know an object, to know an event, is not simply to look at it and make a mental copy or image of it. To know an object is to act on it. To know is to modify, to transform the object, and to understand the process of this transformation, and as a consequence to understand the way the object is constructed. (Piaget, 1964, p. 8)

This active experience, even at the earliest school levels, should not be limited to the physical manipulation of objects. It should also include mental manipulation of ideas that arise out of class projects or experiments (Gredler, 2005). For example, after a social studies lesson on different jobs, a primary-grade teacher might show the students a picture of a woman and ask, "What could this person be?" After answers such as "teacher," "doctor," "secretary," "lawyer," "saleswoman," and so on, the teacher could suggest, "How about a daughter?" Answers such as "sister," "mother," "aunt," and "granddaughter" may follow. This should help the children switch dimensions in their classification and centre on another aspect of the situation. Next, the teacher might suggest "Canadian," "jogger," or "blonde." With older children, hierarchical classification might be involved: "It is a picture of a woman, who is a human being; a human being is a primate, which is a mammal, which is an animal, which is a life form."

All students need to interact with teachers and peers in order to test their thinking, to be challenged, to receive feedback, and to watch how others work out problems. Disequilibrium is often set in motion quite naturally when the teacher or another student suggests a new way of thinking about something. As a general rule, students should act, manipulate, observe, and then talk and/or write (to the teacher and each other) about what they have experienced. Concrete experiences provide the raw materials for thinking. Communicating with others makes students use, test, and sometimes change their thinking abilities.

The Value of Play. Maria Montessori once noted, and Piaget would agree, that "play is children's work." We saw that the brain develops with stimulation, and that play provides some of that stimulation at every age. Babies in the sensorimotor stage learn by exploring, sucking, pounding, shaking, throwing—acting on their environments. Preoperational preschoolers love pretend play, and through pretending they form symbols, use language, and interact with others. They are beginning to play simple games with predictable rules. During their elementary school years, children also like fantasy, but they are beginning to play more complex games and sports and thus learn cooperation, fairness, negotiation, winning, and losing, as well as developing language. As children grow into adolescents, play continues to be part of their physical and social development (Meece, 2002).

Piaget taught us that children do not think like adults, but discussions about the implications of Piaget's theory often centre on the question of whether cognitive development can be accelerated.

This issue is at the heart of many discussions about the nature of programming in preschool and kindergarten. Many provinces across Canada have implemented, or are in the process of implementing, full-day kindergarten, including British Columbia, Ontario, Quebec, Nova Scotia, and New Brunswick. Some provinces have begun a targeted implementation, focusing on particular groups of children who are believed to be disadvantaged in terms of their readiness for school (e.g., Aboriginal children, immigrant children, and children with disabilities). Others, like British Columbia and Ontario, are quickly moving to universal programs (universally available, although not universally required). These provinces are promoting a play-based approach to instruction, emphasizing that through play children can develop language and literacy, math and science skills, and social competence (BC Ministry of Education, n.d.; Elementary Teachers' Federation of Ontario, 2008). But some proponents of all-day kindergarten would like to see a more academic approach. The *Point/Counterpoint* box examines this question.

POINT / COUNTERPOINT

Can Cognitive Development Be Accelerated?

EVER SINCE PIAGET described his stages of cognitive development, people have asked if progress through the stages could be accelerated. More recently, the question has focused on whether we should accelerate learning for young children who are at risk of academic failure. Can learning be accelerated, and if so, is this a good idea?

POINT

Every child deserves a head start.

Some of the strongest arguments in favour of "speeding up" cognitive development are based on the results of cross-cultural studies of children (studies that compare children growing up in different cultures). These results suggest that certain cognitive abilities are indeed influenced by the environment and education. Children of pottery-making families in one area of Mexico, for example, learn conservation of substance earlier than their peers in families that do not make pottery (Ashton, 1978). Furthermore, children in non-Western cultures appear to acquire conservation operations later than children in Western cultures. It seems likely that factors in the environment contribute to the rate of cognitive development.

But even if cognitive development can be accelerated, is this a good idea? Two of the most vocal (and heavily criticized) advocates of early academic training are Siegfried and Therese Engelmann (1981). In their book *Give Your Child a Superior Mind*, they suggest that children who learn academic skills as preschoolers will be smarter throughout their school years, are less likely to fail, and are more likely to enjoy school. They contend,

> *Children respond to the environment. Their capacity to learn and what they learn depends on what the environment teaches. . . . Instead of relying on the traditional environment that is rich in learning opportunities for the child, we can take the environment a step further and mold it into a purposeful instrument that teaches and that guarantees your child will have a superior mind. (p. 10)*

COUNTERPOINT

Acceleration is ineffective and may be harmful.

The position of psychologists who attempt to apply Piaget's theory to education is that development should not be accelerated. This traditional view has been well summarized by Wadsworth (1978):

> *The function of the teacher is not to accelerate the development of the child or speed up the rate of movement from stage to stage. The function of the teacher is to insure that development within each stage is thoroughly integrated and complete. (p. 117)*

According to Piaget, cognitive development is based on the self-selected actions and thoughts of the student, not on the teacher's action. If you try to teach a student something the student is not ready to learn, he or she may learn to give the "correct" answer, but this will not really affect the way the student thinks about the problem. Therefore, why spend a long time teaching something at one stage when students will learn it by themselves much more rapidly and thoroughly at another stage?

Today, the pressure is on parents and preschool teachers to create "superkids," 3-year-olds who read, write, and speak a second language. David Elkind (1991), author of a best-selling parent-help book, asserts that pushing children can be harmful. He believes that preschool children who are given formal instruction in academic subjects often show signs of stress, such as headaches. These children may become dependent on adults for guidance, and an early focus on "right" and "wrong" answers can lead to competition and loss of self-esteem.

According to the Elementary Teachers' Federation of Ontario (2008), it is crucial that early-years programming be based on developmentally appropriate, research-based philosophies and teaching practices and that the efficacy of play-based learning be supported by research.

Vygotsky: What Can We Learn?

There are at least three ways in which cultural tools can be passed from one individual to another: imitative learning (where one person tries to imitate the other), instructed learning (where learners internalize the instructions of the teacher and use these instructions to self-regulate), and collaborative learning (where peers strive to understand each other and learning occurs in the process) (Tomasello, Kruger, & Ratner, 1993). Vygotsky was most concerned with instructed learning through direct teaching or through structuring experiences that support another's learning, but his theory supports the other forms of cultural learning as well. Thus, Vygotsky's ideas are relevant for educators who teach directly and who also create learning environments (Das, 1995; Wink & Putney, 2002). One major aspect of teaching in either situation is assisted learning.

The Role of Adults and Peers. Vygotsky believed that the child is not alone in the world "discovering" the cognitive operations of conservation or classification. This discovery is *assisted* or *mediated* by family members, teachers, peers, and even software (Puntambekar & Hubscher, 2005). Most of this guidance is communicated through language, at least in Western cultures. In some cultures, observing a skilled performance, not talking about it, guides the child's learning (Rogoff, 1990). Some people have called this adult assistance scaffolding, taken from Wood, Bruner, and Ross (1976). The idea is that children use the help for support while they build a firm understanding that will eventually allow them to solve the problems on their own. Actually, when Wood and his colleagues introduced the term *scaffolding*, they were talking about how teachers set up or structure learning environments, but Vygotsky's theory implies more dynamic exchanges between students and teachers that allow teachers to support students in the parts of a task they cannot do alone. In the section below, we offer an example of how one teacher scaffolds her students' learning about math concepts and problem solving.

SCAFFOLDING LEARNING According to Vygotsky, much of children's learning is assisted or mediated by teachers or parents and tools in their environment, and most of this guidance is communicated through language.

Assisted Learning. Vygotsky's theory suggests that teachers need to do more than just arrange the environment so that students can discover on their own. He believed that children cannot and should not be expected to reinvent or rediscover knowledge already available in their cultures. Rather, they should be guided and assisted in their learning—so, Vygotsky saw teachers, parents, and other adults as central to the child's learning and development (Karpov & Haywood, 1998).

Assisted learning, or guided participation in the classroom, requires scaffolding—giving information, prompts, reminders, and encouragement at the right time and in the right amounts, and then gradually allowing the students to do more and more on their own. Teachers can assist learning by adapting materials or problems to students' current levels; demonstrating skills or thought processes; walking students through the steps of a complicated problem; doing part of the problem (for example, in algebra, the students set up the equation and the teacher does the calculations or vice versa); giving detailed feedback and allowing revisions; or asking questions that refocus students' attention (Rosenshine & Meister, 1992). Cognitive apprenticeships, reciprocal teaching, and instructional conversations (described in Chapter 9) are other examples. Table 2.3 gives examples of assisted learning strategies that can be used in any lesson.

Scaffolding Support for learning and problem solving; the support could be clues, reminders, encouragement, breaking the problem down into steps, providing an example, or anything else that allows the student to grow in independence as a learner.

Assisted learning Learning by having strategic help provided in the initial stages; the help gradually diminishes as students gain independence.

Teaching With Technology. Vygotsky's sociocultural perspective has had a great influence on developing strategies for enhancing learning using computer technology. The advancement of information technology in our society has greatly increased the opportunity for social interaction. In fact, between talking or texting on cell phones, instant messaging, and emailing, today's children can be constantly connected to their peer groups (Rideout, Roberts, & Foehr, 2005). As noted earlier, Vygotsky felt that humans use tools, such as speech and writing, to learn from their social environments. Learning theorists have begun to view the computer, and in particular the social connectivity of this technology, as a tool that can be harnessed to create powerful learning environments. The underlying notion is that students will have unique opportunities to collaborate and share their ideas with other learners. Sometimes students also interact with these learners in face-to-face settings, while at other times they may know them only in an online capacity.

TABLE 2.3

Assisted Learning: Strategies to Scaffold Complex Learning

- *Using procedural facilitators.* These provide a "scaffold" to help students learn implicit skills. For example, a teacher might encourage students to use "signal words" such as *who, what, where, when, why,* and *how* to generate questions after reading a passage.
- *Modelling use of facilitators.* The teacher, in the above example, might model the generation of questions about the reading.
- *Thinking out loud.* This models the teacher's expert thought processes, showing students the revisions and choices the learner makes in using procedural facilitators to work on problems.
- *Anticipating difficult areas.* During the modelling and presentations phase of instruction, for example, the teacher anticipates and discusses potential student errors.
- *Providing prompt or cue cards.* Procedural facilitators are written on "prompt cards" that students keep for reference as they work. As students practise, the cards gradually become unnecessary.
- *Regulating the difficulty.* Tasks involving implicit skills are introduced by beginning with simpler problems, providing for student practice after each step, and gradually increasing the complexity of the task.
- *Providing half-done examples.* Giving students half-done examples of problems and having them work out the conclusions can be an effective way to teach them how to ultimately solve problems on their own.
- *Utilizing reciprocal teaching.* This means having the teacher and students rotate the role of teacher. The teacher provides support to students as they learn to lead discussions and ask their own questions.
- *Providing checklists.* Students can be taught self-checking procedures to help them regulate the quality of their responses.

Source: "Effective Teaching Redux," by John O'Neil. In the 1990 issue of *ASCD Update, 32*(6), p. 5. Learn more about ASCD at www.ascd.org.

Teaching and the "Magic Middle." Both Piaget and Vygotsky probably would agree that students need to be taught in the magic middle (Berger, 2006) or the place of the "match" (Hunt, 1961)—where they are neither bored nor frustrated. Students should be put in situations where they have to reach to understand, but where support from other students or the teacher is also available. Sometimes the best teacher is another student who has just figured out how to solve the problem, because this student is probably operating in the learner's *zone of proximal development.* When a student works with another student who is a bit better at the activity, both students benefit in the exchange of explanations, elaborations, and questions. In addition, students should be encouraged to use language to organize their thinking and to talk about what they are trying to accomplish. Dialogue and discussion are important avenues to learning (Karpov & Bransford, 1995; Kozulin & Presseisen, 1995; Wink & Putney, 2002). The *Guidelines* box on page 52 gives more ideas for how to apply Vygotsky's ideas in the classroom.

Reaching Every Student: Scaffolding Learning

Here is an example of how a teacher named Tamara supported her students' learning about math concepts and problem solving.

> Tamara announces, "To prepare for our museum trip, there's something very important I need to do: Write a check for our entrance fees." She tears a check from a checkbook and holds it up. "It's two dollars a person, and we have twenty-two children. How much would that be?"
>
> When none of the children responds, Tamara modifies her question: "How much for ten people to get into the museum? Let's have ten people stand up so we can see." Tamara asks Kara to tap ten people on the shoulder. After they form a line she continues, "Now, if each ticket costs two dollars and we have ten people, how much will it cost? How could we find out?"
>
> Several children chorus, "We can count by twos!"
>
> Tamara nods and says, "Let's count," as she taps each child in the line. When she reaches "twenty" she asks ten more people to stand. The children continue counting, reaching "forty."
>
> "Now, our last two people. Randy and Michael, please stand up."
>
> A child calls out, "Forty-four dollars in all. That's a lot!" Tamara writes the check, pointing out the dollar signs, followed by numerals 4-4. (Berk, 2001, pp. 186–187)

GUIDELINES: Applying Vygotsky's Ideas to Teaching

Tailor scaffolding to the needs of students.

EXAMPLES

1. When students are beginning new tasks or topics, provide models, prompts, sentence starters, coaching, and feedback. As the students grow in competence, give less support and more opportunities for independent work.
2. Give students choices about the level of difficulty or degree of independence in projects; encourage them to challenge themselves but to seek help when they are really stuck.

Make sure that students have access to powerful tools that support thinking.

EXAMPLES

1. Teach students to use learning and organizational strategies, research tools, language tools (dictionaries or computer searches), spreadsheets, and word-processing programs.
2. Model the use of tools; show students how you use an appointment book or electronic notebook to make plans and manage time, for example.

Capitalize on dialogue and group learning.

EXAMPLES

1. Experiment with peer tutoring; teach students how to ask good questions and how to give helpful explanations.
2. Experiment with cooperative learning strategies, described in Chapters 9 and 11, including using the internet to create communities of learners.

For more information about Vygotsky and his theories, see **http://tip.psychology.org/vygotsky.html**.

The scaffolding that Tamara provided—making the problem more concrete, breaking it into steps, using the students as "counters," using the familiar process of counting by twos—allowed her students to understand and solve this problem that they could not solve alone.

Clearly, language plays a major role in learning, inside and outside the classroom. Let's look at this human capability more closely.

THE DEVELOPMENT OF LANGUAGE

All children in every culture master the complicated system of their native language, unless severe deprivation or physical problems interfere. This knowledge is remarkable. To have a conversation, children must coordinate sounds, meanings, words and sequences of words, volume, voice tone, inflection, and turn-taking rules. Yet, by about age 4, most children have a vocabulary of thousands of words and knowledge of the grammar rules of conversations (Colledge et al., 2002).

What Develops: Language and Cultural Differences

There are over 6000 natural languages in the world (Tomasello, 2006). In general, cultures develop words for the concepts that are important to them. For example: How many different shades of green can you name—mint, olive, emerald, teal, sea foam, chromium, turquoise, chartreuse, lime, apple? An oil painting artist can add cobalt titanate green, cinnabar green, phthalo yellow green, viridian green, and many others. English-speaking countries have over 3000 words for colours. In contrast, the Himba people of Namibia and a tribe in Papua New Guinea have five words for colours, even though they can recognize many colour variations. But whether there are few or many colour terms, children gradually acquire the colour categories that are appropriate for their culture (Roberson, Davidoff, Davies, & Shapiro, 2004).

Languages also change over time to indicate changing cultural needs and values. For example, the Shoshoni Native Americans have one word that means "to make a crunching sound walking on the sand." This word was valuable in the past to communicate about hunting, but today new words describing technical tools have been added to the Shoshoni language, as their life moves away from nomadic hunting. To hear hundreds of new 21st-century tool words, listen to techies talk about computers (Price & Crapo, 2002).

The Puzzle of Language. It is likely that many factors—biological, cultural, and experiential—play a role in language development. To master a language, children must (a) read the intentions of others so the children can acquire the words, phrases, and concepts of their language and also (b) find patterns in the ways other people use these words and phrases to construct the grammar of their language (Tomasello, 2006). The important point is that children develop language as they develop other cognitive abilities by actively trying to make sense of what they hear and by looking for patterns and making up rules to put together the jigsaw puzzle of language.

In this process, humans may have built-in biases, rules, and constraints about language that restrict the number of possibilities considered. For example, young children seem to have a constraint specifying that a new label refers to a whole object, not just a part. Another built-in bias leads children to assume that the label refers to a class of similar objects. So the child learning about the rabbit is equipped naturally to assume that *rabbit* refers to the whole animal (not just its ears) and that other similar-looking animals are also rabbits (Jaswal & Markman, 2001; Markman, 1992). Reward and correction play a role in helping children learn correct language use, but the child's thinking in putting together the parts of this complicated system is very important (Waxman & Lidz, 2006).

When and How Does Language Develop?

Table 2.4 shows the milestones of language development, ages 2 to 6, in Western cultures, along with ideas for encouraging development.

Sounds and Pronunciation. By about age 5, most children have mastered the sounds of their native language, but a few may remain unconquered. In English, generally the *j* and *v* sounds and the consonant clusters of *th, zh, str, sl,* and *dr* are the last to develop (Owens, 2005). Young children may understand and be able to use many words, but prefer to use the words they can pronounce easily. As young children learn to hear differences in the sounds of language, they enjoy rhymes, songs, and general sound silliness. Young children like stories by Dr. Seuss partly because of the sounds, as is evident by book titles, such as *All Aboard the Circus McGurkus* or *Wet Pet, Dry Pet, Your Pet, My Pet*. The young son of a friend of Anita's, one of the authors of this text, wanted to name his new baby sister *Brontosaurus* "just because it's fun to say."

Vocabulary and Meaning. As you can see in Table 2.4, children between ages 2 and 3 can *use* about 450 words (expressive vocabulary) even though they can *understand* many more (receptive vocabulary). By age 6, children know more than 10 000 words. In fact, some researchers estimate that students in the early grades learn up to 20 words a day (Berger, 2003). In the early elementary years, some children may have trouble with abstract words such as *justice* or *economy*. They also may not understand the subjunctive case ("If I were a butterfly") because they lack the cognitive ability to reason about things that are not true ("But you aren't a butterfly"). They may interpret all statements literally and thus misunderstand sarcasm or metaphor. Fables are understood concretely simply as stories instead of as moral lessons, for example. Many children are in their preadolescent years before they are able to distinguish being teased from being taunted or before they know that a sarcastic remark is not meant to be taken literally. But by adolescence, students are able to use their developing cognitive abilities to learn abstract word meanings and to use poetic, figurative language (Owens, 2005).

Bilingual children who are learning two languages at once tend to have smaller vocabularies in each language compared to children learning only one, at least during childhood, but these size differences depend on the bilingual children's exposure to each language—more exposure leads to a larger vocabulary (Hoff, 2006). In addition, the vocabulary of bilingual children is linked to the context in which they use each language, so children are more likely to know more academic words in the language they use in school. If you combine vocabulary knowledge for bilingual children—the total number of concepts that they have words for from both languages—their vocabulary size likely is the same as children who use just one language (Pearson, Fernandez, Lewedeg, & Oller, 1997).

Young children begin to elaborate their simple language by adding plurals; endings for verbs such as *-ed* and *–ing*; small words like *and, but,* and *in*; articles (*a, the*); and possessives (the girl's hair). A classic study by Jean Berko (1958) demonstrated that children could even apply these rules for making plurals, possessives, or past tense verbs to words that they had never encountered. For

Expressive vocabulary The words a person can speak.

Receptive vocabulary The words a person can understand in spoken or written words.

Bilingual Speaking two languages and dealing appropriately with the two different cultures.

TABLE 2.4 **Milestones in Language in the First Six Years and Ways to Encourage Development**

Age Range	Milestone	Strategies to Encourage Development
By age 1	Says one to two words; recognizes name; imitates familiar sounds; understands simple instructions	• Respond to coos, gurgles, and babbling. • Tell nursery rhymes and sing songs. • Teach the names of everyday items and familiar people. • Play simple games such as peek-a-boo and pat-a-cake.
Between 1 and 2	Uses five to twenty words, including names; says two-word sentences; has a growing vocabulary; waves goodbye; makes "sounds" of familiar animals; uses words (like "more") to make wants known; understands "no"	• Reward and encourage early efforts at saying new words. • Talk about everything you're doing while you're with the child. • Talk simply, clearly, and slowly. • Look at the child when he or she talks to you. • Describe what the child is doing, feeling, hearing. • Let the child listen to children's records and tapes.
Between 2 and 3	Identifies body parts; calls self "me" instead of name; combines nouns and verbs; has a 450-word vocabulary; uses short sentences; matches three to four colours; knows "big" and "little"; likes to hear same story repeated; forms some plurals; answers "where" questions	• Help the child listen and follow instructions by playing simple games. • Repeat new words over and over. • Describe what you are doing, planning, thinking. • Have the child deliver simple messages for you. • Show the child you understand what he or she says by answering, smiling, and nodding your head. • Expand what the child says. Child: "More juice." You say, "Chris wants more juice."
Between 3 and 4	Can tell a story; uses sentences of four to five words; has a vocabulary of about 1000 words; knows last name, name of street, several nursery rhymes	• Talk about how objects are the same or different. • Help the child to tell stories using books and pictures. • Encourage play with other children. • Talk about places where you've been or will be going.
Between 4 and 5	Uses sentences of four to five words; uses past tense; has a vocabulary of about 1500 words; identifies colours, shapes; asks many questions like "why?" and "who?"	• Help the child sort objects and things (e.g., things to eat, animals). • Teach the child how to use the telephone. • Let the child help you plan activities. • Continue talking about the child's interests. • Let the child tell and make up stories for you.
Between 5 and 6	Uses sentences of five to six words; average 6-year-old has a vocabulary of about 10 000 words; defines objects by their use; knows spatial relations (like "on top" and "far") and opposites; knows address; understands "same" and "different"; uses all types of sentences	• Praise children when they talk about feelings, thoughts, hopes, fears. • Sing songs, rhymes. • Talk with a child as you would an adult.
At every age		• Listen and show your pleasure when the child talks to you. • Carry on conversations with the child. • Ask questions to get the child to think and talk. • Read books to the child every day, increasing in length as the child develops.

Source: Adapted from www.ldonline.org/ld_indepth/speech-language/lda_milestones.html and www.med.umich.edu/1libr/yourchild/devmile.htm.

example, when shown a picture of a single "wug," the preschool children in the study could answer correctly "wugs" when the researcher said, "Now there is another one. There are two of them. There are two _____." In the process of figuring out the rules governing these aspects of language, children make some very interesting mistakes.

Grammar and Syntax. For a brief time, children may use irregular forms of particular words properly, as if they are saying what they have heard. Then, as they begin to learn rules, they overregularize words by applying the rules to everything. Children who once said, "Our car is broken" begin to insist, "Our car is broked." A child who once talked about her feet may discover the *s* for plurals and refer to her foots or feets, then learn about *es* for plurals (horses, kisses) and describe her footses, before she finally returns to talking about her feet (Flavell et al., 2002). Parents often wonder why their child seems to be "regressing." Actually, these "mistakes" show how logical and rational children can be as they try to assimilate new words into existing schemes. Apparently these overregularizations happen in all languages including American Sign Language. Because most languages have many irregular words, accommodation is necessary in mastering language. According to one interesting recent finding, girls tend to overregularize verb tenses more than boys, so they are more likely to say "holded" instead of "held." Joshua Hartshore and Michael Ullman (2006) speculate that, because girls may have better memory for words, they have better access to similar words (folded, moulded, scolded) and generalize to "holded."

Children master the basics of word order, or syntax, in their native language early. Another aspect of overregularizing language involves syntax. Because the usual order in English is subject–verb–object, preschoolers just mastering the rules of language have trouble with sentences in any different order. For example, if 4-year-old Justin hears a statement in the passive voice, like "The truck was bumped by the car," he probably thinks the truck did the bumping to the car because "truck" came first in the sentence. Interestingly, however, in languages where the passive voice is more important, such as the South African language Sesotho, children use this construction much earlier, as young as 3 or 4 (Demuth, 1990). So in talking with young children, in English at least, it is generally better to use direct language. By early elementary school, many children can understand the meaning of passive sentences, but they do not use such constructions in their normal conversations, unless the passive construction is common in their culture.

Pragmatics: Using Language in Social Situations. Pragmatics involves the appropriate use of language to communicate in social situations—how to enter a conversation, tell a joke, interrupt, keep a conversation going, or adjust your language for the listener. Children show an understanding of pragmatics when they talk in simpler sentences to younger children or command their pets to "Come here!" in louder, deeper voices, or when they provide more detail describing an event to a parent who did not participate in the event (Flavell et al., 2002; Rice, 1989). So even young children do seem quite able to fit their language to the situation, at least with familiar people.

Metalinguistic Awareness. Around the age of 5, children begin to develop metalinguistic awareness. This means their understanding about language and how it works becomes explicit. They have knowledge about language itself. They are ready to study and extend the rules that have been implicit—understood but not consciously expressed. This process continues throughout life, as we all become better able to use language.

The next section examines other kinds of diversity in language development.

Diversity in Language Development

Some children learn two or more languages growing up. In fact, about half the children in the world live in environments where two or more languages are spoken (Hoff, 2006). Canada has two official languages, French and English, and unofficially the United States is moving more in that direction with a sizeable minority of their citizens speaking Spanish in their homes.

Dual Language Development. Are children at a disadvantage if they are learning two languages at once? That depends. Children exposed to two languages from birth reach the language milestones in both languages on the same schedule as monolingual children (children learning only

Overregularize To apply a rule of syntax or grammar in situations where the rule does not apply; for example, "the bike was broked."

Syntax The order of words in phrases or sentences.

Pragmatics The rules for when and how to use language to be an effective communicator in a particular culture.

Metalinguistic awareness Understanding about one's own use of language.

Monolingual Speaking only one language.

one language). Initially, bilingual children may have a larger vocabulary in the language that they are learning from the person with whom they spend the most time or have the closest bond, so a child who stays home all day with a French-speaking parent will likely use more French words. But over time, these children can become fully and equally bilingual if the dual language exposure (a) begins early in life, (b) occurs across a wide and rich range of contexts, and (c) is consistent and sustained (Petitto & Kovelman, 2003). Another requirement is that the second language must provide more than 25 percent of the child's language input—with less exposure, the child is unlikely to learn the second language (Pearson et al., 1997). Bilingual children may mix vocabularies of the two languages when they speak, but this is not a sign that they are confused because their bilingual parents often intentionally mix vocabularies as well, selecting the word that best expresses their intent. So with consistent and sustained engagement in two languages, children can be fully bilingual.

Benefits of Bilingualism. There is no cognitive penalty for children who learn and speak two languages. In fact, there are benefits. Higher degrees of bilingualism are correlated with increased cognitive abilities in such areas as concept formation, creativity, theory of mind, cognitive flexibility, and understanding that printed words are symbols for language. In addition, these children have more advanced metalinguistic understanding of how language works; for example, they are more likely to notice grammatical errors. These findings seem to hold as long as there is no stigma attached to being bilingual and as long as children are not expected to abandon their first language to learn the second (Bialystok, 2001; Bialystok, Majumder, & Martin, 2003; Galambos & Goldin-Meadow, 1990; Hamers & Blanc, 2000). In addition, speaking two languages is an asset when graduates enter the business world (Mears, 1998).

Even though the advantages of bilingualism seem clear, many children and adults are losing their heritage language. This is particularly problematic for many First Nation peoples whose intergenerational language transmission ceased as a result of the children being sent to residential schools during the first half of the 20th century. Dr. Nicole Rosen at the University of Lethbridge is currently attempting to document one such language, called Michif, which is spoken by a few hundred Métis in Saskatchewan and Manitoba. As part of these efforts, she is involved in a language revitalization project with the Manitoba Métis Federation. The revitalization process follows a multi-pronged approach, with language learning targeted to both adults and children and taking place in both school and the home (Rosen, 2004).

Second Language Learning. What if you didn't learn two languages as you were growing up? When and how should you learn a second language? It is a misconception that young children learn a second language faster than adolescents or adults. In fact, older children go through the stages of language learning faster than young children. Adults have more learning strategies and greater knowledge of language in general to bring to bear in mastering a second language (Diaz-Rico & Weed, 2002). Age is a factor in learning language, but "not because of any critical period that limits the possibility of language learning by adults" (Marinova-Todd, Marshall, & Snow, 2000, p. 28).

As you saw earlier in this chapter, however, there appears to be a critical period for learning accurate language *pronunciation*. The earlier people learn a second language, the more their pronunciation is near-native. After adolescence it is difficult to learn a new language without speaking with an accent (Anderson & Graham, 1994). Even if a child overhears a language, without actually learning the language, this can improve later learning. After studying college students learning Spanish, Terry Au and colleagues concluded that, "Although waiting until adulthood to learn a language almost guarantees a bad accent, having overheard the target language during childhood seems to lessen this predicament substantially" (Au, Knightly, Jun, & Oh, 2002, p. 242). So the best time to teach a second language probably is during early or middle childhood, but the best time to acquire two languages on your own through exposure (and to learn native pronunciation for both languages) is early childhood.

Emergent Literacy

Today, in most languages, reading is a cornerstone of learning, and the foundation for reading is built in early childhood. But young children vary greatly in their knowledge and skills related to reading, so research has expanded to study what supports these emerging literacy skills (often called emergent literacy). Look at the picture of a 4-year-old's story and grocery list (see Figure 2.5) to see some emerging literacy skills.

Heritage language The language spoken in the student's home or by members of the family.

Emergent literacy The skills and knowledge, usually developed in the preschool years, that are the foundation for the development of reading and writing.

FIGURE 2.5 **A Story and a Grocery List**

This child knows quite a bit about reading and writing—letters make words that communicate meaning, writing goes from left to right and lists go down the page, and stories look different from shopping lists.

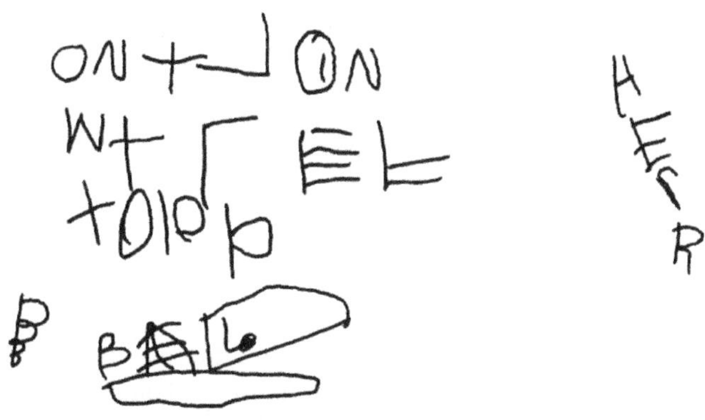

Source: From Lea M. McGee & Donald J. Richgels, *Literacy's Beginnings: Supporting Young Writers and Readers,* 2e. Published by Allyn and Bacon, Boston, MA. Copyright © 1995 by Pearson Education. Adapted by permission of the publisher.

What are the most important skills that help literacy emerge? Here the answers are not certain, but research has identified two broad categories of skills that are important for later reading: (1) skills related to understanding sounds and codes such as knowing that letters have names, that sounds are associated with letters, and that words are made up of sounds, and (2) oral language skills such as expressive and receptive vocabulary, knowledge of syntax, and the ability to understand and tell stories, for example (Dickinson, McCabe, Anastopoulos, Peisner-Feinberg, & Poe, 2003; Storch & Whitehurst, 2002).

Some educators have emphasized code skills, others oral language, but a study by the National Institute of Child Health and Human Development (NICHD) Early Childhood Research Network (2005b) that followed over 1000 children in the United States from age 3 through grade 3 found that oral language skills at age 4 ½ predicted word decoding in grade 1 and reading comprehension in grade 3. The NICHD researchers concluded, "most recent investigations find that preschool oral language skills [for example, size of vocabulary, ability to use syntax, ability to understand and tell stories] play an important role alongside code skills in predicting reading in the transition to school" (p. 439). Because this was not an experimental design (see Chapter 1) we cannot be sure that early code and oral language skills *cause* later reading achievement. But the results of this study suggest that code and oral language skills are likely an important part of the puzzle; these skills often support each other. Beware of either/or choices between emphasizing code versus oral language, however—both are important.

Building a Foundation. What builds this foundation of emergent literacy skills? Two related activities are critical—conversations with adults that develop knowledge about language, and joint reading, using books as supports for talk about sounds, words, pictures, and concepts (NICHD Early Childhood Research Network, 2005a). Especially in the early years, the children's home experiences are central in the development of language and literacy (Burgess, Hecht, & Lonigan, 2002; Sénéchal & LeFevre, 2002). In homes that promote literacy, parents and other adults value reading as a source of pleasure, and there are books and other printed materials everywhere. Parents read to their children, take them to bookstores and libraries, limit the amount of television everyone watches, and encourage literacy-related play such as setting up a pretend school or writing "letters" (Pressley, 1996; Snow, 1993; Whitehurst et al., 1994). For example, when Spanish-speaking and bilingual parents are more involved with their young children in literacy activities, the children's oral language improves in both English and Spanish (Farver, 2007). Child-care workers and teachers can help. In a study that followed almost 300 low-income children from kindergarten to grade 5, researchers found that the more families were involved with the school, the better their children's literacy development. School involvement was especially valuable when mothers had less education themselves (Dearing, Kreider, Simpkins, & Weiss, 2006). The *Family and Community Partnerships Guidelines* box gives some ideas for how to involve families in their children's language and literacy acquisition.

FAMILY AND COMMUNITY PARTNERSHIPS

GUIDELINES: Supporting Language and Promoting Literacy

FOR FAMILIES

Read with your children.

EXAMPLES

1. Help children understand that books contain stories, that they can visit the stories as often as they like, that the pictures in the books go along with the story meaning, and that the words are always the same when they visit the story—that's reading! (Hulit & Howard, 2006)
2. Have a night-time reading ritual.

Choose appropriate books and stories.

EXAMPLES

1. Books should have simple plots and clear illustrations.
2. Illustrations should precede the text related to the illustration. This helps children learn to predict what is coming next.
3. Language should be repetitive, rhythmic, and natural.

FOR TEACHERS

Use stories as a springboard for conversations.

EXAMPLES

1. Retell stories you have read with your students.
2. Talk about the words, activities, and objects in the books. Do the students have anything like these in their home or classroom?

Identify and build on strengths the families already have (Delpit, 2003).

EXAMPLES

1. What are the histories, stories, and skills of family members? Students can draw or write about these.
2. Show respect for the student's language by celebrating poems or songs from the language.

Provide home activities to be shared with family members.

EXAMPLES

1. Encourage family members to work with children to read and follow simple recipes, to play language games, to keep diaries or journals for the family, and to visit the library. Get feedback from families or students about the activities.
2. Give families feedback sheets and ask them to help evaluate the child's school work.
3. Provide lists of good children's literature available locally—work with libraries, clubs, and churches to identify sources.

FOR SCHOOL COUNSELLORS AND ADMINISTRATORS

Communicate with families about the goals and activities of your program.

EXAMPLES

1. Have someone from the school district or community, or even an older student, translate into the language of the child's family any material you plan to send home.
2. At the beginning of school, send home a description of the goals to be achieved in your class—make sure it is in a clear and readable format.
3. As you start each unit, send home a newsletter describing what students will be studying—give suggestions for home activities that support the learning.

Involve families in decisions about curriculum.

EXAMPLES

1. Have planning workshops at times family members can attend—provide child care for younger siblings, but let children and families work together on projects.
2. Invite parents to come to class to read to students, take dictation of stories, tell stories, record or bind books, and demonstrate skills.

Make it easier for families to come to school.

EXAMPLES

1. Provide babysitting for younger children while families meet with teachers.
2. Consider transportation needs of families—can they get to school?

For more information on Family Literacy Partnerships, see **www.famlit.org.**

Source: From *Born to talk: An introduction to speech and language development* (4th ed.) by L. M. Hulit & M. R. Howard. Published by Allyn & Bacon, Boston, MA. Copyright © 2006 by Pearson Education. Reprinted by permission of the publisher.

DIVERSITY AND CONVERGENCES IN COGNITIVE DEVELOPMENT

Research across different cultures has confirmed that Piaget was accurate in the sequence of stages he described, but there is diversity in the age ranges for the stages.

Diversity

Western children typically move to the next stage about two to three years earlier than children in non-Western societies. When a culture or context emphasizes a cognitive ability, children growing up in that culture tend to acquire the ability sooner. In a study that compared Chinese students in grade 1, grade 3, and grade 5 to American students in the same grades, the Chinese students mastered a Piagetian task that involved distance, time, and speed relationships about two years ahead of American students. The Chinese education system puts more emphasis on math and science in the early grades (Zhou, Peverly, Beohm, & Chongde, 2001).

MyEducationLab Go to the Teacher Talk section in Chapter 2 of MyEducationLab and watch a video of Isabel Rodriguez, 2007 Teacher of the Year from Puerto Rico, talking about teaching students from diverse cultural backgrounds.

There is also diversity in language development. Developing an understanding of the sounds and patterns that make up language may take a different path for children who learn languages like Spanish and Finnish, where the letter symbols of the language map easily to the sounds of the language (Silven, Poskiparta, Niemi, & Voeten, 2007). Children in every culture and context learn their native language, but they may assimilate a different set of rules for language use—pragmatics. For example, Shirley Brice Heath (1989) spent many hours observing white middle-class parents and African American families who were poor. She found that the adults asked different kinds of questions and encouraged different kinds of "talk." White parents asked test-like questions with right answers, such as "How many cars are there?" or "Which car is bigger?" These questions would seem odd to African American children whose families didn't ask about what they already knew. The African American child might wonder "Why would my aunt ask me how many cars? She can see there are three." Instead, African American families encouraged rich storytelling and also teasing that honed their children's quick wit and assertive responses.

Convergences

In spite of these cross-cultural differences in cognitive development, there are some convergences. Piaget, Vygotsky, and more recent researchers studying cognitive development and the brain probably would agree with the following main ideas:

1. Cognitive development requires both physical and social stimulation.
2. To develop thinking, children have to be mentally, physically, and linguistically active. They need to experiment, talk, describe, reflect, write, and solve problems. But they also benefit from teaching, guidance, questions, explanations, demonstrations, and challenges to their thinking.
3. Teaching students what they already know is boring. Trying to teach what the student isn't ready to learn is frustrating and ineffective.
4. Challenge with support will keep students engaged but not fearful.
5. One conclusion of years of research is that children in social environments with "more adult-produced, child-directed speech—particularly speech that uses rich vocabulary and complex structure—acquire language more rapidly" (Hoff, 2006).

MyEducationLab Go to the Teacher Talk section in Chapter 2 of MyEducationLab and watch a video of Melanie Teemant, 2007 Teacher of the Year from Nevada, discussing her desire to inspire in her middle school students a lifelong love of literature.

SUMMARY TABLE

A Definition of Development (pp. 26–31)

What are the different kinds of development? Human development can be divided into physical development (changes in the body), personal development (changes in an individual's personality), social development (changes in the way an individual relates to others), and cognitive development (changes in thinking).

What are three questions about development and three general principles? For decades, psychologists and the public have debated whether development is shaped more by nature or nurture, whether change is a continuous process or involves qualitative differences or stages, and whether there are critical times for the development of certain abilities. We know today that these simple either/or distinctions cannot capture the complexities of human development where coactions and interactions are the rule. Theorists generally agree that people develop at different rates, that development is an orderly process, and that development takes place gradually.

What part of the brain is associated with higher mental functions? The cortex is a crumpled sheet of neurons that serves three major functions: receiving signals from sense organs (such as visual or auditory signals), controlling voluntary movement, and forming associations. The part of the cortex that controls physical motor movement develops or matures first, followed by the areas that control complex senses such as vision and hearing, and then the frontal lobe, which controls higher-order thinking processes.

What is lateralization and why is it important? Lateralization is the specialization of the two sides, or hemispheres, of the brain. The brain begins to lateralize soon after birth. For most people, the left hemisphere is the major factor in language, and the right hemisphere is prominent in spatial and visual processing. Even though certain functions are associated with certain parts of the brain, the various parts and systems of the brain work together to learn and perform complex activities such as reading and to construct understanding.

Development Orderly, adaptive changes that humans (or animals) go through from conception to death.

Physical development Changes in body structure that take place as one grows.

Social and emotional development Changes over time in the ways in which one relates to others and the self.

Cognitive development Gradual, orderly changes by which mental processes become more complex and sophisticated.

Maturation Genetically programmed, naturally occurring changes over time.

Coactions Joint actions of individual biology and environment—each shapes and influences the other.

Sensitive periods Times when a person is especially ready for or responsive to certain experiences.

Neurons Nerve cells that store and transfer information.

Synapses The tiny space between neurons; chemical messages are sent across these gaps.

Myelination The process by which neural fibres are coated with a fatty sheath called *myelin* that makes message transfer more efficient.

Lateralization The specialization of the two hemispheres (sides) of the brain cortex.

Plasticity The brain's tendency to remain somewhat adaptable or flexible.

Piaget's Theory of Cognitive Development (pp. 31–41)

What are the main influences on cognitive development? Piaget's theory of cognitive development is based on the assumption that people try to make sense of the world and actively create knowledge through direct experience with objects, people, and ideas. Maturation, activity, social transmission, and the need for equilibrium all influence the way thinking processes and knowledge develop. In response to these influences, thinking processes and knowledge develop through changes in the organization of thought (the development of schemes) and through adaptation—including the complementary processes of assimilation (incorporating new information into existing schemes) and accommodation (changing existing schemes).

What are schemes? Schemes are the basic building blocks of thinking. They are organized systems of actions or thought that allow us to mentally represent or "think about" the objects and events in our world. Schemes may be very small and specific (grasping, recognizing a square), or they may be larger and more general (using a map in a new city). People adapt to their environment as they increase and organize their schemes.

As children move from sensorimotor to formal operational thinking, what are the major changes? Piaget believed that young people pass through four stages as they develop: sensorimotor, preoperational, concrete operational, and formal operational. In the sensorimotor stage, infants explore the world through their senses and motor activity and work toward mastering object permanence and performing goal-directed activities. In the preoperational stage, symbolic thinking and logical operations begin. Children in the stage of concrete operations can think logically about tangible situations and can demonstrate conservation, reversibility, classification, and seriation. The ability to perform hypothetico-deductive reasoning, coordinate a set of variables, and imagine other worlds marks the stage of formal operations.

How do neo-Piagetian and information processing views explain changes in children's thinking over time? Information processing theories focus on attention, memory capacity, learning strategies, and other processing skills to explain how children develop rules and strategies for making sense of the world and solving problems. Neo-Piagetian approaches also look at attention, memory, and strategies and at how thinking develops in different domains such as numbers or spatial relations.

What are some limitations of Piaget's theory? Piaget's theory has been criticized because children and adults often think in ways that are inconsistent with the notion of invariant stages. It also appears that Piaget underestimated children's cognitive abilities; he insisted that children could not be taught the operations of the next stage, but had to develop them on their own. Alternative explanations place greater emphasis on students' developing information processing skills and ways teachers can enhance their development. Piaget's work is also criticized for overlooking cultural factors in child development.

Organization Ongoing process of arranging information and experience into mental systems or categories.

Adaptation Adjustment to the environment.

Schemes Mental systems or categories of perception and experience.

Assimilation Fitting new information into existing schemes.

Accommodation Altering existing schemes or creating new ones in response to new information.

Equilibration Search for mental balance between cognitive schemes and information from the environment.

Disequilibrium In Piaget's theory, the "out-of-balance" state that occurs when a person realizes that his or her current ways of thinking are not working to solve a problem or understand a situation.

Sensorimotor Involving the senses and motor activity.

Object permanence The understanding that objects have a separate, permanent existence.

Goal-directed actions Deliberate actions toward a goal.

Operations Actions that a person carries out by thinking them through instead of literally performing them.

Preoperational The stage of development before a child masters logical mental operations.

Semiotic function The ability to use symbols—language, pictures, signs, or gestures—to represent actions or objects mentally.

Reversible thinking Thinking backward, from the end to the beginning.

Conservation Principle that some characteristics of an object remain the same despite changes in appearance.

Decentring Focusing on more than one aspect at a time.

Egocentric Assuming that others experience the world the way you do.

Concrete operations Mental tasks tied to concrete objects and situations.

Identity The principle that a person or object remains the same over time.

Compensation The principle that changes in one dimension can be offset by changes in another dimension.

Reversibility A characteristic of Piagetian logical operations—the ability to think through a series of steps, then mentally reverse the steps and return to the starting point; also called reversible thinking.

Classification Grouping objects into categories.

Seriation Arrangement of objects in sequential order according to one aspect, such as size, weight, or volume.

Formal operations Mental tasks involving abstract thinking and coordination of a number of variables.

Hypothetico-deductive reasoning A formal-operations problem-solving strategy in which an individual begins by identifying all the factors that might affect a problem and then deduces and systematically evaluates specific solutions.

Adolescent egocentrism Assumption that everyone else is interested in one's thoughts, feelings, and concerns.

Neo-Piagetian theories More recent theories that integrate findings about attention, memory, and strategy use with Piaget's insights about children's thinking and the construction of knowledge.

Vygotsky's Sociocultural Perspective (pp. 42–47)

According to Vygotsky, what are three main influences on cognitive development? Vygotsky believed that human activities must be understood in their cultural settings. He believed that our specific mental structures and processes can be traced to our interactions with others; that the tools of the culture, especially the tool of language, are key factors in development; and that the zone of proximal development is the area where learning and development are possible.

What are psychological tools and why are they important? Psychological tools are signs and symbol systems such as numbers and mathematical systems, codes, and language that support learning and cognitive development—they change the thinking process by enabling and shaping thinking. Many of these tools are passed from adult to child through formal and informal interactions and teachings.

Explain how interpsychological development becomes intrapsychological development. Higher mental processes appear first between people as they are co-constructed during shared activities. As children engage in activities with adults or more capable peers, they exchange ideas and ways of thinking about or representing concepts. These co-created ideas are internalized by children. Thus children's knowledge, ideas, attitudes, and values develop through appropriating, or "taking for themselves," the ways of acting and thinking provided by their culture and by the more capable members of their group.

What are the differences between Piaget's and Vygotsky's perspectives on private speech and its role in development? Vygotsky's sociocultural view asserts that cognitive development hinges on social interaction and the development of language. As an example, Vygotsky described the role of children's self-directed talk in guiding and monitoring thinking and problem solving, while Piaget suggested that private speech was an indication of the child's egocentrism. Vygotsky, more than Piaget, emphasized the significant role played by adults and more able peers in children's learning. This adult assistance provides early support while students build the understanding necessary to solve problems on their own.

What is a student's zone of proximal development? At any given point in development, there are certain problems that a child is on the verge of being able to solve and others that are beyond the child's capabilities. The zone of proximal development is the area where the child cannot solve a problem alone, but can be successful under adult guidance or in collaboration with a more advanced peer.

What are two criticisms or limitations of Vygotsky's theory? Vygotsky may have overemphasized the role of social interaction in cognitive development—children figure out quite a bit on their own. Also, because he died so young, Vygotsky was not able to develop and elaborate on his theories. His students and others since have taken up that work.

Sociocultural theory Theory that emphasizes the role in development of cooperative dialogues between children and more knowledgeable members of society; children learn the culture of their community (ways of thinking and behaving) through these interactions.

Co-constructed Constructed through a social process in which people interact and negotiate (usually verbally) to create an understanding or to solve a problem; the final product is shaped by all participants.

Cultural tools The real tools (computers, scales, etc.) and symbol systems (numbers, language, graphs, etc.) that allow people in a society to communicate, think, solve problems, and create knowledge.

Collective monologue Form of speech in which children in a group talk but do not really interact or communicate.

Private speech Children's self-talk, which guides their thinking and action; eventually, these verbalizations are internalized as silent inner speech.

Zone of proximal development (ZPD) Phase at which a child can master a task if given appropriate help and support.

Implications of Piaget's and Vygotsky's Theories for Teachers (pp. 47–52)

What is the "problem of the match" described by Hunt? The "problem of the match" is that students must be neither bored by work that is too simple nor left behind by teaching they cannot understand. According to Hunt, disequilibrium must be carefully balanced to encourage growth. Situations that lead to errors can help create an appropriate level of disequilibrium.

What is active learning? Why is Piaget's theory of cognitive development consistent with active learning? Piaget's fundamental insight was that individuals *construct* their own understanding; learning is a constructive process. At every level of cognitive development, students must be able to incorporate information into their own schemes. To do this, they must act on the information in some way. This active experience, even at the earliest school levels, should include both physical manipulation of objects and mental manipulation of ideas. As a general rule, students should act, manipulate, observe, and then talk and/or write about what they have experienced. Concrete experiences provide the raw materials for thinking. Communicating with others makes students use, test, and sometimes change their thinking abilities.

What is assisted learning, and what role does scaffolding play? Assisted learning, or guided participation in the classroom, requires scaffolding—giving information, prompts, reminders, and encouragement at the right time and in the right amounts, and then gradually allowing the students to do more and more on their own. Teachers can assist learning by adapting materials or problems to students' current levels, demonstrating skills or thought processes, walking students through the steps of a complicated problem, doing part of the problem, giving detailed feedback and allowing revisions, or asking questions that refocus students' attention.

Scaffolding Support for learning and problem solving; the support could be clues, reminders, encouragement, breaking the problem down into steps, providing an example, or anything else that allows the student to grow in independence as a learner.

Assisted learning Learning by having strategic help provided in the initial stages; the help gradually diminishes as students gain independence.

The Development of Language (pp. 52–58)

How are humans predisposed to develop language? What role does learning play? Children develop language as they develop other cognitive abilities by actively trying to make sense of what they hear, looking for patterns, and making up rules. In this process, built-in biases and rules may limit the search and guide the pattern recognition. Reward and correction play a role in helping children learn correct language use, but the child's thought processes are very important. Metalinguistic awareness begins around age 5 or 6 and grows throughout life.

What are the elements of language? By age 5, most children have mastered almost all the sounds of their native language. In terms of vocabulary, we understand more words than we use. By age 6, children know more than 10 000 words. Understanding of words that express abstract ideas and hypothetical situations comes later as cognitive abilities develop. As children develop an understanding of grammar, they may apply new rules too widely, saying "broked" for "broken," for example. Understanding the passive voice in syntax develops after understanding active voice.

What are pragmatics and metalinguistic awareness? Pragmatics is knowledge about how to use language—when, where, how, and to whom to speak. Metalinguistic awareness refers to explicit knowledge about how language works. This awareness emerges around age 5 or 6 and grows throughout life.

What is involved in learning two languages? Children can learn two languages at once if they have adequate opportunities to speak in both languages. There are cognitive advantages to learning more than one language, so it is valuable to retain your heritage language even as you learn another. The best time to learn accurate pronunciation is early childhood, but people of any age can learn a new language. Having overheard a language as a child can improve your ability to learn that language as an adult.

What are the most important skills that help literacy emerge? Research has identified two broad categories of skills that are important for later reading: (1) understanding sounds and codes such as knowing that letters have names, that sounds are associated with letters, and that words are made up of sounds, and (2) having oral language skills such as expressive and receptive vocabulary, knowledge of syntax, and the ability to understand and tell stories. Parents and teachers can support emerging literacy by reading with children, retelling stories and talking about them, and limiting time spent watching television.

Expressive vocabulary The words a person can speak.

Receptive vocabulary The words a person can understand in spoken or written words.

Bilingual Speaking two languages and dealing appropriately with the two different cultures.

Overregularize To apply a rule of syntax or grammar in situations where the rule does not apply; for example, "the bike was broked."

Syntax The order of words in phrases or sentences.

Pragmatics The rules for when and how to use language to be an effective communicator in a particular culture.

Metalinguistic awareness Understanding about one's own use of language.

Monolingual Speaking only one language.

Heritage language The language spoken in the student's home or by members of the family.

Emergent literacy The skills and knowledge, usually developed in the preschool years, that are the foundation for the development of reading and writing.

PEARSON myeducationlab

MyEducationLab is an interactive, virtual learning tool that will help improve your understanding of the concepts taught in this textbook and in your course. Through this engaging resource, you will have access to simulations of real classroom experiences, exercises that will help you improve your knowledge of key concepts, and additional resources that will help you in your teaching career. Use this online tool with your textbook to help you succeed in your studies and beyond!

TEACHERS' CASEBOOK

The provincial curriculum guide calls for a unit on poetry, including lessons on *symbolism* in poems. You are concerned that many of your grade 5 students may not be ready to understand this abstract concept. To test the waters, you ask a few students to describe a symbol.

"It's sorta like a big metal thing that you bang together." Tracy waves her hands like a drum major.

"Yeah," Sean adds, "my sister plays one in the high school band."

You realize they are on the wrong track here, so you try again. "I was thinking of a different kind of symbol, like a ring as a symbol of marriage or a heart as a symbol of love, or . . ."

You are met with blank stares.

Trevor ventures, "You mean like the Olympic torch?"

"And what does that symbolize, Trevor?" you ask.

"Like I said, a torch." Trevor wonders how you could be so dense.

What Would *They* Do?

Here is how two practising teachers responded to the teaching situation described above.

Janet E. Gettings **Elementary Educator,**
Willoughby Elementary School, Langley, BC
Faculty Adviser and Sessional Instructor, University of British Columbia

The students of the class have indicated a need for scaffolded learning to enhance their understanding of the concept of symbolism.

To introduce the concept, I would build on the children's prior knowledge of homonyms by doing a quick review of commonly used word pairs, such as bear/bare, stare/stair, I/eye, pair/pear, two/to/too, followed by cymbal/symbol. With the latter example, I would explain that Tracy had defined "cymbal." I would then invite suggestions for "symbol," summarizing with a formal definition, such as "something that stands for or represents something else."

I would follow the discussion with a "Think, Pair, Share" activity. Students would be asked to think about symbols independently, and then pair with a partner to share ideas. Next, the partners would be invited to go on a "detective search" of the room and their desks for symbols they could share with the class. For example, when I hang an umbrella on the door, students know they can stay in the classroom at lunch.

Another follow-up activity would be a modified game of Pictionary. The class would be divided into teams of five or six and take turns being artists. Each team would send a student to the teacher to view a phrase, which the student then has to represent pictorially. Sample phrases might include "the house had not been lived in for a long time" or "her face reflected pain and sadness."

At this stage, the students might be ready to move to usage of symbolism in written language. Sections of a familiar novel that includes symbolic phrases to describe feelings and emotions could be shared. For example, the phrase "thunderclouds passed over her face" describes the feelings of a character in a story in language that students understand easily. I would engage the class in a discussion to share the author's message and intent.

Reading aloud humorous poetry, such as that of Jack Prelutsky, might be used to move toward the final goal of identifying the use of symbolism in poetry. Students could demonstrate their understanding by researching the use of symbolic language in the genre of poetry and by writing their own poems, incorporating symbolism into their products.

Mary Lightly

Terry Fox Secondary School, Port Coquitlam, BC

In planning activities for the classroom, I try to be mindful of research on effective teaching. In particular, I draw on the work of Anita Archer at the University of Oregon and Barrie Bennet at the University of Toronto. Both these researchers have written texts that summarize current research, and both relate that research to actual classroom situations.

To develop the concept of symbol, I would first design activities in which students could engage independently or in small groups. For example, I might engage students in a matching activity that requires them to identify the symbolic meaning of concrete, or real-life, objects. I might create a worksheet that includes two lists: one list would include real-world objects, such as a dove or a heart (this list might be presented as pictures); the second list would include descriptions of the symbolic meaning for each object. Students would match the picture of the dove with peace, and the picture of the heart with love. I might ask students to generate their own symbols. For example, a red rose could symbolize passion, a sword could symbolize war. Students could colour their images and display them in the classroom as a reminder of how real-life objects can have symbolic meaning.

After introducing the concept in this manner, I would take the class through one or two concept attainment lessons, a strategy in which students are presented with "yes" and "no" examples of a concept, in this case examples and non-examples of symbols and/or symbolism. I would begin with very clear and simple examples and then increase the level of difficulty as students become more confident and skilled at recognizing symbols and symbolism.

It might take many trials and a variety of strategies, but eventually students would be ready to look for symbolic meaning in literature.

3 Self and Social and Moral Development

Family Portrait II © Diana Ong/SuperStock

Overview

TEACHERS' CASEBOOK

WHAT WOULD YOU DO?

You have seen it before, but this year the situation in your middle school classroom seems especially vicious. A clique of popular girls has made life miserable for one of their former friends, Stephanie, who is now rejected. Stephanie committed the social sin of not fitting in—wearing the wrong clothes or not being pretty enough or not being interested in boys yet. To keep the status distinctions clear between themselves and Stephanie, the popular girls spread gossip about their former friend, often disclosing the intimate secrets revealed when Stephanie was still considered a close friend, which was only a few months ago. However, these girls are not using traditional methods of spreading gossip—instead of passing notes or whispering in the hallways, they are using the internet to humiliate Stephanie. First they forwarded a long, heart-baring email from Stephanie to her former best friend Alison to the entire school. More recently, one of them used a cell phone to take a picture of Stephanie while she was changing after gym class and then emailed it to the students in the whole school. Stephanie has been absent for three days since this latest incident.

CRITICAL THINKING

- How would you respond to the girls?
- Would you say anything to your other students? If so, what would you say?
- In your teaching, are there ways you can address the issues raised by this situation?
- Reflecting on your years in school, were your experiences more like those of Alison or Stephanie?

Schooling involves more than cognitive development. As you remember your years in school, what stands out—memories of academic knowledge or memories of feelings, friendships, and fears? In this chapter, we examine personal, social, and moral development.

We begin with Urie Bronfenbrenner's bioecological theory and use it as a framework for examining the three major influences on children's personal and social development: families, peers, and teachers. Families today have gone through many transitions, and these changes affect the roles of teachers. Then we look at a basic aspect of development that affects all the others—physical changes as students mature. Next, we explore ideas about how we come to understand ourselves by looking at self-concept and identity, including ethnic identity. Erikson's theory of psychosocial development provides a lens for viewing these developments. One major aspect of self and identity involves gender development and sexual identity—two topics we also examine in this chapter. Finally, we look at moral development. What factors determine our views about morality? What can teachers do to foster such personal qualities as honesty and cooperation? Why do students cheat in their academic work and what can be done about it?

By the time you have completed this chapter, you should be able to answer these questions:

- How does Bronfenbrenner's framework describe the social systems that influence development?
- How do parents' discipline styles affect their children?
- What are the roles of peers, cliques, and friendships in students' lives?
- What can teachers do to deal with aggression and bullying in schools?
- How do relationships with teachers support student development?

- How does physical development affect personal and social development during adolescence?
- What are Erikson's stages of psychosocial development, and what are the implications of his theory for teaching?
- How can teachers foster genuine and appropriate self-esteem in their students?
- How does ethnic identity develop?
- How do children develop gender roles and sexual identity?
- What are Kohlberg's stages of moral reasoning, and what are some of the challenges to his work?
- What encourages cheating in classrooms, and how can teachers respond to it?

BRONFENBRENNER: THE SOCIAL CONTEXT FOR DEVELOPMENT

Connect and Extend
Go to the "Connect and Extend" section in Chapter 3 of MyEducationLab to find further content that links to teaching, students' thinking, research, and the news.

This chapter moves beyond cognitive development to examine other important kinds of development that affect learning and motivation—physical, personal, and moral development. But first, we put the developing person in *context* by exploring the work of Urie Bronfenbrenner.

Educational and developmental psychologists are increasingly interested in the role of **context**. There are contextual effects on learning and motivation that are both internal and external to the developing individual. In this book, however, we focus on the contexts outside the person. Children grow up in families and are members of particular ethnic, religious, economic, and language communities. They live in neighbourhoods, attend schools, and are members of classes, teams, or choirs. The social and educational programs and policies of governments affect their lives. These contexts influence the development of behaviours, beliefs, and knowledge by providing resources, supports, incentives and punishments, expectations, teachers, models, and tools—all the building blocks of learning and development (Lerner, Theokas, & Bobek, 2005).

Contexts also affect how actions are interpreted. For example, when a stranger approaches a 7-month-old infant, the baby is likely to cry if the setting is unfamiliar, but not cry when the stranger approaches in the baby's home. Adults are more likely to help a stranger in need in small towns as opposed to larger cities (Kagan & Herschkowitz, 2005). Another example, standing on your seat and screaming means one thing at a football game and another on an airplane. Think about a ringing telephone. Is it 3:00 in the afternoon or 3:00 a.m.? Did you just call someone and leave a message asking for a return call? Has the phone been ringing off the hook, or is this the first call in days? Did you just sit down to dinner? The meaning of the ring and the feelings you have about it will vary, depending on the context.

As you saw in Chapter 1, Urie Bronfenbrenner's **bioecological model** of development (Bronfenbrenner, 1989; Bronfenbrenner & Evans, 2000) recognizes that the social contexts in which we develop are ecosystems because they are in constant interaction and influence each other. Look at Figure 3.1. Every person lives within a *microsystem*, inside a *mesosystem*, embedded in an *exosystem*, all of which are a part of the *macrosystem*—like a set of Russian painted dolls, nested one inside the other.

In the microsystem are the person's immediate relationships and activities. For a child, it might be the immediate family, friends, or teachers and the activities of play and school. Relationships in the microsystem are reciprocal—they flow in both directions. The child affects the parent and the parent influences the child, for example. The mesosystem is the set of interactions and relationships among all the elements of the microsystem—the family members interacting with each other or with the teacher. Again, all relationships are reciprocal—the teacher influences the parents and the parents affect the teacher, and these interactions affect the child. The exosystem includes all the social settings that affect the child, even though the child is not a direct member of the systems. Examples are the teachers' relations with administrators and the school board; parents' jobs; the community resources for health, employment, or recreation; or the family's religious affiliation. The macrosystem is the larger society—its values, laws, conventions, and traditions.

Context The total setting or situation that surrounds and interacts with a person or event. It includes internal and external circumstances and situations that interact with the individual's thoughts, feelings, and actions to shape development and learning.

Bioecological model Bronfenbrenner's theory describing the nested social and cultural contexts that shape development. Every person develops within a *microsystem*, inside a *mesosystem*, embedded in an *exosystem*, all of which are a part of the *macrosystem* of the culture.

FIGURE 3.1

Urie Bronfenbrenner's Bioecological Model of Human Development

Every person develops within a microsystem (family, friends, school activities, teachers, etc.) inside a mesosystem (the interactions among all the microsystem elements), embedded in an exosystem (social settings that affect the child, even though the child is not a direct member—community resources, parents' workplace, etc.); all are part of the macrosystem (the larger society with its laws, customs, values, etc.).

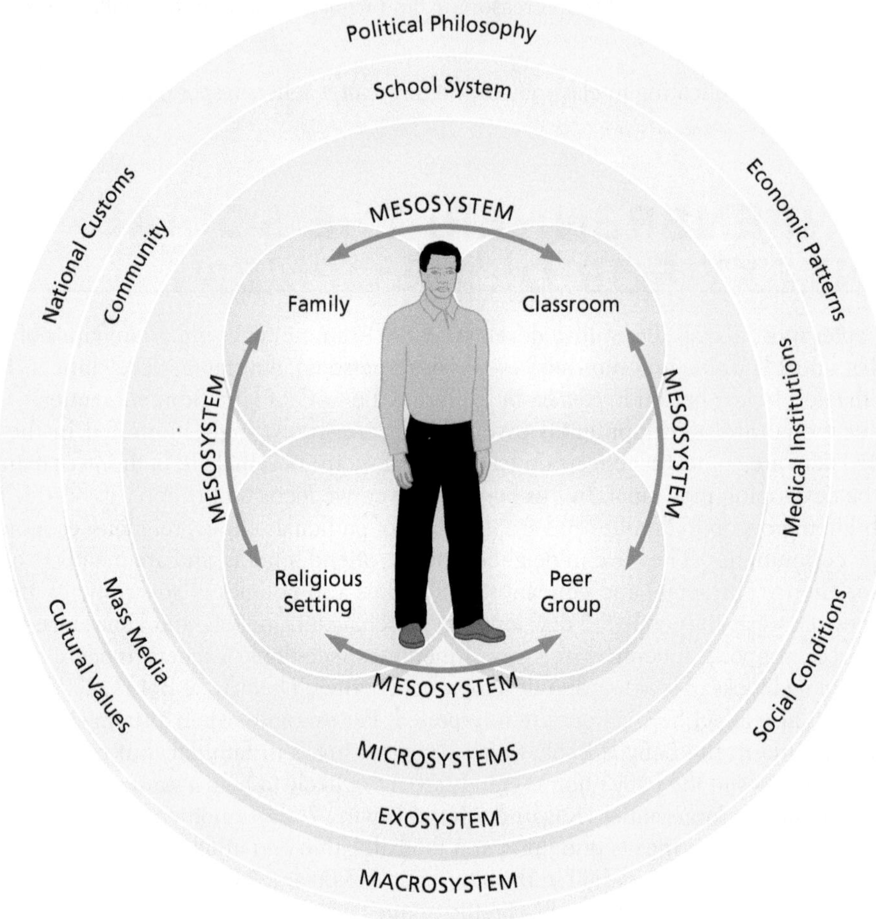

Source: Adapted from K. S. Berger (2004). *The developing person through the lifespan.* New York: Worth, p. 3. With permission of Worth Publishers.

For another example, think of the teacher's own bioecological system. The teacher is influenced by the microsystem of the principal, colleagues, and students; the mesosystem of the interactions among those people; the exosystem of government educational policies, and the macrosystem of cultural norms and values (Woolfolk Hoy, Pape, & Davis, 2006).

Bronfenbrenner's theory has at least two lessons for teachers. First, influences in all social systems are reciprocal. Second, there are many dynamic forces that interact to create the context for individual development. Next, we look at three important social contexts—families, peers, and teachers.

Families

Blended families Parents, children, and stepchildren merged into families through remarriages.

The most appropriate expectation to have about your students' families is no expectation at all. Increasingly, students today have only one or no sibling, or they may be part of blended families, with stepbrothers or stepsisters who move in and out of their lives. Some of your students may live with an aunt, with grandparents, with one parent, in foster or adoptive homes, or with an older brother or sister. In some cultures (e.g., Asian, Latin American, or African), children are more likely to grow up in

FAMILY AND COMMUNITY PARTNERSHIPS

GUIDELINES: Connecting with Families

1. Work with families to co-create methods for family involvement. Offer a range of possible participation methods. Make sure the plans are realistic and fit the lives of the families you are dealing with.
2. Remember that some students' families have had negative experiences with schools or may fear or mistrust schools and teachers. Find other places to collaborate: before or after extracurricular activities, or at a local church or recreation centre. Go where families go; don't always expect them to come to school.
3. Maintain regular home–school contact through telephone calls or notes. If a family has no telephone, identify a contact person (relative or friend) who can take messages. If literacy is a problem, use pictures, symbols, and codes for written communication.
4. Make all communications positive, emphasizing growth, progress, and accomplishments.
5. With the families, design family–student celebrations of the student's efforts and successes (a movie, special meal, trip to the park or library, or going out for ice cream or pizza).
6. On a regular basis, send home a note in word or picture form that describes the student's progress. Ask families to indicate how they celebrated the success and to return the note.
7. Follow up with a telephone call to discuss progress, answer questions, solicit family suggestions, and express appreciation for the families' contributions.
8. Make sure families feel welcome if they visit the classroom.

For more information on family school partnerships, see **www.gse.harvard.edu/hfrp/projects/family.html.**

Source: From "Effects of Parent Involvement in Isolation or in Combination with Peer Tutoring on Student Self-Concept and Mathematics Achievement," by J. Fantuzzo, G. Davis, and M. Ginsburg, *Journal of Educational Psychology*, *87*, pp. 272–281. Copyright © 1995 by the American Psychological Association. Adapted with permission of the APA.

extended families, with grandparents, aunts, uncles, and cousins living in the same household or at least in daily contact with each other. Childcare and economic support often are shared among family members. The best advice is to avoid the phrases "your parents" and "your mother and father" and to speak instead of "your family" when talking to students. The *Family and Community Partnerships Guidelines* box provides some suggestions about how to connect with families.

No matter who is doing the parenting, research has identified characteristic differences in parenting styles.

Parenting Styles. One well-known description of parenting is based on the research of Diane Baumrind (1991). Her early work focused on a careful longitudinal study of 100 (mostly European American, middle-class) preschool children. Through observation of children and parents and interviews with parents, she and Maccoby and Martin (1983), who built on her findings, identified four parenting styles that characterize parents' interactions with children in terms of levels of warmth and control:

- *Authoritative* parents are high in warmth but they also exert firm control. They monitor their children closely, setting clear standards and communicating high expectations for behaviour. These parents are firm without being harsh or unreasonable. Authoritative parents are rational and supportive in their approach to discipline, willing to negotiate in disciplinary matters.
- *Authoritarian* parents tend to be high in control and low in warmth and responsiveness, setting firm limits and expecting children to follow orders, because they say so, often without explanation or negotiation. Authoritarian approaches to discipline can be harsh and punitive—the explanation and negotiation that characterize authoritative approaches to parenting often are not present in interactions between authoritarian parents and their children.
- *Permissive* parents are warm but have little control. They have few rules or consequences for their children and expect little in the way of mature behaviour because "they're just kids." Rather than actively trying to shape their children's behaviour, these parents view themselves as resources for their children to use as they wish.
- *Rejecting/neglecting* parents are low in warmth and control. Maccoby and Martin (1983) referred to these parents as "uninvolved." They put little effort into parenting and, often, are more focused on their own needs than the needs of their children. They may fail to set schedules for sleeping and eating, and react harshly to children's advances or requests for attention. Often these parents have significant problems of their own, which limit or inhibit their ability to meet the needs of their children. Parents who are depressed or who have drug or alcohol problems may become neglecting or rejecting.

Extended families Parents, children, grandparents, aunts, uncles, and cousins living in the same household or in close proximity so they can have daily contact with one another.

Parenting styles The ways of interacting with and disciplining children.

In broad strokes, there are different outcomes for children associated with the four parenting styles. At least in North American, middle-class families, children of authoritative parents are more likely to be happy with themselves and to relate well to others. They do well in school and maintain positive relationships with parents. On average, children of authoritarian parents perform less well in school, are more hostile and less popular with peers, and have lower levels of self-control than children raised by authoritative parents (Baumrind, 1971; Thompson, Hollis, & Richards, 2003).

Children raised by permissive parents tend to be immature and demanding. Also, they tend to be more impulsive, rebellious, and aggressive than children raised by authoritative parents, and less socially competent and confident (Baumrind, 1971; Parke & Buriel, 2006). Of course, the extreme of permissiveness becomes indulgence. Indulgent parents cater to their children's every whim—perhaps it is easier than being the adult who must make unpopular decisions. Both indulgent and rejecting/neglecting parenting styles are harmful, but children of rejecting/neglecting parents fare worst of all. They tend to be insecure in their relationships, non-compliant, aggressive, and withdrawn (Baumrind, 1991; Parke & Buriel, 2006). In adolescence, these children are more likely to engage in risky and delinquent behaviour, suffer disruptions in social and cognitive development, and perform poorly in school.

STUDYING CULTURAL DIFFERENCES IN PARENTING The results of Ruth Chao's studies of Asian American parenting styles have challenged models of parenting based on European American parents and children. She is also studying whether serving as a translator or "language broker" for parents who do not speak English has an impact on the child's psychological well-being and relationship with the parents.

Research on parenting styles is extensive and appeals to North American and Western European cultures. However, it is important to note that most of this research is correlational—we cannot claim that parenting styles cause the observed outcomes for children. Also, the differences observed among parenting styles, although statistically reliable, are generally small. The largest effects are observed between authoritative and rejecting/neglecting parents (Lamborn, Mounts, Steinberg, & Dornbusch, 1991). Finally, research findings about parenting styles are not universal. Outcomes for children raised by authoritarian parents have been found to differ across cultural and socioeconomic status (SES), and across religious communities.

Culture and Parenting. Research indicates that higher control and more authoritarian parenting are linked to better grades for African American and some Asian students (Leung, Lau, & Lam, 1998; Spera, 2005). Parenting that is strict and directive, with clear rules and consequences, combined with high levels of warmth and emotional support, is associated with higher academic achievement and greater emotional maturity for inner-city children (Garner & Spears, 2000; Jarrett, 1995). Differences in cultural values and in the danger level of some urban neighbourhoods may make tighter parental control appropriate, and even necessary (Smetana, 2000). In addition, in cultures that have a greater respect for elders and a more group-centred rather than individualist philosophy, it may be a misreading of the parents' actions to perceive their demand for obedience as "authoritarian" (Lamb & Lewis, 2005; Nucci, 2001). In fact, research by Ruth Chao (Chao, 2001; Chao & Tseng, 2002) has challenged Baumrind's conclusions for Asian families. Chao finds that an alternative parenting style of *chiao shun* (a Chinese term that Chao translates to mean "training") better characterizes parenting in Asian and Asian American families.

Attachment and Parenting Styles. The emotional bond that forms between people is called **attachment**. The first attachment is between the child and parents or other caregivers. The quality of this bond appears to have implications for forming relationships throughout life (Thompson & Raikes, 2003). Children who form what are called *secure attachments* with caregivers receive comfort when needed and are more confident to explore their world, perhaps because they know they can count on the caregiver. Children who form insecure or disorganized attachments can be fearful, sad, anxious, clinging, rejecting, or angry in interactions with the caregivers. Some research indicates that authoritarian parenting styles are related to forming insecure attachments, but as we saw above, many factors influence the effects of parenting styles (Roeser, Peck, & Nasir, 2006).

The quality of attachment children experience has implications for teachers. For example, in preschools, children who have formed secure attachments with parents are less dependent on teachers and interact with other children appropriately. Secure attachment is positively related to achievement test scores, teacher assessments of social competence throughout the school years, and even to lower dropout rates (Roeser et al., 2006).

Attachment Forming an emotional bond with another person, initially a parent or family member.

Divorce. According to 2004 census data, approximately 38 percent of marriages in Canada in any given year will end in divorce before the couple's 30th anniversary (Institute of Marriage and Family Canada, 2010). The risk of divorce decreases the longer couples remain married and the divorce rate for first marriages is lower than for second and subsequent marriages (first-time marriages have a 67 percent chance of lasting a lifetime). As many of us know from experiences in our own families, separation and divorce are stressful events for all participants, even under the best circumstances. The actual separation of the parents may have been preceded by years of conflict in the home or may come as a shock to all, including friends and children. During the divorce itself, conflict may increase as property and custody rights are being decided.

After the divorce, more changes may disrupt the children's lives. Today, as in the past, the mother is most often the custodial parent, even though the number of households headed by fathers has been increasing, to about 20 percent by 2006 (Statistics Canada, 2010b). The parent who has custody may have to move to a less-expensive home, find new sources of income, go to work for the first time, or work longer hours. For the child, this can mean leaving behind important friendships in the old neighbourhood or school, just when support is needed the most. Even in cases where few conflicts arise, when ample resources are available, and when the continuing support of friends and extended family is present, divorce is never easy for anyone, though it can be a better alternative for children than growing up in a home filled with conflict and discord: "Destructive conflict in any type of family undermines the well-being of parents and children" (Hetherington, 2006, p. 232).

The first two years after a divorce seem to be the most difficult period for both boys and girls. Children may have problems in school or just skip school, lose or gain an unusual amount of weight, have trouble sleeping, or experience other difficulties. However, adjustment to divorce is an individual matter; some children respond with increased responsibility, maturity, and coping skills (Amato, 2006; Amato, Loomis, & Booth, 1995). Over time, about 75 to 80 percent of children in divorced families adapt and become reasonably well adjusted (Hetherington & Kelly, 2002). See the *Guidelines* box for ideas about how to help students who are dealing with divorce.

Peers

STOP & THINK Think back to high school—did you have friends in any of these groups: normals, populars, brains, jocks, partyers, druggies, others? What were the main "crowds" at your school? How did your friends influence you?

Peers and friendships are central to students' lives. Positive peer relationships are associated with adaptive development, and children and adolescents who experience peer rejection or who have difficulty forming or maintaining friendships are at risk for maladjustment (Rubin, Coplan, Chen, & Buskirk, 2005). When there has been a falling-out or an argument, when one child is not invited to a sleepover, when rumours are started and pacts are made to ostracize someone (as with Alison and Stephanie at the beginning of the chapter), the results can be devastating.

Peer Groups. Peer groups are social groups formed on the basis of shared interests and values. They typically comprise children with similar characteristics (e.g., same age, sex, race/ethnicity; similar achievement levels, popularity, athletic ability). Rubin et al. (2005) distinguish between two kinds of peer groups: *cliques* and *crowds*. Cliques are relatively smaller friendship-based groups (typically between three and a dozen children), which predominate in middle childhood, whereas crowds are less intimate, more loosely organized groups where members may or may not interact with one another. Affiliation with crowds becomes salient during adolescence and provides a sense of identity within a larger social structure (e.g., membership in a "jock" crowd or a "popular" crowd). Peer groups can be formal, as is the case with organizations such as Girl Guides, after-school clubs, and church groups, or they can be informal.

Participation in peer groups is associated with positive outcomes for children, including learning how to cooperate and how to control negative emotions and hostile impulses (Berndt, 2004; Leets & Sunwolf, 2005; Ruben et al., 2005). Peer groups provide support that helps children cope with stress in their lives. However, peer groups also can become exclusive societies that rebuff children who don't conform to certain dress codes and behaviour (Leets & Sunwolf, 2005). Hence, peer groups have a powerful influence on children's development.

Peer Cultures. Different groups of students who have a set of "rules"—how to dress, talk, style their hair, and interact with others—are called peer cultures. The group determines which

Peer cultures Groups of children or adolescents with their own rules and norms, particularly about such things as dress, appearance, music, language, social values, and behaviour.

GUIDELINES: Helping Children of Divorce

Take note of any sudden changes in behaviour that might indicate problems at home.

EXAMPLES

1. Be alert to physical symptoms such as repeated headaches or stomach pains, rapid weight gain or loss, fatigue, or excess energy.
2. Be aware of signs of emotional distress, including moodiness, temper tantrums, and difficulty in paying attention or concentrating.
3. Let parents know about the students' signs of stress.

Talk individually to students about their attitude or behaviour changes. This gives you a chance to find out about unusual stress such as divorce.

EXAMPLES

1. Be a good listener. Students may have no other adult willing to hear their concerns.
2. Let students know you are available to talk, and then let students who approach you set the agenda.

Watch your language to make sure you avoid stereotypes about "happy" (two-parent) homes.

EXAMPLES

1. Simply say "your families" instead of "your mothers and fathers" when addressing the class.
2. Avoid statements such as "We need volunteers for room mother" or "Your father can help you."

Help students maintain self-esteem.

EXAMPLES

1. Recognize a job well done.
2. Make sure the student understands the assignment and can handle the workload. This is not the time to pile on new and very difficult work.
3. Don't take the student's anger personally. The student may be angry at his or her parents but may direct the anger at teachers.

Find out what resources are available at your school.

EXAMPLES

1. Talk to the school psychologist, guidance counsellor, social worker, or principal about students who seem to need outside help.
2. Consider establishing a discussion group, led by a trained adult, for students going through a divorce.

Be sensitive to both parents' rights to information.

EXAMPLES

1. When parents have joint custody, both are entitled to receive information and attend parent–teacher conferences.
2. The non-custodial parent may still be concerned about the child's school progress. Check with your principal about provincial laws regarding the non-custodial parent's rights.

Be aware of long-term problems for students moving between two households.

EXAMPLES

1. Books, assignments, and gym clothes may be left at one parent's house when the student is currently on visitation with the other parent.
2. Parents may not show up for their turn to pick up their child at school or may miss a parent–teacher conference because the note about the conference never made it home.

For ideas about how to help children understand divorce, see **http://muextension.missouri.edu/xplor/hesguide/humanrel/gh6600.htm.**

activities, music, or other students are in or out of favour. For example, when Jessica, a popular high school student, was asked to explain the rules that her group lives by, she had no trouble:

> OK. No. 1: clothes. You cannot wear jeans any day but Friday, and you cannot wear a ponytail or sneakers more than once a week. Monday is fancy day—like black pants or maybe you bust out with a skirt. You have to remind people how cute you are in case they forgot over the weekend. No. 2: parties. Of course we sit down and discuss which ones we're going to because there is no point in getting all dressed up for a party that's going to be lame. (Talbot, 2002, p. 28)

These peer cultures encourage conformity to the group rules. When another girl in Jessica's group wore jeans on Monday, Jessica confronted her: "Why are you wearing jeans today? Did you forget it was Monday?" (Talbot, 2002, p. 28). Jessica explained that the group had to suspend this "rebel" several times, not allowing her to sit with them at lunch.

To understand the power of peers, we have to look at situations where the values and interests of parents clash with those of peers, and then see whose influence dominates. In these comparisons, peers usually win. But not all aspects of peer cultures are bad or cruel. The norms in some groups are positive and support achievement in school. Peer cultures are more powerful in defining issues of style and socializing. Parents and teachers still are influential in matters of morality, career choice, and religion (Harris, 1998).

DRESS CODES AND MORE Peer cultures may set "rules" for how to dress and behave and in so doing determine which activities, music, or other students are in or out of favour.

Friendships. With some peers, children share a close, mutual, and dyadic relationship, a friendship. Key features of friendship are reciprocity and equality. Friendships deepen as children mature (Davies, 2004; Rubin, Bukowski, & Parker, 2006). Whereas young children (ages 6–8) choose friends who live near them and like the same activities (e.g., riding bikes, playing house), older children choose friends with common values and commitments, and who offer mutual support and loyalty.

Beyond the immediate trauma of being "in" or "out" of the group, friendships can influence motivation and achievement in school (Ryan, 2001). In one study, grade 6 students without friends showed lower levels of academic achievement and positive social behaviours and were more emotionally distressed, even two years later, than students with at least one friend (Wentzel, Barry, & Caldwell, 2004). The characteristics of friends and the quality of the friendships matter, too. Having stable, supportive relationships with friends who are socially competent and mature enhances social development, especially during difficult times such as parents' divorce or transition to new schools (Hartup & Stevens, 1999). Children who are rejected by their peers are less likely to participate in classroom learning activities, they are more likely to drop out of school as adolescents, and they may even evidence more problems as adults. For example, rejected aggressive students are more likely to commit crimes as they grow older (Buhs, Ladd, & Herald, 2006; Dodge, Coie, & Lynam, 2006; Fredricks, Blumenfeld, & Paris, 2004).

Who Is Likely to Have Problems With Peers? Children and adolescents are not always tolerant of differences. New students who are physically, intellectually, ethnically, racially, economically, or linguistically different may be rejected in classes with established peer groups. Students who are aggressive, withdrawn, and inattentive-hyperactive are also more likely to be rejected. But classroom context matters too, especially for aggressive or withdrawn students. In classrooms where the general level of aggression is high, being aggressive is less likely to lead to peer rejection. And in classrooms where solitary play and work are more common, being withdrawn is not as likely to lead to rejection. Thus, part of being rejected is being too different from the norm. Also, pro-social behaviours such as sharing, cooperating, and friendly interactions are associated with peer acceptance, no matter what the classroom context. Many aggressive and withdrawn students lack these social skills; inattentive-hyperactive students often misread social cues or have trouble controlling impulses, so their social skills suffer, too (Coplan, Prakash, O'Neil, & Armer, 2004; Stormshak et al., 1999). A teacher should be aware of how each student gets along with the group. Are there outcasts? Do some students play the bully role? Careful adult intervention can often correct such problems, especially when students are at the late elementary and middle school levels (Pearl, Leung, Acker, Farmer, & Rodkin, 2007).

Peer Aggression. There are several forms of aggression. The most common form is **instrumental aggression**, which is intended to gain an object or privilege, such as shoving to get in line first or snatching a toy from another child. The intent is to get what one wants, not to hurt the other child, but the hurt may happen anyway. A second kind is **hostile aggression**—inflicting intentional harm. Hostile aggression can be either the **overt aggression** of threats or physical attacks (as in, "I'm gonna beat you up!") or **relational aggression**, which involves threatening or damaging social relationships (as in, "I'm never going to speak to you again!"). Boys are more likely to use overt aggression and girls, like Alison in the opening case, are more likely to use relational aggression (Berk, 2005). Aggression should not be confused with assertiveness, which means affirming or maintaining a legitimate right. As Helen Bee (1981) explains, "A child who says, 'That's my toy!' is showing assertiveness. If he bashes his playmate over the head to reclaim it, he has shown aggression" (p. 350).

Instrumental aggression Strong actions aimed at claiming an object, place, or privilege—not intended to harm, but may lead to harm.

Hostile aggression Bold, direct action that is intended to hurt someone else; unprovoked attack.

Overt aggression A form of hostile aggression that involves physical attack.

Relational aggression A form of hostile aggression that involves verbal attacks and other actions meant to harm social relationships.

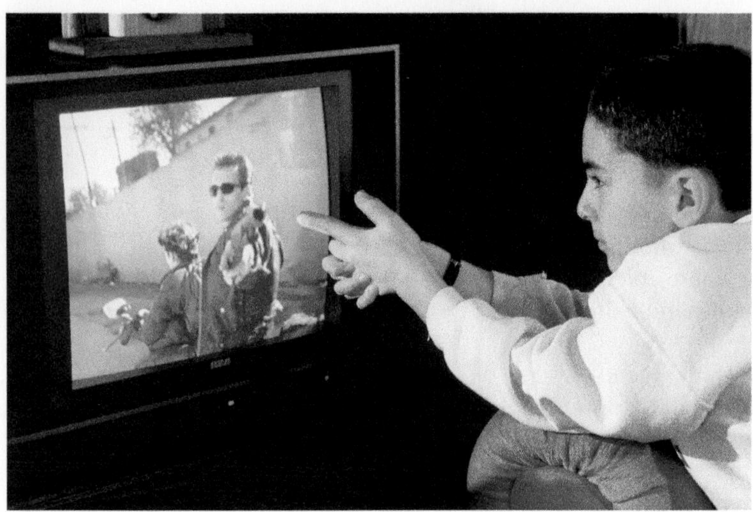

MODELS OF AGGRESSION One very real source of aggressive models is television programming with a high degree of violent content.

In a now seminal study, Albert Bandura and colleagues (Bandura, Ross, & Ross, 1963) showed how modelling plays an important role in the expression of aggression. They arranged for a group of children to watch a film in which an adult interacted aggressively with an inflatable doll (e.g., punching the "Bobo" doll) while another group of children watched an adult playing appropriately with a set of Tinkertoys. After watching the film, both groups of children were given opportunities to play with Bobo dolls and Tinkertoys. The researchers observed that children who had witnessed the aggressive interactions with the Bobo dolls played more aggressively than their peers who had observed the more appropriate play with Tinkertoys.

Similarly, Canadian researchers (Cote, Vaillancourt, LeBlanc, Nagin, & Tremblay, 2006; Craig, Peters, & Konarski, 1998; Pepler, Craig, Jiang, & Connolly, 2008; Tremblay et al., 1996), working with data from the National Longitudinal Study of Children and Youth, have demonstrated strong associations between family membership and family functioning and aggressive behaviour. Children who grow up in homes filled with harsh punishment and family violence are more likely to use aggression to solve their own problems. One very real source of aggressive models found in virtually every home in North America is the television. Rowell Huesmann and colleagues examined the relationship between exposure to violence on television from ages 6 to 10 and aggressive behaviour in adulthood 15 years later for over 300 people. Their conclusion? "Childhood exposure to media violence predicts young adult aggressive behaviour for both males and females. . . . These relations persist even when the effects of socioeconomic status, intellectual ability, and a variety of parenting factors are controlled" (Huesmann, Moise-Titus, Podolski, & Eron, 2003, p. 201). When the children identified with aggressive TV characters (they said they acted like those characters) and when they thought the violence on TV was like real life, they were more likely to be violent as adults.

You can reduce the negative effects of TV violence by stressing three points with your students: (1) most people do not behave in the aggressive ways shown on television, (2) the violent acts on television are not real, but are created by special effects and stunts, and (3) there are better ways to resolve conflicts, and these better ways are the ways that most real people solve their problems (Huesmann et al., 2003). Also, avoid using TV viewing as a reward or punishment because that makes television even more attractive to children (Slaby, Roedell, Arezzo, & Hendrix, 1995).

Television is not the only source of violent media models. Many popular films and video games also are filled with graphic depictions of violence, often performed by the "hero." Students growing up in the inner cities see gangs and drug deals. Finally, the news media is filled with stories of murders, rapes, and robberies.

Bullying. Canadian researchers, including Wendy Craig, Debra Pepler, Tracy Vaillancourt, and Shelley Hymel, are among the leading experts on one type of aggressive behaviour in schools—bullying. Craig and Pepler (1997, p. 42) characterized bullying as a form of social interaction in which a more dominant individual (the bully) exhibits aggressive behaviour that is intended to cause distress or harm to a less dominant individual (the victim). Bullying can include relational forms of aggression (e.g., calling someone names or gossiping behind his or her back) as well as physical forms of aggression, and can occur in virtual (i.e., through the internet) as well as face-to-face interactions. We describe more about cyberbullying below.

In one survey (Charach, Pepler, & Ziegler, 1995), 19 percent of students in Canadian schools reported being bullied twice a term, and 8 percent of students indicated that they experience aggression in school at least once each week. Subsequently, Craig and Pepler (1998) observed 65 elementary school children playing in the schoolyard at recess and lunch. During 48 hours of observations, they observed a total of 314 bullying episodes, approximately 6.5 episodes every hour. They rated 84 percent of the episodes they observed as overt and occurring when peers and/or adults were present. According to their ratings, school staff intervened in only 25 percent of the episodes they witnessed. These studies revealed how serious a problem aggressive behaviour was in

Canadian schools. Currently, Craig and Pepler are co-directors of PREVNet, a Network Centre of Excellence focused on "Promoting Relationships and Eliminating Violence." PREVNet involves 62 researchers from 27 universities across Canada, as well as community, government, and industry partners. Together the network develops and implements strategies designed to stop bullying and to promote healthy relationships among children and youth in school and community settings (PREVNet, 2010).

Aggressive children tend to believe that violence will be rewarded, and they use aggression to get what they want. They are more likely to believe that violent retaliation is acceptable: "It's okay to shove people when you're mad" (Craig et al., 1998; Egan, Monson, & Perry, 1998). Seeing violent acts go unpunished probably affirms and encourages these beliefs. In addition to being surrounded by violence and believing that violent "payback" is appropriate when you are insulted or harmed, some children, particularly boys, have difficulty reading the intentions of others (Dodge & Pettit, 2003; Porath, 2001). They assume that another child "did it on purpose" when their block tower is toppled, they are pushed on the bus, or some other mistake is made. Retaliation follows and the cycle of aggression continues.

Helping children handle aggression properly can make a lasting difference in their lives. Sandra Graham (1996) has successfully experimented with approaches that help aggressive African American boys in grades 5 and 6 become better judges of others' intentions. Strategies include engaging in role play, participating in group discussions of personal experiences, interpreting social cues from photographs, playing pantomime games, making videos, and writing endings to unfinished stories. Boys in a 12-session training group showed clear improvement in reading the intentions of others and responding with less aggression.

MyEducationLab
Go to the Activities and Applications section in Chapter 3 of MyEducationLab and complete Activity 3. As you look for media reports about school violence, consider ways in which recent events have affected your view of school violence.

Relational Aggression. Insults, gossip, exclusion, taunts—all these are forms of relational aggression, sometimes called *social aggression* because the intent is to harm social connections. As children mature, they become less likely to respond to problem situations with overt physical aggression but more likely to respond with less direct forms of relational aggression. Also, whereas boys at all ages are more physically aggressive than girls, research findings are more equivocal about whether girls engage in more relational aggression than boys. Some research supports this view (Crick & Zahn-Waxler, 2003), but other studies indicate boys and girls engage in similar rates of relational aggression (Underwood, 2003). Girls may appear more relationally aggressive because they rely on relational tactics more than physical aggression. Boys, in contrast, use both physical and relational tactics. What is clear is that relational aggression can be even more damaging than overt physical aggression—both to the victim and to the aggressor. Victims, like Stephanie in this chapter's casebook, can be devastated. Also, relational aggressors can be viewed as even more problematic than physical aggressors by teachers and other students (Berger, 2003; Crick, Casas, & Mosher, 1997).

Victims. While some students tend to be bullies, other children are victims. Sullivan (2000) identified three types of victims. *Passive victims* tend to be anxious, physically weak, unpopular, and have low self-esteem. These children do not provoke attacks and do little to defend themselves when attacks occur. *Provocative victims* tend to have their own set of problems that draws negative attention to them. They tend to be physically stronger than passive victims and more actively engaged in incidents that lead to bullying. *Bully/victims* often provoke bullying in others and initiate aggressive acts. It's also true that some groups of children are at higher risk for being bullied than others. More likely victims include children who are obese, children who don't belong to a peer group, children in remedial education, and children with disabilities (Swearer, Espelage, Vaillancourt, & Hymel, 2010).

There are severe consequences associated with being a victim (Entenman, Murnen, & Hendricks, 2006; Garbarino & DeLara, 2002; Swearer et al., 2010). Children who are victims may develop a strong disliking for going to school, may distrust peers, and may have difficulty making friends. Over the long term, children who are chronic victims of bullying through elementary and middle school suffer from anxiety, embarrassment, guilt, loneliness, and loss of self-esteem. In extreme cases, they may experience sleep, speech, and dissociative disorders; panic attacks; paranoia; obsessive compulsive disorder; self-mutilation; delays in mental, social-emotional, and physical development; or even post-traumatic stress disorder (PTSD). In recent years, we have seen tragic consequences when victims of bullying have turned guns on their tormentors in schools in Canada, the United States, and Europe.

Bystanders. What about bystanders? A recent study of over 2000 children in the United Kingdom (Rivers, Voret, Pote, & Ashurst, 2009) found that 63 percent had witnessed bullying in or around their schools within the current school term. **Bystanders** are children who witness bullying behaviour and may or may not do anything about it. They may unintentionally encourage bullying when they watch but don't help the victim, but some take a more active role, condoning the actions of the bully by laughing and harassing the victim. Either way, bystanders have an important role to play in the bully-victim dynamic. One problem for bystanders is knowing what to do or who to tell. Also, they may fear reprisals from the bully if they report an attack. Not surprisingly, observing bullying is associated with risks to mental health, including elevated levels of anxiety, depression, and substance use (Bonnano & Hymel, 2010; Rivers et al., 2009).

Cyberbullying. The use of the internet for communicating with others has become a part of everyday life for adolescents (Bargh, McKenna, & Fitzsimmons, 2002; Gross, Juvonen, & Gable, 2002; Roberts, Foehr, & Rideout, 2005). In 2005, 94 percent of Canadian youth reported having access to the internet from their homes (Media Awareness Network, 2005). While some research shows that access to this media may help some individuals overcome shyness and enhance their social skills (Maczewski, 2002; Valkenburg, Schouten, & Peter, 2005), there is also evidence that it is being used as a venue for bullying activities. *Cyberbullying* has been defined as a form of intentional aggression where an individual, or a group of individuals, uses information technologies, such as email, websites (developed specifically for the purpose of humiliating or degrading others), instant messaging (IM), and/or text messaging on cell phones to inflict harm on others by embarrassing them or gossiping about them (Ybarra & Mitchell, 2004). There is very little research on this topic, so it is not known whether the impact of cyberbullying is as devastating as schoolyard bullying. Also not known is whether the same individuals who bully in person are the ones who are more likely to bully online. But given the anonymous nature of the internet, and the sense of protection one might feel from being behind a screen, it is possible that individuals may feel more free to bully online than in person.

What should schools do about bullying? Experts recommend school-wide, classroom, and individual approaches that focus on prevention, targeted intervention, and development of self-discipline (Osher, Bear, Sprague, & Doyle, 2010; Swearer et al., 2010). For example, Swearer et al. recommend a social-ecological framework that considers all systems directly affecting students, including families, peer groups, teacher–student relationships, parent–school relationships, neighbourhoods, and cultural expectations. Focusing on these factors can help teachers to design meaningful activities and foster positive classroom climates, which will enhance student cooperation, motivation, and learning. Experts caution against punitive and exclusionary approaches, such as zero-tolerance policies, which have actually exacerbated problems in many cases (e.g., by increasing anti-social behaviour and contributing to school disengagement and school dropout). School-wide positive behaviour support (SWPBS) systems teach rules and reward students for following them (see Osher et al., 2010). In schools that implement SWPBS, problem behaviour is analyzed from a functional perspective (i.e., what purpose does it serve?) and interventions address the root of the problem. Finally, schools that emphasize social-emotional learning (SEL) help students to develop self-awareness, self-control, social awareness, relationship skills, and responsible decision making.

Interviews with adolescents reveal how much they count on their teachers and other adults in the school to protect them (Garbarino & deLara, 2002). The *Guidelines* box may give you ideas for how to handle aggression and encourage cooperation in the classroom.

Teachers

Because they are the main adults in students' lives for many hours each week, teachers have the opportunity to play a significant role in students' personal and social development. For students facing emotional or interpersonal problems, teachers are sometimes the best source of help. When students have chaotic and unpredictable home lives, they need a caring, firm structure in school. They need teachers who set clear limits, are consistent, enforce rules firmly but not punitively, respect students, and show genuine concern. Being liked by teachers can offset the negative effects of peer rejection in middle school. And students who have few friends, but are not rejected—simply ignored by other students—can remain well adjusted academically and socially when they are liked and supported by teachers.

Bystanders Children who witness bullying behaviour and may or may not do anything about it.

GUIDELINES: Dealing With Aggression and Encouraging Cooperation

Present yourself as a non-aggressive model.

EXAMPLES

1. Do not use threats of aggression to win obedience.
2. When problems arise, model non-violent conflict-resolution strategies.

Ensure that your classroom has enough space and appropriate materials for every student.

EXAMPLES

1. Prevent overcrowding.
2. Make sure prized toys or resources are plentiful.
3. Remove or confiscate materials that encourage personal aggression, such as toy guns.
4. Avoid highly competitive activities and evaluations.

Make sure students do not profit from aggressive behaviours.

EXAMPLES

1. Comfort the victim of aggression and ignore the aggressor.
2. Use reasonable punishment, especially with older students.

Teach directly about positive social behaviours.

EXAMPLES

1. Incorporate lessons on social ethics and morality through reading selections and discussions.
2. Discuss the effects of anti-social actions such as stealing, bullying, and spreading rumours.
3. Provide models and encouragement—role-play appropriate conflict resolution.
4. Build self-esteem by building skills and knowledge.
5. Seek help for students who seem especially isolated and victimized.

Provide opportunities for learning tolerance and cooperation.

EXAMPLES

1. Emphasize the similarities among people rather than the differences.
2. Set up group projects that encourage cooperation.

For more ideas, see the National Youth Violence Prevention Resource Center at **www.safeyouth.gov/Pages/Home.aspx** or see **www.prevnet.ca/**.

Academic and Personal Caring. When researchers ask students to describe a "good teacher," three qualities are at the centre of their descriptions. First, good teachers have positive interpersonal relationships—they care about their students. Second, good teachers can keep the classroom organized and maintain authority without being rigid or "mean." Finally, good teachers are good motivators—they can make learning fun by being creative and innovative (Noguera, 2005; Woolfolk Hoy & Weinstein, 2006). We will look at motivation in Chapter 11 and management in Chapter 12, so for now let's focus on caring and teaching.

For the past 15 years, research has documented the value and importance of positive relationships with teachers for students at every grade level (Davis, 2003). For example, one of Anita's doctoral graduates studied middle school mathematics classes and found that students' perceptions of their teachers' affective support and caring were related to the effort they invested in learning math (Sakiz, Pape, & Woolfolk Hoy, 2008). Tamera Murdock and Angela Miller (2003) found that grade 8 students' perceptions that their teachers cared about them were significantly related to the students' academic motivation, even after taking into account the motivational influences of parents and peers.

Students define caring in two ways. One is *academic caring*—setting high but reasonable expectations and helping students to reach those goals. The second is *personal caring*—being patient, respectful, humorous, willing to listen, and interested in students' issues and personal problems. For higher-achieving students, academic caring is especially important, but for students who are at risk of experiencing academic, social, or behavioural difficulties and who often are alienated from school, personal caring is critical (Cothran & Ennis, 2000; Woolfolk Hoy & Weinstein, 2006). In fact, in one study of a Texas high school, the Mexican and Mexican American students saw teacher caring as a prerequisite for their own caring about school; in other words, they needed to be *cared for* before they could *care about* school (Valenzuela, 1999). Unfortunately, in the same school, the mostly non-Latino teachers expected the students to care about school before they would invest their caring in the students. And for many teachers, caring about school meant behaving in more "middle-class" ways.

These contrasting student and teacher views can lead to a downward spiral of mistrust. Students withhold their cooperation until teachers "earn it" with their authentic caring. Teachers withhold caring until students "earn it" with respect for authority and cooperation. Marginalized students expect unfair treatment and behave defensively when they sense any unfairness. Teachers get tough and punish. Students feel correct in mistrusting, and become more guarded and defiant. Teachers feel correct in mistrusting and become more controlling and punitive, and so it goes (Woolfolk Hoy & Weinstein, 2006).

Of course, students need both academic and personal caring. Katz (1999) interviewed eight immigrant students in a middle school and concluded the following:

> High expectations without caring can result in setting goals that are impossible for the student to reach without adult support and assistance. On the other hand, caring without high expectations can turn dangerously into paternalism in which teachers feel sorry for "underprivileged" youth but never challenge them academically. High expectations and caring in tandem, however, can make a powerful difference in students' lives. (p. 814)

In short, caring means not giving up on students as well as demonstrating and teaching kindness in the classroom (Davis, 2003).

Reaching Every Student: Teachers and Child Abuse

Certainly, one critical way to care about students is to protect their welfare and intervene in cases of abuse. Accurate information about the number of abused children in Canada is difficult to find because many cases go unreported. That said, an estimated 235 315 child maltreatment investigations were conducted in Canada in 2003, a rate of 38.33 investigations per 1000 children aged 0–15 (Government of Canada, 2006). In approximately half of these investigations (49 percent, or 114 606 cases), the maltreatment allegations were substantiated. Parents are the most likely perpetrators in familial physical and sexual abuse cases, but parents are not the only people who abuse children. Siblings, other relatives, and even teachers have been responsible for the physical and sexual abuse of children. And today, there is another source of abuse—the internet. Table 3.1 lists some ways children can protect themselves from predators on the internet. Share these with your students.

TABLE 3.1 **Safety on the Internet**

Provide these guidelines to your students so that they can protect themselves when using the internet.

1. Never give identifying data such as your name, address, phone number, school name, and so on to anyone on the internet unless you check with a parent or teacher first.
2. Never share your password with anyone, even a best friend.
3. Never tell anyone online where you will be or what you will be doing at a certain time without a parent's or teacher's permission.
4. Never give out your picture over the internet.
5. Choose a name that is not your own name for an email address.
6. Check with a parent or teacher before you enter a chat room.
7. Never agree to meet in person anyone whom you have met on the internet. If someone asks to meet you, tell a parent or a teacher.
8. If you receive pictures or messages that make you uncomfortable, tell an adult at home or at school immediately.
9. If someone makes suggestive comments to you on the internet, stop talking to him or her immediately. Tell an adult at home or at school.
10. Never fill out a questionnaire or give a credit card number online without checking with a parent or teacher.
11. If you unintentionally come across nude or obscene pictures, tell someone immediately.
12. Never open or respond to an email message from someone you do not know.
13. Be open with parents or teachers about what you are accessing on the internet.
14. Be careful when anyone offers you anything free on the internet.
15. Do not do things online that you would hesitate to do in real life.

Source: From Crosson-Tower, C. (2002). *When children are abused: An educator's guide to intervention.* Boston: Allyn & Bacon. Copyright © 2002 by Pearson Education. Reprinted by permission of the publisher. See also Hughes, 1998; Monteleone, 1998; http://encarta.msn.com/schoolhouse/safety.asp; and www.missingkids.com

TABLE 3.2 Types of Child Maltreatment and Examples of Abusive Behaviours

Category	Definition	Examples of Abusive Behaviours
1. Physical abuse (assault)	The application of unreasonable force by an adult or youth to any part of a child's body	Harsh physical discipline, forceful shaking, pushing, grabbing, throwing, hitting with a hand, punching, kicking, biting, hitting with an object, choking, strangling, stabbing, burning, shooting, poisoning, and the excessive use of restraints
2. Sexual abuse	Involvement of a child, by an adult or youth, in an act of sexual gratification, or exposure of a child to sexual contact, activity, or behaviour	Penetration, attempted penetration, oral sex, fondling, sex talk, voyeurism, and sexual exploitation
3. Neglect	Failure by a parent or caregiver to provide the physical or psychological necessities of life to a child	Failure to supervise, leading to physical harm or to sexual harm; permitting criminal behaviour; physical neglect; medical neglect; failure to provide psychological treatment; abandonment; and educational neglect
4. Emotional harm	Adult behaviour that harms a child psychologically, emotionally, or spiritually	Hostile or unreasonable and abusive treatment, frequent or extreme verbal abuse (that may include threatening and demeaning or insulting behaviours), causing non-organic failure to thrive*, emotional neglect, and direct exposure to violence between adults other than primary caregivers
5. Exposure to family violence	Circumstances that allow a child to be aware of violence occurring between a caregiver and his/her partner or between other family members	Allowing a child to see, hear, or otherwise be exposed to signs of the violence (e.g., to see bruises or physical injuries on the caregiver or to overhear violent episodes)

* "Non-organic failure to thrive" is a diagnostic term applied in cases of children less than three years of age who have suffered a slowing or cessation of growth for which no physical or physiological causes can be identified.

Source: Government of Canada. (2006). Child maltreatment in Canada: Overview paper. Table 1. Prepared by Susan Jack, et al. Ottawa: Public Health Agency of Canada.

There are five types of child maltreatment. These are defined with examples in Table 3.2 (Government of Canada, 2006). As a teacher, you must alert your principal, school counsellor, or a school social worker if you suspect a child is being abused or neglected. Child protection is a provincial responsibility, so be sure you understand the laws in your province concerning this important role. In British Columbia, the *Child, Family, and Community Service Act* clearly states that *anyone* who has reason to believe that a child (defined as any individual under the age of 19) has been or is likely to be physically or sexually abused, exploited, or neglected, has a legal responsibility to report the matter to a child-protection social worker (British Columbia Ministry for Children and Families, 1998). Sometimes, people don't report their suspicions because they think they need proof. This is not true. All that is required is a reasonable belief that a child is in emotional or physical danger. What should you look for as indicators of abuse? Table 3.3 lists some indicators.

Now that we have a good sense of the many interacting contexts that influence development, let's turn to the developing individual. First, we look at a very basic aspect of every person—physical development.

TABLE 3.3 **Indicators of Child Abuse**

The following are some of the signs of abuse. Not every child who exhibits these signs is abused, but these indicators should be investigated.

Type of Abuse	Physical Indicators	Behavioural Indicators
Physical abuse	• Unexplained bruises (in various stages of healing), welts, human bite marks, bald spots • Unexplained burns, especially cigarette burns or immersion-burns (glovelike) • Unexplained fractures, lacerations, or abrasions	• Self-destructive • Withdrawn and aggressive—behavioural extremes • Uncomfortable with physical contact • Arrives at school early or stays late, as if afraid • Chronic runaway (adolescents) • Complains of soreness or moves uncomfortably • Wears clothing inappropriate to weather, to cover body
Physical neglect	• Abandonment • Unattended medical needs • Consistent lack of supervision • Consistent hunger, inappropriate dress, poor hygiene • Lice, distended stomach, emaciation	• Regularly displays fatigue or listlessness, falls asleep in class • Steals food, begs from classmates • Reports that no caretaker is at home • Frequently absent or tardy • Self-destructive • School dropout (adolescents)
Sexual abuse	• Torn, stained, or bloodied underclothing • Pain or itching in genital area • Difficulty walking or sitting • Bruises or bleeding in external genitalia • Venereal disease • Frequent urinary or yeast infections	• Withdrawn, chronic depression • Excessive seductiveness • Role reversal, overly concerned for siblings • Poor self-esteem, self-devaluation, lack of confidence • Peer problems, lack of involvement • Massive weight change • Suicide attempts (especially adolescents) • Hysteria, lack of emotional control • Sudden school difficulties • Inappropriate sex play or premature understanding of sex • Threatened by physical contact, closeness • Promiscuity

Source: "Supporting Victims of Child Abuse" by Thelma Bear, Sherry Schenk & Lisa Buckner. In the December 2002/January 2003 issue of *Educational Leadership, 50*(4), p. 44. © 1992 by ASCD. Used with permission. Learn more about ASCD at www.ascd.org.

PHYSICAL DEVELOPMENT

STOP & THINK How tall are you? What grade were you in when you reached that height? Were you one of the tallest or shortest students in your middle or high school, or were you about average? Did you know students who were teased because of something about their physical appearance? How important was your physical development to your feelings about yourself?

This chapter is about personal and social development, but we begin with a kind of development that is a basic concern of all individuals and families—physical development. As you may have remembered when you considered the *Stop & Think* questions above, physical development can affect conceptions of self and interactions with others.

Physical and Motor Development

For most children, at least in the early years, growing up means getting bigger, stronger, and more coordinated. It also can be a frightening, disappointing, exciting, and puzzling time.

The Early Years. Preschool children are very active. Their gross-motor (large muscle) skills improve greatly over the years from ages 2 to 5. Between ages 2 and about 4 or 5, preschoolers' muscles grow stronger and their brains develop to better integrate information about movements. Their balance improves, and their centre of gravity moves lower, so they are able to run, jump, climb, and hop. Most of these movements develop naturally if the child has normal physical abilities and the opportunity to play. Children with physical problems, however, may need special training to develop these skills. For young children, as for many adolescents and adults, physical activity can be an end in itself. It is fun just to improve. Because they can't always judge when to stop, preschoolers may need interludes of rest scheduled after periods of physical exertion (Darcey & Travers, 2006; Thomas & Thomas, 2008).

Fine-motor skills such as tying shoes or fastening buttons, which require the coordination of small movements, also improve greatly during the preschool years. Children should be given the chance to work with large paintbrushes, fat pencils and crayons, large pieces of drawing paper, large Lego blocks, and soft clay or playdough to accommodate their developing skills. During this time, children will begin to develop a lifelong preference for their right or left hand. By age 5, about 90 percent of students prefer their right hand for most skilled work, and 10 percent or so prefer their left hand, with more boys than girls being left-handed (Feldman, 2004). This is a genetically based preference, so don't try to make children switch.

The Elementary School Years. During the elementary school years, physical development is fairly steady for most children. They become taller, leaner, and stronger, so they are better able to master sports and games. There is tremendous variation, however. A particular child can be much larger or smaller than average and still be perfectly healthy. Because children at this age are very aware of physical differences but are not the most tactful people, you may hear comments such as, "You're too little to be in grade 5. What's wrong with you?" or "How come you're so fat?"

Throughout elementary school, many of the girls are likely to be as large as or larger than the boys in their classes. Between the ages of 11 and 14, girls are, on the average, taller and heavier than boys of the same age (Cook & Cook, 2005). The size discrepancy can give the girls an advantage in physical activities, although some girls may feel conflict over this and, as a result, downplay their physical abilities.

The Adolescent Years. Puberty marks the beginning of sexual maturity. It is not a single event, but rather a series of changes involving almost every part of the body. The sex differences in physical development observed during the later elementary years become even more pronounced at the beginning of puberty. Generally, girls begin puberty between ages 10 and 11, about two years ahead of boys, and reach their final height by age 16 or 17; most boys continue growing until about age 18, but both boys and girls can continue to grow slightly until about 25 (Thomas & Thomas, 2008; Wigfield, Byrnes, & Eccles, 2006). Around 80 percent of North American girls have their first menstrual period between the ages of 11 and 14. One tension for adolescents is that they are physically and sexually mature years before they are psychologically or financially ready to shoulder the adult responsibilities of marriage and child-rearing.

The physical changes of adolescence have significant effects on the individual's identity. Psychologists have been particularly interested in the academic, social, and emotional differences they have found between adolescents who mature early and those who mature later. Early maturation seems to have certain special advantages for boys—their taller, broader-shouldered body type fits the cultural stereotype for the male ideal. Early-maturing boys are more likely to have advantages in sports and enjoy high social status, though at least one study also found early-maturing boys in grade 5 to have more symptoms of depression (Wigfield et al., 2006). Early-maturing boys also tend to engage in more delinquent behaviour (Cota-Robles, Neiss, & Rowe, 2002). On the other hand, boys who mature late may have a more difficult time. However, some studies show that in adulthood, males who matured later tend to be more creative, tolerant, and perceptive. Perhaps the trials

Puberty The physiological changes during adolescence that lead to the ability to reproduce.

STUDENTS COME IN ALL SIZES The physical changes of adolescence have significant effects on the individual's identity. Psychologists have been particularly interested in the academic, social, and emotional differences they have found between adolescents who mature early and those who mature later.

and anxieties of maturing late teach some boys to be better problem solvers (Brooks-Gunn, 1988; Steinberg, 2005).

For girls, these effects are reversed. Maturing way ahead of classmates can be a definite disadvantage. Being larger than everyone else in the class is not a valued characteristic for girls in many cultures (Jones, 2004). A girl who begins to mature early probably will be the first in her peer group to display the changes of puberty. Early maturation is associated with emotional difficulties such as depression, anxiety, and eating disorders, especially in societies that define thin as attractive (Steinberg, 2005). Later-maturing girls seem to have fewer problems, but they may worry that something is wrong with them. All students can benefit from knowing that the "normal" range in rates of maturation is great and that there are advantages for both early and late maturers.

Play, Recess, and Physical Activity

Maria Montessori once noted, "Play is children's work," and Piaget and Vygotsky would agree. More recently, the American Academy of Pediatrics stated, "Play is essential to development because it contributes to the cognitive, physical, social, and emotional well-being of children and youth" (Ginsburg, 2007, p. 182). We saw that the brain develops with stimulation, and play provides some of that stimulation at every age. In fact, some neuroscientists suggest that play might help in the important process of pruning brain synapses during childhood (Pellis, 2006). Other psychologists believe play allows children to experiment safely as they learn about their environment, try out new behaviours, solve problems, and adapt to new situations (Pellegrini, Dupusis, & Smith, 2007). Babies in the sensorimotor stage learn by exploring, sucking, pounding, shaking, and throwing—acting on their environments. Preoperational preschoolers love pretend play and use pretending to form symbols, use language, and interact with others. They are beginning to play simple games with predictable rules. Elementary-school-age children also like fantasy, but begin to play more complex games and sports, and thus learn cooperation, fairness, negotiation, winning, and losing as well as develop more sophisticated language. As children grow into adolescents, play continues to be part of their physical and social development (Meece & Daniels, 2008).

LEARNING FROM PLAY Psychologists believe play allows children to experiment safely as they learn about their environment, try out new behaviours, solve problems, and adapt to new situations.

Recess. The National Association for the Education of Young Children (2006) in the United States lists these positive outcomes of recess and outdoor play:

- Play is an active form of learning that unites the mind, body, and spirit. Until at least the age of 9, children's learning occurs best when the whole self is involved.
- Play reduces the tension that often comes with having to achieve or needing to learn. During play, adults do not interfere and children relax.

- Children express and work out emotional aspects of everyday experiences through unstructured play.
- Children permitted to play freely with peers develop skills for seeing things through another person's point of view—cooperating, helping, sharing, and solving problems.
- The development of children's perceptual abilities may suffer when so much of their experience is acquired through television, computers, books, worksheets, and media that require only two senses. The senses of smell, touch, and taste, and the sense of motion through space are powerful modes of learning.
- Children who are less restricted in their access to the outdoors gain competence in moving through the larger world. Developmentally, they should gain the ability to navigate their immediate environments (in safety) and to lay the foundation for the courage that will enable them eventually to lead their own lives.

Other researchers note that students in Asian countries, who consistently outperform U.S. students on international tests, have more frequent recess breaks throughout the school day. These breaks may be especially important for students with attention-deficit/hyperactivity disorders (ADHD). In fact, with more breaks there might be fewer students, especially boys, diagnosed with ADHD (Pellegrini & Bohn, 2005).

Given the value of recess and play, many people worry that we are overlooking play as an important aspect of human development. Children and adolescents spend many of their waking hours in school. Because most children do not get much physical activity in their daily lives today, schools have a role in promoting active play. This can be especially important for students living in poverty and for children with disabilities. The federal government has recognized the value of physical activity and recommends that children engage in 90 minutes of moderate to vigorous physical activity every day. However, the Canadian Fitness and Lifestyle Research Institute (CFLRI, 2008) reports that only about 23 percent of Canadian children reach this benchmark. From 2005 through 2008, the institute studied more than 10 000 children (ages 5–19) using pedometers to count their daily steps. A goal was set for children to take 16 500 steps each day, which translates roughly to 90 minutes of physical activity over and above that required for incidental daily living. Figure 3.2 shows the proportion of children who reached this criterion in each year of the study. On average, boys took more steps than girls, and children aged 5–10 were almost twice as likely to meet the criterion as those aged 15–19. Differences across regions of the country also were found. The amount of physical activity increased from east to west, and children in higher SES communities engaged in more physical activity than children living in low SES communities. One reason for concern about physical activity for children is the increase in childhood obesity, as you will see next.

FIGURE 3.2 Proportion of Children Who Met the Canadian Fitness and Lifestyle Research Institute Criterion From 2005–2008

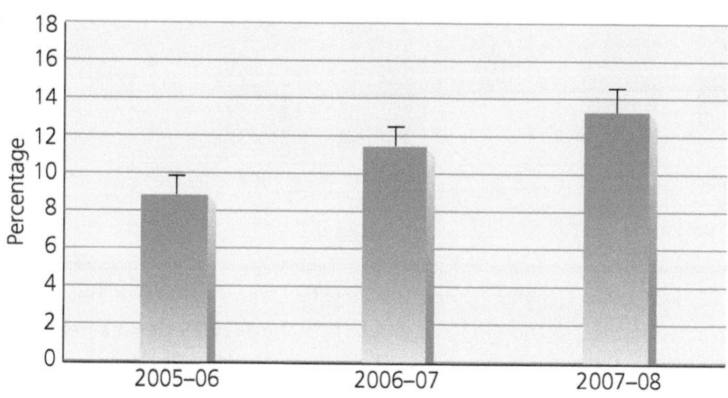

Source: Canadian Fitness and Lifestyle Research Institute. (2008). Kids can play! Encouraging children to be active at home, at school, and in their communities. Retrieved August 26, 2010, from www.cflri.ca/eng/provincial_data/canplay_bulletins/canplay_canada.php

Challenges in Physical Development

Physical development is public—everyone sees how tall, short, heavy, thin, muscular, or coordinated you are. As students move into adolescence, they feel as if they are "on stage" (i.e., as if everyone is evaluating them); physical development is part of what is evaluated. So there are psychological consequences to physical development too (Thomas & Thomas, 2008).

Childhood Overweight and Obesity. If you have seen the news lately, you know that obesity is a growing problem in North America, especially for children. Childhood obesity usually is defined in terms of body mass index, or BMI, which calculates weight in relation to height. Children with BMIs between the 85th and 95th percentiles (i.e., 85 percent of children the same age and sex weigh less than they do) are considered overweight, and children with BMIs above the 95th percentile are considered obese. Although the BMI provides a good screening tool for identifying overweight and obese children, children with BMIs at the 85th percentile or higher should be assessed by a health care professional who will consider other factors, such as diet, physical activity, and family history, to determine whether excess fat is a problem. Figure 3.3 shows how the trend toward childhood obesity is increasing.

The consequences of obesity are serious for children and adolescents: diabetes, strain on bones and joints, respiratory problems, and greater chance of heart problems as adults. Playing with friends or participating in sports can be affected negatively. In addition, children with obesity often are the targets of cruel teasing. Like everything involving children's development, there probably are many interacting causes for this increase in obesity rates including poor diet, genetic factors, increased hours in front of the television and video games, and lack of exercise (Meece & Daniels, 2008). Programs that address this problem emphasize healthy eating, increased physical activity, and decreased television viewing.

There is another challenge in physical development for many children that involves not too much weight, but too little.

FIGURE 3.3 **Increase in Childhood Obesity**
Survey results show increasing overweight and obesity rates in Canada, excluding territories, for 1978–1979 and 2004. Results are shown by age group, household population aged 2 to 17.

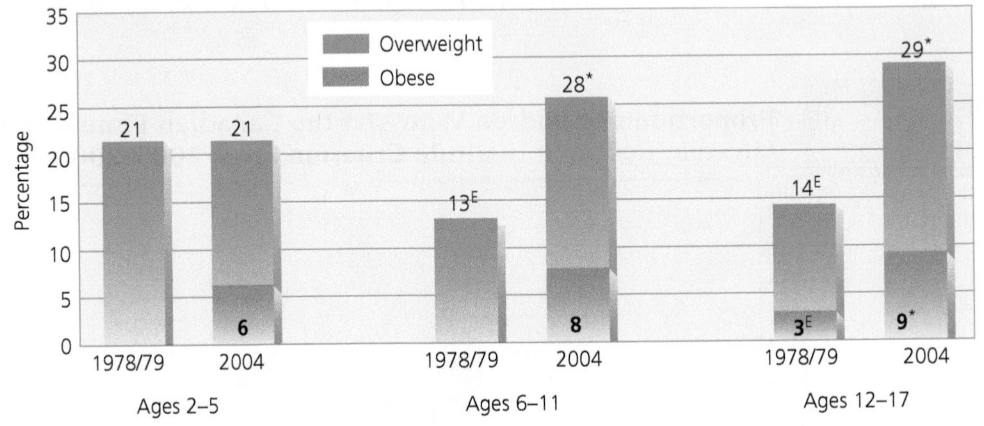

Note 1: Data from 2004 Canadian Community Health Survey: Nutrition; and Canada Health Survey 1978/79.

Note 2: The obesity rates for the 2–5 and 6–11 age groups from the 1978/79 Canada Health Survey have coefficients of variation greater than 33.3 percent; therefore, the estimates are not releasable.

E Coefficient of variation between 16.6 percent and 33.3 percent (interpret with caution).

*Significantly different from estimate for 1978–1979 ($p < 0.05$).

Source: Shields, M. (2005). Measured obesity: Overweight Canadian children and adolescents. Nutrition: Findings from the Canadian Community of Health Survey, 1, 23. Statistics Canada—Cat. No. 82-620-MWE. Also available at www.statcan.gc.ca/pub/82-620-m/2005001/pdf/4193660-eng.pdf or at www.statcan.gc.ca/pub/82-620-m/2005001/article/child-enfant/8061-eng.htm

Body mass index (BMI) A calculation of weight in relation to height.

Eating Disorders. Many adolescents who experience the changes of puberty are very concerned about their bodies. This has always been true, but today, the emphasis on fitness and appearance makes adolescents even more likely to worry about how their bodies "measure up." Both boys and girls can become dissatisfied with their bodies during adolescence—boys because they do not match the muscular models they see in the media and girls because they don't match the cultural ideals either. For girls, it also appears that conversations with friends about appearance can make dissatisfactions worse (Jones, 2004). For some, the concern becomes excessive. One consequence is the development of an eating disorder such as bulimia (binge eating) and anorexia nervosa (self-starvation), both of which are more common in females than in males. People who are bulimic often binge, eating a huge carton of ice cream or a whole cake. Then, to avoid gaining weight, they force themselves to vomit, or they use strong laxatives, to purge themselves of the extra calories. Bulimics tend to maintain a normal weight, but their digestive systems can be permanently damaged by the forced purging.

Anorexia is an even more dangerous disorder—people who are anorexic either refuse to eat or eat practically nothing while often exercising obsessively. In the process, they may lose 20 to 25 percent of their body weight, and some (about 20 percent) literally starve themselves to death. Anorexic students become very thin, and may appear pale, have brittle fingernails, and develop fine dark hairs all over their bodies. They are easily chilled because they have so little fat to insulate their bodies. They are often depressed, insecure, moody, and lonely. Girls may stop having their menstrual period. These eating disorders often begin in adolescence and are becoming more common—about 1 percent of adolescents (mostly, but not all, girls) become anorexic (Rice & Dolgin, 2002). These students usually require professional help. Don't ignore the warning signs—less than one-third of people with eating disorders actually receive treatment (Stice & Shaw, 2004). A teacher may be the person who begins the chain of help for students with these tragic problems. The *Guidelines* box gives a few ideas for how to deal with physical differences in the classroom.

DON'T TURN AWAY FROM ME Students with anorexia usually require professional help—don't ignore the warning signs. A teacher may be the person who begins the chain of help for students with these tragic disorders.

The Brain and Adolescent Development

Along with all the other changes during puberty come changes in the brain and neurological system that affect personal and social development. Throughout adolescence, changes in the brain increase students' computational skills as well as their ability to control behaviour in both low-stress and high-stress situations, to be more purposeful and organized, and to inhibit impulsive behaviour (Wigfield et al., 2006). But these abilities are not fully developed until the early 20s, so adolescents may "seem" like adults, at least in low-stress situations, but their brains are not fully developed. They may have trouble controlling emotions and avoiding risky behaviours. In fact, adolescents appear to need more intense emotional stimulation than either children or adults, so these young people are set up for taking risks or seeking thrills. Teachers can take advantage of their adolescent students' intensity by helping them devote their energy to areas such as politics, the environment, or social causes (Price, 2005) or by guiding them to explore emotional connections with characters in history or literature.

Other changes in the neurological system during adolescence affect sleep; students need about nine hours of sleep per night, but many students' biological clocks are reset so that it is difficult for them to fall asleep before midnight. Getting nine hours of sleep per night during the school week is very difficult, and as a result students can be continually sleep-deprived. Classroom settings that force students to remain in their seats, taking notes for the full period, may literally put students to sleep. And with no time for breakfast, and little for lunch, these students' nutrition is often deprived as well (Sprenger, 2005).

Bulimia Eating disorder characterized by overeating, then getting rid of the food by self-induced vomiting or use of laxatives.

Anorexia nervosa Eating disorder characterized by very limited food intake.

GUIDELINES: Dealing With Physical Differences in the Classroom

Address students' physical differences in ways that do not call unnecessary attention to the variations.

EXAMPLES

1. Try to seat smaller students so they can see and participate in class activities, but avoid seating arrangements that are obviously based on height.
2. Balance sports and games that rely on size and strength with games that reflect cognitive, artistic, social, or musical abilities, such as charades or drawing games.
3. Don't use or allow students to use nicknames based on physical traits.
4. Make sure there is a good supply of left-handed scissors for preschool classes.

Help students obtain factual information about differences in physical development.

EXAMPLES

1. Assign science projects that explore sex differences in growth rates.
2. Have readings available that focus on differences between early and late maturers. Make sure that you present the positives and the negatives of each.
3. Find out the school policy on sex education and on informal guidance for students. Some schools, for example, encourage teachers to talk to girls who are upset about their first menstrual period, while other schools expect teachers to send the girls to talk to the school nurse (if your school still has one—budget cuts have eliminated many).
4. Give the students models in literature or in their community of accomplished and caring individuals who do not fit the culture's ideal physical stereotypes.

Accept that concerns about appearance and the opposite sex will occupy much time and energy for adolescents.

EXAMPLES

1. Allow some time at the end of class for socializing.
2. Deal with issues related to physical differences in curriculum-related materials.

For more information about accommodations for physical differences in your classroom, see **http://dos.claremontmckenna.edu/PhysicalLearningDiff.asp.**

SELF-CONCEPT AND IDENTITY

What is self-concept? Is self-concept different from self-esteem or identity? How do we come to understand other people and ourselves? In this section we look at the individual's sense of self and how that understanding develops. You will see patterns similar to those noted in Chapter 2 for cognitive development. Children's understandings of themselves are concrete at first. Early views of self and friends are based on immediate behaviours and appearances. Children assume that others share their feelings and perceptions. Their thinking about themselves and others is simple, segmented, and rule-bound, not flexible or integrated into organized systems. In time, children are able to think abstractly about internal processes—beliefs, intentions, values, and motivations. With these developments in abstract thinking, knowledge of self, others, and situations can incorporate more abstract qualities (Berk, 2005; Harter, 2003).

PSYCHOSOCIAL THEORY Erik Erikson proposed a theory of psychosocial development that describes tasks to be accomplished at different stages of life.

In this section you will encounter several *self*-terms: identity, self-concept, self-esteem, and self-worth. The distinctions among these terms are not always sharp and there is disagreement even among psychologists about what each term means (Roeser et al., 2006). In general, identity is a broader concept than the other self-terms. Identity includes people's general sense of themselves with all their beliefs and attitudes about themselves. Identity integrates all the different aspects and roles of the self (Wigfield et al., 2006). But it is common for researchers to use self-concept and identity interchangeably. To make matters easier, we will too. We begin our consideration of self-concept/identity within the framework of Erik Erikson.

Erikson: Stages of Individual Development

Like Jean Piaget, Erik Erikson did not start out as a psychologist. In fact, Erikson never graduated from high school. He spent his early adult years studying art and travelling around

Europe. A meeting with Sigmund Freud in Vienna led to an invitation from Freud to study psychoanalysis, and Erikson later created an influential alternative to Freud's stage theory of psychosexual development.

Erikson offered a basic framework for understanding the needs of young people in relation to the society in which they grow, learn, and ultimately make their contributions. Erikson's psychosocial theory emphasized the emergence of the self, the search for identity, the individual's relationships with others, and the role of culture throughout life. Like Piaget, Erikson saw development as a passage through a series of stages, each with its particular goals, concerns, accomplishments, and dangers. The stages are interdependent: accomplishments at later stages depend on how conflicts are resolved in the earlier years. At each stage, Erikson suggests, the individual faces a developmental crisis—a conflict between a positive alternative and a potentially unhealthy alternative. The way in which the individual resolves each crisis has a lasting effect on that person's self-image and view of society. We will look briefly at all eight stages in Erikson's theory—or, as he called them, the "eight ages of man." Table 3.4 presents the stages in summary form.

Psychosocial Describing the relation of the individual's emotional needs to the social environment.

Developmental crisis A specific conflict whose resolution prepares the way for the next stage.

TABLE 3.4 **Erikson's Eight Stages of Psychosocial Development**

Stage	Approximate Age	Important Event	Description
1. Basic trust versus basic mistrust	Birth to 12–18 months	Feeding	The infant must first form a loving, trusting relationship with the caregiver or develop a sense of mistrust.
2. Autonomy versus shame and doubt	18 months to 3 years	Toilet training	The child's energies are directed toward the development of physical skills, including walking, grasping, controlling the sphincter. The child learns control but may develop shame and doubt if not handled well.
3. Initiative versus guilt	3 to 6 years	Independence	The child continues to become more assertive and to take more initiative but may be too forceful, which can lead to feelings of guilt.
4. Industry versus inferiority	6 to 12 years	School	The child must deal with demands to learn new skills or risk a sense of inferiority, failure, or incompetence.
5. Identity versus role confusion	Adolescence	Peer relationships	The teenager must achieve identity in occupation, gender roles, politics, and religion.
6. Intimacy versus isolation	Young adulthood	Love relationships	The young adult must develop intimate relationships or suffer feelings of isolation.
7. Generativity versus stagnation	Middle adulthood	Parenting/ mentoring	Each adult must find some way to satisfy and support the next generation.
8. Ego integrity versus despair	Late adulthood	Reflection on and acceptance of one's life	The culmination is a sense of acceptance of oneself as one is and a sense of fulfillment.

Source: Adapted from Lefton, L. A. (1994). *Psychology* (5th ed.). Needham Heights, MA: Allyn & Bacon.

The Preschool Years: Trust, Autonomy, and Initiative. Erikson identifies *trust versus mistrust* as the basic conflict of infancy. According to Erikson, the infant will develop a sense of trust if its needs for food and care are met with comforting regularity and responsiveness from caregivers. In this first year, infants are in Piaget's sensorimotor stage and are just beginning to learn that they are separate from the world around them. This realization is part of what makes trust so important: infants must trust the aspects of their world that are beyond their control (Isabella & Belsky, 1991; Posada et al., 2002). Having a secure attachment (described earlier in this chapter) helps young children develop trust.

Erikson's second stage, *autonomy versus shame and doubt*, marks the beginning of self-control and self-confidence as young children begin to assume responsibilities for self-care such as feeding, going to the toilet, and dressing. During this period parents must tread a fine line; they must be protective—but not overprotective. If parents do not maintain a reassuring, confident attitude and do not reinforce the child's efforts to master basic motor and cognitive skills, children may begin to feel shame; they may learn to doubt their abilities to manage the world on their own terms. According to Erikson, children who experience too much doubt at this stage will lack confidence in their own powers throughout life.

For Erikson, the next stage of initiative *versus guilt* "... adds to autonomy the quality of undertaking, planning, and attacking a task for the sake of being active and on the move" (Erikson, 1963, p. 255). The challenge of this period is to maintain a zest for activity and at the same time understand that not every impulse can be acted on. Again, adults must tread a fine line, this time in providing supervision without interference. If children are not allowed to do things on their own, a sense of guilt may develop; they may come to believe that what they want to do is always "wrong." The *Guidelines* box suggests ways of encouraging initiative in your students.

Elementary and Middle School Years: Industry Versus Inferiority. Let's set the stage for the next phase. Between the ages of 5 and 7, when most children start school, cognitive development proceeds rapidly. Children can process more information faster and their memory spans increase. They are moving from preoperational to concrete operational thinking. As these internal changes progress, the children spend hours every weekday in the new physical and social world of school. They must now re-establish Erikson's stages of psychosocial development in the unfamiliar school

Initiative Willingness to begin new activities and explore new directions.

Autonomy Independence.

GUIDELINES: Encouraging Initiative in Preschool Children

Encourage children to make and to act on choices.

EXAMPLES

1. Have a free-choice time when children can select an activity or game.
2. Try to avoid interrupting children who are very involved in what they are doing.
3. When children suggest an activity, try to follow their suggestions or incorporate their ideas into ongoing activities.
4. Offer positive choices: instead of saying, "You can't have the cookies now," ask, "Would you like the cookies after lunch or after naptime?"

Make sure that each child has a chance to experience success.

EXAMPLES

1. When introducing a new game or skill, teach it in small steps.
2. Avoid competitive games that highlight differences in children's abilities.

Encourage make-believe with a wide variety of roles.

EXAMPLES

1. Have costumes and props that go along with stories the children enjoy. Encourage the children to act out the stories or make up new adventures for favourite characters.
2. Monitor the children's play to be sure no one monopolizes playing "teacher," "Mommy," "Daddy," or other heroes.

Be tolerant of accidents and mistakes, especially when children are attempting to do something on their own.

EXAMPLES

1. Use cups and pitchers that make it easy to pour and hard to spill.
2. Recognize the attempt, even if the result is unsatisfactory.
3. If mistakes are made, show children how to clean up, repair, or redo.
4. Most important, help children to view errors as opportunities to learn and let them know that everyone makes mistakes (even adults, even you).

For more ideas, see **www.vtaide.com/png/ERIK3.htm.**

setting. They must learn to *trust* new adults, to act *autonomously* in this more complex situation, and to *initiate* actions in ways that fit the new rules of school.

The new psychosocial challenge for the school years is what Erikson calls industry *versus inferiority*. In this stage, students are beginning to see the relationship between perseverance and the pleasure of a job completed. In modern societies, children's ability to move between the worlds of home, neighbourhood, and school and to cope with academics, group activities, and friends will lead to a growing sense of competence. Difficulty with these challenges can result in feelings of inferiority. Children must master new skills and work toward new goals while being compared with others and risking failure.

The skills and concepts children learn in preschool and the early grades are critical. They set students on pathways toward achievement or failure in the rest of their school years (Paris, Morrison, & Miller, 2006). In fact, Entwisle and Alexander (1998) claim, "How well students do in the primary grades matters more for their future success than does their school performance at any other time" (p. 354). Because schools tend to reflect middle-class values and norms, making the transition to school may be especially difficult for children who differ economically or culturally. The *Guidelines* box gives ideas for how to encourage industry in the classroom.

In the transition from elementary to middle school and then high school, students confront an increased focus on grades and performance as well as more competition on all fronts—academic, social, and athletic. Just when they are eager to make decisions and assume more independence, these developing minds encounter more rules, required courses, and assignments. Students change from having a close connection with one teacher all year to having more impersonal relations with many teachers in many different subjects across the year. They also go from being regarded as the most mature and highest status students in a small, familiar elementary school to being regarded as the "babies" in what may seem like a large, impersonal middle or high school (Meece, 2002; Murdock, Hale, & Weber, 2001; Rudolph, Lambert, Clark, & Kurlakowsky, 2001; Wigfield, Eccles, MacIver, Rueman, & Midgley, 1991). In the midst of this challenging context, students face the next hurdle—search for identity.

Adolescence: The Search for Identity. As students move into adolescence, they develop capabilities for abstract thinking and understanding the perspectives of others. Even greater physical changes are taking place as students approach puberty. So, with developing minds and bodies, young adolescents must confront the central issue of constructing an identity that will provide a firm basis for adulthood. Individuals begin developing a sense of self during infancy. But adolescence marks the first time that a conscious effort is made to answer the now-pressing question, "Who am I?" The conflict defining this stage is *identity versus role confusion*. Identity refers to the organization of the individual's drives, abilities, beliefs, and history into a consistent image of self. It involves deliberate choices and decisions, particularly about work, values, ideology, and commitments to people and ideas (Marcia, 1987; Penuel & Wertsch, 1995). If adolescents fail to integrate all these aspects and choices, or if they feel unable to choose at all, they may experience role confusion.

Industry Eagerness to engage in productive work.

Identity The complex answer to the question, "Who am I?"

GUIDELINES: Encouraging Industry

Make sure that students have opportunities to set and work toward realistic goals.

EXAMPLES

1. Begin with short assignments, then move on to longer ones. Monitor student progress by setting up progress checkpoints.
2. Teach students to set reasonable goals. Write down goals and have students keep a journal of their progress toward them.

Give students a chance to show their independence and responsibility.

EXAMPLES

1. Tolerate honest mistakes.
2. Delegate to students tasks such as watering class plants, collecting and distributing materials, monitoring the computer lab, grading homework, keeping records of forms returned, and so on.

Provide support to students who seem discouraged.

EXAMPLES

1. Use individual charts and contracts that show student progress.
2. Keep samples of earlier work so that students can see their improvements.
3. Provide awards for those who are most improved, most helpful, or most hard-working.

For more ideas, see **www.vtaide.com/png/ERIK4.htm.**

STOP & THINK Have you decided on your career? What alternatives did you consider? Who or what was influential in shaping your decision?

CONSTRUCTING AN IDENTITY With developing minds and bodies, young adolescents must confront the central issue of developing an identity that will provide a firm basis for adulthood. With adolescence comes the pressing question, "Who am I?"

James Marcia suggests that there are four identity alternatives for adolescents, depending on whether they have *explored* options and made *commitments* (Marcia, 1991, 1994, 1999). The first, identity diffusion, occurs when individuals do not explore any options or commit to any actions. They reach no conclusions about who they are or what they want to do with their lives; they have no firm direction. Adolescents experiencing identity diffusion may be apathetic and withdrawn, with little hope for the future, or they may be openly rebellious. These adolescents often go along with the crowd, so they are more likely to abuse drugs (Archer & Waterman, 1990; Berger & Thompson, 1995; Kroger, 2000).

Identity foreclosure is commitment without exploration. Foreclosed adolescents have not experimented with different identities or explored a range of options but simply committed themselves to the goals, values, and lifestyles of others, usually their parents but sometimes cults or extremist groups. Foreclosed adolescents tend to be rigid, intolerant, dogmatic, and defensive (Frank, Pirsch, & Wright, 1990).

Adolescents in the midst of struggling with choices experience what Erikson called a moratorium. Erikson used this term to describe exploration with a delay in commitment to personal and occupational choices. This delay is very common, and probably healthy, for modern adolescents. Erikson believed that adolescents in complex societies have an *identity crisis* during moratorium. Today, the period is no longer referred to as a crisis because, for most people, the experience is a gradual exploration rather than a traumatic upheaval (Grotevant, 1998; Wigfield et al., 2006).

Identity achievement means that after exploring the realistic options, the individual has made choices and is committed to pursuing them. It appears that few students achieve this status by the end of high school; students who attend university or college may take a bit longer to decide. Because so many people today go on to university or other continuing education after high school, it is not uncommon for the explorations of moratorium to continue into the early 20s. About 80 percent of students change their majors at least once. And some adults may achieve a firm identity at one period in their lives, only to reject that identity and achieve a new one later. So identity, once achieved, may not be unchanging for everyone (Kroger, 2000; Nurmi, 2004).

Both moratorium and identity-achieved statuses are considered healthy. Schools that give adolescents experiences with community service, real-world work, internships, and mentoring help to foster identity formation (Cooper, 1998). See the *Guidelines* box for other ideas about how to support identity formation in your students.

Identity diffusion Uncentredness; confusion about who one is and what one wants.

Identity foreclosure Commitment without exploration—committing to the goals, values, and lifestyles of others without exploring the range of possibilities for oneself.

Moratorium Identity crisis; suspension of choices because of struggle.

Identity achievement Strong sense of commitment to life choices after free consideration of alternatives.

Generativity Sense of concern for future generations.

Integrity Sense of self-acceptance and fulfillment.

Beyond the School Years. The crises of Erikson's stages of adulthood all involve the quality of human relations. *Intimacy versus isolation* refers to a willingness to relate to another person on a deep level, to have a relationship based on more than mutual need. Someone who has not achieved a sufficiently strong sense of identity tends to fear being overwhelmed or swallowed up by another person and may retreat into isolation. Generativity *versus stagnation* extends the ability to care for another person and involves concern and guidance for both the next generation and future generations. Productivity and creativity are essential features. Finally, achieving integrity *versus*

GUIDELINES: Supporting Identity Formation

Give students many models for career choices and other adult roles.

EXAMPLES

1. Point out models from literature and history. Have a calendar with the birthdays of eminent women, minority leaders, or people who made a little-known contribution to the subject you are teaching. Briefly discuss the person's accomplishments on her or his birthday.
2. Invite guest speakers to describe how and why they chose their professions. Make sure all kinds of work and workers are represented.

Help students find resources for working out personal problems.

EXAMPLES

1. Encourage students to talk to school counsellors.
2. Discuss potential services available outside the school setting.

Be tolerant of teenage fads as long as they don't offend others or interfere with learning.

EXAMPLES

1. Discuss the fads of earlier eras (e.g., neon hair, powdered wigs, love beads).
2. Don't impose strict dress or hair codes.

Give students realistic feedback about themselves.

EXAMPLES

1. When students misbehave or perform poorly, make sure they understand the consequences of their behaviour—the effects on themselves and others.
2. Give students model answers or show them other students' completed projects so that they can compare their work with good examples.
3. Since students are "trying on" roles, keep the roles separate from the person. You can criticize behaviour without criticizing the student.

despair means consolidating your sense of self and fully accepting its unique and now unalterable history. It involves coming to terms with death.

Erikson's work helped start the lifespan development approach, and his theories have been especially useful in understanding adolescence and developing concepts of self. But feminists have criticized his notion that identity precedes intimacy, because their research indicates that for women, identity achievement is fused with achieving intimacy (Miller, 2002). And, as you will see next, recent research has focused on identity issues not fully explored by Erikson—ethnic and racial identity.

Ethnic and Racial Identity

Because ethnic minority students are members of both majority and minority group cultures, it is complicated for them to establish a clear identity. Values, learning styles, and communication patterns of the students' ethnic culture may be inconsistent with the expectations of the school and the larger society. Embracing the values of mainstream culture may seem to require rejecting ethnic values. Ethnic minority students have to "sift through two sets of cultural values and identity options" to achieve a firm identity, so they may need more time to explore possibilities—a longer *moratorium* in Erikson's terms (Markstrom-Adams, 1992, p. 177). But the exploration is important; some psychologists consider ethnic identity a "master status," one that dominates all other identity concerns when judging the self (Herman, 2004).

KNOWING YOURSELF When majority adolescents are knowledgeable and secure about their own heritage, they are also more respectful of the heritage of others.

Ethnic Identities: Outcome and Process. Jean Phinney (1990, 2003) describes four outcomes for ethnic minority youth in their search for identity. They can try *assimilation*, fully adopting the values and behaviours of the majority culture and rejecting their ethnic culture. At the opposite end, they can be *separated*, associating only with members of their ethnic culture. A third possibility is *marginality*, living in the majority culture, but feeling alienated and uncomfortable in it and disconnected from the minority culture as well. The final alternative is *biculturalism* (sometimes called integration), maintaining ties to both cultures. And there are at least three ways to be bicultural. Minority youth can alternate between the two cultures, being fully "majority" in their behaviour in one situation and fully "minority" in other situation. Or they can blend the two cultures by finding values and behaviours that are common to both and acting on them. Finally, minority youth can fuse the two cultures by truly merging them into a new and complete whole (Phinney & Devich-Nevarro, 1997). No matter what your identity outcome is, an important factor for good mental health seems to be having strong positive feelings about your own ethnic group (Steinberg, 2005).

Some psychologists have used James Marcia's identity statuses to understand the process of forming an ethnic identity. Children may begin with an *unexamined ethnic identity*, either because they have not explored at all (diffusion) or because they have accepted the identity encouraged by others (foreclosure). Many European American adolescents could fit the unexamined category. A period of *ethnic identity exploration* (moratorium) might be followed by a *resolution* of the conflict (identity achieved).

Racial and Ethnic Pride. For all students, pride in family and community is part of the foundation for a stable identity. Special efforts to encourage **racial and ethnic pride** are particularly important, so that students examining their identities do not get the message that differences are deficits (Spencer & Markstrom-Adams, 1990). Jim Cummins (1989), at the University of Toronto, encourages schools to make special efforts to foster ethnic pride. For example, he suggests schools display bilingual and multilingual signs, provide opportunities for students to use their first languages, and arrange for parents and community members who represent ethnic minorities to be involved in school events.

Each of us has an ethnic heritage. Janet Helms (1995) has written about stages in white identity development. Richard Milner (2003) has pointed to the importance of racial identity development and awareness, especially in teaching. When majority adolescents are knowledgeable and secure about their own heritage, they are also more respectful of the heritage of others. Thus, exploring the racial and ethnic roots of all students should foster both pride in self and acceptance of others (Rotherham-Borus, 1994).

In the next sections we move from overarching considerations of identity to the more specific conception of self. In 1970, about 1 in every 20 publications in psychology was related to the self. By 2000, the ratio was 1 in every 7 (Tesser, Stapel, & Wood, 2002). In educational psychology, much research is focused on self-concept and self-esteem.

Self-Concept

The term *self-concept* is part of our everyday conversation. We talk about people who have a "low" self-concept or individuals whose self-concept is not "strong," as if the notion of self-concept were like fluid levels in a car or a muscle to be developed. These are actually misuses of the term. In psychology, **self-concept** generally refers to individuals' knowledge and beliefs about themselves—their ideas, feelings, attitudes, and expectations (Pajares & Schunk, 2001). We could consider self-concept to be our attempt to explain ourselves to ourselves, to build a scheme (in Piaget's terms) that organizes our impressions, feelings, and attitudes about ourselves. But this model or scheme is not permanent, unified, or unchanging. Our perceptions of ourselves vary from situation to situation and from one phase of our lives to another.

The Structure of Self-Concept. A student's overall self-concept is made up of other, more specific concepts, including academic and non-academic self-concepts. Herbert Marsh and his colleagues (2006) have identified up to 17 different self-concepts in non-academic areas (e g., physical appearance, popularity, trustworthiness, relations with parents, emotional stability) and academic areas (verbal, mathematics, problem solving, art, computers). For older adolescents and adults, the separate, specific self-concepts are not necessarily integrated into an overall self-concept, so self-concept is more situation-specific in adults (Marsh & Ayotte, 2003; Schunk, Pintrich, & Meece, 2008).

Racial and ethnic pride A positive self-concept about one's racial or ethnic heritage.

Self-concept Individuals' knowledge and beliefs about themselves—their ideas, feelings, attitudes, and expectations.

How Self-Concept Develops. The self-concept evolves through constant self-evaluation in different situations. Children and adolescents are continually asking themselves, in effect, "How am I doing?" They gauge the verbal and non-verbal reactions of significant people—parents and other family members in the early years and friends, schoolmates, and teachers later—to make judgments (Harter, 1998).

Younger children tend to have positive and optimistic views of themselves. In one study, over 80 percent of grade 1 students surveyed thought they were the best students in class (Stipek, 1981). With more experience in school, children make self-concept appraisals based on their own improvement. For example, researchers in New Zealand followed 60 students from the time they started school until the middle of their third year (Chapman, Tunmer, & Prochnow, 2000). In the first two months of school, differences in reading self-concept began to develop, based on the ease or difficulty students had learning to read. Students who entered school with good knowledge about sounds and letters learned to read more easily and developed more positive reading self-concepts. Over time, differences in the reading performance of students with high and low reading self-concepts grew even greater. Thus, the early experiences with the important school task of reading had strong impact on reading self-concept.

CHOICES SHAPE FUTURES The courses selected in high school put students on a path toward the future, so self-concepts about particular academic subjects can be life-changing influences.

During the middle school years, students become more self-conscious. At this age, self-concepts are tied to physical appearance and social acceptance as well as to school achievement (Shapka & Keating, 2005), so these years can be exceedingly difficult for students such as Stephanie, described at the opening of this chapter (Wigfield, Eccles, & Pintrich, 1996). In academics, students compare their performance with their own standards—their performance in math with their performance in English and science, for example—to form self-concepts in these areas. But social comparisons are becoming more influential, too, at least in Western cultures. Students' self-concepts in math are shaped by how their performance compares with that of other students in their math classes and even by comments their classmates make about them (Altermatt, Pomerantz, Ruble, Frey, & Greulich, 2002; Schunk et al., 2008). Students who are strong in math in an average school feel better about their math skills than do students of equal ability in high-achieving schools. Marsh (1990) calls this the "Big-Fish-Little-Pond" effect (BFLP). Research that surveyed over 100 000 15-year-olds around the world found the BFLP effect in every one of the 26 participating countries (Marsh & Hau, 2003). Participation in a program for gifted and talented students seems to have an opposite "Little-Fish-Big-Pond" effect: Students who participate in gifted programs, compared with similar students who remain in regular classes, tend to show *declines* in academic self-concepts over time, but no changes in non-academic self-concepts (Marsh & Craven, 2002).

Self-Concept and Achievement. Many psychologists consider self-concept to be the foundation of both social and emotional development. Research has linked self-concept to a wide range of accomplishments—from performance in competitive sports to job satisfaction and achievement in school (Byrne, 2002; Davis-Kean & Sandler, 2001; Marsh & Hau, 2003; Shapka & Keating, 2003). Some evidence for the link between self-concept and school achievement is that performance in academic subjects is correlated with specific self-concepts in those areas, but not with social or physical self-concepts. For example, in one study, math self-concept correlated .77 with math test scores, .59 with grades, and .51 with coursework selection (Marsh et al., 2006; O'Mara, Marsh, Craven, & Debus, 2006).

That last correlation of math self-concept with course selection points to an important way that self-concept affects learning in school. Think back to high school. When you had a chance to choose courses, did you pick your worst subjects—those where you felt least capable? Probably not. Herbert Marsh and Alexander Yeung (1997) examined how 246 boys in early high school in Sydney, Australia, chose their courses. Academic self-concept for a particular subject (mathematics, science, etc.) was the most important predictor of course selection—more important than previous grades in the subject or overall self-concept. In fact, having a positive self-concept in a particular subject was an even bigger factor in selecting courses when self-concept in other subjects was low. The courses selected in high school put students on a path toward the future, so self-concepts about particular academic subjects can be life-changing influences. Canadian researcher Jennifer Shapka also has found that self-concept is one of the biggest predictors of post-secondary enrolment, particularly in the area of math and science (Shapka & Keating, 2003).

MyEducationLab
Go to the Podcasts section of Chapter 3 in MyEducation Lab and listen to PODCAST—Self-Concepts in Learning and Teaching. What is the difference between self-concept and self-esteem? Should teachers focus on building self-esteem? Is there a better approach to helping students build a positive sense of self? Listen to Anita Woolfolk describe the findings on self-concept, self-esteem, and self-efficacy and explain the differences among these important concepts in educational psychology.

Self-Esteem

STOP & THINK How strongly do you agree or disagree with these statements?

On the whole, I am satisfied with myself.
I feel that I have a number of good qualities.
I wish I could have more respect for myself.
At times, I think that I am no good at all.
I certainly feel useless at times.
I take a positive attitude toward myself.

These *Stop & Think* questions are taken from a widely used measure of self-esteem (Rosenberg, 1979; Hagborg, 1993). Self-esteem is an affective reaction—an overall judgment of self-worth that includes feeling confident and proud of yourself as a person. If people judge themselves positively—if they "like what they see"—we say that they have high self-esteem (Schunk et al., 2008). Can you see the judgments of self-worth in the *Stop & Think* questions?

Self-concept and *self-esteem* are often used interchangeably, even though they have distinct meanings. Self-concept is a cognitive structure—a belief about who you are. Self-esteem is an overall, general feeling of self-worth that incorporates your self-concepts in all areas of your life, so it is the "summary judgment" about your worth as a person (O'Mara et al., 2006). You can see in the *Stop & Think* items above that the questions are pretty general; no specific areas such as academics or appearance are targeted. Self-esteem is influenced by whether the culture around you values your particular characteristics and capabilities (Bandura, 1997; Schunk et al., 2008). So, although some writers use self-concept and self-esteem interchangeably, a conceptual difference between these terms exists—thinking versus feeling about yourself.

For teachers, there are at least two questions to ask about self-esteem: (1) How does self-esteem affect a student's behaviour in school? (2) How does life in school affect a student's self-esteem? In answer to the first question, in longitudinal studies, more positive beliefs about one's self are related to higher academic achievement, especially when the beliefs are specific to the subject studied. But the sizes of the relationships generally are small (Valentine, DuBois, & Cooper, 2004). Of course, as we discussed in Chapter 1, knowing that two variables are related (correlated) does not tell us that one is causing the other. It may be that high achievement and popularity lead to self-esteem, or vice versa. In fact, it probably works both ways (Guay, Larose, & Boivin, 2004; Marsh & Ayotte, 2003; Schunk et al., 2008).

What about the second question of how school affects self-esteem—is school important? As you can see from the *Point/Counterpoint* box, the school's role in student self-esteem has been hotly debated. A study that followed 322 grade 6 students for two years would say yes, school is important. Hoge, Smit, and Hanson (1990) found that students' satisfaction with the school, their sense that classes were interesting and that teachers cared, and teacher feedback and evaluations all influenced students' self-esteem. In physical education, teachers' opinions were especially powerful in shaping students' conceptions of their athletic abilities. Being placed in a low-ability group or being held back in school seems to have a negative impact on students' self-esteem, but learning in collaborative and cooperative settings seems to have a positive effect (Covington, 1992; Deci & Ryan, 1985). Interestingly, special programs such as "student of the month" or admission to advanced math classes had little effect on self-esteem. (Relate this to the BFLP effect.)

More than 100 years ago, William James (1890) suggested that self-esteem is determined by how *successful* we are in accomplishing tasks or reaching goals we *value*. If a skill or accomplishment is not important, incompetence in that area doesn't threaten self-esteem. Susan Harter (1990) has found evidence that James was right. Children who believe an activity is important and who feel capable in that area have higher self-esteem than students who think the activity is important but question their competence. Students must have legitimate success with tasks that matter to them. The way individuals explain their successes or failures is also important. Students must attribute their successes to their own actions, not to luck or to special assistance, in order to build self-esteem.

Self-esteem The value each of us places on our own characteristics, abilities, and behaviours.

POINT / COUNTERPOINT

What Should Schools Do to Encourage Students' Self-Esteem?

MORE THAN 2000 BOOKS about how to increase self-esteem have been published. Schools and mental-health facilities continue to develop self-esteem programs (Slater, 2002). The attempts to improve students' self-esteem have taken three main forms: personal development activities such as sensitivity training; self-esteem programs where the curriculum focuses directly on improving self-esteem; and structural changes in schools that place greater emphasis on cooperation, student participation, community involvement, and ethnic pride.

POINT

The self-esteem movement has problems.

Many of the self-esteem courses are commercial packages—costly for schools but without solid evidence that they make a difference for students (Crisci, 1986; Leming, 1981). Some people have accused schools of developing programs where the main objective is "to dole out a huge heaping of praise, regardless of actual accomplishments" (Slater, 2002, p. 45). But Erik Erikson (1980) warned years ago: "Children cannot be fooled by empty praise and condescending encouragement. They may have to accept artificial bolstering of their self-esteem in lieu of something better. . . ." Erikson went on to explain that a strong and positive identity comes only from "wholehearted and consistent recognition of real accomplishment, that is, achievement that has meaning in their culture" (p. 95).

Frank Pajares and Dale Schunk (2002) point to another problem. "[W]hen what is communicated to children from an early age is that nothing matters quite as much as how they feel or how confident they should be, one can rest assured that the world will sooner or later teach a lesson in humility that may not easily be learned. An obsession with one's sense of self is responsible for an alarming increase in depression and other mental difficulties" (p. 16). Another problem was revealed in a large study of adolescents, where global self-esteem did not correlate with any of the nine academic outcomes measured (Marsh et al., 2006).

Sensitivity training and self-esteem courses assume that we encourage self-esteem by changing the individual's beliefs, making the young person work harder against the odds. But what if the student's environment is truly unsafe, debilitating, and unsupportive? Some people have overcome tremendous problems, but to expect everyone to do so "ignores the fact that having positive self-esteem is almost impossible for many young people, given the deplorable conditions under which they are forced to live by the inequities in our society" (Beane, 1991, p. 27). Worse yet, some psychologists are now contending that low self-esteem is not a problem, whereas high self-esteem may be. For example, they contend, people with high self-esteem are more willing to inflict pain and punishment on others (Baumeister, Campbell, Krueger, & Vohs, 2003; Slater, 2002). And when people set self-esteem as a main goal, they may pursue that goal in ways that are harmful over the long run. They may, for example, avoid constructive criticisms or challenging tasks (Crocker & Park, 2004).

COUNTERPOINT

The self-esteem movement has promise.

Beyond the "feel-good psychology" of some aspects of the self-esteem movement is a basic truth: "Self-esteem is a central feature of human dignity and thus an inalienable human entitlement. As such, schools and other agencies have a moral obligation to help build it and avoid debilitating it" (Beane, 1991, p. 28). If we view self-esteem accurately as a product of our thinking and our actions—our values, ideas, and beliefs as well as our interactions with others—then we see a significant role for the school. Practices that allow authentic participation, cooperation, problem solving, and accomplishment should replace policies that damage self-esteem, such as tracking and competitive grading.

In her article "The Trouble with Self-Esteem," psychologist Lauren Slater (2002) suggests we rethink self-esteem and move toward honest self-appraisal that will lead to self-control:

> *Maybe self-control should replace self-esteem as a primary peg to reach for. Ultimately, self-control need not be experienced as a constriction; restored to its original meaning, it might be experienced as the kind of practiced prowess an athlete or artist demonstrates, muscles not tamed but trained, so that the leaps are powerful, the spine supple and the energy harnessed and shaped. (p. 47)*

One possibility is to refocus on more specific self-concepts, because self-concepts in specific areas such as math are related to learning in math (O'Mara et al., 2006). Because self-concept and achievement probably affect each other, Marsh et al. concluded:

> *In summary, whereas the optimal way to improve self-concept over the short-term is to focus interventions directly on self-concept enhancement, interventions that combine direct self-concept enhancement in concert with performance enhancement, coupled with appropriate feedback and praise, are likely to be advantageous when the goals of the intervention are to improve both self-concept and performance. (Marsh et al., 2006, p. 198)*

Source: From "The Trouble with Self-Esteem," by L. Slater, *The New York Times Magazine,* February 3, 2002, pp. 44–47 and "Sorting Out the Self-Esteem Controversy," by J. A. Beane, 1991, *Educational Leadership, 49*(1), pp. 25–30. © 1991 by ASCD. Used with permission. Learn more about ASCD at www.ascd.org

Sex Differences in Self-Concept and Self-Esteem

Do girls and boys differ in their self-concepts? A recent study followed 761 middle-class, primarily European American students from grade 1 through high school (Jacobs, Lanza, Osgood, Eccles, & Wigfield, 2002). It is difficult to obtain longitudinal data on the subject of sex differences in self-concept and self-esteem, so this is a valuable study. In grade 1, girls and boys had comparable perceptions of their own abilities in language arts, but boys felt significantly more competent in math and sports. As you can see in Figure 3.4, competence beliefs declined for both boys and girls across the grades, but boys fell faster in math so that by high school, math competence beliefs were about the same for boys and girls. In language arts, boys' competence ratings fell more sharply than those of girls after grade 1, but both levelled off during high school. In sports, competence ratings for both boys and girls dropped, but boys remained significantly more confident in their competence in sports throughout the entire 12 years.

Other studies have also found that girls tend to see themselves as more able than boys in reading and developing close friendships, and that boys are more confident about their abilities in math and athletics. Of course, some of these differences in self-confidence may reflect actual differences in achievement—girls tend to be better readers than boys, for example. It is likely that confidence and achievement are reciprocally related—each affects the other (Cole, Martin, Peeke, Seroczynski,

FIGURE 3.4 **Gender Differences in Changes in Self-Competence Beliefs Over the School Years**

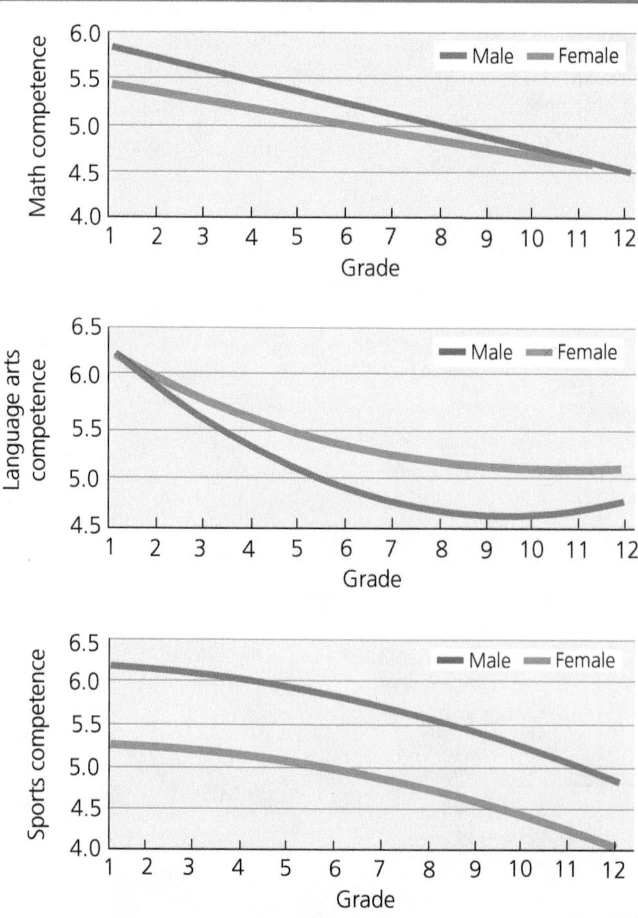

Source: Jacobs, J. E., Lanza, S., Osgood, D. W., Eccles, J. S., & Wigfield, A. (2002). Changes in children's self-competence and values: Gender and domain differences across grades 1 through 12. *Child Development, 73,* 516. Copyright © 2002 by the Society for Research in Child Development, University of Michigan Center for Growth & Human Development. Reprinted with permission of the SRCD.

& Fier, 1999; Eccles, Wigfield, & Schiefele, 1998; Shapka & Keating, 2005). For most ethnic groups (except African Americans), males are more confident about their abilities in math and science. Differences between males and females are generally small, but consistent across studies (Kling, Hyde, Showers, & Buswell, 1999; Shapka & Keating, 2003). Unfortunately, there are no long-term studies of other ethnic groups, so these patterns may be limited to European North Americans.

How do students feel about themselves in general during the school years? Jean Twenge and Keith Campbell (2001) analyzed over 150 samples of students from studies conducted between 1968 and 1994, looking at general self-esteem, not subject-specific competence. They found that self-esteem decreased slightly for both girls and boys in the transition to junior high. Then boys' general self-esteem increased dramatically during high school, while girls' self-esteem stayed about the same, leaving girls with significantly lower general self-esteem than boys by the end of high school. When these results are examined together with the findings by Jacobs et al. above that boys and girls differ in their academic self-concepts in various subjects and Marsh and Yeung's (1997) results that academic self-concept influences course selection, it seems that many students make decisions about courses that forever limit their future options.

Teachers' feedback, grading practices, evaluations, and communication of caring for students can make a difference in how students feel about their abilities in particular subjects. But the greatest increases in self-esteem come when students grow more competent in areas they value—including the social areas that become so important in adolescence. *Thus, a teacher's greatest challenge is to help students achieve important understandings and skills.*

One big factor that influences personal and social development is gender. We turn to that topic now.

GENDER DEVELOPMENT

In this section, we examine the development of two related identities—sexual identity and gender-role identity. We particularly focus on how men and women are socialized and the role of teachers in providing an equitable education for both sexes.

Sex and Gender

The word *gender* usually refers to traits and behaviours that a particular culture judges to be appropriate for men and for women. In contrast, *sex* refers to biological differences (Brannon, 2002; Deaux, 1993). An individual's identity in terms of gender and sex has three components: gender identity, sexual orientation, and gender-role behaviours (Berger, 2006; Patterson, 1995). **Gender identity** is a person's self-identification as male or female. *Gender-role behaviours* are those behaviours and characteristics that the culture associates with each gender, and **sexual orientation** involves the person's choice of a sexual partner.

Relations among these three elements are complex. For example, a woman may identify herself as a female (gender identity), but behave in ways that are not consistent with the gender role (play football), and may be heterosexual, bisexual, or homosexual in her sexual orientation. So sexual identity is a complicated construction of beliefs, attitudes, and behaviours. Erikson and many other earlier psychologists thought that identifying your gender identity was straightforward; you simply realized that you were male or female and acted accordingly. But today, we know that some people experience conflicts about their gender. For example, transsexuals often report feeling trapped in the wrong body; they experience themselves as female, but their biological sex is male or vice versa (Berger, 2006; Yarhouse, 2001).

Sexual Orientation. During adolescence, about 8 percent of boys and 6 percent of girls report engaging in some same-sex activity or feeling strong attractions to same-sex individuals. Males are more likely than females to experiment with same-sex partners as adolescents, but females are more likely to experiment later, often in college or university. Fewer adolescents actually have a homosexual or bisexual orientation—about 4 percent of adolescents identify themselves as gay (males who chose male partners), lesbian (females who chose female partners), or bisexual (people who have partners of both sexes). This number increases to about 8 percent for adults (Savin-Williams & Diamond, 2004; Steinberg, 2005).

Gender identity A person's self-identification as male or female.

Sexual orientation A complex combination of beliefs and orientations about gender roles and sexual orientation.

Scientists debate the origins of homosexuality. Most of the research has been with men, so less is known about women. Evidence so far suggests that both biological and social factors are involved. For example, sexual orientation is more similar for identical twins than for fraternal twins, but not all identical twins have the same sexual orientation (Berger, 2006). There are quite a few models describing the development of sexual orientation. Most focus on how adolescents develop an identity as gay, lesbian, or bisexual. Generally, the models include the following or similar stages (Yarhouse, 2001):

- *Feeling different*—Beginning around age 6, the child may be less interested in the activities of other children who are the same sex. Some children may find this difference troubling and fear being "found out." Others do not experience these anxieties.
- *Feeling confused*—In adolescence, as they feel attractions for the same sex, students may be confused, upset, lonely, and unsure of what to do. They may lack role models and try to change to activities and dating patterns that fit heterosexual stereotypes.
- *Acceptance*—As young adults, many of these youth sort through sexual orientation issues and identify themselves as gay, lesbian, or bisexual. They may or may not make their sexual orientation public, but might share the information with a few friends.

The problem with phase models of identity development is that the identity achieved is assumed to be final. Actually, newer models emphasize that sexual orientation can be flexible, complex, and multi-faceted; it can change over the lifetime. For example, people may have dated or married opposite-sex partners at one point in their lives, but have same-sex attractions or partners later in their lives, or vice versa (Garnets, 2002).

Parents and teachers are seldom the first people to hear about the adolescent's sexual identity concerns. But if a student does seek your counsel, Table 3.5 has some ideas for how to reach out to him or her.

TABLE 3.5

Reaching Out to Help Students Struggling With Sexual Identity

These ideas come from the *Attic Speakers Bureau*, a program of The Attic Youth Center, where trained peer educators reach out to youth and youth-service providers in schools, organizations, and health care facilities.

Reaching Out

If a lesbian, gay, bisexual, or transgender youth or a youth questioning his or her own sexual orientation should come to you directly for assistance, remember the following simple, five-point plan:

LISTEN. It seems obvious, but the best thing that you can do in the beginning is allow that individual to vent and express what is going on in his or her life.

AFFIRM. Tell them, "You are not alone." This is crucial. A lot of l/g/b/t/q youth feel isolated and lack peers with whom they can discuss issues around sexual orientation. Letting them know that there are others dealing with the same issues is invaluable. This statement is also important because it does not involve a judgment call on your part.

REFER. You do not have to be the expert. A referral to someone who is trained to deal with these issues is a gift you are giving to that student, not a dismissal of responsibility.

ADDRESS. Deal with harassers—do not overlook issues of verbal or physical harassment around sexual orientation. It is important to create and maintain an environment where all youth feel comfortable and welcome.

FOLLOW-UP. Be sure to check in with the individual to see if the situation has improved and if there is anything further you may be able to do.

There are also some things that you as an individual can do to better serve l/g/b/t/q youth and youth dealing with issues around sexual orientation:

- Work on your own sense of comfort around issues of sexual orientation and sexuality.
- Get training on how to present information on sexual orientation effectively.
- Dispel myths around sexual orientation by knowing facts and sharing that information.
- Work on setting aside your own personal biases to better serve students dealing with issues around sexual orientation and sexuality.

Source: From Figure 3.

Gender Roles

Gender roles are expectations about how males and females should behave—about what is masculine and what is feminine. Gender roles vary by culture, time, and place. What was expected of women definitely has changed since the 1700s in much of the Western world, even though women generally still are the primary caregivers and in charge of the home.

When and how do children develop gender roles? As early as age 2, children are aware of gender differences—they know whether they are girls or boys and that mommies are girls and daddies are boys. By age 3 or so they realize that their sex cannot be changed; they will always be male or female. Biology plays a role in gender role development. Very early, hormones affect activity level and aggression, with boys tending to prefer active, rough, noisy play. Play styles lead young children to prefer same-sex play partners with similar styles, so by age 4, children spend three times as much play time with same-sex playmates as with opposite-sex playmates; by age 6, the ratio is 11 to 1 (Benenson, 1993; Hines, 2004; Maccoby, 1998).

But biology is not the whole story; boys and girls may be treated differently too. Researchers have found that boys are given more freedom to roam the neighbourhood and are allowed to tackle potentially dangerous activities earlier, such as crossing the street alone. Thus, independence and initiative seem to be encouraged more in boys than in girls. In fact, parents, peers, and teachers may reward behaviours that seem gender appropriate—gentle kindness in girls and strong assertiveness in boys (Brannon, 2002).

And then there are the toys! Walk through any store's toy section and see what is offered to girls and boys. Dolls and kitchen sets for girls and toy weapons for boys have been with us for decades, but what about even more subtle messages? Margot Mifflin went shopping for a toy for her 4-year-old that was not gender-typed and found a Wee Waffle farm set. Then she discovered that "the farmer plugged into a round hole in the driver's seat of the tractor, but the mother—literally a square peg in a round hole—didn't" (Mifflin, 1999, p. 1). But we cannot blame the toy makers alone. Adults buying for children favour gender-typed toys and fathers tend to discourage young sons from playing with "girls'" toys (Brannon, 2002).

Through their interactions with family, peers, teachers, toys, and the environment in general, children begin to form gender schemas, or organized networks of knowledge about what it means to be male or female. Gender schemas help children make sense of the world and guide their behaviour (see Figure 3.5). So a young girl whose schema for "girls" includes "girls play with dolls and not with trucks" or "girls can't be scientists" will pay attention to, remember, and interact more with dolls than trucks, and she may avoid science activities (Berk, 2005; Leaper, 2002; Liben & Signorella, 1993). Of course, these are averages and individuals do not always fit the average. In addition, many other factors—social and cognitive—affect gender role behaviours.

By age 4, children have a beginning sense of gender roles and by around age 5, they have developed a gender schema that describes what clothes, games, toys, behaviours, and careers are

FIGURE 3.5 **Gender Schema Theory**

According to gender schema theory, children and adolescents use gender as an organizing theme to classify and understand their perceptions about the world.

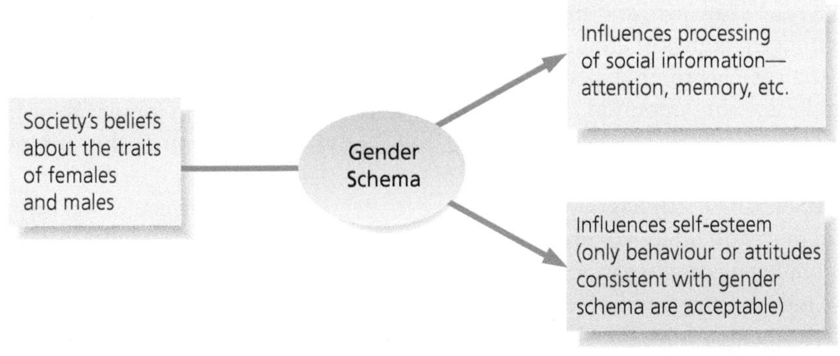

Gender schemas Organized networks of knowledge about what it means to be male or female.

"right" for boys and girls—and these ideas can be quite rigid (Brannon, 2002). Even in this era of great progress toward equal opportunity, a preschool girl is more likely to tell you she wants to become a nurse than to say she wants to be an engineer. After she had given a lecture on the dangers of sex stereotyping in schools, a colleague of Anita's brought her young daughter to her college class. The students asked the little girl, "What do you want to be when you grow up?" The child immediately replied, "A doctor," and her professor/mother beamed with pride. Then the girl whispered to the students in the front row, "I really want to be a nurse, but my Mommy won't let me." Actually, this is a common reaction for young children. Preschoolers tend to have more stereotyped notions of sex roles than older children, and all ages seem to have more rigid and traditional ideas about male occupations than about what females do (Berger, 2006). Later, as adolescents go through puberty, they may become even more focused on behaving in "masculine" or "feminine" ways, as defined by their peer culture. So many factors from biology to cultural norms play a role in gender role development. Beware of either/or explanations.

UNDERSTANDING OTHERS AND MORAL DEVELOPMENT

As we seek our own identity and form images of ourselves, we are also seeking and forming ways to understand the "significant others" around us—this is one aspect of moral development. How do we learn to interpret what others are thinking and feeling?

Theory of Mind and Intention

By age 2 or 3, children begin to develop a theory of mind, an understanding that other people are people too, with their own minds, thoughts, feelings, beliefs, desires, and perceptions (Flavell, Miller, & Miller, 2002). Children need a theory of mind to make sense of other people's behaviour. Why is Sarah crying? Does she feel sad because no one will play with her? You will see in Chapter 4 that one explanation for autism is that children with this condition lack a theory of mind to help them understand their own or other people's emotions and behaviours.

Around the age of 2, children have a sense of intention, at least of their own intentions. They will announce, "I wanna peanut butter sandwich." They can say firmly, "I didn't break it on purpose!" By two and a half or three years of age, children extend the understanding of intention to others. Older preschoolers who get along well with their peers are able to separate intentional from unintentional actions and react accordingly. For example, they will not get angry when other children accidentally knock over their block towers.

With a developing theory of mind, children are increasingly able to understand that other people have different feelings and experiences, and therefore may have a different viewpoint or perspective. This perspective-taking ability develops over time until it is quite sophisticated in adults. Being able to understand how others might think and feel is important in fostering cooperation and moral development, reducing prejudice, resolving conflicts, and encouraging positive social behaviours in general (Gehlbach, 2004). Marion Porath (2001, 2003), at the University of British Columbia, has conducted research about young children's social understanding. Her findings indicate that preschool girls engage in more sophisticated reasoning about social situations than do boys the same age, and they are better able to interpret subtle social cues. Also, she finds children's understandings of others' intentions to be a statistically significant predictor of children's ability to analyze classroom experiences. Other research indicates that aggressive children have more trouble assessing intention. They are likely to attack anyone who topples their towers, even accidentally (Berk, 2002; Dodge & Somberg, 1987). As children mature, they are more able to assess and consider the intentions of others.

Robert Selman (1980) has developed a stage model to describe perspective-taking. As children mature and move toward formal operational thinking, they take more information into account and realize that different people can react differently to the same situation. At some point between the ages of 10 and 15, most children develop the ability to analyze the perspectives of several people involved in a situation from the viewpoint of an objective bystander. Finally, older adolescents and adults can even imagine how different cultural or social values would influence the perceptions of

Theory of mind An understanding that other people are people too, with their own minds, thoughts, feelings, beliefs, desires, and perceptions.

Perspective-taking ability Understanding that others have different feelings and experiences.

the bystander. Even though children move through these stages, there can be great variation among children of the same age. Students who have difficulty taking the perspective of others may feel little remorse when they mistreat peers or adults. Some coaching in perspective-taking from the teacher might help if the mistreatment is not part of a deeper emotional or behavioural disorder (Berk, 2005).

Moral Development

Along with a more advanced theory of mind and an understanding of intention, children also develop a sense of right and wrong. In this section we focus on children's moral reasoning, their *thinking* about right and wrong and their *active construction* of moral judgments. Some of the earliest moral issues in classrooms involve dividing and sharing materials or distributive justice (Damon, 1994). For young children (ages 5 to 6), fair distribution is based on *equality;* thus, teachers often hear, "Tristan got more than I did—that's not fair!" In the next few years, children come to recognize that some people should get more based on *merit*—they worked harder or performed better. Finally, around age 8, children are able to take need into account and to reason based on *benevolence;* they can understand that some students may get more time or resources from the teacher because those students have special needs.

MyEducationLab Go to the Activities and Applications sections in Chapter 3 of MyEducationLab and complete Activity 2, an exercise asking you to create developmental profiles for different age groups.

Another area that involves moral development is an understanding of rules. If you have spent time with young children, you know that there is a period when you can say, "Eating in the living room is not allowed!" and get away with it. For young children, rules simply exist. Piaget (1965) called this the state of moral realism. At this stage, the child of 5 or 6 believes that rules about conduct or rules about how to play a game are absolute and can't be changed. If a rule is broken, the child believes that the punishment should be determined by how much damage is done, not by the intention of the child or by other circumstances. So, accidentally breaking three cups is worse than intentionally breaking one, and in the child's eyes, the punishment for the three-cup offence should be greater.

As children interact with others and see that different people have different rules, there is a gradual shift to a morality of cooperation. Children come to understand that people make rules and people can change them. When rules are broken, both the damage done and the intention of the offender are taken into account.

Kohlberg's Theories of Moral Development. Lawrence Kohlberg's (1963, 1975, 1981) theory of moral development is based in part on Piaget's ideas, described earlier.

STOP & THINK A man's wife is dying. There is one drug that could save her, but it is very expensive, and the druggist who invented it will not sell it at a price low enough for the man to buy it. Finally, the man becomes desperate and considers stealing the drug for his wife. What should he do, and why?

Kohlberg has evaluated the moral reasoning of both children and adults by presenting them with moral dilemmas, or hypothetical situations in which people must make difficult decisions and justify them. Based on the individual's reasoning, Kohlberg proposed a detailed sequence of stages of moral reasoning, or judgments about right and wrong. He divided moral development into three levels: (1) preconventional, where judgment is based solely on a person's own needs and perceptions; (2) conventional, where the expectations of society and law are taken into account; and (3) postconventional, where judgments are based on abstract, more personal principles of justice that are not necessarily defined by society's laws. Look at Table 3.6 to see how each of these three levels is then subdivided into stages. Can you find your reasons for your answer to the *Stop & Think* question above in Table 3.6?

Moral reasoning is related to both cognitive and emotional development. As we have seen, abstract thinking becomes increasingly important in the higher stages of moral development, as children move from decisions based on absolute rules to decisions based on abstract principles such as justice and mercy. The ability to see another's perspective, to judge intentions, and to use formal operational thinking to imagine alternative bases for laws and rules also enters into judgments at the higher stages.

Moral reasoning The thinking process involved in judgments about questions of right and wrong.

Distributive justice Beliefs about how to divide materials or privileges fairly among members of a group; follows a sequence of development from equality to merit to benevolence.

Moral realism Stage of development wherein children see rules as absolute.

Morality of cooperation Stage of development wherein children realize that people make rules and people can change them.

Moral dilemmas Situations in which no choice is clearly and indisputably right

TABLE 3.6 Kohlberg's Stage Theory of Moral Reasoning

Level 1. Preconventional Moral Reasoning	
Judgment is based on personal needs and others' rules.	
Stage 1	Punishment–Obedience Orientation Rules are obeyed to avoid punishment. A good or bad action is determined by its physical consequences.
Stage 2	Personal Reward Orientation Personal needs determine right and wrong. Favours are returned along the lines of "you scratch my back; I'll scratch yours."
Level 2. Conventional Moral Reasoning	
Judgment is based on others' approval, family expectations, traditional values, the laws of society, and loyalty to country.	
Stage 3	Good Boy–Nice Girl Orientation Good means "nice." It is determined by what pleases, aids, and is approved by others.
Stage 4	Law and Order Orientation Laws are absolute. Authority must be respected and the social order maintained.
Level 3. Postconventional Moral Reasoning	
Stage 5	Social Contract Orientation Good is determined by socially agreed-upon standards of individual rights.
Stage 6*	Universal Ethical Principle Orientation Good and right are matters of individual conscience and involve abstract concepts of justice, human dignity, and equality.

*In later work, Kohlberg questioned whether stage 6 exists separately from stage 5.

Source: From Kohlberg, L. (1975). The cognitive-developmental approach to moral education. *Phi Delta Kappan, 56,* 671. Adapted by permission of the *Journal of Philosophy.*

Criticisms of Kohlberg's Theory. Even though there is evidence that the different levels of reasoning identified by Kohlberg do form a hierarchy, with each stage representing an advancement in reasoning over the one before (Boom, Brugman, & van der Heijden, 2001), his stage theory has been criticized. First, in reality, the stages do not seem to be separate, sequenced, and consistent. People often give reasons for moral choices that reflect several different stages simultaneously. Or a person's choices in one instance may fit one stage, while his or her decisions in a different situation may reflect another stage. When asked to reason about helping someone else versus meeting their own needs, both children and adolescents reason at higher levels than when they are asked to reason about breaking the law or risking punishment (Arnold, 2000; Eisenberg et al., 1987; Sobesky, 1983).

Second, in everyday life, making moral choices involves more than reasoning. Emotions, competing goals, relationships, and practical considerations all affect choices. People may be able to reason at higher levels but may make choices at lower levels based on these other factors (Carpendale, 2000). Kohlberg emphasized cognitive reasoning about morality, but he overlooked other aspects of moral maturity, such as character and virtue, that operate to solve moral problems in everyday life (Walker & Pitts, 1998).

Gender Differences: The Morality of Caring. One of the most hotly debated criticisms of Kohlberg's theory is that the stages are biased in favour of male values that emphasize individualism. His stages do not represent the way moral reasoning develops in women or in other cultures, because the stage theory was based on a longitudinal study of American men only (Gilligan, 1982; Gilligan & Attanucci, 1988).

Carol Gilligan (1982) has proposed a different sequence of moral development, an "ethic of care." Gilligan suggests that individuals move from a focus on self-interests to moral reasoning based on commitment to specific individuals and relationships, and then to the highest level of morality based on the principles of responsibility and care for all people (which is a bit like Kohlberg's stage 3). If women never reach what Kohlberg considers the higher stages of justice, are they morally immature?

Actually, studies find few significant differences between men and women, or boys and girls, in their level of moral reasoning as measured by Kohlberg's procedures (Eisenberg, Martin, & Fabes, 1996; Turiel, 1998). Walker and his colleagues (Walker, 1991; Walker, Pitts, Hennig, & Matsuba, 1995) asked children, adolescents, and adults to describe a personal moral problem and to analyze a traditional moral dilemma. For both types of problems, males and females revealed both a morality of caring *and* a concern with justice. When they read fables to boys and girls in grades 1 and 3, Andrew Garrod and his colleagues (1990) found no differences in their moral reasoning. However, a few boys in grade 5 (but no girls) suggested solutions involving violence or tricks. So justice and caring seem to be important bases for moral reasoning for both genders. But even though men and women both seem to value caring and justice, there is some evidence that in everyday life, women feel more guilty about violating caring norms (being inconsiderate or untrustworthy) and men feel more guilty when they show violent behaviours (fighting or damaging property) (Williams & Bybee, 1994). Women are somewhat more likely to use a care orientation, but both men and women *can* use both orientations (Skoe, 1998).

Caring for students and helping students learn to care has become a theme for many educators. For example, Nel Noddings (1995) urged that "themes of care" be used to organize the curriculum. Possible themes include "Caring for Self," "Caring for Family and Friends," and "Caring for Strangers and the World." Using the theme of "Caring for Strangers and the World," there could be units on crime, war, poverty, tolerance, ecology, or technology. Table 3.7 shows how a focus on crime and caring for strangers could be integrated into several high school classes.

TABLE 3.7

Using "Caring for Strangers and the World" as a Teaching Theme

As part of a unit on "Caring for Strangers and the World," high school students examine the issue of crime in several classes. In every class, the study of aspects of crime would be continually tied to the theme of caring and to discussions of safety, responsibility, trust in each other and in the community, and commitment to a safer future.

Subject	Elements
Mathematics	Statistics: Gather data on the location and rates of crimes, ages of offenders, and costs of crime to society. Is there a correlation between severity of punishment and incidence of crime? What is the actual cost of a criminal trial?
English and social studies	Read *Oliver Twist.* Relate the characters to their social and historical context. What factors contributed to crime in 19th-century England? Read popular mysteries. Are they literature? Are they accurate depictions of the criminal justice system?
Science	Genetics: Are criminal tendencies heritable? Are there sex differences in aggressive behaviour? Are women less competent than men in moral reasoning (and why did some social scientists think so)? How would you test this hypothesis?
Arts	Is graffiti art really art?

Source: From Noddings, N. Teaching themes of care. *Phi Delta Kappan, 76,* 675–679.

Moral Judgments, Social Conventions, and Personal Choices

STOP & THINK

1. If there were no law against it, would it be okay to blind someone?
2. If there were no rule against it, would it be okay to chew gum in class?
3. Who should decide your favourite vegetable or how to style your hair?

We probably could agree that it is wrong to blind someone, wrong to break class rules, and wrong to dictate food preferences or hairstyles for other people—but it is a different kind of wrong in each case. The first question is about actions that are inherently immoral. The answer to the question is concerned with conceptions of justice, fairness, human rights, and human welfare. Even young children know that it is not okay to hurt other people or steal from them—law or no law. But some rules, like no gum chewing in question 2, are social conventions—agreed-upon rules and ways of doing things in a particular situation. Students (mostly) avoid chewing gum when the class rules (conventions) say so. It is not inherently immoral to chew gum—it is just against the rules. Some classes—in college or university, for example—work well using different rules. And it is not immoral to dislike lima beans (at least we hope not) or to wear your hair short if you are a female; these are personal choices—individual preferences and private issues.

Other criticisms of Kohlberg's stages are that they mix up moral judgments with decisions about social conventions and also overlook personal choice. Larry Nucci (2001) offers an explanation of moral development that covers all three domains or areas: moral judgments, social conventions, and personal choice. Children's thinking and reasoning develops across all domains, but the pace of development may not be the same in every area.

Moral Versus Conventional Domains. For teachers, the most common "right and wrong" situations involve the moral and conventional domains. In the moral domain, beginning with a few basic ideas about right and wrong ("It is wrong to hurt others"), children move through the following stages: a sense that justice means equal treatment for all, an appreciation of equity and special needs, a more abstract integration of equity and equality along with a sense of caring in social relations, and finally, a sense as adults that morality involves beneficence and fairness and that moral principles are independent of the norms of any particular group.

In the conventional domain, children begin by believing that the regularities they see are real and right—men have short hair, women have longer hair, for example, so that is the way it should be. As they mature, children see the exceptions (men with ponytails, women with very short cuts) and realize that conventions are arbitrary. Next, children understand that rules, even though they are arbitrary, are made to maintain order and that people in charge make the rules. But by early adolescence, students begin to question these rules. Because they are arbitrary and made by others, maybe rules are "nothing but" social expectations. As they move through adolescence, there is another swing—from understanding conventions as the appropriate way things have to operate in a social system to seeing them as nothing but society's standards that have become set because they are used. Finally, adults realize that conventions are useful in coordinating social life, but changeable, too. So, compared with young children, older adolescents and adults are generally more accepting of others who think differently about conventions and customs.

Implications for Teachers. Nucci (2001) offers several suggestions for creating a moral atmosphere in your classroom. First, it is important to establish a community of mutual respect and warmth with a fair and consistent application of the rules. Without that kind of community, all your attempts to create a moral climate will be undermined. Second, teachers' responses to students should be appropriate to the domain of the behaviour—moral or conventional. For example, here are some responses to *moral issues* (Nucci, 2001, p. 146):

1. When an act is inherently hurtful or unjust, emphasize the harm done to others: "John, that really hurt Jamal."
2. Encourage perspective-taking: "Chris, how would you feel if someone stole from you?"

Social conventions Agreed-upon rules and ways of doing things in a particular situation.

Here are two responses to rule or *conventional issues*:

3. Restate the rule: "Lisa, you are not allowed to be out of your seat during announcements."
4. Command: "Howie, stop swearing!"

In all four cases, the teacher's response fits the domain. To create an inappropriate response, just switch responses 1 or 2 with 3 or 4. For example, "Lisa, how would you feel if other people got out of their seat during announcements?" Lisa might feel just fine. And it is a weak response to a moral transgression to say, "John, it is against the rules to hit." It is more than against the rules—it hurts and it is wrong.

In the third domain of moral development—personal choice—children must sort out what decisions and actions are their personal choices and what decisions are outside personal choice. This process is the foundation for developing moral concepts related to individual rights, fairness, and democracy. Here, different cultures may have very different understandings about individual choice, privacy, and the role of individuality in the larger society. For example, some research has shown that both the parents in cultures that emphasize individualism and the parents in cultures that emphasize group membership believe that children need to be given choices to develop their ability to make good decisions. But middle-class parents tend to encourage making choices earlier, before adolescence. For children living in poverty, making too many choices early may be a bad idea, given the very real dangers they face in their neighbourhoods (Nucci, 2001).

CREATING MORAL CLIMATES Educators can create a moral climate in their schools and classrooms by promoting and reinforcing a community of mutual respect.

Diversity in Moral Reasoning

There are a number of broad cultural distinctions that might influence moral reasoning. Some cultures can be considered more traditional, with greater emphasis on customs and rituals that change slowly over time. In contrast, traditions and customs tend to change more rapidly in modern cultures. Nucci (2001) suggests that in more traditional cultures, customs may become "moralized." For example, not wearing head coverings in some cultures may seem to be in the conventional domain to outsiders, but is closer to the moral domain for members of the culture, especially when religious beliefs are involved. Consider the findings of one study described by Nucci that asked devout Hindus to rate 35 behaviours that violated community norms. An eldest son eating chicken a day after his father's death was considered the worst violation and beating a disobedient wife was the least offensive. What seems like a convention (eating chicken) is a moral issue because the Hindus believed that the son's behaviour would prevent his father from receiving salvation—a terrible and eternal fate. So, to understand what is conventional and what is moral, we need to know about the beliefs of the culture.

In cultures that are more family-centred or group-oriented (often called *collectivist cultures*), the highest moral value might involve putting the opinions of the group before decisions based on individual conscience. Research has found that children's reasoning about moral, conventional, and personal domains is similar across cultures (Berk, 2005). Even in societies that encourage deference to authority, such as in China, children agree with Western children that adults have no right to dictate how children spend their free time. And people without authority, including children, should be obeyed when what they want you to do is fair and just, but disobeyed when what they dictate is immoral or unjust (Helwig, Arnold, Tan, & Boyd, 2003; Kim, 1998).

In the last years of his life, Kohlberg studied moral behaviour in schools. We turn to that topic now.

Moral Behaviour

Three important influences on moral behaviour are modelling, internalization, and self-concept. First, children who have been consistently exposed to caring, generous adult models will tend to be more concerned for the rights and feelings of others (Cook & Cook, 2005; Eisenberg & Fabes, 1998). Second, most theories of moral behaviour assume that young children's moral behaviour is first controlled by others through direct instruction, supervision, rewards and punishments, and correction. But in time, children internalize the moral rules and principles of the authority figures who have guided them; that is, children adopt the external standards as their own. If children are given reasons that they can understand when they are corrected—particularly reasons that highlight the effects of actions on others—then they are more likely to internalize moral principles. They learn to behave morally even when "no one is watching" (Berk, 2002; Hoffman, 2000). And finally, we must integrate moral beliefs and values into our total sense of who we are, our self-concept.

> The tendency for a person to behave morally is largely dependent on the extent to which moral beliefs and values are integrated in the personality, and in one's sense of self. The influence our moral beliefs have on our lives, therefore, is contingent on the personal importance that we as individuals attach to them—we must identify and respect them as our own (Arnold, 2000, p. 372).

Internalize Process whereby children adopt external standards as their own.

The *Guidelines* box gives ideas for how to support personal and moral development in the classroom. Next, we will consider a moral issue that arises in classrooms—cheating.

GUIDELINES: Supporting Personal and Moral Development

Help students examine the kinds of dilemmas they are currently facing or will face in the near future.

EXAMPLES

1. In elementary school, discuss sibling rivalries, teasing, stealing, prejudice, treatment of new students in the class, or behaviour toward classmates with disabilities.
2. In high school, discuss cheating, letting friends drive when they are intoxicated, conforming to be more popular, or protecting a friend who has broken a rule.

Help students see the perspectives of others.

EXAMPLES

1. Ask a student to describe his or her understanding of the views of another, and then have the other person confirm or correct the perception.
2. Have students exchange roles and try to "become" the other person in a discussion.

Help students make connections between expressed values and actions.

EXAMPLES

1. Follow a discussion of "What should be done?" with "How would you act? What would be your first step? What problems might arise?"
2. Help students see inconsistencies between their values and their own actions. Ask them to identify inconsistencies, first in others, then in themselves.

Safeguard the privacy of all participants.

EXAMPLES

1. Remind students that in a discussion they can "pass" and not answer questions.
2. Intervene if peer pressure is forcing a student to say more than he or she might like.
3. Don't reinforce a pattern of telling "secrets."

Make sure students are really listening to each other.

EXAMPLES

1. Keep groups small.
2. Be a good listener yourself.
3. Recognize students who pay careful attention to each other.

Make sure that your class reflects concern for moral issues and values as much as possible.

EXAMPLES

1. Make clear distinctions between rules based on administrative convenience (keeping the room orderly) and rules based on moral issues.
2. Enforce standards uniformly. Be careful about showing favouritism.

Source: Adapted with permission from Eiseman, J. W. (1981). What criteria should public school moral education programs meet? *The Review of Education, 7*, 226–227.

Cheating. About 80 to 90 percent of high school and college and university students cheat at some point in school. In fact, the rates of academic cheating have been rising for the past 30 years, perhaps in response to increased pressures and high-stakes testing. Until high school, older students cheat more than younger students, but in college and university the pattern is reversed—older students cheat less than younger ones (Murdock & Anderman, 2006).

There are some individual differences in cheating. Most studies of adolescent and college- or university-age students find that males are more likely to cheat than females and lower-achieving students are more likely to cheat than higher achievers. Students focusing on performance goals (making good grades, looking smart) as opposed to learning goals, and students with a low sense of academic self-efficacy (a belief that they probably can't do well in school) are more likely to cheat (Murdock & Anderman, 2006). But cheating is not all about individual differences—the situation plays a role as well. In one study, the level of cheating decreased when students moved from math classes that emphasized competition and grades to classes that emphasized understanding and mastery (Anderman & Midgley, 2004). Students are also particularly likely to cheat when they are behind or "cramming for tests" or when they believe that their teachers do not care about them. For example, one student had this perspective:

> I am a high school honors student, and I think there are different degrees of cheating. I'm a dedicated student, but when my history teacher bombards me with 50 questions due tomorrow or when a teacher gives me a fill-in-the-blanks worksheet on a night when I have swim practice, church, aerobics—and other homework—I'm going to copy from a friend! . . . Since I only do this when I need to, it isn't a habit. Every kid does this when they're in a pinch. (Jensen, Arnett, Feldman, & Cauffman, 2002, p. 210)

MyEducationLab Go to the Activities and Applications section in Chapter 3 of MyEducationLab and complete Activity 1. As you watch the video and answer the accompanying questions, reflect upon ways in which students at different stages of development react to the idea of cheating.

Tamera Murdock and Eric Anderman (2006) have proposed a model to integrate what we know about cheating with research to learn more about cheating. They suggest that in deciding to cheat, students ask three questions: What is my goal? Can I do it? What are the costs? See Table 3.8 for some example answers to these questions that might be associated with decisions to cheat or not to cheat, and some example strategies to support not cheating.

The implications for teachers are straightforward. To prevent cheating, try to avoid putting students in high-pressure situations. Make sure they are well prepared for tests, projects, and assignments so that they can do reasonably well without cheating. Focus on learning and not on grades. Encourage collaboration on assignments and experiment with open-book, collaborative, or take-home tests. We often tell students what concepts will be on the test and encourage them to discuss the concepts and their applications before the test. You might also make extra help available for those who need it. Be clear about your policies in regard to cheating, and enforce them consistently. Help students resist temptation by monitoring them carefully during testing.

TABLE 3.8 **When Do Students Cheat?**
Tamera Murdock and Eric Anderman have developed a model of academic cheating based on the answers to three questions.

Questions	Less Likely to Cheat: Example Answers	More Likely to Cheat: Example Answers	What Can the Teacher Do? Example Strategies
What is my goal?	The goal is to learn, get smarter, and be the best I can be.	The goal is to look good, outperform others. The goal is imposed on me.	Communicate that the point of the class is to learn—everyone can get better.
Can I do it?	I can do it with reasonable effort.	I doubt my ability to do it.	Build students' confidence by helping them take small but successful steps. Point out students' past accomplishments.
What are the costs?	I will get caught and punished if I cheat. I will feel morally wrong or dishonoured if I cheat.	I probably won't get caught and punished if I cheat. Everyone does it, so it can't be wrong. The pressure is too great—I can't fail. I have to cheat.	Make mistakes an opportunity to learn. Take the pressure out of assignments with the chance to revise. Monitor to prevent cheating and follow through with reasonable penalties.

Source: Adapted from Murdock, T. A., & Anderman, E. M. (2006). Motivational perspectives on student cheating: Toward an integrated model of academic dishonesty. *Educational Psychologist, 42*, 129–145.

DIVERSITY AND CONVERGENCES IN PERSONAL AND SOCIAL DEVELOPMENT

In the areas of physical, personal, and social development, we would expect diversity based on differences in social and cultural contexts, but there are also some convergences.

Diversity

MyEducationLab
Go to the Teacher Talk section in Chapter 3 of MyEducationLab and watch a video of Tamra Tiang, 2007 Teacher of the Year from New Mexico, explaining why she teaches, and the ways in which she hopes to promote her students' moral and personal development.

Differences in social and cultural contexts lead to diversity in areas of physical, personal, and social development:

- Girls enter puberty earlier than boys.
- Parenting styles vary by culture and SES. Parents may be stricter when they perceive the need to protect their children from unsafe environments or when they want to promote a tradition of respect for elders.
- The needs of the family group are elevated over individual concerns in some cultures.

In their relationships with teachers, high-achieving, middle-class students see caring expressed in help with academic work, whereas students who have been alienated from school value personal caring—teachers who are concerned with the lives and futures of their students. Students may not risk caring about school until the school risks caring about them, and the care should be personal. You will see in Chapter 12 that a teaching style of warmth and caring, coupled with high demands for compliance, is effective for the majority of students. This sounds like the authoritative parenting style discussed earlier.

In terms of self-concept, we saw different patterns for boys and girls across the school years in their sense of competence in math, sports, and language arts. In addition, girls tend to see themselves as more able than boys in reading and close friendships; boys are more confident about their abilities in math and athletics. Unfortunately, there are no long-term studies of other ethnic groups, so these patterns may be limited to European Americans. In terms of self-esteem, the family can play a significant role.

When we looked at identity, we saw that white students often deny that they have an ethnic identity, whereas ethnic minority groups have to reconcile two identities and may move through stages from not being aware of or denying differences to finally reaching an integration of the two cultures.

When we turned to moral reasoning, we saw that in some cultures, conventions and customs are seen as rules made to make social life smoother, but in other more traditional societies, social conventions may take on a moral meaning. And the range for personal choice also varies by culture, with individualist cultures valuing more personal choice in a wider range of areas.

Convergences

In spite of these differences, there are some convergences in many areas of personal and social development. Certainly both Erikson and Bronfenbrenner stress that individuals are influenced by their social and cultural contexts. For example, here are a few big ideas we've discussed:

1. Students whose parents are divorcing can benefit from authoritative teachers who are both warm and clear about requirements.
2. For all students, self-concepts are increasingly differentiated over time—students may feel competent in one subject, but not in others or very capable as friends or family members, but not as students.
3. For all students, it is a challenge to forge a meaningful identity that integrates their decisions about career, religion, ethnicity, gender roles, and connection to society. Teachers are in a position to support this quest.
4. Being rejected by peers is harmful for all students. Many students need guidance in developing social skills, in more accurately reading the intentions of others, in resolving conflicts, and in coping with aggression. Again, teachers can provide guidance.
5. When working under high pressure, with unreasonable workloads, and with little chance of being caught, many students will cheat. It is up to teachers and schools to do their best to avoid putting students in these unfavourable conditions.

SUMMARY TABLE

Bronfenbrenner: The Social Context for Development (pp. 67–80)

Describe Bronfenbrenner's bioecological model of development. This model takes into account both the biological aspects internal to the individual and the nested social and cultural contexts that shape development. Every person develops within a *microsystem* (immediate relationships and activities), inside a *mesosystem* (relationships among microsystems), embedded in an *exosystem* (larger social settings such as communities); all of these are part of the *macrosystem* (culture).

What are some aspects of the family that affect students in school? Students probably have experienced different parenting styles and these styles can influence their social adjustment. At least in North American middle-class families, children of authoritative parents are more likely to be happy with themselves and relate well to others, whereas children of authoritarian parents have lower levels of self-control and may be less popular with peers. Children of permissive and rejecting/neglecting parents often have trouble in their relationships and are more likely to engage in risky and delinquent behaviour. But the research findings for parenting styles are not universal. Outcomes for children raised by authoritarian parents can differ across cultural, SES, and religious communities.

How does divorce affect students? During the divorce itself, conflict may increase as property and custody rights are being decided. After the divorce, the custodial parent may have to move to a less expensive home, go to work for the first time, or work longer hours. For the child, this can mean leaving behind important friendships just when support is needed the most, having only one parent who has less time than ever to be with them, or adjusting to new family structures when parents remarry.

Why are peer relations important? Peer relationships play a significant role in healthy personal and social development. There is strong evidence that adults who had close friends as children have higher self-esteem and are more capable of maintaining intimate relationships than adults who had lonely childhoods. Adults who were rejected as children tend to have more problems, such as dropping out of school or committing crimes.

What are peer cultures and how can aggression develop? Groups of students develop their own norms for appearance and social behaviour. Group loyalties can lead to rejection for some students, leaving them upset and unhappy. Peer aggression can be instrumental (intended to gain an object or privilege) or hostile (intended to inflict harm). Hostile aggression can be either overt threats or physical attacks or relational aggression, which involves threatening or damaging social relationships. Boys are more likely to use physical aggression than girls, and girls are more likely to use relational aggression than physical aggression.

How can teachers' academic and personal caring affect students? Students value caring in teachers. Caring can be expressed as support for academic learning and as concern for personal problems. For higher-achieving and higher SES students, academic caring may be more important, but for students who are alienated from school, personal caring may be more important.

What are some signs of child abuse? Signs of abuse or neglect include unexplained bruises, burns, bites, or other injuries, and fatigue, depression, frequent absences, poor hygiene, inappropriate clothing, problems with peers, and many others. Teachers must report suspected cases of child abuse and can be instrumental in helping students cope with other risks as well.

Context The total setting or situation that surrounds and interacts with a person or event. It includes internal and external circumstances and situations that interact with the individual's thoughts, feelings, and actions to shape development and learning.

Bioecological model Bronfenbrenner's theory describing the nested social and cultural contexts that shape development. Every person develops within a *microsystem*, inside a *mesosystem*, embedded in an *exosystem*, all of which are a part of the *macrosystem* of the culture.

Blended families Parents, children, and stepchildren merged into families through remarriages.

Extended families Parents, children, grandparents, aunts, uncles, and cousins living in the same household or in close proximity so they can have daily contact with one another.

Parenting styles The ways of interacting with and disciplining children.

Attachment Forming an emotional bond with another person, initially a parent or family member.

Peer cultures Groups of children or adolescents with their own rules and norms, particularly about such things as dress, appearance, music, language, social values, and behaviour.

Instrumental aggression Strong actions aimed at claiming an object, place, or privilege—not intended to harm, but may lead to harm.

Hostile aggression Bold, direct action that is intended to hurt someone else; unprovoked attack.

Overt aggression A form of hostile aggression that involves physical attack.

Relational aggression A form of hostile aggression that involves verbal attacks and other actions meant to harm social relationships.

Bystanders Children who witness bullying behaviour and may or may not do anything about it.

Physical Development (pp. 80–86)

Describe the changes in physical development in the preschool, elementary, and secondary grades. During the preschool years, there is rapid development of children's gross- and fine-motor skills. Physical development continues throughout the elementary school years, with girls often ahead of boys in size. With adolescence comes puberty and emotional struggles to cope with all the related changes.

What are some of the consequences of early and late maturation for boys and girls? Females mature about two years ahead of males. Early-maturing boys are more likely to enjoy high social status; they tend to be popular and to be leaders. But they also tend to engage in more delinquent behaviour, and this finding applies across cultures. Early maturation is not generally beneficial for girls.

What role does recess and physical activity play in development? Play supports brain development, language, and social development. Children release tensions, learn to solve problems, adapt to new situations, cooperate, and negotiate. The increase in childhood obesity is linked to inactivity and increased time spent watching TV and playing passive games such as video and internet games.

What are some of the signs of eating disorders? Anorexic students may appear pale, have brittle fingernails, and have fine dark hairs developing all over their bodies. They are easily chilled because they have so little fat to insulate their bodies. They often are depressed, insecure, moody, and lonely. Girls may stop having their menstrual period.

Puberty The physiological changes during adolescence that lead to the ability to reproduce.

Body mass index (BMI) A calculation of weight in relation to height.

Bulimia Eating disorder characterized by overeating, then getting rid of the food by self-induced vomiting or use of laxatives.

Anorexia nervosa Eating disorder characterized by very limited food intake.

Self-Concept and Identity (pp. 86–97)

What are Erikson's stages of psychosocial development? Erikson's emphasis on the relationship between society and the individual is a psychosocial theory of development—a theory that connects personal development (psycho) to the social environment (social). Erikson believed that people go through eight life stages, each of which involves a central crisis. Adequate resolution of each crisis leads to greater personal and social competence and a stronger foundation for solving future crises. In the first two stages, an infant must develop a sense of trust over mistrust and a sense of autonomy over shame and doubt. In early childhood, the focus of the third stage is on developing initiative and avoiding feelings of guilt. In the child's elementary school years, the fourth stage involves achieving a sense of industry and avoiding feelings of inferiority. In the fifth stage, identity versus role confusion, adolescents consciously attempt to solidify their identity. According to Marcia, these efforts may lead to identity diffusion, foreclosure, moratorium, or achievement. Erikson's three stages of adulthood involve struggles to achieve intimacy, generativity, and integrity

Describe the formation of ethnic and racial identities. Ethnic and racial minority students are confronted with the challenge of forming an identity while living in two worlds—the values, beliefs, and behaviours of their group and of the larger culture. Most explanations for identity development describe stages moving from being unaware of differences between minority group and majority cultures, to different ways of negotiating the differences, and finally to an integration of cultures.

How does self-concept change as children develop? Self-concept (what we know about ourselves) becomes increasingly complex, differentiated, and abstract as we mature. Self-concept evolves through constant self-reflection, social interaction, and experiences in and out of school. Students develop a self-concept by comparing themselves to personal (internal) standards and social (external) standards. High self-esteem (how we feel about ourselves) is related to better overall school experience, both academically and socially. Gender and ethnic stereotypes are significant factors as well.

Distinguish between self-concept and self-esteem. Both self-concept and self-esteem are beliefs about the self. Self-concept is our attempt to build a scheme that organizes our impressions, feelings, and attitudes about ourselves. But this model is not stable. Self-perceptions vary from situation to situation and from one phase of our lives to another. Self-esteem is an evaluation of your self-worth. If people evaluate their worth positively, we say that they have high self-esteem. Self-concept and self-esteem are often used interchangeably, even though they have distinct meanings. Self-concept is a cognitive structure and self-esteem is an affective evaluation.

Are there differences in self-concepts for girls and boys? From grade 1 to grade 12, competence beliefs decline for both boys and girls in math, language arts, and sports. By high school, boys and girls express about the same competence in math, girls are higher in language arts, and boys are higher in sports. In terms of general self-esteem, both boys and girls report declines in the transition to middle school, but boys' self-esteem goes up in high school while girls' self-esteem stays the same.

Psychosocial Describing the relation of the individual's emotional needs to the social environment.

Developmental crisis A specific conflict whose resolution prepares the way for the next stage.

Initiative Willingness to begin new activities and explore new directions.

Autonomy Independence.

Industry Eagerness to engage in productive work.

Identity The complex answer to the question, "Who am I?"

Identity diffusion Uncentredness; confusion about who one is and what one wants.

Identity foreclosure Commitment without exploration—committing to the goals, values, and lifestyles of others without exploring the range of possibilities for oneself.

Moratorium Identity crisis; suspension of choices because of struggle.

Identity achievement Strong sense of commitment to life choices after free consideration of alternatives.

Generativity Sense of concern for future generations.

Integrity Sense of self-acceptance and fulfillment.

Racial and ethnic pride A positive self-concept about one's racial or ethnic heritage.

Self-concept Individuals' knowledge and beliefs about themselves—their ideas, feelings, attitudes, and expectations.

Self-esteem The value each of us places on our own characteristics, abilities, and behaviours.

Gender Development (pp. 97–100)

What are the stages for achieving a sexual orientation for gay and lesbian youth? Stages of achieving a sexual orientation for gay and lesbian students can also follow a pattern from discomfort to confusion to acceptance. Some researchers contend that sexual identity is not always permanent and can change over the years.

What are gender roles and how do they develop? Gender role is the image each individual has of himself or herself as masculine or feminine in characteristics—a part of self-concept. Biology (hormones) plays a role, as does the differential behaviour of parents and teachers toward male and female children. Through their interactions with family, peers, teachers, and the environment in general, children begin to form gender schemas, or organized networks of knowledge about what it means to be male or female.

Gender identity A person's self identification as male or female.

Sexual identity A complex combination of beliefs and orientations about gender roles and sexual orientation.

Gender schemas Organized networks of knowledge about what it means to be male or female.

Understanding Others and Moral Development (pp. 100–107)

What is a theory of mind and why is it important? A theory of mind is an understanding that other people are people too, with their own minds, thoughts, feelings, beliefs, desires, and perceptions. Children need a theory of mind to make sense of other people's behaviour. As children develop a theory of mind, they also are able to understand that other people have intentions of their own.

How do perspective-taking skills change as students mature? An understanding of intentions develops as children mature, but aggressive students often have trouble understanding the intentions of others. Social perspective-taking also changes as we mature. Young children believe that everyone has the same thoughts and feelings they do. Later, they learn that others have separate identities and therefore separate feelings and perspectives on events.

What are the key differences among the preconventional, conventional, and postconventional levels of moral reasoning? Kohlberg's theory of moral development includes three levels: (1) a preconventional level, where judgments are based on self-interest; (2) a conventional level, where judgments are based on traditional family values and social expectations; and (3) a postconventional level, where judgments are based on more abstract and personal ethical principles. Critics suggest that Kohlberg's view does not account for possible cultural differences in moral reasoning or differences between moral reasoning and moral behaviour.

Describe Gilligan's levels of moral reasoning. Carol Gilligan has suggested that because Kohlberg's stage theory was based on a longitudinal study of men only, it is very possible that the moral reasoning of women and the stages of women's development were not adequately represented. She has proposed an "ethic of care." Gilligan believes that individuals move from a focus on self-interests to moral reasoning based on commitment to specific individuals and relationships, and then to the highest level of morality based on the principles of responsibility and care for all people. Women are somewhat more likely to use a care orientation, but studies also show that both men and women *can* use both orientations.

How does thinking in the moral and conventional domains change over time? Beliefs about morality move from the young child's sense that justice means equal treatment for all to the adult's understanding that morality involves beneficence and fairness and that moral principles are independent of the norms of any particular group. In thinking about social conventions, children begin by believing that the regularities they see are real and right. After going through several stages, adults realize that conventions are useful in coordinating social life, but changeable too.

What influences moral behaviour? Adults first control young children's moral behaviour through direct instruction, supervision, rewards and punishments, and correction. A second important influence on the development of moral behaviour is modelling. Children who have been consistently exposed to caring and generous adult models will tend to be more concerned for the rights and feelings of others. The world and the media provide many negative models of behaviour. In time, children internalize the moral rules and principles of the authority figures who have guided them. If children are given reasons—particularly reasons that highlight the effects of actions on others—they can understand when they are corrected and they are more likely to internalize moral principles. Some schools have adopted programs to increase students' capacity to care for others. In schools, cheating is a common behavioural problem that involves moral issues.

Theory of mind An understanding that other people are people too, with their own minds, thoughts, feelings, beliefs, desires, and perceptions.

Perspective-taking ability Understanding that others have different feelings and experiences.

Moral reasoning The thinking process involved in judgments about questions of right and wrong.

Distributive justice Beliefs about how to divide materials or privileges fairly among members of a group; follows a sequence of development from equality to merit to benevolence.

Moral realism Stage of development wherein children see rules as absolute.

Morality of cooperation Stage of development wherein children realize that people make rules and people can change them.

Moral dilemmas Situations in which no choice is clearly and indisputably right.

Social conventions Agreed-upon rules and ways of doing things in a particular situation.

Internalize Process whereby children adopt external standards as their own.

TEACHERS' CASEBOOK

You have seen it before, but this year the situation in your middle school classroom seems especially vicious. A clique of popular girls has made life miserable for one of their former friends, Stephanie, who is now rejected. Stephanie committed the social sin of not fitting in—wearing the wrong clothes or not being pretty enough or not being interested in boys yet. To keep the status distinctions clear between themselves and Stephanie, the popular girls spread gossip about their former friend, often disclosing the intimate secrets revealed when Stephanie was still considered a close friend, which was only a few months ago. However, these girls are not using traditional methods of spreading gossip—instead of passing notes or whispering in the hallways, they are using the internet to humiliate Stephanie. First they forwarded a long, heart-baring email from Stephanie to her former best friend Alison to the entire school. More recently, one of them used a cell phone to take a picture of Stephanie while she was changing after gym class and then emailed it to the students in the whole school. Stephanie has been absent for three days since this latest incident.

What Would *They* Do?

Here is how some practising teachers responded to the teaching situation described above.

Meagan Mano

The Prince Charles School, Napanee, ON

To determine my actions in dealing with social issues in development, I would consider who was affected and how students could avoid problem situations and effectively deal with them in the future.

The actions of Alison and her clique are a form of harassment. I would make sure that my health program was geared toward educating the class, especially this group of girls, on harassment. Topics covered would include identifying ways of dealing with harassment and resources that can support someone experiencing it. As part of my program, I would arrange for a guest speaker to talk about relationships and about decision-making skills.

Harassment is not the only issue, as the girls seem to have found themselves in cliques. Again, to reach all students, I would analyze different case scenarios using an age-related film that involved several different cliques. In groups, I would have the students discuss the feelings of the characters in the film and brainstorm the characteristics of a true friend.

Since the email was forwarded to the entire school, it is important that the issues of harassment and bullying be addressed in every classroom. I would discuss the situation with the staff. One approach to ensure that all students were being exposed to these issues would be to set up a school-based program informing students about social skills.

I would speak one-on-one with Stephanie and Alison about friendship. They should both understand that although they were friends in the past, choosing different friends now was acceptable. It is common to hang out with people that share the same interests—and interests change. Alison should be made aware that there are ways of dealing with people that do not involve ridiculing them. I would have both of the girls brainstorm (on their own) different ways in which they could have dealt with the situation. Their ideas would help guide the discussion in my health program.

Finally, I would speak with Alison's and Stephanie's parents to inform them of the situation and of how I plan to address it at school. I would also suggest some topics they could raise at home to follow up my own conversations with the two girls.

Kathleen Barter

Seycove Secondary School, North Vancouver, BC

This situation of cyberbullying is, unfortunately, all too commonplace in school today. The biggest problem associated with cyberbullying is that often, as educators, we are unaware when it is occurring. And by the time we find out, the situation has often gone beyond the scope of the classroom teacher. Nevertheless, when a situation like this is exposed, teachers must respond to it in a timely manner. If the situation were not so severe, I would deal with the issue in a class discussion that focused on conflict resolution as a solution to bullying. Depending on the group and how many kids in the class know of the situation or were involved in it, I would do a lesson on ethics. I might find a short story about a bullying situation and have the students discuss responses and possible solutions. However, given the severity of the situation with Stephanie and Alison, this is a problem for the administrators in the school.

The administrators would start by using some conflict resolution strategies with the girls. They would speak separately to Stephanie and Alison and the group to get the story from each girl. Following the individual conversations, they would bring all the girls in together and have each girl speak about why she did the bullying or how she felt as a victim or as a bully. The administrator's challenge is to make the girls understand how Stephanie felt as a result of being bullied and how these girls would feel if they were the victims. The girls need to understand that Stephanie might not be interested in the same things they are, but that doesn't mean they have to malign their past friendship.

The administrative team would also decide at what point in these discussions the girls' parents would be called and asked to come into the school. As well, the girls need to understand very clearly that it is a criminal offence to photograph people against their knowledge. At this point perhaps the school's police liaison officer should also be brought in to talk to the girls.

4 Learner Differences and Learning Needs

International Trio © *Christian Pierre/SuperStock*

TEACHERS' CASEBOOK

WHAT WOULD YOU DO?

It is a new school year and you scan the list of students who will be registered in your classroom. It's a bit overwhelming. Since your district follows the policy of inclusion, you always expect to have students whose academic abilities, social skills, and motivation for learning vary widely. However, this year you will also have a student who is deaf, two students who are new to Canada and just learning to speak English, and a student who has severe learning disabilities. In principle, you believe in the policy of inclusion, but your new class represents a challenge.

CRITICAL THINKING

- How will you design tasks and structure interactions with students to ensure that they *all* make progress and learn to their full potential?
- What can you do to address the specific needs of students who are identified as having exceptional learning needs?

To answer the questions above, you need to understand that learners can differ in their learning strengths and needs. So far, we have talked little about students as individuals. We have discussed principles of development that apply to everyone—stages, processes, conflicts, and tasks. Our development as human beings is similar in many ways, but not in every way. Even among members of the same family, there are marked contrasts in appearance, interests, abilities, and temperament, and these differences have important implications for teaching. We will spend some time analyzing the concepts of intelligence and learning styles because these terms are so often misunderstood. Because you probably will have at least one student with special needs in your class, whichever grade you teach, in this chapter, we also explore both common and less frequently occurring learning problems that students may have. As we discuss each problem area, we will consider how a teacher might recognize problems, seek help, and plan instruction, including how to use the recent "Response to Instruction" approach.

By the time you have completed this chapter, you should be able to answer these questions:

- What are the potential problems associated with categorizing and labelling students?
- What is your personal concept of intelligence?
- Should you adapt lessons for students with varying learning styles?
- What are the implications of the *Canadian Charter of Rights and Freedoms* for your teaching?
- In your classroom, how will you plan your teaching to include a wide range of student interests and abilities?
- What is "response to intervention" and how will you use this three-tier process in your class?

Connect and Extend
Go to the "Connect and Extend" section in Chapter 4 of MyEducationLab to find further content that links to teaching, students' thinking, research, and the news.

LANGUAGE AND LABELLING

Every child has a distinctive collection of strengths and challenges that relate to learning and development. In that sense, all children are regarded as "exceptional." Some **exceptional students** have high abilities in particular areas (e.g., music, art, or math). Others have disabilities that impact learning and may require special education or other services. Students may have developmental delays, learning disabilities, communication disorders, emotional or behavioural disorders, physical disabilities, autism, traumatic brain injury, impaired hearing, impaired vision, or advanced abilities and

Exceptional students Students who have high abilities in particular areas or disabilities that impact learning and may require special education or other services.

LABELS MAY PROMOTE FALSE STEREOTYPES When labels take precedence over individual characteristics, the labels themselves constitute a handicap. Stereotypes about people who use wheelchairs might interfere with recognition of this young girl's other characteristics and her individuality.

talents. Even though we will use these terms throughout the chapter, a caution is in order because labelling students is a controversial issue.

A label does not tell a teacher which methods to use with individual students. For example, few specific "treatments" automatically follow from a "diagnosis" of a learning disability or high ability—instead, many different teaching strategies and materials are appropriate. Furthermore, the labels can become self-fulfilling prophecies. Everyone—teachers, parents, classmates, and even the students themselves—may see a label as a stigma that cannot be changed. Finally, labels are mistaken for explanations, as is evident in this line of thinking: "Chris gets into fights because he has a behaviour disorder." "How do you know he has a behaviour disorder?" "Because he gets into fights."

On the other hand, some educators argue that applying a label protects the child. For example, if classmates know that a student has a disability, they will be more willing to accept his or her behaviour. Labels still open doors to some special programs, useful information, special technology and equipment, or financial assistance. In truth, labels probably both stigmatize *and* help students (Hallahan, Lloyd, Kauffman, Weiss, & Martinez, 2005). Therefore, labels should be applied judiciously.

Disabilities and Handicaps

A **disability** is just what the word implies—an inability to do something specific such as see or walk. A **handicap** is defined as a disadvantage in certain situations. Some disabilities lead to handicaps, but not in all contexts. For example, being blind (a visual disability) is a handicap if you want to drive a car. But blindness is not a handicap when you are composing music or talking on the telephone. Stephen Hawking, the greatest living physicist, has Lou Gehrig's disease and no longer can walk or talk. He once said he is lucky that he became a theoretical physicist "because it is all in the mind. So my disability has not been a serious handicap." It is important that we do not create handicaps for people by the way we react to their disabilities. Some educators have suggested that we drop the word *handicap* altogether because the source of the word is demeaning. Handicap came from the phrase "cap-in-hand," used to describe people with disabilities who once were forced to beg just to survive (Hardman, Drew, & Egan, 2005).

We can think of all human characteristics as falling somewhere on a continuum. For instance, some people have very acute hearing while others are completely deaf. Not only do all of us have human characteristics that fall somewhere on that continuum, but also the location of those characteristics on the continuum changes over our lifetimes. As we age, for example, we are likely to experience changes in hearing, vision, and even some aspects of intellectual ability, as you will see later in this chapter.

People-First Language

Because everyone has a range of abilities, it makes sense to avoid using labels such as "emotionally disturbed student" or "at-risk student." Describing a complex person with one or two words implies that the condition labelled is the most important aspect of the person. Actually, the individual has many abilities, and to focus exclusively on the disability or high ability is to misrepresent the individual. An alternative is to use "people-first" language—to refer to "students with developmental disabilities" or "students placed at risk." Here the emphasis is on the students first, not on the special challenges these students face.

Examples of terminology to use when referring to students with disabilities are below:

USE	Students with learning disabilities	NOT	Learning disabled students
USE	Students receiving special education	NOT	Special education students
USE	A person with epilepsy	NOT	An epileptic
USE	A child with a physical disability	NOT	A crippled child
USE	Children diagnosed with autism	NOT	Autistic children or autistics

Disability The inability to do something specific, such as walk or hear.

Handicap A disadvantage in a particular situation, sometimes caused by a disability.

Another suggestion is to avoid the language of pity, as appears in phrases such as "confined to a wheelchair" or "victim of AIDS." Wheelchairs are not confining. They allow people to get around. Using "victim of" or "suffering with" makes the person seem powerless. Finally, when the person with the disability is present, talk *to* the person with a disability, not *about* him or her with a companion or interpreter.

In the next section, we consider a concept that has provided the basis for many labels—intelligence.

INTELLIGENCE

Because the concept of intelligence is so important to education, so controversial, and so often misunderstood, we will spend quite a few pages discussing it. Let us begin with the basic question, "What does intelligence mean?"

What Does Intelligence Mean?

STOP & THINK Who was the most intelligent person in your high school? Write down a name and the first four or five words that come to mind when you see that person in your mind's eye. What made you pick this individual?

The idea that people vary in what we call intelligence has been with us for a long time. Plato discussed similar variations over 2000 years ago. Most early theories about the nature of intelligence involved one or more of the following three themes: (1) the capacity to learn; (2) the total knowledge a person has acquired; and (3) the ability to adapt successfully to new situations and to the environment in general.

In 1986 at a symposium on intelligence, 24 psychologists offered 24 different views about the nature of intelligence (Neisser et al., 1996; Sternberg & Detterman, 1986). Over half of the experts mentioned higher-level thinking processes such as abstract reasoning, problem solving, and decision making as important aspects of intelligence, but they disagreed about the structure of intelligence. Is it a single ability or many separate abilities (Gustafsson & Undheim, 1996)?

Intelligence: One Ability or Many? Because there are moderate to high correlations among scores on all mental tests, some believe intelligence is a basic ability that affects performance on all cognitively oriented tasks, from solving mathematical problems, to analyzing poetry, to completing history essay examinations. In fact, this positive intercorrelation among scores for all cognitive tasks "is arguably both the best established and the most striking phenomenon in the psychological study of intelligence" (van der Mass et al., 2006, p. 855). What could explain these results? Charles Spearman (1927) suggested that mental energy, which he called *g* or general intelligence, is used to perform any mental test, but that each test also requires some specific abilities in addition to g. More recent research suggests that g is closely related to working memory (Waterhouse, 2006), an aspect of brain functioning that we will explore in Chapter 7. Today, psychologists generally agree that we can mathematically compute a common factor across cognitive tests, but knowing this isn't much help in understanding specific human abilities; in other words, the notion of g does not have much explanatory power (Blair, 2006).

Raymond Cattell and John Horn's theory of fluid and crystallized intelligence is more helpful in providing explanations of human abilities (Cattell, 1963, 1998; Horn, 1998). Fluid intelligence is defined as pertaining to mental efficiency and reasoning ability. The neurophysiological underpinnings of fluid intelligence may be related to changes in brain volume, myelinization (coating of neural fibres that makes processing faster), the density of dopamine receptors, or processing abilities in the prefrontal lobe of the brain such as selective attention and working memory. This aspect of intelligence increases until late adolescence (about age 22) because it is grounded in brain development, then declines gradually with age. Fluid intelligence is sensitive to injuries and diseases.

In contrast, crystallized intelligence is the ability to apply the problem-solving methods appropriate in your cultural context. Crystallized intelligence can increase throughout the lifespan because it includes the learned skills and knowledge such as reading, facts, and how to hail a cab, make a quilt, or design a unit on symbolism in poetry. By *investing fluid intelligence* in solving

Intelligence Ability or abilities to acquire and use knowledge for solving problems and adapting to the world.

General intelligence *(g)* A general factor in cognitive ability that is related in varying degrees to performance on all mental tests.

Fluid intelligence Mental efficiency that is culture-free and nonverbal and is grounded in brain development.

Crystallized intelligence Ability to apply culturally approved problem-solving methods.

FIGURE 4.1 **An Example of a Hierarchical Model of Intelligence**
The specific abilities at the third level are just some of the possibilities. Carroll identified over 70 specific abilities.

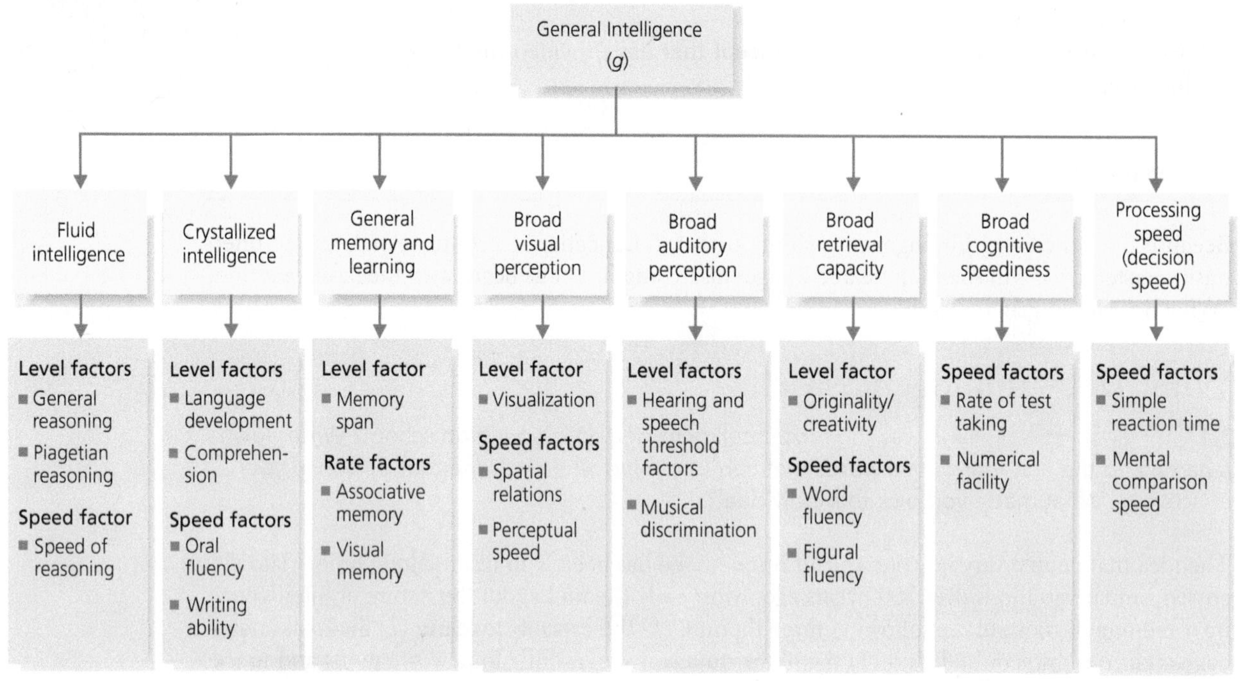

Source: *Contemporary Intellectual Assessment: Theories, Tests, and Issues* by J. B. Carroll in text by D. B. Flanagan, J. L. Genshaft, and P. L. Harrison. Copyright 1996 by Guilford Publications, Inc. Reproduced with permission of Guilford Publications, Inc. in the formats Textbook and Other book via Copyright Clearance Center.

problems, we *develop our crystallized intelligence*, but many tasks in life such as mathematical reasoning draw on both fluid and crystallized intelligence (Ferrer & McArdle, 2004; Finkel, Reynolds, McArdle, Gatz, & Peterson, 2003; Hunt, 2000).

The most widely accepted view today is that intelligence, like self-concept, has many facets and is a hierarchy of abilities, with general ability positioned at the top and more specific abilities appearing at lower levels of the hierarchy (Carroll, 1997; Sternberg, 2000). Look at Figure 4.1 to see an example of this three-level view of intelligence. John Carroll (1997) identifies one general ability, a few broad abilities (such as fluid and crystallized abilities, learning and memory, visual and auditory perception, and processing speed), and at least 70 specific abilities (such as language development, memory span, and simple reaction time). General ability may be related to the maturation and functioning of the frontal lobe of the brain, while specific abilities may be connected to other parts of the brain (Byrnes & Fox, 1998).

Multiple Intelligences

In spite of the correlations among the various tests of different abilities, some psychologists insist that there are several separate mental abilities (Gardner, 1983; Guilford, 1988). According to Gardner's (1983, 2003) theory of multiple intelligences, there are at least eight separate intelligences.

Theory of multiple intelligences In Gardner's theory of intelligence, a person's eight separate abilities: linguistic, musical, spatial, logical-mathematical, bodily-kinesthetic, interpersonal, intrapersonal, and naturalist.

What Are These Intelligences? The eight intelligences in multiple intelligence (MI) theory are linguistic (verbal), musical, spatial, logical-mathematical, bodily-kinesthetic (movement), interpersonal (understanding others), intrapersonal (understanding self), and naturalist (observing and understanding natural and human-made patterns and systems). Gardner stresses that there may be more kinds of intelligence—eight is not a magic number. Recently, he has speculated that there may be a spiritual intelligence and an existential intelligence, or the abilities to contemplate

TABLE 4.1 Eight Intelligences

Howard Gardner's theory of multiple intelligences suggests that there are eight kinds of human abilities. An individual might have strengths or weaknesses in one or several areas.

Intelligence	End States	Core Components
Linguistic	Poet Journalist	Sensitivity to the sounds, rhythms, and meanings of words; sensitivity to the different functions of language.
Musical	Composer Violinist	Abilities to produce and appreciate rhythm, pitch, and timbre; appreciation of the forms of musical expressiveness.
Spatial	Navigator Sculptor	Capacities to perceive the visual-spatial world accurately and to perform transformations on one's initial perceptions.
Logical-mathematical	Scientist Mathematician	Sensitivity to, and capacity to discern, logical or numerical patterns; ability to handle long chains of reasoning.
Bodily-kinesthetic	Dancer Athlete	Abilities to control one's body movements and to handle objects skilfully.
Interpersonal	Therapist Salesperson	Capacities to discern and respond appropriately to the moods, temperaments, motivations, and desires of other people.
Intrapersonal	Person with detailed, accurate self-knowledge	Access to one's own feelings and the ability to discriminate among them and draw on them to guide behaviour; knowledge of one's own strengths, weaknesses, desires, and intelligence.
Naturalist	Botanist Farmer Hunter	Abilities to recognize plants and animals, to make distinctions in the natural world, to understand systems and define categories (perhaps even categories of intelligence).

Source: From "Multiple Intelligences Go to School," by H. Gardner and T. Hatch, *Educational Researcher, 18*(8), p. 6. Copyright © 1989 by the American Educational Research Association. Reproduced by permission of the publisher. Also *Educational Information and Transformation*, edited by J. Kane. Published by Prentice Hall. Copyright © 2002 by Prentice Hall. Reprinted by permission of Pearson Education, Inc., Upper Saddle River, NJ.

big questions about the meaning of life (Gardner, 2003). Gardner bases his notion of separate abilities on evidence that brain damage (from a stroke, for example) often interferes with functioning in one area, such as language, but does not affect functioning in other areas. Also, individuals may excel in one of these eight areas but have no remarkable abilities in the other seven. Table 4.1 summarizes these eight intelligences.

Gardner believes that intelligence has a biological base. An intelligence is a "biopsychological potential to process information that can be activated in a cultural setting to solve problems or create products that are of value in a culture" (Gardner & Moran, 2006, p. 227). Varying cultures and eras of history place different values on the eight intelligences. A naturalist intelligence is critical in farming cultures, whereas verbal and mathematical intelligences are important in technological cultures.

Evaluations of MI Theory. Gardner's MI theory has not received wide acceptance in the scientific community, even though many educators have embraced it. Lynn Waterhouse (2006) concluded that there have been no published studies that validate multiple intelligence theory. The eight intelligences are not independent; there are correlations among the abilities. In fact, logical-mathematical and spatial intelligences are highly correlated (Sattler, 2001). So, these "separate abilities" may not be so separate after all. Recent evidence linking musical and spatial abilities has prompted Gardner to consider that there may be connections among the intelligences (Gardner, 1998). In addition, some critics suggest that several intelligences are really talents (bodily-kinesthetic skill, musical ability) or personality traits (interpersonal ability). Other "intelligences" are not new at all. Many researchers have identified verbal and spatial abilities as elements of intelligence. Daniel Willingham (2004) has been even more blunt: "In the end, Gardner's theory is not that helpful. For scientists the theory is almost certainly incorrect. For educators, the daring applications forwarded by others in Gardner's name (and of which he disapproves) are unlikely to help students" (p. 24). So there is not yet strong research evidence that adopting a multiple intelligences approach will enhance learning. In one of the few carefully designed evaluations, Callahan, Tomlinson, and Plucker (1997) found no significant gains in either achievement or self-concept for students who participated in START, a multiple intelligences approach to identifying and promoting talent in students who were at risk of failing.

MyEducationLab
Go to the Activities and Applications section in Chapter 4 of MyEducationLab and complete Activity 1. As you watch the video and answer the questions, consider the challenges for teachers as they divide students into learning groups based on multiple intelligences.

In response to these criticisms, defenders of MI theory say that the critics have a very narrow view of intelligence and research about intelligence. They believe that newer research methods that look at dynamic models and study intelligence in cultural contexts will support MI theory (Chen, 2004; Gardner & Moran, 2006). In addition, Gardner (2003) has responded to critics by identifying a number of myths and misconceptions about multiple intelligences theory and schooling. One myth is that intelligences are the same as learning styles. (Gardner doesn't believe that people actually have consistent learning styles.) Another misconception is that multiple intelligences theory disproves the idea of g. Gardner does not deny the existence of a general ability, but does question how useful g is as an explanation for human achievements. Stay tuned for more developments.

Multiple Intelligences Go to School. An advantage of the multiple intelligences perspective is that it expands teachers' thinking about abilities and avenues for teaching, but the theory has been misused. Some teachers embrace a simplistic version of Gardner's theory. They include every "intelligence" in every lesson, no matter how inappropriate. A better way to use the theory is to focus on six *entry points*—narrative, logical-quantitative, aesthetic, experiential, interpersonal, and existential/foundational—in designing a curriculum (Gardner, 1991). For example, to teach about evolution, teachers might use the entry points as follows (Kornhaber, Fierros, & Veenema, 2004):

Narrative: Provide rich stories about Darwin's voyage to the Galapagos Islands or traditional folktales about the different plants and animals.

Logical-quantitative: Examine Darwin's attempts to map the distributions of the species or pose logical problems about what would happen to the ecosystem if one species disappeared.

Aesthetic: Examine Darwin's drawings of the species he studied on the Galapagos Islands.

Experiential: Do laboratory activities such as breeding fruit flies or completing virtual simulations of evolutionary processes.

Interpersonal: Form research teams or hold debates.

Existential/foundational: Consider questions about why species die out or the purpose for variation in species.

Many educators and schools have embraced Gardner's ideas and believe that multiple intelligences practices increase achievement for all students and improve both student discipline and parent participation (Kornhaber et al., 2004). But Gardner himself stresses that his theory is not an educational intervention. Learning is still hard work, even if there are multiple paths to knowledge.

Intelligence as a Process

As you can see, the theories of Spearman, Cattell and Horn, Carroll, and Gardner tend to describe how individuals differ in the content of intelligence—the different abilities. Recent work in cognitive psychology has emphasized instead the thinking processes that may be common to all people. How do humans gather and use information to solve problems and behave intelligently? New views of intelligence are growing out of this work. For example, the debates in the 2006 issue of *Behavioral and Brain Sciences* emphasized working memory capacity, the abilities to focus attention and inhibit impulses, and emotional self-regulation as aspects of fluid cognitive abilities.

Robert Sternberg's (1985, 2004) **triarchic theory of intelligence** is a cognitive process approach to understanding intelligence, or *successful intelligence*—the term Sternberg prefers. Sternberg uses the term *successful intelligence* to stress that intelligence is more than what is tested by mental abilities measures—intelligence is about life success based on your own definition of success in your cultural context. As you might guess from the name, this theory has three parts—analytic, creative, and practical intelligence.

Analytic intelligence involves the mental processes of the individual that lead to more or less intelligent behaviour. Some processes are specific; that is, they are necessary for only one kind of task, such as solving analogies. Other processes such as monitoring progress and switching strategies are very general and may be necessary in almost every cognitive task. This may help to explain the persistent correlations among all types of mental tests. People who are effective in selecting good problem-solving strategies, monitoring progress, and moving to a new approach when the first one fails are more likely to be successful on all types of tests.

Triarchic theory of intelligence A three-part description of the mental abilities (thinking processes, coping with new experiences, and adapting to context) that lead to more or less intelligent behaviour.

The second part of Sternberg's theory, *creativity*, involves coping with new experiences. Intelligent behaviour is marked by two characteristics: (1) insight, or the ability to deal effectively with novel situations and find new solutions to problems, and (2) automaticity, the ability to become efficient and automatic in thinking and problem solving—the ability to quickly make the new solutions part of your cognitive tool kit, so to speak.

The third part of the triarchic theory, *practical* intelligence, highlights the importance of choosing an environment in which you can succeed, adapting to that environment, and reshaping it if necessary. People who are successful often seek situations in which their abilities will be valuable, and then work hard to capitalize on those abilities and compensate for any weaknesses. Thus, intelligence in this third sense involves practical matters such as career choice or social skills (Grigorenko & Sternberg, 2001; Sternberg, Wagner, Williams, & Horvath, 1995). In a field study in a Russian city, Elena Grigorenko and Robert Sternberg (2001) found that adults with higher practical and analytical intelligence coped better both mentally and physically with the stresses caused by rapid changes in that part of the world.

WHAT'S SMART? There has been considerable controversy over the meaning of intelligence, whether there is more than one way to be "smart," and how we should measure intelligence.

Principals, teachers, and parents are most familiar with intelligence as a number or score on an IQ test.

Measuring Intelligence

STOP & THINK What is the capital of France? How are an inch and a mile alike? What does *obstreperous* mean? Repeat these numbers backwards: 8 5 7 3 0 2 1 9 7. In what two ways is a lamp better than a candle? If a suit costs $123 and that is 45 percent off the original price, what was the original price of the suit?

These items, taken from Sattler (2001, p. 222), are similar to the verbal questions from a common individual intelligence test for children. Another part of the test asks the child to tell what is missing in a picture, put pictures in order to tell a story, copy a design using blocks, assemble part of a puzzle, complete mazes, and copy symbols. Even though psychologists do not agree on what intelligence is, they do agree that the intelligence recorded in standard tests is related to learning in school. Why is this so? It has to do in part with the way intelligence tests were first developed.

Binet's Dilemma. In 1904, Alfred Binet was confronted with the following problem by the minister of public instruction in Paris: How can students who will need special teaching and extra help be identified early in their school careers, before they fail in regular classes? Binet was also a political activist, very concerned with the rights of children. He believed that having an objective measure of learning ability could protect students from poor families who might be forced to leave school because they were the victims of discrimination and assumed to be slow learners.

Binet and his collaborator Theophile Simon wanted to measure not merely school achievement but the intellectual skills that students needed to do well in school. After trying many different tests and eliminating items that did not allow discrimination between successful and unsuccessful students, Binet and Simon finally identified 58 tests, several for each age group from 3 to 13. Binet's tests allowed the examiner to determine a mental age of a child. A child who succeeded on the items passed by most 6-year-olds, for example, was considered to have a mental age of 6, whether the child was actually 4, 6, or 8 years of age.

The concept of intelligence quotient, or IQ, was added after Binet's test was brought to North America and revised at Stanford University to give us the Stanford-Binet test. An IQ score was computed by comparing the mental-age score with the person's actual chronological age. The formula was as follows:

$$\text{Intelligence quotient} = \text{Mental age}/\text{Chronological age} \times 100$$

Insight The ability to deal effectively with novel situations.

Automaticity The result of learning to perform a behaviour or thinking process so thoroughly that the performance is automatic and does not require effort.

Mental age In intelligence testing, a score based on average abilities for that age group.

Intelligence quotient (IQ) Score comparing mental and chronological ages.

The early Stanford-Binet test has been revised five times, most recently in 2003 (Roid, 2003). The practice of computing a mental age has been problematic because IQ scores calculated on the basis of mental age do not have the same meaning as children get older. To cope with this problem, the concept of deviation IQ was introduced. The deviation IQ score is a number that tells exactly how much above or below the average a person scored on the test, compared with others in the same age group.

What Does an IQ Score Mean? Most intelligence tests are designed so that they have certain statistical characteristics. For example, the average score is 100; 50 percent of the people from the general population who take the tests will score 100 or above, and 50 percent will score below 100. About 68 percent of the general population will earn IQ scores between 85 and 115. Only about 16 percent will receive scores below 85, and only 16 percent will score above 115. Note, however, that these figures hold true for white, native-born Canadian children (assuming the use of Canadian versions of tests) whose first language is English. Whether IQ tests should even be used with ethnic and linguistic minority-group students is hotly debated.

Group Versus Individual IQ Tests. The Stanford-Binet test is an individual intelligence test. It has to be administered to one student at a time by a trained psychologist and takes about 2 hours to complete. Most of the questions are asked orally and do not require reading or writing. A student usually pays closer attention and is more motivated to do well when working directly with an adult.

Psychologists also have developed group tests that can be given to whole classes or schools. Compared with an individual test, a group test is much less likely to yield an accurate picture of any one person's abilities. When students take tests in a group, they may do poorly because they do not understand the instructions, because their pencils break, because other students distract them, or because they do not shine on paper-and-pencil tests (Sattler, 2001). As a teacher, you should be wary of IQ scores based on group tests. The accompanying *Guidelines* box will help you to interpret students' IQ scores realistically.

Deviation IQ Score based on statistical comparison of individuals' performance with the average performance of others in that age group.

GUIDELINES: Interpreting IQ Scores

Check to see if the score is based on an individual or a group test. Be wary of group test scores.

EXAMPLES

1. Individual tests include the Wechsler Scales (WPPSI, WISC-III, WAIS-R), the Stanford-Binet, the McCarthy Scales of Children's Abilities, the Woodcock-Johnson Psycho-Educational Battery, and the Kaufman Assessment Battery for Children.
2. Group tests include the Otis-Lennon School Abilities Tests, Slosson Intelligence Test, Raven Progressive Matrices, Naglieri Nonverbal Ability Test—Multiform, Differential Abilities Scales, and Wide Range Intelligence Test.

Remember that IQ tests are only estimates of general aptitude for learning.

EXAMPLES

1. Ignore small differences in scores among students.
2. Bear in mind that even an individual student's scores may change over time for many reasons, including measurement error.
3. Be aware that a total score is usually an average of scores on several kinds of questions. A score in the middle or average range may mean that the student performed at the average on every kind of question or that the student did quite well in some areas (for example, on verbal tasks) and rather poorly in other areas (for example, on quantitative tasks).

Remember that IQ scores reflect a student's past experiences and learning.

EXAMPLES

1. Consider these scores as predictors of school abilities, not measures of innate intellectual abilities.
2. If a student is doing well in your class, do not change your opinion or lower your expectations just because one score seems low.
3. Be wary of IQ scores for ethnic-minority students and for students whose first language is not English. Even scores on "culture-free" tests are lower for disadvantaged students.
4. Check to see if Canadian versions of the tests are used. Use caution when interpreting a student's scores acquired on American tests and normed for American students.

For more about interpreting IQ scores, see **http://wilderdom.com/intelligence/IQUnderstandingInterpreting.html**.

The Flynn Effect: Are We Getting Smarter? Ever since IQ tests were introduced in the early 1900s, scores in 20 different industrialized countries and in some more traditional cultures have been rising (Daley, Whaley, Sigman, Espinosa, & Neumann, 2003). In fact, in a generation, the average score goes up about 18 points on standardized IQ tests—maybe you really are smarter than your parents! This is called the **Flynn effect** after James Flynn, a political scientist who documented the phenomenon. Some explanations include better nutrition and medical care for children and parents, increasing complexity in the environment that stimulates thinking, the preponderance of smaller families who give more attention to their children, increased literacy of parents, more and better schooling, and better preparation for taking tests. One result of the Flynn effect is that the norms used to determine scores (you will read more about norms in Chapter 14) must be continually revised. In other words, to keep a score of 100 as the average, the test questions have to be made more difficult. This increasing difficulty has implications for any program that uses IQ scores as part of the entrance requirements. For example, some "average" students of the previous generation now might be identified as having intellectual disabilities because the test questions are harder (Kanaya, Scullin, & Ceci, 2003).

Intelligence and Achievement. Scoring higher on IQ tests is related to school achievement for children in all ethnic groups. But what about life after school? Do people who score high on IQ tests achieve more in life? Here the answer is less clear because life success and education are intertwined. On average, high school graduates earn more in their lifetime than non-graduates; college and university graduates and those with professional degrees earn even more (Ceci & Williams, 1997). People with higher intelligence test scores tend to complete more years of school and to have higher-status jobs. However, when the number of years of education is held constant, the correlation decreases between IQ scores and income and success in later life. Other factors such as motivation, social skills, and luck may make the difference (Goleman, 1995; Neisser et al., 1996; Sternberg & Wagner, 1993).

MyEducationLab Go to the Activities and Applications section in Chapter 4 of MyEducationLab and complete Activity 2, which asks you to take two different IQ tests, reflect upon your experience, and consider how you might use IQ results in your future teaching.

Sex Differences in Intelligence

From infancy through the preschool years, most studies find few differences between boys and girls in overall mental and motor development or in specific abilities. During the school years and beyond, psychologists find no differences in general intelligence on the standard measures—these tests have been designed and standardized to minimize sex differences. However, scores on some tests of specific abilities show sex differences. The scores of males tend to be more variable in general, so there are more males than females with very high *and* very low scores on tests (Halpern et al., 2007; Willingham & Cole, 1997). There also are more boys diagnosed with learning disabilities, attention-deficit/hyperactivity disorder (ADHD), and autism. Diane Halpern and her colleagues (2007) summarize the research in the passage below:

> By the end of grade school and beyond, females perform better on assessments of verbal abilities when assessments are heavily weighted with writing and the language-usage items cover topics with which females are familiar; sex differences favoring females are much larger in these conditions than when assessments of verbal abilities do not including writing. In contrast, males excel on certain visuospatial-ability measures. Yet, of all the sex differences in cognitive abilities, differences in quantitative abilities have received the most attention because of the marked differences favoring males at the highest end of the ability distribution and because of their importance in so many occupations. (p. 40)

One note of caution, however: in most studies of sex differences, race and socioeconomic status are not taken into account. When racial groups are studied separately, African American females outperform African American males in high school mathematics; there is little or no difference in the performance of Asian girls and boys in math or science (Grossman & Grossman, 1994; Yee, 1992). Girls in general tend to get higher grades than boys in mathematics classes (Halpern et al., 2007). Also, international studies of 15-year-olds in 41 countries show no sex differences in mathematics for half of the countries tested (Angier & Chang, 2005). The *International Comparisons in Fourth-Grade Reading Literacy* findings (Mullis, Martin, Gonzalez, & Kennedy, 2003) revealed that in 34 countries, boys in grade 4 scored below girls in reading literacy.

What is the basis for the differences? The answers are complex. For example, males on average score better on tests that require mental rotation of a figure in space, prediction of the trajectories

Flynn effect A steady rise in IQ test scores because of better health, smaller families, increased complexity in the environment, and more and better schooling.

of moving objects, and navigating. Some researchers argue that evolution has favoured these skills in males (Buss, 1995; Geary, 1995, 1999), but others relate these skills to males' more active play styles and to their participation in athletics (Linn & Hyde, 1989; Newcombe & Baenninger, 1990; Stumpf, 1995). The cross-cultural comparisons suggest that much of the difference in mathematics scores comes from learning, not biology. And studies showing that adults rated a math paper attributed to "John T. McKay" a full point higher on a 5-point scale than the same paper attributed to "Joan T. McKay" suggests that discrimination plays a role as well (Angier & Chang, 2005).

Heredity or Environment? Nowhere, perhaps, has the nature versus nurture debate raged so hard as in the area of intelligence. Should intelligence be seen as a potential, limited by our genetic makeup? Or does intelligence simply refer to an individual's current level of intellectual functioning, as fed and influenced by experience and education? In fact, it is almost impossible to separate intelligence "in the genes" from intelligence "due to experience." Today, most psychologists believe that differences in intelligence are due to both heredity and environment, probably in about equal proportions for children (Petrill & Wilkerson, 2000). "Genes do not fix behaviour. Rather they establish a range of possible reactions to the range of possible experiences that the environment can provide" (Weinberg, 1989, p. 101). And environmental influences include everything from the health of a child's mother during pregnancy to the amount of lead in the child's home to the quality of teaching a child receives.

For all adults caring for children—parents, teachers, administrators, counsellors, medical workers—it is especially important to realize that cognitive skills, like any other skills, can always be improved. *Intelligence is a current state of affairs*, affected by past experiences and open to future changes. Even if intelligence is a limited potential, the potential is still quite large, and it presents a challenge to all teachers. For example, Japanese and Chinese students know much more mathematics than North American students do, but their intelligence test scores are quite similar. This superiority in math is probably related to differences in the way mathematics is taught and studied in these countries and to the self-motivation skills of many Asian students (Baron, 1998; Stevenson & Stigler, 1992).

Now that you have a sense of what intelligence means, let's consider another kind of individual difference that often is misused and misunderstood in education—learning styles.

LEARNING AND THINKING STYLES

Research in psychology over many years has focused on individual differences in "styles"—cognitive styles, learning styles, problem-solving styles, thinking styles, decision-making styles . . . the list goes on. Li-fang Zhang and Robert Sternberg (2005) organized the work on individual styles into three traditions. Cognitive-centred styles assess ways people process information, for example by being reflective or impulsive in responding (Kagan, 1976). Personality-centred styles assess more stable personality traits such as being extroverted versus introverted or relying on thinking versus feeling (Myers & McCaully, 1988). Activity-centred styles assess a combination of cognition and personality that affects how people approach activities, so these styles may be of special interest to teachers.

One theme in activity-centred approaches is the differences between surface and deep approaches to processing information in learning situations (Snow, Corno, & Jackson, 1996). Students who take a ***surface-processing*** approach focus on memorizing the learning materials, not understanding them. These students tend to be motivated by rewards, grades, external standards, and the desire to be evaluated positively by others. Individuals who adopt the ***deep-processing*** approach see the learning activities as a means for understanding some underlying concepts or meanings. These students tend to learn for the sake of learning and are less concerned about how their performance is evaluated. Of course, the situation can encourage deep or surface processing, but there is evidence that individuals have tendencies to approach learning situations in characteristic ways (Biggs, 2001; Coffield, Moseley, Hall, & Ecclestone, 2004; Pintrich & Schrauben, 1992; Tait & Entwistle, 1998).

Learning Styles and Preferences

Learning styles The way a person approaches learning and studying.

Here is another "style" term. You may have heard about learning styles or used the phrase yourself. Learning style usually is defined as the way a person approaches learning and studying. But beware—some conceptions of learning style have little research support; others are based on solid studies. First, the cautions.

Cautions About Learning Styles. Since the late 1970s, a great deal has been written about differences in students' learning styles (Dunn & Dunn, 1978, 1987; Dunn & Griggs, 2003; Gregorc, 1982; Keefe, 1982). But we believe **learning preferences** is a more accurate label because most of this work describes preferences for particular learning environments. For example, where, when, with whom, or with what lighting, food, or music do you like to study? The authors of this text have different learning preferences. Anita likes to study and write using large blocks of time, late at night. She usually makes some kind of commitment or deadline every week, so that she has to work under pressure in long stretches to finish the work. Then she takes a day off. Phil and Nancy like to write very early in the morning, but they also like to set goals.

There are a number of instruments for assessing students' learning preferences. Be aware, however, that many lack evidence of reliability and validity. In fact, research that has assessed children's learning styles and then tried to match instructional methods to them have failed to show any effect on learning (Stahl, 2002, p. 99), leading Snider (1990) to conclude the following:

> . . . people are different, and it is good practice to recognize and accommodate individual differences. It is also good practice to present information in a variety of ways through more than one modality, but it is not wise to categorize learners and prescribe methods solely on the basis of tests with questionable technical qualities. The idea of learning styles is appealing, but a critical examination of this approach should cause educators to be skeptical. (p. 53)

So before you try to accommodate all your students' learning styles, remember that students, especially younger ones, may not be the best judges of how they should learn. Sometimes students, particularly students who have difficulty, prefer what is easy and comfortable; real learning can be hard-won and uncomfortable. Sometimes students prefer to learn in a certain way because they have no alternatives; it is the only way they know how to approach the task. These students may benefit from developing new—and perhaps more effective—ways to learn.

The Value of Considering Learning Styles. Even though much of the work on matching learning styles and preferences to teaching is suspect, with unreliable measures and inflated claims, there is some value in thinking about students' approaches to and preferences for learning. First, by helping students think about how they learn, you can develop thoughtful self-monitoring and self-awareness. In upcoming chapters, we will look at the value of such self-knowledge for learning and motivation. Second, looking at individual students' approaches to learning might help you appreciate, accept, and accommodate student differences (Coffield et al., 2004; Rosenfeld & Rosenfeld, 2004).

So far, we have focused mostly on teachers' responses to variability in students' abilities and learning preferences apart from specific exceptionalities. For the rest of the chapter, we will consider the needs of students whose high abilities and disabilities create particular challenges for teaching and learning.

STUDENTS WHO ARE GIFTED AND TALENTED

Consider the following situation, a true story.

> Latoya was already an advanced reader when she entered 1st grade in a large urban school district. Her teacher noticed the challenging chapter books Latoya brought to school and read with little effort. After administering a reading assessment, the school's reading consultant confirmed that Latoya was reading at the 5th grade level. Latoya's parents reported with pride that she had started to read independently when she was 3 years old and "had read every book she could get her hands on." (Reis et al., 2002)

In her struggling urban school, Latoya received no particular accommodations, and by grade 5, she was still reading at just above the grade 5 level. Her grade 5 teacher had no idea that Latoya had ever been an advanced reader.

Learning preferences Preferred ways of studying and learning, such as using pictures instead of text, working with other people versus alone, learning in structured or in unstructured situations, and so on.

Latoya is not alone. There is a group of students with special needs that is often overlooked by the schools: students with gifts and talents. In the past, providing an enriched education for extremely bright or talented students was seen as undemocratic and elitist. Now there is a growing recognition that **gifted students** are being poorly served by most public schools. Lupart and Pyryt (1996) at the University of Calgary estimated that, in a sample of 373 students they identified as having gifts and talents, 21 percent were underachieving in school. Because Lupart and Pyryt applied a very narrow definition of giftedness (referring to intellectual/academic talent), they claim that their estimate was fairly low. A more accurate estimate, according to these researchers, would be somewhere between 40 and 50 percent. Current research about this issue is hard to find, but experts believe the situation has not changed (M. Porath, personal communication, August 31, 2010).

Who Are These Students?

There are many definitions of the term *gifted* because individuals can have many different gifts. Remember that Gardner (2003) identified eight separate kinds of "intelligences," and that Sternberg suggested a triarchic model. Recent provincial definitions reflect the research of Dan Keating (1990, 1991), formerly at the University of Toronto and now at the University of Michigan, and Dona Matthews (1996), at the University of Toronto. These scholars emphasize that gifts and talents are often located in specific domains (i.e., individuals typically are not advanced in all areas).

Children who are truly gifted are not the students who simply learn quickly with little effort. The work of gifted students is original, extremely advanced for their age, and potentially of lasting importance. These children may read fluently with little instruction by the age of 3 or 4. They may play a musical instrument as would a skilful adult, turn a visit to the grocery store into a mathematical puzzle, and become fascinated with algebra when their friends are having trouble carrying in addition (Winner, 2000). Recent conceptions widen the view of giftedness to include attention to the children's culture, language, and other exceptionalities (Association for the Gifted, 2001).

What do we know about these remarkable individuals? A classic study of the characteristics of individuals with gifts was started decades ago by Lewis Terman and colleagues (1925, 1947, 1959). This huge project has followed the lives of 1528 gifted males and females, continuing, at least, through the year 2010. The subjects were identified on the basis of teacher recommendations, and all have IQ scores in the top 1 percent of the population (140 or above on the Stanford-Binet individual test of intelligence).

Terman and colleagues found that these children were larger, stronger, and healthier than the norm. Often, they began walking sooner and were more athletic. They were more emotionally stable than their peers and became better-adjusted adults than the average. They had lower rates of delinquency, emotional difficulty, divorce, drug problems, and so on. Of course, the teachers in Terman's study who made the nominations may have selected students who were better adjusted initially. And remember, Terman's study describes academically gifted students only. There are many other kinds of gifts.

ORIGINS OF GIFTEDNESS For years, researchers have debated the nature versus nurture question about people with extraordinary abilities and talents. Studies of prodigies and geniuses in many fields document that deep and prolonged practice is necessary to achieve at the highest levels.

What Is the Origin of These Gifts? For years, researchers have debated the nature versus nurture question about people with extraordinary abilities and talents. As usual, there is evidence that it takes both. Studies of prodigies and geniuses in many fields document that deep and prolonged practice is necessary to achieve at the highest levels. For example, it took Newton 20 years to move from his first ideas to his ultimate contribution (Howe, Davidson, & Sloboda, 1998; Winner, 2000).

Anita remembers listening to the early reports of Bloom's study of talent (1982). His research team had interviewed, among others, the top tennis players in the world and their coaches, parents, siblings, and friends. One coach said that he would make a suggestion to a young tennis athlete, and a few days later the athlete would have mastered the move. Then the parents told how the child had practised that move for hours on end after getting the coach's tip. So, focused, intense

Gifted student A very bright, creative, and talented student.

practice plays a role. Also, the families of prodigies tend to be child-centred and to devote hours to supporting the development of their child's gifts. Bloom's research team described tremendous sacrifices made by families: rising before dawn to drive their child to a coach in another city, working two jobs, or even moving the whole family to another part of the country to find the best teachers or coaches. The children responded to the family's sacrifices by working harder and the families responded to the child's hard work by sacrificing more—an upward spiral of investment and achievement.

But hard work will never make Anita a world-class tennis player or a Newton. There is a role for nature as well. The children studied by Bloom showed early and clear talent in the areas they later developed. As children, great sculptors were constantly drawing and mathematicians were fascinated with dials, gears, and gauges. Parents' investments in their children came after the children showed early high-level achievement (Winner, 2000, 2003). Recent research suggests that gifted children, at least those with extraordinary abilities in mathematics, music, and visual arts, may have unusual brain organization—which can have both advantages and disadvantages. Giftedness in mathematics, music, and visual arts appears to be associated with superior visual-spatial abilities and enhanced development of the right side of the brain. Children with these gifts are also more likely not to have right-hand dominance—they may have left-hand dominance or mixed dominance. Also, this group is more likely to have language-related problems. These brain differences are evidence that "gifted children, child prodigies, and savants are not made from scratch but are born with unusual brains that enable rapid learning in a particular domain" (Winner, 2000, p. 160).

What Problems Do the Gifted Face? In spite of Bloom's and Terman's findings, it would be incorrect to say that every student with gifts and talents is superior in adjustment and emotional health. In fact, gifted adolescents, especially girls, are more likely to be depressed and to report social and emotional problems (Berk, 2005). Schoolmates may be consumed with baseball or worried about failing math, while the gifted child is fascinated with Mozart, focused on a social issue, or totally absorbed in computers, drama, or geology. Children who are gifted may also be impatient with friends, parents, and even teachers who do not share their interests or abilities. If their language is highly developed, they may be seen as show-offs when they are simply expressing themselves. If they are highly sensitive to expectations and feelings of others, these students may be very vulnerable to criticisms and taunts. Because they are goal-directed and focused, these students may seem stubborn and uncooperative. Also, their keen sense of humour can be used as a weapon against teachers and other students. Adjustment problems seem to be greatest for children with the greatest gifts—those in the highest range of academic ability (i.e., above 180 IQ) (Hardman et al., 2005; Robinson & Clinkenbeard, 1998).

Identifying and Teaching Students Who Are Gifted

Identifying gifted children is not always easy, and teaching them well may be even more challenging. Many parents provide early educational experiences for their children. Even very advanced reading ability in the early grades does not guarantee that students will still be outstanding readers years later (Mills & Jackson, 1990). In middle and high school, some very able students deliberately earn lower grades, making their abilities even harder to recognize. Girls are especially likely to hide their abilities (Berk, 2005; Lupart & Barva, 1998).

Recognizing Students' Special Abilities. Teachers are successful only about 10 to 50 percent of the time in picking out children with gifts and talents in their classes (Fox, 1981). Here are a few questions to guide identification, suggested by Marilyn Friend (2006):

- Who can easily manipulate abstract symbol systems such as mathematics?
- Who can concentrate for long periods of time on personal interests?
- Who remembers easily?
- Who developed language and reading early (as did Latoya, described at the beginning of this section)?
- Who is curious and has many interests?
- Whose work is original and creative?

Students who are gifted may also prefer to work alone, have a keen sense of justice and fairness, be energetic and intense, form strong commitments to friends—often older students—and struggle with perfectionism.

Group achievement and intelligence tests tend to underestimate the IQs of very bright children. Group tests may be appropriate for screening, but they are not appropriate for making decisions about instruction. Many psychologists recommend a case study approach to identifying students with gifts and talents. This means gathering many kinds of information, including test scores, grades, examples of work, projects and portfolios, letters or ratings from teachers, self-ratings, and so on (Renzulli & Reis, 2003; Sisk, 1988). Especially for recognizing artistic talent, experts in the field can be called in to judge the merits of a child's creations. Science projects, exhibitions, performances, auditions, and interviews are all possibilities. Creativity tests may identify some children not picked up by other measures, particularly students from minority groups who may be at a disadvantage on the other types of tests (Maker, 1987). Remember, students with remarkable abilities in one area may have much less impressive abilities in others. In fact, some students with gifts and talents also have learning disabilities.

Teaching Gifted Students. Some educators believe that students who are gifted should be accelerated—moved quickly through the grades or through particular subjects. Other educators prefer enrichment—giving the students additional, more sophisticated, and more thought-provoking work, but keeping them with their age group in school. Actually, both may be appropriate (Torrance, 1986). One strategy, called *curriculum compacting*, involves assessing students' knowledge of the material in an instructional unit, then teaching only for those goals not yet reached (Reis & Renzulli, 2004). Using curriculum compacting, teachers may be able to eliminate about half of the usual curriculum content for some gifted students without any loss of learning. The time saved can be used for learning goals that include enrichment, sophistication, and novelty (Werts, Culatta, & Tompkins, 2007). Look at Table 4.2 to see examples of how content can be modified through acceleration, enrichment, sophistication, and novelty.

Many people object to acceleration, but most careful studies indicate that students who are truly gifted and who begin elementary school, junior high school, high school, college or university, or even graduate school, early do as well as, and usually better than, other students who are progressing at the normal pace. Social and emotional adjustment does not appear to be impaired. Students who are gifted tend to prefer the company of older playmates and may be miserably bored if kept with children of their own age. Skipping grades may not be the best solution for a particular student, but it does not deserve the bad name it has received (Jones & Southern, 1991; Kulik & Kulik, 1984; Richardson & Benbow, 1990). An alternative to skipping grades is to accelerate students in one or two particular subjects but keep them with peers for most classes (Robinson & Clinkenbeard, 1998). However, for students who are extremely advanced intellectually (for example, those scoring 160 or

TABLE 4.2 Examples of How to Modify Content for Students With Gifts and Talents

	Subject			
Modification	**Math**	**Science**	**Language Arts**	**Social Studies**
Acceleration	Algebra in grade 5	Early chemistry and physics	Learning grammatical structure early	Early introduction to world history
Enrichment	Changing bases in number systems	Experimentation and data collection	Short story and poetry writing	Reading biographies for historical insight
Sophistication	Mastering the laws of arithmetic	Learning the laws of physics	Mastering the structural properties of plays, sonnets, and so on	Learning and applying the principles of economics
Novelty	Probability and statistics	Science and its impact on society	Rewriting Shakespeare's tragedies with happy endings	Creating future societies and telling how they are governed

Source: From Gallagher, J. J., & Gallagher, S. (1994). *Teaching the gifted child* (4th ed.). Boston: Allyn & Bacon. Copyright © 1994 by Pearson Education. Adapted by permission of the publisher.

higher on an individual intelligence test), the only practical solution may be to accelerate their education (Hardman et al., 2005; Hunt & Marshall, 2002).

Teaching methods for students who are gifted should encourage abstract thinking (formal operational thought), creativity, and independence, not just the learning of greater quantities of facts. One approach that does *not* seem promising with gifted students is cooperative learning in mixed ability groups. Gifted students tend to learn more when they work in groups with other high-ability peers (Fuchs, Fuchs, Hamlett, & Karns, 1998; Robinson & Clinkenbeard, 1998). In working with students who are gifted and talented, teachers must be imaginative, flexible, and unthreatened by the capabilities of these students. The teacher must ask the following questions: What does this child need most? What is she ready to learn? Who can help me to challenge her? Answers might come from faculty members at nearby colleges and universities; from books, museums, planetariums, and aquariums; from retired professionals; or from older students. Strategies might be as simple as letting the child do math with the next grade. Other options include summer institutes; courses at nearby colleges and universities; classes with local artists, musicians, or dancers; independent research projects; selected classes in high school for younger students; honours classes; and special-interest clubs (Rosenberg, Westling, & McLeskey, 2008).

In the midst of providing challenge, don't forget the support. We have all seen the ugly sights of parents, coaches, or teachers forcing the joy out of talented children by demanding practice and perfection beyond the child's interest. Just as we should not force children to stop investing in their talent ("Oh Michelangelo, quit fooling around with those sketches and go outside and play"), we should also avoid destroying intrinsic motivation with heavy doses of pressure and external rewards.

MyEducationLab
Go to the Teacher Talk section in Chapter 1 of MyEducationLab and watch a video of Connie Dahn, 2007 Teacher of the Year from Florida, discussing teaching every student in inclusive classrooms.

HIGH-INCIDENCE DISABILITIES

Teachers are more likely to encounter students with certain disabilities. These higher-incidence groups include children with learning disabilities, communication disorders, developmental disabilities, and emotional or behavioural disorders. As you can see in Table 4.3, most provinces and territories have adopted inclusive policies that place students with disabilities in their neighbourhood schools within general education classrooms. As a result of these policies, you will have children from all these categories in your classes.

More than half of all students receiving some kind of special education services in Canada are diagnosed as having learning disabilities. This is by far the largest category of students with disabilities.

IPRC Identification Categories:
1. Behaviour
2. Communication
3. Intellectual
4. Physical
5. Multiple

Students With Learning Disabilities

How do you explain what is wrong with a student who struggles to read, write, spell, or learn math, even though she is not developmentally delayed, emotionally disturbed, or educationally deprived and has normal vision, hearing, and language capabilities? The student likely has a **learning disability**, but there is no fully agreed upon definition of learning disabilities (Wong, 1996), and there are slight differences in emphasis in the definitions used across Canada (Hutchinson, 2007). Many scholars believe that, in practice, too much emphasis is given to the discrepancy between students' IQ, as measured by an intelligence test, and their achievement in school. They would like to see equal, if not greater, emphasis placed on the psychological processing problems these students experience (e.g., phonological processing problems, memory problems, and problems with number sense). Linda Siegel, at the University of British Columbia, has written extensively about this topic (1989, 1999). Most educational psychologists suggest that there are both physiological and environmental bases for learning disabilities, such as brain injury, exposure to toxins before birth by mothers who smoked or drank while pregnant, poor nutrition, lead-based paint in the home, or even poor instruction (Smith, 2004). Genetics plays a role as well. If parents have a learning disability, their children have a 30 to 50 percent chance of having a learning disability too (Friend, 2008).

The official definition of learning disabilities, adopted by the Learning Disabilities Association of Canada on January 30, 2002, emphasizes processing problems as the primary characteristic of students with learning disabilities. See the excerpt below, taken from the association's website.

> "Learning Disabilities" refer to a number of disorders which may affect the acquisition, organization, retention, understanding or use of verbal or nonverbal information. These disorders affect learning in individuals who otherwise demonstrate at least average abilities essential for thinking and/or reasoning. As such, learning disabilities are distinct from global intellectual deficiency.

Learning disability Problem with acquisition and use of language; may show up as difficulty with reading, writing, reasoning, or math.

TABLE 4.3 Summary of Provincial and Territorial Approaches to Education of Exceptional Learners

Province or Territory	IEP or Equivalent	Description of Policy	Review of Special Ed.
British Columbia	Individual Education Plan	Inclusive education	1990s
Yukon	Individual Education Plan	Inclusive philosophy	1990s
Alberta	Individualized Program Plan	Most appropriate placement	1990s, 2000
Northwest Territories	Individual Education Plan	Inclusive schooling	1990s
Nunavut	Individual Education Plan (of NT)	Inclusive schooling (of NT)	Created in 1999
Saskatchewan	Personal Program Plan	Inclusive settings	Ongoing
Manitoba	Individual Education Plan	Philosophy of inclusion	Ongoing
Ontario	Individual Education Plan and Identification, Placement, and Review Committee	Regular class first	1990s
Quebec	Individual Education Plan	Integration, neighbourhood schools	Ongoing
New Brunswick	Individual Education Plan	Inclusive education	1990s
Nova Scotia	Individual Program Plan	Regular instructional settings	1990s
Prince Edward Island	Individual Education Plan	Most enabling environment	Ongoing
Newfoundland and Labrador	Individual Support Services Plan	Regular classrooms and continuum of service	1990s

Source: Hutchinson, N. L. (2007). *Inclusion of exceptional learners in Canadian schools: A practical handbook for teachers* (2nd ed., p. 12). Toronto: Pearson Education. Reprinted with permission by Pearson Education Canada Inc.

Learning disabilities result from impairments in one or more processes related to perceiving, thinking, remembering or learning. These include, but are not limited to: language processing; phonological processing; visual spatial processing; processing speed; memory and attention; and executive functions (e.g., planning and decision-making).

Learning disabilities range in severity and may interfere with the acquisition and use of one or more of the following:

- oral language (e.g., listening, speaking, understanding);
- reading (e.g., decoding, phonetic knowledge, word recognition, comprehension);
- written language (e.g., spelling and written expression); and
- mathematics (e.g., computation, problem solving).

Learning disabilities may also involve difficulties with organizational skills, social perception, social interaction and perspective taking.

Learning disabilities are lifelong. The way in which they are expressed may vary over an individual's lifetime, depending on the interaction between the demands of the environment and the individual's strengths and needs. Learning disabilities are suggested by unexpected academic underachievement or achievement which is maintained only by unusually high levels of effort and support.

Learning disabilities are due to genetic and/or neurobiological factors or injury that alters brain functioning in a manner which affects one or more processes related to learning. These disorders are not due primarily to hearing and/or vision problems, socioeconomic factors, cultural or linguistic differences, lack of motivation or ineffective teaching, although these factors may further complicate the challenges faced by individuals with learning disabilities. Learning disabilities may co-exist with various conditions including attentional, behavioural and emotional disorders, sensory impairments or other medical conditions.

Student Characteristics. Students with learning disabilities are not all alike. The most common characteristics are specific difficulties in one or more academic areas; poor coordination; problems paying attention; hyperactivity and impulsivity; problems organizing and interpreting visual and auditory information; disorders of thinking, memory, speech, and hearing; and difficulties making and keeping friends (Hallahan, Kauffman, & Pullen, 2009; Hunt & Marshall, 2002). Also, many students with other disabilities (such as ADHD) and many students without disabilities may have some of the same characteristics. To complicate the situation even more, not all students with learning disabilities will have these problems, and few will have all of these problems.

Most students with learning disabilities have difficulties reading. Table 4.4 lists some of the most common problems, although these problems are not always signs of learning disabilities. For English-speaking students, these difficulties appear to be caused by problems with relating sounds to letters that make up words, making spelling hard as well (Lyon, Shaywitz, & Shaywitz, 2003; Willcutt et al., 2001). For Chinese speakers, reading disabilities seem to be related to *morphological awareness* or the ability to combine morphemes into words. Morphemes are the smallest units of meaning that makes sense alone. For example, "books" has two morphemes: "*book*" and "*s*"—the "*s*" has meaning because it makes *book* plural. Recognizing units of meaning in Chinese characters is helpful in learning the language (Shu, McBride-Chang, Wu, & Liu, 2006).

Math, both in terms of computation and problem solving, is the second most common problem for students with learning disabilities. Whereas students with reading disabilities have trouble

TABLE 4.4

Reading Habits and Errors of Students With Learning Disabilities

Do any of your students show these signs? They could be indications of learning disabilities.

Poor Reading Habits

- Frequently loses his or her place
- Jerks head from side to side
- Expresses insecurity by crying or refusing to read
- Prefers to read with the book held within inches from face
- Shows tension while reading, such as reading in a high-pitched voice, biting lips, and fidgeting

Word Recognition Errors

- Omitting a word (e.g., "He came to the park," is read, "He came to park")
- Inserting a word (e.g., "He came to the [beautiful] park")
- Substituting a word for another (e.g., "He came to the *pond*")
- Reversing letters or words (e.g., *was* is read *saw*)
- Mispronouncing words (e.g., *park* is read *pork*)
- Transposing letters or words (e.g., "The dog ate fast," is read, "The dog fast ate")
- Not attempting to read an unknown word by breaking it into familiar units
- Slow, laborious reading, less than 20 to 30 words per minute

Comprehension Errors

- Recalling basic facts (e.g., cannot answer questions directly from a passage)
- Recalling sequence (e.g., cannot explain the order of events in a story)
- Recalling main theme (e.g., cannot give the main idea of a story)

Source: From *Child and Adolescent Development for Educators*, by J. L. Meece. Published by McGraw-Hill. Copyright © 1997 McGraw-Hill. Reprinted with permission from The McGraw-Hill Companies.

FIGURE 4.2 **Writing Sample From a Student With Learning Disabilities**

2/6/02
4P

If I could leave class
early, I would...

go home and
Do my work. I work on
my faster truck and
rebelild the moter. fix
my moter on my rider.
or whatch my TV in my
room. play with my farit.
She is a lot of fun
to play with she will
bite your feet or get
in your stuff... I can
go out and puch the
puncing bag. cline a tree.
run around the block
coup ol times. it is fun
for me to do that.
I would play with
a dog that is half
my sise and runing with
him.

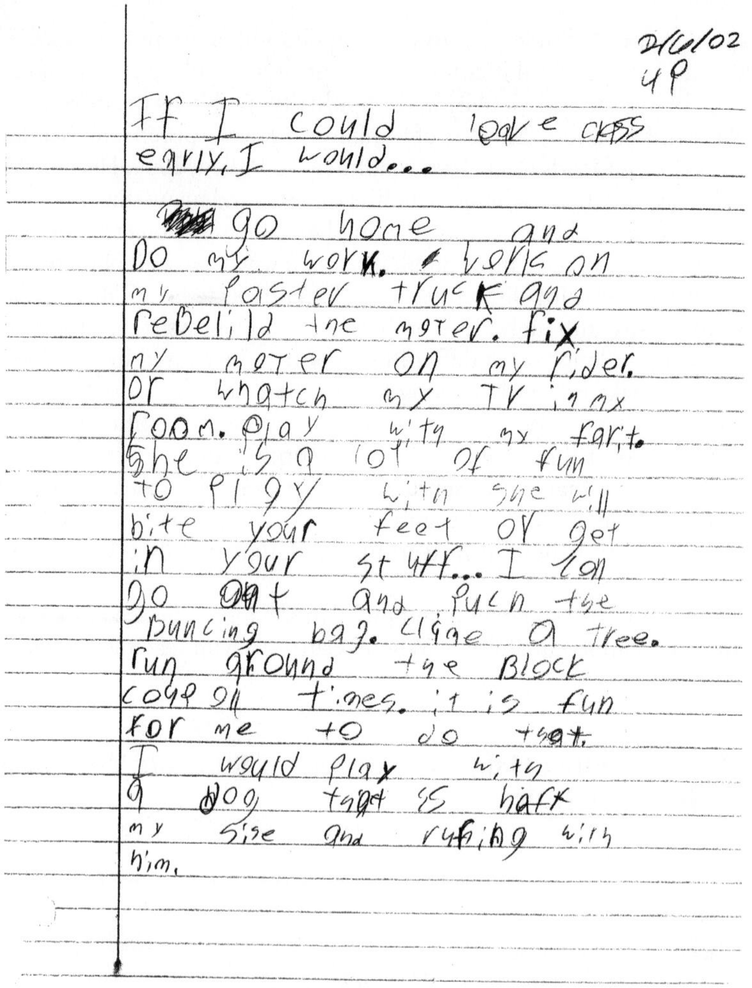

Source: From Friend, Marilyn, *Special Education: Contemporary Perspectives for School Professionals*, 2e. Published by Allyn and Bacon, Boston, MA. Copyright 2008 by Pearson Education. Adapted by permission of the publisher.

associating sounds with letters, students with some math disabilities have difficulty automatically associating numerals (1, 2, 3, etc.) with the correct magnitude—how many is 28, for example. So before young students learn math computations, some may need extra practice to become automatic in associating numerals with the quantities they represent (Rubinsten & Henik, 2006). As well, the writing of some students with learning disabilities is virtually unreadable (as you can see in Figure 4.2), and their spoken language can be halting and disorganized.

Students with learning disabilities often lack effective ways of approaching academic tasks. They don't know how to focus on the relevant information, get organized, apply learning strategies and study skills, change strategies when one isn't working, or evaluate their learning. They tend to be passive learners, in part because they don't know *how* to learn—they have failed so often. Working independently is especially trying, so homework and seatwork are often left incomplete (Hallahan et al., 2005).

Teaching Students With Learning Disabilities. Nancy Perry (see Perry et al., 2001) has argued that early diagnosis is important in order that students with learning disabilities get the remediation they need and do not become terribly frustrated and discouraged. Also, it is important to help students understand their disabilities. When students do not understand why they are having such trouble, they may become victims of learned helplessness. Students who experience learned helplessness believe that they cannot control or improve their own learning. This is a powerful belief.

Learned helplessness The expectation, based on previous experiences involving lack of control, that all of one's efforts will lead to failure.

The students never exert the effort to discover that they can make a difference in their own learning, so they remain passive and helpless. This becomes a greater problem as students move through school and into life beyond school. These students need to understand their disability and the accommodations they need to advocate for themselves.

Students with learning disabilities may also try to compensate for their problems and develop bad learning habits in the process, or they may begin avoiding certain subjects out of fear of not being able to handle the work. Research by Nancy Heath (1996; Heath & Ross, 2000) at McGill University indicates that students with learning disabilities are at risk for social withdrawal and even depression. To prevent these things from happening, teachers must be sensitive to the emotional and motivational impact of students' academic difficulties. Some strategies for supporting students with learning disabilities are listed below (Hardman et al., 2005):

Preschool years

- Keep verbal instructions short and simple.
- Match the level of content carefully to the child's developmental level.
- Give multiple examples to clarify meaning.
- Allow more practice than usual, especially when material is new.

Elementary school years

- Keep verbal instructions short and simple; have students repeat directions back to you to be sure they understand.
- Use mnemonics (memory strategies) in instruction to teach students how to remember.
- Repeat main points several times.
- Provide additional time for learning and practice—reteach when necessary.

Secondary school and transition years

- Directly teach self-monitoring strategies, such as cueing students to ask, "Was I paying attention?"
- Connect new material to knowledge students already have.
- Teach students to use external memory strategies and devices (tape-recording, note taking, creating to-do lists, etc.).

In general, emphasizing study skills and methods for processing information in a given subject, such as reading or math, seems to be effective. Many of the principles of cognitive learning described in Chapters 7 and 8 can be applied to help students improve their attention, memory, and problem-solving abilities (Sawyer, Graham, & Harris, 1992). Strategic Content Learning, developed by Deborah Butler at the University of British Columbia, is one example of this approach (Butler, 1998; Wong, Harris, Graham, & Butler, 2003). You may be thinking that these are good ideas for many students who need more support and direct teaching of study skills. You are right.

In teaching reading, a combination of teaching letter-sound (phonological) knowledge and word identification strategies appears to be effective. For example, Maureen Lovett at the University of Toronto and her colleagues (Lovett et al., 2000) taught students with severe reading disabilities to use the four different word identification strategies: (1) word identification by analogy, (2) seeking the part of the word that you know, (3) attempting different vowel pronunciations, and (4) "peeling off" prefixes and suffixes in a multi-syllabic word. Teachers worked one-on-one with the students to learn and practise these four strategies, along with analysis of word sounds and blending sounds into words (phonological knowledge). Explicit and intensive teaching of skills and strategies is especially helpful for students with reading disabilities. However, reading instruction should not focus solely on low-level skills. Students with learning disabilities should also be learning and using higher-order comprehension skills and strategies. One example of how teachers can accomplish this is described in the next section.

Reaching Every Student: Higher-Order Comprehension and Severe Learning Disabilities. Joanna Williams (2002) developed the Theme Identification Program to help middle school students with severe learning disabilities understand and use the abstract idea of themes in literature.

Teachers taught 12 different lessons using 12 stories. In summary, the process for each lesson was as follows:

Prereading: The teacher defines the idea of theme and leads a discussion on the value of themes, drawing on students' personal experiences.

Reading: The teacher reads the story and inserts questions while reading to help students connect what they know to the story. At the end of the reading, the class discusses the main point in the story, and the teacher reads a summary highlighting the points.

Discussion using the Theme Scheme: The teacher and students discuss the important information using six organizing questions. The first four questions focus on the content of the story:

- Who was the main character?
- What was her or his problem?
- What did she or he do?
- What happened at the end of the story?

The last two questions encourage students to make judgments in order to identify a theme:

- Was what happened good or bad?
- Why was it good or bad?

Identification of the theme: The students then state the theme in a standard format:

- [The main character] learned that she (he) should (not) ___________.
- We should (not) ___________.
- The theme of the story is ___________.

Application of theme: The students learn to ask three questions to generalize the theme:

- Can you name someone who should (not) ___________?
- When is it important for (that person) to do (or not do) ___________?
- In what situation will this help?

Multimodal activity: Every lesson after the first one includes a role play of the story theme where the students act out the characters in the story, an art activity to show the theme, or a music activity such as writing a rap song that communicates the theme.

Review: The class does a recap of the Theme Scheme and previews the next lesson.

For a summary of research about teaching higher-order skills to students with learning disabilities, see Swanson (2001).

Students With Hyperactivity and Attention Disorders

STOP & THINK If a student is struggling with time management and organization issues, what kind of accommodations would you provide?

You have probably heard and may even have used the term hyperactivity. The notion is a modern one; there were no hyperactive children 50 to 60 years ago. Today, if anything, the term is applied too often and too widely. Actually, hyperactivity is not one particular condition, but two kinds of problems that may or may not occur together—attention disorders and impulsive-hyperactivity problems.

Hyperactivity Behaviour disorder marked by atypical, excessive restlessness and inattentiveness.

Attention-deficit/hyperactivity disorder (ADHD) Current term for disruptive behaviour disorders marked by overactivity, excessive difficulty sustaining attention, or impulsiveness.

Characteristics of Students With Hyperactivity and Attention Disorders. Today, most psychologists agree that the main problem for children who are labelled hyperactive is directing and maintaining attention, not simply controlling their restlessness and physical activity. The American Psychiatric Association has established the diagnostic category of attention-deficit/hyperactivity disorder (ADHD) to identify children with this problem. Table 4.5 lists some indicators of ADHD used by this group.

TABLE 4.5 **Indicators of ADHD: Attention-Deficit/Hyperactivity Disorder**

Do any of your students show these signs? They could be indicators of ADHD.

Problems with *Inattention*

- Often does not give close attention to details or makes careless mistakes
- Has difficulty sustaining attention in tasks or play activities
- Does not seem to listen when spoken to directly
- Does not follow through on instructions and fails to finish school work (not due to oppositional behaviour or failure to understand instructions)
- Has difficulty organizing tasks or activities
- Avoids, dislikes, or is reluctant to engage in tasks that require sustained mental effort (such as school work or homework)
- Loses things necessary for tasks or activities
- Is easily distracted by extraneous stimuli
- Is forgetful in daily activities

Problems with *Impulse Control*

- Often blurts out answers before questions have been completed
- Has difficulty awaiting his or her turn
- Often interrupts or intrudes on others in conversations or games

Hyperactivity

- Fidgets with hands or feet or squirms in seat
- Often gets up from seat when remaining seated is expected
- Often runs about or climbs excessively in situations in which it is inappropriate (in adolescents, may be limited to subjective feelings of restlessness)
- Often has difficulty playing or engaging in leisure activities quietly
- Talks excessively
- Often acts as if "driven by a motor" and cannot remain still

Source: Reprinted with permission from *Diagnostic and Statistical Manual of Mental Disorders*, Fourth Edition, Text Revision. (Copyright 2000). American Psychiatric Association.

Children with ADHD are not only more physically active and inattentive than other children; they also have difficulty responding appropriately and working steadily toward goals (even their own goals). In addition, they may not be able to control their behaviour on command, even for a brief period. The problem behaviour is generally evident in all situations and with every teacher. It is difficult to know how many children should be classified as hyperactive. The most common estimate is 3 to 5 percent of the elementary school population in Canada (Hutchinson, 2007). About three to four times more boys than girls are identified as hyperactive, but the gap appears to be narrowing (Hallahan et al., 2005). Girls have the same symptoms as boys, but often they show the symptoms in less obvious ways, so they may not get identified as often and could miss getting appropriate support (Friend, 2008).

ADHD usually is diagnosed in elementary school, but problems with attention and hyperactivity may begin to show up much earlier (Friedman-Weieneth, Harvey, Youngswirth, & Goldstein, 2007). Just a few years ago, most psychologists thought that ADHD diminished as children entered adolescence, but now experts agree that the problems can persist into adulthood (Hallowell & Ratey, 1994). Adolescence—with the increased stresses of puberty, transition to middle or high school, more demanding academic work, and more engrossing social relationships—can be an especially difficult time for students with ADHD (Taylor, 1998).

Treatment and Teaching Students With ADHD. The most common intervention for students with ADHD is drug therapy. Ritalin and other prescribed drugs such as Adderall, Focalin,

Dexedrine, and Cylert are stimulants, but in particular dosages, they tend to have paradoxical effects on many children with ADHD: Short-term effects include possible improvements in social behaviours such as cooperation, attention, and compliance. Research suggests that about 70 to 80 percent of children with ADHD are more manageable when on medication. (Batschaw, 1997; Hutchinson, 2007). In general, students with ADHD who take stimulant medication engage in less stimulant-seeking behaviour and are more able to benefit from educational and social interventions (Hutchinson, 2007; Zentall, 1993). Of course, these drugs need to be carefully administered and their effects carefully monitored. Some children experience side effects such as loss of appetite or nausea, headaches, insomnia, and increased heart rate and blood pressure. For most children, these side effects are mild and can be controlled by adjusting the dosage. However, little is known about the long-term effects of drug therapy, so parents and teachers need to keep up with the research on treatments for ADHD. Table 4.6 lists some questions parents and teachers should ask about medication for children with ADHD.

While stimulant medications can improve the attention and behaviour of students with ADHD, in and of themselves they will not improve students' learning and achievement in school. For learning to occur, medication needs to be paired with other effective interventions. The methods that have proven most successful for helping students with ADHD are based on behavioural principles of learning such as those described in Chapter 6. One promising approach is positive behaviour support (PBS). According to Joe Lucyshyn (Lucyshyn et al., 2002) at the University of British Columbia, PBS, which is linked to applied behaviour analysis, helps families, educators, and psychologists identify and understand the full range of variables (e.g., personal, ecological) influencing problem behaviour. The goal of PBS is to foster more adaptive behaviour that supports learning. The bottom line is that even if students in your class are on medication, it is critical that they also learn the academic and social skills they will need to succeed. They need to learn how and when to apply learning strategies and study skills. Also, they need to be encouraged to persist when challenged by difficult tasks and to see themselves as having control over their learning and behaviour. Medication alone will not make this happen (Kneedler, 1984).

The notion of being in control is part of a new strategy for dealing with ADHD, one that stresses personal agency (Nylund, 2000). Rather than focusing on the child's problems, Nylund's

TABLE 4.6

Questions for Teachers and Parents to Ask About Medication for Children With ADHD

The most commonly prescribed medications for children and adolescents with ADHD are Ritalin (methylphenidate) and Dexedrine (dextroamphetamine). Parents and teachers should be well informed about these medications.

1. What is the medication? What information can I read about it?
2. Why is this medication prescribed for this adolescent? What changes should we expect to see at home? At school?
3. What behavioural program or behavioural therapy is being implemented in conjunction with this drug therapy?
4. How long will this medication be prescribed for this adolescent?
5. What are the side effects in the short term? In the long term?
6. What is the dosage? What is the schedule on which the medication will be taken?
7. How often will the adolescent be seen by the prescribing physician for re-evaluation?
8. Should the medication be stopped for a short period of time to see if it is still required? When?
9. Are there foods, beverages, or other substances that should not be consumed when one is taking this medication?
10. What kind of communication is necessary among home, school, and the adolescent to evaluate whether the medication is having the desired effect?
11. What procedures should be followed if the adolescent accidentally ingests an overdose?
12. Who explains all of this to the adolescent and what should the adolescent be told?

Source: Hutchinson, N. L. (2004). *Teaching exceptional children and adolescents: A Canadian casebook.* Toronto: Prentice Hall. Reprinted by permission.

idea is to enlist the child's strengths to conquer the child's problems—to put the child in control. New metaphors for the situation are developed. Rather than seeing the problems as inside the child, Nylund helps everyone see ADHD, trouble, boredom, and other enemies of learning as outside the child—demons to be conquered or unruly spirits to be enlisted in the service of what *the child* wants to accomplish. The focus is on solutions. The steps of Nylund's SMART approach are as follows:

Separating the problem of ADHD from the child;
Mapping the influence of ADHD on the child and family;
Attending to the exceptions to the ADHD story;
Reclaiming special abilities of children diagnosed with ADHD;
Telling and celebrating the new story.
(Nylund, 2000, p. xix)

As a teacher, you can look for times when the student is engaged—even short times. What is different about these times? Discover the student's strengths and allow yourself to be amazed by them. Make changes in your teaching that support the changes the student is trying to make. Nylund gives the following example. Nine-year-old Chris and his teacher, Ms. Baker, became partners in putting Chris in control of his concentration in school. Ms. Baker moved Chris's seat to the front of the room. The two designed a subtle signal to get Chris back on track, and Chris organized his messy desk. When Chris's concentration improved, Chris received the award shown in Figure 4.3 at a party in his honour. Chris described how he was learning to listen in class: "You just have to have a strong mind and tell ADHD and Boredom not to bother you" (Nylund, 2000, p. 166). See Table 4.7 for suggestions that came from students working with Nylund, telling how their teachers can help them gain control.

Students With Language and Communication Disorders

Language is a complex learned behaviour. Language disorders may arise from many sources, because so many different aspects of the individual are involved in learning language. A child with a hearing impairment may not learn to speak normally. Injuries can cause neurological problems that interfere with speech or language. Children who are not listened to, or whose perception of

FIGURE 4.3 **Conquering Boredom: Putting Students in Charge**
Notice how the words in the certificate recognize the child as being in control of his own life.

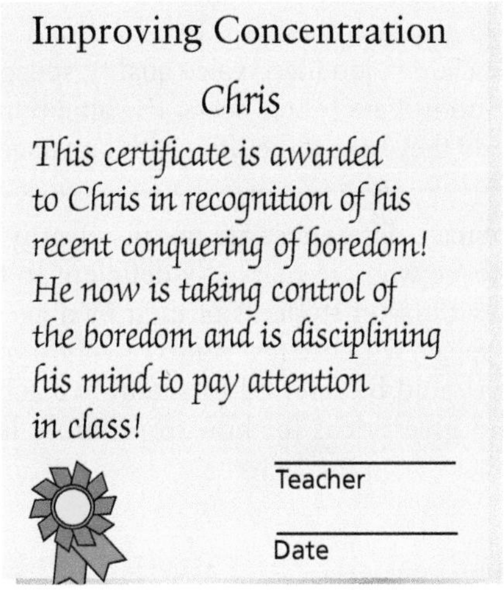

Improving Concentration

Chris

This certificate is awarded
to Chris in recognition of his
recent conquering of boredom!
He now is taking control of
the boredom and is disciplining
his mind to pay attention
in class!

Teacher

Date

Source: From Nylund, D. (2000). *Treating Huckleberry Finn: A new narrative approach to working with kids diagnosed ADD/ADHD.* San Francisco: Jossey-Bass. Copyright © 2000 by Jossey-Bass. This material is adapted by permission of John Wiley & Sons, Inc.

TABLE 4.7 Students With ADHD Give Teachers Advice
Students with ADHD make these recommendations for their teachers (Nylund, 2000).

- Use lots of pictures (visual clues) to help me learn.
- Recognize cultural and racial identity.
- Know when to bend the rules.
- Notice when I am doing well.
- Don't tell the other kids that I am taking Ritalin.
- Offer us choices.
- Don't just lecture—it's boring!
- Realize that I am intelligent.
- Let me walk around the classroom.
- Don't give tons of homework.
- More recess!
- Be patient.

the world is distorted by emotional problems, will reflect these problems in their language development. Because speaking involves movements, any impairment of the motor functions involved with speech can cause language disorders. And because language development and thinking are so interwoven, any problems in cognitive functioning can affect ability to use language.

Speech Impairments. Students who cannot produce sounds effectively for speaking are considered to have a **speech impairment**. Winzer (2006), at the University of Lethbridge, estimates that between 5 and 8 percent of school-aged children have some form of speech impairment. Articulation problems and stuttering are the two most common problems, and about two-thirds of all children with communication disorders are boys (Winzer, 2006).

Articulation disorders include substituting one sound for another (*thunthine* for *sunshine*), distorting a sound (*shoup* for *soup*), adding a sound (*ideer* for *idea*), or omitting sounds (*po-y* for *pony*) (Smith, 1998). Keep in mind, however, that most children are 6 to 8 years old before they can successfully pronounce all English sounds in normal conversation. The sounds of the consonants *l, r, y, s,* and *z* and the consonant blends *sh, ch, zh,* and *th* are the last to be mastered. Also, there are dialect differences based on geography that do not represent articulation problems. A student from Newfoundland might say *ideer* for *idea* but have no speech impairment.

Stuttering generally appears between the ages of 3 and 4. Causes of stuttering are unclear, but might include emotional or neurological problems or learned behaviour. Whatever the cause, stuttering can lead to embarrassment and anxiety. If stuttering continues more than a year or so, the child should be referred to a speech therapist. Early intervention can make a big difference (Hardman et al., 2005).

Voicing problems, a third type of speech impairment, include speaking with an inappropriate pitch, quality, or loudness, or in a monotone (Hallahan et al., 2009). A student with any of these problems should be referred to a speech therapist. Recognizing the problem is the first step. Be alert for students whose pronunciation, loudness, voice quality, speech fluency, expressive range, or speaking rate is very different from that of their peers. Pay attention also to students who seldom speak. Are they simply shy, or do they have difficulties with language?

Speech impairment Inability to produce sounds effectively for speaking.

Articulation disorders Any of a variety of pronunciation difficulties.

Stuttering Repetitions, prolongations, and hesitations that block flow of speech.

Voicing problems Speech impairments involving inappropriate pitch, quality, loudness, or intonation.

Developmental disabilities Significantly below-average intellectual and adaptive social behaviour evident before the age of 18.

Language Disorders. Language differences are not necessarily language disorders. Students with language disorders are those who are markedly deficient in their ability to understand or express language, compared with other students of their own age and cultural group (Owens, 1999). Students who seldom speak, who use few words or very short sentences, or who rely only on gestures to communicate should be referred to a qualified school professional for observation or assessment. Table 4.8 gives ideas for how to promote language development in all students.

Students With Developmental Disabilities

The term **developmental disabilities** refers to disabilities that affect all aspects of development and is used widely in Canada to replace the term *mental retardation,* which is still used in the United States (Hutchinson, 2007). Students with developmental delays have significant limitations in

TABLE 4.8

Encouraging Language Development

- Talk about things in which the child is interested.
- Follow the child's lead. Reply to the child's initiations and comments. Share his or her excitement.
- Don't ask too many questions. If you must, use questions that result in longer explanatory answers such as "How did/do . . . ?" "Why did/do . . . ?" and "What happened?"
- Encourage the child to ask questions. Respond openly and honestly. If you don't want to answer a question, say so and explain why (e.g., "I don't think I want to answer that question; it's very personal").
- Use a pleasant tone of voice. You need not be a comedian, but you can be light and humorous. Children love it when adults are a little silly.
- Don't be judgmental or make fun of a child's language. If you are overly critical of the child's language or try to catch and correct all errors, he or she will stop talking to you.
- Allow enough time for the child to respond.
- Treat the child with courtesy by not interrupting when he or she is talking.
- Include the child in family and classroom discussions. Encourage participation and listen to the child's ideas.
- Be accepting of the child and of the child's language. Hugs and acceptance can go a long way.
- Provide opportunities for the child to use language and to have that language work for him or her to accomplish his or her goals.

Source: From Owens, R. E., Jr. (1999). *Language disorders: A functional approach to assessment and intervention* (3rd ed.). Boston: Allyn & Bacon. Copyright © 1999 by Pearson Education. Reprinted by permission.

cognitive abilities and adaptive behaviour. In general, these individuals learn at a far slower rate than other students, and they may reach a point at which their learning plateaus. Often, these individuals have difficulties maintaining skills without ongoing practice and generalizing skills learned in one context to another. Also, many of these students have difficulties carrying out tasks that involve combining or integrating multiple skills (e.g., doing the laundry).

Intelligence tests are typically used to identify developmental delays. An IQ score below 70 to 75 is one indicator of a developmental delay, but it is not enough evidence to diagnose a child as having a developmental disability. There must also be problems with adaptive behaviour, day-to-day independent living, and social functioning. This caution is especially important when interpreting the scores of students from different cultures. Defining developmental disabilities based on test scores alone can create what some critics call "six-hour retardates"—students who are seen as developmentally disabled only for that part of the day when they are in school.

Given the limitations of formal assessments, advocates for individuals with developmental disabilities are beginning to argue that it is better to focus efforts on identifying the amount and types of services these individuals require. In Canada, a distinction is made between two levels of developmental disabilities, mild and severe (Hutchinson, 2007). This distinction is made primarily on the basis of the level of support required for adaptive functioning. As a general education teacher, you may not have contact with children needing extensive or pervasive support, but you will probably work with children with mild developmental disabilities. In the early grades, these students may simply learn more slowly than their peers. They need more time and more practice to learn and have difficulty transferring learning from one setting to another or putting small skills together to accomplish a more complex task.

Teaching Students With Developmental Disabilities. For many students with developmental disabilities between the ages of 9 and 13, learning goals include basic reading, writing, arithmetic, learning about the local environment, social behaviour, and personal interests. In junior and senior high school, the emphasis is on vocational and domestic skills, literacy for living (using the telephone book; reading signs, labels, and newspaper ads; completing a job application), job-related behaviours such as courtesy and punctuality, health self-care, and citizenship skills. Today, there is a growing emphasis on **transition programming**—preparing the student to live and work in the

Transition programming Gradual preparation of exceptional students to move from high school into further education or training, employment, or community involvement.

community. Nancy Hutchinson and her colleagues at Queen's University, Kingston, are researching the benefits of cooperative education and on-the-job training for high school students with developmental disabilities. Their research shows that these students benefit from workplace experiences that gradually increase demands for independence and productivity (Hutchinson et al., 2005). As you will see later in the chapter, schools need to design an IEP, or individualized educational program, for every child with disabilities. An ITP, or individualized transition plan, may be part of the IEP for students with retardation (Friend, 2008).

The accompanying *Guidelines* box lists suggestions for teaching students with below-average general intelligence.

Students With Emotional or Behavioural Disorders

Students with emotional and behavioural disorders can be among the most challenging to teach in general education classrooms, and are a source of concern for many prospective teachers (Avramidis, Bayliss, & Burden, 2000). Behaviour becomes a problem when it deviates so greatly from what is appropriate for the child's age group that it significantly interferes with the child's own growth and development and/or the lives of others. Clearly, deviation implies a difference from some standard, and standards of behaviour differ from one situation, age group, culture, and historical period to another. Thus, what passes for team spirit in the football bleachers might be seen as disturbed behaviour in a bank or restaurant. In addition, the deviation must be more than a temporary response to stressful events; it must be consistent across time and in different situations (Forness & Knitzer, 1992). Table 4.9 describes a few of the specific disorders covered by the *Diagnostic and Statistical Manual of Mental Disorders* (4th edition, revised), also called the *DSM-IV-TR*.

Emotional and behavioural disorders Behaviours or emotions that deviate so much from the norm that they interfere with the child's own growth and development and/or the lives of others—inappropriate behaviours, unhappiness or depression, fears and anxieties, and trouble with relationships.

Children who have *conduct disorders* are aggressive, destructive, disobedient, uncooperative, distractible, disruptive, and persistent. They have been corrected and punished for the same misbehaviour countless times. Often, these children are disliked by the adults and even by the other children in their lives. They can be bullies or they can be the ones being bullied. The most successful strategies for helping these children include behaviour management approaches such as those described in Chapter 6 and PBS (described earlier in this chapter). These students need very clear rules and consequences, consistently enforced. Nancy Hutchinson (2007) at Queen's University recommends that students with behaviour disorders have the following supports in their classrooms

GUIDELINES: Teaching Children With Below-Average General Intelligence

1. Be clear about your instructional objectives and expectations. Use instructional approaches that match those expectations and, whenever possible, make adaptations that are appropriate for the student and that become a natural part of your instructional environment.
2. Use heterogeneous classroom groups to support and include students with moderate and severe disabilities. Using strategies such as peer tutoring, cooperative learning, and friend support systems fosters a sense of community in the classroom and helps students learn to value and respect one another.
3. Sometimes students with disabilities need specialized instruction about skills that are not a part of your regular curriculum. Identify optimal times for this instruction to occur (e.g., when students are working on independent projects) and, when appropriate, involve other students in the classroom.
4. Enlist natural support systems such as older students, parents, volunteers, and teaching assistants. These individuals can reinforce your instructional objectives and support students' development of appropriate social skills.
5. Involve the students' families whenever possible. Family members can provide valuable tips about how their children learn and can reinforce your goals and objectives at home.
6. Take advantage of technology. For example, students who cannot use language to communicate can be supported by various forms of augmentative communication (e.g., electronic communication boards).

Source: Adapted from Friend, M., Bursuck, W., & Hutchinson, N. (1998). *Including exceptional students: A practical guide for classroom teachers.* Scarborough, ON: Allyn & Bacon Canada.

TABLE 4.9 Examples of Emotional and Behavioural Disorders From the *Diagnostic and Statistical Manual of Mental Disorders*

Many specific emotional and behavioural disorders have been identified, and these are included in the *Diagnostic and Statistical Manual of Mental Disorders* (fourth edition, text revision) (*DSM-IV-TR*). Instead of being called emotional and behaviour disorders, they are referred to as mental disorders. The following list, although not complete, includes examples of mental disorders listed in that publication that educators would consider emotional and behaviour disorders:

- **Anxiety disorders.** Anxiety disorders occur when students experience an overwhelming sense of fear or dread. One example is obsessive-compulsive disorder (OCD) in which students cannot stop themselves from worrying excessively about a specific concern, for example, germs. Other examples include phobias (fear of specific items, such as spiders, or fear of certain activities, such as going to school) and post-traumatic stress disorder (PTSD) in which students re-live in nightmares or flashbacks a traumatic event that they witnessed.
- **Disruptive behaviour disorders.** This category includes three types of disorders:
  - *Attention-deficit/hyperactivity disorder* . . . is characterized by inattention, a high level of activity and impulsivity, or a combination of these. Note, though, that it often is not considered a disability.
  - *Oppositional defiant disorder* (ODD) is diagnosed when students are defiant with adults and vindictive or blaming with peers to an excessive degree over a long period of time.
  - *Conduct disorders* are diagnosed when students fight, bully, display cruelty to animals or people, or otherwise repeatedly break serious rules.
- **Eating disorders.** The most common eating disorder is anorexia nervosa in which students believe they are overweight and refuse to eat, even when they are near starvation.
- **Mood disorders.** Also called affective disorders, this group includes depression . . . and bipolar disorder, also called manic depression, in which students' moods swing from extreme highs (manic) to extreme lows (depression).
- **Tic disorders.** Tics are involuntary, rapid, stereotyped movements of specific muscle groups. Students with tics may blink their eyes or repeatedly sniff. The most well known tic disorder is Tourette syndrome, a disorder that ranges from mild to severe and includes both facial or other physical tics as well as vocal tics, often "barking" or profanity.

Source: From Friend, Marilyn. *Special Education: Contemporary Perspectives for School Professionals.* Published by Allyn and Bacon, Boston, MA. Copyright © 2006 by Pearson Education. Reprinted by permission of the publisher.

to enhance their self-confidence, sense of responsibility and independence, and engagement in positive problem solving:

- structure, predictability, and consistency;
- immediate, frequent, and specific feedback with consequences;
- opportunities for academic success;
- positive alternatives to current behaviours;
- positive school-to-home support systems;
- evidence that the student is making a change for the better.

Early intervention and the classroom and school-wide initiatives described in Chapter 3 are also effective (Osher, Bear, Sprague, & Doyle, 2010; Sprague & Walker, 2000; Swearer, Espelage, Vaillancourt, & Hymel, 2010). Importantly, most students with behavioural problems need challenging and cognitively engaging work. According to Hutchinson (2007), we should not lower our expectations or excuse these students from learning. The future is not promising for those who never learn to control their behaviour and who also fail academically, so waiting for the students to "outgrow" their problems is seldom effective. In fact, doing nothing may result in the problem behaviours of the individual becoming more socialized. Students with behavioural problems are drawn to gangs and get involved in anti-social behaviour, such as stealing and vandalism, because their peer culture expects it.

Children who are extremely anxious, withdrawn, shy, depressed, and hypersensitive, or who cry easily and have little confidence, may have an *anxiety-withdrawal disorder*. These children have few social skills and consequently very few friends. The most successful approaches with them appear to involve the direct teaching of social skills (Gresham, 1981).

Many exceptional students—those with learning disabilities, developmental disabilities, or ADHD, for example—may also have emotional or behavioural problems as they struggle in school. In Chapter 12, we will consider how to help all students cope with social and emotional challenges that threaten both their own learning and the learning of others in the classroom.

No set of teaching techniques can be effective for every child. You should work with the special education teachers in your school to design appropriate instruction for individual students. Also, you will need to continue your professional development in this area throughout your teaching career. One way to do this is to read professional journals. Table 4.10 lists professional journals that may help you understand your students.

Let's consider an area where teachers may be able to detect problems and make a difference—suicide.

Suicide. The Canadian Institutes of Health Research (CIHR, 2006) rates suicide as the second leading cause of death among youth aged 13–18, and for every youth who successfully dies by suicide there are another 200 who attempt to kill themselves. The rate of death by suicide is higher for boys than girls, but non-fatal, self-inflicted injuries are more common among girls. Some minority groups, including youth with disabilities and youth who are gay or lesbian (Galliher et al., 2004; Wilson, Armstrong, Furrie, & Walcot, 2009), are at higher risk for suicide than others. Suicide in Aboriginal youth populations is especially high compared with other groups. In 2006, Health Canada estimated the rates of suicide for First Nations youth were five to seven times that for non-Aboriginal youth, and rates of suicide for Inuit youth were among the highest in the world (11 times the national average).

Suicide is often regarded by youth as a response to life problems—problems that parents and teachers sometimes dismiss. There are many warning signs that trouble is brewing. Watch for changes in eating or sleeping habits, weight, grades, disposition, activity level, or interest in friends. Students at risk of suicide sometimes suddenly give away prized possessions such as cell phones, iPods, clothing, or pets. They may seem depressed or hyperactive and may say things like, "Nothing matters anymore," "You won't have to worry about me anymore," or "I wonder what dying is like." They may start missing school or quit doing work. The situation is especially dangerous if the student not only talks about suicide but also has a plan for carrying out a suicide attempt.

If you suspect that there is a problem, talk to the student directly. One feeling shared by many people who attempt suicide is that no one really takes them seriously. "A question about suicide does not provoke suicide. Indeed, teens (and adults) often experience relief when someone finally

TABLE 4.10 **Reading the Journals**

Special Education Journals	General Education Journals
Education and Training in Mental Retardation	*Canadian Journal of Education*
Exceptional Children	*Education Canada*
Exceptionality Education Canada	*Educational Leadership*
Focus on Exceptional Children	*Journal of Reading*
Intervention in School and Clinic	*Phi Delta Kappan*
Journal of Learning Disabilities	*Reading Research Quarterly*
Journal of Special Education	*Reading Teacher*
Learning Disabilities Research and Practice	*Review of Educational Research*
Learning Disability Quarterly	
Remedial and Special Education	
Teaching Exceptional Children	

Source: Hutchinson, N. L. (2007). *Inclusion of exceptional learners in Canadian schools: A practical handbook for teachers* (2nd ed.) (p. 29). Toronto: Prentice Hall. Reprinted with permission by Pearson Education Canada Inc.

TABLE 4.11

Myths and Facts About Suicide

Myth:	People who talk about suicide don't kill themselves.
Fact:	Eight out of 10 people who commit suicide tell someone that they're thinking about hurting themselves before they actually do it.
Myth:	Only certain types of people commit suicide.
Fact:	All types of people commit suicide—male and female, young and old, rich and poor, country people and city people. It happens in every racial, ethnic, and religious group.
Myth:	When a person talks about suicide, you should change the subject to get his or her mind off it.
Fact:	You should take them seriously. Listen carefully to what they are saying. Give them a chance to express their feelings. Let them know you are concerned. And help them get help.
Myth:	Most people who kill themselves really want to die.
Fact:	Most people who kill themselves are confused about whether they want to die. Suicide is often intended as a cry for help.

Source: From Bell, R. (1980). *Changing bodies, changing lives: A book for teens on sex and relationships.* New York: Random House, p. 142.

cares enough to ask" (Range, 1993, p. 145). Be realistic, not poetic, about suicide. Ask about specifics, and take the student seriously. Also, be aware that teenage suicides often occur in clusters. After one student acts or when stories about a suicide are reported in the media, other teens are more likely to copy the suicide (Lewinsohn, Rohde, & Seeley, 1994; Rice & Dolgin, 2002). Table 4.11 lists common myths and facts about suicide.

Drug Abuse. Although drug abuse is not always associated with emotional or behavioural problems and people without these challenges may abuse drugs, many adolescents with emotional problems also abuse drugs. Modern society makes growing up a very confusing process. Celebrities who are attractive and popular with youth drink alcohol and smoke cigarettes with seemingly little concern for their health. We have over-the-counter drugs for almost every common ailment. Coffee wakes us up, and a pill helps us sleep. And then we tell our youth to "say no" to drugs.

For many reasons, not just because of these contradictory messages, drug use has become a problem for students. Accurate statistics are hard to find, but one survey conducted by Health Canada (2004/05) indicates that 21 percent of youths in grades 5 to 9 have tried tobacco. While this is alarming, given all the information available about the harmful effects of smoking, it represents a 50 percent reduction in the prevalence of youth smoking over the past 10–15 years. Data from the Canadian Centre on Substance Abuse (2007) found that 83 percent of 15- to 24-year-olds either were current drinkers or had consumed alcohol within the previous year. Marijuana is the most popular illicit drug. In fact, it is more popular than tobacco among youth, used by 17 percent of students in grades 7 to 9. Significantly, these behaviours are associated with peer groups. Two-thirds of youths who reported having been drunk once also indicated that their peers drank alcohol. Drug use among secondary school students has been gradually declining or holding steady since 2001, with the exception of inhalants. Inhalants (glues, paint thinners, nail polish remover, aerosol sprays, etc.) are inexpensive and available. Also, students don't realize that they are risking injury or death when they use inhalants. One study found that the proportion of students in grades 8 and 10 who believe that inhalants are dangerous is actually declining (Johnston, O'Malley, Bachman, & Schulenberg, 2004).

Prevention. What can be done about preventing drug use among our students? First, we should distinguish between experimentation and abuse. Many students try a drug at a party but do not become regular users. The best way to help students who have trouble saying no appears to be through peer programs that teach how to say no assertively. Also, the older students are when they experiment with drugs, the more likely they are to make responsible choices, so helping younger students say no is a clear benefit.

LOW-INCIDENCE DISABILITIES

In this section, we discuss students with disabilities that are less common in the general population. Low-incidence disabilities include severe developmental disabilities, such as autism, and sensory impairments having to do with hearing and vision. They also include physical disabilities and chronic health concerns that can range from allergies and asthma to diabetes, cystic fibrosis, HIV and AIDS, and cancer. Over the course of your teaching career, it is likely that you will encounter only a few students with low-incidence disabilities. However, you can still make a difference in their lives. For more information about these and other disabilities, we refer you to the descriptions in Table 4.12 and to the professional journals listed in Table 4.10 on page 142.

TABLE 4.12 Students With Low-Incidence Exceptionalities, Physical Disabilities, and Chronic Medical Conditions

Exceptionality	Description
	Low-Incidence Exceptionalities
Severe developmental disabilities	Severe limitation in both intellectual functioning and adaptive behaviour; focus is on the individual's need for support to function in the community
Autism	Impairments in verbal and non-verbal communication and reciprocal social interaction; restricted, repetitive patterns of behaviour; and intellectual disability
Asperger syndrome	Severe and sustained impairment in social interaction, and development of restricted, repetitive patterns of behaviour and interests
Hearing impairments	Hearing loss that has significantly affected development of speech and/or language and has caused students to need adaptations to learn
Visual impairments	Blind or partially sighted students who need adaptations to learn through channels other than visual
	Physical Disabilities and Chronic Medical Conditions
Nervous system impairment	
Cerebral palsy	Disorders affecting body movement and muscle coordination resulting from damage to brain during pregnancy or first three years
Spina bifida	Neural tube defect that occurs during first four weeks of pregnancy causing vertebrae or spinal cord to fail to develop properly
Epilepsy	Neurological disorder involving sudden bursts of electrical energy in the brain
Tourette syndrome	Neurological disorder characterized by tics
Brain injury	Damage to brain tissue that prevents it from functioning properly
Fetal alcohol syndrome	Neurological disorder caused by significant prenatal exposure to alcohol
Musculoskeletal conditions	
Muscular dystrophy	Genetically based muscle disorders that result in progressive muscle weakness
Juvenile arthritis	Continuous inflammation of joints in young people under 16
Chronic health impairments	
Diabetes	Condition in which the body does not make enough insulin and has problems absorbing and storing sugars
Allergies	Sensitivity or abnormal immune response to normal substance, which can cause anaphylactic shock
Asthma	Chronic lung condition, characterized by difficulty breathing, in which airways are obstructed by inflammation, muscle spasms, and excess mucus
Cystic fibrosis	Incurable disorder caused by inherited genetic defect, affecting mainly the lungs and the digestive system
HIV and AIDS	Human immunodeficiency virus and acquired immune deficiency syndrome are virus-caused illnesses resulting in the breakdown of the immune system; currently no known cure exists

Students With Physical Disabilities and Chronic Health Concerns

Some students must have special devices, such as braces, special shoes, crutches, or wheelchairs, to participate in school programs. If the school has the necessary architectural features, such as ramps, elevators, and accessible washrooms, and if teachers allow for the physical limitations of students, little needs to be done to alter the usual educational program. Other students have chronic health concerns that require moment-to-moment accommodations.

Cerebral Palsy. Cerebral palsy (CP) is a disorder that affects muscle tone, movement, and motor skills—children with cerebral palsy have difficulty moving in a coordinated way (Kids Health, 2009). Other vital functions that also involve motor skills and muscles may be involved and cause difficulty breathing, controlling bladder and bowel, and eating. The most common cause of cerebral palsy is lack of oxygen causing brain damage at or before birth. However, cerebral palsy also can develop during the first three to five years of a child's life if, for example, a child contracts meningitis or viral encephalitis (American Academy of Family Physicians, 2009). Cerebral palsy can be mild or severe. For example, a child with mild CP may have awkward movements but require very little in the way of adaptations and accommodations. A child who has severe cerebral palsy may not be able to walk or may have trouble speaking. Some children with cerebral palsy will require lifelong care and assistance. Cerebral palsy is not degenerative; that is, it does not worsen over time (American Academy of Family Physicians, 2009). The most common form of cerebral palsy is characterized by spasticity (overly tight or tense muscles).

Many children with cerebral palsy have additional disabilities (KidsHealth, 2009). For example, many children with cerebral palsy also have hearing impairments, speech problems, or mild developmental disabilities. In classrooms, and other settings, these secondary handicaps may create the greatest challenges. The strategies we describe for other children with language and learning disabilities and sensory impairments can work for these children too. Assistive technologies, like those described near the end of this chapter, can help them do their work. Exercise and muscle training are critical, so physical and occupational therapy may be part of their individualized family or education plans. Importantly, professionals working as a multidisciplinary team with a coordinated plan can provide a wide range of resources to support development and learning in children with cerebral palsy and other physical disabilities.

INSTRUCTIONAL ACCOMMODATIONS Physical and instructional accommodations can enable students with many kinds of disabilities to participate in general education classrooms. A specially designed desk enables this young girl with cerebral palsy to work independently in class.

Seizure Disorders (Epilepsy). A seizure is a cluster of behaviour that occurs in response to abnormal neurochemical activities in the brain (Hardman et al., 2005). The effects of the seizure depend on where the discharge of energy starts in the brain and how far it spreads. People with epilepsy have recurrent seizures, but not all seizures are the result of epilepsy; temporary conditions such as high fevers or infections can also trigger seizures. Seizures take many forms and differ with regard to the length, frequency, and movements involved. A partial seizure involves only a small part of the brain, whereas a generalized seizure includes much more of the brain.

Most generalized seizures (once called *grand mal*) are accompanied by uncontrolled jerking movements that ordinarily last from 2 to 5 minutes, possible loss of bowel or bladder control, and irregular breathing, followed by a deep sleep or coma. On regaining consciousness, the student may

Cerebral palsy Condition involving a range of motor or coordination difficulties due to brain damage.

Spasticity Overly tight or tense muscles, characteristic of some forms of cerebral palsy.

Epilepsy Disorder marked by seizures and caused by abnormal electrical discharges in the brain.

Generalized seizure A seizure involving a large portion of the brain.

be very weary, confused, and in need of extra sleep. Most seizures can be controlled by medication. If a student has a seizure accompanied by convulsions in class, the teacher must take action so that the student will not be injured. The major danger to a student having a seizure is getting hurt by striking a hard surface during the violent jerking.

For this or any other medical emergency, it is important to stay calm and reassure the rest of the class. Do not try to restrain the child's movements; you can't stop the seizure once it starts. Lower the child gently to the floor, away from furniture or walls. Move hard objects away. Loosen scarves, ties, or anything that might make breathing difficult. Turn the child's head gently to the side and put a soft coat or blanket under the student's head. Never put anything in the student's mouth—it is not true that people having seizures can swallow their tongues. Don't attempt artificial respiration unless the student does not start breathing again after the seizure stops. Find out from the student's parents how the seizure is usually dealt with. If one seizure follows another and the student does not regain consciousness in between, if the student is pregnant, if the student has a medical ID that does not say "epilepsy, seizure disorder," if there are signs of injury, or if the seizure goes on for more than 5 minutes, get medical help right away (Friend, 2008). For more ideas and information, see **www.epilepsy.ca**.

Not all seizures are dramatic. Sometimes the student just loses contact briefly. The student may stare, fail to respond to questions, drop objects, and miss what has been happening for 1 to 30 seconds. These partial seizures or absence seizures, which were once called *petit mal*, can easily go undetected. If a child in your class appears to daydream frequently, does not seem to know what is going on at times, or cannot remember what has just happened when you ask, you should consult the school psychologist or nurse. The major problem for students with partial seizures is that they miss the continuity of the class interaction—these seizures can occur as often as 100 times a day. If their seizures are frequent, students will find the lessons confusing. Question these students to be sure they are understanding and following the lesson. Be prepared to repeat yourself periodically.

Other Serious Health Concerns. There are many other health problems that affect students' learning, in great part because they cause students to miss school, leading to lost instructional time and missed opportunities for friendships. Consider the following health concerns that you may have to deal with in your classroom:

- Asthma is a chronic lung condition affecting more than half a million Canadian children and youth—it is the leading cause of school absences (Asthma Society of Canada, 2009). Since there is no cure for asthma, the goal is to control the symptoms. This can be done with medication and by helping children avoid what "triggers" their symptoms. Common triggers include pollens, pet dander, and especially second-hand smoke.
- Diabetes is a metabolic disorder that occurs when the pancreas does not produce enough insulin to deal with sugar in the bloodstream. This disease is becoming increasingly common in children, especially those who are overweight or obese. Diabetes can be controlled through diet and regular doses of insulin (Rosenberg et al., 2008; Werts et al., 2007).
- What once were terminal diseases in children are now illnesses they can survive or learn to live with. For example, the current survival rate from common childhood cancers (e.g., leukemia and brain and central nervous system tumours) exceeds 80 percent (Canadian Cancer Society, 2008; Daly, Kral, & Brown, 2008; National Cancer Institute, 2009). Unfortunately, the treatments (e.g., chemotherapy and radiation) often have negative long-term effects on development and learning.

In the case of each health condition, teachers need to talk to parents to know how the problems are handled, what the signs are that dangerous situations might be developing, and what resources are available for the student. Keep records of any incidents—they may be useful in the student's medical diagnosis and treatment, and consider appropriate accommodations on a case-by-case basis (e.g., some children may just need additional time on assignments, others will need emotional support and/or support for learning much like students with other disabilities).

Students With Sensory Impairments

Partial seizure or absence seizure A seizure involving only a small part of the brain.

Students With Hearing Impairments and Students Who Are Deaf. You will hear the term *hearing impaired* used to describe students who have difficulties hearing. The deaf community and researchers prefer the terms *deaf* and *hard of hearing*. The number of deaf students has been declining over the past three decades, but when the problem does occur, the consequences for learning are serious (Hunt & Marshall, 2002). Signs of hearing problems are turning one ear toward the speaker, favouring one ear in conversation, or misunderstanding conversation when the speaker's face cannot be seen. Other indications include not following directions, seeming distracted or confused at times, frequently asking people to repeat what they have said, mispronouncing new words or names, and being reluctant to participate in class discussions. Take note particularly of students who have frequent earaches, sinus infections, or allergies.

In the past, educators have debated whether oral or manual approaches are better for children who are deaf or hard of hearing. Oral approaches involve speech reading (also called lip reading) and training students to use whatever limited hearing they may have. Manual approaches include sign language and finger spelling. Research indicates that children who learn some manual method of communicating perform better in academic subjects and are more socially mature than students who are exposed only to oral methods. Today, the trend is to combine both approaches (Hallahan et al., 2009).

Another perspective suggests that people who are deaf are part of a different culture with a different language, values, social institutions, and literature. Hunt and Marshall (2002) quote one deaf professional: "How would women like to be referred to as male-impaired, or whites like to be called black-impaired? I'm not impaired; I'm deaf!" (p. 348). From this perspective, a goal is to help deaf children become bilingual and bicultural, to be able to function effectively in both cultures. Technological innovations such as teletypewriters in homes and public phones and the many avenues of communication possible through email and the internet have expanded communication possibilities for all people with hearing problems.

Students Who Are Visually Impaired. Approximately 1 in 1000 students in Canada is visually impaired (Hutchinson, 2007). The majority of these students will be print users versus Braille users (American Printing House for the Blind, 2009). Students who have difficulty seeing often hold books either very close to or very far from their eyes. They may squint, rub their eyes frequently, or complain that their eyes burn or itch. Students with vision problems may misread material on the board, describe their vision as being blurred, be very sensitive to light, or hold their heads at an odd angle. They may become irritable when they have to work at a desk or lose interest if they have to follow an activity happening across the room (Hunt & Marshall, 2002). Any of these signs should be reported to a qualified school professional.

Mild vision problems can be overcome with corrective lenses. However, students with more significant visual impairments probably require special materials and equipment to function in general education classrooms. Most of these students have partial or low vision; that is, they have some useful vision between 20/70 and 20/200 (on the Snellen scale, where 20/20 is considered normal). For example, a person with 20/70 vision can only see at 6 metres what individuals with normal vision see at 21.3 metres. An individual with 20/200 vision is considered legally and educationally blind. Students who are educationally blind must use hearing and touch as their primary learning channels (Kirk, Gallagher, & Anastasiow, 1993).

Special materials and equipment that help these students function in regular classrooms include large-print typewriters; software that converts printed material to speech or to Braille; electronic organizers that have talking appointment books or address books; variable-speed tape recorders (which allow teachers to make time-compressed tape recordings that can be sped up in a way that changes the rate of speech without changing the voice pitch); special calculators; the abacus; three-dimensional maps, charts, and models; and special measuring devices. For students with visual problems, the quality of the print is often more important than the size, so watch out for hard-to-read handouts and blurry copies. Make yourself aware of local, provincial, and national resource centres (e.g., Special Education Technology, SET-BC, in British Columbia, and the Canadian National Institute for the Blind, CNIB) that have resource materials and assistive technologies for students with sensory impairments.

The arrangement of your classroom is also an issue. Students with low vision or blindness need to know where things are, so consistency matters—a place for everything and everything in its place. Leave plenty of space for moving around the room and make sure to monitor possible obstacles and safety hazards, such as garbage cans in aisles and open cabinet doors. If you rearrange the room, give students with visual problems a chance to learn the new layout. Make sure that each student has a buddy for fire drills or other emergencies (Friend, Bursuck, & Hutchinson, 1998).

Speech reading Using visual cues to understand language.

Sign language Communication system of hand movements that symbolize words and concepts.

Finger spelling Communication system that "spells out" each letter with a hand position.

Low vision Vision limited to close objects.

Educationally blind Needing Braille materials in order to learn.

Students With Autism Spectrum Disorders

You may be familiar with the term *autism*. According to the American Psychiatric Association (2000), autism is a developmental disability that significantly affects verbal and non-verbal communication, social interaction, and imaginative creativity, and is characterized by restrictive, repetitive, and stereotypic patterns of behaviour, interests, and activities. Generally, autism is evident before age 3. We use the term autism spectrum disorders to emphasize that autism includes a range of disorders, from mild to major. From an early age, children with autism spectrum disorders may have difficulties in social relations. They do not form connections with others, avoid eye contact, or don't share feelings such as enjoyment or interest with others. Communication is impaired. About half of these students are non-verbal; they have very few or no language skills. Others make up their own language. They may obsessively insist on regularity and sameness in their environments—change is very disturbing. They may repeat behaviours and have restricted interests, watching the same DVD over and over, for example. They may be very sensitive to light, sound, touch, or other sensory information—sounds may be painful, for example. They may be able to memorize words or steps in problem solving, but not use them appropriately or be very confused when the situation changes or questions are asked in a different way (Friend, 2006).

Asperger syndrome is one of the disabilities included in the autistic spectrum. These children have many of the characteristics described above, but their greatest trouble is with social relations. Language is less affected. Their speech may be fluent, but unusual, mixing up "I" and "you" pronouns, for example (Friend, 2006; Hutchinson, 2007). Many students with autism also have moderate to severe intellectual disabilities, but those with Asperger syndrome usually have average to above average intelligence.

Theory of Mind. One current explanation for autism and Asperger syndrome is that children with these disorders lack a theory of mind—an understanding that they and other people have minds, thoughts, and emotions. They have difficulty explaining their own behaviours, appreciating that other people might have different feelings, and predicting how behaviours might affect emotions. So, for example, a student may not understand why classmates are bored by his constant repetition of stories or obscure facts about topics he finds fascinating. Or the student may stand too close or too far away when interacting, not realizing that she is making other people uncomfortable (Friend, 2006; Hutchinson, 2007; Wellman et al., 2002).

Autism and autism spectrum disorders Developmental disability significantly affecting verbal and non-verbal communication, social interaction, and imaginative creativity, generally evident before age 3 and ranging from mild to major.

Interventions. Early and intense interventions that focus on communication and social relations are particularly important for children with autism spectrum disorders. As they move into elementary school, some of these students will be in inclusive settings, others in specialized classes, and many in some combination of these two. Collaboration among teachers and the family is

SOME FACES OF ASPERGER SYNDROME In his book, *The Genesis of Artistic Creativity: Asperger Syndrome and the Arts*, Michael Fitzgerald (2005) speculates that the famous musicians Beethoven and Mozart and the artists van Gogh and Warhol display behaviours associated with Asperger syndrome.

particularly important. Supports such as smaller classes, structured environments, providing a safe "home base" for times of stress, consistency in instruction, assistive technologies, and the use of visual supports may be part of a collaborative plan (Friend, 2006). Through adolescence and the transition to adulthood, life, work, and social skills are important educational goals.

EXCEPTIONAL EDUCATION AND INCLUSION

We have been discussing in detail the many needs of exceptional learners because, no matter what grade or subject you teach, you will encounter these students in your classroom. The trend toward including exceptional students in general education classrooms began in the early 1970s.

Education Laws and Policies Pertaining to Exceptional Students

Canada does not have a national office of education, unlike Britain and the United States. Instead, each province has the authority to make its own laws concerning education, including exceptional education, and each province and territory has an education or school act that governs education in its elementary and secondary schools. As a teacher, you will need to become familiar with the laws and policies that govern education in your province or territory.

Inclusion is the current policy of the ministries of education in all of Canada's provinces and territories (Hutchinson, 2007). However, provinces vary in their definitions of inclusion. In British Columbia, for example, the principle of inclusion supports "equitable access to learning by all students and the opportunity for all students to pursue their goals in all aspects of their education" (British Columbia Special Education Branch, 1995, Section A, p. 2). However, the British Columbia Ministry of Education clarifies that integration—exceptional students' participation in activities with non-exceptional peers—is only one way to achieve inclusion, the preferred way. This definition of inclusion means that exceptional students may not spend 100 percent of every school day in general education activities or classrooms. The emphasis is on meeting the educational needs of all students, and this "does not preclude the appropriate use of resource rooms, self-contained classrooms, community-based training, or other specialized settings" (British Columbia Special Education Branch, 1995, Section A, p. 3). Consistent with British Columbia's policy in this regard, no jurisdiction uses the expression "full inclusion" and all provide alternatives to the general education classroom when that choice clearly does not meet the student's needs.

There is one national piece of legislation that has an impact on education across Canada—the *Canadian Charter of Rights and Freedoms*, which is part of the Constitution. Section 15.1 of the *Charter* outlines the equality provisions that apply to education:

> Every individual is equal before and under the law and has the right to equal protection and equal benefit of the law without discrimination and, in particular, without discrimination based on race, national or ethnic origin, colour, religion, sex, age, or mental or physical disability.

William MacKay (1986), a law professor at Dalhousie University in Nova Scotia, interpreted that there are three dimensions of "equality rights"—non-discrimination, equal opportunity, and equal outcomes. For some students, having equal opportunities and achieving equal outcomes requires differential treatment—that is, a program that attends to and supports their exceptional learning needs.

Exceptional education in Canada has also been influenced by American legislation. In particular, Canadian practices in special education have embraced American practices of providing exceptional learners with a least restrictive placement and an individualized education program (IEP) and of protecting the rights of exceptional students and their families.

Least Restrictive Placement. In the United States, federal law requires that students be educated in the least restrictive environment possible. Typically, this is interpreted to mean that exceptional students should be educated in general educational settings whenever possible or in settings

Education or school act Provincial or territorial legislation that governs education in elementary and secondary schools.

Inclusion The practice of integrating exceptional students into regular education classrooms; the emphasis is on participation rather than placement.

Integration The practice of having exceptional students participate in activities with their non-exceptional peers.

Canadian Charter of Rights and Freedoms Legislation that protects the rights of all Canadians and, in particular, Canadians who are members of minority groups, including Canadians with disabilities.

Least restrictive placement The practice of placing exceptional students in the most regular educational settings possible while ensuring that they are successful and receive support appropriate to their special needs.

that provide as close a match as possible to general educational settings. This practice is referred to as **least restrictive placement**. While there is no law requiring least restrictive placement in Canada, the principle is embodied in our practices. Some provinces (e.g., Prince Edward Island) refer to placement in the "most enabling environment" rather than the least restrictive environment (Hutchinson, 2007). Consistent with Canada's goal of becoming an inclusive society, it is generally accepted that the most enabling environment for most learners most of the time is the general education classroom. But as you can see in the *Point/Counterpoint* box, inclusion challenges our education systems.

POINT / COUNTERPOINT

Is Inclusion a Reasonable Approach to Teaching Exceptional Students?

SURVEYS INDICATE THE majority of Canadians and, in particular, teachers agree with the principle of inclusion (Human Resources and Social Development Canada, 2004). "People with exceptionalities ought to be part of the mainstream of society and all its institutions from birth onward. . . . They [should] be ensured full social, educational, and economic participation in society and on their own terms as much as possible" (Hutchinson, 2007, p. 18). However, many teachers feel unprepared and unsupported in their efforts to meet the needs of these students in their classrooms. For this reason, inclusion continues to be a controversial issue in education in Canada.

POINT

Inclusion makes sense.

Proponents of inclusion argue their case along two lines (Perry, Mirenda, & Siegel, 2007). Both in terms of human rights and effective instruction for all students, they argue it is the right thing to do. On the second point, they cite research indicating exceptional learners' academic performance is better in general versus special education settings (Katz & Mirenda, 2002; Stevens & Slavin, 1995). They argue that students receive higher quality instruction in general education classrooms compared with special education classrooms, where teachers' expectations tend to be lower and curriculum coverage less comprehensive. Furthermore, they argue that exceptional learners develop better communication and social skills and experience a greater sense of belonging in general education classrooms. Finally, they cite research showing that inclusion has no deleterious effects on the learning or behaviour of students without disabilities and, in fact, enhances their understandings about disabilities and commitment to inclusion.

COUNTERPOINT

Inclusion is not working.

Although research points to the benefits of inclusion, there is plenty of anecdotal evidence concerning inclusion failures (Perry et al., 2007). Also, some research indicates that academic achievement and long-term life outcomes have not dramatically improved for individuals with disabilities, even after a quarter century of emphasis on inclusion in our public schools (Frattura & Capper, 2006). School dropout rates for special education students are still twice as high as for the general population and, when they leave school, they are significantly more likely to have difficulty finding and keeping employment and, therefore, living independently.

In defence of general education teachers, some skeptics ask: Is it reasonable to expect general education teachers who are already overburdened with responsibilities for low-achieving students, students coping with family crises, and students who speak little or no English to also handle the wide range of disabilities that could confront them? Currently, teacher preparation programs do little to prepare teacher candidates for the diversity of today's classrooms, and budgets for professional development have been cut for in-service teachers. The idea that extra support and consultation will be provided is good in theory, but it has been lacking in practice. Nancy Hutchinson (2007) agrees that effective inclusion has been an elusive goal in education. Perhaps it's prudent to ask what characterizes classroom and school contexts where inclusion is "working"? According to Perry et al. (2007, p. 8), inclusion works when students receive excellent instruction from knowledgeable teachers in the context of coordinated and comprehensive approaches to programming. Ideally there is collaboration between general and special educators to produce plans for (a) remedial, tutorial, and skill-building instruction, and (b) adapting, modifying, and supplementing curricula, instruction, and classroom materials. In addition, inclusion works when children's learning challenges are identified early and support for inclusion is provided at all levels of the education system (i.e., school, district, province). Contexts like these do exist and, in them, *all* students learn and thrive and parents and teachers report positive perceptions of inclusion (Fisher, Roach, & Frey, 2002).

Individualized Education Program. Each student with exceptional learning needs must have an educational program tailored to his or her unique needs. The individualized education program (IEP) is written by a team that includes the student's teacher or teachers, a qualified school psychologist or special education supervisor, the parent(s) or guardian(s), and (when possible) the student. The program should be reviewed and updated each year and should address the following issues:

1. The student's present level of functioning.
2. Goals for the year and short-term measurable instructional objectives leading to those goals.
3. A list of specific services to be provided to the student and details of when those services will be initiated.
4. A description of how fully the student will participate in the general education program.
5. A schedule telling how the student's progress toward the objectives will be evaluated and approximately how long the services described in the plan will be needed.
6. Beginning at the age of 16 (and as young as 14 for some students), a statement of needed transitional services to move the student toward further education or work in adult life.

MyEducationLab Go to the Activities and Applications section in Chapter 4 of MyEducationLab and complete Activity 3. As you watch the video and answer the accompanying questions, consider ways in which IEPs can facilitate educational success for students with different abilities.

The Ontario Ministry of Education posts sample IEPs on its website at **www.ontariodirectors.ca/IEP-PEI/en.html**.

The Rights of Students and Parents or Guardians. As a teacher, you need to be aware of the expectations for the participation of parents and guardians in education in your province. Typically, parents and guardians are viewed as partners in the education of exceptional learners. They must approve any testing and special placements concerning their child, and they have the right to see all records kept by the school board that concern their child. They may obtain an independent evaluation, and they have the right to participate in planning their children's IEPs. Schools must maintain the confidentiality of students' records and ensure that testing practices do not discriminate against students from minority groups. Furthermore, schools should communicate with parents and guardians in their native languages (i.e., through interpreters and translators) and must have processes in place for them to appeal any decisions made by the school about their children. Finally, students are entitled to see all records that the school board keeps about them, and should, whenever possible, be involved in planning their educational programs. See the *Family and Community Partnerships Guidelines* box for suggestions about how to conduct productive conferences with parents or guardians and students.

RESPONSE TO INTERVENTION (RTI) One of the main goals of the response to intervention (RTI) process is to identify students who may have learning difficulties as early as possible so that they don't fall too far behind before their problems are recognized. A second goal is to document what works and what doesn't with each student for planning.

Individualized education program (IEP) Annually revised program for an exceptional student detailing present achievement level, goals, and strategies, drawn up by teachers, family members, specialists, and (if possible) the student.

Response to intervention (RTI) A process in which one of the main goals is to identify students who may have learning difficulties as early as possible so that they don't fall too far behind before their problems are recognized. A second goal is to document what works and what doesn't with each student for planning.

Response to Intervention (RTI)

One of the problems for students with serious learning problems is that they have to struggle through the early grades, often falling further and further behind, until they are identified and assessed, meet criteria for a special education category, receive an IEP, and finally get appropriate help. A process called response to intervention (RTI) gives educators a new option for assessing and educating students who might have serious learning problems early in their educational careers. The main goal of RTI is to make sure students get appropriate research-based instruction and support as soon as possible, in kindergarten if they need it, before they have fallen too far behind. A second goal is to make sure teachers are systematic in documenting what they have tried with these students and how well each intervention worked (Friend, 2008).

FAMILY AND COMMUNITY PARTNERSHIPS

GUIDELINES: Productive Conferences

Plan and prepare for a productive conference.

EXAMPLES

1. Have a clear purpose and gather the needed information. If you want to discuss student progress, have work samples available.
2. Send home a list of questions and ask families to bring the information to the conference. The following are sample questions from Friend and Bursuck (2002):
   - What is your child's favourite class activity?
   - Does your child have worries about any class activities? If so, what are they?
   - What are your priorities for your child's education this year?
   - What questions do you have about your child's education in my class this year?
   - How could we at school help make this the most successful year ever for your child?
   - Are there any topics you want to discuss at the conference that I might need to prepare for? If so, please let me know.
   - Would you like other individuals to participate in the conference? If so, please give me a list of their names.
   - Is there particular school information you would like me to have available? If so, please let me know.

During the conference, create and maintain an atmosphere of collaboration and respect.

EXAMPLES

1. Arrange the room for private conversation. Put a sign on your door to avoid interruptions. Meet around a conference table for better collaboration. Have tissues available.
2. Address families as "Mr." and "Ms.," not "Mom" and "Dad" or "Grandma." Use students' names.
3. Listen to families' concerns and build on their suggestions for their children.

After the conference, keep good records and follow up on decisions.

EXAMPLES

1. Make notes to yourself and keep them organized.
2. Summarize any actions or decisions in writing and send a copy to the family and any other teachers or professionals involved.
3. Communicate with families on other occasions, especially when there is good news to share.

For more information about parent conferences, see **http://content.scholastic.com/browse/home.jsp** and search using "parent teacher conference."

MyEducationLab
Go to the Activities and Applications section in Chapter 4 of MyEducationLab and complete Activity 4, included in the **IRIS MODULE: RTI (Part 2): Assessment.** This module outlines the differences between the IQ-achievement discrepancy model and the RTI model. It also offers a brief overview of each tier in the RTI model and explains its benefits.

One common way of reaching these RTI goals is to use a three-tiered system (Fuchs & Fuchs, 2007). The *first tier* is to use a strong, well-researched way of teaching all the students (we will look at these kinds of approaches in Chapter 13). Students who do not do well with these methods are moved to the *second tier* by getting extra support and additional small-group instruction. If some students still make limited progress, they move to the *third tier* for one-to-one intensive help and perhaps a special needs assessment. The approach has at least two advantages—students get extra help right away and the information gained based on their responses to the different interventions can be used for IEP planning, if the students reach the third stage of RTI.

If you decide that students in your class might benefit from special services, the first step is making a referral. How would you begin? Table 4.13 guides you through the referral process. In Chapter 12, when we discuss effective teaching, we will look at more ways to reach all of your students.

Technology and Exceptional Students

Assistive technology is any product, piece of equipment, or system that is used to increase, maintain, or improve the functional capabilities of individuals with disabilities (Goldman, Lawless, Pellegrino, & Plants, 2006). Computers have improved the education of exceptional children in countless ways. Teachers can use computers for record keeping, program planning, and managing instruction. For students who require small steps and many repetitions to learn a new concept, computers are the perfect patient tutors, repeating steps and lessons as many times as necessary. A well-designed computer-based instructional program is engaging and interactive—two important qualities for students who have problems paying attention or a history of failure that has eroded motivation. For example, a math or spelling program might use images, sounds, and game-like features to maintain the attention of a student with ADHD. Interactive videodisc programs are

Assistive technology Devices, systems, and services that support and improve the capabilities of individuals with disabilities.

TABLE 4.13

Making a Referral

1. Contact the student's parents. It is very important that you discuss the student's problems with the parents *before* you refer.
2. Before making a referral, check *all* the student's school records. Has the student ever
   - had a psychological evaluation?
   - qualified for special services?
   - been included in other special programs (e.g., for disadvantaged children; speech or language therapy)?
   - scored far below average on standardized tests?
   - been retained?

   Do the records indicate
   - good progress in some areas but poor progress in others?
   - any physical or medical problem?
   - that the student is taking medication?
3. Talk to the student's other teachers and professional support personnel about your concern for the student. Have other teachers also had difficulty with the student? Have they found ways of dealing successfully with the student? Document the strategies you have used in your class to meet the student's educational needs. Your documentation will provide evidence that will be helpful to or required by the team of professionals who will evaluate the student. Demonstrate your concern by keeping written records. Your notes should include items such as
   - exactly what you are concerned about;
   - why you are concerned about it;
   - dates, places, and times you have observed the problem;
   - precisely what you have done to try to resolve the problem;
   - who, if anyone, helped you devise the plans or strategies you have used;
   - evidence that the strategies have been successful or unsuccessful.

Remember that you should refer a student only if you can make a convincing case that the student may have a handicapping condition and probably cannot be served appropriately without special education. Referral for special education begins a time-consuming, costly, and stressful process that is potentially damaging to the student and has many legal ramifications.

Source: Pullen, P. L., & Kaufmann, J. M. (1987). *What should I know about special education? Answers for classroom teachers.* Austin, TX: Pro-Ed. Reprinted by permission.

being developed to teach hearing people how to use sign language. Many programs do not involve sound, so students with hearing impairments can get the full benefit from the lessons. Students who have trouble reading can use programs that will "speak" a word for them if they touch the unknown word with a light pen or the cursor. With this immediate access to help, the students are much more likely to get the reading practice they need to prevent falling further and further behind. Other devices actually convert printed pages and typed texts to spoken words or Braille for students who are blind.

With these tremendous advances in technology have come new barriers, however. Many computers have graphic interfaces. To manipulate the programs requires precise "mouse movements," as you may remember when you first learned to point and click. These manoeuvres are difficult for students with motor problems or visual impairments. And the information available on the internet is often unusable for students with visual problems. Researchers are trying to devise ways for people to access the information non-visually, but the adaptations are not perfected yet (Hallahan et al., 2009). One current trend is universal design—considering the needs of all users in the design of new tools, learning programs, or websites (Pisha & Coyne, 2001).

ASSISTIVE TECHNOLOGY The use of assistive technology to help students participate in general education classrooms is an important component of a student's individualized educational program (IEP).

For gifted students, computers can be a connection with databases and computers in universities, museums, and research labs. Computer networks allow students to work on projects and share information with others across the country. It is also possible to have gifted students write programs for students and teachers. These are just a few examples of what technology can do. Check with the resource teachers in your district to find out what is available in your school.

Universal design Considering the needs of all users in the design of new tools, learning programs, or websites.

DIVERSITY AND CONVERGENCES IN LEARNING ABILITIES

Diversity

Even though there are many good tests and careful procedures available for making special education placement decisions, some racial and ethnic minority students are over-represented in the disability categories and under-represented in gifted programs. This situation is particularly true for Aboriginal students in Canada and African American and Native American students in the United States. Educators have struggled to understand the causes of these over- and under-representations. Explanations include the higher poverty rates among minority youth, which lead to poorer prenatal care, nutrition, and health care; systematic biases in teachers' attitudes, curriculum, instruction, and the referral process itself; and lack of preparation for teachers to work effectively with ethnic minority students (Friend, 2008). To deal with the referral problem, educators have recommended gathering more information about a student before a formal referral is made. How long has the student been in Canada? What about proficiency with English? Are there unusual stressors such as being homeless? Does the curriculum build on the student's funds of cultural knowledge? Is the classroom culturally compatible (Chapter 5) and engaging (Chapter 11)? Is the teacher knowledgeable about and respectful of the student's culture? Can the student's abilities be assessed through alternative approaches such as creativity tests and portfolios or performances (Chapter 14)? Having more knowledge about the student and his or her circumstances outside of school should help teachers make better decisions about what programs are appropriate. In fact, instruction should be differentiated to better match the needs of all students, as we will see in Chapter 13.

Girls and Giftedness. As young girls develop their identities in adolescence, they often reject being labelled as gifted—being accepted and popular and "fitting in" may become more important than achievement (Basow & Rubin, 1999; Stormont, Stebbins, & Holliday, 2001). How can teachers reach girls who are gifted?

- Notice when girls' test scores seem to decline in middle or high school.
- Encourage assertiveness, achievement, high goals, and demanding work from all students.
- Provide models of achievement through speakers, internships, or readings.
- Look for and support gifts in arenas other than academic achievement.

Gifted Students With Learning Disabilities: Twice-Exceptional. Here are some ideas for supporting twice-exceptional students (McCoach, Kehle, Bray, & Siegle, 2001):

- Identify these students by looking longitudinally at achievement.
- Remediate skill deficits, but also identify and develop talents and strengths.
- Provide emotional support; it is important for all students, but especially for this group.
- Help students learn to compensate directly for their learning problems, and assist them in "tuning in" to their own strengths and difficulties.

Gifted Students Who Live in Poverty. Health problems, lack of resources, homelessness, fears about safety and survival, frequent moves, and responsibilities for the care of other family members all make achievement in school more difficult for students who live in poverty. To identify students with gifts:

- Use alternative assessment, teacher nomination, and creativity tests.
- Be sensitive to the demands on students' time that may interfere with their ability to focus on school work.
- Ethnicity and culture are linked to poverty, so be sensitive to cultural differences in values about cooperative or solitary achievement (Ford, 2000), and use multicultural strategies to encourage both achievement and the development of racial identities.

Convergences

This chapter is about diversity—the many differences among individuals in abilities and disabilities, learning preferences, strengths, and challenges. But even with this diversity, differences among individuals are very small compared to all the characteristics we share.

Another convergence should be in the uses of testing. We saw that intelligence tests originally were developed, in part, to protect the rights of children from poorer families who might be denied an education on the false grounds that they weren't able to learn. We also saw that intelligence tests predict school success similarly for students of different races and income levels. Even so, these tests can never be free of cultural content, so they always will have some biases built in. Keep this in mind when you see your students' scores on any test. Finally, remember that the results of every assessment for every student should be used to support that student's learning and development and to identify effective practices, not to deny the student resources or appropriate teaching.

SUMMARY TABLE

Language and Labelling (pp. 115–117)

What are the advantages of and problems with labels? Labels and diagnostic classifications of students with exceptionalities can easily become both stigmas and self-fulfilling prophecies, but they can also open doors to special programs and help teachers develop appropriate instructional strategies.

What is people-first language? People-first language ("students with developmental disabilities," "students with gifts and talents," etc.) is an alternative to labels that describe a complex person with one or two words, implying that the condition labelled is the most important aspect of the person. With person-first language, the emphasis is on the students first, not on the special challenges these students face.

Distinguish between a disability and a handicap. A disability is an inability to do something specific, such as see or walk. A handicap is a disadvantage in certain situations. Some disabilities lead to handicaps, but not in all contexts. Teachers must avoid imposing handicaps on learners who are disabled.

Exceptional students Students who have high abilities in particular areas or disabilities that impact learning and may require special education or other services.

Disability The inability to do something specific, such as walk or hear.

Handicap A disadvantage in a particular situation, sometimes caused by a disability.

Intelligence (pp. 117–124)

What is *g*? Spearman suggested that there is one mental attribute, which he called g, or general intelligence, that is used to perform any mental test, but that each test also requires some specific abilities in addition to g. Spearman assumed that individuals vary in both general intelligence and specific abilities, and that together these factors determine performance on mental tasks. A current version of the general-plus-specific-abilities theory is Carroll's work identifying a few broad abilities (such as learning and memory, visual perception, verbal fluency) and at least 70 specific abilities.

What is Gardner's view of intelligence and his position on *g*? Gardner contends that an intelligence is a biological and psychological potential to solve problems and create products or outcomes that are valued by a culture. These intelligences are realized to a greater or lesser extent as a consequence of experiential, cultural, and motivational factors. There are at least eight separate intelligences: linguistic, musical, spatial, logical-mathematical, bodily-kinesthetic, interpersonal, intrapersonal, naturalist, and perhaps existential. Gardner does not deny the existence of a general ability, but he does question how useful g is as an explanation for human achievements.

What are the elements of Sternberg's theory of intelligence? Sternberg's triarchic theory of intelligence is a cognitive process approach to understanding intelligence that has three parts: analytic, creative, and practical. Analytic/componential intelligence involves the mental processes that are defined in terms of components: metacomponents, performance components, and knowledge-acquisition components. Creative/experiential intelligence involves coping with new experiences through insight or automaticity. Practical/contextual intelligence involves choosing to live and work in a context where success is likely, adapting to that context, and reshaping it if necessary. Practical intelligence is made up mostly of action-oriented tacit knowledge learned during everyday life rather than through formal schooling.

How is intelligence measured, and what does an IQ score mean? Intelligence is measured through individual tests (Stanford-Binet, Wechsler, Woodcock-Johnson, etc.) and group tests (Otis-Lennon School Abilities Tests, Slosson Intelligence Test, etc.). Compared with an individual test, a group test is much less likely to yield an accurate picture of any one person's abilities. The average score is 100. About 68 percent of the general population will earn IQ scores between 85 and 115. Only about 16 percent of the population will receive scores below 85, and only 16 percent will score above 115. These figures hold true for white, native-born North Americans whose first language is Standard English. Intelligence test scores predict success in school, but they are less predictive of success in life when level of education is taken into account.

What is the Flynn effect and what are its implications? Since the early 1900s, IQ scores have been rising. To keep 100 as the average for IQ test scores, questions have to be made more difficult. This increasing difficulty has implications for any program that uses IQ scores as part of the entrance requirements. For example, students who were not identified as having intellectual disabilities a generation ago might be identified as disabled now because the test questions are harder.

Are there sex differences in cognitive abilities? Girls seem to be better on verbal tests, especially when writing is involved. Males seem to be superior on tasks that require mental rotation of objects. The scores of males tend to be more variable in general, so there are more males than females with very high *and* very low scores on tests. Research on the causes of these differences has been inconclusive, except to indicate that academic socialization and teachers' treatment of male and female students in mathematics classes may play a role.

Intelligence Ability or abilities to acquire and use knowledge for solving problems and adapting to the world.

General intelligence *(g)* A general factor in cognitive ability that is related in varying degrees to performance on all mental tests.

Fluid intelligence Mental efficiency that is culture-free and non-verbal and is grounded in brain development.

Crystallized intelligence Ability to apply culturally approved problem-solving methods.

Theory of multiple intelligences In Gardner's theory of intelligence, a person's eight separate abilities: linguistic, musical, spatial, logical-mathematical, bodily-kinesthetic, interpersonal, intrapersonal, and naturalist.

Triarchic theory of intelligence A three-part description of the mental abilities (thinking processes, coping with new experiences, and adapting to context) that lead to more or less intelligent behaviour.

Insight The ability to deal effectively with novel situations.

Automaticity The result of learning to perform a behaviour or thinking process so thoroughly that the performance is automatic and does not require effort.

Mental age In intelligence testing, a score based on average abilities for that age group.

Intelligence quotient (IQ) Score comparing mental and chronological ages.

Deviation IQ Score based on statistical comparison of individuals' performance with the average performance of others in that age group.

Flynn effect A steady rise in IQ test scores because of better health, smaller families, increased complexity in the environment, and more and better schooling.

Learning and Thinking Styles (pp. 124–125)

Distinguish between learning styles and learning preferences. Learning styles are the characteristic ways a person approaches learning and studying. Learning preferences are individual preferences for particular learning modes and environments. Even though learning styles and learning preferences are not related to intelligence or effort, they can affect school performance.

What are the advantages and disadvantages of matching teaching to individual learning styles? Results of some research indicate that students learn more when they study in their preferred setting and manner, but most research does not show a benefit. Many students would benefit from developing new—and perhaps more effective—ways to learn.

What learning style distinctions are the most well-supported by research? One distinction that is repeatedly supported by the research is deep versus surface processing. Individuals who have a *deep-processing* approach see learning activities as a means for understanding some underlying concepts or meanings. Students who take a *surface-processing* approach focus on memorizing the learning materials, not understanding them. A second distinction is Mayer's visualizer–verbalizer dimension, which has three facets: *cognitive spatial ability* (low or high), *cognitive style* (a visualizer versus a verbalizer), and *learning preference* (a verbal learner versus a visual learner).

Learning styles The way a person approaches learning and studying.

Learning preferences Preferred ways of studying and learning, such as using pictures instead of text, working with other people versus alone, learning in structured or in unstructured situations, and so on.

Students Who Are Gifted and Talented (pp. 125–129)

What are the characteristics of students who are gifted? Students who are gifted learn easily and rapidly and retain what they have learned; use common sense and practical knowledge; know about many things that the other children don't; use a large number of words easily and accurately; recognize relations and comprehend meaning; are alert and keenly observant and respond quickly; are persistent and highly motivated on some tasks; and are creative or make interesting connections. Most students have gifts and talents in particular areas. Teachers should make special efforts to support students who are under-represented in gifted programs—girls, students who also have learning disabilities, students from minority cultures, and students who are living in poverty.

Is acceleration a useful approach with gifted students? Many people object to acceleration, but most careful studies indicate that truly gifted students who are accelerated do as well as, and usually better than, other students who are progressing at the normal pace.

Students who are gifted tend to prefer the company of older playmates and may be bored if kept with children their own age. Skipping grades may not be the best solution for a particular student, but for students who are extremely advanced intellectually (with a score of 160 or higher on an individual intelligence test), the only practical solution may be to accelerate their education.

Gifted student A very bright, creative, and talented student.

High-Incidence Disabilities (pp. 129–143)

What is a learning disability? Specific learning disabilities involve significant difficulties in the acquisition and use of listening, speaking, reading, writing, reasoning, or mathematical abilities. These difficulties are intrinsic to the individual, presumed to be the result of central nervous system dysfunction, and may occur throughout the lifespan. Students with learning disabilities may become victims of learned helplessness when they come to believe that they cannot control or improve their own learning and therefore cannot succeed. A focus on learning strategies often helps students with learning disabilities.

What is ADHD, and how is it handled in school? *Attention-deficit/hyperactivity disorder (ADHD)* is the term used to describe individuals of any age with hyperactivity and attention difficulties. Use of medication to address ADHD is effective for 70 to 90 percent of individuals who have the disorder; however, it is controversial. There can be negative side effects, such as headaches and nausea, but modifying the dosage can typically control these. Also, little is known about the long-term effects of drug therapy. The drugs alone will not lead to improvements in academic learning or peer relationships, two areas in which children with ADHD have great problems. Instructional methods that have proven most successful for helping students with ADHD are based on behavioural principles of learning such as those described in Chapter 6. One promising approach is positive behaviour support (PBS).

What are the most common communication disorders? Common communication disorders include speech impairments (articulation disorders, stuttering, and voicing problems) and oral language disorders. If these problems are addressed early, great progress is possible.

What defines intellectual disabilities? Before age 18, students must score below about 70 on a standard measure of intelligence and must have problems with adaptive behaviour, day-to-day independent living, and social functioning.

What are the best approaches for students with emotional and behavioural disorders? Methods from applied behaviour analysis and direct teaching of social skills are two useful approaches. Students also may respond to structure and organization in the environment, schedules, activities, and rules.

What are some warning signs of potential suicide? Students at risk of suicide may show changes in eating or sleeping habits, weight, grades, disposition, activity level, or interest in friends. They sometimes suddenly give away prized possessions such as cell phones, iPods, clothing, or pets. They may seem depressed or hyperactive and may start missing school or quit doing work. It is especially dangerous if the student not only talks about suicide, but also has a plan for carrying it out.

Learning disability Problem with acquisition and use of language; may show up as difficulty with reading, writing, reasoning, or math.

Learned helplessness The expectation, based on previous experiences involving lack of control, that all of one's efforts will lead to failure.

Hyperactivity Behaviour disorder marked by atypical, excessive restlessness and inattentiveness.

Attention-deficit/hyperactivity disorder (ADHD) Current term for disruptive behaviour disorders marked by overactivity, excessive difficulty sustaining attention, or impulsiveness.

Speech impairment Inability to produce sounds effectively for speaking.

Articulation disorders Any of a variety of pronunciation difficulties.

Stuttering Repetitions, prolongations, and hesitations that block flow of speech.

Voicing problems Speech impairments involving inappropriate pitch, quality, loudness, or intonation.

Developmental disabilities Significantly below-average intellectual and adaptive social behaviour evident before the age of 18.

Transition programming Gradual preparation of exceptional students to move from high school into further education or training, employment, or community involvement.

Emotional and behavioural disorders Behaviours or emotions that deviate so much from the norm that they interfere with the child's own growth and development and/or the lives of others—inappropriate behaviours, unhappiness or depression, fears and anxieties, and trouble with relationships.

Low-Incidence Disabilities (pp. 144–149)

How can schools accommodate the needs of physically disabled students? If the school has the necessary architectural features, such as ramps, elevators, and accessible washrooms, and if teachers allow for the physical limitations of students, little needs to be done to alter the usual educational program. Identifying a peer to help with movements and transitions can be useful.

How would you handle a seizure in class? Do not restrain the child's movements. Lower the child gently to the floor, away from furniture or walls. Move hard objects away. Turn the child's head gently to the side, put a soft coat or blanket under the student's head, and loosen any tight clothing. Never put anything in the student's mouth. Find out from the student's parents how the seizure is usually dealt with. If one seizure follows another and the student does not regain consciousness in between, if the student is pregnant, or if the seizure goes on for more than 5 minutes, get medical help *right away*.

What are some signs of hearing and visual impairment? Signs of hearing problems are turning one ear toward the speaker, favouring one ear in conversation, or misunderstanding conversation when the speaker's face cannot be seen. Other indications include not following directions, seeming distracted or confused at times, frequently asking people to repeat what they have said, mispronouncing new words or names, and being reluctant to participate in class discussions. Students who have frequent earaches, sinus infections, or allergies should be scrutinized particularly closely. Holding books very close or far away, squinting, rubbing eyes, misreading the chalkboard, and holding the head at an odd angle are possible signs of visual problems.

How does autism differ from Asperger syndrome? Asperger syndrome is one of the autism spectrum disorders. Many students with autism also have moderate to severe intellectual disabilities, but those with Asperger syndrome usually have average to above average intelligence and better language abilities than other children with autism.

Cerebral palsy Condition involving a range of motor or coordination difficulties due to brain damage.

Spasticity Overly tight or tense muscles, characteristic of some forms of cerebral palsy.

Epilepsy Disorder marked by seizures and caused by abnormal electrical discharges in the brain.

Generalized seizure A seizure involving a large portion of the brain.

Partial seizure or absence seizure A seizure involving only a small part of the brain.

Speech reading Using visual cues to understand language.

Sign language Communication system of hand movements that symbolize words and concepts.

Finger spelling Communication system that "spells out" each letter with a hand position.

Low vision Vision limited to close objects.

Educationally blind Needing Braille materials in order to learn.

Autism and autism spectrum disorders Developmental disability significantly affecting verbal and non-verbal communication, social interaction, and imaginative creativity, generally evident before age 3 and ranging from mild to major.

Exceptional Education and Inclusion (pp. 149–153)

What legislation affects special education across Canada? Each province and territory has an education or school act that governs education in its elementary and secondary schools. Inclusion is the current policy of all provinces and territories in Canada. Also, educating students in the least restrictive or most enabling environment, developing an individualized education plan (IEP) that meets the unique needs of each exceptional learner, and protecting the rights of students with exceptionalities and their families are principles shared by ministries of education across Canada. Only one piece of legislation has an impact on education across the country: the *Canadian Charter of Rights and Freedoms*, which is part of the Constitution.

What is response to intervention (RTI)? RTI is an approach to supporting students with learning problems as early as possible, not waiting for years to assess, identify, and plan a program. One RTI process is a three-tiered system. The *first tier* is to use a strong, well-researched way of teaching all the students. Students who do not do well with these methods are moved to the *second tier* by getting extra support and additional small-group instruction. If some students still make limited progress, they move to the *third tier* for one-to-one intensive help and perhaps a special needs assessment.

Education or school act Provincial or territorial legislation that governs education in elementary and secondary schools.

Inclusion The practice of integrating exceptional students into regular education classrooms; the emphasis is on participation rather than placement.

Integration The practice of having exceptional students participate in activities with their non-exceptional peers.

Canadian Charter of Rights and Freedoms Legislation that protects the rights of all Canadians and, in particular, Canadians who are members of minority groups, including Canadians with disabilities.

Least restrictive placement The practice of placing exceptional students in the most regular educational settings possible while ensuring that they are successful and receive support appropriate to their special needs.

Individualized education program (IEP) Annually revised program for an exceptional student detailing present achievement level, goals, and strategies, drawn up by teachers, family members, specialists, and (if possible) the student.

Response to intervention (RTI) A process in which one of the main goals is to identify students who may have learning difficulties as early as possible so that they don't fall too far behind before their problems are recognized. A second goal is to document what works and what doesn't with each student for planning.

Assistive technology Devices, systems, and services that support and improve the capabilities of individuals with disabilities.

Universal design Considering the needs of all users in the design of new tools, learning programs, or websites.

PEARSON myeducationlab

MyEducationLab is an interactive, virtual learning tool that will help improve your understanding of the concepts taught in this textbook and in your course. Through this engaging resource, you will have access to simulations of real classroom experiences, exercises that will help you improve your knowledge of key concepts, and additional resources that will help you in your teaching career. Use this online tool with your textbook to help you succeed in your studies and beyond!

TEACHERS' CASEBOOK

It is a new school year and you scan the list of students who will be registered in your classroom. It's a bit overwhelming. Since your district follows the policy of inclusion, you always expect to have students whose academic abilities, social skills, and motivation for learning vary widely. However, this year you will also have a student who is deaf, two students who are new to Canada and just learning to speak English, and a student who has severe learning disabilities. In principle, you believe in the policy of inclusion, but your new class represents a challenge.

What Would *They* Do?

Here is how two practising teachers responded to the teaching situation described above.

Barb Cadel

Poplar Bank Public School, Newmarket, ON

When setting up a classroom and planning programming, I find it beneficial to think about using universal design for learning. This way of thinking helps teachers design their classrooms to make the learning accessible for all students. Looking at learning as a continuum allows each student in the class, regardless of ability, to progress toward his or her learning goals in the most appropriate way, and to be assessed and evaluated fairly and accurately. Every student in every classroom is unique; recognizing this will help to ensure that every student will benefit. Assessing students' learning preferences will also help in planning a program that will help each to learn.

The physical set-up of the classroom will be important to ensure that the student with a hearing impairment and the English language learners will have the supports they require. I post a visual schedule of the day, which includes words and pictures to help all students understand what will happen during the course of the day. Labels throughout the classroom also assist with language development and allow students to "read the room."

The students identified as having a hearing impairment and a learning disability will have individualized education plans (IEPs), which will outline the specific program accommodations and modifications they require to be successful in the classroom. The IEPs will outline teaching, learning, and assessment strategies that will be beneficial to those students. It will also be important to have a sound understanding of any assistive technology the students may require (e.g., hearing aids, interpreter, computer technology).

When planning tasks and learning opportunities for the students, I would ensure that each student would be engaged each week working in a variety of groupings. Working in a small group will allow all students an opportunity to participate in meaningful discussion about their learning and to learn from and with each other. Tiered activities also provide all students with opportunities for success. With tiered instruction, the teacher plans a variety of activities around a central essential skill or concept that has varying degrees of complexity. All students will learn the basic skill or concept, but the students will achieve a variety of learning outcomes based on their learning strengths and needs.

It will also be important to consider the needs of all learners when planning assessments. Students should have the opportunity to be assessed in ways that allow them to best demonstrate their understanding; instead of traditional pen-and-paper tasks, many students will share their ideas orally; through art, drama, or music; using technology; or through an appropriate graphic organizer.

By looking first at a student's strengths and focusing on what the student can do, a teacher can plan appropriate programs to benefit all students and help them to learn in the most appropriate way.

Karen Noel-Bentley

Choice School for Gifted Children, Vancouver, BC

In a diverse classroom, it is important that all students feel like they belong and that they can learn. Every student has something to offer in a community of learners. In the first weeks of school, I would design activities that foster a sense of community and cooperation. I would give all students the opportunity to demonstrate their areas of interest and strength, celebrating their diversity while finding areas of common interest and aspirations. This would provide me with insight into their learning preferences and would facilitate an atmosphere of acceptance and camaraderie.

To accommodate the unique learning needs of my students with exceptionalities, I would try to learn more about their needs and what support is available before the start of the year. How does my deaf student communicate? Sign language? Lip reading? Is there technology available to facilitate communication? Is there an audiologist or doctor with whom I can collaborate to support my deaf student? Does my school have a teacher with expertise in teaching English as a second language? Is a pullout program offered for ESL at my school? Are there other students in my class who speak the same language as the students who are learning to speak English? What are the needs of my student with a learning disability? Will he or she be in the classroom every day, and for how long? Will a Special Education Assistant be involved? I would hope to be able to work as a team with these experts, involving them in planning and consulting with them as needed.

The best way to manage planning for a diverse class is to design complex tasks that involve opportunities to differentiate content, process, and product. When designing a task for my diverse class, I would start with determining the big idea. What do all students need to learn? This is the main concept of the task, which all students would be expected to learn. What do most of the students need to learn? This would involve deeper learning that most students would be required to achieve, but would be optional for the students with exceptional learning needs. Finally, what do some students need to learn? This would include further enrichment for those students who are highly able and need advanced work to stay challenged. All students would be offered the choice to attempt a higher level of learning.

To differentiate the process of learning, I would consider what I know about how students in my class prefer to learn. For example, I would be sure to include a variety of visual and kinesthetic strategies that would be beneficial to my students with special needs, along with many other students who learn best visually or through direct manipulation. I would offer opportunities for cooperative learning, independent projects, and learning centres.

Learning materials would include books, videos, manipulatives, and discussions. All students would be exposed to a variety of learning tactics and strategies and would be offered choices for how they would acquire their information.

To provide all students with opportunities to demonstrate their learning, I would differentiate the products required from the learning tasks. For example, my student with a learning disability may not be able to write, but he may be able to dictate his thoughts to a scribe, type them on a computer, or draw a picture. Choices for some tasks could include drawing a map, creating a puppet show, or writing a diary. I would conduct regular and ongoing assessments with all students, using techniques such as interviews and observation. The students would maintain portfolios, indicating growth in their learning and giving them control over content. A variety of products and assessment strategies would ensure that all students can demonstrate their learning in ways that meet their unique needs.

The choices offered in all phases of learning and assessment give students control and understanding of their own learning. All students benefit when they understand their own strengths and areas of need. Students with exceptional needs become part of a continuum of learners within the classroom community. When teachers plan for this continuum, they can adjust the edges of the continuum to accommodate the specific needs of individual learners without feeling overwhelmed.

6 Behavioural Views of Learning

Programmers © Diana Ong/SuperStock

TEACHERS' CASEBOOK

WHAT WOULD YOU DO?

You were hired in January to take over the classes of a teacher who moved away. This is a great district and a terrific school. If you do well, you might be in line for a full-time opening next fall. As you are introduced around the school, you get a number of sympathetic looks and many—too many—offers of help: "Let me know if I can do anything for you."

After the first hour, you begin to understand why so many teachers volunteered their help. Evidently the previous teacher had no management system—no order. Several students walk around the room while you are talking to the class, interrupt you when you are working with a group, torment each other, and open their lunches (or those of other students) for a self-determined snack. There is one very charismatic leader who causes regular disruptions, resists your authority, and destroys your efforts to develop a community of learners. Simply taking attendance and introducing the first activity lasts 10 minutes. You end the first day exhausted and discouraged, having lost both your voice and your patience. You wonder how you can possibly establish a workable management system and still teach students what they will need to know in order to complete the province-wide spring reading, writing, and mathematics proficiency tests.

CRITICAL THINKING

- How would you approach the situation?
- Which problem behaviours would you tackle first?
- Would giving rewards or administering punishments be useful in this situation?
- Why or why not?

We begin this chapter with a general definition of learning that takes into account the opposing views of different theoretical groups. We will highlight one group, the behavioural theorists, in this chapter. In Chapters 7 and 8 we will look at another major group, the cognitive theorists. Then we will look at constructivism in Chapter 9 and social cognitive views in Chapter 10. As you can see, there are many ways to look at how learning takes place, and each has something to offer educators.

Our discussion in this chapter will focus on four behavioural learning processes—contiguity, classical conditioning, operant conditioning, and observational learning—with the greatest emphasis on the last two processes. After examining the implications of applied behaviour analysis for teaching, we look at a recent direction in behavioural approaches to learning—self-management.

By the time you have completed this chapter, you should be able to answer these questions:

- What is learning?
- What are the similarities and differences among contiguity, classical conditioning, operant conditioning, and observational learning?
- What are examples of four different kinds of consequences that can follow any behaviour, and what effect is each likely to have on future behaviour?
- How could you use applied behaviour analysis (group consequences, contingency contracts, token economies, or functional behavioural assessment) to solve common academic or behavioural problems?

Connect and **Extend**
Go to the "Connect and Extend" section in Chapter 6 of MyEducationLab to find further content that links to teaching, students' thinking, research, and the news.

UNDERSTANDING LEARNING

When we hear the word *learning*, most of us think of studying and school. We think about subjects or skills we intend to master, such as algebra, French or English, chemistry, or karate. But learning is not limited to taking place in school. We learn every day of our lives. Babies learn to kick their
nobile above their cribs move, young girls learn the lyrics to all their favourite
;s, middle-aged people learn to change their diet and exercise patterns, and every
arn to find a new style of dress attractive when the old styles (the ones we once
ıshion. This last example shows that learning is not always intentional. We don't
les and dislike old ones; it just seems to happen that way. We don't intend to
hen we hear the sound of a dentist's drill or when we step onto a stage, yet many
is this powerful phenomenon called learning?

st sense, learning occurs when experience (including practice) causes a relatively
e in an individual's knowledge or behaviour. The change may be deliberate or
better or for worse, correct or incorrect, and conscious or unconscious (Schunk,
ıs learning, this change must be brought about by experience—by the interaction
iis or her environment. Changes simply caused by maturation, such as growing
turning grey, do not qualify as learning. Temporary changes resulting from illness,
ıunger are also excluded from a general definition of learning. A person who has
for two days does not learn to be hungry, and a person who is ill does not learn to
Of course, learning plays a part in how we respond to hunger or illness.

ı specifies that the changes resulting from learning take place in the individual's
ıaviour. Most psychologists would agree with this statement, but some tend to
change in knowledge, others the change in behaviour. Cognitive psychologists, who focus on changes in knowledge, believe learning is an internal mental activity that cannot be observed directly. As you will see in the next chapter, cognitive psychologists who study learning are interested in unobservable mental activities such as thinking, remembering, and solving problems (Schwartz, Wasserman, & Robbins, 2002).

L
e
ir

B
Explanations of learning that focus on external events as the cause of changes in observable behaviours.

The psychologists discussed in this chapter, on the other hand, favour behavioural learning theories. The behavioural view generally assumes that the outcome of learning is a change in behaviour, and it emphasizes the effects of external events on the individual. Some early behaviourists such as J. B. Watson took the radical position that because thinking, intentions, and other internal mental events could not be seen or studied rigorously and scientifically, these "mentalisms," as he called them, should not even be included in an explanation of learning.

WHAT IS LEARNING? Behavioural views of learning generally assume that the outcome of learning is a change in behaviour. The focus is on what can be observed.

Neuroscience of Behavioural Learning

You saw in Chapter 2 that we are learning more and more about the brain. Researchers who study behavioural views have discovered quite a bit about the parts of the brain that are involved with learning new behaviours, especially in animal studies. For example, researchers found that parts of the cerebellum are involved in simple reflex learning, like learning to blink following a particular tone, and that other parts of the brain are involved in learning how to avoid painful stimulation such as shock (Schwartz, Wasserman, & Robbins, 2002). Other lines of research ask why animals and people will behave in certain ways to gain stimulation or reinforcers. Stimulation to certain parts of the brain will cause hungry rats to ignore food and keep doing whatever it takes to keep the stimulation coming. These same brain systems are associated with the pleasures people experience from many things, including food and music. It is likely that many parts of the brain and complex patterns of activity allow us to enjoy some experiences and "learn to want them, and learn how to get them" (Bernstein & Nash, 2008, p. 187).

Before we look in depth at behavioural explanations of learning, let's step into an actual classroom and note the possible results of learning.

Learning Is Not Always What It Seems

Elizabeth Chan was beginning her first day of solo teaching. After weeks of working with her cooperating teacher in a grade 8 social studies class, she was ready to take over. As she moved from behind the desk to the front of the room, she saw another adult approach the classroom door. It was B. J. Ross, her university supervisor. Elizabeth's neck and facial muscles suddenly became very tense and her hands trembled.

"I've stopped by to observe your teaching," Dr. Ross said. "This will be my first of six visits. I tried to reach you last night to tell you."

Elizabeth tried to hide her reaction, but her hands trembled as she gathered the notes for the lesson.

"Let's start today with a kind of game. I will say some words, then I want you to tell me the first words you can think of. Don't bother to raise your hands. Just say the words out loud, and I will write them on the board. Don't all speak at once, though. Wait until someone else has finished to say your word. Okay, here is the first word: Métis."

"Red River." "Louis Riel." "Rebellion." The answers came very quickly, and Elizabeth was relieved to see that the students understood the game.

"All right, very good," she said. "Now try another one: Batoche."

"Duck Lake." "Fish Creek." "John A. Macdonald." "Big Mac." "Sir Ronald McDonald!" With this last answer, a ripple of laughter moved across the room.

"Ronald McDonald?" Elizabeth sighed wearily. "Get serious." Then she laughed too. Soon, all the students were laughing. "Okay, settle down," Elizabeth said. "These ideas are getting a little off base!"

"Off base? Baseball," shouted the boy who had first mentioned Ronald McDonald. He stood up and started throwing balls of paper to a friend in the back of the room, simulating the style of pitcher Roger Clemens.

"Red Sox." "No, the Blue Jays." "The Rogers Centre." "Hot dogs." "Popcorn." "Hamburgers." "Ronald McDonald." The responses now came too fast for Elizabeth to stop them. For some reason, the Ronald McDonald line got an even bigger laugh the second time around, and Elizabeth suddenly realized she had lost the class.

"Okay, since you know so much about the Rebellion, close your books and take out a pen," Elizabeth said, obviously angry. She passed out the worksheet that she had planned as a cooperative, open-book project. "You have 20 minutes to finish this test!"

"You didn't tell us we were having a test!" "This isn't fair!" "We haven't even covered this stuff yet!" "I didn't do anything wrong!" There were moans and disgusted looks, even from the most mellow students. "I'm reporting you to the principal; it's a violation of students' rights!"

This last comment hit hard. The class had just finished discussing human rights as preparation for this unit on the Northwest Rebellion. As she listened to the protests, Elizabeth felt terrible. How was she going to grade these "tests"? The first section of the worksheet involved facts about events leading up to the Northwest Rebellion, and the second section asked students to create a news-style program interviewing ordinary people touched by the war.

"All right, all right, it won't be a test. But you do have to complete this worksheet for a grade. I was going to let you work together, but your behaviour this morning tells me that you are not ready for group work. If you can complete the first section of the sheet working quietly and seriously, you may work together on the second section." Elizabeth knew that her students would like to work together on writing the script for the news interview program.

It appears, on the surface at least, that very little learning of any sort was taking place in Elizabeth's classroom. Elizabeth had some good ideas, but she also made some mistakes in her application of learning principles. We will return to this episode later in the chapter to analyze various aspects of what took place. To get us started, three events can be singled out, each possibly related to a different learning process.

First, Elizabeth's hands trembled when her university supervisor entered the room. Second, the students were able to associate the phrases *Red River* and *Louis Riel* with the word *Métis*.

Third, one student continued to disrupt the class with inappropriate responses. The three learning processes represented are classical conditioning, contiguity, and operant conditioning. In the following pages, we will examine these three kinds of learning.

EARLY EXPLANATIONS OF LEARNING: CONTIGUITY AND CLASSICAL CONDITIONING

One of the earliest explanations of learning came from Aristotle (384–322 BC). He said that we remember things together (1) when they are similar, (2) when they contrast, and (3) when they are *contiguous*. This last principle is the most important, because it is included in all explanations of *learning by association*. The principle of contiguity states that whenever two or more sensations occur together often enough, they will become associated. Later, when only one of these sensations (a stimulus) occurs, the other will be remembered too (a response) (Rachlin, 2004; Schwartz et al., 2002). Contiguity also plays a major role in another learning process best known as *classical conditioning*.

STOP & THINK Close your eyes and focus on a vivid recollection of the following: The smell of french fries cooking. A time you were really embarrassed in school. The taste of chocolate fudge. The sound of a dentist's drill. What did you notice as you formed these mental images?

If you are like Nancy, imagining the sound of the dentist's drill tightens your neck muscles. Phil actually salivates when he imagines salty fries or mocha smoothie (especially when it's 12:50 p.m. and he hasn't had lunch yet). Classical conditioning focuses on the learning of *involuntary* emotional or physiological responses such as fear, increased muscle tension, salivation, or sweating. These are sometimes called respondents because they are automatic responses to stimuli. Through the process of classical conditioning, humans and animals can be trained to react involuntarily to a stimulus that previously had no effect—or a very different effect—on them. The stimulus comes to *elicit*, or bring forth, the response automatically.

Classical conditioning was discovered in the 1920s by Ivan Pavlov, a Russian physiologist who was trying to determine how long it took a dog to secrete digestive juices after it had been fed. But the intervals of time kept changing. At first, the dogs salivated as expected while they were being fed. Then the dogs began to salivate as soon as they saw the food and then as soon as they heard the scientists walking toward the lab. Pavlov decided to make a detour from his original experiments and examine these unexpected interferences or "psychic reflexes" as he called them at first.

In one of his first experiments, Pavlov began by sounding a tuning fork and recording a dog's response. As expected, there was no salivation. At this point, the sound of the tuning fork was a neutral stimulus because it brought forth no salivation. Then Pavlov fed the dog. The response was salivation. The food was an unconditioned stimulus (US) because no prior training or "conditioning" was needed to establish the natural connection between food and salivation. The salivation was an unconditioned response (UR), again because it was elicited automatically—no conditioning required.

Using these three elements—the food, the salivation, and the tuning fork—Pavlov demonstrated that a dog could be conditioned to salivate after hearing the tuning fork. He did this by contiguous pairing of the sound with food. He sounded the fork and then quickly fed the dog. After Pavlov repeated this several times, the dog began to salivate after hearing the sound but before receiving the food. Now the sound had become a conditioned stimulus (CS) that could bring forth salivation by itself. The response of salivating after the tone was now a conditioned response (CR).

If you think that Pavlovian conditioning is of historical interest only, consider this news story describing an advertising campaign for products aimed at "Gen Y," those people born between 1977 and 1994:

> Mountain Dew executives have their own term for this [advertising strategy]: the Pavlovian connection. By handing out samples of the brand at surfing, skateboard and snowboard tournaments, "There's a Pavlovian connection between the brand and the exhilarating experience," says Dave Burwich, a top marketing executive at Pepsi, which makes Mountain Dew. (Horovitz, 2002, p. B2)

Contiguity Association of two events because of repeated pairing.

Stimulus Event that activates behaviour.

Response Observable reaction to a stimulus.

Classical conditioning Association of automatic responses with new stimuli.

Respondents Responses (generally automatic or involuntary) elicited by specific stimuli.

Neutral stimulus Stimulus not connected to a response.

Unconditioned stimulus (US) Stimulus that automatically produces an emotional or physiological response.

Unconditioned response (UR) Naturally occurring emotional or physiological response.

Conditioned stimulus (CS) Stimulus that evokes an emotional or physiological response after conditioning.

Conditioned response (CR) Learned response to a previously neutral stimulus.

Maybe they could hand out math homework too!

It is possible that many of our emotional reactions to situations are learned in part through classical conditioning. Physicians have a term, *white coat syndrome,* that describes people whose blood pressure (an involuntary response) goes up when it is tested in the doctor's office, usually by someone in a white coat. Another example, Elizabeth's trembling hands when she saw her university supervisor, might be traced to previous unpleasant experiences during past evaluations of her performance. Now just the thought of being observed elicits a pounding heart and sweaty palms. Classical conditioning has implications for teachers as well as marketing executives. Remember that emotions and attitudes as well as facts and ideas are learned in classrooms. This emotional learning can sometimes interfere with academic learning. Procedures based on classical conditioning also can be used to help people learn more adaptive emotional responses, as the *Guidelines* box suggests.

GUIDELINES: Applying Classical Conditioning

Associate positive, pleasant events with learning tasks.

EXAMPLES

1. Emphasize group competition and cooperation over individual competition. Many students have negative emotional responses to individual competition that may generalize to other occasions for learning.
2. Make division drills fun by having students decide how to divide refreshments equally and then letting them eat and drink the results.
3. Make voluntary reading appealing by creating a comfortable reading corner with pillows, colourful displays of books, and reading props such as puppets (see Morrow & Weinstein, 1986, for more ideas).

Help students to risk anxiety-producing situations voluntarily and successfully.

EXAMPLES

1. Assign a shy student the responsibility of teaching two other students how to distribute materials for map study.
2. Devise small steps toward a larger goal. For example, give ungraded practice tests daily, and then weekly, to students who tend to "freeze" in test situations.
3. If a student is afraid of speaking in front of the class, let the student read a report to a small group while seated, then read it while standing, then give the report from notes instead of reading it verbatim. Next, move in stages toward having the student give a report to the whole class.

Help students recognize differences and similarities among situations so they can discriminate and generalize appropriately.

EXAMPLES

1. Explain that it is appropriate to avoid strangers who offer gifts or rides, but safe to accept favours from adults when parents are present.
2. Assure students who are anxious about taking post-secondary entrance exams that these types of tests are like all the other achievement tests they have taken.

If you would like to learn more about classical conditioning, see these sites: **www.class.uidaho.edu/psyc390/lessons/lesson02/lesson2.htm** and **www.scholarpedia.org/article/Classical_conditioning**

OPERANT CONDITIONING: TRYING NEW RESPONSES

So far, we have concentrated on the automatic conditioning of reflex-like responses such as salivation and fear. Clearly, not all human learning is so unintentional and not all behaviours are so automatic. People actively "operate" on their environment. These deliberate actions are called operants. The learning process involved in operant behaviour is called operant conditioning because we learn to behave in certain ways as we operate on the environment.

The person generally thought to be responsible for developing the concept of operant conditioning is B. F. Skinner (1953). Skinner began with the belief that the principles of classical conditioning account for only a small portion of learned behaviours. Many human behaviours are operants, not respondents. Classical conditioning describes only how existing responses might be paired with new stimuli; it does not explain how new operant behaviours are acquired.

Operants Voluntary (and generally goal-directed) behaviours emitted by a person or an animal.

Operant conditioning Learning in which voluntary behaviour is strengthened or weakened by consequences or antecedents.

Behaviour, like response or action, is simply a word for what a person does in a particular situation. Conceptually, we may think of a behaviour as sandwiched between two sets of environmental influences: those that precede it (its antecedents) and those that follow it (its consequences) (Skinner, 1950). This relationship can be shown very simply as antecedent–behaviour–consequence, or A–B–C (Kazdin, 2008). As behaviour is ongoing, a given consequence becomes an antecedent for the next A–B–C sequence. Research in operant conditioning shows that operant behaviour can be altered by changes in the antecedents, the consequences, or both. Early work focused on *consequences*, often using rats or pigeons as subjects.

Types of Consequences

STOP & THINK Think back about teachers you have had who used rewards or punishments. *Try to remember different types of rewards such as the following:*

- Concrete rewards (stickers, food, prizes, certificates)
- Activity rewards (free time, puzzles, free reading)
- Exemption rewards (no homework, no weekly test)
- Social rewards (praise, recognition)

What about punishments? Think back about punishments such as these:

- Loss of privileges (cannot sit where you want, cannot work with friends)
- Fines (lost points, grades, money)
- Extra work (homework, laps, push-ups)

MyEducationLab Go to the Activities and Applications section in Chapter 6 of MyEducationLab and complete Activity 1. ... artifa... nyin... beha... of re... beha...

According to the behavioural view, consequences determine to a great extent whether a person will repeat the behaviour that led to the consequences. The type and timing of consequences can ... behaviours. We will look first at consequences that strengthen behaviour.

Case where social isolation is not serving goal (making sit better → escape an adversive experience is a reward for acting out

... lthough reinforcement is commonly understood to mean "reward," this term ... ning in psychology. A reinforcer is any consequence that strengthens the ... So, by definition, reinforced behaviours increase in frequency or duration. ... behaviour persisting or increasing over time, you can assume the conse... viour are reinforcers for the individual involved (Landrum & Kauffman, ... nent process can be diagrammed as follows:

	CONSEQUENCE	EFFECT
... →	Reinforcer →	Strengthened or repeated behaviour

... ertain that food will be a reinforcer for a hungry animal, but what about rein... not clear why an event acts as a reinforcer for an individual, but there are ... hy reinforcement works. For example, as you saw earlier, some psychologists ... are preferred activities or that they satisfy needs, whereas other psycholo... orcers reduce tension or stimulate a part of the brain (Rachlin, 1991; ... Whether the consequences of any action are reinforcing probably depends on the individual's perception of the event and the meaning it holds for her or him. For example, students who repeatedly get themselves sent to the principal's office for misbehaving may be indicating that something about this consequence is reinforcing for them, even if it doesn't seem desirable to you. By the way, Skinner did not speculate about why reinforcers increase behaviour. He believed that it was useless to talk about "imaginary constructs" such as meaning, expectations, needs, or tensions. Skinner simply described the tendency for a given operant to increase after certain consequences (Hill, 2002; Skinner, 1953, 1989).

There are two types of reinforcement. The first, called positive reinforcement, occurs when the behaviour produces a new stimulus. Examples include pigeons pecking on the red key that produces food for them, a student wearing a new outfit that produces many compliments, or a student falling out of her chair and receiving cheers and laughter from classmates.

Notice that positive reinforcement can occur even when the behaviour being reinforced (falling out of a chair) is not "positive" from the teacher's point of view. In fact, positive reinforcement of inappropriate behaviours occurs unintentionally in many classrooms. Teachers help maintain problem behaviours by inadvertently reinforcing them. For example, Elizabeth may

and lis... Reinfo... to read... textbo... continu... this ne... tive rei... Woolfo... simplify... forceme... find diff...

Antecedents Events that precede an action.

Consequences Events that follow an action.

Reinforcement Use of consequences to strengthen behaviour.

Reinforcer Any event that follows a behaviour and increases the chances that the behaviour will occur again.

Positive reinforcement Strengthening behaviour by presenting a desired stimulus after the behaviour.

have unintentionally reinforced problem behaviour in her class by laughing the first time the boy answered, "Ronald McDonald." The problem behaviour may have persisted for other reasons, but the consequence of Elizabeth's laughter could have played a role.

When the consequence that strengthens a behaviour is the *appearance (addition)* of a new stimulus, the situation is defined as positive reinforcement. In contrast, when the consequence that strengthens a behaviour is the *disappearance (subtraction)* of a stimulus, the process is called negative reinforcement. If a particular action leads to avoiding or escaping an aversive situation, the action is likely to be repeated in a similar situation. A common example is the sound that rings in a car when passenger seatbelts have not been fastened. As soon as you put on your seatbelt, the irritating sound stops. You are likely to *repeat* this "buckling up" action in the future (so the process is *reinforcement*) because the behaviour made an aversive ringing stimulus *disappear* (so the kind of reinforcement is *negative*).

Consider students who continually "get sick" right before a test and are sent to the nurse's office. The behaviour allows the students to escape aversive situations—tests—so getting "sick" is being maintained, in part, through negative reinforcement. It is negative because the stimulus (the test) disappears; it is reinforcement because the behaviour that caused the stimulus to disappear (getting "sick") increases or repeats. It is also possible that classical conditioning plays a role; the students may have been conditioned to experience unpleasant physiological reactions to tests.

The "negative" in negative reinforcement does not imply that the behaviour being reinforced is necessarily negative or bad. The meaning is closer to that of the negation operation used in arithmetic—something is subtracted. Try to associate *positive* and *negative* reinforcement with *adding* or *subtracting* something following a behaviour that strengthens (reinforces) the behaviour.

Punishment. Negative reinforcement is often confused with punishment. The process of reinforcement (positive or negative) always involves strengthening behaviour. Punishment, on the other hand, involves *decreasing or suppressing behaviour*. A behaviour followed by a punisher is *less* likely to be repeated in similar situations in the future. Again, it is the effect that defines a consequence as punishment, and different people have different perceptions of what constitutes punishment. One student may interpret suspension from school as punishment, whereas another student may not. The process of punishment is diagrammed as follows:

	CONSEQUENCE	EFFECT
Behaviour ⟶	Punisher ⟶	Weakened or decreased behaviour

Like reinforcement, punishment may take one of two forms. The first type has been called Type I punishment, but this name isn't very informative, so we use the term presentation punishment. It occurs when the appearance of a stimulus following the behaviour suppresses or decreases the behaviour. When teachers reprimand students, assign extra work, or make students run extra laps, and so on, they are using presentation punishment. We call the other type of punishment (Type II punishment) removal punishment because it involves removing a stimulus. When teachers or parents take away privileges after a young person has behaved inappropriately, they are applying removal punishment. With both types, the effect is to decrease the behaviour that led to the punishment. Figure 6.1 summarizes the processes of reinforcement and punishment.

Reinforcement Schedules

When people are learning a new behaviour, they will learn it faster if they are reinforced for every correct response. This is a continuous reinforcement schedule. Then, when the new behaviour has been mastered, they will maintain it best if they are reinforced intermittently rather than every time. An intermittent reinforcement schedule helps students to maintain skills without expecting constant reinforcement.

There are two basic types of intermittent reinforcement schedules. One—called an interval schedule—is based on the amount of time that passes between reinforcers. The other—a ratio schedule—is based on the number of responses learners give between reinforcers. Interval and ratio schedules may be either *fixed* (predictable) or *variable* (unpredictable). Table 6.1 on page 204 summarizes the five possible reinforcement schedules (the continuous schedule and the four kinds of intermittent schedules).

Negative reinforcement Strengthening behaviour by removing an aversive stimulus when the behaviour occurs.

Aversive Irritating or unpleasant.

Punishment Process that weakens or suppresses behaviour.

Presentation punishment Decreasing the chances that a behaviour will occur again by presenting an aversive stimulus following the behaviour; also called Type I punishment.

Removal punishment Decreasing the chances that a behaviour will occur again by removing a pleasant stimulus following the behaviour; also called Type II punishment.

Continuous reinforcement schedule Presenting a reinforcer after every appropriate response.

Intermittent reinforcement schedule Presenting a reinforcer after some but not all responses.

Interval schedule Reinforcement schedule based on the length of time between reinforcers.

Ratio schedule Reinforcement schedule based on the number of responses between reinforcers.

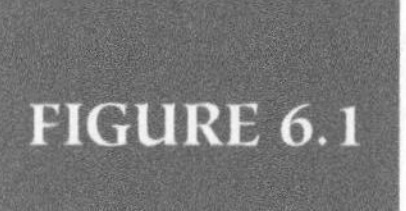

FIGURE 6.1

Kinds of Reinforcement and Punishment
Negative reinforcement and punishment are often confused. It may help you to remember that reinforcement is always associated with increases in behaviours, and punishment always involves decreasing or suppressing behaviour.

	Behaviour Encouraged	Behaviour Suppressed
Stimulus presented	POSITIVE REINFORCEMENT ("Reward") Example: high grades	PRESENTATION PUNISHMENT (Type I punishment) Example: after-school detention
Stimulus removed or withheld	NEGATIVE REINFORCEMENT ("Escape") Example: excused from chores	REMOVAL PUNISHMENT (Type II punishment) Example: no TV for a week

TABLE 6.1

Reinforcement Schedules

Schedule	Definition	Example	Response Pattern	Reaction When Reinforcement Stops
Continuous	Reinforcement after every response	Turning on the television	Rapid learning of response	Very little persistence; rapid disappearance of response
Fixed-interval	Reinforcement after a set period of time	Weekly quiz	Response rate increases as time for reinforcement approaches, then drops after reinforcement	Little persistence; rapid drop in response rate when time for reinforcement passes and no reinforcer appears
Variable-interval	Reinforcement after varying lengths of time	Pop quizzes	Slow, steady rate of responding; very little pause after reinforcement	Greater persistence; slow decline in response rate
Fixed-ratio	Reinforcement after a set number of responses	Piece work Bake sale	Rapid response rate; pause after reinforcement	Little persistence; rapid drop in response rate when expected number of responses are given and no reinforcer appears
Variable-ratio	Reinforcement after a varying number of responses	Slot machines	Vary high response rate; little pause after reinforcement	Greatest persistence; response rate stays high and gradually drops off

Source: From *Achieving Educational Excellence: Behavior Analysis for School Personnel* (Figure, p. 89), by B. Sulzer-Azaroff and G. R. Mayer, 1994, San Marcos, CA: Western Image, P.O. Box 427.

What are the effects of different schedules? Speed of performance depends on control. If reinforcement is based on the number of responses you give, then you have more control over the reinforcement: The faster you accumulate the correct number of responses, the faster the reinforcement will come. A teacher who says, "As soon as you complete these 10 problems correctly, you may listen to your music," can expect higher rates of performance than a teacher who says, "Work on these 10 problems for the next 20 minutes. Then I will check your papers and those with 10 correct may listen to their music."

Persistence in performance depends on unpredictability. Continuous reinforcement and both kinds of fixed reinforcement (ratio and interval) are quite predictable. We come to expect reinforcement at certain points and are generally quick to give up when the reinforcement does not meet our expectations. To encourage persistence of response, variable schedules are most appropriate. A newspaper recently provided a great example of student persistence on a variable schedule in an article about Valorie Lewis, a recognized teacher. Describing Lewis's grade 3 class, one of her colleagues said that the students are "afraid to be absent because they don't want to take the chance they will miss anything. Mrs. Lewis doesn't tell them when she is planning something special, so they have to be there every day just in case" (Johnson, 2008, p. 7D). In fact, if the reinforcement schedule is gradually changed until it becomes very "lean"—meaning that reinforcement occurs only after many responses or after a long time interval—then people can learn to work for extended periods without any reinforcement at all. Just watch people playing slot machines to see how powerful a lean reinforcement schedule can be.

Reinforcement schedules influence how persistently we will respond when reinforcement is withheld. What happens when reinforcement is completely withdrawn?

Extinction. In classical conditioning, the conditioned response is extinguished (disappears) when the conditioned stimulus appears but the unconditioned stimulus does not follow (e.g., tone, but no food). In operant conditioning, a person or an animal will not persist in a certain behaviour if the usual reinforcer is withheld long enough. The behaviour will eventually be extinguished (stop). For example, if you repeatedly email a professor but never get a reply, you may give up. Removal of reinforcement altogether leads to extinction. The process may take a while, however, as you may already know if you have ever tried to extinguish a child's tantrums by withholding your attention. Often the child wins—you give up ignoring and, instead of extinction, intermittent reinforcement occurs. This, of course, may encourage even more persistent tantrums in the future.

INTERMITTENT REINFORCEMENT Casino slot machines are a good example of the effectiveness of intermittent reinforcement: People "learn" to persist in losing their money, because they might be rewarded with a jackpot, albeit infrequently and unpredictably.

Antecedents and Behaviour Change

In operant conditioning, antecedents—the events preceding behaviours—provide information about which behaviours will lead to positive consequences and which will lead to unpleasant ones. For example, Skinner's pigeons learned to peck for food when a light was on, but not to bother when the light was off, because no food followed pecking when the light was off. In other words, they learned to use the antecedent light as a cue to discriminate the likely consequence of pecking. The pigeons' pecking was under stimulus control, controlled by the discriminative stimulus of the light. This happens with humans too. For example, Anita found herself (more than once) about to turn into her old office parking lot, even after the department had been relocated to a new building across town. As she drove, the old landmark cues kept her heading automatically to the old office. Another example is the supposedly true story of a getaway car driver in a bank robbery who sped through town, only to be caught by the police when she dutifully stopped at a red light. The stimulus of the red light had come to have automatic control.

We all learn to discriminate, or to "read" situations. When should you ask to borrow your roommate's car—after a major disagreement or after you both have had a great time at a party? The antecedent cue of a school principal standing in the hall helps students discriminate the probable consequences of running in the halls or attempting to break into a locker. We often respond to

Extinction The disappearance of a learned response.

Stimulus control Capacity for the presence or absence of antecedents to cause behaviours.

such antecedent cues without fully realizing that they are influencing our behaviour. But teachers can use cues deliberately in the classroom.

Effective Instruction Delivery (EID). One important antecedent to increase positive student responses is the type of instructions teachers give. Research on **effective instruction delivery** has found that concise, clear, and specific instructions that communicate an expected result are more effective than vague directions. Statements work better than questions. Teachers should provide concise instructions within a few feet of the students; directions shouted from across the room are less likely to work. Ideally, teachers should also make eye contact with students before giving instructions (Roberts, Tingstrom, Olmi, & Bellipanni, 2008).

Cueing. By definition, **cueing** is the act of providing an antecedent stimulus just before a specific behaviour is supposed to take place. Cueing is particularly useful in setting the stage for behaviours that must occur at a given time but are easily forgotten. In working with young people, teachers often find themselves correcting behaviours after the fact. For example, they may ask students, "When are you going to start remembering to . . . ?" These reminders often lead to irritation. The mistake is already made, and the young person is left with only two choices: to promise to try harder or to say, "Why don't you leave me alone?" Neither response is very satisfying. Presenting a non-judgmental cue can help prevent such negative confrontations. When a student performs the appropriate behaviour after a cue, the teacher can reinforce the student's accomplishment instead of punishing failure.

Effective instruction delivery Instructions that are concise, clear, and specific, and that communicate an expected result. Statements work better than questions.

Cueing Providing a stimulus that "sets up" a desired behaviour.

Prompt A reminder that follows a cue to make sure a person reacts to the cue.

Prompting. Sometimes students need help learning to respond to a cue in an appropriate way so the cue becomes a discriminative stimulus. One approach is to provide an additional cue, called a **prompt**, following the first cue. There are two principles for using a cue and a prompt to teach a new behaviour. First, make sure the environmental stimulus that you want to become a cue occurs immediately before the prompt you are using, so students will learn to respond to the cue and not rely only on the prompt. Second, fade the prompt as soon as possible so students do not become dependent on it (Alberto & Troutman, 2006).

An example of cueing and prompting is providing students with a checklist or reminder sheet. Figure 6.2 is a checklist for the steps involved in effective peer tutoring. Working in pairs is the cue; the checklist is the prompt. As students learn the procedures, the teacher may stop using the

FIGURE 6.2 **Written Prompts: A Peer-Tutoring Checklist**

By using this checklist, students are reminded how to be effective tutors. As they become more proficient, the checklist may be less necessary.

Remember to...

____ 1. Have the lesson ready.

____ 2. Talk clearly.

____ 3. Be friendly.

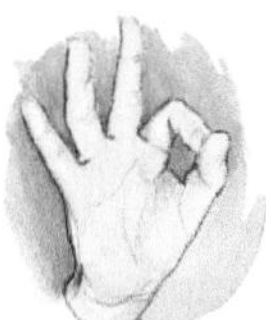

____ 4. Tell the student when the answer is right.

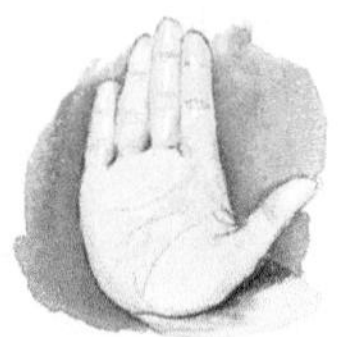

____ 5. STOP! Correct mistakes.

____ 6. Praise good work!

____ 7. Make the lesson fun.

____ 8. Do not give TOO MUCH help.

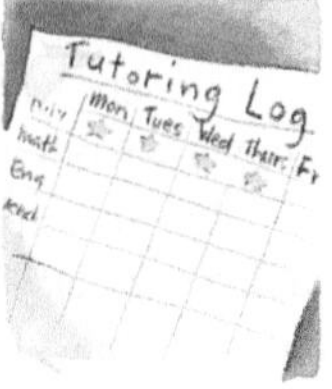

____ 9. Fill out the daily sheet.

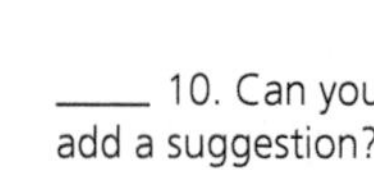

____ 10. Can you add a suggestion?

Source: From *Achieving Educational Excellence: Behavior Analysis for School Personnel* (Figure, p. 89), by B. Sulzer-Azaroff and G. R. Mayer, 1994, San Marcos, CA: Western Image, P.O. Box 427. Copyright © 1994 by Beth Sulzer-Azaroff and G. Roy Mayer. Reprinted by permission of the authors.

checklist, but may remind the students of the steps. When no written or oral prompts are necessary, the students have learned to respond appropriately to the environmental cue of working in pairs—they have learned how to behave in tutoring situations. However, the teacher should continue to monitor the process, recognize good work, and correct mistakes. Before a tutoring session, the teacher might ask students to close their eyes and "see" the checklist, focusing on each step. As students work through a tutoring session, the teacher could listen to their interactions and continue to coach students as they improve their tutoring skills.

What would these principles look like in action? We turn to that next.

APPLIED BEHAVIOUR ANALYSIS

Applied behaviour analysis is the application of behavioural learning principles to change behaviour. The method is sometimes called behaviour modification, but this term has negative connotations for many people and is often misunderstood (Alberto & Troutman, 2006; Kazdin, 2001, 2008).

Ideally, applied behaviour analysis requires clear specification of the behaviour to be changed, careful measurement of the behaviour, analysis of the antecedents and reinforcers that might be maintaining inappropriate or undesirable behaviour, interventions based on behavioural principles to change the behaviour, and careful measurement of changes. In research on applied behaviour analysis, an ABAB design (described in Chapter 1) is common. That is, researchers take a baseline measurement of the behaviour (A), then apply the intervention (B), then stop the intervention to see if the behaviour goes back to the baseline level (A), and then reintroduce the intervention (B).

In classrooms, teachers usually cannot follow all the ABAB steps, but they can do the following:

1. Clearly specify the behaviour to be changed and note the current level. For example, if a student is "careless," does this mean 2, 3, 4, or more computation errors for every 10 problems?
2. Plan a specific intervention using antecedents, consequences, or both. For example, offer the student one extra minute of computer time for every problem completed with no errors.
3. Keep track of the results, and modify the plan if necessary.

Let's consider some specific methods for accomplishing step 2—the intervention.

Methods for Encouraging Behaviours

As we discussed earlier, to encourage behaviour is to reinforce it. There are several specific ways to encourage existing behaviours or to teach new ones. These include teacher attention and praise, the Premack principle, shaping, and positive practice, as we describe in the sections that follow.

Reinforcing With Teacher Attention. Many psychologists advise teachers to "accentuate the positive"—praise students for good behaviour, while ignoring misbehaviour. In fact, some researchers believe that "the systematic application of praise and attention may be the most powerful motivational and classroom management tool available to teachers" (Alber & Heward, 1997, p. 277; Alber & Heward, 2000). A related strategy is *differential reinforcement*, or ignoring inappropriate behaviours, while being sure to reinforce appropriate behaviours as soon as they occur. For example, if a student is prone to making irrelevant comments (such as "When is the game this Friday?"), you should ignore the off-task comment, but recognize a task-related contribution as soon as it occurs (Landrum & Kauffman, 2006).

MyEducationLab Go to the Activities and Applications section in Chapter 6 of MyEducationLab and complete Activity 2. As you read the article and answer the questions, consider situations when praising students may not be a good idea.

This *praise-and-ignore approach* can be helpful, but don't expect it to solve all classroom management problems. Several studies have shown that disruptive behaviours persist when teachers use positive consequences (mostly praise) as their only classroom management strategy (McGoey & DuPaul, 2000; Pfiffner & O'Leary, 1987; Sullivan & O'Leary, 1990). Also, if attention from other students is maintaining the problem behaviours, the teacher ignoring the students who are disruptive won't help much.

There is a second point to consider when using praise. The positive results found in research occur when teachers carefully and systematically praise their students (Landrum & Kauffman, 2006). Merely "handing out compliments" will not improve behaviour. To be effective, praise must (1) be contingent on the behaviour to be reinforced, (2) specify clearly the behaviour being

Applied behaviour analysis The application of behavioural learning principles to understand and change behaviour.

Behaviour modification Systematic application of antecedents and consequences to change behaviour.

reinforced, and (3) be believable (O'Leary & O'Leary, 1977). In other words, the praise should be sincere recognition of a well-defined behaviour so students understand what they did to warrant the recognition. Teachers who have not received special training often violate these conditions (Brophy, 1981). Ideas for using praise effectively, based on Brophy's extensive review of the subject and Alan Kazdin's (2008) work with parents and teachers, are presented in the *Guidelines* box.

Some psychologists have suggested that teachers' use of praise tends to focus students on learning to win approval rather than on learning for its own sake. Perhaps the best advice is to be aware of the potential dangers of the overuse or misuse of praise and to navigate accordingly.

Selecting Reinforcers: The Premack Principle. In most classrooms, there are many readily available reinforcers other than teacher attention, such as the chance to talk to other students, work at computers, or water the class plants. However, teachers tend to offer these opportunities in a rather haphazard way. Just as is the case with praise, by making privileges and rewards directly contingent on learning and positive behaviour, the teacher can greatly increase both learning and desired behaviour.

A helpful guide for choosing the most effective reinforcers is the Premack principle, named for David Premack (1965). According to the Premack principle, a high-frequency behaviour (a preferred activity) can be an effective reinforcer for a low-frequency behaviour (a less-preferred activity). This is sometimes referred to as "Grandma's rule": First, do what I want you to do, and then you may do what you want to do. Elizabeth used this principle in her class when she told students they could work together on the second section of their worksheets after they quietly completed the first section on their own.

Premack principle Principle stating that a more-preferred activity can serve as a reinforcer for a less-preferred activity.

GUIDELINES: Using Praise Appropriately

Be clear and systematic when giving praise.

EXAMPLES

1. Make sure praise is tied directly to appropriate behaviour.
2. Make sure the student understands the specific action or accomplishment that is being praised. Say, "I am impressed that you made sure everyone in your group got a chance to speak," not, "Good job leading the group."

Make praise "appreciative" not "evaluative" (Ginott, 1972).

EXAMPLES

1. Praise and appreciate the student's efforts, accomplishments, and actions—especially when the actions help others.
2. Don't evaluate the student's character or personality—praise the action, not the person.

Set standards for praise based on individual abilities and limitations.

EXAMPLES

1. Praise progress or accomplishment in relation to the individual student's past efforts.
2. Focus the student's attention on his or her own progress, not on comparisons with others.

Attribute the student's success to effort and ability so the student will gain confidence that success is possible again.

EXAMPLES

1. Don't imply that the success may be based on luck, extra help, or easy material.
2. Ask students to describe the problems they encountered and how they solved them.

Be sure praise is really a reinforcer.

EXAMPLES

1. Don't attempt to influence the rest of the class by singling out some students for praise. This tactic frequently backfires because students know what's really going on. In addition, you risk embarrassing the student you have chosen to praise.
2. Don't give undeserved praise to students simply to balance failures. It is seldom consoling and calls attention to the student's inability to earn genuine recognition.
3. Don't use "caboosing"—tacking a criticism on at the end, as in "Good job on completing your homework this week. Why can't you do that every week?" (Kazdin, 2008).

Recognize genuine accomplishments.

EXAMPLES

1. Reward the attainment of specified goals, not just participation.
2. Do not reward uninvolved students just for being quiet and not disrupting the class.
3. Tie praise to students' improving competence or to the value of their accomplishment. Say, "I noticed that you double-checked all your problems. Your score reflects your careful work."

For more information on teacher praise, see **http://moodle.ed.uiuc.edu/wiked/index.php/Praise.**

If students didn't have to study, what would they do? The answers to this question may suggest many possible reinforcers. For most students, talking, moving around the room, sitting near a friend, being exempt from assignments or tests, reading magazines, using the computer, or playing games are preferred activities. The best way to determine appropriate reinforcers for your students may be to watch what they do in their free time.

For the Premack principle to be effective, the low-frequency (less-preferred) behaviour must happen first. In the following dialogue, notice how the teacher loses a perfect opportunity to use the Premack principle:

Students: Oh, no! Do we have to work on grammar again today? The other classes got to discuss the play we saw in the auditorium this morning.

Teacher: But the other classes finished the lesson on sentences yesterday. We're almost finished too. If we don't finish the lesson, I'm afraid you'll forget the rules we reviewed yesterday.

Students: Why don't we finish the sentences at the end of the period and talk about the play now?

Teacher: Okay, if you promise to complete the sentences later.

GRANDMA'S RULE "First, do what I want you to do, and then you may do what you want to do." According to the Premack principle, by making preferred activities contingent on learning and positive behaviour, teachers can greatly increase both.

Discussing the play could have served as a reinforcer for completing the lesson. As it is, the class may well spend the entire period discussing the play. Or, just as the discussion becomes interesting, the teacher will have to end it and insist that the class return to the grammar lesson.

Shaping. What happens when students continually fail to gain reinforcement because they simply cannot perform a skill in the first place? Consider these examples:

- A grade 4 student looks at the results of the latest mathematics test. "No credit on almost half of the problems again because I made one dumb mistake in each problem. I hate math!"
- A grade 10 student finds some excuse each day for avoiding the softball game in gym class. The student cannot catch a ball and now refuses to try.

In both situations, the students receive no reinforcement for their work because the end product of their efforts is not good enough. A safe prediction is that the students will soon learn to dislike the class, the subject, and perhaps the teacher and school in general. One way to prevent this problem is the strategy of shaping, also called successive approximations. Shaping involves reinforcing progress instead of waiting for perfect behaviour to occur before providing reinforcement.

In order to use shaping, the teacher must take the final complex behaviour the student is expected to master and break it down into a number of small steps. One approach that identifies the small steps is task analysis, originally developed by R. B. Miller (1962) to help the armed services train personnel. Miller's system begins with a definition of the final performance requirement, what the trainee (or student) must be able to do at the end of the program or unit. Then, the steps that will lead to the final goal are specified. The procedure simply breaks skills and processes down into subskills and subprocesses—small steps to success.

Consider an example of task analysis in which students must write a position paper based on library research. If the teacher assigned the position paper without analyzing the task, what could happen? Some of the students might not know how to do systematic computer research. They might read one or two entries in *Wikipedia*, then write about their position based only on this brief research. Another group of students might know how to use computers and search engines to do research online and how to find information from indexes in books, but they may have difficulty integrating information to reach conclusions. They might hand in lengthy papers listing summaries of different ideas without any synthesis or conclusions. Another group of students might be able to draw conclusions, but their written presentations might be so confusing and grammatically incorrect that the teacher won't be able to understand what they were trying to say. Each of the groups would have failed to fulfill the assignment, but for different reasons.

Shaping Reinforcing each small step of progress toward a desired goal or behaviour.

Successive approximations Small components that make up a complex behaviour.

Task analysis System for breaking down a task hierarchically into basic skills and subskills.

A task analysis gives a picture of the logical sequence of steps leading toward the final goal. An awareness of this sequence can help teachers make sure that students have the necessary skills before they move to the next step. In addition, when students have difficulty, the teacher can pinpoint problem areas. Many behaviours can be improved through shaping, especially skills that involve persistence, endurance, increased accuracy, greater speed, or extensive practice to master. Because shaping is a time-consuming process, however, it should not be used if success can be attained through simpler methods such as cueing.

Positive Practice. In positive practice, students replace one behaviour with another. This approach is especially appropriate for dealing with academic errors. When students make a mistake, they must correct it as soon as possible and practise the correct response. The same principle can be applied when students break classroom rules. Instead of being punished, the student might be required to practise the correct alternative action. This process is sometimes called *positive practice overcorrection* because the correct behaviour is practised until it becomes almost automatic (Cole, Montgomery, Wilson, & Milan, 2000; Gibbs & Luyben, 1985; Kazdin, 1984).

Positive practice Practising correct responses immediately after errors.

The *Guidelines* box summarizes approaches for encouraging positive behaviour.

GUIDELINES: Encouraging Positive Behaviours

Make sure you recognize positive behaviour in ways that students value.

EXAMPLES

1. When presenting class rules, set up positive consequences for following rules as well as negative consequences for breaking rules.
2. Recognize honest admissions of mistakes by giving students a second chance: "Because you admitted that you copied your paper from a book, I'm giving you a chance to rewrite it."
3. Offer desired rewards for academic efforts, such as extra recess time, exemptions from homework or tests, or extra credit on major projects.

When students are tackling new material or trying new skills, give plenty of reinforcement.

EXAMPLES

1. Find and comment on something positive in every student's first life drawing.
2. Reinforce students for encouraging each other. "French pronunciation is difficult and awkward at first. Let's help each other by eliminating all giggles when someone is brave enough to attempt a new word."

After new behaviours are established, give reinforcement on an unpredictable schedule to encourage persistence.

EXAMPLES

1. Offer surprise rewards for good participation in class.
2. Start classes with a short, written extra-credit question. Students don't have to answer, but a good answer offered by a student will add points to his or her total for the semester.
3. Make sure successful students get compliments for their work from time to time. Don't take students who are thriving in school for granted.

Use the Premack principle to identify effective reinforcers.

EXAMPLES

1. Watch what students do with their free time.
2. Notice which students like to work together. The chance to work with friends is often a good reinforcer.

Use cueing to help establish new behaviours.

EXAMPLES

1. Put up humorous signs in the classroom to remind students of rules.
2. At the beginning of the year, as students enter class, call their attention to a list on the board of the materials they should have with them when they come to class.

Make sure all students, even those who often cause problems, receive some praise, privileges, or other rewards when they do something well.

EXAMPLES

1. Review your class list occasionally to make sure all students are receiving some reinforcement.
2. Set standards for reinforcement so that all students will have a chance to be rewarded.
3. Check your biases. Are boys getting more opportunities for reinforcement than girls, or vice versa? How about students of different ethnicities?

Establish a variety of reinforcers.

EXAMPLES

1. Let students suggest their own reinforcers or choose from a "menu" of reinforcers with "weekly specials."
2. Talk to other teachers or parents about ideas for reinforcers.

For more ideas about building positive behaviours, see **www.afcec.org/tipsforteachers/tips_c4.html.**

Handling Undesirable Behaviour

No matter how successful you are at accentuating the positive, there are times when you must cope with undesirable behaviour, either because other methods fail or because the behaviour itself is dangerous and calls for direct action. For this purpose, negative reinforcement, reprimands, response cost, and social isolation all offer possible solutions.

Negative Reinforcement. Recall the basic principle of negative reinforcement: If a behaviour stops or avoids something unpleasant, then that behaviour is likely to occur again in similar situations. Negative reinforcement was operating in Elizabeth's classroom. When students moaned and complained, Elizabeth cancelled the test and they escaped it. So, negative reinforcement probably increased the frequency of students complaining in the future.

Negative reinforcement can also be used to enhance learning. To do this, teachers place students in mildly unpleasant situations so they can "escape" when their behaviour improves. Consider the following examples:

> **Teacher to a grade 3 class:** "When the supplies are put back in the cabinet and each of you is sitting quietly, we will go outside. Until then, we will miss our recess."
>
> **High school teacher to a student who seldom finishes in-class assignments:** "As soon as you complete the assignment, you may join the class in the auditorium. But until you finish, you must work in the study hall."
>
> **Antonio Banderas in the film *Take the Lead*:** Working with a group of totally uncooperative students, Banderas blasts the students with music they hate, only turning it off when the entire class is lined up and ready to practise their ballroom dance moves.

Actually, a true behaviourist might object to identifying these situations as examples of negative reinforcement because too much student thinking and understanding is required to make the negative reinforcers work. Teachers cannot treat students like lab animals, delivering a mild shock to their feet until they give a correct answer, then turning off the shock briefly. But teachers can make sure that unpleasant situations improve when student behaviour improves.

You may wonder why the negative reinforcement examples above are not considered punishment. Surely staying in during recess, not accompanying the class to a special program, or being subjected to unpleasant music is punishing. But the focus in each case is on strengthening a specific behaviour (putting away supplies, finishing in-class assignments, lining up and cooperating with the teacher). The teacher strengthens (reinforces) the behaviour by removing something aversive *as soon as the desired behaviour occurs*. Because the consequence involves removing or "subtracting" a stimulus, the reinforcement is negative.

Negative reinforcement also gives students a chance to exercise control. Missing recess and staying behind in study hall are unpleasant situations, but in each case the students retain control. As soon as they perform the appropriate behaviour, the unpleasant situation ends. In contrast, punishment occurs after the fact, and a student cannot so easily control or terminate it.

There are several rules for using negative reinforcement effectively: Describe the desired change in a positive way. Don't bluff. Make sure you can enforce your unpleasant situation. Follow through despite complaints. Insist on action, not promises. If the unpleasant situation ends when students *promise* to be better next time, you have reinforced making promises, not making changes (Alberto & Troutman, 2006; O'Leary, 1995).

DELIVERING REPRIMANDS Research has shown that scolding a student in front of the entire class may actually reinforce his or her disruptive behaviour by drawing more attention to it; thus, calm and private reprimands may be more effective.

Reprimands. In the *Junction Journal*, Anita's daughter's elementary school newspaper, the following lines appeared in a story called "Why I Like School," written by a grade 4 student: "I also like my teacher. She helps me understand and learn. She is nice to everyone. I like it when she gets mad at somebody, but she doesn't yell at them in front of the class, but speaks to them privately."

Soft, calm, private reprimands are more effective than loud, public reprimands in decreasing disruptive behaviour (Landrum & Kauffman, 2006). Research has shown that when reprimands are loud enough for the entire class to hear, disruptions increase or continue at a constant level. Some students enjoy public recognition for misbehaviour, or they don't want classmates to see them "lose" to the teacher. If they are not used too often, and if the classroom is generally a positive, warm environment, students usually respond quickly to private reprimands (Kaplan, 1991; Van Houten & Doleys, 1983).

Response Cost. The concept of response cost is familiar to anyone who has ever paid a fine. For certain infractions of the rules, people must lose some reinforcer—money, time, privileges (Walker, Shea, & Bauer, 2004). In a classroom, the concept of response cost can be applied in a number of ways. The first time a student breaks a class rule, the teacher gives a warning. The second time, the teacher makes a mark beside the student's name in the grade book. The student loses 2 minutes of recess for each mark accumulated. For older students, a certain number of marks might mean losing the privilege of working in a group or using the computers.

Social Isolation. One of the most controversial behavioural methods for decreasing undesirable behaviour is the strategy of social isolation, often called time out from reinforcement. The process involves removing a highly disruptive student from the classroom for 5 to 10 minutes. The student is placed in an empty, uninteresting room alone—the punishment is brief isolation from other people. A trip to the principal's office or confinement to a chair in the corner of the regular classroom does not have the same effect as sitting alone in an empty room. But beware. If a brief time out does not help improve the situation, don't try a longer time out. Alan Kazdin (2008), who has been helping teachers and parents work positively with children for decades, says, "If you are giving longer and longer time-outs, it means your strategy is failing. The answer is not to escalate—just the opposite in fact. If you are giving more and longer time-outs, this should tell you that you need to do more to positively reinforce good behaviors to replace the unwanted behaviors" (p. 10)—good advice for any form of punishment.

Some Cautions About Punishment. Unfortunately, punishment seems to be a very common part of parenting and schooling. We say *unfortunately* because study after study shows that punishment by itself, as usually practised in homes and schools, just doesn't work. It tells children what to stop doing (often, they knew that already), but it does not teach them what to do instead (Kazdin, 2008). Whenever you consider the use of punishment, you should make it part of a two-pronged attack. The first goal is to carry out the punishment and suppress the undesirable behaviour. The second goal is to make clear what the student should be doing instead and to provide reinforcement for those desirable actions. Thus, while the problem behaviours are being suppressed, positive alternative responses are being strengthened. As you will see in the next section, recent approaches to teaching really emphasize supporting positive behaviours. The *Guidelines* box gives ideas for using punishment for positive purposes.

Let us repeat. Punishment in and of itself does not lead to any positive behaviour. Harsh punishment communicates to students that "might makes right" and may encourage retaliation. In addition, punishment works best when the potential punisher—the teacher—is around. Students learn to "be good" when the teacher is in the room, but when the teacher leaves or when a substitute teacher is present, the system might fall apart. Punishment tends to focus students on the consequences of their actions for themselves instead of thinking about the impact of their behaviour on others; as a result, punishment does not instill compassion or empathy for others. Finally, punishment can interfere with developing a caring relationship with your students (Alberto & Troutman, 2006; Hardin, 2008; Kohn, 1996a, 2005; Walker et al., 2004).

Reprimands Criticisms for misbehaviour; rebukes.

Response cost Punishment by loss of reinforcers.

Social isolation Removal of a disruptive student for 5 to 10 minutes.

Time out Technically, the removal of all reinforcement. In practice, isolation of a student from the rest of the class for a brief time.

GUIDELINES: Using Punishment

Try to structure the situation so you can use negative reinforcement rather than punishment.

EXAMPLES

1. Allow students to escape unpleasant situations (completing additional workbook assignments, writing weekly math tests) when they reach a level of competence.
2. Insist on actions, not promises. Don't let students convince you to change the terms of the agreement.

If you do use punishment, keep it mild and brief—then pair it with doing the right thing.

EXAMPLES

1. Use strategies such as a time out for young children (i.e., no more than 2 to 5 minutes) or a loss of points (i.e., no more than one sticker if the student can earn five in a day) (Kazdin, 2008).
2. Pair the brief, mild punishment with reinforcement for doing the right thing or restitution. If a student writes graffiti in the restroom, use brief punishment plus cleaning off the graffiti.

Be consistent in your application of punishment.

EXAMPLES

1. Avoid inadvertently reinforcing the behaviour you are trying to punish. Keep confrontations private, so that students don't become heroes for standing up to the teacher in a public showdown.
2. Let students know in advance the consequences of breaking the rules by posting major class rules for younger students or outlining rules and consequences in a course syllabus for older students.
3. Tell students they will receive only one warning before punishment is given. Give the warning in a calm manner, and then follow through.
4. Make punishment as unavoidable and immediate as is reasonably possible.
5. Don't punish when you are angry—you may be too harsh and then need to take it back later, which shows a lack of consistency.

Focus on the students' actions, not on the students' personal qualities.

EXAMPLES

1. Reprimand in a calm but firm voice.
2. Avoid vindictive or sarcastic words or tones of voice. You might hear your own angry words later when students imitate your sarcasm.
3. Stress the need to end the problem behaviour instead of expressing any dislike you might feel for the student.
4. Be aware that students from visible minorities are disproportionately punished, sent to detention, and expelled from school—are your policies fair?

Adapt the punishment to the infraction.

EXAMPLES

1. Ignore minor misbehaviours that do not disrupt the class, or stop these misbehaviours with a disapproving glance or a move toward the student.
2. Make sure the punishment isn't worse than the crime—don't take away all the free time a student has earned for one infraction of the rules, for example (Landrum & Kauffman, 2006). Less punishment is more effective, as long as it is paired with reinforcement for doing the right thing.
3. Don't use homework as a punishment for misbehaviours such as talking during class.
4. When a student misbehaves to gain peer acceptance, removal from the group of friends can be effective, because this is really time out from a reinforcing situation.
5. If problem behaviours continue, analyze the situation and try a new approach. Your "punishment" may not actually be a punisher, or you may be inadvertently reinforcing the misbehaviour.

For more information on punishment, see **www.ext.vt.edu/pubs/family/350-111/350-111.html**.

PUTTING IT ALL TOGETHER: BEHAVIOURAL APPROACHES TO TEACHING AND MANAGEMENT

The behavioural approach to learning has made several important contributions to instruction, including systems for specifying learning objectives and direct instruction (we will look at these topics in Chapter 13 when we discuss teaching) and class management systems such as group consequences, contingency contracts, and token economies (Landrum & Kauffman, 2006). These approaches are useful when the goal is to learn *explicit information* or change *behaviours* and when the material is *sequential* and *factual*.

First, let's consider one element that is part of every behavioural learning program—specific practice of correct behaviours. Contrary to popular wisdom, practice does not make *perfect*.

Instead, practice makes permanent the behaviours practised, so practising accurate behaviours is important. Describing Tiger Woods in a magazine article, Devin Gordon (2001) said,

> Tiger's habit of pounding golf ball after golf ball long into the twilight—often during tournament play—has already become part of his legend. During his so-called slump earlier this year, Woods claimed he was simply working on shots he would need for the Masters in April. People rolled their eyes. Until he won the Masters. (p. 45)

No doubt Tiger has continued specific practice of the shots he needs for each tournament.

As examples of behavioural approaches, consider group consequences, contingency contracts, and token reinforcement.

Group Consequences

A teacher can base reinforcement for the class on the behaviour of selected target students (for example, "If Jamarcus, Evan, and Mei don't get off their mats until the end of nap time, then we will have a special snack"). Also, the class can earn rewards based on the collective behaviour of everyone in the class, usually by adding each student's points to a class or a team total. The good behaviour game is an example of this approach. Teachers and students discuss what would make the classroom a better place. Then, they identify behaviours that get in the way of learning. Based on this discussion, class rules are developed and the class is divided into two or three teams. Each time a student breaks one of the rules, that student's team is given a mark. The team with the fewest marks at the end of the period receives a special reward or privilege (longer recess, first to lunch, the team "spaceship" is moved closer to the "moon," and so on). If all teams earn fewer than a pre-established number of marks, all receive the reward. Sometimes a class needs a "no tattling" rule so the teams don't spend all their time pointing out each other's mistakes. Most studies indicate that even though the game generates only small improvements in academic achievement, it can produce definite improvements in the behaviours listed in the good behaviour rules and it can prevent many behavioural problems (Embry, 2002; Tingstrom, Sterling-Turner, & Wilczynski, 2006).

You can also use group consequences without dividing the class into teams; that is, you can base reinforcement on the behaviour of the whole class. However, caution is needed when using group approaches—the whole group should not suffer for the misbehaviour or mistakes of one individual if the group has no real influence over that person. Anita once saw an entire class break into cheers when the teacher announced that one boy was transferring to another school. The chant "No more points! No more points!" filled the room. The "points" referred to the teacher's system of giving one point to the whole class each time anyone broke a rule. Every point meant 5 minutes of recess lost. The boy who was transferring had been responsible for the loss of many recess periods. He was not very popular to begin with, and the point system, though quite effective in maintaining order, had made the boy an outcast in his own class.

Peer pressure in the form of support and encouragement, however, can be a positive influence. Group consequences are recommended when students care about the approval of their peers (Theodore, Bray, Kehle, & Jenson, 2001). If the misbehaviour of several students seems to be encouraged by the attention and laughter of other students, then group consequences could be helpful. Teachers might show students how to give support and constructive feedback to classmates. If a few students seem to enjoy sabotaging the system, those students may need separate arrangements such as putting all the saboteurs together in their own group.

Contingency Contracts and Token Reinforcement

In a contingency contract program, the teacher draws up an individual contract with each student, describing exactly what the student must do to earn a particular privilege or reward. In some programs, the students suggest the behaviours to be reinforced and the rewards that can be gained. The negotiating process itself can be an educational experience, as students learn to set reasonable goals and abide by the terms of a contract. And, if students participate in setting the goals, they often are more committed to reaching them (Locke & Latham, 2002; Schunk, 2008; Schunk, Pintrich, & Meece, 2008).

An example of a contract for completing assignments that is appropriate for intermediate and upper-level students is presented in Figure 6.3. This chart serves as a contract, assignment sheet, and progress record. Information about progress can support student motivation. Something like this might even help you keep track of assignments and due dates in your university classes.

Good behaviour game Arrangement where a class is divided into teams and each team receives demerit points for breaking agreed-upon rules of good behaviour.

Group consequences Rewards or punishments given to a class as a whole for adhering to or violating rules of conduct.

Contingency contract A contract between the teacher and a student specifying what the student must do to earn a particular reward or privilege.

FIGURE 6.3

A Contingency Contract for Completing Assignments

The teacher and student agree on the due dates for each assignment, marking them in blue on the chart. Each time an assignment is turned in, the date of completion is marked in black on the chart. As long as the actual completion line is above the planned completion line, the student earns free time or other contracted rewards.

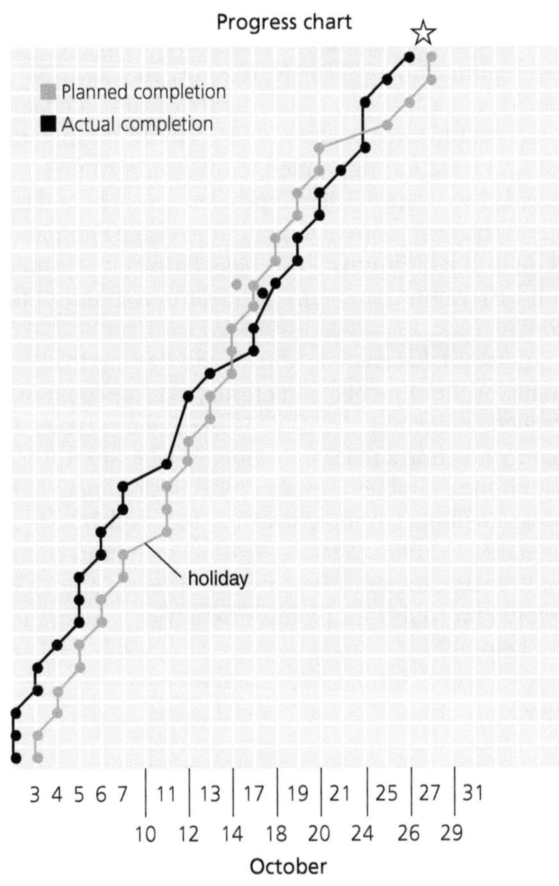

Source: From *Achieving Educational Excellence: Behavior Analysis for School Personnel* (Figure, p. 89), by B. Sulzer-Azaroff and G. R. Mayer, 1994, San Marcos, CA: Western Image, P.O. Box 427. Copyright © 1994 by Beth Sulzer-Azaroff and G. Roy Mayer. Reprinted by permission of the authors.

STOP & THINK Have you ever participated in a program where you earned points or credits that you could exchange for a reward? Are you a member of a frequent flyer club, or do you get points on your credit card? Do you get one free rental movie for every 10 rentals or a free smoothie when you fill a punch card? Does being a part of such a program affect your buying habits? How? Some people pay for everything they can with a credit card to accumulate points and then always try fly on one airline for the same reason. Go to **www.bookitprogram.com** and see a reading incentive club for pizza eaters.

Often, it is difficult to provide positive consequences for all the students who deserve them. A token reinforcement system can help solve this problem by allowing all students to earn tokens for both academic work and positive classroom behaviour. The tokens may be points, check marks, holes punched in a card, chips, play money, or anything else that is easily identified as the student's property. Periodically, the students exchange the tokens they have earned for some desired reward (Alberto & Troutman, 2006; Kazdin, 2001).

Token reinforcement system System in which tokens earned for academic work and positive classroom behaviour can be exchanged for some desired reward.

Depending on the age of the student, the rewards could be small toys, school supplies, free time, special class jobs, positive notes sent home, time to listen to music, or other privileges. When a *token economy*, as this kind of system is called, is first established, the tokens should be given out on a fairly continuous schedule, with chances to exchange the tokens for rewards available early and often. Once the system is working well, however, tokens should be distributed on an intermittent schedule and saved for longer periods of time before they are exchanged for rewards.

Another variation is to allow students to earn tokens in the classroom and then exchange them for rewards at home. These plans are very successful when parents are willing to cooperate. Usually a note or report form is sent home daily or twice a week. The note indicates the number of points earned in the preceding time period. The points may be exchanged for minutes of television viewing, access to special toys, or private time with parents. Points can also be saved up for larger rewards such as trips. Do not use this procedure, however, if you suspect the child might be punished for poor reports (Jurbergs, Palcic, & Kelly, 2007).

Because token reinforcement systems are complicated and time-consuming, generally, they should be used in only three situations: (1) to motivate students who are completely uninterested in their work and have not responded to other approaches; (2) to encourage students who have consistently failed to make academic progress; and (3) to deal with a class that is out of control. Some groups of students seem to benefit from token economies more than others. Students with intellectual disabilities, children who have failed often, students with few academic skills, and students with behavioural problems all seem to respond to the concrete, direct nature of token reinforcement.

Before you try a token system, you should be sure that your teaching methods and materials are appropriate for the students. Sometimes, class disruptions or lack of motivation indicate that teaching practices need to be changed. Maybe the class rules are unclear or are enforced inconsistently. Perhaps your instructions are vague. Maybe the text is too easy or too hard or the pace is inappropriate. If these problems exist, a token system may improve the situation temporarily, but the students will still have trouble learning the academic material. Improve your teaching first. The few pages devoted here to token reinforcement and contingency contracts can offer only an introduction to these programs. If you want to set up a large-scale reward program in your classroom, you should probably seek professional advice. Often, the school psychologist, counsellor, or principal can help.

The next section describes two examples of successfully applied behavioural principles to improve behaviours of students with special needs.

Reaching Every Student: Severe Behavioural Problems

Students with severe behavioural problems provide some of the most difficult challenges for teachers. Two studies show how behavioural principles can be useful in helping these students.

Lea Theodore and her colleagues (2001) worked with the teacher of five adolescent males who were diagnosed as having severe emotional disorders. A short list of clear rules was established (e.g., no obscene words, comply with teacher's requests within 5 seconds, no verbal putdowns). The rules were written on index cards taped to each student's desk. The teacher had a checklist on his desk with each student's name to note any rule-breaking. This checklist was easily observable, so students could monitor their own and each other's performance. At the end of the 45-minute period, a student chose a "criterion" from a jar. The possible criteria were performance of the whole group, student with the highest score, student with the lowest score, the average of all students, or a random single student. If the student or students selected to be the criterion had five check marks or fewer for rule-breaking, then the whole class got a reward, also chosen randomly from a jar. The possible rewards were things like a power drink, a late-to-class pass, or a snack. An ABAB design was used—that is, baseline, two-week intervention, two-week withdrawal of intervention, and two-week return to group consequences. All students showed clear improvement in following the rules when the reward system was in place, as you can see in Figure 6.4, which illustrates a chart for one of the students. Students liked the approach and the teacher found it easy to implement.

In the second study, Kara McGoey and George DuPaul (2000) worked with teachers in three preschool classrooms to address the problem behaviours of four students diagnosed as having attention-deficit/hyperactivity disorder (ADHD). The teachers tried both a token reinforcement program (students earned small and large buttons on a chart for following class rules) and a response cost system (students began with five small buttons and one large button per activity each day and lost buttons for not following rules). Both procedures were effective in lowering rule-breaking, but the teachers found the response cost system easier to implement.

FIGURE 6.4 **Using an ABAB Design to Evaluate an Improvement Strategy With a Student Who Exhibited Severe Behavioural Problems**

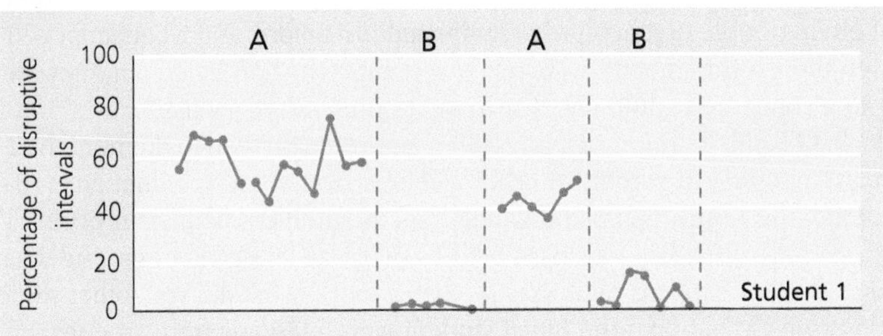

Source: For details of both of these approaches see: "Randomization of Group Contingencies and Reinforcers to Reduce Classroom Disruptive Behavior" by L. A. Theodore, M. A. Bray, T. J. Kehle, & W. R. Jenson, 2001, *Journal of School Psychology, 39,* 267–277 and "Token Reinforcement and Response Cost Procedures: Reducing Disruptive Behaviour of Preschool Children with Attention-Deficit/Hyperactive Disorder" by K. E. McGoey & G. J. DuPaul, 2000, *School Psychology Quarterly, 15,* 330–343. Reprinted with permission from Elsevier.

What's New? Functional Behavioural Assessment and Positive Behaviour Supports

Teachers in both regular and special education classes have had success with a new approach that begins by asking, "What are students getting out of their problem behaviours—what functions do these behaviours serve?" The focus is on the *why* of the behaviour, not on the *what* (Lane, Falk, & Wehby, 2006; Warren et al., 2006). The reasons that children engage in problem behaviours generally fall into one, or more, of four categories (Barnhill, 2005; Maag & Kemp, 2003). Students act out to:

1. Receive attention from others—teachers, parents, or peers.
2. Escape from some unpleasant situation, such as an academic or social demand.
3. Obtain a desired item or activity.
4. Meet sensory needs, such as stimulation from rocking or flapping arms, in the cases of some children with autism.

If the reason for the behaviour is known, the teacher can devise ways of supporting positive behaviours that will serve the same "why" function. For example, Anita once worked with a middle school principal who was concerned about a boy who had lost his father a few years earlier and was having trouble with a number of subjects, especially math. The student disrupted math class at least twice a week and ended up in the principal's office. When he arrived, the boy got the principal's undivided attention. After a scolding, they talked about sports because the principal liked the student and was concerned that he had no male role models in his life. It is easy to spot the function of the classroom disruptions—they always led to (1) escape from math class (negative reinforcement) and (2) one-on-one time with the principal (positive reinforcement after a little bit of reprimanding). Together, the principal, the teacher, and Anita developed a way to support the student's positive behaviours in math by arranging for some extra tutoring and by giving him time with the principal when he completed math problems, instead of when he acted up in class. The new positive behaviours served many of the same functions as the old problem behaviours.

FUNCTIONAL BEHAVIOURAL ASSESSMENT These approaches focus on the "why" of student behaviour . . . or misbehaviour. Teachers observe student behaviours in context and may interview the student, peers, and parents to determine the reason for the student's behaviour.

Discovering the "Why": Functional Behavioural Assessments. The process of understanding the "why" of a problem behaviour is known as functional behavioural assessment (FBA). Using a wide range of procedures to map the A–B–Cs of the situation—the antecedents, behaviours, and consequences—teachers try to identify the reason for or the function of the behaviour (Barnhill, 2005). You can begin by interviewing the students about their behaviours. In one study, students were asked to describe what they did that got them in trouble in school, what happened just before, and what happened right after they acted out. Even though the students were not always sure why they acted out, they seemed to benefit from talking to a concerned adult who was trying to understand their situation, not just reprimand them (Murdock, O'Neill, & Cunningham, 2005). But you will need to do more than just talk to students. You might also talk to parents or other teachers. You could conduct an A–B–C observation with these questions in mind: When and where does the problem behaviour occur? What people or activities are involved? What happens right before—what do others do or say and what did the target student do or say? What happens right after the behaviour—what did you, other students, or the target student do or say? What does the target student gain or escape from by engaging in the behaviour—what changes after the student acts out? A more structured approach is shown in Figure 6.5, which illustrates an observation and planning worksheet for functional behavioural assessment.

Remember, too, that the same behaviours may serve different functions for different students. For example, a functional behavioural assessment of three preschool students found that two of the students were aggressive and uncooperative in order to gain the teacher's attention, but the third child was trying to escape or avoid teacher attention (Dufrene, Doggett, Henington, & Watson, 2007). With information from a functional behavioural assessment, teachers developed an intervention package, including positive behaviour supports (PBS) for each child. Two students met specific standards to get the teacher attention they wanted, but the third child got to be "left alone" as long as he met certain standards.

Positive Behaviour Supports. Positive behaviour supports are interventions designed to replace problem behaviours with new actions that serve the same purpose for the student. These approaches can help students with disabilities succeed in inclusion classrooms. For example, in one study, the disruptive behaviour of a 5-year-old boy with an intellectual disability was nearly eliminated in a relatively short time through a PBS intervention that was based on a functional assessment conducted by the regular teaching staff and the special education teacher. The intervention included making sure the tasks assigned were at the appropriate difficulty level, providing assistance with these tasks, teaching the student how to request assistance, and teaching the student how to request a break from assigned work (Soodak & McCarthy, 2006; Umbreit, 1995).

But these approaches are not only for students with special needs. Research shows that disciplinary referrals decrease when the whole school uses these approaches for all students (Lewis, Sugai, & Colvin, 1998). Because about 5 percent of students account for about 50 percent of the disciplinary referrals, it makes sense to develop interventions for those students. Positive behaviour interventions based on functional assessments can reduce these behavioural problems by 80 percent (Crone & Horner, 2003). At the classroom level, teachers are encouraged to use such preventive strategies as precorrection, which involves identifying the context for a student's misbehaviour, clearly specifying the alternative expected behaviour, modifying the situation to make the problem behaviour less likely—for example, providing a cue or moving the student away from tempting distractions—then rehearsing the expected positive behaviours in the new context and providing powerful reinforcers when the behaviours occur. There is an emphasis on keeping students engaged, providing a positive focus, consistently enforcing school or class rules, correcting disruptive behaviour proactively, and planning for smooth transitions (Freiberg, 2006; U.S. Department of Education, 2010).

Positive behaviour supports also can be part of a school-wide program. At the school level, the teachers and administrators can:

- Agree on a common approach for supporting positive behaviours and correcting problems.
- Develop a few positively stated, specific behavioural expectations and procedures for teaching these expectations to all students.
- Identify a continuum of ways (from small and simple, to more complex and stronger) to acknowledge appropriate behaviours and correct behavioural errors.
- Integrate the positive behaviour support procedures with the school's discipline policy.

Functional behavioural assessment (FBA) Procedures used to obtain information about antecedents, behaviours, and consequences to determine the reason for or function of the behaviour.

Positive behaviour supports (PBS) Interventions designed to replace problem behaviours with new actions that serve the same purpose for the student.

Precorrection A tool for positive behaviour support that involves identifying the context for a student's misbehaviour, clearly specifying the alternative expected behaviour, modifying the situation to make the problem behaviour less likely, then rehearsing the expected positive behaviours in the new context and providing powerful reinforcers.

FIGURE 6.5

A Structured Observation Guide for Functional Behavioural Assessment

Student Name: ______________________ **Date:** __________

Target behaviour: Operationally define the behaviour that most interferes with the student's functioning in the classroom. Include intensity (high, medium, or low), frequency, and duration.

____

____

When, where, with whom, and in what condition is the target behaviour *least* likely to occur?

____

Setting events or context variables (i.e., hunger, lack of sleep, medications, problems on bus):

____

Immediate Antecedents & Consequences

Antecedents	***Problematic Settings***	***Consequences***
___ Demand/request	___ Unstructured setting	___ Behaviour ignored
___ Difficult task	___ Unstructured activity	___ Reprimanded
___ Time of day	___ Individual seat work	___ Verbal redirection
___ Interruption in routine	___ Group work	___ Time-out (duration: ___)
___ Peer tease/provoked	___ Specials	___ Loss of incentives
___ No materials/activities	___ Specific subject/task	___ Physical redirection
___ Could not get desired item	___ Crowded setting	___ Physical restraint
___ People ________	___ Noisy setting	___ Sent to office
___ Alone	___ Other ________	___ Suspension
___ Other ________	___ Other ________	___ Other ________

What function(s) does the target behaviour seem to serve for the student?

___ Escape from:	___ demand/request	___ person	___ activity/task	___ school	___ other ________
___ Attention from:	___ adult	___ peer	___ other ________		
___ Gain desired:	___ item	___ activity	___ area	___ other ________	

___ Automatic sensory stimulation: ______________________

Hypothesis:

When ______________ (antecedent) occurs in the context of ______________ (problematic setting)

the student exhibits ______________ (target behaviour) in order to ______________ (perceived function).

This behaviour is more likely to occur when ______________ (setting event/context variables).

Replacement or competing behaviour that could still serve the same function for the student:

____

Is the replacement behaviour in the student's repertoire, or will it need to be taught directly? ______________

If so, how will it be taught? ______________

List some potential motivators for student: ______________

____

Source: From "Functional behavior assessment in schools" by G. P. Barnhill, *Intervention in School and Clinic*, 40, p. 138. Copyright 2005 by PRO-ED, Inc. Reprinted by permission of SAGE Publications.

Research on school-wide positive behaviour supports is limited, but results so far have been encouraging. A study comparing middle school students in a behaviour support program with students outside the program showed that students who were in the program reported more positive reinforcement for appropriate behaviour. Disciplinary referrals as well as verbal and physical aggression significantly decreased. In addition, students' perceptions of school safety improved (Metzler, Biglan, Rusby, & Sprague, 2001). Studies of school-wide PBS efforts also indicate decreases in disciplinary referrals (Lewis, Sugai, & Colvin, 1998; Soodak & McCarthy, 2006).

Even with new approaches such as PBS, in recent years, most behavioural psychologists have found that operant conditioning offers too limited an explanation of learning. As behavioural approaches to learning developed, some researchers added a new element—thinking about behaviour.

CHALLENGES TO BEHAVIOURAL VIEWS: THINKING ABOUT BEHAVIOUR

Today, many learning theorists have expanded their view of learning to include the study of cognitive processes that cannot be directly observed, such as expectations, thoughts, mental maps, and beliefs. Two examples of this expanded view are observational learning and self-management.

Social Learning Theory

Over 30 years ago, Albert Bandura, a native of Alberta, noted that the traditional behavioural views of learning were accurate but incomplete because they gave only a partial explanation of learning and overlooked important elements, particularly social influences. His early work on learning was grounded in the behavioural principles of reinforcement and punishment, but he added a focus on *learning from observing others*. This expanded view was labelled social learning theory and was considered a *neobehavioural approach* (Bandura, 1977; Hill, 2002; Zimmerman & Schunk, 2003).

Learning and Performance. To explain some limitations of the behavioural model, Bandura distinguished between the *acquisition of knowledge* (learning) and the *observable performance based on that knowledge* (behaviour). In other words, Bandura suggested that we all may know more than we show. An example is found in one of Bandura's early studies (1965). Preschool children saw a film of a model kicking and punching an inflatable "Bobo" doll. One group saw the model rewarded for the aggression, another group saw the model punished, and a third group saw no consequences. When they were moved to a room with the Bobo doll, the children who had seen the punching and kicking reinforced on the film were the most aggressive toward the doll. Those who had seen the attacks punished were the least aggressive. But when the children were promised rewards for imitating the model's aggression, all of them demonstrated that they had learned the behaviour.

Thus, incentives can affect performance. Even though learning may have occurred, it may not be demonstrated until the situation is appropriate or there are incentives to perform. This might explain why some students don't perform the "bad" behaviours, such as swearing or smoking cigarettes, that they all see modelled by adults, peers, and the media. Personal consequences may discourage them from performing the behaviours. In other examples, children may have learned how to write the alphabet, but perform poorly because their fine motor coordination is limited, or they may have learned how to simplify fractions, but perform poorly on a test because they are feeling anxious. In these cases, the children's performance is not an accurate indication of the learning that took place earlier.

MyEducationLab Go to the Activities and Applications section in Chapter 6 of MyEducationLab and complete Activity 3. As you watch the video and answer the questions, consider what behaviourists would say about the interplay of enactive and vicarious learning in the classroom, as well as the use of praise and routines in the classroom.

Enactive and Vicarious Learning. In his later work, Bandura focused on cognitive factors such as beliefs, self-perceptions, and expectations, so his theory is now called a *social cognitive theory* (Hill, 2002). Social cognitive theory (discussed in Chapter 10) distinguishes between enactive and vicarious learning. *Enactive learning* is learning by doing (acting) and experiencing the consequences of your actions. This may sound like operant conditioning all over again, but it is not, and the difference has to do with the role of consequences. Proponents of operant conditioning believe that consequences strengthen or weaken behaviour. In enactive learning, however, consequences are seen as providing information. Our interpretations of the consequences create expectations, influence motivation, and shape beliefs (Schunk, 2008). We will see many examples of enactive learning—learning by doing—throughout this book.

Vicarious learning is learning by observing others, so it often is called observational learning. People and animals can learn merely by observing another person or animal learn, and this fact challenges the behaviourist idea that cognitive factors are unnecessary in an explanation of learning.

Social learning theory Theory that emphasizes learning through observation of others.

Social cognitive theory Theory that adds concern with cognitive factors such as beliefs, self-perceptions, and expectations to social learning theory.

Observational learning Learning by observation and imitation of others.

If people can learn by watching, they must be focusing their attention, constructing images, remembering, analyzing, and making decisions that affect learning. Thus, much is going on mentally before performance and reinforcement can even take place. Cognitive apprenticeships, discussed in Chapter 9, are examples of vicarious learning—learning by observing others.

Elements of Observational Learning

STOP & THINK Your interview for a position in the middle school is going well. The next question is "Who are your models as teachers? Do you hear yourself saying or see yourself doing things that other teachers have done? Are there teachers from films or books that you would like to be like?" How would you answer?

Through observational learning, we learn not only how to perform a behaviour but also what will happen to us in specific situations if we do perform it. Observation can be a very efficient learning process. The first time children hold hairbrushes, cups, or tennis rackets, they usually brush, drink, or swing as well as they can, given their current muscle development and coordination. Let's take a closer look at how observational learning occurs. Bandura (1986) notes that observational learning includes four elements: *paying attention, retaining information or impressions, producing behaviours*, and *being motivated* to repeat the behaviours.

Attention. In order to learn through observation, we have to pay attention. In teaching, you will have to ensure students' attention to the critical features of the lesson by making clear presentations and highlighting important points. In demonstrating a skill (for example, threading a sewing machine or operating a lathe), you may need to have students look over your shoulder as you work. Seeing your hands from the same perspective as they see their own directs their attention to the right features of the situation and makes observational learning easier.

Retention. In order to imitate the behaviour of a model, you have to remember it. This involves mentally representing the model's actions in some way, probably as verbal steps (e.g., "Hwa-Rang, the eighth form in Tae Kwon Do karate, is a palm-heel block, then a middle riding stance punch, then . . ."), or as visual images, or both. Retention can be improved by mental rehearsal (imagining imitating the behaviour) or by actual practice. In the retention phase of observational learning, practice helps us remember the elements of the desired behaviour, such as the sequence of steps.

Production. Once we "know" how a behaviour should look and remember the elements or steps, we still may not perform it smoothly. Sometimes, we need a great deal of practice, feedback, and coaching about subtle points before we can reproduce the behaviour of the model. In the production phase, practice makes the behaviour smoother and more expert.

Motivation and Reinforcement. As mentioned earlier, social learning theory distinguishes between acquisition and performance. We may acquire a new skill or behaviour through observation, but we may not perform that behaviour until there is some motivation or incentive to do so. Reinforcement can play several roles in observational learning. If we anticipate being reinforced for imitating the actions of a model, we may be more motivated to pay attention, remember, and reproduce the behaviours. In addition, reinforcement is important in maintaining learning. A person who tries a new behaviour is unlikely to persist without reinforcement (Ollendick, Dailey, & Shapiro, 1983; Schunk, 2008). For example, if an unpopular student adopted the style of dress of the "in" group, but was ignored or ridiculed, it is unlikely that the imitation would continue.

OBSERVATIONAL LEARNING Observational theories of learning consider the importance of learning by doing and of learning by observing others.

Bandura identifies three forms of reinforcement that can encourage observational learning. In the first form, the observer may reproduce the behaviours of the model and receive direct reinforcement, as when a gymnast successfully executes a front flip/round-off combination and the coach/model says, "Excellent!"

But the reinforcement need not be direct—it may be vicarious reinforcement. The observer may simply see others reinforced for a particular behaviour and then increase his or her production of that behaviour. For example, if you compliment two students on the attractive illustrations in their lab reports, several other students who observe your compliments may turn in illustrated lab reports next time. Most TV ads hope for this kind of effect. People in commercials become deliriously happy when they drive a particular car or drink a specific energy drink, and the viewer is supposed to do the same; the viewer's behaviour is reinforced vicariously by the actors' obvious pleasure. Punishment can also be vicarious: You may slow down on a stretch of highway after seeing several people get speeding tickets there.

The final form of reinforcement is self-reinforcement, or controlling your own reinforcers. This sort of reinforcement is important for both students and teachers. In fact, if one goal of education is to produce people who are capable of educating themselves, then students must learn to manage their own lives, set their own goals, and provide their own reinforcement. In adult life, rewards are sometimes vague and goals often take a long time to reach. Think about how many small steps are required to complete an education and find your first job. As a teacher, sometimes self-reinforcement is all that keeps you going. Life is filled with tasks that call for this sort of self-management (Rachlin, 2004).

Self-Management

STOP & THINK What area of your own life needs some self-management? Write down one behaviour you would like to increase and one behaviour you would like to eliminate.

As you will see throughout this book, the role of students as architects of their own learning is a major concern of psychologists and educators today. This concern is not restricted to any one group or theory. Different areas of research and theory all converge on one important idea: that responsibility and the ability to learn rest within the student. Students must be active—no one can learn for someone else (Mace, Belfiore, & Hutchinson, 2001; Manning & Payne, 1996; Winne, 1995; Zimmerman & Schunk, 2004). From a behavioural perspective, students may be involved in any or all of the steps in a basic behaviour change program. They may help set goals, observe their own work, keep records of it, and evaluate their own performance. Finally, they can select and deliver reinforcement.

Goal Setting. It appears that the goal-setting phase is very important in self-management (Reeve, 1996; Schunk, Pintrich, & Meece, 2008). In fact, some research suggests that setting specific goals and making them public may be the critical elements of self-management programs. For example, S. C. Hayes and his colleagues identified university students who had serious problems with studying and taught them how to set specific study goals. Students who set goals and announced them to the experimenters performed significantly better on tests covering the material they were studying than students who set goals privately and never revealed them to anyone (Hayes, Rosenfarb, Wulfert, Munt, Korn, & Zettle, 1985).

Higher standards tend to lead to higher performance (Locke & Latham, 2002). Unfortunately, student-set goals have a tendency to reflect increasingly lower expectations. Teachers can help students maintain high standards by monitoring the goals set and reinforcing high standards.

Monitoring and Evaluating Progress. Students may also participate in the monitoring and evaluation phases of a behaviour change program (Mace, Belfiore, & Hutchinson, 2001). Some examples of behaviours that are appropriate for self-monitoring are the number of assignments completed, time spent practising a skill, number of books read, number of correct problems, and time taken to run a mile. Tasks that must be accomplished without teacher supervision, such as homework or private study, are also good candidates for self-monitoring. Students keep a chart, diary, or checklist that records the frequency or duration of the behaviours in question. A progress record card can help older students break down assignments into small steps, determine the best sequence for completing the steps, and keep track of daily progress by setting goals for each day. The record card itself serves as a prompt that can be faded out.

Self-evaluation is somewhat more difficult than simple self-recording because it involves making a judgment about quality. Students can evaluate their behaviour with reasonable accuracy, especially

Vicarious reinforcement Increasing the chances that a person repeats a behaviour by observing another person being reinforced for that behaviour.

Self-reinforcement Controlling your own reinforcers.

Self-management Use of behavioural learning principles to change your own behaviour.

if they learn standards for judging a good performance or product. For example, Sweeney, Salva, Cooper, and Talbert-Johnson (1993) taught secondary students how to evaluate their handwriting for size, slant, shape, and spacing. One key to accurate self-evaluation seems to be for the teacher to periodically check students' assessments and give reinforcement for accurate judgments. Older students may learn accurate self-evaluation more readily than younger students. Again, bonus points can be awarded when the teachers' and students' evaluations match (Kaplan, 1991). Self-correction can accompany self-evaluation. Students first evaluate, then alter and improve their work, and finally, compare the improvements to the standards again (Mace et al., 2001).

Self-Reinforcement. The last step in self-management is self-reinforcement. There is some disagreement, however, as to whether this step is actually necessary. Some psychologists believe that setting goals and monitoring progress alone are sufficient and that self-reinforcement adds nothing to the effects (Hayes et al., 1985). Others believe that rewarding yourself for a job well done can lead to higher levels of performance than simply setting goals and keeping track of progress (Bandura, 1986). If you are willing to be tough and really deny yourself something you want until your goals are reached, then perhaps the promise of the reward can provide extra incentive for work. With that in mind, you may want to think of some way to reinforce yourself when you finish reading this chapter. A similar approach helped us write the chapter in the first place.

Sometimes, teaching students self-management can solve a problem for teachers and provide fringe benefits as well. For example, the coaches of a competitive swim team with members aged 9 to 16 were having difficulty persuading swimmers to maintain high work rates. Then the coaches drew up four charts indicating the training program to be followed by each member and posted the charts near the pool. The swimmers were given the responsibility of recording both their numbers of laps and their completion of each training unit. Because the recording was public, swimmers could see their own progress and their teammates' progress and keep accurate track of the work units completed. Work output increased by 27 percent. The coaches also liked the system because swimmers could begin to work immediately without waiting for instructions (McKenzie & Rushall, 1974).

At times, families can be enlisted to help their children develop self-management abilities. Working together, teachers and parents can focus on a few goals and, at the same time, support the growing independence of the students. The *Family and Community Partnerships Guidelines* box gives some ideas for how to encourage families and communities to help children develop self-management skills.

MyEducationLab Go to the Teacher Talk section of Chapter 6 of MyEducationLab and watch a video of Gary Carmichael, 2007 Teacher of the Year from Montana, explaining his goals for his students to become successful on their own, and to be able to think for themselves and evaluate different situations and new ideas.

FAMILY AND COMMUNITY PARTNERSHIPS

GUIDELINES: Student Self-Management

Introduce the system to parents and students in a positive way.

EXAMPLES

1. Invite family participation and stress possible benefits to all family members.
2. Consider starting the program with only volunteers.
3. Describe how you use self-management programs yourself.

Help families and students establish reachable goals.

EXAMPLES

1. Have examples of possible self-management goals for students such as starting homework early in the evening, or keeping track of books read.
2. Show families how to post goals and keep track of progress. Encourage everyone in the family to work on a goal.

Give families ways to record and evaluate their child's progress (or their own).

EXAMPLES

1. Divide the work into easily measured steps.
2. Provide models of good work where judgments are more difficult, such as in creative writing.
3. Give families a record form or checklist to keep track of progress.

Encourage families to check the accuracy of student records from time to time and to help their children to develop forms of self-reinforcement.

EXAMPLES

1. Conduct many checkups when students are beginning to learn, and fewer later.
2. Ask siblings to check one another's records.
3. Where appropriate, test the skills that students are supposed to be developing at home and reward students whose self-evaluations match their test performances.
4. Ask students to brainstorm ideas with their families for rewarding themselves for jobs well done.

For more about self-management, see **www.lehigh.edu/projectreach/teachers/self-managemnt/self-manage_open.htm**.

PROBLEMS AND ISSUES

The preceding sections provide an overview of several strategies for changing student behaviour in the classroom. However, you should be aware that these strategies are tools that can be used either responsibly or irresponsibly. What, then, are some issues you should keep in mind?

Criticisms of Behavioural Methods

STOP & THINK During your job interview, the principal asks, "A teacher last year got in trouble for bribing his students with homework exemptions to get them to behave in class. What do you think about using rewards and punishments in teaching?" What do you say?

While you think about your answer to this question, look at the *Point/Counterpoint* box on "Should Students Be Rewarded for Learning?" to see two different perspectives. Properly used, the strategies in this chapter can be effective tools to help students learn academically and grow in self-sufficiency. Effective tools, however, do not automatically produce excellent work, and behavioural strategies are often implemented haphazardly, inconsistently, incorrectly, or superficially (Landrum & Kauffman, 2006). The indiscriminate use of even the best tools can lead to difficulties.

Some psychologists fear that rewarding students for all learning will cause them to lose interest in learning for its own sake (Deci, 1975; Deci & Ryan, 1985; Kohn, 1993, 1996; Lepper & Greene, 1978; Lepper, Keavney, & Drake, 1996; Ryan & Deci, 1996). Studies have suggested that using reward programs with students who are already interested in the subject matter may, in fact, cause students to be less interested in the subject when the reward program ends, as you can see in the *Point/Counterpoint* box. In addition, there is some evidence that praising students for being intelligent when they succeed can undermine their motivation if they do not perform as well the next time. After they fail, students who had been praised for being smart may be less persistent and enjoy the task less compared to students who had been praised earlier for working hard (Mueller & Dweck, 1998).

"Hey wait a minute! You're cleaning erasers as a punishment? I'm cleaning them as a reward!"

Just as you must take into account the effects of a reward system on the individual, you must also consider its impact on other students. Using a reward program or giving one student increased attention may have a detrimental effect on the other students in the classroom. Is it possible that other students will learn to be "bad" in order to be included in the reward program? Most of the evidence on this question suggests that using individual adaptations, such as reward programs, does not have any adverse effects on students who are not participating if the teacher believes in the program and explains the reasons for using it to the non-participating students. After interviewing 98 students in grades 1 through 6, Cindy Fulk and Paula Smith (1995) concluded, "Teachers may be more concerned about equal treatment of students than students are" (p. 416). If the conduct of some students does seem to deteriorate when their peers are involved in special programs, many of the same procedures discussed in this chapter should help them return to previous levels of appropriate behaviour (Chance, 1992, 1993).

Ethical Issues

The ethical questions related to the use of the strategies described in this chapter are similar to those raised by any process that seeks to influence people. What are the goals? How do these goals fit with those of the school as a whole? What effect will a strategy have on the individuals involved? Is too much control being given to the teacher, or to the views of a majority group in society?

Goals. The strategies described in this chapter could be applied exclusively to teaching students to sit still, raise their hands before speaking, and remain silent at all other times (Winett & Winkler, 1972). This certainly would be an unethical use of the techniques. It is true that a teacher may need to establish some organization and order, but limiting improvements to student behaviours like these will not ensure academic learning. On the other hand, in some situations, reinforcing academic skills may lead to improvements in student conduct. Whenever possible, emphasis should be placed on academic learning. Academic improvements generalize to other situations more successfully than do changes in students' classroom conduct.

Strategies. Punishment can have negative side effects: It can serve as a model for aggressive responses, and it can encourage negative emotional reactions. Punishment is unnecessary and even

POINT / COUNTERPOINT

Should Students Be Rewarded for Learning?

FOR YEARS, EDUCATORS and psychologists have debated whether students should be rewarded for school work and academic accomplishments. In the early 1990s, Paul Chance and Alfie Kohn exchanged opinions on this subject in several issues of *Phi Delta Kappan* (March 1991, November 1992, June 1993). Then, University of Alberta professors Judy Cameron and W. David Pierce (1996) published an article on reinforcement in the *Review of Educational Research* that precipitated extensive criticisms and rebuttals in the same journal from Mark Lepper, Mark Keavney, Michael Drake, Alfie Kohn, Richard Ryan, and Edward Deci. Many of the same people exchanged opinions in the November 1999 issue of *Psychological Bulletin*. What are the arguments?

POINT

Students are punished by rewards.

Alfie Kohn (1993) argues, "Applied behaviourism, which amounts to saying, 'do this and you'll get that,' is essentially a technique for controlling people. In the classroom it is a way of doing things *to* children rather than working *with* them" (p. 784). He contends that rewards are ineffective because when the praise and prizes stop, the behaviours stop too. After analyzing 128 studies of extrinsic rewards, Edward Deci, Richard Koestner, and Richard Ryan (1999) concluded that "tangible rewards tend to have a substantial effect on intrinsic motivation, with the limiting conditions we have specified. Even when tangible rewards are offered as indicators of good performance, they typically decrease intrinsic motivation for interesting activities" (pp. 658–659).

The problem with rewards does not stop here. According to Kohn, rewarding students for learning actually makes them less interested in the material:

> *All of this means that getting children to think about learning as a way to receive a sticker, a gold star, or a grade—or even worse, to get money or a toy* for *a grade, which amounts to an extrinsic motivator for an extrinsic motivator—is likely to turn learning from an end into a means. Learning becomes something that must be gotten through in order to receive the reward. Take the depressingly pervasive program by which children receive certificates for pizzas when they have read a certain number of books. John Nicholls of the University of Illinois comments, only half in jest, that the likely consequence of this program is "a lot of fat kids who don't like to read." (p. 785)*

COUNTERPOINT

Learning should be rewarding.

According to Paul Chance (1993):

> *Behavioral psychologists in particular emphasize that we learn by* acting *on our environment. As B. F. Skinner put it: "[People] act on the world, and change it, and are changed in turn by the consequences of their actions." Skinner, unlike Kohn, understood that people learn best in a responsive environment. Teachers who praise or otherwise reward student performance provide such an environment. . . . If it is immoral to let students know they have answered questions correctly, to pat students on the back for a good effort, to show joy at a student's understanding of a concept, or to recognize the achievement of a goal by providing a gold star or a certificate—if this is immoral, then count me a sinner. (p. 788)*

Do rewards undermine interest? In their review of research, Cameron and Pierce (1994) concluded, "When tangible rewards (e.g., gold star, money) are offered contingent on performance on a task [not just on participation] or are delivered unexpectedly, intrinsic motivation is maintained" (p. 49). In a later review of research, Eisenberg, Pierce, and Cameron (1999) added: "Reward procedures requiring specific high task performance convey a task's personal or social significance, increasing intrinsic motivation" (p. 677). Even psychologists such as Edward Deci and Mark Lepper who suggest that rewards might undermine intrinsic motivation agree that rewards can also be used positively. When rewards provide students with information about their growing mastery of a subject or when the rewards show appreciation for a job well done, then the rewards bolster confidence and make the task more interesting to the students, especially students who lacked ability or interest in the task initially. Nothing succeeds like success. As Chance points out, if students master reading or mathematics with the support of rewards, they will not forget what they have learned when the praise stops. Would they have learned without the rewards? Some would, but some might not. Would you continue working for a company that didn't pay you, even though you liked the work? Will freelance writer Alfie Kohn, for that matter, lose interest in writing because he gets paid fees and royalties?

unethical when positive approaches, which have fewer potential dangers, might work as well. When simpler, less-restrictive procedures fail, then more complicated procedures should be tried.

A second consideration to take into account when selecting a strategy to encourage learning is the impact of the strategy on the individual student. For example, some teachers arrange for students to be rewarded at home with a gift or special activities based on good work in school. But if a student has a history of being severely punished at home for bad reports from school, a home-based reinforcement program might be very harmful to that student. Be mindful that reports of unsatisfactory progress at school could lead to increased abuse of students at home.

DIVERSITY AND CONVERGENCES IN BEHAVIOURAL LEARNING

Diversity

There is great diversity in the learning histories of students. Every person in your class will come to you with different fears and anxieties. Some students may be terrified of speaking in public or of failing at competitive sports. Others will be anxious about working closely with peers in small groups. Different activities or objects will serve as reinforcers for some students, but not others. Some students will work for the promise of good grades—others couldn't care less. All of your students will have learned different behaviours in their homes, neighbourhoods, churches, or communities.

The research and theories presented in this chapter should help you understand how the learning histories of your students might have taught them to respond to tests automatically with sweaty palms and racing hearts—possible classical conditioning at work. Their learning histories might have included being reinforced for persistence or for whining—operant conditioning at work. The chance to work in a group may be a reinforcer for some students and a punisher for others. Some teachers use questionnaires such as the one in Table 6.2 to identify effective reinforcers for

TABLE 6.2 **What Do You Like? Reinforcer Ideas From Students**

This reinforcer survey for middle or high school students is adapted from an example generated using *Jackpot!* Surveys can also be personalized for individual students by using their names.

Reinforcer Survey: What Would You Like to Do in School?

Directions: Read each item and mark how much you would like to do it in school.
1= Not liked at all, 5=Liked

Not Liked		/		Liked	Activity
1	2	3	4	5	Spend time (with appropriate supervision) on the internet at academic sites.
1	2	3	4	5	Read a book of my choice.
1	2	3	4	5	Listen to books-on-tape.
1	2	3	4	5	Have first choice in seating assignments.
1	2	3	4	5	Be praised privately by the teacher or other adult.
1	2	3	4	5	Receive praise during school-wide announcements.
1	2	3	4	5	Receive a pass to get out of one homework assignment of my choice.
1	2	3	4	5	Deliver school-wide announcements.
1	2	3	4	5	Work in the school store.
1	2	3	4	5	Get extra gym time with another class.
1	2	3	4	5	Be excused from one gym class of my choice.
1	2	3	4	5	Select friends to sit with to complete a cooperative learning activity.
1	2	3	4	5	Post drawings or other artwork in a public place such as on a hall bulletin board.
1	2	3	4	5	Sit at a reserved table in the lunchroom.
1	2	3	4	5	Be given a raffle ticket for a prize drawing.

Source: Jackpot!: Online Reinforcer Survey Generator available at www.jimwrightonline.com/php/jackpot/jackpot.php.

their students. Remember, what works for one student may not be appropriate for another. And students can get "too much of a good thing"—reinforcers can lose their potency if they are overused.

Convergences

Even though your classroom will be filled with students who have many different learning histories, there are some convergences—that is, principles that apply to all learners:

1. No one eagerly repeats behaviours that have been punished or ignored. Without some sense of progress, students are unlikely to persist with inappropriate behaviours.
2. When actions lead to consequences that are positive for the person involved, those actions are likely to be repeated.
3. Teachers often fail to use reinforcement to recognize appropriate behaviour; they respond instead to inappropriate behaviours, sometimes providing reinforcing attention in the process.
4. To be effective, praise must be a sincere recognition of a real accomplishment.
5. Whatever their current level of functioning, students can learn to be more self-managing.

MyEducationLab
Go to the Teacher Talk section of Chapter 6 of MyEducationLab and watch a video of Katie Sullivan, a 2007 Teacher of the Year, explaining how feedback from her students and their families encourages her to persevere as a teacher.

SUMMARY TABLE

Understanding Learning (pp. 198–200)

What is learning? Although theorists disagree about the definition of learning, most would agree that learning occurs when experience causes a change in a person's knowledge or behaviour. Changes caused by maturation, illness, fatigue, or hunger are excluded from a general definition of learning. Behavioural theorists emphasize the role of environmental stimuli in learning and focus on behaviour—observable responses. Behavioural learning processes include contiguity learning, classical conditioning, operant conditioning, and observational learning.

Learning Process through which experience causes permanent change in knowledge or behaviour.

Behavioural learning theories Explanations of learning that focus on external events as the cause of changes in observable behaviours.

Early Explanations of Learning: Contiguity and Classical Conditioning (pp. 200–201)

How does a neutral stimulus become a conditioned stimulus? In classical conditioning, which was discovered by Pavlov, a previously neutral stimulus is repeatedly paired with a stimulus that evokes an emotional or physiological response. Later, the previously neutral stimulus alone evokes the response—that is, the neutral stimulus is conditioned to bring forth a conditioned response. The neutral stimulus has become a conditioned stimulus.

What are some everyday examples of classical conditioning? Here are a few examples (you can add your own): Salivating when you smell your favourite foods, feeling tension when you hear a dentist's drill, becoming nervous when you step on stage . . .

Contiguity Association of two events because of repeated pairing.

Stimulus Event that activates behaviour.

Response Observable reaction to a stimulus.

Classical conditioning Association of automatic responses with new stimuli.

Respondents Responses (generally automatic or involuntary) elicited by specific stimuli.

Neutral stimulus Stimulus not connected to a response.

Unconditioned stimulus (US) Stimulus that automatically produces an emotional or physiological response.

Unconditioned response (UR) Naturally occurring emotional or physiological response.

Conditioned stimulus (CS) Stimulus that evokes an emotional or physiological response after conditioning.

Conditioned response (CR) Learned response to a previously neutral stimulus.

Operant Conditioning: Trying New Responses (pp. 201–207)

What defines a consequence as a reinforcer? As a punisher? According to Skinner's concept of operant conditioning, people learn through the effects of their deliberate responses. For an individual, the effects of consequences following an action may serve as either reinforcers or punishers. A consequence is defined as a reinforcer if it strengthens or maintains the response that brought it about, but as a punishment if it decreases or suppresses the response that brought it about.

Negative reinforcement is often confused with punishment. How are they different? The process of reinforcement (positive or negative) always involves strengthening behaviour. The teacher strengthens (reinforces) desired behaviours by removing something aversive *as soon as the desired behaviours occur*. Because the consequence involves removing or "subtracting" a stimulus, the reinforcement is negative. Punishment, on the other hand, involves *decreasing or suppressing behaviour*. A behaviour followed by a "punisher" is *less* likely to be repeated in similar situations in the future.

How can you encourage persistence of a behaviour? Ratio schedules (based on the number of responses) encourage higher rates of response, and variable schedules (based on varying numbers of responses or varying time intervals) encourage persistence of responses.

What is the difference between a prompt and a cue? A cue is an antecedent stimulus that occurs just before a particular behaviour is to take place. A prompt is an additional cue following the first cue. Make sure the environmental stimulus that you want to become a cue occurs immediately before the prompt you are using, so students will learn to respond to the cue and not rely only on the prompt. Then, fade the prompt as soon as possible so students do not become dependent on it.

Operants Voluntary (and generally goal-directed) behaviours emitted by a person or an animal.

Operant conditioning Learning in which voluntary behaviour is strengthened or weakened by consequences or antecedents.

Antecedents Events that precede an action.

Consequences Events that follow an action.

Reinforcement Use of consequences to strengthen behaviour.

Reinforcer Any event that follows a behaviour and increases the chances that the behaviour will occur again.

Positive reinforcement Strengthening behaviour by presenting a desired stimulus after the behaviour.

Negative reinforcement Strengthening behaviour by removing an aversive stimulus when the behaviour occurs.

Aversive Irritating or unpleasant.

Punishment Process that weakens or suppresses behaviour.

Presentation punishment Decreasing the chances that a behaviour will occur again by presenting an aversive stimulus following the behaviour; also called Type I punishment.

Removal punishment Decreasing the chances that a behaviour will occur again by removing a pleasant stimulus following the behaviour; also called Type II punishment.

Continuous reinforcement schedule Presenting a reinforcer after every appropriate response.

Intermittent reinforcement schedule Presenting a reinforcer after some but not all responses.

Interval schedule Reinforcement schedule based on the length of time between reinforcers.

Ratio schedule Reinforcement schedule based on the number of responses between reinforcers.

Extinction The disappearance of a learned response.

Stimulus control Capacity for the presence or absence of antecedents to cause behaviours.

Effective instruction delivery Instructions that are concise, clear, and specific, and that communicate an expected result. Statements work better than questions.

Cueing Providing a stimulus that "sets up" a desired behaviour.

Prompt A reminder that follows a cue to make sure the person reacts to the cue.

Applied Behaviour Analysis (pp. 207–213)

What are the steps in applied behaviour analysis? The steps are as follows: (1) Clearly specify the behaviour to be changed and note the current level. (2) Plan a specific intervention using antecedents, consequences, or both. (3) Keep track of the results, and modify the plan if necessary.

How can the Premack principle help you identify reinforcers? The Premack principle states that a high-frequency behaviour (a preferred activity) can be an effective reinforcer for a low-frequency behaviour (a less-preferred activity). The best way to determine appropriate reinforcers for your students may be to watch what they do in their free time. For most students, talking, moving around the room, sitting near a friend, being exempt from assignments or tests, reading magazines, or playing games are preferred activities.

When is shaping an appropriate approach? Shaping helps students develop new responses a little at a time, so it is useful for building complex skills, working toward difficult goals, and increasing persistence, endurance, accuracy, or speed. Because shaping is a time-consuming process, however, it should not be used if success can be attained through simpler methods such as cueing.

What are some cautions associated with using punishment? Punishment in and of itself does not lead to any positive behaviour or compassion for others and it may interfere with developing caring relationships with students. Thus, whenever you consider the use of punishment, you should make it part of a two-pronged attack. First, carry out the punishment and suppress the undesirable behaviour. Second, make clear what the student should be doing instead and provide reinforcement for those desirable actions. Thus, while the problem behaviours are being suppressed, positive alternative responses are being strengthened.

Applied behaviour analysis The application of behavioural learning principles to understand and change behaviour.

Behaviour modification Systematic application of antecedents and consequences to change behaviour.

Premack principle Principle stating that a more-preferred activity can serve as a reinforcer for a less-preferred activity.

Shaping Reinforcing each small step of progress toward a desired goal or behaviour.

Successive approximations Small components that make up a complex behaviour.

Task analysis System for breaking down a task hierarchically into basic skills and subskills.

Positive practice Practising correct responses immediately after errors.

Reprimands Criticisms for misbehaviour; rebukes.

Response cost Punishment by loss of reinforcers.

Social isolation Removal of a disruptive student for 5 to 10 minutes.

Time out Technically, the removal of all reinforcement. In practice, isolation of a student from the rest of the class for a brief time.

Putting It All Together: Behavioural Approaches to Teaching and Management (pp. 213–220)

Describe the managerial strategies of group consequences, contracts, and token programs. Using group consequences involves basing reinforcement for the whole class on the behaviour of the whole class. In a contingency contract program, the teacher draws up an individual contract with each student, describing exactly what the student must do to earn a particular privilege or reward. In token programs, students earn tokens (points, check marks, holes punched in a card, chips, etc.) for both academic work and positive classroom behaviour. Periodically, the students exchange the tokens they have earned for some desired reward. A teacher must use these programs with caution, emphasizing learning and not just "good" behaviour.

How can functional behavioural assessment and positive behaviour supports be used to improve student behaviours? In doing a functional behavioural assessment, a teacher studies the antecedents and consequences of problem behaviours to determine the reason for or function of the behaviour. Then, positive behaviour supports are designed to replace problem behaviours with new actions that serve the same purpose for the student, but do not have the same problems.

Good behaviour game Arrangement where a class is divided into teams and each team receives demerit points for breaking agreed-upon rules of good behaviour.

Group consequences Rewards or punishments given to a class as a whole for adhering to or violating rules of conduct.

Contingency contract A contract between the teacher and a student specifying what the student must do to earn a particular reward or privilege.

Token reinforcement system System in which tokens earned for academic work and positive classroom behaviour can be exchanged for some desired reward.

Functional behavioural assessment (FBA) Procedures used to obtain information about antecedents, behaviours, and consequences to determine the reason for or function of the behaviour.

Positive behaviour supports (PBS) Interventions designed to replace problem behaviours with new actions that serve the same purpose for the student.

Precorrection A tool for positive behaviour support that involves identifying the context for a student's misbehaviour, clearly specifying the alternative expected behaviour, modifying the situation to make the problem behaviour less likely, then rehearsing the expected positive behaviours in the new context and providing powerful reinforcers.

Challenges to Behavioural Views: Thinking About Behaviour (pp. 220–223)

Distinguish between social learning and social cognitive theories. Social learning theory was an early neobehavioural theory that expanded behavioural views of reinforcement and punishment. From the behavioural perspective, reinforcement and punishment directly affect behaviour. In social learning theory, seeing another person, a model, reinforced or punished can have similar effects on the observer's behaviour. Social learning theory recognized the differences between learning and performance—you can learn something, but not perform it until the situation and incentives are appropriate. Social cognitive theory expanded social learning theory to include cognitive factors such as beliefs, expectations, and perceptions of self.

Distinguish between enactive and vicarious learning. *Enactive learning* is learning by doing and experiencing the consequences of your actions. *Vicarious learning* is learning by observing, which challenges the behaviourist idea that cognitive factors are unnecessary in an explanation of learning. Much is going on mentally before performance and reinforcement can even take place.

What are the elements of observational learning? In order to learn through observation, we have to pay attention to aspects of the situation that will help us learn. To imitate the behaviour of a model, we have to retain the information. This involves mentally representing the model's actions in some way, probably as verbal steps. In the production phase, practice makes the behaviour smoother and more expert. Sometimes, we need a great deal of practice, feedback, and coaching about subtle points before we can reproduce the behaviour of the model. Finally, motivation shapes observational learning through incentives and reinforcement. We may not perform a learned behaviour until there is some motivation or incentive to do so. Reinforcement can focus attention, encourage reproduction or practice, and maintain the new learning.

What are the steps in self-management? Students can apply behavioural analysis on their own to manage their own behaviour. Teachers can encourage the development of self-management skills by allowing students to participate in setting goals, keeping track of progress, evaluating accomplishments, and selecting and giving their own reinforcers. Teachers can also use cognitive behaviour modification, a behaviour change program described by Meichenbaum, a professor emeritus at the University of Western Ontario, in which students are directly taught how to use self-instruction.

Social learning theory Theory that emphasizes learning through observation of others.

Social cognitive theory Theory that adds concern with cognitive factors such as beliefs, self-perceptions, and expectations to social learning theory.

Observational learning Learning by observation and imitation of others.

Vicarious reinforcement Increasing the chances that a person repeats a behaviour by observing another person being reinforced for that behaviour.

Self-reinforcement Controlling your own reinforcers.

Self-management Use of behavioural learning principles to change your own behaviour.

Problems and Issues (pp. 224–226)

What are the main criticisms of behavioural approaches? The misuse or abuse of behavioural learning methods is unethical. Critics of behavioural methods also point out the danger that reinforcement could decrease interest in learning by overemphasizing rewards and could have a negative impact on other students. Teachers can use behavioural learning principles appropriately and ethically.

TEACHERS' CASEBOOK

You were hired in January to take over the classes of a teacher who moved away. This is a great district and a terrific school. If you do well, you might be in line for a full-time opening next fall. As you are introduced around the school, you get a number of sympathetic looks and many—too many—offers of help: "Let me know if I can do anything for you."

After the first hour, you begin to understand why so many teachers volunteered their help. Evidently the previous teacher had no management system—no order. Several students walk around the room while you are talking to the class, interrupt you when you are working with a group, torment each other, and open their lunches (or those of other students) for a self-determined snack. There is one very charismatic leader who causes regular disruptions, resists your authority, and destroys your efforts to develop a community of learners. Simply taking attendance and introducing the first activity lasts 10 minutes. You end the first day exhausted and discouraged, having lost both your voice and your patience. You wonder how you can possibly establish a workable management system and still teach students what they will need to know in order to complete the province-wide spring reading, writing, and mathematics proficiency tests.

What Would *They* Do?

Here is how some practising teachers responded to the teaching situation described above.

Janice Farrell Colby

St. Joseph School, Sydney, NS

Accentuate the Positive—Eliminate the Negative

What goes on in our classrooms can be productive or destructive in relation to a child's self-image. I would like children to work with me in a cooperative, positive learning environment. I would use several strategies so that children learn such skills as responsibility, cooperation, and problem solving. These skills can help students come to terms with their own behaviour, knowing what they need to do rather than being told what to do.

I would use basic life skills in what I do every day. These skills are valuable ways to pass the ownership and responsibility of actions to each individual. Through a positive, cooperative learning plan, I would be flexible in my expectations while still adhering to some basic principles. These life skills are easily integrated in all subject areas. Working within this model, children would understand they are unique, important, and special and would develop their own self-worth and self-esteem. The strengths of each child would be emphasized.

Teachers shouldn't be afraid to be *human*. We assume many roles in a classroom but, most importantly, the roles of teacher and friend. We learn from one another; involving the students in decisions that affect them helps them feel important and worthwhile. Look at teaching as a daily adventure in humanity. Developing the basic life skills will help students prepare for the future.

Get to know your students and their strengths. Students and teachers should establish and achieve positive goals that will help promote a healthy learning environment. As educators, we all have the opportunity to plant a seed, but we must also be willing to nurture it so that each child will grow and develop to full potential in a safe and caring environment. Learning is ongoing, and as teachers we need to facilitate this learning process to encourage and develop the positive while making efforts to eliminate the negative. We must all try as teachers to remember that *the art of teaching lies in teaching from the heart!*

My Golden Rule
by Janice Farrell Colby
May I always have the strength
To stand tall and be ever so strong
So that the children I teach will realize
That I too can be wrong.
May I always have the insight
To not let the opportunity pass
To help the child that needs me
Each day within my class.
May I always have a sense of caring
Down deep within my heart
For each and every child I teach
So that I can always do my part.
May I always be ready to listen
And use love and guidance to try
To be there for my children
And to hear their gentle silent cry.
May I always value what they can offer
And know they may just need me near
To guide them along as they struggle
And help them ease away any fear.
May I always have the strength
To stand tall and be ever so strong
So that the children I teach will realize
That I too can be wrong.
May we always be ready to help one another
So that we can come to realize
When we walk along hand in hand
We all have our silent cries.

Rosemary Dixon

Retired, Ottawa, ON

This situation requires the use of both short- and long-term strategies. Positive behaviour must be rewarded immediately—with positive verbal statements and, initially, with a system of token rewards for which a larger reward, such as free time, will be given later. Whenever possible, negative behaviour must be ignored, as these children must be accepting negative attention as desirable.

Clear, explicit rules must be instituted immediately. These children should be involved in the making of these rules and in deciding on consequences for the infraction of rules. I would try to have as few rules as possible and insist that they be adhered to with absolute consistency. I would have to remind myself that learning would not take place in this class until the behaviour improved. I must not be afraid to stop the class at any time, send all the children to their seats, or call the children into a circle to discuss problems that are arising.

My first long-term strategy would be to get to know as many of the parents as possible. They could become invaluable allies. The teacher might have become a faceless name about whom horror stories were told. The parents would naturally feel more positive toward a friendly, concerned educator who had their children's best interests at heart and who was willing to involve them in the learning process.

How much help can I expect from my principal or vice-principal? It would be a good idea to find out if these colleagues would be willing to support my rewards program. A visit from the principal to the class or by the children to the principal's office so that praise and rewards could be given for appropriate behaviour would probably be a pleasant and reinforcing change. For these children, previous encounters with administration have likely been mostly negative.

Finally, I would take up offers of help from my colleagues. Perhaps my class, or groups from the class, could be involved in cooperative or friendly competitive activities with another class.

These strategies should lead to improved self-esteem, an improved reputation within the school, increased motivation, and a return to appropriate classroom behaviour.

7 Cognitive Views of Learning

Madame Joseph Michele Ginoux, Vincent Van Gogh. Photo: Superstock

TEACHERS' CASEBOOK

WHAT WOULD YOU DO?

The students in your senior history classes seem to equate understanding with memorizing. They prepare for each unit test by memorizing the exact words of the textbook. Even the best students seem to think that the use of flash cards is the only learning strategy possible. In fact, when you try to encourage students to think about history by reading some original sources, debating issues in class, or examining art and music from the time period you are studying, they rebel. "Will this be on the test?" "Why are we looking at these pictures—will we have to know who painted them and when?" "What's this got to do with history?" Even the students who participate in the debates seem to use words and phrases straight from the textbook without knowing what they are saying.

CRITICAL THINKING

- What are these students' beliefs and expectations, and how do these affect their learning?
- Why do you think they insist on using the rote memory approach?
- How would you use what the students already know to help them learn in better, more meaningful ways?
- How will these issues affect the grade levels you will teach?

In this chapter, we turn from behavioural theories of learning to the cognitive perspective. This means a shift from "viewing the learners and their behaviours as products of incoming environmental stimuli" to seeing the learners as "sources of plans, intentions, goals, ideas, memories, and emotions actively used to attend to, select, and construct meaning from stimuli and knowledge from experience" (Wittrock, 1982, pp. 1–2). We will begin with a discussion of the general cognitive approach to learning and memory and the importance of knowledge in learning. To understand memory, we will consider a widely accepted cognitive model, information processing, which suggests that information is manipulated in different storage systems. Next, we will explore metacognition, a field of study that may provide insights into individual and developmental differences in learning. Then, we turn to ideas about how teachers can help their students become more knowledgeable.

By the time you have completed this chapter, you should be able to answer these questions:

- What is the role of knowledge in learning?
- What is the human information processing model of memory?
- How do perception, attention, schemas, and scripts influence learning and remembering?
- What are declarative, procedural, and conditional knowledge?
- Why do students forget what they have learned?
- What is the role of metacognition in learning and remembering?
- What are the stages in the development of cognitive skills?

Connect and **Extend**
Go to the "Connect and Extend" section in Chapter 7 of MyEducationLab to find further content that links to teaching, students' thinking, research, and the news.

ELEMENTS OF THE COGNITIVE PERSPECTIVE

The cognitive perspective is both the oldest and one of the youngest members of the psychological community. It is old because discussions of the nature of knowledge, the value of reason, and the contents of the mind date back at least to the ancient Greek philosophers (Gluck, Mercado, & Myers, 2008). From the late 1800s until several decades ago, however, cognitive studies fell from favour and behaviourism thrived. Then, several factors—research during the Second World War on the development of complex human skills, the computer revolution, and breakthroughs in understanding language development—all stimulated a resurgence in cognitive research. Evidence accumulated indicating that people plan their responses, use strategies to help themselves remember, and organize the material they are learning in their own unique ways (Miller, Galanter, & Pribram, 1960; Shuell, 1986). Educational psychologists became interested in how people think, learn concepts, and solve problems (e.g., Ausubel, 1963; Bruner, Goodnow, & Austin, 1956).

Interest in concept learning and problem solving soon gave way, however, to interest in how knowledge is represented in the mind and particularly how it is remembered. Remembering and forgetting became major topics for investigation in cognitive psychology in the 1970s and 1980s, and the information processing model of memory dominated research.

Today, there is renewed interest in learning, thinking, and problem solving. The cognitive view of learning can be described as a generally agreed-upon philosophical orientation. This means that cognitive theorists share basic notions about learning and memory. Most importantly, cognitive psychologists assume that mental processes exist, that they can be studied scientifically, and that humans are active participants in their own acts of cognition (Ashcraft, 2006).

Comparing Cognitive and Behavioural Views

The cognitive and behavioural views differ in their assumptions about what is learned. According to the cognitive view, knowledge is learned, and changes in knowledge make changes in behaviour possible. According to the behavioural view, the new behaviours themselves are learned (Shuell, 1986). Both behavioural and cognitive theorists believe reinforcement is important in learning, but for different reasons. The strict behaviourist maintains that reinforcement strengthens responses; cognitive theorists see reinforcement as a source of information about what is likely to happen if behaviours are repeated or changed.

Cognitive view of learning
A general approach that views learning as an active mental process of acquiring, remembering, and using knowledge.

View of Learning. The cognitive view sees learning as extending and transforming the understanding we already have, not simply writing associations on the blank slates of our brains (Greeno, Collins, & Resnick, 1996). Instead of being passively influenced by environmental events, people actively choose, practise, pay attention, ignore, reflect, and make many other decisions as they pursue goals. Earlier cognitive views emphasized the *acquisition* of knowledge, but newer approaches stress its *construction* (Anderson, Reder, & Simon, 1996; Greeno, Collins, & Resnick, 1996; Mayer, 1996).

COGNITIVE VIEWS These students are literally building their understanding as they try to construct models and solve problems.

Methods. The methods of cognitive and behavioural researchers also differ. Much of the work on behavioural learning principles has been with animals in controlled laboratory settings. But cognitive psychologists study people, and educational psychologists in the cognitive camp tackle messy, complicated questions about learning in real life. Patricia Alexander (2006b) captures these interests below:

> I have a passion for playing with messy problems situated within dynamic educational contexts. I do not want to study animals because they are easier to control or work within the confines of a sterile laboratory so the noises of everyday learning can be muffled or silenced. I want to experience learning in all its messiness. . . . (p. 258)

Goals. The goal of behavioural researchers is to identify a small set of general laws of learning that apply to all higher organisms—including humans—regardless of age, intelligence, or other individual differences. Cognitive psychologists, on the other hand, study a wide range of learning situations. Because of their focus on individual and developmental differences in cognition, they have not been as concerned with general laws of learning. This is one of the reasons that there is no single cognitive model or theory of learning that is representative of the entire field.

The Brain and Cognitive Learning

The brain continues to change throughout life, and learning affects those changes. One study found that part of the brain's hippocampus is larger in taxi drivers than in non-taxi drivers, and that the increase in size is related to the length of time the person has been driving a taxi. The explanation is that part of the brain grew larger because it was used more in navigating around the city (Maguire et al., 2000). In another study, when people learned to read musical notations, they developed an automatic response to looking at a sheet of music—they read it without being told to and their motor cortex prepared to play the notes (Stewart et al., 2003). Observing and visualizing also support learning because the brain automatically responds. For example, when observing someone perform an action, the area of the observer's brain that would be involved in that action is activated just by watching—the brain rehearses the action it sees another person perform (Rizzolatti, Fadiga, Gallese, & Fogassi, 1996). When you look at an object, a certain area of the brain is activated. Just mentally visualizing the object activates at least two-thirds of the same area of the brain (Ganis, Thompson, & Kosslyn, 2004).

MyEducationLab Go to the Podcasts section of Chapter 7 in MyEducation Lab and listen to PODCAST—Learning. In this podcast, Anita Woolfolk discusses not only the differences between behavioural, co[illegible] and constructivist learning th[illegible] importance of u[illegible]

Clearly the brain is involved whenever learning takes place. As Blakemore and Firth (2005) note in their book on lessons for education from research in neuroscience: "We start with the idea that the brain has evolved to educate and be educated, often instinctively and effortlessly" (p. 459). The brain shapes and is shaped by cognitive processing activities. Even at the neural level, new synapses are formed a few minutes after a child is unsuccessful at processing information. So unsuccessful processing triggers development too (Siegler, 2004).

Because of the continuing development of the brain, particularly as the prefrontal cortex matures, children become more able to integrate past and present experiences. An infant or a toddler reacts impulsively, but the 8-year-old can remember and reflect. Analysis, control, abstraction, memory space, speed of processing, and interconnection of information make self-regulation and continuing cognitive development possible. By about age 7, most children have developed these cognitive abilities (Kagan & Herschkowitz, 2005). They can:

- *Integrate the present with the past* to connect an experience in the past with something that is happening to them now.
- *Anticipate the future.* Children develop a better sense of what is "sooner" and what is "later."
- *Appreciate causality.* If something unfamiliar happens, children aged 7 and older usually want to know why.
- *Rely on semantic categories.* Children increasingly organize and remember their experiences using words and networks of meaning (concept and categories).
- *Detect relationships between events and concepts.* Children are increasingly able to understand abstract relationships such as *larger, smaller, shorter,* and *taller* and apply these flexibly.

Many of these developmental and brain changes involve knowledge—a key element in the cognitive perspective.

The Importance of Knowledge in Learning

STOP & THINK Quickly, list 10 terms that pertain to educational psychology. Now list 10 terms that relate to ceramic engineering.

Unless you are studying ceramic engineering, it probably took you longer to list 10 terms from that field than from educational psychology. Or, maybe you're still asking, "What is ceramic engineering anyway?" Your answers depend on your knowledge. (*Hint:* Think fibre optics, ceramic teeth and bones, ceramic semiconductors for computers, and heat-shielding tiles for space shuttles.)

Knowledge and knowing are the outcomes of learning. When we learn the history of cognitive psychology, the products of ceramic engineering, or the rules of tennis, we know something new. However, knowing is more than the end product of previous learning; it also guides new learning. The cognitive approach suggests that one of the most important elements in the learning process is what the individual brings to new learning situations. What we already know is the foundation and frame for constructing all future learning. Knowledge determines to a great extent what we will pay attention to, perceive, learn, remember, and forget (Bransford, Brown, & Cocking, 2000; Sawyer, 2006b).

An Example Study. A study by Recht and Leslie (1988) shows the importance of knowledge in understanding and remembering new information. These psychologists identified middle school students who were either very good or very poor readers. They tested the students on their knowledge of baseball and found that knowledge of baseball was not related to reading ability. So the researchers were able to identify four groups of students: *good readers/high baseball knowledge, good readers/low baseball knowledge, poor readers/high baseball knowledge,* and *poor readers/low baseball knowledge.* Then, students in all four groups read a passage describing a baseball game and were tested in a number of ways to see if they understood and remembered what they had read.

The results demonstrated the power of knowledge. Poor readers who knew baseball remembered more than good readers with little baseball knowledge and almost as much as good readers who knew baseball. Poor readers who knew little about baseball remembered the least of what they had read. Thus, a good basis of knowledge can be more important than good reading skills in understanding and remembering—but having extensive knowledge plus good reading skills is even better.

General and Specific Knowledge. Knowledge in the cognitive perspective includes subject-specific understandings in math, history, soccer, and so on, as well as general cognitive skills, such as planning, solving problems, and comprehending language (Greeno et al., 1996). We refer to domain-specific knowledge when knowledge pertains to a particular task or subject. For example, knowing that the shortstop plays between second and third base is specific to the domain of base-[illegible] that applies to many different situations—for example, how to read or write [illegible] called general knowledge. Of course, there is no absolute line between [illegible]ecific knowledge. When you were first learning to read, you may have studied [illegible]e sounds of letters. At that time, knowledge about letter sounds was specific to the domain of reading. But now you can use both knowledge about sounds and the ability to read in more general ways (Alexander, 1992; Schunk, 2008).

What we know exists in our memory. To know something is to remember it over time and to be able to find it when you need it. Cognitive psychologists have studied memory extensively and have learned more about knowledge in the process. Let's see what they have learned.

COGNITIVE VIEWS OF MEMORY

There are a number of theories about how memory works, but the most common are the information processing explanations (Ashcraft, 2006; Hunt & Ellis, 1999; Sternberg, 1999). We will use this well-researched framework to examine learning and memory.

Early information processing views of memory used the computer as a model. Like the computer, the human mind takes in information, performs operations on it to change its form and content, stores the information, retrieves it when needed, and generates responses to it. For most cognitive psychologists, the computer model is only a metaphor for human mental activity. But other cognitive scientists, particularly those studying artificial intelligence, have tried to design and program computers to "think" and solve problems like human beings (Anderson, 2005; Sawyer, 2006). Some theorists suggest that the operation of the brain resembles a large number of very slow computers, all operating in parallel (at the same time), with each computer dedicated to a different, specific task (Ashcraft, 2006).

Figure 7.1 is a schematic representation of a typical information processing model of memory, derived from the ideas of several theorists (Atkinson & Shiffrin, 1968; R. Gagné; 1985; Neisser, 1976). In order to understand this model, let's examine each element.

Domain-specific knowledge Information that is useful in a particular situation or that applies mainly to one specific topic.

General knowledge Information that is useful in many different kinds of tasks or that applies to many situations.

Information processing The human mind's activity of taking in, storing, and using information.

FIGURE 7.1 **The Information Processing System**

Information is encoded in sensory memory where perception and attention determine what will be held in working memory for further use. In working memory, new information connects with knowledge from long-term memory. Thoroughly processed and connected information becomes part of long-term memory and can be activated to return to working memory. Implicit memories are formed without conscious effort.

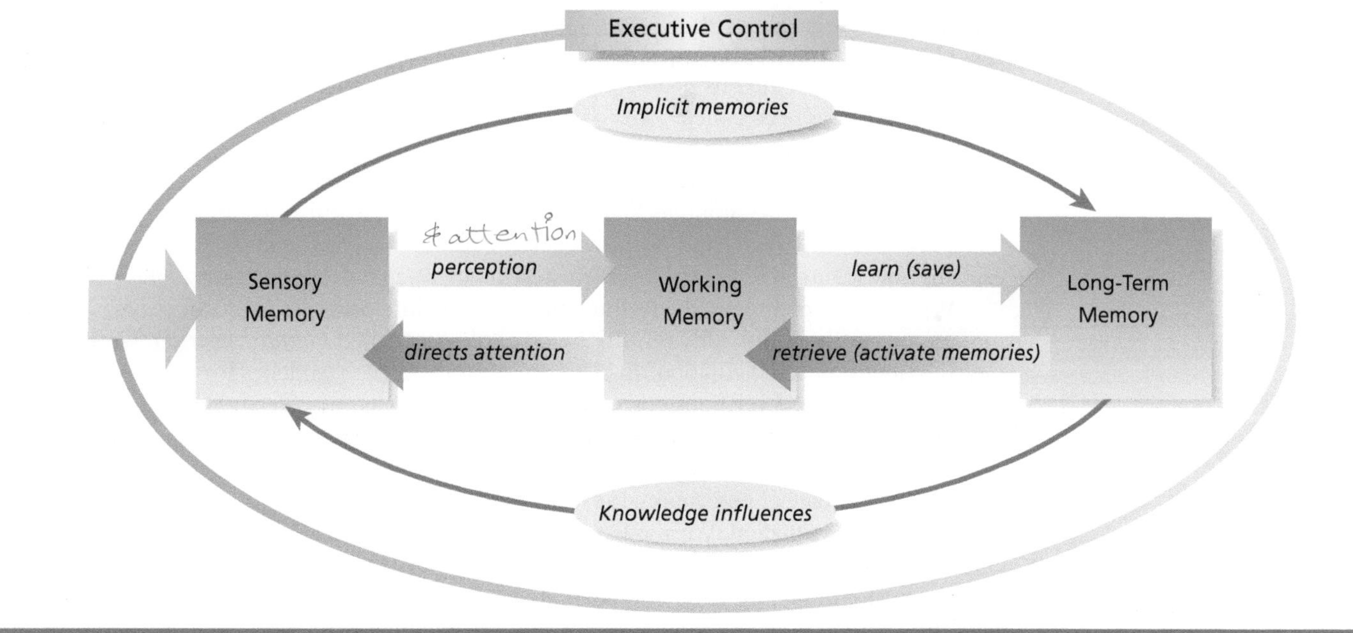

Sensory Memory

Stimuli from the environment (sights, sounds, smells, etc.) constantly bombard our body's mechanisms for seeing, hearing, tasting, smelling, and feeling. Sensory memory is the initial processing that transforms these incoming stimuli into information so we can make sense of them. Even though sights and sounds may last only fractions of a second, the transformations (information) that represent these sensations are briefly held in the *sensory register* or *sensory information store* so that this initial processing can take place (Driscoll, 2005; Sperling, 1960).

MyEducationLab Go to the Activities and Applications section in Chapter 7 of MyEducation Lab and complete Activity 1, in which you will take The Stroop Test, which demonstrates the power and complexity of sensory memory.

Capacity, Duration, and Contents of Sensory Memory. The *capacity* of sensory memory is very large; sensory memory can take in more information than we can possibly handle at once. But this vast amount of sensory information is fragile in *duration*—it lasts between 1 and 3 seconds.

STOP & THINK Wave a pencil (or your finger) back and forth before your eyes while you stare straight ahead. What exactly do you see? Pinch your arm and let go. What do you feel just after you let go?

You just experienced this brief holding of sensory information in your own sensory register. You could see a trace of the pencil after the actual stimulus had been removed and feel the pinch after you let go. The sensory register held information about the stimuli very briefly after the actual stimulus was removed (Lindsay & Norman, 1977).

The information *content* of sensory memory resembles the sensations from the original stimulus. Visual sensations are coded briefly by the sensory register as images, almost like photographs. Auditory sensations are coded as sound patterns, similar to echoes. It may be that the other senses also have their own codes. Thus, for a second or so, a wealth of data from sensory experience remains intact. In these instants, we have a chance to select and organize information for further processing. Perception and attention are critical at this stage.

Sensory memory System that holds sensory information very briefly.

Perception. The process of detecting a stimulus and assigning meaning to it is called perception. This meaning is constructed based on both physical representations from the world and our existing knowledge. For example, consider these marks: 13. If asked what the letter is, you would say "B." If asked what the number is, you would say "13." The actual marks remain the same; their meaning changes in keeping with your expectation to recognize a letter or a number and your knowledge of what Arabic numbers and the Latin alphabet look like. To a child without appropriate knowledge, the marks would probably be meaningless (F. Smith, 1975).

The path from sensory input to recognized objects probably goes through several stages (Anderson, 2005). In the first phase, features are extracted or analyzed to give a rough sketch. This *feature analysis* has been called bottom-up processing because the stimulus must be analyzed into features or components and assembled into a meaningful pattern "from the bottom up." For example, a capital letter A consists of two relatively straight lines joined at a 45-degree angle and a horizontal line through the middle. Whenever we see these features, or anything close enough, including, A, A, **A**, A, A, and A, we are on the road to recognizing an A (Anderson, 2005). This explains how we are able to read words written in other people's handwriting.

As perception continues, the features are organized into patterns. These processes were studied in Germany early in the 20th century by psychologists called *Gestalt theorists.* Gestalt, which means "pattern" or "configuration" in German, refers to people's tendency to organize sensory information into patterns or relationships. Instead of perceiving bits and pieces of unrelated information, we usually perceive organized, meaningful wholes. Figure 7.2 presents a few Gestalt principles.

If all perception relied only on feature analysis and Gestalt principles, learning would be very slow. At the last stage of perception, the features and patterns detected are combined in relation to the context of the situation. We also have a prototype (a best example or classic case) of input such as the letter A stored in memory to use to help us perceive patterns quickly (Driscoll, 2005). So to recognize patterns rapidly, in addition to noting features, we use context and what we already know about the situation—what we know about words or pictures or the way the world generally operates. When we use prior knowledge to develop perceptions, we engage in top-down processing. For example, you would not have seen the marks above as the letter A if you had no knowledge of the Latin alphabet. So, what you know also affects what you are able to perceive. The role of knowledge in perception is represented by the arrows pointing left in Figure 7.1 from long-term memory (stored knowledge) to working memory and then to sensory memory.

Perception Interpretation of sensory information.

Bottom-up processing Perceiving based on noticing separate defining features and assembling them into a recognizable pattern.

Gestalt German for *pattern* or *whole*. Gestalt theorists hold that people organize their perceptions into coherent wholes.

Prototype A best example or best representative of a category.

Top-down processing Perceiving based on context and knowledge that jointly predict patterns expected in a situation.

Attention Focus on a stimulus.

The Role of Attention. If every variation in colour, movement, sound, smell, temperature, and so on ended up in working memory, life would be impossible. But attention is selective. By paying attention to selected stimuli and ignoring others, we limit the possibilities that we will perceive and process. What we pay attention to is guided to a certain extent by what we already know and what we need to know, so attention is involved in and influenced by all three memory processes in Figure 7.1. Attention is also affected by what else is happening at the time, by the complexity of the task, and by our ability to control or focus our attention (Driscoll, 2005). Some students with attention-deficit/hyperactivity disorder have great difficulty focusing attention or ignoring competing stimuli.

FIGURE 7.2 Examples of Gestalt Principles

Gestalt principles of perception explain how we "see" patterns in the world around us.

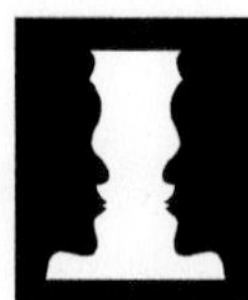

a. Figure-ground
What do you see? Faces or a vase? Make one figure—the other ground.

b. Proximity
You see these lines as three groups because of the proximity of the lines.

c. Similarity
You see these lines as an alternating pattern because of the similarity in height of lines.

d. Closure
You perceive a circle instead of a series of curved lines.

Source: From *Learning Theories: An Educational Perspective* (4th ed.), by D. H. Schunk. Published by Prentice Hall. Copyright © 2004 by Prentice Hall. Reprinted by permission of Pearson Education, Inc., Upper Saddle River, NJ.

But attention takes effort and is a limited resource. We imagine you might have to work a bit to pay attention to these words about attention! People can pay attention to only one cognitively demanding task at time (Anderson, 2005). For example, when Nancy was learning to drive, she couldn't listen to the radio and drive at the same time. After some practice, she could listen, but she had to turn the radio off when traffic was heavy. After years of practice, she can plan a class, listen to the radio, and carry on a conversation as she drives. This is possible because many processes that initially require attention and concentration become automatic with practice. Actually, automaticity probably is a matter of degree; we are not completely automatic, but rather more or less automatic in our performances depending on how much practice we have had and the situation and whether we are intentionally focusing our attention and directing our own cognitive processing. For example, even experienced drivers might become very attentive and focused during a blinding blizzard (Anderson, 2005; Sinatra & Mason, 2008).

Attention and Teaching. The first step in learning is paying attention. Students cannot process information that they do not recognize or perceive (Lachter, Forster, & Ruthruff, 2004). Many factors in the classroom influence student attention. Eye-catching or startling displays or actions can draw attention at the beginning of a lesson. A teacher might begin a science lesson on air pressure by blowing up a balloon until it pops. Bright colours, underlining, highlighting of written or spoken words, calling students by name, surprise events, intriguing questions, variety in tasks and teaching methods, and changes in voice level, lighting, or pacing can all be used to gain attention. And students have to maintain attention—they have to stay focused on the important features of the learning situation. The *Guidelines* box offers additional ideas for ways to capture and maintain students' attention in the classroom.

Automaticity The ability to perform thoroughly learned tasks without much mental effort.

GUIDELINES: Gaining and Maintaining Attention

Use signals.

EXAMPLES

1. Develop a signal that tells students to stop what they are doing and focus on you. Some teachers move to a particular spot in the room, flick the lights, tap the table, or play a chord on the class piano. Mix visual and auditory signals.
2. Avoid distracting behaviours, such as tapping a pencil while talking, that interfere with both signals and attention to learning.
3. Give short, clear directions before, not during, transitions.
4. Be playful with younger children: Use a dramatic voice, sensational hat, or clapping game (Miller, 2005).

Reach out rather than call out (Miller, 2005).

EXAMPLES

1. Walk to the child and look into his or her eyes.
2. Speak in a firm but non-threatening voice.
3. Use the child's name.

Make sure the purpose of the lesson or assignment is clear to students.

EXAMPLES

1. Write the goals or objectives on the board and discuss them with students before starting the lesson or activity. Ask students to summarize or restate the goals.
2. Explain the reasons for learning, and ask students for examples of how they will apply their understanding of the material.
3. Tie the new material to previous lessons—show an outline or map of how the new topic fits with previous and upcoming material.

Incorporate variety, curiosity, and surprise.

EXAMPLES

1. Arouse curiosity with questions such as "What would happen if . . . ?"
2. Create shock by staging an unexpected event such as a loud argument just before a lesson on communication.
3. Alter the physical environment by changing the arrangement of the room or moving to a different setting.
4. Shift sensory channels by giving a lesson that requires students to touch, smell, or taste.
5. Use movements, gestures, and voice inflection—walk around the room, point, and speak softly and then more emphatically. (Anita's husband has been known to jump up on his desk to make an important point in his college classes!)

Ask questions and provide frames for answering.

EXAMPLES

1. Ask students why the material is important, how they intend to study, and what strategies they will use.
2. Give students self-checking or self-editing guides that focus on common mistakes or have them work in pairs to improve each other's work—sometimes it is difficult to pay attention to your own errors.

For more ideas about gaining student attention, see **www.inspiringteachers.com/classroom_resources/tips/classroom_management_and_discipline/getting_student_attention.html.**

Working Memory

Working memory is the "workbench" of the memory system, the interface where new information is held temporarily and combined with knowledge from long-term memory, to solve problems or comprehend a lecture, for example. Working memory "contains" what you are thinking about at the moment. For this reason, some psychologists consider the working memory to be synonymous with "consciousness" (Sweller, van Merriënboer, & Paas, 1998). Unlike sensory memory or long-term memory, working memory capacity is very limited—something many of your professors seem to forget as they race through a lecture while you work to hold and make sense of the information.

You may have heard the term short-term memory. Short-term memory is not exactly the same as working memory. Working memory includes both temporary storage and active processing—the workbench of memory—where active mental effort is applied to both new and old information. But short-term memory usually means just storage—the immediate memory for new information that can be held for about 15 to 20 seconds (Baddeley, 2001). Early experiments suggested that the capacity of short-term memory was only about five to nine (the "magic 7 + or − 2") separate new items at once (Miller, 1956). Later, we will see that this limitation can be overcome using strategies such as chunking or grouping, but the five-to-nine-item limit generally holds true in everyday life. It is quite common to remember a new phone number after looking it up, as you make the call. But what if you have two phone calls to make in succession? Two new phone numbers (14 digits—or 20 digits in cities like Vancouver, where you have to dial the area code as well as the number) are difficult to store simultaneously.

A current view of working memory is that it is composed of at least three elements: the central executive that controls attention and other mental resources (the "worker" of working memory), the phonological loop that holds verbal and acoustical (sound) information, and the visuospatial sketchpad for visual and spatial information (Gathercole, Pickering, Ambridge, & Wearing, 2004; Reed, 2006).

STOP & THINK Solve this problem from Ashcraft (2006, p. 190) and pay attention to how you go about the process:

$$\frac{(4 + 5) \times 2}{3 + (12/4)}$$

The Central Executive. As you solved the problem above, the central executive of your working memory focused attention on the facts that you needed (what is 4 + 5? 9 × 2?), retrieved rules for which operations to do first, and recalled how to divide. The central executive supervises attention, makes plans, and retrieves and integrates information. Language comprehension, reasoning, rehearsing information to transfer to long-term memory—all these activities and more are handled by the central executive, as you can see in Figure 7.3. Two systems help out and support the central executive—the phonological loop and the visuospatial sketchpad.

The Phonological Loop. The phonological loop is a system for rehearsing words and sounds for short-term memory. It is the "place" you put the 18 (4 + 5 = 9 × 2 = 18) from the top line of the problem above while you calculated the 3 + (12/4) on the bottom of the problem. Baddeley (1986, 2001) suggests that we can hold as much in the phonological loop as we can rehearse (say to ourselves) in 1.5 to 2 seconds. A seven-digit telephone number fits this limitation. But what if you tried to hold these seven words in mind: *disentangle appropriation gossamer anti-intellectual preventative foreclosure prorogue* (Gray, 2002)? Besides being a mouthful, these words take longer than 2 seconds to rehearse and are more difficult to hold in working memory than seven single digits or seven short words. In addition, some of the words may be unfamiliar to you, so they are harder to rehearse.

Remember—put in your working memory—that we are discussing temporarily holding *new information.* In daily life we certainly can hold more than five to nine bits or 1.5 seconds of information at once. While you are dialing that seven-digit phone number you just looked up, you are bound to have other things "on your mind"—in your memory—such as how to use a telephone, whom you are calling, and why. You don't have to pay attention to these things; they are not new knowledge. Some of the processes, such as dialing the phone, have become automatic. However, because of the working memory's limitations, if you were in a foreign country and were attempting

Working memory The information that you are focusing on at a given moment.

Short-term memory Component of the memory system that holds information for about 20 seconds.

Central executive The part of working memory that is responsible for monitoring and directing attention and other mental resources.

Phonological loop Part of working memory; a memory rehearsal system for verbal and sound information of about 1.5 to 2 seconds.

FIGURE 7.3

Three Parts of Working Memory

The central executive system is the pool of mental resources for such cognitive activities as focusing attention, reasoning, and comprehension. The phonological loop holds verbal and sound information, and the visuospatial sketchpad holds visual and spatial information. The system is limited and can be overwhelmed if too much information, or information that is too difficult, is presented.

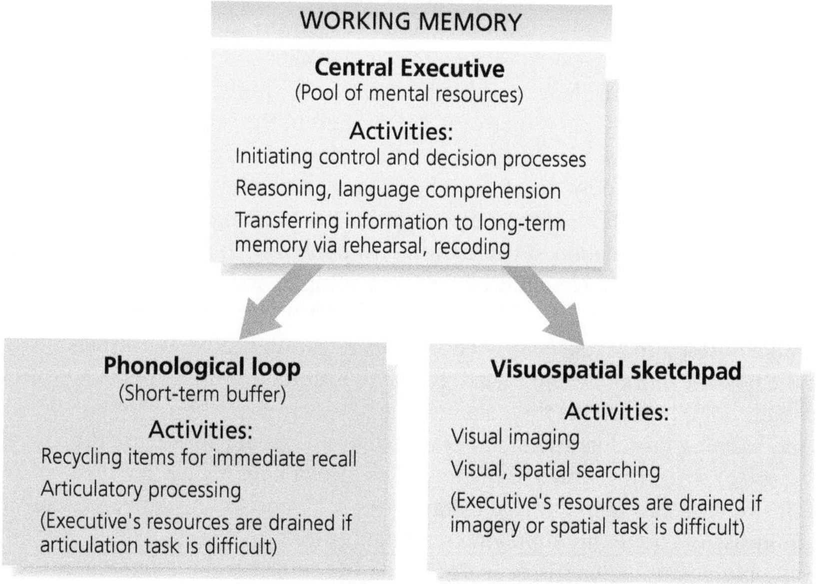

WORKING MEMORY

Central Executive
(Pool of mental resources)

Activities:
Initiating control and decision processes
Reasoning, language comprehension
Transferring information to long-term memory via rehearsal, recoding

Phonological loop
(Short-term buffer)

Activities:
Recycling items for immediate recall
Articulatory processing
(Executive's resources are drained if articulation task is difficult)

Visuospatial sketchpad

Activities:
Visual imaging
Visual, spatial searching
(Executive's resources are drained if imagery or spatial task is difficult)

Source: From *Cognition* (3rd ed.), by M. H. Ashcraft. Published by Prentice Hall. Copyright © 2002 by Prentice Hall. Reprinted by permission of Pearson Education, Inc., Upper Saddle River, NJ.

to use an unfamiliar telephone system, you might very well have trouble remembering the phone number because your central executive was trying to figure out the phone system at the same time. Even a few bits of new information can be too much to remember if the new information is very complex or unfamiliar or if you have to integrate several elements to make sense of a situation (Sweller, van Merriënboer, & Paas, 1998).

STOP & THINK Try this problem from Gray (2002): If you rotate a *p* 180 degrees, do you get a *b* or a *d*?

The Visuospatial Sketchpad. Most people answer the question above by creating a visual image of a "p" and rotating it. The visuospatial sketchpad is the place where you manipulated the image (after your central executive retrieved the meaning of "180 degrees," of course). Working in the visuospatial sketchpad has some of the same aspects as actually looking at a picture or object. If you have to solve the "p" problem and also pay attention to an image on a screen, you will be slowed down just like you would be if you had to look back and forth between two different objects. But if you had to solve the "p" problem while repeating digits, there is little slowdown. You can use your phonological loop and your visuospatial sketchpad at the same time, but each is quickly filled and easily overburdened. In fact, each kind of task—verbal and visual—appears to happen in different areas of the brain. As we will see later, there are some individual differences in the capacities of these systems, too (Ashcraft, 2006; Gray, 2002).

Duration and Contents of Working Memory. It is clear that the *duration* of information in the working memory system is short, about 5 to 20 seconds, unless you keep rehearsing the information or process it some other way. It may seem to you that a memory system with a 20-second time limit is not very useful, but, without this system, you would have already forgotten what you read in the first part of this sentence before you came to these last few words. This would clearly make understanding sentences difficult.

Visuospatial sketchpad Part of working memory; a holding system for visual and spatial information.

The *contents* of information in working memory may be in the form of sounds and images that resemble the representations in sensory memory, or the information may be structured more abstractly, based on meaning.

Cognitive Load. Let's get back to that professor who raced through a lecture, taxing your working memory. Some tasks make more demands than others on working memory. **Cognitive load** is a term for the amount of mental resources, mostly working memory, required to perform a particular task. The concept is only about 20 years old, but in 2004 one search found almost 300 studies that examined how cognitive load is related to learning (Nesbit & Hadwin, 2006). The cognitive load of a task is not an absolute "weight." The extent of cognitive load in a given situation depends on many things including what the person already knows about the task and what resources are available. There are three kinds of cognitive load—one is unavoidable, one gets in the way, and one is valuable.

Intrinsic cognitive load is unavoidable—it is the amount of cognitive processing required to figure out the material. That amount depends on how many elements you have to take into account and how complicated the interactions among the elements are. Even though working memory can *hold* five to nine new bits of information, it can *process* only about two to four at a time. So, if you have to understand how many separate elements interact in a complex system, such as grasping the structure and function of DNA, you will be in trouble unless you already understand some of the parts—vocabulary, concepts, procedures, and so on (van Merriënboer & Sweller, 2005). Intrinsic cognitive load is *intrinsic* to the task—it cannot be eliminated. But good instruction can help manage intrinsic load.

Extraneous cognitive load is the cognitive capacity you use when dealing with problems not related to the learning task, like trying to get your roommate (or spouse, children, partner) to quit interrupting you or struggling with a disorganized lecture or a poorly written textbook (not this one, we hope!). Instruction can help manage extraneous load by providing supports, focusing attention on the main ideas, and generally supplying scaffolding (see Chapter 2).

The valuable cognitive load is called *germane* because it is directly related to (germane to) high-quality learning. **Germane cognitive load** comes from deep processing of relevant information—organizing and integrating the material with what you already know and forming new understandings. Instruction can support this process by asking students to explain the material to each other or to themselves, draw or chart their understandings, take useful notes, and use other strategies we will discuss in upcoming chapters (Mayer, 2008; Reed, 2006).

Retaining Information in Working Memory. Because information in working memory is fragile and easily lost, it must be kept activated to be retained. Activation is high as long as you are focusing on information, but activation decays or fades quickly when attention shifts away. Holding information in working memory is like keeping a series of plates spinning on top of poles in a circus act. The performer gets one plate spinning, moves to the next plate, and the next, but has to return to the first plate before it slows down too much and falls off its pole. If we don't keep the information "spinning" in working memory—keep it activated—it will "fall off" (Anderson, 2005, 1995). When activation fades, forgetting follows, as shown in Figure 7.4.

FIGURE 7.4 **Working Memory: Holding, Processing, and Forgetting**
Information in working memory can be kept activated through maintenance rehearsal or transferred into long-term memory by being connected with information in long-term memory (elaborative rehearsal).

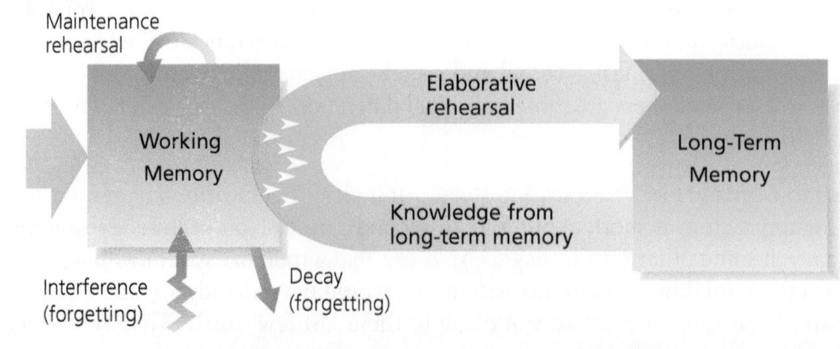

Cognitive load The volume of resources necessary to complete a task.

Intrinsic cognitive load The resources required by the task itself, regardless of other stimuli.

Extraneous cognitive load The resources required to process stimuli irrelevant to the task.

Germane cognitive load Deep processing of information related to the task, including the application of prior knowledge to a new task or problem.

To keep information activated, most people keep rehearsing the information mentally. There are two types of rehearsal (Craik & Lockhart, 1972). Maintenance rehearsal involves repeating the information in your mind. As long as you repeat the information, it can be maintained in working memory indefinitely. Maintenance rehearsal is useful for retaining something you plan to use and then forget, such as a phone number or a location on a map.

Elaborative rehearsal involves connecting the information you are trying to remember with something you already know—with knowledge from long-term memory. For example, if you meet someone at a party whose name is the same as your brother's, you don't have to repeat the name to keep it in memory; you just have to make the association. This kind of rehearsal not only retains information in working memory but also helps move information to long-term memory. Rehearsal is a process the central executive controls to manage the flow of information through the information processing system.

The limited capacity of working memory can also be somewhat circumvented by the process of chunking. Because the number of bits of information, not the size of each bit, is a limitation for working memory, you can retain more information if you can group individual bits of information. You can experience this effect of chunking by trying to hold these letters in memory:

BMOLOLPMODNACTV

Now try these:

BMO LOL PMO DNA CTV

You just used chunking to group the string of letters into memorable (and meaningful) chunks, so you could hold more in memory. Also, you brought your knowledge of the world to bear on the memory task. Chunking helps you remember a password or social insurance number (Driscoll, 2005).

Forgetting. Information may be lost from working memory through interference or decay (see Figure 7.4). Interference is fairly straightforward: Processing new information interferes or gets confused with old information. As new thoughts accumulate, old information is lost from working memory. Information is also lost by time decay. If you don't continue to pay attention to information, the activation level decays (weakens) and finally drops so low that the information cannot be reactivated—it disappears altogether.

Actually, forgetting is very useful. Without forgetting, people would quickly overload their working memories and learning would cease. Also, it would be a problem if you remembered permanently every sentence you ever read, every sound you ever heard, every picture you ever saw . . . you get the idea. Finding a particular bit of information in all that sea of knowledge would be impossible. It is helpful to have a system that provides temporary storage and that "weeds out" some information from everything you experience.

We turn next to long-term memory. Because this is such an important topic for teachers, we will spend quite a bit of time on it.

LONG-TERM MEMORY

Working memory holds the information that is currently activated, such as the name of the person you just met. Long-term memory holds the information that is well learned, such as the names of all the people you know.

Capacity, Duration, and Contents of Long-Term Memory

There are a number of differences between working and long-term memory, as you can see in Table 7.1 on page 244. Information enters working memory very quickly but it takes time and effort to store memories for the long term. Whereas the capacity of working memory is limited, the capacity of long-term memory appears to be, for all practical purposes, unlimited. In addition, once information is securely stored in long-term memory, it can remain there permanently. Our access to information in working memory is immediate because we are thinking about the information at that very moment. But access to information in long-term memory requires time and effort. Recently, some psychologists have suggested that there are not two separate memory

Maintenance rehearsal Keeping information in working memory by repeating it to yourself.

Elaborative rehearsal Keeping information in working memory by associating it with something else you already know.

Chunking Grouping individual bits of data into meaningful larger units.

Decay The weakening and fading of memories with the passage of time.

Long-term memory Permanent store of knowledge.

TABLE 7.1 Working and Long-Term Memory

Type of Memory	Input	Capacity	Duration	Contents	Retrieval
Working	Very fast	Limited	Very brief: 5–20 sec.	Words, images, ideas, sentences	Immediate
Long-term	Relatively slow	Practically unlimited	Practically unlimited	Propositional networks, schemata, productions, episodes, perhaps images	Depends on representation and organization

Source: From *Comprehension and Learning: A Conceptual Framework for Teachers,* by F. Smith, 1975, New York: Holt, Rinehart, and Winston. Copyright © Holt, Rinehart, and Winston. Adapted with permission of the author.

stores (working and long-term). Rather, working memory is the part of long-term memory that works on (processes) currently activated information—so working memory is more about processing than storage (Wilson, 2001).

MyEducationLab Go to the Activities and Applications section in Chapter 7 of MyEducation Lab and complete Activity 3. As you watch the video and answer the accompanying questions, note the differences in memory strategies used by early and late adolescent students.

Contents of Long-Term-Memory: Declarative, Procedural, and Self-Regulatory Knowledge. Earlier, we talked about general and specific knowledge. Another way to categorize knowledge is as declarative, procedural, or self-regulatory (Schraw, 2006).

Declarative knowledge is knowledge that can be declared, through words and symbol systems of all kinds—Braille, sign language, dance or musical notation, mathematical symbols, and so on (Farnham-Diggory, 1994). Declarative knowledge is "knowing that" something is the case. The history students in the opening "What Would You Do?" situation were focusing exclusively on declarative knowledge about history. The range of declarative knowledge is tremendous. You can know very specific facts (the atomic weight of gold is 196.967), or generalities (leaves of some trees change colour in autumn), or personal preferences (I don't like lima beans), or rules (to divide fractions, invert the divisor and multiply). Small units of declarative knowledge can be organized into larger units; for example, principles of reinforcement and punishment can be organized in your thinking into a theory of behavioural learning (Gagné, Yekovich, & Yekovich, 1993).

Procedural knowledge is "knowing how" to do something such as divide fractions or clean a carburetor—it is knowledge in action. Procedural knowledge must be demonstrated. Notice that repeating the rule "to divide fractions, invert the divisor and multiply" shows *declarative* knowledge—the student can state the rule. But to show *procedural* knowledge, the student must act. When faced with a fraction to divide, the student must divide correctly. Students demonstrate procedural knowledge when they translate a passage into French or Spanish, correctly categorize a geometric shape, or craft a coherent paragraph.

Self-regulatory knowledge is knowing how to manage your learning—knowing how and when to use your declarative and procedural knowledge (Schraw, 2006; Winne, in press). It takes self-regulatory knowledge to know when to read every word in a text and when to skim, or when to apply a strategy for overcoming procrastination. Self-regulatory knowledge has also been called *conditional* knowledge (Paris & Cunningham, 1996; Paris, Lipson, & Wixson, 1983). For many students, this kind of knowledge is a stumbling block on the path to learning. They have the facts and can do the procedures, but they don't seem to understand how to apply what they know at the appropriate time. Self-regulatory knowledge can be specific to a subject area (when to use the formula for calculating area, not perimeter, in geometry) or more general (how to summarize key points or use diagrams to organize information). In fact, all three kinds of knowledge—declarative, procedural, and self-regulatory—can be either general or domain-specific, as you can see in Table 7.2 (Schraw, 2006).

Most cognitive psychologists distinguish two categories of long-term memory, explicit and implicit, with subdivisions under each category, as shown in Figure 7.5. Explicit memory is knowledge from long-term memory that can be recalled and consciously considered. We are aware of these memories—we know we have remembered them. Implicit memory, on the other hand, is

Declarative knowledge Verbal information; facts; "knowing that" something is the case.

Procedural knowledge Knowledge that is demonstrated when we perform a task; "knowing how."

Self-regulatory knowledge Knowing how to manage your learning, or knowing how and when to use your declarative and procedural knowledge.

Explicit memory Long-term memories that involve deliberate or conscious recall.

Implicit memory Knowledge that we are not conscious of recalling, but that influences behaviour or thought without our awareness.

TABLE 7.2 Kinds of Knowledge

	General Knowledge	Domain-Specific Knowledge
Declarative	Hours the library is open Rules of grammar	The definition of "hypotenuse" The lines of the poem "The Raven"
Procedural	How to use your cell phone How to drive	How to solve an oxidation-reduction equation How to throw a pot on a potter's wheel
Conditional	When to give up and try another approach When to skim and when to read carefully	When to use the formula for calculating volume When to rush the net in tennis

knowledge that we are not conscious of recalling, but that influences behaviour or thought without our awareness. These different kinds of memory are associated with different parts of the brain (Ashcraft, 2006).

Explicit Memories: Semantic and Episodic

In Figure 7.5, you will see that explicit memories can be either semantic (based on meaning) or episodic (based the sequence of events). Semantic memory, very important in schools, is memory for meaning, including words, facts, theories, and concepts—declarative knowledge. These memories are not tied to particular experiences and are represented and stored as *propositions*, *images*, *concepts*, and *schemas* (Anderson, 2005; Schraw, 2006; Winne, in press).

Propositions and Propositional Networks. How do we represent the meaning of sentences and pictures in our memories? One answer is with propositions connected in networks. A *proposition* is the smallest unit of knowledge that can be judged true or false. Here is an example of a statement with three propositions: "The Prime Minister, who is head of Canada's government and lives at 24 Sussex Drive, is appointed by the Governor General." The three basic propositions are:

1. The Prime Minister is head of Canada's government.
2. The Prime Minister lives at 24 Sussex Drive.
3. The Prime Minister is appointed by the Governor General.

FIGURE 7.5 Long-Term Memory: Explicit and Implicit

Explicit and implicit memory systems follow different rules and involve different neural systems of the brain. The subdivisions of each kind of memory also may involve different neural systems.

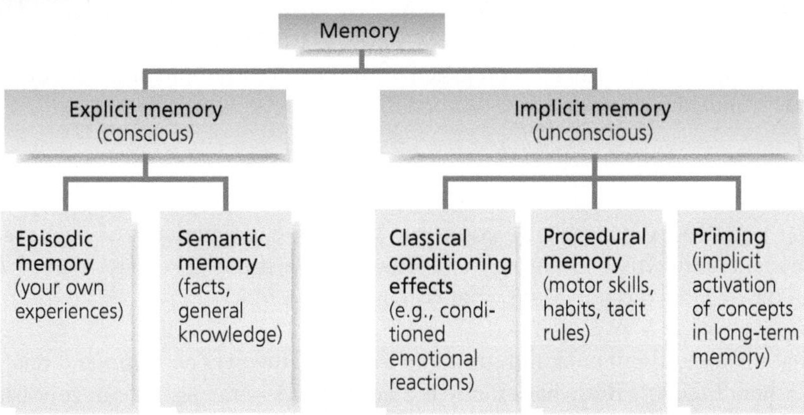

Source: From *Psychology* by Peter Gray. Published by Worth Publishers. Copyright © 1991, 1994, 1999, 2002 by Worth Publishers. Adapted with permission of the publisher.

Semantic memory Memory for meaning.

Propositions that share information are linked in what cognitive psychologists call propositional networks. It is the meaning, not the exact words or word order, that is stored in the network. The same propositional network would apply to this sentence: "Appointed as Canada's head of government by the Governor General, the Prime Minister lives at 24 Sussex Drive." The meaning is the same, and it is this *meaning* that is stored in memory as a set of relationships among propositions.

It is possible that most information is stored and represented in propositional networks. When we want to recall a bit of information, we can translate its meaning (as represented in the propositional network) into familiar phrases and sentences, or mental pictures. Also, because propositions are networked, recall of one bit of information can trigger or *activate* recall of another. We are not aware of these networks, for they are not part of our conscious memory (Anderson, 2005). In much the same way, we are not aware of underlying grammatical structure when we form a sentence in our own language; we don't have to diagram a sentence in order to say it.

Images. Images are representations based on the structure or appearance of the information (Anderson, 2005). As we form images (like you did in the "p" problem), we try to remember or recreate the physical attributes and spatial structure of information. For example, when asked how many windowpanes are in their living room, most people call up an image of the windows "in their mind's eye" and count the panes—the more panes, the longer it takes to respond. If the information were represented only in a proposition such as "my living room has seven windowpanes," then everyone would take about the same time to answer, whether the number was 1 or 24 (Mendell, 1971). However, researchers don't agree on exactly how images are stored in memory. Some psychologists believe that images are stored as pictures; others believe that we store propositions in long-term memory and convert to pictures in working memory when necessary.

There probably are features of each process involved—some memory for images and some verbal or propositional descriptions of the image. Seeing images "in your mind's eye" is not exactly the same as seeing the actual image. It is more difficult to perform complicated transformations on mental images than on real images (Driscoll, 2005; Matlin & Foley, 1997). For example, if you had a plastic "p" magnet on your refrigerator, you could very quickly rotate it. Rotating mentally takes more time for most people. Nevertheless, images are useful in making many practical decisions such as how a sofa might look in your living room or how to line up a golf shot. Images may also be helpful in abstract reasoning. Physicists, such as Faraday and Einstein, report creating images to reason about complex new problems. Einstein claimed that he was visualizing chasing a beam of light and catching up to it when the concept of relativity came to him (Kosslyn & Koenig, 1992).

Two Are Better Than One: Words and Images. Allan Paivio (1986; Clark & Paivio, 1991), recently of the University of Western Ontario, suggests that information is stored in long-term memory as either visual images or verbal units, or both. Psychologists who agree with this point of view believe that information coded both visually and verbally is easiest to learn (Butcher, 2006; Mayer & Sims, 1994). This may be one reason why explaining an idea with words and representing it visually in a figure, as we do in textbooks, has proved helpful to students. For example, Richard Mayer and his colleagues (Mautone & Mayer, 2001; Mayer, 1999a, 2001) have found that illustrations like the one in Figure 7.9 on page 255 are helpful in improving students' understanding of science concepts.

Concepts.

STOP & THINK What makes a cup a cup? List the characteristics of *cupness*. What is a fruit? Is a banana a fruit? Is a tomato a fruit? How about a squash? A watermelon? A sweet potato? An olive? How did you learn what makes a fruit a fruit?

Most of what we know about cups and fruits and the world involves concepts and relations among concepts (Ashcraft, 2006). But what exactly is a concept? A concept is a category used to group similar events, ideas, objects, or people. When we talk about a particular concept such as *student*, we refer to a category of people who are similar to one another—they all study a subject. The people may be old or young, in school or not; they may be studying basketball or Bach, but they all can be

Propositional network Set of interconnected concepts and relationships in which long-term knowledge is held.

Images Representations based on the physical attributes—the appearance—of information.

Concept A category used to group similar events, ideas, objects, or people.

categorized as students. Concepts are abstractions. They do not exist in the real world. Only individual examples of concepts exist. Concepts help us organize vast amounts of information into manageable units. For instance, there are about 7.5 million distinguishable differences in colours. By categorizing these colours into some dozen or so groups, we manage to deal with this diversity quite well (Bruner, 1973).

In early research, psychologists assumed that concepts share a set of defining attributes, or distinctive features. For example, books all contain pages that are bound together in some way (but what about electronic "books"?). Your concept of a cat might include *defining attributes* such as a round head on a small body, triangle-shaped ears, whiskers, four legs, and fur. This concept enables you to identify cats whether they are calico or Siamese without re-learning "cat" each time you encounter a new cat. The defining attributes theory of concepts suggests that we recognize specific examples by noting key required features.

Since about 1970, however, these views about the nature of concepts have been challenged (Ashcraft, 2006). Although some concepts, such as equilateral triangle, have clear-cut defining attributes, most concepts do not. Take the concept of *party*. What are the defining attributes? You might have difficulty listing these attributes, but you probably recognize a party when you see or hear one (unless, of course we are talking about political parties, or the other party in a lawsuit, where the sound might not help you recognize the "party"). What about the concept of *bird*? Your first thought might be that birds are animals that fly. But is an ostrich a bird? What about a penguin? A bat?

Prototypes and Exemplars. Current views of concept learning suggest that we have in our minds a prototype of a party or a bird or the letter A—an image that captures the essence of each concept. As we described earlier, a prototype is the best representative of its category. For instance, the best representative of the "birds" category for many Canadians might be a robin (Rosch, 1973). Other members of the category may be very similar to the prototype (sparrow) or similar in some ways but different in others (chicken, ostrich). At the boundaries of a category, it may be difficult to determine if a particular instance really belongs. For example, is a telephone "furniture"? Is an elevator a "vehicle"? Is an olive a "fruit"? Whether something fits into a category is a matter of degree. Thus, categories have fuzzy boundaries. Some events, objects, or ideas are simply better examples of a concept than others (Ashcraft, 2006).

Defining attribute Qualities that connect members of a group to a specific concept.

Exemplar An actual memory of a specific object.

Another explanation of concept learning suggests that we identify members of a category by referring to exemplars. Exemplars are our actual memories of specific birds, parties, furniture, and so on that we use to compare with an item in question to see if that item belongs in the same category as our exemplar. For example, if you see a strange steel-and-stone bench in a public park, you may compare it to the sofa in your living room to decide if the uncomfortable-looking creation is still for sitting on or if it has crossed a fuzzy boundary into "sculpture." Prototypes probably are built from experiences with many exemplars. This happens naturally because memories of particular events (episodic memories) tend to blur together over time, creating an average or typical sofa prototype from all the sofa exemplars you have experienced (Schwartz & Reisberg, 1991).

Jacob Feldman (2003) suggests a final aspect of concept formation—the *simplicity principle*. Feldman theorizes that when humans are confronted with examples, they induce the simplest category or rule that would cover all the examples. Sometimes it is easy to come up with a simple rule (triangles) and sometimes it is more difficult (fruit), but humans seek a simple hypothesis for collecting all the examples under one concept. Feldman suggests that this simplicity principle is one of the oldest ideas in cognitive psychology: "organisms seek to understand their environment by reducing incoming information to a simpler, more coherent, and more useful form" (p. 231). Does this remind you of the Gestalt principles of perception?

CHANGING CONCEPTS Concepts have many attributes and may not remain constant. Recent technological applications such as text messaging have changed the concept of "conversation."

Schemas. Propositions and single images are fine for representing single ideas and relationships, but often our knowledge about a topic combines many concepts, images, and propositions. To explain this kind of complex knowledge, psychologists developed the idea of a schema (Gagné, Yekovich, &

Yekovich, 1993). Schemas (sometimes called *schemata*) are abstract knowledge structures that organize vast amounts of information. A schema (the singular form) is a mental framework that guides our perception and helps us make sense of our experience based on what we already know and what we expect to happen (Schraw, 2006). For example, Figure 7.6 is a partial representation of a schema for knowledge about "reinforcement."

The schema tells you what features are typical of a category, what to expect about an object or situation. The pattern has "slots" that are filled with specific information as we apply the schema in a particular situation. And schemas are personal. For example, our schemas of reinforcement are less richly developed than Skinner's schema must have been. You encountered a very similar concept of scheme in the discussion of Piaget's theory of cognitive development in Chapter 2.

When you hear the sentence, "The Prime Minister, who is head of Canada's government and lives at 24 Sussex Drive, is appointed by the Governor General," you know even more about it than the three propositions. You probably can infer that being head of government requires quite a lot of negotiating with the other political parties. Your schema for "political parties" gives you some sense of the sorts of topics they negotiate. None of this information was explicitly stated in the sentence.

Schematic knowledge helps us to form and understand concepts. How do we know that counterfeit money is not "real" money, even though it perfectly fits our "money" prototype and exemplars and looks like real money? We know because of its history. The "wrong" people printed the money. So our understanding of the concept of money is connected with concepts of crime, forgery, the federal treasury, and many others in a larger schema for "money."

Another type of schema, a story grammar (sometimes called a schema for text or story structure) helps students to understand and remember stories (Gagné, Yekovich, & Yekovich, 1993; Rumelhart & Ortony, 1977). A story grammar could be something like this: murder discovered, search for clues carried out, murderer's fatal mistake identified, trap set to trick suspect into confessing, murderer takes the bait—mystery solved! In other words, a story grammar is a typical general structure that could fit many specific stories. To comprehend a story, we select a schema that seems appropriate. Then, we use this framework to decide which details are important, what information to seek, and what to remember. It is as though the schema is a theory about what should occur in the story. The schema guides us in "interrogating" the text, pointing to the specific information we expect to find so that the story makes sense. If we activate our "murder mystery schema,"

Schemas (singular, schema) Basic structures for organizing information; concepts.

Story grammar Typical structure or organization for a category of stories.

FIGURE 7.6 **A Partial Schema for "Reinforcement"**

The concept of "reinforcement" is under the general category of "consequence." It is related to other concepts, such as eating in restaurants or bouncing babies on your lap, depending on the individual's experiences.

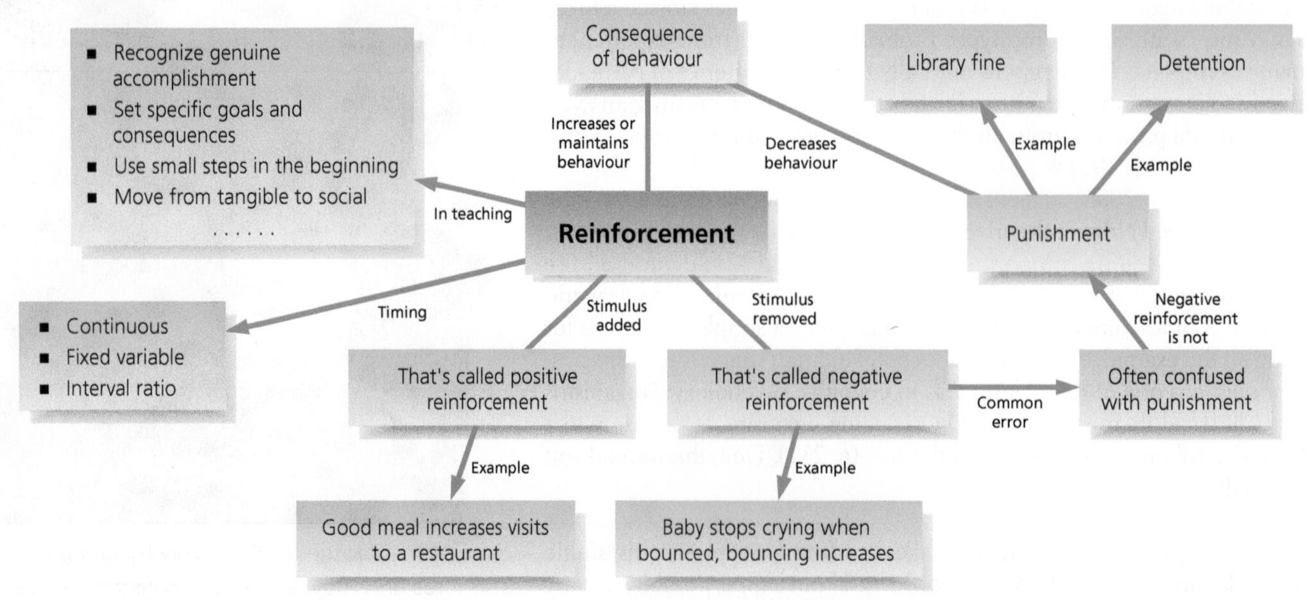

we may be alert for clues or a murderer's fatal mistake. Without an appropriate schema, trying to understand a story, textbook, or classroom lesson is a very slow, difficult process, something like finding your way through a new town without a map.

Now that we've examined semantic memory, let's turn to the second kind of explicit memory, *episodic memory*.

Episodic Memory. Memory for information tied to a particular place and time, especially information about the events or *episodes* of your own life, is called *episodic* memory. **Episodic memory** is about events we have experienced, so we often can explain *when* the event happened. In contrast, we usually can't describe when we acquired a semantic memory. For example, you may have a difficult time remembering when you developed semantic memories for the meaning of the word *injustice*, but you can easily remember a time that you felt unjustly treated. Episodic memory also keeps track of the order of things, so it is a good place to store jokes, gossip, or plots from films.

Memories for dramatic or emotional moments in your life are called **flashbulb memories**. These memories are vivid and complete, as if your brain demanded that you "record this moment." Under stress, more glucose energy goes to fuel brain activity, while stress-induced hormones signal the brain that something important is happening (Myers, 2005). So when we have strong emotional reactions, memories are stronger and more lasting. Many people have vivid memories of very positive or very negative events in school, winning a prize or being humiliated, for example. You probably know just where you were and what you were doing on 9/11 or when the Canadian hockey team defeated the U.S. team to win Olympic gold.

Episodic memory Long-term memory for information tied to a particular time and place, especially memory of the events in a person's life.

Flashbulb memories Clear, vivid memories of emotionally important events in your life.

Procedural memory Long-term memory for how to do things.

Script Schema or expected plan for the sequence of steps in a common event such as buying groceries or ordering a pizza.

Productions The contents of procedural memory; rules about what actions to take, given certain conditions.

Implicit Memories

Look back at Figure 7.5. You see that there are three kinds of implicit or out-of-awareness memories: classical conditioning, procedural memory, and priming effects. In classical conditioning, as we saw in Chapter 6, some out-of-awareness memories may cause you to feel anxious as you take a test or may make your heart rate increase when you hear a dentist's drill.

The second type of implicit memory is **procedural memory** for skills, habits, and how to do things—in other words, memory for procedural knowledge. It may take a while to learn a procedure—such as how to ski, factor an equation, or design a teaching portfolio—but once learned, this knowledge tends to be remembered for a long time. Procedural knowledge is represented as *scripts* and *condition-action rules*, sometimes called productions.

Scripts are action sequences or plans for actions stored in memory (Schraw, 2006). We all have scripts for events like ordering food in restaurants, and these scripts differ depending on whether the restaurant is a four-star bistro or a fast-food drive-through. Even young children have scripts for how to behave during snack time at preschool or during a friend's birthday party, as you can see in Figure 7.7 on page 250. In fact, for very young children, scripts seem to help them organize and remember the predictable aspects of their world. This frees up some working memory to learn new things and recognize when something is out of place in the situation. In terms of human survival, it probably is useful to remember what is likely to keep happening and to notice when something is out of place. (Nelson, 2004)

Productions specify what to do under certain conditions: If A occurs, then do B. A production might be something like, "If you want to snow ski faster, lean back slightly," or "If your goal is to increase student attention and a student has been paying attention a bit longer than usual, then praise the student." People can't necessarily state all their scripts and condition-action rules, and don't even know that they are following these rules, but they act on them nevertheless. The more practised the procedure, the more automatic the action and the more implicit the memory (Schraw, 2006).

PROCEDURAL MEMORY Procedural memory applies to skills, habits, and "how to do things." It may take a while to learn a procedure, such as serving a tennis ball, but once learned, the procedure tends to be remembered for a long time.

FIGURE 7.7 **A Child's Script for a Fast-Food Restaurant**

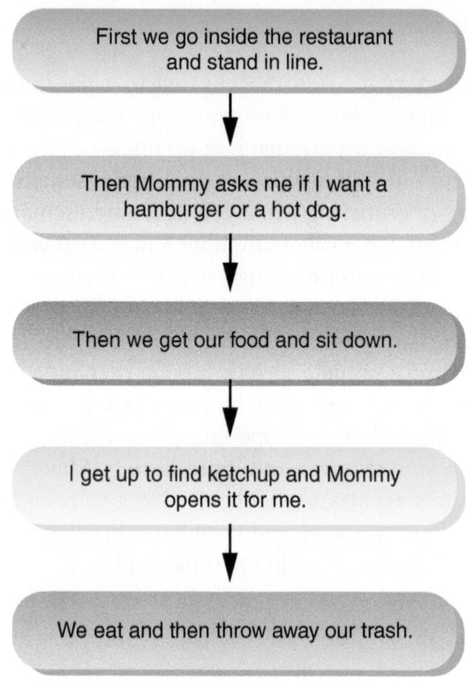

STOP & THINK Fill in these blanks: MEM _ _ _

The final type of implicit memory involves priming, or activating information that already is in long-term memory through some out-of-awareness process. You might have seen an example of priming in the fill-in-the-blank question above. If you wrote MEMORY instead of MEMOIR or MEMBER, or other ME words, then priming may have played a role because the word *memory* has occurred many times in this chapter. Priming may be the fundamental process for retrieval as associations are activated and spread through the memory system (Ashcraft, 2006).

Storing and Retrieving Information in Long-Term Memory

Just what is done to "save" information permanently—to create explicit and implicit memories? How can we make the most effective use of our practically unlimited capacity to learn and remember? *The way you learn information in the first place*—the way you process it in working memory at the outset—strongly affects its recall later. One important requirement is that you integrate new information with existing knowledge as you construct an understanding. Here, *elaboration*, *organization*, and *context* play a role.

Elaboration is adding meaning to new information by connecting it with already existing knowledge. In other words, we apply our schemas and draw on already existing knowledge to construct an understanding. Frequently, we change our existing knowledge in the process. We often elaborate automatically. For example, a paragraph about a historic figure in ancient Rome tends to activate our existing knowledge about that period; we use the old knowledge to understand the new information.

Material that is elaborated when first learned will be easier to recall later. First, as we saw earlier, elaboration is a form of rehearsal. It keeps the information activated in working memory long enough to have a chance for the new information to be linked with knowledge in long-term memory. Second, elaboration builds extra links to existing knowledge. The more one bit of information or knowledge is associated with other bits, the more routes there are to follow to get to the original bit. To put it another way, you have several "handles" or priming/retrieval cues to "pick up" or recognize the information you might be seeking (Schunk, 2004).

Priming Activating a concept in memory or the spread of activation from one concept to another.

Elaboration Adding and extending meaning by connecting new information to existing knowledge.

The more students elaborate new ideas, the more they "make them their own," the deeper their understanding and the better their memory for the knowledge will be. We help students to elaborate when we ask them to translate information into their own words, create examples, explain to a peer, draw or act out the relationships, or apply the information to solve new problems. Of course, if students elaborate new information by developing misguided explanations, these misconceptions will be remembered too.

Organization is a second element of processing that improves learning. Material that is well organized is easier to learn and to remember than bits and pieces of information, especially if the material is complex or extensive. Placing a concept in a structure will help you learn and remember both general definitions and specific examples. The structure serves as a guide back to the information when you need it. For example, Table 7.1 gives an organized view of the capacity, duration, contents, and retrieval of information from working and long-term memory; Table 7.2 organizes information about types of knowledge; and Figure 7.6 organizes knowledge about reinforcement.

Context is a third element of processing that influences learning. Aspects of physical and emotional context—places, rooms, moods, who is with us—are learned along with other information. Later, if you try to remember the information, it will be easier if the current context is similar to the original one. Context is a kind of priming that activates the information. This has been demonstrated in the laboratory. Students who learned material in one type of room performed better on tests taken in a similar room than they did on comparable tests taken in a very different-looking room (Smith, Glenberg, & Bjork, 1978). So, studying for a test under "test-like" conditions may result in improved performance. Of course, you can't always go back to the same place or a similar one in order to recall something. But if you can picture the setting, the time of day, and your companions, you may eventually reach the information you seek.

Levels of Processing Theory. Craik and Lockhart (1972), psychologists at the University of Toronto, first proposed their levels of processing theory as an alternative to short- and long-term memory models, but levels of processing theory is particularly related to the notion of elaboration described earlier. Craik and Lockhart suggested that what determines how long information is remembered is *how extensively* the information is analyzed and connected with other information. The more completely information is processed, the better are our chances of remembering it. For example, according to the levels of processing theory, if we ask you to sort pictures of dogs based on the colour of their coats, you might not remember many of the pictures later. But if we ask you to rate each dog on how likely it is to chase you as you jog, you probably would remember more of the pictures. To rate the dogs, you must pay attention to details in the pictures, relate features of the dogs to characteristics associated with danger, and so on. This rating procedure requires "deeper" processing and more focus on the *meaning* of the features in the photos.

Retrieving Information From Long-Term Memory. When we need to use information from long-term memory, we search for it. Sometimes the search is conscious, as when you see a friend approaching and search for her name. At other times, locating and using information from long-term memory is automatic, as when you dial a telephone or solve a math problem without having to search for each step, or when the word *memory* pops to mind when you see MEM _ _ _. Think of long-term memory as a huge cabinet full of tools (skills, procedures) and supplies (knowledge, concepts, schemas) ready to be brought to the workbench of working memory to accomplish a task. The cabinet (long-term memory) stores an incredible amount, but it may be hard to find what you are looking for quickly. The workbench (working memory) is small, but anything on it is immediately available. Because it is small, however, supplies (bits of information) sometimes are lost when the workbench overflows or when one bit of information covers (interferes with) another (E. Gagné, 1985). Of course you have to walk into the room through the door of attention in order to get to the workbench and the cabinet.

Spreading Activation. The size of the network in long-term memory is huge, but only small parts of it are activated at any one time. Only the information we are currently thinking about is in working memory. Information is retrieved in this network through spreading activation. When a particular proposition or image is active—when we are thinking about it—other closely associated knowledge can be *primed* or triggered as well, and activation can spread through the network

Organization Ordered and logical network of relations.

Context The physical or emotional backdrop associated with an event.

Levels of processing theory Theory that recall of information is based on how deeply it is processed.

Spreading activation Retrieval of pieces of information based on their relatedness to one another. Remembering one bit of information activates (stimulates) recall of associated information.

(Anderson, 2005; Gagné, Yekovich, & Yekovich, 1993). Thus, if you focus on the propositions, "I'd like to go for a drive to see the fall leaves," related ideas such as "I should rake leaves" and "The car needs an oil change," come to mind. As activation spreads from the "car trip" to the "oil change," the original thought, or active memory, disappears from working memory because of the limited space. Thus, retrieval from long-term memory occurs partly through the spreading of activation from one bit of knowledge to related ideas in the network. We often use this spreading in reverse to retrace our steps in a conversation, as in, "Before we got onto the topic of where to get the oil changed, what were we talking about? Oh yes, seeing the leaves." The learning and retrieving processes of long-term memory are diagrammed in Figure 7.8.

Reconstruction. In long-term memory, the information is still available, even when it is not activated—that is, even when you are not thinking about it at the moment. If spreading activation does not "find" the information we seek, then we might still come up with an answer through reconstruction, a cognitive tool or problem-solving process that makes use of logic, cues, and other knowledge to *construct* a reasonable answer by filling in any missing parts (Koriat, Goldsmith, & Pansky, 2000). Sometimes reconstructed recollections are incorrect. For example, in 1932, F. C. Bartlett conducted a series of famous studies on remembering stories. He read a complex, unfamiliar First Nations tale to students at England's Cambridge University and, after various lengths of time, asked the students to recall the story. Stories the students recalled were generally shorter than the original and were translated into the concepts and language of the Cambridge student culture. The story told of a seal hunt, for instance, but many students remembered (reconstructed) a "fishing trip," an activity closer to their experiences and more consistent with their schemas.

One area where reconstructed memory can play a major role is eyewitness testimony. Elizabeth Loftus and her colleagues have conducted a number of studies showing that misleading questions or other information during questioning can affect memory. For example, in a classic study, Loftus and Palmer (1974) showed subjects slides of a car wreck. Later, the experimenters asked some subjects, "How fast were the cars going when they *hit* each other?" while other subjects who saw the same slides were asked, "How fast were the cars going when they *smashed* into each other?" The difference in verbs was enough to bias the subjects' memories—the subjects who heard the word *hit* estimated the cars were travelling an average of 55 kilometres per hour, but the subjects who heard the word *smashed* estimated almost 66 kilometres per hour. And one week later, 32 percent of the subjects who heard the word *smashed* remembered seeing broken glass at the scene of the wreck, while only 14 percent of the subjects who heard the word *hit* remembered glass. (There was no broken glass visible in any of the slides.)

Retrieval Process of searching for and finding information in long-term memory.

Reconstruction Recreating information by using memories, expectations, logic, and existing knowledge.

Forgetting and Long-Term Memory. Information in working memory that is lost before it has a chance to integrate into the network of long-term memory truly disappears. No amount of effort or searching will bring it back. But information stored in long-term memory may be available,

FIGURE 7.8

Long-Term Memory

We activate information from long-term memory to help us understand new information in working memory. With mental work and processing (elaboration, organization, context) the new information can be stored permanently in long-term memory. Forgetting is caused by interference and time decay.

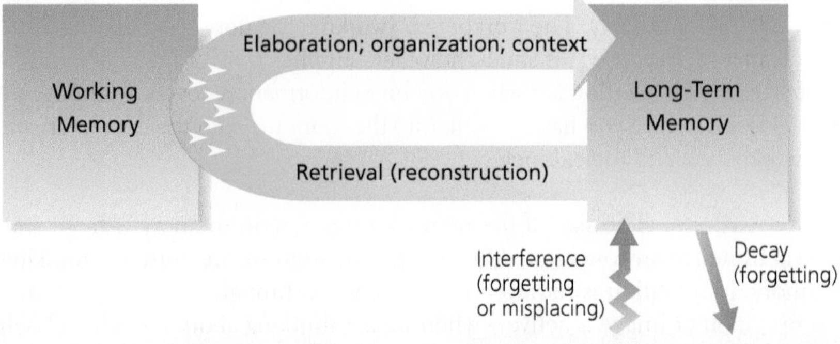

given the right cues. Some people believe that nothing is ever lost from long-term memory; however, research casts doubts on this assertion (Schwartz, Wasserman, & Robbins, 2002).

Information appears to be lost from long-term memory through time decay and interference. For example, study has shown that memory for Spanish–English vocabulary decreases for about 3 years after a person's last course in Spanish, then stays level for about 25 years, then drops again for the next 25 years. One explanation for this decline is that neural connections, like muscles, grow weak without use. After 25 years, it may be that the memories are still somewhere in the brain, but they are too weak to be reactivated (Anderson, 2005). And some neurons simply die. Finally, newer memories may interfere with or obscure older memories, and older memories may interfere with memory for new material.

Even with decay and interference, long-term memory is remarkable. In a review of almost 100 studies of memory for knowledge taught in school, George Semb and John Ellis (1994) concluded that, "contrary to popular belief, students retain much of the knowledge taught in the classroom" (p. 279). It appears that teaching strategies that encourage student engagement and lead to higher levels of *initial* learning (such as frequent reviews and tests, elaborated feedback, high standards, mastery learning, and active involvement in learning projects) are associated with longer retention.

Now that we have examined the information processing explanation of how knowledge is represented and remembered, let's turn to the really important question: How can teachers support the development of knowledge?

BECOMING KNOWLEDGEABLE: SOME BASIC PRINCIPLES

MyEducationLab
Go to the Activities and Applications section in Chapter 7 of MyEducation Lab and complete Activity 2. As you view the artifact and complete the accompanying activities, consider the different uses of declarative versus procedural knowledge.

Understanding a concept such as "reinforcement" involves *declarative knowledge* about characteristics and images as well as *procedural knowledge* about how to apply rules to categorize specific consequences. We will discuss the development of declarative and procedural knowledge separately, but keep in mind that real learning is a combination and integration of these elements. We look at the process of developing self-regulatory knowledge in the next chapter when we discuss metacognition.

Development of Declarative Knowledge

As you have seen, people learn best when they have a good base of knowledge in the area they are studying (remember the baseball study described earlier in this chapter). When people have well-elaborated schemas and scripts to guide them, new material makes more sense, and there are many possible spots in the long-term memory network for connecting new information with old.

What are some possible strategies? Perhaps the best single method for helping students learn is to make each lesson as meaningful as possible.

Making It Meaningful. Meaningful lessons are presented in vocabulary that makes sense to the students. New terms are clarified through ties with more familiar words and ideas. Meaningful lessons are well organized, with clear connections between the different elements of the lesson. Finally, meaningful lessons make natural use of old information to help students understand new information through examples or analogies.

The importance of meaningful lessons is emphasized below in an example presented by Smith (1975).

STOP & THINK Look at the three lines below. Begin by covering all but the first line. Look at it for a second, close the book, and write down all the letters you remember. Then repeat this procedure with the second and third lines.

1. KBVODUWGPJMSQTXNOGMCTRSO
2. READ JUMP WHEAT POOR BUT SEEK
3. KNIGHTS RODE HORSES INTO WAR

Interference The process that occurs when remembering certain information is hampered by the presence of other information.

Each line has the same number of letters, but the chances are great that you remembered all the letters in the third line, a good number of letters in the second line, and very few in the first line. The first line makes no sense. There is no way to organize it in a brief glance. Working memory is simply not able to hold and process all that information quickly. The second line is more meaningful. You do not have to see each letter because your long-term memory brings prior knowledge of spelling rules and vocabulary to the task. The third line is the most meaningful. Just a glance and you can probably remember all of it because you bring to this task prior knowledge not only of spelling and vocabulary but also of rules about syntax and probably some historical information about knights (they didn't ride in tanks). This sentence is meaningful because you have existing schemas for assimilating it (Sweller, van Merriënboer, & Paas, 1998).

The challenge for teachers is to make lessons less like learning the first line and more like learning the third line. Although this may seem obvious, think about the times when *you* have read a sentence in a text or heard an explanation from a professor that might just as well have been KBVODUWGPJMSQTXNOGMCTRSO. But beware, attempts to change the ways that students are used to learning—moving from memorizing to meaningful activities as in the opening "What Would You Do?" situation—are not always greeted with student enthusiasm. Students may be concerned about their grades; at least when memorization gains an A, they know what is expected. Meaningful learning can be riskier and more challenging. In Chapters 8, 9, 10, and 13 we will examine a variety of ways in which teachers can support meaningful learning and understanding.

Visual Images and Illustrations. Is a picture worth 1000 words in teaching? Richard Mayer (2001, 2005) has studied this question for several years and found that the right combination of pictures and words can make a significant difference in students' learning. Mayer's cognitive theory of multimedia learning includes three ideas:

Dual Coding: Visual and verbal materials are processed in different systems (Clark & Paivio, 1991).

Limited Capacity: Working memory for verbal and visual material is severely limited. Cognitive load has to be managed (Baddeley, 2001; van Merriënboer & Sweller, 2005).

Generative Learning: Meaningful learning happens when students focus on relevant information and generate or build connections (Mayer, 2008).

The problem: How to build complex understandings that integrate information from visual (pictures, diagrams, graphs, films) and verbal (text, lecture) sources, given the limitations of working memory. The answer: Make sure the information is available at the same time or in focused small bites. Mayer and Gallini (1990) provide an example. They used three kinds of texts to explain how a bicycle pump works. One text used only words, the second had pictures that just showed the parts of the pump system and the steps, and the third (this one improved student learning and recall) showed both the "on" and the "off" states of the pumps with labels for each step, as in Figure 7.9.

The moral of the story? Give students multiple ways to understand—pictures *and* explanations. But don't overload working memory—"package" the visual and verbal information together in bite-size (or memory-size) pieces.

What can you do when students don't have a good base of knowledge? In the early phases of learning, students of any age must grope around the landscape a bit, searching for landmarks and direction. Even experts in an area must use some learning strategies when they encounter unfamiliar material or new problems (Alexander, 1996, 1997; Garner, 1990; Perkins & Salomon, 1989; Shuell, 1990). Mnemonics are memory strategies for getting started.

Mnemonics. Mnemonics are systematic procedures for improving memory (Atkinson et al., 1999; Levin, 1994; Rummel, Levin, & Woodward, 2003). When information has little inherent meaning, mnemonic strategies build in meaning by connecting what is to be learned with established words or images.

The loci method derives its name from the plural of the Latin word *locus*, meaning "place." To use loci, you must first imagine a very familiar place, such as your own house or apartment, and pick out particular locations to serve as "pegs" on which to "hang" memories. For instance, let's say you want to remember to buy milk, bread, butter, and cereal at the store. Imagine a giant bottle of milk blocking the entry hall, a lazy loaf of bread sleeping on the living room couch, a stick of butter melting all over the dining room table, and cereal covering the kitchen floor. When you want to remember the items, all you have to do is take an imaginary walk through your house.

If you need to remember information for long periods of time, an acronym may be the answer. An acronym is a form of abbreviation—a word formed from the first letter of each word in a phrase,

Mnemonics Techniques for remembering; the art of memory.

Loci method Technique of associating items with specific places.

Acronym Technique for remembering names, phrases, or steps by using the first letter of each word to form a new, memorable word.

FIGURE 7.9

Images and Words That Help Students Understand

Is a picture worth 1000 words in teaching? The right combination of pictures and words, like the labelled illustrations here, can make a significant difference in students' learning.

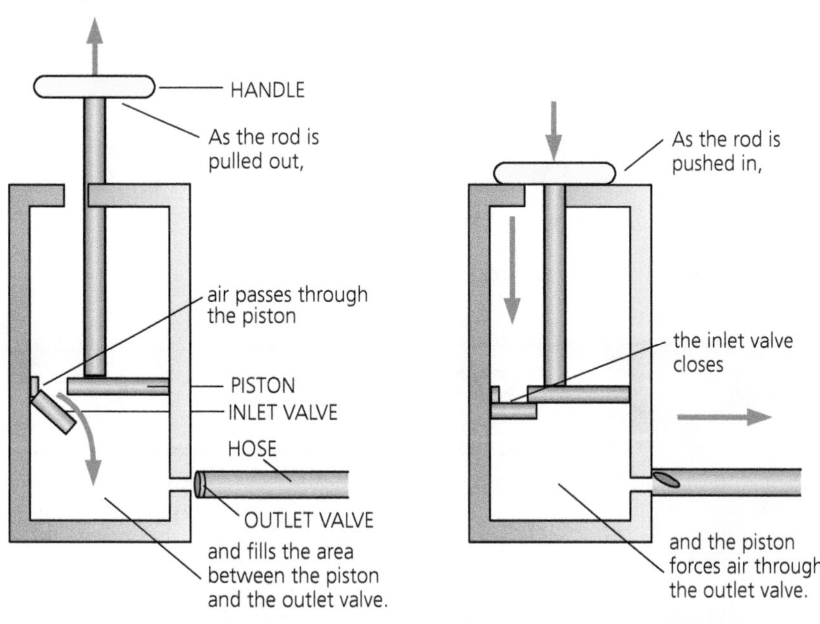

Source: Adapted from *The World Book Encyclopedia*. © 2003 World Book, Inc. By permission of the publisher. www.worldbook.com

for example, HOMES to remember the Great Lakes (Huron, Ontario, Michigan, Erie, Superior). Another method forms phrases or sentences out of the first letter of each word or item in a list, for example, Every Good Boy Does Fine to remember the lines on the G clef—E, G, B, D, F. Because the words must make sense as a sentence, this approach also has some characteristics of chain mnemonics, methods that connect the first item to be memorized with the second, the second item with the third, and so on. In one type of chain method, each item on a list is linked to the next through some visual association or story. Another chain-method approach is to incorporate all the items to be memorized into a jingle such as "*i* before *e* except after *c*."

The mnemonic system that has been most extensively researched in teaching is the keyword method. Joel Levin and his colleagues use a mnemonic (the 3 *Rs*) to teach the keyword mnemonic method:

- *Recode* the to-be-learned vocabulary item as a more familiar, concrete keyword—this plays the role of the keyword.
- *Relate* the keyword clue to the vocabulary item's definition through a sentence.
- *Retrieve* the desired definition.

For example, to remember that the English word *carlin* means *old woman*, you might recode *carlin* as the more familiar keyword *car*. Then, make up a sentence such as *The old woman was driving a car*. When you are asked for the meaning of the word *carlin*, you think of the keyword *car*, which triggers the sentence (or image) about the car and the *old woman*, the meaning (Jones, Levin, Levin, & Beitzel, 2000).

The keyword method has been used extensively in foreign language learning. For example, the French word *carte* (meaning "map") sounds like the English word *cart*. *Cart* becomes the keyword: You imagine a shopping cart being used to move a huge collection of old maps, or you make up a sentence such as "The cart with all the maps tipped over" (Pressley, Levin, & Delaney, 1982). A similar approach has been used to help students connect artists with particular aspects of their paintings. For example, students are told to imagine that the heavy dark lines of paintings by Rouault are made with a *ruler* (Rouault) dipped in black paint (Carney & Levin, 2000, 2002).

Vocabulary learned with keywords can be easily forgotten if students are given keywords and images instead of being asked to supply words and images that are relevant to them. When the

Chain mnemonics Memory strategies that associate one element in a series with the next element.

Keyword method System of associating new words or concepts with similar-sounding cue words and images.

teacher provides the memory links, these associations may not fit the students' existing knowledge and may be forgotten or confused later; as a result, remembering suffers (Wang & Thomas, 1995; Wang, Thomas, & Ouelette, 1992). Younger students have some difficulty forming their own images. For them, memory aids that rely on auditory cues—rhymes such as "Thirty days hath September" seem to work better (Willoughby, Porter, Belsito, & Yearsley, 1999).

Many teachers use a mnemonic system to quickly learn their students' names. Until we have some knowledge to guide learning, it may help to use some mnemonic approaches to build vocabulary and facts. Not all educators agree, however, as you will see in the *Point/Counterpoint* box.

POINT/COUNTERPOINT

What's Wrong With Memorizing?

FOR YEARS, STUDENTS have relied on memorization to learn vocabulary, procedures, steps, names, and facts. Is this a bad idea?

POINT

Rote memorization creates inert knowledge.

Years ago, William James (1912) described the limitations of rote learning by telling a story about what can happen when students memorize but do not understand:

> *A friend of mine, visiting a school, was asked to examine a young class in geography. Glancing at the book, she said: "Suppose you should dig a hole in the ground, hundreds of feet deep, how should you find it at the bottom—warmer or colder than on top?" None of the class replying, the teacher said: "I'm sure they know, but I think you don't ask the question quite rightly. Let me try." So, taking the book, she asked: "In what condition is the interior of the globe?" And received the immediate answer from half the class at once. "The interior of the globe is in a condition of igneous fusion." (p. 150)*

The students had memorized the answer, but they had no idea what it meant. Perhaps they didn't understand the meaning of "interior," "globe," or "igneous fusion." At any rate, the knowledge was useful to them only when they were answering test questions, and only then when the questions were phrased exactly as they had been memorized. Students often resort to memorizing the exact words of definitions when they have no hope for actually understanding the terms or when teachers deduct marks for definitions that are not exact.

Howard Gardner has been a vocal critic of rote memorization and a champion of "teaching for understanding." In an interview in *Phi Delta Kappan* (Siegel & Shaughnessy, 1994), Gardner says:

> *. . . even our better students in our better schools are just going through the motions of education. In* The Unschooled Mind, *I review ample evidence that suggests an absence of understanding—the inability of students to take knowledge, skills, and other apparent attainments and apply them successfully in new situations. In the absence of such flexibility and adaptability, the education that the students receive is worth little. (pp. 563–564)*

COUNTERPOINT

Rote memorization can be effective.

Memorization may not be such a bad way to learn new information that has little inherent meaning, such as foreign language vocabulary. Alvin Wang, Margaret Thomas, and Judith Ouellette (1992) compared learning Tagalog (the national language of the Philippines) using either rote memorization or the keyword approach. The keyword method is a way of creating connections and meaning for associating new words with existing words and images. In their study, even though the keyword method led to faster and better learning initially, long-term forgetting was *greater* for students who had used the keyword method than for students who had learned by rote memorization.

There are times when students must memorize and we do them a disservice if we don't teach them how. Every discipline has its own terms, names, facts, and rules. As adults, we want to work with physicians who have memorized the correct names for the bones and organs of the body or the drugs needed to combat particular infections. Of course, they can look up some information or research certain conditions, but they have to know where to start. We want to work with accountants who give us accurate information about the new tax codes, information they probably had to memorize because it changes from year to year in ways that are not necessarily rational or meaningful. We want to deal with computer salespeople who have memorized their stock and know exactly which printers will work with our computer. Just because something was learned through memorization does not mean it is inert knowledge. The real question, as Gardner points out, is whether you can *use* the information flexibly and effectively to solve new problems.

Rote Memorization. *Very few things need to be learned by rote.* The greatest challenge teachers face is to help students think and understand, not just memorize. Unfortunately, many students, including those featured in the scenario opening this chapter, see rote memorizing and learning as the same thing (Iran-Nejad, 1990).

However, on rare occasions we have to memorize something word-for-word, such as lines in a song, poem, or play. How would you do it? If you have tried to memorize a list of items that are all similar to one another, you may have found that you tended to remember items at the beginning and at the end of the list, but forgot those in the middle. This is called the serial-position effect. Using part learning—breaking the list into smaller segments—can help prevent this effect, because breaking a list into several shorter lists means there will be fewer middle items to forget.

Another strategy for memorizing a long selection or list is the use of distributed practice. A student who studies Hamlet's soliloquy intermittently throughout the weekend will probably do much better than a student who tries to memorize the entire speech on Sunday night. Studying for an extended period is called massed practice. Massed practice leads to cognitive overload, fatigue, and lagging motivation. Distributed practice gives time for deeper processing (Mumford, Costanza, Baughman, Threlfall, & Fleishman, 1994). What is forgotten after one session can be relearned in the next with distributed practice. Table 7.3 gives some other tips for improving your memory.

Rote memorization Remembering information by repetition without necessarily understanding the meaning of the information.

Serial-position effect The tendency to remember the beginning and the end but not the middle of a list.

Part learning Breaking a list of items into shorter lists.

Distributed practice Practice in brief periods with rest intervals.

Massed practice Practice for a single extended period.

TABLE 7.3

Top 10 Tips for a Better Memory

1. *Pay attention.* Often when we "forget" something, it's not that we've lost the memory but that we didn't learn the thing properly in the first place. If you pay full attention to what you are trying to learn, you'll be more likely to remember it later.
2. *Create associations.* Associate what you're trying to learn with other information you already know. For example, while memorizing the periodic table for a chemistry class, it will be easier to remember that Ag = silver if you know that *argentum* is the Latin for "silver." It might also help if you knew that Argentina got its name from early European explorers who thought the region was rich in silver (in fact, the native populations had imported their silver from elsewhere).
3. *A picture is worth a thousand words.* Information such as names and dates is more memorable if you can link it to an image. The effort you expend generating an image strengthens the memory. For example, in an art history course, you might have to remember that Manet specialized in painting figures and his contemporary, Monet, is famous for paintings of haystacks and water lilies. Picture the human figures lined up acrobat-style to form a letter "A" for Manet, and the water lilies arranged in a daisy chain to form the letter "O" for Monet.
4. *Practice makes perfect.* There's a reason kindergarteners drill on their ABCs and elementary school children drill on their multiplication tables. Memories for facts are strengthened by repetition. The same principle holds for memories for skills such as bike riding and juggling: they are improved by practice.
5. *Use your ears.* Instead of just reading information silently, read it aloud. You will encode the information aurally as well as visually. You can also try writing it out; the act of writing activates sensory systems and also forces you to think about the words you're copying.
6. *Reduce overload.* If you're having trouble remembering everything, use memory aids such as Post-It notes, calendars, or electronic schedulers to remember dates and obligations, freeing you to focus on remembering items in situations where written aids won't work—say, during an exam!
7. *Time-travel.* Remembering information for facts doesn't depend on remembering the exact time and place where you acquired it. Nevertheless, if you can't remember a fact, try to remember where you first heard it. If you can remember your high school history teacher lecturing on Napoleon, perhaps what she said about the causes of the Napoleonic Wars will also come to mind.
8. *Get some sleep.* Two-thirds of Americans don't get enough sleep and consequently are less able to concentrate during the day, which makes it harder for them to encode new memories and retrieve old ones (see Tip 1). Sleep is also important for helping the brain organize and store memories.
9. *Try a rhyme.* Do you have to remember a long string of random information? Create a poem (or better yet, a song) that includes the information. Remember the old standard: "'I' before 'E,' except after 'C,' or sounded as 'A,' as in 'neighbour' or 'weigh'"? This ditty uses rhythm and rhyme to make it easier to remember a rule of English spelling.
10. *Relax.* Sometimes trying hard to remember is less effective than turning your attention to something else; often, the missing information will pop into your awareness later. If you are stumped by one question on a test, skip the troublesome question and keep working; come back to it later, and perhaps the missing information won't be so hard to retrieve.

Source: Gluck, M. A., Mercado, E., & Myers, C. E. (2008). *Learning and memory: From brain to behavior.* New York: Worth, p. 3. With permission of Worth Publishers.

EXPERT KNOWLEDGE Driving a car employs both automated basic skills and domain-specific strategies.

Development of Procedural Knowledge

One characteristic that distinguishes experts from novices in every arena, from reading to medical diagnosis, is that the expert's declarative knowledge has become "proceduralized"—that is, incorporated into routines they can apply automatically without making many demands on working memory. Explicit memories have become implicit and the expert is no longer aware of them. Skills that are applied without conscious thought are called automated basic skills. An example is shifting gears in a standard transmission car. At first you have to think about every step, but as you become more expert (if you do), the procedure becomes automatic. But not all procedures can be automatic, even for experts in a particular domain. For example, no matter how expert you are at driving, you still have to consciously watch the traffic around you. This kind of conscious procedure is called a *domain-specific strategy*. Automated basic skills and domain-specific strategies are learned in different ways (Gagné, Yekovich, & Yekovich, 1993).

Automated Basic Skills. Most psychologists identify three stages in the development of an automated skill: *cognitive, associative,* and *autonomous* (Anderson, 2005; Fitts & Posner, 1967). At the *cognitive stage,* when we are first learning, we rely on declarative knowledge and general problem-solving strategies to accomplish our goal. For example, to learn to assemble a bookshelf, we might try to follow steps in the instruction manual, putting a check mark beside each step as we complete it to keep track of progress. At this stage, we have to "think about" every step and perhaps refer back to the pictures of parts to see what a "10-cm metal bolt with locknut" looks like. The cognitive load on working memory is heavy. There can be quite a bit of trial-and-error learning at this stage—for example, if the bolt we have chosen doesn't fit.

At the *associative stage,* individual steps of a procedure are combined or "chunked" into larger units. We reach for the right bolt and put it into the right hole. One step smoothly cues the next. With practice, the associative stage moves to the *autonomous stage,* where the whole procedure can be accomplished without much attention. So if you assemble enough bookshelves, you can have a lively conversation as you do, paying little attention to the assembly task. This movement from the cognitive to the associative to the autonomous stage holds for the development of basic cognitive skills in any area, but science, medicine, chess, and mathematics have been most heavily researched. One thing is clear—it takes many hours of successful practice to make skills automatic.

What can teachers do to help their students pass through these three stages and become more expert learners? In general, it appears that two factors are critical: *prerequisite knowledge* and *practice with feedback.* First, if students don't have the essential prior knowledge (concepts, schemas, skills, etc.), the cognitive load on working memory will be too great. In order to compose a poem in a foreign language, for example, you must know some of the vocabulary and grammar of that language, and you must have some understanding of poetry forms. To learn the vocabulary, grammar, *and* forms as you also try to compose the poem would be too much.

Second, practice with feedback allows you to form associations, recognize cues automatically, and combine small steps into larger condition-action rules or *productions.* Even from the earliest stage, some of this practice should include a simplified version of the whole process in a real context. Practice in real contexts helps students learn not only *how* to do a skill but also *why* and *when* (Collins, Brown, & Newman, 1989; Gagné, Yekovich, & Yekovich, 1993). Of course, as every athletic coach knows, if a particular step, component, or process is causing trouble, that element might be practised alone until it is more automatic, and then put back into the whole sequence, to lower the cognitive load on working memory (Anderson, Reder, & Simon, 1996).

Automated basic skills Skills that are applied without conscious thought.

Domain-Specific Strategies. As we saw earlier, some procedural knowledge, such as monitoring the traffic while you drive, is not automatic because conditions are constantly changing. Once you decide to change lanes, the manoeuvre may be fairly automatic, but the decision to change lanes was conscious, based on the traffic conditions around you. **Domain-specific strategies** are consciously applied skills that organize thoughts and actions to reach a goal. To support this kind of learning, teachers need to provide opportunities for practice in many different situations—for example, they may have their students practise reading with newspapers, package labels, magazines, books, letters, operating manuals, and so on. In the next chapter's discussion of problem-solving and studying strategies, we will examine other ways to help students develop domain-specific strategies. For now, we summarize these ideas for developing declarative and procedural knowledge in the accompanying *Guidelines* box. We will spend quite a bit of time in the next chapter discussing how to develop self-regulatory knowledge.

So far we have talked about attention, knowledge, and memory, without considering individual differences. In the last section of this chapter, we consider diversity and convergence in cognitive learning.

Domain-specific strategies Consciously applied skills to reach goals in a particular subject or problem area.

GUIDELINES: Helping Students Understand and Remember

Make sure you have the students' attention.

EXAMPLES

1. Develop a signal that tells students to stop what they are doing and focus on you. Make sure students respond to the signal—don't let them ignore it. Practise using the signal.
2. Move around the room, use gestures, and avoid speaking in a monotone voice.
3. Begin a lesson by asking a question that stimulates interest in the topic.
4. Regain the attention of individual students by walking closer to them, using their names, or asking them a question.

Help students separate essential from non-essential details and focus on the most important information.

EXAMPLES

1. Summarize instructional objectives to indicate what students should be learning. Relate the material you are presenting to the objectives as you teach: "Now I'm going to explain exactly how you can find the information you need to meet Objective One on the board—determining the tone of the story."
2. When you make an important point, pause, repeat, ask a student to paraphrase, note the information on the board in coloured chalk, or tell students to highlight the point in their notes or readings.

Help students make connections between new information and what they already know.

EXAMPLES

1. Review prerequisites to help students bring to mind the information they will need to understand new material: "Who can tell us the definition of a quadrilateral? Now, what is a rhombus? Is a square a quadrilateral? Is a square a rhombus? What did we say yesterday about how you can tell? Today we are going to look at some other quadrilaterals."
2. Use an outline or diagram to show how new information fits with the framework you have been developing. For example, "Now that you know the duties of the Canadian Space Agency, where would you expect to find it in this diagram of the Canadian government?"
3. Give an assignment that specifically calls for the use of new information along with information already learned.

Provide for repetition and review of information.

EXAMPLES

1. Begin the class with a quick review of the homework assignment.
2. Give frequent, short tests.
3. Build practice and repetition into games, or have students work with partners to quiz each other.

Present material in a clear, organized way.

EXAMPLES

1. Make the purpose of the lesson very clear.
2. Give students a brief outline to follow. Put the same outline on an overhead transparency so you can keep yourself on track. When students ask questions or make comments, relate these to the appropriate section of the outline.
3. Use summaries in the middle and at the end of the lesson.

Focus on meaning, not memorization.

EXAMPLES

1. In teaching new words, help students associate the new word to a related word they already understand: "*Enmity* is from the same base as *enemy*."
2. In teaching about remainders, have students group 12 objects into sets of 2, 3, 4, 5, and 6, and ask them to count the "leftovers" in each case.

For more information on information processing, see **www.edpsycinteractive.org/topics/cogsys/infoproc.html**.

DIVERSITY AND CONVERGENCES IN COGNITIVE LEARNING

Many of the concepts and processes discussed in this chapter—the importance of knowledge in learning and the sensory, working, and long-term memory systems—apply to all students. But there are developmental and individual differences in what students know and how their memory processes are used.

Diversity: Individual Differences and Working Memory

As you might expect, there are both developmental and individual differences in working memory. Let's examine a few.

Developmental Differences. There are three basic aspects of memory: *memory span*, or the amount of information that can be held in working memory, *memory processing efficiency*, and *speed of processing*. As they get older, children can process many different kinds of information—verbal, visual, mathematical, and so on—faster, so increased speed of processing seems to be a general factor of the cognitive system. In addition, the increase in speed with age is the same for North American and Korean children, so increasing processing speed with age may be universal (Kail, 2000; Kail & Park, 1994).

These three basic capacities act together and influence each other—more efficient processing allows greater amounts of information to be held in memory, for example (Demetriou, Christou, Spanoudis, & Platsidou, 2002). You experienced this effect of efficient processing when you remembered BMOLOLPMODNACTV by chunking the letters into BMO LOL PMO DNA CTV. Your more efficient and faster processing expanded your memory span. Young children have fewer strategies and less knowledge, so they have more trouble with memorizing a longer series. But as they grow older, children develop more effective strategies for remembering information. Most children spontaneously discover rehearsal around age 5 or 6 and continue to use it. Also around age 6, most children discover the value of using organizational strategies, and by age 9 or 10, they use these strategies spontaneously. So, given the following words to learn,

couch, orange, rat, lamp, pear, sheep, banana, rug, pineapple, horse, table, dog

an older child or an adult might organize the words into three short lists of furniture, fruit, and animals. Younger children can be taught to use rehearsal or organization to improve memory, but they probably won't apply the strategies unless they are reminded. Children also become more able to use elaboration as they mature, but this strategy develops late in childhood. Creating images or stories to remember ideas is more likely for older elementary school students and adolescents (Siegler, 1998).

Changes in the brain that support memory affect how efficiently memories can be encoded, consolidated, stored, and then retrieved (Bauer, 2006). In terms of strategies, for young children, using a new strategy or operation—such as reaching for a toy, counting, or finding a word—takes up a large portion of their working memory. But once an operation is mastered and becomes more automatic, there is more working memory available for short-term storage of new information (Johnson, 2003). Children may use reasonable but incorrect strategies to solve problems because of their limited memories. They may try to simplify a task by ignoring important information or by skipping steps to reach a correct solution. This puts less strain on memory. For example, when comparing quantities, young children may consider only the height of the water in a glass, not the diameter of the glass, because this approach demands less of their memory. This may explain young children's inability to solve the classic Piagetian conservation problem (Case, 1998). (See Figure 2.3 on page 36.)

DEVELOPMENTAL DIFFERENCES There are several developmental differences in how students process information in working and long-term memory.

So, through changes in the brain, faster processing of information, the development and automating of strategies, and the addition of knowledge, working memory increases in capacity from ages 4 through adolescence (Alloway, Gathercole, & Pickering, 2006; Gathercole, Pickering, Ambridge, & Wearing, 2004). Children are 10 to 11 years old before they have adult-like memories (Bauer, 2006).

Besides developmental differences, there are other individual variations in working memory, and these differences have implications for learning. Try this:

STOP & THINK Read the following sentences and words in capital letters out loud once:

For many years my family and friends have been working on the farm. SPOT
Because the room was stuffy, Bob went outside for some fresh air. TRAIL
We were fifty kilometres out to sea before we lost sight of the land. BAND

Now cover the sentences and answer these questions (be honest):
Name the words that were in capital letters. Who was in the stuffy room? Who worked on the farm?

You have just taken a few items from a test of working memory span (Engle, 2001). The test required you to both process and store—process the meaning of the sentences and store the words (Ashcraft, 2006). How did you do?

Individual Differences. The correlation between scores on a test of working memory span (like the one you just took in the *Stop & Think* exercise above) and the verbal portion of the standardized tests of achievement that American students take to compete for university admission is about .59. But there is no correlation between those test scores and simple short-term memory span (repeating digits). Working memory span is also related to scores on intelligence tests. If a task requires controlled attention or higher-level thinking, then working memory span probably is a factor in performing that task (Ackerman, Beier, & Boyle, 2005; Ashcraft, 2006; Hambrick, Kane, & Engle, 2005; Unsworth & Engle, 2005).

Some people seem to have more efficient working memories than others (Cariglia-Bull & Pressley, 1990; DiVesta & Di Cintio, 1997; Jurden, 1995), and differences in working memory may be associated with giftedness in math and verbal areas. For example, subjects in one research study were asked to remember lists of numbers, the locations of marks on a page, letters, and words (Dark & Benbow, 1991). Subjects who excelled in mathematics remembered numbers and locations significantly better than subjects who excelled in verbal areas. The verbally talented subjects, on the other hand, had better memories for words. Based on these results, Dark and Benbow believe that basic differences in information processing abilities play a role in the development of mathematical and verbal talent.

Diversity: Individual Differences and Long-Term Memory

Features of long-term memory also vary significantly among people. Let's look at three major sources of these differences.

Knowledge. The major individual difference that affects long-term memory is knowledge. When students have more *domain-specific declarative* and *procedural knowledge,* they are better at learning and remembering material in that domain (Alexander, 1997). Think about what it is like to read a very technical textbook in an area you know little about. Every line is difficult. You have to stop and look up words or turn back to read about concepts you don't understand. It is hard to remember what you are reading because you are trying to understand and remember at the same time. But with a good basis of knowledge, learning and remembering become easier; the more you know, the easier it is to know more. This may be why classes in your major seem easier than the required classes outside your major. Another factor could be interest. To develop expert understanding and recall in a domain requires the "continuous interplay of skill (i.e., knowledge) and thrill (i.e., interest)" (Alexander, Kulikowich, & Schulze, 1994, p. 334).

As we have seen throughout this book, because people grow up in different cultural contexts, they have different funds of knowledge (Gonzales, Moll, & Amanti, 2005; Nieto, 2004). Remember the baseball study earlier in this chapter—attention, learning, and memory are supported when teaching builds on the prior knowledge of students.

MyEducationLab
Go to the Teacher Talk section in Chapter 7 of MyEducation Lab and watch a video of Lee-Ann Stephens, 2007 Teacher of the Year from Minnesota, explaining what teaching means to her, and how she is creating memories for her students.

Cultural Differences in Event Memories. Adults provide scaffolding and guide how children talk about the past, present, and future, so memories are socially constructed, as Vygotsky would say. This social construction leads to gender and cultural differences in early memories. As adults, women have earlier, longer, and more detailed first memories than men. Individuals from Western cultures have earlier, longer, and more detailed first memories than people from Asian cultures. One reason suggested by Fivush and Nelson (2004) is that young children's discussions about the past with adults in Western cultures tend to focus on the child's actions (for boys and girls) and feelings (more for girls), whereas Asian parents are less likely to talk about the child separate from the group and tend to downplay emotions such as anger that would interfere with group membership. So when Asian parents reminisce with their children, they tend not to scaffold early memories of the child separate from the group.

Developmental Differences in Event Memories. During the preschool years, children develop an autobiographical or personal memory for the events in their own lives. Their memories begin to include what happened to them and how they felt; for example, "I fell down and *was so embarrassed* because everyone was watching me" (Bauer, 2006, p. 398, emphasis in the original). There are more time markers, such as "last summer" or "at Thanksgiving" (Nelson & Fivush, 2004). There is more detail and description, and maybe even quoted dialogue—"And then I said . . . and then Jamal said . . ." So children develop richer narratives—stories—about their own lives during their preschool years (Bauer, 2006). As these narratives grow, children begin to realize that they might have experienced the past events differently than they remember them—they remember different details or have different feelings compared to others who were there. As they sort out these differences, children are developing their *theory of mind*—the realization that others have different minds, thoughts, feelings, and beliefs (Fivush & Nelson, 2004).

Convergences: Connecting With Families

The last several sections of this chapter have described many ideas for helping students become knowledgeable—memory strategies, mnemonics, and cognitive skills. Some students have an advantage in school because they learn these strategies and skills at home. One way to capitalize on this diversity is to connect with the family in support of the child's learning. The *Family and Community Partnerships Guidelines* box gives ideas for how to work with families to give all your students more support and practice developing these skills.

FAMILY AND COMMUNITY PARTNERSHIPS

GUIDELINES: Organizing Learning

Give families specific strategies to use to help their children practise and remember information.

EXAMPLES

1. Develop "super learner" homework assignments that include material to be learned and a "parent coaching card" with a description of a simple memory strategy—appropriate for the material—that parents can teach their child.
2. Provide a few comprehension-check questions so a family member can review reading assignments and check the child's understanding.
3. Describe the value of distributed practice and give family members ideas for how and when to work skills practice into home conversations and projects.

For a website on high school study skills that might help parents, see **www.mtsu.edu/~studskl/hsindex.html**.

Ask family members to share their strategies for organizing and remembering.

EXAMPLES

1. Create a family calendar.
2. Encourage planning discussions in which family members help students to break large tasks into smaller jobs, to identify goals, and to find resources.

Discuss the importance of attention in learning.

EXAMPLES

1. Encourage families to create study spaces that are away from distractions.
2. Make sure parents know the purpose of homework assignments.

For help with parent involvement, see **www.nea.org/tools/14659.htm**.

SUMMARY TABLE

Elements of the Cognitive Perspective (pp. 234–236)

Contrast cognitive and behavioural views of learning in terms of what is learned and the role of reinforcement. In the cognitive view, knowledge is learned, and changes in knowledge make changes in behaviour possible. In the behavioural view, the new behaviours themselves are learned. Both behavioural and cognitive theorists believe reinforcement is important in learning, but for different reasons. The strict behaviourist maintains that reinforcement strengthens responses; cognitive theorists see reinforcement as a source of feedback about what is likely to happen if behaviours are repeated or changed—that is, as a source of information.

How does knowledge affect learning? The cognitive approach suggests that one of the most important elements in the learning process is the knowledge the individual brings to the learning situation. What we already know determines to a great extent what we will pay attention to, perceive, learn, remember, and forget.

What is the brain's role in cognition? The human brain seems to both affect and be affected by learning. For example, individuals who regularly complete tasks such as taxi driving develop certain parts of the brain. Research also suggests that learning changes communication among neurons. These changes enable children to engage in complex tasks such as integrating past and present experiences by approximately age 7.

Cognitive view of learning A general approach that views learning as an active mental process of acquiring, remembering, and using knowledge.

Domain-specific knowledge Information that is useful in a particular situation or that applies mainly to one specific topic.

General knowledge Information that is useful in many different kinds of tasks or that applies to many situations.

Cognitive Views of Memory (pp. 236–243)

Give two explanations for perception. The Gestalt principles are valid explanations of certain aspects of perception, but there are two other kinds of explanations in information processing theory for how we recognize patterns and give meaning to sensory events. The first is called *feature analysis*, or *bottom-up processing*, because the stimulus must be analyzed into features or components and assembled into a meaningful pattern. The second type of perception, *top-down processing*, is based on knowledge and expectation. To recognize patterns rapidly, in addition to noting features, we use what we already know about the situation and prototypes.

What is working memory? Working memory is both short-term storage in the phonological loop and visuospatial sketchpad, and processing guided by the central executive—it is the workbench of conscious thought. To keep information activated in working memory for longer than 20 seconds, people use maintenance rehearsal (mentally repeating) and elaborative rehearsal (making connections with knowledge from long-term memory). Elaboration rehearsal also helps move new information to long-term memory. The limited capacity of working memory can also be somewhat circumvented by the control process of chunking.

What is cognitive load and how does it impact information processing? Cognitive load refers to the volume of cognitive resources—including perception, attention, and memory—necessary to perform a task. These resources must be devoted not only to organizing and understanding the task, but also to analyzing the solution and ignoring irrelevant stimuli. If cognitive load is high, it can decrease or even inhibit one's ability to perform a task.

Information processing The human mind's activity of taking in, storing, and using information.

Sensory memory System that holds sensory information very briefly.

Perception Interpretation of sensory information.

Bottom-up processing Perceiving based on noticing separate defining features and assembling them into a recognizable pattern.

Gestalt German for *pattern* or *whole*. Gestalt theorists hold that people organize their perceptions into coherent wholes.

Prototype A best example or best representative of a category.

Top-down processing Perceiving based on context and knowledge that jointly predict patterns expected in a situation.

Attention Focus on a stimulus.

Automaticity The ability to perform thoroughly learned tasks without much mental effort.

Working memory The information that you are focusing on at a given moment.

Short-term memory Component of the memory system that holds information for about 20 seconds.

Central executive The part of working memory that is responsible for monitoring and directing attention and other mental resources.

Phonological loop Part of working memory; a memory rehearsal system for verbal and sound information of about 1.5 to 2 seconds.

Visuospatial sketchpad Part of working memory; a holding system for visual and spatial information.

Cognitive load The volume of resources necessary to complete a task.

Intrinsic cognitive load The resources required by the task itself, regardless of other stimuli.

Extraneous cognitive load The resources required to process stimuli irrelevant to the task.

Germane cognitive load Deep processing of information related to the task, including the application of prior knowledge to a new task or problem.

Maintenance rehearsal Keeping information in working memory by repeating it to yourself.

Elaborative rehearsal Keeping information in working memory by associating it with something else you already know.

Chunking Grouping individual bits of data into meaningful larger units.

Decay The weakening and fading of memories with the passage of time.

Long-Term Memory (pp. 243–253)

Compare declarative, procedural, and conditional knowledge. Declarative knowledge is knowledge that can be declared, usually in words or other symbols. Declarative knowledge is "knowing that" something is the case. Procedural knowledge is "knowing how" to do something; it must be demonstrated. Conditional knowledge is "knowing when and why" to apply your declarative and procedural knowledge.

How is information represented in long-term memory, and what role do schemas play? Memories may be explicit (semantic or episodic) or implicit (procedural, classical conditioning, or priming). In long-term memory, bits of information may be stored and interrelated in terms of propositional networks, images, concepts, and schemas. A concept is a category used to group similar events, ideas, objects, or people such as books, students, or cats. Concepts provide a manner of organizing diversity among members of a group. Concepts are often represented by *prototypes* (an ideal example) and *exemplars* (a representative memory). Long-term memories include concepts that enable people to identify and recognize members of a group. To organize propositions, images, and concepts, we have schemas, which are data structures that allow us to represent large amounts of complex information, make inferences, and understand new information.

What learning processes improve long-term memory? The way you learn information in the first place affects its recall later. One important requirement is to integrate new material with knowledge already stored in long-term memory using elaboration, organization, and context. Another view of memory is the levels of processing theory, in which recall of information is determined by how completely it is processed.

Why do we forget? Information lost from working memory truly disappears, but information in long-term memory may be available, given the right cues. Information appears to be lost from long-term memory through time decay (neural connections, like muscles, grow weak without use) and interference (newer memories may obscure older memories, and older memories may interfere with memory for new material).

Long-term memory Permanent store of knowledge.

Declarative knowledge Verbal information; facts; "knowing that" something is the case.

Procedural knowledge Knowledge that is demonstrated when we perform a task; "knowing how."

Self-regulatory knowledge Knowing how to manage your learning, or knowing how and when to use your declarative and procedural knowledge.

Explicit memory Long-term memories that involve deliberate or conscious recall.

Implicit memory Knowledge that we are not conscious of recalling, but that influences behaviour or thought without our awareness.

Semantic memory Memory for meaning.

Propositional network Set of interconnected concepts and relationships in which long-term knowledge is held.

Images Representations based on the physical attributes—the appearance—of information.

Concept A category used to group similar events, ideas, objects, or people.

Defining attribute Qualities that connect members of a group to a specific concept.

Prototype A best example or best representative of a category.

Exemplar An actual memory of a specific object.

Schemas (singular, **schema)** Basic structures for organizing information; concepts.

Story grammar Typical structure or organization for a category of stories.

Episodic memory Long-term memory for information tied to a particular time and place, especially memory of the events in a person's life.

Flashbulb memories Clear, vivid memories of emotionally important events in your life.

Procedural memory Long-term memory for how to do things.

Script Schema or expected plan for the sequence of steps in a common event such as buying groceries or ordering a pizza.

Productions The contents of procedural memory; rules about what actions to take, given certain conditions.

Priming Activating a concept in memory or the spread of activation from one concept to another.

Elaboration Adding and extending meaning by connecting new information to existing knowledge.

Organization Ordered and logical network of relations.

Context The physical or emotional backdrop associated with an event.

Levels of processing theory Theory that recall of information is based on how deeply it is processed.

Spreading activation Retrieval of pieces of information based on their relatedness to one another. Remembering one bit of information activates (stimulates) recall of associated information.

Retrieval Process of searching for and finding information in long-term memory.

Reconstruction Recreating information by using memories, expectations, logic, and existing knowledge.

Interference The process that occurs when remembering certain information is hampered by the presence of other information.

Becoming Knowledgeable: Some Basic Principles (pp. 253–259)

Describe three ways to develop declarative knowledge. Declarative knowledge develops as we integrate new information with our existing understanding. The most useful and effective way to learn and remember is to understand and use new information. Making the information to be remembered meaningful is important and often is the greatest challenge for teachers. Mnemonics are memorization aids: They include approaches such as the loci method, acronyms, chain mnemonics, and the keyword method. A powerful but limiting way to accomplish this is rote memorization, which can best be supported by part learning and distributed practice.

Describe some methods for developing procedural knowledge. Automated basic skills and domain-specific strategies—two types of procedural knowledge—are learned in different ways. There are three stages in the development of an automated skill: cognitive (following steps or directions guided by declarative knowledge), associative (combining individual steps into larger units), and autonomous (accomplishing the whole procedure without paying much attention). Prerequisite knowledge and practice with feedback help students move through these stages. Domain-specific strategies are consciously applied skills of organizing thoughts and actions to reach a goal. To support this kind of learning, teachers need to provide opportunities for practice and application in many different situations.

Mnemonics Techniques for remembering; the art of memory.

Loci method Technique of associating items with specific places.

Acronym Technique for remembering by using the first letter of each word to form a new, memorable word.

Chain mnemonics Memory strategies that associate one element in a series with the next element.

Keyword method System of associating new words or concepts with similar-sounding cue words and images.

Rote memorization Remembering information by repetition without necessarily understanding the meaning of the information.

Serial-position effect The tendency to remember the beginning and the end but not the middle of a list.

Part learning Breaking a list of items into shorter lists.

Distributed practice Practice in brief periods with rest intervals.

Massed practice Practice for a single extended period.

Automated basic skills Skills that are applied without conscious thought.

Domain-specific strategies Consciously applied skills to reach goals in a particular subject or problem area.

TEACHERS' CASEBOOK

The students in your senior history classes seem to equate understanding with memorizing. They prepare for each unit test by memorizing the exact words of the textbook. Even the best students seem to think that the use of flash cards is the only learning strategy possible. In fact, when you try to encourage students to think about history by reading some original sources, debating issues in class, or examining art and music from the time period you are studying, they rebel. "Will this be on the test?" "Why are we looking at these pictures—will we have to know who painted them and when?" "What's this got to do with history?" Even the students who participate in the debates seem to use words and phrases straight from the textbook without knowing what they are saying.

What Would *They* Do?

Here is how two practising teachers responded to the teaching situation described above.

Judith Rutledge

Eastern High School of Commerce, Toronto, ON

I'd recognize the importance of marks, first of all. Frequently, students have to produce a piece of writing that asks them for much more than memorized facts. While memorizing has many advantages, I'd also explore the limitations of using that as a primary learning strategy. In fact, for an interim period, I'd guarantee students their old marks and hold out the possibility of higher ones if they were willing to expand their ways of thinking.

People who are very concerned with marks often have high aspirations. They are also interested in other people who have achieved remarkable goals and in how they did it; it's not hard to demonstrate the advantages of creative and critical thinking and to set up some exercises that let the students experiment deliberately with a variety of thinking techniques. I'd explore the kind of thinking that goes on at the highest levels of human endeavour. We'd look at the factors that go into decision making, intellectual breakthroughs and discoveries, wise government, and good citizenship. Contemporary events invariably offer excellent case studies.

It's also interesting to examine the idea of what constitutes a "fact"—that is, what can be memorized with perfect assurance that it won't subsequently be challenged. Dividing the class into different groups and getting them to present the views of various people involved in a historical moment can be pretty illuminating. It provides an opportunity to think about who writes history; which views and values prevail; and whose voices are not heard at all. This kind of reflection can be very meaningful for students as they wonder about their own position and purpose in the world. They can see that it's fun and ultimately more useful and rewarding than attempting to simply memorize what one textbook has presented. They are in control of their learning, not just blind consumers.

Claire Frankel-Salama

Bishops College, St. John's, NL

Most students are motivated to obtain good marks and, for many, these have been achieved through rote learning. True learning through the association of ideas has not been part of their school experience. Why is this the case? Why is the rote memory approach still the favoured method of "learning"?

In many schools, teachers have to deal with the unpleasant logistical realities of extremely large classes, multiple preparations, heavy course loads, and extracurricular activities. In the interest of expedience, there is a strong emphasis on multiple-choice and factually strict questioning techniques that afford little room for independent thinking and development of good writing skills. In fact, the increased use of standardized testing has served only to exacerbate this problem by precluding more pedagogically sound qualitative forms of evaluation and feedback. Teachers feel increasingly pressured to prepare students for the exam rather than to develop keen, critical minds.

How can we, as educators, deal with these realities and still work toward a more synthetic approach to learning?

Certainly it is valuable to consider an interdisciplinary approach to teaching, especially at the high school level, where courses tend to be taught as separate units. Meetings between departments should take place, and multidisciplinary projects should be encouraged. For example, it may be possible to accommodate a history presentation or essay in a literature, or even a science, assignment. This should not be considered cheating; indeed, such an effort should have the cooperation of all departments involved. In this way, the student begins to realize the impact of science on literature, of music on history, of mathematics on art, and so on. A co-directed paper on socialism in literature will surely have more intellectual impact than a simple research paper in one restricted area.

Another effective way to encourage analysis and synthesis involves the use of authentic documents and oral histories. A reading of Rabelais's recommendation of a good Renaissance education helps us question our own. The study of caricatures from different sources regarding the same historical event deepens understanding of different political viewpoints. A survivor's account of the Triangle Shirtwaist Factory fire helps us "feel" the need for labour reform. A study of socialist art and its relationship to an economic system will explain what the ideology is really about. The comprehension of contextualities will certainly deepen understanding.

Teachers should neither despair nor think that these efforts will bear no fruit. After all, wisdom comes with age and experience. It is not unusual to receive visits or letters from former students thanking a teacher for introducing a particular author, some interesting paintings, a meaningful destination, or previously unheard music. Germination requires a confluence of several seemingly unrelated conditions. Eventually, some seeds will bloom, perhaps even beyond expectations.

8 Complex Cognitive Processes

SuperStock/Stockbyte

TEACHERS' CASEBOOK

WHAT WOULD YOU DO?

This year's class is worse than ever. You assigned a research paper and you are finding that more and more students are using the web for their sources. In itself, using the web is not wrong, but the students appear to be completely uncritical about what they find on the internet. "If it is on the web, it must be right" is the attitude of most students. Their first drafts are filled with quotes that seem very biased to you, but there are no sources cited or listed. It is not just that students don't know how to reference their work. You are more concerned that they cannot critically evaluate what they are reading. And all they are reading is information on the internet!

CRITICAL THINKING

- How would you help your students evaluate the information they find on the internet?
- Beyond this immediate issue, how will you help students think more critically about the subjects you are teaching?
- How will you take into account the cultural beliefs and values of your students as you support their critical thinking?

In the previous chapter, we focused on the development of knowledge—how people make sense of and remember information and ideas. In this chapter, we consider complex cognitive processes that lead to understanding. Understanding is more than memorizing. It is more than retelling in your own words. Understanding involves appropriately *transforming* and *using* knowledge, skills, and ideas. These understandings are considered "higher-level cognitive objectives" in a commonly used system of educational objectives (Anderson & Krathwohl, 2001; Bloom, Engelhart, Frost, Hill, & Krathwohl, 1956). We will focus on the implications of cognitive theories for the day-to-day practice of teaching.

Because the cognitive perspective is a philosophical orientation and not a unified theoretical model, teaching methods derived from it are varied. In this chapter, we will first examine the complex cognitive process of metacognition—using knowledge and skills about learning, motivation, and yourself to plan and regulate your own learning. Next we explore four important areas in which cognitive theorists have made suggestions for learning and teaching: problem solving, creativity, learning strategies and tactics, and critical thinking. Finally, we will consider the question of how to encourage the transfer of learning from one situation to another to make learning more useful.

By the time you have completed this chapter, you should be able to answer these questions:

- What is the role of metacognition in learning and remembering?
- How could you apply new learning strategies and tactics to prepare for tests and assignments in your current courses?
- What are the steps in solving complex problems?
- How can you help students learn from worked-out examples?
- What are the roles of problem representation, algorithms, and heuristics in problem solving?
- How can teachers encourage creativity in their students?
- What are three ways a teacher might encourage positive transfer of learning?

In the previous chapter we saw that there are three types of knowledge: declarative (things that can be "declared"—knowing *that* . . .), procedural (how to do things—knowing *how* . . .), and self-regulatory (knowledge about managing knowledge). Metacognition is the higher-level cognitive process that orchestrates all three kinds of knowledge and skills to accomplish goals, learn, and remember.

METACOGNITION

Look back to Figure 7.1 on page 237. The executive control processes shown in Figure 7.1 guide the flow of information through the information processing system. In Chapter 7 we discussed a number of control processes, including attention, rehearsal, organization, and elaboration. These executive control processes are sometimes called *metacognitive skills* because they can be intentionally used to regulate cognition.

Connect and Extend
Go to the "Connect and Extend" section in Chapter 8 of MyEducationLab to find further content that links to teaching, students' thinking, research, and the news.

Metacognitive Knowledge and Regulation

Donald Meichenbaum, professor emeritus at the University of Waterloo, and his colleagues described metacognition as people's "awareness of their own cognitive machinery and how the machinery works" (Meichenbaum, Burland, Gruson, & Cameron, 1985, p. 5). Metacognition literally means cognition about cognition—or knowledge about knowing and learning. Metacognition is cognition used to monitor and regulate cognitive processes such as reasoning, comprehension, problem solving, and so on (Metcalfe & Shimamura, 1994). Because people differ in their metacognitive knowledge and skills, they differ in how well and how quickly they learn (Brown, Bransford, Ferrara, & Campione, 1983; Morris, 1990).

Metacognition involves all three kinds of knowledge we discussed earlier: (1) *declarative knowledge* about yourself as a learner, the factors that influence your learning and memory, and the skills, strategies, and resources needed to perform a task—knowing what to do; (2) *procedural knowledge* or knowing how to use the strategies; and (3) *self-regulatory knowledge* to ensure the completion of the task—knowing the conditions and when and why to apply the procedures and strategies (Bruning, Schraw, Norby, & Ronning, 2004). Metacognition is the strategic application of this declarative, procedural, and self-regulatory knowledge to accomplish goals and solve problems (Schunk, 2004). Metacognition also includes knowledge about the *value* of applying cognitive strategies in learning (Pressley & Harris, 2006).

Executive control processes Processes such as selective attention, rehearsal, elaboration, and organization that influence encoding, storage, and retrieval of information in memory.

Metacognition Knowledge about our own thinking processes.

Metacognition is used to regulate thinking and learning (Brown, 1987; Nelson, 1996). Three essential skills allow us to do this: planning, monitoring, and evaluating. *Planning* involves deciding how much time to give to a task, which strategies to use, how to start, what resources to gather, what order to follow, what to skim and what to give intense attention to, and so on. *Monitoring* is the real-time awareness of "how I'm doing." Monitoring entails asking, "Is this making sense? Am I trying to work too fast? Have I studied enough?" *Evaluating* involves making judgments about the processes and outcomes of thinking and learning: "Should I change strategies? Get help? Give up for now? Is this paper (painting, model, poem, plan, etc.) finished?" The notion of *reflection* in teaching—thinking back on what happened in class and why, and thinking forward to what you might do next time—is really about metacognition in teaching (Sawyer, 2006b).

Of course, we don't have to be metacognitive all the time. Some actions become routine. Metacognition is most useful when tasks are challenging, but not too difficult. Then, planning, monitoring, and evaluating can be helpful. And even when we are planning, monitoring, and evaluating, these processes are not necessarily conscious, especially in adults. We may use them automatically without being aware of our efforts (Perner, 2000). Experts in a field of study tend to plan, monitor, and evaluate as second nature; they have difficulty describing their metacognitive knowledge and skills (Pressley & Harris, 2006; Reder, 1996).

METACOGNITION Metacognition involves choosing the best way to approach a learning task. Students with good metacognitive skills set goals, organize their activities, select among various approaches to learning, and change strategies if needed.

Sources of Individual Differences in Metacognition

Some differences in metacognitive abilities are the result of development. Younger children, for example, may not be aware of the purpose of a lesson—they may think the point is simply to finish. They also may not be good at gauging the difficulty of a task—they may think that reading for fun and reading a science book are the same (Gredler, 2009). As children grow older, they are more able to exercise executive control over strategies. For example, they are more able to determine if they have understood instructions (Markman, 1977, 1979) or if they have studied enough to remember a set of items (Flavell, Friedrichs, & Hoyt, 1970). Metacognitive abilities begin to develop around ages 5 to 7 and improve throughout school (Flavell, Green, & Flavell, 1995; Garner, 1990). In her work with students in grade 1 and grade 2, Nancy found that asking students two questions helped them become more metacognitive. The questions were "What did you learn about yourself as a reader/writer today?" and "What did you learn that you can do again and again and again?" When teachers asked these questions regularly during class, even young students demonstrated fairly sophisticated levels of metacognitive understanding and action (Perry, VandeKamp, & Mercer, 2000).

Not all differences in metacognitive abilities have to do with age or maturation, however. Some individual differences in metacognitive abilities are probably caused by biological differences or by variations in learning experiences. Students can vary greatly in their ability to attend selectively to information in their environment. In fact, many students diagnosed as having learning disabilities actually have attention disorders (Hallahan & Kauffman, 2006), particularly with respect to completing long tasks (Pelham, 1981). Working to improve metacognitive skills can be especially important for students who often have trouble in school (Schunk, 2008; Swanson, 1990).

You may remember that metacognition includes knowledge about the *value* of using strategies in learning. In the next section we will explore learning strategies.

LEARNING STRATEGIES

Most teachers will tell you that they want their students to "learn how to learn." Years of research indicate that using good learning strategies helps students to learn and that these strategies can be taught (Hamman, Berthelot, Saia, & Crowley, 2000; Pressley & Harris, 2006). But were you taught "how to learn"? Powerful and sophisticated learning strategies and study skills are seldom taught directly until high school or even college or university, so students have little practice with these powerful strategies. In contrast, early on, students usually discover repetition and rote learning on their own, so they have extensive practice with these strategies. And, unfortunately, some teachers think that memorizing is learning (Hofer & Pintrich, 1997; Woolfolk Hoy & Murphy, 2001). This may explain why many students cling to flash cards and memorizing—they don't know what else to do (Willoughby, Porter, Belsito, & Yearsley, 1999).

As we saw in Chapter 7, the way something is learned in the first place greatly influences how readily we remember, and how appropriately we can apply, the knowledge later. First, students must be *cognitively engaged* in order to learn—they have to focus attention on the relevant or important aspects of the material. Second, they have to *invest effort*, make connections, elaborate, translate, invent, organize, and reorganize in order to *think and process deeply*—the greater the practice and processing, the stronger the learning. Finally, students must *regulate and monitor* their own learning—they have to keep track of what is making sense and notice when a new approach is needed. The emphasis today is on helping students develop effective learning strategies and tactics that focus *attention and effort*, *process information deeply*, and *monitor understanding*.

Learning Strategies and Tactics

Learning strategies are flexible outlines for accomplishing learning goals, a kind of overall plan of attack. **Learning tactics** are the specific techniques that make up the plan (Derry, 1989; Winne, 2001). Your *strategy* for learning the material in this chapter might include the *tactics* of using mnemonics to remember key terms, skimming the chapter to identify the organization, and then writing answers to possible essay questions. Your use of strategies and tactics reflects metacognitive knowledge. Using learning strategies and study skills is related to higher grade point averages (GPAs) in high school and persistence in post-secondary education (Robbins et al., 2004). Researchers have identified several important principles about these skills and strategies:

1. Students must be exposed to a number of *different strategies*—not only general learning strategies but also very specific tactics for particular subjects, such as the graphic strategies described later in this section.

Learning strategies General plans for approaching learning tasks.

Learning tactics Specific techniques for learning, such as using mnemonics or outlining a passage.

2. Students should be taught *self-regulatory (conditional) knowledge* about when, where, and why to use various strategies. Although this may seem obvious, teachers often neglect this step. A strategy is more likely to be maintained and employed if students know when, where, and why to use it.
3. Students may know when and how to use a strategy, but unless they also *develop the desire to employ these skills*, general learning ability will not improve. Several learning strategy programs include a motivational training component. In Chapter 11 we look more closely at this important issue of motivation.
4. Students should receive *direct instruction in schematic knowledge*; this is often an important component of strategy training. In order to identify main ideas—a critical skill for a number of learning strategies—students must have an appropriate schema for making sense of the material—they need knowledge. It will be difficult for students to summarize a paragraph about ichthyology, for example, if they don't know much about fish. Table 8.1 summarizes several tactics for learning declarative (verbal) knowledge and procedural skills (Derry, 1989).

Deciding What Is Important. You can see from the first entry in Table 8.1 that learning begins with focusing attention—deciding what is important. But distinguishing the main idea from less important information is not always easy. Often students focus on the "seductive details" or the concrete examples, perhaps because they are more interesting (Gardner, Brown, Sanders, & Menke, 1992). You may have had the experience of remembering a joke or an intriguing example from a lecture, but not being clear about the larger point the professor was trying to make. Finding the central idea is especially difficult if you lack prior knowledge in an area and the amount of new information provided is extensive. Teachers can give students practice in locating signals authors use in textbooks such as headings, bold words, outlines, or other indicators that identify key concepts and main ideas (Lorch, Lorch, Ritchey, McGovern, & Coleman, 2001).

TABLE 8.1 Examples of Learning Tactics

	Examples	Use When?
Tactics for learning verbal information	1. Attention focusing	
	• Making outlines, underlining	• With easy, structured materials; for good readers
	• Looking for headings and topic sentences	• With more difficult materials; for poorer readers
	2. Schema building	
	• Story grammars • Theory schemas • Networking and mapping	• With poor text structure; goal is to encourage active comprehension
	3. Idea elaboration	
	• Self-questioning • Imagery	• To understand and remember specific ideas
Tactics for learning procedural information	1. Pattern learning	
	• Hypothesizing	• To learn attributes of concepts
	• Identifying reasons for actions	• To match procedures to situations
	2. Self-instruction	
	• Comparing own performance to expert model	• To tune or improve complex skills
	3. Practice	
	• Part practice	• When few specific aspects of a performance need attention
	• Whole practice	• To maintain and improve skill

Source: Based on "Putting Learning Strategies to Work," by S. Derry, 1989. *Educational Leadership*, 47(5), pp. 5–6.

Summaries. Creating summaries can help students learn, but students have to be taught how to summarize (Byrnes, 1996; Palincsar & Brown, 1984). Jeanne Ormrod (2004) provides these suggestions for helping students create summaries. Ask students to:

- Find or write a *topic sentence* for each paragraph or section.
- Identify *big ideas* that cover several specific points.
- Find some *supporting information* for each big idea.
- Delete any *redundant information* or unnecessary details.

Begin by asking students to summarize short, easy, well-organized readings. Introduce longer, less organized, and more difficult passages gradually. Ask students to compare their summaries and to discuss what ideas they thought were important and why—that is, to describe their evidence.

Two other study strategies that are based on identifying key ideas are *underlining* texts and *taking notes*.

STOP & THINK How do you make notes as you read? Look back over the past several pages of this chapter. Are any words highlighted? Are there marks or drawings in the margins and, if so, do the notes pertain to the chapter content or are they grocery lists and email addresses?

Underlining and Highlighting. Do you underline or highlight key phrases in textbooks? Underlining and note taking are probably two of the most commonly but ineffectively used strategies among college and university students. One common problem is that students underline or highlight too much. It is far better to be selective. In studies that limited how much students could underline—for example, only one sentence per paragraph—learning improved (Snowman, 1984). In addition to being selective, students also should actively transform the information into their own words as they underline or take notes. Relying on the words of the book isn't enough—connections need to be forged between information in the text and prior knowledge. Diagrams are helpful to illustrate relationships. Finally, students should look for organizational patterns in the material and use them to guide underlining and note taking (Irwin, 1991; Kiewra, 1988).

Taking Notes. Taking good lecture notes is not an easy task. You have to hold the lecture information in working memory; select, organize, and transform the important ideas and themes before the information "falls off" your working memory workbench; and write down the ideas and themes—all while still following the lecture (Peverly et al., 2007). As you fill your notebook with words and try to keep up with a lecturer, you may wonder if taking notes makes a difference. It does, if done well, as the evidence below illustrates:

- Taking notes focuses attention during class. As students record key ideas in their own words, they build memories by translating, connecting, elaborating, and organizing information. Even if students don't review notes before a test, taking them in the first place appears to aid learning, especially for those who lack prior knowledge in an area. Of course, if taking notes distracts a student from actually listening to and making sense of the lecture, then note taking may not be effective (Kiewra, 1989; Van Meter, Yokoi, & Pressley, 1994).
- Notes provide extended external storage that allows you to return and review content. Students who use their notes to study tend to perform better on tests, especially if they take many high-quality notes—more is better as long as you are capturing key ideas, concepts, and relationships, not just intriguing details (Kiewra, 1985, 1989; Peverly, Brobst, Graham, & Shaw, 2003).
- Expert students match notes to their anticipated use and modify strategies after tests or assignments, use personal codes to flag material that is unfamiliar or difficult, fill in holes by consulting relevant sources (including other students in the class), and record information verbatim only when a verbatim response will be required. In other words, they are *strategic* about taking and using notes (Van Meter, Yokoi, & Pressley, 1994).
- To help students organize their note taking, some teachers provide tables or maps. When students are first learning to use these maps, you might fill in some of the spaces for them. If you use maps and tables with your students, encourage them to exchange their filled-in worksheets and explain their thinking to each other.

Visual Tools for Organizing

To effectively take notes and use underlining, you must identify main ideas. In addition, you must understand the *organization* of the text or lecture—the connections and relationships among ideas. Some visual strategies have been developed to help students with this key element (Van Meter, 2001). A concept map is a drawing that charts the relationships among ideas, as shown in Figure 8.1, which is a concept map describing a website for creating concept maps! You may have referred to these interconnected ideas as *webs*. There is some evidence that creating graphic organizers, such as maps or charts, is more effective than outlining when learning from texts (Robinson, 1998; Robinson & Kiewra, 1995). "Mapping" relationships by noting causal connections, comparison/contrast connections, and examples improved recall. To be even more effective, students should compare their filled-in "maps" and discuss the differences in their thinking with each other.

In a review of 55 studies with students—from grade 4 to graduate school—and with subjects ranging from science to statistics to nursing, Simon Fraser University researchers John Nesbit and Olusola Adesope (2006) concluded that, "in comparison with activities such as reading text passages, attending lectures, and participating in class discussions, concept mapping activities are more effective for attaining knowledge retention and transfer" (p. 434). Using concept maps may be effective because students have to be more cognitively engaged to create maps or webs.

Joseph Novak invented concept mapping in the 1970s at Cornell University. Recently he has worked with researchers at the Institute for Human Machine Cognition (IHMC) to develop Cmaps, free downloadable software tools for creating concept maps. Look at Figure 8.1 again to see an example. We know of several students who use these tools—one even planned his dissertation and organized all the reading for his doctoral examinations with tools from the website. Cmaps can be linked to the internet, and students in different classrooms and schools all over the world can collaborate on them.

Concept map A drawing that charts the relationships among ideas.

Cmaps Tools for concept mapping, developed by the Institute for Human Machine Cognition, that are connected to many knowledge maps and other resources on the internet.

FIGURE 8.1 **The Website for the Institute for Human Machine Cognition Cmap Tools at http://cmap.ihmc.us/**

At this site, you can download concept mapping tools to construct, share, and criticize knowledge on any subject.

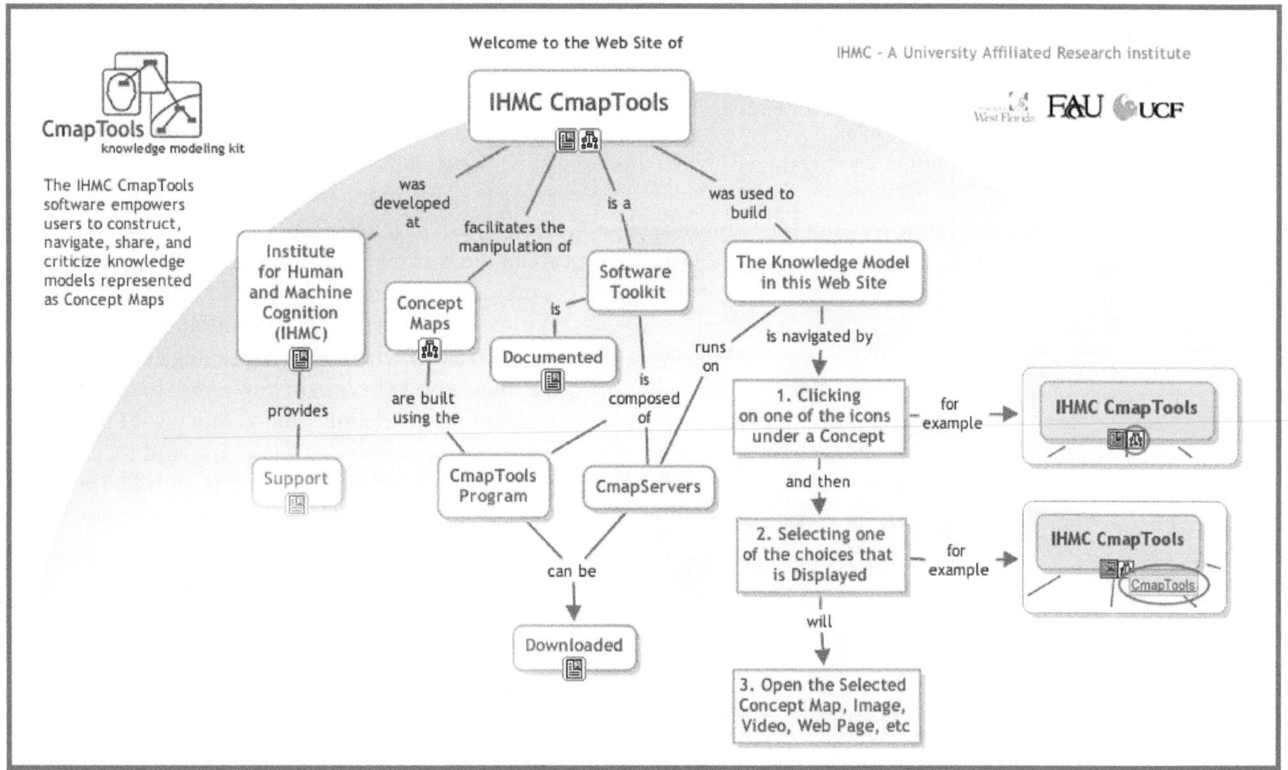

Source: Institute for Human and Machine Cognition Cmap Tools home page. http://cmap.ihmc.us. Reprinted with permission from the IHMC.

There are other ways to visualize organization, such as *Venn diagrams*, which show how ideas or concepts overlap, and *tree diagrams*, which show how ideas branch off each other. *Timelines* organize information in sequence and are useful in classes such as history or geology.

Reading Strategies

As we saw above, effective learning strategies and tactics should help students focus attention, invest effort (elaborate, organize, summarize, connect, translate) so they process information deeply, and monitor their understanding. There are a number of strategies that support these processes in reading. Many use mnemonics to help students remember the steps involved. For example, one strategy for any grade above later elementary is READS, which is described below:

R *Review* headings and subheadings.
E *Examine* boldface words.
A *Ask*, "What do I expect to learn?"
D *Do* it—Read!
S *Summarize* in your own words. (Friend & Bursuck, 2009)

A strategy that can be used in reading literature is CAPS, described below:

C Who are the *characters*?
A What is the *aim* of the story?
P What *problem* happens?
S How is the problem *solved*?

READS A five-step reading strategy: *Review* headings; *Examine* boldface words; *Ask*, "What do I expect to learn?"; *Do* it—Read; *Summarize* in your own words.

CAPS A strategy that can be used in reading literature; involves identifying *characters*, *aim* of story, *problem*, and *solution*.

KWL A strategy to guide reading and inquiry: Before—What do I already *know*? What do I *want* to know? After—What have I *learned*?

Many of the cooperating teachers we work with use a strategy called KWL to guide reading and inquiry in general. This strategy can be used with most grade levels. The steps are as follows:

K What do I already *know* about this subject?
W What do I *want* to know?
L At the end of the reading or inquiry, what have I *learned*?

There are several reasons why strategies such as the ones described above are effective. First, following the steps makes students more aware of the organization of a given chapter. How often have you skipped reading headings entirely and thus missed major clues about the way the information was organized? Next, these steps require students to study the chapter in sections instead of trying to learn all the information at once. This makes use of distributed practice. Creating and answering questions about the material forces students to process the information more deeply and with greater elaboration (Doctorow, Wittrock, & Marks, 1978; Hamilton, 1985).

KWL One cooperative learning strategy used by many teachers to guide reading and inquiry is called KWL: What do I *know*? What do I *want* to know? What have I *learned*?

No matter which learning strategies you want students to use, they have to be taught how to use them. Direct teaching, explanation, modelling, and practice with feedback are necessary. Direct teaching of learning and reading strategies is especially important for students with learning challenges and students whose first language is not English. Marilyn Friend and William Bursuck (2009) describe how one teacher uses modelling and discussion to teach the KWL strategy. After reviewing the steps, the teacher models an example and a non-example of using KWL to learn about "crayons."

Teacher: What do we do now that we have a passage assigned to read? First, I brainstorm, which means I try to think of anything I already know about the topic and write it down.

The teacher writes on the board or overhead known qualities of crayons, such as "made of wax," "come in many colors," "can be sharpened," "several different brands."

Teacher: I then take this information I already know and put it into categories, like "what crayons are made of" and "crayon colors." Next, I write down any questions I would like to have answered during my reading, such as "Who invented crayons? When were they invented? How are crayons made? Where are they made?" At this point, I'm ready to read, so I read the passage on crayons. Now I must write down what I learned from this passage. I must include any information that answers the questions I wrote down before I read and any additional information. For example, I learned that colored crayons were first made in the United States in 1903 by Edwin Binney and E. Harold Smith. I also learned that the Crayola Company owns the company that made the original magic markers. Last, I must organize this information into a map so I can see the different main points and any supporting points.

At this point, the teacher draws a map on the chalkboard or overhead.

Teacher: Let's talk about the steps I used and what I did before and after I read the passage.

A class discussion follows.

Teacher: Now I'm going to read the passage again, and I want you to evaluate my textbook reading skills based on the KWL Plus strategy we've learned.

The teacher then proceeds to demonstrate the strategy *incorrectly*.

Teacher: The passage is about crayons. Well, how much can there really be to know about crayons besides there are hundreds of colors and they always seem to break in the middle? Crayons are for little kids, and I'm in junior high so I don't need to know that much about them. I'll just skim the passage and go ahead and answer the question. Okay, how well did I use the strategy steps?

The class continues to discuss the teacher's inappropriate use of the strategy. Notice how the teacher provides both an example and a non-example—this is a good teaching strategy.

Applying Learning Strategies

One of the most common findings in research on learning strategies is something called production deficiencies—students learn strategies, but do not apply them when they could or should (Pressley & Harris, 2006). To ensure that students actually use the strategies they know, several conditions must be met (Ormrod, 2004). First, of course, the learning task must be appropriate. Why would students use more complex learning strategies when the task set by the teacher is to "learn and return" the exact words of the text or lecture? With these tasks, memorizing will be rewarded and the best strategies involve distributed practice and perhaps mnemonics (described in Chapter 7). But we hope that there are few of these kinds of tasks in contemporary teaching, so if the task is understanding, not memorizing, what else is necessary?

Valuing Learning. The second condition for using sophisticated learning strategies is that students must care about learning and understanding—they must have goals that can be reached using effective strategies (Zimmerman & Schunk, 2001). Anita was reminded of this one semester when she enthusiastically shared with her educational psychology class an article from a newspaper about study skills. The gist of the article was that students should continually revise and rewrite their notes from a course, so that by the end, all their understanding could be captured in one or two pages. Of course, the majority of the knowledge at that point would be reorganized and connected well with other knowledge. "See," she told the class, "these ideas are real—not just trapped in texts. They can help you study smarter in college." After a heated discussion, one of the best students said in exasperation, "I'm carrying 18 hours—I don't have time to *learn* this stuff!" The student did not believe that her goal—to survive all her courses—could be reached by using time-consuming study strategies. In other words, this student did not value learning enough to apply the effort needed to succeed.

Production deficiency When students learn problem-solving strategies, but do not apply them when they could or should.

Effort and Efficacy. The student above also was concerned about effort. The third condition for applying learning strategies is that students must believe the effort and investment required to apply the strategies are *reasonable*, given the likely return (Winne, 2001). And of course, students must believe that they are capable of using the strategies; that is, they must have self-efficacy for using the strategies to learn the material in question (Schunk, 2008). This is related to another condition. Students must have a base of knowledge and/or experience in the area. No learning strategies will help students accomplish tasks that are completely beyond their current understandings.

The *Guidelines* box provides a summary of ideas you can give to students to promote expertise and nourish motivation to become an expert student.

Reaching Every Student: Learning Strategies for Students With Learning Disabilities

For students with learning disabilities, executive control processes that manage metacognitive strategies such as planning, organizing, monitoring progress, and making adaptations are especially important but often underdeveloped (Kirk, Gallagher, Anastasiow, & Coleman, 2006). It makes sense to teach these strategies directly. Some approaches make use of mnemonics to remember the

GUIDELINES: Becoming an Expert Student

Make sure you have the necessary declarative knowledge (facts, concepts, ideas) to understand new information.

EXAMPLES

1. Keep definitions of key vocabulary available as you study.
2. Review required facts and concepts before attempting new material.

Find out what type of test the teacher will give (essay, short answer), and study the material with that in mind.

EXAMPLES

1. For a test with detailed questions, practise writing answers to possible questions.
2. For a multiple-choice test, use mnemonics to remember definitions of key terms.

Make sure you are familiar with the organization of the materials to be learned.

EXAMPLES

1. Preview the headings, introductions, topic sentences, and summaries of the text.
2. Be alert for words and phrases that signal relationships, such as *on the other hand, because, first, second, however, since.*

Know your own cognitive skills and use them deliberately.

EXAMPLES

1. Use examples and analogies to relate new material to something you care about and understand well, such as sports, hobbies, or films.
2. If one study technique is not working, try another—the goal is to stay involved, not to use any particular strategy.

Study the right information in the right way.

EXAMPLES

1. Be sure you know exactly what topics and readings the test will cover.
2. Spend your time on the important, difficult, and unfamiliar material that will be required for the test or assignment.
3. Keep a list of the parts of the text that give you trouble and spend more time on those pages.
4. Process the important information thoroughly by using mnemonics, forming images, creating examples, answering questions, making notes in your own words, and elaborating on the text. Do not try to memorize the author's words—use your own.

Monitor your own comprehension.

EXAMPLES

1. Use questioning to check your understanding.
2. When reading speed slows down, decide if the information in the passage is important. If it is, note the problem so you can reread or get help to understand. If it is not important, ignore it.
3. Check your understanding by working with a friend and quizzing one another.

For more resources on studying, see **www.ucc.vt.edu/stdysk/stdyhlp.html** or **www.d.umn.edu/student/loon/acad/strat**.

Source: From "Research Synthesis on Study Skills" by B. B. Armbruster and T. H. Anderson. *Educational Leadership*, 39. The Association for Supervision and Curriculum Development is a worldwide community of educators advocating sound policies and sharing best practices to achieve the success of each learner. To learn more, visit ASCD at www.ascd.org.

TABLE 8.2

Teaching Strategies for Improving Students' Metacognitive Knowledge and Skills

These eight guidelines taken from Pressley and Woloshyn (1995) should help you in teaching any metacognitive strategy.

- Teach a few strategies at a time, intensively and extensively as part of the ongoing curriculum.
- Model and explain new strategies.
- If parts of the strategy were not understood, model again and re-explain strategies in ways that are sensitive to those confusing or misunderstood aspects of strategy use.
- Explain to students where and when to use the strategy.
- Provide plenty of practice, using strategies for as many appropriate tasks as possible.
- Encourage students to monitor how they are doing when they are using strategies.
- Increase students' motivation to use strategies by heightening their awareness that they are acquiring valuable skills—skills that are at the heart of competent functioning.
- Emphasize reflective processing rather than speedy processing; do all possible to eliminate high anxiety in students; encourage students to shield themselves from distractions so they can attend to academic tasks.

For a list of strategies and how to teach them, see **www.unl.edu/csi/bank.html**.

Source: Adapted from Pressley, M., & Woloshyn, V. (1995). *Cognitive strategy instruction that really improves children's academic performance.* Cambridge, MA: Brookline Books, p. 18.

steps. For example, teachers can help older students use a writing strategy called DEFENDS (Deshler, Ellis, & Lenz, 1996), described below:

- Decide on audience, goals, and position.
- Estimate main ideas and details.
- Figure the best order of main ideas and details.
- Express your position in the opening.
- Note each main idea and supporting points.
- Drive home the message in the last sentence.
- Search for errors and correct.

Of course, you have to do more than just tell students about the strategy—you have to teach it. Michael Pressley and his colleagues (1995) developed the *Cognitive Strategies Model* as a guide for teaching students to improve their metacognitive strategies. Table 8.2 describes the steps in teaching these strategies.

PROBLEM SOLVING

STOP & THINK You're interviewing with the district superintendent for a position as a school psychologist. The superintendent is known for his unorthodox interview questions. He hands you a pad of paper and a ruler and says, "Tell me, what is the exact thickness of a single sheet of paper?"

This is a true story—Anita was asked the paper thickness question in an interview years ago. The answer was to measure the thickness of the entire pad and divide that figure by the number of pages in the pad. She figured out the correct answer and got the job, but what a tense moment that was. Perhaps the superintendent was interested in determining Anita's problem solving ability under pressure!

A problem has an initial state (the current situation), a goal (the desired outcome), and a path for reaching the goal (including operations or activities that move you toward the goal). Problem solvers often have to set and reach subgoals as they move toward the final solution. For example, if your goal is to drive to the beach, but at the first stop sign you skid through the intersection, you may have to reach a subgoal of fixing your brakes before you can continue toward the original goal (Schunk,

Problem Any situation in which you are trying to reach some goal and must find a means to do so.

2008). Also, problems can range from *well-structured* to *ill-structured*, depending on how clear-cut the goal is and how much structure is provided for solving the problem. Most arithmetic problems are well-structured, but selecting the right college or university major is ill-structured—many different solutions and paths to solutions are possible. Life presents many ill-structured problems.

Problem solving is usually defined as formulating new answers, going beyond the simple application of previously learned rules to achieve a goal. Problem solving is what happens when no solution is obvious—when, for example, you can't afford new brakes for the car that skidded on the way to the beach (Mayer & Wittrock, 2006). Some psychologists suggest that most human learning involves problem solving (Anderson, 1993).

There is a debate about problem solving. Some psychologists believe that effective problem-solving strategies are specific to the problem area. That is, the problem-solving strategies in mathematics are unique to math, the strategies in art are unique to art, and so on. The other side of the debate claims that some general problem-solving strategies can be useful in many areas. Actually, there is evidence for both sides of the argument. In their research with 8- to 12-year-olds, Robert Kail and Lynda Hall (1999) found that both domain-specific and general factors affected performance on arithmetic word problems. The influences were *arithmetic knowledge*—assessed by the time needed and errors produced in solving simple addition and subtraction problems—and *general information processing skills*, including reading and information processing time and, to a lesser extent, memory span. Another study in grade 3 found that both specific *arithmetic knowledge* and general *attention-focusing* skills were related to arithmetic problem solving (Fuchs et al., 2006).

It appears that people move between general and specific approaches, depending on the situation and their level of expertise. Early on, when we know little about a problem area or domain, we can rely on general learning and problem-solving strategies to make sense of the situation. As we gain more domain-specific knowledge (particularly procedural knowledge about how to do things in the domain), we consciously apply the general strategies less and less; our problem solving becomes more automatic. But if we encounter a problem outside our current knowledge, we may return to relying on general strategies to attack the problem (Alexander, 1992, 1996; Shuell, 1990).

Let's consider general problem-solving strategies first. Think of a general problem-solving strategy as a beginning point, a broad outline. Such strategies usually have five stages (Derry, 1991; Gallini, 1991; Gick, 1986). John Bransford and Barry Stein (1993) use the acronym IDEAL to identify the five steps:

I *Identify* problems and opportunities.
D *Define* goals and represent the problem.
E *Explore* possible strategies.
A *Anticipate* outcomes and *Act*.
L *Look* back and *Learn*.

We will examine each of these steps because they are found in many approaches to problem solving.

Identifying: Problem Finding

The first step, identifying that a problem exists and treating the problem as an opportunity, begins the process. This is not always straightforward. There is a story about tenants who were angry because the elevators in their building were slow. Consultants hired to "fix the problem" reported that the elevators were no worse than average and that improvements would be very expensive. One day, as the building supervisor watched people waiting impatiently for an elevator, he realized that the problem was not slow elevators, but the fact that people were bored; they had nothing to do while they waited. When the boredom problem was identified and seen as an opportunity to improve the "waiting experience," the simple solution of installing a mirror by the elevator on each floor eliminated complaints.

Identifying the problem is a critical first step. Research indicates that people often hurry through this important step and "leap" to naming the first problem that comes to mind ("the elevators are too slow!"). Experts in a field are more likely to spend time carefully considering the nature of the problem (Bruning, Schraw, Norby, & Ronning, 2004). Finding a solvable problem and turning it into an opportunity is the process behind many successful inventions, such as the ballpoint pen, appliance timer, alarm clock, self-cleaning oven, and thousands of others.

Once a *solvable* problem is identified, what next?

Problem solving Creating new solutions for problems.

Defining Goals and Representing the Problem

Let's take a real problem: The machines designed to pick tomatoes are damaging the tomatoes. What should we do? If we represent the problem as a faulty machine design, then the goal is to improve the machine. But if we represent the problem as a faulty design of the tomatoes, then the goal is to develop a tougher tomato. The problem-solving process follows two entirely different paths, depending on which representation and goal are chosen (Bransford & Stein, 1993). To represent the problem and set a goal, you have to *focus attention* on relevant information, *understand* the words of the problem, and *activate the right schema* to understand the whole problem.

STOP & THINK If you have black socks and white socks in your drawer, mixed in the ratio of four to five, how many socks will you have to take out to make sure you have a pair the same colour (adapted from Sternberg & Davidson, 1982)?

Focusing Attention. Representing the problem often requires finding the relevant information and ignoring the irrelevant details. For example, what information was relevant in solving the above sock problem? Did you realize that the information about the four-to-five ratio of black socks to white socks is irrelevant? As long as you have only two different colours of socks in the drawer, you will have to remove only three socks before two of them have to match.

Understanding the Words. The second task in representing a problem presented as a story is understanding the meaning of the words and sentences (Mayer, 1992). For example, the main stumbling block in representing many word problems is the students' understanding of *part-whole relations* (Cummins, 1991). Students have trouble figuring out what is part of what, as is evident in this dialogue between a teacher and a student in grade 1:

> **Teacher:** Pete has three apples. Ann also has some apples. Pete and Ann have nine apples altogether. How many apples does Ann have?
>
> **Student:** Nine.
>
> **Teacher:** Why?
>
> **Student:** Because you just said so.
>
> **Teacher:** Can you retell the story?
>
> **Student:** Pete had three apples. Ann also had some apples. Ann had nine apples. Pete also has nine apples. (Adapted from De Corte & Verschaffel, 1985, p. 19)

The student interprets "altogether" (the whole) as "each" (the parts). Sometimes, students are taught to search for key words (more, less, greater, etc.), pick a strategy or formula based on the key words (more means "add"), and apply the formula. Actually, this gets in the way of forming a conceptual understanding of the whole problem.

Understanding the Whole Problem. The third task in representing a problem is to assemble all the relevant information and sentences into an accurate understanding or translation of the total problem. This means that students need to form a conceptual model of the problem—they have to understand what the problem is really asking (Jonassen, 2003). Consider the following example.

STOP & THINK Two train stations are 80 kilometres apart. At 2 p.m. one Saturday afternoon, two trains start toward each other, one from each station. Just as the trains pull out of the stations, a bird springs into the air in front of the first train and flies ahead to the front of the second train. When the bird reaches the second train it turns back and flies toward the first train. The bird continues to do this until the trains meet. If both trains travel at the rate of 40 kilometres per hour and the bird flies at 160 kilometres per hour, how many miles will the bird have flown before the trains meet? (Posner, 1973)

Your interpretation of the problem is called a *translation* because you translate the problem into a schema that you understand. If you translate this as a *distance* problem and set a goal ("I have to figure out how far the bird travels before it meets the oncoming train and turns around, then how far it travels before it has to turn again, and finally add up all the trips back and forth"), then you have a very difficult task on your hands. But there is a better way to structure the problem. You can represent it as a question of *time* and focus on the time the bird is in the air. The solution could be stated like this:

> The trains are going the same speed so they will meet in the middle, 40 kilometres from each station. This will take *one hour* because they are travelling 40 kilometres per hour. In an hour, the bird will cover 160 kilometres because it is flying at 160 kilometres per hour. Easy!

Research shows that students can be too quick to decide what a problem is asking. Once a problem is categorized—"Aha, it's a distance problem!"—a particular schema is activated. The schema directs attention to relevant information and sets up expectations for what the right answer should look like (Kalyuga, Chandler, Tuovinen, & Sweller, 2001; Reimann & Chi, 1989).

When students lack the necessary schemas to represent problems, they often rely on surface features of the situation and represent the problem incorrectly, like the student who wrote "15 + 24 = 39" as the answer to the question, "Joan has 15 bonus points and Baljit has 24. How many more does Baljit have?" This student saw two numbers and the word *more*, so he applied the *add to get more* procedure. When students use the wrong schema, they overlook critical information, use irrelevant information, and may even misread or misremember critical information so that it fits the schema. But when students use the proper schema to represent a problem, they are less likely to be confused by irrelevant information or tricky wording, such as *more* in a problem that really requires *subtraction* (Fenton, 2007; Resnick, 1981). Figure 8.2 gives examples of different ways students might represent a simple mathematics problem.

Translation and Schema Training. How can students who lack a good base of knowledge improve their translation and schema selection? To answer this question, we often have to move from general to area-specific problem-solving strategies because schemas are specific to content areas. In mathematics and physics, for example, it appears that in the early stages of learning students benefit from seeing many different kinds of example problems worked out correctly for them. These worked examples reflect all the stages of problem solving—identifying the problem, setting goals, taking steps to the solution, and finally reaching a correct answer (Schworm & Renkl, 2007). The common practice of showing students a few examples, then having students work out many problems on their own, is less effective.

FIGURE 8.2

Four Different Ways to Represent a Problem

A teacher asks, "How many wildlife stamps will Jane need to fill her book if there are three pages and each page holds 30 stamps?" The teacher gives the students supplies such as squared paper, number lines, and place-value frames and encourages them to think of as many ways as possible to solve the problem. Here are four different solutions, based on four different but correct representations.

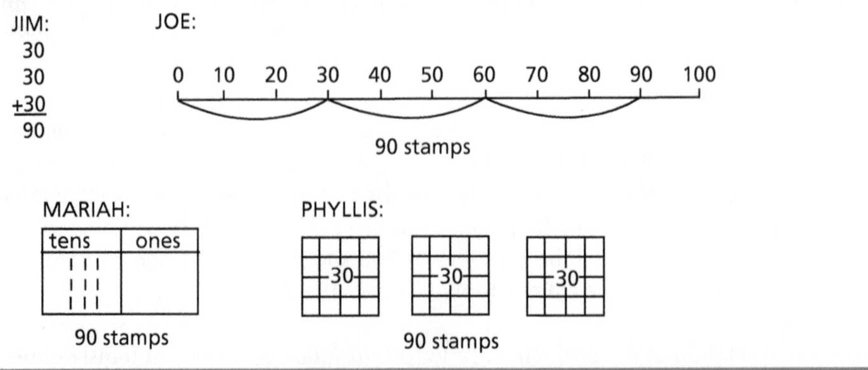

Source: From James E. Schwartz & C. Alan Riedesel, *Essentials of Classroom Teaching: Elementary Mathematics.* Published by Allyn and Bacon, Boston, MA. Copyright © 1994 by Pearson Education. Adapted by permission of the publisher.

Worked examples are useful in other subjects too. Adrienne Lee and Laura Hutchinson (1998) found that undergraduate students learned more when they had examples of chemistry problem solutions that were annotated to show an expert problem solver's thinking at critical steps. In Australia, Slava Kalyuga and colleagues (2001) found that worked examples helped apprentices to learn about electrical circuits when the apprentices had less experience in the area. Silke Schworm and Alexander Renkl (2007) used video examples to help student teachers learn how to make convincing arguments for or against a position.

WORKED EXAMPLES Students benefit from seeing many different kinds of example problems worked out correctly for them, especially when the examples show an expert problem solver's thinking at critical steps.

To get the most benefit from worked examples, however, students have to actively engage with information in the examples—just "looking over" examples is not enough. This is not too surprising when you think about what supports learning and memory. You need to pay attention, process deeply, and connect with what you already know. Students should explain the examples to themselves. This self-explanation component is critical to make learning from worked examples active rather than passive. Examples of self-explanation strategies include trying to predict the next step in a solution, then checking to see if you are right, or trying to identify an underlying principle that explains how to solve the problem. In the study with student teachers, Schworm and Renkl (2007) embedded prompts that required the student teachers to think about and explain elements of the arguments they saw on the tape, for example, "*Which argumentative elements does this sequence contain? How is it related to Kirsten's statement?*"(p. 289). Students have to be mentally engaged in making sense of the examples—self-explanation is one key to engagement (Atkinson & Renkl, 2007; Atkinson, Renkl, & Merrill, 2003).

Another way to use worked examples is to have students compare examples that reach a right answer, but that are worked out in different ways. What is the same about each solution? What is different? Why? (Rittle-Johnson & Star, 2007). Also, worked examples should deal with one source of information at a time rather than having students move between text passages, graphs, tables, and so on. The cognitive load will be too heavy for beginners if they have to integrate many sources of information to make sense of the worked examples (Marcus, Cooper, & Sweller, 1996). But remember, we are talking about students without much knowledge in an area. Students with advanced knowledge improve when they solve new problems. Worked examples can actually interfere with the learning of more expert students (Atkinson & Renkl, 2007).

Familiar examples can serve as analogies or models for solving new problems. But beware. Without explanations and coaching, novices may remember the surface features of an example or case instead of the deeper meaning or the structure. It is the meaning or structure, not the surface similarities, that helps in solving new, analogous problems (Gentner, Lowenstein, & Thompson, 2003). We have heard students complain that the test preparation problems in their math classes were about boats and river currents, but the test asked about airplanes and wind speed. They protested, "There were no problems about boats on the test!" In fact, the problems on the test about wind speed were solved in exactly the same way as the "boat" problems, but the students were focusing only on the surface features. One way to overcome this tendency is to have students compare examples or cases so they can develop a general problem-solving schema that captures the common structure, not the surface features, of the cases (Gentner et al., 2003).

How else might students develop the schemas they will need to represent problems in a particular subject area? Mayer (1983b) has recommended giving students practice in the following: (1) recognizing and categorizing a variety of problem types; (2) representing problems—either concretely in pictures, symbols, or graphs, or in words; and (3) selecting relevant and irrelevant information in problems.

The Results of Problem Representation. There are two main outcomes of the problem representation stage of problem solving, as shown in Figure 8.3. If your representation of the problem suggests an immediate solution, your task is done. In one sense, you haven't really solved a new

FIGURE 8.3 **Diagram of the Problem-Solving Process**
There are two paths to a solution. In the first, the correct schema is activated and the solution is apparent. But if no schema is available, searching and testing may become the path to a solution.

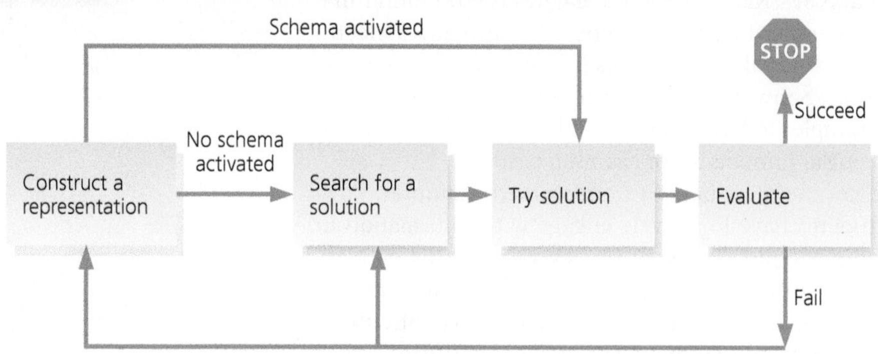

Source: From "Problem-Solving Strategies," by M. L. Gick, *Educational Psychologist*, 21, 1986, p.101. Adapted with permission of Lawrence Erlbaum Associates, Inc. and the author.

problem; you have simply recognized the new problem as a "disguised" version of an old problem that you already know how to solve. This has been called schema-driven problem solving. In terms of Figure 8.3, you have taken the *schema-activated route* and have proceeded directly to a solution. But what if you have no existing way of solving the problem or if your activated schema fails? Time to search for a solution!

Exploring Possible Solution Strategies

If you do not have existing schemas that suggest an immediate solution, then you must take the *search-based route* indicated in Figure 8.3. Obviously, this path is not as efficient as activating the right schema, but sometimes it is the only way. In conducting your search for a solution, you have available two general kinds of procedures: algorithmic and heuristic. Both of these are forms of *procedural* knowledge (Schraw, 2006).

Algorithms. An algorithm is a step-by-step prescription for achieving a goal. It usually is domain-specific; that is, it is tied to a particular subject area. In solving a problem, if you choose an appropriate algorithm (e.g., to find the arithmetic mean, you add all the scores, then divide by the number of scores) and implement it properly, a right answer is guaranteed. Unfortunately, students often apply algorithms unsystematically. They try first this, then that. They may even happen on the right answer but not understand how they found it. For some students, applying algorithms haphazardly could be an indication that formal operational thinking and the ability to work through a set of possibilities systematically, as described by Piaget, is not yet developed.

Many problems cannot be solved by algorithms. What then?

Heuristics. A heuristic is a general strategy that might lead to the right answer. Because many of life's problems (careers, relationships, etc.) are not straightforward and have ill-defined problem statements and no apparent algorithms, the discovery or development of effective heuristics is important (Korf, 1999). Let's examine a few.

In means-ends analysis, the problem is divided into a number of intermediate goals or subgoals, and then a means of solving each intermediate subgoal is figured out. For example, writing a 20-page term paper can loom as an insurmountable problem for some students. They would be better off breaking this task into several intermediate goals, such as selecting a topic, locating sources of information, reading and organizing the information, making an outline, and so on. As they attack a particular intermediate goal, they may find that other goals arise. For example, locating information may require that they find someone to refresh their memory about how to use the library computer search system. Keep in mind that psychologists have yet to discover an effective heuristic for students who are just starting their term paper the night before it is due.

Schema-driven problem solving Recognizing a problem as a "disguised" version of an old problem for which you already have a solution.

Algorithm Step-by-step procedure for solving a problem; prescription for solutions.

Heuristic General strategy used in attempting to solve problems.

Means-ends analysis Heuristic in which a goal is divided into subgoals.

A second aspect of means-ends analysis is *distance reduction*, or pursuing a path that moves directly toward the final goal. People tend to look for the biggest difference between the current state of affairs and the goal and then search for a strategy that reduces the difference. We resist taking detours or making moves that are indirect as we search for the quickest way to reach the goal. So when you realize that reaching the goal of completing a term paper may require a detour of relearning the library computer search system, you may resist at first because you feel as though you are not moving directly and quickly toward your final objective (Anderson, 1993).

Some problems lend themselves to a working-backward strategy, in which you begin at the goal and move back to the unsolved initial problem. Working backward is sometimes an effective heuristic for solving geometry proofs. It can also be a good way to set intermediate deadlines ("Let's see, if I have to submit this chapter in three weeks, then it has to be in the mail by the 28th, so I should have a first draft finished by the 11th").

Another useful heuristic is analogical thinking (Copi, 1961; Gentner et al., 2003), which limits your search for solutions to situations that have something in common with the one you currently face. When submarines were first designed, for example, engineers had to figure out how battleships could determine the presence and location of vessels hidden in the depths of the sea. Studying how bats solve an analogous problem of navigating in the dark led to the invention of sonar.

Analogical reasoning can lead to faulty problem solving, too. When word processors first came out, some people used the analogy of the typewriter and failed to take advantage of the computer's features. They were focusing on the surface similarities. It seems that people need knowledge in both the problem domain and the analogy domain in order to use an analogy effectively (Gagné, Yekovich, & Yekovich, 1993). In addition, they must focus on meaning, not surface similarities, when forming the analogies.

Putting your problem-solving plan into words and giving reasons for selecting it can lead to successful problem solving (Lee & Hutchinson, 1998). You may have discovered the effectiveness of this verbalization process accidentally, when a solution popped into your head as you were explaining a problem to someone else.

Anticipating, Acting, and Looking Back

After representing the problem and exploring possible solutions, the next step is to select a solution and *anticipate the consequences*. For example, if you decide to solve the damaged tomato problem by developing a tougher tomato, how will consumers react? If you take time to learn a new graphics program to enhance your term paper (and your grade), will you still have enough time to finish the paper?

After you choose a solution strategy and implement it, evaluate the results by checking for evidence that confirms or contradicts your solution. Many people tend to stop working before reaching the best solution and simply accept an answer that works in some cases. In mathematical problems, evaluating the answer might mean applying a checking routine such as adding to check the result of a subtraction problem or, in a long addition problem, adding the column from bottom to top instead of top to bottom. Another possibility is estimating the answer. For example, if the computation was 11×21, the answer should be approximately 200, because 10×20 is 200. A student who reaches an answer of 2311 or 32 or 562 should quickly realize these answers cannot be correct. Estimating an answer is particularly important when students rely on calculators or computers, because they cannot go back and spot an error in the figures.

Factors That Hinder Problem Solving

STOP & THINK You enter a room. There are two ropes suspended from the ceiling. You are asked by the experimenter to tie the two ends of the ropes together and are assured that the task is possible. On a nearby table are a few tools, including a hammer and pliers. You grab the end of one of the ropes and walk toward the other rope. You immediately realize that you cannot possibly reach the end of the other rope. You try to extend your reach using the pliers but still cannot grasp the other rope. What can you do? (Maier, 1933)

Fixation. Problem solving requires seeing things in new ways. The rope problem can be solved if you tie the hammer or the pliers to the end of one rope and start swinging it like a pendulum. Then you will be able to catch it while you are standing across the room holding the other rope.

Working-backward strategy Heuristic in which you start with the goal and move backward to solve the problem.

Analogical thinking Heuristic in which you limit the search for solutions to situations that are similar to the one at hand.

Verbalization Putting your problem-solving plan and its logic into words.

You can use the weight of the tool to make the rope come to you instead of trying to stretch the rope. People often fail to solve this problem, because they fixate on conventional uses for materials. This difficulty is called functional fixedness (Duncker, 1945). In your everyday life, you may often exhibit functional fixedness. Suppose a screw on a dresser-drawer handle is loose. Will you spend 10 minutes searching for a screwdriver or will you fix it with a ruler edge or a dime?

Another kind of fixation that blocks effective problem solving is response set, getting stuck on one way of representing a problem. Try this:

> In each of the four matchstick arrangements below, move only one stick to change the equation so that it represents a true equality such as V = V.
>
> V = VII   VI = XI   XII = VII   VI = II

You probably figured out how to solve the first example quite quickly. You simply move one matchstick from the right side over to the left to make VI = VI. Examples two and three can also be solved without too much difficulty by moving one stick to change the V to an X or vice versa. But the fourth example (taken from Raudsepp & Haugh, 1977) probably has you stumped. To solve this problem, you must change your response set or switch schemas, because what has worked for the first three problems will not work this time. The answer here lies in changing from Roman numerals to Arabic numbers and using the concept of square root. By overcoming response set, you can move one matchstick from the right to the left to form the symbol for square root; the solution reads $\sqrt{1} = 1$, which is simply the symbolic way of saying that the square root of 1 equals 1. Recently, a creative reader of this text emailed some other solutions. Jamaal Allan, then a master's student at Pacific University, pointed out that you could use any of the matchsticks to change the = sign to ≠. Then, the last example would be V ≠ II or 5 does not equal 2, an accurate statement. He suggested that you also might move one matchstick to change = to < (less than) or > (greater than), and the statements would still be true (but not equalities as specified in the problem above). Bill Wetta, a student at Ashland University, offered another solution that used both Arabic and Roman numerals. You can move one matchstick to make the first V an X. Then VI = II becomes XI = II, or eleven (in Roman numerals) equals 11 (in Arabic numerals). Can you come up with any other solutions?

Some Problems With Heuristics. We often apply heuristics automatically to make quick judgments; that saves us time in everyday problem solving. The mind can react automatically and instantaneously, but the price we often pay for this efficiency may be bad problem solving, which can be costly. Making judgments by invoking stereotypes leads even smart people to make poor decisions. For example, we might use representativeness heuristics to make judgments about possibilities based on our prototypes—what we think is representative of a category. Consider this:

> If I ask you whether a slim, short stranger who enjoys poetry is more likely to be a truck driver or a university classics professor, what would you say?

You might be tempted to answer based on your prototypes of truck drivers or professors. But consider the odds. Depending how you count, there are about 200 universities and colleges in Canada with perhaps an average of 2 or so classics professors per school. So, we have 400 professors. Say about 20 percent are both short and slim—that's 80; and half of those like poetry—we are left with 40. Suppose there are 200 000 truck drivers in Canada. If only 1 in every 1000 of those truck drivers were short, slim, poetry lovers, we have 200 truck drivers who fit the description. With 40 professors versus 200 truck drivers, it's five times more likely that our stranger is a truck driver (Myers, 2005).

Teachers and students are busy people, and they often base their decisions on what they have in their minds at the time. When judgments are based on the availability of information in our memories, we are using the availability heuristic. If instances of events come to mind easily, we think they are common occurrences, but that is not necessarily the case; in fact, it is often wrong. People remember vivid stories and quickly come to believe that such events are the norm, but again, they often are wrong. For example, you may have been surprised to read in Chapter 4 that accelerating gifted students' pace through the grades does not undermine their social development. Data may not support a judgment, but belief perseverance, or the tendency to hold on to our beliefs, even in the face of contradictory evidence, may make us resist change.

The confirmation bias is the tendency to search for information that confirms our ideas and beliefs: this arises from our eagerness to find a good solution. You have often heard the saying

Functional fixedness Inability to use objects or tools in a new way.

Response set Rigidity; tendency to respond in the most familiar way.

Representativeness heuristic Judging the likelihood of an event based on how well the events match your prototypes—what you think is representative of the category.

Availability heuristic Judging the likelihood of an event based on what is available in your memory; assuming those easily remembered events are common.

Belief perseverance The tendency to hold on to beliefs, even in the face of contradictory evidence.

Confirmation bias Seeking information that confirms our choices and beliefs, while disconfirming evidence.

"Don't confuse me with the facts." This aphorism captures the essence of the confirmation bias. Most people seek evidence that supports their ideas more readily than they search for facts that might refute them (Myers, 2005). For example, once you decide to buy a certain car, you are likely to notice reports about the good features of the car you chose, not the good news about the cars you rejected. Our automatic use of heuristics to make judgments, our eagerness to confirm what we like to believe, and our tendency to explain away failure combine to generate *overconfidence*. Students usually are overconfident about how quickly they can write their papers; it typically takes twice as long as they estimate (Buehler, Griffith, & Ross, 1994). In spite of their underestimation of their completion time, they remain overly confident of their next prediction.

The Importance of Flexibility. Functional fixedness, response set, the confirmation bias, and belief perseverance point to the importance of flexibility in understanding problems. If you get started with an inaccurate or inefficient representation of the true problem, it will be difficult—or at least very time-consuming—to reach a solution. Sometimes, it is helpful to "play" with the problem. Ask yourself, "What do I know? What do I need to know to answer this question? Can I look at this problem in other ways?" Try to think conditionally rather than rigidly, and divergently rather than convergently. Ask "What could this be?" instead of "What is it?" (Benjafield, 1992).

If you open your mind to multiple possibilities, you may have what the Gestalt psychologists called an insight. **Insight** is the sudden reorganization or reconceptualization of a problem that clarifies the problem and suggests a feasible solution. The supervisor described earlier, who suddenly realized that the problem in his building was not slow elevators but impatient, bored tenants, had an insight that allowed him to reach the solution of installing mirrors by the elevators. The *Guidelines* box gives some ideas for how to help students become good problem solvers.

Expert Knowledge and Problem Solving

Most psychologists agree that effective problem solving is based on an ample store of knowledge about the problem area. In order to solve the matchstick problem, for example, you had to understand Roman and Arabic numbers as well as the concept of square root. You also had to know that the square root of 1 is 1. Let's take a moment to examine this expert knowledge.

Insight Sudden realization of a solution.

GUIDELINES: Problem Solving

Ask students if they are sure they understand the problem.

EXAMPLES

1. Can they separate relevant from irrelevant information?
2. Are they aware of the assumptions they are making?
3. Can they visualize the problem by diagramming or drawing it?
4. Can they explain the problem to someone else? What would a good solution look like?

Encourage attempts to see the problem from different angles.

EXAMPLES

1. Suggest several different possibilities yourself, and then ask students to offer some.
2. Give students practice in taking and defending different points of view on an issue.

Let students do the thinking; don't just hand them solutions.

EXAMPLES

1. Offer individual problems as well as group problems, so that each student has the chance to practise.
2. Give partial credit if students have good reasons for "wrong" solutions to problems.
3. If students are stuck, resist the temptation to give too many clues. Let them think about the problem overnight.

Help students develop systematic ways of considering alternatives.

EXAMPLES

1. Think out loud as you solve problems.
2. Ask, "What would happen if . . . ?"
3. Keep a list of suggestions.

Teach heuristics.

EXAMPLES

1. Use analogies to solve the problem of limited parking in the downtown area. How are other "storage" problems solved?
2. Use the working backward strategy to plan a party.

For more resources on problem solving, see **www.hawaii.edu/suremath/home.html**.

Memory for Patterns. The modern study of expertise began with investigations of chess masters (Simon & Chase, 1973). Results indicated that chess masters can quickly recognize about 50 000 different arrangements of chess pieces. They can look at one of these patterns for a few seconds and remember where every piece on the board was placed. It is as though they have a "vocabulary" of 50 000 patterns. Michelene Chi (1978) demonstrated that chess experts in grades 3 through 8 had a similar ability to remember chess piece arrangements. For all the masters, patterns of chess pieces are like words. If you were shown a word from your vocabulary store for just a few seconds, you would be able to remember every letter in the word in the right order (assuming you could spell the word).

But a series of letters arranged randomly is hard to remember, as you saw in Chapter 7. An analogous situation holds for chess masters. When chess pieces are placed on a board randomly, masters are no better than average players at remembering the positions of the pieces. The master's memory is for patterns that make sense or could occur in a game.

A similar phenomenon occurs in other fields. There may be an intuition about how to solve a problem based on recognizing patterns and knowing the "right moves" for those patterns. Experts in physics, for example, organize their knowledge around central principles, whereas beginners organize their smaller amounts of physics knowledge around the specific details stated in the problems (Ericsson, 1999). For instance, when asked to sort physics problems from a textbook in any way they wanted, novices sorted based on superficial features such as the kind of apparatus mentioned—a lever or a pulley—whereas the experts grouped problems according to the underlying physics principle needed to solve the problem, such as Boyle's or Newton's laws (Fenton, 2007; Hardiman, Dufresne, & Mestre, 1989).

Procedural Knowledge. In addition to representing a problem very quickly, experts know what to do next and can do it. They have a large store of *productions* or if-then schemas about what action to take in various situations. Thus, the steps of understanding the problem and choosing a solution happen simultaneously and fairly automatically (Ericsson & Charness, 1999). Of course, this means that they must have many, many schemas available. A large part of becoming an expert is simply acquiring a great store of *domain knowledge* or knowledge that is particular to a field (Alexander, 1992). To do this, you must encounter many different kinds of problems in that field, see problems solved by others, and practise solving many yourself. Some estimates are that it takes 10 years or 10 000 hours of deliberate, focused, sustained practice to become an expert in most fields (Ericsson & Charness, 1994; Simon, 1995).

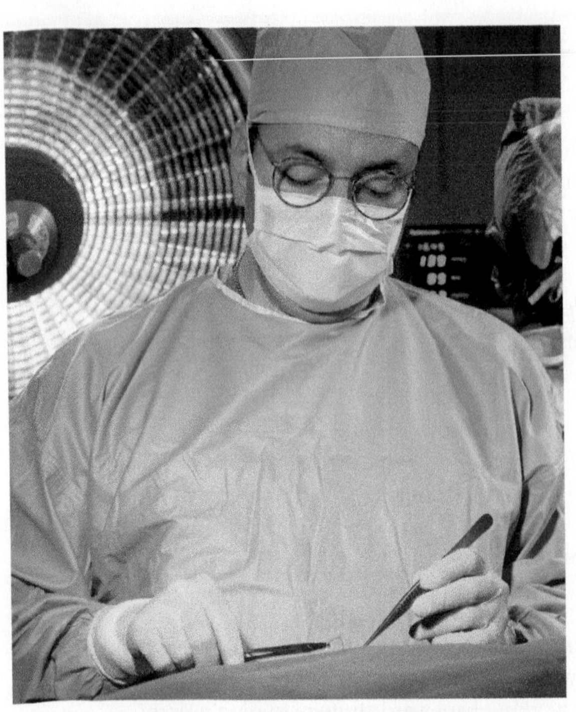

EXPERT KNOWLEDGE A large part of becoming an expert is simply acquiring a great store of domain knowledge or knowledge that is particular to a field. This surgeon has likely invested years of deliberate, focused, sustained practice to become an expert in his field.

Organization. Experts' rich store of knowledge is *elaborated* and *well practised*, so that it is easy to retrieve from long-term memory when needed (Anderson, 1993). Experts can use their extensive knowledge to *organize* information for easier learning and retrieval. In one study, grade 4 students who were soccer experts learned and remembered far more new soccer terms than peers who had little knowledge of soccer, even though the abilities of the two groups to learn and remember non-soccer terms were the same. The soccer experts organized and clustered the soccer terms to aid in recall (Schneider & Bjorklund, 1992). Even very young children who are experts on a topic can use strategies to organize their knowledge. A good example of the use of category knowledge about dinosaurs was provided by Anita's nephews, Lucas and Geoffrey (4 and 3 years old at the time). They promptly ran down the list of large and small plant- and meat-eating dinosaurs (their organizing categories), from the well-known stegosaurus (large, plant eater) to the less familiar ceolophysis (small, meat eater).

Monitoring. With organization comes planning and monitoring. Experts spend more time analyzing problems, drawing diagrams, breaking large problems down into subproblems, and making plans. Whereas a novice might begin immediately—writing equations for a physics problem or drafting the first paragraph of a paper, experts plan out the whole solution and often make the task simpler in the process. As they work, experts monitor progress, so time is not lost pursuing dead ends or weak ideas (Schunk, 2008).

Chi, Glaser, and Farr (1988) summarize the superior capabilities of experts. Experts (1) perceive large, meaningful patterns in given information,

(2) perform tasks quickly and with few errors, (3) deal with problems at a deeper level, (4) hold more information in working and long-term memories, (5) take a great deal of time to analyze a given problem, and (6) are better at monitoring their performance. When the area of problem solving is fairly well defined, such as chess or physics or computer programming, then these skills of expert problem solvers hold fairly consistently. But when the problem-solving area is less well defined and has fewer clear underlying principles, such as problem solving in economics or psychology, then the differences between experts and novices are not as clear-cut (Alexander, 1992).

CREATIVITY AND CREATIVE PROBLEM SOLVING

STOP & THINK Consider this student: He had severe dyslexia—a learning disability that made reading and writing exceedingly difficult. He described himself as an "underdog." In school, he knew that if the reading assignment would take others an hour to complete, he had to allow two or three hours. He knew that he had to keep a list of all his most frequently misspelled words in order to be able to write at all. He spent hours alone in his room. Would you expect this student's writing to be creative? Why or why not?

The person described in the box above is John Irving, celebrated author of what one critic called "wildly inventive" novels such as *The World According to Garp*, *The Cider House Rules*, and *A Prayer for Owen Meany* (Amabile, 2001). How do we explain his amazing creativity? What is creativity?

Defining Creativity

Let's start with what creativity is not. Here are four myths about creativity (Plucker, Beghetto, & Dow, 2004):

1. **People are born creative.** Actually, years of research show that creativity can be developed, enhanced, and supported by the individual's or group's environment.
2. **Creativity is intertwined with negative qualities.** It is true that some creative people are nonconforming or that some may have mental or emotional problems, but so do many people who are not creative. The danger with this myth is that teachers may expect creative students to be troublemakers and treat these students in a biased way (Scott, 1999).
3. **Creativity is a fuzzy, soft construct.** In contrast to seeing a creative person as mentally unbalanced, some people think creative individuals are wildly eccentric. Actually, even though creative people may be open to new experiences and may be generally nonconforming, they also may be focused, organized, and flexible.
4. **Creativity is enhanced within a group.** It is true that brainstorming in a group can lead to creative ideas, but these group efforts tend to be more creative if individuals brainstorm on their own first.

So what is creativity? Creativity is the ability to produce work that is original, but still appropriate and useful (Berk, 2005). Most psychologists agree that there is no such thing as "all-purpose creativity"; people are creative *in a particular area*, as John Irving is in writing fiction. But to be creative, the "invention" must be intended. An accidental spilling of paint that produces a novel design is not creative unless the artist recognizes the potential of the "accident" or uses the spilling technique intentionally to create new works (Weisberg, 1993). Although we frequently associate the arts with creativity, any subject can be approached in a creative manner.

A definition that combines many aspects of creativity (Plucker et al., 2004) suggests that creativity

- often involves more than one person,
- happens when people apply their abilities as part of a helpful process in a supportive environment, and
- results in an identifiable product that is new and useful in a particular culture or situation.

Creativity Imaginative, original thinking or problem solving.

SOCIAL ACCEPTANCE OF CREATIVITY History is filled with examples of creative breakthroughs rejected in their time (for example, Galileo's theory of the sun's position at the centre of the solar system). Is today's society ready to welcome creative contributions in the field of alternative energies?

What Are the Sources of Creativity?

Researchers have studied cognitive processes, personality factors, motivational patterns, and background experiences to explain creativity (Simonton, 2000). But to truly understand creativity, we must look at the social environment too. Both intrapersonal (cognition, personality) and social factors support creativity (Amabile, 1996, 2001; Simonton, 2000). Teresa Amabile (1996) proposes a three-component model of creativity. In her view, individuals or groups must have the following attributes to be creative:

1. *Domain-relevant skills* including talents and competencies that are valuable for working in the domain. An example would be Michelangelo's skills in shaping stone, developed when he lived with a stonecutter's family as a child.
2. *Creativity-relevant processes* including work habits and personality traits such as a John Irving's habit of working 10-hour days to write and rewrite and rewrite until he perfected his stories.
3. *Intrinsic task motivation* or a deep curiosity and fascination with the task. This aspect of creativity can be greatly influenced by the social environment (as we will see in Chapter 11), and by supporting autonomy, stimulating curiosity, encouraging fantasy, and providing challenge.

Another social factor that influences creativity is whether the field is ready and willing to acknowledge the creative contribution (Nakamura & Csikszentmihalyi, 2001). History is filled with examples of creative breakthroughs rejected at the time (for example, Galileo's theory of the sun's position at the centre of the solar system) and of rivalries between creators that led each to push the edges of creativity (for example, the friendly and productive rivalry between Picasso and Matisse).

Creativity and Cognition. Having a rich store of knowledge in an area is the basis for creativity, but something more is needed. For many problems, that "something more" is the ability to break set—restructuring the problem to see things in a new way, which leads to a sudden insight. Often this happens when a person has struggled with a problem or project and then sets it aside for a while. Some psychologists believe that time away from the problem allows for *incubation*, a kind of unconscious working through of the problem. It is more likely that leaving the problem for a time interrupts rigid ways of thinking so you can restructure your view of the situation (Gleitman, Fridlund, & Reisberg, 1999). So it seems that creativity requires extensive knowledge, flexibility, and the continual reorganizing of ideas. And we have seen that motivation, persistence, and social support play important roles in the creative process as well.

Assessing Creativity

STOP & THINK How many uses can you list for a brick? Take a moment and brainstorm—write down as many as you can.

Like the author John Irving, Paul Torrance also had a learning disability; he became interested in educational psychology when he was a high school English teacher (Neumeister & Cramond, 2004). Torrance was known as the "father of creativity." He developed two types of creativity tests: verbal and graphic (Torrance, 1972; Torrance & Hall, 1980). In the verbal test, you might be instructed to think of as many uses as possible for a brick (as you did above) or be asked how a particular toy might be changed to make it more fun. On the graphic test, you might be given 30 circles and be asked to create 30 different drawings, with each drawing including at least one circle. Figure 8.4 shows the creativity of an 8-year-old girl in completing this task.

Restructuring Conceiving a problem in a new or different way.

Divergent thinking Coming up with many possible solutions.

Convergent thinking Narrowing possibilities to a single answer.

These tests require divergent thinking, an important component of many conceptions of creativity. Divergent thinking is the ability to propose many different ideas or answers. Convergent thinking is the more common ability to identify only one answer. Responses to all these creativity tasks are scored for originality, fluency, and flexibility—three aspects of divergent thinking. *Originality* is usually

FIGURE 8.4 **A Graphic Assessment of the Creativity of an 8-Year-Old**

The titles she gave her drawings, from left to right, are as follows: "Dracula," "one-eyed monster," "pumpkin," "hula-hoop," "poster," "wheelchair," "earth," "moon," "planet," "movie camera," "sad face," "picture," "stoplight," "beach ball," "the letter O," "car," "glasses."

Source: "A Graphic Assessment of the Creativity of an Eight-Year-Old," from *The Torrance Test of Creative Thinking* by E.P. Torrance, 1986, 2000. Reprinted with permission of Scholastic Testing Service, Inc., Bensonville, IL 60106 USA.

determined statistically. To be original, a response must be given by fewer than 5 or 10 people out of every 100 who take the test. *Fluency* is the number of different responses. *Flexibility* is generally measured by the number of different categories of responses. For instance, if you listed 20 uses of a brick, but each was to build something, your fluency score might be high, but your flexibility score would be low. Of the three measures, fluency—the number of responses—is the best predictor of divergent thinking, but there is more to real-life creativity than divergent thinking (Plucker et al., 2004).

Teachers are not always the best judges of creativity. In fact, Torrance (1972) reports data from a 12-year follow-up study indicating no relationship between teachers' judgments of their students' creative abilities and the actual creativity these students revealed in their adult lives. A few possible indicators of creativity in students are curiosity, concentration, adaptability, high energy, humour (sometimes bizarre), independence, playfulness, nonconformity, risk taking, attraction to the complex and mysterious, willingness to fantasize and daydream, intolerance for boredom, and inventiveness (Sattler, 1992).

Creativity in the Classroom

Today's and tomorrow's complex problems require creative solutions. And creativity is important for an individual's psychological, physical, social, and career success (Plucker et al., 2004). How can teachers promote creative thinking? All too often, in the crush of day-to-day classroom life, teachers stifle creative ideas without realizing what they are doing. Teachers are in an excellent position to encourage or discourage creativity through their acceptance or rejection of the unusual and imaginative. The *Guidelines* box on page 290, adapted from Fleith (2000) and Sattler (1992), describes other possibilities for encouraging creativity in the classroom.

Agnes is able to think divergently.
By permission of Tony Cochran and Creative Syndicate, Inc.

GUIDELINES: Encouraging Creativity

Accept and encourage divergent thinking.

EXAMPLES

1. During class discussion, ask, "Can anyone suggest a different way of looking at this question?"
2. Reinforce attempts at unusual solutions to problems, even if the final product is not perfect.
3. Offer choices in topics for projects or modes of presentation (written, oral, visual or graphic, using technology).

Tolerate dissent.

EXAMPLES

1. Ask students to support dissenting opinions.
2. Make sure nonconforming students receive an equal share of classroom privileges and rewards.

Encourage students to trust their own judgment.

EXAMPLES

1. When students ask questions you think they can answer, rephrase or clarify the questions and direct them back to the students.
2. Give ungraded assignments from time to time.

Emphasize that everyone is capable of creativity in some form.

EXAMPLES

1. Avoid describing the feats of great artists or inventors as if they were superhuman accomplishments.
2. Recognize creative efforts in each student's work. Have a separate grade for originality on some assignments.

Provide time, space, and materials to support creative projects.

EXAMPLES

1. Collect "found" materials for collages and creations—buttons, stones, shells, paper, fabric, beads, seeds, drawing tools, clay—try asking flea markets and friends for donations. Have mirrors and pictures for drawing faces.
2. Make a well-lighted space available where children can work on projects, leave them, and come back to finish them.
3. Follow up on memorable occasions (field trips, news events, holidays) with opportunities to draw, write, or make music.

Be a stimulus for creative thinking.

EXAMPLES

1. Use a class brainstorming session whenever possible.
2. Model creative problem solving by suggesting unusual solutions for class problems.
3. Encourage students to delay judging a particular suggestion for solving a problem until all the possibilities have been considered.

For more ideas, see **http://ceep.crc.uiuc.edu/eecearchive/digests/1995/edward95.html**.

Source: Adapted from Fleith (2000) and Sattler (1992).

In addition to encouraging creativity through everyday interactions with students, teachers can try brainstorming. The basic tenet of brainstorming is to separate the process of creating ideas from the process of evaluating them because evaluation often inhibits creativity (Osborn, 1963). Evaluation, discussion, and criticism are postponed until all possible suggestions have been made. In this way, one idea inspires others; people do not withhold potentially creative solutions out of fear of criticism. John Baer (1997, p. 43) gives these rules for brainstorming:

1. Defer judgment.
2. Avoid ownership of ideas. When people feel that an idea is "theirs," egos sometimes get in the way of creative thinking. They are likely to be more defensive later when ideas are critiqued, and they are less willing to allow their ideas to be modified.
3. Feel free to "hitchhike" on other ideas. This means that it's okay to borrow elements from ideas already on the table, or to make slight modifications of ideas already suggested.
4. Encourage wild ideas. Impossible, totally unworkable ideas may lead someone to think of other, more possible, more workable ideas. It's easier to take a wildly imaginative bad idea and tone it down to fit the constraints of reality than it is to take a boring bad idea and make it interesting enough to be worth thinking about.

Individuals as well as groups may benefit from brainstorming. In writing this book, for example, we have sometimes found it helpful to list all the different topics that could be covered in a chapter and then leave the list and return to it later to evaluate the ideas.

Brainstorming Generating ideas without stopping to evaluate them.

The Big C: Revolutionary Innovation

Ellen Winner (2000) describes the "big-C creativity" or innovation that establishes a new field or revolutionizes an old one. Even child prodigies do not necessarily become adult innovators. Prodigies have mastered well-established domains very early, but innovators change the entire domain. "Individuals who ultimately make creative breakthroughs tend from their earliest days to be explorers, innovators, and tinkerers. Often this adventurousness is interpreted as insubordination, though more fortunate tinkerers receive from teachers or peers some form of encouragement for their experimentation" (Gardner, 1993, pp. 32–33). What can parents and teachers do to encourage these potential creators? Winner (2000) lists four dangers to avoid:

1. Avoid pushing so hard that the child's intrinsic passion to master a field becomes a craving for extrinsic rewards.
2. Avoid pushing so hard that the child later looks back on a missed childhood.
3. Avoid freezing the child into a safe, technically perfect way of performing that has led to lavish rewards.
4. Be aware of the psychological wounds that can follow when the child who can perform perfectly becomes the forgotten adult who can do nothing more than continue to perform perfectly—without ever creating something new.

Finally, teachers and parents can encourage students who have outstanding abilities and creative talents to give back to the society that has provided the extra support and resources that they needed. Service learning, discussed in Chapter 9, provides one opportunity for creative students to give back to society.

We may not all be revolutionary in our creativity, but we all can be experts in one area—critical thinking, our next topic.

CRITICAL THINKING

Many educational psychologists believe that good thinking can and should be developed in school. But clearly, teaching thinking entails much more than the standard classroom practices of answering "thought" questions at the end of the chapter or participating in teacher-led discussions. What else is needed? One approach has been to focus on the development of *thinking skills*, either through stand-alone programs that teach skills directly, or through indirect methods that embed development of thinking in the regular curriculum. The advantage of **stand-alone thinking skills programs** is that students do not need extensive subject matter knowledge to master the skills. Students who have had trouble with the traditional curriculum may achieve success—and perhaps enhanced self-esteem—through these programs. The disadvantage is that the general skills often are not used outside the program unless teachers make a concerted effort to show students how to apply the skills in specific subjects (Mayer & Wittrock, 2006; Prawat, 1991).

Another way to develop students' thinking is to emphasize analysis, problem solving, and reasoning through the regular lessons of the curriculum. David Perkins and his colleagues (Perkins, Jay, & Tishman, 1993) propose that teachers do this by creating a culture of thinking in their classrooms. This means that there is a spirit of inquisitiveness and critical thinking, a respect for reasoning and creativity, and an expectation that students will learn and understand. In such a classroom, education is seen as *enculturation*, a broad and complex process of acquiring knowledge and understanding consistent with Vygotsky's theory of mediated learning. Just as our home culture taught us lessons about the use of language, the culture of a classroom can teach lessons about thinking by giving us models of good thinking, providing direct instruction in thinking processes, and encouraging practice of those thinking processes through interactions with others.

Developing Critical Thinking

Critical thinking skills are useful in almost every life situation—even in evaluating the media ads that constantly bombard us. When you see a group of gorgeous people extolling the virtues of a particular brand of orange juice as they frolic in skimpy bathing suits, you must decide if sex appeal is a relevant factor in choosing a fruit drink (remember Pavlovian advertising from Chapter 6). As

Stand-alone thinking skills programs Programs that teach thinking skills directly without need for extensive subject matter knowledge.

Critical thinking Evaluating conclusions by logically and systematically examining the problem, the evidence, and the solution.

POINT/COUNTERPOINT

Should Schools Teach Critical Thinking and Problem Solving?

THE QUESTION OF WHETHER schools should focus on process or content, problem-solving skills or core knowledge, higher-order thinking skills or academic information has been debated for years. Some educators suggest that students must be taught how to think and solve problems, while other educators assert that students cannot learn to "think" in the abstract. They must be thinking about something—some content. Should teachers focus on knowledge or thinking?

POINT

Problem solving and higher-order thinking can and should be taught.

An article in the April 28, 1995, issue of the *Chronicle of Higher Education* makes this claim:

> *Critical thinking is at the heart of effective reading, writing, speaking, and listening. It enables us to link together mastery of content with such diverse goals as self-esteem, self-discipline, multicultural education, effective cooperative learning, and problem solving. It enables all instructors and administrators to raise the level of their own teaching and thinking. (p. A-71)*

How can students learn to think critically? Some educators recommend teaching thinking skills directly with widely used techniques such as the Productive Thinking Program or Cognitive Research Trust (CoRT). Other researchers argue that learning computer programming languages such as LOGO will improve students' minds and teach them how to think logically. For example, Papert (1980) believes that when children learn through discovery how to give instructions to computers in LOGO, "powerful intellectual skills are developed in the process" (p. 60). Finally, because expert readers automatically apply certain metacognitive strategies, many educators and psychologists recommend directly teaching novice or poor readers how to apply these strategies. Michael Pressley's Good Strategy User model and Palincsar and Brown's (1984) reciprocal teaching approach are successful examples of direct teaching of metacognitive skills. Research on these approaches generally shows improvements in achievement and comprehension for students of all ages who participate (Pressley, Barkowski, & Schneider, 1987; Rosenshine & Meister, 1994).

COUNTERPOINT

Thinking and problem-solving skills do not transfer to new contexts.

According to E. D. Hirsch (1996), a vocal critic of critical thinking programs:

> *. . . whether such direct instruction of critical thinking or self-monitoring does in fact improve performance is a subject of debate in the research community. For instance, the research regarding critical thinking is not reassuring. Instruction in critical thinking has been going on in several countries for over a hundred years. Yet researchers found that students from nations as varied as Israel, Germany, Australia, the Philippines, and the United States, including those who have been taught critical thinking continue to fall into logical fallacies. (p. 136)*

The CoRT program has been used in over 5000 classrooms in 10 nations. But Polson and Jeffries (1985) report that "after 10 years of widespread use we have no adequate evidence concerning the effectiveness of the program" (p. 445). In addition, Mayer and Wittrock (1996) note that field studies of problem solving in real situations show that people often fail to apply the mathematical problem-solving approaches they learn in school to actual problems encountered in the "real world," such as problems people face in the grocery store or at home.

Even though educators have been more successful in teaching metacognitive skills, critics still caution that there are times when such teaching hinders rather than helps learning. Robert Siegler (1993) suggests that teaching self-monitoring strategies to low-achieving students can interfere with the students' development of adaptive strategies. Forcing students to use the strategies of experts may put too much burden on working memory as the students struggle to use an unfamiliar strategy and miss the meaning or content of the lesson. For example, rather than teach students strategies for figuring out words from context, it may be helpful for students to focus on learning more vocabulary words.

you can see in the *Point/Counterpoint* box, educators don't necessarily agree about the best way to foster critical thinking skills in schools.

No matter what approach you use to develop critical thinking, it is important to follow up with additional practice. One lesson is not enough. For example, if your class examined a particular historical document to determine if it reflected bias or propaganda, you should follow up by analyzing

TABLE 8.3 **Examples of Critical Thinking Skills**

Defining and Clarifying the Problem

1. Identify central issues or problems.
2. Compare similarities and differences.
3. Determine which information is relevant.
4. Formulate appropriate questions.

Judging Information Related to the Problem

5. Distinguish among fact, opinion, and reasoned judgment.
6. Check consistency.

other written historical documents, contemporary advertisements, or news stories. Until thinking skills become overlearned and relatively automatic, they are not likely to be transferred to new situations (Mayer & Wittrock, 2006). Instead, students will use these skills only to complete the lesson in social studies, not to evaluate the claims made by friends, politicians, toy manufacturers, or those promoting diet plans. Table 8.3 provides a representative list of critical thinking skills.

The Language of Thinking

STOP & THINK How many different words can you list that describe aspects of thinking? Try to "think" of at least 20.

Phil's computer's thesaurus found over 100 more words when he highlighted "thinking." The language of thinking consists of natural language terms that refer to mental processes and mental products—"words like think, believe, guess, conjecture, hypothesis, evidence, reasons, estimate, calculate, suspect, doubt, and theorize—to name just a few" (Tishman, Perkins, & Jay, 1995, p. 8). The classroom should be filled with a clear, precise, and rich vocabulary of thinking. Rather than saying, "What do you think about Jamie's answer?" the teacher might ask questions that expand thinking such as, "What evidence can you give to refute or support Jamie's answer?" "What assumptions is Jamie making?" "What are some alternative explanations?" Students surrounded by a rich language of thinking are more likely to think deeply about thinking. Students learn more when they engage in talk that is interpretive and that analyzes and gives explanations. Talk that just describes is less helpful in learning than talk that explains, gives reasons, identifies parts, makes a case, defends a position, or evaluates evidence (Palincsar, 1998).

"We did that last year—how come we have to do it again this year?"

Critical Thinking in Specific Subjects

Many of the strategies we have discussed, such as note taking or highlighting, can be applied to almost any subject. But some strategies are specific to one subject, such as using particular strategies for solving word problems in algebra. For example, Jeffrey Nokes and his colleagues investigated using traditional texts versus multiple readings and direct teaching of critical thinking skills versus no direct teaching of skills (Nokes, Dole, & Hacker, 2007). The multiple texts included historical fiction, excerpts from speeches, government documents, photographs, charts and historical data, and short sections from texts. The critical thinking skills required to master the subject of history were as follows:

- **Sourcing:** Looking at the source of the document before reading and using that information to help interpret and make inferences about the reading. Is the source biased? Can I trust it?

- **Corroboration:** Making connections between the information in different texts and noting similarities and contradictions.
- **Contextualization:** Imaging the time, place, people, and culture that is the context for the event, with all the political and social forces that might be operating.

Students who learned with multiple texts instead of traditional textbooks actually learned more history content. Also, students were able to learn and apply two of the three critical thinking skills, sourcing and corroboration, when they were directly taught how to use the skills. Contextualization proved more difficult, perhaps because the students lacked the background knowledge to fill in contextual information. So critical thinking for specific subjects can be taught along with the subject.

Here is an important question: What is the purpose of all this critical thinking? Will students be able to transfer it to other situations?

TEACHING FOR TRANSFER

STOP & THINK Think back for a moment to a subject you studied in high school that you have not studied in university. Imagine the teacher, the room, and the textbook you used. Now remember what you actually learned in class. If it was a science class, what were some of the formulas you learned? Oxidation reduction? Boyle's law?

If you are like most of us, you may remember that you learned these things, but you will not be quite sure exactly what you learned. Were those hours wasted? These questions are about the transfer of learning. We turn to that important topic next. Let's begin with a definition of transfer.

Whenever something previously learned influences current learning or when solving an earlier problem affects how you solve a new problem, transfer has occurred. Erik De Corte (2003) calls transfer "the productive use of cognitive tools and motivations" (p. 142). This meaning of transfer emphasizes doing something new (productive), not just reproducing a previous application of the tools. If students learn a mathematical principle in one class and use it to solve a physics problem days or weeks later in another class, then transfer has taken place. However, the effect of past learning on present learning is not always positive. *Functional fixedness* and *response set* (described earlier in this chapter) are examples of negative transfer because they are attempts to apply familiar but *inappropriate* strategies to a new situation.

Actually, there are several dimensions of transfer (Barnett & Ceci, 2002). You can transfer learning across subjects (math skills used in science problems), across physical contexts (learned in school, used on the job), across social contexts (learned alone, used with your family or team), across time periods (learned in college or university, used months or years later), across functions (learned for academics, used for hobbies and recreation), and across modalities (learned from watching the Home and Garden cable channel, used to discuss ideas for a patio with a landscape architect). So transfer can refer to many different examples of applying knowledge and skills beyond where, when, and how you learned them.

The Many Views of Transfer

Transfer has been a focus of research in educational psychology for over 100 years. After all, the productive use of knowledge, skills, and motivations across a lifetime is a fundamental goal of education (Pugh & Bergin, 2006). Early work focused on specific transfer of skills and the general transfer of *mental discipline* gained from studying rigorous subjects such as Latin or mathematics. But in 1924, E. L. Thorndike demonstrated that there was no mental discipline benefit from learning Latin. Learning Latin just helped you learn more Latin. So, thanks to Thorndike, you were not required to take Latin in high school.

More recently, researchers distinguish between the automatic, direct use of skills such as reading or writing in everyday applications versus the extraordinary transfer of knowledge and strategies to arrive at creative solutions to problems (Bereiter, 1995; Bransford & Schwartz, 1999; Salomon & Perkins, 1989). Gabriel Salomon and David Perkins (1989) describe these two kinds of transfer, termed low-road and high-road transfer. Low-road transfer "involves the spontaneous, automatic

Transfer Influence of previously learned information, skills, and motivation on learning new information or completing new tasks successfully.

Low-road transfer Spontaneous and automatic transfer of highly practised skills.

TABLE 8.4

Kinds of Transfer

	Low-Road Transfer (Direct-Application)	High-Road Transfer (Preparation for Future Learning)
Definition	Automatic transfer of highly practised skills	Conscious application of abstract knowledge to a new situation Productive use of cognitive tools and motivations
Key conditions	Extensive practice Variety of settings and conditions Overlearning to automaticity	Mindful focus on abstracting a principle, main idea, or procedure that can be used in many situations Learning in powerful teaching-learning environments
Examples	Driving many different cars Finding your gate in an airport	Applying KWL or READS strategies Applying procedures from math in designing a page layout for the school newspaper

transfer of highly practiced skills, with little need for reflective thinking" (p. 118). Low-road transfer builds the automated basic skills discussed in Chapter 7. The key is practising a skill often, in a variety of situations, until your performance becomes automatic. So if you worked one summer for a temporary secretarial service and were sent to many different offices to work on all kinds of computers, by the end of the summer you probably would be able to handle most machines easily. Your practice with many machines would let you transfer your skill automatically to a new situation. Bransford and Schwartz (1999) refer to this kind of transfer as *direct-application transfer*.

High-road transfer, on the other hand, involves consciously applying abstract knowledge or strategies learned in one situation to a different situation. This can happen in one of two ways. First, you may learn a principle or a strategy, intending to use it in the future—*forward-reaching transfer*. For example, if you plan to apply what you learn in anatomy class this semester to work in a drawing course you will take next semester, you may search for principles about human proportions, muscle definition, and so on. Second, when you are faced with a problem, you may look back on what you have learned in other situations to help you in this new one—*backward-reaching transfer*. Analogical thinking is an example of this kind of transfer. You search for other, related situations that might provide clues to the current problem. Bransford and Schwartz (1999) consider this kind of high-road transfer to be *preparation for future learning*.

The key to high-road transfer is *mindful abstraction*, or the deliberate identification of a principle, main idea, strategy, or procedure that is not tied to one specific problem or situation, but could apply to many. Such an abstraction becomes part of your metacognitive knowledge, available to guide future learning and problem solving. Bransford and Schwartz (1999) add another key—a resource-rich environment that supports productive, appropriate transfer. Table 8.4 summarizes the types of transfer.

Teaching for Positive Transfer

Years of research and experience show that students will master new knowledge, problem-solving procedures, and learning strategies, but usually they will not use them unless prompted or guided. For example, studies of real-world mathematics show that people do not always apply math procedures learned in school to solve practical problems that arise in their homes or in grocery stores (Lave, 1988; Lave & Wenger, 1991). This happens because learning is *situated*; that is, learning happens in specific situations. We learn solutions to particular problems, not general, all-purpose solutions that can fit any problem. Because knowledge is learned as a tool to solve particular problems, we may not realize that the knowledge is relevant when we encounter a problem that seems different, at least on the surface (Driscoll, 2005; Singley & Anderson, 1989). How can you make sure your students will use what they learn, even when situations change?

High-road transfer Application of abstract knowledge learned in one situation to a different situation.

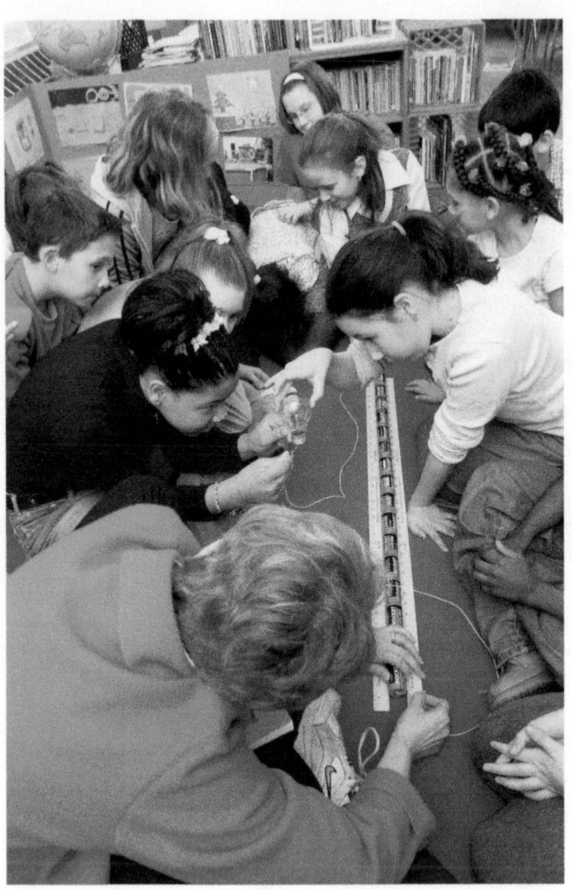

HIGHER-LEVEL TRANSFER Students will be more likely to transfer knowledge to new situations if they have been actively involved in the learning process. They should be encouraged to form abstractions that they will apply later, so they know transfer is an important goal.

What Is Worth Learning? First, you must answer the question "What is worth learning?" The learning of basic skills such as reading, writing, computing, cooperating, and speaking will definitely transfer to other situations, because these skills are necessary for later work both in and out of school—writing job applications, reading novels, paying bills, working on a team, locating and evaluating health care services, and so on. All later learning depends on positive transfer of these basics to new situations.

Teachers must also be aware of what the future is likely to hold for their students, both as a group and as individuals. What will society require of them as adults? As children, neither Anita nor Phil nor Nancy studied anything about computers; yet now we spend hours using them; Phil even designs software for researching how people learn. Computer programming and word processing were not part of our high school studies, but we learned to use a slide rule. Now, calculators and computers have made this skill obsolete. We were encouraged to take advanced math and chemistry instead of typing in high school. Those were great classes, but now we type every day at our computers—who knew? Undoubtedly, changes as extreme and unpredictable as these await the students you will teach. For this reason, the general transfer of principles, attitudes, learning strategies, motivations, and problem solving will be just as important for your students as the specific transfer of basic skills.

How Can Teachers Help? For basic skills, greater transfer can also be ensured by overlearning, practising a skill past the point of mastery. Many of the basic facts students learn in elementary school, such as the multiplication tables, are traditionally overlearned. Overlearning helps students develop automated basic skills as we saw in Chapter 7.

For higher-level transfer, students must first learn and understand. Students will be more likely to transfer knowledge to new situations if they have been actively involved in the learning process. They should be encouraged to form abstractions that they will apply later, so they know transfer is an important goal. It also helps if students form deep connections between the new knowledge and their existing structures of knowledge as well as connections to their everyday experiences (Pugh & Bergin, 2006). Erik De Corte (2003) believes that teachers support transfer, the productive use of cognitive tools and motivations, when they create powerful teaching-learning environments using these design principles:

- The environments should support constructive learning processes in all students.
- The environments should encourage the development of student self-regulation, so that teachers gradually give over more and more responsibilities to the students.
- Learning should involve interaction and collaboration.
- Learners should deal with problems that have personal meaning for them, problems they will face in the future.
- The classroom culture should encourage students to become aware of and develop their cognitive and motivational processes. In order to be productive users of these tools, students must know about and value them.

The next three chapters delve in depth into how to support constructive learning, motivation, self-regulation, collaboration, and self-awareness in all students. For now, the *Family and Community Partnerships Guidelines* box gives ideas for how to enlist the support of families in encouraging transfer in students.

There is one last kind of transfer that is especially important for students—the transfer of the learning strategies we encountered in the previous section. Learning strategies and tactics are meant to be applied across a wide range of situations, but this often does not happen, as you will see below.

Stages of Transfer for Strategies. Sometimes students simply don't understand that a particular strategy applies in new situations or they don't know how to adapt it to fit. As we saw earlier, they may think that using the strategy will take too much time (Schunk, 2004).

Overlearning Practising a skill past the point of mastery.

FAMILY AND COMMUNITY PARTNERSHIPS

GUIDELINES: Promoting Transfer

Keep families informed about their child's curriculum so they can support learning.

EXAMPLES

1. At the beginning of units or major projects, send a letter summarizing the key goals, a few of the major assignments, and some common problems students have in learning the material for that unit.
2. Ask parents for suggestions about how their child's interests could be connected to the curriculum topics.
3. Invite parents to school for an evening of "strategy learning." Have the students teach their family members one of the strategies they have learned in school.

Give families ideas for how they might encourage their children to practise, extend, or apply learning from school.

EXAMPLES

1. To extend writing, ask parents to encourage their children to write letters or email messages to companies or civic organizations asking for information or free products. Provide a shell letter form for structure and ideas and include addresses of companies that provide free samples or information.
2. Ask family members to include their children in some projects that require measurement, halving or doubling recipes, or estimating costs.
3. Suggest that students work with grandparents to create a family memory book. Combine historical research and writing.

Show connections between learning in school and life outside school.

EXAMPLES

1. Ask families to talk about and show how they use the skills their children are learning in jobs, hobbies, or community involvement projects.
2. Ask family members to come to class to demonstrate how they use reading, writing, science, math, or other knowledge in their work.

Make families partners in practising learning strategies.

EXAMPLES

1. Focus on one learning tactic at a time—ask families to simply remind their children to use a particular tactic with homework that week.
2. Develop a lending library of books and videotapes to teach families about learning strategies.
3. Give parents a copy of the "Becoming an Expert Student" Guidelines on page 276, rewritten for the appropriate grade level.

For more information on promoting transfer see **www.kidsource.com/education/motivation.lang.learn.html#2**.

Gary Phye (1992, 2001; Phye & Sanders, 1994) suggests that we think of the transfer of learning strategies as a tool to be used in a "mindful" way to solve academic problems. He describes three stages in developing strategic transfer. In the *acquisition phase*, students should not only receive instruction about a strategy and how to use it, but also rehearse the strategy and practise being aware of when and how they are using it. In the *retention phase*, more practice with feedback helps students hone their strategy use. In the *transfer phase*, the teacher should provide new problems that can be solved with the same strategy, even though the problems appear different on the surface. To enhance motivation, point out to students how using the strategy will help them solve many problems and accomplish different tasks. These steps help build both procedural and conditional knowledge—how to use the strategy as well as when and why.

DIVERSITY AND CONVERGENCES IN COMPLEX COGNITIVE PROCESSES

This chapter has covered quite a bit of territory, partly because the cognitive perspective has so many implications for instruction. Although they vary, you can see that most of the cognitive ideas for teaching concepts, creative problem-solving skills, and learning strategies emphasize the role of the student's prior knowledge and the need for active, mindful learning.

Diversity

Problem solving and strategy-learning processes may be similar for all students, but the prior knowledge, beliefs, and skills they bring to the classroom are bound to vary, based on their experience and culture. For example, Zhe Chen and his colleagues (2004) wondered if university students might use familiar folk tales—one kind of cultural knowledge—as analogies to solve problems. In fact, that is precisely what happened. Chinese students were better at solving a problem of weighing a statue because the problem was similar to the Chinese folk tale about how to weigh an elephant (by using water displacement). North American students were better at solving a problem of finding the way out of a cave (by leaving a trail), by using an analogy to *Hansel and Gretel*, a common folk tale. In another study in Australia, Volet (1999) found that some culturally based knowledge and motivation strategies of Asian students—such as high achievement motivation, a deep processing and effortful approach to learning, and a recognition of the benefits of collaboration—transferred well to Western-oriented schools. Other culturally based beliefs, however, such as valuing rote memorization or solitary learning, might cause conflicts with the expectations of some schools. For example, we saw in Chapter 5 that the native Hawaiian style of interacting was seen as "interrupting" by non-Hawaiian teachers until the teachers learned more about the family communication styles of their students.

Creativity and Diversity. Even though creativity has been studied for centuries, as Dean Simonton said, "Psychologists still have a long way to go before they come anywhere close to understanding creativity in women and minorities" (2000, p. 156). The focus of research and writing on creativity over the years has centred on white males. Patterns of creativity in other groups are complex—sometimes matching and sometimes diverging from patterns found in traditional research.

In another connection between creativity and culture, research suggests that being on the outside of mainstream society, being bilingual, or being exposed to other cultures might encourage creativity (Simonton, 1999, 2000). In fact, true innovators often break rules. "Creators have a desire to shake things up. They are restless, rebellious, and dissatisfied with the status quo" (Winner, 2000, p. 167). In addition, even for those who are not outside the mainstream, it appears that participation in multicultural experiences fosters creativity. Angela Ka-Yee Leung and her colleagues (2008) reviewed theory and research, including experimental studies that exposed participants to information and images about other cultures. The researchers concluded that multicultural experiences support both creative processes, such as retrieving novel or unconventional ideas from memory, and creative performance, such as generating insightful solutions to problems. These effects are especially strong when people open themselves up to divergent ideas and when the situation does not emphasize finding quick, firm answers. So your students may not be able to travel to Tibet or Turkey, but they could become more creative problem solvers if they learned about different cultures.

Convergences

As you have seen throughout this chapter, in the beginning, as students learn problem solving or try to transfer cognitive tools to new situations, there is a tendency to focus on surface features. For all novices, their challenge is to grasp the abstractions: underlying principles, structures, strategies, or big ideas. It is those larger ideas that lead to understanding and serve as a foundation for future learning (Chen & Mo, 2004).

A second convergence: For all students, there is a positive relationship between using learning strategies and academic gains such as high school GPA and retention in post-secondary educational environments (Robbins, Le, & Lauver, 2005). Some students will learn productive strategies on their own, but all students can benefit from direct teaching, modelling, and practice of learning strategies and study skills. This is one important way to prepare all your students for their futures. Newly mastered concepts, principles, and strategies must be applied in a wide variety of situations and problems (Chen & Mo, 2004). Positive transfer is encouraged when skills are practised under authentic conditions, similar to those that will exist when the skills are needed later. Students can learn to write by corresponding with email "pen pals" in other countries. They can learn historical research methods by researching their own families. Some of these applications should involve complex, ill-defined, unstructured problems, because many of the problems to be faced in later life, both in and out of school, will not come to students complete with instructions.

SUMMARY TABLE

Metacognition (pp. 269–270)

What are the three metacognitive skills? The three metacognitive skills used to regulate thinking and learning are planning, monitoring, and evaluating. Planning involves deciding how much time to give to a task, which strategies to use, how to start, and so on. Monitoring is the awareness of "how I'm doing." Evaluating involves making judgments about the processes and outcomes of thinking and learning, and acting on those judgments.

What are some sources of individual differences in metacognition? Individual differences in metacognition may result from different paces of development (maturation) or biological differences among learners. For example, young students may not be able to understand a lesson's purpose as well as older students.

How can using better metacognitive strategies improve children's working and long-term memories? Younger children can be taught to use organization to improve memory, but they probably won't apply the strategy unless they are reminded. Children also become more able to use elaboration as they mature, but this strategy is developed late in childhood. Creating images or stories to remember ideas is more likely for older elementary school students and adolescents.

Executive control processes Processes such as selective attention, rehearsal, elaboration, and organization that influence encoding, storage, and retrieval of information in memory.

Metacognition Knowledge about our own thinking processes.

Learning Strategies (pp. 270–277)

Distinguish between learning strategies and tactics. Learning strategies are ideas for accomplishing learning goals, a kind of overall plan of attack. Learning tactics are the specific techniques that make up the plan. A strategy for learning might include several tactics such as mnemonics to remember key terms, skimming to identify organization, and then writing answers to possible essay questions. Use of strategies and tactics reflects metacognitive knowledge.

What key functions do learning strategies play? First, learning strategies help students *become cognitively engaged*—focus attention on the relevant or important aspects of the material. Second, they encourage students to *invest effort*, make connections, elaborate, translate, organize, and reorganize in order to *think and process deeply*—the greater the practice and processing, the stronger the learning. Finally, strategies help students *regulate and monitor* their own learning—keep track of what is making sense and notice when a new approach is needed.

Describe some procedures for developing learning strategies. Expose students to a number of different strategies, not only general learning strategies but also very specific tactics, such as the graphic strategies. Teach conditional knowledge about when, where, and why to use various strategies. Develop motivation to use the strategies and tactics by showing students how their learning and performance can be improved. Provide direct instruction in content knowledge needed to use the strategies.

When will students apply learning strategies? If they have appropriate strategies, students will apply them if they are faced with a task that requires good strategies, value doing well on that task, think the effort to apply the strategies will be worthwhile, and believe that they can succeed using the strategies. Also, to apply deep processing strategies, students must assume that knowledge is complex and takes time to learn and that learning requires their own active efforts.

Learning strategies General plans for approaching learning tasks.

Learning tactics Specific techniques for learning, such as using mnemonics or outlining a passage.

Concept map A drawing that charts the relationships among ideas.

Cmaps Tools for concept mapping, developed by the Institute for Human Machine Cognition, that are connected to many knowledge maps and other resources on the internet.

READS A five-step reading strategy: *Review* headings; *Examine* boldface words; *Ask*, "What do I expect to learn?"; *Do* it—Read; *Summarize* in your own words.

CAPS A strategy that can be used in reading literature; involves identifying *characters*, *aim* of story, *problem*, and *solution*.

KWL A strategy to guide reading and inquiry: Before—What do I already *know*? What do I *want* to know? After—What have I *learned*?

Production deficiency When students learn problem-solving strategies, but do not apply them when they could or should.

Problem Any situation in which you are trying to reach some goal and must find a means to do so.

Problem Solving (pp. 277–287)

What are the steps in the general problem-solving process? Problem solving is both general and domain-specific. The five stages of problem solving are contained in the acronym IDEAL: *Identify* problems and opportunities; *Define* goals and represent the problem; *Explore* possible strategies; *Anticipate* outcomes and *Act*; *Look* back and *Learn*.

Why is the representation stage of problem solving so important? To represent the problem accurately, you must understand both the whole problem and its discrete elements. Schema training may improve this ability. The problem-solving process follows entirely different paths, depending on what representation and goal are chosen. If your representation of the problem suggests an immediate solution, the task is done; the new problem is recognized as a "disguised" version of an old problem with a clear solution. But if there is no existing way of solving the problem or if the activated schema fails, then you must search for a solution. The application of algorithms and heuristics—such as means-ends analysis, analogical thinking, working backward, and verbalization—may help students solve problems.

Describe factors that can interfere with problem solving. Factors that hinder problem solving include functional fixedness or rigidity (response set). These disallow the flexibility needed to represent problems accurately and to have insight into solutions. Also, as we make decisions and judgments, we may overlook important information because we base judgments on what seems representative of a category (representativeness heuristic) or what is available in memory (availability heuristic), then pay attention only to information that confirms our choices (confirmation bias) so that we hold on to beliefs, even in the face of contradictory evidence (belief perseverance).

What are the differences between expert and novice knowledge in a given area? Expert problem solvers have a rich store of declarative, procedural, and conditional knowledge. They organize this knowledge around general principles or patterns that apply to large classes of problems. They work faster, remember relevant information, and monitor their progress better than novices.

Problem Any situation in which you are trying to reach some goal and must find a means to do so.

Problem solving Creating new solutions for problems.

Schema-driven problem solving Recognizing a problem as a "disguised" version of an old problem for which you already have a solution.

Algorithm Step-by-step procedure for solving a problem; prescription for solutions.

Heuristic General strategy used in attempting to solve problems.

Means-ends analysis Heuristic in which a goal is divided into subgoals.

Working-backward strategy Heuristic in which you start with the goal and move backward to solve the problem.

Analogical thinking Heuristic in which you limit the search for solutions to situations that are similar to the one at hand.

Verbalization Putting your problem-solving plan and its logic into words.

Functional fixedness Inability to use objects or tools in a new way.

Response set Rigidity; tendency to respond in the most familiar way.

Representativeness heuristic Judging the likelihood of an event based on how well the events match your prototypes—what you think is representative of a category.

Availability heuristic Judging the likelihood of an event based on what is available in your memory; assuming those easily remembered events are common.

Belief perseverance The tendency to hold on to beliefs, even in the face of contradictory evidence.

Confirmation bias Seeking information that confirms our choices and beliefs, while disconfirming evidence.

Insight Sudden realization of a solution.

Creativity and Creative Problem Solving (pp. 287–291)

What are some myths about creativity? These four statements are completely or partly wrong: Creativity is determined at birth. Creativity comes with negative personality traits. Creative people are disorganized hippie types. Working in a group enhances creativity. These are the facts: Creativity can be developed. A few but not all creative people are nonconforming or have emotional problems. Many creative people are focused, organized, and part of the mainstream. Finally, groups can limit as well as enhance creativity.

What is creativity and how is it assessed? Creativity is a process that involves independently restructuring problems to see things in new, imaginative ways. Creativity is difficult to measure, but tests of divergent thinking can assess originality, fluency, and flexibility. Originality is usually determined statistically. To be original, a response must be given by fewer than 5 or 10 people out of every 100 who take the test. Fluency is the number of different responses. The number of different categories of responses measures flexibility. Teachers can encourage creativity by providing opportunities for play, using brainstorming techniques, and accepting divergent ideas.

What can teachers do to support creativity in the classroom? Teachers can encourage creativity in their interactions with students by accepting unusual, imaginative answers, modelling divergent thinking, using brainstorming, and tolerating dissent.

Creativity Imaginative, original thinking or problem solving.

Restructuring Conceiving a problem in a new or different way.

Divergent thinking Coming up with many possible solutions.

Convergent thinking Narrowing possibilities to a single answer.

Brainstorming Generating ideas without stopping to evaluate them.

Critical Thinking (pp. 291–294)

What is meant by thinking as enculturation? *Enculturation* is a broad and complex process of acquiring knowledge and understanding consistent with Vygotsky's theory of mediated learning. Just as our home culture taught us lessons about the use of language, the culture of a classroom can teach lessons about thinking by giving us *models* of good thinking, providing *direct instruction* in thinking processes, and encouraging *practice* of those thinking processes through *interactions* with others.

What is critical thinking? Critical thinking skills include defining and clarifying the problem, making judgments about the consistency and adequacy of the information related to a problem, and drawing conclusions. No matter what approach you use to develop critical thinking, it is important to follow up activities with additional practice. One lesson is not enough.

Stand-alone thinking skills programs Programs that teach thinking skills directly without need for extensive subject matter knowledge.

Critical thinking Evaluating conclusions by logically and systematically examining the problem, the evidence, and the solution.

Teaching for Transfer (pp. 294–297)

What is transfer? Transfer occurs when a rule, fact, or skill learned in one situation is applied in another situation; for example, applying rules of punctuation to write a job application letter. Transfer also involves applying to new problems the principles learned in other, often dissimilar situations.

What are some dimensions of transfer? Information can be transferred across a variety of contexts. Some examples include transfer from one subject to another, one physical location to another, or one function to another. These types of transfer make it possible to use skills developed in one area for many other tasks.

Distinguish between low-road and high-road transfer. Transfer involving spontaneity and automaticity in familiar situations has been called *low-road transfer*. *High-road transfer* involves reflection and conscious application of abstract knowledge to new situations. Learning environments should support active constructive learning, self-regulation, collaboration, and awareness of cognitive tools and motivational processes. In addition, students should deal with problems that have meaning in their lives. Teachers can help students transfer learning strategies by teaching strategies directly, providing practice with feedback, and then expanding the application of the strategies to new and unfamiliar situations.

Transfer Influence of previously learned information, skills, and motivation on learning new information or completing new tasks successfully.

Low-road transfer Spontaneous and automatic transfer of highly practised skills.

High-road transfer Application of abstract knowledge learned in one situation to a different situation.

Overlearning Practising a skill past the point of mastery.

PEARSON myeducationlab

MyEducationLab is an interactive, virtual learning tool that will help improve your understanding of the concepts taught in this textbook and in your course. Through this engaging resource, you will have access to simulations of real classroom experiences, exercises that will help you improve your knowledge of key concepts, and additional resources that will help you in your teaching career. Use this online tool with your textbook to help you succeed in your studies and beyond!

TEACHERS' CASEBOOK

This year's class is worse than ever. You assigned a research paper and you are finding that more and more students are using the web for their sources. In itself, using the web is not wrong, but the students appear to be completely uncritical about what they find on the internet. "If it is on the web, it must be right" is the attitude of most students. Their first drafts are filled with quotes that seem very biased to you, but there are no sources cited or listed. It is not just that students don't know how to reference their work. You are more concerned that they cannot critically evaluate what they are reading. And that all they are reading is information available on the internet!

What Would *They* Do?

Here is how one practising teacher responded to the teaching situation described above.

John Baldassarre

Archbishop Oscar Romero High School, Edmonton, AB

When assigning a "research" paper, I find it extremely valuable to start the process early in the year by presenting students with a website that features a fake news story that appears to be real. I ask students to begin to discuss and evaluate the story that is presented and to discuss any similar events that are taking place in the world at the time. After a lengthy discussion, I reveal to the students the fact that the website and the news story are fake and begin to show them how to establish the validity of a website or author. I ask students to consider the following basic questions:

- Who is the author of the news story or website and what is his or her background? Is there anything on the site that could bias the information?
- What is the purpose of the website? Is it affiliated with any other sites (political parties, social action groups, etc.)? Is it associated with a specific domain or is it a personal site?
- How active and recent is the website?
- Is the content based on opinions or on studies and/or articles? Can those studies or articles be accessed?
- Can you find the same information stated on other websites or within more traditional, print-based research materials?

I then ask students to apply the above criteria to each research paper that I assign. Students come to realize that they need to research more than one source of information and that they must develop the ability to discern information and to filter bias and opinions from the objective facts. In teaching and advocating this type of methodology and critical thinking process, I also try to function as a role model and demonstrate to students how to filter through a plethora of information to find the sources that are best suited to the task.

9 The Learning Sciences and Constructivism

Parts Equal the Whole I © DianaOng/SuperStock

TEACHERS' CASEBOOK

WHAT WOULD YOU DO?

You have finally landed a job teaching English and writing in a high school. The first day of class, you discover that a number of students appear to be just beginning to learn English. You make a mental note to meet with them to determine how much and what kind of reading they can handle. To get a sense of the class's interest, you ask them to write a "review" of the last book they read, as if they were on TV doing a "Book Talk" program. There is a bit of grumbling, but the students seem to be writing, so you take a few minutes to try to talk with one of the students who seems to have trouble with English.

That night you look over the "book reviews." Either the students are giving you a hard time, or no one has read anything lately. Several students mention a text from another class, but their reviews are one-sentence evaluations—usually containing the words *lame* or *useless* (often misspelled). In stark contrast are the papers of three students—they are a pleasure to read, worthy of publication in the school literary magazine (if there were one), and they reflect a fairly sophisticated understanding of some good literature.

CRITICAL THINKING

- How would you adapt your lesson plans for this group?
- What will you do tomorrow?
- What teaching approaches do you think will work with this class?
- How will you work with the three students who are more advanced and with the students who are just learning English?

For the past three chapters, we have analyzed different aspects of learning. We considered behavioural and information processing explanations of what and how people learn. We also examined complex cognitive processes such as metacognitive skills and problem solving. These explanations of learning focus on the individual and what is happening in his or her "head." In this chapter, we expand our investigation of learning to include insights from a relatively recent interdisciplinary approach called *the learning sciences*. This approach brings together work from many fields that are dedicated to study learning including educational psychology, computer science, neuroscience, and anthropology. One of the foundations of the learning sciences is constructivism, a broad perspective that calls attention to two critical aspects of learning: social and cultural factors. In this chapter, we examine the role of other people in, and the cultural context of, learning. Sociocultural constructivist theories have roots in cognitive perspectives, but have moved well beyond these early explanations. We will explore a number of teaching strategies and approaches that are consistent with cognitive perspectives—inquiry, problem-based learning, cooperative learning, cognitive apprenticeships, and service learning. Finally, we will examine learning in this digital age, including the considerations associated with learning in technology-rich environments.

By the time you have completed this chapter, you should be able to answer these questions:

- What are the assumptions of those who embrace the interdisciplinary approach called learning sciences?
- What are three constructivist perspectives on learning?

- How could you incorporate inquiry, problem-based learning, cooperative learning, and cognitive apprenticeships in your teaching?
- What dilemmas do constructivist teachers face?
- How can service learning encourage student engagement and academic learning?
- How can technology-rich learning environments scaffold student learning and motivation?

Connect and Extend Go to the "Connect and Extend" section in Chapter 9 of MyEducationLab to find further content that links to teaching, students' thinking, research, and the news.

THE LEARNING SCIENCES

In the previous three chapters, psychologists were responsible for most of the theory and research we discussed. But many other people have also studied learning: today, multiple perspectives are included in the learning sciences.

What Are the Learning Sciences?

Recently, a new interdisciplinary science of learning has emerged, based on research in psychology, education, computer science, philosophy, sociology, anthropology, neuroscience, and other fields that study learning. This collaboration of fields is known as the **learning sciences**. You already have explored some of the foundations of the learning sciences in Chapters 7 and 8, including the study of how information is represented in complex structures such a schema, what experts know and how their knowledge is different from novices, metacognition, problem solving, thinking and reasoning, and how knowledge transfers (or doesn't transfer) from the classroom to the world beyond.

No matter what their focus, all knowledge workers in the learning sciences are interested in how deep knowledge in subjects like science, mathematics, and literacy is actually learned and applied in the real world of scientists and mathematicians and writers. In the *Cambridge Handbook of Learning Sciences*, R. Keith Sawyer compares what it takes for deep learning to occur with how learning takes place in the context of traditional classroom practices that have dominated schooling in many countries for decades. Look at Table 9.1 to see the differences.

Learning sciences A new interdisciplinary science of learning, based on research in psychology, education, computer science, philosophy, sociology, anthropology, neuroscience, and other fields that study learning.

Basic Assumptions of the Learning Sciences

Even though experts in different fields of the learning sciences approach their study from varying perspectives, there is growing agreement about some basic assumptions (Sawyer, 2006b):

- ***Experts have deep conceptual knowledge.*** Experts know many facts and procedures, but just learning facts and procedures will not make you an expert. Experts have deep conceptual

TABLE 9.1 **Deep Learning Versus Traditional Classroom Practices**

Learning Knowledge Deeply (Findings from Cognitive Science)	Traditional Classroom Practices (Instructionism)
Deep learning requires that learners relate new ideas and concepts to previous knowledge and experience.	Learners treat course material as unrelated to what they already know.
Deep learning requires that learners integrate their knowledge into interrelated conceptual systems.	Learners treat course material as disconnected bits of knowledge.
Deep learning requires that learners look for patterns and underlying principles.	Learners memorize facts and carry out procedures without understanding how or why.
Deep learning requires that learners evaluate new ideas, and relate them to conclusions.	Learners have difficulty making sense of new ideas that are different from what they encountered in the textbook.
Deep learning requires that learners understand the process of dialogue through which knowledge is created, and they examine the logic of an argument critically.	Learners treat facts and procedures as static knowledge, handed down from an all-knowing authority.
Deep learning requires that learners reflect on their own understanding and their own process of learning.	Learners memorize without reflecting on the purpose or on their own learning strategies.

Source: Sawyer, K. (2006). The new science of learning. In R. K. Sawyer (Ed.). *The Cambridge handbook of the learning sciences* (p. 4). New York: The Cambridge University Press. New York: Oxford University Press.

understanding that allows them to put their knowledge into action; they are able to apply and modify their knowledge to fit each situation. Experts' deep conceptual knowledge generates problem finding and problem solving.

- ***Learning comes from the learner.*** Better instruction alone will not transfer deep understandings from teachers to students. Learning is more than receiving and processing information transmitted by teachers or texts. Rather, students must actively participate in their own personal construction of knowledge (de Kock, Sleegers, & Voeten, 2004).

Agnes is an advocate of deep knowledge. She resists the traditional approach to schooling—but maybe memorizing the principal's name would be a good idea.
By permission of Tony Cochran and Creators Syndicate, Inc.

- ***Schools must create effective learning environments.*** It is the job of the school to create environments where students can be active in constructing their own deep understandings so they can reason about real-world problems and transfer their learning from school to their lives beyond the school walls.
- ***Prior knowledge is key.*** Students come into our classrooms filled with knowledge and beliefs about how the world works. Some of these preconceptions are correct, some are partly correct, and some are incorrect. If teaching does not begin with what the students "know," then the students will learn what it takes to pass the test, but their knowledge and beliefs about the world will not change.
- ***Reflection is necessary to develop deep conceptual knowledge.*** Students need to express and use their developing knowledge through writing, conversations, drawings, projects, skits, portfolios, reports, and so on. But the performance is not enough. To develop deep conceptual knowledge, students need to reflect—that is, they need to thoughtfully analyze their own work and progress.

Neuroscience: Teaching With the Brain in Mind

Research from animal and human studies shows that both experiences and direct teaching cause changes in the organization and structure of the brain (Varma, McCandliss, & Schwartz, 2008). For example, people who are hearing-impaired and use sign language have different patterns of electrical activity in their brains than people who are hearing-impaired and do not use sign language. Also, the intensive instruction and practice provided to rehabilitate stroke victims can help them regain functioning by forming new connections and using new areas of the brain (Bransford, Brown, & Cocking, 2000). In the next section we explore connections between the brain and instruction.

Instruction and Brain Development. Several studies have shown differences in brain activity associated with instruction. For example, Margarete Delazer and her colleagues (2005) compared students' brain activity as they learned new arithmetic operations, either by just memorizing the answers or by learning an algorithm strategy. Using functional magnetic resonance imaging (fMRI), the researchers found that students who simply memorized answers showed greater activity in the area of the brain that specializes in retrieving verbal information, whereas the students who used a strategy showed greater activity in the visual-spatial processing portion of the brain. Bennett Shaywitz and his colleagues (2004) reported another dramatic demonstration of brain changes in children following instruction. The researchers studied 28 children ages 6 to 9 who were good readers and 49 children who were poor readers. Again fMRIs showed differences in the brain activity of the two groups. The poor readers underused parts of their brains' left hemisphere and sometimes overused their right hemispheres. After over 100 hours of intensive instruction in letter–sound combinations, reading ability improved and the brains of the poor readers started to function more like those of the good readers and continued this functioning a year later. Poor readers who received the standard school remediation did not show changes in brain function. In

Functional magnetic resonance imaging (fMRI) A form of MRI (an imaging technique that uses a magnetic field along with radio waves and a computer to create detailed pictures of the inside of the body) used to measure the tiny changes during brain activity.

POINT/COUNTERPOINT

Brain-Based Education

EDUCATORS ARE HEARING more and more about brain-based education, the importance of early stimulation for brain development, the "Mozart effect," and right- and left-brain activities. In fact, based on some research findings that listening to 10 minutes of Mozart can briefly improve spatial reasoning (Rauscher & Shaw, 1998; Steele, Bass, & Crook, 1999), a former governor of the U.S. state of Georgia established a program to give a Mozart CD to every newborn. The scientists who had done the work couldn't believe how their research had been "applied" (Katzir & Paré-Blagoev, 2006). In fact, the governor apparently had confused experiments on infant brain development with studies that involved adult participants (Pinker, 2002). Are there clear educational implications from the neuroscience research on the brain?

POINT

No, the implications are not clear.

John Bruer, president of the James S. McDonnell Foundation, has written articles that are critical of the brain-based education craze (Bruer, 1999, 2002). He notes that many so-called applications of brain research begin with solid science, but then move to unwarranted speculation, and end in a sort of appealing folk tale about the brain and learning. He suggests that for each claim, the educator should ask, "Where does the science end and the speculation begin?" For example, one claim that Bruer questions is the notion of right-brain, left-brain learning.

> *"Right brain versus left brain" is one of those popular ideas that will not die. Speculations about the educational significance of brain laterality have been circulating in the education literature for 30 years. Although repeatedly criticized and dismissed by psychologists and brain scientists, the speculation continues. David Sousa devotes a chapter of* How the Brain Learns *to explaining brain laterality and presents classroom strategies that teachers might use to ensure that both hemispheres are involved in learning. . . . Now let's consider the brain sciences and how or whether they offer support for some of the particular teaching strategies Sousa recommends. To involve the right hemisphere in learning, Sousa writes, teachers should encourage students to generate and use mental imagery. . . . What brain scientists currently know about spatial reasoning and mental imagery provides counterexamples to such simplistic claims as these. Such claims arise out of a folk theory about brain laterality, not a neuroscientific one. . . . Different brain areas are specialized for different tasks, but that specialization occurs at a finer level of analysis than "using visual imagery." Using visual imagery may be a useful learning strategy, but if it is useful it is not because it involves an otherwise underutilized right hemisphere in learning. (Bruer, 1999, pp. 653–654)*

No teacher doubts that the brain is important in learning. As Steven Pinker (2002), professor of psychology at Harvard University, observed, does anyone really think learning takes place somewhere else like the pancreas? But knowing that learning affects the brain does not tell us how to teach. Virtually all of the so-called best practices for brain-based education are simple restatements of good teaching based on understandings of how people learn, not how their brain works. All learning affects the brain. ". . . this should be obvious, but nowadays any banality about learning can be dressed up in neurospeak and treated like a great revelation of science" (p. 86).

COUNTERPOINT

Yes, teaching should be brain-based.

In their article "Applying Cognitive Neuroscience Research to Education" in *Educational Psychologist*, Tami Katzir and Juliana Paré-Blagoev (2006) concluded, "When applied correctly, brain science may serve as a vehicle for advancing the application of our understanding of learning and development. . . . Brain research can challenge common-sense views about teaching and learning by suggesting additional systems that are involved in particular tasks and activities" (p. 70). Brain research is leading to much better understandings about learning disabilities. For example, neuroscience studies of people with reading disabilities have found that these individuals may have trouble with sounds and sound patterns or with retrieving the names of very familiar letters, so there may be different bases for the reading disabilities (Katzir & Paré-Blagoev, 2006).

There are examples of applying knowledge of brain research to education. A reading improvement product called *FastForword* was developed by two neuroscientists, Dr. Michael Merzenich and Dr. Paula Tallal, and is already in use today in classrooms around the country (see **www.scilearn.com/our-approach/brain-fitness-in-education/**). It specifically uses discoveries in neural plasticity to change the brain's ability to read the printed word (Tallal & Miller, 2003).

Schools should not be run on curriculums based solely on the biology of the brain. However, to ignore what we do know about the brain would be equally irresponsible. Brain-based learning offers some direction for educators who want more purposeful, informed teaching.

other research, several studies have found that children and adults with attention-deficit/hyperactivity disorder (ADHD) have smaller frontal lobes, basal ganglia, and cerebellums than people without ADHD. These areas are involved with self-regulation of behaviour, coordination, and control of motor behaviour (Hallahan, Kauffman, & Pullen, 2009).

There are even cultural differences in brain activity. For example, in one study, when Chinese speakers added and compared Arabic numbers, they showed brain activity in the motor (movement) areas of their brains, whereas English speakers doing the same tasks demonstrated activity in the language areas of their brains (Tang et al., 2006). One explanation is that Chinese children are taught arithmetic using an abacus—a calculation tool that involves movement and spatial positions. As adults, these children retain a kind of visual-motor sense of numbers (Varma et al., 2008).

Implications for Teachers

As you have seen, the brain and learning are intimately related—this is not a surprise—but what does this mean for teachers? There has been quite a debate lately between enthusiastic advocates of brain-based education and skeptical neuroscience researchers who caution that studies of the brain do not really address major educational questions. See the *Point/Counterpoint* box for a slice of this debate.

So what can we learn from neuroscience? We can draw these teaching implications:

1. Many cognitive functions are differentiated—that is, they are associated with different parts of the brain. Thus, learners may have preferred modes of processing (visual or verbal, for example) as well as different capabilities in these different modes. Using different modalities for instruction and activities that draw on different senses may match preferences—for example, using maps and songs to teach geography—but recent evidence indicates that different modalities do not necessarily provide advantages for learning (Krätzig & Arbuthnott, 2006; Mayer & Massa, 2003).
2. The brain is relatively plastic, so enriched active environments and flexible instructional strategies may differentially support cognitive development in young children and learning in adults.
3. Some learning disorders may have a neurological basis; neurological testing may assist in diagnosing and treating these disorders, as well as in evaluating the effects of various treatments.

MyEducationLab
Go to the Podcasts section of Chapter 9 in MyEducation Lab and listen to PODCAST The Brain and Education. There is a lot of talk about brain-based education. What does this mean? Are there some clear implications for teachers or is it still too early to say?

Finally, another clear connection between the brain and classroom learning is in the area of emotions and stress. As you will see in Chapter 11, anxiety interferes with learning, whereas challenge, interest, and curiosity can support learning. If students feel unsafe and anxious, they are not likely to be able to focus attention on academics (Sylvester, 2003). But if students are not challenged or interested, learning suffers too. Keeping the level of challenge and support "just right" is a challenge for teachers. And helping students learn to regulate their own emotions and motivation is an important goal for education (see Chapter 10).

One of the most important foundations of the learning sciences is constructivism, an explanation of learning that we will explore for the rest of this chapter.

COGNITIVE AND SOCIAL CONSTRUCTIVISM

Consider this situation:

> A young child who has never been to the hospital is in her bed in the pediatric wing. The nurse at the station down the hall calls over the intercom above the bed, "Hi Chelsea, how are you doing? Do you need anything?" The girl looks puzzled and does not answer. The nurse repeats the question with the same result. Finally, the nurse says emphatically, "Chelsea, are you there? Say something!" The little girl responds tentatively, "Hello wall—I'm here."

Chelsea encountered a new situation—a talking wall. The wall is persistent. It sounds like a grown-up wall. She knows that she shouldn't talk to strangers, but she is not sure about walls. She uses what she knows and what the situation provides to *construct* meaning and to act.

Here is another example of constructing meaning taken from Berk (2001, p. 31). This time, a father and his 4-year-old son Ben co-construct understandings as they walk along a California beach, collecting litter after a busy day:

Ben: (*Running ahead and calling out*) Some bottles and cans. I'll get them.

Mel: If the bottles are broken, you could cut yourself, so let me get them. (*Catches up and holds out the bag as Ben drops items in*)

Ben: Dad, look at this shell. It's a whole one, really big. Colors all inside!

Mel: Hmmm, might be an abalone shell.

Ben: What's abalone?

Mel: Do you remember what I had in my sandwich on the wharf yesterday? That's abalone.

Ben: You eat it?

Mel: Well, you can. You eat a meaty part that the abalone uses to stick to rocks.

Ben: Ewww. I don't want to eat it. Can I keep the shell?

Mel: I think so. Maybe you can find some things in your room to put in it. (*Points to the shell's colors*) Sometimes people make jewelry out of these shells.

Ben: Like mom's necklace?

Mel: That's right. Mom's necklace is made out of a kind of abalone with a very colourful shell—pinks, purples, blues. It's called Paua. When you turn it, the colours change.

Ben: Wow! Let's look for Paua shells!

Mel: You can't find them here, only in New Zealand.

Ben: Where's that? Have you been there?

Mel: No, someone brought Mom the necklace as a gift. But I'll show you New Zealand on the globe. It's far away, halfway around the world.*

Look at the knowledge being co-constructed about sea creatures and their uses for food or decoration; safety; environmental responsibility; and even geography. Constructivist theories of learning focus on how people make meaning, both on their own, like Chelsea, and during interaction with others, like Ben.

Constructivist Views of Learning

Constructivism is a broad term used by philosophers, curriculum designers, psychologists, educators, and others. Ernst Von Glasersfeld calls it "a vast and woolly area in contemporary psychology, epistemology, and education" (1997, p. 204). Constructivist perspectives are grounded in the research of Piaget, Vygotsky, the Gestalt psychologists, Bartlett, Bruner, and Rogoff, as well as the philosophy of John Dewey and the work in anthropology of Jean Lave, to mention just a few intellectuals.

There is no single constructivist theory of learning, but most constructivist theorists agree on two central ideas:

Central Idea #1: Learners are active in constructing their own knowledge.

Central Idea #2: Social interactions are important in this knowledge construction process (Bruning, Schraw, Norby, & Ronning, 2004).

Constructivist approaches in science and mathematics education, in educational psychology and anthropology, and in computer-based education all embrace these two ideas. But, even though many psychologists and educators use the term *constructivism*, they often mean very different things (Driscoll, 2005; McCaslin & Hickey, 2001; Phillips, 1997).

One way to organize constructivist views is to talk about two forms of constructivism: psychological and social construction (Palincsar, 1998; Phillips, 1997). We could oversimplify a bit and say that psychological constructivists focus on how individuals use information, resources, and even help

Constructivism View that emphasizes the active role of the learner in building understanding and making sense of information.

*From p. 31 of *Awakening Children's Minds: How Parents and Teachers Can Make a Difference* by L. E. Berk (2004). Used by permission of Oxford University Press.

from others to build and improve their mental models and problem-solving strategies—see Central Idea #1 above. In contrast, social constructivists see learning as increasing our abilities to participate with others in activities that are meaningful in the culture—see Central Idea #2 above (Windschitl, 2002). Let's take a closer look at each type of constructivism.

CONSTRUCTIVIST VIEWS Constructivist theories are based on the ideas that learners actively develop their knowledge by participating in social interactions, rather than passively receive it in package-form from teachers or outside sources.

Psychological/Individual/Cognitive Constructivism. Many psychological theories include some type of constructivism concept because these theories embrace the idea that individuals construct their own cognitive structures as they interpret their experiences in particular situations (Palincsar, 1998). These psychological constructivists "are concerned with how individuals build up certain elements of their cognitive or emotional apparatus" (Phillips, 1997, p. 153). Because they study individual knowledge, beliefs, self-concept, or identity, they are sometimes called individual constructivists or cognitive constructivists; they all focus on the inner psychological life of individuals. When Chelsea talked to the wall in the previous section, she was making meaning using her own individual knowledge and beliefs about how to respond when someone (or something) talks to you. She was using what she knew to impose intellectual structure on her world (Piaget, 1971; Windschitl, 2002). When children observe that most plants need soil to grow and then conclude that plants "eat dirt," they are using what they know about how eating supports life to make sense of plant growth (Linn & Eylon, 2006).

Using these standards, the most recent information processing theories are constructivist because they are concerned with how individuals construct internal representations (propositions, images, concepts, schemas) that can be remembered and retrieved (Mayer, 1996). The outside world is seen as a source of input, but once the sensations are perceived and enter working memory, the important work is assumed to be happening "inside the head" of the individual (Schunk, 2008; Vera & Simon, 1993). Some psychologists, however, believe that information processing is "trivial" or "weak" constructivism because the individual's only constructive contribution is to build accurate internal representations of the outside world (Derry, 1992; Garrison, 1995; Marshall, 1996; Windschitl, 2002).

In contrast, Piaget's psychological (cognitive) constructivist perspective is less concerned with "correct" representations and more interested in meaning as it is constructed by the individual. As we saw in Chapter 2, Piaget proposed that as children develop, their thinking becomes more organized and adaptive and less tied to concrete events. Piaget's special concern was with logic and the construction of universal knowledge that cannot be learned directly from the environment—knowledge such as conservation or reversibility (Miller, 2002). Such knowledge comes from reflecting on and coordinating our own cognitions or thoughts, not from mapping external reality. Piaget saw the social environment as an important factor in development, but did not believe that social interaction was the main mechanism for changing thinking (Moshman, 1997). Some educational and developmental psychologists have referred to Piaget's kind of constructivism as first wave constructivism or "solo" constructivism, with its emphasis on Central Idea #1, individual meaning-making (De Corte, Greer, & Verschaffel, 1996; Paris, Byrnes, & Paris, 2001).

MyEducationLab Go to the Activities and Applications section in Chapter 9 of MyEducationLab and complete Activity 1. As you read the article and complete the accompanying activity, consider the limitations of learning by memorization alone, and the benefits of bringing knowledge to life through authentic learning tasks.

At the extreme end of individual constructivism is the notion of radical constructivism. This perspective holds that there is no reality or truth in the world, only the individual's perceptions and beliefs. Each of us constructs meaning from our own experiences, but we have no way of understanding or "knowing" the reality of others (Woods & Murphy, 2002). A difficulty with this position is that, when pushed to the extreme of relativism, all knowledge and all beliefs are equal because they are all valid individual perceptions. There are problems with this type of thinking for educators. First, teachers have a professional responsibility to emphasize some values, such as honesty or justice, over others such as bigotry and deception. For educators, all perceptions and beliefs are not equal. As teachers, we ask students to work hard to learn. If learning cannot advance understanding because all understandings are equally good, then, as David Moshman (1997) notes, "we might just as well let students continue to believe whatever they believe" (p. 230). Also, it appears that some knowledge, such as counting and one-to-one correspondence, is not constructed, but universal (Geary, 1995; Schunk, 2008).

First wave constructivism A focus on the individual and psychological sources of knowing, as in Piaget's theory.

Radical constructivism Knowledge is assumed to be the individual's construction; it cannot be judged right or wrong.

Vygotsky's Social Constructivism. As you also saw in Chapter 2, Vygotsky emphasized Central Idea #2—that social interaction, cultural tools, and activity shape individual development and learning, just as Ben's interactions on the beach with his father shaped Ben's learning about sea creatures, safety, environmental responsibility, and geography (Martin, 2006). By participating in a broad range of activities with others, learners appropriate the outcomes produced by working together; these outcomes could include both new strategies and knowledge. Appropriation means being able to reason, act, and participate using cultural tools—for example, using conceptual tools such as "force" and "acceleration" to reason in physics (Mason, 2007). In psychological (cognitive) constructivism, learning means individually possessing knowledge, but in social constructivism, learning means belonging to a group and participating in the social construction of knowledge (Mason, 2007). Putting learning in social and cultural context is known as second wave constructivism (Paris et al., 2001).

Because Vygotsky's theory relies heavily on social interactions and the cultural context to explain learning, most psychologists classify him as a social constructivist (Palincsar, 1998; Prawat, 1996). However, some theorists categorize him as a psychological constructivist because he was primarily interested in development within the individual (Moshman, 1997; Phillips, 1997). In a sense, Vygotsky was both. One advantage of Vygotsky's theory of learning is that it gives us a way to consider both the psychological and the social: He bridges both camps. For example, Vygotsky's concept of the zone of proximal development—the area where a child can solve a problem with the help (scaffolding) of an adult or more able peer—has been called a place where culture and cognition create each other (Cole, 1985). Culture creates cognition when the adult uses tools and practices from the culture (language, maps, computers, looms, or music) to steer the child toward goals the culture values (reading, writing, weaving, dance). Cognition creates culture as the adult and child together generate new practices and problem solutions to add to the cultural group's repertoire (Serpell, 1993). So people are both products and producers of their societies and cultures (Bandura, 2001). One way of integrating individual and social constructivism is to think of knowledge as both individually constructed and socially mediated (Windschitl, 2002).

The term constructionism is sometimes used to describe how public knowledge is created. Although this is not our main concern in educational psychology, it is worth a brief discussion.

Constructionism. *Social* constructionists do not focus on individual learning. Their concern is with how public knowledge in disciplines such as science, math, economics, or history is constructed. Beyond this kind of academic knowledge, constructionists also are interested in how common-sense ideas, everyday beliefs, and commonly held understandings about people and the world are communicated to new members of a sociocultural group (Gergen, 1997; Phillips, 1997). Questions raised might include who determines what constitutes history, what is the proper way to behave in public, or how to get elected class president. Social constructionists believe all knowledge is socially constructed, and, more important, that some people have more power than others to define what constitutes such knowledge. Relationships between and among teachers, students, families, and the community are the central issues. Collaboration to understand diverse viewpoints is encouraged, and traditional bodies of knowledge often are challenged (Gergen, 1997). The philosophies of Jacques Derrida and Michel Foucault are important sources for constructionists. Vygotsky's theory, with its attention to how cognition creates culture, has some elements in common with constructionism.

These different perspectives on constructivism raise some general questions, and they disagree on the answers. These questions can never be fully resolved, but different theories tend to favour different positions. Let's consider the questions next.

MyEducationLab
Go to the Podcasts section of Chapter 9 in MyEducationLab and listen to PODCAST—Learning. In this podcast, Anita Woolfolk discusses not only the differences between behavioural, cognitive, and constructivist learning theories, but also the importance of understanding and appreciating all three when thinking about learning.

Appropriation Being able to internalize or take for yourself knowledge and skills developed during interaction with others or with cultural tools.

Second wave constructivism A focus on the social and cultural sources of knowing, as in Vygotsky's theory.

Constructionism How public knowledge in disciplines such as science, math, economics, or history is constructed.

How Is Knowledge Constructed?

One tension among different approaches to constructivism is based on how knowledge is constructed. Moshman (1982) provides three explanations.

1. *The realities and truths of the external world direct knowledge construction.* Individuals *reconstruct* outside reality by building accurate mental representations such as propositional networks, concepts, cause-and-effect patterns, and condition-action production rules that reflect "the way things really are." The more the person learns, the deeper and broader his or her experience is, the closer that person's knowledge will reflect objective reality. Information processing holds this view of knowledge (Cobb & Bowers, 1999).

2. *Internal processes such as Piaget's organization, assimilation, and accommodation direct knowledge construction.* New knowledge is abstracted from old knowledge. Knowledge is not a mirror of reality, but rather an abstraction that grows and develops with cognitive activity. Knowledge is not true or false; it just grows more internally consistent and organized with development.
3. *Both external and internal factors direct knowledge construction.* Knowledge grows through the *interactions* of internal (cognitive) and external (environmental and social) factors. Vygotsky's description of cognitive development through the appropriation and use of cultural tools such as language is consistent with this view (Bruning et al., 2004). Another example is Bandura's theory of reciprocal interactions among people, behaviours, and environments described in Chapter 10 (Schunk, 2000). Table 9.2 summarizes the three general explanations about how knowledge is constructed.

Knowledge: Situated or General?

A second question that cuts across many constructivist perspectives is whether knowledge is internal, general, and transferable or bound to the time and place in which it is constructed. Psychologists who emphasize the social construction of knowledge and situated learning affirm Vygotsky's notion that learning is inherently social and embedded in a particular cultural setting (Cobb & Bowers, 1999). What is true in one time and place—such as the "fact" before Columbus's time that the earth was flat—becomes false in another time and place. Particular ideas may be useful within a specific community of practice, such as 15th-century navigation, but useless outside that community. What counts as new knowledge is determined in part by how well the new idea fits with current accepted practice. Over time, the current practice may be questioned and even overthrown, but until such major shifts occur, current practice will shape what is considered valuable.

Situated learning emphasizes that learning in the real world is not like studying in school. It is more like an apprenticeship where novices, with the support of an expert guide and model, take on more and more responsibility until they are able to function independently. Proponents of this view believe situated learning explains learning in factories, around the dinner table, in high school halls, in street gangs, in the business office, and on the playground.

Situated learning is often described as "enculturation," or adopting the norms, behaviours, skills, beliefs, language, and attitudes of a particular community. The community might be mathematicians, gang members, writers, students in your grade 8 class, or soccer players—any group that has particular ways of thinking and doing. Knowledge is seen *not* as individual cognitive structures

Community of practice Social situation or context in which ideas are judged useful or true.

Situated learning The idea that skills and knowledge are tied to the situation in which they were learned and are difficult to apply in new settings.

TABLE 9.2 How Knowledge Is Constructed

Type	Assumptions About Learning and Knowledge	Example Theories
External direction	Knowledge is acquired by constructing a representation of the outside world. Direct teaching, feedback, and explanation affect learning. Knowledge is accurate to the extent that it reflects the "way things really are" in the outside world.	Information processing
Internal direction	Knowledge is constructed by transforming, organizing, and reorganizing previous knowledge. Knowledge is not a mirror of the external world, even though experience influences thinking and thinking influences knowledge. Exploration and discovery are more important than teaching.	Piaget
Both external and internal direction	Knowledge is constructed based on social interactions and experience. Knowledge reflects the outside world as filtered through and influenced by culture, language, beliefs, interactions with others, direct teaching, and modelling. Guided discovery, teaching, models, and coaching as well as the individual's prior knowledge, beliefs, and thinking affect learning.	Vygotsky

but as a creation of the community over time. The practices of the community—the ways of interacting and getting things done, as well as the tools the community has created—constitute the knowledge of that community. Learning means becoming more able to participate in those practices and to use the tools (Greeno, Collins, & Resnick, 1996; Mason, 2007; Rogoff, 1998).

At the most basic level, "situated learning emphasizes the idea that much of what is learned is specific to the situation in which it is learned" (Anderson, Reder, & Simon, 1996, p. 5). Thus, some would argue, learning to do calculations in school may help students do more school calculations, but it may not help them balance a chequebook, because the skills can be applied only in the context in which they were learned, namely school (Lave, 1997; Lave & Wenger, 1991). But it also appears that knowledge and skills can be applied across contexts that were not part of the initial learning situation, as when you use your ability to read and calculate to complete your income taxes, even though learning how to use income tax forms was not part of your high school curriculum (Anderson et al., 1996).

MyEducationLab Go to the Teacher Talk section of Chapter 9 of MyEducationLab and watch a video of Terry Kaldhusdal, 2007 Teacher of the Year from Wisconsin, explaining how he teaches his students to think using real-life situations.

Learning that is situated in school does not have to be doomed or irrelevant (Bereiter, 1997). As you saw in Chapter 8, a major question in educational psychology—and education in general—concerns the *transfer* of knowledge from one situation to another. How can you encourage this transfer from one situation to another? Help is on the way in the next section.

Common Elements of Constructivist Student-Centred Teaching

STOP & THINK What makes a lesson student-centred? List the characteristics and features that put the student at the centre of learning.

We have looked at some areas of disagreement among the constructivist perspectives, but what about areas of agreement? All constructivist theories assume that knowledge develops as learners, like Chelsea and Ben, try to make sense of their experiences. "Learners, therefore, are not empty vessels waiting to be filled, but rather active organisms seeking meaning" (Driscoll, 2005, p. 487). These learners construct mental models or schemas and continue to revise them to make better sense of their experiences. Their constructions do not necessarily resemble external reality; rather, they are the unique interpretations of the learner, like Chelsea's friendly, persistent wall. This doesn't mean that all constructions are equally useful or viable. Learners test their understandings against experience and the understandings of other people—they negotiate and co-construct meanings like Ben did with his father.

Constructivists share similar goals for learning. They emphasize knowledge in use rather than the storing of inert facts, concepts, and skills. Learning goals include developing abilities to find and solve ill-structured problems, critical thinking, inquiry, self-determination, and openness to multiple perspectives (Driscoll, 2005). Even though there is no single constructivist theory, many constructivist approaches recommend the following five conditions for learning:

1. Embed learning in complex, realistic, and relevant learning environments.
2. Provide for social negotiation and shared responsibility as a part of learning.
3. Support multiple perspectives and use multiple representations of content.
4. Nurture self-awareness and an understanding that knowledge is constructed.
5. Encourage ownership of learning. (Driscoll, 2005; Marshall, 1992)

Before we discuss particular teaching approaches, let's look more closely at these dimensions of constructivist teaching.

Complex Learning Environments and Authentic Tasks. Constructivists believe that students should not be given stripped-down, simplified problems and basic skills drills, but instead should encounter **complex learning environments** that deal with "fuzzy," ill-structured problems. The world beyond school presents few simple problems or step-by-step directions, so schools should be sure that every student has experience solving complex problems. Complex problems are not simply difficult ones; they have many parts. There are multiple, interacting elements in complex problems and multiple possible solutions. There is no one right way to reach a conclusion, and each solution may bring a new set of problems. These complex problems should be embedded in authentic tasks and activities,

Complex learning environments Problems and learning situations that mimic the ill-structured nature of real life.

the kinds of situations that students would face as they apply what they are learning to the real world (Needles & Knapp, 1994). Students may need support (scaffolding) as they work on these complex problems, with teachers helping them find resources, keeping track of their progress, breaking larger problems down into smaller ones, and so on. This aspect of constructivist approaches is consistent with situated learning in the sense that it emphasizes learning in situations where it will be applied.

AUTHENTIC TASKS AND SOCIAL INTERACTIONS Constructivist approaches recommend that educators emphasize complex, realistic, and relevant learning environments, as well as the importance of social interactions in the learning process. For example, the students here are collaborating to create a household budget.

Social Negotiation. Many constructivists share Vygotsky's belief that higher mental processes develop through social negotiation and interaction, so collaboration in learning is valued. The Language Development and Hypermedia Group (1992) suggests that a major goal of teaching is to develop students' abilities to establish and defend their own positions while respecting the positions of others and working together to negotiate or co-construct meaning. To accomplish this exchange, students must talk and listen to each other. It is a challenge for children in cultures that are individualistic and competitive, such as those in the United States, to adopt what has been called an intersubjective attitude—a commitment to build shared meaning by finding common ground and exchanging interpretations.

Multiple Perspectives and Representations of Content. When students encounter only one model, one analogy, one way of understanding complex content, they often oversimplify as they try to apply that one approach to every situation. Anita saw this happen in her educational psychology class when six students presented an example of guided discovery learning. The students' presentation was a near copy of a guided discovery demonstration that she had given earlier in the semester, but with some major misconceptions. The students knew only one way to represent discovery learning. Resources for the class should have provided multiple representations of content using different analogies, examples, and metaphors.

Rand Spiro and his colleagues (1991) suggest that "revisiting the same material, at different times, in rearranged contexts, for different purposes, and from different conceptual perspectives is essential for attaining the goals of advanced knowledge acquisition" (p. 28). This idea is consistent with Jerome Bruner's (1966) spiral curriculum, a structure for teaching that introduces the fundamental structure of all subjects—the "big ideas"—early in the school years, then revisits the subjects in more and more complex forms over time.

Understanding the Knowledge Construction Process. Constructivist approaches emphasize making students aware of their own role in constructing knowledge (Cunningham, 1992). The assumptions we make, our beliefs, and our experiences shape what each of us comes to "know" about the world. Different assumptions and different experiences lead to different knowledge. If students are aware of the influences that shape their thinking, they will be more able to choose, develop, and defend positions in a self-critical way while respecting the positions of others.

Student Ownership of Learning. "While there are several interpretations of what [constructivist] theory means, most agree that it involves a dramatic change in the focus of teaching, putting the students' own efforts to understand at the center of the educational enterprise" (Prawat, 1992, p. 357). Student ownership does not mean that the teacher abandons responsibility for instruction. Because the design of teaching is a central issue in this book, we will spend the rest of this chapter discussing examples of ownership of learning and of student-centred instruction.

Social negotiation Aspect of the learning process that relies on collaboration with others and respect for different perspectives.

Intersubjective attitude A commitment to build shared meaning with others by finding common ground and exchanging interpretations.

Multiple representations of content Considering problems using various analogies, examples, and metaphors.

Spiral curriculum Bruner's design for teaching that introduces the fundamental structure of all subjects early in the school years, then revisits the subjects in more and more complex forms over time.

APPLYING CONSTRUCTIVIST PERSPECTIVES

Even though there are many applications of constructivist views of learning, we can recognize constructivist approaches by the activities of the teacher and the students. Mark Windschitl (2002) suggests that the following activities encourage meaningful learning:

- Teachers elicit students' ideas and experiences in relation to key topics, then fashion learning situations that help students elaborate on or restructure their current knowledge.
- Students are given frequent opportunities to engage in complex, meaningful, problem-based activities.
- Teachers provide students with a variety of information resources as well as the tools (technological and conceptual) necessary to mediate learning.
- Students work collaboratively and are given support to engage in task-oriented dialogue with one another.
- Teachers make their own thinking processes explicit to learners and encourage students to do the same through dialogue, writing, drawings, or other representations.
- Students are routinely asked to apply knowledge in diverse and authentic contexts, explain ideas, interpret texts, predict phenomena, and construct arguments based on evidence, rather than focus exclusively on the acquisition of predetermined "right answers."
- Teachers encourage students' reflective and autonomous thinking in conjunction with the conditions listed above.
- Teachers employ a variety of assessment strategies to understand how students' ideas are evolving and to give feedback on the processes as well as the products of their thinking. (p. 137)

In addition, constructivist approaches include *scaffolding* to support students' developing expertise. One implication of Vygotsky's theory of cognitive development is that deep understanding requires that students grapple with problems in their zone of proximal development; they need scaffolding in order to work in that zone. Here is a definition of scaffolding that emphasizes the knowledge that both teacher and student bring—both are experts on something: "Scaffolding is a powerful conception of teaching and learning in which teachers and students create meaningful connections between teachers' cultural knowledge and the everyday experience and knowledge of the student" (McCaslin & Hickey, 2001, p. 137). Look back at the conversation on the beach between Ben and his father at the beginning of the previous section. Notice how the father used the abalone sandwich and the necklace—connections to Ben's experience and knowledge—to scaffold Ben's understanding.

In this section, we will examine three specific teaching approaches that put the student at the centre of learning: inquiry and problem-based learning, cognitive apprenticeships, and cooperative learning. Another approach, conceptual change, is discussed in Chapter 13.

Inquiry and Problem-Based Learning

John Dewey described the basic inquiry learning format in 1910. There have been many adaptations of this strategy, but the form usually includes the following elements (Echevarria, 2003; Lashley, Matczynski, & Rowley, 2002). The teacher presents a puzzling event, question, or problem. The students then

- formulate hypotheses to explain the event or solve the problem,
- collect data to test the hypotheses,
- draw conclusions, and
- reflect on the original problem and the thinking processes needed to solve it.

Inquiry learning Approach in which the teacher presents a puzzling situation and students solve the problem by gathering data and testing their conclusions.

Examples of Inquiry. Shirley Magnusson and Annemarie Palincsar have developed a teachers' guide for planning, implementing, and assessing different phases of inquiry science units (Palincsar, Magnusson, Marano, Ford, & Brown, 1998). The model, called *Guided Inquiry supporting Multiple Literacies*, or GIsML, is shown in Figure 9.1.

FIGURE 9.1 **A Model to Guide Teacher Thinking About Inquiry-Based Science Instruction**

The straight lines show the sequence of phases in instruction and the curved lines show cycles that might be repeated during instruction.

Source: From "Designing a Community of Practice: Principles and Practices of the GIsML Community," by A. S. Palincsar, S. J. Magnusson, N. Marano, D. Ford, and N. Brown, 1998, *Teaching and Teacher Education, 14,* p. 12. Adapted with permission from Elsevier.

Based on this model, the teacher first identifies a curriculum area and some general guiding questions, puzzles, or problems. For example, the teacher chooses *communication* as the area and asks this general question: "How and why do humans and animals communicate?" Next, several specific focus questions are posed. "How do whales communicate?" "How do gorillas communicate?" The focus questions have to be carefully chosen to guide students toward important understandings. One key idea in understanding animal communication is the relationship among the animals' physiological structures, survival functions, and habitat. Animals have specific *structures* such as large ears or echo-locators, which *function* to find food or attract mates or identify predators, and these structures and functions are related to the animals' *habitats.* Thus, focus questions must ask about animals with different structures for communication, different functional needs for survival, and different habitats. Questions about animals with the same kinds of structures or the same habitats would not be good focus points for inquiry (Magnusson & Palincsar, 1995).

The next phase is to engage students in the inquiry, perhaps by playing different animal sounds, having students make guesses and claims about communication, and asking the students questions about their guesses and claims. Then, the students conduct both first-hand and second-hand investigations. *First-hand investigations* are direct experiences and experiments, for example, measuring the size of bats' eyes and ears in relation to their bodies (using pictures or videos—not real bats!). In *second-hand investigations*, students consult books, the internet, interviews with experts, and other resources to find specific information or get new ideas. As part of their investigating, the students begin to identify patterns. The curved lines in Figure 9.1 show that cycles can be repeated. In fact, students might go through several cycles of investigating, identifying patterns, and reporting results before moving on to constructing explanations and making final reports. Another possible cycle is to evaluate explanations before reporting by making and then checking predictions, applying the explanation to new situations.

Inquiry teaching allows students to learn content and process at the same time. In the examples above, students learned about how animals communicate and how physiological structures are related to habitats. In addition, they learned the inquiry process itself—how to solve problems, evaluate solutions, and think critically.

Problem-Based Learning. Whereas inquiry learning grew out of practices in science, problem-based learning grew out of research on expert knowledge in medicine. The goals of problem-based learning are to help students develop flexible knowledge that can be applied in many situations, in contrast to inert knowledge. Inert knowledge is information that is memorized but seldom applied (Cognition and Technology Group at Vanderbilt [CTGV], 1996; Whitehead, 1929). Other goals of problem-based learning are to enhance intrinsic motivation and skills in problem solving, collaboration, evidence-based decision making, and self-directed lifelong learning.

In problem-based learning, students are confronted with a problem that launches their inquiry as they collaborate to find solutions. The students identify and analyze the problem based on the facts from the scenario, and then they begin to generate hypotheses about solutions. As they suggest hypotheses, they identify missing information—what do they need to know to test their solutions? This launches a phase of research. Then, students apply their new knowledge, evaluate their problem solutions, recycle to research again if necessary, and finally reflect on the knowledge and skills they have gained. Throughout the entire process, students are not alone or unguided. Their thinking and problem solving is scaffolded by the teacher, computer software supports, models, coaching, expert hints, guides and organizational aids, or other students in the collaborative groups—so working memory is not overloaded. For example, as students work, they may have to fill in a diagram that helps them distinguish between "claims" and "reasons" in a scientific argument (Derry, Hmelo-Silver, Nagarajan, Chernobilsky, & Beitzel, 2006; Hmelo-Silver, Ravit, & Chinn, 2007).

In true problem-based learning, the problem is real and the students' actions matter. In one example, a teacher capitalized on current affairs to encourage student reading, writing, and social studies problem solving:

> Cathie's elementary class learned about the Exxon Valdez oil spill in the Gulf of Alaska. She brought a newspaper article to class that sequenced in logbook fashion the events of the oil spill in Prince William Sound. To prepare her students to understand the article, she had her students participate in several background-building experiences. First, they used a world map, an encyclopedia, and library books to gather and share relevant information. Next, she simulated an oil spill by coating an object with oil. By then, the class was eager to read the article. (Espe, Worner, & Hotkevich, 1990, p. 45)*

After asking students to read and discuss the newspaper article, the teacher asked the class to imagine how the problem might have been prevented. Students had to explain and support their proposed solutions. The next week, the students read another newspaper article about how people were helping with the cleanup efforts associated with the oil spill. The teacher asked if the students wanted to help, and they replied with an enthusiastic "Yes!" The students designed posters and made speeches requesting donations of clean towels to be used to clean the oil-soaked animals in Prince William Sound. The class sent four large bags of towels to Alaska to help in the cleanup. The teacher's and the students' reading, writing, research, and speaking were directed toward solving a real-life problem (Espe et al., 1990). Other authentic problems that might be the focus for student projects include reducing pollution in local rivers, resolving student conflicts in school, raising money for tsunami or hurricane relief, or building a playground for young children.

Some problems are not authentic in the sense that they directly affect students' lives, but they are engaging. For example, the Cognition and Technology Group at Vanderbilt University (1993) has developed a problem-based approach called anchored instruction. The *anchor* is a rich, interesting, and challenging situation. This anchor provides a focus—a reason for sorting out ideas to solve the problem. The intended outcome is to develop knowledge that is useful and flexible, not inert. For example, in a computer simulation called the *River of Life Challenge* (Sherwood, 2002), students meet Billy and his lab partner Suzie who are analyzing the quality of water from a local

Problem-based learning Methods that provide students with realistic problems that don't necessarily have "right" answers.

Anchored instruction A type of problem-based learning that uses a complex, interesting situation as an anchor for learning.

*Source: "Whole Language—What a Bargain" by C. Espe, C. Worner, & M. Hotkevich. *Educational Leadership*, 47(6), p. 45.

FIGURE 9.2

The STAR Legacy Problem-Based Learning Cycle
This is the learning cycle based on work at the Learning Technology Center at Vanderbilt University and used by the Vanderbilt, Northwestern, Texas, Harvard/MIT Engineering Research Center (VaNTH-ERC) to design learning challenges in bioengineering/biomedical engineering. The cycle can be adapted for many subjects and grades.

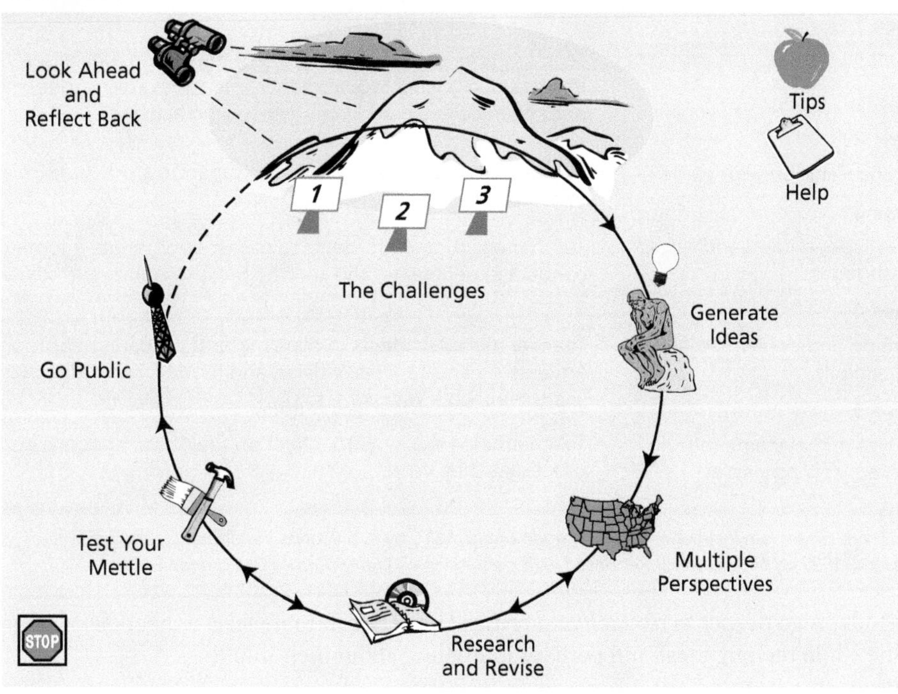

Source: *Instructional Design Theories and Models, Vol. II: A New Paradigm of Instructional Theory* by Schwartz, D.L., Lin, X., Brophy, S., & Bransford, J.D., in text edited by C.M. Reigelut. Copyright 1999 by Taylor & Francis Group, LLC-Books. Reproduced with permission of Taylor & Francis Group LLC—Books in the formats Textbook and Other Book via the Copyright Clearance Center.

river. Suzie is concerned that Billy's conclusions are careless and incomplete. Billy is challenged to research in more depth by the *Legacy League*, a multi-ethnic group of characters who raise questions and direct Billy and Suzie to resources so they can research the answers. The format for the challenge is the STAR Legacy Cycle shown in Figure 9.2. The phases of the cycle are as follows: encounter the challenge, generate ideas, consider multiple perspectives, research and revise your ideas, test your mettle (check your understanding), and go public about your conclusions. Undergraduate science education students who used this simulation improved their graph-reading skills as well as their conceptual understanding of several topics such as the composition of air and the classes of organisms in a river ecosystem (Kumar & Sherwood, 2007).

Let's look at these phases more closely as they might take place in an upper-level science class (Klein & Harris, 2007).

1. The cycle begins with an intriguing *challenge* to the whole class. For example, in biomechanics it might be "Assume you are a living cell in a bioreactor. What things will influence how long you live?" or "Your grandmother is recovering from a broken hip. In which hand should she hold the cane to help her balance?" The question is framed in a way that makes students bring to bear their current knowledge and preconceptions.
2. Next, students *generate ideas* to compile what they currently know and believe using individual, small group, or whole group brainstorming or other activities.
3. Then, *multiple perspectives* are added to the process in the form of outside experts (live, on video, or from texts), websites, magazine or journal articles, or a CD on the subject. In the river challenge above, the *Legacy League* guided Billy and Suzie to explore multiple perspectives.

TABLE 9.3

The Teacher's Role in Problem-Based Learning

Phase	Teacher Behaviour
Phase 1	
Orient students to the problem	Teacher goes over the objectives of the lesson, describes important logistical requirements, and motivates students to engage in self-selected problem-solving activity.
Phase 2	
Organize students for study	Teacher helps students define and organize study tasks related to the problem.
Phase 3	
Assist independent and group investigation	Teacher encourages students to gather appropriate information, conduct experiments, and search for explanations and solutions.
Phase 4	
Develop and present artifacts and exhibits	Teacher assists students in planning and preparing appropriate artifacts such as reports, videos, and models and helps them share their work with others.
Phase 5	
Analyze and evaluate the problem-solving process	Teacher helps students to reflect on their investigations and the processes they used.

Source: From *Classroom Instruction and Management* (p. 161), by R. I. Arends. Published by McGraw-Hill. Copyright © 1997 by McGraw-Hill. Reprinted with permission of The McGraw-Hill Companies, Inc.

4. Students go deeper to *research and revise*. They consult more texts or hear class lectures, all the while revising ideas and perhaps journaling about their thinking.
5. Students *test their mettle* by getting feedback from other students or the teacher about their tentative conclusions. Some formative (ungraded) tests might check their understanding at this point.
6. Students *go public* with their final conclusions and solutions in the form of an oral presentation, poster/project, or final exam.

Project-based science is an approach to teaching similar to problem-based learning that focuses on the middle grades (Krajcik & Czerniak, 2007). The teacher's role in methods based on problem-based learning is summarized in Table 9.3.

Research on Inquiry and Problem-Based Learning. Inquiry methods must be carefully planned and organized, especially for less-prepared students who may lack the background knowledge and problem-solving skills needed to benefit. When they are well planned and scaffolded, inquiry learning activities can lead to greater achievement. For example, using an open-ended and software-supported inquiry science approach called GenScope that explores genetics, students in high school science classrooms learned significantly more compared to students in traditional classrooms (Hickey, Kindfield, Horwitz, & Christie, 1999; Hickey, Wolfe, & Kindfield, 2000). In a study of almost 20 000 middle school students in a large urban district who used inquiry-based materials, those who participated in inquiry learning had significantly higher passing rates on standardized tests. African American males especially benefited from these methods (Geier et al., in press). Several other studies point to increases in student engagement and motivation with inquiry learning (Hmelo-Silver et al., 2007).

Much of the research on problem-based learning has taken place in medical schools and results have been mixed. In one study, students learning through problem-based instruction performed better at clinical skills such as problem formation and reasoning than students studying in usual ways, but they were worse in their basic knowledge of science and felt less prepared in science (Albanese & Mitchell, 1993). In another study, medical students who learned with problem-based approaches created more accurate and coherent solutions to medical problems (Hmelo, 1998). In another study, MBA students who learned a concept using problem-based methods better explained the concept than students who had learned the concept from lecture and discussion

(Capon & Kuhn, 2004). Although students who are better at self-regulation may benefit more from problem-based methods (Evensen, Salisbury-Glennon, & Glenn, 2001), using problem-based methods over time can help *all* students to develop self-directed learning skills.

Cindy Hmelo-Silver (2004; Hmelo-Sliver et al., 2007) reviewed the research and found evidence that problem-based learning supports the construction of flexible knowledge and the development of problem-solving and self-directed learning skills, but less evidence exists that participating in problem-based learning is intrinsically motivating or that it teaches students to collaborate. In studies of high school economics and mathematics classes, recent research favours problem-based approaches for learning more complex concepts and for solving multi-step word problems.

Beware of Either/Or. Bear in mind that you don't have to choose between inquiry or content-focused teaching methods. The best approach for use in elementary and secondary schools may be a balance of content-focused and inquiry or problem-based methods (Arends, 2007). For example, Eva Toth, David Klahr, and Zhe Chen (2000) tested a balanced approach for teaching grade 4 students how to use the controlled variable strategy in science to design good experiments. The method involved three phases: (1) in small groups, students conducted exploratory experiments to identify variables that made a ball roll farther down a ramp; (2) the teacher led a discussion, explained the controlled variable strategy, and modelled good thinking about experiment design; and (3) the students designed and conducted application experiments to isolate which variables caused the ball to roll farther. The combination of inquiry, discussion, explanation, and modelling was successful in helping the students to understand the concepts. Clearly scaffolding supports are key factors in successful inquiry and problem-based learning.

Another constructivist approach that relies heavily on scaffolding is cognitive apprenticeships.

Cognitive Apprenticeships and Reciprocal Teaching

Over the centuries, apprenticeships have proved to be an effective form of education. By working alongside a master and perhaps other apprentices, young people have learned many skills, trades, and crafts. Knowledgeable guides provide models, demonstrations, and corrections, as well as a personal bond that is often motivating. The performances required of the learner are real and important and grow more complex as the learner becomes more competent (Collins, 2006; Linn & Eylon, 2006; Hung, 1999). With *guided participation* in real tasks comes *participatory appropriation*—students appropriate the knowledge, skills, and values involved in doing the tasks (Rogoff, 1995, 1998). In addition, both the newcomers to learning and those with more experience contribute to the community of practice by mastering and remastering skills—sometimes improving these skills in the process (Lave & Wenger, 1991).

Allan Collins (2006) suggests that knowledge and skills learned in school have become too separated from their use in the world beyond school. To correct this imbalance, some educators recommend that schools adopt many of the features of apprenticeships. But rather than learning to sculpt or dance or build a cabinet, apprenticeships in school would focus on cognitive objectives such as reading comprehension, writing, or mathematical problem solving. There are many **cognitive apprenticeship** models, but most share six features:

- Students observe an expert (usually the teacher) *model* the performance.
- Students receive external support through *coaching* or tutoring (including hints, feedback, models, and reminders).
- Students receive conceptual *scaffolding*, which is then gradually faded as the student becomes more competent and proficient.
- Students continually *articulate* their knowledge—putting into words their understanding of the processes and content being learned.
- Students *reflect* on their progress, comparing their problem solving to an expert's performance and to their own earlier performances.
- Students are required to *explore* new ways to apply what they are learning—ways that they have not practised at the expert's side.

As students learn, they are challenged to master more complex concepts and skills and to perform them in many different settings (Roth & Bowen, 1995; Shuell, 1996).

MyEducationLab Go to the Activities and Applications section in Chapter 9 of MyEducationLab and complete Activity 2. As you watch the video and answer the accompanying questions, consider ways in which both students and teachers benefit from classroom dialogue.

Cognitive apprenticeship A relationship in which a less experienced learner acquires knowledge and skills under the guidance of an expert.

NURTURING INDEPENDENT READERS The concept of scaffolding and gradually moving the student toward independent and fluid reading comprehension is a critical component in reciprocal teaching and cognitive apprenticeships.

How can teaching provide cognitive apprenticeships? Teaching through mentoring is one example. Another is cross-age grouping. For example, in the Key School, an inner-city public elementary school in Indianapolis, Indiana, students of different ages work side by side for part of every day on a "pod" designed to have many of the qualities of an apprenticeship. The pods might focus on a craft or a discipline. Examples include gardening, architecture, and "making money." Many levels of expertise are evident in the students of different ages, so students can move at a comfortable pace, but still have the model of a master available. Community volunteers, including many parents, visit to demonstrate a skill that is related to the pod topic.

Alan Schoenfeld's (1989, 1994) proposed method of teaching mathematical problem solving is another example of the cognitive apprenticeship instructional model. Teachers asks students three important questions: What are you doing? Why are you doing it? How will success in what you are doing help you to find a solution to the problem? The teacher's role is not to evaluate students' answers. Rather, the teacher moderates a discussion and gently steers it to help students understand how the problem is structured and alternative paths that can be taken toward solving it.

Cognitive Apprenticeships in Reading: Reciprocal Teaching. The goal of **reciprocal teaching** is to help students understand and think deeply about what they read (Palincsar, 1986; Palincsar & Brown, 1984, 1989). To accomplish this goal, students in small reading groups learn four strategies: *summarizing* the content of a passage, *asking a question* about the central point, *clarifying* the difficult parts of the material, and *predicting* what will come next. These are strategies skilled readers apply almost automatically, but poor readers seldom do—or they don't know how. To use the strategies effectively, poorer readers need direct instruction, modelling, and practice in actual reading situations.

First, the teacher introduces these strategies, perhaps focusing on one strategy each day. As the expert, the teacher explains and models each strategy and encourages student apprentices to practise it. Next, the teacher and the students read a short passage silently. Then, the teacher again provides a model by summarizing, questioning, clarifying, or predicting based on the reading. Everyone reads a second passage, and the students gradually begin to assume the teacher's role. The teacher becomes a member of the group, and may finally leave, as the students take over the teaching. Often, the students' first attempts are halting and incorrect. But the teacher gives clues, guidance, encouragement, support in accomplishing parts of the task (such as providing question stems; explained later in the chapter), modelling, and other forms of scaffolding to help the students master these strategies. The goal is for students to learn to apply these strategies independently as they read so they can make sense of the text on their own.

Applying Reciprocal Teaching. Although reciprocal teaching seems to work with students of almost any age, most of the research has been done with younger adolescents who can read aloud fairly accurately, but who fall far below average in reading comprehension. After 20 hours of practice with this approach, many students who were in the bottom quarter of their class moved up to the average level, or higher, on tests of reading comprehension. Palincsar has identified three guidelines for effective reciprocal teaching (1986):

1. *Shift gradually.* The shift in responsibility from teacher to student must occur gradually.
2. *Match demands to abilities.* The difficulty of the task and the level of responsibility must match the abilities of each student and increase as the student's abilities develop.
3. *Diagnose thinking.* Teachers should carefully observe the "teaching" of each student for clues about how the student is thinking and what kind of instruction the student needs.

Reciprocal teaching A teaching strategy designed to help students understand and think deeply about what they read.

In contrast to some approaches that try to teach 40 or more strategies, an advantage of reciprocal teaching is that it focuses attention on four powerful strategies: summarizing, asking a question, clarifying, and predicting. But these strategies must be taught—not all students will develop them on their own. One study of reciprocal teaching spanning over three years found that questioning was the strategy used most often, but that students had to be taught how to ask higher-level questions because most questions posed by students were literal or superficial (Hacker & Tenent, 2002). Another advantage of reciprocal teaching is that it emphasizes practising these four strategies in the context of actual reading—reading literature and reading texts. Finally, the idea of scaffolding and gradually moving the student toward independent and fluid reading comprehension is a critical component of reciprocal teaching and of cognitive apprenticeships in general (Rosenshine & Meister, 1994).

COOPERATION: A WORTHY GOAL While academics are the key goal, a structured education also prepares students to live and work cooperatively with all kinds of people. Studies of cooperative learning indicate its positive influence on students' empathy, tolerance, friendships, self-confidence, and even school attendance.

Collaboration and Cooperation

Even with all the concern today about academic standards, performance on proficiency tests, and international comparisons of student achievement, schooling has always been about more than academic learning. Of course, academics are the prime directive but, in addition, an education prepares students to live and work cooperatively with all kinds of people. Elliot Aronson sheds some light on this in the excerpt below:

> Most corporations are looking for employees who are not only good at the mastery of a particular set of academic skills but who also have the ability to work harmoniously with a wide variety of coworkers as a cooperative team, to demonstrate initiative and responsibility, and to communicate effectively. (Aronson, 2000, p. 91)

For the past three decades, researchers have examined collaboration and cooperation among students in schools. Although there are some inconsistencies, the majority of the studies indicate that truly cooperative groups have positive effects on students' empathy, tolerance for differences, feelings of acceptance, friendships, self-confidence, and even school attendance (Solomon, Watson, & Battistich, 2001). It is argued that cooperative learning experiences are crucial in preventing many of the social problems that plague children and adolescents (Gillies, 2003, 2004).

Collaboration, Group Work, and Cooperative Learning. The terms *collaboration*, *group work*, and *cooperative learning* often are used as if they mean the same thing. Certainly there is some overlap, but there are differences as well. The distinctions between collaboration and cooperation are not always clear. Ted Panitz (1996) suggests collaboration is a philosophy about how to relate to others—that is, how to learn and work. Collaboration is a way of dealing with people that respects differences, shares authority, and builds on the knowledge that is distributed among other people. Cooperation, on the other hand, is a way of working with others to attain a shared goal (Gillies, 2003). Collaborative learning has roots in the work of British teachers who wanted their students to respond to literature in more active ways as they learned. Cooperative learning has American roots in the work of psychologists John Dewey and Kurt Lewin. You could say that cooperative learning is one way to collaborate in schools.

Group work, on the other hand, is simply several students working together—they may or may not be cooperating. Many activities can be completed in groups. For example, students can work together to conduct a local survey. How do people feel about the plan to build a new mall that will bring more shopping and more traffic? Would the community support or oppose the building of a nuclear power plant? If students must learn 10 new definitions in a biology class, why not let them divide up the terms and definitions and teach one another? Be sure, however, that everyone in the group can handle the task. Sometimes, one or two students end up doing the work of the entire group.

Collaboration A philosophy about how to relate to others—how to learn and work.

Cooperation A way of working with others to attain a shared goal.

Group work can be useful, but true cooperative learning requires much more than simply putting students in groups and dividing up the work. Angela O'Donnell and Jim O'Kelly describe a teacher who claimed to be using "cooperative learning" by asking students to work in pairs on a paper, each writing one part. Unfortunately, the teacher allowed no time to work together and provided no guidance or preparation in cooperative social skills. Students received a grade for their individual part and a group grade for the whole project. One student received an A for his part, but a C for the group project because his partner earned an F—he never turned in any work. So one student was punished with a C for a situation he could not control while the other was rewarded with a C for doing no work at all. This was not cooperative learning—it wasn't even group work (O'Donnell & O'Kelly, 1994).

Beyond Groups to Cooperation. Cooperative learning has a long history in American education, moving in and out of favour over the years. Today, evolving constructivist perspectives have fuelled "a heightened interest in situations where elaboration, interpretation, explanation, and argumentation are integral to the activity of the group and where learning is supported by other individuals" (Webb & Palincsar, 1996, p. 844).

MyEducationLab Go to the Podcasts section of Chapter 9 in MyEducationLab and listen to PODCAST—Cooperative Learning. In this podcast Anita Woolfolk shares some ways that she has used cooperative learning in her university classes to take advantage of students as experts in technology.

Different approaches to learning theory favour cooperative learning for different reasons (O'Donnell, 2002, 2006). Information processing theorists point to the value of group discussion in helping participants rehearse, elaborate, and expand their knowledge. As group members question and explain, they have to organize their knowledge, make connections, and review—all processes that support information processing and memory. Advocates of a Piagetian perspective suggest the interactions in groups can create the cognitive conflict and disequilibrium that lead an individual to question his or her understanding and try out new ideas—or, as Piaget (1985) said, "to go beyond his current state and strike out in new directions" (p. 10). Those who favour Vygotsky's theory suggest that social interaction is important for learning because higher mental functions such as reasoning, comprehension, and critical thinking originate in social interactions and are then internalized by individuals. Students can accomplish mental tasks with social support before they can do them alone. Thus, cooperative learning provides the social support and scaffolding students need to move learning forward.

Table 9.4 summarizes the functions of cooperative learning from different theoretical perspectives, and describes some of the elements of each kind of group. To benefit from these dimensions of cooperative learning, groups must be *cooperative*—all members must participate. But, as any teacher or parent knows, cooperation is not automatic when students are put into groups.

Cooperative learning Situations in which elaboration, interpretation, explanation, and argumentation are integral to the activity of the group and in which learning is supported by other individuals.

What Can Go Wrong: Misuses of Group Learning. Without careful planning and monitoring by the teacher, group interactions can hinder learning and reduce rather than improve social relations in classes. For example, if there is pressure in a group for conformity—perhaps because

TABLE 9.4 Different Forms of Cooperative Learning for Different Purposes

Different forms of cooperative learning (Elaboration, Piagetian, and Vygotskian) fit different purposes, need different structures, and have their own potential problems and possible solutions.

Considerations	Elaboration	Piagetian	Vygotskian
Group size	Small (2–4)	Small	Dyads
Group composition	Heterogeneous/homogeneous	Homogeneous	Heterogeneous
Tasks	Rehearsal/integrative	Exploratory	Skills
Teacher role	Facilitator	Facilitator	Model/guide
Potential problems	Poor help-giving Unequal participation	Inactive No cognitive conflict	Poor help-giving Providing adequate time/dialogue
Averting problems	Direct instruction in help-giving Modelling help-giving Scripting interaction	Structuring controversy	Direct instruction in help-giving Modelling help-giving

Source: From *Educational Psychology Review, 6*, p. 327, "Learning from Peers: Beyond the Rhetoric of Positive Results," by A. M. O'Donnell and J. O'Kelly.

rewards are being misused or one student dominates the others—interactions can be unproductive and unreflective. Misconceptions might be reinforced, or the worst, not the best, ideas may be combined to construct a superficial understanding (Battistich, Solomon, & Delucci, 1993). Students who work in groups but arrive at incorrect answers may be *more* confident that they are correct—a case of "two heads are worse than one" (Puncochar & Fox, 2004). Also, the ideas of students with low status may be ignored or even ridiculed while the contributions of high-status students are accepted and reinforced, regardless of the merit of either set of ideas (Anderson, Holland, & Palincsar, 1997; Cohen, 1986). Mary McCaslin and Tom Good (1996) provide several other disadvantages of group learning, as listed below:

- Students often value the process or procedures over the learning. Speed and finishing early may take precedence over thoughtfulness and learning.
- Rather than challenging and correcting misconceptions, students may support and reinforce misunderstandings.
- Socializing and interpersonal relationships may take precedence over learning.
- Students may simply shift from dependency on the teacher to dependency on the "expert" in the group—learning is still a passive activity and the knowledge that is learned can be incorrect.
- Status differences may be increased rather than decreased. Some students learn to "loaf" because the group progresses with or without their contributions. Others become even more convinced that they are unable to understand without the support of the group.

The next sections examine how teachers can avoid these problems and encourage true cooperation among learners.

Tasks for Cooperative Learning

Like other decisions in teaching, plans for using cooperative groups begin with a goal. What are the students supposed to accomplish? What is the task? Is it a true group task—one that builds on the knowledge and skills of several students—or is the task more appropriate for individuals (Cohen, 1994; O'Donnell, 2006)?

Tasks for cooperative groups may be more or less structured. Highly structured tasks include work that has specific answers—drill and practice, applying routines or procedures, answering questions from readings, computations in mathematics, and so on. Ill-structured complex tasks have multiple answers and unclear procedures, requiring problem finding and higher-order thinking. These ill-structured problems are true group tasks; that is, they are likely to require the resources (knowledge, skills, problem-solving strategies, creativity) of all the group members to accomplish the task, whereas individuals often can accomplish highly structured tasks just as effectively on their own. These distinctions are important because ill-structured, complex, true group tasks appear to require more and higher-quality interactions than routine tasks if learning and problem solving are to occur (Cohen, 1994; Gillies, 2004).

Highly Structured, Review, and Skill-Building Tasks. A relatively structured task such as reviewing previously learned material for an exam might be well served by a structured technique such as STAD (Student Teams Achievement Divisions), in which teams of four students compete to determine which team's members can amass the greatest improvement over previous achievement levels (Slavin, 1995). Praise, recognition, or extrinsic rewards can enhance motivation, effort, and persistence under these conditions, and thus increase learning. Focusing the dialogue by assigning narrow roles also may help students stay engaged when the tasks involve practice or review.

Ill-Structured, Conceptual, and Problem-Solving Tasks. If the task is ill-structured and more cognitive in nature, then an open exchange and elaborated discussion will be more helpful (Cohen, 1994; Ross & Raphael, 1990). Thus, strategies that encourage extended and productive interactions are appropriate when the goal is to develop higher-order thinking and problem solving. In these situations, a tightly structured process, competition among groups for rewards, and rigid assignment of roles are likely to *inhibit* the richness of the students' interactions and to *interfere* with progress toward the goal. Open-ended techniques such as reciprocal questioning

(King, 1994), reciprocal teaching (Palincsar & Brown, 1984; Rosenshine & Meister, 1994), pair-share (Kagan, 1994), or Jigsaw should be more productive because, when used appropriately, they encourage more extensive interaction and elaborate thought in situations where students are exposed to complex materials. In these instances, the use of rewards may well divert the group away from the goal of in-depth cognitive processing. When rewards are offered, the goal often shifts from cognitive processing to achieving the reward as efficiently as possible (Webb & Palincsar, 1996).

Social Skills and Communication Tasks. When the goal of peer learning is enhanced social skills or increased intergroup understanding and appreciation of diversity, the assignment of specific roles and functions within the group might support communication (Cohen, 1994; Kagan, 1994). In these situations, it can be helpful to rotate leadership roles so that minority group students and females have the opportunity to demonstrate and develop leadership skills; in addition, all group members can experience the leadership capabilities of each individual (Miller & Harrington, 1993). Rewards probably are not necessary, and they may actually get in the way because the goal is to build community, a sense of respect, and responsibility for all team members.

Preparing Students for Cooperative Learning

David and Roger Johnson (1999a) list the following five elements as defining true cooperative learning groups:

- Face-to-face interaction
- Positive interdependence
- Individual accountability
- Collaborative skills
- Group processing

Students *interact face-to-face* and close together, not across the room from each other. Group members experience *positive interdependence*—they need each other for support, explanations, and guidance. Even though they work together and help each other, members of the group must ultimately demonstrate learning on their own; they are held *individually accountable* for learning, often through individual tests or other assessments. *Collaborative skills* are necessary for effective group functioning. Often, these skills, such as giving constructive feedback, reaching consensus, and involving every member, must be taught and practised before the groups tackle a learning task. Finally, members monitor *group processes* and relationships to make sure the group is working effectively and to learn about the dynamics of groups. They take time to ask, "How are we doing as a group? Is everyone working together?"

Research on students in grades 8 through 12 in Australia found that the children in cooperative groups structured to require positive interdependence and mutual helping learned more in math, science, and English than students in unstructured learning groups (Gillies, 2003). In addition, compared to students in the unstructured groups, students in the structured groups also said learning was more fun.

Setting Up Cooperative Groups. How large should a cooperative group be? Again, the answer depends on the goals you set for learning. Whether the purpose is for group members to review, rehearse information, or practise, or to encourage each student to participate in discussions, problem solving, or computer learning, groups of two to four members work best. Also, when setting up cooperative groups, it often makes sense to balance the number of boys and girls. Some research indicates that when there are just a few girls in a group, they tend to be left out of the discussions unless they are the most able or assertive members. By contrast, when there are only one or two boys in the group, they tend to dominate and be "interviewed" by the girls unless these boys are less able than the girls or are very shy. In some studies of mixed-gender groups, girls avoided conflict and boys dominated discussion (O'Donnell & O'Kelly, 1994; Webb & Palincsar, 1996). Whatever the case, teachers must monitor groups to make sure every member is contributing and learning.

TABLE 9.5 Levels of Help in Cooperative Groups
Students are more likely to learn if they give and receive higher-level help.

Level	Description and Example
Highest	
6	Verbally labelled explanation of how to solve part or all of the problem ("Multiply 13 cents by 29, because 29 minutes are left after the first minute.")
5	Numerical rule with no verbal labels for the numbers ("This is 30, so you minus 1.")
4	Numerical expression or equation ("13 times 29.")
3	Numbers to write or copy ("Put 13 on top, 29 on the bottom. Then you times it.")
2	Answer to part or all of the problem ("I got $3.77.")
1	Non-content or non-informational response ("Just do it the way she said.")
0	No response
Lowest	

Source: From "Productive helping in cooperative groups," by N. M. Webb, S. H. Farviar, & A. M. Mastergeorge. *Theory in Practice,* 41(1), p. 14.

Giving and Receiving Explanations. In practice, the effects of learning in a group vary, depending on what actually happens in the group and who is in it. If only a few people take responsibility for the work, these people will learn, but the non-participating members probably will not. Students who ask questions, get answers, and attempt explanations are more likely to learn than students whose questions go unasked or unanswered. In fact, there is evidence that the more a student provides elaborated, thoughtful explanations to other students in a group, the more the *explainer* learns. Giving good explanations appears to be even more important for learning than receiving explanations (O'Donnell, 2006; Webb, Farivar, & Mastergeorge, 2002; Webb & Palincsar, 1996). In order to explain, you have to organize the information, put it into your own words, think of examples and analogies (which connect the information to things you already know), and test your understanding by answering questions. These are excellent learning strategies (King, 1990, 2002; O'Donnell & O'Kelly, 1994).

Good explanations are relevant, timely, correct, and elaborated enough to help the listener correct misunderstandings; the best explanations tell why (Webb et al., 2002; Webb & Mastergeorge, 2003). For example, in a middle school mathematics class, students worked in groups on the following problem:

> Find the cost of a 30-minute telephone call to the area code 604 where the first minute costs $0.22 and each additional minute costs $0.13.

The level of explanation and help students received was significantly related to learning; the higher the level, the more learning that took place. Table 9.5 shows the different levels of help. Of course, the students must pay attention to and use the help in order to learn. And the receiver of the help also has responsibilities if learning is to go well. For example, if a helper says, "13 cents times 29," then the receiver should say, "Why is it 29?" Asking good questions and giving clear explanations are critical, and usually these skills must be taught.

Assigning Roles. Some teachers assign roles to students to encourage cooperation and full participation. Several roles are described in Table 9.6 on page 326. If you use roles, be sure that the roles support learning. In groups that focus on social skills, roles should support listening, encouragement, and respect for differences. In groups that focus on practice, review, or mastery of basic skills, roles should support persistence, encouragement, and participation. In groups that focus on higher-order problem solving or complex learning, roles should encourage thoughtful discussion, sharing of explanations and insights, probing, brainstorming, and creativity. Make sure that you don't communicate to students that the major purpose of the groups is simply to do the procedures—the roles. Roles are supports for learning, not ends in themselves (Woolfolk Hoy & Tschannen-Moran, 1999).

TABLE 9.6

Possible Student Roles in Cooperative Learning Groups
Depending on the purpose of the group and the age of the participants, having these assigned roles might help students cooperate and learn. Of course, students may need to be taught how to enact each role effectively, and roles should be rotated so students can participate in different aspects of group learning.

Role	Description
Encourager	Encourages reluctant or shy students to participate
Praiser/cheerleader	Shows appreciation of others' contributions and recognizes accomplishments
Gate keeper	Equalizes participation and makes sure no one dominates
Coach	Helps with the academic content, explains concepts
Question commander	Makes sure all students' questions are asked and answered
Checker	Checks the group's understanding
Taskmaster	Keeps the group on task
Recorder	Writes down ideas, decisions, and plans
Reflector	Keeps the group aware of progress (or lack of progress)
Quiet captain	Monitors noise level
Materials monitor	Picks up and returns materials

Source: From *Cooperative Learning* by S. Kagan. Published by Kagan Publishing, San Clemente, CA. Copyright © 1994 by Kagan Publishing. Adapted with permission. 1-800-WEE CO-OP.

Often, cooperative learning strategies include group reports to the entire class. If you have been on the receiving end of these class reports, you know that they can be deadly dull. To make the process more useful for the audience as well as the reporters, Annemarie Palincsar and Leslie Herrenkohl (2002) taught class members to use intellectual roles as they listened to reports. These roles were based on the scientific strategies of predicting and theorizing, summarizing results, and relating predictions and theories to results. Some audience members were assigned the role of checking the reports for clear relationships between predictions and theories. Other students in the audience listened for clarity in the findings. And the rest of the students were responsible for evaluating how well the group reports linked prediction, theories, and findings. Research shows that using these roles promotes class dialogue, thinking and problem solving, and conceptual understanding (Palincsar & Herrenkohl, 2002). Table 9.7 summarizes the considerations to take into account when designing cooperative learning, based on the goals of the group.

MyEducationLab
Go to the Activities and Applications section in Chapter 9 of MyEducationLab and complete Activity 3. As you watch the video and answer the accompanying questions, look for ways in which the teacher fosters student confidence and self-regulation.

Designs for Cooperation

Developing deep understandings in cooperative groups requires that all the group members participate in high-quality discussions. Discussions that support learning include talk that interprets, connects, explains, and uses evidence to support arguments. We now turn to different strategies that build in structures to support both participation and high-quality discussions.

Reciprocal Questioning. Reciprocal questioning requires no special materials or testing procedures and can be used with students in a wide range of ages. After a lesson or presentation by the teacher, students work in pairs or triads to ask and answer questions about the material (King, 1990, 1994, 2002). The teacher provides question stems (see Table 9.8 on page 328), and then students are taught how to develop specific questions about the lesson material using the generic question stems. The students create questions, and then take turns asking and answering. This process has proved more effective than traditional discussion groups because it seems to encourage deeper thinking about the material. Questions such as those listed in Table 9.8, which encourage students to make connections between the lesson and previous knowledge or experience, seem to be the

Reciprocal questioning Students working in pairs or triads to ask and answer questions about lesson material.

TABLE 9.7

What Should You Consider in Planning and Using Cooperative Learning Methods?

Considerations	Social Skills Tasks: Team Building, Cooperation Skills	Structured Tasks: Review, Practice Facts, and Skills	Unstructured Tasks: Conceptual, Problem Solving, Thinking and Reasoning
Group size and composition	Groups of 2–5, common interest groups, mixed groups, random groups	Groups of 2–4, mixed ability, high-medium/medium-low or high-low/medium-medium	Groups of 2–4, select members to encourage interaction
Why assign roles?	To monitor participation and conflict, rotate leadership	To monitor engagement and ensure low-status students have resources to offer, i.e., Jigsaw	Only to encourage interaction, divergent thinking, and extended, connected discourse, i.e., debate sides, group facilitator
Extrinsic rewards/incentives	Not necessary, may be helpful	To support motivation, effort, persistence	Not necessary
Teacher's role	Model, encourager	Model, director, coach	Model, facilitator
Student skills needed	Listening, turn-taking, encouraging, managing conflict	Questioning, explaining, encouraging, content knowledge, learning strategies	Questioning, explaining, elaborating, probing, divergent thinking, providing rationales, synthesizing
What supports learning? Watch and listen for . . .	Modelling and practice	Giving multiple, elaborated explanations, attention and practice	Quantity and quality of interactions, using and connecting knowledge resources, probing, and elaboration
Potential problems	Unproductive conflict, non-participation	Poor help-giving skills, disengaged or excluded students	Disengaged or excluded students, cognitive loafing, superficial thinking, avoiding controversy
Averting problems	Simpler task, direct teaching of social skills, team building, conflict resolution skills, discuss group process	Structure interdependence and individual accountability, teach helping and explaining	Structure controversy, assign "thinking roles," allow adequate time
Small start	One or two skills, i.e., listening and paraphrasing	Pairs of students quizzing each other	Numbered heads together

Source: From "Implications of cognitive approaches to peer learning for teacher education," by A. Woolfolk Hoy & M. Tschannen-Moran in *Cognitive perspectives on peer learning*, A. O'Donnell and A. King (Eds.), 1999, p. 278. Adapted with permission of Taylor and Francis Group, LLC, a division of Informa plc.

most helpful. For example, using the question stems in Table 9.8, a small group in Mr. Garcia's grade 9 world cultures class had the following discussion about the concept of *culture*:

Sally: In your own words, what does *culture* mean?

Jim: Well, Mr. Garcia said in the lesson that a culture is the knowledge and understandings shared by the members of a society. I guess it's all the things and beliefs and activities that people in a society have in common. It includes things like religion, laws, music, medical practices, stuff like that.

Sally: And dance, art, family roles.

Barry: Knowledge includes language. So, I guess cultures include language, too.

Jim: I guess so. Actually, I have a question about that: How does a culture influence the language of a society?

Barry: Well, for one thing, the language is made up of words that are important to the people of that culture. Like, the words name things that the people care about, or need, or use. And so, different cultures would have different vocabularies. Some cultures may not even have a word for *telephone*, because they don't have any. But, phones are important in our culture, so we have lots of different words for phones, like *cell phone*, *digital phone*, *desk phone*, *cordless phone*, *phone machine*, and . . .

TABLE 9.8 Question Stems to Encourage Dialogue in Reciprocal Questioning

After studying materials or participating in a lesson, students use these question stems to develop questions and share answers.

What is a new example of . . .?
How would you use . . . to . . .?
What would happen if . . .?
What are the strengths and weaknesses of . . .?
How does . . . tie in with what we learned before?
Explain why . . . Explain how . . .
How does . . . affect . . .?
What is the meaning of . . .?
Why is . . . important?
How are . . . and . . . similar? How are . . . and . . . different?
What is the best . . . and why?
Compare . . . and . . . with regard to . . .
What do you think causes . . .?
What conclusions can you draw about . . .?
Do you agree or disagree with this statement . . .? Support your answer.

Source: From "Structuring peer interaction to promote high-level cognitive processing," by A. King. *Theory in Practice*, 41(1), pp. 34–35.

Jim (laughing): I'll bet desert cultures don't have any words for *snow* or *skiing*.

Sally (turning to Barry): What's your question?

Barry: I've got a great question! You'll never be able to answer it. What would happen if there was a group somewhere without any spoken language? Maybe they were all born not being able to speak, or something like that. How would that affect their culture, or could there even *be* a culture?

Sally: Well, it would mean they couldn't communicate with each other.

Jim: And they wouldn't have any music! Because they wouldn't be able to sing.

Barry: But wait! Why couldn't they communicate? Maybe they would develop a nonverbal language system, you know, the way people use hand signals, or the way deaf people use sign language. (King, 2002, pp. 34–35)

Jigsaw. Elliot Aronson and his graduate students invented the concept of the Jigsaw Classroom when he was a professor of social psychology at the University of Texas at Austin. Some of Anita's friends worked on his research team. Aronson developed the approach "as a matter of absolute necessity to help defuse a highly explosive situation" (Aronson, 2000, p. 137). The Austin schools had just been desegregated by court order. White, African American, and Hispanic students were together in classrooms for the first time. Hostility and turmoil ensued with fistfights in corridors and classrooms. Aronson's answer to the volatile situation was the Jigsaw Classroom.

Jigsaw Classroom A learning process in which each student is part of a group and each group member is assigned part of the material to be learned by the whole group. Students become "experts" on their piece of the puzzle and then teach it to the others in their group.

In Jigsaw, each group member is given part of the material to be learned by the whole group. Students become "expert" on their piece of the "puzzle." Because students need to learn and be tested on every piece of the larger puzzle, everyone's contribution is important—the students truly are interdependent. A more recent version, Jigsaw II, adds expert groups in which the students who are responsible for the same material from each learning group confer to make sure they understand their assigned part and then plan ways to teach the information to their learning group members. Next, students return to their learning groups, bringing their expertise to the sessions. In the end,

TABLE 9.9 Letter From a Student Who Participated in a Jigsaw Classroom

Years after inventing the Jigsaw strategy, Elliot Aronson received the following letter:

Dear Professor Aronson:

I am a senior at _____ University. Today I got a letter admitting me to the Harvard Law School. This may not seem odd to you but, let me tell you something. I am the sixth of seven children my parents had—and I am the only one who ever went to college, let alone graduate, or go to law school.

By now, you are probably wondering why this stranger is writing to you and bragging to you about his achievements. Actually, I'm not a stranger although we never met. You see, last year I was taking a course in social psychology and we were using a book you wrote called The Social Animal, *and when I read about prejudice and jigsaw it all sounded very familiar—and then, I realized that I was in that very first class you ever did jigsaw in—when I was in the 5th grade in Austin. And as I read on, it dawned on me that I was the boy that you called* **CARLOS**. *And then I remembered you when you first came to our classroom and how I was scared and how I hated school and how I was so stupid and didn't know anything. And you came in—it all came back to me when I read your book—you were very tall—about 6 feet—and you had a big black beard and you were funny and made us all laugh.*

And, most important, when we started to do work in jigsaw groups, I began to realize that I wasn't really that stupid. And the kids I thought were cruel and hostile became my friends and the teacher acted friendly and nice to me and I actually began to love school, and I began to love to learn things and now I'm about to go to Harvard Law School.

You must get a lot of letters like this but I decided to write anyway because let me tell you something. My mother tells me that when I was born I almost died. I was born at home and the cord was wrapped around my neck and the midwife gave me mouth to mouth and saved my life. If she were still alive, I would write to her too, to tell her that I grew up smart and good and I'm going to law school. But she died a few years ago. I'm writing to you because, no less than her, you saved my life too.

Source: From *Nobody Left to Hate: Teaching Compassion after Columbine*, by E. Aronson. Published by Worth Publishers. Copyright © 2001 by Worth Publishers. Reprinted with permission from Henry Holt and Company, LLC.

students take an individual test covering all the material and earn points for their learning team score. Teams can work for rewards or simply for recognition (Aronson, 2000; Slavin, 1995). But in Aronson's eyes, an even greater lesson is learned about respect and compassion. See Table 9.9 for a letter that Aronson received from an EAL (English as an additional language) student who participated in one of those early Jigsaw classes in Austin.

Judy Pitts (1992) describes a lesson about how to do library research that has a Jigsaw format. The overall project for each group is to educate the class about a different country. Groups have to decide what information to present and how to make it interesting for their classmates. In the library, each group member is responsible for mastering a particular resource (Readers' Guide, NewsBank, reference sets, almanacs, etc.) and teaching other group members how to use it, if the need arises. Students learning about each resource meet first in expert groups to be sure all the "teachers" know how to use the resource.

In this class, students confront complex, real-life problems, and not simplified worksheets. They learn by doing and by teaching others. The students must take positions and argue for them—how should our group educate the class about Turkey, for example—all the time being open to the ideas of others. They may encounter different representations of the same information—graphs, databases, maps, interviews, or encyclopedia articles—and they may need to integrate information from a variety of sources. This lesson exemplifies many of the characteristics of constructivist approaches described earlier in this chapter. The students have a good chance of learning how to do library research by actually doing it.

Structured Controversies. Constructive conflict resolution is essential in classrooms because conflicts are inevitable and even necessary for learning. Piaget's theory tells us that developing knowledge requires cognitive conflict. One study of students in grade 10 found that students who were wrong, but for different reasons, were sometimes able to correct their misunderstandings if they argued together about their conflicting wrong answers (Schwarz, Neuman, & Biezuner, 2000). Individuals trying to exist in groups will have interpersonal conflicts, too, which also can lead to learning. Table 9.10 on page 330 shows how academic and interpersonal conflicts can be positive forces in a learning community.

As you can see in Table 9.10, the structured part of structured controversies is that students work in pairs within their four-person cooperative groups to research a particular controversy, such

Structured controversy Students working in pairs within their four-person cooperative groups to research a particular controversy.

TABLE 9.10 **Structured Controversies: Learning From Academic and Interpersonal Conflicts**
Conflict, if handled well, can support learning. Academic conflicts can lead to critical thinking and conceptual change. Conflicts of interest are unavoidable, but can be handled so no one is the loser.

Academic Controversy	Conflicts of Interest
One person's ideas, information, theories, conclusions, and opinions are incompatible with those of another, and the two seek to reach an agreement.	The actions of one person attempting to maximize benefits prevents, blocks, or interferes with another person maximizing her or his benefits.
Controversy Procedure	*Integrative (Problem-Solving) Negotiations*
Research and prepare positions	Describe wants
Present and advocate positions	Describe feelings
Refute opposing position and refute attacks on own position	Describe reasons for wants and feelings
Reverse perspectives	Take the other's perspective
Synthesize and integrate best evidence and reasoning from all sides	Invent three optional agreements that maximize joint outcomes Choose one and formalize agreement

Source: From "The Three Cs of School and Classroom Management," by D. Johnson and R. Johnson. In H. J. Freiberg (Ed.), *Beyond Behaviorism: Changing the Classroom Management Paradigm.* Boston: Allyn and Bacon. Copyright © 1999 by Allyn & Bacon. Adapted with permission.

as whether lumber companies should be allowed to cut down trees in national forests. Each pair of students researches the issue, develops a *pro* or *con* position, presents their position and evidence to the other pair, discusses the issue, and then reverses positions and argues for the other perspective. Then, the group develops a final report that summarizes the best arguments for each position and reaches a consensus (Johnson & Johnson, 1999a; O'Donnell, 2006).

In addition to these approaches, Spencer Kagan (1994) has developed many cooperative learning structures designed to accomplish different kinds of academic and social tasks. The *Guidelines* box on the next page gives you ideas for incorporating cooperative learning into your classes.

Reaching Every Student: Using Cooperative Learning Wisely

Using cooperative learning as an effective learning strategy in the classroom always involves careful organization and forethought. However, using this strategy when students with special needs are involved requires doubling your efforts when planning and preparing lessons. For example, cooperative structures such as scripted questioning and peer tutoring depend on a balanced interaction between the person taking the role of questioner or explainer and the student who is answering or being taught. In these interactions, you want to see and hear explaining and teaching, not just telling or giving correct answers. But many students with learning disabilities have difficulties understanding new concepts, so both the person doing the explaining and the student can get frustrated, and social rejection for the student with learning disabilities might follow. Because students with learning disabilities often have difficulties with social relations, it is not a good idea to put them in situations where more rejection is likely. So, when you are teaching new or difficult-to-grasp concepts, cooperative learning might not be the best choice for students with learning disabilities (Kirk, Gallagher, Anastasiow, & Coleman, 2006). In fact, research has found that cooperative learning in general is not always effective for students with learning disabilities (Smith, 2006).

Gifted students also may not benefit from cooperative learning, especially when groups of students are mixed in ability. For gifted students, the pace often is too slow, the tasks are too simple, and too much repetition is involved to sustain a gifted student's interest. In addition, gifted students often fall into the role of teacher or just end up doing the work quickly for the whole group. If you use mixed-ability groups and include gifted students in them, your challenge will be to use complex tasks that allow students to work at different levels and to keep gifted students engaged without losing the interest of the rest of the class (Smith, 2006).

GUIDELINES: Using Cooperative Learning

Fit group size and composition to your learning goals.

EXAMPLES

1. For social skills and team-building goals, use groups of two to five, with common interest groups, mixed groups, or random groups.
2. For structured fact and skill-based practice and review tasks, use groups of two to four, with mixed ability such as high-middle and middle-low or high-low and middle-middle group compositions.
3. For higher-level conceptual and thinking tasks, use groups of two to four; select members to encourage interaction.

Assign appropriate roles.

EXAMPLES

1. For social skills and team-building goals, assign roles to monitor participation and conflict; rotate leadership of the group.
2. For structured fact and skill-based practice and review tasks, assign roles to monitor engagement and ensure low-status students have resources to offer, as in Jigsaw activities.
3. For higher-level conceptual and thinking tasks, assign roles only to encourage interaction, divergent thinking, and extended and connected discourse, as in debate teams, or group facilitator. Don't let roles get in the way of learning.

Make sure you assume a supporting role as the teacher.

EXAMPLES

1. For social skills and team-building goals, be a model and encourager.
2. For structured fact and skill-based practice and review tasks, be a model, director, or coach.
3. For higher-level conceptual and thinking tasks, be a model and facilitator.

Move around the room and monitor the groups.

EXAMPLES

1. For social skills and team-building goals, watch for listening, turn-taking, encouraging, and managing conflict.
2. For structured fact and skill-based practice and review tasks, watch for questioning, giving multiple elaborated explanations, attention, and practice.
3. For higher-level conceptual and thinking tasks, watch for questioning, explaining, elaborating, probing, divergent thinking, providing rationales, synthesizing, and using and connecting knowledge sources.

Start small and simple until you and the students know how to use cooperative methods.

EXAMPLES

1. For social skills and team-building goals, try one or two skills, such as listening and paraphrasing.
2. For structured fact and skill-based practice and review tasks, try pairs of students quizzing each other.
3. For higher-level conceptual and thinking tasks, try reciprocal questioning using pairs and just a few question stems.

For more information on cooperative learning, see **http://edtech.kennesaw.edu/intech/cooperativelearning.htm**.

Source: Adapted from "Implications of Cognitive Approaches to Peer Learning for Teacher Education," by A. Woolfolk Hoy and M. Tschannen-Moran, 1999. In A. O'Donnell and A. King (Eds.), *Cognitive Perspectives on Peer Learning* (pp. 257–284). Mahwah, NJ: Lawrence Erlbaum.

Cooperative learning may be an excellent choice, however, for English as an additional language learners (EAL). The Jigsaw cooperative structure is especially helpful for these students because all students in the group, including the EAL students, have information that the group needs, so they also must participate (talk, explain, and interact). In fact, the Jigsaw approach was developed in response to the need for high interdependence among diverse groups of students. You saw the value of Jigsaw for Carlos in Table 9.9. In many classrooms today, there are four, five, six, or more languages represented. Teachers can't be expected to master every heritage language spoken by all their students every year. In these classrooms, using a cooperative learning strategy can help as students work together on academic tasks. Students who speak two languages can help translate and explain lessons to others in the group. Speaking in a smaller group may also be less anxiety-provoking for students who are just beginning to learn English; thus, EAL students may get more language practice with feedback in these groups (Smith, 2006).

As you can see, cooperative learning is only as good as its design and implementation. Cooperative learning methods are likely both misused and underused in schools, in part because using cooperative learning successfully requires the teacher to invest time and effort in teaching students how to learn in groups (Blatchford, Baines, Rubie-Davis, Bassett, & Chowne, 2006).

An Integrated Constructivist Program: Fostering Communities of Learners

Fostering communities of learners (FCL) is "a system of interacting activities that results in a self-consciously active and reflective learning environment" (Brown & Campione, 1996, p. 292). This is an entire instructional program grounded in constructivist learning theories.

It is tempting to reduce the complex processes and understandings of FCL into a simple set of steps or procedures. But the inventors, Ann Brown and Joseph Campione, caution that when considering FCL, the emphasis should be on philosophy and principles, not procedures and steps. At the heart of FCL is a three-part process: (1) Students engage in independent and group research on one aspect of the topic of class inquiry—for example, animal adaptation and survival. The goal is for the entire class to develop a deep understanding of the topic. Because the material is complex, class mastery requires that students become experts on different aspects of the larger topic and that they (2) share their expertise with others. The sharing is motivated by a consequential task (3)—a performance that is meaningful. The task may be completing a traditional test or it may be delivering a public performance, participating in a competition, or delivering a social service. Thus, the heart of FCL is *research*, in order to *share* information, in order to *perform* a consequential task (Brown, 1997; Brown & Campione, 1996; Collins, 2006).

This inquiry cycle may not seem that new, but what sets FCL apart, among other things, is having a variety of research-based ways of accomplishing each phase and paying careful attention to teaching students how to benefit intellectually and socially from each step. *Research* can take many forms, such as reading, studying, participating in research seminars, guided writing, consulting with experts or peers face-to-face or electronically, and cross-age tutoring. In order to do research, students are taught and coached in powerful comprehension-monitoring and comprehension-extending strategies such as summarizing and predicting for younger students, and for older students, forming analogies, giving causal explanations, providing evidence, and making sound arguments and predictions. Students are taught explicitly how to *share* information by asking for and providing help, majoring (i.e., developing special interest and expertise in an area), learning from each others' exhibitions, participating in cooperative groups, and joining in whole-class sessions to check the progress of each of the research groups. *Performing* consequential tasks includes publishing; designing; creating solutions to real problems; setting up exhibitions; staging performances; and taking tests, quizzes, and authentic assessments that can hardly be distinguished from ongoing teaching.

Thoughtful reflection and deep disciplinary content surround and support the *research, share, perform* cycle. FCL teachers create a culture of thinking—self-conscious reflection about important and complex disciplinary units. As Brown and Campione (1996) point out, we "cannot expect students to invest intellectual curiosity and disciplined inquiry on trivia" (p. 306). In FCL classrooms, the teachers' main ploy is to "trap students into thinking deeply" about complex content (Brown & Campione, 1996, p. 302).

Dilemmas of Constructivist Practice

Years ago, Larry Cremin (1961) observed that progressive, innovative pedagogies require exceptionally skilled teachers. Today, the same could be said about constructivist teaching. We have already seen that there are many varieties of constructivism and many practices that flow from these different conceptions. We also know that all teaching today happens in a context of high-stakes testing and accountability. In these situations, constructivist teachers face many challenges. Mark Windschitl (2002) identified four dilemmas which are summarized in Table 9.11. The first is conceptual: How do I make sense of cognitive versus social conceptions of constructivism and reconcile these different perspectives with my practice? The second dilemma is pedagogical: How do I teach in truly constructivist ways that honour my students' attempts to think for themselves, but still ensure that they learn the academic material? Third are cultural dilemmas: What activities, cultural knowledge, and ways of communicating will build a community in a classroom that includes students from diverse backgrounds? Finally, there are political dilemmas: How can I teach in ways that will encourage deep understanding and critical thinking, but that will still satisfy the accountability demands of parents?

Fostering communities of learners (FCL) A system of interacting activities that results in a self-consciously active and reflective learning environment and uses a research, share, and perform learning cycle.

TABLE 9.11 **Teachers' Dilemmas of Constructivism in Practice**

Teachers face conceptual, pedagogical, cultural, and political dilemmas as they implement constructivist practices. Here are explanations of these dilemmas and some representative questions that teachers face as they confront them.

Teachers' Dilemma Category	Representative Questions of Concern
I. *Conceptual dilemmas:* Grasping the underpinnings of cognitive and social constructivism; reconciling current beliefs about pedagogy with the beliefs necessary to support a constructivist learning environment.	Which version of constructivism is suitable as a basis for my teaching? Is my classroom supposed to be a collection of individuals working toward conceptual change or a community of learners whose development is measured by participation in authentic disciplinary practices? If certain ideas are considered correct by experts, should students internalize those ideas instead of constructing their own?
II. *Pedagogical dilemmas:* Honouring students' attempts to think for themselves while remaining faithful to accepted disciplinary ideas; developing deeper knowledge of subject matter; mastering the art of facilitation; managing new kinds of discourse and collaborative work in the classroom.	Do I base my teaching on students' existing ideas rather than on prescribed learning objectives? What skills and strategies are necessary for me to become a facilitator? How do I manage a classroom in which students talk to one another rather than to me? Should I place limits on students' construction of their own ideas? What types of assessments will capture the learning I want to foster?
III. *Cultural dilemmas:* Becoming conscious of the culture of your classroom; questioning assumptions about what kinds of activities should be valued; taking advantage of experiences, discourse patterns, and local knowledge of students with varied cultural backgrounds.	How can we contradict traditional, efficient classroom routines and generate new agreements with students about what is valued and rewarded? How do my own past images of what is proper and possible in a classroom prevent me from seeing the potential for a different kind of learning environment? How can I accommodate the worldviews of students from diverse backgrounds while at the same time transforming my own classroom culture? Can I trust students to accept responsibility for their own learning?
IV. *Political dilemmas:* Confronting issues of accountability with various stakeholders in the school community; negotiating with key others the authority and support to teach for understanding.	How can I gain the support of administrators and parents for teaching in such a radically different and unfamiliar way? Should I make use of approved curriculums that are not sensitive enough to my students' needs, or should I create my own? How can diverse problem-based experiences help students meet specific state and local standards? Will constructivist approaches adequately prepare my students for high-stakes testing associated with college admissions?

Source: M. Windschitl (2002). Framing constructivism in practice as the negotiation of dilemmas: An analysis of the conceptual, pedagogical, cultural, and political challenges facing teachers. *Review of Educational Research, 72*, p. 133. Copyright © 2002 by the American Educational Research Association. Reproduced with permission of the publisher.

SERVICE LEARNING

Service learning combines academic learning with personal and social development for secondary and post-secondary students (Woolfolk Hoy, Demerath, & Pape, 2002). A more formal definition of service learning is "a teaching and learning strategy that integrates meaningful community service with instruction and reflection to enrich the learning experience, teach civic responsibility, and strengthen communities" (National Service Learning Clearing House, n.d.). In Canada and the United States, service learning activities share common characteristics. The activities:

- Coordinate with and meet actual community needs.
- Integrate into the student's curriculum.
- Provide time for students to reflect and write about the service experience.
- Provide opportunities for students to apply newly learned academic skills and knowledge.
- Enhance both academic learning and a sense of caring for others.

MyEducationLab
Go to the Teacher Talk section in Chapter 9 of MyEducationLab and watch a video of Christopher Poulos, 2007 Teacher of the Year from Connecticut, describing how he transfers a love of learning to his students by sharing with them parts of the world much different from their own.

Service learning Combines academic learning with personal and social development for secondary and post-secondary students.

SERVICE LEARNING Community service projects can promote adolescents' moral development, feelings of competence and agency, and tolerance of differences, and encourage them to reflect critically on their roles in society.

Service learning activities may involve direct service (tutoring, serving meals at homeless shelters), indirect service (collecting food for shelters, raising money), or advocacy (designing and distributing posters about a food drive, writing newspaper articles) (Johnson & Notah, 1999). Service learning also could be a form of problem-based learning.

Participation in service learning can promote political and moral development for adolescents. Through service learning projects, adolescents experience their own competence and agency by working with others in need. Students see themselves as political and moral agents, rather than merely as good citizens (Youniss & Yates, 1997). In addition, service learning can help adolescents think in new ways about their relationships with people who are unlike them, and thus can lead them to become more tolerant of differences (Tierney, 1993). Finally, service learning experiences foster an "ethic of care" that can result in a growing commitment to confront difficult social problems (Rhodes, 1997). In this sense, student involvement in service learning can motivate and empower adolescents to critically reflect on their role in society (Yates & Youniss, 1999; Woolfolk Hoy et al., 2002). A number of schools now have participation in service learning as a graduation requirement, but some educators question if "required" service is fair or appropriate. At least three of the school requirements have been challenged in the American court system but, so far, the requirements have been upheld (Johnson & Notah, 1999).

Studies of the impact of service learning on the political and moral development of students have produced mixed results. Some studies have found modest gains on measures of social responsibility, tolerance for others, empathy, attitude toward adults, and self-esteem (Solomon et al., 2001). A case study at an urban religious high school describes a successful service learning experience (Yates & Youniss, 1999). This program was required for juniors at the school and was part of a year-long course on social justice. In the class, students examined the moral implications of current events such as homelessness, poverty, exploitation of immigrant labourers, and urban violence. Students also were required to serve four times (approximately 20 hours) at an inner-city soup kitchen. The researchers concluded that students emerged from the course with "a deeper awareness of social injustice, a greater sense of commitment to confront these injustices, and heightened confidence in their abilities overall" (Yates & Youniss, 1999, p. 64).

If you decide to use service learning strategies in your teaching, consider the suggestions in the *Guidelines* box, many of which are taken from Richard Sagor (2003) and Elias and Schwab (2006).

LEARNING IN A DIGITAL WORLD

It seems that computers, cell phones, personal digital assistants (PDAs), iPods, video games, and other digital media have changed our lives. A recent Ipsos Reid poll found that, in early 2010, Canadians spent slightly more than 18 hours per week online and that they watched television for just under 17 hours per week (Ipsos Reid Interactive Group, 2010). Among older students, completing homework often involves using digital technology—exchanging messages via email, sending instant messages, using cell phones, or searching the internet and downloading resources—all while simultaneously listening to music from an iPod or to a television program (Roberts, Foehr, & Rideout, 2005).

Television

Almost every Canadian has access to a television. Furthermore, Statistics Canada reports that Canadian children watched a lot of TV in 2004 —about 14.1 hours per week for 2- to 11-year-olds and 12.9 hours per week for 12- to 17-year-olds (Statistics Canada, 2006). If we're like Americans, the television is on all

GUIDELINES: Using Service Learning

Ensure the service is ongoing, not just a brief project.

EXAMPLES

1. Instead of having a two-week food drive with a celebration party for the class that collected the most, involve students in a longer commitment to cook or serve food at shelters for homeless families.
2. Contact local agencies to identify real needs that your students could address or search online: **www.youth.gc.ca/eng/topics/jobs/volunteer.shtml** or **www.communityservicelearning.ca/en/**

Consider virtual volunteering.

EXAMPLES

1. Encourage students who are fluent in a language other than English to translate a document into another language.
2. Invite students to post multimedia presentations online.
3. Prompt students to design an agency's newsletter or brochure or to copyedit an agency's publication or proposal.
4. Motivate students to proofread drafts of papers and online publications.
5. Encourage students to research and write articles for brochures, newsletters, and websites.
6. Invite students to design a logo for an agency or program or to fill other illustration needs.

Make sure learning is at the centre of service learning.

EXAMPLES

1. Provide clear learning objectives for each project.
2. Examine grade-level standards in science, history, health, literature, and other areas to see how some might be met by completing service projects. For example, how might concepts in biology be learned by designing a nutrition education program for senior citizens or preschool students?
3. Ask students to reflect over time about their experiences, to keep journals, and to write or draw what they have learned, and then include these reflections in class discussions.

Make sure the service draws on the students' talents and skills so that it is actually valuable to the recipients and so that the students, in turn, gain a sense of accomplishment and usefulness from applying their skills to help others.

EXAMPLES

1. Students who have artistic talents might help to redecorate a recreation room at a senior citizens' centre.
2. Students who are good storytellers could work with children at a daycare centre or in a children's clinic.
3. Students who are bilingual could help teachers translate school newsletters into the languages of fellow students' families or might serve as translators at local clinics.

Design service learning opportunities so they are inclusive (Dymond, Renzaglia, & Chun, 2007).

EXAMPLES

1. Consider the transportation needs of students with disabilities.
2. Link service learning projects to life skills such as developing social skills on the job, being mindful of safety issues, and practising punctuality.
3. Monitor interactions in groups comprising students with mixed abilities and ethnicities; be aware of how students with special needs are included.

For more ideas, see **www.communityservicelearning.ca/en/**, **www.service-learningpartnership.org/site/PageServer**, and **www.fiu.edu/~time4chg/Library/bigdummy.html**

day or during most of the day in about one-third of homes (Vandewater et al., 2005). In those homes, parents read less to their children and the children are less likely to be able to read.

But television has also been used to improve the emergent literacy skills of young children. For example, Linebarger and her colleagues showed kindergarten and grade 1 children 17 episodes of the educational television program *Between the Lions* (Linebarger, Kosanic, Greenwood, & Doku, 2004). The program focused on whole processes such as reading and writing in different contexts and learning specific skills such as letter-sound correspondences and the alphabet. The children who viewed the program improved in word recognition and reading test scores, but the ones who improved the most were the kindergarten students who were at no risk, or were only at moderate risk, for developing reading problems. So children who were on track and developing as readers benefitted the most from exposure to the television program. Kindergartners at greatest risk for developing

MEDIA MULTITASKERS For older students, completing homework often involves exchanging messages via email, sending instant messages, using cell phones, or searching the internet and downloading resources—all while listening to music from an iPod or to a television program.

reading problems and grade 1 children did not benefit as much—so the lessons clearly need to be adjusted to fit the needs and readiness of the child. Exposing children to programs that are too advanced or too easy for them won't be as helpful—as Vygotsky would remind us.

Computers

According to Statistics Canada, 79.4 percent of Canadian households reported owning a computer in 2008. Almost everyone uses email (93 percent) but people also use computers to check road conditions (74.6 percent), to search for health-related information (69.9 percent), and to conduct research in general (72.7 percent) (Statistics Canada, 2010a).

With the proliferation of technology, there is growing interest in technology-rich learning environments, or TREs, to help students learn. These environments include virtual worlds, computer simulations that support problem-based learning such as the *River of Life Challenge* described earlier, intelligent tutoring systems, educational games, audio recordings, hand-held wireless devices, and multimedia environments—to name just a few. Debates have emerged about whether technology-rich learning environments should teach students directly (as in tutoring systems) or provide support for learning activities (as in problem-based learning simulations). These arguments mirror the debates about whether teachers should be "sages on the stage" or "guides by the side." As you can imagine, constructivist approaches favour TREs that scaffold student learning and engagement—giving students more control over their own learning. TREs situate learning in authentic contexts and support the social construction of knowledge by providing models and coaching as well as support for collaboration. TREs can even encourage students to collaborate with peers around the world (Lajoie & Azevedo, 2006; Pea & Maldonado, 2006).

In the next few pages we look at the uses of computers, a common feature of many TREs (Sawyer, 2006b).

Developmentally Appropriate Computer Activities. Digital media are appealing, but are they appropriate for preschool children? This is a hotly debated issue. The Alliance for Children (2000) argues that we should stop using computers in early childhood education until we learn more about their long-term effects. These researchers believe computers take children away from the physical activities and social interactions they require for their development. Before about age 3, children learn best by being active. They are in the sensorimotor stage and need to use their hands, mouths, ears, eyes, arms, and legs to act on their environments. Expecting preschool students to sit in front of computers or to stand still for any reason will not support their development (Hohman, 1998). Also, children who play alone in front of a computer are not having conversations with adults about a story or cooperating with peers to build with blocks. Furthermore, preschoolers who use computers may be exposed to violence and to sexual content that is completely inappropriate.

But it is likely that digital media are here to stay and that their use in classrooms will only expand in the future. So, are there appropriate uses for computers with young children? Developmentally appropriate software for preschoolers should include simple spoken directions. The computer activities should be open-ended and encourage discovery, exploration, problem solving, and understanding of cause and effect; computers should not be used for solitary drill and practice activities. Children should be able to remain in control of the activities through a variety of responses. Finally, the content should be appropriate for and respectful of diverse cultures, ages, and abilities (Fischer & Gillespie, 2003; Frost, Wortham, & Reifel, 2005). Linda Tsantis and her colleagues (2003) suggest that you ask this question about any digital media program you are considering: "Does this software program help create learning opportunities that did not exist without it?" One danger is that programs will include attractive visuals or sound-effects interruptions that actually interfere with the development of important concepts. For example, in describing a Peter Rabbit storytelling software program that includes the sound effects of a buzz saw and the thud of a tree falling, Tsantis et al. (2003) cautioned:

> How do these cute asides fit into a child's construction of the notion of story sequence and plot? Perhaps these digressions foster lack of focus and distractibility for youngsters who already have such tendencies. Further, how does this interruption affect the comprehension of the plot, action, and characters? (p. 6)

In fact, some research suggests that expecting preschoolers to deal with sensory stimulation might make them better at multitasking, but it might also make them worse at deeper thought processes such as developing perspective-taking skills and understanding the plot, theme, and sequence of the story. So some children may learn to do several things at once, but they may develop only a superficial understanding of what they are doing (Carpenter, 2000).

Computers and Older Students. There is evidence that older students' use of computers—especially games that require multiple activities, visual attention, imagery, and fast action—supports the development of their visual skills, as long as the tasks correspond with the student's level of ability (Subrahmanyam, Greenfield, Kraut, & Gross, 2001). But does computer use support academic learning? The answer is complex and even surprising. After reviewing hundreds of studies, including five other research reviews, Roschelle, Pea, Hoadley, Gordon, and Means (2000) concluded that there were no strong conclusions. Using computer tutorial programs appeared to improve achievement test scores for students in kindergarten through grade 12, but simulations and enrichment programs had few effects—perhaps another example that when you teach and test specific skills, children learn the skills. Computers may be more useful in improving mathematics and science skills than those associated with other subjects. Like any teaching tool, a computer can be effective if used well, but simply asking students to use a computer will not automatically increase their academic achievement. Roschelle and colleagues concluded that computers are more likely to increase achievement if they support the basic processes that lead to learning: active engagement, frequent interaction with feedback, authenticity and real-world connection, and productive group work (Jackson et al., 2006). See the *Guidelines* box on page 338 for more ideas about using computers.

Having access to computers, calculators, and word processing programs at home certainly can be an advantage for students. Is it an unfair advantage? We look at this topic next.

Home Resources and the Digital Divide

Studies have found that home computer availability is a strong predictor of academic achievement in math and science, but these studies have not separated home computer usage from socioeconomic status, so it is difficult to say if computers alone make a difference. Many other resources besides computers tend to accompany higher socioeconomic status (Jackson et al., 2006). In terms of reading, however, home computer access is associated with higher achievement, even when family income is taken into account (Atwell, 2000). Some of the advantages associated with reading online, at least for children with internet access, may be the result of the reading practice that comes with using the internet. Students mostly use the internet to search for information for school projects, followed by communicating with friends (girls tend to communicate with friends more than boys do), but this research is generally based on self-reports. It is difficult to ascertain exactly how students use the internet at home (Jackson et al., 2006).

We do know that internet use differs among groups of Canadians. Among Canadians with less than a high school education, Statistics Canada (2010c) data show that 50.7 percent access the internet. This figure rises to 83.4 percent for Canadians with high school or college degrees and to 94.7 percent among Canadians with a university degree. When income is used to group Canadians, 76.2 percent in the lowest quartile use the internet while 92.1 percent of those who are in the highest income quartile use the internet. This split in access to technology has been called the **digital divide**.

"HomeNetToo" was a longitudinal study conducted in the United States to address the digital divide and to examine the effects of home internet use on children in low-income families (Jackson et al., 2006). The participants—mostly 10- to 18-year-old African American boys in single-parent homes—received a computer, internet access, and in-home technical support for 16 months. The participants' computer use was monitored and all participants completed surveys and interviews along the way. The families were allowed to keep the computers after the project ended and the researchers helped them find low-cost internet service. Compared to children who used the internet less, participants who used it more had higher grade point averages (GPAs) and higher scores on standardized reading tests at the end of the project. The children used the internet more for researching school projects than for emailing or instant messaging (though the reason for this phenomenon may be that the participants' friends may not have had access to computers or the internet).

Digital divide A split in access to technologies between those who fall into high versus low socioeconomic status.

GUIDELINES: Using Computers

IF YOU HAVE ONLY ONE COMPUTER IN YOUR CLASSROOM

Provide convenient access.

EXAMPLES

1. Find a central location if the computer is used to display material for the class.
2. Find a spot on the side of the room that allows seating and a view of the screen, but does not crowd or disturb other students, especially if the computer is used as a workstation for several individuals or for small groups.

Be prepared.

EXAMPLES

1. Check to be sure that software needed for a lesson or assignment is installed and working.
2. Make sure instructions for using the software or doing the assignment are clear and posted in a visible location.
3. Provide a checklist for completing assignments.

Create "trained experts" to help with computers.

EXAMPLES

1. Train students to become "experts," and rotate the role of expert.
2. Involve adult volunteers—parents, grandparents, aunts and uncles, older siblings—anyone who cares about the students.

Develop systems for using the computer.

EXAMPLES

1. Make up a schedule to ensure that each student has access to the computer and that no single student (or group of students) monopolizes the equipment.
2. Create standard ways for students to save their work.

IF YOU HAVE MORE THAN ONE COMPUTER IN YOUR CLASSROOM

Plan the physical arrangement of the computers to fit your instructional goals.

EXAMPLES

1. For cooperative groups, arrange the setting so students can cluster around their group's computer.
2. For students completing different projects at different computer stations, allow for easy rotation from one station to another.

Experiment with other models of teaching that involve using computers.

EXAMPLES

1. *Navigator model*—Four students per computer: One student is the (mouse and keyboard) "driver," another is the "navigator." "Back-seat driver 1" manages the group's progress and "back-seat driver 2" serves as the timekeeper. The navigator attends a 10- to 20-minute training session in which the facilitator provides an overview of the basics of a particular software program. Navigators cannot touch the mouse. Driver roles are rotated.
2. *Facilitator model*—Six students per computer: The facilitator has more experience, expertise, or training—he or she serves as the guide or teacher.
3. *Collaborative group model*—Seven students per computer: Each small group is responsible for creating some component of the whole group's final product. For example, one part of the group writes a report, another creates a map, and a third uses the computer to gather and graph census data.

NO MATTER HOW MANY COMPUTERS YOU HAVE IN YOUR CLASSROOM

Select developmentally appropriate programs that encourage learning, creativity, and social interaction.

EXAMPLES

1. Encourage two children to work together, rather than expecting or encouraging children to work alone.
2. Check the implicit messages some computer programs convey. For example, some drawing programs allow children to "blow up" their projects if they don't like them, so instead of working hard to solve a problem, the students can simply elect to destroy it. Tsantis et al. (2003) recommend using a recycle metaphor instead of a "blow it up" option.
3. Look for programs that encourage discovery, exploration, problem solving, and multiple responses.

Closely monitor children as they work at computers.

EXAMPLES

1. Ensure that computers are stationed in areas where an adult can observe them.
2. Discuss with children why some programs or websites are "off limits."
3. Balance computer time with active play such as hands-on projects (such as creating art or playing with blocks, sand, or water).

Keep children safe as they work at computers.

EXAMPLES

1. Teach children to shield their identities on the internet, to be careful about accepting invitations from those who have requested to be Facebook "friends," and to be cautious about sharing information with anyone else.
2. Install filtering software to protect children from exposure to inappropriate content.

For more ideas about older students, see **www.internet4classrooms.com/classroom_organization.htm#one**.

Suggestions are taken from Frost, J. L., Wortham, S. C., & Reifel, S. (2005). *Play and child development* (2nd ed.). Upper Saddle River, NJ: Prentice-Hall, pp. 76–80 and Tsantis, L. A., Bewick, C. J., & Thouvenelle, S. (2003, November). Examining some common myths about computer use in the early years. *Beyond the Journal: Young Children on the Web.* (pp. 1–9).

Media/Digital Literacy

DIGITALLY DISADVANTAGED? Many students have limited access to technology at home or in their communities. This split in access to technology has been called the digital divide.

With the advent of digital media comes a new concern about literacy—the need for media or digital literacy. Today, to be literate—that is, to be able to read, write, and communicate—children need to read and write in many media, not just the printed word. Media literacy generally is defined as "the ability to access, analyze, evaluate and communicate messages in a wide variety of forms" (Aufderheide & Firestone, 1993, p. 7). Media such as films, videos, DVDs, computers, photographs, artwork, magazines, music, television, and billboards communicate messages through images and sounds. How do children read these messages? This is a new area of research and application in educational and developmental psychology (Hobbs, 2004).

As an example of such research, consider *Project Look Sharp*, directed by Cynthia Scheibe, a developmental psychologist (**www.ithaca.edu/looksharp/**). The goal of the project is to provide materials, training, and support as teachers integrate media literacy and critical thinking about media into their class lessons. Teachers participating in the project help their students become critical readers of media. One group of elementary school students studied ants in science, and then viewed the animated film, *Antz*. In the discussion after the movie, students were challenged to describe what was accurate and inaccurate in the film's portrayal of ants. What were the messages of the film? How was product placement (e.g., an ant drinking a bottle of Pepsi) used? Tests immediately and six months later indicated that the children performed best on the questions related to the discussion about the accuracy of the film (Scheibe, 2005). *Project Look Sharp* suggests that teachers use the following questions to guide discussion of media:

1. Who made—and who sponsored—this message, and what is their purpose?
2. Who is the target audience and how is the message specifically tailored to that audience?
3. What are the different techniques used to inform, persuade, entertain, and attract attention?
4. What messages are communicated (and/or implied) about certain people, places, events, behaviours, lifestyles, and so forth?
5. How current, accurate, and credible is the information in this message?
6. What is left out of the message that might be good to know? (p. 63)

The *Guidelines* box on page 340 gives more ideas from Scheibe and Rogow (2004) about how to support the development of media literacy in your students.

DIVERSITY AND CONVERGENCES IN THE LEARNING SCIENCES AND CONSTRUCTIVISM

Diversity

The power and value of diversity is part of the theoretical framework of constructivist theories of learning. By its very nature, constructivism expects and respects diversity because a major tenet of constructivist theories is that knowing is socially constructed—it is shaped by the culture and the families in which the "knowers" learn, develop, and create their identities. We saw that the cultural contexts for learning to do arithmetic become part of the knowers, even in terms of their brain activity. Because the cultures and contexts for learning are widely diverse, the knowledge constructed individually and socially in those settings will be diverse.

Finally, one of the political dilemmas for teachers, indicated earlier in Table 9.11, is that families often question and criticize educational reforms, especially if the families have had different

GUIDELINES: Supporting the Development of Media Literacy

Use media to practise general observation, critical thinking, analysis, perspective-taking, and production skills.

EXAMPLES

1. Ask students to think critically about the information presented in advertising, "news" programs, and textbooks—would different people interpret the messages in differing ways?
2. Foster creativity by having students produce their own media on a topic you are studying.
3. Ask students to compare ways information might be presented in a documentary, TV news report, advertisement, public service announcement, and so on.
4. Give examples of how word selection, background music, camera angles, and colour can be used to set a mood or to bias a message.

Use media to stimulate interest in a new topic.

EXAMPLES

1. Encourage students to analyze a magazine article about the topic.
2. Encourage students to read sections from a novel or view film clips on the topic.

Help students identify what they already know or believe about a topic based on popular media content. Help them to identify erroneous beliefs.

EXAMPLES

1. Ask students what they "know" about space travel.
2. Ask students what they have they learned about biology from advertisements.

Use media as a standard pedagogical tool.

EXAMPLES

1. Provide information about a topic through many different media sources—the internet, books, DVDs, audio recordings, online newspapers, and so on.
2. Assign homework that makes use of different media.
3. Ask students to express opinions or to attempt to persuade using different media such as photographs, collages, videos, poems, songs, or animated films.

Analyze the effects of different media on certain historical events.

EXAMPLES

1. Ask students to investigate how Aboriginals were portrayed in art and films during certain periods.
2. Encourage students to learn more about what sources of information were available 50 years ago and 100 years ago.

For more ideas, see **www.ithaca.edu/looksharp/**.

experiences with schooling. Many teachers using non-traditional approaches to learning find they must explain these approaches to students' families. The *Family and Community Partnerships Guidelines* box on the next page gives ideas for how to communicate about innovative constructivist methods of teaching and learning.

Convergences

Even though all students bring different knowledge and beliefs to the classroom, we can end this chapter by reaffirming the points of agreements across the learning sciences about constructing understanding:

- ***Experts have deep conceptual knowledge.*** Experts have deep understanding that allows them to put their knowledge into action; they are able to apply and modify their knowledge to fit each situation.
- ***Learning comes from the learner.*** Learning is more than receiving and processing information transmitted by teachers or texts. Students must actively participate in their own personal construction of knowledge.
- ***Schools must create effective learning environments.*** It is the job of the school to create environments in which students are able to actively construct their own deep understandings so they can reason about real-world problems and transfer the knowledge they acquired in school to their lives beyond the school walls.
- ***Prior knowledge is key.*** Students come into our classrooms filled with knowledge and beliefs about how the world works. To develop deep understanding, teachers must begin with what the students already know.
- ***Reflection is necessary to develop deep conceptual knowledge.*** Students need to express, perform, and reflect on their developing knowledge in many forms. Technology that is used appropriately can support these performances and reflections.

FAMILY AND COMMUNITY PARTNERSHIPS

GUIDELINES: Communicating About Innovations

Be confident and honest.

EXAMPLES

1. Write out your rationale for the methods you use, then consider likely objections and craft your responses to those imagined objections.
2. Admit mistakes or oversights and explain what you have learned from them.

Treat parents and caregivers as equal partners.

EXAMPLES

1. Listen carefully to families' objections, take notes, and follow up on requests or suggestions—remember, you both want the best for the child.
2. Give parents or caregivers the telephone number of an administrator who will answer their questions about a new program or initiative.
3. Invite families to visit your classroom or to assist with the project in some way.

Communicate effectively.

EXAMPLES

1. Use plain language and avoid jargon. If you must use a technical term, define it in accessible ways. Use your best teaching skills to educate families about the new approach.
2. Encourage local newspapers or television stations to feature stories about the "great learning" going on in your classroom or school.
3. Create a lending library of articles and references about the new strategies.

Provide examples of projects and assignments when families visit your class.

EXAMPLES

1. Encourage parents or caregivers to try math activities themselves. If they have trouble, show them how your students (and their children!) are successful with the activities and highlight the strategies the students have learned.
2. Keep a library of students' favourite activities to demonstrate to family members.

Develop family involvement packages.

EXAMPLES

1. Once a month, send families, via their children, descriptions and examples of the math, science, or language skills to be learned in the upcoming unit. Include activities children can complete with their families.
2. Make the family project meaningful (for example, ensure the project counts for a homework grade).

Source: From "Addressing Parents' Concerns over Curriculum Reform," by Margaret R. Meyer, Mary L. Delgardelle, and James A. Middleton. In the April 1996 issue of *Educational Leadership*, 53(7), pp. 54–57. Learn more about ASCD at www.ascd.org.

SUMMARY TABLE

The Learning Sciences (pp. 304–307)

What are some basic assumptions of the learning sciences? Key assumptions in the learning sciences are that experts develop deep conceptual knowledge, learning comes from the learner, creating learning environments is the responsibility of the school, students' prior knowledge is key, and reflection is a critical component of learning. These common assumptions enable researchers from a variety of disciplines to address the same issues of learning from a variety of perspectives. Recent advances in both methods and findings in the neurosciences provide exciting information about brain activity during learning and about differences in brain activity among people with varying abilities and challenges. There are some basic implications for teaching based on these findings, but many of the strategies offered by "brain-based" advocates simply involve good teaching. Perhaps we now know more about why these strategies work.

Learning sciences A new interdisciplinary science of learning based on research in psychology, education, computer science, philosophy, sociology, anthropology, neuroscience, and other fields that study learning.

Functional magnetic resonance imaging (fMRI) A form of MRI (an imaging technique that uses a magnetic field along with radio waves and a computer to create detailed pictures of the inside of the body) used to measure the tiny changes during brain activity.

Cognitive and Social Constructivism (pp. 307–313)

Describe two kinds of constructivism and distinguish these from constructionism. *Psychological* constructivists such as Piaget are concerned with how *individuals* make sense of their world, based on individual knowledge, beliefs, self-concept, or identity—also called *first wave constructivism*. *Social* constructivists such as Vygotsky believe that social interaction, cultural tools, and activity shape individual development and learning—also called *second wave constructivism*. By participating in a broad range of activities with others, learners appropriate the outcomes produced by working together; they acquire new strategies and knowledge of their world. Finally, constructionists are interested in how public knowledge in academic disciplines is constructed as well as how everyday beliefs about the world are communicated to new members of a sociocultural group.

In what ways do constructivist views differ about knowledge sources, accuracy, and generality? Constructivists debate whether knowledge is constructed by mapping external reality, by adapting and changing internal understandings, or by an interaction of external forces and internal understandings. Most psychologists believe there is a role for both internal and external factors, but differ in how much they emphasize one or the other. Also, there is discussion about whether knowledge can be constructed in one situation and applied to another, or whether knowledge is situated, that is, specific and tied to the context in which it was learned.

What is meant by thinking as enculturation? *Enculturation* is a broad and complex process of acquiring knowledge and understanding consistent with Vygotsky's theory of mediated learning. Just as our home culture taught us lessons about the use of language, the culture of a classroom can teach lessons about thinking by giving us *models* of good thinking, providing *direct instruction* in thinking processes, and encouraging *practice* of those thinking processes through *interactions* with others.

What are some common elements in most constructivist views of learning? Even though there is no single constructivist theory, many constructivist approaches recommend complex, challenging learning environments and authentic tasks; social negotiation and co-construction; multiple representations of content; understanding that knowledge is constructed; and student ownership of learning.

Constructivism View that emphasizes the active role of the learner in building understanding and making sense of information.

First wave constructivism A focus on the individual and psychological sources of knowing, as in Piaget's theory.

Radical constructivism Knowledge is assumed to be the individual's construction; it cannot be judged right or wrong.

Appropriation Being able to internalize or take for yourself knowledge and skills developed in interaction with others or with cultural tools.

Second wave constructivism A focus on the social and cultural sources of knowing, as in Vygotsky's theory.

Constructionism How public knowledge in disciplines such as science, math, economics, or history is constructed.

Community of practice Social situation or context in which ideas are judged useful or true.

Situated learning The idea that skills and knowledge are tied to the situation in which they were learned and are difficult to apply in new settings.

Complex learning environments Problems and learning situations that mimic the ill-structured nature of real life.

Social negotiation Aspect of the learning process that relies on collaboration with others and respect for different perspectives.

Intersubjective attitude A commitment to build shared meaning with others by finding common ground and exchanging interpretations.

Multiple representations of content Considering problems using various analogies, examples, and metaphors.

Spiral curriculum Bruner's design for teaching that introduces the fundamental structure of all subjects early in the school years, then revisits the subjects in more and more complex forms over time.

Applying Constructivist Perspectives (pp. 314–333)

Distinguish between inquiry methods and problem-based learning. The inquiry strategy begins when the teacher presents a puzzling event, question, or problem. The students ask questions (only yes-no questions in some kinds of inquiry) and then formulate hypotheses to explain the event or solve the problem, collect data to test the hypotheses about causal relationships, form conclusions and generalizations, and reflect on the original problem and the thinking processes needed to solve it. Problem-based learning may follow a similar path, but the learning begins with an authentic problem—one that matters to the students. The goal is to learn math, science, history, or some other important subject while seeking a real solution to a real problem.

Describe six features that most cognitive apprenticeship approaches share. Students observe an expert (usually the teacher) *model* the performance, get external support through *coaching* or tutoring, and receive conceptual *scaffolding*, which is then gradually faded as the student becomes more competent and proficient. Students continually *articulate* their knowledge—putting into words their understanding of the processes and content being learned. They *reflect* on their progress, comparing their problem solving to an expert's performance and to their own earlier performances. Finally, students *explore* new ways to apply what they are learning—ways that they have not practised at the expert's side.

Describe the use of dialogue in reciprocal teaching. The goal of reciprocal teaching is to help students understand and think deeply about what they read. To accomplish this goal, students in small reading groups learn four strategies: *summarizing* the content of a passage, *asking a question* about the central point, *clarifying* the difficult parts of the material, and *predicting* what will come next. These strategies are practised in a classroom dialogue about the readings. Teachers first take a central role, but as the discussion progresses, the students take more and more control.

What are the differences between collaboration and cooperation? One view is that collaboration is a philosophy about how to relate to others—how to learn and work. Collaboration is a way of dealing with people that respects differences, shares authority, and builds on the knowledge that is distributed among other people. Cooperation, on the other hand, is a way of working together with others to attain a shared goal.

What are the learning theory underpinnings of cooperative learning? Learning can be enhanced in cooperative groups through rehearsal and elaboration (information processing theories), creation and resolution of disequilibrium (Piaget's theory), or scaffolding of higher mental processes (Vygotsky's theory).

Describe five elements that define true cooperative learning. Students *interact face-to-face* and close together, not across the room from each other. Group members experience *positive interdependence*—they need each other for support, explanations, and guidance. Even though they work together and help each other, members of the group must ultimately demonstrate learning on their own—they are held *individually accountable* for learning, often through individual tests or other assessments. If necessary, the *collaborative skills* important for effective group functioning—such as giving constructive feedback, reaching consensus, and involving every member—are taught and practised before the groups tackle a learning task. Finally, members monitor *group processes* and relationships to make sure the group is working effectively and to learn about group dynamics.

How should tasks match design in cooperative learning? A relatively structured task works well with a structured technique; extrinsic rewards can enhance motivation, effort, and persistence under these conditions; and roles, especially those that focus attention on the work to be accomplished, also may be productive. On the other hand, strategies that encourage extended and productive interactions are appropriate when the goal is to develop higher-order thinking and problem solving. The use of rewards may well divert the group away from the goal of in-depth cognitive processing. When the goal of peer learning is enhanced social skills or increased intergroup understanding and appreciation of diversity, the assignment of specific roles and functions within the group might support communication. Rewards probably are not necessary and may actually get in the way because the goal is to build community, a sense of respect, and responsibility for team members.

What are some possible strategies for cooperative learning? Strategies include reciprocal questioning, Jigsaw, structured controversy, and many cooperative structures described by Spencer Kagan.

What is FCL? Fostering communities of learners (FCL) is an approach to organizing classrooms and schools. The heart of FCL is *research*, in order to *share* information, in order to *perform* a consequential task that involves deep disciplinary content. Students engage in independent and group research so the entire class can develop an understanding of the topic. Because the material is complex, class mastery requires that students become experts on different aspects of the larger topic and share their expertise. The sharing is motivated by a consequential task—a performance that matters.

Inquiry learning Approach in which the teacher presents a puzzling situation and students solve the problem by gathering data and testing their conclusions.

Problem-based learning Methods that provide students with realistic problems that don't necessarily have "right" answers.

Anchored instruction A type of problem-based learning that uses a complex, interesting situation as an anchor for learning.

Cognitive apprenticeship A relationship in which a less experienced learner acquires knowledge and skills under the guidance of an expert.

Reciprocal teaching A teaching strategy designed to help students understand and think deeply about what they read.

Collaboration A philosophy about how to relate to others—how to learn and work.

Cooperation A way of working with others to attain a shared goal.

Cooperative learning Situations in which elaboration, interpretation, explanation, and argumentation are integral to the activity of the group and in which learning is supported by other individuals.

Reciprocal questioning Students working in pairs or triads to ask and answer questions about lesson material.

Jigsaw Classroom A learning process in which each student is part of a group and each group member is assigned part of the material to be learned by the whole group. Students become "experts" on their piece of the puzzle and then teach it to the others in their group.

Structured controversy Students working in pairs within their four-person cooperative groups to research a particular controversy.

Fostering communities of learners (FCL) A system of interacting activities that results in a self-consciously active and reflective learning environment and uses a research, share, and perform learning cycle.

Service Learning (pp. 333–335)

What are some key characteristics of service learning? Service learning activities should (1) be organized around and designed to meet actual community needs, (2) be integrated into the student's curriculum, (3) provide time to reflect and write about the service experience, (4) provide opportunities to apply newly learned academic skills and knowledge, and (5) enhance both academic learning and a sense of caring for others. Service learning activities ought not be supplementary to students' regular activities, but an integral part of their school-based learning.

Service learning Combines academic learning with personal and social development for secondary and post-secondary students.

Learning in a Digital World (pp. 335–339)

What are some possible uses of technology in the classroom? Technology such as computers, iPods, PDAs, and interactive gaming systems are becoming increasingly popular among young people. In fact, the many new ways of communicating and interacting with others through technology may even shape the way students think about what it means to socialize.

These technologies can be useful teaching tools, but they do have limitations. First, technology cannot necessarily replace the teacher when it comes to direct instruction (and not all programs are able to bring about learning). Second, not all students have equal access to or experience with technology such as computers.

Digital divide A split in access to technologies between those who fall into high versus low socioeconomic status.

TEACHERS' CASEBOOK

You have finally landed a job teaching English and writing in a high school. The first day of class, you discover that a number of students appear to be just beginning to learn English. You make a mental note to meet with them to determine how much and what kind of reading they can handle. To get a sense of the class's interest, you ask them to write a "review" of the last book they read, as if they were on TV doing a "Book Talk" program.

That night you look over the "book reviews." Either the students are giving you a hard time, or no one has read anything lately. Several students mention a text from another class, but their reviews are one-sentence evaluations—usually containing the words *lame* or *useless* (often misspelled). In stark contrast are the papers of three students—they are a pleasure to read, worthy of publication in the school literary magazine (if there were one), and they reflect a fairly sophisticated understanding of some good literature.

What Would *They* Do?

Here is how some practising teachers responded to the teaching situation described above.

Elaine A. Tan

Lakeview Elementary School, Burnaby, BC

As a new teacher myself, I understand the initial excitement this teacher was feeling. Rather than feel helpless at this point, remember that these book reviews reflect only one type of assessment—the written form. Today's multi-ability-level classrooms require a variety of assessment methods to address diverse backgrounds and learning styles and to give students more opportunities to demonstrate progress. The key here is to focus less on what needs to be covered and more on how it will be covered—process over content!

The first assignment might have caused some students to feel incapable because they lacked English grammar and writing skills and used an underdeveloped vocabulary. The key for English language learners is to provide lower-language and higher-interest visuals; for example, to use key words that connect ideas, sentence frames, or line maps. All students will benefit from vocabulary building. Select key vocabulary in each lesson and ask students to discuss, use, and apply those words.

The teacher should also adapt various instructional methods. For example, supplement long novels with videos or short stories written at appropriate levels to access students' different learning styles and means of understanding; integrate fine art to appeal to another type of learning style. Try the same activity again by grouping students in twos and threes, providing each with an interesting article she or he can relate to and write about. Prepare in advance a set of sentence frames to be completed for the students' articles.

Make use of the capable students, since all students benefit from shared learning experiences. Ask these three students to function as peer tutors in small groups. Cooperative learning groups assist with the inherent behavioural management challenge and help to reduce the isolation, boredom, and fear of sharing some students feel. Small groups also give the English language learner access to a fluent English speaker while simultaneously building the confidence and self-esteem of the peer tutor.

Where possible, assign world literature selections based on students' countries of origin to heighten interest and attention span. English language learners may want to write responses in their first languages. Ask peer tutors to assist these students in translating their ideas into English. This provides major language and interpersonal benefits for both groups of students, along with challenges for the advanced students.

Lesley Peterson

Sister High School, Winnipeg, MB

The first thing to determine is whether this writing task was a reasonably reliable diagnostic tool. Did you check that the students were familiar with the conventions of the review form and/or ensure that your expectations were clearly articulated to students? It might be worth assigning another writing task before deciding that the students whose papers were lacking in coherence were, in fact, unable to write coherent papers. However, in my experience, weak students tend to interpret every writing task as an invitation to retell the story. If these students have failed to do even that coherently, the problem is probably a real one.

Determining how to proceed with the very weak students, then, assuming that their weaknesses are validated, requires reference to the program policy and course outline. Also, if the course is required for university entrance or is a prerequisite for such a course, you cannot solely grade on effort and improvement. There must be standards. You should be prepared to differentiate your teaching in terms of the material that students read, the assignments they may choose, and the criteria by which they are evaluated. Differentiating instruction is still a good strategy for the standards-driven curriculum while retaining the same evaluation criteria for all students.

Central to the design of courses like this is a strong emphasis on the writing process. You should plan to teach writing, reading, and revision strategies that will be helpful to all or most students. If this is your goal, however, I strongly suggest changing this first assignment. Instead, ask the students to write reviews of the "best" book they have ever read. Knowing what they consider to be the "best" books is invaluable for planning a wide range of readings that engage students' interest. If you're well and widely read in world literature, you'll be able to find novels, short stories, and poems that intersect with what engages students. It's that basic old principle of teaching that needs to be put into action here: Find out where they are, then meet them, and take them forward from there.

If this is a university-entrance course, you should gather more data about the students who appear weak. Check their final marks in the prerequisite course and talk to previous English teachers. If you still feel a student does not have the reading, writing, and thinking skills necessary for success in this course, consider requesting conferences with the student's parents. Advise parents that this course will be a struggle for their child. An early recommendation to see a guidance counsellor or to change a timetable can turn into a real favour to the student. Better that the student enrol in an appropriate course now than sit in the wrong one, have her or his self-esteem battered for months, and then drop the course.

As for the really advanced writers, they need to be recognized, supported, and challenged. Nurture and challenge their love of literature and writing. Assigning advanced students assignments that are too easy can hurt students' self-esteem and lead to underachievement (not to mention boredom). Encourage these students to get involved in whatever writing communities are available. If a school magazine doesn't exist, encourage them to start one. Many cities have organizations similar to the Manitoba Writers' Guild, which sponsors readings and open-microphone sessions, organizes workshops, and so on, that can be very helpful to advanced writers.

Teaching a separate, gifted program to three students is more work than most English teachers have time for. But there are community resources you can access. Does your town library, university, or college have a "writer in residence?" If your school has a work experience coordinator, can he or she hook up these students with a professional journalist? Our local theatre gave one of my students a volunteer position reading and making recommendations on scripts. It changed her life.

Find out what kind of writing these students are most interested in and introduce them to other people who care about it as much as they do. You definitely shouldn't "punish" these students for their ability by giving them extra work. It might be possible for them to earn a separate credit for their extra involvement—talk to a guidance counsellor, work experience coordinator, or administrator to find out what's available. And have the grace to admit that these students might learn more if you let them spend part of your class time in the library. They'll respect you more for it, not less.

10 Social Cognitive Views of Learning and Motivation

Bedtime Story © *Diana Ong/SuperStock*

TEACHERS' CASEBOOK

WHAT WOULD YOU DO?

You know that your students need to be organized and self-regulating to do well in both their current and future classes. But many of the students just don't seem to know how to take charge of their own learning. They have trouble completing larger projects—many wait until the last minute. They can't organize their work or decide what is most important. Some can't even keep up with assignments. The students' book bags are disaster areas, containing long overdue assignments and class handouts from last semester crumpled in with school newsletters and permission slips for field trips. You are concerned because the students will need to be much more organized and on top of their work as they progress through their education. You have so much material to cover to meet the provincial curriculum, but many of your students are just drowning in the amount of work they already have, and you don't know how you'll be able to prepare them properly for the province-wide exams.

CRITICAL THINKING

- What organizational skills do students need for your subject or class?
- What could you do to teach these skills, while still covering the material that will be on the proficiency or achievement tests some students are required to take in the spring?

For the past four chapters, we have analyzed different aspects of how students learn. We considered behavioural and information processing explanations of what and how people learn. We examined complex cognitive processes such as concept learning and problem solving. These explanations of learning focus on the individual and what is happening in his or her "head." Recent perspectives have called attention to two other aspects of learning that are critically important: social and cultural factors. In the previous chapter, we examined social constructivism and the interdisciplinary learning sciences. In this chapter, we look at social cognitive theory—a current view of learning and motivation that discusses dynamic interactions among many of the behavioural, personal, and cultural factors involved in learning and motivation.

Social cognitive theory has its roots in Bandura's early theories of observational learning and vicarious reinforcement. You read about these early theories in Chapter 6, but social cognitive theory moved beyond behaviourism to focus on humans as self-directed agents who make choices and marshal resources to reach goals. Concepts such as self-efficacy and self-regulated learning are key to social cognitive theories. These concepts are important to understanding motivation as well, so this chapter provides a good path from the discussion of how people learn to that of motivation in the next chapter. We conclude with a look back at our tour through different models of instruction. Rather than debating the merits of each approach, we will consider the contributions of these different models of instruction, which are grounded in different theories of learning. Don't feel that you must choose the "best" approach—there is no such thing. Even though theorists argue about which model is best, excellent teachers don't debate. Instead, they apply each of the approaches to suit the needs of their students.

By the time you have completed this chapter, you should be able to answer these questions:

- What is triadic reciprocal causality and what role does it play in social cognitive theory?
- What is self-efficacy and how does it affect learning in school?
- What are the sources of self-efficacy?

- What is a teacher's sense of efficacy?
- How does self-regulated learning work—what are the phases?
- How can teachers support students in developing self-efficacy and self-regulated learning?

Connect and **Extend**
Go to the "Connect and Extend" section in Chapter 10 of MyEducationLab to find further content that links to teaching, students' thinking, research, and the news.

SOCIAL COGNITIVE THEORY

As we saw in Chapter 6, in the early 1960s, Albert Bandura demonstrated that people can learn by observing the actions of others and the consequences of those actions. Most of what we know today as *social cognitive theory* is based on the work begun by Bandura in the 1950s. Before we talk about the theory, let's meet the man.

ALBERT BANDURA Albert Bandura expanded on behavioural theories to emphasize observational learning. Most of what we know today as social cognitive theory is based on the work he began in the 1950s at Stanford University.

A Self-Directed Life: Albert Bandura

Albert Bandura's life story should be chronicled in a movie. Born in Alberta, his parents were immigrants from Eastern Europe; they chose to settle their family farm on the rugged land in the northern part of the province. Bandura's parents never went to school, but they valued education. His father taught himself to read in three languages, providing young Albert with a great model of self-regulated learning—a concept that figures prominently in social cognitive theory today. On the way to finishing high school, Bandura worked many jobs including a stint as a carpenter at a furniture factory and one as a road worker on the Alaska Highway in the Yukon. He finished his undergraduate degree at the University of British Columbia in three years, even though he had to cram all his classes into the morning so that the afternoon would be available to work at his jobs. Because he needed a morning class to fill one time slot, he enrolled in introductory psychology and found his future profession (Bandura, 2007, p. 46). His next stop was graduate school at the epicentre of psychological research in 1950—the University of Iowa. After earning his Ph.D. (again, in three years), Bandura joined the faculty at Stanford in 1953—he was 28 years old. He is still a faculty member at Stanford over 50 years later, and now teaches some of the children of his former students.

Bandura's autobiography (see **www.des.emory.edu/mfp/bandurabio.html** for a summary with pictures) highlights how much his theories reflected his life as a self-directed, self-regulating learner who grew up in a challenging environment. Describing his experiences in his two-teacher high school, Bandura said:

> We had to take charge of our own learning. Self-directed learning was an essential means of academic self-development, not a theoretical abstraction. The paucity of educational resources turned out to be an enabling factor that has served me well rather than an insurmountable handicapping one. The content of courses is perishable, but self-regulatory skills have lasting functional value whatever the pursuit might be. (p. 45)

In the next section we will look at the key features of Bandura's work and of social cognitive theory by considering four topics: the theory's evolution beyond behaviourism, the concept of triarchic reciprocal causality, the key beliefs of agency and self-efficacy, and the power of observational learning.

Beyond Behaviourism

Bandura's early social learning theory emphasized modelling and seeing others reinforced or punished for particular behaviours. But he found basic behaviourism to be too limited. In his autobiography, Bandura (2007) describes the shortcomings of behaviourism and the need to put people in social context:

Social learning theory Theory that emphasizes learning through observation of others.

> I found this behavioristic theorizing discordant with the obvious social reality that much of what we learn is through the power of social modeling. I could not imagine a culture in which its language; mores; familial customs and practices; occupational competencies; and educational, religious, and political practices were gradually shaped in each new member by rewarding and punishing consequences of their trial-and-error performances. (p. 55)

Over time, Bandura's explanations of learning included more attention to cognitive factors such as expectations and beliefs in addition to the social influences of models. His current perspective is called social cognitive theory (Bandura, 1986, 1997, 2001). Bandura relabelled his theory for two reasons. First, at the time, at least four other theories existed that were called *social learning theory* and they differed both from each other and from Bandura's work. To escape this confusion, he chose a new name for his theory. Second, his theory was broader than a theory of learning—it included cognitive factors and motivation. So *social cognitive theory* today retains an emphasis on the role of other people serving as models and teachers (the social part of social cognitive theory), but also includes the impact on learning of cognitive factors such as thinking, believing, expecting, anticipating, self-regulating, and making comparisons and judgments (the cognitive part).

Current social cognitive theory is a dynamic system that explains human adaptation, learning, and motivation. The theory addresses how people develop social, emotional, cognitive, and behavioural capabilities; how people regulate their own lives; and what motivates them (Bandura, 2007; Bandura & Locke, 2003). In fact, social cognitive theory is a major current explanation for motivation, so it is a good way to round out our discussion of learning and move toward the topic of motivation in Chapter 11. Many of the concepts that you will learn in this chapter will help you understand motivation.

Triarchic Reciprocal Causality

Social cognitive theory describes a system called triarchic reciprocal causality—that is, the dynamic interplay among three kinds of influences: personal, environmental, and behavioural, as shown in Figure 10.1. Personal factors (beliefs, expectations, attitudes, and knowledge), the physical and social environment (resources, consequences of actions, other people, models and teachers, and physical settings), and behaviour (individual actions, choices, and verbal statements) all influence and are influenced by each other.

Figure 10.1 shows the interaction of person, environment, and behaviour in learning settings (Schunk, Pintrich, & Meece, 2008). External factors such as models, instructional strategies, or teacher feedback (elements of the *environment* for students) can affect student's *personal* factors such as goals, sense of efficacy for the task (described in the next section), attributions (beliefs about causes for success and failure), and processes of self-regulation such as planning, monitoring,

Social cognitive theory Theory that adds concern with cognitive factors such as beliefs, self-perceptions, and expectations to social learning theory.

Triarchic reciprocal causality An explanation of behaviour that emphasizes the mutual effects of the individual and the environment on each other.

FIGURE 10.1 **Reciprocal Influences**
All three forces—personal, social/environmental, and behavioural—are in constant interaction. They influence and are influenced by each other.

Source: From "Social-Self Interaction and Achievement Behavior" by D. H. Schunk, 1999, *Educational Psychologist, 34*, p. 221. Adapted with permission of Lawrence Erlbaum Associates, Inc. and the author.

and controlling distractions. For example, teacher feedback can lead students to feel either more confident or more discouraged, and then students adjust their goals accordingly. Environmental and personal factors encourage the *behaviours* such as effort and persistence that lead to learning. But these behaviours also reciprocally impact personal factors. For example, as students achieve through increased effort (behaviour), their confidence and interest increase (personal). And behaviours also affect the social environment. For example, if students do not persist or if they seem to misunderstand, teachers may change instructional strategies or group assignments.

Think for a minute about the power of reciprocal causality in classrooms. If personal factors, behaviours, and the environment are in constant interaction, then cycles of events are progressive and self-perpetuating. Suppose a student who is new to the school walks into class late because he got lost in the unfamiliar building. The student has a tattoo and several visible pierced body parts. The student is anxious about his first day and hopes to do better at this new school, but the teacher's initial reaction to his late entry and dramatic appearance is a bit hostile. The student feels insulted and responds in kind, so the teacher begins to form expectations about him and acts more vigilant and less trusting. The student senses the distrust. He decides that this school will be just as worthless as his previous one—and he wonders why he should even bother to try harder in this new environment. The teacher sees the student's disengagement, invests less effort in teaching him, and the cycle continues.

Self-Efficacy and Agency

Self-efficacy A person's sense of being able to deal effectively with a particular task.

Human agency The capacity to coordinate learning skills, motivation, and emotions to reach your goals.

Bandura (1986, 1994, 1997) suggests that predictions about possible outcomes of behaviour are critical for learning because they affect goals, effort, persistence, strategies, and resilience. "Will I succeed or fail?" "Will I be liked or laughed at?" "Will I be more accepted by teachers in this new school?" These predictions are affected by self-efficacy—our beliefs about our personal competence or effectiveness *in a given area*. Bandura (1994) defines self-efficacy as "people's beliefs about their capabilities to produce designated levels of performance that exercise influence over events that affect their lives" (p. 71).

Recently, Bandura's (2006) efforts and the work of many other researchers have focused on the role of self-efficacy in human agency—the "exercising influence over life events" part of the definition above. Agency involves the ability to make intentional choices and action plans, design appropriate courses of action, and then motivate and regulate the execution of these plans and actions. When we discuss self-regulation later in the chapter, you will see how students and teachers can become more *agentic*—more self-directing and in charge of their own learning and motivation.

CAN I DO IT? Self-efficacy refers to the knowledge of one's own ability to successfully accomplish a particular task with no need for comparisons with others' ability—the question is "Can I do it?" not "Are others better than I am?"

Self-Efficacy, Self-Concept, and Self-Esteem. Most people assume self-efficacy is the same as self-concept or self-esteem, but it isn't. Self-efficacy is future-oriented, "a context-specific assessment of competence to perform a specific task" (Pajares, 1997, p. 15). Self-concept is a more global construct that contains many perceptions about the self, including self-efficacy. Self-concept is developed as a result of external and internal comparisons, using other people or other aspects of the self as frames of reference. But self-efficacy focuses on *your* ability to successfully accomplish a particular task with no need for comparisons—the question is whether *you* can do it, not whether others would be successful. Also, self-efficacy beliefs are strong predictors of behaviour, but self-concept has weaker predictive power (Anderman & Anderman, 2009; Bandura, 1997).

Self-efficacy is "context specific," which means it varies, depending on the subject or task. For example, Anita's sense of efficacy for singing is really low, but she feels confident in her ability to read a map and to navigate (except in certain cities that are hopeless). Even young students hold different efficacy beliefs for different tasks. One study found that by grade 1, students already differentiated among their sense of efficacy for reading, for writing, and for spelling (Wilson & Trainin, 2007).

Self-efficacy is concerned with judgments of personal competence; self-esteem is concerned with judgments of self-worth. There is no direct relationship between self-esteem and self-efficacy. It is possible to feel highly efficacious in one area and still not have a high level of self-esteem, or vice versa (Valentine, DuBois, & Cooper, 2004). For example, even though Anita has very low self-efficacy for singing, her self-esteem is not affected, probably because her life does not require singing. But if her self-efficacy for teaching a particular class started dropping after several bad experiences, she is certain her self-esteem would suffer because of how much she values teaching.

Sources of Self-Efficacy. Bandura identified four sources of self-efficacy expectations: mastery experiences, physiological and emotional arousal, vicarious experiences, and social persuasion. Mastery experiences are our own direct experiences—the most powerful source of efficacy information. Successes raise efficacy beliefs, while failures lower those beliefs. Level of arousal also affects self-efficacy, depending on how the arousal is interpreted. For example, as you face a task, are you anxious and worried (lowers efficacy) or excited and "psyched" (raises efficacy) (Bandura, 1997; Schunk et al., 2008)?

In vicarious experiences, someone else models accomplishments. The more closely the observer identifies with the model, the greater the impact on self-efficacy will be. When the model performs well, the observer's efficacy is enhanced, but when the model performs poorly, efficacy expectations decrease. Although mastery experiences generally are acknowledged as the most influential source of efficacy beliefs in adults, Keyser and Barling (1981) found that children (grade 6 students in this study) rely more on modelling as a source of self-efficacy information.

Social persuasion can take the form of a "pep talk" or specific performance feedback. Social persuasion alone can't create enduring increases in self-efficacy, but a persuasive boost in self-efficacy can lead a student to make an effort, attempt new strategies, or try hard enough to succeed (Bandura, 1982). Social persuasion can counter occasional setbacks that might have instilled self-doubt and interrupted persistence. The potency of persuasion depends on the credibility, trustworthiness, and expertise of the persuader (Bandura, 1997). Table 10.1 summarizes the sources of self-efficacy.

Modelling: Learning From Others

Learning by observing others is a key element of social cognitive theory. We just saw that modelling can be a vicarious experience and a source of self-efficacy. What causes an individual to learn and perform modelled behaviours and skills? Several factors play a role. First, the developmental level of the observer makes a difference in learning. As children grow older, they are able to focus attention for longer periods of time, to use memory strategies to retain information, and to motivate themselves to practise, as you can see in Table 10.2 on page 352. A second influence is the status of the model. Children are more likely to imitate the actions of others who seem competent, powerful, prestigious, and enthusiastic, so parents, teachers, older siblings, athletes, action heroes, rock stars,

Mastery experiences Our own direct experiences—the most powerful source of efficacy information.

Arousal Physical and psychological reactions causing a person to feel alert, excited, or tense.

Vicarious experiences Accomplishments that are modelled by someone else.

Modelling Changes in behaviour, thinking, or emotions that occur by observing another person—a model.

Social persuasion A "pep talk" or specific performance feedback—one source of self-efficacy.

TABLE 10.1 Sources of Self-Efficacy

Source	Example
Mastery experiences	Your past successes and failures in similar situations. To increase efficacy, the success must be attributed to your ability, effort, choices, and strategies—not to luck or to extensive help from others.
Vicarious experiences	Seeing other people like you succeed in completing a task or accomplishing a goal that is similar to the one you face.
Social persuasion	Encouragement, informational feedback, and/or useful guidance from a trusted source.
Physiological arousal	Positive or negative arousal—excitement and a feeling of being "psyched" and ready (increases efficacy) or a sense of anxiety and foreboding (decreases efficacy).

TABLE 10.2 Factors That Affect Observational Learning

Characteristic	Effects on Modelling Process
Developmental status	Improvements with development include longer attention and increased capacity to process information, use strategies, compare performances with memorial representations, and adopt intrinsic motivators.
Model prestige and competence	Observers pay greater attention to competent, high-status models. Consequences of modelled behaviours convey information about functional value. Observers attempt to learn actions they believe they will need to perform.
Vicarious consequences	Consequences to models convey information about behavioural appropriateness and likely outcomes of actions. Valued consequences motivate observers. Similarity in attributes or competence signals appropriateness and heightens motivation.
Outcome expectations	Observers are more likely to perform modelled actions that they believe are appropriate and will result in rewarding outcomes.
Goal setting	Observers are likely to attend to models who demonstrate behaviours that help observers attain goals.
Self-efficacy	Observers attend to models when they believe they are capable of learning or performing the modelled behaviour. Observation of similar models affects self-efficacy (e.g., "If they can do it, I can too").

Source: From *Learning Theories: An Education Perspective* (4th ed.), by D. H. Schunk. Published by Prentice Hall.

MyEducationLab
Go to the Activities and Applications section in Chapter 10 of MyEducationLab and complete Activity 1. As you watch the video and answer the accompanying questions, consider how the teacher supports the development of self-efficacy for her students through social persuasion and positive mastery experiences.

or film personalities may serve as models, depending on the age and interests of the child. Third, by watching others, we learn about what behaviours are appropriate for people like ourselves, so models who are seen as similar to ourselves are more readily imitated (Schunk et al., 2008). All students, regardless of their ethnicity, socioeconomic status, or gender, need to see successful, capable models who look and sound like them.

Look at Table 10.2. The last three influences involve goals and expectations. If observers expect that certain actions of models will lead to particular outcomes (such as particular practice regimens leading to improved athletic performance) and the observers value those outcomes or goals, then the observers are more likely to pay attention to the models and to try to reproduce their behaviours. Finally, observers are more likely to learn from models if the observers have a high level of self-efficacy—that is, if they believe they are capable of doing the actions needed to reach the goals, or at least capable of learning how to do so (Bandura, 1997; Schunk et al., 2008).

In the next section we examine how to apply social cognitive theory to the classroom environment, beginning with what we just discussed—modelling or learning by observation.

MyEducationLab
Go to the Podcasts section of MyEducationLab and listen to PODCAST—Sources of Self-Efficacy. Self-efficacy is a future-oriented, context-specific assessment of competence to perform a specific task. Why is the belief about yourself so important and where does it come from? Listen to Anita Woolfolk explain the sources of self-efficacy and how teachers might use this information to invent ways of supporting their students' sense of efficacy for learning.

APPLYING SOCIAL COGNITIVE THEORY

Social cognitive theory has some powerful implications for the teaching profession. In this section, we will look more closely at using observational learning in teaching, developing students' self-efficacy, and building teachers' own sense of efficacy.

Observational Learning in Teaching

STOP & THINK How would you incorporate observational learning into your teaching? What are the skills, attitudes, and strategies you can use that will serve as models for your students?

In the classroom, five possible outcomes of observational learning can emerge: directing attention, encouraging existing behaviours, changing inhibitions, teaching new behaviours and attitudes, and arousing emotions. Let's look at each of these as they occur in classroom settings.

Directing Attention. By observing others, we not only learn about actions but also notice the objects involved in the actions. For example, in a preschool class, when one child plays enthusiastically with a toy that has been ignored for days, many other children may want to have the toy, even if they play with it in different ways or simply carry it around. This happens, in part, because the children's attention has been drawn to that particular toy.

Fine-Tuning Already-Learned Behaviours. All of us have had the experience of looking for cues from other people when we find ourselves in unfamiliar situations. Observing the behaviour of others tells us which of our already-learned behaviours to use: for example, which fork to use when eating salad, when to leave a gathering, what kind of language is appropriate, and so on. Students who copy the dress and grooming styles of TV or music idols is another example of this kind of effect.

Strengthening or Weakening Inhibitions. If class members witness one student breaking a class rule and getting away with it, they may learn that undesirable consequences do not always follow rule-breaking. If the rule breaker is a well-liked, high-status class leader, the effect of the modelling on other students may be even more pronounced. This **ripple effect** (Kounin, 1970) can work to the teacher's benefit. When the teacher deals effectively with a rule breaker, especially a class leader, the idea of breaking this rule may be inhibited for the other students viewing the interaction. This does not mean that teachers must reprimand each student who breaks a rule, but once a teacher has called for a particular action, following through with it is an important part of capitalizing on the ripple effect.

Ripple effect "Contagious" spreading of behaviours through imitation.

Teaching New Behaviours. Modelling has long been used, of course, to teach dance, sports, and crafts, as well as skills in subjects such as food science, chemistry, and welding. Modelling can also be applied deliberately in the classroom to teach mental skills and to broaden horizons—that is, to teach new ways of thinking. Teachers serve as models for a vast range of behaviours, from how to pronounce vocabulary words, to how to react when a student with epilepsy has a seizure, to how to promote genuine enthusiasm for learning. For example, a teacher might model sound critical thinking skills by thinking "out loud" about a student's question. Or a high school teacher concerned about girls who appear to have stereotyped ideas about certain careers might invite women with non-traditional jobs to speak to the class. Studies indicate that modelling can be most effective when the teacher makes use of all the elements of observational learning described in Chapter 6, especially reinforcement and practice.

Models who are the same age as the students may be particularly effective. For example, Schunk and Hanson (1985) compared two methods for teaching subtraction to grade 2 students who had difficulties learning this skill. One group of students observed other grade 2 students learning the procedures, while another group watched a teacher's demonstration. Then, both groups participated in the same instructional program. The students who observed peer models not only scored higher on tests of subtraction after instruction, but also gained more confidence in their own ability to learn. For students who doubt their own abilities, a particularly effective model is a low-achieving student who keeps trying and finally masters the material (Schunk, 2004).

DO AS I DO Modelling has long been used to teach dance, sports, and crafts, and skills such as cooking, chemistry, and welding. Modelling can also be applied deliberately in the classroom to teach mental skills and to broaden horizons—to teach new ways of thinking.

Arousing Emotion. Finally, through observational learning, people may develop emotional reactions to situations they have never experienced personally, such as flying or driving. A child who watches a friend fall from a swing and

GUIDELINES: Using Observational Learning

Model the behaviours and attitudes that you want your students to learn.

EXAMPLES

1. Show enthusiasm for the subject you teach.
2. Be willing to demonstrate both the mental and the physical tasks you expect the students to perform. Anita once saw a teacher sit down in the sandbox while her 4-year-old students watched her demonstrate the difference between "playing with sand" and "throwing sand."
3. When reading to students, model methods that improve comprehension. Stop and say, "Now let me see if I remember what happened so far," or "That was a hard sentence. I'm going to read it again."
4. Model good problem solving—think out loud as you work through a difficult problem.

Use peers, especially class leaders, as models.

EXAMPLES

1. In group work, pair students who do well with those who are having difficulties.
2. Ask students to demonstrate the difference between concepts; for example, the difference between "whispering" and "silence—no talking."

Make sure students see that positive behaviours lead to reinforcement for others.

EXAMPLES

1. Point out the connections between positive behaviour and positive consequences in stories.
2. Be fair when giving reinforcement. The same rules for gaining rewards should apply to both the students who tend to behave problematically and the students who do not behave problematically.

Enlist the help of class leaders to serve as models for behaviours you would like the entire class to adopt.

EXAMPLES

1. Ask a well-liked student to be friendly to an isolated, fearful student.
2. Let high-status students lead an activity when you need class cooperation or when students are likely to be reluctant at first. Popular students can model dialogues in foreign-language classes or be the first to tackle dissection procedures in biology.

For more information on observational learning, see **www.readwritethink.org/lessons/lesson_view.asp?id=275**.

break an arm may become fearful of swings. After the terrible events of September 11, 2001, children may become anxious when they see airplanes flying close to the ground. News reports of shark attacks make many of us anxious about swimming in the ocean. Note that hearing and reading about a situation are also forms of observation. Some terrible examples of modelling occur with the "copycat killings" that sometimes take place in schools. When frightening things happen to people who are similar in age or circumstances to your students, the students may need to be given an opportunity to talk about their emotions.

The *Guidelines* box will give you some ideas about how to use observational learning in the classroom.

Self-efficacy is a key element of social cognitive theory that is especially important to learning and teaching effectively.

Self-Efficacy in Learning and Teaching

STOP & THINK On a scale from 1 to 100, how confident are you that you will finish reading this chapter today?

Let's assume your sense of efficacy is around 90 for reading this chapter in its entirety today. Greater efficacy leads to greater effort and persistence in the face of setbacks, so even if you are interrupted during your reading, you are likely to return to the task. The thinking is something along these lines: "I believe I can finish writing this section today, so I have returned to working on it after meeting with some students about their research projects. Of course, completing the task today could make for a late night, because I have a faculty meeting yet to attend and a class lecture to prepare for tomorrow." Self-efficacy also influences motivation through goal setting. If we have a high sense of efficacy in a given area, we will set higher goals, be less afraid of failure, and find new strategies when old ones fail. If your sense of efficacy for reading this chapter is high, you are likely to set high goals for completing the chapter—maybe you will take some notes, too. If your sense of efficacy is low, however, you may avoid the reading altogether or give up easily when problems arise or when you are interrupted with a better offer (Bandura, 1993, 1997; Pajares & Schunk, 2001).

What is the most motivating level of efficacy? Should students be accurate, optimistic, or pessimistic in their predictions? There is evidence that a higher sense of self-efficacy supports motivation, even when the efficacy is an overestimation. Children and adults who are optimistic about the future are more mentally and physically healthy, less depressed, and more motivated to achieve (Flammer, 1995; Seligman, 2006). After examining almost 140 studies of motivation, Sandra Graham concluded that these qualities characterize many African Americans. She found that the African Americans studied had strong self-concepts and high expectations, even in the face of difficulties (Graham, 1994, 1995).

Agnes provides her teacher with an "efficacy correction."
By permission of Tony Cochran and Creators Syndicate.

MyEducationLab
Go to the Activities and Applications section in Chapter 10 of MyEducationLab and complete Activity 2. As you read the article and answer the accompanying questions, consider the relationship between mastery experiences and self-efficacy.

As you might expect, there are dangers associated with underestimating abilities because then students are more likely to put out a weak effort and to give up easily. But there are dangers with continually overestimating performance as well. Students who think that they are better readers than they actually are may not be motivated to go back and repair misunderstandings as they read. They don't discover that they did not really understand the material until it is too late (Pintrich & Zusho, 2002).

In schools, we are particularly interested in self-efficacy for learning mathematics, writing, history, science, sports, and other subjects, as well as for using learning strategies and for the many other challenges that classrooms present. For example, in research with students, self-efficacy is related to academic achievement in math for middle school students (Kenney-Benson, Pomerantz, Ryan, & Patrick, 2006), to life satisfaction for adolescents (Vecchio, Gerbino, Pastorelli, Del Bove, & Caprara, 2007), to writing and math performance for students from grade 3 through high school (Pajares, 2002), to choice of university major (Pajares, 2002), and to performance in university for older students (Elias & MacDonald, 2007). So, maybe you are thinking, sure, higher self-efficacy is related to higher achievement because students who have more ability have higher self-efficacy. But these relationships between self-efficacy and achievement hold even when we take ability into account. For example, when students with the same ability in math are compared, those with higher self-efficacy for math perform better in math (Wigfield & Wentzel, 2007).

Research indicates that performance in school is improved and self-efficacy is increased when students (a) adopt short-term goals so it is easier to judge progress; (b) are taught to use specific learning strategies, such as outlining or summarizing, that help them focus their attention; and (c) receive rewards based on achievement, not just on engagement, because achievement rewards signal increasing competence (Graham & Weiner, 1996). The *Guidelines* box on page 356 gives more ideas about how to encourage self-efficacy in your students.

MyEducationLab
Go to the Podcasts section of MyEducationLab and listen to PODCAST—Increasing Student, Teacher, and Collective Efficacy. There are three kinds of efficacy judgments at work in schools, and all three are related to student achievement. In this podcast Anita Woolfolk describes each kind of efficacy and gives ideas for how to increase them.

Teachers' Sense of Efficacy

Much of Anita's research has focused on a particular kind of self-efficacy—teachers' sense of efficacy (Knoblauch & Woolfolk Hoy, 2008; Tschannen-Moran & Woolfolk Hoy, 2001, 2007; Tschannen-Moran, Woolfolk Hoy, & Hoy, 1998; Woolfolk & Hoy, 1990; Woolfolk Hoy & Burke-Spero, 2005; Woolfolk Hoy, Hoy, & Davis, 2009). Teachers' sense of efficacy—a teacher's belief that he or she can reach even difficult students and help them to learn—appears to be one of the few personal characteristics of teachers that is correlated with student achievement. Self-efficacy theory predicts that teachers

Teachers' sense of efficacy A teacher's belief that he or she can reach even the most difficult students and help them learn.

GUIDELINES: Encouraging Self-Efficacy

Emphasize students' progress in a particular area.

EXAMPLES

1. When reviewing content with the class, return to earlier material and show students how "easy" that content seems now.
2. Encourage students to improve previously submitted or completed projects when they have learned more about the subject of those projects.
3. Keep examples of particularly good work in portfolios.

Set learning goals for your students, and model a mastery orientation for them.

EXAMPLES

1. Recognize progress and improvement.
2. Share examples of how you have developed your abilities in a given area and provide other models of achievement who are similar to your students. Avoid inviting "supermen" or "superwomen" whose accomplishments seem unattainable to speak to the class.
3. Assign reading assignments about students who overcame physical, mental, or economic challenges.
4. Don't excuse failure because a student has problems outside school. Instead, help the student succeed inside school.

Make specific suggestions for improvement, and revise grades when improvements are made.

EXAMPLES

1. Return work with comments noting what the students did correctly, what they did incorrectly, and why they might have made the mistakes.
2. Experiment with peer editing (i.e., asking students' peers to read and comment on their work).
3. Show students how their revised, higher grade reflects greater competence and raises their class average.

Stress connections between past efforts and past accomplishments.

EXAMPLES

1. Have individual goal-setting and goal-review conferences with students, in which you ask students to reflect on how they solved difficult problems.
2. Confront self-defeating, failure-avoiding strategies directly.

For more information on self-efficacy, see **www.emory.edu/EDUCATION/mfp/self-efficacy.html**.

TEACHER SELF-EFFICACY Research shows that teachers' sense of efficacy grows from real success with students. Experience or training that helps teachers succeed in the day-to-day tasks of teaching will contribute to their sense of efficacy.

with a high sense of efficacy work harder and persist longer even when students are difficult to teach, in part because these teachers believe in themselves and in their students. Also, teachers with a high sense of efficacy are less likely to experience burn-out (Fives, Hamman, & Olivarez, 2005).

Anita and her colleagues found that prospective teachers tend to increase their personal sense of efficacy as a consequence of completing student teaching stints. But teachers' sense of efficacy may go down after their first year teaching, perhaps because the support that was there for them as beginning teachers often disappears once they become full-time staff (Woolfolk Hoy & Burke-Spero, 2005). Teachers' sense of efficacy is also higher in schools in which the other teachers and administrators have high expectations for students and in which teachers receive help from their principals in solving instructional and management problems (Capa, 2005; Hoy & Woolfolk, 1993). Another important conclusion from the research is that efficacy grows from real success with students, not just from the moral support or cheerleading of fellow professors and colleagues. Any experience or training that helps you succeed in the day-to-day tasks of teaching will give you a foundation for developing a high sense of efficacy in your career.

As with any kind of efficacy, there may be both benefits and dangers associated with teachers overestimating their abilities. Optimistic teachers probably set higher goals, work harder, reteach when necessary, and persist in the face of problems. But some benefits might also follow from having doubts about your efficacy. The *Point/Counterpoint* box looks at both sides of teachers' judgments of their own teaching efficacy.

POINT / COUNTERPOINT

Are High Levels of Teacher Efficacy Beneficial?

BASED ON BANDURA'S research on self-efficacy, we probably would assume that a high sense of efficacy for teachers is a good thing. But not everyone agrees. Here is the debate.

POINT

Higher efficacy is better than lower efficacy.

The research on teachers' sense of efficacy points to many positive outcomes related to higher efficacy. Anita, her husband, and a colleague summarized this research (Woolfolk Hoy, Hoy, & Davis, 2009). Here are a few of the findings that they identified. Teachers with a strong sense of efficacy tend to be more enthusiastic and spend more time teaching in subject areas in which their sense of efficacy is higher, and they tend to avoid subjects in which their sense of efficacy is lower. Teachers with higher efficacy judgments tend to be more open to new ideas, more willing to experiment with new methods to better meet the needs of their students, more likely to use powerful but potentially difficult-to-manage methods such as inquiry and small group work, and less likely to use easy-to-adopt but weaker methods such as lecture. Teachers with higher efficacy are less likely to criticize students and more persistent in following up on incorrect student answers. They also tend to select strategies that support student learning rather than those that simply cover the curriculum. Compared to low efficacy teachers, those who report a higher sense of efficacy tend to be more active in monitoring seatwork and maintaining academic focus, and they respond quickly to student misbehaviour by redirecting attention without showing anger or becoming threatened. What about the students? In addition to being related to student achievement, teachers' sense of efficacy has been associated with other student outcomes such as motivation and students' own sense of efficacy.

COUNTERPOINT

There are problems with high efficacy.

In spite of the large body of literature describing positive outcomes associated with higher self-efficacy, several researchers have questioned whether higher is always better. For example, Karl Wheatley (2002, 2005) suggested that several forms of teacher self-efficacy might be problematic. One is the excessive optimism that some beginning teachers adopt that interferes with their ability to accurately judge their own effectiveness. In an analysis of students who were about to begin their student teaching, Carol Weinstein (1988) found a strong sense of "unrealistic optimism"—the tendency to believe that problems experienced by others would not happen to them. Interestingly, the unrealistic optimism was greatest for activities having to do with controlling students (e.g., maintaining discipline and establishing and enforcing class rules). These findings are consistent with Emmer and Hickman's (1991) observations that student teachers who had trouble managing the students in their classes still reported high levels of classroom management efficacy. Another problematic consequence of higher efficacy is resistance to learning new knowledge and skills and a tendency to "stick with what works"—that is, stick with the ways of teaching that have provided a sense of mastery in the past. Overconfident efficacy may quickly be followed by giving up if the task proves more difficult than first thought. Wheatley (2002) believes "lower efficacy beliefs are essential for teacher learning; doubt motivates change" (p. 18).

It is true that persistently high efficacy perceptions in the face of poor performance (unrealistic optimism) can produce avoidance rather than action and can interfere with teacher learning, but we believe that a sense of *efficacy for learning to teach* would be necessary to respond to the doubts described above.

As you may remember from the discussion at the beginning of this chapter, Albert Bandura said that his early education in a tiny school in Canada had given him self-regulation skills that lasted a lifetime. He also noted the following:

> A major goal of formal education is to equip students with the intellectual tools, self-beliefs, and self-regulatory capabilities to educate themselves throughout their lifetime. The rapid pace of technological change and accelerated growth of knowledge are placing a premium on capability for self-directed learning. (Bandura, 2007, p. 10)

We turn to this issue next as we explore how you can help your students lead a self-directed life.

MyEducationLab
Go to the Podcasts section of MyEducationLab and listen to PODCAST—Academic Optimism. In the podcast Anita Woolfolk discusses a new concept she developed with her husband, Wayne Hoy, a professor of educational administration who works with principals and superintendents.

SELF-REGULATED LEARNING

Today, people change jobs an average of seven times before they retire. Many of these career changes require new learning that must be self-initiated and self-directed (Martinez-Pons, 2002; Weinstein, 1994). Thus, one goal of teaching, as Bandura noted, should be to free students from the need for teachers, so students can continue to learn independently throughout their lives. To continue learning independently throughout life, people must be self-regulated—what we refer to in conversations as a *self-starter*.

STOP & THINK Think about the class you are taking in which you are using this textbook. On a 7-point scale—with 1 meaning *not at all true of me*, and 7 meaning *very true of me*—answer the following questions:

1. When I study for a test, I try to put together the information from class and from the book.
2. When I do homework, I try to remember what the teacher said in class so I can answer the questions correctly.
3. I know I will be able to learn the material for this class.
4. I expect to do well in this class.
5. I ask myself questions to make sure I know the material I have been studying.
6. Even when study materials are dull and uninteresting, I keep working until I finish.

You have just responded to six items from the *Motivated Strategies for Learning Questionnaire* (MSLQ) (Midgley et al., 1998; Pintrich & De Groot, 1990). This questionnaire has been used in hundreds of studies to assess students' perceptions of their self-regulated learning and motivation. How did you describe yourself? The first two questions assess your view about how you use cognitive strategies, like those we discussed in Chapter 8. The second two questions assess your sense of efficacy for this class. But the last two questions specifically assess your sense of self-regulation, defined by Barry Zimmerman (2002) as the process we use to activate and sustain our thoughts, behaviours, and emotions in order to reach our goals. Bandura (2007) summarizes the concept of self-regulation as setting goals and mobilizing the efforts and resources needed to reach those goals. When the goals involve learning, we talk about *self-regulated learning*.

Self-regulation Process of activating and sustaining thoughts, behaviours, and emotions in order to reach goals.

Self-regulated learners have a combination of academic learning skills and self-control that makes learning more productive, so they are more motivated; in other words, they have the *skill* and the *will* to learn (Murphy & Alexander, 2000; Schunk, 2005). Self-regulated learners transform their mental abilities, whatever they are, into academic skills and strategies (Zimmerman, 2002). Many studies link strategy use to different measures of academic achievement, especially for middle and high school students (Fredricks, Blumenfeld, & Paris, 2004).

THE SKILL AND THE WILL Self-regulated learners have a combination of academic learning skills and self-control that makes learning more productive; they have the skill and the will to learn.

What Influences Self-Regulation?

The concept of self-regulated learning integrates much of what is known about effective learning and motivation. As you can see from the processes described above, three factors influence skill and will: knowledge, motivation, and self-discipline or volition.

Knowledge. To be self-regulated learners, students need *knowledge* about themselves, the subject, the task, strategies for learning, and the contexts in which they will apply their learning. "Expert" students know about *themselves* and about how they learn best. For example, they know their preferred learning approaches, what is easy and what is hard for them, how to cope with the difficult parts, what their interests and talents are, and how to use their strengths (see Chapter 4 of this book). These experts also know quite a bit about the *subject* being studied—and the more they know, the easier it is for them to learn more (Alexander, 2006a). They probably understand that different *learning tasks* require

metacognition / reflection

different approaches on their part. A simple memory task, for example, might require a mnemonic strategy (see Chapter 7), whereas a complex comprehension task might be approached by means of creating concept maps of the key ideas (see Chapter 8). Also, these self-regulated learners know that learning is often difficult and that knowledge is seldom absolute; they understand that there usually are different ways of looking at problems as well as different solutions (Pressley, 1995; Winne, 1995).

Expert students not only know what each task requires but also can apply the *strategy* needed. They can skim content or read it carefully. They can use memory strategies or reorganize the material. As they become more knowledgeable in a field, they apply many of these strategies automatically. In short, they have mastered a large, flexible repertoire of learning strategies and tactics as described in Chapter 8 (Winne, in press). Finally, self-regulated learners think about the *contexts* in which they will apply their knowledge—when and where they will use their learning—so they can set motivating goals and connect present work to future accomplishments (Wang & Palincsar, 1989; Weinstein, 1994; Winne & Hadwin, 1998).

MyEducationLab Go to the Activities and Applications section in Chapter 10 of MyEducationLab and complete Activity 3. As you view the artifact and complete the accompanying activities, think about what students need to become self-regulated learners.

Motivation. Self-regulated learners are *motivated* to learn (see Chapter 11). They find many tasks in school interesting because they value learning, not just performing well in the eyes of others. Even if self-regulated learners are not intrinsically motivated by a particular task, they are serious about obtaining the intended benefit from it. They know *why* they are studying, so their actions and choices are self-determined and not controlled by others. However, knowledge and motivation are not always enough. Self-regulated learners need volition or self-discipline. According to Corno, "Where motivation denotes commitment, volition denotes follow-through" (Corno, 1992, p. 72).

Volition. It is early Friday afternoon, the first really sunny day just after the summer solstice. Phil's eyes keep drifting to the bay he can spy from his study, but he wants to keep working because the deadline for the submission of this chapter is very near. He has knowledge and motivation, but to keep going he needs a good dose of *volition*. Volition is an old-fashioned word for willpower. The more technical definition for volition is *planning for and protecting opportunities to reach goals*. Self-regulated learners know how to protect themselves from distractions—where to study, for example, so they are not interrupted. They know how to cope when they feel anxious, drowsy, or lazy (Corno, 1992, 1995; Snow, Corno, & Jackson, 1996). And they know what to do when they are tempted to stop working and have (another) cup of coffee—the temptation that Phil is facing now—that, and his dog, Abby, is begging for a walk.

Models of Self-Regulated Learning and Agency

Albert Bandura may have gone from high school graduate to professor at one of the world's leading universities in six years by using his self-regulated learning knowledge and skills, but not all of your students will have the same abilities as Bandura. In fact, some psychologists suggest that we think of this capacity as one of many characteristics that distinguish individuals (Snow et al., 1996). Some students are much better at self-regulation than others. How can you help more students become self-regulated learners in school? What is involved in being self-regulated?

Theoretical models of self-regulated learning describe how learners—like you!—set goals and mobilize the efforts and resources needed to reach those goals. There are several models of self-regulated learning (Puustinen & Pulkkinen, 2001). Let's look at one developed by Phil and his colleague Allyson Hadwin (1998; Winne & Hadwin, 2010), shown in Figure 10.2. This depiction of self-regulated learning has many facets, as it should when the topic at hand is how you manage your academic life.

The model of self-regulated learning illustrated in Figure 10.2 is based on the belief that learners are *agents*. As we saw earlier, agency is the capacity to coordinate learning skills, motivation, and emotions to reach your goals. Agents are not puppets on strings held by teachers, textbook authors, or webpage designers. Instead, agents control many factors that influence how they learn. Self-regulating learners exercise agency as they engage in a cycle involving four main phases: analyzing the task, setting goals and designing plans, engaging in learning, and adjusting their approach to improve the effectiveness of learning.

1. *Analyzing the learning task.* You are familiar with this stage of self-regulated learning. What do you do when a professor announces there will be a test? You ask about conditions you believe will influence how you'll study for it. Will it feature essay questions or multiple-choice questions?

Volition Willpower; self-discipline; work styles that plan for and protect opportunities to reach goals by applying self-regulated learning.

Self-regulated learning A view of learning as skills and will applied to analyzing a learning task, setting goals and planning how to do the task, applying skills, and especially making adjustments about how learning is carried out.

FIGURE 10.2 **The Cycle of Self-Regulated Learning**

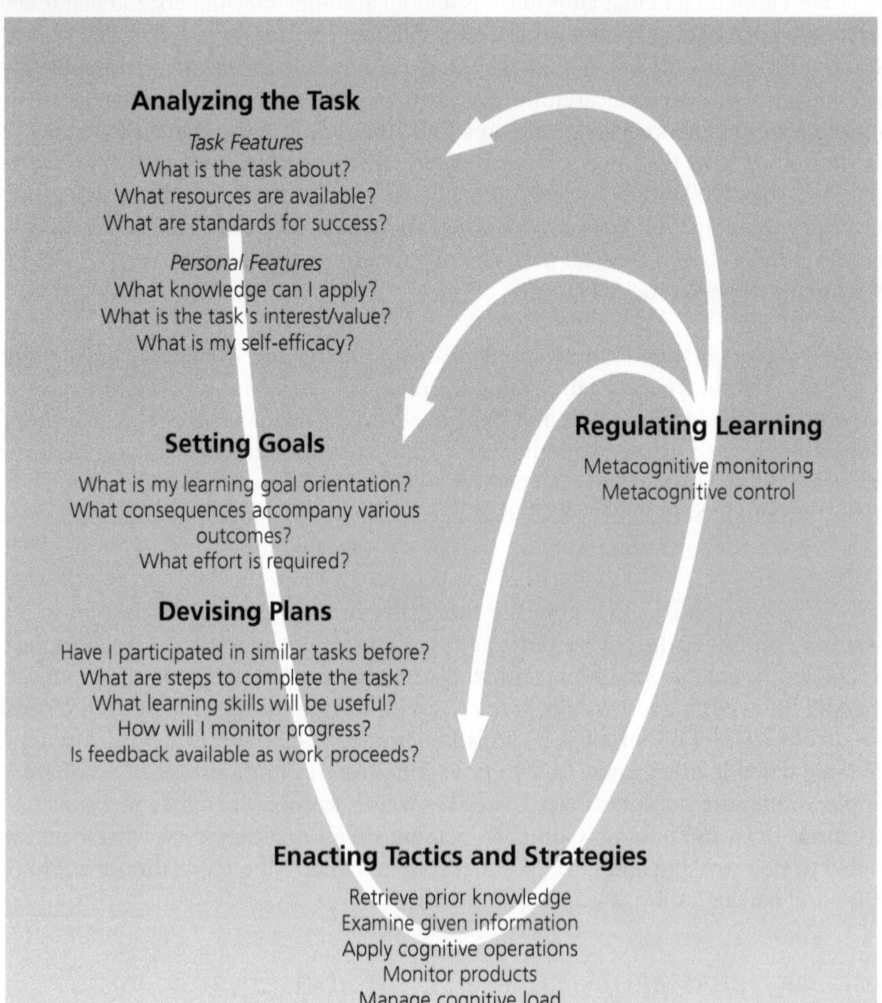

Source: "The cycle of self-regulated learning" from *Educational Psychology* (3rd Canadian ed.) by A. E. Woolfolk, P. H. Winne, and N. E. Perry. Toronto: Pearson, 2006, p. 307, Fig. 8.9. Adapted with permission of Pearson Education Canada and Philip Winne.

Is your best friend up to date on the material to be tested and available to study with you? In general, learners examine whatever information they think is relevant in order to construct a sense of what the task is about, what resources to bring to bear, and how they feel about the work to be done—are they interested? confident? anxious? knowledgeable? clueless?

2. *Setting goals and designing plans.* Knowing the conditions that influence work on tasks provides information that learners use to create goals for learning. Then, they can develop plans for how to reach those goals. What goals for studying might you set for a quiz covering only one chapter that counts just 3 percent toward your course grade? Would your goals change if the test covered the last six chapters and counted 30 percent toward your course grade? What targets are identified in these goals—repeating definitions, being able to discuss how a teacher could apply findings from key research studies described in the textbook, or critiquing theoretical positions? Choosing goals affects the shape of a learner's plans for how to study. Is cramming (massed practice) the best approach? Is a better plan to study a half-hour each day, overlapping content a bit from one day to the next (distributed practice)?
3. *Enacting tactics and strategies to accomplish the task.* In this phase, self-regulated learners consider what they know or need to know to help them be successful with these tactics and

strategies. As they enact their plan, self-regulated learners are especially alert in monitoring how well the plan is working. They ask themselves these questions: Is the cognitive load too great? Am I feeling overwhelmed? What can I do to manage all this complex information? Is the approach I'm taking too effortful for the results I am achieving? Am I reaching my goals? Is my progress rate fast enough to be prepared for the test?

4. *Regulating learning.* This is metacognitive monitoring and control (see Chapter 8). In this phase, learners come to decisions about whether changes are needed in any of the three preceding phases. For example, if learning is slow, they ask these questions: Should I study with my best friend? Do I need to review some prior material that provides the foundation for the content I am now studying? Do I need to start over—identifying what the task really is and then setting new (higher, lower, different) goals?

An Individual Example of Self-Regulated Learning

Students today are faced with constant distractions. In the following quotation, Barry Zimmerman (2002) describes Tracy, a high school student who is devoted to MTV:

> An important mid-term math exam is two weeks away, and she had begun to study while listening to popular music "to relax her." Tracy has not set any study goals for herself—instead she simply tells herself to do as well as she can on the test. She uses no specific learning strategies for condensing and memorizing important material and does not plan out her study time, so she ends up cramming for a few hours before the test. She has only vague self-evaluative standards and cannot gauge her academic preparation accurately. Tracy attributes her learning difficulties to an inherent lack of mathematical ability and is very defensive about her poor study methods. However, she does not ask for help from others because she is afraid of "looking stupid," or seek out supplementary materials from the library because she "already has too much to learn." She finds studying to be anxiety-provoking, has little self-confidence in achieving success, and sees little intrinsic value in acquiring mathematical skill. (p. 64)

Clearly, Tracy is unlikely to do well on the test. What would help? For an answer, let's consider Zimmerman's cycle of self-regulated learning. His model has three stages—*forethought, performance, reflection*—and is consistent with the Winne and Hadwin model described above. In Zimmerman's phase 1, the *forethought phase* (a combination of Winne and Hadwin's phases 1 and 2 of analyzing the task and setting goals), Tracy needs to set clear, reasonable goals and plan a few strategies for accomplishing those goals. And Tracy's beliefs about motivation make a difference at this point, too. If Tracy had a sense of self-efficacy for applying the strategies that she planned, if she believed that using those strategies would lead to math learning and success on the test, if she saw some connections between her own interests and the math learning, and if she were trying to master the material—not just look good or avoid looking bad—then she would be on the road to self-regulated learning.

Moving from forethought to Zimmerman's *performance phase* (similar to Winne and Hadwin's phase 3, which concerns enacting the strategies) brings new challenges. Now Tracy must have a repertoire of self-control (volitional) and learning strategies, including the use of imagery, mnemonics, attention focusing, and other techniques such as those described in Chapters 7 and 8 (Kiewra, 2002). She also will need to self-observe, that is, monitor how things are going so she can change strategies if needed. Actual recording of time spent, problems solved, or pages written may provide clues about when or how to make the best use of study time. Turning off the music would likely help, too.

Finally, Tracy needs to move to Zimmerman's phase 3 of *reflection* (similar to phase 4 of regulating learning in Winne and Hadwin's model) by looking back on her performance and reflecting on what happened. It will help her to develop a sense of efficacy if she attributes successes to effort and good strategy use and avoids self-defeating actions and beliefs such as making weak efforts, pretending not to care, or assuming she is "no good at math."

Both Zimmerman's and Winne and Hadwin's models emphasize the cyclical nature of self-regulated learning: Each phase flows into the next, and the cycle continues as students encounter new learning challenges. Both models begin with the concept of being informed about the task so the learner can set appropriate goals. Having access to a repertoire of learning strategies and tactics also is necessary in both models. And self-monitoring of progress followed by modifying plans if necessary are critical to both models. Notice also that the way students think about the task and their ability to do it—their sense of efficacy for self-regulation—is key as well.

Two Classrooms

Students differ in their self-regulation knowledge and skills. But teachers must work with an entire classroom of students and still "reach every student." Here are two examples of real situations in which teachers did just that. The first involves writing, the second mathematical problem solving—both complex tasks.

Writing. Carol is a grade 2 student described by Nancy and her colleague Lynn Drummond (Perry & Drummond, 2002). Lynn was Carol's teacher; she characterized Carol as "a very weak writer." Carol had difficulty finding facts, and then transforming those facts into meaningful prose for a research report. Also, she had difficulty with the mechanics of writing, which, according to Lynn, "held her back."

Over the course of the year, Lynn involved her grade 2 and 3 students in three projects about animals. Through the writing exercise, she wanted students to learn how to (a) do research, (b) write expository text, (c) edit and revise their writing, and (d) use the computer as a tool for researching and writing. For the first report, the class worked on one topic together (chipmunks). The students did the fact-finding and writing together, because Lynn needed to show them how to do research and write a report. Also, the class developed frameworks for working collaboratively as a community of learners. When the students wrote the second report (on penguins), Lynn offered students many more choices and encouraged them to depend more on themselves and on one another. Finally, for the third report, students chose an animal, conducted a self-regulated research project, and wrote a report. Because the students now understood how to conduct research and to write a report, they could work alone or together and achieve success at this complex task.

Carol, who was in grade 2, worked with a student in grade 3 who was doing research on a related topic. He showed Carol how to use a table of contents, and offered advice about how to phrase ideas in her report. Also, Carol underlined words she thought were misspelled so she could check them later when she met with Lynn to edit her report. Unlike many low-achieving students who have not learned strategies for self-regulating learning, Carol was not afraid to attempt challenging tasks, and she was confident about her ability to develop as a writer. Reflecting on her progress across the school year, Carol said, "I learned a lot from when I was in grade 1 because I had a lot of trouble then."

Mathematical Problem Solving. Lynn Fuchs and her colleagues (2003) assessed the value of incorporating self-regulated learning strategies into mathematical problem-solving lessons in real classrooms. The researchers worked with 24 teachers. All of the teachers taught the same content in their grade 3 classes. Some of these teachers (randomly chosen) taught in their usual way. Another randomly chosen group of teachers incorporated strategies to encourage problem-solving *transfer*—using skills and knowledge learned in the lessons to solve problems in other situations and classes. The third group of teachers added transfer and self-regulated learning strategies to their units on mathematical problem solving. Here are a few of the transfer and self-regulated learning strategies taught:

- Using a key, students scored their homework and gave it to a homework collector (a peer).
- Students graphed their completion of homework on a class report.
- Students used individual thermometer graphs that were kept in folders to chart their daily scores on individual problems.
- At the beginning of each session, students inspected their previous charts and set goals to beat their previous scores.
- Students discussed with partners how they might apply problem-solving strategies outside class.
- Before some lessons, students reported to the group about how they had applied problem-solving skills outside class.

Both transfer and self-regulated learning strategies helped students to learn mathematical problem solving and to apply this knowledge to new problems. The addition of self-regulated learning strategies was especially effective when students were asked to solve problems that were very different from those they encountered in the lessons. Students at every achievement level as well as students with learning disabilities benefited from learning the strategies.

Technology and Self-Regulation

SELF-REGULATION BEGINS AT HOME Parents can teach and support self-regulated learning through modelling, encouragement, facilitation, and providing rewards for goal setting, in order to help children become more self-regulating.

In the previous chapter, we saw some examples of how to use technology-rich environments to teach and to foster learning about complex concepts. But to learn in these environments, students need metacognitive and self-regulatory skills so they won't get lost in a sea of information. If the concepts that students are learning are challenging and complicated, then some scaffolding is usually needed to support the students' developing understandings (Azevedo, 2005). For example, Roger Azevedo, a professor at McGill University, and his colleagues (2004) studied undergraduate students who were learning about the circulatory system using a hypermedia-enabled encyclopedia. The materials available to them included texts, diagrams, photographs, video clips, and animated examples of how the circulatory system works. Three different learning conditions were used. One group of students was told just to learn all they could about the circulatory system. A second group received the same instructions, but, in addition, they were provided with a list of 10 subgoals to guide their learning. The third group received the list of subgoals plus a self-regulation "coach," who helped them plan their learning, monitor their developing understanding, try different strategies, and handle problems when they arose. Students in all three conditions were asked to "think out loud" as they used the hypermedia materials—that is, to describe what they were thinking as they read through the materials. Students who received the support of a self-regulation coach and focused on analyzing the task, setting goals, using strategies, and monitoring progress developed more complete and complex mental models of the circulatory system.

How could you provide this kind of support for self-regulated learning and coaching for your students? Enlisting peer coaches would be one way of incorporating this method into your teaching style, or asking for the help of families.

Reaching Every Student: Families and Self-Regulation

Children begin to learn the skills needed for self-regulated learning in their homes. Families can teach and support self-regulated learning through modelling, encouragement, facilitation, providing rewards for goal setting, good strategy use, and other processes described in the next section (Martinez-Pons, 2002). The *Family and Community Partnerships Guidelines* box on page 364 gives some additional ideas for how to help students become more self-regulating.

Another Approach to Self-Regulation: Cognitive Behaviour Modification

When some psychologists were studying a behaviour modification approach called *self-management*—using reinforcement and punishment to manage your own behaviour—Donald Meichenbaum, now retired from the University of Waterloo, was achieving success teaching impulsive students to "talk themselves through" tasks (Meichenbaum, 1977). He called his method *cognitive behaviour modification* (Manning & Payne, 1996). **Cognitive behaviour modification** focuses on self-talk to regulate behaviour.

You may remember from Chapter 2 that there is a stage in cognitive development when young children seem to guide themselves through a task using private speech. They talk to themselves, often repeating the words of a parent or teacher. In cognitive behaviour modification, students are taught directly how to use this **self-instruction**. Meichenbaum (1977) outlined the following steps:

1. An adult model performs a task while talking to him- or herself out loud (cognitive modelling).
2. The child performs the same task under the direction of the model's instructions (overt, external guidance).

Cognitive behaviour modification Procedures based on both behavioural and cognitive learning principles for changing your own behaviour by using self-talk and self-instruction.

Self-instruction Talking oneself through the steps of a task.

FAMILY AND COMMUNITY PARTNERSHIPS

GUIDELINES: Supporting Self-Regulation at Home and in School

Emphasize the value of encouragement.

EXAMPLES

1. Teach students to encourage each other.
2. Tell families about the areas that are most challenging for their child—those that will be the most in need of encouragement at home.

Model self-regulation.

EXAMPLES

1. Target small steps for improving an academic skill. Tailor goals to the student's current achievement level.
2. Discuss with your students how you set goals and monitor progress.
3. Ask parents and caregivers to show their children how they set goals for the day or week, write to-do lists, or keep appointment books.

Make families a source of good strategy ideas.

EXAMPLES

1. Provide short, simple materials describing a "strategy of the month" that students can practise at home.
2. Create a lending library of books students can take home about goal setting, motivation, learning, and time-management strategies.
3. Encourage families to help their children complete homework by focusing on problem-solving processes rather than by consulting the answers at the back of the textbook.

Provide self-evaluation guidelines.

EXAMPLES

1. Develop rubrics for self-evaluation with students (see Chapter 14). Model how to use them.
2. Provide record-keeping sheets for assignments early in the year, then gradually ask students to develop their own sheets.
3. Encourage parents and caregivers to model self-evaluation as they focus on areas in which they want their children to improve.
4. For family conferences, provide examples of materials other families have successfully used to keep track of their children's progress.

For more ideas to share with parents and caregivers, see **www.pbs.org/wholechild/parents/building.html**.

3. The child performs the task while instructing him- or herself aloud (overt, self-guidance).
4. The child whispers the instructions to him- or herself as he/she goes through the task (faded, overt self-guidance).
5. The child performs the task while guiding his/her performance via private speech (covert self-instruction). (p. 32)

Brenda Manning and Beverly Payne (1996) list four skills that can increase students' ability to learn: *listening*, *planning*, *working*, and *checking*. How might cognitive self-instruction help students develop these skills? One possibility is to use personal booklets or class posters that prompt students to "talk to themselves" about these skills. For example, the teacher and students in one grade 5 class collaboratively designed a set of prompts for each of the four skills and posted the prompts around the classroom. The prompts for listening included "Does this make sense?" "Am I getting this?" "I need to ask a question now before I forget." "Pay attention!" "Can I do what he's saying to do?" Planning prompts included "Do I have everything together?" "Do I have my friends tuned out for right now?" "Let me get organized first." "What order will I do this in?" "I know this stuff!" Posters for these and the other two skills, working and checking, are shown in Figure 10.3. Part of the power of this process is involving students in thinking about and creating their own guides and prompts. Having the discussion and posting the ideas makes students more self-aware and in control of their own learning.

Actually, cognitive behaviour modification as it is practised by Meichenbaum and others has many more components than just teaching students to use self-instruction. Meichenbaum's methods also include dialogue and interaction between teacher and student, modelling, guided discovery, motivational strategies, feedback, careful matching of the task with the student's developmental level, and other principles of effective teaching. The student is even involved in designing the learning program (Harris, 1990; Harris & Pressley, 1991). Given all this, it is no surprise that students seem to be able to generalize the skills developed through cognitive behaviour modification to new learning situations (Harris, Graham, & Pressley, 1992).

FIGURE 10.3 Posters to Remind Students to "Talk Themselves Through" Listening, Planning, Working, and Checking in School

These four posters were designed by the teacher and students in a grade 5 class to help them remember to use self-instruction. Some of the reminders reflect the unique world of these preadolescents.

Poster 1

While Listening:

1. Does this make sense?
2. Am I getting this?
3. I need to ask a question now before I forget.
4. Pay attention.
5. Can I do what he's saying to do?

Poster 2

While Planning:

1. Do I have everything together?
2. Do I have my friends tuned out for right now?
3. Let me get organized first.
4. What order will I do this in?
5. I know this stuff!

Poster 3

While Working:

1. Am I working fast enough?
2. Stop staring at my girlfriend and get back to work.
3. How much time is left?
4. Do I need to stop and start over?
5. This is hard for me, but I can manage.

Poster 4

While Checking:

1. Did I finish everything?
2. What do I need to recheck?
3. Am I proud of this work?
4. Did I write all the words? Count them.
5. I think I finished. I organized myself. Did I daydream too much?

Source: From *Self-Talk for Teachers and Students: Metacognitive Strategies for Personal and Classroom Use* by Brenda H. Manning, Beverly D. Payne. Published by Allyn and Bacon, Boston, MA. Copyright © 1996 by Pearson Education. Adapted by permission of the publisher.

Today, there are entire school intervention programs based on cognitive behaviour modification. For example, the *Coping Power Program* includes training for both parents and their children, beginning in the last half of one academic year and continuing through the entire following school year. The training for students often focuses on how to manage anger and aggression. Different training sessions emphasize setting personal goals, fostering awareness of feelings (especially anger), learning to relax and to change the focus away from the angry feelings, creating coping self-statements, developing organizational and study skills, seeing the perspectives of others, developing social problem-solving skills, and managing peer pressure by practising how to say no (Lochman & Wells, 2003). Another similar approach is the *Tools for Getting Along* program (Daunic, Smith, Brank, & Penfield, 2006). Both programs have been effective in helping aggressive middle school students to learn to "get along" with their classmates and teachers. In addition, in psychotherapy sessions, tools based on cognitive behaviour modification have proved to be some of the most effective ways for people to deal with psychological problems such as depression. Figure 10.4 on page 366 includes two slides from a *Tools for Getting Along* lesson designed to help middle school students reflect on their actions and use self-talk to be more self-regulating.

Both the *Coping Power Program* and the *Tools for Getting Along* program include the use of emotional self-regulation skills. We turn to this area of self-regulation next.

Emotional Self-Regulation

Social and emotional competences and self-regulation are critical for both academic and personal development. Table 10.3 describes four skills associated with emotional self-regulation.

FIGURE 10.4

Tools for Getting Along

Tools for Getting Along are materials for late elementary and middle school teachers to use in helping students to become more self-regulating, to deal with conflict and emotion, and to solve social problems in productive ways. The two slides below are from a lesson on evaluating choices of action.

How Did I Do?

Did I make the right choice?

If YES, . . . nice job!

If NO, . . . why?

- Did I choose the wrong solution?
- Did I choose the right solution but didn't carry it out well?

When Things Don't Go Right

USE SELF-TALK

Tell yourself. . .

- I messed up, but I know why.
- I won't make that mistake again.
- I'll think more carefully about my choices.
- Nobody's perfect. I'll do better next time.

Remember, every problem is another opportunity for success!

Source: "Tools for Getting Along," by Daunic, A. P., Smith, S. W., Brank, E. M., & Penfield, R. D. (2006). Classroom based cognitive–behavioral intervention to prevent aggression: Efficacy and social validity. *Journal of School Psychology, 44*, 123–29 with permission from Elsevier.

TABLE 10.3

Essential Social and Emotional Self-Regulation Skills

Here are examples of four important social/emotional skills and the competencies needed for each. The list was developed by the Collaborative for Academic, Social, and Emotional Learning [CASEL] at **www.casel.org/home.php**.

Know Yourself and Others

- *Identify feelings*—Recognize and label feelings in yourself and in others.
- *Be responsible*—Understand and act upon obligations to engage in ethical, safe, and legal behaviours.
- *Recognize strengths*—Identify and cultivate positive qualities.

Make Responsible Decisions

- *Manage emotions*—Regulate feelings so that they aid rather than impede the handling of situations.
- *Understand situations*—Accurately understand the circumstances you are in.
- *Set goals and plans*—Establish and work toward the achievement of specific short- and long-term outcomes.
- *Solve problems creatively*—Engage in a creative, disciplined process of exploring alternative possibilities that lead to responsible, goal-directed action, including overcoming obstacles to plans.

Care for Others

- *Show empathy*—Identify and understand the thoughts and feelings of others.
- *Respect others*—Act on the belief that, as part of our shared humanity, others deserve to be treated with kindness and compassion.
- *Appreciate diversity*—Understand that individual and group differences complement one another and add strength and adaptability to the world around us.

Know How to Act

- *Communicate effectively*—Use verbal and non-verbal skills to express yourself and to promote effective exchanges with others.
- *Build relationships*—Establish and maintain healthy and rewarding connections with individuals and with groups.
- *Negotiate fairly*—Strive to achieve mutually satisfactory resolutions to conflict by addressing the needs of all concerned.
- *Refuse provocations*—Convey and follow through effectively with decisions not to engage in unwanted, unsafe, and unethical behaviour.
- *Seek help*—Identify your need for help and access appropriate assistance and support in pursuit of your needs and goals.
- *Act ethically*—Guide decisions and actions by a set of principles or standards derived from recognized legal/professional codes of conduct or moral or faith-based systems of conduct.

Source: From "Handbook of Classroom Management: Research, Practice, and Contemporary Issues" (paper) by M. J. Elias and Y. Schwab in text by C. Evertson & C. Weinstein. Copyright 2006 by Taylor & Francis Group LLC—Books. Reproduced with permission of Taylor & Francis Group LLC—Books in the formats Textbook and Other book via Copyright Clearance Center.

GUIDELINES: Encouraging Emotional Self-Regulation

Create a climate of trust in your classroom.

EXAMPLES

1. Avoid listening to students who tell "tattle tale" stories about other students.
2. Follow through with delivering fair consequences.
3. Avoid unnecessary comparisons and give students opportunities to improve their work.

Help students to recognize and to express their feelings.

EXAMPLES

1. Provide students with a vocabulary of emotions and point out for students descriptions of emotions that appear in characters or stories.
2. Be clear and descriptive about your own emotions.
3. Encourage students to write in journals about their own feelings. Protect the privacy of these writings (see trust above).

Help students to recognize emotions in others.

EXAMPLES

1. For young children, use questions like these: "Look at Chandra's face. How do you think she feels when you say those things?"
2. For older students, use readings analyses of characters in literature and films, and role-play exercises where they reverse roles to help students identify the emotions of others.

Provide strategies for coping with emotions.

EXAMPLES

1. Discuss or practise alternatives such as stopping to consider how the other person feels, seeking help, and using anger management strategies such as self-talk or leaving the scene.
2. Model coping strategies for students. Talk about how you handle anger, disappointment, or anxiety.

Help students to recognize cultural differences in emotional expression.

EXAMPLES

1. Ask students to write about or discuss how they show emotions in their family.
2. Teach students to "check it out"—that is, to ask the other people how they are feeling.

For ideas about promoting emotional competence, see **http://csefel.vanderbilt.edu/resources/strategies.html#teachingskills.**

A number of studies that followed students over several years in the United States and in Italy have found that prosocial behaviours and social competence in the early grades are related to academic achievement and to popularity with peers as many as five years later (Elias & Schwab, 2006). How can teachers help students develop these skills? The *Guidelines* box gives some ideas about how to do so in the classroom.

TEACHING TO PROMOTE SELF-EFFICACY AND SELF-REGULATED LEARNING

STOP & THINK How are you studying right now? What goals have you set for your reading today? What is your plan for learning, and what strategies are you using right now to learn? How did you learn those strategies?

Most teachers agree that students need to develop skills and attitudes for independent, lifelong learning (i.e., for self-regulated learning and for a sense of efficacy for learning). Fortunately, there is a growing body of research that offers guidance about how to design tasks and structure classroom interactions to support students' development of and engagement in self-regulated learning (Neuman & Roskos, 1997; Perry, 1998; Wharton-McDonald et al., 1997; Woolfolk, Perry, & Winne, 2006; Zimmerman, 2002). This research indicates that students develop academically effective forms of self-regulated learning (SRL) and a sense of efficacy for learning when teachers involve them in complex, meaningful tasks that extend over long periods of time, much like the constructivist activities described in Chapter 9. Also, to develop SRL and self-efficacy for learning, students need to have some control over their learning processes and products—that is, they need

MyEducationLab
Go to the Podcasts section of MyEducationLab and listen to PODCAST—Procrastination. Recent surveys of American adults indicate that the habit of procrastination is getting worse. Are you a procrastinator? In this podcast Anita Woolfolk discusses how you can improve your work habits and those of your students.

to make choices. And because self-monitoring and self-evaluation are key to effective SRL and a sense of efficacy, teachers can help students develop SRL by involving them in setting criteria for evaluating their learning processes and products, and then giving them opportunities to make judgments about their progress using those standards. Finally, it helps to work collaboratively with peers and to seek feedback from them. Let's examine each of these skills more closely.

Complex Tasks

Teachers don't want to assign students to tasks that are too difficult and that lead to frustration. This is especially true when the students you are teaching have learning difficulties or disabilities. In fact, research indicates that the most motivating and academically beneficial tasks for students are those that challenge, but don't overwhelm them (Rohrkemper & Corno, 1988; Turner, 1997); complex tasks need not be overly difficult for students.

The term *complex* refers to the design of tasks, not their level of difficulty. From a design point of view, tasks are complex when they address multiple goals and involve large chunks of meaning, such as projects and thematic units. Furthermore, complex tasks extend over long periods of time, engage students in a variety of cognitive and metacognitive processes, and allow for the production of a wide range of products (Perry, VandeKamp, Mercer, & Nordby, 2002; Wharton-McDonald et al., 1997). For example, a study of the Egyptian pyramids might result in the production of a variety of items, including written reports, maps, diagrams, and models.

Even more important, complex tasks provide students with information about their learning progress. These tasks require them to engage in deep, elaborative thinking and problem solving. In the process, students develop and refine their cognitive and metacognitive strategies. Furthermore, succeeding at complex tasks increases students' self-efficacy and intrinsic motivation (McCaslin & Good, 1996; Turner, 1997). Rohrkemper and Corno (1988) advised teachers to design complex tasks that provide opportunities for students to modify the learning conditions in order to cope with challenging problems. Learning to cope with stressful situations and make adaptations is an important educational goal. As you will recall from Chapter 4, according to Sternberg, one aspect of intelligence involves choosing, or adapting to, environments so that you can succeed.

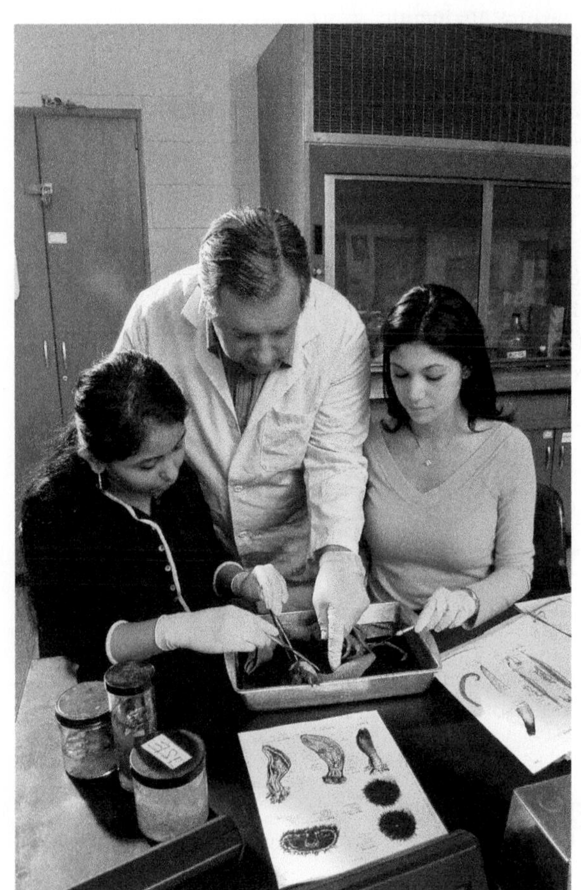

DEVELOPING STUDENT CONTROL In order to develop self-regulated learning and self-efficacy for learning, students need to have some control over their learning processes and products; teachers can help by involving students in evaluating their learning processes, products, and progress.

Control

Teachers can share control with students by giving them choices. When students have choices (e.g., about what to produce, how to produce it, where to work, whom to work with), they are more likely to anticipate a successful outcome (increased self-efficacy) and consequently to increase effort and persist when difficulty arises (Turner & Paris, 1995). Also, by involving students in making decisions, teachers invite them to take responsibility for learning by planning, setting goals, monitoring progress, and evaluating outcomes (Turner, 1997). These are qualities of highly effective, self-regulating learners.

Giving students choices creates opportunities for them to adjust the level of challenge that a particular task presents (they can choose easy or more challenging reading materials, determine the nature and amount of writing in a report, or supplement writing with other expressions of learning). But what if students make poor academic choices? Nancy and her colleagues have discovered that highly effective, high-SRL teachers carefully consider the choices they give to students. They make sure students have the knowledge and skills they need to operate independently and to make sound decisions (Perry & Drummond, 2002). For example, when students are learning new skills or routines, teachers can offer choices with constraints (e.g., students must write a minimum of four sentences/paragraphs/pages, but they can choose to write more; they must demonstrate their understanding of an animal's habitat, food, and babies, but they can share that knowledge in writing, through drawings, or orally).

Highly effective teachers also teach and model good decision making. For example, when students are asked to choose partners, teachers can ask the students to consider what they need from their partners (shared interest and commitment, knowledge or skills that they need to develop, etc.). When students are invited to make choices about how best to use their time, effective teachers can ask, "What can you do when you're finished? What can you do if you are waiting for my help?" Often, students generate lists they can refer to while they work. Finally, highly effective teachers give students feedback about the choices they make and then customize future choices they offer to suit the unique characteristics of particular learners. For example, the teachers might encourage some students to select research topics for which resources are readily available and which are written at a level that is accessible to the learner. Alternatively, the teachers might encourage some students to work collaboratively versus independently to ensure that learners have the support they need to be successful.

Self-Evaluation

Evaluation practices that support SRL are non-threatening. They are embedded in ongoing activities, emphasize process as well as products, focus on personal progress, and help students to interpret errors as opportunities for learning to occur. In these contexts, students enjoy and actually seek challenging tasks because the cost of participation is low (Paris & Ayres, 1994). Involving students in generating evaluation criteria and in evaluating their own work also reduces the anxiety that often accompanies assessment by giving students a sense of control over the outcome. Students can judge their work in relation to a set of qualities both they and their teachers have identified as "good" work. They can also consider the effectiveness of their approaches to learning and then alter their behaviours in ways that enhance it (Winne & Perry, 2000).

In the high-SRL classrooms that Nancy has studied, both formal and informal opportunities are available for students to evaluate their learning. For example, one student teacher asked grade 4 and 5 students to submit reflections journals describing the games they designed with a partner or small group of collaborators in a probability and statistics unit (Perry, Phillips, & Dowler, 2004). Their journals explained their contribution to the group's process and product, and described what they learned from participating. The student teacher took these reflections into account when she evaluated the games. More informally, teachers ask students "What have you learned about yourself as a writer today?" "What do good researchers and writers do?" "What can we do that we couldn't do before?" Questions like these, posed to individuals or embedded in class discussions, prompt students' metacognition, motivation, and strategic action—the components of SRL.

Collaboration

The Committee on Increasing High School Students' Engagement and Motivation to Learn (2004) concluded that when students can put their heads together, they are more receptive to challenging assignments—that is, to the very kind of complex task that develops self-regulation. The Committee added:

> Collaborative work also can help students develop skills in cooperation. Furthermore, it helps create a community of learners who have responsibility for each other's learning, rather than a competitive environment, which is alienating to many students, particularly those who do not perform as well as their classmates. (p. 51)

The most effective uses of cooperative/collaborative relationships to support SRL in classrooms Nancy has studied are those that reflect a climate of community and shared problem solving (Perry & Drummond, 2002; Perry, VandeKamp, Mercer, & Nordby, 2002). In these contexts, teachers and students actually co-regulate one another's learning (McCaslin & Good, 1996), offering support, whether working alone, in pairs, or in small groups. This support is instrumental to individuals' development and use of metacognition, intrinsic motivation, and strategic action (e.g., sharing ideas, comparing strategies for solving problems, identifying *everyone's* area of expertise). High-SRL teachers spend time at the start of each school year teaching routines and establishing norms of participation; for example, teaching how to give constructive feedback and how to interpret and respond to peers' suggestions. As you will see in Chapter 12, developing useful management and learning procedures and routines takes time at the beginning of the year, but it is time well spent. Once routines and patterns of interaction are established, students can focus on learning and teachers can attend to teaching academic skills and the curriculum.

DIVERSITY AND CONVERGENCES IN THEORIES OF LEARNING

Diversity

The power and value of diversity is part of the theoretical framework of social cognitive theories of learning and motivation. Social cognitive theory describes the unique reciprocal interactions among personal, environmental, and behavioural factors that shape the individual's learning and motivation. Culture, social context, personal history, ethnicity, language, and racial identity—to name only a few factors—all shape personal characteristics such as knowledge and self-efficacy beliefs, environmental features such as resources and challenges, and behavioural actions and choices. For example, there are cultural differences in self-efficacy. Males and African American students in the United States are more likely to be overconfident in their academic abilities, so their predictions of future achievement are less accurate than the predictions of Asian American students and female students, who are much less likely to express overconfidence in their abilities. Gifted male students are less likely to be overconfident, and gifted female students are likely to actually underestimate their abilities, whereas students with disabilities tend to be overconfident in their sense of efficacy (Pajares, 2000).

Convergences

MyEducationLab Go to the Teacher Talk section of Chapter 10 of MyEducationLab and watch a video of Cameron McKinley, 2007 Teacher of the Year from Alabama, explaining her motivation to teach and to inspire her students.

Even though there are cultural and gender differences in self-efficacy, these efficacy judgments are related to academic outcomes across cultures (Bandura, 2002). For example, self-efficacy is related to math and science goals, and interest in the subject, for Mexican American youth (Navarro, Flores, & Worthington, 2007), to the academic achievement in math for both male and female middle school students (Kenney-Benson et al., 2006), and to mathematics achievement for both Anglo-Canadian and South Asian Canadian middle school students (Klassen, 2004).

How can we make sense of the diversity of perspectives we have explored in the last four chapters? We have considered behavioural, cognitive, constructivist (individual and social), and social cognitive explanations of what people learn and how they learn it. Table 10.4 presents a summary of several of these perspectives about learning.

Rather than debating the merits of each approach, consider instead their contributions to our understanding of how learning takes place and to how teaching can be improved. Don't feel that you must choose the "best" approach—no such thing exists. Just as chemists, biologists, and nutritionists rely on different theories, and combinations of theories, to explain and improve health, so too can different views of learning be used together to create productive learning environments for the diverse students you will teach. Behavioural theory helps us understand the role of cues in setting the stage for behaviours and the role of consequences and practice in encouraging or discouraging particular behaviours. But much of humans' lives and learning involves more than behaviours. Language and higher-order thinking require complex information processing and memory—something the cognitive models help us to understand. And what about the person as a creator and constructor of knowledge, not just a processor of information? Here, constructivist perspectives have much to offer. Finally, social cognitive theory highlights the important role of agency and self-direction. Life requires self-regulated learners.

We like to think of the four main learning theories in Table 10.4 as four pillars for teaching. Students must first understand and make sense of the material (constructivist theory); then, they must remember what they have understood (cognitive—information processing theory); and then, they must practise and apply (behavioural) their new skills and understanding to make them more fluid and automatic—a permanent part of their repertoire. Finally, students must take charge of their own learning (social cognitive theory). Failure to attend to any part of the process results in lower-quality learning.

TABLE 10.4 **Four Views of Learning**

There are variations within each of these views of learning and overlaps as well, especially in relation to constructivist views.

	Behavioural	Cognitive	Constructivist		Social Cognitive
	Applied Behaviour Analysis *B.F. Skinner*	***Information Processing*** *J. Anderson*	***Individual*** *Jean Piaget*	***Social/Situated*** *Lev Vygotsky*	***Social Cognitive Theory*** *Albert Bandura*
Knowledge	• a fixed body of knowledge exists for learners to acquire • knowledge is stimulated from the environment	• a fixed body of knowledge exists for learners to acquire • knowledge is stimulated from the environment • prior knowledge influences how information is processed	• a changing body of knowledge is individually constructed in a social world • knowledge is built on prior knowledge	• knowledge is socially constructed • knowledge is built on what participants contribute and construct together	• a changing body of knowledge is constructed through interactions with others and with the environment
Learning	• learning is the acquisition of facts, skills, and concepts • learning occurs through drill and guided practice	• learning is the acquisition of facts, skills, concepts, and strategies • learning occurs through effective application of strategies	• learning is the active construction of and restructuring of prior knowledge • learning occurs through multiple opportunities and diverse processes that extend what is already known	• learning is a collaborative construction of socially defined knowledge and values • learning arises in socially constructed interaction	• learning is the active construction of knowledge • learning arises from observing and interacting with the physical and social world • agency transforms through increasingly effective self-regulation
Teaching	• teaching is telling students what they should learn and providing appropriate consequences for responses	• teaching is telling students what they should learn and guiding them toward more "accurate" and complete knowledge	• teaching is challenging and guiding thinking toward more complete understanding	• teaching is co-constructing knowledge with students	• teaching is modelling and facilitating changes in knowledge • supporting self-efficacy and self-regulation are key
Role of teacher	• the teacher is the manager and supervisor • the teacher corrects wrong answers	• the teacher presents information and models effective strategies • the teacher extends knowledge and corrects misconceptions	• the teacher listens to students' current conceptions, ideas, and thinking • the teacher facilitates and guides students' growth	• the teacher is a co-participant with students in the teaching process • the teacher facilitates and guides students' growth, co-constructs multiple interpretations of knowledge, and listens to socially constructed conceptions	• the teacher models new skills, facilitates students' exploration, and motivates • the teacher supports students' choices and self-regulated learning
Role of peers	• peers are sources of reinforcement and punishment	• peers are not necessary but can influence an individual's information processing	• peers are not necessary but can stimulate thinking and raise questions	• peers are ordinary in and necessary to the process of co-constructing knowledge	• peers are ordinary in and necessary to the process of building knowledge
Role of student	• the student actively searches for reinforcement and avoids punishment	• the student actively processes information and applies strategies for learning • the student organizes and reorganizes information in memory	• the student actively constructs knowledge, seeks explanations, and interprets events in the world	• the student participates in co-constructing knowledge through social interaction with others • the student is an active thinker, explainer, interpreter, and questioner	• the student participates in co-constructing knowledge through social interaction with others • the student is an active thinker, explainer, interpreter, and questioner

SUMMARY TABLE

Social Cognitive Theory (pp. 348–352)

Distinguish between social learning and social cognitive theories. Social learning theory expanded behavioural views of reinforcement and punishment. From the behavioural perspective, reinforcement and punishment directly affect behaviour. From the perspective of social learning theory, seeing another person, a model, reinforced or punished can have similar effects on the observer's behaviour. Social cognitive theory expands social learning theory to include cognitive factors such as beliefs, expectations, and perceptions of self. Current social cognitive theory is a dynamic system that explains human adaptation, learning, and motivation. The theory addresses how people develop social, emotional, cognitive, and behavioural capabilities; how people regulate their own lives; and what motivates them.

What is triarchic reciprocal causality? Triarchic reciprocal causality is the dynamic interplay among three kinds of influences: personal, environmental, and behavioural. Personal factors (beliefs, expectations, attitudes, and knowledge), the physical and social environment (resources, consequences of actions, other people, models and teachers, and physical settings), and behaviours (individual actions, choices, and verbal statements) all influence and are influenced by each other.

What is self-efficacy, and how is it different from other self-schemas? Self-efficacy is distinct from other self-schemas in that it involves judgments of capabilities *specific to a particular task*. Self-concept is a more global construct that contains many perceptions about the self, including self-efficacy. Compared to self-esteem, self-efficacy is concerned with judgments of personal capabilities; self-esteem is concerned with judgments of self-worth.

What are the sources of self-efficacy? The four sources of self-efficacy are mastery experiences (direct experiences), level of arousal as you face the task, vicarious experiences (accomplishments modelled by someone else), and social persuasion (a "pep talk" or specific performance feedback).

What is modelling? Learning by observing others is a key element of social cognitive theory. Modelling is influenced by the developmental characteristics of the observer, the status and prestige of the model, the consequences of the model's actions as seen by the observer, the observer's expectations about performing the observed behaviours (will I be rewarded?), the links that the observer perceives between his or her goals and the model's behaviours (will doing what the model does get me what I want?), and the observer's self-efficacy (can I do it?).

Social learning theory Theory that emphasizes learning through observation of others.

Social cognitive theory Theory that adds concern with cognitive factors such as beliefs, self-perceptions, and expectations to social learning theory.

Triarchic reciprocal causality An explanation of behaviour that emphasizes the mutual effects of the individual and the environment on each other.

Self-efficacy A person's sense of being able to deal effectively with a particular task.

Human agency The capacity to coordinate learning skills, motivation, and emotions to reach your goals.

Mastery experiences Our own direct experiences—the most powerful source of efficacy information.

Arousal Physical and psychological reactions causing a person to feel alert, excited, or tense.

Vicarious experiences Accomplishments that are modelled by someone else.

Modelling Changes in behaviour, thinking, or emotions that occur by observing another person—a model.

Social persuasion A "pep talk" or specific performance feedback—one source of self-efficacy.

Applying Social Cognitive Theory (pp. 352–357)

What kinds of outcomes can observational learning encourage? Observational learning can lead to five possible outcomes, including directing attention, encouraging existing behaviours, changing inhibitions, teaching new behaviours and attitudes, and arousing emotions. By directing attention, we gain insight into how others do things and what objects are involved in their actions. Encouraging or fine-tuning existing behaviours can lead to the development of good habits or make work more efficient. Observing others also has the capacity to cue us in to others' attention, which can cause us to become more or less "self-conscious" about our behaviour; when others are doing something, it's easier for us to do the same. Young children in particular learn by watching and emulating others, but everyone can gain insight into how something is done well (or poorly) by observing someone else do it. Finally, observing can lead to the association of emotions with certain activities. If others are observed enjoying an activity, the observer may learn to enjoy the activity as well.

How does self-efficacy affect motivation? Greater efficacy leads to greater effort, persistence in the face of setbacks, higher goals, and finding new strategies when old ones fail. If sense of efficacy is low, however, people may avoid a task altogether or give up easily when problems arise.

What is teacher's sense of efficacy? One of the few personal characteristics of teachers related to student achievement is a teacher's efficacy belief that he or she can reach even difficult students to help them learn. Teachers with a high sense of efficacy work harder, persist longer, and are less likely to experience burnout. Teachers' sense of efficacy is higher in schools where the other teachers and administrators have high expectations of students and where teachers receive help from their principals to solve instructional and management problems. Efficacy grows from real success with students, so any experience or training that helps you succeed in the day-to-day tasks of teaching will give you a foundation for developing a sense of efficacy in your career.

Ripple effect "Contagious" spreading of behaviours through imitation.

Teachers' sense of efficacy A teacher's belief that he or she can reach even the most difficult students and help them learn.

Self-Regulated Learning (pp. 358–367)

What factors are involved in self-regulated learning? One important goal of teaching is to prepare students for lifelong learning. To reach this goal, students must be self-regulated learners; that is, they must have a combination of the knowledge, motivation to learn, and volition that provides the skill and will to learn independently and effectively. Knowledge includes an understanding of self, subject, task, learning strategy, and contexts for application. Motivation to learn provides the commitment, and volition is the follow-through that combats distraction and protects persistence.

What is the self-regulated learning cycle? There are several models of self-regulated learning. Winne and Hadwin describe a four-phase model: analyzing the task, setting goals and designing plans, enacting tactics to accomplish the task, and regulating learning. Zimmerman notes three similar phases: forethought (which includes setting goals, making plans, self-efficacy, and motivation); performance (which involves self-control and self-monitoring); and reflection (which includes self-evaluation and adaptations, leading to the forethought/planning phase again).

What are some examples of self-regulating behaviours that instructors can teach? Self-regulating learners engage in four types of activities: analyzing the task, setting goals and designing plans, engaging in learning, and adjusting their approach to learning. Teaching students to be more self-regulating might take the form of providing opportunities to identify and analyze the task at hand. Students should ask themselves: What is the task? What is an ideal outcome of the task? Students may also benefit from goal-setting practice; they may ask: What are my short-term goals? What are my long-term goals? Learning strategies such as identifying important details and developing a big picture of material is the next step in the process. Finally, students need to reflect on whether they were successful and to devise strategies for overcoming shortcomings in their self-regulation process. They may ask themselves: Where was I successful? Where do I need to improve in order to meet my goals in the future?

What is cognitive behaviour modification? Cognitive behaviour modification is a process in which self-talk is used to regulate behaviour. Cognitive behaviour modification may take many forms in the classroom, including helping to keep students engaged in learning or helping them deal effectively with anger and aggression. Some research has identified four skills that are particularly helpful self-talk strategies: listening, planning, working, and checking. Cognitive behaviour modification can be used with students of all ages, but helping students engage in self-talk may require more adult assistance and guidance for younger children, or for those who have not had opportunities to practise good self-regulation strategies.

What are the skills involved in emotional self-regulation? Emotionally self-regulating individuals are aware of their own emotions and the feelings of others—realizing that inner emotions can differ from outward expressions. They can talk about and express emotions in ways that are appropriate for their cultural group. They can feel empathy for others in distress and also cope with their own distressing emotions—they can handle stress. These individuals know that relationships are defined in part by how emotions are communicated within the relationship. All these skills come together to produce a capacity for emotional self-regulation.

Self-regulation Process of activating and sustaining thoughts, behaviours, and emotions in order to reach goals.

Volition Willpower; self-discipline; work styles that plan for and protect opportunities to reach goals by applying self-regulated learning.

Self-regulated learning A view of learning as skills and will applied to analyzing a learning task, setting goals and planning how to do the task, applying skills, and especially making adjustments about how learning is carried out.

Cognitive behaviour modification Procedures based on both behavioural and cognitive learning principles for changing your own behaviour by using self-talk and self-instruction.

Self-instruction Talking oneself through the steps of a task.

Teaching to Promote Self-Efficacy and Self-Regulated Learning (pp. 367–370)

How can teachers support the development of self-efficacy and self-regulated learning? Teachers should involve students in complex, meaningful tasks that extend over long periods of time and provide students with control over their learning processes and products—students need to make choices. Involve students in setting criteria for evaluating their learning processes and products, then give them opportunities to make judgments about their progress using those standards. Finally, encourage students to work collaboratively with and seek feedback from peers.

TEACHERS' CASEBOOK

You know that your students need to be organized and self-regulating to do well in both their current and future classes. But many of the students just don't seem to know how to take charge of their own learning. They have trouble completing larger projects—many wait until the last minute. They can't organize their work or decide what is most important. Some can't even keep up with assignments. The students' book bags are disaster areas, containing long overdue assignments and class handouts from last semester crumpled in with school newsletters and permission slips for field trips. You are concerned because the students will need to be much more organized and on top of their work as they progress through their education. You have so much material to cover to meet the provincial curriculum, but many of your students are just drowning in the amount of work they already have, and you don't know how you'll be able to prepare them properly for the province-wide exams.

What Would *They* Do?

Here is how some practising teachers responded to the teaching situation described above.

James Hathaway

Stephen Lewis Secondary School, Thornhill, ON

In order to help students learn to become more organized in general, I build organizational skills into daily lessons. For example, I post a classroom agenda, drawn up on chart paper, on one wall so that the students can refer to it on a daily basis. It includes the date, a page number for their binder, and the topic of the day. Students can update their own binders at the same time as the wall agenda is updated, and this takes only a few moments from every day. Besides keeping the class on the same "page," encouraging students to use their own binders also becomes habit forming, something that they can use in other courses.

When it comes to helping students stay on top of large projects, I break the project into smaller and more manageable parts that they complete throughout the course or over several weeks. This way the students won't be overwhelmed by the amount of work to be done; it also provides me with checkpoints to monitor student progress. In addition, if students fall behind on a smaller task, it isn't too hard for them to catch up, and they are less likely to just give up and not complete the work.

Sarah MacNeil **High School Social Studies,**

Park View Education Centre, Bridgewater, NS

At the high school level, students spend a lot of time travelling from classroom to classroom, which means the possibility of them losing important papers and materials is quite high. The need to stay organized is paramount. I ask students to bring a three-ring binder when they attend my class and to use dividers to indicate when we move from unit to unit. In the first few days of class, I spend a lot of time introducing students to my classroom. There are various plastic bins (labelled by class) around the room which are used for handouts and for handing in homework. Teacher course materials are also readily visible in my classroom so students can observe how materials can be organized. They see me use the materials on a daily basis and can recognize how easy it is for me to locate certain items because they are organized. Binders are labelled by subject and topic area. Other resource materials (i.e., books) are organized by topic. I also make an effort to discuss timelines for assignment completion with my students. Together we assess what a fair timeline is and, in some cases (depending on the size of the assignment), we set up various due dates for different stages of the assignment. I also discuss my own timelines for having assignments marked and returned to students. I find this is an effective way to let students know that timelines are important for both students and teachers. Being consistent with routines for organization helps students to become more self-reliant.

11 Motivation in Learning and Teaching

Nights in Tunisia © *Gil Meyers/SuperStock*

TEACHERS' CASEBOOK

WHAT WOULD YOU DO?

It is July and you have finally been offered a teaching position. The district wasn't your first choice, but job openings were really scarce, so you're pleased to have a job in your field. You are discovering that the teaching resources in your school are slim to none; the only resources are some aging texts and the workbooks that go with them. Every idea you have suggested for software, simulation games, visual aids, or other more active teaching materials has been met with the same response, "There's no money in the budget for that." As you look over the texts and workbooks, you wonder how the students could be anything but bored by them. To make matters worse, the texts look pretty high-level for your students. But the objectives in the workbooks are important. Besides, the provincial curriculum requires these units. Students will be tested on them in the province-wide assessments next spring required by the Ministry.

CRITICAL THINKING

- How would you arouse student curiosity and interest about the topics and tasks in the workbooks?
- How would you establish the value of learning this material?
- How would you handle the difficulty level of the texts?
- What do you need to know about motivation to solve these problems?
- What do you need to know about your students in order to motivate them?

Most educators agree that motivating students is one of the critical tasks of teaching. In order to learn, students must be cognitively, emotionally, and behaviourally engaged in productive class activities. We begin with the question "What is motivation?" and examine many of the answers that have been proposed, including a discussion of intrinsic and extrinsic motivation and five general theories of motivation: behavioural, humanistic, cognitive, social cognitive, and sociocultural. Next, we consider more closely several personal factors that frequently appear in discussions of motivation: needs, goal orientations, beliefs and self-perceptions, interests and curiosity, emotions, and anxiety.

How do we put all this information together when teaching? How do we create environments, situations, and relationships that encourage motivation and engagement in learning? First, we consider how the personal influences on motivation come together to support motivation to learn. Then, we examine how motivation is influenced by the academic work of the class, the value of the work, and the setting in which the work must be done. Finally, we discuss a number of strategies for developing motivation as a constant state in your classroom and as a permanent trait in your students.

By the time you have completed this chapter, you should be able to answer these questions:

- What is the difference between intrinsic and extrinsic motivation?
- How is motivation conceptualized in the behavioural, humanistic, cognitive, social cognitive, and sociocultural perspectives?
- What are the roles of needs, goals, interests and curiosity, emotions, and anxiety in motivation?
- What are the possible motivational effects of attributions for successes and failures, and how do these effects relate to beliefs about ability?
- What external factors can teachers influence that will encourage students' motivation to learn?
- What is your strategy for teaching your subject to an uninterested student?

We began examining motivation in the previous chapter when we explored students' beliefs about their capabilities—their self-efficacy. We will spend another chapter on motivation because students' motivation has a direct and powerful impact on their social interactions and academic achievement in your classroom. Students with the same abilities and prior knowledge may perform quite differently, based on their motivation (Wigfield & Wentzel, 2007). So how does that work? Let's start with a basic question.

WHAT IS MOTIVATION?

Motivation is usually defined as *an internal state that arouses, directs, and maintains behaviour.* Psychologists studying motivation tend to focus on five basic questions:

1. *What choices do people make about their behaviour?* Why do some students, for example, focus on their homework while others watch television instead?
2. *How long does it take to get started?* Why do some students start their homework right away, while others procrastinate?
3. *What is the intensity or level of involvement in the chosen activity?* Once the backpack is opened, is the student absorbed and focused or just going through the motions?
4. *What causes a person to persist or to give up?* Will a student read the entire Shakespeare assignment or just a few pages?
5. *What is the person thinking and feeling while engaged in the activity?* Is the student enjoying Shakespeare, feeling competent, or worrying about an upcoming test (Graham & Weiner, 1996; Pintrich, Marx, & Boyle, 1993)?

Connect and Extend
Go to the "Connect and Extend" section in Chapter 11 of MyEducationLab to find further content that links to teaching, students' thinking, research, and the news.

Meeting Some Students

Many factors influence motivation and engaged learning. To get a sense of the complexity of the concept of motivation, let's step into a high school science classroom just after the teacher has given directions for a lab activity. The student profiles below are adapted from Stipek (2002).

Hopeless Hunter won't even start the assignment—as usual. He just keeps saying, "I don't understand," or "This is too hard." When he answers your questions correctly, he "guessed" and he "doesn't really know." Hunter spends most of his time staring into space; he is falling farther and farther behind.

Safe Sara checks with you about every step—she wants to be perfect. You once gave her bonus points for doing an excellent colour drawing of the apparatus, and now she produces a work of art for lab every time. But Sara won't risk getting a B. If it isn't required or on the test, Sara isn't interested.

Satisfied Sean, on the other hand, is interested in this project. In fact, he knows more than you do about it. Evidently he spends hours reading about chemistry and performing experiments. But his overall grade in your class is between B– and C+ because he never turns in homework. Sean is satisfied with the C he can get on tests without even trying.

Defensive Dana doesn't have her lab manual—again, so she has to share with another student. Then she pretends to be working, but spends most of her time making fun of the assignment or trying to get answers from other students when your back is turned. She is afraid to try because if she makes an effort and fails, she fears that everyone will think she is "dumb."

Anxious Alexis is a good student in most subjects, but she freezes on science tests and "forgets" everything she knows when she has to answer questions in class. Her parents are scientists and expect her to become one too, but her prospects for this future profession look dim.

STOP & THINK Each of these students has problems with at least one of the five areas of motivation: choices, getting started, intensity, persistence, or thoughts and feelings. Can you diagnose the problems? The answers are on page 379.

Motivation An internal state that arouses, directs, and maintains behaviour.

Each student presents a different motivational challenge, yet you are expected to motivate and teach the entire class. In the next few pages, we will look more closely at the meaning of motivation so we can better understand these students.

Intrinsic and Extrinsic Motivation

We all know how it feels to be motivated, to move energetically toward a goal or to work hard, even if we are bored by the task. What energizes and directs our behaviour? The explanation could be drives, basic desires, needs, incentives, fears, goals, social pressure, self-confidence, interests, curiosity, beliefs, values, expectations, and more. Some psychologists have explained motivation in terms of personal *traits* or individual characteristics. Certain people, so the theory goes, have a strong *need* to achieve, a *fear* of tests, a *curiosity* about mechanical objects, or an enduring *interest* in art, so they work hard to achieve, avoid tests, tinker endlessly in their garages, or spend hours in art galleries. Other psychologists see motivation more as a *state*, a temporary situation. If, for example, you are reading this paragraph because you have a test tomorrow, you are motivated (at least for now) by the situation. Of course, the motivation we experience at any given time usually is a combination of trait and state. You may be studying because you value learning *and* because you are preparing for a test.

MyEducationLab Go to the Activities and Applications section in Chapter 11 of MyEducationLab and complete Activity 1. As you watch the video and complete the accompanying activity, consider how teachers motivate students at different ages and grade levels.

As you can see, some explanations of motivation rely on internal, personal factors such as needs, interests, and curiosity. Other explanations point to external, environmental factors—rewards, social pressure, punishment, and so on. A classic distinction in motivation is between intrinsic and extrinsic varieties. **Intrinsic motivation** is the natural human tendency to seek out and conquer challenges as we pursue personal interests and exercise our capabilities. When we are intrinsically motivated, we do not need incentives or punishments, because *the activity itself is satisfying and rewarding* (Anderman & Anderman, 2009; Deci & Ryan, 2002; Reiss, 2004). Satisfied Sean studies chemistry outside school simply because he loves learning about chemistry; no one makes him do it.

In contrast, when we do something in order to earn a grade, avoid punishment, please the teacher, or for some other reason that has very little to do with the task itself, we experience **extrinsic motivation**. We are not really interested in the activity for its own sake; we care only about what it will gain us. Safe Sara works for the grade; she has little interest in the subject itself.

According to psychologists who adopt the intrinsic/extrinsic concept of motivation, it is impossible to tell just by observing it if a behaviour is intrinsically or extrinsically motivated. The essential difference between the two types of motivation is the student's reason for acting, that is, whether the **locus of causality** for the action (the location of the cause) is internal or external—inside or outside the person. Students who read or practise their backstroke or paint may be reading, swimming, or painting because they freely chose the activity based on personal interests (*internal locus* of causality/intrinsic motivation), or because someone or something else outside is influencing them (*external locus* of causality/extrinsic motivation) (Reeve, 2002; Reeve & Jang, 2006).

Intrinsic motivation Motivation associated with activities that are their own reward.

Extrinsic motivation Motivation created by external factors such as rewards and punishments.

Locus of causality The location—internal or external—of the cause of behaviour.

As you think about your own motivation, you probably realize that the dichotomy between intrinsic and extrinsic motivation is too either/or—that is, too all-or-nothing. There are two explanations that avoid either/or thinking. One is that our activities fall along a continuum from fully *self-determined* (intrinsic motivation) to fully *determined by others* (extrinsic motivation). For example, students may freely choose to work hard on activities that they don't find particularly enjoyable because they know the activities are important to reaching a valued goal—such as spending hours studying educational psychology in order to become an effective teacher. Is this intrinsic or extrinsic motivation? Actually, it is somewhere in between—the person is freely choosing to accept outside causes such as licensure requirements and then is trying to get the most benefit from the requirements. The person has *internalized an external cause* (Vansteenkiste, Lens, & Deci, 2006).

FOR THE MEDAL ONLY? Is this athlete motivated just by a piece of metal hanging from a ribbon, or is he also likely intrinsically motivated to achieve what he has in his sport?

A second explanation for motivation that avoids either/or thinking is based on the idea that intrinsic and extrinsic forms of motivation do not represent opposing ends of a continuum. Instead, this second explanation is that intrinsic and extrinsic tendencies are two independent possibilities, and, at any given time, we can be motivated by some of each (Covington & Mueller, 2001). Teaching can create intrinsic motivation by connecting to students' interests and supporting growing competence. But you know this won't work all the time. Did you find long division inherently interesting? Was your curiosity piqued by irregular verbs? If teachers count on intrinsic motivation to energize all their students all of the time, they will be disappointed. There are situations where incentives and external supports are necessary. Teachers must encourage and nurture intrinsic motivation, while making sure that extrinsic motivation supports learning (Anderman & Anderman, 2009; Brophy, 2003; Deci, Koestner, & Ryan, 1999). To do this, they need to know about the factors that influence motivation.

Five General Approaches to Motivation

STOP & THINK Why are you reading this chapter? Are you curious about motivation and interested in the topic? Or is there a test in your near future? Do you need this course to graduate? Maybe you believe that you will do well in this class, and that belief keeps you working. Perhaps it is some combination of these reasons. What motivates you to study motivation?

Motivation is a vast and complicated subject encompassing many theories. Some theories were developed through work with animals in laboratories. Others are based on research with humans in situations that used games or puzzles. Some theories grew out of the work done in clinical or industrial psychology. Our examination of the field will be selective; otherwise we would never finish reviewing the topic.

Behavioural Approaches to Motivation. According to the behavioural view, an understanding of student motivation begins with a careful analysis of the incentives and rewards present in the classroom. A reward is an attractive object or event supplied as a consequence of a particular behaviour. For example, Safe Sara was rewarded with bonus points when she drew an excellent diagram. An incentive is an object or event that encourages or discourages behaviour. The promise of an A+ was an incentive to Sara. Actually receiving the grade was a reward.

If we are consistently reinforced for certain behaviours, we may develop habits or tendencies to act in certain ways. For example, if a student is repeatedly rewarded with affection, money, praise, or privileges for accomplishments in baseball, but receives little recognition for studying, the student will probably work longer and harder on perfecting her fastball than on understanding geometry. Providing students with grades, stars, stickers, and other reinforcers for learning—or demerits for misbehaviour—is an attempt to motivate students by extrinsic means of incentives, rewards, and punishments.

STOP & THINK ANSWERS **Hopeless Hunter** has trouble with getting started (2) and with a sense of despair (5); during the activity he feels defeated and helpless. **Safe Sara** makes good choices (1), gets started right away (2), and persists (3). But she is not really engaged and takes little pleasure in the work (4 and 5). As long as he is following his own choices (1), **Satisfied Sean** is prompt in getting started (2), engaged (3), persistent (4), and enjoys the task (5). **Defensive Dana** makes poor choices (1), procrastinates (2), avoids engagement (3), and gives up easily (4) because she is so concerned about how others will judge her (5). **Anxious Alexis**'s problems have to do with what she thinks and how she feels as she works (5). Her worry and anxiety may lead her to make poor choices (1) and to procrastinate (2), which only makes her more anxious at test time.

Humanistic Approaches to Motivation. In the 1940s, proponents of humanistic psychology such as Carl Rogers argued that neither of the dominant schools of psychology, behavioural or Freudian, adequately explained why people act as they do. Humanistic interpretations of motivation emphasize such intrinsic sources of motivation as a person's needs for "self-actualization" (Maslow, 1968, 1970), the inborn "actualizing tendency" (Rogers & Freiberg, 1994), or the need for "self-determination" (Deci, Vallerand, Pelletier, & Ryan, 1991). So, from the humanistic perspective, to motivate means to encourage people's inner resources—their sense of competence, self-esteem, autonomy, and self-actualization. Maslow's theory and Deci and Ryan's self-determination theory, discussed later, are influential humanistic explanations of motivation.

Reward An attractive object or event supplied as a consequence of a behaviour.

Incentive An object or event that encourages or discourages behaviour.

Humanistic interpretation Approach to motivation that emphasizes personal freedom, choice, self-determination, and striving for personal growth.

Cognitive Approaches to Motivation. From the perspective of cognitive theorists, people are viewed as active and curious, in search of information to solve personally relevant problems. Thus, cognitive theorists emphasize intrinsic motivation. In many ways, cognitive theories of motivation also developed as a reaction to the behavioural views. Cognitive theorists believe that behaviour is determined by our thinking, not simply by whether we have been rewarded or punished for the behaviour in the past (Stipek, 2002). Behaviour is initiated and regulated by plans (Miller, Galanter, & Pribram, 1960), goals (Locke & Latham, 2002), schemas (Ortony, Clore, & Collins, 1988), expectations (Vroom, 1964), and attributions (Weiner, 2000). We will look at goals and attributions later in this chapter.

Social Cognitive Theories. Social cognitive theories of motivation are integrations of behavioural and cognitive approaches: They take into account both the behaviourists' concern with the consequences of behaviour and the cognitivists' interest in the impact of individual beliefs and expectations. Many influential social cognitive explanations of motivation can be characterized as expectancy × value theories. This means that motivation is seen as the product of two main forces: the individual's expectation of reaching a goal and the value of that goal to him or her. In other words, the important questions are, "If I try hard, can I succeed?" and "If I succeed, will the outcome be valuable or rewarding to me?" Motivation is a product of these two forces, because if either factor is zero, no motivation exists to work toward the goal. For example, if I believe I have a good chance of making the basketball team (high expectation), and if making the team is very important to me (high value), then my motivation should be strong. But if either factor is zero (I believe I haven't a prayer of making the team, or I couldn't care less about playing basketball), then my motivation level will be zero, too (Tollefson, 2000).

Jacqueline Eccles and Allan Wigfield add the element of *cost* to the expectancy × value equation. Values must be considered in relation to the cost of pursuing them. How much energy will be required? What could I be doing instead? What are the risks if I fail? Will I look stupid (Eccles & Wigfield, 1985)? Bandura's theory of self-efficacy, discussed in Chapter 10, is a social cognitive expectancy × value approach to motivation (Feather, 1982; Schunk, Pintrich, & Meece, 2008).

Sociocultural Conceptions of Motivation. Finish this sentence: I am a/an _____. What is your identity? With what groups do you identify most strongly? Sociocultural views of motivation emphasize participation in communities of practice. From this perspective, people engage in activities to maintain their identities and their interpersonal relations within the community. Thus, students are motivated to learn if they are members of a classroom or school community that values learning. Just as we learn through socialization how to speak or to dress or to order food in restaurants—by watching and learning from more capable members of the culture—we also learn to be students by watching and learning from members of our school community. In other words, we learn by the company we keep (Hickey, 2003; Rogoff, Turkanis, & Bartlett, 2001). When we see ourselves as soccer players, or sculptors, or engineers, or teachers, or psychologists, we are claiming an identity within a group. When building an identity in the group, we move from legitimate peripheral participation to central participation. Legitimate peripheral participation means that beginners are genuinely involved in the work of the group, even if their abilities are undeveloped and their contributions are small. The novice weaver learns to dye wool before spinning and weaving, and the novice teacher learns to tutor one person before working with the whole group. Each task is a piece of the real work of the expert. The identities of both the novice and the expert are bound up in their participation in the community. They are motivated to learn the values and practices of the community to maintain their identity as community members (Lave & Wenger, 1991; Wenger, 1998).

Some classrooms are intentionally structured as learning communities. For example, Brown and Campione (1996) developed learning communities for middle school students around research projects in science, as we saw in Chapter 9. Marlene Scardamalia and Carl Bereiter (1996) at the University of Toronto designed a learning community using a computer system called CSILE—Computer-Supported Intentional Learning Environment—that encourages collaboration among students about questions, hypotheses, and findings. The challenge associated with these approaches is to be sure that all students are fully participating members of the community, because motivation comes from both identity *and* legitimate participation.

Expectancy × value theories Explanations of motivation that emphasize an individual's expectations for success combined with the value of the goal to him or her.

Sociocultural views of motivation Perspectives that emphasize participation, identities, and interpersonal relations within communities of practice.

Legitimate peripheral participation Genuine involvement in the work of the group, even if your abilities are undeveloped and your contributions are small.

TABLE 11.1

Five Views of Motivation

	Behavioural	Humanistic	Cognitive	Social Cognitive	Sociocultural
Source of motivation	Extrinsic	Intrinsic	Intrinsic	Intrinsic and extrinsic	Intrinsic
Important influences	Reinforcers, rewards, incentives, and punishers	Need for self-esteem, self-fulfillment, and self-determination	Beliefs, attributions for success and failure, expectations	Goals, expectations, intentions, self-efficacy	Engaged participation in learning communities; maintaining identity through participation in activities of group
Key theorists	Skinner	Maslow, Deci	Weiner, Graham	Locke and Latham, Bandura	Lave, Wenger

The behavioural, humanistic, cognitive, social cognitive, and sociocultural approaches to motivation are summarized in Table 11.1. These theories differ in their answers to the question, "What is motivation?" but each contributes in its own way toward a comprehensive understanding of the concept.

To organize the many ideas about motivation in a way that is useful for teaching, let's examine four broad areas. Most contemporary explanations for motivation include a discussion of needs, goals, self-perceptions, and finally, the emotional "hot" side of motivation—interests, curiosity, emotions, and anxiety (Murphy & Alexander, 2000).

NEEDS

Early research in psychology conceived of motivation in terms of trait-like needs or consistent personal characteristics. Three of the main needs studied extensively in this earlier work were the needs for achievement, power, and affiliation (Pintrich, 2003). Abraham Maslow's influential theory emphasized a hierarchy that included all these needs and more.

Maslow's Hierarchy of Needs

Maslow (1970) suggested that humans have a hierarchy of needs ranging from lower-level needs for survival and safety to higher-level needs for intellectual achievement and finally self-actualization. Self-actualization is Maslow's term for self-fulfillment, the realization of personal potential. Each of the lower needs must be met before the next higher need can be addressed.

Maslow (1968) called the four lower-level needs—for survival, followed by safety, then belonging, and then self-esteem—deficiency needs. When these needs are satisfied, the motivation for fulfilling them decreases. He labelled the three higher-level needs—intellectual achievement, then aesthetic appreciation, and finally self-actualization—being needs. When these needs are met, a person's motivation does not cease; instead, it increases to seek further fulfillment. Unlike the deficiency needs, being needs can never be completely filled. For example, the more successful you are in your efforts to develop as a teacher, the harder you are likely to strive for even greater improvement.

Maslow's theory has been criticized for the very obvious reason that people do not always appear to behave as the theory would predict. Most of us move back and forth among different types of needs and may even be motivated by many needs at the same time. Some people deny themselves safety or friendship in order to achieve knowledge, understanding, or greater self-esteem.

Criticisms aside, Maslow's theory does give us a way of looking at the whole student, whose physical, emotional, and intellectual needs are all interrelated. A child whose feelings of safety and sense of belonging are threatened by divorce may have little interest in learning how to divide fractions. If school is a fearful, unpredictable place where neither teachers nor students know where

Hierarchy of needs Maslow's model of seven levels of human needs, from basic physiological requirements to the need for self-actualization.

Self-actualization Fulfilling one's potential.

Deficiency needs Maslow's four lower-level needs, which must be satisfied first.

Being needs Maslow's three higher-level needs, sometimes called growth needs.

they stand, both are likely to be more concerned with security and less with teaching and learning. Belonging to a social group and maintaining self-esteem within that group, for example, are important to students. If doing what the teacher says conflicts with group rules, students may choose to ignore the teacher's wishes or even to defy the teacher.

Self-determination theory is a more recent approach to motivation that focuses on human needs (Deci & Ryan, 2002).

Self-Determination: Need for Competence, Autonomy, and Relatedness

Self-determination theory suggests that we all need to feel competent and capable in our interactions in the world, to have some choices and a sense of control over our lives, and to be connected to others—to belong to a social group. Notice that these are similar to earlier conceptions of basic needs: competence (achievement), autonomy and control (power), and relatedness (affiliation).

Need for autonomy is central to self-determination because it represents the desire to have our own wishes, rather than external rewards or pressures, determine our actions (Deci & Ryan, 2002; Reeve, Deci, & Ryan, 2004; Ryan & Deci, 2000). People strive to have authority in their lives and to be in charge of their own behaviour. They constantly struggle against pressure from external controls such as the rules, schedules, deadlines, orders, and limits imposed by others. Sometimes, even help is rejected so that the individual can remain in command (deCharms, 1983).

Self-Determination in the Classroom. Classroom environments that support students' self-determination and autonomy are associated with greater student interest and curiosity, sense of competence, creativity, conceptual learning, and preference for challenge. These relationships appear to hold from grade 1 through graduate school (Deci & Ryan, 2002; Moller, Deci, & Ryan, 2006; Shih, 2008). When students have the authority to make choices, they are more likely to believe that the work is important, even if it is not "fun." Thus, they tend to internalize educational goals and take them as their own.

Need for autonomy The desire to have our own wishes, rather than external rewards or pressures, determine our actions.

Cognitive evaluation theory Suggests that events affect motivation through the individual's perception of the events as controlling behaviour or providing information.

In contrast to autonomy-supporting classrooms, controlling environments tend to improve performance only on rote recall tasks. When students are pressured to perform, they often seek the quickest, easiest solution. One discomforting finding, however, is that both students and parents seem to prefer more controlling teachers, even though the students learn more when their teachers support autonomy (Flink, Boggiano, & Barrett, 1990). Assuming you are willing to risk going against popular images, how can you support student autonomy? One answer is to focus on *information*, not *control*, in your interactions with students.

SELF-DETERMINED STUDENTS Classroom environments that support student self-determination and autonomy are associated with greater student interest and curiosity, sense of competence, creativity, conceptual learning, and preference for challenge.

Information and Control. Many things happen to students throughout the school day. They are praised or criticized, reminded of deadlines, assigned grades, given choices, lectured about rules, and on and on. Cognitive evaluation theory (Deci & Ryan, 2002) explains how these events can influence the students' intrinsic motivation by affecting their sense of self-determination and competence. According to this theory, all events have two aspects: controlling and informational. If an event is highly controlling, that is, if it pressures students to act or to feel a certain way, then students will experience less control and their *intrinsic motivation* will be diminished. If, on the other hand, the event provides information that increases the students' sense of competence, then intrinsic motivation will increase. Of course, if the information provided makes students feel less competent, it is likely that motivation will decrease (Pintrich, 2003).

For example, a teacher might praise a student by saying, "Good for you! You got an A because you finally followed my instructions correctly." This is a highly controlling statement, giving the credit to the teacher and thus undermining the student's sense of self-determination and intrinsic motivation. The teacher could praise the same work by saying, "Good for you! Your understanding of the author's use of metaphors has improved tremendously. You earned an A." This statement provides information about the student's growing competence and should increase the student's intrinsic motivation.

As a teacher, what can you do to support student needs for autonomy and competence? An obvious first step is to limit your controlling messages to students because controlling language (*must, ought, have to, should*...) can undermine student motivation (Vansteenkiste, Simons, Lens, Sheldon, & Deci, 2004). Make sure the information you provide highlights students' growing competence. The *Guidelines* box provides some suggestions for ways you can support autonomy and self-determination in the classroom.

GUIDELINES: Supporting Self-Determination and Autonomy

Allow and encourage students to make choices.

EXAMPLES

1. Design several different ways to meet a learning objective (e.g., writing an essay, conducting and compiling interviews, taking a test, summarizing a news broadcast) and let students choose one. Encourage them to explain the reasons for their choice.
2. Appoint student committees to make suggestions about how to streamline procedures such as organizing a class project or distributing equipment.
3. Provide time for independent and extended projects.
4. Allow students to choose work partners as long as they focus on the task.

Help students plan actions to accomplish self-selected goals.

EXAMPLES

1. Experiment with using goal cards. Students list their short- and long-term goals and then record three or four specific actions that will move them toward those goals. Goal cards are personal—like credit cards.
2. Encourage middle and high school students to set goals in each subject area, to record them in a goal book or on a computer flash drive, and to check their progress toward the goals on a regular basis.

Hold students accountable for the consequences of their choices.

EXAMPLES

1. If students choose to work with partners and do not finish a project because they spent too much time socializing, grade the project as it deserves and help the students see the connection between lost time and poor performance.
2. When students choose a topic that captures their imaginations, discuss the connections between their investment in the work and the quality of the products that follow.

Provide rationales for limits, rules, and constraints.

EXAMPLES

1. Explain reasons for rules.
2. As a teacher, respect rules and constraints in your own behaviour.

Acknowledge that negative emotions are valid reactions to teacher control.

EXAMPLES

1. Explain that it is okay (and normal) to feel bored while waiting for a turn, for example.
2. Communicate that sometimes important learning involves frustration, confusion, and weariness.
3. Acknowledge students' perspective: "Yes, this problem is difficult." Or "I can understand why you might feel that way."

Use non-controlling, positive feedback.

EXAMPLES

1. See poor performance or behaviour as a problem to be solved, rather than as a target of criticism.
2. Avoid controlling language, such as "should," "must," "have to."

For more information on self-determination theory, see **www.psych.rochester.edu/SDT/**.

Source: From *150 Ways to Increase Intrinsic Motivation in the Classroom*, by James P. Raffini. Published by Allyn and Bacon, Boston, MA. Copyright © 1996 by Pearson Education and from *Motivating Others: Nurturing Inner Motivational Resources* by Johnmarshall Reeve. Published by Allyn and Bacon, Boston, MA. Copyright © 1996 by Pearson Education. Adapted by permission of the publisher.

The Need for Relatedness. The need for relatedness is the desire to establish close emotional bonds and attachments with others. When teachers and parents are responsive and demonstrate that they care about the children's interests and well-being, the children show high intrinsic motivation. Students who feel a sense of relatedness to teachers, parents, and peers are more emotionally engaged in school (Furrer & Skinner, 2003). All students need caring teachers, but students placed at risk for failure need this kind of teacher even more. Positive relationships with teachers increase the likelihood that students will succeed in high school and go on to pursue a post-secondary education (Stipek, 2006; Thompson, 2008; Woolfolk Hoy & Weinstein, 2006). In addition, emotional and physical problems—ranging from eating disorders to suicide—are more common among people who lack social relationships (Baumeister & Leary, 1995). The need for relatedness is similar to the need for a sense of belonging, discussed in Chapter 3 (Osterman, 2000).

The importance of social connections to supporting engaged learning is nicely summed up in the following quotation from the report of the Committee on Increasing High School Students' Engagement and Motivation to Learn (2004):

> Although learning involves cognitive processes that take place within each individual, motivation to learn also depends on the student's involvement in a web of social relationships that supports learning. The likelihood that students will be motivated and engaged is increased to the extent that their teachers, family, and friends effectively support their purposeful involvement in learning in school. Thus a focus on engagement calls attention to the connection between a learner and the social context in which learning takes place. Engaging schools promote a sense of belonging by personalizing instruction, showing an interest in students' lives, and creating a supportive, caring social environment. (p. 3)

Needs: Lessons for Teachers

From infancy to old age, people want to be both competent and connected. Students are more likely to participate in activities that help them grow more competent, and they are less likely to engage in activities that hold the possibility of failure. This means that the students need appropriately challenging tasks—not too easy, but not impossible either. Students also benefit from ways of watching their competence grow, perhaps through self-monitoring systems or portfolios. To be connected, students need to feel that people in school care about them and can be trusted to help them learn.

What else matters in motivation? Many theories include goals as key elements.

GOAL ORIENTATIONS

STOP & THINK On a scale from 1 (strongly agree) to 5 (strongly disagree), how would you answer these questions:

I feel really pleased in school when

___ I solve problems by working hard
___ I know more than the others
___ I don't have to work hard
___ I keep busy
___ I finish first
___ All the work is easy
___ I learn something new
___ I am the only one who gets an A
___ I am with my friends

A goal is an outcome or attainment that an individual is striving to accomplish (Locke & Latham, 2002). When students strive to read a chapter or to make a superior grade point average (GPA), they are involved in *goal-directed behaviour*. When pursuing goals, students are generally aware of some current condition (I haven't even opened my textbook), some ideal condition (I have understood every page), and the discrepancy between the current and ideal situations. Goals motivate people to act in order to reduce the discrepancy between "where they are" and "where they want to be." Goal setting is usually effective for Anita, for instance. In addition to the routine tasks, such as eating lunch, which will happen without much attention, she often sets goals for each day. For example,

Goal What an individual strives to accomplish.

today she intends to finish this section, to walk on the treadmill, to talk with the air conditioning contractor about why her AC keeps freezing up, and to wash another load of clothes. Having decided to do these things, she will feel uncomfortable if she is unable to complete them.

According to Edwin Locke of the University of Toronto and his colleague Gary Latham (2002), there are four main reasons why goal setting improves performance. Goals:

1. *Direct our attention* to the task at hand and away from distractions. Every time Anita's mind wanders from this chapter, her goal of finishing the section helps direct her attention back to the writing.
2. *Energize effort*. The more challenging the goal, to a point, the greater the effort.
3. *Increase persistence*. When we have a clear goal, we are less likely to give up until we reach the goal: Hard goals demand effort and tight deadlines lead to faster work.
4. *Promote the development of new knowledge and strategies* when old strategies fall short. For example, if your goal is making an A and you don't reach that goal on your first quiz, you might try a new study approach for the next quiz, such as explaining the key points to a friend.

Types of Goals and Goal Orientations

The types of goals we set influence the amount of motivation we have to reach them. Goals that are specific, moderately difficult, and likely to be reached in the near future tend to enhance motivation and persistence (Schunk et al., 2008; Stipek, 2002). Specific goals provide clear standards for judging performance. If performance falls short, we keep going. For example, Anita decided to "finish this section" instead of deciding to "work on the book." Anything short of having the section ready to mail means that she will need to "keep working" (looks like another late night!). Moderate difficulty provides a challenge, but not an unreasonable one. For instance, Anita can finish this section if she stays with it. Finally, goals that can be reached fairly soon are not likely to be pushed aside by more immediate concerns. Groups such as Alcoholics Anonymous show they are aware of the motivating value of short-term goals when they encourage their members to stop drinking "one day at a time."

Goal orientations Patterns of beliefs about goals related to achievement in school.

Mastery goal A personal intention to improve abilities and learn, no matter how performance suffers.

Task-involved learners Students who focus on mastering the task or solving the problem.

Four Achievement Goal Orientations in School. Goals are specific targets. Goal orientations are patterns of beliefs about goals related to achievement in school. Goal orientations include the reasons we pursue goals and the standards we use to evaluate progress toward those goals. For example, your target might be to make an A in this course. Are you doing so in order to master educational psychology—to learn all about it—or are you doing so to perform—to look good in the eyes of your friends and family? There are four main goal orientations: mastery (learning), performance (looking good), work-avoidance, and social (Murphy & Alexander, 2000; Schunk et al., 2008). In the *Stop & Think* exercise on page 384, can you tell which goal orientations are reflected in the different answers? Most of the questions were adapted from a study on students' theories about learning mathematics (Nicholls, Cobb, Wood, Yackel, & Patashnick, 1990).

The most common distinction in research on students' goals is between mastery goals (also called *task goals* or *learning goals*) and performance goals (also called *ability goals* or *ego goals*). The point of a mastery goal is to improve and to learn, no matter how awkward you appear. When students set mastery goals, the quality of their engagement in the task is higher—they are more invested. Students who set mastery goals tend to seek challenges, to persist when they encounter difficulties, and to feel better about their work (Midgley, 2001). Because they focus on the task at hand and are not worried about how their performance "measures up" in comparison to others in the class, these students have been called task-involved learners. We often say that these people "get lost in their work." In addition, task-involved learners are more likely to seek appropriate help, to report using deeper cognitive processing strategies, to apply better study strategies, and generally to approach academic tasks with confidence (Kaplan & Maehr, 2007; Midgley, 2001; Young, 1997).

"MEASURING UP" ISN'T THE POINT When students set mastery goals, the quality of their engagement in the task is higher—they are more invested. They are less worried about how their performance compares to others in the class.

The second kind of goal is a performance goal. Students who set performance goals care about demonstrating their ability to others. They may be focused on getting good test scores and grades, or they may be more concerned with winning and beating other students (Wolters, Yu, & Pintrich, 1996). Students whose goal is outperforming others may do things to look smart, such as reading easy books in order to "read the most books" (Young, 1997). The evaluation of their performance by others, not what they learn, is what matters. Students who set performance goals have been called ego-involved learners because they are preoccupied with themselves. They may act in ways that actually interfere with learning. For example, they may cheat or use short-cuts to complete the task, work hard only on graded assignments, feel upset about and hide papers with low grades, choose tasks that are easy, and be very uncomfortable with assignments that have unclear evaluation criteria (Stipek, 2002).

Wait—Are Performance Goals Always Bad? Performance goals sound pretty dysfunctional, don't they? Earlier research indicated that performance goals generally were detrimental to learning, but like extrinsic motivation, a performance goal orientation may not be all bad, all of the time. In fact, some research indicates that both mastery and performance goals are associated with using active learning strategies and high self-efficacy (Midgley, Kaplan, & Middleton, 2001; Stipek, 2002). And, as is the case with intrinsic and extrinsic motivation, students can, and often do, pursue mastery and performance goals at the same time.

To account for these recent findings, educational psychologists have added the distinction of *approach/avoidance* to the mastery/performance distinction. In other words, students may be motivated to either approach mastery or avoid misunderstanding. They may approach performance or avoid looking dumb. Table 11.2 shows examples and the effects of each kind of goal orientation. Where do you see the most problems? Do you agree that the real problems are with avoidance? Students who fear misunderstanding (mastery avoidance) may be perfectionist—focused on getting it exactly right. Students who avoid looking dumb (performance avoidance) may adopt defensive, failure-avoiding strategies like those adopted by Defensive Dana described earlier—they pretend not to care, they make a show of "not really trying," or they cheat (Harackiewiz, Barron, Pintrich, Elliot, & Thrash, 2002; Harackiewiz & Linnenbrink, 2005).

One final caution—performance-approach goals can turn into performance-avoidance goals if students are not successful in looking smart or winning. The path might lead from performance approach (trying to win), to performance avoidance (saving face and trying not to look dumb), to learned helplessness (I give up!). So teachers are wise to avoid trying to motivate students with competition and social comparisons (Brophy, 2005).

Performance goal A personal intention to seem competent or perform well in the eyes of others.

Ego-involved learners Students who focus on how well they perform and how they are judged by others.

Work-avoidant learners Students who don't want to learn or to look smart, but just want to avoid work.

Social goals A wide variety of needs and motives to be connected to others or part of a group.

Beyond Mastery and Performance. Some students don't want to learn, look smart, or avoid looking dumb; they just want to finish fast or avoid work altogether. These students try to complete assignments and activities as quickly as possible without exerting much effort (Schunk et al., 2008). John Nicholls called these students work-avoidant learners—they feel successful when they don't have to try hard, when the work is easy, or when they can "goof off" (Nicholls & Miller, 1984).

A final category of goals—social goals—becomes more important as students get older. As students move into adolescence, their social networks change to include more peers. Non-academic

TABLE 11.2 Goal Orientations

Students may have either an approach or an avoidance focus for mastery and performance goal orientations.

Goal Orientation	Approach Focus	Avoidance Focus
Mastery	*Focus:* Mastering the task, learning, understanding *Standards used:* Self-improvement, progress, deep understanding (task-involved)	*Focus:* Avoiding misunderstanding or not mastering the task *Standards used:* Just don't be wrong; perfectionists don't make mistakes
Performance	*Focus:* Being superior, winning, being the best *Standards used:* Normative—getting the highest grade, winning the competition (ego-involved goal)	*Focus:* Avoiding looking stupid, avoiding losing *Standards used:* Normative—don't be the worst, get the lowest grade, or be the slowest (ego-involved goal)

Source: From Pintrich, Paul R. and Dale H. Schunk. *Motivation in Education: Theory, Research and Applications,* 2e. Published by Allyn and Bacon, Boston, MA.

activities such as athletics, dating, and "hanging out" compete with school work. Social goals include a wide variety of needs and motives that have different relationships to learning—some help, but some hinder learning. For example, adolescents' goal of maintaining friendly relations can get in the way of learning when cooperative learning group members don't challenge incorrect answers or misconceptions because they are afraid to hurt each other's feelings (Anderson, Holland, & Palincsar, 1997). Certainly, pursuing social goals such as having fun with friends or avoiding being labelled a "nerd" can get in the way of learning. But the goal of bringing honour to your family or team by working hard or being part of a peer group that values academics certainly can support learning (Pintrich, 2003; Ryan, 2001; Urdan & Maehr, 1995).

We talk about goals in separate categories, but students can and do pursue several goals at once. Students need to coordinate their goals so they can make decisions about what to do and how to act. But what if social and academic goals are incompatible? For example, if students do not see a connection between achievement in school and success in life, particularly because discrimination prevents them from succeeding, then those students are not likely to set academic achievement as a goal. Such anti-academic peer groups probably exist in every high school (Committee on Increasing High School Students' Engagement and Motivation to Learn, 2004; Wentzel, 1999). Sometimes, succeeding in the peer group means not succeeding in school—and succeeding in the peer group is important. The need for social relationships is basic and strong for most people.

Goals in Social Context. You have seen in other chapters that current thinking in educational psychology puts people in context. Goal orientation theory is no exception. The people in the situation socially construct the meaning of an activity, such as an assignment in a biology class; goals set for the activity will reflect the participants' understanding of "what they are doing." So, in a highly competitive classroom climate, students might be more likely to adopt performance goals. In contrast, in a supportive, learner-centred classroom, even a student with a lower sense of self-efficacy might be encouraged to aim for higher mastery goals. Goals are constructed as part of the triadic reciprocal interaction of person, environment, and behaviour described by social cognitive theory—"interlocking perceptions of 'meaning,' 'purpose,' and 'self' in guiding and framing action, thought and emotion" (Kaplan & Maehr, 2007).

Feedback, Goal Framing, and Goal Acceptance

Besides having specific goals and creating supportive social relationships, three additional factors make goal setting in the classroom effective. The first is *feedback*. In order to be motivated by a discrepancy between "where you are" and "where you want to be," you must have an accurate sense of both your current status and how far you have to go. There is evidence that feedback emphasizing progress is the most effective. In one study, feedback to adults emphasized either that they had accomplished 75 percent of the standards set or that they had fallen short of the standards by 25 percent. When the feedback highlighted accomplishment, the subjects' self-confidence, analytic thinking, and performance were all enhanced (Bandura, 1997).

The second factor affecting motivation to pursue a goal is *goal framing*. Activities or assignments can be explained or framed as helping students reach intrinsic goals, such as becoming more competent, increasing self-determination, establishing positive relationships with friends or teachers, or increasing well-being. The alternative is portraying activities as helping students reach extrinsic goals such as working for a grade, meeting requirements, getting ready for classes next year, and so on. When activities are linked to students' intrinsic goals of becoming more competent, self-directed, and connected with others, then the students process information more deeply and persist longer to gain a conceptual (not superficial) understanding. Linking activities to the extrinsic goals of meeting someone else's standards promotes rote learning, but not deep understanding or persistence (Vansteenkiste et al., 2006).

The third factor that affects motivation in the pursuit of goals is *goal acceptance*. Commitment matters: The relationship between higher goals and better performance is strongest when people are committed to the goals (Locke & Latham, 2002). If students reject goals set by others or refuse to set their own goals, then their motivation will suffer. Generally, students are more willing to commit to the goals of others if the goals seem realistic, reasonably difficult, and meaningful—and if good reasons are given for the value of the goals by connecting activities to students' intrinsic interests, as noted above (Grolnick, Gurland, Jacob, & Decourcey, 2002).

Goals: Lessons for Teachers

Students are more likely to work toward goals that are clear, specific, reasonable, moderately challenging, and attainable within a relatively short period of time. If teachers focus on student performance, high grades, and competition, they may encourage students to set performance goals. This could undermine the students' ability to learn and to become task-involved and set them on a path toward alienation from learning in school and learned helplessness (Anderman & Maehr, 1994; Brophy, 2005). Students may not yet be expert at setting their own goals or keeping these goals in mind, so encouragement and accurate feedback are necessary. If you use any reward or incentive systems, be sure the goal you set is to *learn and improve* in some area, not just to perform well or look smart. And be sure the goal is not too difficult. Students, like adults, are unlikely to stick with tasks or to respond well to teachers who make them feel insecure or incompetent, which leads us to our next topic—the power of beliefs in explanations of motivation.

BELIEFS AND SELF-PERCEPTIONS

Thus far, we have talked about needs and goals, but another important factor must be considered when explaining motivation. What do students believe about learning and about themselves—that is, their competence and the causes for success or failure? Let's start with a basic question: What do students believe about learning and knowledge?

Beliefs About Knowing: Epistemological Beliefs

What students believe about knowledge and learning (their **epistemological beliefs**) will influence their motivation and the kinds of strategies that they use.

STOP & THINK How would you answer these questions taken from Chan and Sachs (2001)?

1. What is the most important thing when learning math? (a) remember what the teacher has taught you, (b) practise lots of problems, (c) understand the problems you work on.
2. What is the most important thing to do when learning science? (a) faithfully do the work the teacher tells you, (b) try to see how the explanation makes sense, (c) try to remember everything you are supposed to know.
3. If you wanted to know everything there is about something, say animals, how long would you have to study it? (a) less than a year if you study hard, (b) about one or two years, (c) forever.
4. What happens when you learn more and more about something? (a) the questions get more and more complex, (b) the questions get easier and easier, (c) the questions all get answered.

Using questions like those above, researchers have identified several dimensions of epistemological beliefs (Chan & Sachs, 2001; Schommer, 1997; Schommer-Aikins, 2002; Schraw & Olafson, 2002) that characterize what knowledge is and how it is learned:

- *Structure of knowledge*: Is knowledge in a field a simple set of facts or a complex structure of concepts and relationships?
- *Stability/certainty of knowledge*: Is knowledge fixed or does it evolve over time?
- *Ability to learn*: Is the ability to learn fixed (based on innate ability) or changeable?
- *Speed of learning*: Can we gain knowledge quickly or does it take time to develop knowledge?
- *Nature of learning*: Does learning mean memorizing facts passed down from authorities and keeping the facts isolated, or does it mean developing your own integrated understandings?

Epistemological beliefs Beliefs about the structure, stability, and certainty of knowledge, and how knowledge is best learned.

Students' beliefs about knowing and learning affect their use of learning strategies. For example, if you believe that knowledge should be gained quickly, you are likely to try one or two quick strategies (read the text once, spend 2 minutes trying to solve the word problem) and then stop. If you believe that learning means developing integrated understandings, you will process the material more deeply, connect to existing knowledge, create your own examples or draw diagrams, and generally elaborate the information to make it your own (Hofer & Pintrich, 1997; Kardash & Howell, 2000). In one study, elementary school students (grades 4 and 6) who believed that learning is "understanding" processed science texts more deeply than students who believed that learning is "reproducing facts" (Chan & Sachs, 2001). The *Stop & Think* questions you just answered were used in that study to assess the students' beliefs. The answers associated with a belief in complex, evolving knowledge that takes time to understand and grows from active learning are 1c, 2b, 3c, and 4a.

Beliefs about one dimension discussed above—ability to learn—are particularly powerful. Read on.

Beliefs About Ability

STOP & THINK Rate these statements taken from Dweck (2000) on a scale from 1 (strongly agree) to 6 (strongly disagree).

____ You have a certain amount of intelligence and you really can't do much to change it.
____ You can learn new things, but you can't really change your basic intelligence.
____ No matter who you are, you can change your intelligence a lot.
____ No matter how much intelligence you have, you can always change it quite a bit.

Some of the most powerful beliefs affecting motivation in school are about *ability*. By examining these beliefs and how they affect motivation, we will understand why some people set inappropriate, unmotivating goals; why some students adopt self-defeating strategies; and why some students seem to give up altogether.

Adults tend to adopt one of two basic concepts of ability (Dweck, 2002, 2006). An **entity view of ability** assumes that ability is a *stable, uncontrollable* trait—a characteristic of the individual that cannot be changed. According to this view, some people have more ability than others, but the amount each person has is set. An **incremental view of ability**, on the other hand, suggests that ability is *unstable and controllable*—that is, that ability represents "an ever-expanding repertoire of skills and knowledge" (Dweck & Bempechat, 1983, p. 144). By hard work, study, or practice, knowledge can be increased and thus ability can be improved. What is your view of ability? Look back at your answers to the *Stop & Think* questions.

Young children tend to hold an exclusively incremental view of ability. Through the early elementary grades, most students believe that effort is the same as intelligence. Smart people try hard, and trying hard makes you smart. If you fail, you aren't smart and you didn't try hard (Dweck, 2000; Stipek, 2002). At around age 11 or 12, children can differentiate among effort, ability, and performance. About this time, they come to believe that someone who succeeds without working at all must be *really* smart. This is when beliefs about ability begin to influence motivation (Anderman & Maehr, 1994).

Students who hold an entity (unchangeable) view of intelligence tend to set performance goals to avoid looking bad in the eyes of others. They seek situations where they can look smart and protect their self-esteem. Like Safe Sara, they keep doing what they can do well without expending too much effort or risking failure, because either one—working hard or failing—indicates (to them) low ability. To work hard but still fail would be devastating. Students with learning disabilities are more likely to hold an entity view.

Teachers who hold entity views are quicker to form judgments about students and slower to modify their opinions when confronted with contradictory evidence (Stipek, 2002). Teachers who hold incremental views, in contrast, tend to set mastery goals and to seek situations in which students can improve their skills, because improvement means getting smarter. Failure is not devastating; it simply indicates more work is needed. Ability is not threatened. Incremental theorists tend to set moderately difficult goals—the kind we have learned are the most motivating.

Beliefs about ability are related to other beliefs about what you can and cannot control when learning.

Entity view of ability Belief that ability is a fixed characteristic that cannot be changed.

Incremental view of ability Belief that ability is a set of skills that can be changed.

Beliefs About Causes and Control: Attribution Theory

One well-known explanation of motivation begins with the assumption that we try to make sense of our own behaviour and the behaviour of others by searching for explanations and causes. To understand our own successes and failures, particularly unexpected ones, we all ask, "Why?" Students ask themselves, "Why did I flunk my midterm?" or "Why did I do so well this grading period?" They may attribute their successes and failures to ability, effort, mood, knowledge, luck, help, interest, clarity of instructions, the interference of others, unfair policies, and so on. To understand the successes and failures of others, we also make attributions—that the others are smart or lucky or work hard, for example. Attribution theories of motivation describe how the individual's explanations, justifications, and excuses about him- or herself or others influence motivation (Anderman & Anderman, 2009).

Bernard Weiner is one of the main educational psychologists responsible for relating attribution theory to school learning (Weiner, 1994a, 1994b, 2000; Weiner & Graham, 1989). According to Weiner, most of the attributed causes for successes or failures can be characterized in terms of three dimensions:

1. *locus* (location of the cause—internal or external to the person),
2. *stability* (whether the cause of the event is the same across time and in different situations), and
3. *controllability* (whether the person can control the cause).

Every cause for success or failure can be categorized in terms of these three dimensions. For example, luck is external (locus), unstable (stability), and uncontrollable (controllability). Table 11.3 shows some common attributions for success or failure on a test. Notice that ability is usually considered stable and uncontrollable, but incremental theorists (described earlier) would argue that ability is unstable and controllable. Weiner's locus and controllability dimensions are closely related to Deci's concept of *locus of causality*.

Weiner believes that these three dimensions have important implications for motivation because they affect expectancy and value. The *stability* dimension, for example, seems to be closely related to expectations about the future. If students attribute their failure to stable factors such as the difficulty of the subject, they will expect to fail in that subject in the future. But if they attribute the outcome to unstable factors such as mood or luck, they can hope for better outcomes next time. The *internal/external locus* seems to be closely related to feelings of self-esteem (Weiner, 2000). If success or failure is attributed to internal factors, success will lead to pride and increased motivation, whereas failure will diminish self-esteem. The *controllability* dimension is related to emotions such as anger, pity, gratitude, or shame. If we feel responsible for our failures, we may feel guilt; if we feel responsible for successes, we may feel proud. Failing at a task we cannot control can lead to shame or anger.

Feeling in control of your own learning seems to be related to choosing more difficult academic tasks, to putting out more effort, to using better strategies, and to persisting longer when completing

TABLE 11.3

Weiner's Theory of Causal Attribution

There are many explanations students can give for why they fail a test. Below are eight reasons representing the eight combinations of locus, stability, and responsibility in Weiner's model of attributions.

Dimension Classification	Reason for Failure
Internal-stable-uncontrollable	Low aptitude
Internal-stable-controllable	Never studies
Internal-unstable-uncontrollable	Sick the day of the exam
Internal-unstable-controllable	Did not study for this particular test
External-stable-uncontrollable	School has hard requirements
External-stable-controllable	Instructor is biased
External-unstable-uncontrollable	Bad luck
External-unstable-controllable	Friends failed to help

Source: From *Human Motivation: Metaphors, Theories and Research*, by B. Weiner. Published by Sage Publications, Newbury Park, CA. Copyright © 1992 by Sage Publications. Adapted with permission of the publisher.

Attribution theories Descriptions of how individuals' explanations, justifications, and excuses influence their motivation and behaviour.

school work (Schunk, 2000; Weiner, 1994a, 1994b). Factors such as continuing discrimination against women, people from visible minorities, and individuals with special needs can affect these individuals' perceptions of their ability to control their lives (Beane, 1991; van Laar, 2000).

UNMOTIVATED? The greatest motivational problems arise when students attribute failures to uncontrollable causes and focus on their own inadequacy. Apathy is a logical reaction if students believe the causes of failure are beyond their control.

Attributions in the Classroom. People with a strong sense of self-efficacy (see Chapter 10) for a given task ("I'm good at math") tend to attribute their failures to lack of effort ("I should have double-checked my work"), misunderstanding directions, or just not studying enough. These are internal, controllable attributions. As a consequence, students with a strong sense of self-efficacy usually focus on strategies for succeeding next time. This response often leads to achievement, pride, and a greater feeling of control. But people with a low sense of self-efficacy ("I'm terrible at math") tend to attribute their failures to lack of ability ("I'm just dumb").

The greatest motivational problems arise when students attribute failures to stable, uncontrollable causes. Such students may seem resigned to failure, depressed, helpless—what we generally call "unmotivated" (Weiner, 2000). These students respond to failure by focusing even more on their own inadequacy; their attitudes toward school work may deteriorate even further. Apathy is a logical reaction to failure if students believe the causes are stable, unlikely to change, and beyond their control. In addition, students who view their failures in this light are less likely to seek help; they believe nothing and no one can help, so they conceal their need for help. This creates a downward spiral of failure and concealment—"the motivationally 'poor' children, by concealing their difficulties, become 'poorer'" (Marchland & Skinner, 2007). You can see that if a student held an entity view of ability (ability cannot be changed) and a low sense of self-efficacy, motivation would be destroyed when failures were attributed to lack of ability ("I just can't do this and I'll never be able to learn") (Bandura, 1997; Schunk et al., 2008; Stipek, 2002).

Teacher Actions and Student Attributions. How do students determine the causes of their successes and failures? Remember, we also make attributions about the causes of other people's successes and failures. When a teacher assumes that student failure is attributable to forces beyond the student's control, the teacher tends to respond with sympathy and to avoid giving punishments. If, however, the failures are attributed to a controllable factor such as lack of effort, the teacher's response is more likely to be irritation or anger, and reprimands may follow. These tendencies seem to be consistent across time and cultures (Weiner, 1986, 2000).

What do students make of these reactions from their teachers? Sandra Graham (1991, 1996) gives some surprising answers. Evidence exists that when teachers respond to students' mistakes with pity, praise for a "good try," or unsolicited help, the students are more likely to attribute their failure to an uncontrollable cause—usually lack of ability. For example, Graham and Barker (1990) asked subjects of various ages to rate the effort and ability of two boys who were depicted on videotape. On the tape, a teacher circulated around the class while students worked. The teacher stopped to look at two boys' papers, did not make any comments to the first boy, but said to the second, "Let me give you a hint. Don't forget to carry your tens." The second boy had not asked for help and did not appear to be stumped by the problem. All of the age groups who watched the tapes, even the youngest, perceived the boy who received help as being lower in ability than the boy who did not receive help. It is as if the subjects read the teacher's behaviour as meaning, "You poor child, you just don't have the ability to do this hard work, so I will help."

Does this mean that teachers should be critical and withhold help? Of course not! But it is a reminder that "praise as a consolation prize" for failing (Brophy, 1985) or over-solicitous help can convey unintended messages. Graham (1991) suggests that many minority-group students could be the victims of well-meaning pity from teachers. Seeing the very real problems that the students face, teachers may "ease up" on requirements so the students will "experience success." But a subtle communication may accompany the pity, praise, and extra help: "You don't have the ability to do this, so I will overlook your failure." Graham says, "The pertinent question for blacks is whether

Self-efficacy A person's sense of being able to deal effectively with a particular task.

their own history of academic failure makes them more likely to be the targets of sympathetic feedback from teachers and thus the recipients of low-ability cues" (1991, p. 28). This kind of benevolent feedback, even if well intended, can be a subtle form of racism.

Beliefs About Self-Worth

Whatever the label, most theorists agree that a sense of efficacy, control, or self-determination is critical if people are to feel intrinsically motivated.

Learned Helplessness. When people come to believe that the events and outcomes in their lives are mostly uncontrollable, they have developed learned helplessness (Seligman, 1975). To understand the power of learned helplessness, consider this experiment (Hiroto & Seligman, 1975): In the first phase of the experiment, subjects received either solvable or unsolvable puzzles. In the next phase, all subjects were given a series of solvable puzzles. The subjects who struggled with unsolvable problems in the first phase of the experiment usually solved significantly fewer puzzles in the second phase. They had learned that they cannot control the outcome, so they seemed to adopt the attitude "why even try?"

Learned helplessness appears to cause three types of deficits: *motivational*, *cognitive*, and *affective*. Students who feel hopeless will be unmotivated and reluctant to attempt work. Like Hopeless Hunter described earlier, students who have developed learned helplessness expect to fail, so they tend to adopt the attitude "why should I even try?"—thus motivation suffers. Because they are pessimistic about learning, these students miss opportunities to practise and to improve skills and abilities, so they develop cognitive deficits. Finally, students who exhibit learned helplessness often suffer from affective problems such as depression, anxiety, and listlessness (Alloy & Seligman, 1979). Once established, it is very difficult to reverse the effects of learned helplessness.

Self-Worth. What are the connections between attributions and beliefs about ability, self-efficacy, and self-worth? Covington and his colleagues suggest that these factors come together in three kinds of motivational sets: *mastery-oriented*, *failure-avoiding*, and *failure-accepting*, as shown in Table 11.4 (Covington, 1992; Covington & Mueller, 2001).

Mastery-oriented students tend to value achievement and to perceive ability as improvable (an incremental view), so they focus on mastery goals in order to increase their skills and abilities. They are not fearful of failure, because failing does not threaten their sense of competence and self-worth. This allows them to set moderately difficult goals, to take risks, and to cope with failure constructively. Students who are mastery-oriented generally attribute success to their own effort, and thus they assume responsibility for learning and have a strong sense of self-efficacy. They perform best in competitive situations, learn fast, have more self-confidence and energy, are more aroused, welcome concrete feedback (it does not threaten them), and are eager to learn "the rules of the game" so that they can succeed. All of these factors make for persistent, successful learning (Covington & Mueller, 2001; McClelland, 1985).

Learned helplessness The expectation, based on previous experiences involving lack of control, that all of one's efforts will lead to failure.

Mastery-oriented students Students who focus on learning goals because they value achievement and see ability as improvable.

TABLE 11.4 Mastery-Oriented, Failure-Avoiding, and Failure-Accepting Students

	Attitude Toward Failure	Goals Set	Attributions	View of Ability	Strategies
Mastery-oriented	Low fear of failure	Learning goals; moderately difficult and challenging	Effort, use of right strategy, sufficient knowledge is cause of success	Incremental; improvable	Adaptive strategies; e.g., try another way, seek help, practise/study more
Failure-avoiding	High fear of failure	Performance goals; very hard or very easy	Lack of ability is cause of failure	Entity; set	Self-defeating strategies; e.g., make a feeble effort, pretend not to care
Failure-accepting	Expectation of failure; depression	Performance goals or no goals	Lack of ability is cause of failure	Entity; set	Learned helplessness; likely to give up

Failure-avoiding students tend to hold an entity view of ability, so they set performance goals. They lack a strong sense of their own competence and self-worth separate from their performance. In other words, they feel only as smart as their last test grade, so they never develop a solid sense of self-efficacy. In order to feel competent, students who practise failure-avoidance must protect themselves (and their self-worth) from failure. If they have been generally successful, they may avoid failure like Safe Sara, simply by taking few risks and "sticking with what they know." If, on the other hand, failure-avoiding students have experienced a good bit of failure, then they, like Defensive Dana, may adopt self-defeating strategies such as feeble efforts, setting very low or ridiculously high goals, or claiming not to care. Just before a test, a student might say, "I didn't study at all!" or "All I want to do is pass." Then, any grade above a pass becomes a success. Some evidence suggests that blaming anxiety for poor test performance can also be a self-protective strategy (Covington & Omelich, 1987). Procrastination is another example. Low grades do not imply low ability if the student can claim, "I did okay considering I didn't start the term paper until last night." All these are self-handicapping strategies because the students are imposing handicaps on their own achievement. Very little learning is going on.

Unfortunately, failure-avoiding strategies generally lead to the very failure the students were trying to avoid. If failures continue and excuses wear thin, the students may finally decide that they are incompetent. Their sense of self-worth and self-efficacy deteriorates. They give up and thus become failure-accepting students. They are convinced that their problems are due to low ability. As we saw earlier, those students who attribute failure to low ability and believe ability is fixed are likely to become depressed, apathetic, and helpless. Like Hopeless Hunter, they have little hope for believing their abilities can be improved.

Teachers may be able to prevent some failure-avoiding students from becoming failure-accepting students by helping them to find new and more realistic goals. Also, some students may need support in aspiring to higher levels in the face of sexual or ethnic stereotypes about what they "should" want or what they "should not" be able to do well. Providing this kind of support to failure-avoiding students could make all the difference in terms of their success. Instead of pitying or excusing these students, teachers can teach them how to learn and then hold them accountable. This will help the students to develop a sense of self-efficacy for learning and to avoid learned helplessness. The *Guidelines* box discusses how to encourage self-worth in the classroom.

Failure-avoiding students Students who avoid failure by sticking to what they know, by not taking risks, or by claiming not to care about their performance.

Self-handicapping When students engage in behaviour that blocks their own success in order to avoid testing their true ability.

Failure-accepting students Students who believe their failures are due to low ability and there is little they can do about it.

GUIDELINES: Encouraging Self-Worth

Emphasize that abilities are not predetermined or set, but instead can be improved.

EXAMPLES

1. Share examples of how you have improved your knowledge and skills. You might describe, for example, how you have improved your writing skills, skills involved in a particular sport, or skills associated with a favourite craft.
2. Describe your own failures that became successes when you tried new strategies or received appropriate help.
3. Save the first drafts and finished products from students in previous classes to show how much the students improved with effort and support.

Teach directly about the difference between learning goals and performance goals.

EXAMPLES

1. Encourage students to set a small-step goal for one subject.
2. Recognize improvements often with private authentic praise.
3. Use personal best goals, rather than between-student competition.

Make the classroom a place where failure is regarded as just diagnostic—that is, failure tells students which areas need improvement.

EXAMPLES

1. If a student gives an incorrect answer in class, say something to this effect: "I bet others would give that answer too. Let's examine why that is not the best answer. This gives us a chance to dig deeper—excellent!"
2. Encourage revising, improving, polishing, and redoing with an emphasis on improvement.
3. Show students connections between their revised work and a higher grade, but also be sure to emphasize their growing competence.

Encourage students to seek help and to give it.

EXAMPLES

1. Teach students how to ask explicit questions about what they do not understand.
2. Recognize students who are helpful to others.
3. Train class experts for some ongoing needs such as technology guides or progress checkers.

For more information on self-worth, see **http://honolulu.hawaii.edu/intranet/committees/FacDevCom/guidebk/teachtip/motiv.htm**.

Beliefs and Attributions: Lessons for Teachers

If students believe they lack the ability to deal with higher mathematics, they will probably act on this belief even if their actual abilities are well above average. These students are likely to have little motivation to tackle trigonometry or calculus, because they expect to do poorly in these areas. If students believe that failing means they are stupid, they are likely to adopt many self-handicapping, but also self-defeating, strategies. And teachers who stress performance, grades, and competition can encourage self-handicapping without realizing they are doing so (Anderman & Anderman, 2009). Simply telling students to "try harder" is not particularly effective. Students need real evidence that effort will pay off, that setting a higher goal will not lead to failure, that they can improve, and that abilities can be changed. In other words, they need authentic mastery experiences.

What else do we know about motivation? Feelings matter.

INTERESTS, CURIOSITY, EMOTIONS, AND ANXIETY

Do you remember starting school? Were you curious about what might be in store, excited about your new world, and interested and challenged? Many children are. But a common concern of parents and teachers is that this curiosity and excitement about learning is replaced by a sense of drudgery and disinterest. School becomes a job you have to do—a workplace where the work is not that interesting (Wigfield & Wentzel, 2007). What do we know about interest and curiosity in school?

Tapping Interests

STOP & THINK As part of your interview for a job in a large high school, the principal asks, "How would you get students interested in learning? Could you tap their interests in your teaching?" How would you answer?

When Walter Vispoel and James Austin (1995) surveyed over 200 middle school students, "lack of interest in the topic" received the highest rating as the reason for school failures. Interest was second only to effort as a choice for explaining successes. In fact, results of research on learning in school show that interest is related to students' attention, goals, and depth of learning (Guthrie et al., 2006; Hidi & Renninger, 2006).

There are two kinds of interests—personal (individual) and situational—the trait and state distinction again. *Personal* or *individual interests* are the more long-lasting aspects of the person, such as an enduring tendency to be attracted to or to enjoy subjects such as languages, history, or mathematics, or activities such as sports, music, or films. Students with individual interests in learning in general seek new information and exhibit more positive attitudes toward learning in school. *Situational interests* can be described as the more short-lived aspects of the activity, text, or materials that catch and keep the student's attention. Both personal and situational interests are related to learning from texts—greater interest leads to more positive emotional responses to the material, then to greater persistence in learning, deeper processing, better recall of the material, and higher achievement (Ainley, Hidi, & Berndorf, 2002; Pintrich, 2003). And interests increase when students feel competent, so even if students are not initially interested in a subject or activity, they may develop interests as they experience success (Stipek, 2002).

Suzanne Hidi and Ann Renninger (2006) describe a four-phase model of interest development:

situational interest triggered → situational interest maintained →
emerging individual interest → well-developed individual interest

For example, consider Julia, a graduating senior in university described by Suzanne Hidi of the University of Toronto and her colleague Ann Renninger (2006). As Julia waits nervously in the dentist's office flipping through a magazine, her attention is drawn (*situational interest triggered*) to an article about a man who left his engineering job to become a facilitator in legal conflict resolution. When she is called to the dentist's chair, Julia is still reading the article, so she marks her place and returns to finish reading the article after her appointment is finished (*situational interest maintained*). She takes notes, and, over the next weeks, searches the internet, visits the library, and meets with her advisor to get more information about this career option (*emerging individual interest*). Four years later, Julia is enjoying her job as a facilitator as she handles more and more arbitration cases for a law firm (*well-developed, enduring individual interest*).

In the early stages of this four-phase model, emotions play a big role—feelings of excitement, pleasure, fun, and curiosity. Situational interest may be triggered by positive feelings, as when Julia started reading the magazine article. Curiosity followed and helped Julia stay engaged as she learned more about becoming a facilitator. As Julia added knowledge to her curiosity and positive feelings, her personal interest emerged, and the cycle of positive feelings, curiosity, and knowledge continued to build enduring interest.

INTEREST AND EXCITEMENT Students' interest in and excitement about what they're learning are two of the most important factors in education.

Catching and Holding Interests. Whenever possible, it helps to connect academic content to students' enduring individual interests. But given that the content you will teach in most classrooms today is determined by standards, it will be difficult to tailor lessons to each student's interests. You will need to rely more on triggering and maintaining situational interest. Here, the challenge is to not only *catch* but also *hold* students' interest (Pintrich, 2003). For example, Mathew Mitchell (1993) found that using computers, groups, and puzzles *caught* students' interest in secondary mathematics classes but that the interests did not *hold*. Lessons that held the students' interest over time included math activities that were related to real-life problems and active participation in laboratory activities and projects. Another source of interest is fantasy. For example, Cordova and Lepper (1996) found that students learned more math facts during a computer exercise in which they were challenged, as captains of starships, to navigate through space by solving math problems. The students were given the opportunity to name their ships, to stock the (imaginary) galley with their favourite snacks, and to name each of the crew members after their friends. In a study of math learning with older adolescents, Durik and Harackiewicz (2007) concluded that *catching* interest by using colourful learning materials with pictures was helpful for students with low initial interest in mathematics, but not for students who were already interested in the subject. For the interested students, *holding* interest by showing how math could be personally useful was more effective.

Other cautionary points about responding to students' interests are described in the *Point/Counterpoint* box.

Curiosity: Novelty and Complexity

Almost 40 years ago, psychologists suggested that individuals are naturally motivated to seek novelty, surprise, and complexity (Berlyne, 1966). Exploration probably is innate; infants must explore the world to learn about it (Bowlby, 1969). More recently, Reiss (2004) listed curiosity as one of the 16 basic human motivations, and Flum and Kaplan (2006) made the case that schools should target developing an exploratory orientation in students as a major goal.

Interest and curiosity are related. Curiosity could be defined as a tendency to be interested in a wide range of areas (Pintrich, 2003). According to Hidi and Renninger's (2006) four-phase model of interest described in the previous section, our individual interests begin to emerge as we raise and answer "curiosity questions" that help us organize our knowledge about a topic. In order for situational interests to develop into long-term individual interests, curiosity and the desire for exploration are necessary.

POINT / COUNTERPOINT

Does Making Learning Fun Make for Good Learning?

WHEN MANY BEGINNING teachers are asked about how to motivate students, they often say, "make learning fun." But is it necessary for learning to be fun?

POINT

Teachers should make learning fun.

When Phil searched "making learning fun" on Google.ca, Google returned more than 52 000 resources and references. Clearly, there is interest in making learning fun. Research shows that passages in texts that are perceived as more interesting are remembered better (Schunk et al., 2008). For example, in one study, students who read books that interested them spent more time reading, read more words in the books, and felt more positively about reading (Guthrie & Alao, 1997). Games and simulations can make learning more fun, too.

For example, when Anita's daughter was in grade 8, all the students in her class spent three days playing a game her teachers had designed called ULTRA. Students were divided into groups and formed their own "countries." Each country had to choose a name, symbol, national flower, and bird. They wrote and sang a national anthem and elected government officials. The teachers allocated different resources to the countries. To get all the materials needed for the completion of assigned projects, the countries had to establish trade with one another. There was a monetary system and a stock market. Students had to work with their fellow citizens to complete cooperative learning assignments. Some countries "cheated" in their trades with other nations, and this provoked debate about international relations, trust, and war. Anita's daughter says she had fun—but she also learned how to work in a group without the teacher's supervision and gained a deeper understanding of world economics and international conflicts.

A highly motivating grade 3 teacher in another study had her class set up a post office for the whole school. Each classroom in the school had an address and postal code. Students had jobs in the post office, and everyone in the school used the post office to deliver letters to students and teachers. Students designed their own stamps and set postal rates. The teacher said that the system "improves their creative writing without them knowing it" (Dolezal, Welsh, Pressley, & Vincent, 2003, p. 254).

COUNTERPOINT

Fun can get in the way of learning.

As far back as the early 1900s, educators warned about the dangers of focusing on fun in learning. None other than John Dewey, who wrote extensively about the role of interest in learning, cautioned that you can't make boring lessons interesting by mixing in fun like you can make bad chili good by adding some spicy hot sauce. Dewey wrote, "When things have to be made interesting, it is because interest itself is wanting. Moreover, the phrase itself is a misnomer. The thing, the object, is no more interesting than it was before" (Dewey, 1913, pp. 11–12).

A good deal of research now exists indicating that adding interest by incorporating fascinating but irrelevant details actually gets in the way of learning the important information. These "seductive details," as they have been called, divert the readers' attention from the less interesting main ideas (Harp & Mayer, 1998). For example, students who read biographies of historical figures remembered more very interesting but unimportant information about the figures compared to interesting main ideas (Wade, Schraw, Buxton, & Hayes, 1993).

Shannon Harp and Richard Mayer (1998) found similar results with high school science texts. These texts added emotional interest and seductive details about swimmers and golfers who are injured by lightning to a lesson on the process of lightning. The researchers concluded that, "in the case of emotional interest versus cognitive interest, the verdict is clear. Adjuncts aimed at increasing emotional interest failed to improve understanding of scientific explanations" (p. 100). The seductive details may have disrupted students' attempts to follow the logic of the explanations and thus interfered with comprehending the text. Harp and Mayer conclude that "the best way to help students enjoy a passage is to help them understand it" (p. 100).

GUIDELINES: Building on Students' Interests and Curiosity

Relate content objectives to student experiences.

EXAMPLES

1. With a teacher in another school, establish "pen pals" across the classes. Through emails and tweets, students exchange personal experiences, photos, drawings, written work, and ask and answer questions (e.g., "Have you learned cursive writing yet?" "What are you doing in math now?" "What are you reading?").
2. Identify classroom experts for different assignments or tasks. To identify experts, you could ask your students questions like these: Who knows how to use the computer for graphics? How to search the internet? How to cook? How to use an index?
3. Hold a "Switch Day" when students exchange roles with a member of the school staff or a support person. Students should research the role in advance by interviewing their staff member, prepare for the job, dress the part for the day they take over, and then evaluate their success after the switch.

Identify student interests, hobbies, and extracurricular activities that can be incorporated into class lessons and discussions.

EXAMPLES

1. Ask students to design and conduct interviews and surveys to learn about each other's interests.
2. Keep the class library stocked with books that connect to students' interests and hobbies.
3. Allow choices (e.g., of stories in language arts or of projects in science) based on students' interests.

Support instruction with humour, personal experiences, and anecdotes that show the human side of the content.

EXAMPLES

1. Share your own hobbies, interests, and favourite activities.
2. Tell students there will be a surprise visitor; then dress up as the author of a story and tell them about "yourself" and your writing.

Use original source material with interesting content or details.

EXAMPLES

1. Consider using letters and diaries during history lessons.
2. Consider sharing Darwin's notes during biology.

Create surprise and curiosity.

EXAMPLES

1. Ask students to predict what will happen in an experiment, then show them whether they were right or wrong.
2. Provide quotes from historical figures and ask students to guess who said them.

For more information on students' interests and motivation, see **http://mathforum.org/~sarah/Discussion.Sessions/biblio.motivation.html**.

Source: From *150 Ways to Increase Intrinsic Motivation in the Classroom*, by James P. Raffini. Published by Allyn and Bacon, Boston, MA. Copyright © 1996 by Pearson Education. Adapted by permission of the publisher. Also *Motivation in Education* (2nd ed.) by P. Pintrich and D. Schunk, 2002, Merrill/Prentice-Hall, pp. 298–299.

Research on teaching has found that variety in teaching approaches and tasks can support learning (Brophy & Good, 1986; Stipek, 2002). For younger students, the chance to manipulate and explore objects relevant to what is being studied may be the most effective way to keep curiosity stimulated. For older students, well-constructed questions, logical puzzles, and paradoxes can have the same effect. But remember that you have to do more than catch students' interest—you have to hold it—so the questions and puzzles should be related to meaningful learning.

George Lowenstein (1994) suggests that curiosity arises when attention is focused on a gap in knowledge. "Such information gaps produce the feeling of deprivation labeled *curiosity*. The curious person is motivated to obtain the missing information to reduce or eliminate the feeling of deprivation" (p. 87). This idea is similar to Piaget's concept of disequilibrium, discussed in Chapter 2, and has a number of implications for teaching. First, students need some base of knowledge before they can experience gaps in that knowledge leading to curiosity. Second, students must be aware of the gaps in order for curiosity to result. In other words, they need a metacognitive awareness of what they know and don't know (Hidi, Renninger, & Krapp, 2004). Asking students to make guesses and then providing feedback to them can be helpful. Also, proper handling of mistakes can stimulate curiosity by pointing to missing knowledge. Finally, the more we learn about a topic, the more curious we may become about that subject. As Maslow (1970) predicted, fulfilling the need to know increases, not decreases, the need to know more. See the *Guidelines* box for more suggestions about how to build interest and curiosity in the classroom.

Emotions and Anxiety

How do you feel about learning? Excited, bored, curious, or fearful? Today, researchers emphasize that learning is not just about the *cold cognition* of reasoning and problem solving. Learning and information processing also are influenced by emotion, so *hot cognition* plays a role in learning as well (Miller, 2002; Pintrich, 2003). Research on emotions, learning, and motivation is expanding, in part because we know more about how the brain works and how emotion influences learning.

Neuroscience and Emotion. In mammals, including humans, stimulation to a small area of the brain called the amygdala seems to trigger emotional reactions such as the "fight or flight" response. The responses in non-human animals can be strong. But human emotions are the outcome of physiological responses triggered by the brain, combined with interpretations of the situation and other information. So, startling sounds heard during an action movie might cause a brief emotional reaction, but the same sounds heard in the middle of the night as you are walking through a dark alley could lead to stronger and more lasting emotional reactions. Even though the amygdala plays a key role in generating emotions, many other brain regions are also involved. Emotions are a "constant interplay between cognitive assessments, conscious feelings, and bodily responses, with each able to influence the other" (Gluck, Mercado, & Myers, 2007, p. 418). Humans are more likely to pay attention to, learn about, and remember events, images, and readings that provoke emotional responses (Alexander & Murphy, 1998; Cowley & Underwood, 1998; Reisberg & Heuer, 1992). Emotions can affect learning by changing brain dopamine levels that influence long-term memory and by directing attention toward one aspect of the situation (Pekrun, Elliott, & Maier, 2006). Sometimes, emotions interfere with learning by taking up attention or working memory space that could be used for learning (Pekrun, Goetz, Titz, & Perry, 2002).

In teaching, we are concerned about a particular kind of emotions—those related to achievement in school. Experiences of success or failure can provoke *achievement emotions* such as pride, hope, boredom, anger, or shame (Pekrun et al., 2006). How can we use these findings to support learning in school?

Achievement Emotions. In the past, with the exception of anxiety, emotions generally were overlooked in research on learning and motivation. But as you saw above, research in the neurosciences has shown that emotions are both causes and consequences of learning processes. Reinhard Pekrun and his colleagues (2006) tested a model that relates different goal orientations to emotions in older adolescents from the United States and Germany. The goal orientations are those we discussed earlier: mastery, performance approach, and performance avoidance. With a mastery goal, students focused on an activity. They valued the activity as a way to become smarter and they felt in control. They were not afraid of failing, so they could focus on the task at hand. The researchers found that having mastery goals predicted enjoyment in learning, hope, and pride. Students who set mastery goals were less likely to feel bored or angry about learning. In the case of performance-approach goals, students wanted to look good or to be the best and focused their attention on positive outcomes. Performance-approach goals were related mostly to pride. Students who set performance-avoidance goals focused on the fear of failing and the possibility of looking stupid. Performance-avoidance goals predicted feelings of anxiety, hopelessness, and shame. These findings about achievement emotions are summarized in Table 11.5.

TABLE 11.5 How Different Achievement Goals Influence Achievement Emotions

Different goals are associated with different emotions that can have an impact on motivation.

Goal Orientation	Student Emotions
Mastery Focus on activity, controllability, positive value of activity	Increases enjoyment of activity, pride, hope Decreases boredom, anger
Performance approach Focus on outcome, controllability, positive outcome value	Increases pride
Performance avoidance Focus on outcome, lack of controllability, negative outcome value	Increases anxiety, hopelessness, shame

Source: Adapted from Pekrun, R., Elliot, A. J., & Maier, M. A. (2006). Achievement goals and discrete achievement emotions: A theoretical model and prospective test. *Journal of Educational Psychology, 98*, 583–597.

How can you increase students' positive achievement emotions associated with the subject you teach? One way is to increase student achievement in that subject, because achievement emotions are domain-specific. In other words, the fact that students enjoy and feel proud of their work in math does not mean they will necessarily enjoy other subjects like English or history (Goetz, Frenzel, Hall, & Pekrun, 2008).

Arousal and Anxiety. Just as we all know how it feels to be motivated, we all know what it is like to be aroused. **Arousal** involves both psychological and physical reactions—changes in brain wave patterns, blood pressure, heart rate, and breathing rate. We feel alert, wide awake, even excited.

To understand the effects of arousal on motivation, think of two extremes. The first scenario unfolds late at night. You are trying for the third time to understand a required reading, but you are feeling sleepy, and your attention drifts as your eyelids droop. You decide to go to bed and to get up early the next morning to continue studying (a plan that you know seldom works). At the other extreme, imagine that you have a critical test tomorrow—one that determines whether or not you will be accepted into the school you desire. You feel tremendous pressure from everyone to do well. You know that you need a good night's sleep, but you are wide awake. In the first case, arousal is too low and in the second, too high. Psychologists have known for years that there is an optimum level of arousal for most activities (Yerkes & Dodson, 1908). Generally speaking, higher levels of arousal are helpful on simple tasks such as sorting laundry, but lower levels of arousal are better for complex tasks such as taking the Law School Admission Test.

Anxiety in the Classroom. At one time or another, everyone has experienced **anxiety**, or a general uneasiness, a feeling of self-doubt, and sense of tension. The effects of anxiety on school achievement are clear. "From the time of the earliest work on this problem, starting with the pioneering work of Yerkes and Dodson (1908), to the present day, researchers have consistently reported a negative correlation between virtually every aspect of school achievement and a wide range of anxiety measures" (Covington & Omelich, 1987, p. 393). Anxiety can be both a cause and an effect of school failure—students do poorly because they are feeling anxious, and their poor performance increases their anxiety. Anxiety probably is both a trait and a state. Some students tend to be anxious in many situations (trait anxiety), but some situations are especially anxiety provoking (state anxiety) (Covington, 1992; Zeidner, 1998).

Anxiety seems to have both cognitive and affective components. The cognitive side includes worry and negative thoughts—thinking about how bad it would be to fail and worrying that you will, for example. The affective side involves physiological and emotional reactions such as sweaty palms, upset stomach, racing heartbeat, or fear (Schunk et al., 2008; Zeidner, 1995, 1998). Whenever there are pressures to perform, severe consequences for failure, and competitive comparisons among students, anxiety may be encouraged (Wigfield & Eccles, 1989). Research with school-age children shows a relationship between the quality of sleep (how quickly and how well you sleep) and anxiety. Better-quality sleep is associated with positive arousal or an "eagerness" to learn. Poor-quality sleep, on the other hand, is related to debilitating anxiety and decreased school performance. You may have discovered these relationships for yourself in your own school career (Meijer & van den Wittenboer, 2004).

How Does Anxiety Interfere With Achievement? Anxiety interferes with achievement at three points: focusing attention, learning, and testing. When students are learning new material, they must pay attention to it. Highly anxious students evidently divide their attention between the new material and their preoccupation with how worried and nervous they are feeling. Instead of concentrating, they keep noticing the tight feelings in their chest, thinking, "I'm so tense, I'll never understand this stuff!" From the beginning, anxious students may miss much of the information they are supposed to learn because their thoughts are focused on their own worries (Cassady & Johnson, 2002; Paulman & Kennelly, 1984).

But the problems do not end there. Even if they are paying attention, many anxious students have trouble learning material that is somewhat disorganized and difficult—material that requires them to rely on their memory. Unfortunately, much material presented in school could be described this way. In addition, many highly anxious students have poor study habits. Simply learning to be more relaxed will not automatically improve these students' performance; their learning strategies and study skills must be improved as well (Naveh-Benjamin, 1991).

Arousal Physical and psychological reactions causing a person to feel alert, excited, or tense.

Anxiety General uneasiness; a feeling of tension.

Finally, anxious students often know more than they can demonstrate on a test. They may lack critical test-taking skills, or they may have learned the material, but "freeze and forget" on tests (Naveh-Benjamin, McKeachie, & Lin, 1987).

Reaching Every Student: Coping With Anxiety

Some students, particularly those with learning disabilities or emotional disorders, may be especially anxious in school. When students face stressful situations such as tests, they can use three kinds of coping strategies: *problem solving*, *emotional management*, and *avoidance*. Problem-focused strategies might include planning a study schedule, borrowing good notes, or finding a protected place to study. Emotion-focused strategies are attempts to reduce the anxious feelings, for example, by using relaxation exercises or by describing the feelings to a friend. Of course, the latter might become an avoidance strategy, along with going out for pizza or suddenly launching an all-out desk-cleaning attack (can't study until you get organized!). Different strategies are helpful at different points—for example, problem solving before an exam and emotion management during an exam. Different strategies fit different people and situations (Zeidner, 1995, 1998).

Teachers should help highly anxious students to set realistic goals, because these individuals often have difficulty making wise choices. Anxious students tend to select either extremely difficult or extremely easy tasks. In the first case, they are likely to fail, which will increase their sense of hopelessness and anxiety about school. In the second case, anxious students will probably succeed on the easy tasks, but they will miss the sense of satisfaction that could encourage greater effort and ease their fears about school work. Using goal cards, progress charts, or goal-planning journals may help reduce anxiety in students like these.

Curiosity, Interests, and Emotions: Lessons for Teachers

Make efforts to keep the level of arousal appropriate for the task at hand. If students look like they are about to fall asleep, energize them by introducing variety, piquing their curiosity, surprising them, or giving them a brief chance to be physically active. Learn about their interests and incorporate these interests into lessons and assignments. If arousal is too great, follow the suggestions in the *Guidelines* box for dealing with anxiety.

How can we put together all this information about motivation? How can teachers create environments, situations, and relationships that encourage motivation? We address these questions next.

MOTIVATION TO LEARN IN SCHOOL: ON TARGET

Motivation to learn The tendency to find academic activities meaningful and worthwhile and to try to benefit from them.

MyEducationLab Go to the Activities and Applications section in Chapter 11 of MyEducationLab and complete Activity 2. As you view the artifact and complete the accompanying activities, reflect upon why giving students a choice in their activities may influence their motivation, and then think about how Maslow and Weiner might explain this.

Teachers are concerned about developing a particular kind of motivation in their students—the **motivation to learn**, defined as "a student tendency to find academic activities meaningful and worthwhile and to try to derive the intended academic benefits from them" (Brophy, 1988, pp. 205–206). Motivation to learn involves more than wanting or intending to learn; it includes the quality of the student's mental efforts. For example, reading the text 11 times may indicate persistence, but motivation to learn implies the use of more thoughtful, active study strategies, such as summarizing, elaborating the basic ideas, outlining in your own words, drawing graphs of the key relationships, and so on (Brophy, 1988).

It would be wonderful if all our students came to us filled with the motivation to learn, but they don't. As teachers, we have three major goals. The first is to get students productively involved with the work of the class; in other words, to catch their interest and to create a *state* of motivation to learn. The second and longer-term goal is to develop in our students enduring individual interests and the *trait* of being motivated to learn so they will be able to educate themselves for the rest of their lives. And finally, we want our students to be cognitively engaged—to think deeply about what they study. In other words, we want them to be *thoughtful* (Blumenfeld, Puro, & Mergendoller, 1992).

GUIDELINES: Coping With Anxiety

Use competition carefully.

EXAMPLES

1. Monitor activities to make sure no students are being put under undue pressure.
2. During competitive games, make sure all students involved have a reasonable chance of succeeding.
3. Experiment with cooperative learning activities.

Avoid situations in which highly anxious students will be required to perform in front of large groups.

EXAMPLES

1. Ask anxious students questions that can be answered with a simple yes or no, or some other brief reply.
2. Encourage anxious students to practise their public speaking skills in front of smaller groups.

Make sure all instructions are clear. Uncertainty can lead to anxiety.

EXAMPLES

1. Provide written test instructions on the board or on the test itself, instead of delivering them orally.
2. Check with students to make sure they understand the instructions. Ask several students how they would do the first question, exercise, or sample question on a test. Correct any misconceptions.
3. If you are using a new format or starting a new type of task, give students examples or models to show how it is done.

Avoid setting unnecessary time pressures.

EXAMPLES

1. Assign occasional take-home tests.
2. Make sure all students can complete classroom tests within the period given.

Remove some of the pressures associated with completing major tests and exams.

EXAMPLES

1. Teach test-taking skills, administer practice tests, and provide study guides.
2. Avoid basing most of the grade on a single test.
3. Make "extra-credit" work available so that students can add points to their course grades.
4. Test knowledge using several different test formats (e.g., multiple-choice questions, short-answer questions, matching questions, labelling questions, essay questions) because some students experience performance difficulties with certain test formats.

Develop alternatives to written tests.

EXAMPLES

1. Try administering oral, open-book, or group tests.
2. Ask students to complete projects, to organize portfolios of their work, to make oral presentations, or to create a finished product as an alternative to written tests.

Teach students self-regulation strategies (Schutz & Davis, 2000).

EXAMPLES

1. Before the test, encourage students to see the test as an important and challenging task that they have the capabilities to prepare for. Help students stay focused on the task of obtaining as much information as possible about the test in advance.
2. During the test, remind students that the test is important (but not overly important). Encourage students to use task focusing skills, such as picking out the main idea in the question, slowing down, and staying relaxed.
3. After the test, think back on what went well and what could be improved. Focus on helping students develop controllable attributions (e.g., study strategies, effort, careful reading of questions, relaxation strategies).

For more information about test anxiety, see **www.counselingcenter.uiuc.edu/?page_id=193**.

In this chapter we examined the roles of intrinsic and extrinsic motivation, attributions, goals, interests, curiosity, emotions, and self-perceptions in motivation. Table 11.6 on page 402 shows how each of these factors contributes to motivation to learn.

The central question for the remainder of the chapter is this: How can teachers use their knowledge about attributions, goals, interests, emotions, beliefs, and self-perceptions to increase students' motivation to learn? To organize our discussion, we will use the TARGET model.

Carol Ames (1990, 1992) has identified six areas in which teachers make decisions that can influence student motivation to learn: the nature of the *task* that students are asked to do, the *autonomy* or authority students are allowed when performing the task, how students are *recognized* for their accomplishments, *grouping* practices, *evaluation* procedures, and the scheduling of *time* in the classroom. Epstein (1989) coined the acronym TARGET to organize these six areas of possible teacher influence, as shown in Table 11.7 on page 403.

TABLE 11.6 Building a Concept of Motivation to Learn

Motivation to learn is encouraged when the following six elements come together.

	Optimum Characteristics of Motivation to Learn	Characteristics That Diminish Motivation to Learn
Source of motivation	*Intrinsic:* Personal factors such as needs, interests, curiosity, enjoyment	*Extrinsic:* Environmental factors such as rewards, social pressure, punishment
Type of goal set	*Learning goal:* Personal satisfaction in meeting challenges and improving; tendency to choose moderately difficult and challenging goals	*Performance goal:* Desire for approval for performance in others' eyes; tendency to choose very easy or very difficult goals
Type of involvement	*Task-involved:* Concerned with mastering the task	*Ego-involved:* Concerned with self in others' eyes.
Achievement motivation	*Motivation to achieve:* Mastery orientation	*Motivation to avoid failure:* Prone to anxiety
Likely attributions	Success and failure attributed to *controllable* effort and ability	Success and failures attributed to *uncontrollable* causes
Beliefs about ability	*Incremental view:* Belief that ability can be improved through hard work and added knowledge and skills	*Entity view:* Belief that ability is a stable, uncontrollable trait

Tasks for Learning

To understand how an academic task can affect students' motivation, we need to analyze the task. Tasks have different values for students.

Task Value. As you probably recall, many theories suggest that the strength of our motivation in a particular situation is determined by both our *expectation* that we can succeed and the *value* of that success to us. Perceptions of task value predict the choices students make, such as whether to enrol in advanced science classes or to join a team. Efficacy expectations predict achievement in actually doing the task (e.g., how well the students will perform in the advanced science class or on the varsity team) (Wigfield & Eccles, 2002b).

We can think of task value as having four components: importance, interest, utility, and cost (Eccles & Wigfield, 1985; Eccles, Wigfield, & Schiefele, 1998). Importance or attainment value is the significance of doing well on the task; this is closely tied to the needs of the individual (the need to be well-liked, to be regarded as athletic, etc.). For instance, if someone has a strong need to appear smart and believes that receiving a high grade on a test demonstrates that he or she is smart, then the test has high attainment value for that person. A second component is interest or intrinsic value. This is simply the enjoyment one receives from the activity itself. Some people like the experience of learning. Others enjoy the feeling of hard physical effort or the challenge of solving puzzles. Tasks also can have utility value; that is, they help us to achieve a short-term or long-term goal such as earning a degree. Finally, tasks have costs—negative consequences that might follow from doing the task, such as not having time to do other things or looking awkward as you perform the task.

You see from our discussion of task value that personal and environmental influences on motivation interact constantly. The task we ask students to accomplish is an aspect of the environment; it is external to the student. But the value of accomplishing the task is bound up with the internal needs, beliefs, and goals of the individual. Because task value has to do with choices, positive values toward academic tasks can be life-changing because, for example, choices about which courses to take in high school and what sort of education to pursue after high school affect career and life opportunities (Durik, Vida, & Eccles, 2006).

Academic tasks The work a student must accomplish, including the content covered and the mental operations required.

Importance/attainment value The importance of doing well on a task; how success on the task meets personal needs.

Interest or intrinsic value The enjoyment a person receives from a task.

Utility value The contribution of a task to meeting one's goals.

Authentic task Tasks that have some connection to real-life problems the students will face outside the classroom.

Authentic Tasks. Recently, there has been a great deal written about the use of authentic tasks in teaching. An authentic task is one that has some connection to the real-life problems and situations that students will face outside the classroom, both now and in the future. If you ask students to memorize definitions they will never use, to learn the material only because it will appear on the test, or to repeat work they already understand, then there can be little motivation to learn. But if

TABLE 11.7 **The TARGET Model for Supporting Student Motivation to Learn**

Teachers make decisions in many areas that can influence motivation to learn. The TARGET acronym highlights task, autonomy, recognition, grouping, evaluation, and time.

TARGET Area	Focus	Objectives	Examples of Possible Strategies
Task	How learning tasks are structured—what the student is asked to do	Enhance intrinsic attractiveness of learning tasks Make learning meaningful	Encourage instruction that relates to students' backgrounds and experience Avoid payment (monetary and other) for attendance, grades, or achievement Foster goal setting and self-regulation
Autonomy/ responsibility	Student participation in learning/school decisions	Provide optimal freedom for students to make choices and to take responsibility	Provide alternatives when creating assignments Ask for student comments on school life—and take them seriously Encourage students to take initiative and to evaluate their own learning Establish leadership opportunities for *all* students
Recognition	The nature and use of recognition and reward in the school setting	Provide opportunities for all students to be recognized for learning Recognize *progress* in goal attainment Recognize challenge seeking and innovation	Foster "personal best" awards Reduce emphasis on "honour rolls" Recognize and publicize a wide range of students' school-related activities
Grouping	The organization of school learning and experiences	Build an environment of acceptance and appreciation of all students Broaden the range of social interaction, particularly of students at risk for failing Enhance social skills development	Provide opportunities for cooperative learning, problem solving, and decision making Encourage multiple group membership to increase range of peer interaction Eliminate ability-grouped classes
Evaluation	The nature and use of evaluation and assessment procedures	Establish grading and reporting processes Use practices associated with standardized testing Define goals and standards	Reduce emphasis on social comparisons of achievement Give students opportunities to improve their performance (e.g., study skills, classes) Establish grading and reporting practices that highlight student progress in learning Encourage student participation in the evaluation process
Time	The scheduling of the school day	Provide opportunities for extended and significant student involvement in learning tasks Allow the learning task and student needs to dictate scheduling	Allow students to *progress at their own rate* whenever possible Encourage flexibility in the scheduling of learning experiences Give teachers greater control over time usage through, for example, block scheduling

Source: From "Reinventing Schools for Early Adolescents: Emphasizing Task Goals," by M. L. Maehr and E. M. Anderman, *The Elementary School Journal, 93.5*, pp. 604–605. Copyright © 1993 by The University of Chicago Press. Adapted with permission.

the tasks are authentic, students are more likely to see the genuine utility value of the work and are also more likely to find the tasks meaningful and interesting. **Problem-based learning** (Chapter 9) is one example of the use of authentic tasks in teaching. For example, a physics teacher might use skateboarding activities as a basis for problems and examples, knowing that skateboarding is an authentic task for many of her students (Anderman & Anderman, 2009). For examples of two very different authentic tasks created for younger students, compare the approaches, described by

Problem-based learning Methods that provide students with realistic problems that don't necessarily have correct answers.

Anderman and Anderman (2009), of the following two teachers who have taught nearly identical introductory lessons about halves and quarters:

> Mrs. Byrnes . . . divides her students into groups of three and provides each group with two Twinkies and a plastic knife. She then tells each group to cut one Twinkie into two equal-size pieces and the other Twinkie into four equal-size pieces. She then tells each group that they are to use the Twinkie pieces to demonstrate whether one-half (1/2) or three-fourths (3/4) is the bigger fraction. Mrs. Byrnes then visits each group, and the members must explain their work to her. When they are correct, they get to eat the Twinkies.
>
> Mr. Fletcher . . . provides each student with a worksheet with a few simple questions that are designed to help the students to learn about fractions. For these questions, the students are supposed to imagine that they have several pieces of paper and that they cut the paper with scissors into various quantities (e.g., they cut one paper into four equal size pieces, they cut another paper into two equal-size pieces). The students are then asked to demonstrate whether one-half (1/2) or three-fourths (3/4) is the bigger fraction. They then have to write down their answer, along with a brief explanation. (p. 9)

The students in Mrs. Byrnes's class were involved in a more authentic (and tasty) task involving cutting and dividing food, cooperating with others, and enjoying the fruits (or Twinkies) of their labour. Mrs. Byrnes's students also had to figure out how to share two halves and four quarters equally among three people—advanced cooperation.

Supporting Autonomy and Recognizing Accomplishment

The second area in the TARGET model involves how much choice and autonomy students are allowed. Providing choice to students in schools is not the norm. Children and adolescents spend literally thousands of hours in schools where other people decide what will happen. Yet we know that self-determination and a sense of internal locus of causality are critical to maintaining intrinsic motivation (Reeve, Nix, & Hamm, 2003). What can teachers do to support student choice without creating chaos?

Supporting Choices. Offering students choices isn't always motivating. Choices should provide a range of selections that allow students to follow their interests and to pick an option that is important and relevant to them (Katz & Assor, 2007). But beware of giving students too many choices. Like totally unguided discovery or aimless discussions, unstructured or unguided choices can be counterproductive for learning (Garner, 1998). For example, Dyson (1997) found that children become anxious and upset when directed by teachers to draw or write about anything they want in any way they want. Dyson says that students see this *unbounded choice* as a "scary void." According to Anita, graduate students in her classes find it disconcerting if they are asked to design a final project that will determine their grade, just as Anita would experience feelings of panic if she were asked to give a lecture on "whatever you want."

The alternative to unbounded choice is *bounded choice*—giving students a range of options that set valuable tasks for them, but also allow them to follow personal interests. The balance must be just right: "too much autonomy is bewildering and too little is boring" (Guthrie et al., 1998, p. 185). Guthrie describes how students in a grade 5 class were able to exercise their choices about researching and writing. The class was studying the life cycle of the Monarch butterfly. Each child worked in a heterogeneous team and each team was given a chrysalis to observe as it grew. The class had organized a library of multi-level expository books, trade books, literary books, reference books, maps, electronic databases, and other resources. In this case, the teacher had taught specific skills that would be needed—using an index and table of contents, setting goals, and writing summaries—but the students were able to choose the topics and appropriate resources for crafting their own chapter.

Calvin and Hobbes **by Bill Watterson**

Students can provide input into work partners, seating arrangements, how to display work, or class rules. But the most important kind of autonomy support teachers can provide probably is cognitive autonomy support—giving students opportunities to discuss different cognitive strategies for learning, approaches to solving problems, or positions on an issue (Stefanou, Perencevich, DiCinto, & Turner, 2004). Students also can exercise autonomy about how they receive feedback from the teacher or from classmates. Figure 11.1 describes a strategy called "Check It Out," in which students specify the skills that they want to be evaluated in a particular assignment. Over the course of a unit, all the skills need to be "checked out," but students can choose when each one should be evaluated.

Recognizing Accomplishment. The third TARGET area is *recognition* for accomplishments. Students should be recognized for improving their own "personal best," for tackling difficult tasks, for persistence, and for creativity—not just for performing better than others. In Chapter 6 we noted that giving students rewards for activities that they already enjoy can undermine intrinsic motivation. But nothing in teaching is simple. At times, praise can have paradoxical effects. For example, if two students succeed and the teacher praises only one of them, the message, to other children at least, may be that the praised student had less ability and had to work harder to succeed, thus earning praise. So students may use the teacher's praise or criticism as cues about capabilities—praise means I'm not very smart, so when I succeed, I deserve recognition. Criticism means my teacher thinks I'm smart and could do better (Stipek, 2002).

What sort of recognition leads to engagement? One answer comes from a study by Ruth Butler (1987). Students in grades 5 and 6 were given interesting divergent thinking tasks followed by either individual personalized comments, standardized praise ("very good"), grades, or no feedback. Interest, performance, attributions to effort, and task involvement were higher after personalized comments. Ego-involved motivation (the desire to look good or to do better than others) was greater after grades and standard praise.

FIGURE 11.1

Student Autonomy: Check It Out

Using this technique to support student autonomy, the teacher decides on a set of skills that will be developed over the course of a unit, but the student decides which skill(s) will be evaluated on any given assignment. Over the course of the unit, all the skills need to be "checked out" by the teacher; however, the decision about which skills to "check out" is determined by the student. This student has indicated that she wants the teacher to "check out" her creativity and use of verb tense.

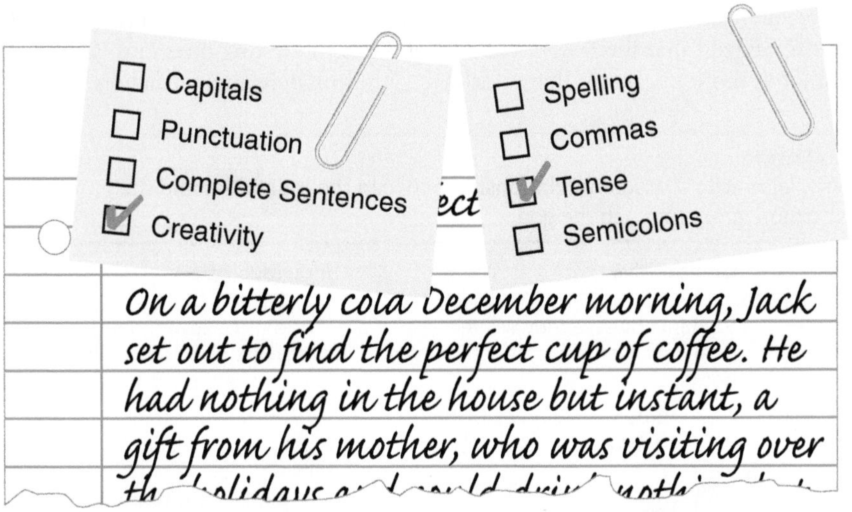

Source: From James P. Raffini, *150 Ways to Increase Intrinsic Motivation to the Classroom*. Published by Allyn and Bacon, Boston, MA. Copyright © 1996 by Pearson Education. Reprinted/Adapted by permission of the publisher.

Grouping, Evaluation, and Time

You may remember a teacher who made you want to work hard—someone who made a subject come alive. Or you may remember how many hours you spent practising as a member of a team, an orchestra, a choir, or a theatre troupe. If you do, then you understand the motivational power of relationships with other people.

Grouping and Goal Structures. Motivation can be greatly influenced by the ways we relate to the other people who are also involved in accomplishing a particular goal. Johnson and Johnson (1999a) have labelled this interpersonal factor the **goal structure** of the task. There are three such structures: cooperative, competitive, and individualistic, as shown in Table 11.8.

When the task involves complex learning and problem-solving skills, cooperation leads to higher achievement than competition, especially for students with lower abilities. Students learn to set attainable goals and to negotiate. They become more altruistic. The interaction with peers that students enjoy so much becomes a part of the learning process. The result? The need for belonging described by Maslow is more likely to be met and motivation increases (Stipek, 2002; Webb & Palincsar, 1996). There are many approaches to peer learning or group learning, as you saw in Chapter 10. For example, to encourage motivation with a cooperative goal structure, form reading groups based on student interests instead of abilities, and change the composition of the groups every month (Anderman & Anderman, 2009). Bette Chambers and Philip Abrami (1991) of Concordia University in Montreal found that members of successful teams learned more than members of unsuccessful teams. Successful team members were also happier about the outcome and rated their ability higher than members of losing teams. For low-achieving students who tend to be anxious, failure-accepting, or helpless, being a member of a losing team could make matters worse. Chambers and Abrami suggest experimenting with cooperation both within and between teams. For example, consider recognizing the whole class, if each team reaches a specified level of learning.

Evaluation. The greater the emphasis on competitive evaluation and grading, the more students will focus on performance goals rather than mastery. And low-achieving students who have little hope of either performing well or mastering the task may simply want to get it over with (Brophy, 2005). One study of grade 1 students found that low-achieving students made up answers, filled in the page with patterns, or copied from other students, just to get through their seatwork. As one student said when she finished a word/definition matching exercise, "I don't know what it means, but I did it" (Anderson, Brubaker, Alleman-Brooks, & Duffy, 1985, p. 132). On closer examination, the researchers found that the work was much too hard for these students, which led the students to connect words and definitions at random.

How can teachers prevent students from simply focusing on the grade or doing the work "just to get finished"? The most obvious answer is to de-emphasize grades and to emphasize learning in the class. Students need to understand the value of the work. Instead of saying, "You will need to know this for the test," tell students how the information will be useful in solving problems they want to solve. Suggest that the lesson will answer some interesting questions. Communicate that understanding is more important than finishing. Unfortunately, many teachers do not follow this

Goal structure The way students relate to others who are also working toward a particular goal.

TABLE 11.8 Different Goal Structures

Each goal structure is associated with a different relationship between the individual and the group. This relationship influences the motivation to reach the goal.

	Cooperative	Competitive	Individualistic
Definition	Students believe their goal is attainable only if other students will also reach the goal.	Students believe they will reach their goal if, and only if, other students do not reach the goal.	Students believe that their own attempt to reach a goal is not related to other students' attempts to reach the goal.
Examples	Team victories—each player wins only if all the team members win: a relay race, a quilting bee, a barn raising, a symphony, a play.	Golf tournament, singles tennis match, a 100-metre dash, class valedictorian.	Lowering your handicap in golf, jogging, learning a new language, enjoying a museum, losing or gaining weight, stopping cigarette smoking.

Source: Based on *Learning Together and Alone: Cooperation, Competition, and Individualization* (5th ed.), by D. Johnson & R. Johnson. Published by Allyn and Bacon, Boston, MA. Copyright © 1999 by Pearson Education.

advice. Jere Brophy (1988) reports that when he and several colleagues spent about 100 hours observing how six teachers introduced their lessons, they found that most introductions were routine oriented, apologetic, or unenthusiastic. The introductions described procedures, made threats, emphasized finishing, or promised tests on the material.

One way to emphasize learning rather than grades is to use self-evaluation. This strategy also supports autonomy. Figure 11.2 illustrates a self-evaluation and goal-planning sheet that could be adapted for use in almost any grade.

Time. Most experienced teachers know that there is too much work and not enough time to complete it in the school day. Even if they become engrossed in a project, students must stop and turn their attention to another class when the bell rings or when the teacher's schedule indicates it's time to move on to a new subject. Furthermore, students must progress as a group. If particular individuals can move faster or if they need more time, they may still have to follow the pace of the whole group. So scheduling often interferes with motivation by making students move faster or slower than would be appropriate or by interrupting their involvement in the task. It is difficult to develop persistence and a sense of self-efficacy when students are not allowed to stick with a challenging activity.

As a teacher, will you be able to make time for engaged and persistent learning? Some elementary classrooms have *DEAR* time—Drop Everything And Read—to provide extended periods when everyone, even the teacher, reads. Some middle schools and high schools use block scheduling in which teachers work in teams to plan larger blocks of class time.

We can see how these motivational elements come together in real classrooms. Sara Dolezal and her colleagues observed and interviewed grade 3 teachers in eight Catholic schools and determined

FIGURE 11.2 **Self-Evaluation and Goals Planning**

By completing this form, students evaluate their own work in relation to their own goals and set new goals for the future.

Name ______________________ Advisor ______________

Subject ______________________ Quarter ______________

1. Self-Evaluation:

a. How am I doing in this course? ______________________

b. What difficulties have I been having? ______________________

c. How much time and effort have I been spending in this course?

____

d. Do I need more help in this course? ________ If yes, how have I tried to get it?

2. Academic Goal:

a. My goal to achieve before the end of the quarter is ______________

b. I want to work on this goal because ______________________

c. I will achieve this goal by ______________________

3. Behaviour or Social Goal:

a. My goal to achieve before the end of the quarter is ______________

b. I want to work on this goal because ______________________

c. I will achieve this goal by ______________________

Variations

Advisors may choose to use this activity at the beginning of each quarter and adapt self-evaluation and goal-planning sheets to specific grade levels. Follow-up conferences are also useful for helping students evaluate their plans.

Source: From James P. Raffini, *150 Ways to Increase Intrinsic Motivation to the Classroom*. Published by Allyn & Bacon, Boston, MA. Copyright © 1996 by Pearson Education. Adapted by permission of the publisher.

whether their students were low, moderate, or high in their level of motivation (Dolezal et al., 2003). Table 11.9 summarizes the dramatic differences in these classrooms between strategies that support motivation and those that undermine it. Students in the low-engagement classes were restless and chatty as they faced their easy, undemanding seatwork. The classrooms were bare, unattractive, and filled with management problems. Instruction was disorganized. The class atmosphere was generally negative. The moderately engaged classrooms were organized to be "student friendly," with reading areas, group work areas, posters adorning the walls, and student artwork decorations. The teachers were warm and caring, and they connected lessons to students' background knowledge. Management routines were smooth and organized, and the class atmosphere was positive. The teachers were effective at catching student attention and encouraging students to become more self-regulating, but the teachers in moderately engaging classrooms had trouble holding attention, probably because the tasks students were given were regarded as too easy. Highly engaging teachers provided all the positive qualities of student-friendly classrooms—positive atmosphere, smooth management routines, support for student self-regulation, and effective instruction—but they added more challenging tasks along with the support the students needed to succeed. These excellent motivators did not rely on one or two approaches to motivate their students; they applied a large repertoire of strategies, such as those that appear in Table 11.9.

TABLE 11.9 **Strategies That Support and Undermine Motivation in the Classroom**

Strategies That Support Motivation	
Strategy	**Example**
Deliver messages of accountability and set high expectations.	The teacher asks students to submit some assignments to their parents for the parents' review and signatures.
Communicate the importance of work.	The teacher says, "We need to check our work for at least 1 minute, which means looking over it carefully."
Provide clear goals and directions.	The teacher explains exactly how the students should separate into groups and submit their nominations for their favourite book.
Establish connections across the curriculum.	The teacher relates the concept of ratios in math to the compare-and-contrast skills used when reading.
Provide opportunities to learn about and to practise dramatic arts.	After studying about historical figures, students write and produce their own plays.
Attribute learning to students' effort.	During a word game, the teacher asks a student, "Did you study last night?" The student nods. The teacher says, "See how it helps?"
Encourage students to be risk-takers.	The teacher says, "I need a new shining face. Someone I haven't called on yet. I need a risk-taker."
Use games and play to reinforce concepts or review the material.	During a math lesson on the concept of balance, students spend 5 minutes weighing the favourite toy they were asked to bring in that day.
Build connections between home and school.	As part of the math science unit, a teacher organizes a recycling activity that asks families to keep a chart of everything they recycle in a week.
Provide multiple representations for learning a task.	The teacher uses four ways to teach multiplication: "magic multipliers," sing-along multiplication facts, whole-class flash card review, and the "Around-the-World" game.
Use positive classroom management, praise, and private reprimands appropriately.	The teacher says, "Thumbs up when you are ready to work. Table 7 has thumbs up. I like the way table 7 is waiting patiently."
Stimulate creative thought.	The teacher says, "We are going to use our imaginations today. We are going to take a trip to an imaginary theatre in our minds."
Provide opportunities for students to make choices.	Students can choose to use prompts for their journal writing or they can pick their own topic.
Communicate to students that they can handle challenging tasks.	The teacher says, "This is hard stuff and you are doing great. I know adults who have trouble with this."
Value students and communicate caring.	The teacher allows a new student to sit with a "buddy" for the day.

continued

TABLE 11.9 **Strategies That Support and Undermine Motivation in the Classroom** (*Continued*)

A Few Strategies That Undermine Motivation	
Strategy	**Example**
Attribute students' learning to intellect rather than to effort.	When students remark during a lesson, "I'm stupid" or "I'm a dork," the teacher says nothing, then replies, "Let's ask someone who is smart."
Emphasize competition rather than working together.	The teacher conducts a poetry contest in which students read poems to the class and the class members then hold up cards with scores rating how well each student performed.
Post few displays of student work around the classroom.	The teacher uses public bulletin boards for posting grades.
Avoid scaffolding when teaching students a new skill.	The teacher is loud and critical when students have trouble: "Just look back in the glossary and don't miss it because you are too lazy to look it up."
Provide ineffective or negative feedback.	The teacher asks, "Does everyone understand?" A few students say yes and the teacher moves on.
Miss opportunities to establish real-world connections when teaching lessons.	The day before Remembrance Day, the teacher reminds students about where to buy poppies without discussing the origin and meaning of wearing poppies on this national holiday.
Assign easy tasks for students.	The teacher provides easy work and "fun" activities that teach students very little.
Encourage a negative class atmosphere.	The teacher says, "Excuse me, I said page number 135. If you follow and listen, you would know."
Use punitive classroom management techniques.	The teacher threatens to give bad grades to students who do not look up words in the glossary.
Assign work that is much too difficult for students.	The teacher assigns independent math work that only one or two students can complete.
Adopt a very slow teaching pace.	The teacher sets the pace to accommodate the slowest students—others finish and have nothing to do.
Emphasize the importance of finishing work more than learning.	The teacher communicates that the purpose is to finish the vocabulary test, not to learn the words or to use the vocabulary.
Design a sparse, unattractive classroom.	The teacher does not decorate bulletin boards or post maps, charts, and other displays of student work.
Plan lessons poorly.	The teacher discovers during a lesson that not enough handouts are available, forcing the teacher to establish larger instead of smaller work groups.
Punish students in front of their peers.	The teacher asks all students to stand, and then calls out a list of students who finished the assignment and can therefore be seated. The teacher proceeds to give a public lecture on responsibility to the students left standing.

Source: Adapted from "How do nine third-grade teachers motivate their students?" by S. E. Dolezal, L. M. Welsh, M. Pressley, & M. Vincent. *Elementary School Journal*, 2003, 103, pp. 247–248.

DIVERSITY AND CONVERGENCES IN MOTIVATION TO LEARN

We have seen that motivation to learn grows from the individual's needs, goals, interests, emotions, beliefs, and attributions in interaction with the tasks set, autonomy and recognition provided, grouping structures, evaluation procedures, and time allowed. This leads to great diversity in individual motivation.

Diversity: Motivation to Learn

Because students differ in terms of language, culture, economic privilege, personality, knowledge, and experience, they will also differ in their needs, goals, interests, emotions, and beliefs. Teachers can encourage motivation to learn by taking this diversity into account using TARGET— designing

MyEducationLab
Go to the Teacher Talks section of Chapter 11 of MyEducationLab and watch a video of Buffy Murphy, 2007 Teacher of the Year from South Carolina, explaining how she motivates all of her students.

tasks, supporting autonomy, recognizing accomplishments, grouping, making evaluations, and managing time. Take interest, for example. Embedding student writing tasks in cultural contexts is one way to *catch* and *hold* situational interest (Alderman, 2004; Bergin, 1999). For example, in a study conducted by Rueda and Moll, when Latin American immigrant students in junior-high classes moved from writing using worksheets and standard assignments to writing about such topics as immigration, bilingualism, and gang life—factors that were important to them and to their families—the students' papers became longer and the writing quality increased (Rueda & Moll, 1994).

Language is a central factor in students' connections with the school. When bilingual students are encouraged to draw on both English and their heritage language, motivation and participation can increase. Robert Jimenez (2000) found in his study of Latin American bilingual students that successful readers saw reading as a process of making sense; they used both of their languages to understand the material. For instance, successful readers might look for Spanish word parts in English words to help them translate. Less-successful students had a different goal. They believed that reading just meant saying the words correctly in English. It is likely their interest and sense of efficacy for reading in English would be less, too.

Encouraging students to capitalize on their cultural knowledge can increase motivation and learning in school. But this doesn't happen often enough. "The lack of congruence between students' life experiences and instruction in most schools has been well documented, especially for low income students, students of color, and English language learners" (Committee on Increasing High School Students' Engagement and Motivation to Learn, 2004, p. 66). Review Chapter 5 for ideas about how to build lessons on students' funds of cultural knowledge.

Convergences: Strategies to Encourage Motivation

Until four basic conditions are met for every student and in every classroom, no motivational strategies will succeed. First, the classroom must be relatively organized and free from constant interruptions and disruptions. (Chapter 12 will give you the information you need to make sure this requirement is met.) Second, the teacher must be a patient, supportive person who never embarrasses the students because they made mistakes. Everyone in the class should see mistakes as opportunities for learning (Clifford, 1990, 1991). Third, the work must be challenging, but reasonable. If work is too easy or too difficult, students will have little motivation to learn. They will focus on finishing the task, not on learning. Finally, the learning tasks must be authentic, and what makes a task authentic is influenced by the students' culture, as we have seen (Bergin, 1999; Brophy & Kher, 1986; Stipek, 1993).

Once these four basic conditions are met, the influences on students' motivation to learn in a particular situation can be summarized in four questions: Can I succeed at this task? Do I want to succeed? What do I need to do to succeed? Do I belong? (Committee on Increasing High School Students' Engagement and Motivation to Learn, 2004; Eccles & Wigfield, 1985). We want students to have confidence in their ability so they will approach learning with energy and enthusiasm. We want them to see the value of the tasks involved and to work to learn, not just to get the grade or to complete the task. We want students to believe that success will come when they apply effective learning strategies instead of believing that their only option is to use self-defeating, failure-avoiding, face-saving strategies. When things get difficult, we want students to stay focused on the task, and not to become so worried about failure that they "freeze." And we want students to feel as though they belong in school—that their teachers and classmates care about them and can be trusted.

Can I Do It? Building Confidence and Positive Expectations. No amount of encouragement or "cheerleading" will substitute for real accomplishment. To ensure genuine progress, use these strategies:

1. *Begin work at the students' level and move forward in small steps.* The pace should be brisk, but not so fast that students are forced to move to the next step before they understand the one they are working on. This may require assigning different tasks to different students. One possibility is to have very easy and very difficult questions on every test and assignment, so all students can feel both successful and challenged. When grades are required, make sure all the students in the class have a chance to make at least a C if they work hard.

2. *Make sure learning goals are clear, specific, and possible to reach in the near future.* When long-term projects are planned, break the work into subgoals and then help students to mark their progress toward the long-term goal. If possible, give students a range of goals at different levels of difficulty and let them choose.
3. *Stress self-comparison, not comparison with others.* Help students to see the progress they are making by showing them how to use self-regulation strategies such as those described in Chapter 10. Give students specific feedback and corrections. Tell students what they are doing correctly as well as what they are doing incorrectly and describe why some of their actions are incorrect. Periodically, give students a question or a problem that they once regarded as difficult but will now find easy. Point out to them how much they have improved.
4. *Communicate to students that academic ability is improvable* and specific to the task at hand. In other words, remind students that just because they find a subject like algebra difficult doesn't necessarily mean that geometry or English classes will also be difficult. Don't undermine your efforts to stress the importance of improvement by displaying only the papers that received a perfect or near perfect grade on the classroom bulletin board.
5. *Model good problem solving,* especially when you plan to try several approaches. Students need to see that learning is often not smooth and error-free, even for the teacher.

Do I Want to Do It? Seeing the Value of Learning. Teachers can use intrinsic and extrinsic motivation strategies to help students to see the value of the learning task.

Attainment and Intrinsic Value. To establish attainment value, we must connect the learning task with the needs of the students. First, it must be possible for students to meet their needs for safety, belonging, and achievement in school. The classroom should not be perceived as a frightening or lonely place. Many students are quietly wounded by their teachers' words or by school practices that embarrass, label, or demean. For example, Kirsten Olson (2008) describes Marie, a usually outgoing grade 8 student who became sad and silent in math classes after her advanced math teacher told her that she "wasn't well equipped" and couldn't keep up with her peers in advanced math. "Marie now dreads the many years of math classes ahead of her and rushes through her nightly math homework, which she finds boring and difficult" (p. 46). Second, we must make it clear that both women and men can become high achievers in all subjects and that no subjects are the territory of only one sex. It is not "unfeminine" to be strong in mathematics, science, car mechanics, or sports. It is not "unmasculine" to be a high achiever in subjects like literature, art, music, or French.

There are many strategies for encouraging *intrinsic* (interest) motivation. Several of the following are taken from Brophy (1988).

1. *Tie class activities to student interests* in sports, music, current events, pets, common problems or conflicts with family and friends, fads, television and cinema personalities, or other significant features of their lives (Schiefele, 1991). But be sure you know what you are talking about. For example, if you use a verse from a popular song to make a point, ensure that you have some knowledge of the music and the performer. When possible, give students topic choices when they are expected to write research papers or to complete reading assignments, so that they can follow their own interests.
2. *Arouse curiosity.* Point out puzzling discrepancies between students' beliefs and the facts. For example, Stipek (1993) describes a teacher who asked her grade 5 class if "people" lived on some of the other planets. When the students said yes, the teacher then asked if people need oxygen to breathe. Because the students had just learned this fact, they responded yes to this question also. Then the teacher told them there is no oxygen in the atmosphere of the other planets. This surprising discrepancy between what the children knew about people's need for oxygen and what they believed about life on other planets led to a rousing discussion of the atmospheres of other planets, the kinds of beings that could survive in these atmospheres, and so on. A straight lecture on the atmosphere of the planets might have put the students to sleep, but the discussion the teacher led stimulated genuine interest in the subject.
3. *Make the learning task fun.* Many lessons can be taught through simulations or games, as you saw in the *Point/Counterpoint* box on making learning fun. Used appropriately so that the activity connects with learning, lessons that involve simulations or games can be very worthwhile and fun, too.

4. *Make use of novelty and familiarity*. Don't overuse a few teaching approaches or motivational strategies. We all need some variety. Varying the goal structures of tasks (cooperative, competitive, individualistic) can help, as can using different teaching media. When the material being covered in class is abstract or unfamiliar to students, try to connect it to something they know and understand. For example, talk about the size of a large area, such as the Acropolis in Athens, in terms of football fields. Brophy (1988) describes one teacher who read a brief passage from *Spartacus* to personalize the unit on slavery in the ancient world.

Instrumental Value. Sometimes it is difficult to encourage intrinsic motivation, and so teachers must rely on the utility or "instrumental" value of tasks: It is important for students to learn many skills because they will be needed in more advanced classes and in life outside school.

1. When the connections are not obvious, you should *explain the connections to your students*. Jeanette Abi-Nader (1991) describes one project, the PLAN program, that makes these connections come alive for Hispanic high school students. The three major strategies used in the program to focus students' attention on their future include: (1) working with mentors and models—often PLAN graduates—who give advice about how to choose courses, budget time, take notes, and deal with cultural differences in college; (2) storytelling about the achievements of former students—sometimes the college term papers of former students are posted on PLAN bulletin boards; and (3) filling the classroom with future-oriented talk such as "When you go to college, you will encounter these situations" or, "You're at a parents' meeting—you want a good education for your children—and you are the ones who must speak up; that's why it is important to learn public speaking skills" (p. 548).
2. In some situations, teachers can *provide incentives and rewards for learning* (see Chapter 6). Remember, though, that giving rewards when students are already interested in the activity may undermine intrinsic motivation.
3. Use *ill-structured problems and authentic tasks* in teaching. Connect problems in school to "real" problems outside school, such as buying your first car, weighing claims and making decisions about mobile phone plans, or writing a persuasive letter to a potential employer.

What Do I Need to Do to Succeed? Staying Focused on the Task. When students encounter difficulties, as they must if they are asked to work at a challenging level, they need to keep their attention on the task. If the focus shifts to worries about performance, fear of failure, or concern with looking smart, then motivation to learn is lost. Here are some ideas for keeping the focus on learning:

1. *Give students frequent opportunities to respond* through questions and answers, short assignments, or demonstrations of skills. Make sure you check the students' answers so you can correct problems quickly. You don't want students to practise errors too long. Keep in mind, too, that some computer learning programs give students the immediate feedback they need to correct errors before they become habits.
2. When possible, *create activities in which students are asked to create a finished product*. Students are usually more persistent and focused on the task when the end is in sight. Furthermore, we all have experienced the power of the need for closure. For example, Anita often begins a house-painting project thinking she will work for just an hour or so and then finds herself still painting hours later because she wants to see the finished product.
3. *Avoid heavy emphasis on grades and competition*. An emphasis on grades forces students to be ego-involved rather than task-involved. Anxious students are especially hard hit by highly competitive evaluation.
4. *Reduce the task's risk without oversimplifying the task*. When tasks are risky (failure is likely and the consequences of failing are grave), student motivation suffers. For example, when assigning difficult, complex, or ambiguous tasks, provide students with plenty of time, support, resources, help, and the chance to revise or improve their work.
5. *Model motivation to learn for your students*. Talk about your interest in the subject and how you deal with difficult learning problems.

6. *Teach the particular learning tactics* that students will need to master the material being studied. Show students how to learn and remember so they won't be forced to fall back on self-defeating strategies or rote memory.

Do I Belong in This Classroom? This last question will take more than a page or two to address, so we have devoted a large part of the next chapter (Chapter 12) to the notion of creating learning communities. In the meantime, bear in mind that the support of families can be helpful as you design learning strategies for your students. The *Family and Community Partnerships Guidelines* box provides some suggestions about how to involve students' families in fostering motivation to learn.

FAMILY AND COMMUNITY PARTNERSHIPS

GUIDELINES: Motivation to Learn

Understand the goals that families may set for your students.

EXAMPLES

1. In an informal setting, such as around the coffee or snack table, meet with families individually or in small groups to listen to how they describe goals they set for their children.
2. Mail out questionnaires or send response cards home with students, asking parents what skills they believe their children most need to work on. Pick one goal for each child and develop a plan for working toward the goal both inside and outside school. Share the plan with the children's families and then ask the parents to send you their feedback on the effectiveness of the learning strategy.

Identify student and family interests that can be related to student goals.

EXAMPLES

1. Ask a member of a student's family to share a skill or hobby in the classroom.
2. Identify "family favourites"—favourite foods, music, vacations, sports, activities, hymns, movies, games, snacks, recipes, and memories. Tie class lessons to these popular interests.

Give families a way track their child's progress toward goals.

EXAMPLES

1. Provide simple "progress charts" or goal cards that families can post on the refrigerator and that the child can use to track progress toward a specific goal.
2. Ask for parents' or caregivers' feedback (and mean it!) about your effectiveness as a teacher in helping their children increase motivation to learn.

Work with families to build their children's confidence and positive expectations.

EXAMPLES

1. Avoid comparing one child to another during conferences and discussions with family members.
2. Ask family members to highlight the strong points of a particular homework project you assigned. For example, parents could be asked to attach a note to completed homework assignments describing the three most effective aspects of the homework and one element that could be improved.

Make families partners in demonstrating the value of learning to students.

EXAMPLES

1. Invite family members to the class to demonstrate how they use mathematics or writing in their work.
2. Involve parents or caregivers in identifying skills and knowledge that can be applied at home and would prove helpful to the family immediately. For example, ask students to keep careful records about service agencies, to write letters of complaint to department stores or landlords, or to research vacation destinations.

Provide resources for families for building skill and will to learn in their children.

EXAMPLES

1. Provide family members with simple strategies for helping their children to improve study skills.
2. Ask older students to participate in a "homework hotline" telephone network to help younger students.

Hold frequent celebrations of student learning and progress.

EXAMPLES

1. Invite families to attend a "museum" that your students created at the end of a unit (such as a unit on dinosaurs). After visiting the museum, families could then examine their child's portfolio for the unit.
2. Erect mini-exhibits of student work at local grocery stores, libraries, or community centres, so members of the community can participate in the celebration.

For more information on family partnerships and motivation, see **www.vanderbilt.edu/peabody/family-school/**.

SUMMARY TABLE

What Is Motivation? (pp. 377–381)

Define motivation. Motivation is an internal state that arouses, directs, and maintains behaviour. The study of motivation focuses on how and why people initiate actions directed toward specific goals, how long it takes them to get started in the activity, how intensively they are involved in the activity, how persistent they are in their attempts to reach these goals, and what they are thinking and feeling along the way.

What is the difference between intrinsic and extrinsic motivation? Intrinsic motivation is the natural tendency to seek out and conquer challenges as we pursue personal interests and exercise capabilities—it is motivation to do something when we don't have to. Extrinsic motivation is based on factors not related to the activity itself. We are not really interested in the activity for its own sake; we care only about what it will gain us.

How does locus of causality apply to motivation? The essential difference between intrinsic and extrinsic motivation is the person's reason for acting, that is, whether the locus of causality for the action is inside or outside the person. If the locus is internal, the motivation is intrinsic; if the locus is external, the motivation is extrinsic. Most motivation has elements of both. In fact, intrinsic and extrinsic motivation may be two separate tendencies—both can operate at the same time in a given situation.

What are the key factors in motivation according to a behavioural viewpoint? A humanistic viewpoint? A cognitive viewpoint? A social cognitive viewpoint? A sociocultural viewpoint? Behaviourists tend to emphasize extrinsic motivation caused by incentives, rewards, and punishment. Humanistic views stress the intrinsic motivation created by the need for personal growth, fulfillment, and self-determination. Cognitive views stress a person's active search for meaning, understanding, and competence, and the power of the individual's attributions and interpretations. Social cognitive theories take into account both the behaviourists' concern with the consequences of behaviour and the cognitivists' interest in the impact of individual beliefs and expectations. Many influential social cognitive explanations of motivation can be characterized as expectancy × value theories. Sociocultural views emphasize legitimate engaged participation and identity within a community.

What are expectancy × value theories? Expectancy × value theories suggest that motivation to reach a goal is the product of our expectations for success and the value of the goal to us. If either is zero, our motivation is zero also.

What is legitimate peripheral participation? Legitimate peripheral participation means that beginners are genuinely involved in the work of the group, even if their abilities are undeveloped and their contributions are small. The identities of the novice and the expert are bound up in their participation in the community. They are motivated to learn the values and practices of the community to keep their identity as community members.

Motivation An internal state that arouses, directs, and maintains behaviour.

Intrinsic motivation Motivation associated with activities that are their own reward.

Extrinsic motivation Motivation created by external factors such as rewards and punishments.

Locus of causality The location—internal or external—of the cause of behaviour.

Reward An attractive object or event supplied as a consequence of a behaviour.

Incentive An object or event that encourages or discourages behaviour.

Humanistic interpretation Approach to motivation that emphasizes personal freedom, choice, self-determination, and striving for personal growth.

Expectancy × value theories Explanations of motivation that emphasize an individual's expectations for success combined with the value of the goal to him or her.

Sociocultural views of motivation Perspectives that emphasize participation, identities, and interpersonal relations within communities of practice.

Legitimate peripheral participation Genuine involvement in the work of the group, even if your abilities are undeveloped and contributions are small.

Needs (pp. 381–384)

Distinguish between deficiency needs and being needs in Maslow's theory. Maslow called four lower-level needs—survival, safety, belonging, and self-esteem—deficiency needs. When these needs are satisfied, the motivation for fulfilling them decreases. He labelled the three higher-level needs—intellectual achievement, aesthetic appreciation, and self-actualization—being needs. When they are met, a person's motivation increases to seek further fulfillment.

What are the basic needs that affect motivation and how does self-determination affect motivation? Self-determination theory suggests that motivation is affected by the need for competence, autonomy and control, and relatedness. When students experience self-determination, they are intrinsically motivated—they are more interested in their work, have a greater sense of self-esteem, and learn more. Whether students experience self-determination depends in part on if the teacher's communication with students provides information or seeks to control them. In addition, teachers must acknowledge the students' perspective, offer choices, provide rationales for limits, and treat poor performance as a problem to be solved rather than a target for criticism.

Hierarchy of needs Maslow's model of seven levels of human needs, from basic physiological requirements to the need for self-actualization.

Self-actualization Fulfilling one's potential.

Deficiency needs Maslow's four lower-level needs, which must be satisfied first.

Being needs Maslow's three higher-level needs, sometimes called growth needs.

Need for autonomy The desire to have our own wishes, rather than external rewards or pressures, determine our actions.

Cognitive evaluation theory Suggests that events affect motivation through the individual's perception of the events as controlling behaviour or providing information.

Goal Orientations (pp. 384–388)

What kinds of goals are the most motivating? Goals increase motivation if they are specific, moderately difficult, and able to be reached in the near future.

Describe mastery, performance, work-avoidant, and social goals. A mastery goal is the intention to gain knowledge and master skills, leading students to seek challenges and persist when they encounter difficulties. A performance goal is the intention to get good grades or to appear smarter or more capable than others, leading students to be preoccupied with themselves and how they appear (ego-involved learners). Students can approach or avoid these two kinds of goals—the problems are greatest with avoidance. Another kind of avoidance is evident with work-avoidant learners, who simply want to find the easiest way to handle the situation. Students with social goals can be supported or hindered in their learning, depending on the specific goal (i.e., have fun with friends or bring honour to the family).

What makes goal setting effective in the classroom? For goal setting to be effective in the classroom, students need accurate feedback about their progress toward goals and they must accept the goals set. Generally, students are more willing to adopt goals that seem realistic, reasonably difficult, and meaningful, and for which good reasons are given for the value of the goals.

Goal What an individual strives to accomplish.

Goal orientations Patterns of beliefs about goals related to achievement in school.

Mastery goal A personal intention to improve abilities and learn, no matter how performance suffers.

Task-involved learners Students who focus on mastering the task or solving the problem.

Performance goal A personal intention to seem competent or perform well in the eyes of others.

Ego-involved learners Students who focus on how well they perform and how they are judged by others.

Work-avoidant learners Students who don't want to learn or to look smart, but just want to avoid work.

Social goals A wide variety of needs and motives to be connected to others or part of a group.

Beliefs and Self-Perceptions (pp. 388–394)

What are epistemological beliefs and how do they affect motivation? Epistemological beliefs are ways of understanding how you think and learn. Individuals' epistemological beliefs can impact their approach to learning, their expectations of themselves and the work they do, and the extent to which they engage in academic tasks. Specifically, epistemological beliefs include your understanding of the structure, stability, and certainty of knowledge. A belief that knowledge can be organized into a grand scheme in which all things are related, for example, may lead students to try to connect all new knowledge with previous knowledge in a meaningful way. If the task proves excessively challenging, these students may believe the new information is not relevant to them or worth understanding.

How do beliefs about ability affect motivation? When people hold an entity theory of ability—that is, they believe that ability is fixed—they tend to set performance goals and strive to protect themselves from failure. When they believe ability is improvable (an incremental theory), however, they tend to set mastery goals and handle failure constructively.

What are the three dimensions of attributions in Weiner's theory? According to Weiner, most of the attributed causes for successes or failures can be characterized in terms of three dimensions: *locus* (location of the cause internal or external to the person), *stability* (whether the cause stays the same or can change), and *responsibility* (whether the person can control the cause). The greatest motivational problems arise when students attribute failures to stable, uncontrollable causes. These students may seem resigned to failure, depressed, helpless—what we generally call "unmotivated."

What is learned helplessness and what deficits does it cause? When people come to believe that the events and outcomes in their lives are mostly uncontrollable, they have developed learned helplessness, which is associated with three types of deficits: motivational, cognitive, and affective. Students who feel hopeless will be unmotivated and reluctant to attempt work. They miss opportunities to practise and improve skills and abilities, so they develop cognitive deficits and they often suffer from affective problems such as depression, anxiety, and listlessness.

How does self-worth influence motivation? Mastery-oriented students tend to value achievement and see ability as improvable, so they focus on mastery goals, take risks, and cope with failure constructively. A low sense of self-worth seems to be linked with the failure-avoiding and failure-accepting strategies intended to protect the individual from the consequences of failure. These strategies may seem to help in the short term, but are damaging to motivation and self-esteem in the long run.

Epistemological beliefs Beliefs about the structure, stability, and certainty of knowledge and how knowledge is best learned.

Entity view of ability Belief that ability is a fixed characteristic that cannot be changed.

Incremental view of ability Belief that ability is a set of skills that can be changed.

Attribution theories Descriptions of how individuals' explanations, justifications, and excuses influence their motivation and behaviour.

Self-efficacy A person's sense of being able to deal effectively with a particular task.

Learned helplessness The expectation, based on previous experiences involving lack of control, that all of one's efforts will lead to failure.

Mastery-oriented students Students who focus on learning goals because they value achievement and see ability as improvable.

Failure-avoiding students Students who avoid failure by sticking to what they know, by not taking risks, or by claiming not to care about their performance.

Self-handicapping When students engage in behaviour that blocks their own success in order to avoid testing their true ability.

Failure-accepting students Students who believe their failures are due to low ability and there is little they can do about it.

Interests, Curiosity, Emotions, and Anxiety (pp. 394–401)

How do interests and emotions affect learning? Learning and information processing are influenced by emotion. Students are more likely to pay attention to, learn, and remember events, images, and readings that provoke emotional responses or that are related to their personal interests. However, there are cautions in responding to students' interests. "Seductive details," interesting bits of information that are not central to the learning, can hinder learning.

How does curiosity affect learning and what can teachers do to stimulate curiosity in their subject area? Curiosity is the tendency toward interest in a variety of things. Students' curiosity is guided by their interests, and thus provides them with a self-driven motivation to explore new ideas and concepts. As a result, curiosity can be a powerful motivational tool that captures and maintains students' attention in school. Teachers can foster curiosity by tapping into students' interests, illustrating connections between course material and applications that may be interesting to students, and allowing students to find these connections for themselves. An example might include asking students to identify which simple machines are at work in a skateboard or rollercoaster.

What is the role of arousal in learning? There appears to be an optimum level of arousal for most activities. Generally speaking, a higher level of arousal is helpful on simple tasks, but lower levels of arousal are better for complex tasks. When arousal is too low, teachers can stimulate curiosity by pointing out gaps in knowledge or using variety in activities. Severe anxiety is an example of arousal that is too high for optimal learning.

How does anxiety interfere with learning? Anxiety can be the cause or the result of poor performance; it can interfere with attention to, learning of, and retrieval of information. Many anxious students need help in developing effective test-taking and study skills.

Arousal Physical and psychological reactions causing a person to feel alert, excited, or tense.

Anxiety General uneasiness; a feeling of tension.

Motivation to Learn in School: On TARGET (pp. 401–409)

Define motivation to learn. Teachers are interested in a particular kind of motivation—student motivation to learn. Student motivation to learn is both a trait and a state. It involves taking academic work seriously, trying to get the most from it, and applying appropriate learning strategies in the process.

What does TARGET stand for? TARGET is an acronym for the six areas where teachers make decisions that can influence student motivation to learn: the nature of the *task* that students are asked to do, the *autonomy* students are allowed in working, how students are *recognized* for their accomplishments, *grouping* practices, *evaluation* procedures, and the scheduling of *time* in the classroom.

How do tasks affect motivation? The tasks that teachers assign affect motivation. When students encounter tasks that are related to their interests, stimulate their curiosity, or are connected to real-life situations, they are more likely to be motivated to learn. Tasks can have attainment, intrinsic, or utility value for students. Attainment value is the importance to the student of succeeding. Intrinsic value is the enjoyment the student gets from the task. Utility value is determined by how much the task contributes to reaching short-term or long-term goals.

Distinguish between bounded and unbounded choices. Like totally unguided discovery or aimless discussions, unstructured or unbounded choices can be counterproductive for learning. The alternative is bounded choice—giving students a range of options that set out valuable tasks for them, but also allow them to follow personal interests. The balance must be just right so that students are not bewildered by too much choice or bored by too little room to explore.

How can recognition undermine motivation and a sense of self-efficacy? Recognition and reward in the classroom will support motivation to learn if the recognition is for personal progress rather than competitive victories. Praise and rewards should focus on students' growing competence. At times, praise can have paradoxical effects when students use the teacher's praise or criticism as cues about capabilities.

List three goal structures and distinguish among them. How students relate to their peers in the classroom is influenced by the goal structure of the activities. Goal structures can be competitive, individualistic, or cooperative. Cooperative goal structures can encourage motivation and increase learning, especially for low-achieving students.

How does evaluative climate affect goal setting? The more competitive the grading, the more students set performance goals and focus on "looking competent"—that is, they are more ego-involved. When the focus is on performing rather than learning, students often see the goal of classroom tasks as simply finishing, especially if the work is difficult.

What are some effects of time on motivation? In order to foster motivation to learn, teachers should be flexible in their use of time in the classroom. Students who are forced to move faster or slower than they should, or who are interrupted as they become involved in a project, are not likely to develop persistence for learning.

Motivation to learn The tendency to find academic activities meaningful and worthwhile and to try to benefit from them.

Academic tasks The work a student must accomplish, including the content covered and the mental operations required.

Importance/attainment value The importance of doing well on a task; how success on the task meets personal needs.

Interest or intrinsic value The enjoyment a person receives from a task.

Utility value The contribution of a task to meeting one's goals.

Authentic task Tasks that have some connection to real-life problems the students will face outside the classroom.

Problem-based learning Methods that provide students with realistic problems that don't necessarily have correct answers.

Goal structure The way students relate to others who are also working toward a particular goal.

TEACHERS' CASEBOOK

It is July and you have finally been offered a teaching position. The district wasn't your first choice, but job openings were really scarce, so you're pleased to have a job in your field. You are discovering that the teaching resources in your school are slim to none; the only resources are some aging texts and the workbooks that go with them. Every idea you have suggested for software, simulation games, visual aids, or other more active teaching materials has been met with the same response, "There's no money in the budget for that." As you look over the texts and workbooks, you wonder how the students could be anything but bored by them. To make matters worse, the texts look pretty high-level for your students. But the objectives in the workbooks are important. Besides, the provincial curriculum requires these units. Students will be tested on them in the province-wide assessments next spring required by the Ministry.

What Would *They* Do?

Here is how some practising teachers responded to the teaching situation described above.

Michael Landis

James R. Henderson Public School, Kingston, ON

As a teacher coming into a new classroom and grade, you'll encounter insufficient resources more often than not. Money will always be a problem with education, especially considering how quickly the world changes, making it hard to keep up with the most current resources. Yet in this case I believe the teacher is lucky. Many times you're faced with no resources at all—new or old! In this situation the teacher has a base to start from. Not having even that could be overwhelming.

The district school board uses these units to evaluate their students; therefore, they can be seen as an asset, a tool to prepare students for the district-wide assessments. Students will know what to expect, and in some board-wide assessments teachers don't have that knowledge. As well, even though you may feel that the texts are set at a high grade 3 level, you at least know the level your district school board is striving for.

Having this base, your job is now to expand it into a full, up-to-date grade 3 program. Your love of learning and exploring and your good humour will be your number one motivators. Your second motivator will be your hard work. You'll need to create and/or find resources (using the teachers' resource centre, library, internet, etc.) and to connect with district colleagues to prepare daily activities and projects, locate videos, book guest speakers from the community, buy computer programs, organize field trips, etc. Most of these you'll be able to produce with only your time, others with small funds, and a few through parent and student fundraisers.

This varied learning program will touch all the different styles of learning (auditory, visual, etc.). You'll also touch the different academic levels in the class by modifying the activities' levels of difficulty in order to gear the learning to individual student needs. Have fun with the activities—this will motivate your students to enjoy learning, not only for the year they spend with you, but also for life!

Kate Whitton
Meadowview Public School, Addison, ON

Part of the reality of teaching today is that there never seems to be enough funds for the adoption of stimulating new material. As a result, teachers have had to become even more creative and versatile with the resources that are available. As well, many excellent free resources can be found outside the school. I would begin by searching within the local community for guest speakers and for free programs and materials offered by government and private agencies and by public libraries. Sometimes local industry can offer products, such as paper, that would otherwise be discarded. Other wonderful sources are the internet, the Board Learning Resources centres, and inter-school swaps.

By experiencing concrete results students will begin to comprehend the concept of the value of learning, so these results have to be meaningful for them. Creating assignments that integrate the various learning styles in the classroom will initiate and maintain student interest. One possible approach is to find a common theme that incorporates the objectives in the workbooks and then develop problem-solving projects or assignments based on this theme. The Stability strand in science, for example, could be combined with the social studies Pioneers strand by having students create a 3-D model of pioneer life that includes components of language (skit, written report, brochure) and math (geometry, measurement, and number sense).

Breaking down material into smaller chunks helps students understand it without feeling overwhelmed. Going on to apply it in a more concrete, hands-on way will extend and solidify students' knowledge. The project approach gives students a goal to work toward and acts as an incentive to work through some of the more "boring" workbook material. Furthermore, everyone can be successful on some level with a multi-faceted project. Kids love to problem-solve; however, they do require parameters within which to work, and as they become accustomed to this style of learning these parameters can become less stringent. Another advantage of this approach is that teachers can continue making more connections with other curriculum requirements. The key is to remain flexible and open-minded when it comes to altering your own "gems," even at the last minute!

Motivation is highly individualistic. Setting realistic goals and hooking students on some level will enable them to work through most difficult areas, especially when they can bring their own visions and experiences to a project or assignment. Kids usually enjoy working in groups or pairs as they apply concepts in a more active and creative manner. In short, rather than dictating to students, teachers should be more facilitative.

12 Creating Learning Environments

Playtime © *Diana Ong/SuperStock*

TEACHERS' CASEBOOK

WHAT WOULD YOU DO?

Two boys are terrorizing one of your students. They are larger, stronger, and older than the boy being victimized, who is small and shy. Unfortunately, the bullies are fairly popular, in part because they are successful athletes. There are incidents on the bus before and after school, in the gym, and at lunch, including intimidation, extortion of lunch money, tripping, shoving, and verbal taunts—"fag" is a favourite chant. You do not have the two bullies in any of your classes. Your student has started to miss school routinely, and when he is in class, the quality of his work is declining. The other students in your class see what is going on and know you are aware of the problem too.

CRITICAL THINKING

- How do you handle this situation?
- Who should be involved?
- What would you do about the verbal homophobic insults?
- What if the bullies were members of your classroom?
- What would you do if the bullies and victim were girls?

This chapter looks at the ways that teachers create social and physical environments for learning by examining classroom management—one of the main concerns of teachers, particularly beginning teachers. The very nature of classes, teaching, and students makes good management a critical ingredient of success; we will investigate why this is true. Successful managers create more time for learning, involve more students, and help students to become self-managing.

A positive learning environment must be established and maintained throughout the year. One of the best ways to do this is to try to prevent problems from occurring at all. But when problems arise—as they inevitably do—an appropriate response is important. What will you do when students challenge you openly in class, when one student asks for your advice on a difficult personal problem, or when another withdraws from all participation? We will examine the ways in which teachers can communicate effectively with their students in these and many other situations.

By the time you have completed this chapter, you should be able to answer these questions:

- What are the special managerial demands of classrooms, and how do they relate to the needs of students of different ages?
- How will you establish a list of rules and procedures for a class?
- How will you arrange the physical environment of your classroom to fit your learning goals and teaching methods?
- How will you manage computers in your classroom to fit your learning goals and teaching methods?
- What are Kounin's suggestions for preventing management problems?
- How would you prevent problems by building connections with students?
- What are two different approaches for dealing with a conflict between teacher and student?

THE NEED FOR ORGANIZATION

Connect and Extend
Go to the "Connect and Extend" section in Chapter 12 of MyEducationLab to find further content that links to teaching, students' thinking, research, and the news.

In study after study of the factors related to student achievement, classroom management stands out as the variable with the largest impact (Marzano & Marzano, 2003). Knowledge and expertise in classroom management are marks of expertise in teaching; stress and exhaustion from managerial difficulties are precursors of burnout in teaching (Emmer & Stough, 2001). Why is classroom management so critical?

Classes are particular kinds of environments. They have distinctive features that influence their inhabitants no matter how the students or the desks are organized or what the teacher believes about education (Doyle, 1986, 2006). Classrooms are *multidimensional.* They are crowded with people, tasks, and time pressures. Many individuals, all with differing goals, preferences, and abilities, must share resources, accomplish various tasks, use and reuse materials without losing them, move in and out of the room, and so on. In addition, actions can have multiple effects. Calling on students of low ability may encourage their participation and thinking but may slow the discussion and lead to management problems if the students cannot answer. And events occur *simultaneously*—everything happens at once, and the *pace is fast.* Teachers have literally hundreds of exchanges with students during a single day.

In this rapid-fire existence, events are *unpredictable.* Even when plans are carefully made, the overhead projector is in place, and the demonstration is ready, the lesson can still be interrupted by a burned-out bulb in the projector or a loud, angry discussion right outside the classroom. Because classrooms are *public*, the way the teacher handles these unexpected intrusions is seen and judged by all. Students are always noticing if the teacher is being "fair." Is there favouritism? What happens when a rule is broken? Finally, classrooms have *histories.* The meaning of a particular teacher's or student's actions depends in part on what has happened before. The fifteenth time a student arrives late requires a different response from the teacher than the first late arrival. In addition, the history of the first few weeks of school affects life in the class all year.

The Basic Task: Gain Their Cooperation

No productive activity can take place in a group without the cooperation of all members. This obviously applies to classrooms. Even if some students don't participate, they must allow others to do so. (You have probably seen one or two students bring an entire class to a halt.) So the basic management task for teachers is to achieve order and harmony by gaining and maintaining student cooperation in class activities (Doyle, 2006). Given the multidimensional, simultaneous, immediate, unpredictable, public, and historical nature of classrooms, this is quite a challenge.

Gaining student cooperation means much more than dealing effectively with misbehaviour. It means planning activities, having materials ready, making appropriate behavioural and academic demands on students, giving clear signals, accomplishing transitions smoothly, foreseeing problems and stopping them before they start, selecting and sequencing activities so that flow and interest are maintained—and much more. Also, different activities require different managerial skills. For example, a new or complicated activity may be a greater threat to classroom management than a familiar or simple activity. And appropriate student participation varies across different activities. For example, loud student comments during a hip-hop reading of *Green Eggs and Ham* in an urban classroom are indications of engagement and cooperation, not disorderly call-outs (Doyle, 2006).

COOPERATION IS KEY Gaining student cooperation is the first task of classroom management. There are lessons, materials, time, space, and people to coordinate to keep learning on track.

Obviously, gaining the cooperation of kindergartners is not the same task as gaining the cooperation of students in grade 12. During kindergarten and the first few years of elementary school, direct teaching of classroom rules and procedures is important because these students are still learning how to behave in school. For children in the middle elementary years, many school and classroom routines have become relatively automatic, but new rules and procedures for a particular activity may need to be taught directly, and the entire system still needs monitoring and maintenance. Toward the end of elementary school and middle school and the beginning of high school, some students begin to test and defy authority. The management challenges at this stage are to deal productively with these disruptions and to motivate students who are becoming less concerned with teachers' opinions and more interested in their social lives. By the end of high school, the challenges are to manage the curriculum, fit academic material to students' interests and abilities, and help students become more self-managing. The first few classes each semester may be devoted to teaching particular procedures for using materials and equipment or for keeping track of and submitting assignments. However, most students know what is expected of them (Brophy & Evertson, 1978).

The Goals of Classroom Management

MyEducationLab Go to the Activities and Applications section in Chapter 12 of MyEducationLab and complete Activity 1. As you watch the video and answer the accompanying questions, reflect upon the strategies teachers can use to prevent or minimize classroom misbehaviour and distractions.

STOP & THINK You are interviewing for a job in a great school district—it is known for innovation. The vice principal looks at you for a moment and then asks, "What is classroom management?" How would you answer?

The aim of classroom management is to maintain a positive, productive learning environment. But order for its own sake is an empty goal. As we discussed in Chapter 6, it is unethical to use class management techniques just to keep students docile and quiet. What, then, is the point of working so hard to manage classrooms? There are at least three reasons why management is important.

Access to Learning. Each classroom activity has its own rules for participation. Sometimes these rules are clearly stated by the teacher, but often they are implicit and unstated. Teacher and students may not even be aware that they are following different rules for different activities (Berliner, 1983). The differences are sometimes quite subtle. For example, in a reading group students may have to raise their hands to make a comment, but in a show-and-tell circle in the same class they may simply have to catch the teacher's eye.

As we saw in Chapter 5, the rules defining who can talk; what they can talk about; and when, to whom, and how long they can talk are often called participation structures. In order to participate successfully in a given activity, students must understand the participation structure. Some students, however, seem to come to school less able to participate than others. The participation structures they learn at home in interactions with siblings, parents, and other adults do not match the participation structures of school activities (Tharp, 1989). Teachers are not necessarily aware of this conflict. Instead, the teachers may see that a child doesn't quite fit in, always seems to say the wrong thing at the wrong time, or is very reluctant to participate, and they are not sure why.

What can we conclude? To reach the first goal of classroom management—giving all students access to learning—you must make sure that everyone knows *how to participate* in each specific activity. The key is awareness. What are your rules and expectations? Are they understandable, given your students' cultural backgrounds and home experiences? What unspoken rules or values may be operating? Are you clear and consistent in signalling to students how to participate? For some students, particularly those with behavioural and emotional challenges, direct teaching and practice of the important behaviours may be required (Emmer & Stough, 2001).

An example of being sensitive to participation structures was documented by Adrienne Alton-Lee and her colleagues in a classroom in New Zealand (2001). As a critical part of a unit on children in hospitals, the teacher, Ms. Nikora, planned to have one of her students, a Maori girl named Huhana, describe a recent visit to the hospital. Huhana agreed. But when the time came and the teacher asked her to come to the front of the class and share her experiences, Huhana looked down and shook her head. Rather than confront or scold Huhana, the teacher simply said, "All right. If we sit in a circle . . . Huhana might be able to tell us about what happened." When students were in a circle, the teacher said, "All right, Huhana, after Ms. Nikora called your mum and she . . . Where did she take you to?" As Huhana began to share her experience, the teacher scaffolded her participation by asking questions, providing reminders of details the teacher had learned in previous conversations with Huhana, and waiting patiently for the student's responses. Rather than perceiving the *child* as lacking competence, the teacher saw the *situation* as hindering competent expression.

Classroom management Techniques used to maintain a healthy learning environment, relatively free of behavioural problems.

Participation structures The formal and informal rules for how to take part in a given activity.

More Time for Learning. If you were to use a stopwatch to time the commercials during a TV quiz show, you'd likely find that almost half of the program was devoted to commercials. Then, if you timed all the "small talk," you'd find that very little quizzing takes place. If you used a similar approach in classrooms, timing all the different activities throughout the day, you might be surprised by how little actual teaching takes place. Many minutes are lost each day through interruptions, disruptions, late starts, and rough transitions (Karweit, 1989; Karweit & Slavin, 1981).

Obviously, students will learn only what they encounter. Almost every study examining time and learning has found a significant relationship between time spent on content and student learning (Berliner, 1988). Thus, one important goal of classroom management is to expand the sheer number of minutes available for learning. This time is sometimes called allocated time.

Simply making more time available for learning will not automatically lead to achievement. To be valuable, time must be used effectively. As you saw in the chapters on cognitive learning, how students process information is a central factor in what they learn and remember. Basically, students will learn what they practise and think about. The time spent actively involved in specific learning tasks is often called engaged time, or sometimes time on task.

Again, however, engaged time doesn't guarantee learning. Students may be struggling with material that is too difficult or using the wrong learning strategies. When students are working with a high rate of success—really learning and understanding—we call the time spent academic learning time. So the second goal of class management is to increase academic learning time by keeping students *actively engaged in worthwhile, appropriate learning activities*. Figure 12.1 shows how the 1000+ hours of time mandated for school can become only about 333 hours of high-quality academic learning time for a typical student.

Getting students engaged in learning early in their school careers can make a big difference. Several studies have shown that teachers' rating of students' on-task, persistent engagement in grade 1 predicts achievement test score gains and grades through grade 4, as well as the decision to drop out of high school (Fredricks, Blumenfeld, & Paris, 2004).

Allocated time Time set aside for learning.

Engaged time/time on task Time spent actively engaged in the learning task at hand.

Academic learning time Time when students are actually succeeding at the learning task.

FIGURE 12.1 Who Knows Where the Time Goes?

The over 1000 hours per year of instruction students receive can represent only 300 or 400 hours of high-quality academic learning time.

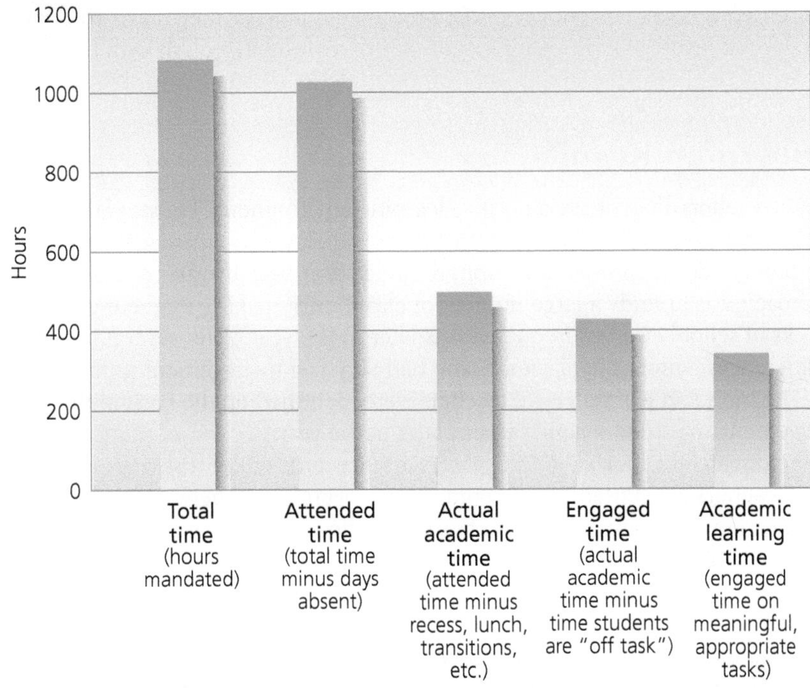

Source: From *Elementary Classroom Management* (4th ed.), by C. S. Weinstein and A. J. Mignano, Jr., New York: McGraw-Hill.

Management for Self-Management. The third goal of any management system is to help students become better able to manage themselves. If teachers focus on student compliance, they will spend much of the teaching/learning time monitoring and correcting. Students come to see the purpose of school as just following rules, not constructing deep understanding of academic knowledge. And complex learning structures such as cooperative or problem-based learning require student self-management. Compliance with rules is not enough to make these learning structures work (McCaslin & Good, 1998).

The movement from demanding obedience to teaching self-regulation and self-control is a fundamental shift in discussions of classroom management today (Weinstein, 1999). Tom Savage (1999) says simply, "the most fundamental purpose of discipline is the development of self-control. Academic knowledge and technological skill will be of little consequence if those who possess them lack self-control" (p. 11). Through self-control, students demonstrate *responsibility*—the ability to fulfill their own needs without interfering with the rights and needs of others (Glasser, 1990). Students learn self-control by making choices and dealing with the consequences, setting goals and priorities, managing time, collaborating to learn, mediating disputes and making peace, and developing trusting relations with trustworthy teachers and classmates (Bear, 2005; Rogers & Frieberg, 1994).

Encouraging self-management requires extra time, but teaching students how to take responsibility is an investment well worth the effort. When elementary and secondary teachers have effective class management systems but neglect to set student self-management as a goal, their students often have trouble working independently after graduating from these "well-managed" classes.

Self-management Management of your own behaviour and acceptance of responsibility for your own actions.

CREATING A POSITIVE LEARNING ENVIRONMENT

In making plans for your class, much of what you have already learned in this book should prove helpful. You know, for example, that problems are prevented when student differences, such as those discussed in Chapters 2, 3, 4, and 5, are taken into account in instructional planning. Sometimes students become disruptive because the work assigned is too difficult. And students who are bored by lessons well below their ability levels may be interested in finding more exciting activities to fill their time.

In one sense, teachers prevent discipline problems whenever they make an effort to motivate students. A student involved in learning is usually not involved in a clash with the teacher or other students at the same time. All plans for motivating students are steps toward preventing problems.

Some Research Results

What else can teachers do to create a positive learning environment? For several years, educational psychologists at the University of Texas at Austin studied classroom management quite thoroughly (Emmer & Stough, 2001; Emmer, Evertson, & Anderson, 1980; Emmer & Gerwels, 2006). Their general approach was to study a large number of classrooms, making frequent observations during the first weeks of school and less frequent visits later in the year. After several months, there were dramatic differences among the classes. Some had very few management problems, while others had many. The most and least effective teachers were identified on the basis of the quality of classroom management and student achievement later in the year.

Next, the researchers looked at their observation records of the first weeks of class to see how the effective teachers got started. Other comparisons were made between the teachers who ultimately had harmonious, high-achieving classes and those whose classes were fraught with problems. On the basis of these comparisons, management principles were developed. The researchers then taught these principles to a new group of teachers; the results were quite positive. Teachers who applied the principles had fewer problems, their students spent more time learning and less time disrupting, and achievement was higher. The findings of these studies formed the basis for two books on classroom management (Emmer & Evertson, 2009; Evertson & Emmer, 2009). Many of the ideas on the following pages are from these books.

Routines and Rules Required

STOP & THINK What are the three or four most important rules you will have for your classroom?

At the elementary school level, teachers must lead 20 to 30 students of varying abilities through many different activities each day. Without efficient rules and procedures, a great deal of time is wasted answering the same question over and over. "My pencil broke. How can I do my math?" "I'm finished with my story. What should I do now?" "Steven hit me!" "I left my homework in my locker."

At the secondary school level, teachers must deal daily with more than 100 students who use dozens of materials and often change rooms for each class. Secondary school students are also more likely to challenge teachers' authority. The effective teachers studied by Emmer, Evertson, and their colleagues had planned procedures and rules for coping with these situations.

Routines and Procedures. How will materials and assignments be distributed and collected? Under what conditions can students leave the room? How will grades be determined? What are the special routines for handling equipment and supplies in science, art, or vocational classes? Procedures and routines describe how activities are accomplished in classrooms, but they are seldom written down; they are simply the ways of getting things done in class. Carol Weinstein and Andy Mignano (Weinstein, 2007; Weinstein & Mignano, 2007) recommend that teachers establish procedures to cover the following areas:

1. *Administrative routines*, such as taking attendance.
2. *Student movement*, such as entering and leaving the classroom or going to the bathroom.
3. *Housekeeping*, such as watering plants or storing personal items.
4. *Routines for accomplishing lessons*, such as how to collect assignments or return homework.
5. *Interactions between teacher and student*, such as how to get the teacher's attention when help is needed.
6. *Talk among students*, such as giving help or socializing.

You might use these six areas as a framework for planning your class procedures and routines. The *Guidelines* box on page 426 should help you as you plan.

Rules. Unlike routines, rules are often written down and posted because rules specify expected and forbidden actions in the class. They are the dos and don'ts of classroom life. In establishing rules, Jack Martin and Jeff Sugarman (1993) at Simon Fraser University in British Columbia recommend considering what kind of atmosphere you want to create. What student behaviour will help you teach effectively? What limits do the students need to guide their behaviour? The rules you set should be consistent with school rules and also in keeping with principles of learning. For example, we know from the research on small-group learning that students benefit when they explain work to peers. They learn as they teach. A rule that forbids students to help each other may be inconsistent with good learning principles. Or a rule that says "No erasures when writing" may make students focus more on preventing mistakes than on communicating clearly in their writing (Burden, 1995; Emmer & Stough, 2001; Weinstein & Mignano, 2007).

Rules should be positive and observable (raise your hand to be recognized). Having a few general rules that cover many specifics is better than listing all the dos and don'ts. But if specific actions, such as chewing gum in class or smoking cigarettes in the bathrooms, are forbidden, a rule should make this clear.

Rules for Elementary School. Evertson and Emmer (2009) give four examples of general rules for elementary school classes:

1. *Respect and be polite to all people.* Give clear explanations of what you mean by "polite," including not hitting, fighting, or teasing. Examples of polite behaviour include waiting your turn, saying "please" and "thank you," and not calling names. This applies to behaviour toward adults (including substitute teachers) and children.

MyEducationLab
Go to the Podcasts section of MyEducationLab and listen to PODCAST—Beliefs About Classroom Management. In this podcast Anita Woolfolk talks about how students and teachers may have beliefs that stand in the way of good classroom relationships.

Procedures/routines Prescribed steps for an activity.

Rules Statements specifying expected and forbidden behaviour; dos and don'ts.

GUIDELINES: Establishing Class Routines

Determine procedures for student upkeep of desks, classroom equipment, and other facilities.

EXAMPLES

1. Set aside a cleanup time each day or once a week in self-contained classes.
2. Demonstrate and have students practise how to push chairs under the desk, take and return materials stored on shelves, sharpen pencils, use the sink or water fountain, assemble lab equipment, and so on.
3. Put a rotating monitor in charge of equipment or materials.

Decide how students will be expected to enter and leave the room.

EXAMPLES

1. Have a procedure for students to follow as soon as they enter the room. Some teachers have a standard assignment ("Have your homework out and be checking it over").
2. Inform students under what conditions they can leave the room, and make sure they understand when they need to ask for permission to do so.
3. Tell students how they should gain admission to the room if they are late.
4. Set up a policy about class dismissal. Many teachers require students to be in their seats and quiet before they can leave at the end of class. The teacher, not the bell, dismisses class.

Establish signals for getting students' attention and teach them to your students.

EXAMPLES

1. In the classroom, flick the lights on and off, sound a chord on a piano or recorder, sound a bell like the "ring bell for service" at a sales counter, move to the podium and stare silently at the class, use a phrase like "Eyes, please," take out your grade book, or move to the front of the class.
2. In the halls, raise a hand, clap once, or use some other signal to indicate "Stop."
3. On the playground, raise a hand or whistle to indicate "Line up."

Set routines for student participation in class.

EXAMPLES

1. Decide whether you will have students raise their hands for permission to speak or simply require that they wait until the speaker has finished.
2. Determine a signal to indicate that you want everyone to respond at once. Some teachers raise a cupped hand to their ear. Others preface the question with "Everyone."
3. Make sure you are clear about differences in procedures for different activities: reading group, learning centre, discussion, teacher presentation, seatwork, video watching, peer learning group, library, and so forth.
4. Establish how many students at a time can be at the pencil sharpener, teacher's desk, learning centre, sink, bookshelves, reading corner, or bathroom.

Determine how you will communicate, collect, and return assignments.

EXAMPLES

1. Establish a place for listing assignments. Some teachers reserve a particular corner of the board for listing assignments. Others write assignments in coloured chalk. For younger students, it may be better to prepare assignment sheets or folders, colour-coding them for math workbook, reading packet, and science kit.
2. Be clear about how and where assignments should be collected. Some teachers collect assignments in a box or bin; others have a student collect work while they introduce the next activity.

For ideas about involving students in developing rules and procedures, see **www.educationworld.com/a_lesson/lesson/lesson274.shtml**.

2. *Be prompt and prepared.* This rule highlights the importance of the academic work in the class. Being prompt includes the beginning of the day and transitions between activities.
3. *Listen quietly while others are speaking.* This applies to the teacher and other students, in both large-class lessons and small-group discussions.
4. *Obey all school rules.* This reminds students that all school rules apply in your classroom. Then students cannot claim, for example, that they thought it was okay to chew gum or listen to music in your class, even though these are against school rules, "because you never made a rule against it for us."

Whatever the rule, students need to be taught the behaviour that the rule includes and excludes. Examples, practice, and discussion will be needed before learning is complete.

As you've seen, different activities often require different rules. This can be confusing for elementary students until they have thoroughly learned all the rules. To prevent confusion, you might consider making signs that list the rules for each activity. Then, before the activity, you can post the appropriate sign as a reminder. This provides clear and consistent cues about participation structures so all students, not just the "well-behaved," know what is expected. Of course, these rules must be explained and discussed before the signs can have their full effect.

RULES PROMOTE RESPECT Classroom rules that are understood clearly by all students can help maintain a classroom environment that is respectful and more conducive to effective learning.

Rules for Secondary School. Emmer and Evertson (2009) suggest six examples of rules for secondary school students:

1. *Bring all needed materials to class.* The teacher must specify the type of pen, pencil, paper, notebook, texts, and so on.
2. *Be in your seat and ready to work when the bell rings.* Many teachers combine this rule with a standard beginning procedure for the class, such as a warm-up exercise on the board or a requirement that students have paper with a proper heading ready when the bell rings.
3. *Respect and be polite to all people.* This rule covers fighting, verbal abuse, and general troublemaking. *All people* includes the teacher.
4. *Listen and stay seated while someone else is speaking.* This applies when the teacher or other students are talking.
5. *Respect other people's property.* This means property belonging to the school, the teacher, or other students.
6. *Obey all school rules.* As with the elementary class rules, this covers a variety of behaviour and situations, so you do not have to repeat every school rule for your class. It also reminds the students that you will be monitoring them inside and outside your class. Make sure that you know all the school rules. Some secondary students are adept at convincing teachers that their misbehaviour "really isn't against the rules."

These rules are more than ways to maintain order. In their study of 34 middle school classrooms, Lindsay Matsumura and her colleagues (2008) found that having explicit rules in the classroom about respecting others predicted the number of students who participated in class discussion, so respect is a gateway to student engagement with the academic material and class dialogue that supports learning.

Consequences. As soon as you decide on your rules and procedures, you must consider what you will do when a student breaks a rule or does not follow a procedure. It is too late to make this decision after the rule has been broken. For many infractions, the logical consequence is having to go back and "do it right." Students who run in the hall may have to return to where they started and walk properly. Incomplete papers can be redone. Materials left out should be put back. You can use natural or logical consequences to support social and emotional development by doing the following (Elias & Schwab, 2006):

- Separate the deed from the doer—the problem is the behaviour, not the student.
- Emphasize to students that they have the power to choose their actions and thus avoid losing control.
- Encourage student reflection, self-evaluation, and problem solving—avoid teacher lecturing.
- Help students identify and give a rationale for what they could do differently next time in a similar situation.

Natural/logical consequences Instead of punishing, having students redo, repair, or in some way face the consequences that naturally flow from their actions.

TABLE 12.1 Seven Categories of Consequences for Students

1. *Expressions of disappointment.* If students like and respect their teacher, then a serious, sorrowful expression of disappointment may cause students to stop and think about their behaviour.
2. *Loss of privileges.* Students can lose free time. If they have not completed homework, for example, they can be required to do it during a free period or recess.
3. *Exclusion from the group.* Students who distract their peers or fail to cooperate can be separated from the group until they are ready to cooperate. Some teachers give a student a pass for 10 to 15 minutes. During this time, the student goes to another class or study hall, where the other students and teachers ignore him or her. Some students may perceive this consequence as a reward.
4. *Written reflections on the problem.* Students can write in journals, write essays about what they did and how it affected others, or write letters of apology—if this is appropriate. Another possibility is to ask students to describe objectively what they did; then the teacher and the student can discuss and sign and date this statement. These records are available if parents or administrators need evidence of the students' behaviour.
5. *Detentions.* Detentions can be very brief meetings after school, during a free period, or at lunch. The main purpose is to talk about what has happened. (In high school, detentions are often used as punishments; suspensions and expulsions are available as more extreme measures.)
6. *Visits to the principal's office.* Expert teachers tend to use this consequence rarely, but they do use it when the situation warrants. Some schools require students to be sent to the office for certain offences, such as fighting. If you tell a student to go to the office and the student refuses, you might call the office saying that the student has been sent. Then the student has the choice of either going to the office or facing the principal's penalty for "disappearing" on the way.
7. *Contact with parents.* If problems become a repeated pattern, most teachers contact the student's family. This is done to seek support for helping the student, not to blame the parents or punish the student.

Source: From *Elementary Classroom Management* (4th ed.), by C. S. Weinstein and A. J. Mignano, Jr., New York: McGraw-Hill. Copyright © 2007 by The McGraw-Hill Companies. Adapted with permission of the McGraw-Hill Companies, Inc.

The main point here is that decisions about penalties (and rewards) must be made early on, so that students know before they break a rule or use the wrong procedure what this will mean for them. Anita encourages her student teachers to get a copy of the school rules and their cooperating teacher's rules, and then plan their own. Sometimes, consequences are more complicated. In their case studies of four expert elementary school teachers, Weinstein and Mignano (2007) found that the teachers' negative consequences fell into seven categories, as shown in Table 12.1.

Who Sets the Rules and Consequences? In Chapter 1, we described Ken, an expert teacher who worked with his students to establish a students' and teacher's "Bill of Rights" instead of defining rules. These "rights" cover most situations that might require a "rule" and help the students move toward the goal of becoming self-managing. The rights for one recent year's class are listed in Table 12.2. Developing rights and responsibilities rather than rules makes a very important point to students. "Teaching children that something is wrong because there is a rule against it is not the same as teaching them that there is a rule against it because it is wrong, and helping them to understand why this is so" (Weinstein, 1999, p. 154). Students should understand that the rules are developed so that everyone can work and learn together. It should be noted that when Ken has had some very difficult classes, he and his students have had to establish some "laws" that protect students' rights.

If you are going to involve students in setting rules or creating a constitution, you may need to wait until you have established a sense of community in your classroom. Before students can contribute meaningfully to the class rules, they need to trust the teacher and the situation (Elias & Schwab, 2006).

Another kind of planning that affects the learning environment is designing the physical arrangement of the class furniture, materials, and learning tools.

TABLE 12.2 A Bill of Rights for Students and Teachers

Mr. Kowalski's Class's Bill of Rights
The right to be treated nicely, politely, respectfully, fairly, kindly, welcomed, equally.
The right to whisper when the teacher isn't talking.
The right to a two-minute break between work periods.
The right to have choices about the day's schedule.
The right to work and learn without being bothered.
The right to talk to the class without anyone else talking.
The right to choose a table.
The right to privacy.
The right to be comfortable.
The right not to have people take your things.
The right to play with anyone during recess.
The right to a snack every day.
The right to stand up for others.
The right to apologies.
The right to learn.
The right to make mistakes.
The right not to be copied.
The right to ask for help.
The right to ask questions.
The right to have fun while learning.
The right to have silence.
The right to work independently.
The right to study.
The right to have feelings.
The right to help other people at the right time.
The right to chew gum without blowing bubbles or making a mess.
The right to go outside almost every day.

Law to Protect Our Rights
1. Follow directions the first time.
2. Speak nicely, be courteous, and respect other people, their feelings and their things. Follow the Bill of Rights.
3. Laugh at the right time for the right time.
4. Respect others' right to learn. Do not distract others. Don't be nosy. Don't yell. Remember to get quiet at countdown.
5. Talk at the right times with the right tone of voice and volume.
6. Transitions and movements are calm, quiet, careful and elegant.
7. Follow all classroom and school procedures, like: bathroom; pencil; lunch and recess; morning; dismissal; and . . .

Source: From *Elementary Classroom Management* (4th ed.), by C. S. Weinstein and A. J. Mignano, Jr., New York: McGraw-Hill. Copyright © 2007 by The McGraw-Hill Companies. Adapted with permission of the McGraw-Hill Companies, Inc.

Planning Spaces for Learning

STOP & THINK Think back over all the classrooms in all the schools you have attended. Which ones stand out as inviting or exciting? Which ones were cold and empty? Did any teachers have designs that let different students do different things at once? How did they accomplish this?

Spaces for learning should invite and support the activities you plan in your classroom, and they should respect the inhabitants of the space. This respect begins at the classroom door for young children by helping them identify their class. One school that has won awards for its architecture paints each classroom door a different bright colour so that young children can find their "home" (Herbert, 1998). Once inside, spaces can be created that invite quiet reading, group collaboration, or independent research. If students are to use materials, they should be able to reach them. In an interview with Marge Scherer (1999), Herb Kohl describes how he creates a positive environment in his classes:

> What I do is put up the most beautiful things I know—posters, games, puzzles, challenges—and let the children know these are provocations. These are ways of provoking them into using their minds. You have to create an environment that makes kids walk in and say, "I really want to see what's here. I would really like to look at this." (p. 9)

MyEducationLab Go to the Activities and Applications section in Chapter 12 of MyEducationLab and complete Activity 2. As you complete the activity, think about the type of classroom you anticipate having.

In terms of classroom arrangements, there are two basic ways of organizing space: one focusing on personal territories and one focusing on interest areas.

Personal Territories. Can the physical setting influence teaching and learning in classrooms organized by territories? Front-seat location does seem to increase participation for students who are predisposed to speak in class, whereas a seat in the back will make it more difficult to participate and easier to sit back and daydream (Woolfolk & Brooks, 1983). But the **action zone**, where participation is greatest, may be in other areas, such as on one side or near a particular learning centre (Good, 1983a; Lambert, 1994). To "spread the action around," Weinstein and Mignano (2007) suggest that teachers move around the room when possible, establish eye contact with and direct questions to students seated far away, and vary the seating so that the same students are not always consigned to the back.

Horizontal rows share many of the advantages of the traditional row and column arrangements. Both are useful for independent seatwork and teacher, student, or media presentations; they encourage students to focus on the presenter and simplify housekeeping. Horizontal rows also permit students to work more easily in pairs. However, this is a poor arrangement for large-group discussion.

Clusters of four or circle arrangements are best for student interaction. Circles are especially useful for discussions but still allow for independent seatwork. Clusters permit students to talk, help one another, share materials, and work on group tasks. Both arrangements, however, are poor for whole-group presentations and may make class management more difficult.

The fishbowl, or stack, special formation, where students sit close together near the focus of attention (the back row may even be standing), should be used only for short periods of time, because it is not comfortable and can lead to discipline problems. On the other hand, the fishbowl can create a feeling of group cohesion and is helpful when the teacher wants students to watch a demonstration, brainstorm on a class problem, or see a small visual aid.

Interest Areas. The design of interest areas can influence the way the areas are used by students. For example, working with a classroom teacher, Weinstein (1977) was able to make changes in interest areas that helped the teacher meet her objectives of having more girls involved in the science centre and having all students experiment more with a variety of manipulative materials. In a second study, changes in a library corner led to more involvement in literature activities throughout the class (Morrow & Weinstein, 1986). If you design areas of interest for your class, keep the suggestions in the *Guidelines* box in mind.

Action zone Area of a classroom where the greatest amount of interaction takes place.

GUIDELINES: Designing Learning Spaces

Note the fixed features and plan accordingly.

EXAMPLES

1. Remember that the audiovisual centre and computers need an electrical outlet.
2. Keep art supplies near the sink, small-group work by a blackboard.

Create easy access to materials and a well-organized place to store them.

EXAMPLES

1. Make sure materials are easy to reach and visible to students.
2. Have enough shelves so that materials need not be stacked.

Provide students with clean, convenient surfaces for studying.

EXAMPLES

1. Put bookshelves next to the reading area, games by the game table.
2. Prevent fights by avoiding crowded work spaces.

Avoid dead spaces and "racetracks."

EXAMPLES

1. Don't have all the interest areas around the outside of the room, leaving a large dead space in the middle.
2. Avoid placing a few items of furniture right in the middle of this large space, creating a "racetrack" around the furniture.

Arrange things so you can see your students and they can see all instructional presentations.

EXAMPLES

1. Make sure you can see over partitions.
2. Design seating so that students can see instruction without moving their chairs or desks.

Make sure work areas are private and quiet.

EXAMPLES

1. Make sure there are no tables or work areas in the middle of traffic lanes; a person should not have to pass through one area to get to another.
2. Keep noisy activities as far as possible from quiet ones. Increase the feeling of privacy by placing partitions, such as bookcases or pegboards, between areas or within large areas.

Provide choices and flexibility.

EXAMPLES

1. Establish private cubicles for individual work, open tables for group work, and cushions on the floor for whole-class meetings.
2. Give students a place to keep their personal belongings. This is especially important if students don't have personal desks.

Try new arrangements, then evaluate and improve.

EXAMPLES

1. Have a "two-week arrangement," then evaluate.
2. Enlist the aid of your students. They have to live in the room, too, and designing a classroom can be a very challenging educational experience.

For more ideas on classroom design, see **www.edfacilities.org/rl/classroom_design.cfm**.

Personal territories and interest areas are not mutually exclusive; many teachers use a design that combines these types of organizations. Individual students' desks—their territories—are placed in the centre, with interest areas in the back or around the periphery of the room. This allows the flexibility needed for both large- and small-group activities. Figure 12.2 on page 432 shows an elementary classroom that combines interest area and personal territory arrangements.

Planning for Computer Uses

Many classrooms today have computers. Some classes have only one, others have several, and some classes are set up as labs with a computer for every student. Using computers productively brings with it management challenges. Computers can be used to connect to powerful knowledge bases around the world; to act as tools for writing, drawing, calculating, and designing; to simulate scientific experiments or life in other times and places; to collaborate and communicate with people across the hall or across the ocean; to publish work or make presentations; and to keep track of appointments, assignments, or grades. To get the greatest benefits from computers in your classroom, teachers must have good management systems. Table 12.3 on page 433 summarizes strategies for managing computer labs.

FIGURE 12.2

An Elementary Classroom Arrangement

This grade 4 teacher has designed a space that allows teacher presentations and demonstrations, small-group work, computer interactions, math manipulatives activities, informal reading, art, and other projects without requiring constant rearrangements.

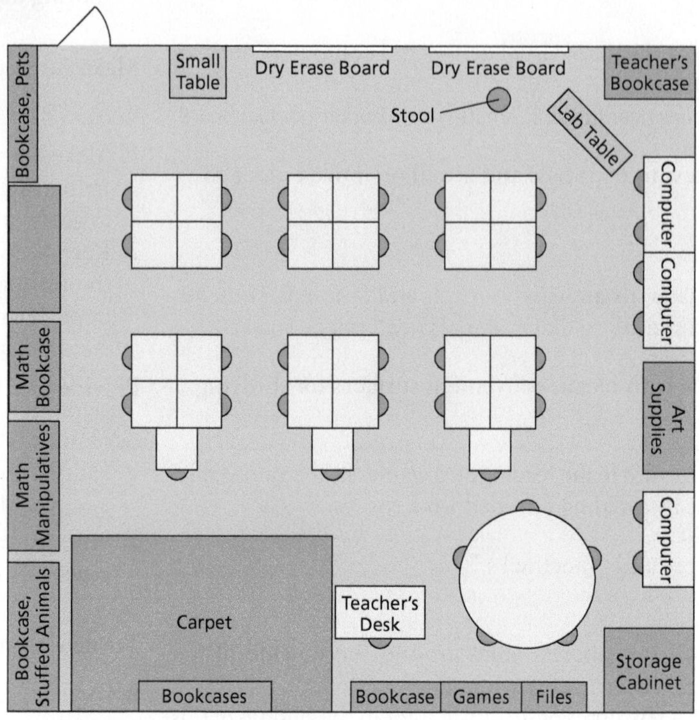

Source: From *Elementary Classroom Management* (4th ed.), by C. S. Weinstein and A. J. Mignano, Jr., New York: McGraw-Hill. Copyright © 2007 by The McGraw-Hill Companies. Adapted with permission of the McGraw-Hill Companies, Inc.

Getting Started: The First Weeks of Class

Determining a room design, rules, and procedures are first steps toward having a well-managed class, but how do effective teachers gain students' cooperation in those first critical days and weeks? One study carefully analyzed the first weeks' activities of effective and ineffective elementary teachers and found striking differences (Emmer et al., 1980). By the second or third week of school, students in the ineffective teachers' classrooms were more and more disruptive, and less and less on task.

Effective Managers for Elementary Students. In the effective teachers' classrooms, the very first day was well organized. Name tags were ready. There was something interesting for each child to do right away. Materials were set up. The teachers had planned carefully to avoid any last-minute tasks that might take them away from their students. These teachers dealt with the children's pressing concerns first. "Where do I put my things?" "How do I pronounce my teacher's name?" "Can I whisper to my neighbour?" "Where is the washroom?" The effective teachers had a workable, easily understood set of rules and taught the students the most important rules right away. They taught the rules as they would any other subject, with a lot of explanation, examples, and practice.

Throughout the first weeks, the effective teachers continued to spend quite a bit of time teaching rules and procedures. Some used guided practice to teach procedures; others used rewards to shape behaviour. Most taught students to respond to a bell or some other signal to gain their attention. These teachers worked with the class as a whole on enjoyable academic activities. They did not rush to get students into small groups or to get them started in readers. This whole-class work gave the teachers a better opportunity to continue monitoring all students' learning of the rules and procedures. Misbehaviour was stopped quickly and firmly, but not harshly.

TABLE 12.3 Tips for Managing a Computer Lab

All these ideas are from Cheryl Bolick and James Cooper (2006).

- Always run through a technology lesson before presenting it to the class—and always have a backup lesson prepared in case the technology fails.
- Type directions for frequently used computer operations—opening programs, inserting clip art, printing documents, and so on—on index cards, laminate them, and connect them with a circle ring. Keep a set next to each computer.
- Have students turn off their monitors when you're giving directions.
- Appoint classroom technology managers. Consider an Attendance Manager, who takes attendance and serves as a substitute teacher helper when necessary; a Materials Manager, who passes out materials and runs errands; a Technical Manager, who helps resolve printer and computer issues; and an End-of-Class Manager, who makes sure work areas are neat—keyboards pushed in, mice straight, and programs closed—before students are dismissed.
- If you have classes filtering in and out of a computer lab each day and have little or no time to set up between classes, arrange for older students to help. Simply end your lesson five minutes early and walk the older students through the process of setting up for the next class.
- When working on lengthy technology projects, print out step-by-step instructions. Include some that say "Save your work; do not go any further until you help your neighbours reach this point." This helps less-proficient students solve problems more quickly, keeps the class at roughly the same point in the project, and fosters collaborative learning.
- Make it a class rule that students can help one another but cannot ever touch another student's computer. That way, you can be sure that learning occurs even when students help one another.
- Keep a red plastic cup at each computer. When students need help, have them place the highly visible cups on top of their monitors.
- Before students leave class, have them turn their mice upside down so that the trackballs are showing. You'll lose fewer trackballs that way.
- Place different coloured sticker dots on the left and the right bottom corners of each monitor. Use these to indicate which side of the screen you are talking about—very helpful when using certain programs, such as the new Kid Pix—and to determine whose turn it is if students share a computer.
- Plug all speakers into a main power bar. Turn the bar off when you're teaching and turn it on when students are working. If the room becomes too noisy, turn off the power bar to get students' attention.
- Use a Video Out card to project a monitor display onto a television screen.
- Type PLEASE WAIT FOR INSTRUCTIONS on 8 by 11 papers, laminate them, and tape one sheet to the top of every monitor. Students flip the signs to the back of the monitor after you've given directions.
- Create a folder in the Start menu and place any programs you use with students in that folder. Students never have to click Programs—everything they use is in one folder.
- When working in a computer lab, assign each student a computer. Students can line up in "computer lab order" in their classrooms. Seating goes very quickly when they get to the lab.
- If you're working on a network, ask your technology coordinator to set up a shared folder for internet resources. Then, when you're planning an internet lesson, simply save a shortcut to the website in that folder. During lab time, students can go to the shared folder, double click the link, and go right to the site without typing the URL. This saves time and stress for both students and teachers.

Source: From Bolick, C. M., & Cooper, J. M. (2006). "Tips for Managing a Computer Lab," Classroom management and technology. In C. Evertson & C. Weinstein (Eds.), *Handbook for classroom management: Research, practice, and contemporary issues.* Reprinted by permission of Lawrence Erlbaum Associates, Inc. and Cheryl Mason Bolick, Ph.D.

In the poorly managed classrooms, the first weeks were quite different. Rules were not workable; they were either too vague or very complicated. For example, one teacher made a rule that students should "be in the right place at the right time." Students were not told what this meant, so their behaviour could not be guided by the rule. Neither positive nor negative behaviour had clear, consistent consequences. After students broke a rule, ineffective teachers might give a vague criticism, such as "Some of my children are too noisy," or issue a warning, but not follow through with the threatened consequence.

In the poorly managed classes, procedures for accomplishing routine tasks varied from day to day and were never taught or practised. Instead of dealing with these obvious needs, ineffective teachers spent time on procedures that could have waited. For example, one teacher had the class practise for a fire drill the first day, but left unexplained other procedures that would be needed every day. Students wandered aimlessly and had to ask each other what they should be doing. Often, the students talked to one another because they had nothing productive to do. Ineffective teachers frequently left the room. Many became absorbed in paperwork or in helping just one student. They had not made plans for how to deal with late-arriving students or other interruptions. One ineffective teacher tried to teach students to respond to a bell as a signal for attention but later let the students ignore it. All in all, the first weeks in these classrooms were disorganized and filled with surprises for teachers and students alike.

Effective Managers for Secondary Students. What about getting started in a secondary school class? It appears that many of the differences between effective and ineffective elementary school teachers hold at the secondary level as well. Again, effective teachers focus on establishing rules, procedures, and expectations on the first day of class. These standards for academic work and class behaviour are clearly communicated to students and consistently enforced during the first weeks of class. Student behaviour is closely monitored, and infractions of the rules are dealt with quickly. In classes with students of lower ability, work cycles are shorter; students are not required to spend long, unbroken periods on one type of activity. Instead, during each period, they are moved smoothly through several different tasks. In general, effective teachers carefully follow each student's progress so that students cannot avoid work without facing consequences (Emmer & Evertson, 1982).

With all this close monitoring and consistent enforcement of the rules, you may wonder if effective secondary teachers have to be grim and humourless. Not necessarily. The effective teachers in one study also smiled and joked more with their students (Moskowitz & Hayman, 1976). As any experienced teacher can tell you, there is much more to smile about when the class is cooperative.

CREATING A LEARNING COMMUNITY

Nel Noddings (1992, 1995) has written about the need to create caring educational environments where students take more responsibility for governing their school and classroom. As we saw in Chapter 11 when we discussed the need for relatedness, students are more intrinsically motivated when they feel that their teachers care about them (Grolnick, Ryan, & Deci, 1991). When Blakeburn Elementary School in Port Coquitlam, British Columbia, opened in 2000, one of its school-wide goals was to develop supportive, caring relationships among colleagues, with parents, and among students (Blakeburn Elementary & Laidlaw, 2001; Laidlaw, 2004). The school focused on helping students become socially responsible. This required consistency and modelling at all levels, and the students learned the language of solving problems, respecting diversity, and contributing to the classroom and the school. In interviews, students talked about feeling safe, included, and happy to be at school. Parents said, "There is a different atmosphere at this school. . . . There is a sense of mutual trust. The expectation is that the kids will manage and get along, and they do" (Blakeburn Elementary & Laidlaw, 2001, p. 1). Historically, however, North American schools have emphasized regulating students' behaviour through rules, not through relationships.

Classroom Community

David and Roger Johnson (1999b) describe three C's for developing the kind of caring and mutually trusting community that exists at Blakeburn Elementary: cooperative community, constructive conflict resolution, and civic values. At the heart of the community is the idea of positive interdependence—individuals working together to achieve mutual goals. Constructive conflict resolution is essential in the community because conflicts are inevitable and even necessary for learning. Piaget's theory of development and the research on conceptual change teaching tell us that true learning requires cognitive conflict. And individuals trying to exist in groups will have interpersonal conflicts; these can lead to learning too. Review Table 9.10 on page 330 for ideas about how to structure constructive conflicts.

The last C stands for civic values—the understandings and beliefs that hold the community together. Values are learned through direct teaching, modelling, literature, group discussions, and the sharing of concerns. Some teachers have a "Concerns Box," where students can put written concerns and comments. The box is opened once a week at a class meeting, and the concerns are discussed. Johnson and Johnson (1999b) give the example of a class meeting about respect. One student told her classmates that she felt hurt during recess the day before because no one listened when she was trying to teach them the rules to a new game. The students discussed what it means to be respectful and why respect is important. Then the students shared personal experiences of times when they felt respected versus not respected.

Getting Started on Community

Whether you are working as an individual or as part of a school-wide team, creating the kind of community that is now visible in the day-to-day routines at Blakeburn Elementary School does not happen automatically (Blakeburn Elementary & Laidlaw, 2001, p. 4). It involves input from many different levels to develop a philosophy and participation structures that will foster self-control and social responsibility on the part of students. At Blakeburn, the "leadership team" met first and talked about how to create a caring and socially responsible learning community. Team members used the provincial ministry's Performance Standards for Social Responsibility as a framework for developing a common language and set of expectations. Then they involved the children and their families. The first week of school was devoted to the articulation of what it means (for all members) to be part of a socially responsible community. Students participated in multi-aged "family" groups on relevant activities. Throughout this process, the staff recognized that this work must be multifaceted and integrated in all the curricula and interactions in their classrooms and at the school. They realized that creating positive classroom and school climates requires more than the implementation of prepackaged programs at a scheduled time in the day. It involves "living the principles of inclusion and responsibility . . . all day, every day" (Blakeburn Elementary & Laidlaw, 2001, p. 4).

MAINTAINING A GOOD ENVIRONMENT FOR LEARNING

A good start is just that—a beginning. Effective teachers build on this beginning. They maintain their management system by preventing problems and keeping students motivated and engaged in productive learning activities. We have discussed several ways to keep students motivated and engaged. In Chapter 11, for example, we considered stimulating curiosity, relating lessons to student interests, encouraging cooperative learning, establishing learning goals instead of performance goals, and having positive expectations. What else can teachers do?

Encouraging Engagement

STOP & THINK What activities keep you completely engaged—the time just seems to disappear? What is it about those activities that keeps you focused?

The format of a lesson affects student involvement. In general, as teacher supervision increases, students' engaged time also increases (Emmer & Evertson, 1981). For example, one study found that elementary students working directly with a teacher were on task 97 percent of the time, while students working on their own were on task only 57 percent of the time (Frick, 1990). This does not mean that teachers should eliminate independent work for students. It simply means that this type of activity usually requires careful monitoring.

When the task provides continuous cues for the student about what to do next, involvement will be greater. Activities with clear steps are likely to be more absorbing, because one step leads naturally to the next. When students have all the materials they need to complete a task, they tend to stay involved. If their curiosity is piqued, students will be motivated to continue seeking an answer. And, as you now know, students will be more engaged if they are involved in authentic tasks—activities that have connections to real life. Also, activities are more engaging when the level

GUIDELINES: Keeping Students Engaged

Make basic work requirements clear.

EXAMPLES

1. Specify and post the routine work requirements for headings, paper size, pen or pencil use, and neatness.
2. Establish and explain rules about late or incomplete work and absences. If a pattern of incomplete work begins to develop, deal with it early; speak with parents if necessary.
3. Make due dates reasonable and stick to them unless the student has a very good excuse for lateness.

Communicate the specifics of assignments.

EXAMPLES

1. With younger students, have a routine procedure for giving assignments, such as writing them on the board in the same place each day. With older students, assignments may be dictated, posted, or given in a syllabus.
2. Remind students of coming assignments.
3. With complicated assignments, give students a sheet describing what to do, what resources are available, due dates, and so on. Explain your grading criteria to older students.
4. Demonstrate how to do the assignment, do the first few questions together, or provide a sample worksheet.

Monitor work in progress.

EXAMPLES

1. When you give an in-class assignment, make sure that each student gets started correctly. If you check only students who raise their hands for help, you will miss those who think they know what to do but don't really understand, those who are too shy to ask for help, and those who don't plan to do the work at all.
2. Check progress periodically. In discussions, make sure that everyone has a chance to respond.

Give frequent academic feedback.

EXAMPLES

1. Elementary students should get papers back the day after they are handed in.
2. Good work can be displayed in class and graded papers sent home to parents each week.
3. Students of all ages can keep records of grades, projects completed, and extra credits earned.
4. For older students, break up long-term assignments into several phases, giving feedback at each point.

For more ideas, see **http://trc.virginia.edu/Publications/Teaching_Concerns/TC_Topic/Engaging_Students.htm**.

of challenge is higher and when students' interests are incorporated into the tasks (Emmer & Gerwels, 2006).

Of course, teachers can't supervise every student all the time, or rely on curiosity. Something else must keep students working on their own. In their study of elementary and secondary teachers, Evertson, Emmer, and their colleagues found that effective class managers at both levels had well-planned systems for encouraging students to manage their own work (Emmer & Evertson, 2009; Evertson & Emmer, 2009). The suggestions in the *Guidelines* box are based on their findings.

Prevention Is the Best Medicine

MyEducationLab Go to the Activities and Applications section in Chapter 12 of MyEducationLab and complete Activity 3. As you view the artifact and complete the accompanying activity, reflect upon your own classroom management philosophy and the relevance of withitness.

The ideal way to manage problems, of course, is to prevent them in the first place. Martin and Sugarman (1993) note that "many difficulties in classroom management can be prevented by effective teaching" (p. 51) that interests students, avoids confusion, and keeps activities moving. In a classic study, Jacob Kounin (1970) examined classroom management by comparing effective teachers, whose classes were relatively free of problems, with ineffective teachers, whose classes were continually plagued by chaos and disruption. Observing both groups in action, Kounin found that the teachers were not very different in the way they handled discipline once problems arose. The difference was that the successful teachers were much better at preventing problems. Kounin concluded that effective classroom teachers were especially skilled in four areas: "*withitness*," *overlapping activities*, *group focusing*, and *movement management* (Doyle, 1977). More recent research confirms the importance of these factors (Emmer & Stough, 2001).

Withitness. Withitness means communicating to students that you are aware of everything that is happening in the classroom, that you aren't missing anything. "With-it" teachers seem to have eyes in the backs of their heads. They avoid becoming absorbed or interacting with only a few students, since such behaviour encourages the rest of the class to wander. They are always scanning the room, making eye contact with individual students, so that the students know they are being monitored (Weinstein & Mignano, 2007).

Withitness According to Kounin, awareness of everything happening in a classroom.

These teachers prevent minor disruptions from becoming major. They also know who instigated the problem, and they make sure that the right people are dealt with. In other words, they do not make what Kounin called *timing errors* (waiting too long before intervening) or *target errors* (blaming the wrong student and letting the real perpetrators escape responsibility for their behaviour).

If two problems occur at the same time, effective teachers deal with the more serious one first. For example, a teacher who tells two students to stop whispering but ignores even a brief shoving match at the pencil sharpener communicates to students a lack of awareness. Students begin to believe that they can get away with almost anything if they are clever (Charles, 2002b).

Overlapping and Group Focus. Overlapping means keeping track of and supervising several activities at the same time. For example, a teacher may have to check the work of an individual and at the same time keep a small group working by saying, "Right, go on," and stop an incident in another group with a quick "look" or reminder (Burden, 1995; Charles, 2002b).

Maintaining a group focus means keeping as many students as possible involved in appropriate class activities and avoiding narrowing in on just one or two students. All students should have something to do during a lesson. For example, the teacher might ask everyone to write the answer to a question, then call on individuals to respond while the other students compare their answers. Choral responses might be required while the teacher moves around the room to make sure everyone is participating (Charles, 2002b). For example, during a grammar lesson the teacher might say, "Everyone who thinks the answer is *have run*, hold up the red side of your card. If you think the answer is *has run*, hold up the green side" (Hunter, 1982). This is one way teachers can ensure that all students are involved and that everyone understands the material.

Movement Management. Movement management means keeping lessons and the group moving at an appropriate (and flexible) pace, with smooth transitions and variety. The effective teacher avoids abrupt transitions, such as announcing a new activity before gaining the students' attention or starting a new activity in the middle of something else. In these situations, one-third of the class will be doing the new activity, many will be working on the old lesson, several will be asking other students what to do, some will be taking the opportunity to have a little fun, and most will be confused. Another transition problem Kounin noted is the *slowdown*, or taking too much time to start a new activity. Sometimes teachers give too many directions. Problems also arise when teachers have students work one at a time while the rest of the class waits and watches.

Student Social Skills as Prevention. But what about the students? What can they do? When students lack social and emotional skills such as being able to share materials, read the intentions of others, or handle frustration, classroom management problems often follow. So all efforts to teach social and emotional self-regulation are steps for preventing management problems. Over the short term, educators can teach and model these skills, then give students feedback and practice using them in a variety of settings. Over the long term, teachers can help to change attitudes that value aggression over cooperation and compromise (Elias & Schwab, 2006). Chapter 3 gave ideas for teaching social and emotional skills and competencies.

Debra Stipek and her colleagues (1999) describe many ways teachers embed social skills lessons into school subjects and informal discussions. For example, class rules emphasize respect ("there are no stupid questions"), students learn to give "put ups" not "put downs," the lives of historical figures provide opportunities to discuss choices and how to deal with stresses, and student conflicts become life lessons in relationships. In addition, students are given a "Toolbox of Coping Skills" that contains concrete objects to be used to address problems. The Toolbox includes Post-it notes to record student concerns and troubling situations so the incidents can be dealt with at an appropriate time. Exit and U-turn signs remind students that the best strategy may be to "exit" the situation. "Exiting to a safe place, without explanation, is taught as one appropriate face-saving, and possibly life-saving, response" (Stipek, de la Sota, & Weishaupt, 1999, p. 443). Early indicators are that students do learn to use these skills.

Caring Relationships: Connections With School

We have talked in other chapters about encouraging student engagement and promoting positive attitudes toward education. We saw in Chapter 5 that culturally responsive teaching can provide access to learning for more students. In Chapter 9 we looked at authentic tasks and problem-based

Overlapping Supervising several activities at once.

Group focus The ability to keep as many students as possible involved in activities.

Movement management Keeping lessons and the group moving at an appropriate (and flexible) pace, with smooth transitions and variety.

"DON'T GIVE UP ON ME" Students who feel connected with school are happier, more self-disciplined, and less likely to engage in negative behaviours. Believing that they matter and that their teachers are "on their side" helps keep students engaged and motivated.

learning as ways to connect with students' lives and interests. We examined the TARGET model in Chapter 11 for ideas about building motivation to learn. Here we consider research that specifically examines what helps students, particularly adolescents, feel connected to school.

All efforts at building positive relationships with students and classroom community are steps toward preventing management problems. Students respect teachers who maintain their authority without being rigid or harsh, who are fair and honest with them, who make sure they understand the materials, who ask if something is wrong when they seem upset, and who use creative instructional practices to "make learning fun." Students also value teachers who show academic and personal caring by acting like real people (not just as teachers), sharing responsibility, minimizing the use of external controls, including everyone, searching for students' strengths, communicating effectively, and showing an interest in their students' lives and pursuits (Elias & Schwab, 2006; Wentzel, 2002; Woolfolk Hoy & Weinstein, 2006). Students who feel connected with school are happier, more self-disciplined, and less likely to engage in dangerous behaviours such as substance abuse, violence, and early sexual activity (Freiberg, 2006; McNeely, Nonnemaker, & Blum, 2002). In fact, in a synthesis of 119 studies in English and German conducted from 1948 to 2004, Jeffrey Cornelius-White (2007) concluded that positive, warm, encouraging relationships with teachers are related to many student outcomes including participation in class, critical thinking, dropout prevention, self-esteem, motivation, less disruptive behaviour, and attendance. When Barbara Bartholomew (2008) asked a veteran special education teacher what keeps students engaged and motivated, the teacher replied without hesitation "Students need to know that no matter what, you will never give up on them" (p. 58).

An example of respect for students and their lives comes from Esme Codell. "Madame Esme" (the name she preferred) had a morning ritual as follows:

> In the morning, three things happen religiously. I say good morning, real chipper, to every single child and make sure they say good morning back. Then I collect "troubles" in a "Trouble Basket," a big green basket into which the children pantomime unburdening their home worries so they can concentrate on school. Sometimes a kid has no troubles. Sometimes a kid piles it in, and I in turn pantomime bearing the burden. This way, too, I can see what disposition the child is in when he or she enters. Finally, before they can come in, they must give me a word, which I print on a piece of tag board and keep in an envelope. It can be any word, but preferably one that they heard and don't really know or one that is personally meaningful. We go over the words when we do our private reading conferences. (Codell, 2001, p. 30)

When students perceive their schools are competitive places where they are treated differently based on race, gender, or ethnicity, then they are more likely to act out or withdraw altogether. But when they feel that they have choices, that the emphasis is on personal improvement and not comparisons, and when they feel respected and supported by teachers, students are more likely to bond with schools (Osterman, 2000). When a large sample of African American, Arab American, European American, and Latin American students, ages 11 to 18, were asked about their relationship with teachers and their beliefs about America, researchers found these students were more likely to believe America is a just society if their teachers were fair, tolerant, and respectful. These results held no matter what the age or ethnic background of the students, so connections to teachers can have an impact on students' basic beliefs about their community and country (Flanagan, Cumsille, Gill, & Gallay, 2007).

DEALING WITH DISCIPLINE PROBLEMS

In 2007, Phi Delta Kappa published the 39th annual Gallup Poll of the public's attitude toward public schools (Rose & Gallup, 2007). From 1969 until 1999, "lack of discipline" was named as the number one problem facing the schools almost every year (Rose & Gallup, 1999). Beginning in 2000, lack of financial support took over the number one place, but lack of discipline remained a close second or third every year. Clearly, the public sees discipline as an important challenge for teachers.

Being an effective manager does not mean publicly correcting every minor infraction of the rules. This kind of public attention may actually reinforce the misbehaviour, as we saw in Chapter 6. Teachers who frequently correct students do not necessarily have the best-behaved classes (Irving & Martin, 1982). The key is being aware of what is happening and knowing what is important so that you can prevent problems.

Stopping Problems Quickly

Most students comply quickly when the teacher gives a desist order (a "stop doing that") or redirects behaviour. But some students are the targets of more than their share of desists. One study found that these disruptive students seldom complied with the first teacher request to stop. Often, the disruptive students responded negatively, leading to an average of four to five cycles of teacher desists and student responses before the student complied (Nelson & Roberts, 2000). Emmer and Evertson (2009) and Levin and Nolan (2000) suggest seven simple ways to stop misbehaviour quickly, moving from least to most intrusive:

- *Make eye contact* with, or move closer to, the offender. Other non-verbal signals, such as pointing to the work students are supposed to be doing, might be helpful. Make sure the student actually stops the inappropriate behaviour and gets back to work. If you do not, students will learn to ignore your signals.
- *Try verbal hints* such as "name-dropping" (simply insert the student's name into the lecture), asking the student a question, or making a humorous (not sarcastic) comment such as, "I must be hallucinating. I swear I heard someone shout out an answer, but that can't be because I haven't called on anyone yet!"
- Ask students *if they are aware* of the negative effects of their actions or send an "I" message, described later in the chapter.
- If they are not performing a class procedure correctly, *remind the students* of the procedure and have them follow it correctly. You may need to quietly collect a toy, comb, magazine, or note that is competing with the learning activities, while privately informing the students that their possessions will be returned after class.
- In a calm, unhostile way, *ask the student to state the correct rule or procedure* and then to follow it. Glasser (1969) proposes three questions: "What are you doing? Is it against the rules? What should you be doing?"
- Tell the student in a clear, assertive, and unhostile way to *stop the misbehaviour*. (Later in the chapter we will discuss assertive messages to students in more detail.) If students "talk back," simply repeat your statement.
- *Offer a choice*. For example, when one student continued to call out answers no matter what the teacher tried, the teacher said, "John, you have a choice. Stop calling out answers immediately and begin raising your hand to answer or move your seat to the back of the room and you and I will have a private discussion later. You decide." (Levin & Nolan, 2000, p. 177).

Many teachers prefer the use of logical consequences, described earlier, as opposed to penalties. For example, if one student has harmed another, you can require the offending student to make an "Apology of Action," which includes a verbal apology plus somehow repairing the damage done. This helps offenders develop empathy and social perspective-taking as they think about what would be an appropriate "repair" (Elias & Schwab, 2006).

If you must impose penalties, the *Guidelines* box on page 440, taken from Weinstein (2007) and Weinstein and Mignano (2007), gives ideas about how to do it. The examples are taken from the actual words of the expert teachers described in their book.

There is a caution about penalties, however. Never use lower achievement status (moving to a lower reading group, giving a lower grade, giving excess homework) as a punishment for breaking class rules. These actions should be done only if the benefit of the action outweighs the possible risk of harm. As Carolyn Orange (2000) notes, "Effective, caring teachers would not use low achievement status, grades, or the like as a means of discipline. This strategy is unfair and ineffective. It only serves to alienate the student" (p. 76).

GUIDELINES: Imposing Penalties

Delay the discussion of the situation until you and the students involved are calmer and more objective.

EXAMPLES

1. Say calmly to a student, "Sit there and think about what happened. I'll talk to you in a few minutes," or, "I don't like what I just saw. Talk to me during your free period today."
2. Say, "I'm really angry about what just happened. Everybody take out journals; we are going to write about this." After a few minutes of writing, the class can discuss the incident.

Impose penalties privately.

EXAMPLES

1. Make arrangements with students privately. Stand firm in enforcing arrangements.
2. Resist the temptation to "remind" students in public that they are not keeping their side of the bargain.
3. Move close to a student who must be disciplined and speak so that only the student can hear.

After imposing a penalty, re-establish a positive relationship with the student immediately.

EXAMPLES

1. Send the student on an errand or ask him or her for help.
2. Compliment the student's work or give a symbolic "pat on the back" when the student's behaviour warrants. Look hard for such an opportunity.

Set up a graded list of penalties that will fit many occasions.

EXAMPLE

1. Establish a list of penalties for not turning in homework: (1) receive reminder; (2) receive warning; (3) hand homework in before close of school day; (4) stay after school to finish work; (5) participate in a teacher–student–parent conference to develop an action plan.

Always teach problem-solving strategies along with penalties to help students learn what to do next time (Elias & Schwab, 2006).

EXAMPLES

1. Use Problem Diaries, where students record what they were feeling, identify the problem and their goal, then think of other possible ways to solve the problem and achieve the goal.
2. Try *Keep Calm* 5-2-5: At the first physical signs of anger, students say to themselves: "Stop. Keep Calm," then take several slow breaths, counting to 5 breathing in, 2 holding breath, and 5 breathing out.

For more ideas, see **www.stopbullyingnow.com or www.cfchildren.org.**

Bullying and Cyberbullying

Teachers tend to underestimate the amount of bullying that takes place in schools. Some research estimates between 10 and 30 percent of students are involved in bullying while others place the figure as high as 43 percent. Typically, these estimates are based on reports from children and youth. The incidence of bullying increases as children become adolescents, and the problem of bullying is worldwide (Cook et al., 2010; Mayer & Furlong, 2010).

Bullying and Teasing. Bullying involves repeated attempts to harm a victim and an imbalance of power between the bully and the victim (Merrell, Isava, Gueldner, & Ross, 2008). The line between good-natured exchanges and hostile teasing may seem thin, but a rule of thumb is that teasing someone who is less powerful or less popular or using any racial, ethnic, or religious slur should not be tolerated.

A longitudinal study that followed a representative sample of students in grades 1 through 6 for two years found that aggressive children whose teachers taught them conflict management strategies were moved away from a life path of aggression and violence (Aber, Brown, & Jones, 2003). But when teachers are silent about aggression and teasing, students may "hear" agreement with the insult (Weinstein, 2007). Table 12.4 presents a list of dos and don'ts about teasing in schools.

Besides following these guidelines, research has shown that having a strong sense of community in your classroom is associated with more student empathy for the victims of bullying and less "blaming the victim" for being attacked (Gini, 2008). So anything you do to develop class community will be a step toward dealing with bullying.

Changing Attributions. Cynthia Hudley and her colleagues (2007) at UCLA have developed a program to reduce physical aggression in elementary school. The program, called *BrainPower*, is grounded in attribution theory, discussed in Chapter 11. The central goal of *BrainPower* is to teach

TABLE 12.4 **Dos and Don'ts About Teasing**

Teasing has led to some tragic situations. Talk about what to do about it in your class.

Do:
1. Be careful of others' feelings.
2. Use humour gently and carefully.
3. Ask whether teasing about a certain topic hurts someone's feelings.
4. Accept teasing from others if you tease.
5. Tell others if teasing about a certain topic hurts your feelings.
6. Know the difference between friendly gentle teasing and hurtful ridicule or harassment.
7. Try to read others' "body language" to see if their feelings are hurt—even when they don't tell you.
8. Help a weaker student when he or she is being ridiculed.
Don't:
1. Tease someone you don't know well.
2. [If you are a boy] tease girls about sex.
3. Tease about a person's body.
4. Tease about a person's family members.
5. Tease about a topic when a student has asked you not to.
6. Tease someone who seems agitated or whom you know is having a bad day.
7. Be thin-skinned about teasing that is meant in a friendly way.
8. Swallow your feelings about teasing—tell someone in a direct and clear way what is bothering you.

Source: From *Middle and Secondary Classroom Management: Lessons from Research and Practice* (4th ed.), by C. S. Weinstein. Published by McGraw-Hill. Copyright © 2007 by McGraw-Hill. Adapted with permission from The McGraw-Hill Companies, Inc.

aggressive students "to *start* from a presumption of accidental causes. When a social encounter with a peer results in a negative outcome (a spilled lunch tray, a bump in the lunch line, missing homework, etc.) the child will begin with the assumption that the outcome was due to accidental causes rather than intentional hostility from peers" (**www.brainpowerprogram.com/index-1.html**). The program also teaches accurate reading of social cues, so that students recognize when aggression against them is intentional. After students become more skilful at judging social cues, they learn and practise appropriate responses such as asking questions, being assertive—not aggressive—or seeking adult help. Two decades of research on this program shows it has been successful in changing many students' attributions and behaviours (Hudley, Graham, & Taylor, 2007).

Cyberbullying. With all the positive possibilities associated with technology come problems too. Now bullies have new ways to torment victims using email, text messaging, cell phones, YouTube, web blogs, online voting booths, and more (Weinstein, 2007). For example, when 16-year-old Denise broke up with her boyfriend, he sought revenge by posting her email address and cell phone number on websites and blogs devoted to sex. For months she got embarrassing and frightening calls and messages (Strom & Strom, 2005). This kind of bullying is difficult to combat because the perpetrators can hide, but the damage can be long-term. Table 12.5 has some ideas for dealing with cyberbullying.

Special Problems With Secondary Students

Many secondary students never complete their work. Besides encouraging student responsibility, what else can teachers do to deal with this frustrating problem? Because students at this age have many assignments and teachers have many students, both teachers and students may lose track of what has and has not been completed. It often helps to teach students how to use a daily planner. In addition, the teacher must keep accurate records. The most important thing is to enforce the established consequences for incomplete work. Do not pass a student because you know that he or

TABLE 12.5 Ideas for Dealing With Cyberbullying

- Develop an explicit policy for acceptable in-school use of the internet and include it in the school handbook (or your class rules). The policy should spell out what constitutes cyberbullying and list consequences.
- Make sure that children and young people are aware that bullying will be dealt with seriously.
- Ensure that parents/guardians who express cyberbullying concerns are taken seriously.
- Explain to students that they
  - Should never share or give out personal information, PIN numbers, phone numbers, etc.
  - Should not delete messages; they do not have to read them, but they should show them to an adult they trust. Messages can be used to take action against cyberbullies.
  - Should not open a message from someone they don't know.
  - Should *never* reply to the message.
  - Can block the sender's message if they are being bullied through email or instant messaging.
  - Can forward the messages to their Internet Service Provider.
  - Should tell an adult.
  - Should show the message to the police if it contains physical threats.
  - Should speak out against cyberbullying.
  - Should never send messages when they are angry.
  - Should never send messages they wouldn't want others to see.
- Make parents aware of the fact that all of the major Internet Service Providers offer some form of parental controls. For example, AOL has developed "AOL Guardian,"* which reports with whom youngsters exchange messages and what websites they visit and monitors chat rooms for children 13 and under.
- Encourage parents to keep computers in a public room in the house.
- Invite members of the local police department to come to school to speak with parents and students about proper internet use.
- Make sure ethics is included in any computer instruction given at your school.

* AOL Canada provides a similar service in Canada.

Source: From *Middle and Secondary Classroom Management: Lessons from Research and Practice* (4th ed.), by C. S. Weinstein. Published by McGraw-Hill. Copyright © 2007 by McGraw-Hill. Adapted with permission from The McGraw-Hill Companies, Inc.

she is "bright enough" to pass. Make it clear to these students that the choice is theirs: they can do the work and pass, or they can refuse to do the work and face the consequences. You might also ask, in a private moment, if there is anything interfering with the student's ability to get to the work.

There is also the problem of students who continually break the same rules—always forgetting materials, for example, or getting into fights. What should you do? Seat these students away from others who might be influenced by them. Try to catch them before they break the rules, but if rules are broken, be consistent in applying established consequences. Do not accept promises to do better next time (Levin & Nolan, 2000). Teach the students how to monitor their own behaviour; some of the self-management techniques described in Chapter 6 should be helpful. Finally, remain friendly with the students. Try to catch them in a good moment so that you can talk to them about something other than their rule breaking.

A defiant, hostile student can pose serious problems. If there is an outbreak, try to get out of the situation as soon as possible; everyone loses in a public power struggle. One possibility is to give the student a chance to save face and cool down by saying, "It's your choice to cooperate or not. You can take a minute to think about it." If the student complies, the two of you can talk later about controlling the outbursts. If the student refuses to cooperate, you can tell him or her to wait in the hall until you get the class started on work, then step outside for a private talk. If the student refuses to leave, send another class member for the assistant principal. Again, follow through. If the student complies before help arrives, do not let him or her off the hook. If outbursts occur frequently, you might have a conference with the counsellor, parents, or other teachers. If the problem is an irreconcilable clash of personalities, the student should be transferred to another teacher. There is quite a bit of discussion today about zero tolerance for rule breaking in the schools. Is this a good idea? The *Point/Counterpoint* box looks at both sides of the issue.

POINT / COUNTERPOINT

Is Zero Tolerance a Good Idea?

WITH THE VERY visible violence in schools today, some districts have instituted "zero-tolerance" policies for rule breaking. One result? A 5-year-old student in Toronto was threatened with suspension because he allegedly violated the school's sexual harassment policy. His offence was showing affection toward his classmates (*National Post*, September 13, 2004). Do zero-tolerance policies make sense?

POINT

Zero tolerance is necessary for now.

The arguments for zero tolerance focus on school safety and the responsibilities of schools and teachers to protect the students and themselves, especially since the much-publicized school shootings in Littleton, Colorado, and even Taber, Alberta (April 28, 1999). Of course, many of the incidents reported in the news seem to be overreactions to childhood pranks, or worse, over-zealous applications of zero tolerance to innocent mistakes or lapses of memory. But how do school officials separate the innocent from the dangerous? For example, it has been widely reported that Andy Williams (the boy who killed two classmates in Santee, California) assured his friends before the shootings that he was only joking about "pulling a Columbine."

On January 13, 2003, Gregg Toppo wrote an article for *USA Today* in which he described how a grade 2 student used his shoe to attack his teacher; a kindergartner hit a pregnant teacher in the stomach; and an 8-year-old threatened to use gasoline to burn down his suburban elementary school. Toppo noted, "Elementary school principals and safety experts say they're seeing more violence and aggression than ever among their youngest students, pointing to what they see as an alarming rise in assaults and threats to classmates and teachers" (p. A2).

Incidents such as these have pressed schools to take a hard line on aggressive behaviour, and their response has often been to adopt the so-called zero-tolerance policy.

COUNTERPOINT

Zero tolerance means zero common sense.

An internet search using the keywords *zero tolerance* and *schools* will locate a wealth of information about the policy—much of it against. For example, in the August 29, 2001, issue of *Salon* magazine, Johanna Wald wrote an article titled "The Failure of Zero Tolerance." Here is one of the examples she cites:

> *A 17-year-old honors student in Arkansas begins his senior year with an even more ominous cloud over his head. His college scholarship is in danger because of a 45-day sentence to an alternative school. His offense? An arbitrary search of his car by school officials in the spring revealed no drugs, but a scraper and pocketknife that his father had inadvertently left there the night before when he was fixing the rearview mirror. Despite anguished pleas of extenuating circumstances by the desperate father, the school system has so far adamantly insisted that automatic punishments for weapon possession in school are inviolate.*

Mary Hall, director of Safe Schools Manitoba and adjunct professor at the University of Manitoba, argues that despite their extensive use, zero-tolerance policies are drawing considerable criticism for a number of reasons (M. Hall, personal communication, April 26, 2005). According to Hall, whose dissertation research was on the topic of violence in schools,

> *These policies treat minor and major incidents of violence with equal severity regardless of extenuating circumstances. [Also], they are deemed to be too prescriptive. Most cases of student violence are too complex to be reduced to a programmed response. [Moreover], the policies are highly punitive. Rigid, punitive responses by schools can destroy educator–student relationships—a key element of resiliency. Such responses can fuel frustration and anger of troubled students, contributing to their disfranchisement from school. Since the introduction of zero-tolerance policies into Canadian school systems, there has been a rapid and alarming increase in student suspensions. In numerous cases, adherence to zero-tolerance policies has led to negative and often ludicrous consequences [as we saw in the previous examples]. Finally, the root causes of the problems are not addressed by zero-tolerance policies and they do not allow for the professional judgment of educators who understand the various factors that contribute to problematic behaviour.*

GUIDELINES: Handling Potentially Explosive Situations

Move slowly and deliberately toward the problem situation.

EXAMPLES

1. Walk slowly, then be as still as possible.
2. Establish eye-level position.

Be respectful.

EXAMPLES

1. Keep a reasonable distance.
2. Do not crowd the student. Do not get "in the student's face."
3. Speak respectfully. Use the student's name.
4. Avoid pointing or gesturing.

Be brief.

EXAMPLES

1. Avoid long-winded statements or nagging.
2. Stay with the agenda. Stay focused on the problem at hand. Do not get sidetracked.
3. Deal with less severe problems later.

Avoid power struggles.

EXAMPLES

1. Speak privately if possible.
2. Do not get drawn into "I won't, you will" arguments.
3. Don't make threats or raise your voice.

Inform the student of the expected behaviour and the negative consequence as a choice or decision for the student to make. Then withdraw from the student and allow some time for the student to decide.

EXAMPLES

1. Say, "Michael, you need to return to your desk, or I will have to send for the principal. You have a few seconds to decide." Then move away, perhaps attending to other students.
2. If Michael does not choose the appropriate behaviour, deliver the negative consequences ("You are choosing to have me call the principal"). Follow through with the consequence.

For more ideas, see **www.njcap.org/templated/Programs.html**.

Source: Adapted from *Middle and Secondary Classroom Management: Lessons from Research and Practice*, 4th ed., by C. S. Weinstein. Copyright © 2007 by McGraw-Hill. Adapted with permission from The McGraw-Hill Companies, Inc.

It is sometimes useful to keep records of the incidents by logging the student's name, words and actions, date, time, place, and teacher's response. These records may help identify patterns and can prove useful in meetings with administrators, parents, or special services personnel (Burden, 1995). Some teachers have students sign each entry to verify the incidents.

Violence or destruction of property is a difficult and potentially dangerous problem, so it needs to be taken seriously. The first step is to send for help and get the names of participants and witnesses. Then get rid of any crowd that may have gathered; an audience will only make things worse. Do not try to break up a fight without help. Make sure that the school office is aware of the incident and follow the school policy in dealing with the situation. What else can you do? Consult the *Guidelines* box for handling potentially explosive situations. The suggestions are taken from Weinstein (2007).

Unfortunately, today schools face more serious concerns about violence. We turn to that next.

VIOLENCE IN SCHOOLS

STOP & THINK Do you remember where you were and what you were doing the day of the W. R. Myers High School shooting in Tabor, Alberta (1999), or on the day of the Dawson College shooting in Montreal (2006)? Do you remember your thoughts and feelings?

Violence in Canadian schools is a serious and growing concern among students, parents, and teachers. In the year of the Canadian Research Institute for Law and the Family's school violence survey, Sillars (1995, p. 37) reported that nearly one-third of junior and senior high school students in Calgary carried a weapon to school. Four-fifths claimed that they had been struck, threatened, or had something stolen at school, and more than half admitted to committing seriously delinquent acts. More recently, we have witnessed tragic loss of life through some highly publicized shootings at schools. The problem of violence has many causes; it is a challenge for every element of society. What can the schools do? Teachers and students need to know the warning signs of potential dangers. Table 12.6 describes two kinds of signs: immediate warning and potential problems.

TABLE 12.6

Recognizing the Warning Signs of Violence

The following lists were developed by the American Psychological Association. Other resources are available at **http://helping.apa.org/warningsigns**.

Often people who act violently have trouble controlling their feelings. They may have been hurt by others. Some think that making people fear them through violence or threats of violence will solve their problems or earn them respect. This isn't true. People who behave violently lose respect. They find themselves isolated or disliked, and they still feel angry and frustrated.

If you see these immediate warning signs, violence is a serious possibility:	If you notice the following signs over a period of time, the potential for violence exists:
• loss of temper on a daily basis	• a history of violent or aggressive behaviour
• frequent physical fighting	• serious drug or alcohol use
• significant vandalism or property damage	• gang membership or strong desire to be in a gang
• increase in use of drugs or alcohol	• access to or fascination with weapons, especially guns
• increase in risk-taking behaviour	• threatening others regularly
• detailed plans to commit acts of violence	• trouble controlling feelings like anger
• announcing threats or plans for hurting others	• withdrawal from friends and usual activities
• enjoying hurting animals	• feeling rejected or alone
• carrying a weapon	• having been a victim of bullying
	• poor school performance
	• history of discipline problems or frequent run-ins with authority
	• feeling constantly disrespected
	• failing to acknowledge the feelings or rights of others

Source: From "Warning Signs." Copyright © 1999 by the American Psychological Association. Adapted with permission of the APA. For more information, consult the website http://apahelpcenter.org/featuredtopics/feature.php?id=38.

Prevention

The best answer to school violence is prevention. As a teacher, you may have little to say about violence on television or in video games, but you have much to say about the way students treat each other and the sense of community created in your classes. You can teach acceptance and compassion and create a culture of belongingness for all your students.

Some gang members have reported that they turned to gang activities when their teachers insulted them, called them names, humiliated them publicly, belittled their culture, ignored them in class, or blamed all negative incidents on particular students. These students reported joining gangs for security and to escape teachers who treated them badly or expected little of them because they were members of minority groups (Padilla, 1992; Parks, 1995). Other studies have found that gang members respected teachers who insisted on academic performance in a caring way (Huff, 1989). Anita once asked a teacher in an urban high school which teachers were most effective with the really tough students. He said that there are two kinds of teachers: teachers who can't be intimidated or fooled and expect their students to learn and teachers who really care about the students. When asked, "Which kind are you?" he answered, "Both!" He is an example of a "warm demander," as you will see later in this chapter.

Reaching Every Student: Peer Mediation and Negotiation

Handling conflict is difficult for most of us—and for young people it can be even harder. Given the public's concern about violence in schools, it is surprising how little we know about conflicts among students (Rose & Gallup, 2001). Over 30 years ago, a major U.S. study of more than 8000 secondary school students and 500 teachers from three major cities concluded that 90 percent of the conflicts among students are resolved in destructive ways or are never resolved at all (DeCecco & Richards, 1974). The few studies conducted since that time have reached similar conclusions. Avoidance, force, and threats seem to be the major strategies for dealing with conflict (Johnson, Johnson, Dudley, Ward, & Magnuson, 1995). But there are better ways—like peer mediation and negotiation strategies that teach lifelong lessons.

David Johnson and his colleagues (1995) provided conflict resolution training to 227 students in grades 2 through 5. Students learned the following five-step negotiating strategy:

1. *Jointly define the conflict.* Separate the person from the problem and the actions involved, avoid win–lose thinking, and get both parties' goals clear.
2. *Exchange positions and interests.* Present a tentative proposal and make a case for it, listen to the other person's proposal and feelings, and stay flexible and cooperative.
3. *Reverse perspectives.* See the situation from the other person's point of view and reverse roles and argue for that perspective.
4. *Invent at least three agreements that allow mutual gain.* Brainstorm, focus on goals, think creatively, and make sure everyone has power to invent solutions.
5. *Reach an integrative agreement.* Make sure both sets of goals are met. If all else fails, flip a coin, take turns, or call in a third party—a mediator.

In addition to learning conflict resolution, all students in Johnson et al.'s study were trained in mediation strategies. The role of the mediator was rotated—every day the teacher chose two students to be the class mediators and to wear the mediators' T-shirts. Johnson and his colleagues found that students learned the conflict resolution and mediation strategies and used them successfully, both in school and at home, to handle conflicts in a more productive way.

Peer mediation has also been successful with older students and those with serious problems (Sanchez & Anderson, 1990). In one program, selected gang members were given mediation training, and then all members were invited to participate voluntarily in the mediation process, supervised by school counsellors. Strict rules governed the process leading to written agreements signed by gang representatives. Sanchez and Anderson (1990) found that gang violence in the school was reduced to a bare minimum—"The magic of the mediation process was communication" (p. 56).

Even if you do not have formal peer mediation training in your school, you can help your students handle conflict more productively. For example, Esme Codell taught her grade 5 students a simple four-step process and posted the steps on a bulletin board: "1. Tell person what you didn't like. 2. Tell person how it made you feel. 3. Tell person what you want in the future. 4. Person responds with what they can do. Congratulations! You are a Confident Conflict Conqueror!" (Codell, 2001, p. 23).

THE NEED FOR COMMUNICATION

STOP & THINK A student says to you, "That book you assigned is really stupid—I'm not reading it!" What do you say?

Communication between teachers and students is essential when problems arise. Communication is more than "teachers talk—students listen." It is more than the words exchanged between individuals. We communicate in many ways. Our actions, movements, voice tone, facial expressions, and other non-verbal behaviour send messages to our students. Many times, the messages we intend to send are not the messages our students receive.

Message Sent—Message Received

Teacher: Carl, where is your homework?

Carl: I left it in my dad's car this morning.

Teacher: Again? You'll have to bring me a note tomorrow from your father saying that you actually did the homework. No grade without the note.

Message Carl receives: I can't trust you. I need proof that you did the work.

Teacher: Sit at every other desk. Put all your things under your desk. Jane and Laurel, you're sitting too close together. One of you move!

Message Jane and Laurel receive: I expect you two to cheat on this test.

A new student comes to Ms. Tung's kindergarten. The child is messy and unwashed. Ms. Tung puts her hand lightly on the girl's shoulder and says, "I'm glad you're here." Her muscles tense, and she leans away from the child.

Message student receives: I don't like you. I think you are bad.

In all interactions, a message is sent and a message is received. Sometimes teachers believe that they are sending one message, but their voices, body positions, choices of words, and gestures may communicate a different message.

Students may hear the hidden message and respond to it. For example, a student may respond with hostility if she or he feels insulted by the teacher (or by another student), but may not be able to say exactly where the feeling of being insulted came from. Perhaps it was in the teacher's tone of voice, not the words actually spoken. In such cases, the teacher may feel attacked for no reason. "What did I say? All I said was . . ." The first principle of communication is that people respond to what they *think* was said or meant, not necessarily to the speaker's intended message or actual words.

There are many exercises for practising sending and receiving messages accurately. Students in Anita's classes have told her about one instructor who encourages accurate communication by using the paraphrase rule. Before any participant, including the teacher, is allowed to respond to any other participant in a class discussion, he or she must summarize what the previous speaker said. If the summary is wrong, indicating that the speaker was misunderstood, the speaker must explain again. The respondent then tries again to paraphrase. The process continues until the speaker agrees that the listener has heard the intended message.

Paraphrasing is more than a classroom exercise. It can be the first step in communicating with students. Before teachers can deal appropriately with any student problem, they must know what the real problem is. A student who says, "This book is really dumb! Why did we have to read it?" may really be saying, "The book was too difficult for me. I couldn't read it, and I feel dumb."

Diagnosis: Whose Problem Is It?

As a teacher, you may find some student behaviour unacceptable, unpleasant, or troubling. It is often difficult to stand back from these problems, take an objective look, and decide on an appropriate response. According to Thomas Gordon (1981), the key to good teacher–student relationships is determining why you are troubled by a particular behaviour and whose problem it is. The teacher must begin by asking who "owns" the problem. The answer to this question is critical. If it is really the student's problem, the teacher must become a counsellor and supporter, helping the student find his or her own solution. But if the teacher "owns" the problem, it is the teacher's responsibility to find a solution through problem solving with the student.

Diagnosing who owns the problem is not always straightforward. Let's look at three troubling situations to get some practice in this skill:

1. A student writes obscene words and draws sexually explicit illustrations in a school encyclopedia.
2. A student tells you that his parents had a bad fight and he hates his father.
3. A student quietly reads a newspaper in the back of the room.

Why is this behaviour troubling? If you cannot accept the student's behaviour because it has a serious effect on you as a teacher—if you are blocked from reaching your goals by the student's action—then you own the problem. It is your responsibility to confront the student and seek a solution. A teacher-owned problem appears to be present in the first situation described above—the young pornographer—because teaching materials are damaged.

If you feel annoyed by the behaviour because it is getting in the student's own way or because you are embarrassed for the child, but the behaviour does not directly interfere with your teaching, it is probably the student's problem. The test question is: Does this student's action tangibly affect you or prevent you from fulfilling your role as a teacher? The student who hates his father would not prevent you from teaching, even though you might wish the student felt differently. The problem is really the student's, and he must find his own solution.

Situation 3 is more difficult to diagnose. There have been lengthy debates about whose problem it is when a student reads a newspaper in class. One argument is that the teacher is not interfered with

Paraphrase rule Policy whereby listeners must accurately summarize what a speaker has said before being allowed to respond.

in any way, so it is the student's problem. Another argument is that teachers might find reading the paper distracting during a lecture, so it is their problem, and they must find a solution. In a grey area such as this, the answer probably depends on how the teacher actually experiences the student's behaviour. After deciding who owns the problem, it is time to act.

Counselling: The Student's Problem

Let's pick up the situation in which the student found the reading assignment "dumb." How might a teacher handle this positively?

Student: This book is really dumb! Why did we have to read it?

Teacher: You're pretty upset. This seemed like a worthless assignment to you. [Teacher paraphrases the student's statement, trying to hear the emotions as well as the words.]

Student: Yeah! Well, I guess it was worthless. I mean, I don't know if it was. I couldn't exactly read it.

Teacher: It was just too hard to read, and that bothers you.

Student: Sure, I felt really dumb. I know I can write a good report, but not with a book this tough.

Teacher: I think I can give you some hints that will make the book easier to understand. Can you see me after school today?

Student: Okay.

Here the teacher used empathetic listening to allow the student to find a solution. (As you can see, this approach relies heavily on paraphrasing.) By trying to hear the student and by avoiding the tendency to jump in too quickly with advice, solutions, criticisms, reprimands, or interrogations, the teacher keeps the communication lines open. Here are a few *unhelpful* responses the teacher might have made:

- I chose the book because it is the best example of this author's style in our library. You will need to have read it before your IB (International Baccalaureate) English class next year. (The teacher justifies the choice; this prevents the student from admitting that this "important" assignment is too difficult.)
- Did you really read it? I bet you didn't do the work, and now you want out of the assignment. (The teacher accuses; the student hears, "The teacher doesn't trust me!" and must defend herself or himself or accept the teacher's view.)
- Your job is to read the book, not ask me why. I know what's best. (The teacher pulls rank, and the student hears, "You can't possibly decide what is good for you!" The student can rebel or passively accept the teacher's judgment.)

Empathetic, active listening can be a helpful response when students bring problems to you. You must reflect back to the student what you hear him or her saying. This reflection is more than a parroting of the student's words; it should capture the emotions, intent, and meaning behind them. Sokolove, Garrett, Sadker, and Sadker (1986, p. 241) have summarized the components of active listening: (1) blocking out external stimuli; (2) attending carefully to both the verbal and non-verbal messages; (3) differentiating between the intellectual and the emotional content of the message; and (4) making inferences regarding the speaker's feelings.

When students realize that they really have been heard and not evaluated negatively for what they have said or felt, they feel freer to trust the teacher and to talk more openly. Sometimes the true problem surfaces later in the conversation.

Confrontation and Assertive Discipline

Now let's assume that a student is doing something that actively interferes with teaching. The teacher decides that the student must stop. The problem is the teacher's. Confrontation, not counselling, is required.

Empathetic listening Hearing the intent and emotions behind what another says and reflecting them back by paraphrasing.

"I" Messages. Gordon (1981) recommends sending an "I" message in order to intervene and change a student's behaviour. Basically, this means telling a student in a straightforward, assertive, and non-judgmental way what she or he is doing, how it affects you as a teacher, and how you feel about it. The student is then free to change voluntarily, and often does so. Here are two "I" messages:

- If you leave your book bags in the aisles, I might trip and hurt myself.
- When you all call out, I can't concentrate on each answer, and I'm frustrated.

EMPATHETIC LISTENING When students realize they really have been heard and not evaluated negatively for what they have said or felt, they begin to trust the teacher and to talk more openly. Sometimes the true problem surfaces later in the conversation.

Assertive Discipline. Lee and Marlene Canter (1992; Canter, 1996) suggest other approaches for dealing with a teacher-owned problem. They call their method assertive discipline. Teachers are assertive when they make their expectations clear and follow through with established consequences. Students then have a straightforward choice: they can follow the rules or accept the consequences. Many teachers are ineffective with students because they are either wishy-washy and passive or hostile and aggressive (Charles, 2002a).

Instead of telling the student directly what to do, teachers with a *passive response style* tell, or often ask, the student to try or to think about the appropriate action. Such a teacher may comment on the problem behaviour without actually telling the child what to do differently: "Why are you doing that? Don't you know the rules?" or "Sam, are you disturbing the class?" Or teachers may clearly state what should happen, but never follow through with the established consequences, giving the students "one more chance" every time. Finally, teachers may ignore behaviour that should receive a response or may wait too long before responding.

A *hostile response style* involves different mistakes. Teachers may make "you" statements that condemn the student without stating clearly what the student should be doing: "You should be ashamed of the way you're behaving!" or "You never listen!" or "You're acting like a baby!" Teachers may also threaten students angrily but follow through too seldom, perhaps because the threats are too vague—"You'll be very sorry you did that when I get through with you!"—or too severe. For example, a teacher tells a student in a physical education class that he will have to "sit on the bench for *three weeks*." A few days later the team is short one member and the teacher allows the student to play, never returning him to the bench to complete the three-week sentence. Often, a teacher who has been passive becomes hostile and explodes when students persist in misbehaving.

In contrast to both the passive and the hostile styles, an *assertive response* communicates to the students that you care too much about them and the process of learning to allow inappropriate behaviour to persist. Assertive teachers clearly state what they expect. To be most effective, the teachers often look into a student's eyes when speaking and address the student by name. Assertive teachers' voices are calm, firm, and confident. They are not sidetracked by accusations such as "You just don't understand!" or "You don't like me!" Assertive teachers do not get into a debate about the fairness of the rules. They expect changes, not promises or apologies.

Not all educators believe that assertive discipline is useful. Earlier critics questioned the penalty-focused approach and emphasized that assertive discipline undermined student self-management (Render, Padilla, & Krank, 1989). John Covaleskie (1992) observed, "What helps children become moral is not knowledge of the rules, or even obedience to the rules, but discussions about the reasons for acting in certain ways" (p. 56). These critics have had an impact. More recent versions of assertive discipline focus on teaching students "in an atmosphere of respect, trust, and support, how to behave responsibly" (Charles, 2002a, p. 47).

Confrontations and Negotiations. If "I" messages or assertive responses fail and a student persists in misbehaving, the teacher and student are in a conflict. Several pitfalls now loom. The two individuals become less able to perceive each other's behaviour accurately. Research has shown that the angrier you get with another person, the more you see the other as the villain and yourself

"I" message Clear, non-accusatory statement of how something is affecting you.

Assertive discipline Clear, firm, unhostile response style.

as an innocent victim. Because you feel that the other person is in the wrong, and he or she feels just as strongly that the conflict is all your fault, very little mutual trust is possible. A cooperative solution to the problem is almost impossible. In fact, by the time the discussion has gone on a few minutes, the original problem is lost in a sea of charges, countercharges, and self-defence (Baron & Byrne, 2003).

There are three methods of resolving a conflict between teacher and student. One is for the teacher to impose a solution. This may be necessary during an emergency, as when a defiant student refuses to go to the hall to discuss a public outbreak, but it is not a good solution for most conflicts. The second method is for the teacher to give in to the student's demands. You might be convinced by a particularly compelling student argument, but again, this method should be used sparingly. It is generally a bad idea to be talked out of a position, unless the position was wrong in the first place. Problems arise when either the teacher or the student gives in completely.

Gordon (1981) recommends a third approach, which he calls the "no-lose method." Here the needs of both the teacher and the students are taken into account in the solution. No one person is expected to give in completely; all participants retain respect for themselves and each other. The no-lose method is a six-step problem-solving strategy:

1. *Define the problem*. What exactly is the behaviour involved? What does each person want? (Use active listening to help students pinpoint the real problem.)
2. *Generate many possible solutions*. Brainstorm, but remember to not allow any evaluations of ideas yet.
3. *Evaluate each solution*. Any participant may veto any idea. If no solutions are found to be acceptable, brainstorm again.
4. *Make a decision*. Choose one solution through consensus, not voting. In the end, everyone must be satisfied with the solution.
5. *Determine how to implement the solution*. What will be needed? Who will be responsible for each task? What is the timetable?
6. *Evaluate the success of the solution*. After trying the solution for a while, ask, "Are we satisfied with our decision? How well is it working? Should we make some changes?"

Many of the conflicts in classrooms can be important learning experiences for all concerned.

DIVERSITY AND CONVERGENCES IN LEARNING ENVIRONMENTS

MyEducationLab
Go to the Teacher Talk section of Chapter 12 of MyEducationLab and watch a video of Dana Boyd, 2007 Teacher of the Year from Texas, explaining how she brings her diverse students together to create a classroom community and achieve success.

We have looked at quite a few perspectives on classroom management. Clearly, there is not a one-size-fits-all strategy for creating social and physical spaces for learning. Let's first consider the role of culture in productive classroom management.

Diversity: Culturally Responsive Management

Research on discipline shows that students from minority groups may be disciplined for behaviours they never meant to be disruptive or disrespectful because of a lack of cultural synchronization between teachers and students. For example, studies involving African Americans, especially males, indicate that these students are punished more often and more harshly than other students. These students lose time from learning as they spend more hours in detention or suspension (Ferguson, 2000; Monroe & Obidah, 2002; Skiba, Michael, Nardo, & Peterson, 2000). Why?

The notion that African American and Latin American students are punished more because they commit more serious offences is NOT supported by the data. Instead, these students are punished more severely for minor offences such as rudeness or defiance—words and actions that are interpreted by teachers as meriting severe punishment. One explanation is a lack of cultural synchronization between teachers and students. "The language, style of walking, glances, and dress of black children, particularly males, have engendered fear, apprehension, and overreaction among many teachers and school administrators" (Irvine, 1990, p. 27). African American students may be disciplined for behaviours that were never intended to be disruptive or disrespectful. According to Joyce Barakett of Concordia University, teachers in Canada also "call upon cultural differences" to explain students' behaviour (Barakett, 1986, p. 98). In interviews, teachers reported that children from Yugoslavia "posed problems of control" and Greek children were more motivated (Barakett, 1986, p. 99). Teachers do their students and themselves a service if they work at becoming bicultural—helping their students to learn how to function in both mainstream and home cultures, but also learning the meaning of their students' words and actions—so they do not misinterpret and then punish their students' unintended insults (Gay, 2006).

Culturally responsive management is simply a part of the larger concept of culturally relevant teaching. Geneva Gay (2006) sums it up:

> If the classroom is a comfortable, caring, embracing, affirming, engaging, and facilitative place for students then discipline is not likely to be much of an issue. It follows then that both classroom management and school achievement can be improved for students from different ethnic, racial, social, and linguistic backgrounds by ensuring that curriculum and instruction are culturally relevant and personally meaningful for them.

The teachers who seem to be most effective with African American students practise culturally responsive management and have been called "warm demanders" (Irvine & Armento, 2001; Irvine & Fraser, 1998). For example, results of one study indicated:

> To a person unfamiliar with African American culture of inner-city life, it could be misconstrued as intimidation or heavy handed but in the minds of these informants, discipline was directly connected to caring. In fact, all viewed lack of discipline as a sign of uncaring and an apathetic teaching force. (Gordon, 1998, p. 427)

Carla Monroe and Jennifer Obidah (2002) studied Ms. Simpson, a grade 8 science teacher. She described herself as having high expectations for academics and behaviour in her classes—so much so that she believed that her students perceived her as "mean." Yet, she often used humour and dialect to communicate her expectations, as in the following exchange:

> **Ms. Simpson [addressing the class]:** If you know you're going to act the fool just come to me and say, "I'm going to act the fool at the pep rally," so I can go ahead and send you to wherever you need to go. [Class laughs.]
>
> **Ms. Simpson:** I'm real serious. If you know you're having a bad day, you don't want anybody touching you, you don't want nobody saying nothing to you, somebody bump into you you're going to snap—you need to come up to me and say, "I'm going to snap and I can't go to the pep rally." [The students start to call out various comments.]
>
> **Ms. Simpson:** Now, I just want to say I expect you to have the best behaviour because you're the most mature students in the building . . . don't make me stop the pep rally and ask the 8th graders to leave.
>
> **Edward:** We'll have silent lunch won't we? [Class laughs.]
>
> **Ms. Simpson:** You don't want to dream about what you're going to have. [Class laughs.] Ok, 15 minutes for warm-ups. [The students begin their warm-up assignment.]

Some students may be more accustomed to a directive kind of management and discipline outside of school. Their families might say, "Put down that candy" or "Go to bed," whereas other parents might ask, "Can we eat candy before dinner?" or "Isn't it time for bed?" As H. Richard Milner (2006) says, "The question should not be which approach is right or wrong but which approach works with and connects with the students' prior knowledge and ways of knowing."

Culturally responsive management Taking cultural meanings and styles into account when developing management plans and responding to students.

Warm demanders Effective teachers who show both high expectations and great caring for their students.

Convergences: Research on Management Approaches

Emmer and Aussiker (1990) conducted a meta-analysis of three general perspectives on management: influencing students through listening and problem solving, as described by Gordon (1981, 1991); group management through class meetings and student discussion, as advocated by Glasser

(1969, 1990); and control through rewards and punishments, as exemplified by Canter and Canter (1992). No clear conclusions could be drawn about the impact of these approaches on student behaviours. However, some evaluations have found positive effects for Freiberg's (1999) Consistency Management program and for programs that use rewards and punishments (Lewis, 2001).

Integrating Ideas. In a study conducted in Australia, Ramon Lewis (2001) found that recognizing and rewarding appropriate student behaviours, talking with students about how their behaviour affects others, involving students in class discipline decisions, and providing non-directive hints and descriptions about unacceptable behaviours were associated with students taking greater responsibility for their own learning. It is interesting that these interventions represent all three of the general approaches reviewed by Emmer and Aussiker—influence, group management, and control. Lewis also concluded that teachers sometimes find using these interventions difficult when students are aggressive—and most in need of the approaches. When teachers feel threatened, it can be difficult to do what students need, but that may be the most important time to act positively.

Communicating With Families About Classroom Management. As we have seen throughout this book, families are important partners in education. This statement applies to classroom management as well. When parents and teachers share the same expectations and support each other, they can create a more positive classroom environment and more time for learning. The *Family and Community Partnerships Guidelines* box gives ideas for how to work with families and the community.

FAMILY AND COMMUNITY PARTNERSHIPS

GUIDELINES: Classroom Management

Make sure that families know the expectations and rules of your class and school.

EXAMPLES

1. At a Family Fun Night, have your students do skits showing the rules—how to follow them and what breaking them "looks like" and "sounds like."
2. Make a poster for the refrigerator at home that describes, in a light way, the most important rules and expectations.
3. For older students, give families a list of due dates for the major assignments, along with tips about how to encourage high-quality work by pacing the effort—avoiding last-minute panic.
4. Communicate in appropriate ways; for example, use the family's first language when possible. Tailor messages to the reading level of the home.

Make families partners in recognizing good citizenship.

EXAMPLES

1. Send positive notes home when students, especially students who have had trouble with classroom management, work well in the classroom.
2. Give ideas for ways in which any family, even one with few economic resources, can celebrate accomplishment—a favourite food; the chance to choose a movie to rent; a comment to a special person such as an aunt, grandparent, or minister; the chance to read to a younger sibling.

Identify talents in the community to help build a learning environment in your class.

EXAMPLES

1. Have students write letters to carpet and furniture stores asking for donations of remnants to carpet a reading corner.
2. Find family members who can build shelves or room dividers, paint, sew, laminate manipulatives, write stories, repot plants, or network computers.
3. Contact businesses for donations of computers, printers, or other equipment.

Seek cooperation from families when behaviour problems arise.

EXAMPLES

1. Talk to families over the phone or in their home. Have good records about the problem behaviour.
2. Listen to family members and solve problems with them.

For more ideas see **www.educationworld.com**.

SUMMARY TABLE

The Need for Organization (pp. 421–424)

What are the challenges of classroom management? Classrooms are by nature multidimensional, full of simultaneous activities, fast-paced and immediate, unpredictable, public, and affected by the history of students' and teachers' actions. A teacher must juggle all these elements every day. Productive classroom activity requires students' cooperation. Maintaining cooperation is different for each age group. Young students are learning how to "go to school" and need to learn the general procedures of school. Older students need to learn the specifics required for working in different subjects. Working with adolescents requires teachers to understand the power of the adolescent peer group.

What are the goals of good classroom management? The goals of effective classroom management are to make ample time for learning; improve the quality of time use by keeping students actively engaged; make sure participation structures are clear, straightforward, and consistently signalled; and encourage student self-management, self-control, and responsibility.

Classroom management Techniques used to maintain a healthy learning environment, relatively free of behavioural problems.

Participation structures The formal and informal rules for how to take part in a given activity.

Allocated time Time set aside for learning.

Engaged time/time on task Time spent actively engaged in the learning task at hand.

Academic learning time Time when students are actually succeeding at the learning task.

Self-management Management of your own behaviour and acceptance of responsibility for your own actions.

Creating a Positive Learning Environment (pp. 424–429)

Distinguish between rules and procedures. Rules are the specific dos and don'ts of classroom life. They usually are written down or posted. Procedures cover administrative tasks, student movement, housekeeping, and routines for accomplishing lessons, interactions between students and teachers, and interactions among students. Rules can be written in terms of rights and students may benefit from participating in establishing these rules. Consequences should be established for following and breaking the rules and procedures so that the teacher and the students know what will happen.

Procedures/routines Prescribed steps for an activity.

Rules Statements specifying expected and forbidden behaviours; dos and don'ts.

Natural/logical consequences Instead of punishing, having students redo, repair, or in some way face the consequences that naturally flow from their actions.

Planning Spaces for Learning (pp. 430–434)

Distinguish between personal territories and interest-areas spatial arrangements. There are two basic kinds of spatial organization, territorial (the traditional classroom arrangement) and functional (dividing space into interest or work areas). Flexibility is often the key. Access to materials, convenience, privacy when needed, ease of supervision, and a willingness to re-evaluate plans are important considerations in the teacher's choice of physical arrangements.

What management issues do computers raise in the classroom? Clear procedures are especially important when there are computers in the classroom. Whether teachers have one, several, or a room full of computers, they need to think through what students will need to know, teach procedures, and provide easy-to-find and easy-to-follow written instructions for common tasks. Students or parent volunteers can be trained as expert support. Different role structures make management of computer tasks easier.

What do effective classroom managers do in the first weeks of classes? Effective classroom managers spent the first days of class teaching a workable, easily understood set of rules and procedures by using a lot of explanation, examples, and practice. In these classes, students were occupied with organized, enjoyable activities and learned to function cooperatively in the group. Quick, firm, clear, and consistent responses to infractions of the rules characterized effective teachers. The teachers had planned carefully to avoid any last-minute tasks that might have taken them away from their students. These teachers dealt with the children's pressing concerns first.

Action zone Area of a classroom where the greatest amount of interaction takes place.

Creating a Learning Community (pp. 434–435)

What are Johnson and Johnson's three C's of establishing a classroom community? The three C's are cooperative community, constructive conflict resolution, and civic values. Classroom management begins by establishing a community based on cooperative learning. At the heart of the community is the idea of positive interdependence—individuals working together to achieve mutual goals. Constructive conflict resolution is essential in the community because conflicts are inevitable and even necessary for learning. The last C stands for civic values—the understandings and beliefs that hold the community together. Values are learned through direct teaching, modelling, literature, group discussions, and the sharing of concerns.

Maintaining a Good Environment for Learning (pp. 435–438)

How can teachers encourage engagement? In general, as teacher supervision increases, students' engaged time also increases. When the task provides continuous cues for the student about what to do next, involvement will be greater. Activities with clear steps are likely to be more absorbing, because one step leads naturally to the next. Making work requirements clear and specific, providing needed materials, and monitoring activities all add to engagement.

Explain the factors identified by Kounin that prevent management problems in the classroom. To create a positive environment and prevent problems, teachers must take individual differences into account, maintain student motivation, and reinforce positive behaviour. Successful problem preventers are skilled in four areas described by Kounin: "withitness," overlapping, group focusing, and movement management. When penalties have to be imposed, teachers should impose them calmly and privately. In addition to applying Kounin's ideas, teachers can prevent problems by establishing a caring classroom community and teaching students to use social skills and emotional self-regulation skills.

How do teachers help students form connections with schools? To get started on building connections, teachers should make expectations for both academic work and student behaviours clear. Respect for students' needs and rights should be at the centre of class procedures. Students know that their teachers care about them when teachers try to make classes interesting, are fair and honest with them, make sure they understand the materials, and have ways to cope with students' concerns and troubles.

Withitness According to Kounin, awareness of everything happening in a classroom.

Overlapping Supervising several activities at once.

Group focus The ability to keep as many students as possible involved in activities.

Movement management Keeping lessons and the group moving at an appropriate (and flexible) pace, with smooth transitions and variety.

Dealing With Discipline Problems (pp. 438–444)

Describe seven levels of intervention in misbehaviour. Teachers can first make eye contact with the student or use other non-verbal signals, then try verbal hints such as simply inserting the student's name into the lecture. Next the teacher asks if the offender is aware of the negative effects of the actions, then reminds the student of the procedure and has her or him follow it correctly. If this does not work, the teacher can ask the student to state the correct rule or procedure and then to follow it, and then move to telling the student in a clear, assertive, and unhostile way to stop the misbehaviour. If this fails too, the teacher can offer a choice—stop the behaviour or meet privately to work out the consequences.

What can teachers do about bullying, teasing, and cyberbullying? Teachers often underestimate the amount of peer conflict and bullying that happens in schools. Bullying involves both an imbalance of power between students and repeated attempts at harm and may take place in a variety of settings—including those in which students are not face-to-face with one another at school. Teachers can think of bullying as a form of violence and approach strategies for overcoming bullying as they would strategies to overcoming other violent acts. For example, prevention of bullying can take the form of developing a respectful classroom community, discussing conflict, and providing venues for students to report attacks against them. Students may also benefit from peer mediation.

What are some challenges in secondary classrooms? Teachers working in secondary schools should be prepared to handle students who don't complete school work, repeatedly break the same rule, or openly defy teachers. These students may also be experiencing new and powerful stressors. As a result, secondary students may benefit if teachers provide opportunities or point out resources for these students to seek out help and support. Teachers might also find consultation with guidance counsellors and parents helpful.

Violence in Schools (pp. 444–446)

What can be done about violence in schools? Violence is actually decreasing in the schools, but incidents such as school shootings bring attention from the media. But young people ages 12 to 24 are the most likely group to be victims of non-fatal violence—often on school property. Possibilities to deal with violence include preventing violence by creating compassionate, respectful classrooms. It is especially important to respect the cultural heritages of the students while also maintaining high expectations for learning, Peer mediation is one good possibility for preventing violence in schools. The steps for peer mediation are as follows: (1) Jointly define the conflict. (2) Exchange positions and interests. (3) Reverse perspectives. (4) Invent at least three agreements that allow mutual gain. (5) Reach an integrative agreement.

The Need for Communication (pp. 446–450)

What is meant by "empathetic listening"? Communication between teacher and student is essential when problems arise. All interactions between people, even silence or neglect, communicate some meaning. Empathetic, active listening can be a helpful response when students bring problems to teachers. Teachers must reflect back to the students what they hear them saying. This reflection is more than a parroting of words; it should capture the emotions, intent, and meaning behind them.

Distinguish among passive, hostile, and assertive response styles. The *passive style* can take several forms. Instead of telling the student directly what to do, the teacher simply comments on the behaviour, asks the student to *think about* the appropriate action, or threatens but never follows through. In a *hostile response style*, teachers may make "you" statements that condemn the student without stating clearly what the student should be doing. An *assertive response* communicates to the students that the teacher cares too much about them and the process of learning to allow inappropriate behaviour to persist. Assertive teachers clearly state what they expect.

Paraphrase rule Policy whereby listeners must accurately summarize what a speaker has said before being allowed to respond.

Empathetic listening Hearing the intent and emotions behind what another says and reflecting them back by paraphrasing.

"I" message Clear, non-accusatory statement of how something is affecting you.

Assertive discipline Clear, firm, unhostile response style.

Culturally responsive management Taking cultural meanings and styles into account when developing management plans and responding to students.

Warm demanders Effective teachers who show both high expectations and great caring for their students.

TEACHERS' CASEBOOK

Two boys are terrorizing one of your students. They are larger, stronger, and older than the boy being victimized, who is small and shy. Unfortunately, the bullies are fairly popular, in part because they are successful athletes. There are incidents on the bus before and after school, in the gym, and at lunch, including intimidation, extortion of lunch money, tripping, shoving, and verbal taunts—"fag" is a favourite chant. You do not have the two bullies in any of your classes. Your student has started to miss school routinely, and when he is in class, the quality of his work is declining. The other students in your class see what is going on and know you are aware of the problem too.

What Would *They* Do?

Here is how a practising teacher responded to the teaching situation described above.

William Wallace

Western Technical and Commercial School, Toronto, ON

You cannot wish bullying away; intervention is essential. Action takes several forms. There are many ways of thinking about how to act, and one way is to think about three steps: being preventative, being proactive, and being persistent.

First is prevention. I work quickly at the beginning of each semester to develop relationships with my students so that as issues, academic or behavioural, arise, I can deal with them as one human being to another. Dealing with bullying is easier if there are relationships in place where each student knows that he or she is seen as a whole human being. When conflict arises, and it will, you can focus on the behaviour without judging the person. It's very hard to get to the person through the negative behaviour. As well, the culture of caring and mutual respect is something that needs to be nurtured and developed in the classroom and in the school. It's not enough to assume that it should be in place. Opportunities for leadership, mentorship, stewardship, and cooperation need to be a part of everyday life at a school. A place where student contributions are not highly valued is a place where bullying is more likely to arise.

Second is being proactive. If there's a one-off incident, I address it with the students involved and, where appropriate, use it in a generic way to discuss broader issues with my classes, for example, homophobia and gay-bashing. If I have any sense that this one incident is serious, or part of a broader pattern, then I immediately involve other teachers who know and work with the students involved, particularly the teachers in guidance, who often have an excellent knowledge of the history of students who might be prone to bullying or to being bullied. If the incidents are ongoing, I would work to develop a joint strategy with my colleagues for how to address them; for example, when to involve parents, the administration, social workers, and so on.

Third is persistence. Bullying and being bullied are usually symptomatic of underlying problems. It provides an opportunity for teachers and schools to respond to the signal students are sending. Checking in with the students involved, and providing opportunities for discussion as well as for the students' personal success, are ways of contributing to a positive outcome from a bullying incident. In addressing bullying directly, we send a strong message that it is not acceptable behaviour; we indicate our concern for the individuals involved, both bullies and bullied; and we help chart a course within the school community to build and strengthen a positive culture.

As you will have gathered, I have talked very little about discipline. Discipline has its place, but wrongly used it will simply alienate the bullies, making them harder to reach. There is no replacement for relationship building, and this is certainly an idea that the bullies themselves need to embrace.

13 Teaching Every Student

SAT © Diana Ong, SuperStock

TEACHERS' CASEBOOK

WHAT WOULD YOU DO?

You have started a new job in a high school in your hometown. When you were in school, the students were fairly similar—white, working to middle class, and English speaking. There was a "special education" class for students who had serious learning or developmental problems. But in the classes you will be teaching, you find a wide range of reading levels, family incomes, and learning problems. Two of your students are virtually ready for post-secondary education, while several can barely read the texts and their writing is impossible to decipher. Reading English texts is a challenge for some of your students, though they seem to speak English with little trouble.

CRITICAL THINKING

- How would you differentiate instruction for these very different students?
- Do different philosophies of teaching provide different answers to this question?
- How will you grade work if you have successfully differentiated instruction?

Much of this text has been about learning and learners. In this chapter, we focus on teachers and teaching. We look first at characteristics of effective teachers and then we examine how teachers plan, including how they use taxonomies of learning objectives or themes as a basis for planning.

With this foundation of knowing how to set goals and make plans, we move to a consideration of some general teacher-centred strategies: lecturing, seatwork, homework, questioning, recitation, and group discussion. The next section focuses on student-centred approaches to teaching in different subjects: reading, writing, mathematics, and science. Educational psychologists have studied how people learn these subjects and identified implications for teaching. Finally, we examine elements of differentiated instruction and effective teaching in inclusive classrooms.

By the time you have completed this chapter, you should be able to answer these questions:

- What are the characteristics of effective teachers?
- When and how should teachers use instructional objectives and themes for planning?
- In what situations would each of the following formats be most appropriate: lecture, seatwork and homework, questioning, and group discussion?
- How does the teacher's role vary in direct and student-centred approaches to teaching?
- What are the merits of student-centred approaches to teaching reading, mathematics, and science?
- How can teachers' expectations affect students' learning?

RESEARCH ON TEACHING

This chapter is about teaching, so we start with findings from several decades of research.

How would you go about identifying the keys to successful teaching? You might ask students, principals, college or university professors of education, or experienced teachers to list the characteristics of good teachers. Or you could do intensive case studies of a few classrooms over a long period. You might observe classrooms, rate different teachers on certain characteristics, and then see which characteristics were associated with teachers whose students either achieved the most or were the most motivated to learn. (To do this, of course, you would have to decide how to assess

Connect and Extend
Go to the "Connect and Extend" section in Chapter 13 of MyEducationLab to find further content that links to teaching, students' thinking, research, and the news.

achievement and motivation.) You could identify teachers whose students, year after year, learned more than students working with other teachers; then you could watch the more successful teachers, and note what they do. You might also train teachers to apply several different strategies to teach the same lesson and then determine which strategy led to the greatest student learning. You could videotape teachers, and then ask them to view the tapes and report what they were thinking about as they taught and what influenced their decisions while teaching. You might study transcripts of classroom dialogue to learn what helped students understand.

All these approaches and more have been used to investigate teaching (Floden, 2001). Often, researchers use the relationships identified between teaching and learning as the basis for developing teaching approaches and testing these approaches in design experiments (Brown, 1992; Greeno, Collins, & Resnick, 1996). Let's examine some of the specific knowledge about teaching gained from these projects.

Characteristics of Effective Teachers

STOP & THINK Think about the most effective teacher you ever had—the one that you learned the most from. What were the characteristics of that person? What made that teacher so effective?

Some of the earliest research on effective teaching focused on the personal qualities of the teachers themselves. Results revealed some lessons about three teacher characteristics: clarity, warmth, and knowledge.

Clarity and Organization. When Barak Rosenshine and Norma Furst (1973) reviewed about 50 studies of teaching, they concluded that clarity was the most promising teacher behaviour for future research on effective teaching. Teachers who provide clear presentations and explanations tend to have students who learn more and who rate their teachers more positively (Comadena, Hunt, & Simonds, 2007; Hines, Cruickshank, & Kennedy, 1985). Teachers with more knowledge of the subject tend to be less vague in their explanations to the class. The less vague the teacher, the more the students learn (Evertson & Emmer, 2009).

Warmth and Enthusiasm. As you are well aware, some teachers are much more enthusiastic than others. Some studies have found that ratings of teachers' enthusiasm for their subject are correlated with student achievement gains (Rosenshine & Furst, 1973), whereas warmth, friendliness, and understanding seem to be the teacher traits most strongly related to students liking the teacher and the class in general (Madsen, 2003; Hamann, Baker, McAllister, & Bauer, 2000; Soar & Soar, 1979). But note that these are correlational studies. The results do not tell us that teacher enthusiasm causes student learning or that warmth causes positive attitudes, only that the two variables tend to occur together. Teachers trained to demonstrate their enthusiasm have students who are more attentive and involved, but not necessarily more successful on tests of content (Gillett & Gall, 1982).

Teachers' Knowledge. Do teachers who know more about their subject have a more positive impact on their students? It depends on the subject. High school students appear to learn more mathematics from teachers with degrees or significant coursework in mathematics (Darling-Hammond, 2000; Wayne & Youngs, 2003). However, when we look at teachers' knowledge of facts and concepts, as measured by test scores and university grades, the relationship to student learning is unclear and may be indirect. Teachers who know more facts about their subject do not necessarily have students who learn more. But teachers who know more may make clearer presentations and recognize student difficulties more readily. They are ready for any student questions and do not have to be evasive or vague in their answers. Thus, knowledge is necessary but not sufficient for effective teaching because being more knowledgeable helps teachers be clearer and more organized.

One caveat—importance can be in the eye of the beholder. In one study, administrators and students agreed that that teacher clarity was very important but differed in their views of teacher knowledge. Students rated knowledge third in importance but administrators rated it nineteenth (Polk, 2006). Teachers' knowledge and expertise has been the focus of quite a bit of research and discussion, as you will see in the next section.

Knowledge for Teaching

As you saw in Chapters 7 and 8, knowledge is the defining characteristic of expertise. Expert teachers have elaborate *systems of knowledge* for understanding problems in teaching. For example, when a beginning teacher is faced with students' wrong answers on math or history tests, all of these answers may seem about the same—wrong. But for an expert teacher, wrong answers are part of a rich system of knowledge that could include how to recognize several types of wrong answers, the misunderstanding or lack of information behind each kind of mistake, the best way to reteach and correct the misunderstanding, materials and activities that have worked in the past, and several ways to test whether the reteaching was successful. In addition, expert teachers have clear goals and take individual differences into account when planning for their students. These teachers are reflective practitioners (Floden & Klinzing, 1990; Hogan, Rabinowitz, & Craven, 2003).

What do expert teachers know that allows them to be so successful? Lee Shulman (1987) has studied this question, and he has identified seven areas of professional knowledge. Expert teachers know:

1. The academic subjects they teach—their content knowledge is deep and interconnected.
2. General teaching strategies that apply in all subjects (such as the principles of classroom management, effective teaching, and evaluation that you will discover in this book).
3. The curriculum materials and programs appropriate for their subject and grade level.
4. Subject-specific knowledge for teaching: special ways of teaching certain students and particular concepts, such as the best ways to explain negative numbers to lower-ability students.
5. The characteristics and cultural backgrounds of learners.
6. The settings in which students learn—pairs, small groups, teams, classes, schools, and the community.
7. The goals and purposes of teaching.

This is quite a list. Obviously, one course cannot give you all the information you need to teach. In fact, a whole program of courses won't make you an expert. That takes time and experience. But studying educational psychology has added to your professional knowledge because at the heart of educational psychology is a concern with learning wherever it occurs. You will be a better teacher by applying the knowledge you have gained in this course: knowledge about your *students* (Part 1 of this book), *learning and motivation* (Part 2), and *teaching and assessing* (Part 3).

Now let's get to the specifics of teaching—the first step is planning.

MyEducationLab Go to the Teacher Talk section in Chapter 13 of MyEducationLab and watch a video of Lois Rebich, 2007 Teacher of the Year from Pennsylvania, explaining her philosophy of teaching children.

THE FIRST STEP: PLANNING

STOP & THINK Greta Morine-Dershimer (2006) asks which of the following are true about teacher planning:

Time is of the essence.	A little planning goes a long way.
Plans are made to be broken.	You can do it yourself.
Don't look back.	One size fits all.

When you thought about the "What Would You Do?" challenge at the beginning of this chapter, you were planning. In the past few years, educational researchers have become very interested in teachers' planning. They have interviewed teachers about how they plan, asked teachers to "think out loud" while planning or to keep journals describing their plans, and even studied teachers intensively for months at a time. What have they found?

First, planning influences what students will learn, since planning transforms the available time and curriculum materials into activities, assignments, and tasks for students—*time is the essence* of planning. When a teacher decides to devote 7 hours to language arts and 15 minutes to science in a given week, the students in that class will learn more language than science. In fact, differences as dramatic as this do occur, with some classes dedicating twice as much time as others

MyEducationLab Go to the Activities and Applications section in Chapter 13 of MyEducationLab and complete Activity 1. Consider the multiple factors that go into effective lesson planning.

Expert teachers Experienced, effective teachers who have developed solutions for classroom problems. Their knowledge of teaching process and content is extensive and well organized.

Reflective Thoughtful and inventive. Reflective teachers think back over situations to analyze what they did and why, and to consider how they might improve learning for their students.

"And then, of course, there's the possibility of being just the slightest bit too organized."

By permission of Glen Dines. From *Phi Delta Kappan*.

to certain subjects (Clark & Yinger, 1988; Karweitt, 1989). Planning done at the beginning of the year is particularly important because many routines and patterns, such as time allocations, are established early. So *a little planning does go a long way* in terms of what will be taught and what will be learned.

Second, teachers engage in several levels of planning—by the year, term, unit, week, and day. All the levels must be coordinated. Accomplishing the year's plan requires breaking the work into terms, the terms into units, and the units into weeks and days. For experienced teachers, unit planning seems to be the most important level, followed by weekly and then daily planning. As you gain experience in teaching, it will become easier to coordinate these levels of planning (Morine-Dershimer, 2006).

Third, plans reduce—but do not eliminate—uncertainty in teaching. Even the best plans cannot (and should not) control everything that happens in class; planning must allow flexibility. There is some evidence that when teachers "overplan"—when they fill every minute and stick to the plan no matter what—their students do not learn as much as students whose teachers are flexible (Shavelson, 1987). So *plans are not made to be broken*—but sometimes they need to be bent a bit.

In order to plan creatively and flexibly, teachers need to have wide-ranging knowledge about students, their interests, and abilities; the subjects being taught; alternative ways to teach and assess understanding; working with groups; the expectations and limitations of the school and community; how to apply and adapt materials and texts; and how to pull all this knowledge together into meaningful activities. The plans of beginning teachers sometimes don't work because the teachers lack knowledge about the students or the subject—they can't estimate how long it will take students to complete an activity, for example, or they stumble when asked for an explanation or a different example (Calderhead, 1996).

In planning, *you can do it yourself*—but *collaboration* is better. Working with other teachers and sharing ideas is one of the best experiences in teaching. Some educators think that a collaborative approach to planning used in Japan called *kenshu* or "mastery through study" is one reason why Japanese students do so well on international tests. A basic part of the *kenshu* process involves a small group of teachers developing a lesson, then videotaping one of the group members teaching the lesson. Next, all members review the tape, analyze student responses, and improve the lesson further. Other teachers try the revised lesson and more improvements follow. At the end of the school year, all the study groups may publish the results of their work. To learn about this approach, search the internet using the keywords "lesson study." While you are out there in cyberspace, explore some of the lesson plans available using the keywords "lesson plans," or search by subject or grade—for example, "math lesson plans" or "4th-grade lesson plans."

But even great lesson plans taken from a terrific website on science have to be adapted to your situation. Some of the adaptation comes before you teach and some comes after. In fact, much of what experienced teachers know about planning comes from looking back—reflecting—on what worked and what didn't, so *do look back* on your plans and grow professionally in the process.

Finally, there is no one model for effective planning. *One size does NOT fit all* in planning. For experienced teachers, planning is a creative problem-solving process. Experienced teachers know how to accomplish many lessons and segments of lessons. They know what to expect and how to proceed, so they don't necessarily continue to follow the detailed lesson-planning models they learned during their

EXPERT PLANNING In planning, you can go it alone, but collaboration is better. Sharing ideas with colleagues can be one of the best experiences in teaching.

teacher-preparation programs. Planning is more informal—"in their heads." However, many experienced teachers think it was helpful to learn this detailed system as a foundation (Clark & Peterson, 1986).

No matter how you plan, you must have a learning goal in mind. In the next section, we consider the range of goals you might have for your students.

Objectives for Learning

We hear quite a bit today about visions, goals, outcomes, and standards. At a very general, abstract level are the grand goals society may have for graduates of public schools (e.g., that all graduates have effective communication and problem-solving skills). However, very general goals are meaningless as potential guidelines for instruction. Therefore, many provinces (e.g., British Columbia, Manitoba, Ontario) are developing standards that provide more specific descriptions of how students will demonstrate progress toward the attainment of grand goals (e.g., students will develop the concept of fractions, mixed numbers, and decimals and use models to relate fractions to decimals and to find equivalent fractions). At this level, the indicators are close to being instructional objectives (Airasian, 2005).

MyEducationLab Go to the Activities and Applications section in Chapter 13 of MyEducationLab and complete Activity 2. After viewing the artifact and completing the accompanying activity, formulate objectives for any number of tasks, including non- academic ones.

Norman Gronlund and Susan Brookhart (2009) define **instructional objectives** as intended learning outcomes, or the types of performance students will demonstrate after instruction to show what they have learned. Objectives written by people with behavioural views focus on observable and measurable changes in the learner. Behavioural objectives use terms such as *list, define, add,* or *calculate.* Cognitive objectives, on the other hand, emphasize thinking and comprehension, so they are more likely to include words such as *understand, recognize, create,* or *apply*. Let us look more closely at two different methods of writing instructional objectives: one that reflects behaviourist views of learning and another based on cognitive views of learning.

Mager: Start With the Specific. Years ago, Robert Mager developed a very influential system for writing instructional objectives (Mager, 1975). His idea is that objectives ought to describe what students will be doing when demonstrating their achievement and how you will know they are doing it, so these are generally regarded as **behavioural objectives**. According to Mager, a good objective has three parts. First, it describes the intended *student behaviour*. What must the student do? Second, it lists the *conditions* under which the behaviour will occur. How will this behaviour be recognized or tested? Third, it gives the *criteria* for acceptable performance on the test. For example, an objective in social studies might be: "Given a recent article from the local newspaper [conditions], the student will mark each statement with an F for fact or an O for opinion [observable student behaviour], with 75 percent of the statement correctly marked [criteria]." With this emphasis on final behaviour, Mager's system requires a very explicit statement. Mager contends that often students can teach themselves if they are given well-stated objectives.

Gronlund: Start With the General. Gronlund and Brookhart (2009) offer a different approach, often used for writing **cognitive objectives**. They believe that an objective should be stated first in general terms (*understand, solve, appreciate,* etc.). Then the teacher should clarify by listing examples of behaviour that would provide evidence that the student has attained the objective. Look at the example in Table 13.1 on page 462. The goal here is *comprehending* a scientific concept. A teacher could never list all the behaviours that might be involved in "presenting and defending," but stating an initial, general objective along with specific examples makes the purpose clear.

The most recent research on instructional objectives tends to favour approaches similar to Gronlund's. James Popham (2005a), a former proponent of very specific objectives, makes this recommendation:

> Strive to come up with a half dozen or so truly salient, broad, yet measurable instructional objectives for your own classroom. Too many small-scope, hyperspecific objectives will be of scant value to you because, if you're at all normal, you'll soon disregard [them]. On the other hand, a small number of intellectually manageable, broad, yet measurable objectives will not only prove helpful to you instructionally but will also help you answer the what-to-assess question. (pp. 104–105)

Instructional objectives Clear statements of what students are intended to learn through instruction.

Behavioural objectives Instructional objectives stated in terms of observable behaviour.

Cognitive objectives Instructional objectives stated in terms of higher-level thinking operations.

TABLE 13.1 A Combined Method for Creating Objectives

General Objective
Comprehends scientific concepts.
Specific Examples
1. Describes the concept in his or her own words. 2. Gives an example of the concept [that is new]. 3. States hypotheses based on the concept. 4. Describes how the process functions in a given situation. 5. Describes an experiment that illustrates the process.

Source: Norman E. Gronlund & Susan M. Brookhart, *Gronlund's writing instructional objectives* (8th ed.), Upper Saddle River, NJ: Pearson © 2009. Adapted by permission of Pearson Education, Inc.

Flexible and Creative Plans—Using Taxonomies

STOP & THINK Think about your assignments for one of your classes. What kind of thinking is involved in doing the assignments?

Remembering facts and terms?

Understanding key ideas?

Applying information to solve problems?

Analyzing a situation, task, or problem?

Making evaluations or giving opinions?

Creating or designing something new?

Fifty years ago, a group of experts in educational evaluation led by Benjamin Bloom set out to improve college and university examinations. The impact of their work has touched education at all levels around the world (Anderson & Sosniak, 1994). Bloom and his colleagues developed a taxonomy, or classification system, of educational objectives. Objectives were divided into three domains: cognitive, affective, and psychomotor. A handbook describing the objectives in each area was eventually published. In real life, of course, behaviour from these three domains occurs simultaneously. While students are writing (psychomotor), they are also remembering or reasoning (cognitive), and they are likely to have some emotional response to the task as well (affective).

The Cognitive Domain. Six basic objectives are listed in Bloom's taxonomy of the thinking or cognitive domain (Bloom, Engelhart, Frost, Hill, & Krathwohl, 1956):

1. *Knowledge:* Remembering or recognizing something without necessarily understanding, using, or changing it.
2. *Comprehension:* Understanding the material being communicated without necessarily relating it to anything else.
3. *Application:* Using a general concept to solve a particular problem.
4. *Analysis:* Breaking something down into its parts.
5. *Synthesis:* Creating something new by combining different ideas.
6. *Evaluation:* Judging the value of materials or methods as they might be applied in a particular situation.

It is common in education to consider these objectives as a hierarchy, each skill building on those below, but such a view is not entirely accurate. Some subjects, such as mathematics, do not fit this structure very well (Kreitzer & Madaus, 1994). Still, you will hear many references to *lower-level* and *higher-level objectives*, with knowledge, comprehension, and application considered lower level and the other categories considered higher level. As a rough way of thinking about

Taxonomy Classification system.

Cognitive domain In Bloom's taxonomy, memory and reasoning objectives.

objectives, this classification can be helpful (Gronlund & Brookhart, 2009). The taxonomy of objectives can also be helpful in planning assessments because different procedures are appropriate for objectives at the various levels.

Bloom 2001. Bloom's taxonomy has guided educators for over 50 years and is considered among the most significant educational writings of the 20th century (Anderson & Sosniak, 1994). In 2001, a group of educational researchers met to discuss revising the taxonomy (Anderson & Krathwohl, 2001). The new version retains the six basic levels in a slightly different order, but the names of three levels have been changed to indicate the cognitive processes involved. The six cognitive processes are remembering (knowledge), understanding (comprehension), applying, analyzing, evaluating, and creating (synthesizing). In addition, the revisers have added a new dimension to the taxonomy to recognize that cognitive processes must process something—you have to remember or understand or apply some form of knowledge. Table 13.2 summarizes the resulting model by showing that six processes—the cognitive acts of remembering, understanding, applying, analyzing, evaluating, and creating—act on four kinds of knowledge—factual, conceptual, procedural, and metacognitive.

Consider how this revised taxonomy might suggest objectives for a social studies or language arts class. For example, an objective that targets *analysis of conceptual knowledge* might be:

> After reading a historical account of the framing of Canada's Constitution, students will be able to recognize the author's point of view or bias.

An objective for evaluating metacognitive knowledge might be:

> Students will reflect on their strategies for identifying the biases of the author.

The Affective Domain. The objectives in the taxonomy of the affective domain, or domain of emotional response, have not yet been revised from the original version. They range from least committed to most committed (Krathwohl, Bloom, & Masia, 1964). At the lowest level, students simply pay attention to a certain idea. At the highest level, students adopt an idea or a value and act consistently with that idea. There are five basic objectives in the affective domain:

1. *Receiving:* Being aware of or attending to something in the environment. This is the "I'll-listen-to-the-concert-but-I-won't-promise-to-like-it" level.
2. *Responding:* Showing some new behaviour as a result of experience. At this level, a person might applaud after the concert or hum some of the music the next day.
3. *Valuing:* Showing some definite involvement or commitment. At this point, a person might choose to go to a concert instead of a film.
4. *Organization:* Integrating a new value into one's general set of values, giving it some ranking among one's general priorities. This is the level at which a person would begin to make long-range commitments to concert attendance.
5. *Characterization by value:* Acting consistently with the new value. At this highest level, a person would be firmly committed to a love of music and demonstrate it openly and consistently.

Affective domain Objectives focusing on attitudes and feelings.

TABLE 13.2 A Revised Taxonomy in the Cognitive Domain

	The Cognitive Process Dimension					
The Knowledge Dimension	**1. Remember**	**2. Understand**	**3. Apply**	**4. Analyze**	**5. Evaluate**	**6. Create**
A. Factual knowledge						
B. Conceptual knowledge						
C. Procedural knowledge						
D. Metacognitive knowledge						

Source: From Anderson, Lorin W., David R. Krathwohl, et al., *A Taxonomy for Learning, Teaching, and Assessing*. Published by Allyn and Bacon, Boston, MA. Copyright © 2001 by Pearson Education. Reprinted by permission of the publisher.

Like the basic objectives in the cognitive domain, these five objectives are very general. To write specific learning objectives, you must state what students will actually be doing when they are receiving, responding, valuing, and so on. For example, an objective for a nutrition class at the valuing level (showing involvement or commitment) might be stated as follows:

> After completing the unit on food contents and labelling, at least 50 percent of the class will commit to a junk-food boycott project by giving up candy for a month.

The Psychomotor Domain. Until recently, the psychomotor domain, or the realm of physical ability objectives, has been mostly overlooked by teachers not directly involved with physical education. There are several taxonomies in this domain (e.g., Harrow, 1972; Simpson, 1972) that generally move from basic perceptions and reflex actions to skilled, creative movements. James Cangelosi (1990) provides a useful way to think about objectives in the psychomotor domain as either (1) voluntary muscle capabilities that require endurance, strength, flexibility, agility, and speed or (2) the ability to perform a specific skill.

Objectives in the psychomotor domain should be of interest to a wide range of educators, including those in fine arts, vocational-technical education, and special education. Many other subjects, such as chemistry, physics, and biology, also require specialized movements and well-developed hand and eye coordination. Using lab equipment, the mouse on a computer, or art materials means learning new physical skills. Here are two examples of psychomotor objectives:

> Four minutes after completing a 1.6-kilometre run in eight minutes or under, your heart rate will be below 120.

> Use a computer mouse effectively to "drag and drop" files.

Whatever your instructional objectives for your students, Terry TenBrink (2006, p. 57) suggests the following four criteria. Objectives should be:

1. Student-oriented (emphasis on what the student is expected to do).
2. Descriptive of an appropriate learning *outcome* (both developmentally appropriate and appropriately sequenced, with more complex objectives following prerequisite objectives).
3. Clear and understandable (not too general or too specific).
4. Observable (avoid outcomes you can't see such as "appreciating" or "realizing").

Psychomotor domain Realm of physical ability and coordination objectives.

The suggestions in the accompanying *Guidelines* box should help you whether you use objectives for every lesson or for just a few assignments.

GUIDELINES: Using Instructional Objectives

Avoid "word magic"—phrases that sound noble and important but say very little, such as, "Students will become deep thinkers."

EXAMPLES

1. Keep the focus on specific changes that will take place in the students' knowledge of skills.
2. Ask students to explain the meaning of the objectives. If they can't give specific examples of what you mean, the objectives are not communicating your intentions to your students.

Suit the activities to the objectives.

EXAMPLES

1. If the goal is the memorization of vocabulary, give the students memory aids and practice exercises.
2. If the goal is the ability to develop well-thought-out positions, consider position papers, debates, projects, or mock trials.
3. If you want students to become better writers, give many opportunities for writing and rewriting.

Make sure that your tests are related to your objectives.

EXAMPLES

1. Write objectives and rough drafts for tests at the same time. Revise these drafts of tests as the units unfold and objectives change.
2. Weight the tests according to the importance of the various objectives and the time spent on each.

For additional ideas, see **www.personal.psu.edu/staff/b/x/bxb11/Objectives/** or **http://edtech.tennessee.edu/~bobannon/objectives.html**.

TABLE 13.3 Some Themes for Integrated Planning for Middle and High School Students

Courage	Time and space
Mystery	Groups and institutions
Survival	Work
Human interaction	Motion
Communities of the future	Cause and effect
Communication/language	Probability and prediction
Human rights and responsibilities	Change and conservation
Identity/coming of age	Diversity and variation
Interdependence	Autobiography

Sources: Adapted from *Toward a Coherent Curriculum* by J. A. Beane (Ed.), 1995. Alexandria, VA: Association for Supervision and Curriculum Development; *Interdisciplinary High School Teaching* by J. H. Clarke and R. M. Agne, 1997, Boston: Allyn & Bacon; and *Teaching through Themes* by G. Thompson, 1991, New York: Scholastic. See Thompson for resources and strategies to develop some of these themes in elementary school and Clarke and Agne for ideas at the high school level.

Planning From a Constructivist Perspective

STOP & THINK Think about the same course assignments you analyzed in the previous *Stop & Think* activity. What are the big ideas that run through all those assignments? What other ways could you learn about those ideas besides completing the assignments?

Traditionally, it has been the teacher's responsibility to do most of the planning for instruction, but new ways of planning are developing. In constructivist approaches, planning is shared and negotiated. The teacher and students together make decisions about content, activities, and approaches. Rather than having specific student behaviour and skills as objectives, the teacher has overarching goals—"big ideas"—that guide planning. These goals are understandings or abilities that the teacher returns to again and again. Today, teaching with themes and integrated content are major elements in planning and designing lessons and units, from kindergarten (Roskos & Neuman, 1998) through high school (Clarke & Agne, 1997). For example, Elaine Homestead and Karen McGinnis (middle school teachers) and Elizabeth Pate (a college professor) designed a unit on "Human Interactions" that included studying racism, world hunger, pollution, and air and water quality. Students researched issues by reading textbooks and outside sources, learning to use databases, interviewing local officials, and inviting guest speakers into class. Students had to develop knowledge in science, mathematics, and social studies. They learned to write and speak persuasively, and in the process, raised money for hunger relief in Africa (Pate, McGinnis, & Homestead, 1995).

Elementary-age students can benefit from integrated planning too. There is no reason to work on spelling skills, then listening skills, then writing skills, and then social studies or science. All these abilities can be developed together if students work to solve authentic problems. Themes for younger children can include, for example, people, pets, gardens as habitats, communities, and patterns. Possibilities for older children are given in Table 13.3.

Let's assume you have an idea of *what* you want students to understand, but *how* do you teach to encourage understanding? You still need to decide what's happening on Monday. You need to design teaching that is appropriate for the objectives.

TEACHING APPROACHES

In this section we will provide some basic formats for putting plans into action. The first challenge is to match your teaching methods to your objectives. We begin with strategies for teaching explicit facts and concepts.

Constructivist approach View that emphasizes the active role of the learner in building understanding and making sense of information.

MyEducationLab Go to the Activities and Applications section in Chapter 13 of MyEducationLab and complete Activity 3. As you watch the video and answer the accompanying questions, consider how the teacher uses class discussions and questioning as advance organizers.

Expository Teaching and Direct Instruction

For many people, the image of teaching is an instructor explaining material to students—lecture is a classic form. Here we look at two models of this traditional teacher-centred approach—expository teaching that grew from theories of verbal learning, and direct instruction that developed from research on effective teaching of basic skills.

Expository Teaching. According to David Ausubel (1963, 1977, 1982), expository teaching stresses meaningful verbal learning—verbal information, ideas, and relationships among ideas, taken together. Rote memorization is not meaningful learning, because material learned by rote is not *connected* with existing knowledge. Ausubel believed that concepts, principles, and ideas are presented and understood using deductive reasoning—from general ideas to specific cases—so the expository approach always begins with a general advance organizer. This is an introductory statement broad enough to encompass all the information that will follow. The organizers can serve three purposes: They direct students' attention to what is important in the coming material, they highlight relationships among ideas that will be presented, and they remind students of relevant information they already have.

Advance organizers fall into one of two categories: *comparative* and *expository* (Mayer, 1984). Comparative organizers *activate* (bring into working memory) already existing schemas. They remind students of what they already know, but may not realize is relevant. A comparative advance organizer for a history lesson on revolutions might be a statement that contrasts military uprisings with the physical and social changes involved in the Industrial Revolution; you could also compare the common aspects of the French, English, Mexican, Russian, Iranian, and American revolutions (Salomon & Perkins, 1989).

Expository teaching Ausubel's method—teachers present material in complete, organized form, moving from broadest to more specific concepts.

Meaningful verbal learning Focused and organized relationships among ideas and verbal information.

Deductive reasoning Drawing conclusions by applying rules or principles; logically moving from a general rule or principle to a specific solution.

Advance organizer Statement of inclusive concepts to introduce and sum up material that follows.

In contrast, *expository organizers* provide *new* knowledge that students will need to understand the upcoming information. In an English class, you might begin a large thematic unit on rites of passage in literature with a very broad statement of the theme and why it has been so central in literature—something like, "A central character coming of age must learn to know himself or herself, often makes some kind of journey of self-discovery, and must decide what in the society is to be accepted and what rejected."

The general conclusion of research on advance organizers is that they do help students learn, especially when the material to be learned is quite unfamiliar, complex, or difficult—if two conditions are met (Corkill, 1992; Langan-Fox, Waycott, & Albert, 2000; Morin & Miller, 1998). First, to be effective, the organizer must be understood by the students. This was demonstrated dramatically in a study by Dinnel and Glover (1985). They found that instructing students to paraphrase an advance organizer—which, of course, requires them to understand its meaning—increased the effectiveness of the organizer. Second, the organizer must really be an organizer: It must indicate relations among the basic concepts and terms that will be used. Concrete models, diagrams, or analogies seem to be especially good organizers (Robinson, 1998; Robinson & Kiewra, 1995).

EXPOSITORY TEACHING Expository methods emphasize the use of advance organizers, based on the assumption that concepts, principles, and ideas are best presented and understood using deductive reasoning—from general ideas to specific cases.

Steps in an Expository Lesson. After the advance organizer, the next step is to present content in terms of similarities and differences using specific examples, perhaps provided by the students themselves. Assume you are teaching the coming-of-age theme in literature, using *The Diary of Anne Frank* and *The Adventures of Huckleberry Finn*. As the students read, you might ask them to compare the central character's growth, state of mind, and position in society with characters from other novels, plays, and films (connect to students' prior knowledge). Then students can compare Anne Frank's inner journey with Huck Finn's trip down the Mississippi. As comparisons are made, you should underscore the goal of the lesson and elaborate the advance organizer.

The best way to point out similarities and differences is with examples. Huck Finn's and Anne Frank's dilemmas must be clear. Finally, when all the material has been

GUIDELINES: Using Advance Organizers and Expository Teaching

Use advance organizers.

EXAMPLES

1. In an English class, use: Shakespeare used the social ideas of his time as a framework for his plays—*Julius Caesar*, *Hamlet*, and *Macbeth* deal with concepts of natural order, a nation as the human body, etc.
2. In a social studies class, use: Geography dictates economy in preindustrialized regions or nations.
3. In a history class, use: Important concepts during the Renaissance were symmetry, admiration of the classical world, the centrality of the human mind.

Use a number of examples.

EXAMPLES

1. In mathematics class, ask students to point out all the examples of right angles that they can find in the room.
2. In teaching about islands and peninsulas, use maps, slides, models, and postcards.

Focus on both similarities and differences.

EXAMPLES

1. In a social studies class, ask students to compare and contrast the political systems in Canada and the United States.
2. In a biology class, ask students how they would transform spiders into insects or an amphibian into a reptile.

For more information on advance organizers, see **http://moodle.ed.uiuc.edu/wiked/index.php/Advance_organizers.**

presented, ask students to discuss how the examples can be used to expand on the original advance organizer. Expository teaching is more developmentally appropriate for students at or above later elementary school, that is, around grade 5 or 6 and up (Luiten, Ames, & Ackerson, 1980). The *Guidelines* box should help you follow the main steps in expository teaching.

Direct Instruction. In the 1970s and 1980s, there was an explosion of research that focused on effective teaching. The results of all this work identified a model of teaching that was related to improved student learning. Barak Rosenshine calls this approach direct instruction (1979) or explicit teaching (1986). Tom Good (1983a) uses the term active teaching for a similar approach.

The direct instruction model fits a specific set of circumstances because it was derived from a particular approach to research. Researchers identified the elements of direct instruction by comparing teachers whose students learned more than expected (based on entering knowledge) with teachers whose students performed at an expected or average level. The researchers focused on existing practices in American classrooms. Because the focus was on traditional forms of teaching, the research could not identify successful innovations. Effectiveness was usually defined as average improvement in standardized test scores for a whole class or school. So the results hold for large groups, but not necessarily for every student in the group. Even when the average achievement of a group improves, the achievement of some individuals may decline (Good, 1996; Shuell, 1996).

Given these conditions, direct instruction applies best to the teaching of basic skills—clearly structured knowledge and essential skills, such as science facts, mathematics computations, reading vocabulary, and grammar rules (Rosenshine & Stevens, 1986). These skills involve tasks that are relatively unambiguous; they can be taught step-by-step and tested objectively. Direct instruction is not necessarily appropriate for objectives such as helping students write creatively, solve complex problems, or mature emotionally. Franz Weinert and Andreas Helmke (1995) describe effective direct instruction as having the following features:

> (a) the teacher's classroom management is especially effective and the rate of student interruptive behaviors is very low; (b) the teacher maintains a strong academic focus and uses available instructional time intensively to initiate and facilitate students' learning activities; (c) the teacher insures that as many students as possible achieve good learning progress by carefully choosing appropriate tasks, clearly presenting subject-matter information and solution strategies, continuously diagnosing each student's learning progress and learning difficulties, and providing effective help through remedial instruction. (p. 138)

How would a teacher turn these themes into actions?

Direct instruction/explicit teaching Systematic instruction for mastery of basic skills, facts, and information.

Active teaching Teaching characterized by high levels of teacher explanation, demonstration, and interaction with students.

Basic skills Clearly structured knowledge that is needed for later learning and that can be taught step by step.

Rosenshine's Six Teaching Functions. Rosenshine and his colleagues (Rosenshine, 1988; Rosenshine & Stevens, 1986) have identified the following six teaching functions based on the research on effective instruction. These can serve as a checklist or framework for teaching basic skills.

1. *Review and check the previous day's work.* Reteach if students misunderstood or made errors.
2. *Present new material.* Make the purpose clear, teach in small steps, and provide many examples and non-examples.
3. *Provide guided practice.* Question students, give practice problems, and listen for misconceptions and misunderstandings. Reteach if necessary. Continue guided practice until students answer about 80 percent of the questions correctly.
4. *Give feedback and correctives* based on student answers. Reteach if necessary.
5. *Provide independent practice.* Let students apply the new learning on their own, in seatwork, cooperative groups, or homework. The success rate during independent practice should be about 95 percent. This means that students must be well prepared for the work by the presentation and guided practice, and that assignments must not be too difficult. The point is for the students to practise until the skills become overlearned and automatic—until the students are confident. Hold students accountable for the work they do—check it.
6. *Review weekly and monthly* to consolidate learning. Include some review items as homework. Test often, and reteach material missed on the tests.

These six functions are not steps to be followed in a particular order, but all of them are elements of effective instruction. For example, feedback, review, or reteaching should occur whenever necessary and should match the abilities of the students. Also, keep in mind the age and prior knowledge of your students. The younger or the less prepared your students, the briefer your explanations should be. Use more and shorter cycles of presentation, guided practice, feedback, and correctives.

Some studies have found that teachers' presentations take up one-sixth to one-fourth of all classroom time. Teacher explanation is appropriate for communicating a large amount of material to many students in a short period of time, introducing a new topic, giving background information, or motivating students to learn more on their own. Teacher presentations are therefore most appropriate for cognitive and affective objectives at the lower levels of the taxonomies described earlier—for remembering, understanding, applying, receiving, responding, and valuing (Arends, 2001; Kindsvatter, Wilen, & Ishler, 1992). The *Guidelines* box gives you ideas for how to apply the best of direct instruction.

Why Do Direct Instruction and Expository Teaching Work? Well-organized presentations with advance organizers, clear explanations, the use of explanatory links, and reviews as described in the *Guidelines* box can all help students perceive connections among ideas. If done well, therefore, a direct instruction lesson may be a resource that students use to construct understanding. For example, reviews activate prior knowledge, so that students are ready to understand. Brief, clear presentations and guided practice avoid overloading the students' information processing systems and taxing their working memories. Numerous examples and explanations give many pathways and associations for building networks of concepts. Guided practice can also give the teacher a snapshot of the students' thinking as well as their misconceptions, allowing the teacher to address them directly as misconceptions rather than simply as "wrong answers."

Every subject, even university-level English or chemistry, can require some direct instruction. Noddings (1990) reminds teachers that students may need some direct instruction in how to use various manipulative materials to get the possible benefits from them. Students working in cooperative groups may need guidance, modelling, and practice in how to ask questions and give explanations. And to solve difficult problems, students may need some direct instruction in possible problem-solving strategies.

Evaluating Direct Instruction. Direct instruction, particularly when it involves extended teacher presentations or lectures, has some disadvantages. You may find that some students have trouble listening for more than a few minutes at a time and that they simply tune you out. Teacher presentations can put the students in a passive position by doing much of the cognitive work for

GUIDELINES: Teaching Effectively

Organize your lessons carefully.

EXAMPLES

1. Provide objectives that help students focus on the purpose of the lesson.
2. Begin lessons by writing a brief outline on the board, or work on an outline with the class as part of the lesson.
3. If possible, break the presentation into clear steps or stages.
4. Review periodically.

Anticipate and plan for difficult parts in the lesson.

EXAMPLES

1. Plan a clear introduction to the lesson that tells students what they are going to learn and how they are going to learn it.
2. Do the exercises and anticipate student problems—consult the teachers' manual for ideas.
3. Have definitions ready for new terms, and prepare several relevant examples for concepts.
4. Think of analogies that will make ideas easier to understand.
5. Organize the lesson in a logical sequence; include checkpoints that incorporate oral or written questions or problems to make sure the students are following the explanations.

Strive for clear explanations.

EXAMPLES

1. Avoid vague words and ambiguous phrases. Steer clear of "the somes"—*something, someone, sometime, somehow;* "the not verys"—*not very much, not very well, not very hard, not very often;* and other unspecific fillers, such as *most, not all, sort of, and so on, of course, as you know, I guess, in fact, or whatever,* and *more or less.*
2. Use specific (and, if possible, colourful) names instead of *it, them,* and *thing.*
3. Refrain from using pet phrases such as *you know, like,* and *Okay?* Another idea is to record a lesson on tape to check yourself for clarity.
4. Give explanations at several levels so that all students, not just the brightest, will understand.
5. Focus on one idea at a time and avoid digressions.

Make clear connections by using explanatory links such as *because, if . . . then,* or *therefore.*

EXAMPLES

1. Use statements, such as, "Explorers found it difficult to get to the west coast of Canada because it was so hard to cross the Rockies."
2. Use helpful explanatory links in labelling visual material such as graphs, concept maps, or illustrations.

Signal transitions from one major topic to another with phrases.

EXAMPLES

1. Use transitional phrases such as, "The next area . . . ," "Now we will turn to . . . ," or "The second step is. . . ."
2. Outline topics by listing key points, drawing concept maps on the board, or using an overhead projector.

Communicate an enthusiasm for your subject and the day's lesson.

EXAMPLES

1. Tell students why the lesson is important. Have a better reason than "This will be on the test" or "You will need to know it next year." Emphasize the value of the learning itself.
2. Be sure to make eye contact with the students.
3. Vary your pace and volume in speaking. Use silence for emphasis.

For more ideas about effective teaching, see **www.effectiveteachingsolutions.com/**.

them and may prevent students from asking or even thinking of questions (Freiberg & Driscoll, 2005). Scripted cooperation is one way to incorporate active learning into lectures. Several times during the presentation, the teacher asks students to work in pairs. One person is the summarizer and the other critiques the summary. This activity gives students a chance to check their understanding, organize their thinking, and translate ideas into their own words. Other possibilities are described in Table 13.4.

Critics also claim that direct instruction is based on a *wrong* theory of learning. Teachers break material into small segments, present each segment clearly, and reinforce or correct, thus *transmitting* accurate understandings from teacher to student. The student is viewed as an "empty vessel" waiting to be filled with knowledge, rather than an active constructor of knowledge (Berg & Clough, 1991; Driscoll, 2005). These criticisms of direct instruction echo the criticisms of behavioural learning theories.

There is ample evidence, however, that direct instruction and explanation can help students learn actively, not passively (Leinhardt, 2001). For younger and less prepared learners, student-controlled learning without teacher direction and instruction can lead to systematic deficits in the students' knowledge. Without guidance, the understandings that students construct may be incomplete and misleading (Sweller, Kirschner, & Clark, 2007). For example, Harris and Graham (1996)

Scripted cooperation Learning strategy in which two students take turns summarizing material and criticizing the summaries.

TABLE 13.4 Active Learning and Teacher Presentations

Here are some ideas for keeping students cognitively engaged in lessons. These suggestions can be adapted for many ages.

Question, All Write: Pose a question, ask everyone to jot an answer, then ask several volunteers to share their answers with the class.

Outcome Sentences: After a segment of presentation, ask students to finish sentences such as, "I learned . . .," "I'm beginning to wonder . . .," "I was surprised. . . ." Share as above. Students may keep their outcome sentences in a learning log or portfolio.

Underexplain with Learning Pairs: Give a brief explanation, then ask students to work in pairs to figure out the process or idea.

Voting: Ask, "How many of you . . ." questions and take a count, e.g., "How many of you agree with Raschon?" "How many of you are ready to move on?" "How many of you got 48 on this problem?"

Choral Response: Have the whole class restate in unison important facts and ideas, such as "The environment is one whole system" or "A 10-sided polygon is called a decagon."

Speak-Write: Tell students you will speak briefly, for three or four minutes. They are to listen but not take notes. At the end of the time, ask them to write the main ideas, a summary, or questions they have about what you said.

Source: Adapted from Harmin, M. (1994). *Inspiring active learning: A handbook for teachers.* Alexandria, VA: Association for Supervision and Curriculum Development.

describe the experiences of their daughter Leah in a whole-language/progressive education school, where the teachers successfully developed their daughter's creativity, thinking, and understanding.

> Skills, on the other hand, have been a problem for our daughter and for other children. At the end of kindergarten, when she had not made much progress in reading, her teacher said she believed Leah had a perceptual problem or a learning disability. Leah began asking what was wrong with her, because other kids were reading and she wasn't. Finally, an assessment was done. (p. 26)

The testing indicated no learning disability, strong comprehension abilities, and poor word attack skills. Luckily, Leah's parents knew how to teach word attack skills. Direct teaching of these skills helped Leah become an avid and able reader in about six weeks. Deep understanding and fluid performance—whether in dance or mathematical problem solving or reading—require models of expert performance and extensive practice with feedback (Anderson, Reder, & Simon, 1995). Guided and independent practice and feedback are at the heart of the direct instruction model.

Seatwork and Homework

Seatwork. The conclusions of the limited research on seatwork (independent classroom-desk work) are clear; this technique is often overused. In fact, one study found that American elementary students spend 51 percent of mathematics time in school working alone, while Japanese students spend 26 percent and Taiwanese students spend only 9 percent of time doing so (Stigler, Lee, & Stevenson, 1987). Some educators point to these differences as part of the explanation for Asian students' superiority in mathematics. A summary of research from 1975 to 2000 found a similar problem in reading instruction for students with disabilities. These students, who often have trouble learning without teacher guidance, spent about 40 percent of their time on individual seatwork (Vaughn, Levy, Coleman, & Bos, 2002).

Seatwork should follow up a lesson and give students supervised practice. It should not be the main mode of instruction. Unfortunately, many workbook pages do little to support the learning of important objectives. Before you assign work, ask yourself, "Does doing this work help students learn anything that matters?" Students should see the connection between the seatwork or homework and the lesson. Tell them why they are doing the work. The objectives should be clear, all the materials that might be needed should be provided, and the work should be easy enough that students can succeed on their own. Success rates should be high—near 100 percent. When seatwork is too difficult, students often resort to guessing or copying just to finish (Anderson, 1985).

Carol Weinstein and Andy Mignano (2007) describe several alternatives to completing workbook assignments, such as reading silently and reading aloud to a partner; writing for a "real" audience; writing letters or journals; transcribing conversations and punctuating them properly; making up problems; working on long-term projects and reports; solving brain teasers and puzzles;

Seatwork Independent classroom work.

and engaging in computer activities. One of our favourites is creating a group story. Two students begin a story on the computer. Then two more add a paragraph. The story grows with each new pair's addition. This allows students to practise reading and writing, editing, and improving.

Any independent work requires careful monitoring. Being available to students doing seatwork is more effective than offering students help before they ask for it. Short, frequent contacts are best (Brophy & Good, 1986). Sometimes you may be working with a small group while other students do seatwork. In these situations, it is especially important for students to know what to do if they need help. Nancy has observed in classrooms where students follow the rule "Ask three, then me." Students have to consult three classmates before seeking help from the teacher. Teachers in these classrooms spend time early in the year showing students *how* to help each other—how to ask questions and how to explain.

SEATWORK Seatwork and homework should follow up a lesson and give students supervised practice, not function as the main mode of instruction.

STOP & THINK Think back to your elementary and high school days. Do you remember any homework assignments? What sticks in your mind about those assignments?

Homework. In contrast to the limited research on seatwork, educators have been studying the effects of homework for over 75 years (Cooper, 2004; Cooper, Robinson, & Patall, 2006; Corno, 2000; Trautwein, 2007). As you can see from the *Point/Counterpoint* box, there continues to be a debate about the value of homework.

To benefit from individual or group seatwork or homework, students must stay involved and do the work. The first step toward involvement is getting students started correctly by making sure that they understand the assignment. It may help to do the first few questions as a class, to clear up any misconceptions. This is especially important for homework assignments because students may have no one at home to consult if they have problems with the assignment. A second way to keep students involved is to hold them accountable for completing the work correctly, not just for filling in the page. This means the work should be checked, the students given a chance to correct the errors or revise work, and the results counted toward the class grade (Brophy & Good, 1986). Expert teachers often have ways of correcting homework quickly during the first minutes of class by having students check each other's or their own work.

If students get stuck on homework, they need help at home from someone who can scaffold their work without just "giving the answer" (Pressley, 1995). But many family members don't know how to help (Hoover-Dempsey et al., 2001; Hoover-Dempsey, Bassler, & Burow, 1995). The *Family and Community Partnerships Guidelines* box includes ideas for helping families deal with homework.

Questioning and Discussion

Teachers pose questions; students answer. This form of teaching, sometimes called *recitation*, has been with us for many years (Stodolsky, 1988). The teacher's questions develop a framework for the subject matter involved. The students' answers are often followed by reactions from the teacher, such as praise, correction, or requests for further information. The pattern from the teacher's point of view consists of *initiation* (teacher asks questions), *response* (student answers), and *evaluation* (praising, correcting, probing, or expanding), or "IRE" (Burbules & Bruce, 2001). These steps are repeated over and over.

Let us consider the heart of recitation—the initiation, or *questioning*, phase. Effective questioning techniques may be among the most powerful tools teachers employ during lessons. An essential element of innovations such as cognitive apprenticeships, peer learning techniques, authentic learning activities, and nearly all other contemporary learning techniques is keeping students cognitively engaged—and that is where skilful questioning strategies are especially effective. Questions play several roles in cognition. They can help students rehearse information for effective recall. They can work to identify gaps in their knowledge base and provoke curiosity and long-term

POINT / COUNTERPOINT

Is Homework a Valuable Use of Time?

LIKE SO MANY METHODS in education, homework has moved in and out of favour. In the early 1900s, homework was seen as an important path to mental discipline, but by the 1940s, homework was criticized as too much drill and low-level learning. Then in the 1950s, homework was rediscovered as a way to catch up with the Soviet Union in science and mathematics, only to be seen as too much pressure on students during the more laid-back 1960s. By the 1980s, homework was in again as a way to improve the standing of American children compared to students around the world (Cooper & Valentine, 2001). Today, homework is increasing in early elementary schools (Hofferth & Sandberg, 2000). Everyone has done homework—were those hours well spent?

POINT

Homework does not help students learn.

No matter how interesting an activity is, students will eventually get bored with it—so why give them work both in and out of school? They will simply grow weary of learning. And important opportunities are lost for community involvement or leisure activities that would create well-rounded citizens. When parents help with homework, they can do more harm than good—sometimes confusing their children or teaching them incorrectly. And students from poorer families often must work, so they miss doing the homework; then the learning discrepancy between the rich and poor grows even greater. Besides, the research is inconsistent about the effects of homework. For example, one study found that in-class work was better than homework in helping elementary students learn (Cooper & Valentine, 2001). In his book, *The Homework Myth: Why Our Kids Get Too Much of a Bad Thing*, Alfie Kohn (2006) suggests the schools adopt no homework as the default policy. "Changing the default to no homework would likely have two practical consequences: The number of assignments would decline and the quality of those assignments would rise. Both of these, I believe, represent significant improvements in our children's education" (p. 168).

COUNTERPOINT

Well-planned homework can work for many students.

Harris Cooper and his colleagues reviewed many studies of homework and concluded that there is little relationship between homework and learning for young students, but the relationship between homework and achievement grows progressively stronger for older students. Most of the studies involved math and reading or English homework, however, not social studies, science, or other subjects. There is recent evidence that students in high school who do more homework (and watch less television after school) have higher grades, even when other factors such as gender, grade level, ethnicity, socioeconomic status (SES), and amount of adult supervision are taken into consideration (Cooper et al., 2006; Cooper & Valentine, 2001a; Cooper, Valentine, Nye, & Kindsay, 1999). The Canadian Council on Learning (CCL, 2009) agrees that homework can be beneficial, but only if it is assigned judiciously and engages students. Specifically, their review of studies on homework conducted between 2003 and 2007 indicates the following:

- homework that asks students to consider alternative strategies for solving problems is more likely to be effective than rote learning;
- homework does not benefit children in the primary grades;
- lower-achieving students benefit the most from homework; and
- homework each day should not exceed a student's grade × 10 (Cooper's rule of thumb)—that is, a student in grade 5 should not do more that 50 minutes of homework each day.

Most research examines the relationship between amount of time spent on homework (as reported by students or parents) and achievement in terms of grades or achievement tests. Another approach is to focus on effort instead of time. Students' self-reported effort on homework is consistently and positively related to student achievement (Trautwein, 2007). "High homework effort means that a student does his or her best to solve the tasks assigned. There need not be a close relationship between effort and time on homework: A student putting as much effort as possible into a homework assignment might finish in 5 min or still be working after an hour" (Trautwein & Lüdtke, 2007, p. 432). So the challenge is to get students to put their best efforts into appropriate homework and to get teachers to assign only high-quality homework.

FAMILY AND COMMUNITY PARTNERSHIPS

GUIDELINES: Homework

Make sure that families know what students are expected to learn.

EXAMPLES

1. At the beginning of a unit, send home a list of the main objectives, examples of major assignments, key due dates, homework "calendar," and a list of resources available for free at libraries or on the internet.
2. Provide a clear, concise description of your homework policy—how homework is counted toward class grades; consequences for late, forgotten, or missing homework; and so on.

Help families find a comfortable and helpful role in their child's homework.

EXAMPLES

1. Remind families that "helping with homework" means encouraging, listening, monitoring, praising, discussing, brainstorming—not necessarily teaching and never doing the work for their child.
2. Encourage families to set aside a quiet time and place for everyone in the family to study. Make this time a regular part of the daily routine.
3. Have some homework assignments that are fun and involve the whole family—puzzles, family albums, watching a television program together and doing a "review."
4. In conferences, ask families what they need to play a helpful role in their child's homework.

Solicit and use suggestions from families about homework.

EXAMPLES

1. Find out what responsibilities the child has at home—how much time is available for homework.
2. Periodically, have a "homework hotline" for call-in questions and suggestions.

If no one is at home to help with homework, set up other support systems.

EXAMPLES

1. Assign study buddies who can be available over the phone.
2. If students have computers, provide lists of internet helplines.
3. Locate free help in public libraries and make these resources known.

Take advantage of family and community "funds of knowledge" to connect homework with life in the community, and life in the community with lessons in school (Moll, Amanti, Neff, & Gonzales, 1992).

EXAMPLES

1. Create a lesson about how family members use math and reading in sewing and in housing construction (Epstein & Van Voorhis, 2001).
2. Design interactive homework projects that families do together to evaluate needed products for their home; for example, deciding on the best buy on shampoo or paper towels.

For more ideas, see **www.ncpie.org/DevelopingPartnerships/**.

For help for parents and an article from teachers' points of view, see **www.parentscanada.com/developing/tweens/articles.aspx?listingid=340www.edu.gov.on.ca/abc123/eng/tips/homework.htmlwww.theglobeandmail.com/life/family-and-relationships/more-teachers-flexing-around-homework/article1370262/**

interest. They can initiate cognitive conflict and promote the disequilibrium that results in a changed knowledge structure. They can serve as cues, tips, or reminders. And students as well as teachers should learn to question effectively. We tell our students that the first step in doing a good research project is asking a good question.

For now, we will focus on teachers' questions and how to make them as helpful as possible for students. Many beginning teachers are surprised to discover how valuable good questions can be and how difficult they are to create.

STOP & THINK Think back to your most recent class. What kinds of questions does your professor ask? What sort of thinking is required to answer the questions? Remembering, understanding, applying, analyzing, evaluating, or creating? How long does the professor wait for an answer?

Kinds of Questions. Some educators have estimated that the typical teacher asks between 30 and 120 questions an hour, or about 1 500 000 questions over a teaching career (Sadker & Sadker, 2006). What sorts of questions do teachers ask? Many can be categorized in terms of Bloom's taxonomy of objectives in the cognitive domain. Table 13.5 on page 474 offers examples of questions at the different taxonomic levels.

TABLE 13.5

Classroom Questions for Objectives in the Cognitive Domain

Thinking at different levels of Bloom's taxonomy in the cognitive domain can be encouraged by different questions. Of course, the thinking required depends on what has gone before in the discussion.

Category	Type of Thinking Expected	Examples
Knowledge (recognition)	Recalling or recognizing information as learned	Define . . . What is the capital of . . .? What did the text say about . . .?
Comprehension	Demonstrating understanding of the materials; transforming, reorganizing, or interpreting	Explain in your own words . . . Compare . . . What is the main idea of . . .? Describe what you saw . . .
Application	Using information to solve a problem with a single correct answer	Which principle is demonstrated in . . .? Calculate the area of . . . Apply the rule of . . . to solve . . .
Analysis	Critical thinking; identifying reasons and motives; making inferences based on specific data; analyzing conclusions to see if supported by evidence	What influenced the writings of . . .? Why was Ottawa chosen . . .? Which of the following are facts and which are opinions . . .? Based on your experiment, what is the chemical . . .?
Synthesis	Divergent, original thinking; original plan, proposal, design, or story	What's a good name for . . .? How could we raise money for . . .? What would Canada be like if the Bloc Québécois were the official opposition?
Evaluation	Judging the merits of ideas, offering opinions, applying standards	Which prime minister was the most effective? Which painting do you believe to be better? Why? Why would you favour . . .?

Source: Adapted from Sadker, M., & Sadker, D. (1986). Questioning skills. In J. Cooper (Ed.), *Classroom teaching skills: A Handbook* (3rd ed., pp. 143–160). Boston: D. C. Heath. Adapted by permission of D. C. Heath.

Another way to categorize questioning is in terms of convergent questions (those with one correct answer only) or divergent questions (those with many possible answers). Questions about concrete facts are convergent: "Who ruled England in 1540?" "Who wrote the original *Peter Pan*?" Questions dealing with opinions or hypotheses are divergent: "In this story, which character is most like you and why?" "In 100 years, which of the past five prime ministers will be most admired?"

Fitting the Questions to the Students. All kinds of questions can be effective (Barden, 1995). Different patterns seem to be better for different students, however. The best pattern for younger students and for lower-ability students of all ages is to use simple questions that allow a high percentage of correct answers, ample encouragement, help when the student does not have the correct answer, and praise. For high-ability students, the successful pattern includes the use of harder questions at both higher and lower levels and more critical feedback (Berliner, 1987; Good, 1988).

Whatever their age or ability, all students should have some exposure to thought-provoking questions and, if necessary, help in learning how to answer them. As we saw in Chapter 8, to master critical thinking and problem-solving skills, students must have a chance to practise the skills. They also need time to think about their answers. But research shows that teachers wait an average of only 1 second for students to answer (Rowe, 1974). Consider the following slice of classroom life (Sadker & Sadker, 2006, pp. 130–131):

Teacher: Who wrote the poem "Stopping by Woods on a Snowy Evening"? Tom?

Tom: Robert Frost.

Teacher: Good. What action takes place in the poem? Sally?

Sally: A man stops his sleigh to watch the woods get filled with snow.

Teacher: Yes. Emma, what thoughts go through the man's mind?

Convergent questions Questions that have a single correct answer.

Divergent questions Questions that have no single correct answer.

Emma: He thinks how beautiful the woods are . . . (*She pauses for a second.*)

Teacher: What else does he think about? Joe?

Joe: He thinks how he would like to stay and watch. (*Pauses for a second.*)

Teacher: Yes—and what else? Rita? (*Waits half a second.*) Come on, Rita, you can get the answer to this. (*Waits half a second.*) Well, why does he feel he can't stay there indefinitely and watch the woods and the snow?

Sarah: Well, I think it might be . . . (*Pauses for a second.*)

Teacher: Think, Sarah. (*Teacher waits for half a second.*) All right then—Mike? (*Waits again for half a second.*) John? (*Waits half a second.*) What's the matter with everyone today? Didn't you do the reading?

Very little thoughtful responding can take place in this situation. When teachers learn to pose a question, then wait at least 3 to 5 seconds before calling on a student to answer, students tend to give longer answers; more students are likely to participate, ask questions, and volunteer appropriate answers; student comments involving analysis, synthesis, inference, and speculation tend to increase; and the students generally appear more confident in their answers (Berliner, 1987; Rowe, 1974; Sadker & Sadker, 2006).

This seems to be a simple method of improving in teaching, but 5 seconds of silence is not that easy to handle. It takes practice. You might try asking students to jot down ideas or even to discuss the question with another student and formulate an answer together. This makes the wait more comfortable and gives students a chance to think. Of course, if it is clear that students are lost or don't understand the question, waiting longer will not help. When your question is met with blank stares, rephrase the question or ask if anyone can explain the confusion. Also, there is some evidence that extending wait times does not affect learning in university classes (Duell, 1994), so with advanced high school students, you may want to conduct your own evaluation of wait time.

A word about selecting students to answer questions. If you call only on volunteers when selecting students to answer questions, you may get the wrong idea about how well students understand the material. Also, the same people volunteer over and over again. Many expert teachers have some systematic way of making sure that they call on everyone; they may pull names from a jar or check names off a list as each student speaks (Weinstein, 2007; Weinstein & Mignano, 2007). Another possibility is to put each student's name on an index card, then shuffle the cards and go through the deck as you call on people. You can use the cards to make notes about students' answers or extra help they may need.

Responding to Student Answers. What do you do after the student answers? The most common response, occurring about 50 percent of the time in most classrooms, is simple acceptance—"Okay" or "Uh-huh" (Sadker & Sadker, 2006). But there are better reactions, depending on whether the student's answer is correct, partly correct, or wrong. If the answer is quick, firm, and correct, simply accept the answer or ask another question. If the answer is correct but hesitant, give the student feedback about why the answer is correct: "That's right, Chris, the Governor General is the Queen's representative in Canada." This allows you to explain the material again. If this student is unsure, others may be confused as well. If the answer is partially or completely wrong but the student has made an honest attempt, you should probe for more information, give clues, simplify the question, review the previous steps, or reteach the material. If the student's wrong answer is silly or careless, however, it is better simply to correct the answer and go on (Good, 1988; Rosenshine & Stevens, 1986).

Group Discussion. Group discussion is in some ways similar to the recitation strategy. A teacher may pose questions, listen to student answers, react, and probe for more information, but in a true group discussion, the teacher does not have a dominant role. Students ask questions, answer each other's questions, and respond to each other's answers (Beck, McKeown, Worthy, Sandora, & Kucan, 1996; Burbules & Bruce, 2001; Parker & Hess, 2001).

There are many advantages to group discussions. The students are directly involved and have the chance to participate. Group discussion helps students learn to express themselves clearly, to justify opinions, and to tolerate different views. Group discussion also gives students a chance to ask for clarification, examine their own thinking, follow personal interests, and assume responsibility

Group discussion Conversation in which the teacher does not have the dominant role; students pose and answer their own questions.

GROUP DISCUSSIONS Small-group discussions allow greater student participation and exchange of ideas, but students may need help to stay focused.

by taking leadership roles in the group. Thus, group discussions help students evaluate ideas and synthesize personal viewpoints. Discussions are also useful when students are trying to understand difficult concepts that go against common sense. As we saw in Chapters 8 and 9, many scientific concepts, such as the role of light in vision or Newton's laws of motion, are difficult to grasp because they contradict common sense notions. By thinking together, challenging each other, and suggesting and evaluating possible explanations, students are more likely to reach a genuine understanding.

Of course, there are disadvantages. Class discussions are quite unpredictable and may easily digress into exchanges of ignorance. Some members of the group may have great difficulty participating and may become anxious if forced to speak. In addition, you may have to do a good deal of preparation to ensure that participants have a background of knowledge on which to base the discussion. And large groups are often unwieldy. In many cases, a few students will dominate the discussion while the others daydream (Arends, 2004; Freiberg & Driscoll, 2005). The *Guidelines* box gives some ideas for how to facilitate a productive group discussion in the classroom.

TEACHING READING, WRITING, ARITHMETIC, AND SCIENCE

Researchers have made great progress in understanding how students learn, or construct understandings, about different subjects. Below we describe approaches to teaching reading, writing, mathematics, and science that are based on these recent research findings.

Teaching Reading and Writing

For years, educators have debated whether students should be taught to read and write through code-based (phonics, skills) approaches that relate letters to sounds and sounds to words or through meaning-based (whole language, literature-based, emergent literacy) approaches that do not dissect words and sentences into pieces but instead focus on the meaning of the text (Barr, 2001; Carlisle, Stahl, & Birdyshaw, 2004; Goodman & Goodman, 1990; Smith, 1994; Stahl & Miller, 1989; Symons, Woloshyn, & Pressley, 1994). Now the consensus is that the best approach to teaching reading and writing balances strategies from both code-based and meaning-based approaches.

Informed by theory and research in the fields of emergent literacy and developmental psychology, advocates of meaning-based approaches, such as whole language, believe that becoming literate is a natural process—much like mastering your native language—that begins long before children enter school. Also, consistent with cognitive and constructivist views of learning, whole language advocates believe that children actively create understandings of what it really means to read and to write by engaging in authentic reading and writing activities. Finally, they stress social aspects of learning to read and write. They emphasize how important it is for parents and teachers to model literate behaviour for developing readers and writers. From this whole language perspective, learning to read and write during the elementary school years is part of a continuum of learning that begins at birth and continues through adulthood (Chapman, 1997). Teachers have to be astute observers of students' literacy development to determine the supports or resources students need to learn.

Whole language perspective A philosophical approach to teaching and learning that stresses learning through authentic, real-life tasks; it emphasizes using language to learn, integrating learning across skills and subjects, and respecting the language abilities of student and teacher.

GUIDELINES: Facilitating Productive Group Discussions

Invite shy children to participate.

EXAMPLES

1. Ask, "What's your opinion, Joel? We need to hear from some other students."
2. Don't wait until there is a deadly silence to ask shy students to reply. Most people, even those who are confident, hate to break a silence.

Direct student comments and questions back to another student.

EXAMPLES

1. Redirect questions: "That's an unusual idea, Steve. Kim, what do you think of Steve's idea?" or "That's an important question, John. Maura, do you have any thoughts about how you'd answer that?"
2. Encourage students to look at and talk to one another rather than wait for your opinion.

Make sure you understand what a student has said. If you are unsure, other students may be unsure as well.

EXAMPLES

1. Ask a second student to summarize what the first student said; then the first student can try again to explain if the summary is incorrect.
2. Provide opportunity for the student to clarify: "Jasdev, I think you're saying. . . . Is that right, or have I misunderstood?"

Probe for more information.

EXAMPLE

1. Ask probing questions: "That's a strong statement. Do you have any evidence to back it up?" or "Tell us how you reached that conclusion. What steps did you go through?"

Bring the discussion back to the subject.

EXAMPLE

1. Remind students where the discussion left off:
   - "Let's see, we were discussing . . . and Sarah made one suggestion. Does anyone have a different idea?"
   - "Before we continue, let me try to summarize what has happened so far."

Give time for thought before asking for responses.

EXAMPLE

1. Ask, "How would your life be different if television had never been invented? Jot down your ideas on paper, and we will share reactions in a minute." After a minute: "Hiromi, will you tell us what you wrote?"

When a student finishes speaking, look around the room to judge reactions.

EXAMPLES

1. If other students look puzzled, ask them to describe why they are confused.
2. If students are nodding assent, ask them to give an example of what was just said.

In many whole language classrooms, teachers and students set goals and design curriculum together. In writing, for instance, students and teachers identify a purpose and an audience. For example, students might decide to write letters to the mayor of their city about her recycling policy. Using such activities is consistent with Lev Vygotsky's (1978) view that "writing should be incorporated in tasks that are necessary and relevant for life. Only then can we be certain that it will develop not as a matter of hand and finger habits but as a really new and complex form of speech" (p. 118). In order to learn to write, students must spend time writing. Table 13.6 describes 10 research-based principles for teaching writing aimed at middle and high school students, but many of these principles apply to teaching younger students as well (Graham & Perin, 2007).

But whole language is not the whole story. There are now three decades of research demonstrating that skill in recognizing sounds and words supports learning to read. Advocates of skill-based approaches cite research showing that being able to identify many words as you read does not depend on using context to guess meaning. In fact, it is almost the other way around—knowing words helps you make sense of context. Identifying words as you read is a highly automatic process. It is the poorest readers who resort to using context to help them understand meaning (Muter, Hulme, Snowling, & Stevenson, 2004; Pressley, 1996). Alphabetic coding and awareness of letter sounds are essential skills for acquiring word identification, so some direct teaching of the alphabet and phonics is helpful in learning to read. But don't forget that reading and writing are for a purpose. Surround students with good literature and create a community of readers and writers. After all, we want our students to be both fluent *and* enthusiastic readers and writers (Reis et al., 2007; Stahl & Yaden, 2004).

TABLE 13.6

Tips for Teaching Middle and High School Students to Write

1. Teach strategies for planning, revising, and editing compositions. Harris and Graham's (1996) self-regulated strategy development model is a potent approach.
2. Teach strategies and procedures for summarizing reading material, because this improves students' abilities to present the information concisely and accurately in writing.
3. Develop instructional arrangements in which students work together to plan, draft, revise, and edit their compositions. Such collaborative activities have a strong impact on the quality of what students write.
4. Set clear and specific goals for what students are to accomplish with their writing product. This includes identifying the purpose of the assignment (e.g., to persuade) as well as characteristics of the final product.
5. Have students use word processing as a primary tool for writing, because it has a positive impact on the quality of their writing.
6. Teach students how to write increasingly complex sentences. Instruction in combining simpler sentences into more sophisticated ones enhances the quality of students' writing.
7. Involve students in writing activities designed to sharpen their inquiry skills. Effective inquiry activities in writing are characterized by a clearly specified goal (e.g., describe the actions of people), analysis of concrete and immediate data (e.g., observe one or more peers during specific activities), use of specific strategies to conduct the analysis (e.g., retrospectively ask the person being observed the reason for their action), and application of what was learned (e.g., write a story where the insights from the inquiry are incorporated into the composition).
8. Engage students in activities that help them gather and organize ideas for their compositions before they write a first draft. This includes activities such as gathering possible information for a paper through reading or developing a visual representation or map of their ideas before writing.
9. Provide adolescents with good models for each type of writing that is the focus of instruction. These examples should be analyzed, and students should be encouraged to imitate the critical elements embodied in the models.
10. Seek out professional development for yourself in learning how to implement the process writing approach.

Source: Adapted from Graham, S., & Perin, D. (2007). A meta-analysis of writing instruction for adolescent students. *Journal of Educational Psychology, 99,* 466–467.

As students develop in reading, **morphological awareness** or understanding how parts of words go together to make meaning becomes more important. A morpheme is the smallest part of a word that has meaning. For example, "beautiful" has two morphemes: "beauty" (a quality) and "ful" (a suffix that makes beauty an adjective) (Kuo & Anderson, 2006). In the later grades, to build reading comprehension, students need background knowledge and vocabulary (think how difficult it is to read a text outside your major), skills in making inferences, and reading strategies. High school students with low reading comprehension especially benefit from instruction that targets background knowledge and vocabulary (Cromley & Azevedo, 2007).

STOP & THINK Think back to the ways that you were taught mathematics. What were your math classes like in elementary school? In high school?

Teaching Arithmetic

Critics of direct instruction believe that traditional mathematics instruction often teaches students an unintended lesson—that they "cannot understand mathematics," or worse, that mathematics doesn't have to make sense, you just have to memorize the formulas. Arthur Baroody and Herbert Ginsburg (1990, p. 62) give this example:

> Sherry, a junior high student, explained that her math class was learning how to convert measurements from one unit to another. The interviewer gave Sherry the following problem:
>
> > To feed data into the computer, the measurements in your report have to be converted to one unit of measurement: metres. Your first measurement, however, is 150 centimetres. What are you going to feed into the computer?
>
> Sherry recognized immediately that the conversion algorithm taught in school applied. However, because she really did not understand the rationale behind the conversion algorithm, Sherry had difficulty in remembering the steps and how to execute them. After some time she came up with an improbable answer (it was less than 1 m). Sherry knew she was in

Morphological awareness Understanding how parts of words go together to make meaning.

> trouble and became flustered. At this point, the interviewer tried to help by asking her if there was any other way of solving the problem. Sherry responded sharply, "No!" She explained, "That's the way it has to be done." The interviewer tried to give Sherry a hint: "Look at the numbers in the problem, is there another way we can think about them that might help us figure out the problem more easily?" Sherry grew even more impatient, "This is the way I learned in school, so it has to be the way."

Sherry believed that there was only one way to solve a problem. Though Sherry knew that 100 centimetres was 1 metre and that shifting the "invisible" decimal at the end of 150 to the left increased the unit size in metric measurements, she did not use this knowledge to solve the problem informally and quickly. Her beliefs prevented her from effectively using her existing mathematical knowledge to solve the problem. Sherry had probably been taught to memorize the steps to convert one measurement to another. How would a constructivist approach teach the same material?

The following excerpt shows how a grade 3 teacher, Ms. Coleman, uses a constructivist approach to teach negative numbers. Notice the use of dialogue and the way the teacher asks students to justify and explain their thinking. The class has been considering one problem: $-10 + 10 = ?$. A student, Marta, has just tried to explain, using a number line, why $-10 + 10 = 0$:

> **Teacher:** Marta says that negative ten plus ten equals zero, so you have to count ten numbers to the right. What do you think, Harold?
>
> **Harold:** I think it's easy, but I don't understand how she explained it.
>
> **Teacher:** OK. Does anybody else have a comment or a response to that? Tessa? (Peterson, 1992, p. 165)

As the discussion progresses, Ms. Coleman encourages students to talk directly to each other:

> **Teacher:** You said you don't understand what she is trying to say?
>
> **Chang:** No.
>
> **Teacher:** Do you want to ask her?
>
> **Chang:** What do you mean by counting to the right?

This dialogue reveals three things about learning and teaching in a constructivist classroom: the thinking processes of the students are the focus of attention; one topic is considered in depth rather than attempting to "cover" many topics; and assessment is ongoing and mutually shared by teacher and students. Conducting these kinds of productive dialogues about mathematics concepts is not easy. You have to continually monitor the dialogue, have a good idea where the discussion is going and if it is productive, and learn when to step in and out of the discussion (Nathan & Knuth, 2003). Also, some studies have found that students with learning disabilities and lower-achieving students benefit more from explicit instruction in mathematics problem-solving strategies (teacher explanation and modelling, practice with feedback) than from constructivist teaching that encourages students to discuss and discover strategies. But both explicit instruction and constructivist methods were better than traditional instruction in at least one study (Kroesbergen, Van Luit, & Maas, 2004).

Conceptual Change Teaching in Science

We have seen a number of times that by high school many students have "learned" some unfortunate lessons in school. Like Sherry, described in the preceding section, they have learned that math is impossible to understand and that you just have to memorize the rules to get the answers. Or they may have developed misconceptions about the world, such as the belief that the Earth is warmer in the summer because it is closer to the sun or that light and sound "die out" as you get farther from the source (Linn & Eylon, 2006).

In order to change these conceptions, students have to integrate new information, usually gained in school, and also restructure their existing representations of knowledge—their schemas. To foster conceptual change, the teaching message has to be comprehensible, plausible, coherent, and compelling. Students cannot be persuaded by a message they do not understand. In addition, motivation plays a role in changing conceptions. Are students dissatisfied with their current understanding? If

Conceptual change teaching A method that helps students understand (rather than memorize) concepts in science by using and challenging the students' current ideas.

not, change is unlikely. Does the new conceptual understanding have personal relevance or emotional meaning? If so, students may engage deeply in understanding and changing their thinking. If motivation is low, students may just memorize superficially, but not change their thinking (Pintrich & Sinatra, 2003; Sinatra, 2005).

Many educators note that the key to understanding in science is for students to directly examine their own theories and confront the shortcomings (Hewson, Beeth, & Thorley, 1998). For conceptual change to take place, students must go through six stages: (a) initial discomfort with their own ideas and beliefs; (b) attempts to explain away inconsistencies between their theories and evidence presented to them; (c) attempts to adjust measurements or observations to fit personal theories; (d) doubt; (e) vacillation; and finally (f) conceptual change (Nissani & Hoefler-Nissani, 1992). You can see Piaget's notions of assimilation, disequilibrium, and accommodation operating here. Students try to make new information fit existing ideas (assimilation), but when the fit simply won't work and disequilibrium occurs, then accommodation or changes in cognitive structures follow.

The goal of conceptual change teaching in science is to help students pass through these six stages of learning. Conceptual change teaching has two central features:

- Teachers are committed to teaching for student understanding rather than "covering the curriculum."
- Students are encouraged to make sense of science using their current ideas—they are challenged to describe, predict, explain, justify, debate, and defend the adequacy of their understanding. Dialogue is key. Only when intuitive ideas prove inadequate can new learning take hold (Anderson & Roth, 1989).

Conceptual change teaching has much in common with inquiry learning described in Chapter 9, with scaffolding and dialogue playing key roles (Mercer, 2007). How would conceptual change teaching look in practice? One answer comes from Michael Beeth's study of a grade 5 classroom. Table 13.7 shows a list of learning goals that the teacher presented to her students. In this classroom, the teacher typically began instruction with questions such as, "Do you have ideas? Can you talk about them? Bring them out into the open? Why do you like your ideas? Why are you attracted to them?" (Beeth, 1998, p. 1095). Notice how the teacher is tapping motivation, personal relevance, and emotional connection to the ideas (Sinatra, 2005).

During her teaching, she constantly asked questions that required explanation and justifications. She summarized the students' answers and sometimes challenged, "But do you really believe what you say?" Studies of the students in the teacher's classroom over the years showed that they had a sophisticated understanding of science concepts.

Canadian researchers Wolf-Michael Roth and Michelle McGinn add that a key to unlocking opportunities for students to construct understandings in science (and mathematics) is posing better problems (Roth & McGinn, 1997). Usually, the problems students are given to solve are uncluttered with the complexities that enrich the real world. Too often, problems have prefigured answers where "students' tasks are to disclose what the texts (or problems) hide . . . as *the* solution" (pp. 19–20) rather than learn how to do science. Roth and McGinn suggest that teachers invite

TABLE 13.7

One Teacher's Learning Goals for Conceptual Change Teaching

The teacher in a grade 5 class gives these questions to her students to support their thinking about science.

1. Can you state your own ideas?
2. Can you talk about why you are attracted to your ideas?
3. Are your ideas consistent?
4. Do you realize the limitations of your ideas and the possibility they might need to change?
5. Can you try to explain your ideas using physical models?
6. Can you explain the difference between understanding an idea and believing in an idea?
7. Can you apply the words *intelligible* and *plausible* as standards for evaluating your ideas?

Source: Adapted from Beeth, M. E. (1998). Teaching science in fifth grade: Instructional goals that support conceptual change. *Journal of Research in Science Teaching, 35,* 1093.

students to bring problems from outside school into the classroom. Then, teachers should support students as students frame hypotheses and explore methods to investigate them. This places problems in context so that students' experiences from outside school are joined with experiences of doing science. This model, called *open inquiry*, transforms what students do to resemble what scientists do. The result? Students construct understandings about science that are genuine rather than textbookish (Roth & Bowen, 1995; Roth & Roychoudhury, 1993).

So far we have talked about approaches to teaching—general strategies. But in today's diverse classrooms, one size does not fit all. Within the general approach, teachers have to fit their instruction to the needs and abilities of their students—they have to differentiate instruction.

DIFFERENTIATED INSTRUCTION

STOP & THINK You are preparing a unit on habitats for your students. You decide to do as your old educational psychology professor recommended and give an alternate form of the final unit test as a pretest to find out what the students already know about the subject. After you reassure them that the test won't be graded—you just want an idea about where to go in developing the lesson—the students settle in and seem to take the task seriously. Looking over the papers that night, you are dismayed. A quarter of the students make over 90 percent on the "final." Quite a few get around half of the questions and problems right, but the rest of the class is clueless. The next day, when you ask Shanequa why she did so well on the test, she explains that in science class last year her group (and several others) chose habitats as the focus of their special project work. You stare at your lesson plans and realize that they fit practically no one in this class. What will you do?

As you have seen throughout this book, today's classrooms are diverse. Students differ in language, SES, culture, race, and ethnicity. They bring different strengths, abilities, and disabilities to the task of learning. Many educators believe that "classes should include students of diverse needs, achievement levels, interests, and learning styles, and instruction should be differentiated to take advantage of the diversity, not ignore it" (Jackson & Davis, 2000, p. 23). Differentiated instruction (Tomlinson, 2005b) is one way of going beyond accommodating these learner differences to seeing diversity as an array of strengths on which to build. The basic idea of differentiated instruction is that teachers must take into account not only the *subjects* they are teaching but also the *students*. In differentiated classrooms, students work at different paces, sometimes exercising varied learning options, and they are assessed using indicators that fit their interests and needs (George, 2005). One way to accomplish differentiation is though grouping—but there are cautions in using some kinds of groups.

Within-Class and Flexible Grouping

Differences like the ones illustrated above are common in most schools and classrooms. It is not unusual to have three- to five-year differences in any given classroom (Castle, Deniz, & Tortora, 2005). But even if you decided to simply forge ahead and teach the same material in the same way to your entire class, you would not be alone. One study found that in 46 different classrooms, 84 percent of the activities were the same for high-achieving and average-achieving students (Westberg, Archambault, Dobyns, & Slavin, 1993). Differences in student prior knowledge are a major challenge for teachers, especially in subjects that build on previous knowledge and skills such as math and science (Loveless, 1998). One answer has been to use the strategy known as ability grouping, but that has problems too.

The Problems With Ability Grouping. Students in many classes and schools are grouped by ability, even though there is no clear evidence that this within-class ability grouping is superior to other approaches. In a random sample of primary-grade teachers in the United States, 63 percent reported using within-class ability groups for reading. Students in lower-ability groups were less likely to be asked critical comprehension questions and given fewer opportunities to make choices about what to read (Chorzempa & Graham, 2006). For schools with lower-SES students, grouping

Differentiated instruction A flexible approach to teaching that matches content, process, and product based on student differences in readiness, interests, and learning needs.

Within-class ability grouping System of grouping in which students in a class are divided into two or three groups based on ability in an attempt to accommodate student differences.

often means that these students are segregated into lower-ability tracks. According to Paul George (2005):

> In my 3 decades of experience with this issue, when homogenous grouping is the primary strategy for organizing students in schools with significant racial and ethnic diversity in the population, the result is almost always deep, and often starkly obvious, division of students on the basis of race, ethnicity, and social class. (p. 187)

Thoughtfully constructed and well-taught ability groups in math and reading can be effective, but the point of any grouping strategy should be to provide appropriate challenge and support—that is, to reach children within their "zone of proximal development" (Vygotsky, 1997). Flexible grouping is one possible answer.

Flexible Grouping. In **flexible grouping**, students are grouped and regrouped based on their learning needs. Assessment is continuous so that students are always working within their zone of proximal development. Arrangements might include small groups, partners, individuals, and even the whole class—depending on which grouping best supports each student's learning of the particular academic content. Flexible grouping approaches include high-level instruction and high expectations for all students, no matter what their group placement. One five-year longitudinal study of flexible grouping in a high-needs urban elementary school (Castle et al., 2005) found 10 to 57 percent increases in students who reached mastery level, depending on the subject area and grade level. Teachers received training and support in the assessment, grouping, and teaching strategies needed, and by the end of the study, 95 percent of the teachers were using flexible grouping. The teachers in the study believed that some of the gains came because students were more focused on learning and more confident.

Another way to use flexible grouping is the non-graded elementary school. Students of several ages (for example, 6, 7, and 8) are together in one class, but they are flexibly grouped within the class for instruction based on achievement, motivation, or interest in different subjects. This cross-grade grouping seems to be effective for students of all abilities as long as the grouping allows teachers to give more direct instruction to the groups. *But be sensible about cross-age grouping.* Mixing students in grades 3, 4, and 5 for math or reading class based on what they are ready to learn makes sense. However, sending a large boy in grade 4 to grade 2, where he is the only older student and stands out like a sore thumb, isn't likely to work well. Also, when cross-age classes are created just because there are too few students for one grade—and not in order to better meet the students' learning needs—the results are not positive (Veenman, 1997). As we have seen repeatedly throughout this text, working at a challenging level, but one you can master with effort and support, is more likely to encourage learning and motivation.

If you ever decide to use flexible grouping in your class, the *Guidelines* box should help you make the approach more effective (Arends, 2007; Good & Brophy, 2008).

The Elements of Differentiated Instruction

Differentiated instruction conceives of all students as seeking purpose, challenge, affirmation, power, and contribution. The teacher responds to these student needs with invitation, investment, persistence, opportunity, and reflection, working to create curriculum and instruction for each student that is focused, engaging, demanding, important, and scaffolded. Carol Ann Tomlinson (2003) describes these characteristics as the "cogs of differentiation." They are called cogs because they are interdependent and interlocking, like the inner working of a clock. To see these interlocking cogs, see Figure 13.1.

What are some examples of differentiation in curriculum and instruction (Tomlinson, 2003)? Let's assume students in a pre-algebra class have varied interests and often have difficulty understanding why they are learning what they are learning in math. The teacher can modify the content and product based on student interests by using examples from sports, business, medicine, technology, and other fields to illustrate how formulas are used. She also might guide students in interviewing people engaged in a range of jobs and hobbies to find out how they use formulas in their work and in sharing those examples with others in the class. As a second example, some students in Advanced Placement History are taking their first advanced course and sometimes feel lost and discouraged by the course's demands. In response, the teacher might modify the learning environment and process

Flexible grouping Grouping and regrouping students based on learning needs.

GUIDELINES: Using Flexible Grouping

Form and re-form groups based on accurate assessments of students' *current performance* in the subject being taught.

EXAMPLES

1. Use scores on the most recent reading assessments to establish reading groups, and rely on current math performance to form math groups.
2. Assess continuously. Change group placement frequently when students' achievements change.

Make sure different groups get appropriately different instruction, not just the same material. Make sure teaching methods and pace are adjusted to fit the needs of the group.

EXAMPLES

1. Vary more than pace; fit teaching to students' interests and knowledge.
2. If all groups are doing research reports, request that some be written, while others are oral or PowerPoint presentations.
3. Organize and teach groups so that low-achieving students get appropriate extra instruction—not just the same material again. Make lower-achieving groups smaller so students get extra attention.
4. Make sure all work is meaningful and respectful—no worksheets for lower-ability groups while the higher-ability groups do experiments and projects.
5. Try alternatives. For example, DeWayne Mason and Tom Good (1993) found that supplementing whole-class instruction in math with remediation and enrichment for students when they needed it worked better than dividing the class into two ability groups and teaching these groups separately.

Discourage comparisons between groups and encourage students to develop a whole-class spirit.

EXAMPLES

1. Don't seat groups together outside the context of their reading or math group.
2. Avoid naming ability groups—save the names for mixed-ability or whole-class teams.

Group by ability for one or, at the most, two subjects.

EXAMPLES

1. Make sure there are many lessons and projects that mix members from the groups.
2. Experiment with learning strategies in which cooperation is stressed (described in Chapter 10).
3. Keep the number of groups small (two or three at most) so that you can provide as much direct teaching as possible—leaving students alone for too long leads to less learning.

For more information about classroom grouping, see these two sites: **www.eduplace.com/science/profdev/articles/valentino.htmlwww.nwrel.org/scpd/sirs/1/cu2.html**

FIGURE 13.1 **The Cogs of Differentiated Instruction**
All students seek purpose, challenge, affirmation, power, and contribution. The teacher responds to these student needs with invitation, investment, persistence, opportunity, and reflection, working to create curriculum and instruction for each student that is focused, engaging, demanding, important, and scaffolded.

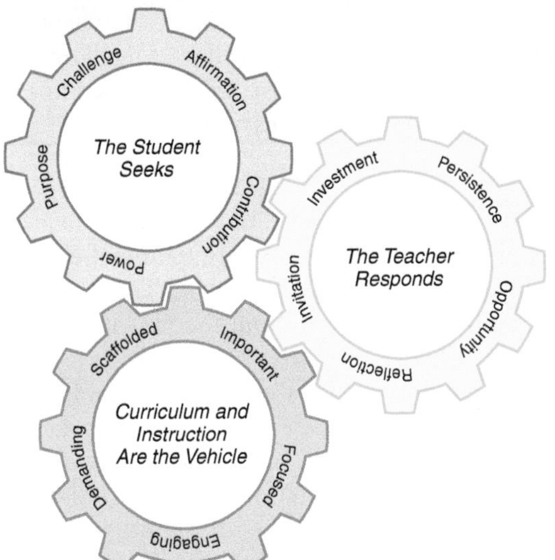

Examples of Enacting Each Element of the Differentiation Cogs		
The Student Seeks	*The Teacher Responds*	*Curriculum and Instruction Are the Vehicle*
Affirmation: People here know how I'm doing and it matters. I am safe here.	**Invitation:** You are unique and valuable; I believe in you.	**Important:** What we study is essential to the structure of the discipline.
Contribution: I bring to this place abilities and perspectives that are unique.	**Opportunity:** I have important things for you to do today. They may be daunting.	**Focused:** Both teacher and student know why we are doing what we are doing.
Power: I make choices that contribute to my success.	**Investment:** It is my job to help you succeed.	**Engaging:** Students most often find the work intriguing.
Purpose: I see the significance in what we do here.	**Persistence:** There is no finishing line in learning.	**Demanding:** Standards for work and behaviour are high.
Challenge: The work here stretches me. I work hard.	**Reflection:** I continually ask, "How can I make this better?"	**Scaffolded:** The teacher uses modelling, organizers, and other strategies to point out success.

Source: From *Fulfilling the Promise of the Differentiated Classroom* (p. 28) by C.A. Tomlinson. Alexandria, VA: ASCD Copyright © by the ASCD. Used with permission. Learn more about ASCD at www.ascd.org.

based on student readiness and emotions by establishing study groups to help students prepare for both oral and written tests. Although much of the work of the study groups takes place outside of class, the teacher conducts whole-class and small-group discussions about how the various groups approach studying, how the different approaches seem to work, and how students feel about their progress. The teacher also provides study guides to ensure focus on critical facets of the content.

Reaching Every Student: Differentiated Instruction in Inclusive Classrooms

STOP & THINK When you think about teaching in an inclusive classroom, what are your concerns? Do you have enough training? Will you get the support you need from school administrators or specialists? Will working with the students with disabilities take time away from your other responsibilities?.

These questions are common, and sometimes concerns are justified. But effective teaching for exceptional students does not require a unique set of skills. It is a combination of good teaching practices and sensitivity to all your students. Students with disabilities need to *learn the academic material*, and they need to be *full participants in the day-to-day life of the classroom*.

To accomplish the first goal of academic learning, students with learning disabilities appear to benefit from using extended practice distributed over days and weeks and from *advance organizers* such as focusing students on what they already know or stating clear objectives (Swanson, 2001).

To accomplish the second goal of integrating students with disabilities into the day-to-day life of the classroom, Marilyn Friend and William Bursuck (2002) recommend the INCLUDE strategy:

Identify the environmental, curricular, and instructional demands of your classroom.
Note students' learning strengths and needs.
Check for potential areas of student success.
Look for potential problem areas.
Use information gathered to brainstorm instructional adaptations.
Decide which adaptations to try.
Evaluate student progress.

Table 13.8 shows how the INCLUDE strategy might be applied to students with learning and behavioural disabilities.

When students have special needs, they may be referred to child study teams, school psychologists, or teachers of students with special needs for evaluation (see Table 4.13 on page 153 for guidelines about referring students for evaluation). The outcome of this process sometimes includes the preparation of an individualized education program, or IEP, as described in Chapter 4. Chapter 4 also describes some ways technology can support student differences in the classroom. Finally, review the section on teaching toward self-regulated learning in Chapter 10. There are some good tips in there about how to differentiate instruction and learning to address the needs of all students.

Teacher Expectations

Nearly 40 years ago, a study by Robert Rosenthal and Lenore Jacobson (1968) captured the attention of the national media in a way that few studies by psychologists have since then. The study also caused great controversy within the professional community. Debate about the meaning of the results continues (Babad, 1995; Rosenthal, 1995; Snow, 1995).

What did Rosenthal and Jacobson say that caused such a stir? They chose several students at random in a number of elementary school classrooms, and then told the teachers that these students probably would make significant intellectual gains during the year. The students did indeed make larger gains than normal that year. The researchers presented data suggesting the existence of a **Pygmalion effect** or self-fulfilling prophecy in the classroom. A **self-fulfilling prophecy** is a groundless expectation that leads to behaviours that then make the original expectation come true (Merton, 1948). An example is a false belief that a bank is failing, leading to a rush to withdraw money that then causes the bank to fail as expected.

Pygmalion effect Exceptional progress by a student as a result of high teacher expectations for that student; named for the mythological king Pygmalion, who made a statue, then caused it to be brought to life.

Self-fulfilling prophecy A groundless expectation that is confirmed because it has been expected.

TABLE 13.8 Making Adaptations for Students With Learning and Behavioural Disabilities Using Steps in the INCLUDE Strategy

Identify Classroom Demands	Note Student Strengths and Needs	Check for Potential Successes; Look for Potential Problems	Decide on Adaptations
Student desks in clusters of four	*Strengths* Good vocabulary skills *Needs* Difficulty attending to task	*Success* Student understands instruction if on task *Problem* Student off task—does not face instructor as she teaches	Change seating so student faces instructor
Small-group work with peers	*Strengths* Good handwriting *Needs* Oral expressive language—problem with word finding	*Success* Student acts as secretary for cooperative group *Problem* Student has difficulty expressing self in peer learning groups	Assign as secretary of group; place into compatible small group; develop social skills instruction for all students
Expect students to attend class and be on time	*Strengths* Good drawing skills *Needs* Poor time management	*Success* Student uses artistic talent in class *Problem* Student is late for class and frequently does not attend at all	Use individualized student contract for attendance and punctuality—if goals met, give student artistic responsibility in class
Textbook difficult to read	*Strengths* Good oral communication skills *Needs* Poor reading accuracy; lacks systematic strategy for reading text	*Success* Student participates well in class; good candidate for class dramatizations *Problem* Student is unable to read text for information	Provide taped textbooks; highlight student text
Lecture on women's suffrage movement to whole class	*Strengths* Very motivated and interested in class *Needs* Lack of background knowledge	*Success* Student earns points for class attendance and effort *Problem* Student lacks background knowledge to understand important information in lecture	Give student video to view before lecture; build points for attendance and working hard into grading system
Whole class instruction on telling time to the quarter hour	*Strengths* Good colouring skills *Needs* Cannot identify numbers 7–12; cannot count by fives	*Success* Student is able to colour clock faces used in instruction *Problem* Student is unable to acquire telling time skills	Provide extra instruction on number identification and counting by fives

Source: From *Including Students with Special Needs: A Practical Guide for Classroom Teachers,* 3/e by Marilyn Friend & William D. Bursuck. Published by Allyn and Bacon, Boston, MA. Copyright © 2002 by Pearson Education. Adapted by permission of the publisher.

STOP & THINK When you thought about the most effective teacher you ever had, was one of the characteristics that the teacher believed in you or demanded the best from you? How did the teacher communicate that belief?

Two Kinds of Expectation Effects. Actually, two kinds of expectation effects can occur in classrooms. In the self-fulfilling prophecy described above, the teacher's beliefs about the students' abilities have no basis in fact, but student behaviour comes to match the initially inaccurate expectation. The second kind of expectation effect occurs when teachers are fairly accurate in their initial reading of students' abilities and respond to students appropriately. The problems arise when students show some improvement, but teachers do not alter their expectations to take account of the improvement. This is called a **sustaining expectation effect**, because the teacher's

Sustaining expectation effect Student performance maintained at a certain level because teachers don't recognize improvements.

SOURCES OF TEACHER EXPECTATIONS Students' extracurricular activities can be sources of expectations. Teachers tend to hold higher expectations for students who participate in extracurricular activities than for students who "just hang out" after school.

unchanging expectation sustains the student's achievement at the expected level. The chance to raise expectations, provide more appropriate teaching, and thus encourage greater student achievement is lost. In practice, self-fulfilling prophecy effects seem to be stronger in the early grades, and sustaining effects are more likely in the later grades (Kuklinski & Weinstein, 2001). And some students are more likely than others to be the recipients of sustaining expectations. For example, withdrawn children provide little information about themselves, so teachers may sustain their expectations about these children for lack of new input (Jones & Gerig, 1994).

Sources of Expectations. There are many possible sources of teachers' expectations including intelligence test scores (especially when not interpreted appropriately), gender (more behaviour problems for boys and higher academic achievement for girls), notes from previous teachers, the medical or psychological reports in students' permanent files, knowledge of older brothers and sisters, appearance (higher expectations for attractive students), previous achievement, socioeconomic status, race and ethnicity, and the actual behaviours of the student (Van Matre, Valentine, & Cooper, 2000). Even the student's after-school activities can be a source of expectations. Teachers tend to hold higher expectations for students who participate in extracurricular activities than for students who do not.

Expectations and beliefs focus attention and organize memory, so teachers may pay attention to and remember the information that fits the initial expectations (Fiske, 1993; Hewstone, 1989). Even when student performance does not fit expectations, the teacher may rationalize and attribute the performance to external causes beyond the student's control. For example, a teacher may assume that the low-ability student who did well on a test must have cheated and that the high-ability student who failed must have been upset that day. In both cases, behaviour that seems out of character is dismissed. It may take many instances of supposedly uncharacteristic behaviour to change the teacher's beliefs about a particular student's abilities. Thus, expectations often remain in the face of contradictory evidence (Brophy, 1998).

Do Teachers' Expectations Really Affect Students' Achievement? The answer to this question is more complicated than it might seem. There are two ways to investigate the issue. One is to give teachers unfounded expectations about their students and note if these baseless expectations have any effects. The other approach is to identify the naturally occurring expectations of teachers and study the effects of these expectations. The answer to the question of whether teacher expectations affect student learning depends in part on which approach is taken to study the question.

The original Rosenthal and Jacobson experiment used the first approach—giving teachers groundless expectations and noting the effects. A careful analysis of the results revealed that even though students in grades 1 through 6 participated in the study, the self-fulfilling prophecy effects could be traced to dramatic changes in just five students in grades 1 and 2. After reviewing the research on teacher expectations, Raudenbush (1984) concluded that these expectations have only a small effect on student IQ scores (the outcome measure used by Rosenthal and Jacobson) and only in the early years of a new school setting—in the first years of elementary school and then again in the first years of junior high school.

But what about the second approach—naturally occurring expectations? Research shows that teachers do indeed form beliefs about students' capabilities. Many of these beliefs are accurate assessments based on the best available data and are corrected as new information is collected. Even so, some teachers do favour certain students (Babad, 1995; Rosenthal, 1987). For example, in a synthesis of over 50 studies, Harriet Tenenbaum and Martin Ruck (2007) found that teachers held higher expectation for and directed more positive questions and encouragement toward European American students compared to African American and Latin American students. The highest expectations were reserved for Asian American students. In another study of 110 students followed from age 4 to age 18, Jennifer Alvidrez and Rhona Weinstein (1999) found that teachers tended to overestimate the abilities of preschool children they rated as independent and interesting and to underestimate the abilities of children perceived as immature and anxious. Teachers' judgments of student ability at age 4 predicted student grade point average at age 18. The strongest predictions were for students whose abilities were *underestimated.* If teachers decide that some students are less able, and if the teachers lack effective strategies for working with lower-achieving students, then students may experience a double threat—low expectations and inadequate teaching (Good & Brophy, 2008). The power of the expectation effect depends on the age of the students (generally speaking, younger students are more susceptible) and on how differently a teacher treats high- versus low-expectation students, an issue we turn to next (Kuklinski & Weinstein, 2001).

Instructional Strategies. Different grouping processes may well have a marked effect on students because different groups get different instruction. And some teachers leave little to the imagination; they make their expectations all too clear. For example, Alloway (1984) recorded comments such as these directed to low-achieving groups:

> "I'll be over to help you slow ones in a minute." "The blue group will find this hard."

In these remarks the teacher not only tells the students that they lack ability, but also communicates that finishing the work, not understanding, is the goal.

Once teachers assign students to ability groups, they usually assign different learning activities. To the extent that teachers choose activities that challenge students and increase achievement, these differences are probably necessary. Activities become inappropriate, however, when students who are ready for more challenging work are not given the opportunity to try it because teachers believe they cannot handle it. This is an example of a sustaining expectation effect.

Teacher–Student Interactions. However the class is grouped and whatever the assignments, the quantity and the quality of teacher–student interactions are likely to affect the students. Students who are expected to achieve tend to be asked more and harder questions, to be given more chances and a longer time to respond, and to be interrupted less often than students who are expected to do poorly. Teachers also give these high-expectation students cues and prompts, communicating their belief that the students can answer the question (Good & Brophy, 2008; Rosenthal, 1995). They tend to smile at these students more often and to show greater warmth through such non-verbal responses as leaning toward the students and nodding their heads as the students speak (Woolfolk & Brooks, 1983, 1985).

In contrast, with low-expectation students, teachers ask easier questions, allow less time for answering, and are less likely to give prompts. They are more likely to respond with sympathetic acceptance or even praise for inadequate answers from low-achieving students, but to criticize these same students for wrong answers. Even more disturbing, low-achieving students receive less praise than high-achieving students for similar correct answers. This inconsistent feedback can be very confusing for low-ability students. Imagine how hard it would be to learn if your wrong answers were sometimes praised, sometimes ignored, and sometimes criticized, and your right answers received little recognition (Good, 1983a, 1983b; Hattie & Timerley, 2007). Even though the effects of these communications may be small each day, there can be huge effects as the expectation differences build year after year with many teachers (Trouilloud, Sarrazin, Bressoux, & Bois, 2006).

Of course, not all teachers form inappropriate expectations or act on their expectations in unconstructive ways (Babad, Inbar, & Rosenthal, 1982). But avoiding the problem may be more difficult than it seems. In general, low-expectation students also tend to be the most disruptive students. (Of course, low expectations can reinforce their desire to disrupt or misbehave.) Teachers may call on these students less, wait a shorter time for their answers, and give them less praise for right answers, partly to avoid the wrong, careless, or silly answers that can cause disruptions, delays, and digressions (Cooper, 1979). The challenge is to deal with these very real threats to classroom management without communicating low expectations to some students or fostering their own low expectations of themselves. And sometimes, low expectations become part of the culture of the school—beliefs shared by teachers and administrators alike (Weinstein, Madison, & Kuklinski, 1995). The *Guidelines* box may help you avoid some of these problems.

GUIDELINES: Avoiding the Negative Effects of Teacher Expectations

Use information about students from tests, cumulative folders, and other teachers very carefully.

EXAMPLES

1. Avoid reading cumulative folders at the beginning of the year.
2. Be critical and objective about the reports you hear from other teachers.

Be flexible in your use of grouping strategies.

EXAMPLES

1. Review work of students often and experiment with new groupings.
2. Use different groups for different subjects.
3. Use mixed-ability groups in cooperative exercises.

Make sure that all the students are challenged.

EXAMPLES

1. Don't say, "This is easy; I know you can do it."
2. Offer a wide range of problems and encourage all students to try a few of the harder ones for extra credit. Find something positive about these attempts.

Be especially careful about how you respond to low-achieving students during class discussions.

EXAMPLES

1. Give them prompts, cues, and time to answer.
2. Give ample praise for good answers.
3. Call on low achievers as often as high achievers.

Use materials that show a wide range of ethnic groups.

EXAMPLES

1. Check readers and library books. Is there ethnic diversity?
2. If few materials are available, ask students to research and create their own, based on community or family sources.

Make sure that your teaching does not reflect racial, ethnic, or sexual stereotypes or prejudice.

EXAMPLES

1. Use a checking system to be sure you call on and include all students.
2. Monitor the content of the tasks you assign. Do boys get the "hard" math problems to work at the board? Do you avoid having students with limited English give oral presentations?

Be fair in evaluation and disciplinary procedures.

EXAMPLES

1. Make sure that equal offences receive equal punishment. Find out from students in an anonymous questionnaire whether you seem to be favouring certain individuals.
2. Try to grade student work without knowing the identity of the student. Ask another teacher to give you a second opinion from time to time.

Communicate to all students that you believe they can learn—and mean it.

EXAMPLES

1. Return papers that do not meet standards with specific suggestions for improvements.
2. If students do not have the answers immediately, wait, probe, and then help them think through an answer.

Involve all students in learning tasks and in privileges.

EXAMPLES

1. Use some system to make sure that you give each student practice in reading, speaking, and answering questions.
2. Keep track of who gets to do what job. Are some students always on the list while others seldom make it?

Monitor your non-verbal behaviour.

EXAMPLES

1. Do you lean away or stand farther away from some students? Do some students get smiles when they approach your desk while others get only frowns?
2. Does your tone of voice vary with different students?

For more information see **http://chiron.valdosta.edu/whuitt/files/teacherexpect.html**.

MyEducationLab
Go to the Podcasts section of MyEducationLab and listen to PODCAST—Academic Optimism. In the podcast Anita Woolfolk discusses a new concept she developed with her husband, Wayne Hoy, a professor of educational administration who works with principals and superintendents.

DIVERSITY AND CONVERGENCES IN TEACHING

The reading and mathematics skills of even young students predict how likely they are to graduate from high school, enrol in college or university, and earn a degree. Inequities in mathematics and reading skills lead to inequities in graduation and finally to inequities in wages. Many chapters in this book addressed the problem of achievement gaps. In this chapter we focused on the teacher and teaching. One study estimated that a child in poverty who had a good teacher five years in a row would learn enough to close the achievement gap (Hanushek, Rivkin, & Kain, 2005).

Diversity: Culture in Your Classroom

A key factor for good teaching is the need to know yourself—your biases, strengths, and blind spots as well as your own cultural identity. Only by having a clear sense of yourself can you understand and respect the cultural identity of your students. Jay Dee and Allan Henkin (2002) note that teachers must be willing to explore beyond their own zone of comfort as members of the majority cultural status quo. To increase the engagement of every student, Richard Sagor (2003) suggests you conduct a cultural audit in your classroom. Table 13.9 shows you how.

Convergences: Beyond the Debates to Outstanding Teaching

In spite of the achievement gaps, criticisms, and debates, there is no one best way to teach. Different goals and student needs require different teaching methods. Direct instruction often leads to better performance on achievement tests, whereas the open, informal methods such as discovery learning or inquiry approaches are associated with better performance on tests of creativity, abstract thinking, and problem solving. In addition, the open methods are better for improving attitudes toward school and for stimulating curiosity, cooperation among students, and lower absence rates (Walberg, 1990). According to these conclusions, when the goals of teaching involve problem solving, creativity, understanding, and mastering processes, many approaches besides direct instruction should be effective. These guidelines are in keeping with Tom Good's conclusion that teaching should become less direct as students mature and when the goals involve affective development and problem solving or critical thinking (Good, 1983a). Every student may require direct, explicit teaching for some learning goals some of the time, but every student also needs to experience more open, constructivist, student-centred teaching as well.

In the midst of all our debates about methods, we have to keep in mind that the first questions are "What should students learn? What is worth knowing today?" Then we can match methods to goals. Deanna Kuhn (2007) said it well:

> As for direct instruction, of course it has a place. Each young student does not need to reinvent knowledge from the ground up. The challenge is to formulate what we want direct instruction to be. In doing so, it is well to keep in mind that it is students who construct meaning from such instruction and decide what it is that they will learn. (p. 112)

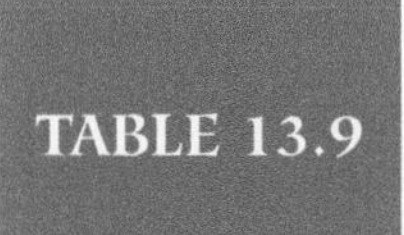

TABLE 13.9

Conducting a Cultural Audit of Your Classroom

Richard Sagor suggests that you conduct a cultural audit to help determine whether your classroom is a place where students from different cultures will feel a sense of belonging. You can do this four-step activity by yourself or with other faculty members.

Step 1. Record and Collect

On a typical day, tape record your lessons and collect all of the instructional materials you used.

Step 2. Review

Review all your lectures, explanations, and discussions and the materials and handouts you used for examples or illustrations drawn from non-majority cultures.

Step 3. Share Your Findings (Optional)

Share your findings with colleagues to see if there is a pattern of multicultural or monocultural perspectives in the school or classroom.

Step 4. Seek Outside Review and Collaboration

If you are not satisfied with the inclusiveness of your instruction and your materials, invite some culturally different parents or school patrons to review your data and to provide suggestions for you on incorporating multiple perspectives into your program.

Source: From *Motivating Students and Teachers in an Era of Standards* by Richard Sagor, pp. 78–79. Alexandria, VA, ASCD. Learn more about ASCD at www.ascd.org.

SUMMARY TABLE

Research on Teaching (pp. 457–459)

What methods have been used to study teaching? For years, researchers have tried to unravel the mystery of effective teaching using classroom observation, case studies, interviews, experimentation with different methods, stimulated recall (teachers view videotapes and explain their teaching), analysis of lesson transcripts, and other approaches to study teaching in real classrooms.

What are the general characteristics of good teaching? A variety of teacher qualities are related to good teaching. Research suggests teachers who receive proper training and certification have more successful students. Although it is important, teacher knowledge of a subject is not sufficient for effective teaching. Thorough knowledge does lead to greater clarity and better organization, which are both tied to good teaching. Teachers who provide clear presentations and explanations tend to have students who learn more and who rate their teachers more positively. Teacher warmth, friendliness, and understanding seem to be the traits most strongly related to positive student attitudes. Interestingly, students and administrators often have differing ideas about what makes a good teacher, which may impact both students' and administrators' perceptions of effective teaching.

What do expert teachers know? It takes time and experience to become an expert teacher. These teachers have a rich store of well-organized knowledge about the many specific situations of teaching. This includes knowledge about the subjects they teach, their students, general teaching strategies, subject-specific ways of teaching, settings for learning, curriculum materials, and the goals of education. Expert teachers also know how to be reflective practitioners—how to use their experience as a way to grow and improve in their teaching.

Expert teachers Experienced, effective teachers who have developed solutions for classroom problems. Their knowledge of teaching process and content is extensive and well organized.

Reflective Thoughtful and inventive. Reflective teachers think back over situations to analyze what they did and why, and to consider how they might improve learning for their students.

The First Step: Planning (pp. 459–465)

What are the levels of planning, and how do they affect teaching? Teachers engage in several levels of planning—by the year, term, unit, week, and day. All the levels must be coordinated. Accomplishing the year's plan requires breaking the work into terms, the terms into units, and the units into weeks and days. The plan determines how time and materials will be turned into activities for students. There is no single model of planning, but all plans should allow for flexibility. Planning is a creative problem-solving process for experienced teachers. It is more informal—that is, "in their heads."

What is an instructional objective? An instructional objective is a clear and unambiguous description of your educational intentions for your students. Mager's influential system for writing behavioural objectives states that a good objective has three parts—the intended student behaviour, the conditions under which the behaviour will occur, and the criteria for acceptable performance. Gronlund's alternative approach suggests that an objective should be stated first in general terms, and then the teacher should clarify by listing sample behaviours that would provide evidence that the student has attained the objective. The most recent research on instructional objectives tends to favour approaches similar to Gronlund's.

Describe the three taxonomies of educational objectives. Bloom and others have developed taxonomies categorizing basic objectives in the cognitive, affective, and psychomotor domains. In real life, of course, behaviours from these three domains occur simultaneously. A taxonomy encourages systematic thinking about relevant objectives and ways to evaluate them. Six basic objectives are listed in the cognitive domain: knowing, understanding, applying, analyzing, evaluating, and creating. A recent revision of this taxonomy adds that these processes can act on four kinds of knowledge: factual, conceptual, procedural, and metacognitive. Objectives in the affective domain run from least committed to most committed. Objectives in the psychomotor domain generally move from basic perceptions and reflex actions to skilled, creative movements.

Describe constructivist planning. In teacher-centred approaches, teachers select learning objectives and plan how to get students to meet those objectives. Teachers control the "what" and "how" of learning. In contrast, planning is shared and negotiated in student-centred, or constructivist, approaches. Rather than having specific student behaviours as objectives, the teacher has overarching goals or "big ideas" that guide planning. Integrated content and teaching with themes are often part of the planning. Assessment of learning is ongoing and mutually shared by teacher and students.

Instructional objectives Clear statements of what students are intended to learn through instruction.

Behavioural objectives Instructional objectives stated in terms of observable behaviour.

Cognitive objectives Instructional objectives stated in terms of higher-level thinking operations.

Taxonomy Classification system.

Cognitive domain In Bloom's taxonomy, memory and reasoning objectives.

Affective domain Objectives focusing on attitudes and feelings.

Psychomotor domain Realm of physical ability and coordination objectives.

Constructivist approach View that emphasizes the active role of the learner in building understanding and making sense of information.

Teaching Approaches (pp. 465–476)

What are the stages of Ausubel's expository teaching? Ausubel believes that learning should progress deductively: from the general to the specific, or from the rule or principle to examples. After presenting an advance organizer, the next step in a lesson using Ausubel's approach is to present content in terms of basic similarities and differences, using specific examples. Finally, when all the material has been presented, the teacher asks students to discuss how the examples can be used to expand on the original advance organizer.

What is direct instruction? Direct instruction is appropriate for teaching basic skills and explicit knowledge. It includes the teaching functions of review/overview, presentation, guided practice, feedback and correctives (with reteaching if necessary), independent practice, and periodic reviews. The younger or less able the students, the shorter the presentation should be with more cycles of practice and feedback.

Distinguish between convergent and divergent and high-level versus low-level questions. Convergent questions have only one right answer. Divergent questions have many possible answers. Higher-level questions require analysis, synthesis, and evaluation—students have to think for themselves. The best pattern for younger students and for lower-ability students of all ages is simple questions that allow a high percentage of correct answers, ample encouragement, help when the student does not have the correct answer, and praise. For high-ability students, the successful pattern includes harder questions at both higher and lower levels and more critical feedback. Whatever their age or ability, all students should have some experience with thought-provoking questions and, if necessary, help in learning how to answer them.

How can wait time affect student learning? When teachers learn to pose a question, then wait at least 3 to 5 seconds before calling on a student to answer, students tend to give longer answers; more students are likely to participate, ask questions, and volunteer appropriate answers; student comments involving analysis, synthesis, inference, and speculation tend to increase; and the students generally appear more confident in their answers.

What are the advantages and disadvantages of group discussion? Group discussion helps students participate directly, express themselves clearly, justify opinions, and tolerate different views. Group discussion also gives students a chance to ask for clarification, examine their own thinking, follow personal interests, and assume responsibility by taking leadership roles in the group. Thus, group discussions help students evaluate ideas and synthesize personal viewpoints. However, discussions are quite unpredictable and may easily digress into exchanges of ignorance.

Expository teaching Ausubel's method—teachers present material in complete, organized form, moving from broadest to more specific concepts.

Meaningful verbal learning Focused and organized relationships among ideas and verbal information.

Deductive reasoning Drawing conclusions by applying rules or principles; logically moving from a general rule or principle to a specific solution.

Advance organizer Statement of inclusive concepts to introduce and sum up material that follows.

Direct instruction/explicit teaching Systematic instruction for mastery of basic skills, facts, and information.

Active teaching Teaching characterized by high levels of teacher explanation, demonstration, and interaction with students.

Basic skills Clearly structured knowledge that is needed for later learning and that can be taught step by step.

Scripted cooperation Learning strategy in which two students take turns summarizing material and criticizing the summaries.

Seatwork Independent classroom work.

Convergent questions Questions that have a single correct answer.

Divergent questions Questions that have no single correct answer.

Group discussion Conversation in which the teacher does not have the dominant role; students pose and answer their own questions.

Teaching Reading, Writing, Arithmetic, and Science (pp. 476–481)

What is a balanced approach to reading and writing? The best approach to teaching reading and writing balances strategies from both code-based and meaning-based approaches. There is extensive research indicating that skill in recognizing sounds and words—phonemic awareness—is fundamental in learning to read. Research also indicates that children are motivated to learn when they are surrounded by good literature and read and write for authentic purposes. Highly effective teachers use a balanced approach combining authentic reading and writing activities with skills instruction when needed.

How do constructivist approaches to mathematics teaching differ from traditional approaches? Critics have characterized historical approaches to teaching math as focusing too strongly on rote memorization and not enough on problem solving. New approaches to mathematics education, informed by constructivist approaches to teaching and learning, emphasize deep understanding of concepts (as opposed to memorization), discussion and explanation, and exploration of students' implicit understandings. Teachers need to monitor students' understanding when using these approaches and be ready to provide explicit instruction about math concepts to students who need it.

What is conceptual change teaching in science? Many educators note that the key to understanding in science is for students to directly examine their own theories and confront the shortcomings. For change to take place, students must go through six stages: initial discomfort with their own ideas and beliefs, attempts to explain away inconsistencies between their theories and evidence presented to them, attempts to adjust measurements or observations to fit personal theories, doubt, vacillation, and finally conceptual change.

Whole language perspective A philosophical approach to teaching and learning that stresses learning through authentic, real-life tasks; it emphasizes using language to learn, integrating learning across skills and subjects, and respecting the language abilities of student and teacher.

Morphological awareness Understanding how parts of words go together to make meaning.

Conceptual change teaching in science A method that helps students understand (rather than memorize) concepts in science by using and challenging the students' current ideas.

Differentiated Instruction (pp. 481–488)

What are the problems with ability grouping? Academic ability groupings can have both disadvantages and advantages for students and teachers. For low-ability students, however, between-class ability grouping generally has a negative effect on achievement, social adjustment, and self-esteem. Teachers of low-achievement classes tend to emphasize lower-level objectives and routine procedures, with less academic focus. Often, there are more student behaviour problems, increased teacher stress, lowered expectations, and decreased enthusiasm. Ability grouping can promote segregation within schools.

What are the alternatives available for grouping in classes, including flexible grouping? Cross-age grouping by subject can be an effective way to deal with ability differences in a school. Within-class ability grouping, if handled sensitively and flexibly, can have positive effects, but alternatives such as cooperative learning may be better.

What are the elements of differentiated instruction? Differentiated instruction can take the form of modifying content, modifying presentation, or modifying learning environments. For example, a teacher might adapt content by applying students' interests to curricular material or change presentation strategies by inviting students to explore alternative sources of information. Learning environments might be modified by moving a class outside the classroom—simply out of doors or even to a location off a school's campus.

What characterizes effective teaching for exceptional students? Effective teaching for exceptional students does not require a unique set of skills. It is a combination of good teaching practices and sensitivity to all students. Students with disabilities need to learn the academic material, and they need to be full participants in the day-to-day life of the classroom.

What resources do teachers have to work effectively with exceptional children? When students have special needs, they may be referred to specialists such as child study teams, school psychologists, or teachers of students with special needs for evaluation. The outcome of this process sometimes includes the preparation of an individualized educational program, or IEP, as described in Chapter 4, which will have teaching ideas and guidelines. In addition, differentiated instruction can improve learning for all students.

What are some sources of teacher expectations? Sources include intelligence test scores, gender, notes from previous teachers and the medical or psychological reports found in cumulative folders, ethnic background, knowledge of older brothers and sisters, physical characteristics, previous achievement, socio-economic status, and the actual behaviours of the student.

What are the two kinds of expectation effects and how do they happen? The first is the self-fulfilling prophecy; the teacher's beliefs about the students' abilities have no basis in fact, but student behaviour comes to match the initially inaccurate expectation. The second is a sustaining expectation effect; teachers are fairly accurate in their initial reading of students' abilities and respond to students appropriately but teachers do not alter their expectations to take account of the improvement. When this happens, the teacher's unchanging expectation can sustain the student's achievement at the expected level. In practice, sustaining effects are more common than self-fulfilling prophecy effects.

What are the different avenues for communicating teacher expectations? Some teachers tend to treat students differently, depending on their own views of how well the students are likely to do. Differences in treatment toward low-expectation students may include setting less challenging tasks, focusing on lower-level learning, giving fewer choices, providing inconsistent feedback, and communicating less respect and trust. Students may behave accordingly, fulfilling teachers' predictions or staying at an expected level of achievement.

Differentiated instruction A flexible approach to teaching that matches content, process, and product based on student differences in readiness, interests, and learning needs.

Within-class ability grouping System of grouping in which students in a class are divided into two or three groups based on ability in an attempt to accommodate student differences.

Flexible grouping Grouping and regrouping students based on learning needs.

Pygmalion effect Exceptional progress by a student as a result of high teacher expectations for that student; named for the mythological king Pygmalion, who made a statue, then caused it to be brought to life.

Self-fulfilling prophecy A groundless expectation that is confirmed because it has been expected.

Sustaining expectation effect Student performance maintained at a certain level because teachers don't recognize improvements.

TEACHERS' CASEBOOK

You have started a new job in a high school in your hometown. When you were in school, the students were fairly similar—white, working to middle class, and English speaking. There was a "special education" class for students who had serious learning or developmental problems. But in the classes you will be teaching, you find a wide range of reading levels, family incomes, and learning problems. Two of your students are virtually ready for post-secondary education, while several can barely read the texts and their writing is impossible to decipher. Reading English texts is a challenge for some of your students, though they seem to speak English with little trouble.

What Would *They* Do?

Here is how two practising teachers responded to the teaching situation described above.

Lenore Klassen **Special Needs Coordinator,**
Edmonton Public School District, Edmonton, AB

This scenario certainly describes many of our classes in a busy urban Alberta school. The teachers in my junior high school face this problem daily, as junior high in our district is the last truly inclusive level, with all students being in the same classroom—in high school our students are streamed according to ability into levelled courses. Thus in most of our classes (grades 7–9) you will find a wide spectrum of students with differing language backgrounds, cultural backgrounds, skill levels, SES, and (dis)abilities.

In order to differentiate teaching, we focus on providing *adaptations* to both the instructional and assessment components of the curriculum. Only in extreme circumstances do we change the learning outcomes (*modifications*) for students. In my school, the four core academic departments (math, language arts, social studies, and science) have determined core learning outcomes for each unit, and have also created a list of the 10 essential learning outcomes for each subject (what the student must learn in order to be successful at the next level). By reducing the curriculum to these 10 essential outcomes, we can focus on teaching the core material to all students, and then supplement the essential material with extra material according to student capabilities.

Adaptations to instruction are crucial for student success. In our school, the core material is taught explicitly. First, key vocabulary is reviewed, and for ESL students, an opportunity to translate into first language is given. Second, background knowledge is given and discussed as a class so that weaker students can learn from stronger students. Our teachers often illustrate key components using a mixed media/smartboard/video format to increase interest and student attention, and teachers provide plenty of classroom time to practise. Assignments can be adapted for length for weaker students, if needed, but the key skills needed for the course are not compromised—instead students practise until mastery is reached. Much of the work done in class is marked as "For Learning" (teacher feedback) and only assignments done in class, under the teacher's direct supervision are used for "Of Learning" (marks for the report card). The analogy is that learning academics is like learning a sport—much practice must occur under a coach's direction before an athlete participates in a real match/event.

Our grading practice has been to assign letter grades according to the level of proficiency and level of adaptations needed for success. A letter grade of C is given if a student demonstrates mastery/knowledge of the basic material. A letter grade of B is given if a student shows mastery of the more complex material. A letter grade of A is given if a student not only shows mastery of the material taught, but also is able to go beyond what is taught and apply it to untaught material. Assessments are written as a department and are designed to follow this grading practice. For example, the first part of a unit final exam will demonstrate basic knowledge items (C-level questions), the second part of the test will ask more difficult questions (B-level questions), and the third part will include a few challenging, never-seen-before questions (A-level questions). Giving a student a grade on an assessment becomes more transparent when you have tests designed on this principle.

If students receive minor adaptations in a course (such as extra time, a quiet space, oral questions), then they are graded using standard grading practices. If they receive major adaptations (open book, A-level questions removed, translator used), then they can receive only a grade of C for that course. The idea is that students need to be "weaned" off major adaptations.

Teaching is becoming more complex as our classrooms become more diverse. Good teaching is always about being willing to make learning work for all students.

Leyton Schnellert **Program Coordinator, Master of Education in Educational Practice Program (and former teacher of elementary, middle, and secondary school students)**
Simon Fraser University, Burnaby, BC

I have been a teacher for 18 years now. I think the first thing that I would do in this scenario is take a deep breath! One of the most important things I can do is tell myself that this might take a little while to figure out and that's okay. Complex situations take time to sort out. Another thing I would do is find out more about the students from their perspective. If I want to develop pathways for information to flow to and from them, then I need to find out what they are interested in, what has worked for them in the past, and what their expectations are of me. I can adjust my teaching without asking these questions, but I have headed in the wrong direction many times before when I just could have asked!

I usually look for trends in what students tell me. I recently had three different Humanities 9 classes with three different profiles: the first was filled with quiet students who were afraid to fail and wanted a lot of structure and visuals; the second was a group of very chatty kids, who knew a lot about popular culture and liked asking questions and having discussions—they wanted to know details; finally, the third class needed movement breaks—lots of kids were into sports, electronics, and art. Across all three classes there were some similarities— students were worried that I would not like them or their work, students liked to read (if not at "grade" level), and none, not even the chatty folks, wanted to give oral presentations. So I took this into account, and while I planned similar lessons for each class, I adjusted my plans with the class "personality" in mind.

Knowing that the students liked to read, I worked with colleagues and the librarian to create "text sets." These are groups of texts on the same theme. I introduced each text with a sales pitch (i.e., a book talk) and then students chose which text to read. Some texts had a lot of visuals or larger print; others were news articles or more factual texts. Many were easier to read. This way, the students had a choice, and I appealed to their need for visuals and different levels of text. What is important is that the students knew what to do with the text. I typically had them process the text in a small group, with support to activate their prior knowledge, and then I had them extract key information and combine what they thought before they read the text with what they learned from reading the text.

One of the most powerful ways I have found to engage diverse classes of students is to offer them more than one way to show what they know. If I am clear with them about the "learning intention" (i.e., outcome) or ask an inquiry question that we develop our knowledge around, they can collect information and show what they know in a variety of ways. I do teach each method (e.g., webbing vs. two column notes vs. flow chart vs. paragraph synthesis), but ultimately it is so students can choose multiple paths to the same outcome.

One of the benefits of having a diverse class is that the class's diversity becomes a strength. If I differentiate instruction with a few kids in mind (e.g., Sarah will need an option to draw), all kids can benefit from seeing and using other ways to synthesize information. In fact, one of the best ways to demonstrate understanding is to show what you know in more than one modality. I have learned to make my classes a place where students can help determine the criteria for an assignment and the options available for demonstrating their learning. While I have the curriculum to refer to, I have found that even my more disengaged learners participate when they have a voice in creating the assignments. When a student asks for an alternative way to show what he or she knows, the route often benefits others—it also reduces the pressure on me. Rather than guessing what students need and want, I co-construct it with them.

Recently, a group of students asked me if they could create a slide show about the Napoleonic Era. I had to refer them back to our shared criteria several times, as they did not have much explanation behind their points. That's been key—being clear that a PowerPoint presentation or painting still needs to be explained, just like any other form of communication. As long as this is in the criteria, I can justify the mark I give. Yet there is differentiation here, too. In this unit, I had students create an artifact for a museum show based on a significant moment in Napoleon's "reign" that showed him to be a hero. Knowing that they had to explain their piece, some students stood beside their artifact and explained it as others came by, others wrote up supporting documents to be placed beside their artifacts, and two students recorded their commentary so that passersby could listen on headphones. All of these were viable options.

REFERENCES

Aber, J. L., Brown, J. L., & Jones, S. M. (2003). Developmental trajectories toward violence in middle childhood: Course, demographic differences, and response to school-based intervention. *Developmental Psychology, 39*, 324–348.

Abi-Nader, J. (1991). Creating a vision of the future: Strategies for motivating minority students. *Phi Delta Kappan, 72*, 546–549.

Aboud, F. E. (2003). The formation of in-group favoritism and out-group prejudice in young children: Are they distinct attitudes? *Developmental Psychology, 39*, 48–60.

Acker, S., & Oatley, K. (1993). Gender issues in education for science and technology: Current situation and prospects for change. *Canadian Journal of Education, 18*, 255–272.

Ackerman, B. P., Brown, E. D., & Izard, C. E. (2004). The relations between contextual risk, earned income, and the school adjustment of children from economically disadvantaged families. *Developmental Psychology, 40*, 204–216.

Ackerman, P. L., Beier, M. E., & Boyle, M. O. (2005). Working memory and intelligence: The same or different constructs? *Psychological Bulletin, 131*, 30–60.

Ainley, M., Hidi, S., & Berndorf, D. (2002). Interest, learning, and the psychological processes that mediate their relationship. *Journal of Educational Psychology, 94*, 545–561.

Airasian, P. W. (2005). *Classroom assessment: Concepts and applications* (5th ed.). New York, NY: McGraw-Hill.

Airasian, P. W., Engemann, J. F., & Gallagher, T. L. (2007). *Classroom assessment: Concepts and applications* (1st Cdn ed.). Toronto, ON: McGraw-Hill Ryerson.

Albanese, M. A., & Mitchell, S. A. (1993). Problem-based learning: A review of literature on its outcomes and implementation issues. *Academic Medicine, 68*, 52–81.

Alber, S. R., & Heward, W. L. (1997). Recruit it or lose it! Training students to recruit positive teacher attention. *Intervention in School and Clinic, 32*, 275–282.

Alber, S. R., & Heward, W. L. (2000). Teaching students to recruit positive attention: A review and recommendations. *Journal of Behavioral Education, 10*, 177–204.

Alberto, P., & Troutman, A. C. (2006). *Applied behavior analysis for teachers: Influencing student performance* (7th ed.). Upper Saddle River, NJ: Prentice-Hall/Merrill.

Alderman, M. K. (2004). *Motivation for achievement: Possibilities for teaching and learning*. Mahwah, NJ: Erlbaum.

Alexander, P. A. (1992). Domain knowledge: Evolving themes and emerging concerns. *Educational Psychologist, 27*, 33–51.

Alexander, P. A. (1996). The past, present, and future of knowledge research: A reexamination of the role of knowledge in learning and instruction. *Educational Psychologist, 31*, 89–92.

Alexander, P. A. (1997). Mapping the multidimensional nature of domain learning: The interplay of cognitive, motivational, and strategic forces. *Advances in Motivation and Achievement, 10*, 213–250.

Alexander, P. A. (2006a). *Psychology in learning and instruction*. Upper Saddle River, NJ: Merrill/Prentice-Hall.

Alexander, P. A. (2006b). Evolution of a learning theory. *Educational Psychologist, 41*, 257–264.

Alexander, P. A., Kulikowich, J. M., & Schulze, S. K. (1994). How subject-matter knowledge affects recall and interest. *American Educational Research Journal, 31*, 313–337.

Alexander, P. A., & Murphy, P. K. (1998). The research base for APA's Learner-Centered Psychological Principles. In N. Lambert & B. McCombs (Eds.), *How students learn: Reforming schools through learner-centered education* (pp. 25–60). Washington, DC: American Psychological Association.

Alexander, P. A., & Winne, P. H. (2006). *Handbook of educational psychology* (2nd ed.). Mahwah, NJ: Erlbaum.

Alliance for a Healthier Generation. [Website]. Retrieved from http://www.healthiergeneration.org/default.aspx

Alliance for Children. (2000, September 12). *Children and computers: A call for action*. Retrieved from http://www.allianceforchildhood.net/projects/computers/computers_articles_call_for_action.htm

Allington, R. L., & McGill-Frazen, A. (2003). The impact of summer setback on the reading achievement gap. *Phi Delta Kappan, 85*(1), 68–75.

Allington, R. L., & McGill-Frazen, A. (2008). *Got books? Educational Leadership, 65*(7), 20–23.

Alloway, N. (1984). *Teacher expectations*. Paper presented at the meetings of the Australian Association for Research in Education, Perth, Australia.

Alloway, T. P., Gathercole, S. E., & Pickering, S. J. (2006). Verbal and visuospatial short-term and working memory in children: Are they separable? *Child Development, 77*, 1698–1716.

Alloy, L. B., & Seligman, M. E. P. (1979). On the cognitive component of learned helplessness and depression. *The Journal of Learning and Motivation, 13*, 219–276.

Altermatt, E. R., Pomerantz, E. M., Ruble, D. N., Frey, K. S., & Greulich, F. K. (2002). Predicting changes in children's self-perceptions of academic competence: A naturalistic examination of evaluative discourse among classmates. *Developmental Psychology, 38*, 903–917.

Alton-Lee, A., Diggins, C., Klenner, L., Vine, E., & Dalton, N. (2001). Teacher management of the learning environment during a social studies discussion in a new-entrant classroom in New Zealand. *The Elementary School Journal, 101*, 549–566.

Alvidrez, J., & Weinstein, R. S. (1999). Early teacher perceptions and later student academic achievement. *Journal of Educational Psychology, 91*, 731–746.

Amabile, T. M. (1996). *Creativity in context*. Boulder, CO: Westview Press.

Amabile, T. M. (2001). Beyond talent: John Irving and the passionate craft of creativity. *American Psychologist, 56*, 333–336.

Amato, L. F., Loomis, L. S., & Booth, A. (1995). Parental divorce, marital conflict, and offspring well-being during early adulthood. *Social Forces, 73*, 895–915.

Amato, P. R. (2006). Marital discord, divorce, and children's well-being. In A. Clarke-Stewart & J. Dunn (Eds.), *Families count: Effects on child and adolescent development* (pp. 179–202). New York, NY: Cambridge University Press.

American Academy of Family Physicians. (2009). Cerebral palsy in children. Retrieved from http://familydoctor.org/online/famdocen/home/children/parents/special/birth/901.html

American Printing House for the Blind. (2009). Distribution of eligible students. Retrieved from http://www.aph.org/fedquotpgm/dist09.html

American Psychiatric Association. (2000). *The diagnostic and statistical manual of mental disorders* (DSM-IV-TR). Washington, DC: Author.

Ames, C. (1990). Motivation: What teachers need to know. *Teachers College Record, 91*, 409–421.

Ames, C. (1992). Classrooms: Goals, structures, and student motivation. *Journal of Educational Psychology, 84*, 261–271.

Anderman, E. M., & Anderman, L. H. (2009). Motivating children and adolescents in schools. Columbus, OH: Merrill/Prentice Hall.

Anderman, E. M., & Maehr, M. L. (1994). Motivation and schooling in the middle grades. *Review of Educational Research, 64*, 287–310.

Anderman, E. M., & Midgley, C. (2004). Changes in self-reported academic cheating across the transition from middle school to high school. *Contemporary Educational Psychology, 29*, 499–517.

Anderson, C. W., Holland, J. D., & Palincsar, A. S. (1997). Canonical and sociocultural approaches to research and reform in science education: The story of Juan and his group. *The Elementary School Journal, 97*, 359–384.

Anderson, C. W., & Roth, K. J. (1989). Teaching for meaningful and self-regulated learning of science. In J. Brophy (Ed.), *Advances in research on teaching*, (Vol. I, pp. 265–306). Greenwich, CT: JAI Press.

Anderson, J. (1995). Listening to parents' voices: Cross cultural perceptions of learning to read and write. *Reading Horizons*, 35, 394–413.

Anderson, J., & Gunderson, L. (1997). Literacy learning from a multicultural perspective. *The Reading Teacher*, 50, 514–516.

Anderson, J. R. (1993). Problem solving and learning. *American Psychologist*, 48, 35–44.

Anderson, J. R. (2005). *Cognitive psychology and its implications*. (6th ed.). New York, NY: Worth.

Anderson, J. R., Reder, L. M., & Simon, H. A. (1995). *Applications and misapplication of cognitive psychology to mathematics education*. Unpublished manuscript. Retrieved from http://www.psy.cmu.edu/~mm4b/misapplied.html

Anderson, J. R., Reder, L. M., & Simon, H. A. (1996). Situated learning and education. *Educational Researcher*, 25, 5–11.

Anderson, L. M. (1985). What are students doing when they do all that seatwork? In C. Fisher & D. Berliner (Eds.), *Perspectives on instructional time* (pp. 189–202). New York, NY: Longman.

Anderson, L. M., Brubaker, N. L., Alleman-Brooks, J., & Duffy, G. G. (1985). A qualitative study of seatwork in first-grade classrooms. *Elementary School Journal*, 86, 123–140.

Anderson, L. W., & Krathwohl, D. R. (Eds.). (2001). *A taxonomy for learning, teaching, and assessing: A revision of Bloom's taxonomy of educational objectives*. New York, NY: Longman.

Anderson, L. W., & Sosniak, L. A. (Eds.). (1994). *Bloom's taxonomy: A forty-year retrospective*. Ninety-third yearbook for the National Society for the Study of Education: Part II. Chicago, IL: University of Chicago Press.

Anderson, P. J., & Graham, S. M. (1994). Issues in second-language phonological acquisition among children and adults. *Topics in Language Disorders*, 14, 84–100.

Anderson, R. C., Nguyen-Jahiel, K., McNurlen, B., Archodidou, A., Kim, S-Y., Reznitskaya, A., . . . Gilbert, L. (2001). The snowball phenomenon: Spread of ways of talking and ways of thinking across groups of children. *Cognition and Instruction*, 19, 1–46.

Anderson, S. M., Klatzky, R. L., & Murray, J. (1990). Traits and social stereotypes: Efficiency differences in social information processing. *Journal of Personality and Social Psychology*, 59, 192–201.

Angier, N., & Chang, K. (2005, January 24). Gray matter and the sexes: Still a scientific gray area. *The New York Times*, A1+.

Anyon, J. (1980). Social class and the hidden curriculum of work. *Journal of Education*, 162, 67–92.

Archer, S. L., & Waterman, A. S. (1990). Varieties of identity diffusions and foreclosures: An exploration of the subcategories of the identity statuses. *Journal of Adolescent Research*, 5, 96–111.

Arends, R. I. (2001). *Learning to teach* (5th ed.). New York, NY: McGraw-Hill.

Arends, R. I. (2004). *Learning to teach* (6th ed.). New York, NY: McGraw-Hill.

Arends, R. I. (2007). *Learning to teach* (7th ed.). New York, NY: McGraw-Hill.

Arnold, M. L. (2000). Stage, sequence, and sequels: Changing conceptions of morality, post-Kohlberg. *Educational Psychology Review*, 12, 365–383.

Aronson, E. (2000). *Nobody left to hate: Teaching compassion after Columbine*. New York, NY: Worth.

Aronson, J. (2002). Stereotype threat: Contending and coping with unnerving expectations. In J. Aronson & D. Cordova (Eds.), *Improving education: Classic and contemporary lessons from psychology* (pp. 279–301). New York, NY: Academic Press.

Aronson, J., Fried, C. B., & Good, C. (2002). Reducing the effects of stereotype threat on African American college students: The role of theories of intelligence. *Journal of Experimental Social Psychology*, 33, 113–125.

Aronson, J., & Inzlicht, M. (2004). The ups and downs of attributional ambiguity: Stereotype vulnerability and the academic self-knowledge of African American college students. *Psychological Science*, 15, 829–836.

Aronson, J., Lustina, M. J., Good, C., Keough, K., Steele, C. M., & Brown, J. (1999). When White men can't do math: Necessary and sufficient factors in stereotype threat. *Journal of Experimental Social Psychology*, 35, 29–46.

Aronson, J., & Steele, C. M. (2005). Stereotypes and the fragility of human competence, motivation, and self-concept. In C. Dweck & E. Elliot (Eds.), *Handbook of competence and motivation*. New York, NY: Guilford.

Aronson, J., Steele, C. M., Salinas, M. F., & Lustina, M. J. (1999). The effect of stereotype threat on the standardized test performance of college students. In E. Aronson (Ed.), *Readings about the social animal* (8th ed.). New York, NY: Freeman.

Ashcraft, M. H. (2006). *Cognition* (4th ed.). Upper Saddle River, NJ: Prentice-Hall.

Ashton, P. T. (1978). Cross-cultural Piagetian research: An experimental perspective. *Harvard Educational Review* (Reprint Series No. 13), 475–506.

Association for the Gifted. (2001). *Diversity and developing gifts and talents: A national action plan*. Arlington, VA: Author.

Asthma Society of Canada. (2009). Asthma at school. Retrieved from http://www.asthma.ca/adults/community/asthmaatschool.php

Atkinson, R. C., & Shiffrin, R. M. (1968). Human memory: A proposed system and its control processes. In K. Spence & J. Spence (Eds.), *The psychology of learning and motivation* (Vol. 2, pp. 89–195). New York, NY: Academic Press.

Atkinson, R. K., Levin, J. R., Kiewra, K. A., Meyers, T., Atkinson, L. A., Renandya, W. A., & Hwang, Y. (1999). Matrix and mnemonic text-processing adjuncts: Comparing and combining their components. *Journal of Educational Psychology*, 91, 242–257.

Atkinson, R. K., & Renkl, A. (2007). Interactive example-based learning environments: Using interactive elements to encourage effective processing of worked examples. *Educational Psychology Review*, 19, 375–386.

Atkinson, R. K., Renkl, A., & Merrill, M. M. (2003). Transitioning from studying examples to solving problems: Combining fading with prompting fosters learning. *Journal of Educational Psychology*, 95, 774–783.

Atwell, P. (2000). *Beyond the digital divide* [Working paper No. 164]. New York, NY: Russell Sage Foundation.

Au, K. H. (1980). Participation structures in a reading lesson with Hawaiian children: Analysis of a culturally appropriate instructional event. *Anthropology and Education Quarterly*, 11, 91–115.

Au, K. T., Knightly, L. M., Jun, S., & Oh, J. S. (2002). Overhearing a language during childhood. *Psychological Science*, 13, 238–243.

Aufderheide, P., & Firestone, C. (1993). *Media literacy: A report of the national leadership conference on media literacy*. Queenstown, MD: Aspen Institute.

Ausubel, D. P. (1963). *The psychology of meaningful verbal learning*. New York, NY: Grune and Stratton.

Ausubel, D. P. (1977). The facilitation of meaningful verbal learning in the classroom. *Educational Psychologist*, 12, 162–178.

Ausubel, D. P. (1982). Schemata, advance organizers, and anchoring ideas: A reply to Anderson, Spiro, and Anderson. *Journal of Structural Learning*, 7, 63–73.

Avramidis, E., Bayliss, P., & Burden, R. (2000). Student teachers' attitudes toward the inclusion of children with special education needs in the ordinary school. Teaching and *Teacher Education*, 16, 277–293.

Azevedo, R. (2005). Using hypermedia as a metacognitive tool for enhancing student learning? The role of self-regulated learning. *Educational Psychologist*, 40, 199–209.

Azevedo, R., Cromley, J. G., & Seibert, D. (2004). Does adaptive scaffolding facilitate students' ability to regulate their learning with hypermedia? *Contemporary Educational Psychology*, 29, 344–370.

Babad, E. Y. (1995). The "Teachers' Pet" phenomenon, students' perceptions of differential behavior, and students' morale. *Journal of Educational Psychology*, 87, 361–374.

Babad, E. Y., Inbar, J., & Rosenthal, R. (1982). Pygmalion, Galatea, and the Golem: Investigations of biased and unbiased teachers. *Journal of Educational Psychology*, 74, 459–474.

Baddeley, A. D. (1986). *Working memory*. Oxford, England: Clarendon Books.

Baddeley, A. D. (2001). Is working memory still working? *American Psychologist*, 56, 851–864.

Baer, J. (1997). *Creative teachers, creative students*. Boston, MA: Allyn & Bacon.

Bailey, S. M. (1993). The current status of gender equity research in American Schools. *Educational Psychologist*, 28, 321–339.

Baillargeon, R. (1999). Yong infants' expectations about hidden objects: A reply to three challenges. *Developmental Psychology*, 2, 115–132.

Bakerman, R., Adamson, L. B., Koner, M., & Barr, R. G. (1990). !Kung infancy: The social context of object exploration. *Child Development*, 61, 794–809.

Baldwin, J. M. (1895). *Mental development in the child and the race: Methods and processes*. New York, NY: Macmillan.

Ball, D. L. (1997). What do students know? Facing challenges of distance, context, and desire in trying to hear children. In B. J. Biddle, T. L. Good, & I. F. Goodson (Eds.), *The international handbook of teachers and teaching* (pp. 769–818). Dordrecht, the Netherlands: Kluwer.

Ball, J. (2008). Promoting equity and dignity for Aboriginal children in Canada. *Choices, 14*(7), 3–27.

Bandura, A. (1965). Influence of models' reinforcement contingencies on the acquisition of imitative responses. *Journal of Personality and Social Psychology, 1*, 589–595.

Bandura, A. (1977). *Social learning theory*. Englewood Cliffs, NJ: Prentice-Hall.

Bandura, A. (1982). Self-efficacy mechanisms in human agency. *American Psychologist*, 37, 122–147.

Bandura, A. (1986). *Social foundations of thought and action*. Englewood Cliffs, NJ: Prentice-Hall.

Bandura, A. (1993). Perceived self-efficacy in cognitive development and functioning. *Educational Psychologist*, 28, 117–148.

Bandura, A. (1994). Self-efficacy. In V. S. Ramachaudran (Ed.), *Encyclopedia of human behavior* (Vol. 4, pp. 71–81). New York, NY: Academic Press.

Bandura, A. (1997). *Self-efficacy: The exercise of control*. New York, NY: Freeman.

Bandura, A. (2001). Social cognitive theory: An agentic perspective. *Annual review of psychology* (Vol. 52, pp. 1–26). Palo Alto, CA: Annual Reviews, Inc.

Bandura, A. (2002). Social cognitive theory in cultural context. *Applied Psychology: An International Review, 51*(2) 269–290.

Bandura, A. (2006). Adolescent development from an agentic perspective. In F. Pajares & T. Urdan (Eds.), *Self-efficacy beliefs of adolescents*. Greenwich, CT: Information Age.

Bandura, A. (2007). Albert Bandura. In L. Gardner & W. M. Runyan (Eds.), *A history of psychology in autobiography* (Vol. IX, pp. 43–75). Washington, DC: American Psychological Association.

Bandura, A., & Locke, E. (2003). Negative self-efficacy and goal effects revisited. *Journal of Applied Psychology, 88*, 87–99.

Bandura, A., Ross, D., & Ross, S. A. (1963). Vicarious reinforcement and imitative learning. *Journal of Abnormal and Social Psychology, 67*, 601–607.

Banks, J. A. (1997). *Teaching strategies for ethnic studies* (6th ed.). Boston, MA: Allyn & Bacon.

Banks, J. A. (1999). *An introduction to multicultural education* (2nd ed.). Boston, MA: Allyn & Bacon.

Banks, J. A. (2002). *An introduction to multicultural education* (3rd ed.). Boston, MA: Allyn & Bacon.

Banks, J. A. (2006). *Cultural diversity and education: Foundations, curriculum, and teaching* (5th ed.). Boston, MA: Allyn & Bacon.

Banks, S. R. (2005). *Classroom assessment: Issues and practice*. Boston, MA: Allyn & Bacon.

Barakett, J. M. (1986). Teachers' theories and methods in structuring routine activities in an inner city school. *Canadian Journal of Education, 11*(2), 91–108.

Barden, L. M. (1995). Effective questioning and the ever-elusive higher-order question. *American Biology Teacher, 57*, 423–426.

Bargh, J. A., McKenna, K. Y. A., & Fitzsimons, G. M. (2002). Can you see the real me? Activation and expression of the "true self" on the Internet. *Journal of Social Issues, 58*(1), 33–48.

Barnett, M. S., & Ceci, S. J. (2002). When and where do we apply what we learn? A taxonomy for far transfer. *Psychological Bulletin, 128*, 612–637.

Barnhill, G. P. (2005). Functional behavioral assessment in schools. *Intervention in School and Clinic, 40*, 131–143.

Baron, R. A. (1998). *Psychology* (4th ed.). Boston, MA: Allyn & Bacon.

Baron, R. A., & Byrne, D. (2003). *Social psychology* (10th ed.). Boston, MA: Allyn & Bacon.

Baroody, A. R., & Ginsburg, H. P. (1990). Children's learning: A cognitive view. In R. Davis, C. Maher, & N. Noddings (Eds.), *Constructivist views on the teaching and learning of mathematics* (pp. 51–64). Monograph 4 of the National Council of Teachers of Mathematics, Reston, VA.

Barr, R. (2001). Research on the teaching of reading. In V. Richardson (Ed.), *Handbook of research on teaching* (4th ed., pp. 390–415). Washington, DC: American Educational Research Association.

Bartholomew, B. (2008). Sustaining the fire. *Educational Leadership, 65*(6), 55–60.

Basow, S. A., & Rubin, L. R. (1999). Gender influences on adolescent development. In N. G. Johnson, M. C. Roberts, & J. Worell (Eds.), *Beyond appearance: A new look at adolescent girls* (pp. 25–52). Washington, DC: American Psychological Association.

Batschaw, M. L. (1997). *Children with disabilities* (4th ed.). Baltimore, ML: Brookes.

Battistich, V., Solomon, D., & Delucci, K. (1993). Interaction processes and student outcomes in cooperative groups. *Elementary School Journal, 94*, 19–32.

Bauer, P. J. (2006). Event memory. In D. Kuhn & R. S. Siegler (Eds.), *Cognition, perception, and language* (6th ed., Vol. 2, pp. 373–425). New York, NY: Wiley.

Baumeister, R. F., Campbell, J. D., Krueger, J. L., & Vohs, K. D. (2003). Does high self-esteem cause better performance, interpersonal success, happiness, or healthier lifestyles? *Psychological Science in the Public Interest, 4*, 1–44.

Baumeister, R. F., & Leary, M. R. (1995). The need to belong: Desire for interpersonal attachments as a fundamental human motivation. Psychological Bulletin, 117, 497–529.

Baumrind, D. (1971). Current patterns of parental authority. *Developmental Psychology, 4*, 1–103.

Baumrind, D. (1991). Effective parenting during early adolescent transitions. In P. A. Cowan & M. Hetherington (Eds.), *Family transitions* (pp. 111–165). Hillsdale, NJ: Erlbaum.

BC College of Teachers. (2008). *Standards for the competence, professional conduct and ethical behaviour of educators in British Columbia* (3rd ed.). Retrieved from http://www.bcct.ca/documents/AboutUs/Standards/edu_stds.pdf

BC Ministry of Education. (n.d.). Full day kindergarten: Program guide. Retrieved from http://www.bced.gov.bc.ca/early_learning/fdk/pdfs/fdk_program_guide.pdf

BCTF. (2003). Summary analysis of the BC College of Teachers' standards for the education competence and professional conduct of educators in BC. Retrieved from www.bctf.ca/

Beane, J. A. (1991). Sorting out the self-esteem controversy. *Educational Leadership, 49*(1), 25–30.

Bear, G. G. (with Cavalier, A. R., & Manning, M. A.). (2005). *Developing self-discipline and preventing and correcting misbehavior*. Boston, MA: Allyn & Bacon.

Beck, C., Hart, D., & Kosnik, C. (2002). The teaching standards movement and current teaching practices. *Canadian Journal of Education, 27*, 175–194.

Beck, I. L., McKeown, M. G., Worthy, J., Sandora, C. A., & Kucan, L. (1996). Questioning the author: A yearlong classroom implementation to engage students with text. *The Elementary School Journal, 96*, 385–414.

Bee, H. (1981). *The developing child* (3rd ed.). New York, NY: Harper & Row.

Beebe-Frankenberger, M., Bocian, K. L., MacMillan, D. L., & Gresham, F. M. (2004). Sorting second grade students with academic deficiencies: Characteristics differentiating those retained in grade from those promoted to third grade. *Journal of Educational Psychology, 96*, 204–215.

Beeth, M. E. (1998). Teaching science in fifth grade: Instructional goals that support conceptual change. *Journal of Research in Science Teaching, 35*, 1091–1101.

Benenson, J. F. (1993). Greater preference among females than males for dyadic interaction in early childhood. *Child Development, 64*, 544–555.

Benjafield, J. G. (1992). *Cognition*. Englewood Cliffs, NJ: Prentice-Hall.

Bennett, C. I. (1995). *Comprehensive multicultural education: Theory and practice* (3rd ed.). Boston, MA: Allyn & Bacon.

Bennett, C. I. (1999). *Comprehensive multicultural education: Theory and practice* (4th ed.). Boston, MA: Allyn & Bacon.

Bereiter, C. (1995). A dispositional view of transfer. In A. McKeough, J. Lupart, & A. Marini (Eds.), *Teaching for mastery: Fostering generalization in learning* (pp. 21–34). Mahwah, NJ: Erlbaum.

Berg, C. A., & Clough, M. (1991). Hunter lesson design: The wrong one for science teaching. *Educational Leadership, 48*(4), 73–78.

Berger, K. S. (2003). *The developing person through childhood and adolescence* (6th ed.). New York, NY: Worth Publishers.

Berger, K. S. (2006). *The developing person through childhood and adolescence* (7th ed.). New York, NY: Worth.

Berger, K. S., & Thompson, R. A. (1995). *The developing person through childhood and adolescence*. New York, NY: Worth.

Bergin, D. (1999). Influences on classroom interest. *Educational Psychologist, 34*, 87–98.

Berk, L. E. (2001). *Awakening children's minds: How parents and teachers can make a difference*. New York, NY: Oxford University Press.

Berk, L. E. (2002). *Infants, children, and adolescents* (4th ed.). Boston, MA: Allyn & Bacon.

Berk, L. E. (2005). *Infants, children, and adolescents* (5th ed.). Boston, MA: Allyn & Bacon.

Berk, L. E., & Spuhl, S. T. (1995). Maternal interaction, private speech, and task performance in preschool children. *Early Childhood Research Quarterly, 10,* 145–169.

Berko, J. (1958). The child's learning of English morphology. *Word, 14,* 150–177.

Berliner, D. C. (1983). Developing concepts of classroom environments: Some light on the T in studies of ATI. *Educational Psychologist, 18,* 1–13.

Berliner, D. C. (1987). But do they understand? In V. Richardson-Koehler (Ed.), *Educators' handbook: A research perspective* (pp. 259–293). New York, NY: Longman.

Berliner, D. C. (1988). Simple views of effective teaching and a simple theory of classroom instruction. In D. Berliner & B. Rosenshine (Eds.), *Talks to teachers* (pp. 93–110). New York, NY: Random House.

Berliner, D. C. (2002). Educational research: The hardest science of all. *Educational Researcher, 31*(8), 18–20.

Berliner, D. C. (2005). Our impoverished view of educational reform. *The Teachers College Record, 108,* 949–995.

Berliner, D. C. (2006). Educational psychology: Searching for essence throughout a century of influence. In P. A. Alexander & P. H. Winne (Eds.), *Handbook of educational psychology* (2nd ed., pp. 3–27). Mahwah, NJ: Erlbaum.

Berlyne, D. (1966). Curiosity and exploration. *Science, 153,* 25–33.

Berndt, T. J. (2004). Children's friendships: Shifts over a half-century in perspectives on their development and their effects. Merrill-Palmer Quarterly: *Journal of Development Sciences, 50,* 206–223.

Berndt, T. J., & Keefe, K. (1995). Friends' influence on adolescents' adjustment to school. *Child Development, 66,* 1312–1329.

Bernstein, D. A., & Nash, P. W. (2008). *Essentials of psychology* (4th ed.). Boston, MA: Houghton-Mifflin.

Betancourt, H., & Lopez, S. R. (1993). The study of culture, ethnicity, and race in American psychology. *American Psychologist, 48,* 629–637.

Bialystok, E. (2001). *Bilingualism in development: Language, literacy, and cognition.* New York, NY: Cambridge University Press.

Bialystok, E., Majumder, S., & Martin, M. M. (2003). Developing phonological awareness: Is there a bilingual advantage? *Applied Linguistics, 24,* 27–44.

Biggs, J. (2001). Enhancing learning: A matter of style of approach. In R. Sternberg & L. Zhang (Eds.), *Perspectives on cognitive, learning, and thinking styles* (pp. 73–102). Mahwah, NJ: Erlbaum.

Blair, C. (2006). How similar are fluid cognition and general intelligence? A developmental neuroscience perspective on fluid cognition as an aspect of human cognition [Main article with commentaries]. *Behavioral and Brain Sciences, 29,* 109–160.

Blakeburn Elementary & Laidlaw, L. (2001). "I can be happy at this school": Creating a socially responsible learning community. *Teacher: Newsmagazine of the British Columbia Teachers Federation, 13*(5), 1–4.

Blakemore, S. K., & Frith, U. (2005). The learning brain: Lessons for education: a precis. Developmental Science, 8, 459–461.

Blatchford, P., Baines, E., Rubie-Davis, C., Bassett, P., & Chowne, A. (2006). The effect of a new approach to group work on pupil-pupil and teacher-interactions. *Journal of Educational Psychology, 98,* 750–765.

Bloom, B. S. (1981). *All our children learning: A primer for parents, teachers, and other educators.* New York, NY: McGraw-Hill.

Bloom, B. S. (1982). The role of gifts and markers in the development of talent. *Exceptional Children, 48,* 510–522.

Bloom, B. S., Engelhart, M. D., Frost, E. J., Hill, W. H., & Krathwohl, D. R. (1956). *Taxonomy of educational objectives. Handbook I: Cognitive domain.* New York, NY: David McKay.

Blumenfeld, P. C., Puro, P., & Mergendoller, J. R. (1992). Translating motivation into thoughtfulness. In H. Marshall (Ed.), *Redefining student learning: Roots of educational change* (pp. 207–240). Norwood, NJ: Ablex.

Bolick, C. M., & Cooper, J. M. (2006). Classroom management and technology. In C. Evertson & C. S. Weinstein (Eds.), *Handbook for classroom management: Research, practice, and contemporary issues.* Mahwah, NJ: Erlbaum.

Bonnano, R. A. & Hymel, S. (2010). Beyond hurt feelings: Investigating why some victims of bullying are at greater risk for suicidal ideation. *Merrill-Palmer Quarterly, 56,* 420–440.

Boom, J., Brugman, D., & van der Heijden, P. G. (2001). Hierarchical structure of moral stages assessed by a sorting task. *Child Development, 72,* 535–548.

Borko, H., & Livingston, C. (1989). Cognition and improvisation: Differences in mathematics instruction by expert and novice teachers. *American Educational Research Journal, 26,* 473–498.

Borman, G. D., & Overman, L. T. (2004). Academic resilience in mathematics among poor and minority students. *The Elementary School Journal, 104,* 177–195.

Bos, C. S., & Reyes, E. I. (1996). Conversations with a Latina teacher about education for language-minority students with special needs. *The Elementary School Journal, 96,* 344–351.

Bowlby, J. (1969). *Attachment and loss: Attachment.* New York, NY: Basic Books.

Brainerd, C. J. (2003). Jean Piaget, learning research, and American education. In B. J. Zimmerman & D. H. Schunk (Eds.), *Educational psychology: A century of contributions* (pp. 251–287). Mahwah, NJ: Erlbaum.

Brannon, L. (2002). *Gender: Psychological perspectives* (3rd ed.). Boston, MA: Allyn & Bacon.

Bransford, J. D., Brown, A. L., & Cocking, R. R. (2000). *How people learn: Brain, mind, experience, and school.* Washington, DC: National Academy Press.

Bransford, J. D., & Schwartz, D. (1999). Rethinking transfer: A simple proposal with multiple implications. In A. Iran-Nejad & P. D. Pearson (Eds.), *Review of research in education* (Vol. 24, pp. 61–100). Washington, DC: American Educational Research Association.

Bransford, J. D., & Stein, B. S. (1993). *The IDEAL problem solver: A guide for improving thinking, learning, and creativity* (2nd ed.). New York, NY: Freeman.

Brantlinger, E. (2004). Who wins and who loses? Social class and students' identities. In M. Sadowski (Ed.), *Adolescents at school: Perspectives on youth, identity, and education* (pp. 107–126). Cambridge, MA: Harvard University Press.

Bredekamp, S., & Copple, C. (1997). *Developmentally appropriate practice in early childhood programs.* Washington, DC: National Association for the Education of Young Children.

British Columbia College of Teachers. (2004, Winter). Aboriginal education initiatives: From parents clubs to teacher education. *Connected,* 9–11.

British Columbia Ministry for Children and Families. (1998). *The BC handbook for action on child abuse and neglect.* Victoria, BC: Crown Publications.

British Columbia Special Education Branch. (1995). *Special education services: A manual of policies, procedures, and guidelines.* Victoria, BC: Author.

Bronfenbrenner, U. (1989). Ecological systems theory. In R. Vasta (Ed.), *Annals of child development* (Vol. 6, pp.187–249). Boston, MA: JAI Press, Inc.

Bronfenbrenner, U., & Evans, G. W. (2000). Developmental science in the 21st century: Emerging theoretical models, research designs, and empirical findings. *Social Development, 9,* 115–125.

Bronfenbrenner, U., McClelland, P., Wethington, E., Moen, P., & Ceci, S. (1996). *The state of Americans: This generation and the next.* New York, NY: Free Press.

Bronfenbrenner, U., & Morris, P. A. (2006). The bioecological model of human development. In W. Damon & R. M. Lerner (Eds.), *Handbook of child psychology: Vol. 1. Theoretical models of human development* (6th ed., pp. 793–827). Hoboken, NJ: Wiley.

Brooks-Gunn, J. (1988). Antecedents and consequences of variations in girls' maturational timing. In M. D. Levin & E. R. McAnarney (Eds.), *Early adolescent transitions* (pp. 101–121). Lexington, MA: Lexington Books.

Brophy, J. E. (1981). Teacher praise: A functional analysis. *Review of Educational Research, 51,* 5–21.

Brophy, J. E. (1985). Teacher–student interaction. In J. Dusek (Ed.), *Teacher expectancies* (pp. 303–328). Hillsdale, NJ: Erlbaum.

Brophy, J. E. (1988). On motivating students. In D. Berliner & B. Rosenshine (Eds.), *Talks to teachers* (pp. 201–245). New York, NY: Random House.

Brophy, J. E. (1998). *Motivating students to learn.* New York, NY: McGraw-Hill.

Brophy, J. E. (2003). An interview with Jere Brophy by B. Gaedke, & M. Shaughnessy. *Educational Psychology Review, 15,* 199–211.

Brophy, J. E. (2005). Goal theorists should move on from performance goals. *Educational Psychologist, 40,* 167–176.

Brophy, J. E., & Evertson, C. (1978). Context variables in teaching. *Educational Psychologist, 12,* 310–316.

Brophy, J. E., & Good, T. (1986). Teacher behavior and student achievement. In M. Wittrock (Ed.), *Handbook of research on teaching* (3rd ed.) (pp. 328–375). New York, NY: Macmillan.

Brophy, J. E., & Kher, N. (1986). Teacher socialization as a mechanism for developing student motivation to learn. In R. Feldman (Ed.), *Social psychology applied to education* (pp. 256–288). New York, NY: Cambridge University Press.

Brown, A. (1987). Metacognition, executive control, self-regulation, and other more mysterious mechanisms. In F. Weinert & R. Kluwe (Eds.), *Metacognition, motivation, and understanding* (pp. 65–116). Hillside, NJ: Erlbaum.

Brown, A. (1997). Transforming schools into communities of thinking and learning about serious matters. *American Psychologist*, 52, 399–413.

Brown, A. L. (1992). Design experiments: Theoretical and methodological challenges in creating complex interventions in classroom settings. *Journal of the Learning Sciences*, 2, 141–178.

Brown, A. L., Bransford, J., Ferrara, R., & Campione, J. (1983). Learning, remembering, and understanding. In P. Mussen (Ed.), *Handbook of child psychology* (Vol. 3, pp. 515–629). New York, NY: Wiley.

Brown, A. L., & Campione, J. C. (1996). Psychological theory and the design of innovative learning environments: On procedures, principles, and systems. In L. Schauble & R. Glaser (Eds.), *Innovations in learning: New environments for education* (pp. 289–325). Mahwah, NJ: Erlbaum.

Bruer, J. T. (1999). In search of . . . brain-based education. *Phi Delta Kappan*, *80*, 648–657.

Bruer, J. T. (2002). Avoiding the pediatrician's error: How neuroscientists can help educators (and themselves). *Nature Neuroscience*, *5*, 1031–1033.

Bruner, J. S. (1966). *Toward a theory of instruction*. New York, NY: Norton.

Bruner, J. S. (1973). *Beyond the information given: Studies in the psychology of knowing*. New York, NY: Norton.

Bruning, R. H., Schraw, G. J., Norby, M. M., & Ronning, R. R. (2004). *Cognitive psychology and instruction* (4th ed.). Columbus, OH: Merrill.

Buhs, E. S., Ladd, G. W., & Herald, S. L. (2006). Peer exclusion and victimization: Processes that mediate the relation between peer group rejection and children's classroom engagement. *Journal of Educational Psychology*, 98, 1–13.

Burbules, N. C., & Bruce, B. C. (2001). Theory and research on teaching as dialogue. In V. Richardson (Ed.), *Handbook of research on teaching* (4th ed., pp. 1102–1121). Washington, DC: American Educational Research Association.

Burden, P. R. (1995). *Classroom management and discipline: Methods to facilitate cooperation and instruction*. White Plains, NY: Longman.

Burgess, S. R., Hecht, S. A., & Lonigan, C. J. (2002). Relations of the home literacy environment (HLE) to the development of reading-related abilities: A one-year longitudinal study. *Reading Research Quarterly*, 37, 408–426.

Buss, D. M. (1995). Psychological sex differences: Origin through sexual selection. *American Psychologist*, 50, 164–168.

Butcher, K. R. (2006). Learning from text with diagrams: Promoting mental model development and inference generation. *Journal of Educational Psychology*, 98, 182–197.

Butler, D. L. (1998). A strategic content learning approach to promoting self-regulated learning by students with learning disabilities. In D. H. Schunk & B. J. Zimmerman (Eds.), *Self-regulated learning: From teaching to self-reflective practice* (pp. 160–183). New York, NY: Guilford Press.

Butler, R. (1987). Task-involving and ego-involving properties of evaluation: Effects of different feedback conditions on motivational perceptions, interest, and performance. *Journal of Educational Psychology*, *79*, 474–482.

Byrne, B. M. (2002). Validating the measurement and structure of self-concept: Snapshots of past, present, and future research. *American Psychologist*, *57*, 897–909.

Byrnes, J. P. (1996). *Cognitive development and learning in instructional contexts*. Boston, MA: Allyn & Bacon.

Byrnes, J. P. (2003). Factors predictive of mathematics achievement in White, Black, and Hispanic 12th graders. *Journal of Educational Psychology*, 95, 316–326.

Byrnes, J. P., & Fox, N. A. (1998). The educational relevance of research in cognitive neuroscience. *Educational Psychology Review*, *10*, 297–342.

Cairns, R. B., & Cairns, B. D. (2006). The making of developmental psychology. In R. M. Lerner (Ed.), *Handbook of child psychology: Vol. 1. Theoretical models of human development* (6th ed., pp. 89–165). New York, NY: Wiley.

Calderhead, J. (1996). Teacher: Beliefs and knowledge. In D. Berliner & R. Calfee (Eds.), *Handbook of educational psychology* (pp. 709–725). New York, NY: Macmillan.

Callahan, C. M., Tomlinson, C. A., & Plucker, J. (1997). *Project START using a multiple intelligences model in identifying and promoting talent in high-risk students*. Storrs, CT: National Research Center for Gifted and Talented. University of Connecticut Technical Report.

Cameron, J., & Pierce, W. D. (1994). Reinforcement, reward, and intrinsic motivation: A meta-analysis. *Review of Educational Research*, *64*, 363–423.

Cameron, J., & Pierce, W. D. (1996). The debate about rewards and intrinsic motivation: Protests and accusations do not alter the results. *Review of Educational Research*, *66*, 39–52.

Campaign 2000. (2009). *2009 Report card on child and family poverty: 1989–2009*. Retrieved from www.campaign2000.ca

Canadian Cancer Society. (2008). Childhood cancer in Canada: Fast facts. Retrieved from http://www.quebec.cancer.ca/quebec/communiques/Stats08_FicheCancerPediatrique_en.pdf

Canadian Centre on Substance Abuse. (2007). *Substance abuse in Canada: Youth in focus*. Retrieved from http://www.ccsa.ca/NR/rdonlyres/5D418288-5147-4CAC-A6E4-6D09EC6CBE13/0/ccsa0115212007e.pdf

Canadian Council on Learning (CCL). (2009). Lessons in learning: Homework helps, but not always. Retrieved from http://ccl-cca.ca/pdfs/LessonsinLearning/50-05_04_09-Lil-Homework-REV-E-meta.pdf

Canadian Fitness and Lifestyle Research Institute (CFLRI). (2008). Kids can play! Encouraging children to be active at home, at school, and in their communities. Retrieved from http://www.cflri.ca/eng/provincial_data/canplay_bulletins/canplay_canada.php

Canadian Institutes of Health Research (CIHR). (2006). Youth suicide: It's time to get involved. Retrieved from http://www.cihr-irsc.gc.ca/e/32154.html

Canadian Teachers Federation. (2009). Supporting education . . . building schools: Child poverty and schools. Retrieved from http://www.ctf-fce.ca/publications/Briefs/FINAL_Hilldayleavebehind_eng.pdf

Cangelosi, J. S. (1990). *Designing tests for evaluating student achievement*. New York, NY: Longman.

Canter, L. (1996). First the rapport—then the rules. *Learning*, *24*(5), 12+.

Canter, L., & Canter, M. (1992). *Lee Canter's Assertive Discipline: Positive behavior management for today's classroom*. Santa Monica, CA: Lee Canter and Associates.

Capa, Y. (2005). *Novice teachers' sense of efficacy* (Doctoral dissertation). The Ohio State University, Columbus, OH.

Capon, N., & Kuhn, D. (2004). What's so good about problem-based learning? *Cognition and Instruction*, 22, 61–79.

Cariglia-Bull, T., & Pressley, M. (1990). Short-term memory differences between children predict imagery effects when sentences are read. *Journal of Experimental Child Psychology*, 49, 384–398.

Carlisle, J. F., Stahl, S. A., & Birdyshaw, D. (Eds.). (2004, November). Lessons from research at the Center for the Improvement of Early Reading Achievement [Special Issue]. *The Elementary School Journal*, *105*(2).

Carney, R. N., & Levin, J. R. (2000). Mnemonic instruction, with a focus on transfer. *Journal of Educational Psychology*, 92, 783–790.

Carney, R. N., & Levin, J. R. (2002). Pictorial illustrations still improve students' learning from text. *Educational Psychology Review*, *14*, 5–26.

Carpendale, J. I. M. (2000). Kohlberg and Piaget on stages and moral reasoning. *Developmental Review*, 20, 181–205.

Carpenter, S. (2000). In the digital age experts pause to examine the effects on kids. *Monitor on Psychology*, *31*(11), 48–49.

Carroll, J. B. (1997). The three-stratum theory of cognitive abilities. In D. P. Flanagan, J. L. Genshaft, & P. L. Harrison (Eds.), *Contemporary intellectual assessment: Theories, tests, and issues* (pp. 122–130). New York, NY: Guilford.

Casanova, U. (1987). Ethnic and cultural differences. In V. Richardson-Koehler (Ed.), *Educators' handbook: A research perspective* (pp. 370–393). New York, NY: Longman.

Case, R. (1985a). *Intellectual development: Birth to adulthood*. New York, NY: Academic Press.

Case, R. (1985b). A developmentally-based approach to the problem of instructional design. In R. Glaser, S. Chipman, & J. Segal (Eds.), *Teaching thinking skills* (Vol. 2, pp. 545–562). Hillsdale, NJ: Erlbaum.

Case, R. (1992). *The mind's staircase: Exploring the conceptual underpinnings of children's thought and knowledge*. Mahwah, NJ: Erlbaum.

Case, R. (1998). The development of conceptual structures. In D. Kuhn & R. S. Siegler (Eds.), *Handbook of child psychology: Vol. 2. Cognition, perception, and language* (pp. 745–800). New York, NY: Wiley.

Cassady, J. C., & Johnson, R. E. (2002). Cognitive anxiety and academic performance. *Contemporary Educational Psychology, 27*, 270–295.

Castellano, J. A., & Diaz, E. I. (Eds.). (2002). *Reaching new horizons. Gifted and talented education for culturally and linguistically diverse students*. Boston, MA: Allyn & Bacon.

Castle, S., Deniz, C. B., & Tortora, M. (2005). Flexible grouping and student learning in a high-needs school. *Education and Urban Society, 37*, 139–150.

Cattell, R. B. (1963). Theory of fluid and crystallized intelligence: A critical experiment. *Journal of Educational Psychology, 54*, 1–22.

Ceci, S. J., & Roazzi, A. (1994). The effects of context on cognition: Postcards from Brazil. In R. J. Sternberg (Ed.), *Mind in context* (pp. 74–101). New York, NY: Cambridge University Press.

Ceci, S. J., & Williams, W. M. (1997). Schooling, intelligence, and income. *American Psychologist, 52*, 1051–1058.

Chambers, B., & Abrami, P. C. (1991). The relationship between student team learning outcomes and achievement, causal attributions, and affect. *Journal of Educational Psychology, 83*, 140–146.

Chamot, A. U., & O'Malley, J. M. (1996). The Cognitive Academic Language Learning Approach: A model for linguistically diverse classrooms. *The Elementary School Journal, 96*, 259–274.

Chan, C. K., & Sachs, J. (2001). Beliefs about learning in children's understanding of science texts. *Contemporary Educational Psychology, 26*, 192–210.

Chance, P. (1992). The rewards of learning. *Phi Delta Kappan, 73*, 200–207.

Chance, P. (1993). Sticking up for rewards. *Phi Delta Kappan, 74*, 787–790.

Chao, R. (2001). Extending research on the consequences of parenting style for Chinese Americans and European Americans. *Child Development, 72*, 1832–1843.

Chao, R., & Tseng, V. (2002). Parenting of Asians. In M. H. Bornstein (Ed.), *Handbook of parenting: Social conditions and applied parenting* (2nd ed., Vol. 4, pp. 59–93). Mahwah, NJ: Erlbaum.

Chapman, J. W., Tunmer, W. E., & Prochnow, J. E. (2000). Early reading-related skills and performance, reading self-concept, and the development of academic self-concept: A longitudinal study. *Journal of Educational Psychology, 92*, 703–708.

Chapman, M. L. (1997). *Weaving webs of meaning: Writing in the elementary school*. Toronto, ON: ITP Nelson.

Charach, A., Pepler, D. J., & Ziegler, S. (1995). Bullying at school: A Canadian perspective. *Education Canada, 35*, 12–18.

Charles, C. M. (2002a). *Essential elements of effective discipline*. Boston, MA: Allyn & Bacon.

Charles, C. M. (2002b). *Building classroom discipline* (7th ed.). Boston, MA: Allyn & Bacon.

Chen, J. Q. (2004). Theory of multiple intelligences: Is it a scientific theory? Teachers *College Record, 106*, 17–23.

Chen, Z., & Mo, L. (2004). Schema induction in problem solving: A multidimensional analysis. *Journal of Experimental Psychology: Learning, Memory, and Cognition, 30*, 583–600.

Chen, Z., Mo, L., & Honomichl, R. (2004). Having the memory of an elephant: long-term retrieval and the use of analogues in problem solving. *Journal of Experimental Psychology: General, 133*, 415–433.

Chi, M. T. H. (1978). Knowledge structures and memory development. In R. Siegler (Ed.), *Children's thinking: What develops?* (pp. 73–96). Hillsdale, NJ: Erlbaum.

Chi, M. T. H., Glaser, R., & Farr, M. (Eds.). (1988). *The nature of expertise*. Hillsdale, NJ: Erlbaum.

Child and Youth Officer for British Columbia. (2007). *Health and well-being of children in care in British Columbia: Educational experience and outcomes*. Victoria, BC: Author.

Chorzempa, B. F., & Graham, S. (2006). Primary-grade teachers' use of within-class ability grouping in reading. *Journal of Educational Psychology, 98*, 529–541.

Citizenship and Immigration Canada. (2007). Refugees in Canada's refugee system. Retrieved from http://www.cic.gc.ca/english/department/media/backgrounders/2007/2007-06-20.asp

Clark, C. M., & Peterson, P. L. (1986). Teachers' thought processes. In M. Wittrock (Ed.), *Handbook of research on teaching* (3rd ed., pp. 255–296). New York, NY: Macmillan.

Clark, C. M., & Yinger, R. (1988). Teacher planning. In D. Berliner & B. Rosenshine (Eds.), *Talks to teachers* (pp. 342–365). New York, NY: Random House.

Clark, J. M., & Paivio, A. (1991). Dual coding theory and education. *Educational Psychology Review, 3*, 149–210.

Clarke, J. H., & Agne, R. M. (1997). *Interdisciplinary high school teaching*. Boston, MA: Allyn & Bacon.

Clement, S. L. (1978). Dual marking system: Simple and effective. *American Secondary Education, 8*, 49–52.

Clifford, M. M. (1990). Students need challenge, not easy success. *Educational Leadership, 48*(1), 22–26.

Clifford, M. M. (1991). Risk taking: Empirical and educational considerations. *Educational Psychologist, 26*, 263–298.

Cobb, P., & Bowers, J. (1999). Cognitive and situated learning: Perspectives in theory and practice. *Educational Researcher, 28*(2), 4–15.

Codell, E. R. (2001). *Educating Esme: Diary of a teacher's first year*. Chapel Hill, NC: Algonquin Books.

Coffield, F. J., Moseley, D. V., Hall, E., & Ecclestone, K. (2004). *Learning styles and pedagogy in post–16 learning: A systematic and critical review*. London, England: Learning and Skills Research Centre/University of Newcastle upon Tyne.

Cognition and Technology Group at Vanderbilt. (1993). Anchored instruction and situated learning revisited. *Educational Technology, 33*(3), 52–70.

Cognition and Technology Group at Vanderbilt. (1996). Looking at technology in context: A framework for understanding technology and educational research. In D. Berliner & R. Calfee (Eds.), *Handbook of educational psychology* (pp. 807–840). New York, NY: Macmillan.

Cohen, E. G. (1986). *Designing group work: Strategies for the heterogeneous classroom*. New York, NY: Teachers College Press.

Cohen, E. G. (1994). *Designing group work* (2nd ed.). New York, NY: Teachers College Press.

Cohen, E. G. (1994). Restructuring the classroom: Conditions for productive small groups. *Review of Educational Research, 64*, 1–35.

Cokley, K. O. (2002). Ethnicity, gender, and academic self-concept: A preliminary examination of academic disidentification and implications for psychologists. *Cultural Diversity and Ethnic Minority Psychology, 8*, 378–388.

Cole, D. A., Martin, J. M., Peeke, L. A., Seroczynski, A. D., & Fier, J. (1999). Children's over- and underestimation of academic competence: A longitudinal study of gender differences, depression, and anxiety. *Child Development, 70*, 459–473.

Cole, G. A., Montgomery, R. W., Wilson, K. M., & Milan, M. A. (2000). Parametric analysis of overcorrection duration effects: Is longer really better than shorter? *Behavior Modification, 24*, 359–378.

Cole, M. (1985). The zone of proximal development: Where culture and cognition create each other. In J. V. Wertsch (Ed.), *Culture, communication, and cognition: Vygotskian perspectives* (pp. 146–161). New York, NY: Cambridge University Press.

Coleman, J. S. (1966). *Equality of educational opportunity*. Washington, DC: U.S. Government Printing Office.

Colledge, E., Bishop, D. V. M., Koeppen-Schomerus, G., Price, T. S., Happe, F., Eley, T., . . . Plomin, R. (2002). The structure of language abilities at 4 Years: A twin study. *Developmental Psychology, 38*, 749–757.

Collins, A. (2006). Cognitive apprenticeship. In R. K. Sawyer (Ed.), *The Cambridge handbook of the learning sciences* (pp. 47–77). New York, NY: Cambridge University Press.

Collins, A., Brown, J. S., & Newman, S. E. (1989). Cognitive apprenticeship: Teaching the crafts of reading, writing, and mathematics. In L. B. Resnick (Ed.), *Knowing, learning, and instruction: Essays in honor of Robert Galser* (pp. 453–494). Hillsdale, NJ: Erlbaum.

Comadena, M. E., Hunt, S. K., & Simonds, C. J. (2007). The effects of teacher clarity, nonverbal immediacy, and caring on student motivation, affective and cognitive learning. *Communication Research Reports, 24*, 241–248.

Comer, J. P., Haynes, N. M., & Joyner, E. T. (1996). The School Development Program. In J. P. Comer, N. M. Haynes, E. T. Joyner, & M. Ben-Avie (Eds.), *Rallying the whole village: The Comer process for reforming education* (pp. 1–26). New York, NY: Teachers College Press.

Committee on Increasing High School Students' Engagement and Motivation to Learn. (2004). *Engaging schools: Fostering high school students' motivation to learn*. Washington, DC: The National Academies Press.

Confrey, J. (1990a). A review of the research on students' conceptions in mathematics, science, and programming. *Review of Research in Education, 16*, 3–56.

Confrey, J. (1990b). What constructivism implies for teaching. In R. Davis, C. Maher, & N. Noddings (Eds.), *Constructivist views on the teaching and learning of mathematics* (pp. 107–122). Monograph 4 of the National Council of Teachers of Mathematics, Reston, VA.

Connell, R. W. (1996). Teaching the boys: New research on masculinity, and gender strategies for schools. *Teachers College Record, 98*, 206–235.

Conway, P. F., & Clark, C. M. (2003). The journey inward and outward: A reexamination of Fuller's concerns-based model of teacher development. *Teaching and Teacher Education, 19*, 465–482.

Cook, C. R., Williams, K. R., Guerra, N. G., Kim, T. E., & Sadek, S. (2010). Predictors of bullying and victimization in childhood and adolescence: A meta-analytic investigation. *School Psychology Quarterly, 25*, 65–83.

Cook, J. L., & Cook, G. (2005). *Child development: Principles and perspectives.* Boston, MA: Allyn & Bacon.

Cooper, C. R. (1998). *The weaving of maturity: Cultural perspectives on adolescent development.* New York, NY: Oxford University Press.

Cooper, H. M. (1979). Pygmalion grows up: A model for teacher expectation communication and performance influence. *Review of Educational Research, 49*, 389–410.

Cooper, H. M. (2004). Homework [Special issue]. *Theory Into Practice, 43*(3).

Cooper, H., & Valentine, J. C. (Eds.). (2001). Homework [Special issue]. *Educational Psychologist, 36*(3).

Cooper, H. M., Robinson, J. C., Patall, E. A. (2006). Does homework improve academic achievement? A synthesis of research, 1987–2003. *Review of Educational Research, 76*, 1–62.

Cooper, H. M., Valentine, J. C., Nye, B., & Kindsay, J. J. (1999). Relationships between five after-school activities and academic achievement. *Journal of Educational Psychology, 91*, 369–378.

Copi, I. M. (1961). Introduction to logic. New York, NY: Macmillan.

Coplan, R. J., Prakash, K., O'Neil, K., & Armer, M. (2004). Do you "want" to play? Distinguishing between conflicted shyness and social disinterest in early childhood. *Developmental Psychology, 40*, 244–258.

Cordova, D. I., & Lepper, M. R. (1996). Intrinsic motivation and the process of learning: Beneficial effects of contextualization, personalization, and choice. *Journal of Educational Psychology, 88*, 715–730.

Corkill, A. J. (1992). Advance organizers: Facilitators of recall. *Educational Psychology Review, 4*, 33–67.

Cornelius-White, J. (2007). Learner-centered teacher–student relationships are effective: A meta-analysis. *Review of Educational Research, 77*, 113–143.

Corno, L. (1992). Encouraging students to take responsibility for learning and performance. *The Elementary School Journal, 93*, 69–84.

Corno, L. (1995). The principles of adaptive teaching. In A. Ornstein (Ed.), *Teaching: Theory into practice.* (pp. 98–115). Boston, MA: Allyn & Bacon.

Corno, L. (2000). Looking at homework differently. *Elementary School Journal, 100*, 529–548.

Cota-Robles, S., Neiss, M., & Rowe, D. C. (2002). The role of puberty in violent and nonviolent delinquency among Anglo American, Mexican American and African American boys. *Journal of Adolescent Research, 17*, 364–376.

Cote, S. Vaillancourt, T., LeBlanc, J. C., Nagin, D. C., & Tremblay, R. E. (2006). The development of physical aggression from toddlerhood to preadolescence: A nation wide longitudinal study of Canadian children. *Journal of Abnormal Child Psychology, 34*, 71–85.

Cothran, D. J., & Ennis, C. D. (2000). Building bridges to student engagement: Communicating respect and care for students in urban high school. *Journal of Research and Development in Education, 33*(2), 106–117.

Covaleskie, J. F. (1992). Discipline and morality: Beyond rules and consequences. *The Educational Forum, 56*(2), 56–60.

Covington, M. V. (1992). *Making the grade: A self-worth perspective on motivation and school reform.* New York, NY: Holt, Rinehart, & Winston.

Covington, M. V., & Mueller, K. J. (2001). Intrinsic versus extrinsic motivation: An approach/avoidance reformulation. *Education Psychology Review, 13*, 157–176.

Covington, M. V., & Omelich, C. (1987). "I knew it cold before the exam": A test of the anxiety-blockage hypothesis. *Journal of Educational Psychology, 79*, 393–400.

Cowley, G., & Underwood, A. (1998, June 15). Memory. *Newsweek, 131*(24), 48–54.

Craig, W. M., & Pepler, D. J. (1997). Observations of bullying and victimization in the school yard. *Canadian Journal of School Psychology, 13*, 41–60.

Craig, W. M., & Pepler, D. J. (1998). Observations of aggressive and nonaggressive children on the school playground. *Merrill-Palmer Quarterly, 44*, 55–76.

Craig, W. M., Peters, R. D., & Konarski, R. (1998, October). *Bullying and victimization among Canadian school children* (Working Paper Series W-98-28E). Hull, QC: Applied Research Branch of Strategic Policy, Human Resources and Development Canada.

Craik, F. I. M., & Lockhart, R. S. (1972). Levels of processing: A framework for memory research. *Journal of Verbal Learning and Verbal Behavior, 11*, 671–684.

Crawford, J. (1997). *Best evidence: Research foundations of the Bilingual Education Act.* Washington, DC: National Clearinghouse for Bilingual Education.

Crealock, C., & Bachor, D. G. (1995). *Instructional strategies for students with special needs* (2nd ed.). Scarborough, ON: Allyn & Bacon Canada.

Cremin, L. (1961). *The transformation of the school: Progressivism in American education*, 1876–1957. New York, NY: Vintage.

Crick, N. R., Casas, J. F., & Mosher M. (1997). Relational and overt aggression in preschool. *Developmental Psychology, 33*, 579–588.

Crick, N. R. & Zahn-Waxler, C. (2003). The development of psychopathology in females and males: Current progress and future challenges. *Development and Psychopathology, 15*, 719–742.

Crisci, P. E. (1986). The Quest National Center: A focus on prevention of alienation. *Phi Delta Kappan, 67*, 440–442.

Crocker, J., & Park, L. E. (2004). Reaping the benefits of pursuing self-esteem without the costs. *Psychological Bulletin, 130*, 392–414.

Cromley. J. G., & Azevedo, R. (2007). Testing and refining the direct and inferential mediation model of reading comprehension. *Journal of Educational Psychology, 99*, 311–325.

Crone, D. A., & Horner, R. H. (2003). *Building positive behavior support systems in schools: Functional behavioral assessment.* New York, NY: Guilford.

Cummins, D. D. (1991). Children's interpretation of arithmetic word problems. *Cognition and Instruction, 8*, 261–289.

Cummins, J. (1989). A theoretical framework for bilingual special education. *Exceptional Children, 56*, 111–119.

Cummins, J. (1994). The acquisition of English as a second language. In K. Spangenberg-Urbschat & R. Prichard (Eds.), *Kids come in all languages: Reading instruction for ESL students* (pp. 36–62). Newark, DE: International Reading Association.

Cunningham, D. J. (1992). Beyond educational psychology: Steps toward an educational semiotic. *Educational Psychology Review, 4*, 165–194.

Daley, T. C., Whaley, S. E., Sigman, M. D., Espinosa, M. P., & Neumann, C. (2003). IQ on the rise: The Flynn Effect in rural Kenyan children. *Psychological Science, 14*(3), 215–219.

Daly, B. P., Kral, M. C., & Brown, R. T. (2008). Cognitive and academic problems associated with childhood cancers and sickle cell disease. *School Psychology Quarterly, 23*, 230–242.

Damon, W. (1994). Fair distribution and sharing: The development of positive justice. In B. Puka (Ed.), Fundamental research in moral development (pp. 189–254). *Moral development: A compendium, Vol. 2.* New York, NY: Garland Publishing.

Darcey, J. S., & Travers, J. F. (2006). *Human development across the lifespan* (6th ed.). New York, NY: McGraw-Hill.

Dark, V. J., & Benbow, C. P. (1991). Differential enhancement of working memory with mathematical versus verbal precocity. *Journal of Educational Psychology, 83*, 48–60.

Darling-Hammond, L. (2000). Teacher quality and student achievement: A review of state policy evidence. *Educational Policy Analysis Archives, 8*, 1–48. Retrieved from http://epaa.asu.edu/epaa/v8n1/

Das, J. P. (1995). Some thoughts on two aspects of Vygotsky's work. *Educational Psychologist, 30*, 93–97.

Daunic, A. P., Smith. S. W., Brank, E. M., & Penfield, R. D. (2006). Classroom based cognitive-behavioral intervention to prevent aggression: Efficacy and social validity. *Journal of School Psychology, 44*, 123–139.

Davies, D. (2004). *Child development: A practitioner's guide.* New York, NY: Guilford Press.

Davies, S. & Guppy, N. (2006). *The schooled society*. Don Mills, ON: Oxford University Press.

Davis, H. A. (2003). Conceptualizing the role and influence of student–teacher relationships on children's social and cognitive development. *Educational Psychologist*, 38, 207–234.

Davis-Kean, P. E., & Sandler, H. M. (2001). A meta-analysis of measures of self-esteem for young children: A framework for future measurers. *Child Development*, 72, 887–906.

De Corte, E. (2003). Transfer as the productive use of acquired knowledge, skills, and motivations. *Current Directions in Psychological Research*, *12*, 142–146.

De Corte, E., Greer, B., & Verschaffel, L. (1996). Mathematics learning and teaching. In D. Berliner & R. Calfee (Eds.), *Handbook of educational psychology* (pp. 491–549). New York, NY: Macmillan.

De Corte, E., & Verschaffel, L. (1985). Beginning first graders' initial representation of arithmetic word problems. *Journal of Mathematical Behavior*, *4*, 3021.

de Kock, A., Sleegers, P., & Voeten, M. J. M. (2004). New learning and the classification of learning environments in secondary education. *Review of Educational Research*, *74*(2), 141–170.

Dearing, E., Kreider, H., Simpkins, S., & Weiss, H. B. (2006). Family involvement in school and low-income children's literacy: Longitudinal associations between and within families. *Journal of Educational Psychology*, *98*, 653–664.

Deaux, K. (1993). Commentary: Sorry, wrong number: A reply to Gentile's call. *Psychological Science*, *4*, 125–126.

DeCecco, J., & Richards, A. (1974). *Growing pains: Uses of school conflicts*. New York, NY: Aberdeen.

deCharms, R. (1983). Intrinsic motivation, peer tutoring, and cooperative learning: Practical maxims. In J. Levine & M. Wang (Eds.), *Teacher and student perceptions: Implications for learning* (pp. 391–398). Hillsdale, NJ: Erlbaum.

Deci, E. L. (1975). *Intrinsic motivation*. New York, NY: Plenum.

Deci, E. L., Koestner, R., & Ryan, R. M. (1999). A meta-analytic review of experiments examining the effects of extrinsic rewards on intrinsic motivation. *Psychological Bulletin*, *125*, 627–668.

Deci, E. L., & Ryan, R. M. (1985). *Intrinsic motivation and self-determination in human behavior*. New York, NY: Plenum.

Deci, E. L., & Ryan, R. M. (Eds.). (2002). *Handbook of self-determination research*. Rochester, NY: University of Rochester Press.

Deci, E. L., Vallerand, R. J., Pelletier, L. G., & Ryan, R. M. (1991). Motivation and education: The self-determination perspective. *Educational Psychologist*, 26, 325–346.

Dee, J. R., & Henkin, A. B. (2002). Assessing dispositions toward cultural diversity among preservice teachers. *Urban Education*, 37(1), 22–40.

Delazer, M., Ischebeck, A., Domahs, F., Zamarian, L., Koppelstaetter, F., Siednetoph, C. M., . . . Felber, S. (2005). Learning by strategies and learning by drill: Evidence from an fMRI study. *NeuroImage*, *25*, 838–849.

Delpit, L. (1995). *Other people's children: Cultural conflict in the classroom*. New York, NY: The New York Press.

Delpit, L. (2003). Educators as "Seed People": Growing a new future. *Educational Researcher*, 7(32), 14–21.

Demetriou, A., Christou, C., Spanoudis, G., & Platsidou, M. (2002). The development of mental processing: Efficiency, working memory and thinking. *Monographs of the Society for Research in Child Development*, *67*(1).

Dempster, F. N. (1991). Synthesis of research on reviews and tests. *Educational Leadership*, *48*(7), 71–76.

Dempster, F. N. (1993). Exposing our students to less should help them learn more. *Phi Delta Kappan*, *74*, 432–437.

Demuth, K. (1990). Subject, topic, and Sesotho passive. *Journal of Child Language*, *17*, 67–84.

Derry, S. J. (1989). Putting learning strategies to work. *Educational Leadership*, *47*(5), 4–10.

Derry, S. J. (1991). Strategy and expertise in solving word problems. In C. McCormick, G. Miller, & M. Pressley (Eds.), *Cognitive strategies research: From basic research to educational applications*. New York, NY: Springer-Verlag.

Derry, S. J. (1992). Beyond symbolic processing: Expanding horizons for educational psychology. *Journal of Educational Psychology*, *84*, 413–419.

Derry, S. J., Hmelo-Silver, C. E., Nagarajan, A., Chernobilsky, E., & Beitzel, B. (2006). Cognitive transfer revisited: Can we exploit new media to solve old problems on a large scale? *Journal of Educational Computing Research*, *35*, 145–162.

Deshler, D., Ellis, E. S., & Lenz, B. K. (1996). *Teaching adolescents with learning disabilities: Strategies and methods* (2nd ed.). Denver, CO: Love Publishing.

Dewey, J. (1913). *Interest and effort in education*. Cambridge, MA: Houghton-Mifflin.

Diaz-Rico, L. T., & Weed, K. Z. (2002). *The crosscultural, language, and academic development handbook* (2nd ed.). Boston, MA: Allyn & Bacon.

Dickinson, D., McCabe, A., Anastopoulos, L., Peisner-Feinberg, E., & Poe, M. (2003). The comprehensive language approach to early literacy: The interrelationships among vocabulary, phonological sensitivity, and print knowledge among preschool-aged children. *Journal of Educational Psychology*, *95*, 465–481.

Dinnel, D., & Glover, J. A. (1985). Advance organizers: Encoding manipulations. *Journal of Educational Psychology*, *77*, 514–522.

DiVesta, F. J., & Di Cintio, M. J. (1997). Interactive effects of working memory span and text comprehension on reading comprehension and retrieval. *Learning and Individual Differences*, 9, 215–231.

Doctorow, M., Wittrock, M. C., & Marks, C. (1978). Generative processes in reading comprehension. *Journal of Educational Psychology*, *70*, 109–118.

Dodge, K. A., Coie, J. D., & Lynam, D. (2006). Aggression and antisocial behaviour in youth. In N. Eisenberg, W. Dammon, & R. M. Lerner (Eds.), *Handbook of child psychology: Vol. 3. Social, emotional, and personality development* (6th ed., pp. 719–788). Hoboken, NJ: John Wiley & Sons.

Dodge, K. A., & Pettit, G. S. (2003). A biopsychosocial model of the development of chronic conduct problems in adolescence. *Developmental Psychology*, 39, 349–371.

Dodge, K. A., & Somberg, D. R. (1987). Hostile attributional biases among aggressive boys are exacerbated under conditions of threats to the self. *Child Development*, 58, 213–224.

Dolezal, S. E., Welsh, L. M., Pressley, M., & Vincent, M. (2003). How do nine third-grade teachers motivate their students? *Elementary School Journal*, *103*, 239–267.

Doll, B., Zucker, S., & Brehm, K. (2005). *Resilient classrooms: Creating healthy environments for learning*. New York, NY: Guilford.

Doyle, A., & Aboud, F. (1995). A longitudinal study of White children's racial prejudice as a social cognitive development. *Merrill-Palmer Quarterly*, *41*, 213–223.

Doyle, W. (1977). The uses of nonverbal behaviors: Toward an ecological model of classrooms. *Merrill-Palmer Quarterly*, 23, 179–192.

Doyle, W. (1986). Classroom organization and management. In M. C. Wittrock (Ed.), *Handbook of research on teaching* (3rd ed., pp. 392–431). New York, NY: Macmillan.

Doyle, W. (2006). Ecological approaches to classroom management. In C. Evertson & C. S. Weinstein (Eds.), *Handbook for classroom management: Research, practice, and contemporary issues*. Mahwah, NJ: Erlbaum.

Driscoll, M. P. (2005). *Psychology of learning for instruction* (3rd ed.). Boston, MA: Allyn & Bacon.

Duell, O. K. (1994). Extended wait time and university student achievement. *American Educational Research Journal*, 31, 397–414.

Dufrene, B. A., Doggett, R. A., Henington, C., & Watson, T. S. (2007). Functional assessment and intervention for disruptive classroom behaviors in preschool and head start classrooms. *Journal of Behavioral Education*, *16*, 368–388.

Duncan, G. J., & Brooks-Gunn, J. (2000). Family poverty, welfare reform, and child development. *Child Development*, *71*, 188–196.

Duncan, R. M., & Cheyne, J. A. (1999). Incidence and functions of self-reported private speech in young adults: A self-verbalization questionnaire. *Canadian Journal of Behavioural Sciences*, 31, 133–136.

Duncker, K. (1945). On solving problems. *Psychological Monographs*, *58*(5, Whole No. 270).

Dunn, K., & Dunn, R. (1978). *Teaching students through their individual learning styles*. Reston, VA: National Council of Principals.

Dunn, K., & Dunn, R. (1987). Dispelling outmoded beliefs about student learning. *Educational Leadership*, *44*(6), 55–63.

Dunn, R., & Griggs, S. (2003). *Synthesis of the Dunn and Dunn Learning-Style Model Research: Who, what, when, where, and so what?* New York, NY: St. John's University.

Durik, A. M., & Harackiewiz, J. M. (2007). Different strokes for different folks: How individual interest moderates the effects of situational factors on task interest. *Journal of Educational Psychology*, 99, 597–610.

Durik, A. M., Vida, M., & Eccles, J. S. (2006). Task values and ability beliefs as predictors of high school literacy choices: A developmental analysis. *Journal of Educational Psychology, 98*(2), 382–393.

Dweck, C. S. (2000). *Self-theories: Their role in motivation, personality, and development.* Philadelphia, PA: Routledge Press.

Dweck, C. S. (2006). *Mindset: The new psychology of success.* New York, NY: Random House.

Dweck, C. S., & Bempechat, J. (1983). Children's theories on intelligence: Consequences for learning. In S. Paris, G. Olson, & W. Stevenson (Eds.), *Learning and motivation in the classroom* (pp. 239–256). Hillsdale, NJ: Erlbaum.

Dymond, S. K., Renzaglia, A., & Chun, E. (2007). Elements of effective high school service learning programs that include students with and without disabilities. *Remedial and Special Education, 28,* 227–243.

Dyson, A. H. (1997). *Writing superheroes: Contemporary childhood, popular culture, and classroom literacy.* New York, NY: Teachers College Press.

Eccles, J., & Wigfield, A. (1985). Teacher expectations and student motivation. In J. Dusek (Ed.), *Teacher expectancies* (pp. 185–226). Hillsdale, NJ: Erlbaum.

Eccles, J., Wigfield, A., & Schiefele, U. (1998). Motivation to succeed. In W. Damon (Series Ed.) & N. Eisenberg (Volume Ed.), *Handbook of child psychology: Vol. 3. Social, emotional, and personality development* (5th ed., pp. 1017–1095). New York, NY: Wiley.

Echevarria, M. (2003). Anomalies as a catalyst for middle school students' knowledge construction and scientific reasoning during science inquiry. *Journal of Educational Psychology, 95,* 357–374.

Edelman, G. M. (1992). *Bright air, brilliant fire: On the matter of the mind.* New York, NY: Basic Books.

Egan, S. K., Monson, T. C., & Perry, D. G. (1998). Social-cognitive influences on change in aggression over time. *Developmental Psychology, 34,* 996–1006.

Eisenberg, N., & Fabes, R. A. (1998). Prosocial development. In W. Damon (Series Ed.) & N. Eisenberg (Vol. Ed.), *Handbook of child psychology: Vol. 3. Social, emotional, and personality development* (5th ed., pp. 701–778). New York, NY: Wiley.

Eisenberg, N., Martin, C. L., & Fabes, R. A. (1996). Gender development and gender effects. In D. Berliner & R. Calfee (Eds.), *Handbook of educational psychology* (pp. 358–396). New York, NY: Macmillan.

Eisenberg, N., Shell, R., Pasernack, J., Lennon, R., Beller, R., & Mathy, R. M. (1987). Prosocial development in middle childhood: A longitudinal study. *Developmental Psychology, 23,* 712–718.

Eisenberg, R., Pierce, W. D., & Cameron, J. (1999). Effects of rewards on intrinsic motivation—Negative, neutral, and positive: Comment on Deci, Koestner, and Ryan (1999). *Psychological Bulletin, 125,* 677–691.

Elementary Teachers' Federation of Ontario. (2008). *Full-day kindergarten: Moving Ontario forward.* Author.

Elias, M. J., & Schwab, Y. (2006). From compliance to responsibility: Social and emotional learning and classroom management. In C. Evertson & C. S. Weinstein (Eds.), *Handbook for classroom management: Research, practice, and contemporary issues.* Mahwah, NJ: Erlbaum.

Elias, S. M., & MacDonald, S. (2007). Using past performance, proxy efficacy, and academic self-efficacy to predict college performance. *Journal of Applied Social Psychology, 37,* 2518–2531.

Elkind, D. (1981). Obituary—Jean Piaget (1896–1980). *American Psychologist, 36,* 911–913.

Elkind, D. (1991). Formal education and early childhood education: An essential difference. In K. M. Cauley, F. Linder, & J. H. MacMillan (Eds.), *Annual Editions: Educational Psychology, 91/92* (pp. 27–37). Guilford, CT: Duskin.

Elrich, M. (1994). The stereotype within. *Educational Leadership, 51*(8), 12–15.

Embry, D. D. (2002). The Good Behavior Game: A best practice candidate as a universal behavior vaccine. *Clinical Child and Family Psychology Review, 5,* 273–297.

Emerson, M. J., & Miyake, A. (2003). The role of inner speech in task switching: A dual-task investigation. *Journal of Memory and Language, 48,* 148–168.

Emmer, E. T., & Aussiker, A. (1990). School and classroom discipline problems: How well do they work? In O. Moles (Ed.), *Student discipline strategies: Research and practice.* Albany, NY: SUNY Press.

Emmer, E. T., & Evertson, C. M. (1981). Synthesis of research on classroom management. *Educational Leadership, 38,* 342–345.

Emmer, E. T., & Evertson, C. M. (1982). Effective classroom management at the beginning of the school year in junior high school classes. *Journal of Educational Psychology, 74,* 485–498.

Emmer, E. T., & Evertson, C. M., (2009). *Classroom management for middle and high school teachers* (8th ed.). Boston, MA: Allyn & Bacon.

Emmer, E. T., Evertson, C. M., & Anderson, L. M. (1980). Effective classroom management at the beginning of the school year. *Elementary School Journal, 80,* 219–231.

Emmer, E. T., & Gerwels, M. C. (2006). Classroom management in middle school and high school classrooms. In C. Evertson & C. S. Weinstein (Eds.), *Handbook for classroom management: Research, practice, and contemporary issues.* Mahwah, NJ: Erlbaum.

Emmer, E., & Hickman, J. (1991). Teacher efficacy in classroom management. *Educational and Psychological Measurement, 51,* 755–765.

Emmer, E. T., & Stough, L. M. (2001). Classroom management: A critical part of educational psychology with implications for teacher education. *Educational Psychologist, 36,* 103–112.

Engelmann, S., & Engelmann, T. (1981). *Give your child a superior mind.* New York, NY: Cornerstone.

Engle, R. W. (2001). What is working memory capacity? In H. Roediger, J. Nairne, I. Neath, & A. Suprenant (Eds.), *The nature of remembering: Essays in honor of Robert G. Crowder* (pp. 297–314). Washington, DC: American Psychological Association.

Entenman, J., Murnen, T. J., & Hendricks, C. (2006). Victims, bullies, and bystanders in K-3 literature. *The Reading Teacher, 59,* 352–364.

Entwisle, D. R., & Alexander, K. L. (1998). Facilitating the transition to first grade: The nature of transition and research on factors affecting it. *The Elementary School Journal, 98,* 351–364.

Epstein, J. L. (1995). School/Family/Community partnerships: Caring for the children we share. *Phi Delta Kappan, 76,* 701–712.

Epstein, J. L., & Van Voorhis, F. L. (2001). More than minutes: Teachers' roles in designing homework. *Educational Psychologist, 36,* 181–193.

Ericsson, K. A. (1999). Expertise. In R. Wilson & F. Keil (Eds.), *The MIT encyclopedia of the cognitive sciences* (pp. 298–300). Cambridge, MA: MIT Press.

Ericsson, K. A., & Charness, N. (1994). Expert performance: Its structure and acquisition. *American Psychologist, 49*(8), 725–747.

Ericsson, K. A., & Charness, N. (1999). Expert performance: Its structure and acquisition. In S. Ceci & W. Williams (Eds.), The nature-nurture debate: The essential readings. *Essential readings in developmental psychology.* Malden, MA: Blackwell.

Erikson, E. H. (1963). *Childhood and society* (2nd ed.). New York, NY: Norton.

Erikson, E. H. (1980). *Identity and the life cycle* (2nd ed.). New York, NY: Norton.

Espe, C., Worner, C., & Hotkevich, M. (1990). Whole language—What a bargain. *Educational Leadership, 47*(6), 45.

Evans, G. W. (2004). The environment of childhood poverty. *American Psychologist, 59,* 77–92.

Evans, L., & Davies, K. (2000). No sissy boys here: A content analysis of the representation of masculinity in elementary school reading texts. *Sex Roles, 42,* 255–270.

Evensen, D. H., Salisbury-Glennon, J. D., & Glenn, J. (2001). A qualitative study of six medical students in a problem-based curriculum: Toward a situated model of self-regulation. *Journal of Educational Psychology, 93,* 659–676.

Evertson, C. M., & Emmer, E. T. (2009). *Classroom management for elementary school teachers* (8th ed.). Boston, MA: Allyn & Bacon.

Farnham-Diggory, S. (1994). Paradigms of knowledge and instruction. *Review of Educational Research, 64,* 463–477.

Farver, J. A. M. (2007). *Family environments and Latino preschoolers' emergent literacy skills.* Paper presented at the biennial meeting of the Society for Research in Child Development, Boston, MA.

Feather, N. T. (1982). *Expectations and actions: Expectancy-value models in psychology.* Hillsdale, NJ: Erlbaum.

Feldman. J. (2003). The simplicity principle in human concept learning. *Current Directions in Psychological Science, 12,* 227–232.

Feldman, R. S. (2004). *Child development* (3rd ed.). Upper Saddle River, NJ: Prentice-Hall.

Fenton, D. F. (2007). The implications of research on expertise for curriculum and pedagogy. *Educational Psychology Review, 19,* 91–110.

Ferguson, A. A. (2000). *Bad boys: Public schools and the making of Black masculinity.* Ann Arbor, MI: University of Michigan Press.

Ferrer, E., & McArdle, J. J. (2004). An experimental analysis of dynamic hypotheses about cognitive abilities and achievement from childhood to early adulthood. *Developmental Psychology, 40,* 935–952.

Fillmore, L.W., & Snow, C. (2000). What teachers need to know about language. [On-line]. Retrieved from http://www.cal.org/ericcll/teachers.pdf

Finkel, D., Reynolds, C. A., McArdle, J. J., Gatz, M., & Pedersen, N. L. (2003). Latent growth curve analyses of accelerating decline in cognitive abilities in adulthood. Developmental Psychology, 39, 535–550.

Fischer, M. A., & Gillespie, C. S. (2003). Computers and young children's development. Young Children, 58(4), 85–91.

Fisher, D., Roach, V., & Frey, N. (2002). Examining the general programmatic benefits of inclusive schools. *International Journal of Inclusive Education, 6,* 63–78.

Fiske, E. B. (1981, October 27). Teachers reward muddy prose, study finds. *The New York Times,* p. C1.

Fiske, S. T. (1993). Social cognition and social perception. *Annual Review of Psychology, 44,* 155–194.

Fitts, P. M., & Posner, M. I. (1967). *Human performance.* Belmont, CA: Brooks Cole.

Fitzgerald, J. (1995). English-as-a-second-language learners' cognitive reading process: A review of the research in the United States. *Review of Educational Research, 62,* 145–190.

Fitzgerald, M. (2005). *The genesis of artistic creativity: Asperger's syndrome and the arts.* London, England: Jessica Kingsley Publishers.

Fives, H. R., Hamman, D., & Olivarez, A. (2005, April). *Does burnout begin with student teaching? Analyzing efficacy, burnout, and support during the student-teaching semester.* Paper presented at the Annual Meeting of the American Educational Research Association, Montreal, QC.

Fivush, R., & Nelson, K. (2004). Culture and language in the emergence of autobiographical memory. *Psychological Science, 15,* 573–577.

Flammer, A. (1995). Developmental analysis of control beliefs. In A. Bandura (Ed.), *Self-efficacy in changing societies* (pp. 69–113). New York, NY: Cambridge University Press.

Flanagan, C. A., Cumsille, P., Gill, S., & Gallay, L. S. (2007). School and community climates and civic commitments: Patterns for ethnic minority and majority students. *Journal of Educational Psychology,* 99, 421–431.

Flavell, J. H., Friedrichs, A. G., & Hoyt, J. D. (1970). Developmental changes in memorization processes. *Cognitive Psychology, 1,* 324–340.

Flavell, J. H., Green, F. L., & Flavell, E. R. (1995). Young children's knowledge about thinking. *Monographs of the Society for Research in Child Development, 60*(1) (Serial No. 243).

Flavell, J. H., Miller, P. H., & Miller, S. A. (2002). *Cognitive development* (4th ed.). Upper Saddle River, NJ: Prentice-Hall.

Fleith, D. (2000). Teacher and student perceptions of creativity in the classroom environment. *Roeper Review,* 22, 148–153.

Flink, C. F., Boggiano, A. K., & Barrett, M. (1990). Controlling teaching strategies: Undermining children's self-determination and performance. *Journal of Personality and Social Psychology,* 59, 916–924.

Floden, R. E. (2001). Research on effects of teaching: A continuing model for research on teaching. In V. Richardson (Ed.), *Handbook of research on teaching* (4th ed., pp. 3–16). Washington, DC: American Educational Research Association.

Floden, R. E., & Klinzing, H. G. (1990). What can research on teacher thinking contribute to teacher preparation? A second opinion. *Educational Researcher, 19*(4), 15–20.

Flum, H., & Kaplan, A. (2006). Exploratory orientation as an educational goal. *Educational Psychologist, 41,* 99–110.

Ford, D. Y. (2000). *Infusing multicultural content into the curriculum for gifted students.* (ERIC EC Digest #E601). Arlington, VA: The ERIC Clearinghouse on Disabilities and Gifted Education.

Forness, S. R., & Knitzer, J. (1992). A new proposed definition and terminology to replace "Serious Emotional Disturbance" in Individuals with Disabilities Education Act. *School Psychology Review, 21,* 12–20.

Foster, W. (1981, August). *Social and emotional development in gifted individuals.* Paper presented at the Fourth World Conference on Gifted and Talented Children, Montreal, QC.

Fox, L. H. (1981). Identification of the academically gifted. *American Psychologist,* 36, 1103–1111.

Frank, S. J., Pirsch, L. A., & Wright, V. C. (1990). Late adolescents' perceptions of their parents: Relationships among deidealization, autonomy, relatedness, and insecurity and implications for adolescent adjustment and ego identity status. *Journal of Youth and Adolescence, 19,* 571–588.

Frattura, E. & Capper, C. A. (2006). Segregated programs versus integrated comprehensive service delivery for all learners. *Remedial and Special Education,* 27, 355–364.

Fredricks, J. A., Blumenfeld, P. C., & Paris, A. H. (2004). School engagement: Potential of the concept, state of the evidence. *Review of Educational Research, 74,* 59–109.

Free the Children. (2005). Child poverty. Retrieved from http://www.freethechildren.com/getinvolved/geteducated/childpoverty.htm

Freiberg, H. J. (1999). Sustaining the paradigm. In H. J. Freiberg (Ed.), *Beyond behaviorism: Changing the classroom management paradigm* (pp. 164–173). Boston, MA: Allyn & Bacon.

Freiberg, H. J. (Ed.). (1999). *Beyond behaviorism: Changing the classroom management.* Boston, MA: Allyn & Bacon.

Freiberg, H. J., & Driscoll, A. (2005). *Universal teaching strategies* (4th ed.). Boston, MA: Allyn & Bacon.

Freiberg, J. (2006). Research-based programs for preventing and solving discipline problems. In C. Evertson & C. S. Weinstein (Eds.), *Handbook for classroom management: Research, practice, and contemporary issues.* Mahwah, NJ: Erlbaum.

Frick, T. W. (1990). Analysis of patterns in time: A method of recording and quantifying temporal relations in education. *American Educational Research Journal,* 27, 180–204.

Friedman-Weieneth, J. L., Harvey, E. A., Youngswirth, S. D., & Goldstein, L. H. (2007). The relation between 3-year-old-children's skills and their hyperactivity, inattention, and aggression. *Journal of Educational Psychology,* 99, 671–681.

Friend, M. (2006). *Special education: Contemporary perspectives for school professionals.* Boston, MA: Allyn & Bacon.

Friend, M. (2008). *Special education: Contemporary perspectives for school professionals* (2nd ed.). Boston, MA: Pearson/Allyn & Bacon.

Friend, M., & Bursuck, W. D. (2002). *Including students with special needs* (3rd ed.). Boston, MA: Allyn & Bacon.

Friend, M., & Bursuck, W. D. (2009). *Including students with special needs: A practical guide for classroom teachers* (5th ed.). Boston, MA: Allyn & Bacon/Pearson.

Friend, M., Bursuck, W., & Hutchinson, N. (1998). *Including exceptional students: A practical guide for classroom teachers.* Scarborough, ON: Allyn & Bacon Canada.

Frost, J. L., Wortham, S. C., & Reifel, S. (2005). *Play and child development* (2nd ed.). Upper Saddle River, NJ: Prentice-Hall.

Fuchs, L. S. & Fuchs, D. (2007, May/June). A model for implementing responsiveness to intervention. *Teaching Exceptional Children,* 39(5), 14–20.

Fuchs, L. S., Fuchs, D., Compton, D. L., Rowell, S. R., Seethaler, P. M., Capizzi, A. M, Schatschneider, C., & Fletcher, J. M. (2006). The cognitive correlates of third-grade skill in arithmetic, algorithmic, computation, and arithmetic work problems. *Journal of Educational Psychology,* 98, 29–43.

Fuchs, L. S., Fuchs, D., Hamlett, C. L., & Karns, K. (1998). High-achieving students' interactions and performance on complex mathematical tasks as a function of homogeneous and heterogeneous pairings. *American Educational Research Journal,* 35, 227–268.

Fuchs, L. S., Fuchs, D., Prentice, K., Burch, M., Hamlett, C. L., Owen, R., & Schroeter, K. (2003). Enhancing third-grade students' mathematical problem solving with self-regulated learning strategies. *Journal of Educational Psychology,* 95(2), 306–315.

Fulk, C. L., & Smith, P. J. (1995). Students' perceptions of teachers' instructional and management adaptations for students with learning or behavior problems. *The Elementary School Journal,* 95, 409–419.

Fuller, F. G. (1969). Concerns of teachers: A developmental conceptualization. *American Educational Research Journal, 6,* 207–226.

Furrer, C., & Skinner, E. (2003). Sense of relatedness as a factor in children's academic engagement and performance. *Journal of Educational Psychology,* 95(11), 148–161.

Gage, N. L. (1991). The obviousness of social and educational research results. *Educational Researcher, 20*(A), 10–16.

Gagné, E. D. (1985). *The cognitive psychology of school learning.* Boston, MA: Little, Brown.

Gagné, E. D., Yekovich, C. W., & Yekovich, F. R. (1993). *The cognitive psychology of school learning* (2nd ed.). New York, NY: Harper-Collins.

Gagné, R. M. (1985). *The conditions of learning and theory of instruction* (4th ed.). New York, NY: Holt, Rinehart & Winston.

Galambos, S. J., & Goldin-Meadow, S. (1990). The effects of learning two languages on metalinguistic development. *Cognition, 34,* 1–56.

Galliher, R. V., Rostosky, S. S., & Hughes, H. K. (2004). School belonging, self-esteem, and depressive symptoms in adolescents: An examination of sex, sexual attraction status, and urbanicity. *Journal of Youth and Adolescence, 33*(3), 235–245.

Gallimore, R., & Goldenberg, C. (2001). Analyzing cultural models and settings to connect minority achievement and school improvement research. *Educational Psychologist, 36,* 45–56.

Gallini, J. K. (1991). Schema-based strategies and implications for instructional design in strategy training. In C. McCormick, G. Miller, & M. Pressley (Eds.), *Cognitive strategies research: From basic research to educational applications.* New York, NY: Springer-Verlag.

Gamoran, A. (1987). The stratification of high school learning opportunities. *Sociology of Education, 60,* 135–155.

Ganis, G., Thompson, W. L., and Kosslyn, S. M. (2004). Brain areas underlying visual mental imagery and visual perception: An fMRI study. *Cognitive Brain Research, 20,* 226–241.

Garbarino, J., & deLara, E. (2002). *And words can hurt forever: How to protect adolescents from bullying, harassment, and emotional violence.* New York, NY: Free Press.

Garcia, E. E. (2002). *Student cultural diversity: Understanding the meaning and meeting the challenge.* Boston, MA: Houghton Mifflin.

Garcia, R. L. (1991). *Teaching in a pluralistic society: Concepts, models, and strategies.* New York, NY: HarperCollins.

Gardner, H. (1983). *Frames of mind: The theory of multiple intelligences.* New York, NY: Basic Books.

Gardner, H. (1991). *The unschooled mind: How children think and how schools should teach.* New York, NY: Basic Books.

Gardner, H. (1998). Reflections on multiple intelligences: Myths and messages. In A. Woolfolk (Ed.), *Readings in educational psychology* (2nd ed., pp. 61–67). Boston, MA: Allyn & Bacon.

Gardner, H. (2003, April 21). *Multiple intelligence after twenty years.* Paper presented at the American Educational Research Association, Chicago, Illinois.

Gardner, H., & Moran, S. (2006). The science of multiple intelligences theory: A response to Lynn Waterhouse. *Educational Psychologist, 41,* 227–232.

Gardner, R., Brown, R., Sanders, S., & Menke, D. J. (1992). "Seductive details" in learning from text. In K. A. Renninger, S. Hidi, & A. Krapp (Eds.), *The role of interest in learning and development* (pp. 239–254). Hillsdale, NJ: Erlbaum.

Garner, P. W., & Spears, F. M. (2000). Emotion regulation in low-income preschool children. *Social Development, 9,* 246–264.

Garner, R. (1990). When children and adults do not use learning strategies: Toward a theory of settings. *Review of Educational Psychology, 60,* 517–530.

Garner, R. (1998). Choosing to learn and not-learn in school. *Educational Psychology Review, 10,* 227–238.

Garnets, L. (2002). Sexual orientations in perspective. *Cultural Diversity and Ethnic Minority Psychology, 8,* 115–129.

Garrison, J. (1995). Deweyan pragmatism and the epistemology of contemporary social constructivism. *American Educational Research Journal, 32,* 716–741.

Garrod, A., Beal, C., & Shin, P. (1990). The development of moral orientation in elementary school children. *Sex Roles, 22,* 13–27.

Gathercole, S. E., Pickering, S. J., Ambridge, B., & Wearing, H. (2004). The structure of working memory from 4 to 15 years of age. *Developmental Psychology, 40,* 177–190.

Gay, G. (2000). *Culturally responsive teaching: Theory, research, and practice.* New York, NY: Teachers College Press.

Gay, G. (2006). Connections between classroom management and culturally responsive teaching. In C. Evertson & C. S. Weinstein (Eds.), *Handbook for classroom management: Research, practice, and contemporary issues.* Mahwah, NJ: Erlbaum.

Geary, D. C. (1995). Sexual selection and sex differences in spatial cognition. *Learning and Individual Differences, 7,* 289–303.

Geary, D. C. (1999). Evolution and developmental sex differences. *Current Directions in Psychological Science, 8,* 115–120.

Geary, D. C., & Bjorklund, D. F. (2000). Evolutionary developmental psychology. *Child Development, 7,* 57–65.

Gehlbach, H. (2004). A new perspective on perspective taking: A multidimensional approach to conceptualizing an aptitude. *Educational Psychology Review, 16,* 207–234.

Geier, R., Blumenfeld, P., Marx, R., Krajcik, J., Fishman, B., & Soloway, E. (in press). Standardized test outcomes for students engaged in inquiry-based science curriculum in the context of urban reform. *Journal of Research in Science Teaching.*

Gelman, R. (2000). The epigenesis of mathematical thinking. *Journal of Applied Developmental Psychology, 21,* 27–37.

Gelman, R., & Cordes, S. A. (2001). Counting in animals and humans. In E. Dupoux (Ed.), *Essay in honor of Jacques Mehler.* Cambridge, MA: MIT Press.

Gentner, D., Loewenstein, J., & Thompson, L. (2003). Learning and transfer: A general role for analogical encoding. *Journal of Educational Psychology, 95,* 393–408.

George, P. S. (2005). A rationale for differentiated instruction in the regular classroom. *Theory Into Practice, 44,* 185–193.

Gergen, K. J. (1997). Constructing constructivism: Pedagogical potentials. *Issues in Education: Contributions from Educational Psychology, 3,* 195–202.

Gersten, R. (1996a). The language-minority students in transition: Contemporary instructional research. *The Elementary School Journal, 96,* 217–220.

Gersten, R. (1996b). Literacy instruction for language-minority students: The transition years. *The Elementary School Journal, 96,* 217–220.

Gibbs, J. W., & Luyben, P. D. (1985). Treatment of self-injurious behavior: Contingent versus noncontingent positive practice overcorrection. *Behavior Modification, 9,* 3–21.

Gick, M. L. (1986). Problem-solving strategies. *Educational Psychologist, 21,* 99–120.

Gillett, M., & Gall, M. (1982, March). *The effects of teacher enthusiasm on the at-task behavior of students in the elementary grades.* Paper presented at the annual meeting of the American Educational Research Association, New York, NY.

Gillies, R. (2003). The behaviors, interactions, and perceptions of junior high school students during small-group learning. *Journal of Educational Psychology, 96,* 15–22.

Gillies, R. (2004). The effects of cooperative learning on junior high school students during small group learning. *Learning and Instruction, 14,* 197–213.

Gilligan, C. (1982). *In a different voice: Psychological theory and women's development.* Cambridge, MA: Harvard University Press.

Gilligan, C., & Attanucci, J. (1988). Two moral orientations: Gender differences and similarities. *Merrill-Palmer Quarterly, 34,* 223–237.

Gini, G. (2008). Italian elementary and middle school students' blaming the victim of bullying and perception of school moral atmosphere. *The Elementary School Journal, 108,* 335–354.

Ginott, H. G. (1972). *Teacher and child: A book for parents and teachers.* New York, NY: Collier Books.

Ginsburg, H., & Opper, S. (1988). *Piaget's theory of intellectual development* (3rd ed.). Englewood Cliffs, NJ: Prentice-Hall.

Ginsburg, K. R. (2007). The importance of play in promoting healthy child development and maintaining strong parent-child bonds. *Pediatrics, 119,* 182–191.

Glasser, W. (1969). *Schools without failure.* New York, NY: Harper & Row.

Glasser, W. (1990). *The quality school: Managing students without coercion.* New York, NY: Harper & Row.

Glassman, M. (2001). Dewey and Vygotsky: Society, experience, and inquiry in educational practice. *Educational Researcher, 30*(4), 3–14.

Gleitman, H., Fridlund, A. J., & Reisberg, D. (1999). *Psychology* (5th ed.). New York, NY: Norton.

Gluck, M. A., Mercado, E., & Myers, C. E. (2008). *Learning and memory: From brain to behavior.* New York, NY: Worth.

Goetz, T., Frenzel, A. C., Hall, N. C., & Pekrun, R. (2008). Antecedents of academic emotions: Testing the internal/external frame of reference model for academic enjoyment. *Contemporary Educational Psychology, 33,* 9–33.

Goldenberg, C. (1996). The education of language-minority students: Where are we, and where do we need to go? *The Elementary School Journal, 96,* 353–361.

Goldman, S. R., Lawless, K., Pellegrino, J. W., & Plants, R. (2006). Technology for teaching and learning with understanding. In J. Cooper (Ed.), *Classroom teaching skills* (8th ed., pp. 104–150). Boston, MA: Houghton-Mifflin.

Goleman, D. (1988, April 10). An emerging theory on blacks' I.Q. scores. *New York Times* (Education Life Section), pp. 22–24.

Goleman, D. (1995). *Emotional intelligence.* New York, NY: Bantam.

Gonzales, N., Moll, L. C., and Amanti, C. (2005). *Funds of knowledge: Theorizing practices in households and classrooms.* Mahwah, NJ: Erlbaum.

Good, C., Aronson, J., & Inzlicht, M. (2003). Improving adolescents' standardized test performance: An intervention to reduce the effects of stereotype threat. *Journal of Applied Developmental Psychology, 24,* 645–662.

Good, T. L. (1983a). Classroom research: A decade of progress. *Educational Psychologist, 18*, 127–144.

Good, T. L. (1983b). Research on classroom teaching. In L. Shulman & G. Sykes (Eds.), *Handbook of teaching and policy* (pp. 42–80). New York, NY: Longman.

Good, T. L. (1988). Teacher expectations. In D. Berliner & B. Rosenshine (Eds.), *Talks to teachers* (pp. 159–200). New York, NY: Random House.

Good, T. L. (1996). Teaching effects and teacher evaluation. In J. Sikula (Ed.), *Handbook of research on teacher education* (pp. 617–665). New York, NY: Macmillan.

Good, T. L., & Brophy, J. (2003). *Looking in classrooms* (9th ed.). Boston, MA: Allyn & Bacon.

Good, T. L., & Brophy, J. E. (2008). *Looking in classrooms* (10th ed.). New York, NY: Allyn & Bacon/Longman.

Goodman, Y. M., & Goodman, K. S. (1990). Vygotsky in a whole-language perspective. In L. Moll (Ed.), *Vygotsky and education: Instructional implications and applications of sociohistorical psychology* (pp. 223–250). New York, NY: Cambridge University Press.

Goodrich, H. (1997). Understanding rubrics. *Educational Leadership, 54*(4), 14–17.

Gordon, D. (2001, June, 18). The dominator. *Newsweek*, 42–47.

Gordon, E. W. (1991). Human diversity and pluralism. *Educational Psychologist, 26*, 99–108.

Gordon, J. A. (1998). Caring through control: Reading urban African American youth. *Journal for a Just and Caring Education, 4*, 418–440.

Gordon, T. (1981). Crippling our children with discipline. *Journal of Education, 163*, 228–243.

Gottlieb, G., Wahlsten, D., & Lickliter, R. (2006). The significance of biology for human development: A developmental psychobiological systems view. In R. M. Lerner (Ed.), *Handbook of child psychology: Vol. 1. Theoretical models of human development* (6th ed., pp. 210–257). New York, NY: Wiley.

Government of Canada (2006). *Child maltreatment in Canada: Overview paper.* Prepared by Susan Jack et al. Ottawa: Public Health Agency of Canada.

Graham, S. (1991). A review of attribution theory in achievement contexts. *Educational Psychology Review, 3*, 5–39.

Graham, S. (1994). Motivation in African Americans. *Review of Educational Research, 64*, 55–117.

Graham, S. (1995). Narrative versus meta-analytic reviews of race differences in motivation. *Review of Educational Research, 65*, 509–514.

Graham, S. (1996). How causal beliefs influence the academic and social motivation of African-American children. In G. G. Brannigan (Ed.), *The enlightened educator: Research adventures in the schools* (pp. 111–126). New York, NY: McGraw-Hill.

Graham, S., & Barker, G. (1990). The downside of help: An attributional developmental analysis of helping behavior as a low ability cue. *Journal of Educational Psychology, 82*, 7–14.

Graham, S., & Perin, D. (2007). A meta-analysis of writing instruction for adolescent students. *Journal of Educational Psychology, 99*, 445–476.

Graham, S., & Weiner, B. (1996). Theories and principles of motivation. In D. Berliner & R. C. Calfee (Eds.), *Handbook of educational psychology* (pp. 63–84). New York, NY: Macmillan.

Gray, P. (2002). *Psychology* (4th ed.). New York, NY: Worth.

Gredler, M. E. (2005). *Learning and instruction: Theory into practice* (5th ed.). Boston, MA: Allyn & Bacon.

Gredler, M. E. (2007). Of Cabbages and Kings: Concepts and inferences curiously attributed to Lev Vygotsky (Commentary on McVee, Dunsmore, and Gavelek, 2005). *Review of Educational Research, 77*, 233–238.

Gredler, M. E. (2009). *Learning and instruction: Theory into practice* (6th ed.). Columbus, OH: Merrill.

Greeno, J. G., Collins, A. M., & Resnick, L. B. (1996). Cognition and learning. In D. Berliner & R. Calfee (Eds.), *Handbook of educational psychology* (pp. 15–46). New York, NY: Macmillan.

Gregorc, A. F. (1982). *Gregorc Style Delineator: Development, technical, and administrative manual*. Maynard, MA: Gabriel Systems.

Gresham, F. (1981). Social skills training with handicapped children. *Review of Educational Research, 51*, 139–176.

Griffins, P. E., & Gray, R. D. (2005). Discussion: Three ways to misunderstand developmental systems theory. *Biology and Philosophy, 20*, 417–425.

Grigorenko, E. L., & Sternberg, R. J. (1998). Dynamic testing. *Psychological Bulletin, 124*, 75–111.

Grissom, J. B., & Shepard, L. A. (1989). Repeating and dropping out of school. In L. A. Shepard & M. L. Smith (Eds.), *Flunking grades: Research and policies on retention* (pp. 34–63). New York, NY: Falmer.

Grolnick, W.S., Gurland, S.T., Jacob, K.F., & DeCourcey, W. (2002). The development of self-determination in middle childhood and adolescence. In A. Wigfield & J. Eccles (Eds.), *Development of achievement motivation* (pp. 147–171). New York, NY: Academic Press.

Grolnick, W. S., Ryan, R. M., & Deci, E. L. (1991). Inner resources for school achievement: Motivational mediators of children's perceptions of their parents. *Journal of Educational Psychology, 83*, 508–517.

Gronlund, N. E., & Brookhart, S. M. (2009). *Gronlund's writing instructional objectives* (8th ed.). Columbus, OH: Pearson.

Gronlund, N. E., & Waugh, C. K. (2009). *Assessment of student achievement* (9th ed.). Columbus, OH: Pearson.

Gross, E. F., Juvonen, J., & Gable, S. L. (2002). Internet use and well-being in adolescence. *Journal of Social Issues, 58*(1), 75–90.

Gross, M. (2005). *Studying Children's Questions: Imposed and Self-Generated Information Seeking at School*. Lanham, MD: The Scarecrow Press.

Grossman, H., & Grossman, S. H. (1994). *Gender issues in education*. Boston, MA: Allyn & Bacon.

Grotevant, H. D. (1998). Adolescent development in family contexts. In N. Eisenberg (Ed.), *Handbook of child psychology: Vol 3. Social, emotional, and personality development* (5th ed., pp. 1097–1149). New York, NY: Wiley.

Guay, F., Larose, S., & Boivin, M. (2004). Academic self-concept and educational attainment level: A ten-year longitudinal study. *Self and Identity, 3*, 53–68.

Guilford, J. P. (1988). Some changes in the Structure-of-Intellect model. *Educational and Psychological Measurement, 48*, 1–4.

Gurian, M., & Henley, P. (2001). *Boys and girls learn differently: A guide for teachers and parents*. San Francisco, CA: Jossey-Bass.

Guskey, T. R. (1994). Making the grade: What benefits students? *Educational Leadership, 52*(2), 14–21.

Guskey, T. R., & Bailey, J. M. (2001). *Developing grading and reporting systems for student learning*. Thousand Oaks, CA: Corwin Press.

Gustafsson, J-E., & Undheim, J. O. (1996). Individual differences in cognitive functioning. In D. Berliner & R. Calfee (Eds.), *Handbook of educational psychology* (pp. 186–242). New York, NY: Macmillan.

Guthrie, J. T., & Alao, S. (1997). Designing contexts to increase motivations of reading. *Educational Psychologist, 32*, 95–105.

Guthrie, J. T., Cox, K. E., Anderson, E., Harris, K., Mazzoni, S., & Rach, L. (1998). Principles of integrated instruction for engagement in reading. *Educational Psychology Review, 10*, 227–238.

Guthrie, J. T., Wigfield, A., Humenick, N. M., Perencivich, K. C., Taboada, A., Barbosa, P. (2006). Influences of stimulating tasks on reading motivation and comprehension. *Journal of Educational Research, 99*(4), 232–245.

Hacker, D. J., & Tenent, A. (2002). Implementing reciprocal teaching in the classroom: Overcoming obstacles and making modifications. *Journal of Educational Psychology, 94*, 699–718.

Haertel, E. H. (1999). Performance assessment and educational reform. *Phi Delta Kappan, 80*, 662–666.

Hagborg, W. J. (1993). Rosenberg Self-Esteem Scale and Harter's Self-Perception Profile for Adolescents: A concurrent validity study. *Psychology in Schools, 30*, 132–136.

Hakuta, K. (1986). *Mirror of language: The debate on bilingualism*. New York, NY: Basic Books.

Hakuta, K., & Garcia, E. E. (1989). Bilingualism and education. *American Psychologist, 44*, 374–379.

Hakuta, K., & Gould, L. J. (1987). Synthesis of research on bilingual education. *Educational Leadership, 44*(6), 38–45.

Haladyna, T. H. (2002). *Essentials of standardized achievement testing: Validity and accountability*. Boston, MA: Allyn & Bacon.

Hallahan, D. P., & Kauffman, J. M. (2006). *Exceptional learners: Introduction to special education* (10th ed.). Boston, MA: Allyn & Bacon.

Hallahan, D. P., Kauffman, J. M., & Pullen, P. C. (2009). *Exceptional learners: Introduction to special education* (11th ed.). Boston, MA: Allyn & Bacon.

Hallahan, D. P., Lloyd, J. W., Kauffman, J. M., Weiss, M. P., & Martinez, E. A. (2005). *Introduction to learning disabilities* (5th ed.). Boston, MA: Allyn & Bacon.

Hallowell, E. M., & Ratey, J. J. (1994). *Driven to distraction*. New York, NY: Pantheon Books.

Halpern, D. F., Benbow, C. P., Geary. D. C., Gur, R. C., Hyde, J. S., & Gernsbacher, M. A. (2007). The science of sex differences in science and mathematics. Psychological Science in the Public Interest, 8, 1–51.

Hamann, D. L., Baker, D. S., McAllister, P. A., & Bauer, W. I. (2000). Factors affecting university music students' perceptions of lesson quality and teaching effectiveness. *Journal of Research in Music Education, 48*, 102–113.

Hambrick, D. Z., Kane, M. J., & Engle, R. W. (2005). The role of working memory in higher-level cognition. In R. Sternberg & J. E. Pretz (Eds.), *Cognition and intelligence: Identifying the mechanisms of the mind* (pp. 104–121). New York, NY: Cambridge University Press.

Hamers, J. F., & Blanc, M. H. A. (2000). *Bilinguality and bilingualism* (2nd ed.). Cambridge, England: Cambridge University Press.

Hamilton, R. J. (1985). A framework for the evaluation of the effectiveness of adjunct questions and objectives. *Review of Educational Research, 55*, 47–86.

Hamman, D., Berthelot, J., Saia, J., & Crowley, E. (2000). Teachers' coaching of learning and its relation to students' strategic learning. *Journal of Educational Psychology, 92*, 342–348.

Hamre, B. K., & Pianta, R. C. (2001). Early teacher–child relationships and the trajectory of children's school outcomes through eighth grade. *Child Development, 72*, 625–638.

Hanushek, E. A., Rivkin, S. G., & Kain, J. J. (2005). Teachers, schools and academic achievement. *Econometrica* 73, 417–458.

Harackiewicz, J. M., Barron, K. E., Pintrich, P. R., Elliot, A. J., & Thrash, T. M. (2002). Revision of achievement goal theory: Necessary and illuminating. *Journal of Educational Psychology, 94*, 562–575.

Harackiewicz, J. M., & Linnenbrink, E. A. (2005). Multiple achievement goals and multiple pathways for learning: The agenda and impact of Paul R. Pintrich. *Educational Psychologist, 40*, 75–84.

Hardiman, P. T., Dufresne, R., & Mestre, J. P. (1989). The relation between problem categorization and problem solving among experts and novices. *Memory & Cognition, 17*, 627–638.

Hardin, C. J. (2008). *Effective classroom management: Models and strategies for today's classrooms* (2nd ed.). Columbus, OH: Merrill/Prentice-Hall.

Hardman, M. L., Drew, C. J., & Egan, M. W. (2005). *Human exceptionality: Society, school, and family* (8th ed.). Boston, MA: Allyn & Bacon.

Harp, S. F., & Mayer, R. E. (1998). How seductive details do their damage: A theory of cognitive interest in science learning. *Journal of Educational Psychology, 90*, 414–434.

Harris, J. R. (1998). *The nurture assumption: Why children turn out the way they do; parents matter less than you think and peers matter more.* New York, NY: Free Press.

Harris, K. R. (1990). Developing self-regulated learners: The role of private speech and self-instruction. *Educational Psychologist, 25*, 35–50.

Harris, K. R., & Graham, S. (1996). Memo to constructivist: Skills count too. *Educational Leadership, 53*(5), 26–29.

Harris, K. R., Graham S., & Pressley, M. (1992). Cognitive-behavioral approaches in reading and written language: Developing self-regulated learners. In N. N. Singh & I. L. Beale (Eds.), *Learning disabilities: Nature, theory, and treatment* (pp. 415–451). New York, NY: Springer-Verlag.

Harris, K. R., & Pressley, M. (1991). The nature of cognitive strategy instruction: Interactive strategy construction. *Exceptional Children, 57*, 392–404.

Harrow, A. J. (1972). *A taxonomy of the psychomotor domain: A guide for developing behavior objectives.* New York, NY: David McKay.

Harter, S. (1990). Issues in the assessment of self-concept of children and adolescents. In A. LaGreca (Ed.), *Through the eyes of a child* (pp. 292–325). Boston, MA: Allyn & Bacon.

Harter, S. (1998). The development of self-representations. In N. Eisenberg (Ed.), *Handbook of child psychology: Vol. 3. Social, emotional, and personality development* (5th ed., pp. 553–618). New York, NY: Wiley.

Harter, S. (2003). The development of self-representation during childhood and adolescence. In M. R. Leary & J. P. Tangney (Eds.), *Handbook of self and identity* (pp. 610–642). New York, NY: Guilford.

Hartshore, J. K., & Ullman, M. T. (2006). Why girls say "holded" more than boys. *Developmental Science, 9*, 21–32.

Hartup, W. W., & Stevens, N. (1999). Friendships and adaptation across the lifespan. *Current Directions in Psychological Science, 8*, 76–79.

Hattie, J., & Timperley, H. (2007). The power of feedback. *Review of Educational Research, 77*, 81–112.

Hayes, S. C., Rosenfarb, I., Wulfert, E., Munt, E. D., Korn, Z., & Zettle, R. D. (1985). Self-reinforcement effects: An artifact of social standard setting? *Journal of Applied Behavior Analysis, 18*, 201–214.

Health Canada. (2004/05). *Summary of results of the 2004–05 Youth Smoking Survey.* Retrieved from http://www.hc-sc.gc.ca/hl-vs/tobac-tabac/research-recherche/stat/survey-sondage/2004-2005/result_e.html

Health Canada. (2006). First Nations, Inuit and Aboriginal Health: Suicide prevention. Retrieved from http://www.hc-sc.gc.ca/fniah-spnia/promotion/suicide/index-eng.php

Heath, N. (1996). The emotional domain: Self-concept and depression in children with learning disabilities. *Advances in Learning and Behavioural Disabilities, 10*, 47–75.

Heath, N. L., & Ross, S. (2000). The prevalence and expression of depressive symptomatology in children with and without learning disabilities. *Learning Disability Quarterly, 23*, 24–36.

Heath, S. B. (1989). Oral and literate traditions among black Americans living in poverty. *American Psychologist, 44*, 367–373.

Helms, J. E. (1995). An update of Helms's White and People of Color racial identity models. In J. G. Ponterotto, J. M. Casas, L. A. Suzuki & C. M. Alexander (Eds.), *Handbook of multicultural counseling* (pp. 181–198). Thousand Oaks, CA: Sage.

Helwig, C. C., Arnold, M. L., Tan, D., & Boyd, D.(2003). Chinese adolescents' reasoning about democratic and authority-based decision making in peer, family, and school contexts. *Child Development, 74*, 783–800.

Herbert, E. A. (1998). Design matters: How school environment affects children. *Educational Leadership, 56*(1), 69–71.

Herman, J., & Winters. L. (1994). Portfolio research: A slim collection. *Educational Leadership, 52*(2), 48–55.

Herman, M. (2004). Forced to choose: Some determinants of racial identification in multi-racial adolescents. *Child Development, 75*, 730–748.

Herzig, A. H. (2004). Becoming mathematicians: Women and students of color choosing and leaving doctoral mathematics. *Review of Educational Research, 74*, 171–214.

Hetherington, E. M. (2006). The influence of conflict, marital problem solving and parenting on children's adjustment in nondivorced, divorced and remarried families. In A. Clarke-Stewart & J. Dunn (Eds.), *Families count: Effects on child and adolescent development* (pp. 203–237). New York, NY: Cambridge University Press.

Hetherington, E. M., & Kelly, J. (2002). *For better or for worse: Divorce reconsidered.* New York, NY: W. W. Norton.

Hewson, P. W., Beeth, M. E., & Thorley, N. R. (1998). Teaching for conceptual change. In B. J. Fraserr & K. G. Tobin (Eds.), *International handbook of science education* (pp. 199–218). New York, NY: Kluwer.

Hewstone, M. (1989). Changing stereotypes with disconfirming information. In D. Bar-Tal, C. Graumann, A. Kruglanski, & W. Stroebe (Eds.), *Stereotyping and prejudice: Changing conceptions* (pp. 207–223). New York, NY: Springer-Verlag.

Hickey, D. T. (2003). Engaged participation vs. marginal non-participation: A stridently sociocultural model of achievement motivation. *Elementary School Journal, 103*(4), 401–429.

Hickey, D. T., Kindfield, A. C. H., Horwitz, P., & Christie, M. A. (1999). Advancing educational theory by enhancing practice in a technology supported genetics learning environment. *Journal of Education, 181*, 25–55.

Hickey, D. T., Wolfe, E. W., & Kindfield, A. C. H. (2000). Assessing learning in a technology-supported genetics environment: Evidential and consequential validity issues. *Educational Assessment, 6*, 155–196.

Hidi, S., & Renninger, K. A. (2006). The four-phase model of interest development. *Educational Psychologist, 41*, 111–127.

Hidi, S., Renninger, K. A., & Krapp, A. (2004). Interest, a motivational variable that combines affective and cognitive functioning. In D. Y. Dai & R. J. Sternberg (Eds.), *Motivation, emotion, and cognition: Integrative perspectives on intellectual functioning and development* (pp. 89–115). Mahwah, NJ: Erlbaum.

Hilgard, E. R. (1996). History of educational psychology. In R. Calfee & D. Berliner (Eds.), *Handbook of educational psychology* (pp. 990–1004). New York, NY: Macmillan.

Hill, W. F. (2002). *Learning: A survey of psychological interpretations* (7th ed.). Boston, MA: Allyn & Bacon.

Hindi, E. R., & Perry, N. (2007). Elementary teachers' application of Jean Piaget's theories of cognitive development during social studies curriculum debates in Arizona. *The Elementary School Journal, 108*, 64–79.

Hines, C. V., Cruickshank, D. R., & Kennedy, J. J. (1985). Teacher clarity and its relation to student achievement and satisfaction. *American Educational Research Journal, 22*, 87–99.

Hines, M. (2004) *Brain gender*. New York, NY: Oxford University Press.

Hiroto, D. S., & Seligman, M. E. P. (1975). Generality of learned helplessness in man. *Journal of Personality and Social Psychology, 31*, 311–327.

Hmelo, C. E. (1998). Problem-based learning: Effects on the early acquisition of cognitive skill in medicine. *Journal of the Learning Sciences, 7*, 173–208.

Hmelo-Silver, C. E. (2004). Problem-based learning: What and how do students learn? *Educational Psychology Review, 16*, 235–266.

Hmelo-Silver, C. E., Ravit, G. D., & Chinn, C. A. (2007). Scaffolding and achievement in problem-based and inquiry learning: A response to Kirschner, Sweller, and Clark (2006). *Educational Psychologist, 42*, 99–107.

Hobbs, R. (2004). A review of school-based initiatives in media literacy education. *American Behavioral Scientist, 48*, 42–59.

Hofer, B. K., & Pintrich, P. R. (1997). The development of epistemological theories: Beliefs about knowledge and knowing and their relation to learning. *Review of Educational Research, 67*, 88–140.

Hoff, E. (2006). How social contexts support and shape language development. *Developmental Review, 26*, 55–88.

Hofferth, S. L., & Sandberg, J. F. (2000). *Changes in American children's time, 1981–1997*. Ann Arbor, MI: University of Michigan Population Studies Center.

Hoffman, M. L. (2000). *Empathy and moral development*. New York, NY: Cambridge University Press.

Hogan, T., Rabinowitz, M., & Craven, J. A. III. (2003). Representation in teaching: Inferences from research of expert and novice teachers. *Educational Psychologist, 38*, 235–247.

Hoge, D. R., Smit, E. K., & Hanson, S. L. (1990). School experiences predicting changes in self-esteem of sixth- and seventh-grade students. *Journal of Educational Psychology, 82*, 117–126.

Hohman, C. (1998). Evaluating and selecting software for children. *Child Care Information Exchange, 123*, 60–62.

Hoover-Dempsey, K. V., Bassler, O. C., & Burow, R. (1995). Parents' reported involvement in students' homework: Strategies and practices. *The Elementary School Journal, 95*, 435–450.

Hoover-Dempsey, K. V., Battiato, A. C., Walker, J. M. T., Reed, R. P., DeJong, J. M., & Jones, K. P. (2001). Parental involvement in homework. *Educational Psychologist, 36*, 195–209.

Horn, J. L. (1998). A basis for research on age differences in cognitive capabilities. In J. J. McArdle & R. W. Woodcock (Eds.), *Human cognitive theories in theory and practice* (pp. 57–87). Mahwah, NJ: Erlbaum.

Horovitz, B. (2002, April 22). Gen Y: A tough crowd to sell. *USA Today*, pp. B1–2.

Howe, M. J. A., Davidson, J. W., & Sloboda, J. A. (1998). Innate talents: Reality or myth? *Behavioral and Brain Sciences, 21*, 399–406.

Hoy, W. K., & Woolfolk, A. E. (1993). Teachers' sense of efficacy and the organizational health of schools. *Elementary School Journal, 93*, 355–372.

Hudley, C., Graham, S., & Taylor, A. (2007). Reducing aggressive behavior and increasing motivation in school: The evolution of an intervention to strengthen school adjustment. *Educational Psychologist, 42*, 251–260.

Hudley, C., & Novak, A. (2007). Environmental influences, the developing brain, and aggressive behavior. *Theory Into Practice, 46*, 121–129.

Huff, C. R. (1989). Youth gangs and public policy. *Crime & Delinquency, 35*, 524–537.

Hughes, D. R. (1998). *Kids online: Protecting your children in cyberspace*. Grand Rapids, MI: Fleming H. Revell.

Huguet, P., & Régner, I. (2007). Stereotype threat among schoolgirls in quasi-ordinary classroom circumstances. *Journal of Educational Psychology, 99*, 345–360.

Hulit, L., & Howard, M. (2006). *Born to talk: An introduction to speech and language development* (4th ed.). Boston, MA: Allyn & Bacon.

Human Resources and Social Development Canada. (2004). Advancing the Inclusion of Persons with Disabilities. Retrieved from http://www.hrsdc.gc.ca/en/hip/odi/documents/advancingInclusion04/index.shtml

Hung, D. W. L. (1999). Activity, apprenticeship, and epistemological appropriation: Implications from the writings of Michael Polanyi. *Educational Psychologist, 34*, 193–205.

Hunt, E. (2000). Let's hear it for crystallized intelligence. *Learning and Individual Differences, 12*, 123–129.

Hunt, J. M. (1961). *Intelligence and experience*. New York, NY: Ronald.

Hunt, N., & Marshall, K. (2002). *Exceptional children and youth: An introduction to special education* (3rd ed.). Boston, MA: Houghton Mifflin.

Hunt, R. R., & Ellis, H. C. (1999). *Fundamentals of cognitive psychology* (6th ed.). New York, NY: McGraw-Hill College.

Hunter, M. (1982). *Mastery teaching*. El Segundo, CA: TIP Publications.

Hutchinson, N. L. (2007). *Inclusion of exceptional learners in Canadian schools*. (2nd ed.). Toronto, ON: Prentice-Hall.

Hutchinson, N. L., Wintermute, J., Munby, H., Versnel, J., Chin, P., & Dalgarno, N. (2005, April). *Negotiating accommodations so that work-based education facilitates career development for youth with disabilities*. Paper presented at the annual meeting of the American Educational Research Association, Montreal, QC.

Institute of Marriage and Family Canada. (2010). Canadian Divorce Statistics. Retrieved from http://www.imfcanada.org/article_files/Canadian%20Divorce%20Statistics.pdf

International Reading Association & National Association for the Education of Young Children. (1998). Learning to read and write: Developmentally appropriate practices for young children. *The Reading Teacher, 52*, 193–216.

Ipsos Reid Interactive Group. (2010) Weekly internet usage overtakes television watching. Retrieved from http://www.ipsos-na.com/news-polls/pressrelease.aspx?id=4720

Iran-Nejad, A. (1990). Active and dynamic self-regulation of learning processes. *Review of Educational Research, 60*, 573–602.

Irvine, J. J. (1990). *Black students and school failure: Policies, practices, and prescriptions*. New York, NY: Praeger.

Irvine, J. J., & Armento, B. J. (2001). *Culturally responsive teaching: Lesson planning for elementary and middle grades*. New York, NY: McGraw-Hill.

Irvine, J. J. & Fraser, J. W. (1998, May). Warm demanders. *Education Week*. Retrieved from http://www.edweek.org/ew/ewstory.cfm?slug=35irvine.h17&keywords=Irvine

Irving, O., & Martin, J. (1982). Withitness: The confusing variable. *American Educational Research Journal, 19*, 313–319.

Irwin, J. W. (1991). *Teaching reading comprehension* (2nd ed.). Boston, MA: Allyn & Bacon.

Isabella, R., & Belsky, J. (1991). Interactional synchrony and the origins of infant–mother attachment: A replication study. *Child Development, 62*, 373–384.

Jackson, A., & Davis, G. (2000). *Turning points 2000: Educating adolescents in the 21st century*. New York, NY: Teachers College Press.

Jackson, L. A., von Eye, A., Biocca, F. A., Barbatsis, G., Zhao, Y., & Fitzgerald, H. E. (2006). Does home Internet use influence the academic performance of low-income children? *Developmental Psychology, 42*, 429–435.

Jacobs, J. E., Lanza, S., Osgood, D. W., Eccles, J. S., & Wigfield, A. (2002). Changes in children's self-competence and values: Gender and domain differences across grades one through twelve. *Child Development, 73*, 509–527.

James, W. (1890). *The principles of psychology* (Vol. 2). New York, NY: Holt.

James, W. (1912). *Talks to teachers on psychology: And to students on some of life's ideals*. New York, NY: Holt.

Jarrett, R. (1995). Growing up poor: The family experiences of socially mobile youth in low-income African American neighborhoods. *Journal of Adolescent Research, 10*, 111–135.

Jaswal, V. K., & Markman, E. M. (2001). Learning proper and common names in inferential versus ostensive contexts. *Child Development, 72*, 787–802.

Jensen, L. A., Arnett, J. J., Feldman, S. S., & Cauffman, E. (2002). It's wrong but everybody does it: Academic dishonesty among high school and college students. *Contemporary Educational Psychology, 27*, 209–228.

Jimenez, R. (2000). Literacy and identity development of Latina/o students who are successful English readers: Opportunities and obstacles. *American Educational Research Journal, 37*, 971–1000.

Jimerson, S. R. (1999). On the failure of failure: Examining the association between early grade retention and education and employment outcomes during late adolescence. *Journal of School Psychology, 37*, 243–272.

Jimerson, S. R., Anderson, G. E., & Whipple, A. D. (2002). Winning the battle and losing the war: Examining the relation between grade retention and dropping out of high school. *Psychology in the Schools, 39*, 441–457.

Johnson, A. (2003). Procedural memory and skill acquisition. In A. F. Healy & R. W. Proctor (Eds.), *Experimental psychology* (Vol. 4, pp. 499–523). New York, NY: Wiley.

Johnson, A. M., & Notah, D. J. (1999). Service learning: History, literature, review, and a pilot study of eighth graders. *The Elementary School Journal, 99*, 453–467.

Johnson, D. W., & Johnson, R. T. (1999a). *Learning together and alone: Cooperation, competition, and individualization* (5th ed.). Boston, MA: Allyn & Bacon.

Johnson, D. W., & Johnson, R. T. (1999b). The three Cs of school and classroom management. In H. J. Freiberg (Ed.), *Beyond behaviorism: Changing the classroom management paradigm* (pp. 119–144). Boston, MA: Allyn & Bacon.

Johnson, D. W., & Johnson, R. T. (2002). *Meaningful assessment: A meaningful and cooperative process*. Boston, MA: Allyn & Bacon.

Johnson, D. W., Johnson, R. T., Dudley, B., Ward, M., & Magnuson, D. (1995). The impact of peer mediation training on the management of school and home conflicts. *American Educational Research Journal, 32*, 829–844.

Johnson, S. (2008, January 14). A childhood in poverty informs her teaching. *USA Today*, p. 7D.

John-Steiner, V., & Mahn, H. (1996). Sociocultural approaches to learning and development: A Vygotskian framework. *Educational Psychologist, 31*, 191–206.

Johnston, L. D., O'Malley, P. M., Bachman, J. G., & Schulenberg, J. E. (2004, December 21). *Overall teen drug use continues gradual decline; but use of inhalants rises*. [Online]. Ann Arbor, MI: University of Michigan News and Information Services. Retrieved from www.monitoringthefuture.org

Jonassen, D. H. (2003). Designing research-based instruction for story problems. *Educational Psychology Review, 15*, 267–296.

Jones, D. C. (2004). Body image among adolescent girls and boys: A longitudinal study. *Developmental Psychology, 40*, 823–835.

Jones, E. D., & Southern, W. T. (1991). Conclusions about acceleration: Echoes of a debate. In W. Southern & E. Jones (Eds.), *The academic acceleration of gifted children* (pp. 223–228). New York, NY: Teachers College Press.

Jones, M. G., & Gerig, T. M. (1994). Silent sixth-grade students: Characteristics, achievement, and teacher expectations. *Elementary School Journal, 95*, 169–182.

Jones, M. S., Levin, M. E., Levin, J. R., & Beitzel, B. D. (2000). Can vocabulary-learning strategies and pair-learning formats be profitably combined? *Journal of Educational Psychology, 92*, 256–262.

Jones, S. M., & Dindia, K. (2004). A meta-analytic perspective on sex equity in the classroom. *Review of Educational Research, 74*, 443–471.

Jurbergs, N., Palcic, J., & Kelly, M. L. (2007). School-home notes with and without response cost: Increasing attention and academic performance in low-income children with attention deficit/hyperactivity disorder. *School Psychology Quarterly, 22*, 358–379.

Jurden, F. H. (1995). Individual differences in working memory and complex cognition. *Journal of Educational Psychology, 87*, 93–102.

Kagan, J. (1976). Commentary on reflective and impulsive children: Strategies of information processing underlying differences in problem solving. *Monograph of the Society for Research in Child Development, 41*(5) (Ser. No. 168).

Kagan, J., & Herschkowitz, N. (2005). *A young mind in a growing brain*. Mahwah, NJ: Erlbaum.

Kagan, S. (1994). *Cooperative learning*. San Juan Capistrano, CA: Kagan Cooperative Learning.

Kail, R. (2000). Speed of processing: Developmental change and links to intelligence. *Journal of School Psychology, 38*, 51–61.

Kail, R., & Hall, L. K. (1999). Sources of developmental change in children's word-problem performance. *Journal of Educational Psychology, 91*, 600–668.

Kail, R., & Park, Y. (1994). Processing time, articulation time, and memory span. *Journal of Experimental Child Psychology, 57*, 281–291.

Kalyuga, S., Chandler, P., Tuovinen, J., & Sweller, J. (2001). When problem solving is superior to studying worked examples. *Journal of Educational Psychology, 93*, 579–588.

Kanaya, T., Scullin, M.H., & Ceci, S. J. (2003). The Flynn effect and U.S. policies: The impact of rising IQ scores on American society via mental retardation diagnoses. *American Psychologist, 58*, 1–13.

Kaplan, A., & Maehr, M. L. (2007). The contributions and prospects of goal orientation theory. *Educational Psychology Review, 19*, 141–184.

Kaplan, J. S. (1991). *Beyond behavior modification* (2nd ed.). Austin, TX: Pro-Ed.

Kardash, C. M., & Howell, K. L. (2000). Effects of epistemological beliefs and topic-specific beliefs on undergraduates' cognitive and strategic processing of dual-positional text. *Journal of Educational Psychology, 92*, 524–535.

Karpov, Y. V., & Bransford, J. D. (1995). L. S. Vygotsky and the doctrine of empirical and theoretical learning. *Educational Psychologist, 30*, 61–66.

Karpov, Y. V., & Haywood, H. C. (1998). Two ways to elaborate Vygotsky's concept of mediation implications for instruction. *American Psychologist, 53*, 27–36.

Karweitt, N. (1989). Time and learning: A review. In R. E. Slavin (Ed.), *School and classroom organization* (pp. 69–95). Hillsdale, NJ: Erlbaum.

Karweitt, N., & Slavin, R. (1981). Measurement and modeling choices in studies of time and learning. *American Educational Research Journal, 18*, 157–171.

Katz, I., & Assor, A. (2007). When choice motivates and when it does not. *Educational Psychology Review, 19*, 429–442.

Katz, J., & Mirenda, P. (2002). Including students with developmental disabilities in general education classrooms: Educational benefits. *International Journal of Special Education, 17*, 86–96.

Katz, P. A. (2003). Racists or tolerant multiculturalists? How do they begin? *American Psychologist, 58*, 897–909.

Katz, S. R. (1999). Teaching in tensions: Latino immigrant youth, their teachers, and the structures of schooling. *Teachers College Record, 100*(4), 809–840.

Katzir, T., & Paré-Blagoev, J. (2006). Applying cognitive neuroscience research to education: The case of literacy. *Educational Psychologist, 4*, 53–74.

Kazdin, A. E. (1984). *Behavior modification in applied settings*. Homewood, IL: Dorsey Press.

Kazdin, A. E. (2001). *Behavior modification in applied settings* (6th ed.). Belmont, CA: Wadsworth.

Kazdin, A. E. (2008). *The Kazdin method for parenting the defiant child*. Boston, MA: Houghton-Mifflin.

Keating, D. P. (1991). Curriculum options for the developmentally advanced: A developmental alternative for gifted education. *Exceptionality Education Canada, 1*, 53–83.

Keefe, J. W. (1982). Assessing student learning styles: An overview. In *Student learning styles and brain behavior*. Reston, VA: National Association of Secondary School Principals.

Kelly, K. (1999). Retention vs. social promotion: Schools search for alternatives. *Harvard Education Letter, 15*(1), 1–3.

Kenney-Benson, G. A., Pomerantz, E. M., Ryan, A. M., & Patrick, H. (2006). Sex differences in math performance: The role of children's approach to school work. *Developmental Psychology, 42*, 11–26.

Kerckhoff, A. C. (1986). Effects of ability grouping in British secondary schools. *American Sociological Review, 51*, 842–858.

Keyser, V., & Barling, J. (1981). Determinants of children's self-efficacy beliefs in an academic environment. *Cognitive Therapy and Research, 5*, 29–40.

KidsHealth. (2009). Cerebral Palsy. Retrieved from http://kidshealth.org/parent/medical/brain/cerebral_palsy.html#

Kiewra, K. A. (1985). Investigating notetaking and review: A depth of processing alternative. *Educational Psychologist, 20*, 23–32.

Kiewra, K. A. (1988). Cognitive aspects of autonomous note taking: Control processes, learning strategies, and prior knowledge. *Educational Psychologist, 23*, 39–56.

Kiewra, K. A. (1989). A review of note-taking: The encoding storage paradigm and beyond. *Educational Psychology Review, 1*, 147–172.

Kiewra, K. A. (2002). How classroom teachers can help students learn and teach them how to learn. *Theory Into Practice, 41*, 71–80.

Kim, K. M. (1998). Korean children's perceptions of adult and peer authority and moral reasoning. *Developmental Psychology, 5*, 310–329.

Kindsvatter, R., Wilen, W., & Ishler, M. (1992). *Dynamics of effective teaching* (2nd ed.). New York, NY: Longman.

King, A. (1990). Enhancing peer interaction and learning in the classroom through reciprocal questioning. *American Educational Research Journal, 27*, 664–687.

King, A. (1994). Guiding knowledge construction in the classroom: Effects of teaching children how to question and how to explain. *American Educational Research Journal, 31*, 338–368.

King, A. (2002). Structuring peer interactions to promote high-level cognitive processing. *Theory Into Practice, 41*, 31–39.

King, G. (1979, June). [Personal communication]. University of Texas at Austin.

Kirk, S., Gallagher, J. J., & Anastasiow, N. J. (1993). *Educating exceptional children* (7th ed.). Boston, MA: Houghton Mifflin.

Kirk, S. A., Gallagher, J. J., Anastasiow, N. J., & Coleman, M. R. (2006). *Educating exceptional children* (11th ed.). Boston, MA: Houghton Mifflin.

Kirst, M. (1991). Interview on assessment issues with James Popham. *Educational Researcher, 20*(2), 24–27.

Klassen, R. M. (2004). A cross-cultural investigation of the efficacy beliefs of South Asian immigrant and Anglo Canadian nonimmigrant early adolescents. *Journal of Educational Psychology, 96*, 731–742.

Klein, S. S., & Harris, A. H. (2007). A users guide to the Legacy Cycle. *Journal of Education and Human Development, 1*. Retrieved from http://www.scientificjournals.org/journals2007/articles/1088.pdf

Kleinfield, J. (2005, May 20). *Culture fuels boys' learning problems*. Alaska Daily News, p. B6.

Kling, K. C., Hyde, J. S., Showers, C. J., & Buswell, B. N. (1999). Gender differences in self-esteem: A meta-analysis. *Psychological Bulletin, 125*, 470–500.

Knapp, M., Turnbull, B. J., & Shields, P. M. (1990). New directions for educating children of poverty. *Educational Leadership, 48*(1), 4–9.

Knapp, M. S., & Woolverton, S. (2003). Social class and schooling. In J. A. Banks & C. A. Banks (Eds.), *Handbook of research on multicultural education*. San Francisco, CA: Jossey-Bass.

Kneedler, R. (1984). *Special education for today*. Englewood Cliffs, NJ: Prentice-Hall.

Knoblauch, D., & Woolfolk Hoy, A. (2008). "Maybe I can teach those kids." The influence of contextual factors on student teachers' sense of efficacy. *Teaching and Teacher Education, 24*, 166–179.

Kohlberg, L. (1963). The development of children's orientations toward moral order: Sequence in the development of moral thought. *Vita Humana, 6*, 11–33.

Kohlberg, L. (1975). The cognitive-developmental approach to moral education. *Phi Delta Kappan, 56*, 670–677.

Kohlberg, L. (1981). *The philosophy of moral development*. New York, NY: Harper & Row.

Kohn, A. (1993). Rewards versus learning: A response to Paul Chance. *Phi Delta Kappan, 74*, 783–787.

Kohn, A. (1996a). *Beyond discipline: From compliance to community*. Alexandria, VA: Association for Supervision and Curriculum Development.

Kohn, A. (1996b). By all available means: Cameron and Pierce's defense of extrinsic motivators. *Review of Educational Research, 66*, 1–4.

Kohn, A. (2005). Unconditional teaching. *Educational Leadership, 62*, 12–17.

Kohn. A. (2006). *The homework myth: Why our kids get too much of a bad thing*. Cambridge, MA: Da Capo Press.

Kolb, G., & Whishaw, I. Q. (1998). Brain plasticity and behavior. In J. T. Spence, J. M. Darley, & D. J. Foss (Eds.), Annual review of psychology (pp. 43–64). Palo Alto, CA: Annual Reviews.

Koppelman, K. (2008). *Understanding human differences: Multicultural education for a diverse America* (2nd ed.). Boston, MA: Pearson/Allyn & Bacon.

Korenman, S., Miller, J., & Sjaastad, J. (1995). Long-term poverty and child development in the United States: Results from the NLSY. *Children and Youth Services Review, 17*, 127–155.

Korf, R. (1999). Heuristic search. In R. Wilson & F. Keil (Eds.), *The MIT encyclopedia of the cognitive sciences* (pp. 372–373). Cambridge, MA: MIT Press.

Koriat, A., Goldsmith, M., & Pansky, A. (2000). Toward a psychology of memory accuracy. In S. Fiske (Ed.), *Annual review of psychology* (pp. 481–537). Palo Alto, CA: Annual Reviews.

Kornhaber, M., Fierros, E., & Veenema, S. (2004). *Multiple intelligences: Best ideas for research and practice*. Boston, MA: Allyn & Bacon.

Kosslyn, S. M., & Koenig, O. (1992). *Wet mind: The new cognitive neuroscience*. New York, NY: Free Press.

Kounin, J. S. (1970). *Discipline and group management in classrooms*. New York, NY: Holt, Rinehart & Winston.

Kozulin, A. (1990). *Vygotsky's psychology: A biography of ideas*. Cambridge, MA: Harvard University Press.

Kozulin, A., (2003). Psychological tools and mediated learning. In A. Kouzlin, B. Gindis, V. Ageyev, & S. M. Miller (Eds.), *Vygotsky's educational theory in cultural context* (pp. 15–38). Cambridge, England: Cambridge University Press.

Kozulin, A. (Ed.). (2003). *Vygotsky's educational theory in cultural context*. Cambridge, England: Cambridge University Press.

Kozulin, A., & Presseisen, B. Z. (1995). Mediated learning experience and psychological tools: Vygotsky's and Feuerstein's perspectives in a study of student learning. *Educational Psychologist, 30*, 67–75.

Krahn, H. & Taylor, A. (2008). "Streaming" in the 10th grade in four Canadian provinces in 2000. *Statistics Canada*. Retrieved from http://www.statcan.gc.ca/pub/81-004-x/2007002/9994-eng.htm

Krajcik, J., & Czerniak, C. (2007). *Teaching science in elementary and middle school classrooms: A project-based approach* (3rd ed.). Mahwah, NJ: Erlbaum.

Krathwohl, D. R., Bloom, B. S., & Masia, B. B. (1964). *Taxonomy of educational objectives. Handbook II: Affective domain*. New York, NY: David McKay.

Krätzig, G. P., & Arbuthnott, K. D. (2006). Perceptual learning style and learning proficiency: A test of the hypothesis. *Journal of Educational Psychology, 98*, 238–246.

Kreitzer, A. E., & Madaus, G. F. (1994). Empirical investigations of the hierarchical structure of the taxonomy. In L. W. Anderson & L. A. Sosniak (Eds.), *Bloom's taxonomy: A forty-year retrospective*. Ninety-third yearbook for the National Society for the Study of Education: Part II (pp. 64–81). Chicago, IL: University of Chicago Press.

Kroesbergen, E. H., Van Luit, J. E. H., & Maas, C. J. M. (2004). Effectiveness of explicit and constructivist mathematics for low-achieving students in the Netherlands. *The Elementary School Journal, 104*, 233–251.

Kroger, J. (2000). *Identity development: Adolescence through adulthood*. Thousand Oaks, CA: Sage.

Krumboltz, J. D., & Yeh, C. J. (1996). Competitive grading sabotages good teaching. *Phi Delta Kappan, 78*, 324–326.

Kuhn, D. (2007). Is direct instruction an answer to the right question? *Educational Psychologist, 42*, 109–113.

Kuklinski, M. R., & Weinstein, R. S. (2001). Classroom and developmental differences in a path model of teacher expectancy effects. *Child Development, 72*, 1554–1578.

Kulik, J. A., & Kulik, C. C. (1984). Effects of accelerated instruction on students. *Review of Educational Research, 54*, 409–425.

Kumar, D. D., & Sherwood, R. D. (2007). Effect of problem-based simulation on the conceptual understanding of undergraduate science educational majors. *Journal of Science Education and Technology, 16*, 239–246.

Kuo, L., & Anderson, R. C. (2006). Morphological awareness and learning to read: A cross-language perspective. *Educational Psychologist, 41*, 161–180.

Lachter, J., Forster, K. I., & Ruthruff, K. I. (2004). Forty-five years after Broadbent (1958): Still no identification without attention. *Psychological Review, 111*, 880–913.

Ladson-Billings, G. (1990). Like lightning in a bottle: Attempting to capture the pedagogical excellence of successful teachers of Black students. *Qualitative Studies in Education*, 3, 335–344.

Ladson-Billings, G. (1992). Culturally relevant teaching: The key to making multicultural education work. In C. A. Grant (Ed.), *Research and multicultural education* (pp. 106–121). London, England: Falmer Press.

Ladson-Billings, G. (1994). *The dream keepers*. San Francisco, CA: Jossey-Bass.

Ladson-Billings, G. (1995). But that is just good teaching! The case for culturally relevant pedagogy. *Theory Into Practice*, 34, 161–165.

Ladson-Billings, G. (2004). Landing on the wrong note: The price we paid for Brown. *Educational Researcher*, 33(7), 3–13.

Laidlaw, L. (2004). The importance of little details: Complexity, emergence, and pedagogy. Retrieved from http://www.ccfi.educ.ubc.ca/publication/insights/v09n01/articles/laidlaw.html

Lajoie, S. P., & Azevedo, R. (2006). Teaching and learning in technology-rich environments. In A. Alexander & P. H. Winne (Eds.), *Handbook of educational psychology* (2nd ed., pp. 803–823). Mahwah, NJ: Erlbaum.

Lamb, M. E., & Lewis, C. (2005). The role of parent-child relationships in child development. In M. H. Bornstein & M. E. Lamb (Eds.), *Developmental science: An advanced textbook* (5th ed., pp. 429–468). Mahwah, NJ: Erlbaum.

Lambert, A. J. (1995). Stereotypes and social judgment: The consequences of group variability. *Journal of Personality and Social Psychology, 68*, 388–403.

Lambert, N. M. (1994). Seating arrangement in classrooms. In *International encyclopedia of education* (2nd ed., Vol. 9, pp. 5355–5359). Oxford, England: Pergamon.

Lamborn, S. D., Mounts, N. S., Steinberg, L., & Dornbusch, S. M. (1991). Patterns of competence and adjustment among adolescents from authoritative, authoritarian, indulgent, and neglectful families. *Child Development*, *63*, 1049–1065.

Landrum, T. J., & Kauffman, J. M. (2006). Behavioral approaches to classroom management. In C. M. Evertson & C. S. Weinstein (Eds.), *Handbook of classroom management: Research, practice, and contemporary issues*. Mahwah, NJ: Erlbaum.

Lane, K., Falk, K., & Wehby, J. (2006). Classroom management in special education classrooms and resource rooms. In C. M. Evertson & C. S. Weinstein (Eds.), *Handbook of classroom management: Research, practice, and contemporary issues*. Mahwah, NJ: Erlbaum.

Langan-Fox, J., Waycott, J. L., & Albert, K. (2000). Linear and graphic organizers: Properties and processing. *International Journal of Cognitive Ergonomics*, *4*(1), 19–34.

Language Development and Hypermedia Group. (1992). "Open" software design: A case study. *Educational Technology*, *32*, 43–55.

Lashley, T. J., II, Matczynski, T. J., & Rowley, J. B. (2002). *Instructional models: Strategies for teaching in a diverse society* (2nd ed.). Belmont, CA: Wadsworth/Thomson Learning.

Lave, J. (1988). *Cognition in practice: Mind, mathematics, and culture in everyday life*. New York, NY: Cambridge University Press.

Lave, J. (1997). The culture of acquisition and the practice of understanding. In D. Kirshner & J. A. Whitson (Eds.), *Situated cognition: Social, semiotic, and psychological perspectives* (pp. 17–35). Mahwah, NJ: Erlbaum.

Lave, J., & Wenger, E. (1991). *Situated learning: Legitimate peripheral participation*. Cambridge, MA: Cambridge University Press.

Leaper, C. (2002). Parenting girls and boys. In M. H. Bornstein (Ed.), *Handbook of parenting, Vol. 1: Children and parenting* (2nd ed., pp. 127–152). Mahwah, NJ: Erlbaum.

Lee, A. Y., & Hutchinson, L. (1998). Improving learning from examples through reflection. *Journal of Experimental Psychology: Applied*, *4*, 187–210.

Lee, R. M. (2005). Resilience against discrimination: Ethnic identity and other-group orientation as protective factors for Korean Americans. *Journal of Counseling Psychology*, *52*, 36–44.

Lee, S. J., Wong, N. W., & Alvarez, A. N. (2009). The model minority and the perpetual foreigner: Stereotypes of Asian Americans. In N. Tewari & A. N. Alvarez (Eds.), *Asian American psychology: Current perspectives* (pp. 69-84). New York, NY: Routledge/Taylor & Francis Group.

Leets, L. & Sunwolf. (2005). Adolescent rules for social exclusion: When is it fair to exclude someone else? *Journal of Moral Education*, *34*, 343–362.

Lehman, D. R., & Nisbett, R. E. (1990). A longitudinal study of the effects of undergraduate training on reasoning. *Developmental Psychology*, *26*, 952–960.

Leinhardt, G. (2001). Instructional explanations: A commonplace for teaching and location for contrasts. In V. Richardson (Ed.), *Handbook of research on teaching* (4th ed., pp. 333–357). Washington, DC: American Educational Research Association.

LeMahieu, P., Gitomer, D. H., & Eresh, J. T. (1993). *Portfolios in large-scale assessment: Difficult but not impossible*. Unpublished manuscript, University of Delaware.

Lemelson, R. (2003). Obsessive-compulsive disorder in Bali. *Transcultural Psychiatry*, *40*, 377–408.

Leming, J. S. (1981). Curriculum effectiveness in value/moral education. *Journal of Moral Education*, *10*, 147–164.

Lepper, M. R., & Greene, D. (1978). *The hidden costs of rewards: New perspectives on the psychology of human motivation*. Hillsdale, NJ: Erlbaum.

Lepper, M. R., Keavney, M., & Drake, M. (1996). Intrinsic motivation and extrinsic reward: A commentary on Cameron and Pierce's meta-analysis. *Review of Educational Research*, *66*, 5–32.

Lerner, R. M., Theokas, C., & Bobek, D. L. (2005). Concepts and theories of human development: Historical and contemporary dimensions. In M. H. Bornstein & M. E. Lamb (Eds.), *Developmental science: An advanced textbook* (5th ed., pp. 3–43). Mahwah, NJ: Erlbaum.

Leung, A. K., Maddux, W. W., Galinsky, A. D., & Chiu, C. (2008). Multicultural experience enhances creativity: The when and how. *American Psychologist*, *63*, 169–181.

Leung, K., Lau, S., & Lam, W. (1998). Parenting styles and academic achievement: A cross-cultural study. *Merrill-Palmer*, *44*, 157–167.

Levin, J. R. (1994). Mnemonic strategies and classroom learning: A twenty-year report card. *Elementary School Journal*, *94*, 235–254.

Levin, J. R., & Nolan, J. F. (2000). *Principles of classroom management: A professional decision-making model*. Boston, MA: Allyn & Bacon.

Lewinsohn, P. M., Rohde, P., & Seeley, J. R. (1994). Psychological risk factors for future attempts. *Journal of Consulting and Clinical Psychology*, *62*, 297–305.

Lewis, R. (2001). Classroom discipline and student responsibility: The students' view. *Teaching and Teacher Education*, *17*, 307–319.

Lewis, T. J., Sugai, G., & Colvin, G. (1998). Reducing problem behavior through a school-wide system of effective behavioral support: Investigation of a school-wide social skills training program and contextual interventions. *School Psychology Review*, *27*, 446–459.

Liben, L. S., & Signorella, M. L. (1993). Gender-schematic processing in children: The role of initial interpretations of stimuli. *Developmental Psychology*, *29*, 141–149.

Lindsay, P. H., & Norman, D. A. (1977). *Human information processing: An introduction to psychology* (2nd ed.). New York, NY: Academic Press.

Linebarger, D. L., Kosanic, A. Z., Greenwood, C. R., & Doku, N. S. (2004). Effects of viewing the television program Between the Lions on the emergent literacy skills of young children. *Journal of Educational Psychology*, *96*, 297–308.

Linn, M. C., & Eylon, B. S. (2006). Science education: Integrating views of learning and instruction. In P. A. Alexander & P. H. Winne (Eds.), *Handbook of educational psychology* (2nd ed., pp. 511–544). Mahwah, NJ: Erlbaum.

Linn, M. C., & Hyde, J. S. (1989). Gender, mathematics, and science. *Educational Researcher*, *18*, 17–27.

Linn, R. L., & Miller, M. D. (2005). *Measurement and assessment in teaching* (9th ed.). Upper Saddle River, NJ: Prentice-Hall/ Merrill.

Lipman, P. (1997). Restructuring in context: A case study of teacher participation and the dynamics of ideology, race, and power. *American Educational Research Journal*, *34*, 3–37.

Liu, W. M., Ali, S. R., Soleck, G., Hopps, J., Dunston, K., & Pickett, T., Jr. (2004). Using social class in counseling psychology research. *Journal of Counseling Psychology*, *51*, 3–18.

Lochman, J. E., & Wells, K. C. (2003a). The Coping Power program for preadolescent aggressive boys and their parents: Effects at the one-year follow-up. *Journal of Consulting and Clinical Psychology*, *72*, 571–578.

Lochman, J. E., & Wells, K. C. (2003b). Effectiveness of the Coping Power program and of classroom intervention with aggressive children: Outcomes at a 1-year follow-up. *Behavior Therapy*, *34*, 403–515.

Locke, E. A., & Latham, G. P. (2002). Building a practically useful theory of goal setting and task motivation: A 35-year odyssey. *American Psychologist*, *57*, 705–717.

Loftus, E., & Palmer, J. C. (1974). Reconstruction of automobile destruction: An example of the interaction between language and memory. *Journal of Verbal Learning and Verbal Behavior*, *13*, 585–589.

Lorch, R. F., Lorch, E. P., Ritchey, K., McGovern, L., & Coleman, D. (2001). Effects of headings on text summarization. *Contemporary Educational Psychology*, *26*, 171–191.

Loveless, T. (1998). The tracking and ability grouping debate. *Fordham Report*, *2*(88), 1–27.

Loveless, T. (1999). Will tracking reform promote social equity? *Educational Leadership*, *56*(7), 28–32.

Lovett, M. W., Lacerenza, L., Borden, S. L., Frijters, J. C., Steinbach, K. A., & De Palma, M. (2000). Components of effective remediation for developmental disabilities: Combining phonological and strategy-based instruction to improve outcomes. *Journal of Educational Psychology*, *92*, 263–283.

Lowenstein, G. (1994). The psychology of curiosity: A review and reinterpretation. *Psychological Bulletin*, *117*, 75–98.

Lucyshyn, J. M., Horner, R. H., Dunlap, G., Albin, R. W., & Ben, K. R. (2002). Positive behavior support with families. In J. M. Lucyshyn, G. Dunlap, & R. W. Albin (Eds.), *Families and positive behavior support: Addressing problem behavior in family contexts* (pp. 3–43). Baltimore, MD: Paul H. Brookes.

Luiten, J., Ames, W., & Ackerson, G. (1980). A meta-analysis of the effects of advance organizers on learning and retention. *American Educational Research Journal*, *17*, 211–218.

Lupart, J., & Barva, C. (1998). Promoting female achievement in the sciences: Research and implications. *International Journal for the Advancement of Counselling*, *20*, 319–338.

Lupart, J. L., & Timmons, V. (2003). Preamble. *Exceptionality Education Canada, 13*, 5–7.

Lupart, J. L., & Pyryt, M. C. (1996). "Hidden gifted" students: Underachiever prevalence and profile. *Journal for the Education of the Gifted, 20*(1), 36–53.

Lyon, G. R., Shaywitz, S. E., & Shaywitz, B. A. (2003). A definition of dyslexia. *Annals of Dyslexia, 53*, 1–14.

Maag, J. W., & Kemp, S. E. (2003). Behavioral intent of power and affiliation: Implications for functional analysis. *Remedial and Special Education, 24*, 57–64.

Mabry, L. (1999). Writing to the rubrics: Lingering effects of traditional standardized testing on direct writing assessment. *Phi Delta Kappan, 80*, 673–679.

Maccoby, E. E. (1998). *The two sexes: Growing up apart, coming together.* Cambridge, MA: Belknap/Harvard University Press.

Maccoby, E. E. & Martin, J. A. (1983). Socialization in the context of the family. In E. M. Heatherington (Ed.), *Handbook of Child Psychology: Vol. 4. Socialization, personality, and social development* (pp. 1–101). New York, NY: Wiley.

Mace, F. C., Belfiore, P. J., & Hutchinson, J. M. (2001). Operant theory and research on self-regulation. In B. Zimmerman & D. Schunk (Eds.), *Self-regulated learning and academic achievement: Theoretical perspectives* (2nd ed.). Mahwah, NJ: Erlbaum.

Macionis, J. J. (2003). *Sociology* (9th ed.). Upper Saddle River, NJ: Prentice-Hall.

MacKay, A. W. (1986). The Charter's equality provisions and education: A structural analysis. *Canadian Journal of Education, 11*, 293–312.

Macrae, C. N., Milne, A. B., & Bodenhausen, C. V. (1994). Stereotypes as energy-saving devices: A peek inside the cognitive toolbox. *Journal of Personality and Social Psychology, 66*, 37–47.

Maczewski, M. (2002). Exploring identities through the Internet: Youth Experiences Online. *Child and Youth Care Forum, 31*(2), pp. 111–129.

Madsen, C. H., Becker, W. C., Thomas, D. R., Koser, L., & Plager, E. (1968). An analysis of the reinforcing function of "sit down" commands. In R. K. Parker (Ed.), *Readings in educational psychology*. Boston, MA: Allyn & Bacon.

Madsen, K. (2003). The effect of accuracy of instruction, teacher delivery, and student attentiveness on musicians' evaluation of teacher effectiveness. *Journal of Research in Music Education, 51*, 38–51.

Mager, R. (1975). *Preparing instructional objectives* (2nd ed.). Palo Alto, CA: Fearon.

Magnusson, S. J., & Palincsar, A. S. (1995). The learning environment as a site of science reform. *Theory Into Practice, 34*, 43–50.

Maguire, E. A., Gadian, D.G., Johnsrude, I. S., Good, C. D., Ashburner, J., Frackowiak, R. S., & Frith, C. D. (2000). Navigation-related structural change in the hippocampi of taxi drivers. *Proceedings of the National Academy of Science, USA, 97*(8), 4398–4403.

Maier, N. R. F. (1933). An aspect of human reasoning. *British Journal of Psychology, 24*, 144–155.

Major, B., & Schmader, T. (1998). Coping with stigma through psychological disengagement. In J. Swim & C. Stangor (Eds.), *Stigma: The target's perspective* (pp. 219–241). New York, NY: Academic Press.

Maker, C. J. (1987). Gifted and talented. In V. Richardson-Koehler (Ed.), Educators' handbook: A *research perspective* (pp. 420–455). New York, NY: Longman.

Manning, B. H., & Payne, B. D. (1996). Self-talk for teachers and students: *Metacognitive strategies for personal and classroom use*. Boston, MA: Allyn & Bacon.

Mantzicopolos, P., & Morrison, D. (1992). Kindergarten retention: Academic and behavioral outcomes through the end of second grade. *American Educational Research Journal, 29*, 182–198.

Marchland, G., & Skinner, E. A. (2007). Motivational dynamics of children's academic help-seeking and concealment. *Journal of Educational Psychology, 99*, 65–82.

Marcia, J. E. (1987). The identity status approach to the study of ego identity development. In T. Honess & K. Yardley (Eds.), *Self and identity: Perspectives across the life span* (pp. 161–171). London, England: Routledge & Kegan Paul.

Marcia, J. E. (1991). Identity and self development. In R. Lerner, A. Peterson, & J. Brooks-Gunn (Eds.), *Encyclopedia of adolescence* (Vol. 1). New York, NY: Garland.

Marcia, J. E. (1994). The empirical study of ego identity. In H. Bosma, T. Graafsma, H. Grotebanc, & D. DeLivita (Eds.), *The identity and development*. Newbury Park, CA: Sage.

Marcia, J. E. (1999). Representational thought in ego identity, psychotherapy, and psychosocial development. In I. E. Sigel (Ed.), Development of mental representation: *Theories and applications*. Mahwah, NJ: Erlbaum.

Marcus, N., Cooper, M., & Sweller, J. (1996). Understanding instructions. *Journal of Educational Psychology, 88*, 49–63.

Marinova-Todd, S., Marshall, D., & Snow, C. (2000). Three misconceptions about age and L2 learning. *TESOL Quarterly, 34*(1), 9–34.

Markman, E. M. (1977). Realizing that you don't understand: A preliminary investigation. *Child Development, 48*, 986–992.

Markman, E. M. (1979). Realizing that you don't understand: Elementary school children's awareness of inconsistencies. *Child Development, 50*, 643–655.

Markman, E. M. (1992). Constraints on word learning: Speculations about their nature, origins, and domain specificity. In M. Gunnar & M. Maratsos (Eds.), *Minnesota symposium on child psychology* (Vol. 25, pp. 59–101). Hillsdale, NJ: Erlbaum.

Markstrom-Adams, C. (1992). A consideration of intervening factors in adolescent identity formation. In G. R. Adams, R. Montemayor, & T. Gullotta (Eds.), *Advances in adolescent development: Vol. 4. Adolescent identity formation* (pp. 173–192). Newbury Park, CA: Sage.

Marsh, H. W. (1990). Influences of internal and external frames of reference on the formation of math and English self-concepts. *Journal of Educational Psychology, 82*, 107–116.

Marsh, H. W., & Ayotte, V. (2003). Do multiple dimensions of self-concept become more differentiated with age? The differential distinctiveness hypothesis. *Journal of Educational Psychology, 95*, 687–706.

Marsh, H. W., & Craven, R. (2002). The pivotal role of frames of reference in academic self-concept formation: The Big Fish Little Pond Effect. In F. Pajares & T. Urdan (Eds.), *Adolescence and Education* (Vol. II, pp. 83–123). Greenwich, CT: Information Age.

Marsh, H. W., & Hau, K-T. (2003). Big-Fish-Little-Pond effect on academic self-concept. *American Psychologist, 58*, 364–376.

Marsh, H. W., Trautwein, U., Lüdtke, O., Köller, O., & Baumert, J. (2006). Integration of multidimensional self-concept and core personality constructs: Construct validation and relations to well-being and achievement. *Journal of Personality, 74*, 403–456.

Marsh, H. W., & Yeung, A. S. (1997). Coursework selection: Relation to academic self-concept and achievement. *American Educational Research Journal, 34*, 691–720.

Marshall, H. H. (Ed.). (1992). *Redefining student learning: Roots of educational change*. Norwood, NJ: Ablex.

Marshall, H. H. (1996). Implications of differentiating and understanding constructivist approaches. *Journal of Educational Psychology, 31*, 235–240.

Martin, J. (2006). Social cultural perspectives in educational psychology. In P. A. Alexander & P. H. Winne (Eds.), *Handbook of educational psychology* (2nd ed., pp. 595–614). Mahwah, NJ: Erlbaum.

Martin, J., & Sugarman, J. (1993). *Models of classroom management: Principles, applications and critical perspectives* (2nd ed.). Calgary, AB: Detselig.

Martinez-Pons, M. (2002). A social cognitive view of parental influence on student academic self-regulation. *Theory Into Practice, 61*, 126–131.

Marzano, R. J., & Marzano, J. S. (2003, September). The key to classroom management. *Educational Leadership, 61*(1), 6–13.

Mascolo, M. F., & Fischer, K. W. (2005). Constructivist theories. In B. Hopkins (Ed.), *The Cambridge encyclopedia of child development*. New York, NY: Cambridge University Press.

Maslow, A. H. (1968). *Toward a psychology of being* (2nd ed.). New York, NY: Van Nostrand.

Maslow, A. H. (1970). *Motivation and personality* (2nd ed.). New York, NY: Harper and Row.

Mason, D. A., & Good, T. L. (1993). Effects of two-group and whole-class teaching on regrouped elementary students' mathematics achievement. *American Educational Research Journal, 30*, 328–360.

Mason, L. (2007). Introduction: Bridging the cognitive and sociocultural approaches in research on conceptual change: Is it possible? *Educational Psychologist, 42*, 1–7.

Matlin, M. W., & Foley, H. J. (1997). *Sensation and perception* (4th ed.). Boston, MA: Allyn & Bacon.

Matsumura, L. C., & Crosson, A. (2008). Classroom climate, rigorous instruction and curriculum, and students' interactions in urban middle schools. *The Elementary School Journal, 108*, 293–312.

Matthews, D. (1996). Giftedness at adolescence: Diverse educational options required. *Exceptionality Education Canada, 6*, 25–49.

Mautone, P. D., & Mayer, R. E. (2001). Signaling as a cognitive guide in multimedia learning. *Journal of Educational Psychology*, 93, 377–389.

Mayer, M. J. & Furlong, M. J. (2010). How safe are our schools? *Educational Researcher*, 39, 16–26.

Mayer, R. E. (1983a). Can you repeat that? Qualitative and quantitative effects of repetition and advance organizers on learning from science prose. *Journal of Educational Psychology, 75*, 40–49.

Mayer, R. E. (1983b). *Thinking, problem solving, cognition.* San Francisco, CA: Freeman.

Mayer, R. E. (1984). Twenty-five years of research on advance organizers. *Instructional Science*, 8, 133–169.

Mayer, R. E. (1992). *Thinking, problem solving, cognition* (2nd ed.). New York, NY: Freeman.

Mayer, R. E. (1996). Learners as information processors: Legacies and limitations of educational psychology's second metaphor. *Journal of Educational Psychology, 31*, 151–161.

Mayer, R. E. (1999a). Multimedia aids to problem-solving transfer. *International Journal of Educational Research*, 31, 611–623.

Mayer, R. E. (1999b). *The promise of educational psychology: Learning in the content areas.* Upper Saddle River, NJ: Prentice-Hall.

Mayer, R. E. (2001). *Multimedia learning.* New York, NY: Cambridge University Press.

Mayer, R. E. (2004). Should there be a three-strikes rule against discovery learning? A case for guided methods of instruction. *American Psychologist*, 59, 14–19.

Mayer, R. E. (2005). Cognitive theory of multimedia learning. In R. E. Mayer (Ed.), *The Cambridge handbook of multimedia learning* (pp. 31–48). New York, NY: Cambridge University Press.

Mayer, R. E. (2008). *Learning and instruction* (2nd ed.). Columbus, OH: Merrill/Prentice-Hall.

Mayer, R. E., & Gallini, J. K. (1990). When is an illustration worth ten thousand words? *Journal of Educational Psychology*, 82, 715–726.

Mayer, R. E., & Massa, L. J. (2003). Three facets of visual and verbal learners: Cognitive ability, cognitive style and learning preference. *Journal of Educational Psychology*, 95(4), 833–846.

Mayer, R. E., & Sims, V. K. (1994). For whom is a picture worth a thousand words? Extensions of a dual-coding theory of multimedia learning. *Journal of Educational Psychology*, 86, 389–401.

Mayer, R. E., & Wittrock, M. C. (1996). Problem-solving transfer. In D. Berliner & R. Calfee (Eds.), *Handbook of educational psychology* (pp. 47–62). New York, NY: Macmillan.

Mayer, R. E., & Wittrock, M. C. (2006). Problem solving. In P. A. Alexander & P. H. Winne (Eds.), *Handbook of educational psychology* (2nd ed., pp. 287–303). Mahwah, NJ: Erlbaum.

McCafferty, S. G. (2004). Introduction. *International Journal of Applied Linguistics*, 14(1), 1–6.

McCaslin, M., & Good, T. (1996). The informal curriculum. In D. Berliner & R. Calfee (Eds.), *Handbook of educational psychology* (pp. 622–670). New York, NY: Macmillan.

McCaslin, M., & Good, T. L. (1998). Moving beyond management as sheer compliance: Helping students to develop goal coordination strategies. *Educational Horizons*, 76, 169–176.

McCaslin, M., & Hickey, D. T. (2001). Self-regulated learning and academic achievement: A Vygotskian view. In B. Zimmerman & D. Schunk (Eds.), *Self-regulated learning and academic achievement: Theoretical perspectives* (2nd ed., pp. 227–252). Mahwah, NJ: Erlbaum.

McClelland, D. (1985). *Human motivation.* Glenview, IL: Scott, Foresman.

McCoach, D. B., Kehle, T. J., Bray, M. L., & Siegle, D. (2001). Best practices in the identification of gifted students with learning disabilities. *Psychology in the Schools*, 38, 403–411.

McDonald, J. P. (1993). Three pictures of an exhibition: Warm, cool, and hard. *Phi Delta Kappan*, 6, 480–485.

McGoey, K. E., & DuPaul, G. J. (2000). Token reinforcement and response cost procedures: Reducing disruptive behavior of children with attention-deficit/hyperactivity disorder. *School Psychology Quarterly*, 15, 330–343.

McKenzie, T. L., & Rushall, B. S. (1974). Effects of self-recording on attendance and performance in a competitive swimming training environment. *Journal of Applied Behavior Analysis*, 7, 199–206.

McKown, C. (2005). Applying ecological theory to advance the science and practice of school-based prejudice reduction interventions. *Educational Psychologist, 40*, 177–189.

McLoyd, V. C. (1998). Economic disadvantage and child development. *American Psychologist*, 53, 185–204.

McMillan, J. H. (2004). *Classroom assessment: Principles and practice for effective instruction* (3rd ed.). Boston, MA: Allyn & Bacon.

McNeely, C. A., Nonnemaker, J. M., & Blum, R. W. (2002). Promoting school connectedness: Evidence from the National Longitudinal Study of Adolescent Health. *Journal of School Health*, 72(4), 138–146.

Mears, T. (1998). Saying 'Si' to Spanish. *Boston Globe*, April 12. Mediascope. (1996). *National television violence study: Executive summary 1994–1995*. Studio City, CA: Author.

Media Awareness Network (2005). Young Canadians in a wired world, phase 2: Student survey report. Retrieved from: http://www.media-awareness.ca/english/research/YCWW/phaseII/upload/YCWWII_Student_Survey.pdf

Meece, J. L. (2002). *Child and adolescent development for educators* (2nd ed.). New York, NY: McGraw-Hill.

Meece, J. L., & Daniels, D. H. (2008). *Child and adolescent development for educators* (3rd ed.). New York, NY: McGraw-Hill.

Meichenbaum, D. (1977). *Cognitive behavior modification: An integrative approach.* New York, NY: Plenum.

Meichenbaum, D., Burland, S., Gruson, L., & Cameron, R. (1985). Metacognitive assessment. In S. Yussen (Ed.), *The growth of reflection in children* (pp. 1–30). Orlando, FL: Academic Press.

Meijer, A. M., & Wittenboer, G. L. H. van den. (2004). The joint contribution of sleep, intelligence and motivation to school performance. *Personality and Individual Differences*, 37, 95–106.

Melnick, S. A., & Meister, D. G. (2008). A comparison of beginning and experienced teacher concerns. *Education Research Quarterly*, 31(3), 39–56.

Mercer, N. (2007). Commentary on the reconciliation of cognitive and sociocultural accounts of conceptual change. *Educational Psychologist*, 42, 75–78.

Merrell, K. W., Isava, D. M., Gueldner, B. A., & Ross, S. W. (2008). How effective are school bullying intervention programs? A meta-analysis of intervention research. *School Psychology Quarterly*, 23, 26–42.

Merton, R. K. (1948). The self-fulfilling prophecy. *Antioch Review*, 8, 193–210.

Messick, S. (1975). The standard problem: Meaning and values in measurement and evaluation. *American Psychologist*, 35, 1012–1027.

Metcalfe, J., & Shimamura, A. P. (Eds.). (1994). *Metacognition: Knowledge about knowing.* Cambridge, MA: MIT Press.

Metzler, C. W., Biglan, A., Rusby, J. C., & Sprague, J. R. (2001). Evaluation of a comprehensive behavior management program to improve school-wide positive behavior support. *Education and Treatment of Children*, 24(4), 448–470.

Midgley, C. (2001). A goal theory perspective on the current status of middle level schools. In T. Urdan & F. Pajares (Eds.), *Adolescence and education* (Vol. I, pp. 33–59). Greenwich, CT: Information Age Publishing.

Midgley, C., Kaplan, A., & Middleton, M. (2001). Performance-approach goals: Good for what, for whom, under what circumstances, and at what cost? *Journal of Educational Psychology*, 93, 77–86.

Midgley, C., Kaplan, A., Middleton, M., Maehr, M. L., Urdan, T., Anderman, L. H., Anderman, E., & Roser, R. (1998). The development and validation of scales assessing students' achievement goal orientations. *Contemporary Educational Psychology*, 23, 113–131.

Mifflin, M. (1999, December 13). *Singing the pink blues. Mothers who think.* Retrieved from http://www.salon.com/mwt/feature/1999/12/13/toys/

Miller, D. M., Linn, R. L., & Gronlund, N. E. (2009). *Measurement and assessment in teaching* (10th ed.). Boston, MA: Allyn & Bacon.

Miller, G. A. (1956). The magical number seven, plus or minus two: Some limits on our capacity for processing information. *Psychological Review, 63*, 81–97.

Miller, G. A., Galanter, E., & Pribram, K. H. (1960). *Plans and the structure of behavior.* New York, NY: Holt, Rinehart & Winston.

Miller, N., & Harrington, H. J. (1993). Social categorization and intergroup acceptance: Principles for the development an design of cooperative learning teams. In R. Hertz-Lasarowitz & N. Miller (Eds.), *Interaction in cooperative groups: The theoretical anatomy of group learning* (pp. 203–227). New York, NY: Cambridge University Press.

Miller, P. H. (2002). *Theories of developmental psychology* (4th ed.). New York, NY: Worth.

Miller, S. A. (2005). Tips for getting children's attention. *Early Childhood Today, 19.*

Mills, J. R., & Jackson, N. E. (1990). Predictive significance of early giftedness: The case of precocious reading. *Journal of Educational Psychology, 82,* 410–419.

Milner, H.R. (2003). Teacher reflection and race in cultural contexts: History, meaning, and methods in teaching. *Theory into Practice* 42(3), 173–180.

Milner, H. R. (2006). Classroom management in urban classrooms. In C. M. Evertson & C. S. Weinstein, (Eds.), *Handbook of classroom management: Research, practice, and contemporary issues* (pp. 491–522). Mahwah, NJ: Erlbaum.

Mitchell, M. (1993). Situational interest: Its multifaceted structure in the secondary school mathematics classroom. *Journal of Educational Psychology, 85,* 424–436.

Moll, L. C., Amanti, C., Neff, D., & Gonzales, N. (1992). Funds of knowledge for teaching: Using a qualitative approach to connect homes and classrooms. *Theory into Practice, 31,* 132–141.

Moller, A. C., Deci, E. L., & Ryan, R. M. (2006). Choice and ego-depletion: The moderating role of autonomy. *Personality and Social Psychology Bulletin,* 32(8), 1024–1036.

Monroe, C. R., & Obidah, J. E. (2002, April). *The impact of cultural synchronization on a teacher's perceptions of disruption: A case study of an African American middle school classroom.* Paper presented at the American Educational Research Association, New Orleans, LA.

Monteleone, J. A. (1998). *Child abuse.* St. Louis, MO: G. W. Medical Publisher.

Moore, M. K., & Meltzoff, A. N. (2004). Object permanence after a 24-hr delay and leaving the locale of disappearance: the role of memory, space, and identity. *Developmental Psychology, 40,* 606–620.

Morin, V. A., & Miller, S. P. (1998). Teaching multiplication to middle school students with mental retardation. *Education & Treatment of Children, 21,* 22–36.

Morine-Dershimer, G. (2006). Instructional planning. In J. Cooper (Ed.), *Classroom teaching skills* (7th ed., pp. 20–54). Boston, MA: Houghton-Mifflin.

Morris, P. F. (1990). Metacognition. In M. W. Eysenck, (Ed.), *The Blackwell dictionary of cognitive psychology* (pp. 225–229). Oxford, England: Basil Blackwell.

Morrow, L. M. (1983). Home and school correlates of early interest in literature. *Journal of Educational Research, 76,* 221–230.

Morrow, L. M., & Weinstein, C. (1986). Encouraging voluntary reading: The impact of a literature program on children's use of library centers. *Reading Research Quarterly, 21,* 330–346.

Moshman, D. (1982). Exogenous, endogenous, and dialectical constructivism. *Developmental Review,* 2, 371–384.

Moshman, D. (1997). Pluralist rational constructivism. *Issues in Education: Contributions from Educational Psychology,* 3, 229–234.

Moskowitz, G., & Hayman, M. L. (1976). Successful strategies of inner-city teachers: A year-long study. *Journal of Educational Research, 69,* 283–289.

Moss, P. A. (1992). Shifting conceptions of validity in educational measurement: Implications for performance assessment. *Review of Educational Research, 62,* 229–258.

Mueller, C. M., & Dweck, C. S. (1998). Praise for intelligence can undermine children's motivation and performance. *Journal of Personality and Social Psychology, 75,* 33–52.

Mullis, I. V. S., Martin, M. O., Gonzalez, E., & Kennedy, A. M. (2003). *PIRLS 2001 International report: IEA's study of reading literacy achievement in primary schools.* Chestnut Hill, MA: Boston College. Retrieved from http://timss.bc.edu/pirls2001i/PIRLS2001_Pubs_IR.html

Mumford, M. D., Costanza, D. P., Baughman, W. A., Threlfall, V., & Fleishman, E. A. (1994). Influence of abilities on performance during practice: Effects of massed and distributed practice. *Journal of Educational Psychology, 86,* 134–144.

Murdock, S. G., O'Neill, R. E., & Cunningham, E. (2005). A comparison of results and acceptability of functional behavioral assessment procedures with a group of middle school students with emotional/behavioral disorders (E/BD). *Journal of Behavioral Education, 14,* 5–18.

Murdock, T. A., & Anderman, E. M. (2006). Motivational perspectives on student cheating: Toward an integrated model of academic dishonesty. *Educational Psychologist,* 42, 129–145.

Murdock, T. B., Hale, N. M., & Weber, M. J. (2001). Predictors of cheating among early adolescents: Academic and social motivations. *Contemporary Educational Psychology, 26,* 96–115.

Murdock, T. B., & Miller, A. (2003). Teachers as sources of middle school students' motivational identity: Variable-centered and person-centered analytic approaches. *Elementary School Journal, 103,* 383–399.

Murphy, P. K., & Alexander, P. A. (2000). A motivated exploration of motivation terminology. *Contemporary Educational Psychology,* 25, 3–53.

Mussen, P., Conger, J. J., & Kagan, J. (1984). *Child development and personality* (6th ed.). New York, NY: Harper & Row.

Muter, V., Hulme, C., Snowling, M. J., & Stevenson, J. (2004). Phonemes, rimes, vocabulary, and grammatical skills as foundation of early reading development: Evidence from a longitudinal study. *Developmental Psychology, 40,* 665–681.

Myers, D. G. (2005). *Exploring psychology* (6th ed. in modules). New York, NY: Worth.

Myers, I. B., & McCaulley, M. H. (1988). *Manual: A guide to the development and use of the Myers-Briggs Type Indicator.* Palo Alto, CA: Consulting Psychologists.

Nakamura, J., & Csikszentmihalyi, M. (2001). Catalytic creativity: The case of Linus Pauling. *American Psychologist, 56,* 337–341.

Nathan, M. J., & Knuth, E. J. (2003). A study of whole class mathematical discourse and teacher change. *Cognition and Instruction, 21,* 175–207.

National Association for the Education of Young Children. (2006). *The value of recess and outdoor play.* Retrieved from http://www.naeyc.org/ece/1998/08.asp

National Cancer Institute (NCI). (2008). Childhood cancers. Retrieved from http://www.cancer.gov/cancertopics/factsheet/Sites-Types/childhood

National Commission on Teaching and America's Future. (2003). *No dream denied: A pledge to America's children.* Washington, DC: Author.

National Science Foundation. (1996, December 31). *Women and underrepresented minority scientists and engineers have lower levels of employment in business and industry, 1996* (14). Available from http://www.nsf.gov/sbe/srs/databrf/sdb96331.htm

National Service Learning Clearinghouse. (n.d.). *Service learning is. . . .* Retrieved from http://www.servicelearning.org/welcome_to_service-learning/service-learning_is/index.php

Navarro, R. L., Flores, L. Y., & Worthington, R. L. (2007). Mexican American middle school students' goal intentions in mathematics and science: A test of social cognitive career theory. *Journal of Counseling Psychology, 54,* 320–335.

Naveh-Benjamin, M. (1991). A comparison of training programs intended for different types of test-anxious students: Further support for an information-processing model. *Journal of Educational Psychology,* 83, 134–139.

Naveh-Benjamin, M., McKeachie, W. J., & Lin, Y. (1987). Two types of test-anxious students: Support for an information processing model. *Journal of Educational Psychology,* 79, 131–136.

Needles, M., & Knapp, M. (1994). Teaching writing to children who are undeserved. *Journal of Educational Psychology, 86,* 339–349.

Neisser, U. (1976). *Cognition and reality.* San Francisco, CA: Freeman.

Neisser, U., Boodoo, G., Bouchard, A., Boykin, W., Brody, N., Ceci, S. J., . . . Urbina, S. (1996). Intelligence: Knowns and unknowns. *American Psychologist, 51,* 77–101.

Nelson, C.A. (2001). The development and neural bases of face recognition. *Infant and Child Development, 10,* 3–18.

Nelson, J. R., & Roberts, M. L. (2000). Ongoing reciprocal teacher-student interactions involving disruptive behaviors in general education classrooms. *Journal of Emotional and Behavioral Disorders, 4,* 147–161.

Nelson, K. (2004). Evolution and the development of human memory systems. In B. J. Ellis & D. Bjorklund (Eds.), *Origins of the social mind: Evolutionary psychology and child development* (pp. 354–382). New York, NY: Guilford.

Nelson, K., & Fivush, R. (2004). The emergence of autobiographical memory: A social cultural developmental theory. *Psychological Review, 111,* 486–511.

Nelson, T. O. (1996). Consciousness and metacognition. *American Psychologist, 51,* 102–116.

Nesbit, J. C., & Adesope, O. O. (2006). Learning with concept and knowledge maps: A meta-analysis. *Review of Educational Research, 76,* 413–448.

Nesbit, J. C., & Hadwin, A. F. (2006). Methodological issues in educational psychology. In P. A Alexander & P. H. Winne (Eds.), *Handbook of educational psychology* (2nd ed., pp. 825–847). Mahwah, NJ: Erlbaum.

Neuman, S. B., & Roskos, K. A. (1997). Literacy knowledge in practice: Contexts of participation for young writers and readers. *Reading Research Quarterly, 32*, 10–32.

Neumeister, K. L. S., & Cramond, B. (2004). E. Paul Torrance (1915–2003). American *Psychologist, 59*, 179.

Neville, H. (2007, March). *Experience shapes human brain development and function*. Paper presented at the biennial meeting of the Society for Research in Child Development, Boston, MA.

Newcombe, N., & Baenninger, M. (1990). The role of expectations in spatial test performance: A meta-analysis. *Sex Roles, 16*, 25–37.

NICHD Early Child Care Research Network. (2005a). *Child care and child development*. New York, NY: Guilford Press.

NICHD Early Child Care Research Network. (2005b). Pathways to reading: The role of oral language in the transition to reading. *Developmental Psychology, 41*(2), 428–442.

Nicholls, J., Cobb, P., Wood, T., Yackel, E., & Patashnick, M. (1990). Assessing student's theories of success in mathematics: Individual and classroom differences. *Journal for Research in Mathematics Education, 21*, 109–122.

Nicholls, J. G., & Miller, A. (1984). Conceptions of ability and achievement motivation. In R. Ames & C. Ames (Eds.), *Research on motivation in education: Vol. 1.Student Motivation* (pp. 39–73). New York, NY: Academic Press.

Nieto, S. (2004). *Affirming diversity: The sociopolitical context of multicultural education* (4th ed.). Boston, MA: Allyn & Bacon.

Nieto, S., & Bode, P. (2008). *Affirming diversity: The sociopolitical context of multicultural education* (5th ed.). Boston, MA: Allyn & Bacon.

Nissani, M., & Hoefler-Nissani, D. M. (1992). Experimental studies of belief dependence of observations and of resistance to conceptual change. *Cognition and Instruction, 9*, 97–111.

Noddings, N. (1990). Constructivism in mathematics education. In R. Davis, C. Maher, & N. Noddings (Eds.), *Constructivist views on the teaching and learning of mathematics* (pp. 7–18). Monograph 4 of the National Council of Teachers of Mathematics, Reston, VA.

Noddings, N. (1992). *The challenge to care in schools: An alternative approach to education*. New York, NY: Teachers College Press.

Noddings, N. (1995). Teaching themes of care. *Phi Delta Kappan, 76*, 675–679.

Noguera, P. (2005). The racial achievement gap: How can we assume an equity of outcomes. In L. Johnson, M. E. Finn, & R. Lewis (Eds.), *Urban education with an attitude*. Albany, NY: SUNY Press.

Nokes, J. D., Dole, J. A., & Hacker, D. J. (2007). Teaching high school students to use heuristics while reading historical texts. *Journal of Educational Psychology, 99*, 492–504.

Norbert, F. (2005). Research findings on early first language attrition: Implications for the discussion of critical periods in language acquisition. *Language Learning, 55*(3), 491–531.

Nucci, L. P. (2001). Education in the moral domain. New York, NY: Cambridge Press.

Nungester, R. J., & Duchastel, P. C. (1982). Testing versus review: Effects on retention. *Journal of Educational Psychology, 74*, 18–22.

Nurmi, J. (2004). Socialization and self-development: Channeling, selection, adjustment, and reflection. In R. Lerner & L. Steinberg (Eds.), *Handbook of adolescent psychology*. New York, NY: Wiley.

Nylund, D. (2000). *Treating Huckleberry Finn: A new narrative approach to working with kids diagnosed ADD/ADHD*. San Francisco, CA: Jossey-Bass.

O'Boyle, M. W., & Gill, H. S. (1998). On the relevance of research findings in cognitive neuroscience to educational practice. *Educational Psychology Review, 10*, 397–410.

O'Donnell, A. M. (Ed.). (2002, Winter). Promoting thinking through peer learning [Special issue]. *Theory Into Practice, 61*(1).

O'Donnell, A. M. (2006). The role of peers and group learning. In P. A. Alexander & P. H. Winne (Eds.), *Handbook of educational psychology* (2nd ed., pp. 781–802). Mahwah, NJ: Erlbaum.

O'Donnell, A. M., & O'Kelly, J. (1994). Learning from peers: Beyond the rhetoric of positive results. *Educational Psychology Review, 6*, 321–350.

O'Leary, K. D., & O'Leary, S. (Eds.). (1977). *Classroom management: The successful use of behavior modification* (2nd ed.). Elmsford, NY: Pergamon.

O'Leary, S. (1995). Parental discipline mistakes. *Current Directions in Psychological Science, 4*, 11–13.

O'Mara, A. J., Marsh, H. W., Craven, R. G., & Debus, R. L. (2006). Do self-concept interventions make a difference? A synergistic blend of construct validation and meta-analysis. *Educational Psychologist, 41*, 181–206.

Oakes, J. (1990a). Opportunities, achievement, and choice: Women and minority students in science and math. *Review of Research in Education, 16*, 153–222.

Oakes, J. (1990b). *Multiplying inequities: The effects of race, social class, and tracking on opportunities to learn mathematics and science*. Santa Monica, CA: Rand.

Oakes, J. (1999). Promotion or retention: Which one is social? *Harvard Education Letter, 15*(1), 8.

Oakes, J., & Wells, A. S. (2002). Detracking for high student achievement. In L. Abbeduto (Ed.), *Taking sides: Clashing views and controversial issues in educational psychology* (2nd ed., pp. 26–30). Guilford, CT: McGraw-Hill Duskin.

Ogbu, J. U. (1987). Variability in minority school performance: A problem in search of an explanation. *Anthropology and Education Quarterly, 18*, 312–334.

Ogbu, J. U. (1997). Understanding the school performance of urban blacks: Some essential background knowledge. In H. Walberg, O. Reyes, & R. P. Weissberg (Eds.), *Children and youth: Interdisciplinary perspectives* (pp. 190–240). Norwood, NJ: Ablex.

Ogden, J. E., Brophy, J. E., & Evertson, C. M. (1977, April). *An experimental investigation of organization and management techniques in first-grade reading groups*. Paper presented at the annual meeting of the American Educational Research Association, New York, NY.

Okagaki, L. (2001). Triarchic model of minority children's school achievement. *Educational Psychologist, 36*, 9–20.

Okagaki, L. (2006). Ethnicity, learning. In P. Alexander & P. Winne (Eds.), *Handbook of educational psychology* (2nd ed., pp. 615–634). Mahwah, NJ: Erlbaum.

Ollendick, T. H., Dailey, D., & Shapiro, E. S. (1983). Vicarious reinforcement: Expected and unexpected effects. *Journal of Applied Behavior Analysis, 16*, 485–491.

Olsen, L. (1988). *Crossing the schoolhouse border: Immigrant students and the California public schools*. San Francisco, CA: California Tomorrow.

Olson, D. R. (2004). The triumph of hope over experience in the search for "what works": *A response to Slavin. Educational Researcher, 33*(1), 24–26.

Olson, K. (2008). The wounded student. *Educational Leadership, 65*(6), 46-48.

Omi, M., & Winant, H. (1994). *Racial formation in the United States: From the 1960s to the 1990s* (2nd ed.). New York, NY: Routledge.

Ontario Ministry of Education (2006). *Language: The Ontario curriculum, grades 1–8*. Retrieved from http://www.edu.gov.on.ca/eng/curriculum/elementary/language18currb.pdf

Oosterhof, A. (2009). *Developing and using classroom assessments* (4th ed.). Columbus, OH: Pearson/Merrill.

Orange, C. (2000). *25 biggest mistakes teachers make and how to avoid them*. Thousand Oaks, CA: Corwin.

Orange, C. (2005). *44 smart strategies for avoiding classroom mistakes*. Thousand Oaks, CA: Corwin Press.

Orlando L., & Machado, A. (1996). In defense of Piaget's theory: A reply to 10 common criticisms. *Psychological Review, 103*, 143–164.

Ormrod, J. E. (2004). *Human learning* (4th ed.). Columbus, OH: Merrill/Prentice-Hall.

Ortony, A., Clore, G. L., & Collins, A. (1988). *The cognitive structure of emotions*. Cambridge, MA: Cambridge University Press.

Osborn, A. F. (1963). *Applied imagination* (3rd ed.). New York, NY: Scribner's.

Osborne, J. W. (2001). Testing stereotype threat: Does anxiety explain race and sex differences in achievement? *Contemporary Educational Psychology, 26*, 291–310.

Osher, D., Bear, G. G., Sprague, J. R., & Doyle, W. (2010). How can we improve school discipline? *Educational Researcher*, 39(1), 48–58.

Osterman, K. F. (2000). Students' need for belonging in the school community. *Review of Educational Research, 70*, 323–367.

Overton, W. F. (2006). Developmental psychology: Philosophy, concepts, and methodology. In R. M. Lerner (Ed.), *Handbook of child psychology: Vol. 1: Theoretical models of human development* (6th ed., pp. 18–88). New York, NY: Wiley.

Owens, R. (1999). *Language disorders: A functional approach to assessment and intervention* (3rd ed.). Boston, MA: Allyn & Bacon.

Owens, R. E. J. (2005). *Language development: An introduction* (6th ed.). Boston, MA: Allyn & Bacon.

Padilla, F. M. (1992). *The gang as an American enterprise*. New Brunswick, NJ: Rutgers University Press.

Pai, Y., & Adler, S. A. (2001). *Cultural foundations of education* (3rd ed.). Upper Saddle River, NJ: Merrill.

Paivio, A. (1986). *Mental representations: A dual-coding approach*. New York, NY: Oxford University Press.

Pajares, F. (1997). Current directions in self-efficacy research. In M. L. Maehr & P. R. Pintrich (Eds.), *Advances in motivation and achievement* (Vol. 10, pp. 1–49). Greenwich, CT: JAI Press.

Pajares, F. (2000, April). *Seeking a culturally attentive educational psychology*. Paper presented at the annual meeting of the American Educational Research Association, New Orleans, LA. Retrieved from http://www.emory.edu/EDUCATION/mfp/AERA2000Discussant.html

Pajares, F. (2002). *Self-efficacy beliefs in academic contexts: An outline*. Retrieved from http://des.emory.edu/mfp/efftalk.html

Pajares, F. (2003). William James: Our father who begot us. In B. J. Zimmerman & D. H. Schunk (Eds.), *Educational psychology: A century of contributions* (pp. 41–64). Mahwah, NJ: Erlbaum.

Pajares, F., & Schunk, D. H. (2001). Self-beliefs and school success: Self-efficacy, self-concept, and school achievement. In R. Riding & S. Rayner (Eds.), *Perception* (pp. 239–266). Westport, CT: Ablex Publishing.

Pajares, F., & Schunk, D. H. (2002). Self and self-belief in psychology and education: An historical perspective. In J. Aronson & D. Cordova (Eds.), *Psychology of education: Personal and interpersonal forces* (pp. 1–19). New York, NY: Academic Press.

Palincsar, A. S. (1986). The role of dialogue in providing scaffolded instruction. *Educational Psychologist, 26*, 73–98.

Palincsar, A. S. (1996). Language-minority students: Instructional issues in school cultures and classroom social systems. *Elementary School Journal, 96*, 221–226.

Palincsar, A. S. (1998). Social constructivist perspectives on teaching and learning. In J. T. Spence, J. M. Darley, & D. J. Foss (Eds.), *Annual Review of Psychology* (pp. 345–375). Palo Alto, CA: Annual Reviews.

Palincsar, A. S., & Brown, A. L. (1984). Reciprocal teaching of comprehension-fostering and monitoring activities. *Cognition and Instruction, 1*, 117–175.

Palincsar, A. S., & Brown, A. L. (1989). Classroom dialogues to promote self-regulated comprehension. In J. Brophy (Ed.), *Advances in research on teaching* (Vol. 1, pp. 35–67). Greenwich, CT: JAI Press.

Palincsar, A. S., & Herrenkohl, L. R. (2002). Designing collaborative learning contexts. *Theory Into Practice, 61*, 26–32.

Palincsar, A. S., Magnuson, S. J., Marano, N., Ford, D., & Brown, N. (1998). Designing a community of practice: Principles and practices of the GIsML community. *Teaching and Teacher Education, 14*, 5–19.

Panitz, T. (1996). *A definition of collaborative vs cooperative learning*. Retrieved from http://www.city.londonmet.ac.uk/deliberations/collab.learning/panitz2.html

Papert, S. (1980). *Mindstorms; Children, computers, and powerful ideas*. New York, NY: Basic Books.

Paris, S. G. & Ayres, L. R. (1994). *Becoming reflective students and teachers: With portfolios and authentic assessment*. Washington, DC: American Psychological Association.

Paris, S. G., Byrnes, J. P., & Paris, A. H. (2001). Constructing theories, identities, and actions of self-regulated learners. In B. J. Zimmerman & D. H. Schunk (Eds.), *Self-regulated learning and academic achievement: Theoretical perspectives* (2nd ed., pp. 253–287). Mahwah, NJ: Erlbaum.

Paris, S. G., & Cunningham, A. E. (1996). Children becoming students. In D. Berliner & R. Calfee, (Eds.), *Handbook of educational psychology* (pp. 117–146). New York, NY: Macmillan.

Paris, S. G., Lipson, M. Y., & Wixson, K. K. (1983). Becoming a strategic reader. *Contemporary Educational Psychology, 8*, 293–316.

Paris, S. G., Morrison, F. J., & Miller, K. F. (2006). Academic pathways from preschool through elementary school. In P. A. Alexander & P. H. Winne (Eds.), *Handbook of educational psychology* (2nd ed., pp. 61–85). Mahwah, NJ: Erlbaum.

Parke, R. D. & Buriel, R. (2006). Socialization in the family: Ethnic and ecological perspectives. In W. Damon & N. Eisenberg (Eds.), *Handbook of child psychology: Vol. 3. Social, emotional, and personality development* (6th ed., pp. 429–504). New York, NY: Wiley.

Parker, W. C., & Hess, D. (2001). Teaching with and for discussion. *Teaching and Teacher Education, 17*, 273–289.

Parks, C. P. (1995). Gang behavior in the schools: Myth or reality? *Educational Psychology Review, 7*, 41–68.

Pate, P. E., McGinnis, K., & Homestead, E. (1995). Creating coherence through curriculum integration. In M. Harmin (1994), *Inspiring active learning: A handbook for teachers* (pp. 62–70). Alexandria, VA: Association for Supervision and Curriculum Development.

Patterson, C. (1995). *Lesbian and gay parents and their children: Summary of research findings*. Retrieved from http://www.apa.org/pi/parent.html

Paulman, R. G., & Kennelly, K. J. (1984). Test anxiety and ineffective test taking: Different names, same construct? *Journal of Educational Psychology, 76*, 279–288.

Pea, R. D., & Maldonado, H. (2006). WILD for learning: Interacting through new computing devices anywhere, anytime. In R. K. Sawyer (Ed.), *The Cambridge handbook of the learning sciences* (pp. 427–441). New York, NY: Cambridge University Press.

Pearl, R., Leung, M. C., Acker, R. V., Farmer, T. W., & Rodkin, P. C. (2007). Fourth- and fifth-grade teachers' awareness of their classrooms' social networks. *The Elementary School Journal, 108*, 25–39.

Pearson, B. Z., Fernandez, S. C., Lewedeg, V., & Oller, D. K. (1997). The relation of input factors to lexical learning by bilingual infants. *Applied Linguistics, 18*, 41–58.

Pekrun, R., Elliot, A. J., & Maier, M. A. (2006). Achievement goals and discrete achievement emotions: A theoretical model and prospective test. *Journal of Educational Psychology, 98*, 583–597.

Pekrun, R., Goetz, T., Titz, W., & Perry, R. P. (2002). Academic emotions in students' self-regulated learning and achievement. A program of qualitative and quantitative research. *Educational Psychologist, 37*, 91–105.

Pelham, W. E. (1981). Attention deficits in hyperactive and learning-disabled children. *Exceptional Education Quarterly, 2*, 13–23.

Pellegrini, A. D., & Bohn, C. M. (2005). The role of recess in children's cognitive performance and school adjustment. *Educational Researcher, 34*, 13–19.

Pellegrini, A. D., Dupuis, D., & Smith, P. K. (2007). Play in evolution and development. *Developmental Review, 27*, 261–276.

Pellis, S. (2006). The effects of orbital frontal cortex damage on the modulation of defensive responses by rats in playful and nonplayful social contexts. *Behavioral Neuroscience, 120*, 72–84.

Peng, S., & Lee, R. (1992, April). *Home variables, parent–child activities, and academic achievement: A study of 1988 eighth graders*. Paper presented at the annual meeting of the American Educational Research Association, San Francisco, CA.

Penuel, W. R., & Wertsch, J. V. (1995). Vygotsky and identity formation: A sociocultural approach. *Educational Psychologist, 30*, 83–92.

Pepler, D., Craig, W., Jiang, D., & Connolly, J. (2008). Developmental trajectories of bullying and associated factors. *Child Development, 79*, 325–338.

Perkins, D. N., Jay, E., & Tishman, S. (1993). New conceptions of thinking: From ontology to education. *Educational Psychologist, 28*, 67–85.

Perkins, D. N., & Salomon, G. (1989). Are cognitive skills context-bound? *Educational Researcher, 18*, 16–25.

Perner, J. (2000). Memory and theory of mind. In E. Tulving & F. I. M. Craik (Eds.), *The Oxford handbook of memory* (pp. 297–312). New York, NY: Oxford.

Perry, N. E. (1998). Young children's self-regulated learning and contexts that support it. *Journal of Educational Psychology, 90*, 715–729.

Perry, N. E., & Drummond, L. (2002). Helping young students become self-regulated researchers and writers. *The Reading Teacher, 56*, 298–310.

Perry, N. E., McNamara, J. K., & Mercer, K. L. (2001). Principles, policies, and practices in special education in British Columbia. *Exceptionality Education Canada, 11*, 63–89.

Perry, N., Mirenda, P., and Siegel, L. (2007, October). Beyond placement: Supporting effective inclusion education. *Educational Leadership Centre at UBC, 1*, 6–9, 12.

Perry, N. E., Phillips, L., & Dowler, J. (2004). Examining features of tasks and their potential to promote self-regulated learning. Teachers College Record, 106, 1854–1878.

Perry, N. E., VandeKamp, K. O., & Mercer, L. K. (2000, April). *Investigating teacher-student interactions that foster self-regulated learning*. In N. E. Perry (Chair), Symposium conducted at the meeting of the American Educational Research Association, New Orleans, LA.

Perry, N. E., VandeKamp, K. O., Mercer, L. K., & Nordby, C. J. (2002). Investigating teacher-student interactions that foster self-regulated learning. *Educational Psychologist, 37*, 5–15.

Peterson, P. L. (1992). Revising their thinking: Keisha Coleman and her third-grade mathematics class. In H. Marshall (Ed.), *Redefining student learning: Roots of educational change* (pp. 151–176). Norwood, NJ: Ablex.

Petitto, L. A., & Kovelman, I. (2003). The bilingual paradox: How signing-speaking bilingual children help us resolve bilingual issues and teach us about the brain's mechanisms underlying all language acquisition. *Language Learning, 8*(3), 5–18.

Peverly, S. T., Ramaswamy, V., Garner, J., Brown, Sumowowski, J., & Alidoost, M. (2007). What predicts skill in lecture note taking? *Journal of Educational Psychology, 99*, 167–180.

Petrill, S. A., & Wilkerson, B. (2000). Intelligence and achievement: A behavioral genetic perspective. *Educational Psychology Review, 12*, 185–199.

Pettigrew, T. (1998). Intergroup contact theory. In J. T. Spence, J. M. Darley, & D. J. Foss (Eds.), *Annual review of psychology* (pp. 65–85). Palo Alto, CA: Annual Reviews.

Peverly, S., Brobst, K., Graham, M., & Shaw, R. (2003). College adults are not good at self-regulation: A study on the relationship of self-regulation, note-taking, and test-taking. *Journal of Educational Psychology, 95*, 335–346.

Pfiffner, L. J., & O'Leary, S. G. (1987). The efficacy of all positive management as a function of the prior use of negative consequences. *Journal of Applied Behavior Analysis, 20*, 265–271.

Phillips, D. (1997). How, why, what, when, and where: Perspectives on constructivism and education. *Issues in Education: Contributions from Educational Psychology, 3*, 151–194.

Phinney, J. (2003). Ethnic identity and acculturation. In K. Chun, P. Ball, & Marin, G. (Eds.), *Acculturation: Advances in theory, measurement, and applied research* (pp. 63–81). Washington, DC: American Psychological Association.

Phinney, J. S. (1990). Ethnic identity in adolescents and adults: Review of research. *Psychological Bulletin, 108*(3), 499–514.

Phinney, J. S., & Devich-Navarro, M. (1997). Variations in bicultural identification among African American and Mexican American adolescents. *Journal of Research on Adolescence, 7*, 3–32.

Phye, G. D. (1992). Strategic transfer: A tool for academic problem solving. *Educational Psychology Review, 4*, 393–421.

Phye, G. D. (2001). Problem-solving instruction and problem-solving transfer: The correspondence issue. *Journal of Educational Psychology, 93*, 571–578.

Phye, G. D., & Sanders, C. E. (1994). Advice and feedback: Elements of practice for problem solving. *Contemporary Educational Psychology, 17*, 211–223.

Piaget, J. (1954). *The construction of reality in the child* (M. Cook, Trans.). New York, NY: Basic Books.

Piaget, J. (1962). *Comments on Vygotsky's critical remarks concerning "The language and thought of the child" and "Judgment and reasoning in the child."* Cambridge, MA: MIT Press.

Piaget, J. (1963). *Origins of intelligence in children.* New York, NY: Norton.

Piaget, J. (1964). Development and learning. In R. Ripple & V. Rockcastle (Eds.), *Piaget rediscovered* (pp. 7–20). Ithaca, NY: Cornell University Press.

Piaget, J. (1965). *The moral judgment of the child.* New York, NY: Free Press.

Piaget, J. (1965/1995). *Sociological studies.* New York, NY: Routledge. (Original work published in 1965.)

Piaget, J. (1969). *Science of education and the psychology of the child.* New York, NY: Viking.

Piaget, J. (1970a). Piaget's theory. In P. Mussen (Ed.), *Handbook of child psychology* (3rd ed., Vol. 1, pp. 703–732). New York, NY: Wiley.

Piaget, J. (1970b). *The science of education and the psychology of the child.* New York, NY: Orion Press.

Piaget, J. (1971). *Biology and knowledge.* Edinburgh, Scotland: Edinburgh Press.

Piaget, J. (1974). *Understanding causality* (D. Miles and M. Miles, Trans.). New York, NY: Norton.

Piaget, J. (1985). *The equilibrium of cognitive structures: The central problem of intellectual development* (T. Brown & K. L. Thampy, Trans.). Chicago, IL: University of Chicago Press.

Pianta, R. C., Belsky, J., Vandergrift, N., Houts, R., & Morrison, F. J. (2008). Classroom effects on children's achievement trajectories in elementary school. *American Educational Research Journal, 45*, 365–397.

Pierson, L. H., & Connell, J. P. (1992). Effect of grade retention on self-system processes, school engagement, and academic performance. *Journal of Educational Psychology, 84*, 300–307.

Pigge, F. L., & Marso, R. N. (1997). A seven-year longitudinal multi-factor assessment of teaching concerns development through preparation and early teaching. *Teaching and Teacher Education, 13*, 225–235.

Pinker, S. (2002). *The blank slate: The modern denial of human nature.* New York, NY: Penguin.

Pintrich, P. R. (2000). Educational psychology at the millennium: A look back and a look forward. *Educational Psychologist, 35*, 221–226.

Pintrich, P. R. (2003). A motivational science perspective on the role of student motivation in learning and teaching. *Journal of Educational Psychology, 95*, 667–686.

Pintrich, R. R., & De Groot, E. V. (1990). Motivational and self-regulated learning components of classroom academic performance. *Journal of Educational Psychology, 82*, 33–40.

Pintrich, P. R., Marx, R. W., & Boyle, R. A. (1993). Beyond cold conceptual change: The role of motivational beliefs and classroom contextual factors in the process of conceptual change. *Review of Educational Research, 63*, 167–199.

Pintrich, P. R., & Schrauben, B. (1992). Students' motivational beliefs and their cognitive engagement in academic tasks. In D. Schunk & J. Meece (Eds.), *Students' perceptions in the classroom: Causes and consequences* (pp. 149–183). Hillsdale, NJ: Erlbaum.

Pintrich, R. R., & Sinatra, G. M. (2003). Future direction for theory and research on intentional conceptual change. In G. M. Sinatra & P. R. Pintrich (Eds.), *Intentional conceptual change* (pp. 429–441). Mahwah, NJ: Erlbaum.

Pintrich, P. R., & Zusho, A. (2002). The development of academic self-regulation: The role of cognitive and motivational factors. In A. Wigfield & J. Eccles (Eds.), *Development of achievement motivation* (pp. 249–284). San Diego, CA: Academic Press.

Pisha, B., & Coyne, P. (2001). Smart for the start: The promise of universal design for learning. *Remedial and Special Education, 22*, 197–203.

Pitts, J. M. (1992). Constructivism: Learning rethought. In J. B. Smith & J. C. Coleman, Jr. (Eds.), *School Library Media Annual* (Vol. 10, pp. 14–25). Englewood, CO: Libraries Unlimited.

Plucker, J. A., Beghetto, R. A., & Dow, G. T. (2004). Why isn't creativity more important to educational psychologists? Potential pitfalls and future directions in creativity research. *Educational Psychology, 39*(2), 83–96.

Polk, J. A. (2006). Traits of effective teachers. *Arts Education Policy Review, 107*(4), 23–29.

Polson, P. G., & Jeffries, R. (1985). Instruction in general problem-solving skills: An analysis of four approaches. In J. Segal, S. Chipman, & R. Glaser (Eds.), *Thinking and learning skills* (Vol. 1, pp. 417–455). Mahwah, NJ: Erlbaum.

Popham, W. J. (2005a). *Classroom assessment : What teachers need to know* (4th ed.). Boston, MA: Allyn & Bacon.

Popham, W. J. (2005b). Instructional quality: Collecting credible evidence. *Educational Leadership, 62*(6), 80–81.

Popham, W. J. (2008). *Classroom assessment: What teachers need to know* (5th ed.). Boston, MA: Allyn & Bacon.

Porath, M. (1996). Narrative performance in verbally gifted children. *Journal for the Education of the Gifted, 19*, 276–292.

Porath, M. (2001). Young girls' social understanding: Emergent interpersonal expertise. *High Ability Studies, 12*, 113–126.

Porath, M. (2003). Social understanding in the first years of school. *Early Childhood Research Quarterly, 18*(4), 468–484.

Posada, G., Jacobs, A., Richmond, M., Carbonell, O. A., Alzate, G., Bustamante, M. R., & Quiceno, J. (2002). Maternal care giving and infant security in two cultures. *Developmental Psychology, 38*, 67–78.

Posner, M. I. (1973). Cognition: An introduction. Glenview, IL: Scott, Foresman.

Prawat, R. S. (1991). The value of ideas: The immersion approach to the development of thinking. *Educational Researcher, 20*, 3–10.

Prawat, R. S. (1992). Teachers beliefs about teaching and learning: A constructivist perspective. *American Journal of Education, 100*, 354–395.

Prawat, R. S. (1996). Constructivism, modern and postmodern. *Issues in Education: Contributions from Educational Psychology, 3*, 215–226.

Premack, D. (1965). Reinforcement theory. In D. Levine (Ed.), *Nebraska symposium on motivation* (Vol. 13, pp. 123–180). Lincoln, NE: University of Nebraska Press.

Pressley, M. (1995). More about the development of self-regulation: complex, long-term, and thoroughly social. *Educational Psychologist, 30,* 207–212.

Pressley, M. (1996, August). *Getting beyond whole language: Elementary reading instruction that makes sense in light of recent psychological research.* Paper presented at the annual meeting of the American Psychological Association, Toronto, ON.

Pressley, M., Allington, R. L., Wharton-McDonald, R., Collins, C. B., & Morrow, L. M. (2001). *Learning to read: Lessons from exemplary first-grade classrooms.* New York, NY: Guilford Press.

Pressley, M., Barkowski, J. G., & Schneider, W. (1987). Cognitive strategies: Good strategy users coordinate metacognition and knowledge. In R. Vasta & G. Whitehurst (Eds.), *Annals of Child Development* (Vol. 5, pp. 89–129). Greenwich, CT: JAI Press.

Pressley, M., & Harris, K. A. (2006). Cognitive strategies instruction: From basic research to classroom instruction. In P. A. Alexander & P. H. Winne (Eds.), *Handbook of educational psychology* (2nd ed., pp. 265–286). Mahwah, NJ: Erlbaum.

Pressley, M., Levin, J., & Delaney, H. D. (1982). The mnemonic keyword method. *Review of Research in Education, 52,* 61–91.

Pressley, M., Rahael, L., Gallagher, J. D. & DiBella, J. (2004). Providence St. Mel School: How a school that works for African American students works. *Journal of Educational Psychology, 96*(2), 216–235.

Pressley, M., & Roehrig, A. (2003). Educational psychology in the modern era: 1960 to the present. In B. J. Zimmerman & D. H. Schunk (Eds.), *Educational psychology: A century of contributions* (pp. 333–366). [A Project of Division 15 (Educational Psychology) of the American Psychological Association]. Mahwah, NJ: Erlbaum.

PREVNet. (2010). *Promoting relationships and eliminating violence.* [Website]. Retrieved from http://prevnet.ca/Home/tabid/36/Default.aspx

Price, L. F. (2005). The biology of risk taking. *Educational Leadership, 62*(7), 22–27.

Price, W. F., & Crapo, R. H. (2002). *Cross-cultural perspectives in introductory psychology* (4th ed.). Pacific Grove, CA: Wadsworth.

Proctor, C. P., August, D., Carlo, M. S., & Snow, C. (2006). The intriguing role of Spanish language vocabulary knowledge in predicting English reading comprehension. *Journal of Educational Psychology, 98,* 159–169.

Pugh, K. J., & Bergin, D. A. (2006). Motivational influences on transfer. *Educational Psychologist, 41,* 147–160.

Puncochar, J., & Fox, P. W. (2004). Confidence in individual and group decision-making: When "Two Heads" are worse than one. *Journal of Educational Psychology, 96,* 582–591.

Puntambekar, S., & Hubscher, R. (2005). Tools for scaffolding students in a complex learning environment: What have we gained and what have we missed? *Educational Psychologist, 40,* 1–12.

Puustinen, M., & Pulkkinen, L. (2001). Models of self-regulated learning: A review. *Scandinavian Journal of Educational Research, 45,* 269–286.

Rachlin, H. (1991). *Introduction to modern behaviorism* (3rd ed.), New York, NY: W. H. Freeman.

Rachlin, H. (2004). *The science of self-control.* Cambridge, MA: Harvard University Press.

Range, L. M. (1993). Suicide prevention: Guidelines for schools. *Educational Psychology Review, 5,* 135–154.

Raudenbush, S. (1984). Magnitude of teacher expectancy effects on pupil IQ as a function of the credibility of expectancy induction: A synthesis of findings from 18 experiments. *Journal of Educational Psychology, 76,* 85–97.

Raudsepp, E., & Haugh, G. P. (1977). *Creative growth games.* New York, NY: Harcourt Brace Jovanovich.

Rauscher, F. H., & Shaw, G. L. (1998). Key components of the Mozart effect. *Perceptual and Motor Skills, 86,* 835–841.

Recht, D. R., & Leslie, L. (1988). Effect of prior knowledge on good and poor readers' memory of text. *Journal of Educational Psychology, 80,* 16–20.

Reder, L. M. (1996). Different research programs on metacognition: Are the boundaries imaginary? *Learning and Individual Differences, 8,* 383–390.

Reed, S., & Sautter, R. C. (1990). Children of poverty: The status of 12 million Americans. *Phi Delta Kappan, 71*(10), K1–K12.

Reed, S. K. (2006). Cognitive architecture for multimedia learning. *Educational Psychologist, 41,* 87–98.

Reeve, J. (1996). *Motivating others: Nurturing inner motivational resources.* Boston, MA: Allyn & Bacon.

Reeve, J. (2002). Self-determination theory applied to educational settings. In E. L. Deci & R. M. Ryan (Eds.), *Handbook of self-determination research* (pp. 183–203). Rochester, NY: University of Rochester Press.

Reeve, J., Deci, E. L., & Ryan, R. M. (2004). *Self-determination theory: A dialectical framework for understanding the sociocultural influences on motivation and learning: Big theories revisited* (Vol. 4, pp. 31–59). Greenwich, CT: Information Age Press.

Reeve, J., & Jang, H. (2006). Teachers as facilitators: What autonomy-supportive teachers do and why their students benefit. *Elementary School Journal, 106,* 225–236.

Reeve, J., Nix, G., & Hamm, D. (2003). The experience of self-determination in intrinsic motivation and the conundrum of choice. *Journal of Educational Psychology, 95,* 347–392.

Reimann, P., & Chi, M. T. H. (1989). Human expertise. In K. J. Gilhooly (Ed.), *Human and machine problem solving* (pp. 161–191). New York, NY: Plenum Press.

Reis, S. M., McCoach, D. B., Coyne, M., Schreiber, F. J., Eckert, R. D., & Gubbins, E. J. (2007). Using planned enrichment strategies with direct instruction to improve reading fluency, comprehension, and attitude toward reading: An evidence-based study. *The Elementary School Journal, 108,* 3–23.

Reis, S. M., & Renzulli, J. S. (2004). Current research on the social and emotional development of gifted and talented students: Good news and future possibilities. *Psychology in the Schools, 41.* Published online in Wiley InterScience (www.interscience.wiley.com).

Reisberg, D., & Heuer, F. (1992). Remembering the details of emotional events. In E. Winograd & U. Neisser (Eds.), *Affect and accuracy in recall: Studies of "flashbulb" memories.* Cambridge, England: Cambridge University Press.

Reiss, S. (2004). Multifaceted nature of intrinsic motivation: The theory of 16 basic desires. *Review of General Psychology, 8,* 179–193.

Render, G. F., Padilla, J. N. M., & Krank, H. M. (1989). What research really shows about assertive discipline. *Educational Leadership, 46*(6), 72–75.

Renzulli, J. S., & Reis, S. M. (2003). The schoolwide enrichment model: Developing creative and productive giftedness. In N. Colangelo & G. A. Davis (Eds.), *Handbook of gifted education* (pp. 184–203). Boston, MA: Allyn & Bacon.

Resnick, L. B. (1981). Instructional psychology. *Annual Review of Psychology, 32,* 659–704.

Reynolds, A. (1992). Grade retention and school adjustment: An explanatory analysis. *Educational Evaluation and Policy Analysis, 14*(2), 101–121.

Rhodes, R. A. (1997). *Community service and higher learning: Explorations of the caring self.* Albany, NY: State University of New York Press.

Rice, F. P., & Dolgin, K. G. (2002). *The adolescent: Development, relationships, and culture* (10th ed.). Boston, MA: Allyn & Bacon.

Richardson, T. M., & Benbow, C. P. (1990). Long-term effects of acceleration on the social-emotional adjustment of mathematically precocious youths. *Journal of Educational Psychology, 82,* 464–470.

Richell, R., Deakin, J., & Anderson, I. (2005). Effect of acute tryptophan depletion on the response to controllable and uncontrollable noise stress. *Biological Psychiatry, 57,* 295–300.

Rideout, V., Roberts, D. F., Foehr, U. G. (2005). *Generation M: Media in the Lives of 8–18 year-olds: Executive Summary.* Menlo Park, CA: Kaiser Family Foundation.

Rittle-Johnson, B., & Star, J. R. (2007). Does comparing solution methods facilitate conceptual and procedural knowledge? An experimental study on learning to solve equations. *Journal of Educational Psychology, 99,* 561–574.

Rivers, I., Voret, V. P., Pote, N., & Ashurst, N. (2009). Observing bullying at school: The mental health implications of witness status. *School Psychology Quarterly, 24,* 211–223.

Rizzolatti, G., Fadiga, L., Gallese, V., & Fogassi, L. (1996). Premotor cortex and the recognition of motor actions. *Brain Research: Cognitive Brain Research, 3*(2), 131–141.

Robbins, S. B., Lauver, K., Davis, H. L., Davis, D., Langley, R., & Carlstrom, A. (2004). Psychosocial and study skill factors predict college outcomes? A *meta-analysis. Psychological Bulletin, 130,* 261–288.

Robbins, S. B., Le, L., & Lauver, K. (2005). Promoting successful college outcomes for all students: Reply to Weissberg and Owen (2005). *Psychological Bulletin, 131,* 410–411.

Roberson, D., Davidoff, J., Davies, I. R. L., & Shapiro, L. R. (2004). The development of color categories in two languages: A longitudinal study. *Journal of Experimental Psychology: General, 133*, 554–571.

Roberts, D. F., Foehr, U. G., & Rideout, V. (2005). *Generation M: Media in the lives of 8–18 year-olds.* Technical Reports 7250/7251. Menlo Park, CA: Kaiser Family foundation. Retrieved from http://www.kff.org/entmedia/7251.cfm.

Roberts, D. S., Tingstrom, D. H., Olmi, D. J., & Bellipanni, K. D. (2008). Positive antecedent and consequent components in child compliance training. *Behavior Modification*, 32, 21–38.

Robinson, A., & Clinkenbeard, P. R. (1998). Giftedness: An exceptionality examined. In J. T. Spence, J. M. Darley, & D. J. Foss (Eds.), *Annual review of psychology* (pp. 117–139). Palo Alto, CA: Annual Reviews.

Robinson, D. H. (1998). Graphic organizers as aids to test learning. *Reading Research and Instruction*, 37, 85–105.

Robinson, D. H., & Kiewra, K. A. (1995). Visual argument: Graphic outlines are superior to outlines in improving learning from text. *Journal of Educational Psychology*, 87, 455–467.

Roeser, R. W., Peck, S. C., & Nasir, N. S. (2006). Self and identity processes in school motivation, learning, and achievement. In P. A. Alexander & P. H, Winne (Eds.), *Handbook of educational psychology* (2nd ed., pp. 391–424). Mahwah, NJ: Erlbaum.

Rogers, C. R., & Freiberg, H. J. (1994). *Freedom to learn* (3rd ed.). Columbus, OH: Charles E. Merrill.

Rogoff, B. (1990). *Apprenticeship in thinking: Cognitive development in social context.* New York, NY: Oxford University Press.

Rogoff, B. (1995). Observing sociocultural activity on three planes: Participatory appropriation, guided participation, and apprenticeship. In J. Wertsch, P. del Rio, & A. Alverez (Eds.), *Sociocultural studies of mind* (pp. 139–164). Cambridge, England: Cambridge University Press.

Rogoff, B. (1998). Cognition as a collaborative process. In W. Damon (Series Ed.) and D. Kuhn & R. S. Siegler (Vol. Eds.), *Handbook of child psychology* (5th ed., Vol. 2, pp. 679–744). New York, NY: Wiley.

Rogoff, B. (2003). *The cultural nature of human development.* New York, NY: Oxford University Press.

Rogoff, B., & Morelii, G. (1989). Perspectives on children's development from cultural psychology. *American Psychologist, 44*, 343–348.

Rogoff, B., Turkanis, C. G., & Bartlett, L. (2001). *Learning together: Children and adults in a school community.* New York, NY: Oxford.

Rohrkemper, M., & Corno, L. (1988). Success and failure on classroom tasks: Adaptive learning and classroom teaching. *Elementary School Journal*, 88, 297–312.

Roid, G. H. (2003). *Stanford-Binet Intelligence Scales, Fifth Edition.* Itasca, IL: Riverside Publishing.

Rosch, E. H. (1973). On the internal structure of perceptual and semantic categories. In T. Moore (Ed.), *Cognitive development and the acquisition of language* (pp. 111–144). New York, NY: Academic Press.

Roschelle, J. M., Pea, R. D., Hoadley, C. M., Gordon, D. N., & Means, B. M. (2000, Fall/Winter). Changing how and what children learn in school with computer-based technologies. *Children and Computer Technology, 10*(2), 76–101.

Rose, L. C., & Gallup, A. M. (1999). The 31st annual Phi Delta Kappa/Gallup Poll of the public's attitude toward the public schools. *Phi Delta Kappan, 81*(1), 41–58.

Rose, L. C., & Gallup, A. M. (2001). The 33rd annual Phi Delta Kappa/Gallup Poll of the public's attitude toward the public schools. *Phi Delta Kappan,* 83(1), 41–58.

Rose, L. C., & Gallup, A. M. (2007). The 39th annual Phi Delta Kappa/Gallup Poll of the public's attitude toward the public schools. *Phi Delta Kappan,* 89(1), 33–45.

Rosen, N. (2004). *Background report and recommendations for setting up adult Michif language classes.* Unpublished Technical Report.

Rosenberg, M. (1979). *Conceiving the self.* New York, NY: Basic Books.

Rosenberg, M. S., Westling, D. L., & McLeskey, J. (2008). *Special education for today's teachers: An introduction.* Boston, MA: Pearson/Allyn & Bacon.

Rosenfeld, M., & Rosenfeld, S. (2004). Developing teacher sensitivities to individual learning differences. *Educational Psychology*, 24, 465–486.

Rosenshine, B. (1979). Content, time, and direct instruction. In P. Peterson & H. Walberg (Eds.), *Research on teaching: Concepts, findings, and implications* (pp. 28–56). Berkeley, CA: McCutchan.

Rosenshine, B. (1988). Explicit teaching. In D. Berliner & B. Rosenshine (Eds.), *Talks to teachers* (pp. 75–92). New York, NY: Random House.

Rosenshine, B., & Furst, N. (1973). The use of direct observation to study teaching. In R. Travers (Ed.), *Second handbook of research on teaching.* Chicago, IL: Rand McNally.

Rosenshine, B., & Meister, C. (1992, April). *The uses of scaffolds for teaching less structured academic tasks.* Paper presented at the annual meeting of the American Educational Research Association, San Francisco, CA.

Rosenshine, B., & Meister, C. (1994). Reciprocal teaching: A review of the research. *Review of Educational Research, 64*, 479–530.

Rosenshine, B., & Stevens, R. (1986). Teaching functions. In M. Wittrock (Ed.), *Handbook of research on teaching* (3rd ed., pp. 376–391). New York, NY: Macmillan.

Rosenthal, R. (1987). Pygmalion effects: Existence, magnitude and social importance. A reply to Wineburg. *Educational Researcher, 16*, 37–41.

Rosenthal, R. (1995). Critiquing Pygmalion: A 25-year perspective. *Current Directions in Psychological Science, 4*, 171–172.

Rosenthal, R., & Jacobson, L. (1968). *Pygmalion in the classroom.* New York, NY: Holt, Rinehart, Winston.

Roskos, K., & Neuman, S. B. (1998). Play as an opportunity for literacy. In O. N. Saracho & B. Spodek (Eds.), *Multiple perspectives on play in early childhood education* (pp. 100–115). Albany, NY: State University of New York Press.

Ross, J. A., & Raphael, D. (1990). Communication and problem solving achievement in cooperative learning groups. *Journal of Curriculum Studies, 22*, 149–164.

Roth, W-M., & Bowen, G. M. (1995). Knowing and interacting: A study of culture, practices, and resources in a grade 8 open-inquiry science guided by an apprenticeship metaphor. *Cognition and Instruction, 13*, 73–128.

Roth, W.-M., & McGinn, M. K. (1997). Toward a new perspective on problem solving. *Canadian Journal of Education*, 22, 18–32.

Roth, W.-M., & Roychoudhury, A. (1993). The development of science process skills in authentic contexts. *Journal of Research on Science Teaching, 30*, 127–152.

Rotherham-Borus, M. J. (1994). Bicultural reference group orientations and adjustment. In M. Bernal & G. Knight (Eds.), *Ethnic identity.* Albany, NY: State University of New York Press.

Rowe, M. B. (1974). Wait-time and rewards as instructional variables: Their influence on language, logic, and fate control. Part 1: Wait-time. *Journal of Research in Science Teaching, 11*, 81–94.

Rubin, K. H., Bukowski, W. M., Parker, J. G. (2006). Peer interactions, relationships, and groups. In N. Eisenberg, W. Dammon, & R. M. Lerner (Eds.), *Handbook of child psychology: Vol. 3. Social, emotional, and personality development* (6th ed., pp. 571–645). Hoboken, NJ: John Wiley & Sons.

Rubin, K. H., Coplan, R., Chen, X, & Buskirk, A. A. (2005). Peer relationships in childhood. In M. H. Borstein & Lamb, M. E. (Eds.), *Developmental science: An advanced textbook* (pp. 469–512). Mahwah, NJ: Lawrence Erlbaum.

Rudolph, K. D., Lambert, S. F., Clark, A. G., & Kurlakowsky, K. D. (2001). Negotiating the transition to middle school: The role of self-regulatory processes. *Child Development*, 72, 926–946.

Rueda, R., & Moll, L. C. (1994) A sociocultural perspective on motivation. In F. O'Neil Jr. & M. Drillings (Eds.), *Motivation: Theory and research* (pp. 117–137). Hillsdale, NJ: Erlbaum.

Rumelhart, D., & Ortony, A. (1977). The representation of knowledge in memory. In R. Anderson, R. Spiro, & W. Montague (Eds.), *Schooling and the acquisition of knowledge* (pp. 99–135). Hillsdale, NJ: Erlbaum.

Rummel, N., Levin, J. R., & Woodward, M. M. (2003). Do pictorial mnemonic text-learning aids give students something worth writing about? *Journal of Educational Psychology*, 95, 327–334.

Ryan, A. (2001). The peer group as a context for development of young adolescents' motivation and achievement. *Child Development*, 72, 1135–1150.

Ryan, K. E., & Ryan, A. M. (2005). Psychological processes underlying stereotype threat and standardized math test performance. *Educational Psychologist, 40*, 53–63.

Ryan, R. M., & Deci, E. L. (1996). When paradigms clash: Comments on Cameron and Pierce's claim that rewards do not undermine intrinsic motivation. *Review of Educational Research, 66*, 33–38.

Ryan, R. M., & Deci, E. L. (2000). Intrinsic and extrinsic motivation: Classic definitions and new directions. *Contemporary Educational Psychology*, 25, 54–67.

Sackett, P. R., Hardison, C. M., & Cullen, M. J. (2004). On the value of correcting mischaracterizations of stereotype threat. *American Psychologist, 59*, 48–49.

Sadker, M., & Sadker, D. (1994). *Failing at fairness: How America's schools cheat girls*. New York, NY: Scribner.

Sadker, M., & Sadker, D. (2006). Questioning skills. In J. Cooper (Ed.), *Classroom teaching skills* (8th ed., pp. 104–150). Boston, MA: Houghton-Mifflin.

Sadker, M., Sadker, D., & Klein, S. (1991). The issue of gender in elementary and secondary education. *Review of Research in Education, 17*, 269–334.

Sagor, R. (2003). *Motivating students and teachers in an era of standards*. Alexandria, VA: Association for Supervision and Curriculum Development.

Sakiz, G., Pape, S., & Woolfolk Hoy, A. (2008, March). *Does teacher affective support matter? The role of affective support in middle school mathematics classrooms*. Paper presented at the annual meeting of the American Educational Research Association, New York, NY.

Salomon, G., & Perkins, D. N. (1989). Rocky roads to transfer: Re-thinking mechanisms of a neglected phenomenon. *Educational Psychologist, 24*, 113–142.

Sanchez, F., & Anderson, M. L. (1990, May). Gang mediation: A process that works. *Principal*, 54–56.

Sattler, J. M. (1992). *Assessment of children* (3rd ed. rev.). San Diego, CA: Jerome M. Sattler.

Sattler, J. M. (2001). *Assessment of children: Cognitive applications* (4th ed.). San Diego, CA: Jerome M. Sattler.

Savage, T. V. (1999). *Teaching self-control through management and discipline*. Boston, MA: Allyn & Bacon.

Savin-Williams, R. C., & Diamond, L. M. (2004). Sex. In R. M. Lerner & L. Steinberg (Eds.), *Handbook of adolescent psychology* (2nd ed., pp. 189–231). New York, NY: John Wiley & Sons.

Sawyer, R. J., Graham, S., & Harris, K. R. (1992). Direct teaching, strategy instruction, and strategy instruction with explicit self-regulation: Effects on the composition skills and self-efficacy of learning disabled students. *Journal of Educational Psychology, 84*, 340–352.

Sawyer, R. K. (2006a). *Explaining creativity: The science of human motivation*. New York, NY: Oxford University Press.

Sawyer, R. K. (2006b). Introduction: The new science of learning. In R. K. Sawyer (Ed.), *The Cambridge handbook of the learning sciences* (pp. 1–16). New York, NY: Cambridge.

Saxe, G. B. (1999). Source of concepts: A cross cultural-developmental perspective. In E. K. Scholnick, K. Nelson, S. A. Gelman, & P. H. Miller (Eds.), *Conceptual development: Piaget's legacy* (pp. 253–267). Mahwah, NJ: Erlbaum.

Scardamalia, M., & Bereiter, C. (1996). Adaptation and understanding: A case for new cultures of schooling. In S. Vosniado, E. De Corte, R. Glasse, & H. Mandl (Eds.), *International perspectives on the design of technology-supported learning environments* (pp. 149–163). Hillsdale, NJ: Erlbaum.

Schacter, D. L., Gilbert, D. T., & Wenger, D. M. (2009). *Psychology*, New York, NY: Worth.

Scherer, M. (1993). On savage inequalities: A conversation with Jonathan Kozol. *Educational Leadership, 50*(4), 4–9.

Scherer, M. (1999). The discipline of hope: A conversation with Herb Kohl. *Educational Leadership, 56*(1), 8–13.

Schiefele, U. (1991). Interest, learning, and motivation. *Educational Psychologist, 26*, 299–324.

Schneider, W., & Bjorklund, D. F. (1992). Expertise, aptitude, and strategic remembering. *Child Development, 63*, 416–473.

Schoenfeld, A. H. (1989). Teaching mathematical thinking and problem solving. In L. B. Resnick & L. E. Klopfer (Eds.), *Toward the thinking curriculum: Current cognitive research* (pp. 83–103). Alexandria, VA: ASCD.

Schoenfeld, A. H. (1994). Mathematics thinking and problem solving. Hillsdale, NJ: Erlbaum.

Schommer, M. (1997). The development of epistemological beliefs among secondary students: A longitudinal study. Journal of Educational Psychology, 89, 37–40.

Schommer-Aikins, M. (2002). An evolving theoretical framework for an epistemological belief system. In B. K. Hofer & P. R. Pintrich (Eds.), Personal epistemology: The psychology of beliefs about knowledge and knowing (pp. 103–118). Mahwah, NJ: Erlbaum.

Schonert-Reichl, K. A. (1994). Gender differences in depressive symptomatology and egocentrism in adolescence. *Journal of Early Adolescence, 14*, 49–65.

Schraw, G. (2006). In P. A Alexander & P. H. Winne (Eds.), *Handbook of educational psychology* (2nd ed., pp. 825–847). Mahwah, NJ: Erlbaum.

Schraw, G., & Olafson, L. (2002). Teachers epistemological world views and educational practices. *Issues in Education, 8*, 99–148.

Schunk, D. H. (2000). *Learning theories: An educational perspective* (3rd ed.). Columbus, OH: Merrill/Prentice-Hall.

Schunk, D. H. (2004). *Learning theories: An educational perspective* (4th ed.). Columbus, OH: Merrill/Prentice-Hall.

Schunk, D. H. (2005). Self-regulated learning: The educational legacy of Paul R. Pintrich. *Educational Psychologist, 40*, 85–94.

Schunk, D. H. (2008). *Learning theories: An educational perspective* (5th ed.). Columbus, OH: Merrill/Prentice-Hall.

Schunk, D. H., & Hanson, A. R. (1985). Peer models: Influence on children's self-efficacy and achievement. *Journal of Educational Psychology, 77*, 313–322.

Schunk, D. H., Pintrich, P. R., & Meece, J. L. (2008). *Motivation in education: Theory, research, and applications* (3rd ed.). Columbus, OH: Merrill/Prentice-Hall.

Schutz, P. A., & Davis, H. A. (2000). Emotions and self-regulations during test-taking. *Educational Psychologist, 35*, 243–256.

Schwab, J. J. (1973). The Practical 3: Translation into curriculum. *School Review, 81*, 501–522.

Schwartz, B., & Reisberg, D. (1991). *Learning and memory*. New York, NY: Norton.

Schwartz, B., Wasserman, E. A., & Robbins, S. J. (2002). *Psychology of learning and behavior* (5th ed.). New York, NY: W. W. Norton.

Schwarz, B. B., Neuman, Y., & Biezuner, S. (2000). Two wrongs may make a right . . . if they argue together! *Cognition and Instruction, 18*, 461–494.

Schworm, S., & Renkl, A. (2007). Learning argumentation skills through the use of prompts for self-explaining examples. *Journal of Educational Psychology, 99*, 285–295.

Scott, C. L. (1999). Teachers' biases toward creative children. *Creativity Research Journal, 12*, 321–337.

Seligman, M. E. P. (1975). *Helplessness: On depression, development, and death*. San Francisco, CA: Freeman.

Seligman, M. E. P. (2006). *Learned optimism: How to change your mind and your life* (2nd ed.). New York, NY: Pocket Books.

Selman, R. L. (1980). *The growth of interpersonal understanding*. New York, NY: Academic Press.

Semb, G. B., & Ellis, J. A. (1994). Knowledge taught in school: What is remembered? *Review of Educational Research, 64*, 253–286.

Sénéchal, M., & LeFevre, J. A. (2002). Parental involvement in the development of children's reading skills: A five-year longitudinal study. *Child Development, 73*, 445–460.

Serpell, R. (1993). Interface between sociocultural and psychological aspects of cognition. In E. Forman, N. Minick, & C. A. Stone (Eds.), *Contexts for learning: Sociocultural dynamics in children's development* (pp. 357–368). New York, NY: Oxford University Press.

Shapka, J. D., & Keating, D.P. (2003). Effects of a girls-only curriculum during adolescence: Performance, persistence, and engagement in mathematics and science. *American Education Research Journal, 40*, 929–960.

Shapka, J. D., & Keating, D. P. (2005). Structure and change in self-concept during adolescence. *Canadian Journal of Behavioural Sciences, 37*, 83–96.

Shavelson, R. J. (1987). Planning. In M. Dunkin (Ed.), *The international encyclopedia of teaching and teacher education* (pp. 483–486). New York, NY: Pergamon Press.

Shaywitz, B. A., Shaywitz, S.E., Blachman, B. A., Pugh, K. R., Fulbright, R. K., Skudlarski, P., . . . Gore, J.C. (2004). Development of left occipitotemporal systems for skilled reading in children after a phonologically-based intervention. *Biological Psychiatry, 55*, 926–933.

Sheets, R. H. (2005). *Diversity pedagogy: Examining the role of culture in the teaching-learning process*. Boston, MA: Allyn & Bacon.

Shepard, L. A., & Smith, M. L. (1989). Academic and emotional effects of kindergarten retention. In L. Shepard & M. Smith (Eds.), *Flunking grades: Research and policies on retention* (pp. 79–107). Philadelphia, PA: Falmer Press.

Sherwood, R. D. (2002). Problem-based multimedia software for middle grades science: Development issues and an initial field study. *Journal of Computers in Mathematics and Science Teaching, 21*, 147–165.

Shields, P., Gordon, J., & Dupree, D. (1983). Influence of parent practices upon the reading achievement of good and poor readers. *Journal of Negro Education*, 52, 436–445.

Shih, S. S. (2008). The relation of self-determination and achievement goals to Taiwanese eighth graders' behavioral and emotional engagement in schoolwork. *The Elementary School Journal*, *108*, 313–334.

Shonkoff, J. P. (2006). A promising opportunity for developmental and behavioral pediatrics at the interface of neuroscience, psychology, and social policy: remarks on receiving the 2005 C. Anderson Aldrich Award. *Pediatrics*, *118*, 2187–2191.

Shu, H., McBride-Chang, C., Wu, S., & Liu, H. (2006). Understanding Chinese developmental dyslexia: Morphological awareness as a core cognitive construct. *Journal of Educational Psychology*, 98, 122–133.

Shuell, T. J. (1986). Cognitive conceptions of learning. *Review of Educational Research*, *56*, 411–436.

Shuell, T. J. (1990). Phases of meaningful learning. *Review of Educational Psychology*, *60*, 531–548.

Shuell, T. J. (1996). Teaching and learning in a classroom context. In D. Berliner & R. Calfee (Eds.), *Handbook of educational psychology* (pp. 726–764). New York, NY: Macmillan.

Shulman, L. S. (1987). Knowledge and teaching: Foundations of the new reform. *Harvard Educational Review*, *19*(2), 4–14.

Shultz, J., & Florio, S. (1979). Stop and freeze: The negotiation of social and physical space in a kindergarten/first grade classroom. *Anthropology and Education Quarterly*, *10*, 166–181.

Siddle Walker, V. (2001). African American teaching in the South: 1940–1960. *Review of Educational Research*, 38, 751–779.

Siegel, J., & Shaughnessy, M. F. (1994). Educating for understanding: An interview with Howard Gardner. *Phi Delta Kappan*, *75*, 536–566.

Siegel, L. S. (1989). IQ is irrelevant to the definition of learning disabilities. *Journal of Learning Disabilities*, 22, 469–479.

Siegel, L. S. (1999). Issues in the definition and diagnosis of learning disabilities. *Journal of Learning Disabilities*, 32, 304–319.

Siegler, R. S. (1993). Adaptive and non-adaptive characteristics of low-income children's mathematical strategy use. In B. Penner (Ed.), *The challenge in mathematics and science education: Psychology's response* (pp. 341–366). Washington, DC: American Psychological Association.

Siegler, R. S. (1998). *Children's thinking* (3rd ed.). Upper Saddle River, NJ: Prentice-Hall.

Siegler, R. S. (2000). The rebirth of children's learning. *Child Development*, *71*, 26–35.

Siegler, R. S. (2004). Turning memory development inside out. *Developmental Review*, 24, 469–475.

Siegler, R. S., & Alibali, M. W. (2005). *Children's thinking* (4th ed.). Upper Saddle River, NJ: Prentice-Hall.

Siegler, R. S., & Crowley, K. (1991). The microgenetic method: A direct means for studying cognitive development. *American Psychologist*, 56, 606–620.

Sillars, L. (1995). Studying crime in school. *Alberta Report*, 22(25), 37.

Silven, M., Poskiparata, E., Niemi, P., & Voeten, M. (2007). Precursors of reading skill from infancy to first grade in Finnish: Continuity and change in a highly inflected language. *Journal of Educational Psychology*, 99, 516–531.

Simon, D. P., & Chase, W. G. (1973). Skill in chess. *American Scientist*, *61*, 394–403.

Simon, H. A. (1995). The information-processing view of mind. *American Psychologist*, 50, 507–508.

Simonton, D. K. (1999). Creativity from a historiometric perspective. In R. J. Sternberg (Ed.), *Handbook of creativity* (pp. 116–133). New York, NY: Cambridge University Press.

Simonton, D. K. (2000). Creativity: Cognitive, personal, developmental, and social aspects. *American Psychologist*, *55*, 151–158.

Simpson, E. J. (1972). *The classification of educational objectives in the psychomotor domain: The psychomotor domain* (Vol. 3). Washington, DC: Gryphon House.

Sinatra, G. M. (2005). The "Warming Trend" in conceptual change research: The legacy of Paul R. Pintrich. *Educational Psychologist*, 40, 107–115.

Sinatra, G. M., & Mason, L. (2008). Beyond knowledge: Learner characteristics influencing conceptual change. In S. Vosniadou (Ed.), *International handbook of research on conceptual change*. Mahwah, NJ: Erlbaum.

Singley, K., & Anderson, J. R. (1989). *The transfer of cognitive skill*. Cambridge, MA: Harvard University Press.

Sirin, S. R. (2005). Socioeconomic status and academic achievement: A meta-analytic review of research. *Review of Educational Research*, *75*, 417–453.

Sisk, D. A. (1988). Children at risk: The identification of the gifted among the minority. *Gifted Education International*, 5, 138–141.

Skiba, R. J., Michael, R. S., Nardo, A. C., & Peterson, R. (2000). *The color of discipline: Sources of racial and gender disproportionality in school punishment* (Report #SRS1). Bloomington, IN: Indiana Education Policy Center.

Skinner, B. F. (1950). Are theories of learning necessary? *Psychological Review*, 57, 193–216.

Skinner, B. F. (1953). Science and human behavior. New York, NY: Macmillan.

Skinner, B. F. (1989). The origins of cognitive thought. *American Psychologist*, *44*, 13–18.

Skoe, E. E. A. (1998). The ethic of care: Issues in moral development. In E. E. A. Skoe & A. L. von der Lippe (Eds.), *Personality development in adolescence* (pp. 143–171). London, England: Routledge.

Slaby, R. G., Roedell, W. C., Arezzo, D., & Hendrix, K. (1995). *Early violence prevention*. Washington, DC: National Association for the Education of Young Children.

Slater, L. (2002, February 3). The trouble with self-esteem. *The New York Times Magazine*, pp. 44–47.

Slavin, R. E. (1995). *Cooperative learning* (2nd ed.). Boston, MA: Allyn & Bacon.

Slavin, R. E. (2002). Evidence-based education policies: Transforming education practice and research. *Educational Researcher*, *31*(7), 15–21.

Smetana, J. G. (2000). Middle-class African American adolescents' and parents' conceptions of parental authority and parenting practices: A longitudinal investigation. *Child Development*, *71*, 1672–1686.

Smith, C. B. (Moderator). (1994). *Whole language: The debate*. Bloomington, IN: EDINFO Press.

Smith, C. R. (2004). *Learning disabilities: The interaction of learner, task, and setting* (5th ed.). Boston, MA: Allyn & Bacon.

Smith, D. D. (1998). *Introduction to special education: Teaching in an age of challenge* (3rd ed.). Boston, MA: Allyn & Bacon.

Smith, D. D. (2006). *Introduction to special education: Teaching in an age of opportunity* (5th ed.). Boston, MA: Allyn & Bacon.

Smith, F. (1975). *Comprehension and learning: A conceptual framework for teachers*. New York, NY: Holt, Rinehart & Winston.

Smith, J. K., Smith, L. F., & De Lisi, R. (2001). *Natural classroom assessment: Designing seamless instruction and assessment*. Thousand Oaks, CA: Corwin Press.

Smith, J. L., Sanson, C., & White, P. H. (2007). The stereotyped task process: The role of interest and achievement motivation. *Journal of Educational Psychology*, 88, 99–114.

Smith, S. M., Glenberg, A., & Bjork, R. A. (1978). Environmental context and human memory. *Memory and Cognition*, *6*, 342–353.

Snider, V. E. (1990). What we know about learning styles from research in special education. *Educational Leadership*, *48*(2), 53.

Snow, C. E. (1993). Families as social contexts for literacy development. In C. Daiute (Ed.), *New directions for child development* (No. 61, pp. 11–24). San Francisco, CA: Josey-Bass.

Snow, R. E. (1995). Pygmalion and intelligence. *Current Directions in Psychological Science*, *4*, 169–171.

Snow, R. E., Corno, L., & Jackson, D. (1996). Individual differences in affective and cognitive functions. In D. Berliner & R. Calfee (Eds.), *Handbook of educational psychology* (pp. 243–310). New York, NY: Macmillan.

Snowman, J. (1984). Learning tactics and strategies. In G. Phye & T. Andre (Eds.), *Cognitive instructional psychology* (pp. 243–275). Orlando, FL: Academic Press.

Soar, R. S., & Soar, R. M. (1979). Emotional climate and management. In P. Peterson & H. Walberg (Eds.), *Research on teaching: Concepts, findings, and implications* (pp. 97–119). Berkeley, CA: McCutchan.

Sobesky, W. E. (1983). The effects of situational factors on moral judgment. *Child Development*, *54*, 575–584.

Sokolove, S., Garrett, J., Sadker, D., & Sadker, M. (1986). Interpersonal communications skills. In J. Cooper (Ed.), *Classroom teaching skills: A handbook* (pp. 233–278). Lexington, MA: D. C. Heath.

Solomon, D., Watson, M. S., & Battistich, V. A. (2001). Teaching and schooling effects on moral/prosocial development. In V. Richardson (Ed.), *Handbook of research on teaching* (4th ed., pp. 566–603). Washington, DC: American Educational Research Association.

Soodak, L. C., & McCarthy, M. R. (2006). Classroom management in inclusive settings. In C. M. Evertson & C. S. Weinstein (Eds.), *Handbook of classroom management: Research, practice, and contemporary issues*. Mahwah, NJ: Erlbaum.

Sotillo, S. M. (2002). Finding our voices, finding ourselves: Becoming bilingual and bicultural. In G. S. Boutte (Ed.), *Resounding voices: School experiences of people from diverse ethnic backgrounds* (pp. 275–307). Boston, MA: Allyn & Bacon.

Spearman, C. (1927). *The abilities of man: Their nature and measurement*. New York, NY: Macmillan.

Spencer, M. B., & Markstrom-Adams, C. (1990). Identity processes among racial and ethnic-minority children in America. *Child Development, 61*, 290–310.

Spencer, M. B., Noll, E., Stoltzfus, J., & Harpalani, V. (2001). Identity and school adjustment: Questioning the "Acting White" assumption. *Educational Psychologist, 36*(1), 21–30.

Spera, C. (2005). A review of the relationship among parenting practices, parenting styles, and adolescent school achievement. *Educational Psychology Review, 17*, 125–146.

Sperling, G. (1960). The information available in brief visual presentations. *Psychological Monographs, 74* (11, Whole No. 498).

Spinelli, C. G. (2002). *Classroom assessment for students with special needs in inclusive classrooms*. Upper Saddle River, NJ: Merrill/Prentice-Hall.

Spiro, R. J., Feltovich, P. J., Jacobson, M. L., & Coulson, R. L. (1991). Cognitive flexibility, constructivism, and hypertext: Random access instruction for advanced knowledge acquisition in ill-structured domains. *Educational Technology, 31*(5), 24–33.

Sprague, J., & Walker, H. (2000). Early identification and intervention for youth with antisocial and violent behavior. *Exceptional Children, 66*, 367–379.

Sprenger, M. (2005). In side Amy's brain. *Educational Leadership, 62*(7), 28–32.

Stahl, S. A. (2002). Different strokes for different folks? In L. Abbeduto (Ed.), *Taking sides: Clashing on controversial issues in educational psychology* (pp. 98–107). Guilford, CT: McGraw-Hill/Duskin.

Stahl, S. A., & Miller, P. D. (1989). Whole language and language experience approaches for beginning reading: A quantitative research synthesis. *Review of Educational Research, 59*, 87–116.

Stahl, S. A., & Yaden, D. B. Jr. (2004). The development of literacy in preschool and primary grades: Work by the Center for the Improvement of Early Reading Achievement. *The Elementary School Journal, 82*, 141–166.

Stanovich, K. E. (1992). *How to think straight about psychology* (3rd ed.). Glenview, IL: Scott, Foresman.

Stanovich, P. J., & Jordan, A. (1998). Canadian teachers' and principals' beliefs about inclusive education as predictors of effective teaching in heterogeneous classrooms. *Elementary School Journal, 98*, 221–238.

STAR Legacy Cycle. Retreived from https://repo.vanth.org/portal/public-content/star-legacy-cycle/star-legacy-cycle/

Starch, D., & Elliot, E. C. (1913a). Reliability of grading work in history. *Scholastic Review, 21*, 676–681.

Starch, D., & Elliot, E. C. (1913b). Reliability of grading work in mathematics. *Scholastic Review, 21*, 254–259.

Statistics Canada. (2006, March 31). Television viewing. *The Daily*. Retrieved from http://www.statcan.gc.ca/daily-quotidien/060331/dq060331b-eng.htm

Statistics Canada. (2008). Socioeconomic status (SES). Retrieved from http://www.statcan.gc.ca/pub/81-004-x/def/4068719-eng.htm#tphp

Statistics Canada. (2010a). Characteristics of individuals using the Internet. Retrieved from http://www40.statcan.gc.ca/l01/cst01/comm35a-eng.htm

Statistics Canada. (2010b). Father's day . . . by the numbers. Retrieved from http://www42.statcan.ca/smr08/2010/smr08_143_2010-eng.htm

Statistics Canada. (2010c). Internet use by individuals, by selected characteristics. Detailed tables from CANSIM. Retrieved from http://cansim2.statcan.gc.ca/cgi- win/cnsmcgi.exe?Lang=E&ResultTemplate=CST&CORCmd=GetCRel&CORId=COMM35A&CORRel=4

Statistics Canada. (2010d). Study: Projections of the diversity of the Canadian population. Retrieved from http://www.statcan.gc.ca/daily-quotidien/100309/dq100309a-eng.htm

Steele, C. (1992). *Race and the schooling of African-Americans*. Atlantic Monthly, 269(4), 68–78.

Steele, K. M., Bass, K. E., & Crook, M. D. (1999). The mystery of the Mozart effect: Failure to replicate. *Psychological Science, 10*, 366–368.

Stefanou, C. R., Perencevich, K. C., DiCintio, M., & Turner, J. C. (2004). Supporting autonomy in the classroom: Ways teachers encourage student decision making and ownership. *Educational Psychologist, 39*, 97–110.

Steinberg, L. (2005). *Adolescence* (7th ed.). New York, NY: McGraw-Hill.

Sternberg, R. J. (1985). *Beyond IQ: A triarchic theory of human intelligence*. New York, NY: Cambridge University Press.

Sternberg, R. J. (1999). *Cognitive psychology* (2nd ed.). Fort Worth, TX: Harcourt Brace.

Sternberg, R. J. (2000). *Handbook of human intelligence*. New York, NY: Cambridge University Press.

Sternberg, R. J. (2004). Culture and intelligence. *American Psychologist, 59*, 325–338.

Sternberg, R. J., & Davidson, J. (1982, June). The mind of the puzzler. *Psychology Today*, 37–44.

Sternberg, R. J., & Detterman, D. L. (Eds.). (1986). *What is intelligence? Contemporary viewpoints on its nature and definition*. Norwood, NJ: Ablex.

Sternberg, R. J., & Wagner, R. K. (1993). The geocentric view of intelligence and job performance is wrong. *Current Directions in Psychological Science, 2*, 1–5.

Sternberg, R. J., Wagner, R. K., Williams, W. M., & Horvath, J. A. (1995). Testing common sense. *American Psychologist, 50*, 912–927.

Stevens, R. J. & Slavin, R. E. (1995). The cooperative elementary school: Effects on students' achievement, attitudes, and social relations. *American Educational Research Journal, 32*, 321–351.

Stevenson, H. W., & Stigler, J. (1992). *The learning gap*. New York, NY: Summit Books.

Stewart, L., Henson, R., Kampe, K., Walsh, V., Turner, R., & Frith, U. (2003). Brain changes after learning to read and play music. *NeuroImage, 20*(1), 71–83.

Stice, E., & Shaw, H. (2004). Eating disorder prevention programs: A meta-analytic review. *Psychological Bulletin, 130*, 206–227.

Stiggins, R. J., & Chappuis, J. (2005). Using student-involved classroom assessment to close achievement gaps. *Theory Into Practice, 44*, 11–18.

Stigler, J. W., Lee, S., & Stevenson, H. W. (1987). Mathematics classrooms in Japan, Taiwan, and the United States. *Child Development, 58*, 1272–1285.

Stinson, D. W. (2006). African American male adolescents, schooling, (an mathematics): Deficiency, rejection, and achievement. *Review of Educational Research, 76*, 477–506.

Stipek, D. J. (1981). Children's perceptions of their own and their peers' academic competence. *Journal of Educational Psychology, 73*, 404–410.

Stipek, D. J. (1993). *Motivation to learn* (2nd ed.). Boston, MA: Allyn & Bacon.

Stipek, D. J. (2002). *Motivation to learn: Integrating theory and practice* (4th ed.). Boston, MA: Allyn & Bacon.

Stipek, D. (2006). Relationships matter. *Educational Leadership, 64*(1), 46–49.

Stipek, D., de la Sota, A., & Weishaupt, L. (1999). Life lessons: An embedded classroom approach to preventing high-risk behaviors among preadolescents. *The Elementary School Journal, 99*, 433–451.

Stodolsky, S. S. (1988). *The subject matters: Classroom activity in math and social studies*. Chicago, IL: University of Chicago Press.

Storch, S., & Whitehurst, G. (2002). Oral language and code-related precursors to reading: Evidence from a longitudinal structural model. *Developmental Psychology, 38*, 934–947.

Stormont, M., Stebbins, M. S., & Holliday, G. (2001). Characteristics and educational support needs of underrepresented gifted adolescents. *Psychology in the Schools, 38*, 413–423.

Stormshak, E. A., Bierman, K. L., Bruschi, C., Dodge, K. A., & Coie, J. D. (1999). The relation between behavior problems and peer preference in different classroom contexts. *Child Development, 70*, 169–182.

Strom, P. S., & Strom, R. D. (2005). Cyberbullying by adolescents: A preliminary assessment. *The Educational Forum, 70*(1), 21–36.

Stumpf, H. (1995). Gender differences on test of cognitive abilities: Experimental design issues and empirical results. *Learning and Individual Differences, 7*, 275–288.

Subrahmanyam, K., Greenfield, P., Kraut, R., & Gross, E. (2001). The impact of computer use on children's and adolescents' development. *Applied Developmental Psychology, 22*, 7–30.

… (2000). *The anti-bullying handbook*. New York, NY: Oxford University Press.

Sullivan, M. A., & O'Leary, S. G. (1990). Maintenance following reward and cost token programs. *Behavior Therapy, 21*, 139–149.

Suzuki, B. H. (1983). The education of Asian and Pacific Americans: An introductory overview. In D. Nakanishi & M. HiranoNakanishi (Eds.), *The education of Asian and Pacific Americans: Historical perspectives and prescriptions for the future* (pp. 1–14). Phoenix, AZ: Oryx Press.

Svoboda, J. S. (2001). Review of *Boys and girls learn differently*.The Men's Resource Network. Retrieved from http://www.themenscenter.com/mensight/reviews/Svoboda/boys and girls.htm

Swanson, H. L. (1990). The influence of metacognitive knowledge and aptitude on problem solving. *Journal of Educational Psychology*, 82, 306–314.

Swanson, H. L. (2001). Research on interventions for adolescents with learning disabilities: A meta-analysis of outcomes related to higher-order processing. *The Elementary School Journal, 101*, 332–348.

Swearer, S. M., Espelage, D. L., Vaillancourt, T. & Hymel, S. (2010). What can be done about school bullying? Linking research to educational practice. *Educational Researcher*, 39(1), 38–47.

Sweeney, W. J., Salva, E., Cooper, J. O., & Talbert-Johnson, C. (1993). Using self-evaluation to improve difficult to read handwriting for secondary students. *Journal of Behavioral Education*, 3, 427–443.

Sweller, J., Kirschner, P. A., & Clark, R. E. (2007). Why minimally guided teaching techniques do not work: A reply to commentaries. *Educational Psychologist, 42*, 115–121.

Sweller, J., van Merriënboer, J. J. G., & Paas, F. G. W. C. (1998). Cognitive architecture and instructional design. *Educational Psychology Review, 10*, 251–296.

Sylvester, R. (2003). *A biological brain in a cultural classroom* (2nd ed.). Thousand Oaks, CA: Sage.

Symons, S., Woloshyn, V., & Pressley, M. (1994). The scientific evaluation of the whole language approach to literacy development [Special issue]. *Educational Psychologist*, 29(4).

Tait, H., & Entwistle, N. J. (1998). Identifying students at risk through ineffective study strategies. *Higher Education, 31*, 97–116.

Talbot, M. (2002, February 24). Girls just want to be mean. *The New York Times Magazine*, pp. 24–29+.

Tallal, P., & Miller, S. L. (2003). How the brain learns to read. *Middle Matters*, 12(1), 7.

Tang, Y., Zhang, W., Chen, K., Feng, S., Ji, Y. Shen, J, . . . Liu, Y. (2006). Arithmetic processing in the brain shaped by cultures. *Proceedings of the National Academy of Sciences USA, 103*, 10775–10780.

Taylor, E. (1998). Clinical foundation of hyperactivity research. *Behavioural Brain Research, 94*, 11–24.

TenBrink, T. D. (2006). Assessment. In J. Cooper (Ed.), *Classroom teaching skills* (8th ed., pp. 55–78). Boston, MA: Houghton-Mifflin.

Tenenbaum, H. R., & Ruck, M.D. (2007). Are teachers' expectations different for racial minority than for European American students? A meta-analysis. *Journal of Educational Psychology*, 99, 253–273.

Terman, L. M., Baldwin, B. T., & Bronson, E. (1925). Mental and physical traits of a thousand gifted children. In L. M. Terman (Ed.), *Genetic studies of genius* (Vol. 1). Stanford, CA: Stanford University Press.

Terman, L. M., & Oden, M. H. (1947). The gifted child grows up. In L. M. Terman (Ed.), *Genetic studies of genius* (Vol. 4). Stanford, CA: Stanford University Press.

Terman, L. M., & Oden, M. H. (1959). The gifted group in mid-life. In L. M. Terman (Ed.), *Genetic studies of genius* (Vol. 5). Stanford, CA: Stanford University Press.

Tesser, A., Stapel, D. A., & Wood, J. V. (2002). *Self and motivation: Emerging psychological perspectives*. Washington, DC: American Psychological Association.

Tharp, R. G. (1989). Psychocultural variables and constants: Effects on teaching and learning in schools. *American Psychologist, 44*, 349–359.

Tharp, R. G., & Gallimore, R. (1988). *Rousing minds to life: Teaching, learning, and schooling in social context*. New York, NY: Cambridge University Press.

Theodore, L. A., Bray, M. A., Kehle, T. J., & Jenson, W. R. (2001). Randomization of group contingencies and reinforcers for reduce classroom disruptive behavior. *Journal of School Psychology*, 39, 267–277.

Thomas, K. T., & Thomas, J. R. (2008). Principles of motor development for elementary school physical education. *The Elementary School Journal, 108*, 181–195.

Thompson, A., Hollis, C., & Richards, D. (2003). Authoritarian parenting attitudes as a risk for conduct problems. *European Child & Adolescent Psychiatry, 12*, 84.

Thompson, G. (2008). Beneath the apathy. *Educational Leadership, 65*(6), 50–54.

Thompson, R. A., & Raikes, H. A. (2003). Toward the next quarter-century: Conceptual and methodological challenges for attachment theory. *Development and Psychopathology, 15*, 691–718.

Tierney, R. J., Readence, J. E., & Dishner, E. K. (1990). *Reading strategies and practices: A compendium* (3rd ed.). Boston, MA: Allyn & Bacon.

Tierney, W. G. (1993). *Building communities of difference: Higher education in the twenty-first century*. Westport, CT: Bergin and Garvey.

Tingstrom, D. H., Sterling-Turner, H. E., & Wilczynski, S. M. (2006). The Good Behavior Game: 1962–2002. *Behavior Modification, 30*, 225–253.

Tishman, S., Perkins, D., & Jay, E. (1995). *The thinking classroom: Creating a culture of thinking*. Boston, MA: Allyn & Bacon.

Tollefson, N. (2000). Classroom applications of cognitive theories of motivation. *Education Psychology Review, 12*, 63–83.

Tomasello, M. (2006). Acquiring linguistic constructions. In D. Kuhn & R. S. Siegler (Eds.), *Handbook of child psychology: Vol. 2. Cognition, language, and perception* (6th ed., pp. 255–298). New York, NY: Wiley.

Tomasello, M., Kruger, A. C., & Ratner, H. H. (1993). Cultural learning. *Behavioral and Brain Sciences, 16*, 495–552.

Tomlinson, C. A. (2003). *Fulfilling the promise of the differentiated classroom*. Alexandria, VA: Association for Supervision and Curriculum Development.

Tomlinson, C. A. (2005a). Grading and differentiation: Paradox or good practice? *Theory Into Practice, 44*, 262–269.

Tomlinson, C. A. (2005b, Summer). Differentiating instruction. *Theory Into Practice, 44*(3).

Toppo, G. (2003, January 13). School violence hits lower grades: Experts who see violent behavior in younger kids blame parents, prenatal medical problems and an angry society; educators search for ways to cope. *USAToday*. Retrieved from http://www.usatoday.com/educate/college/education/articles/20030119.htm

Torrance, E. P. (1972). Predictive validity of the Torrance tests of creative thinking. Journal of Creative Behavior, 6, 236–262. Torrance, E. P. (1986). Teaching creative and gifted learners. In M. Wittrock (Ed.), *Handbook of research on teaching* (3rd ed., pp. 630–647). New York, NY: Macmillan.

Torrance, E. P. (1986). Teaching creative and gifted learners. In M. Wittrock (Ed.), *Handbook of research on teaching* (3rd ed., pp. 630–647). New York, NY: Macmillan.

Torrance, E. P., & Hall, L. K. (1980). Assessing the future reaches of creative potential. *Journal of Creative Behavior, 14*, 1–19.

Toth, E., Klahr, D., & Chen, Z. (2000). Bridging research and practice: A cognitively based classroom intervention for teaching experimentation to elementary school children. *Cognition and Instruction, 18*, 423–459.

Trautwein, U. (2007). The homework–achievement relation reconsidered: Differentiating homework time, homework frequency, and homework effort. *Learning and Instruction, 17*, 372–388.

Trautwein, U., & Lüdtke, O. (2007). Students' self-reported effort and time on homework in six school subjects: Between-students differences and within-student variation. *Journal of Educational Psychology*, 99, 232–234.

Tremblay, R. E., Boulerice, B., Harden, P. W., McDuff, P., Perusse, D., Pihl, R. O., & Zoccolillo, M. (1996). Do children in Canada become more aggressive as they approach adolescence? In *Growing up in Canada: National Longitudinal Survey of Children and Youth*. Ottawa, ON: Statistics Canada, Human Resources Development.

Trouilloud, D., Sarrazin, P., Bressoux, P., & Bois, J. (2006). Relation between teachers' early expectations and students' later perceived competence in physical education classes: autonomy-supportive climate as a moderator. *Journal of Educational Psychology*, 98, 75–86.

Tsantis, L. A., Bewick, C. J., & Thouvenelle, S. (2003). Examining some common myths about computer use in the early years [Electronic version]. *Beyond the Journal: Young Children on the Web, 1–9*. Retrieved from http://www.journal.naeyc.org/btj/200311/CommonTechnoMyths.pdf

Tschannen-Moran, M., & Woolfolk Hoy, A. (2001). Teacher efficacy: Capturing an elusive construct. *Teaching and Teacher Education, 17*, 783–805.

Tschannen-Moran, M., & Woolfolk Hoy, A. (2007). The differential antecedents of self-efficacy beliefs of novice and experienced teachers. *Teaching and Teacher Education, 23*, 944–956.

Tschannen-Moran, M., Woolfolk Hoy, A., & Hoy, W. K. (1998). Teacher efficacy: Its meaning and measure. *Review of Educational Research, 68*, 202–248.

Turiel, E. (1998). The development of morality. In W. Damon (Series Ed.) & N. Eisenberg (Vol. Ed.), *Handbook of child psychology: Vol. 3. Social, emotional, and personality development* (5th ed., pp. 863–932). New York, NY: Wiley.

Turner, J. C. (1997). Starting right: Strategies for engaging young literacy learners. In J. T. Guthrie & A. Wigfield (Eds.), *Reading engagement: Motivating readers through integrated instruction* (pp. 183–204). Newark, DE: International Reading Association.

Turner, J. C., & Paris, S. G. (1995). How literacy tasks influence students' motivation for literacy. *The Reading Teacher, 48*, 662–673.

Twenge, J. M., & Campbell, W. K. (2001). Age and birth cohort differences in self-esteem: A cross temporal meta-analysis. *Journal of Personality and Social Psychology Review, 5*, 321–344.

Uline, C. L., & Johnson, J. F. (2005, Winter). Closing the achievement gap: What will it take? Special Issue of *Theory Into Practice, 44*(1).

Umbreit, J. (1995). Functional analysis of disruptive behavior in an inclusive classroom. *Journal of Early Intervention, 20*(1), 18–29.

Underwood, M. K. (2003). *Social aggression among girls.* New York, NY: Guilford.

Unsworth, N., & Engle, R. W. (2005). Working memory capacity and fluid abilities: Examining the correlation between Operation Span and Raven. *Intelligence, 33*, 67–81.

Urdan, T. C., & Maehr, M. L. (1995). Beyond a two-goal theory of motivation and achievement: A case for social goals. *Review of Educational Research, 65*, 213–243.

U.S. Department of Education. (2010). OSEP center on positive behavioral interventions and supports. [Website]. *Office of Special Education Programs.* Retrieved from http://pbis.org/school/default.aspx

Valentine, J. C., DuBois, D. L., & Cooper, H. (2004). The relations between self-beliefs and academic achievement: A systematic review. *Educational Psychologist, 39*, 111–133.

Valenzuela, A. (1999). *Subtractive schooling: U.S.-Mexican youth and the politics of caring.* Albany, NY: SUNY Press.

Valkenburg, P. M., Schouten, A. P., & Peter, J. (2005). Adolescents' identity experiments on the internet. *New Media & Society, 7*(3), 383–402.

van der Mass, H. L. J., Dolan, C. V., Grasman, R. P., Wicherts, J. M., Huizenga, H. M., & Raijmakers, M. E. J. (2006). A dynamic model of general intelligence: The positive manifold of intelligence by mutualism. *Psychological Review, 113*, 842–861.

Van Der Veer, R. (2007). Vygotsky in context: 1900–1935. In H. Daniels, M. Cole, & J. V. Wertsch (Eds.), *The Cambridge companion to Vygotsky* (pp. 21–49). New York, NY: Cambridge University Press.

Van Houten, R., & Doleys, D. M. (1983). Are social reprimands effective? In S. Axelrod & J. Apsche (Eds.), *The effects of punishment on human behavior.* San Diego, CA: Academic Press.

van Laar, C. (2000). The paradox of low academic achievement but high self-esteem in African American students: An attributional account. *Educational Psychology Review, 12*, 33–61.

Van Matre, J. C., Valentine, J. C., & Cooper, H. (2000). Effect of students' after-school activities on teachers' academic expectations. *Contemporary Educational Psychology, 25*, 167–183.

van Merriënboer, J. J. G., & Sweller, J. (2005). Cognitive load and complex learning: Recent developments and future directions. *Educational Psychology Review, 17*, 147–177.

Van Meter, P. (2001). Drawing construction as a strategy for learning from text. *Journal of Educational Psychology, 93*, 129–140.

Van Meter, P., Yokoi, L., & Pressley, M. (1994). College students' theory of note-taking derived from their perceptions of note-taking. *Journal of Educational Psychology, 86*, 323–338.

Vandewater, E. A., Bickham, D. S., Lee, J. H., Cummings, H. M., Wartella, E. A., & Rideout, V. J. (2005). When the television is always on: Heavy television exposure and young children's development. *American Behavioral Scientist, 48*, 562–567.

Vansteenkiste, M., Lens, W., & Deci, E. L. (2006). Intrinsic versus extrinsic goal contents in self-determination theory: Another look at the quality of academic motivation. *Educational Psychologist, 41*, 19–31.

Vansteenkiste, M., Simons, J., Lens, W., Sheldon, K. M., & Deci, E. L. (2004). Motivating learning, performance, and persistence: The synergistic role of intrinsic goals and autonomy-support. *Journal of Personality and Social Psychology, 87*, 246–260.

Varma, S., McCandliss, B. D., & Schwartz, D. L. (2008). Scientific and pragmatic challenges for bridging education and neuroscience. *Educational Researcher, 37*, 140–152.

Vaughn, S., Levy, S., Coleman, M., & Bos, C. S. (2002). Reading instruction for students with LD and EBD: A synthesis of observation studies. *Journal of Special Education, 36*(1), 2–13.

Vecchio, G. M., Gerbino, M., Pastorelli, C., Del Bove, G., & Caprara, G. V. (2007). Multi-faceted self-efficacy beliefs as predictors of life satisfaction in late adolescence. *Personality and Individual Differences, 43*, 1807–1818.

Veenman, S. (1984). Perceived problems of beginning teachers. *Review of Educational Research, 54*, 143–178.

Veenman, S. (1997). Combination classes revisited. *Educational Research and Evaluation, 65*(4), 319–381.

Vera, A. H., & Simon, H. A. (1993). Situated action: A symbolic interpretation. *Cognitive Science, 17*, 7–48.

Vispoel, W. P., & Austin, J. R. (1995). Success and failure in junior high school: A critical incident approach to understanding students' attributional beliefs. *American Educational Research Journal, 32*, 377–412.

Volet, S. (1999). Learning across cultures: Appropriateness of knowledge transfer. *International Journal of Educational Research, 31*, 625–643.

von Glasersfeld, E. (1997). Amplification of a constructivist perspective. *Issues in Education: Contributions from Educational Psychology, 3*, 203–210.

Vroom, V. (1964). *Work and motivation.* New York, NY: Wiley.

Vygotsky, L. S. (1978). *Mind in society: The development of higher mental process.* Cambridge, MA: Harvard University Press.

Vygotsky, L. S. (1986). *Thought and language.* Cambridge, MA: MIT Press.

Vygotsky, L. S. (1987a). The genetic roots of thinking and speech. In R. W. Rieber & A. S. Carton (Eds.), *Problems of general psychology: Vol. 1. Collected works* (pp. 101–120). New York, NY: Plenum. (Work originally published in 1934.)

Vygotsky, L. S. (1987b). *Problems of general psychology.* New York, NY: Plenum.

Vygotsky, L. S. (1993). *The collected works of L. S. Vygotsky: Vol. 2* (J. Knox & C. Stevens, Trans.). New York, NY: Plenum.

Vygotsky, L. S. (1997). *Educational psychology* (R. Silverman, Trans.). Boca Raton, FL: St. Lucie.

Wade, S. E., Schraw, G., Buxton, W. M., & Hayes, M. T. (1993). Seduction of the strategic reader: Effects of interest on strategies and recall. *Reading Research Quarterly, 28*, 3–24.

Wadsworth, B. J. (1978). *Piaget for the classroom teacher.* Oxford, England: Longman.

Walberg, H. J. (1990). Productive teaching and instruction: Assessing the knowledge base. *Phi Delta Kappan, 72*, 470–478.

Wald, J. (2001, August 29). The failure of zero tolerance. *Salon Magazine.* Retrieved from http://www.salon.com/mwt/feature/2001/08/29/zero_tolerance/index.html?sid=1046257

Walker, J. E., Shea, T. M., & Bauer, A. M. (2004). *Behavior management: A practical approach for educators.* Upper Saddle River, NJ: Merrill/Prentice Hall.

Walker, L. J. (1991). Sex differences in moral reasoning. In W. M. Kurtines & J. L. Gewirtz (Eds.), *Handbook of moral behavior and development* (Vol. 2, pp. 333–362). Hillsdale, NJ: Erlbaum.

Walker, L. J., & Pitts, R. C. (1998). Naturalistic conceptions of moral maturity. *Developmental Psychology, 34*, 403–419.

Walker, L. J., Pitts, R. C., Hennig, K. H., & Matsuba, M. K. (1995). Reasoning about morality and real-life moral problems. In M. Killen & D. Hart (Eds.), *Morality in everyday life: Developmental perspectives* (pp. 371–407). Cambridge, England: Cambridge University Press.

Walker, V. S. (1996). *Their highest potential.* Chapel Hill, NC: University of North Carolina Press.

Wang, A. Y., & Thomas, M. H. (1995). Effects of keywords on long-term retention: Help or hindrance? *Journal of Educational Psychology, 87*, 468–475.

Wang, A. Y., Thomas, M. H., & Ouellette, J. A. (1992). Keyword mnemonic and retention of second-language vocabulary words. *Journal of Educational Psychology, 84*, 520–528.

..., & Palincsar, A. S. (1989). Teaching students to assume an active ...e in their learning. In M. Reynolds (Ed.), *Knowledge base for the beginning teacher* (pp. 71–84). New York, NY: Pergamon.

Ward, L. M. (2004). Wading through the stereotypes: Positive and negative associations between media use and Black adolescents' conception of self. *Developmental Psychology*, *40*, 284–294.

Waterhouse, L. (2006). Multiple intelligences, the Mozart effect, and emotional intelligence: A critical review. *Educational Psychologist*, *41*, 207–225.

Waxman, S. R., & Lidz, J. L. (2006). Early word learning. In D. Kuhn & R. S. Siegler (Eds.), *Handbook of child psychology: Vol. 2. Cognition, perception, and language* (6th ed., pp. 299–335). New York, NY: Wiley.

Wayne, A. J., & Youngs, P. (2003). Teacher characteristics and student achievement gains: A review. *Review of Educational Research*, *73*, 89–122.

Webb, N. M., Farivar, S. H., & Mastergeorge, A. M. (2002). Productive helping in cooperative groups. *Theory Into Practice*, *41*, 13–20.

Webb, N. M., & Mastergeorge, A. M. (2003). The development of students' helping behavior and learning in peer-directed small groups. *Cognition and Instruction*, *21*, 361–428.

Webb, N. M., & Palincsar, A. (1996). Group processes in the classroom. In D. C. Berliner & R. C. Calfee (Eds.), *Handbook of educational psychology* (pp. 841–876). New York, NY: Macmillan.

Weil, E. (2008, March 2). Should boys and girls be taught separately? *The New York Times Magazine*, pp. 33–45+.

Weiner, B. (1979). A theory of motivation for some classroom experiences. *Journal of Educational Psychology*, *71*, 3–25.

Weiner, B. (1986). *An attributional theory of motivation and emotion*. New York, NY: Springer.

Weiner, B. (1994a). Ability versus effort revisited: The moral determinants of achievement evaluation an achievement as a moral system. *Educational Psychologist*, *29*, 163–172.

Weiner, B. (1994b). Integrating social and persons theories of achievement striving. *Review of Educational Research*, *64*, 557–575.

Weiner, B. (2000). Interpersonal and intrapersonal theories of motivation from an attributional perspective. *Educational Psychology Review*, *12*, 1–14.

Weiner, B., & Graham, S. (1989). Understanding the motivational role of affect: Lifespan research from an attributional perspective. *Cognition and Emotion*, *4*, 401–419.

Weinert, F. E., & Helmke, A. (1995). Learning from wise mother nature or big brother instructor: The wrong choice as seen from an educational perspective. *Educational Psychologist*, *30*, 135–143.

Weinstein, C. (1988). Preservice teachers' expectations about the first year of teaching. *Teaching and Teacher Education*, *4*, 31–41.

Weinstein, C. E. (1994). Learning strategies and learning to learn. In *International encyclopedia of education*. New York, NY: Pergamon.

Weinstein, C. S. (1977). Modifying student behavior in an open classroom through changes in the physical design. *American Educational Research Journal*, *14*, 249–262.

Weinstein, C. S. (1999). Reflections on best practices and promising programs: Beyond assertive classroom discipline. In H. J. Freiberg (Ed.), *Beyond behaviorism: Changing the classroom management paradigm* (pp. 147–163). Boston, MA: Allyn & Bacon.

Weinstein, C. S. (2007). *Middle and secondary classroom management: Lessons from research and practice* (3rd ed.). New York, NY: McGraw-Hill.

Weinstein, C. S., & Mignano, A. (2007). *Elementary classroom management: Lessons from research and practice* (4th ed.). New York, NY: McGraw-Hill.

Weinstein, R. S., Madison, S. M., & Kuklinski, M. R. (1995). Raising expectations in schools: Obstacles and opportunities for change. *American Educational Research Journal*, *32*, 121–159.

Weisberg, R. W. (1993). *Creativity: Beyond the myth of genius*. New York, NY: W. H. Freeman.

Wellman, H. M., Baron-Cohen, S., Caswell, R., Gomez, J.C., Swettenham, J., Toye, E., & Lagattuta, K. (2002). Thought bubbles help children with autism acquire an alternative to a theory of mind. *Autism*, *6*, 343–363.

Wenger, E. (1998). *Communities of practice: learning, meaning, and identity*. New York, NY: Cambridge University Press.

Wentzel, K. R. (1999). Social-motivational processes and interpersonal relations: Implications for understanding motivation in school. *Journal of Educational Psychology*, *91*, 76–97.

Wentzel, K. R. (2002). Are effective teachers like good parents? Teaching styles and student adjustment in early adolescence. *Child Development*, *73*, 287–301.

Wentzel, K. R., Barry, C. M., & Caldwell, K. A. (2004). Friendships in middle school: Influences on motivation and school adjustment. *Journal of Educational Psychology*, *96*, 195–203.

Werts, M. G., Culatta, A., & Tompkins, J. R. (2007). *Fundamentals of special education: What every teacher should know* (3rd ed.). Columbus, OH: Pearson/Allyn & Bacon-Merrill.

Wertsch, J. V. (1991). *Voices of the mind: A sociocultural approach to mediated action*. Cambridge, MA: Harvard University Press.

Wertsch, J. V. (2007). Mediation. In H. Daniels, M. Cole, & J. V. Wertsch (Eds.), *The Cambridge companion to Vygotsky* (pp. 178–192). New York, NY: Cambridge University Press.

Wertsch, J. V., & Tulviste, P. (1992). L. S. Vygotsky and contemporary developmental psychology. *Developmental Psychology*, *28*, 548–557.

Westberg, K. L., Archambault, F. X., Dodyns, S. M., & Slavin, T. J. (1993). The classroom practices observation study. *Journal of the Education of the Gifted*, *16*(2), 120–146.

Wharton-McDonald, R., Pressley, M., Rankin, J., Mistretta, J., Yokoi, L., & Ettenberger, S. (1997). Effective primary-grades literacy instruction = Balanced literacy instruction. *The Reading Teacher*, *50*, 518–521.

Wheatley, K. F. (2002). The potential benefits of teacher efficacy doubts for educational reform. *Teaching and Teacher Education*, *18*, 5–22.

White, S., & Tharp, R. G. (1988, April). *Questioning and wait-time: A cross cultural analysis*. Paper presented at the annual meeting of the American Educational Research Association, New Orleans, LA.

Whitehead, A. N. (1929). *The aims of education*. New York, NY: Macmillan.

Whitehurst, G. J. (2003, April). *The Institute of Educational Sciences: New wine, new bottles*. Paper presented at the annual meeting of the American Educational Research Association, Chicago, IL.

Whitehurst, G. J., Epstein, J. N., Angell, A. L., Payne, A. C., Crone, D. A., & Fischel, J. E. (1994). Outcomes of an emergent literacy program in headstart. *Journal of Educational Psychology*, *86*, 542–555.

Wigfield, A., Byrnes, J. P., & Eccles, J. S. (2006). Development during early and middle adolescence. In P. A. Alexander & P. H. Winne (Eds.), *Handbook of educational psychology* (2nd ed., pp. 87–113). Mahwah, NJ: Erlbaum.

Wigfield, A., & Eccles, J. (1989). Test anxiety in elementary and secondary school students. *Educational Psychologist*, *24*, 159–183.

Wigfield, A., & Eccles, J. S. (2002a). Students' motivation during the middle school years. In J. Aronson (Ed.), *Improving academic development: Impact of psychological factors in education* (pp. 159–184). New York, NY: Academic Press.

Wigfield, A., & Eccles, J. S. (2002b). The development of competence beliefs, expectancies of success, and achievement values from childhood through adolescence. In A. Wigfield & J. Eccles (Eds.), *Development of achievement motivation* (pp. 91–120). San Diego, CA: Academic Press.

Wigfield, A., Eccles, J. S., MacIver, D., Rueman, D., & Midgley, C. (1991). Transitions during early adolescence: Changes in children's domain-specific self-perceptions and general self-esteem across the transition to junior high school. *Developmental Psychology*, *27*, 552–565.

Wigfield, A., Eccles, J. S., & Pintrich, P. R. (1996). Development between the ages of 11 and 25. In D. Berliner & R. Calfee (Eds.), *Handbook of educational psychology* (pp. 148–185). New York, NY: Macmillan.

Wigfield, A., & Wentzel, K. R. (2007). Introduction to motivation at school: Interventions that work. *Educational Psychologist*, *42*, 191–196.

Wiggins, G. (1989). Teaching to the authentic test. *Educational Leadership*, *46*(7), 41–47.

Wiggins, G. (1991). Standards, not standardization: Evoking quality student work. *Educational Leadership*, *48*(5), 18–25.

Wiggins, G. (1993). Assessment, authenticity, context, and validity. *Phi Delta Kappan*, *75*, 200–214.

Willcutt, E. G., Pennington, B. F., Boada, R., Ogline, J. S., Tunick, R. A., Chhabidas, N. A., & Olson, R. K. (2001). A comparison of the cognitive deficits in reading disability and attention-deficit/hyperactivity disorder. *Journal of Abnormal Psychology*, *110*, 157–172.

Williams, C., & Bybee J. (1994). What do children feel guilty about? Developmental and gender differences. *Developmental Psychology*, *30*, 617–623.

Williams, J. (2002). Using the Theme Scheme to improve story comprehension. In C. C. Block & M. Pressley (Eds.), *Comprehension instruction: Research-based best practices* (pp. 126–139). New York, NY: Guilford.

Willingham, D. T. (2004). Reframing the mind. *Education Next, 4*(3), 19–24.

Willingham, W. W., & Cole, N. S. (1997). *Gender and fair assessment*. Mahwah, NJ: Erlbaum.

Willis, P. (1977). *Learning to labor*. Lexington, MA: D.C. Heath.

Willoughby, T., Porter, L., Belsito, L., & Yearsley, T. (1999). Use of elaboration strategies by grades two, four, and six. *Elementary School Journal, 99*, 221–231.

Wilson, A. M., Armstrong, C. D., Furrie, A. & Walcot, E. (2009). The mental health of Canadians with self-reported learning disabilities. *Journal of Learning Disabilities, 42*, 24–40.

Wilson, M. (2001). The case for sensorimotor coding in working memory. *Psychonomic Bulletin and Review, 8*, 44–57.

Wilson M., & Trainin, G. (2007). First-grade students' motivation and achievement for reading, writing, and spelling. *Reading Psychology, 28*, 257–282.

Windschitl, M. (2002). Framing constructivism in practice as the negotiation of dilemmas; An analysis of the conceptual, pedagogical, cultural, and political challenges facing teachers. *Review of Educational Research, 72*, 131–175.

Winett, R. A., & Winkler, R. C. (1972). Current behavior modification in the classroom: Be still, be quiet, be docile. *Journal of Applied Behavior Analysis, 15*, 499–504.

Wink, J., & Putney, L. (2002). *A vision of Vygotsky*. Boston, MA: Allyn & Bacon.

Winne, P. H. (1995). Inherent details in self-regulated learning. *Educational Psychologist, 30*, 173–188.

Winne, P. H. (2001). Self-regulated learning viewed from models of information processing. In B. J. Zimmerman & D. H. Schunk (Eds.), *Self-regulated learning and academic achievement: Theoretical perspectives* (2nd ed., pp. 153–189). Mahwah, NJ: Erlbaum.

Winne, P. H. (in press). A cognitive and metacognitive analysis of self-regulated learning. In B. J. Zimmerman and D. H. Schunk (Eds.), *Handbook of self-regulation of learning and performance*. New York, NY: Routledge.

Winne, P. H., & Hadwin, A. F. (1998). Studying as self-regulated learning. In D. J. Hacker, J. Dunlosky, & A. C. Graesser (Eds.), *Metacognition in educational theory and practice* (pp. 277–304). Mahwah, NJ: Erlbaum.

Winne, P. H., & Hadwin, A. F. (2010). Self-regulated learning and sociocognitive theory. In P. Peterson, E. Baker & B. McGaw (Eds.), *International encyclopedia of education* (Vol. 5, pp. 503–508). Amsterdam, the Netherlands: Elsevier.

Winne, P. H., & Perry, N. E. (2000). Measuring self-regulated learning. In P. Pintrich, M. Boekaerts, & M. Zeidner (Eds.), *Handbook of self-regulation* (pp. 531–566). Orlando, FL: Academic Press.

Winner, E. (2000). The origins and ends of giftedness. *American Psychologist, 55*, 159–169.

Winner, E. (2003). Musical giftedness. *Bulletin of Psychology and the Arts, 4*, 1, 2–5.

Winsler, A., Carlton, M. P., & Barry, M. J. (2000). Age-related changes in preschool children's systematic use of private speech in a natural setting. *Journal of Child Language, 27*, 665–687.

Winsler, A., & Naglieri, J. A. (2003). Overt and covert verbal problem-solving strategies: Developmental trends in use, awareness, and relations with task performance in children age 5 to 17. *Child Development, 74*, 659–678.

Winzer, M. A. (2006). *Children with exceptionalities in Canadian classrooms* (6th ed.). Toronto, ON: Prentice-Hall.

Wittrock, M. C. (1982, March). *Educational implications of recent research on learning and memory*. Paper presented at the annual meeting of the American Educational Research Association, New York, NY.

Wittrock, M. C. (Ed.). (1986). *Handbook of research on teaching* (3rd ed.). New York, NY: Macmillan.

Wittrock, M. C. (1992). An empowering conception of educational psychology. *Educational Psychologist, 27*, 129–142.

Wolf, D., Bixby, J., Glenn, J., III, & Gardner, H. (1991). To use their minds well: New forms of student assessment. *Review of Research in Education, 17*, 31–74.

Wolters, C. A., Yu, S. L., & Pintrich, P. R. (1996). The relation between goal orientation and students' motivational beliefs and self-regulated learning. *Learning and Individual Differences, 8*, 211–238.

Wong, B. Y. L. (1996). *The ABCs of learning disabilities*. San Diego, CA: Academic Press.

Wong, B. Y. L., Harris, K. R., Graham, S., & Butler, D. L. (2003). Cognitive strategies instruction research in learning disabilities. In H. L. Swanson, K. R. Harris, & S. Graham (Eds.), *Handbook of learning disabilities* (pp. 383–402). New York, NY: Guilford Press.

Wong, L. (1987). Reaction to research findings: Is the feeling of obviousness warranted? *Dissertation Abstracts International*, 48/12, 3709B. (University Microfilms #DA 8801059)

Wood, D., Bruner, J., & Ross, S. (1976). The role of tutoring in problem solving. *British Journal of Psychology, 66*, 181–191.

Woods, B. S., & Murphy, P. K. (2002). Thickening the discussion: What can William James tell us about constructivism? *Educational Theory, 52*, 443–449.

Woolfolk, A. E., & Brooks, D. (1983). Nonverbal communication in teaching. In E. Gordon (Ed.), *Review of research in education* (Vol. 10, pp. 103–150). Washington, DC: American Educational Research Association.

Woolfolk, A. E., & Brooks, D. (1985). The influence of teachers' nonverbal behaviors on students' perceptions and performance. *Elementary School Journal, 85*, 514–528.

Woolfolk, A. E., & Hoy, W. K. (1990). Prospective teachers' sense of efficacy and beliefs about control. *Journal of Educational Psychology, 82*, 81–91.

Woolfolk, A. E., Perry, N., & Winne, P. (2006). *Educational psychology: Third Canadian edition* (3rd ed.). Toronto, ON: Pearson.

Woolfolk Hoy, A., & Burke-Spero, R. (2005). Changes in teacher efficacy during the early years of teaching: A comparison of four measures. *Teaching and Teacher Education, 21*, 343–356.

Woolfolk Hoy, A., Demerath, P., & Pape, S. (2002). Teaching adolescents: Engaging developing selves. In T. Urdan & F. Pajares (Eds.), *Adolescence and education* (Vol. I, pp. 119–169). Greenwich, CT: Information Age Publishing.

Woolfolk Hoy, A., Hoy, W. K., & Davis, H. (2009). Teachers' self-efficacy beliefs. In K. Wentzel & A. Wigfield (Eds.), *Handbook of motivation in school*. Mahwah, NJ: Erlbaum.

Woolfolk Hoy, A., & Murphy, P. K. (2001). Teaching educational psychology to the implicit mind. In R. Sternberg & B. Torff (Eds.), *Understanding and teaching the implicit mind* (pp. 145–185). Mahwah, NJ: Erlbaum.

Woolfolk Hoy, A., Pape, S., & Davis, H. (2006). Teachers' knowledge, beliefs, and thinking. In P. A. Alexander & P. H, Winne (Eds.), *Handbook of educational psychology* (2nd ed.). Mahwah, NJ: Erlbaum.

Woolfolk Hoy, A., & Tschannen-Moran. M. (1999). Implications of cognitive approaches to peer learning for teacher education. In A. O'Donnell & A. King (Eds.), *Cognitive perspectives on peer learning* (pp. 257–284). Mahwah, NJ: Erlbaum.

Woolfolk Hoy, A., & Weinstein, C. S. (2006). Students' and teachers' perspectives about classroom management. In C. Evertson & C. S. Weinstein (Eds.), *Handbook for classroom management: Research, practice, and contemporary issues*. Mahwah, NJ: Erlbaum.

Wright, S. C., & Taylor, D. M. (1995). Identity and the language of the classroom: Investigating the impact of heritage versus second language instruction on personal and collective self-esteem. *Journal of Educational Psychology, 87*, 241–252.

Wyler, R. S. (1988). Social memory and social judgment. In P. Solomon, G. Goethals, C. Kelly, & B. Stephans (Eds.), *Perspectives on memory research*. New York, NY: Springer-Verlag.

Yarhouse, M. A. (2001). Sexual identity development: The influence of valuative frameworks on identity synthesis. *Psychotherapy, 38*(3), 331–341.

Yates, M., & Youniss, J. (1999). Promoting identity development: Ten ideas for school-based service-learning programs. In J. Claus & C. Ogden (Eds.), *Service learning for youth empowerment and social change* (pp. 43–67). New York, NY: Peter Lang.

Ybarra, M. L., & Mitchell, K. J. (2004). Youth engaging in online harassment: associations with caregiver-child relationships, Internet use, and personal characteristics. *Journal of Adolescence, 27*, 319–336.

Yee, A. H. (1992). Asians as stereotypes and students: Misperceptions that persist. *Educational Psychology Review, 4*, 95–132.

Yerkes, R. M., & Dodson, J. D. (1908). The relation of strength of stimulus to rapidity of habit formation. *Journal of Comparative Neurology, 18*, 459–482.

Young, A. J. (1997). I think, therefore I'm motivated: The relations among cognitive strategy use, motivational orientation, and classroom perceptions over time. *Learning and Individual Differences, 9*, 249–283.

K., & Warrington, M. (2006). Would Harry and Hermione have ...e better in single-sex teaching in coeducational secondary schools in the United Kingdom? *American Educational Research Journal, 43*, 579–620.

Youniss, J., & Yates, M. (1997). *Community service and social responsibility in youth*. Chicago, IL: University of Chicago Press.

Zeidner, M. (1995). Adaptive coping with test situations. *Educational Psychologist, 30*, 123–134.

Zeidner, M. (1998). *Test anxiety: The state of the art*. New York, NY: Plenum.

Zentall, S. S. (1993). Research on the educational implications of attention deficit hyperactivity disorder. *Exceptional Children, 60*, 143–153.

Zhang, L., & Sternberg, R. J. (2005). The threefold model of intellectual styles. *Educational Psychology Review, 17*, 1–53.

Zhou, Z., Peverly, S. T., Beohm, A. E., & Chongde, L. (2001). American and Chinese children's understanding of distance, time, and speed interrelations. *Cognitive Development, 15*, 215–240.

Zimmerman, B. J. (2002). Becoming a self-regulated learner: An overview. *Theory Into Practice, 41*, 64–70.

Zimmerman, B. J., & Schunk, D. H. (Eds.). (2001). *Self-regulated learning and academic achievement: Theoretical perspectives* (2nd ed.). Mahwah, NJ: Erlbaum.

Zimmerman, B. J., & Schunk, D. H. (Eds). (2003). *Educational psychology: A century of contributions* [A Project of Division 15 (Educational Psychology) of the American Psychological Association]. Mahwah, NJ: Erlbaum.

Zimmerman, B. J., & Schunk, D. H. (2004). Self-regulating intellectual processes and outcomes: A social cognitive perspective. In D. Y. Dao & R. J. Sternberg (Eds.), *Motivation, emotion, and cognition: Integrative perspectives on intellectual functioning and development* (pp. 323–350). Mahwah, NJ: Erlbaum.

Zimmerman, D. W. (1981). On the perennial argument about grading "on the curve" in college courses. *Educational Psychologist, 16*, 175–178.

NAME INDEX

C

H

R

SUBJECT INDEX

Page numbers followed by italic *f* indicate figures, and those followed by italic *t* indicate tables.

E

F

Q

R